FDCA STATUTORY SUPPLEMENT, 2018

Edited by Deborah M. Shelton and Joy J. Liu

FDLI

ISBN 978-1-935065-86-9

The following documents are derived or reproduced from publicly available documents. The reader should consult the original publication to ensure the accuracy of the enclosed versions.

For additional information or to order copies of this publication, contact FDLI:

1155 15th Street NW, Suite 910

Washington, D.C. 20005

(800) 956-6293 or (202) 371-1420

info@fdli.org

www.fdli.org

FDCA STATUTORY SUPPLEMENT, 2018

The Federal Food, Drug, and Cosmetic Act (FDCA) has been amended frequently and significantly over the years and is presented here as amended through January 2018. This new 2018 edition is fully updated to reflect, inter alia, the recent amendments to the FDCA by the Food and Drug Administration Reauthorization Act (FDARA), which was signed into law by President Donald Trump in August of 2017. FDARA had the effect of reauthorizing the Prescription Drug User Fee Act (PDUFA), as well as user fees for biosimilars, generic drugs, and medical devices. These amendments are presented in track changes (additions are underlined; deletions are struck-through), making it easy to identify updates and changes to the law.

It is presented in the order, and bearing the section numbers of, the original statute because of the many cross-references within the statute and because of the frequency with which those section numbers are referenced by courts, practitioners, and academics. The bracketed numbers following the FDCA section numbers are the section numbers in Title 21 of the United States Code, where the FDCA sections are codified. For example, the definitions section is presented as "Sec. 201. [321]." A few relevant statutory sections were not passed as amendments to the FDCA, but have been codified within the same range of code section numbers in Title 21. Such sections are presented here in their correct place in the 21 U.S.C. numbering scheme, but without an FDCA section number. For example, 21 U.S.C. 321a, defining butter, appears after Section 201 [321].

As in previous editions, this edition includes an appendix of selected text from other statutes and acts that may be particularly relevant for practitioners in this area of the law. Thus, for example, sections of the Public Health Service Act relating to the approval of biological products are included in the appendix, as are provisions of the FDA Amendments Act of 2007 relating to user fees and postmarket surveillance. The selections in the appendix are not, however, meant to be exhaustive or all-encompassing; FDLI encourages users to seek out the actual statutes and acts when substantive legal review is required.

For access to the electronic version of the FDCA Statutory Supplement, go to http://www.fdli.org/stat2018.

ACKNOWLEDGMENTS

FDLI gratefully acknowledges the contributions of the following individuals for their invaluable work as editors of this book:

Deborah M. Shelton, McCarter & English, LLP
Joy J. Liu, Vertex Pharmaceuticals Incorporated
For copyediting assistance:
Nina Seebeck

TABLE OF CONTENTS
FEDERAL FOOD, DRUG, AND COSMETIC ACT

FEDERAL FOOD, DRUG, AND COSMETIC ACT

(References in brackets [ ] are to title 21, United States Code)

Chapter I — Short Title

Sec. 1. [301] Short Title.

This Act may be cited as the Federal Food, Drug, and Cosmetic Act.

Chapter II — Definitions

Sec. 201. [321] Definitions.

For the purposes of this Act —

(a) —

(1) The term "State", except as used in the last sentence of section 702(a), means any State or Territory of the United States, the District of Columbia, and the Commonwealth of Puerto Rico.

(2) The term "Territory" means any Territory or possession of the United States, including the District of Columbia, and excluding the Commonwealth of Puerto Rico and the Canal Zone.

(b) The term "interstate commerce" means

(1) commerce between any State or Territory and any place outside thereof, and

(2) commerce within the District of Columbia or within any other Territory not organized with a legislative body.

(c) The term "Department" means the Department of Health and Human Services.

(d) The term "Secretary" means the Secretary of Health and Human Services.

(e) The term "person" includes individual, partnership, corporation, and association.

(f) The term "food" means

(1) articles used for food or drink for man or other animals,

(2) chewing gum, and

(3) articles used for components of any such article.

(g) —

(1) The term "drug" means

(A) articles recognized in the official United States Pharmacopeia, official Homeopathic Pharmacopeia of the United States, or official National Formulary, or any supplement to any of them; and

(B) articles intended for use in the diagnosis, cure, mitigation, treatment, or prevention of disease in man or other animals; and

(C) articles (other than food) intended to affect the structure or any function of the body of man or other animals; and

(D) articles intended for use as a component of any articles specified in clause (A), (B), or (C).

A food or dietary supplement for which a claim, subject to sections 403(r)(1)(B) and 403(r)(3) or sections 403(r)(1)(B) and 403(r)(5)(D), is made in accordance with the requirements of section 403(r) is not a drug solely because the label or the labeling contains such a claim. A food, dietary ingredient, or dietary supplement for which a truthful and not misleading statement is made in accordance with section 403(r)(6) is not a drug under clause (C) solely because the label or the labeling contains such a statement.

(2) The term "counterfeit drug" means a drug which, or the container or labeling of which, without authorization, bears the trademark, trade name, or other identifying mark, imprint, or device, or any likeness thereof, of a drug manufacturer, processor, packer, or distributor other than the person or persons who in fact manufactured, processed, packed, or distributed such drug and which thereby falsely purports or is represented to be the product of, or to have been packed or distributed by, such other drug manufacturer, processor, packer, or distributor.

(h) The term "device" (except when used in paragraph (n) of this section and in sections 301(i), 403(f), 502(c), and 602(c)) means an instrument, apparatus, implement, machine, contrivance, implant, in vitro reagent, or other similar or related article, including any component, part, or accessory, which is —

(1) recognized in the official National Formulary, or the United States Pharmacopeia, or any supplement to them,

(2) intended for use in the diagnosis of disease or other conditions, or in the cure, mitigation, treatment, or prevention of disease, in man or other animals, or

(3) intended to affect the structure or any function of the body of man or other animals, and which does not achieve its primary intended purposes through chemical action within or on the body of man or other animals and which is not dependent upon being metabolized for the achievement of its primary intended purposes. The term 'device' does not include software functions excluded pursuant to section 520(o).

(i) The term "cosmetic" means

(1) articles intended to be rubbed, poured, sprinkled, or sprayed on, introduced into, or otherwise applied to the human body or any part thereof for cleansing, beautifying, promoting attractiveness, or altering the appearance, and

(2) articles intended for use as a component of any such articles; except that such term shall not include soap.

(j) The term "official compendium" means the official United States Pharmacopeia, official Homeopathic Pharmacopeia of the United States, official National Formulary, or any supplement to any of them.

(k) The term "label" means a display of written, printed, or graphic matter upon the immediate container of any article; and a requirement made by or under authority of this Act that any word, statement, or other information appear on the label shall not be considered to be complied with unless such word, statement, or other information also appears on the outside container or wrapper, if any there be, of the retail package of such article, or is easily legible through the outside container or wrapper.

(l) The term "immediate container" does not include package liners.

(m) The term "labeling" means all labels and other written, printed, or graphic matter

(1) upon any article or any of its containers or wrappers, or

(2) accompanying such article.

(n) If an article is alleged to be misbranded because the labeling or advertising is misleading, then in determining whether the labeling or advertising is misleading there shall be taken into account (among other things) not only representations made or suggested by statement, word, design, device, or any combination thereof, but also the extent to which the labeling or advertising fails to reveal facts material in the light of such representations or material with respect to consequences which may result from the use of the article to which the labeling or advertising relates under the conditions of use prescribed in the labeling or advertising thereof or under such conditions of use as are customary or usual.

(o) The representation of a drug, in its labeling, as an antiseptic shall be considered to be a representation that it is a germicide, except in the case of a drug purporting to be, or represented as, an antiseptic for inhibitory use as a wet dressing, ointment, dusting powder, or such other use as involves prolonged contact with the body.

(p) The term "new drug" means —

(1) Any drug (except a new animal drug or an animal feed bearing or containing a new animal drug) the composition of which is such that such drug is not generally recognized, among experts qualified by scientific training and experience to evaluate the safety and effectiveness of drugs, as safe and effective for use under the conditions prescribed, recommended, or suggested in the labeling thereof, except that such a drug not so recognized shall not be deemed to be a "new drug" if at any time prior to the enactment of this Act it was subject to the Food and Drugs Act of June 30, 1906, as amended, and if at such time its labeling contained the same representations concerning the conditions of its use; or

(2) Any drug (except a new animal drug or an animal feed bearing or containing a new animal drug) the composition of which is such that such drug, as a result of investigations to determine its safety and effectiveness for use under such conditions, has become so recognized, but which has not, otherwise than in such investigations, been used to a material extent or for a material time under such conditions.

(q) —

(1) —

(A) Except as provided in clause (B), the term "pesticide chemical" means any substance that is a pesticide within the meaning of the Federal Insecticide, Fungicide, and Rodenticide Act, including all active and inert ingredients of such pesticide. Notwithstanding any other provision of law, the term "pesticide" within such meaning includes ethylene oxide and propylene oxide when such substances are applied on food.

(B) In the case of the use, with respect to food, of a substance described in clause (A) to prevent, destroy, repel, or mitigate micro-organisms (including bacteria, viruses, fungi, protozoa, algae, and slime), the following applies for purposes of clause (A):

(i) The definition in such clause for the term "pesticide chemical" does not include the substance if the substance is applied for such use on food, or the substance is included for such use in water that comes into contact with the food, in the preparing, packing, or holding of the food for commercial purposes. The substance is not excluded under this subclause from such definition if the substance is ethylene oxide or propylene oxide, and is applied for such use on food. The substance is not so excluded if the substance is applied for such use on a raw agricultural commodity, or the substance is included for such use in water that comes into contact with the commodity, as follows:

(I) The substance is applied in the field.

(II) The substance is applied at a treatment facility where raw agricultural commodities are the only food treated, and the treatment is in a manner that does not change the status of the food as a raw agricultural commodity (including treatment through washing, waxing, fumigating, and packing such commodities in such manner).

(III) The substance is applied during the transportation of such commodity between the field and such a treatment facility.

(ii) The definition in such clause for the term "pesticide chemical" does not include the substance if the substance is a food contact substance as defined in section 409(h)(6), and any of the following circumstances exist: The substance is included for such use in an object that has a food contact surface but is not intended to have an ongoing effect on any portion of the object; the substance is included for such use in an object that has a food contact surface and is intended to have an ongoing effect on a portion of the object but not on the food contact surface; or the substance is included for such use in or is applied for such use on food packaging (without regard to whether the substance is intended to have an ongoing effect on any portion of the packaging). The food contact substance is not excluded under this subclause from such definition if any of the following circumstances exist: The substance is applied for such use on a semipermanent or permanent food contact surface (other than being applied on food packaging); or the substance is included for such use in an object that has a semipermanent or permanent food contact surface (other than being included in food packaging) and the substance is intended to have an ongoing effect on the food contact surface.

With respect to the definition of the term "pesticide" that is applicable to the Federal Insecticide, Fungicide, and Rodenticide Act, this clause does not exclude any substance from such definition.

(2) The term "pesticide chemical residue" means a residue in or on raw agricultural commodity or processed food of—

(A) a pesticide chemical; or

(B) any other added substance that is present on or in the commodity or food primarily as a result of the metabolism or other degradation of a pesticide chemical.

(3) Notwithstanding subparagraphs (1) and (2), the Administrator may by regulation except a substance from the definition of "pesticide chemical" or "pesticide chemical residue" if—

(A) its occurrence as a residue on or in a raw agricultural commodity or processed food is attributable primarily to natural causes or to human activities not involving the use of any substances for a pesticidal purpose in the production, storage, processing, or transportation of any raw agricultural commodity or processed food; and

(B) the Administrator, after consultation with the Secretary, determines that the substance more appropriately should be regulated under one or more provisions of this Act other than sections 402(a)(2)(B) and 408.

(r) The term "raw agricultural commodity" means any food in its raw or natural state, including all fruits that are washed, colored, or otherwise treated in their unpeeled natural form prior to marketing.

(s) The term "food additive" means any substance the intended use of which results or may reasonably be expected to result, directly or indirectly, in its becoming a component or otherwise affecting the characteristics of any food (including any substance intended for use in producing, manufacturing, packing, processing, preparing, treating, packaging, transporting, or holding food; and including any source of radiation intended for any such use), if such substance is not generally recognized, among experts qualified by scientific training and experience to evaluate its safety, as having been adequately shown through scientific procedures (or, in the case of a substance used in food prior to January 1, 1958, through either scientific procedures or experience based on common use in food) to be safe under the conditions of its intended use; except that such term does not include —

(1) a pesticide chemical residue in or on a raw agricultural commodity or processed food; or

(2) a pesticide chemical; or

(3) a color additive; or

(4) any substance used in accordance with a sanction or approval granted prior to the enactment of this paragraph [September 6, 1958 — Ed.] pursuant to this Act, the Poultry Products Inspection Act (21 U.S.C. 451 and the following) or the Meat Inspection Act of March 4, 1907 (34 Stat. 1260), as amended and extended (21 U.S.C. 71 and the following);

(5) a new animal drug; or

(6) an ingredient described in paragraph (ff) in, or intended for use in, a dietary supplement.

(t) —

(1) The term "color additive" means a material which —

(A) is a dye, pigment, or other substance made by a process of synthesis or similar artifice, or extracted, isolated, or otherwise derived, with or without intermediate or final change of identity, from a vegetable, animal, mineral, or other source, and

(B) when added or applied to a food, drug, or cosmetic, or to the human body or any part thereof, is capable (alone or through reaction with other substance) of imparting color thereto;

except that such term does not include any material which the Secretary, by regulation, determines is used (or intended to be used) solely for a purpose or purposes other than coloring.

(2) The term "color" includes black, white, and intermediate grays.

(3) Nothing in subparagraph (1) of this paragraph shall be construed to apply to any pesticide chemical, soil or plant nutrient, or other agricultural chemical solely because of its effect in aiding, retarding, or otherwise affecting, directly or indirectly, the growth or other natural physiological processes of produce of the soil and thereby affecting its color, whether before or after harvest.

(u) The term "safe", as used in paragraph (s) of this section and in sections 409, 512, 571, and 721, has reference to the health of man or animal.

(v) The term "new animal drug" means any drug intended for use for animals other than man, including any drug intended for use in animal feed but not including such animal feed —

(1) the composition of which is such that such drug is not generally recognized, among experts qualified by scientific training and experience to evaluate the safety and effectiveness of animal drugs, as safe and effective for use under the conditions prescribed, recommended, or suggested in the labeling thereof; except that such a drug not so recognized shall not be deemed to be a "new animal drug" if at any time prior to June 25, 1938, it was subject to the Food and Drug Act of June 30, 1906, as amended, and if at such time its labeling contained the same representations concerning the conditions of its use; or

(2) the composition of which is such that such drug, as a result of investigations to determine its safety and effectiveness for use under such conditions, has become so recognized but which has not, otherwise than in such investigations, been used to a material extent or for a material time under such conditions.

Provided that any drug intended for minor use or use in a minor species that is not the subject of a final regulation published by the Secretary through notice and comment rulemaking finding that the criteria of paragraphs (1) and (2) have not been met (or that the exception to the criterion in paragraph (1) has been met) is a new animal drug.

(w) The term "animal feed", as used in paragraph (w) [probably should be paragraph "(v)" — Ed.] of this section, in section 512, and in provisions of this Act referring to such paragraph or section, means an article which is intended for use for food for animals other than man and which is intended for use as a substantial source of nutrients in the diet of the animal, and is not limited to a mixture intended to be the sole ration of the animal.

(x) The term "informal hearing" means a hearing which is not subject to section 554, 556, or 557 of title 5 of the United States Code and which provides for the following:

(1) The presiding officer in the hearing shall be designated by the Secretary from officers and employees of the Department who have not participated in any action of the Secretary which is the subject of the hearing and who are not directly responsible to an officer or employee of the Department who has participated in any such action.

(2) Each party to the hearing shall have the right at all times to be advised and accompanied by an attorney.

(3) Before the hearing, each party to the hearing shall be given reasonable notice of the matters to be considered at the hearing, including a comprehensive statement of the basis for the action taken or proposed by the Secretary which is the subject of the hearing and a general summary of the information which will be presented by the Secretary at the hearing in support of such action.

(4) At the hearing the parties to the hearing shall have the right to hear a full and complete statement of the action of the Secretary which is the subject of the hearing together with the information and reasons supporting such action, to conduct reasonable questioning, and to present any oral or written information relevant to such action.

(5) The presiding officer in such hearing shall prepare a written report of the hearing to which shall be attached all written material presented at the hearing. The participants in the hearing shall be given the opportunity to review and correct or supplement the presiding officer's report of the hearing.

(6) The Secretary may require the hearing to be transcribed. A party to the hearing shall have the right to have the hearing transcribed at his expense. Any transcription of a hearing shall be included in the presiding officer's report of the hearing.

(y) The term "saccharin" includes calcium saccharin, sodium saccharin, and ammonium saccharin.

(z) The term "infant formula" means a food which purports to be or is represented for special dietary use solely as a food for infants by reason of its simulation of human milk or its suitability as a complete or partial substitute for human milk.

(aa) The term "abbreviated drug application" means an application submitted under section 505(j) for the approval of a drug that relies on the approved application of another drug with the same active ingredient to establish safety and efficacy, and —

(1) in the case of section 306, includes a supplement to such an application for a different or additional use of the drug but does not include a supplement to such an application for other than a different or additional use of the drug, and

(2) in the case of sections 307 and 308, includes any supplement to such an application.

(bb) The term "knowingly" or "knew" means that a person, with respect to information —

(1) has actual knowledge of the information, or

(2) acts in deliberate ignorance or reckless disregard of the truth or falsity of the information.

(cc) For purposes of section 306, the term "high managerial agent" —

(1) means —

(A) an officer or director of a corporation or an association,

(B) a partner of a partnership, or

(C) any employee or other agent of a corporation, association, or partnership,

having duties such that the conduct of such officer, director, partner, employee, or agent may fairly be assumed to represent the policy of the corporation, association, or partnership, and

(2) includes persons having management responsibility for —

(A) submissions to the Food and Drug Administration regarding the development or approval of any drug product,

(B) production, quality assurance, or quality control of any drug product, or

(C) research and development of any drug product.

(dd) For purposes of sections 306 and 307, the term "drug product" means a drug subject to regulation under section 505, 512, or 802 of this Act or under section 351 of the Public Health Service Act.

(ee) The term "Commissioner" means the Commissioner of Food and Drugs.

(ff) The term "dietary supplement" —

(1) means a product (other than tobacco) intended to supplement the diet that bears or contains one or more of the following dietary ingredients:

(A) a vitamin;

(B) a mineral;

(C) an herb or other botanical;

(D) an amino acid;

(E) a dietary substance for use by man to supplement the diet by increasing the total dietary intake; or

(F) a concentrate, metabolite, constituent, extract, or combination of any ingredient described in clause (A), (B), (C), (D), or (E);

(2) means a product that —

(A) —

(i) is intended for ingestion in a form described in section 411(c)(1)(B)(i); or

(ii) complies with section 411(c)(1)(B)(ii);

(B) is not represented for use as a conventional food or as a sole item of a meal or the diet; and

(C) is labeled as a dietary supplement; and

(3) does —

(A) include an article that is approved as a new drug under section 505 or licensed as a biologic under section 351 of the Public Health Service Act (42 U.S.C. 262) and was, prior to such approval, certification, or license, marketed as a dietary supplement or as a food unless the Secretary has issued a regulation, after notice and comment, finding that the article, when used as or in a dietary supplement under the conditions of use and dosages set forth in the labeling for such dietary supplement, is unlawful under section 402(f); and

(B) not include —

(i) an article that is approved as a new drug under section 505, certified as an antibiotic under section 507, or licensed as a biologic under section 351 of the Public Health Service Act (42 U.S.C. 262), or

(ii) an article authorized for investigation as a new drug, antibiotic, or biological for which substantial clinical investigations have been instituted and for which the existence of such investigations has been made public,

which was not before such approval, certification, licensing, or authorization marketed as a dietary supplement or as a food unless the Secretary, in the Secretary's discretion, has issued a regulation, after notice and comment, finding that the article would be lawful under this Act.

Except for purposes of section 201(g) and 417, a dietary supplement shall be deemed to be a food within the meaning of this Act.

(gg) The term "processed food" means any food other than a raw agricultural commodity and includes any raw agricultural commodity that has been subject to processing, such as canning, cooking, freezing, dehydration, or milling.

(hh) The term "Administrator" means the Administrator of the United States Environmental Protection Agency.

(ii) The term "compounded positron emission tomography drug" —

(1) means a drug that —

(A) exhibits spontaneous disintegration of unstable nuclei by the emission of positrons and is used for the purpose of providing dual photon positron emission tomographic diagnostic images; and

(B) has been compounded by or on the order of a practitioner who is licensed by a State to compound or order compounding for a drug described in subparagraph (A), and is compounded in accordance with the State's law, for a patient or for research, teaching, or quality control; and

(2) includes any nonradioactive reagent, reagent kit, ingredient, nuclide generator, accelerator, target material, electronic synthesizer, or other apparatus or computer program to be used in the preparation of such a drug.

(jj) The term "antibiotic drug" means any drug (except drugs for use in animals other than humans) composed wholly or partly of any kind of penicillin, streptomycin, chlortetracycline, chloramphenicol, bacitracin, or any other drug intended for human use containing any quantity of any chemical substance which is produced by a micro-organism and which has the capacity to inhibit or destroy micro-organisms in dilute solution (including a chemically synthesized equivalent of any such substance) or any derivative thereof.

(kk) The term "priority supplement" means a drug application referred to in section 101(4) of the Food and Drug Administration Modernization Act of 1997 (111 Stat. 2298).

(ll) —

(1) The term "single-use device" means a device that is intended for one use, or on a single patient during a single procedure.

(2) —

(A) The term "reprocessed", with respect to a single-use device, means an original device that has previously been used on a patient and has been subjected to additional processing and manufacturing for the purpose of an additional single use on a patient. The subsequent processing and manufacture of a reprocessed single-use device shall result in a device that is reprocessed within the meaning of this definition.

(B) A single-use device that meets the definition under clause (A) shall be considered a reprocessed device without regard to any description of the device used by the manufacturer of the device or other persons, including a description that uses the term "recycled" rather than the term "reprocessed".

(3) The term "original device" means a new, unused single-use device.

(mm) —

(1) The term "critical reprocessed single-use device" means a reprocessed single-use device that is intended to contact normally sterile tissue or body spaces during use.

(2) The term "semi-critical reprocessed single-use device" means a reprocessed single-use device that is intended to contact intact mucous membranes and not penetrate normally sterile areas of the body.

(nn) The term "major species" means cattle, horses, swine, chickens, turkeys, dogs, and cats, except that the Secretary may add species to this definition by regulation.

(oo) The term "minor species" means animals other than humans that are not major species.

(pp) The term "minor use" means the intended use of a drug in a major species for an indication that occurs infrequently and in only a small number of animals or in limited geographical areas and in only a small number of animals annually.

(qq) The term "major food allergen" means any of the following:

(1) Milk, egg, fish (e.g., bass, flounder, or cod), Crustacean shellfish (e.g., crab, lobster, or shrimp), tree nuts (e.g., almonds, pecans, or walnuts), wheat, peanuts, and soybeans.

(2) A food ingredient that contains protein derived from a food specified in paragraph (1), except the following:

(A) Any highly refined oil derived from a food specified in paragraph (1) and any ingredient derived from such highly refined oil.

(B) A food ingredient that is exempt under paragraph (6) or (7) of section 403(w).

(rr) —

(1) The term "tobacco product" means any product made or derived from tobacco that is intended for human consumption, including any component, part, or accessory of a tobacco product (except for raw materials other than tobacco used in manufacturing a component, part, or accessory of a tobacco product).

(2) The term "tobacco product" does not mean an article that is a drug under subsection (g)(1), a device under subsection (h), or a combination product described in section 503(g).

(3) The products described in paragraph (2) shall be subject to chapter V of this Act.

(4) A tobacco product shall not be marketed in combination with any other article or product regulated under this Act (including a drug, biologic, food, cosmetic, medical device, or a dietary supplement).

Sec.____. [321a] "Butter" Defined.

For the purposes of the Food and Drugs Act of June 30, 1906 (Thirty-fourth Statutes at Large, page 768) "butter" shall be understood to mean the food product usually known as butter, and which is made exclusively from milk or cream, or both, with or without common salt, and with or without additional coloring matter, and containing not less than 80 per centum by weight of milk fat, all tolerances having been allowed for.

Sec.____. [321b] "Package" Defined.

The word "package" where it occurs the second and last time in the act entitled "An Act to amend section 8 of an act entitled, 'An act for preventing the manufacture, sale, or transportation of adulterated or misbranded or poisonous deleterious foods, drugs, medicines, and liquors, and for regulating traffic therein, and for other purposes.'" approved March 3, 1913, shall include and shall be construed to include wrapped meats enclosed in papers or other materials as prepared by the manufacturers thereof for sale.

Sec.____. [321c] Nonfat Dry Milk; "Milk" Defined.

For the purposes of the Federal Food, Drug, and Cosmetic Act of June 26, 1938, (ch. 675, sec. 1, 52 Stat. 1040), nonfat dry milk is the product resulting from the removal of fat and water from milk, and contains the lactose, milk proteins, and milk minerals in the same relative proportions as in the fresh milk from which made. It contains not over 5 per centum by weight of moisture. The fat content is not over 1 1/2 per centum by weight unless otherwise indicated.

The term "milk", when used herein, means sweet milk of cows.

Sec.____. [321d] Market Names for Catfish and Ginseng.

(a) Catfish Labeling. —

(1) In General. — Notwithstanding any other provision of law, for purposes of the Federal Food, Drug, and Cosmetic Act (21 U.S.C. 301 et seq.) —

(A) the term "catfish" may only be considered to be a common or usual name (or part thereof) for fish classified within the family Ictaluridae; and

(B) only labeling or advertising for fish classified within that family may include the term "catfish".

(2) [Omitted.]*

(b) Ginseng Labeling. —

(1) In General. — Notwithstanding any other provision of law, for purposes of the Federal Food, Drug, and Cosmetic Act (21 U.S.C. 301 et seq.) —

(A) the term "ginseng" may only be considered to be a common or usual name (or part thereof) for any herb or herbal ingredient derived from a plant classified within the genus Panax; and

(B) only labeling or advertising for herbs or herbal ingredients classified within that genus may include the term "ginseng".

(2) [Omitted.]**

* Subsection (a)(2) added 21 U.S.C. 343(t).

** Subsection (b)(2) added 21 U.S.C. 343(u).

CHAPTER III — PROHIBITED ACTS AND PENALTIES

SEC. 301. [331] PROHIBITED ACTS.

The following acts and the causing thereof are hereby prohibited:

(a) The introduction or delivery for introduction into interstate commerce of any food, drug, device, tobacco product, or cosmetic that is adulterated or misbranded.

(b) The adulteration or misbranding of any food, drug, device, tobacco product, or cosmetic in interstate commerce.

(c) The receipt in interstate commerce of any food, drug, device, tobacco product, or cosmetic that is adulterated or misbranded, and the delivery or proffered delivery thereof for pay or otherwise.

(d) The introduction or delivery for introduction into interstate commerce of any article in violation of section 404, 415, 505, or 564.

(e) The refusal to permit access to or copying of any record as required by section 412, 414, 417(j); 504, 564, 703, or 704(a), 760, or 761; or the failure to establish or maintain any record, or make any report, required under section 412, 414(b), 416, 417, 504, 505 (i) or (k), 512(a)(4)(C), 512 (j), (l) or (m), 572(i), 515(f), 519, 564, 760, 761, 909, or 920 or the refusal to permit access to or verification or copying of any such required record; or the violation of any recordkeeping requirement under section 204 of the FDA Food Safety Modernization Act (except when such violation is committed by a farm).

(f) The refusal to permit entry or inspection as authorized by section 704.

(g) The manufacture within any Territory of any food, drug, device, tobacco product, or cosmetic that is adulterated or misbranded.

(h) The giving of a guaranty or undertaking referred to in section 303(c)(2) which guaranty or undertaking is false, except by a person who relied upon a guaranty or undertaking to the same effect signed by, and containing the name and address of, the person residing in the United States from whom he received in good faith the food, drug, device, tobacco product, or cosmetic; or the giving of a guaranty or undertaking referred to in section 303(c)(3), which guaranty or undertaking is false.

(i) —

> **(1)** Forging, counterfeiting, simulating, or falsely representing, or without proper authority using any mark, stamp, tag, label, or other identification device authorized or required by regulations promulgated under the provisions of section 404 or 721.
>
> **(2)** Making, selling, disposing of, or keeping in possession, control, or custody, or concealing any punch, die, plate, stone, or other thing designed to print, imprint, or reproduce the trademark, trade name, or other identifying mark, imprint, or device of another or any likeness of any of the foregoing upon any drug or container or labeling thereof so as to render such drugs a counterfeit drug.
>
> **(3)** The doing of any act which causes a drug to be a counterfeit drug, or the sale or dispensing, or the holding for sale or dispensing, of a counterfeit drug.

(j) The using by any person to his own advantage, or revealing, other than to the Secretary or officers or employees of the Department, or to the courts when relevant in any judicial proceeding under this Act, any information acquired under authority of section 404, 409, 412, 414, 505, 510, 512, 513, 514, 515, 516, 518, 519, 520, 571, 572, 573, 704, 708, 721, 904, 905, 906, 907, 908, 909, or 920(b) concerning any method or process which as a trade secret is entitled to protection; or the violating of section 408(i)(2) or any regulation issued under that section. This paragraph does not authorize the withholding of information from either House of Congress or from, to the extent of matter within its jurisdiction, any committee or subcommittee of such committee or any joint committee of Congress or any subcommittee of such joint committee.

(k) The alteration, mutilation, destruction, obliteration, or removal of the whole or any part of the labeling of, or the doing of any other act with respect to, a food, drug, device, tobacco product, or cosmetic, if such act is done while such article is held for sale (whether or not the first sale) after shipment in interstate commerce and results in such article being adulterated or misbranded.

(l) [Repealed.]

(m) The sale or offering for sale of colored oleomargarine or colored margarine, or the possession or serving of colored oleomargarine or colored margarine in violation of section 407(b) or 407(c).

(n) The using, in labeling, advertising or other sales promotion of any reference to any report or analysis furnished in compliance with section 704.

(o) In the case of a prescription drug distributed or offered for sale in interstate commerce, the failure of the manufacturer, packer, or distributor thereof to maintain for transmittal, or to transmit, to any practitioner licensed by applicable State law to administer such drug who makes written request for information as to such drug, true and correct copies of all printed matter which is required to be included in any package in which that drug is distributed or sold, or such other printed matter as is approved by the Secretary. Nothing in this paragraph shall be construed to exempt any person from any labeling requirement imposed by or under other provisions of this Act.

(p) The failure to register in accordance with section 510 or 905, the failure to provide any information required by section 510(j), 510(k), 905(i), or 905(j), or the failure to provide a notice required by section 510(j)(2) or 905(i)(3).

(q) —

(1) The failure or refusal to

(A) comply with any requirement prescribed under section 518, 520(g), 903(b), 907, 908, or 915,

(B) furnish any notification or other material or information required by or under section 519, 520(g), 904, 909, or 920; or

(C) comply with a requirement under section 522 or 913.

(2) With respect to any device or tobacco product, the submission of any report that is required by or under this Act that is false or misleading in any material respect.

(r) The movement of a device, drug, or tobacco product, in violation of an order under section 304(g) or the removal or alteration of any mark or label required by the order to identify the device, drug, or tobacco product as detained.

(s) The failure to provide the notice required by section 412(c) or 412(e), the failure to make the reports required by section 412(f)(1)(B), the failure to retain the records required by section 412(b)(4), or the failure to meet the requirements prescribed under section 412(f)(3).

(t) The importation of a drug in violation of section 801(d)(1), the sale, purchase, or trade of a drug or drug sample or the offer to sell, purchase, or trade a drug or drug sample in violation of section 503(c), the sale, purchase, or trade of a coupon, the offer to sell, purchase, or trade such a coupon, or the counterfeiting of such a coupon in violation of section 503(c)(2), the distribution of a drug sample in violation of section 503(d) or the failure to otherwise comply with the requirements of section 503(d), the distribution of drugs in violation of section 503(e), failure to comply with the requirements under section 582, the failure to comply with the requirements under section 584, as applicable, or the failure to otherwise comply with the requirements of section 503(e).

(u) The failure to comply with any requirements of the provisions of, or any regulations or orders of the Secretary, under section 512(a)(4)(A), 512(a)(4)(D), or 512(a)(5).

(v) The introduction or delivery for introduction into interstate commerce of a dietary supplement that is unsafe under section 413.

(w) The making of a knowingly false statement in any statement, certificate of analysis, record, or report required or requested under section 801(d)(3); the failure to submit a certificate of analysis as required under such section; the failure to maintain records or to submit records or reports as required by such section; the release into interstate commerce of any article or portion thereof imported into the United States under such section or any finished product made from such article or portion, except for export in accordance with section 801(e) or 802, or with section 351(h) of the Public Health Service Act; or the failure to so export or to destroy such an article or portions thereof, or such a finished product.

(x) The falsification of a declaration of conformity submitted under section 514(c) or the failure or refusal to provide data or information requested by the Secretary under paragraph (3) of such section.

(y) In the case of a drug, device, or food —

(1) the submission of a report or recommendation by a person accredited under section 523 that is false or misleading in any material respect;

(2) the disclosure by a person accredited under section 523 of confidential commercial information or any trade secret without the express written consent of the person who submitted such information or secret to such person; or

(3) the receipt of a person accredited under section 523 of a bribe in any form or the doing of any corrupt act by such person associated with a responsibility delegated to such person under this Act.

(z) The dissemination of information in violation of section 551.

(aa) The importation of a prescription drug in violation of section 804, the falsification of any record required to be maintained or provided to the Secretary under such section, or any other violation of regulations under such section.

(bb) The transfer of an article of food in violation of an order under section 304(h), or the removal or alteration of any mark or label required by the order to identify the article as detained.

(cc) The importing or offering for import into the United States of an article of food by, with the assistance of, or at the direction of, a person debarred under section 306(b)(3).

(dd) The failure to register in accordance with section 415.

(ee) The importing or offering for import into the United States of an article of food in violation of the requirements under section 801(m).

(ff) The importing or offering for import into the United States of a drug or device with respect to which there is a failure to comply with a request of the Secretary to submit to the Secretary a statement under section 801(o).

(gg) The knowing failure to comply with paragraph (7)(E) of section 704(g); the knowing inclusion by a person accredited under paragraph (2) of such section of false information in an inspection report under paragraph (7)(A) of such section; or the knowing failure of such a person to include material facts in such a report.

(hh) The failure by a shipper, carrier by motor vehicle or rail vehicle, receiver, or any other person engaged in the transportation of food to comply with the sanitary transportation practices by the Secretary under section 416.

(ii) The falsification of a report of a serious adverse event submitted to a responsible person (as defined under section 760 or 761) or the falsification of a serious adverse event report (as defined under section 760 or 761) submitted to the Secretary.

(jj) —

(1) The failure to submit the certification required by section 402(j)(5)(B) of the Public Health Service Act, or knowingly submitting a false certification under such section.

(2) The failure to submit clinical trial information required under subsection (j) of section 402 of the Public Health Service Act.

(3) The submission of clinical trial information under subsection (j) of section 402 of the Public Health Service Act at is false or misleading in any particular under paragraph (5)(D) of such subsection (j).

(kk) The dissemination of a television advertisement without complying with section 503B.

(ll) The introduction or delivery for introduction into interstate commerce of any food to which has been added a drug approved under section 505, a biological product licensed under section 351 of the Public Health Service Act, or a drug or a biological product for which substantial clinical investigations have been instituted and for which the existence of such investigations has been made public, unless —

(1) such drug or such biological product was marketed in food before any approval of the drug under section 505, before licensure of the biological product under such section 351, and before any substantial clinical investigations involving the drug or the biological product have been instituted;

(2) the Secretary, in the Secretary's discretion, has issued a regulation, after notice and comment, approving the use of such drug or such biological product in the food;

(3) the use of the drug or the biological product in the food is to enhance the safety of the food to which the drug or the biological product is added or applied and not to have independent biological or therapeutic effects on humans, and the use is in conformity with —

(A) a regulation issued under section 409 prescribing conditions of safe use in food;

(B) a regulation listing or affirming conditions under which the use of the drug or the biological product in food is generally recognized as safe;

(C) the conditions of use identified in a notification to the Secretary of a claim of exemption from the premarket approval requirements for food additives based on the notifier's determination that the use of the drug or the biological product in food is generally recognized as safe, provided that the Secretary has not questioned the general recognition of safety determination in a letter to the notifier;

(D) a food contact substance notification that is effective under section 409(h); or

(E) such drug or biological product had been marketed for smoking cessation prior to the date of the enactment of the Food and Drug Administration Amendments Act of 2007; or

(4) The drug is a new animal drug whose use is not unsafe under section 512.

(mm) The failure to submit a report or provide a notification required under section 417(d).

(nn) The falsification of a report or notification required under section 417(d).

(oo) The sale of tobacco products in violation of a no-tobacco-sale order issued under section 303(f).

(pp) The introduction or delivery for introduction into interstate commerce of a tobacco product in violation of section 911.

(qq) —

(1) Forging, counterfeiting, simulating, or falsely representing, or without proper authority using any mark, stamp (including tax stamp), tag, label, or other identification device upon any tobacco product or container or labeling thereof so as to render such tobacco product a counterfeit tobacco product.

(2) Making, selling, disposing of, or keeping in possession, control, or custody, or concealing any punch, die, plate, stone, or other item that is designed to print, imprint, or reproduce the trademark, trade name, or other identifying mark, imprint, or device of another or any likeness of any of the foregoing upon any tobacco product or container or labeling thereof so as to render such tobacco product a counterfeit tobacco product.

(3) The doing of any act that causes a tobacco product to be a counterfeit tobacco product, or the sale or dispensing, or the holding for sale or dispensing, of a counterfeit tobacco product.

(rr) The charitable distribution of tobacco products.

(ss) The failure of a manufacturer or distributor to notify the Attorney General and the Secretary of the Treasury of their knowledge of tobacco products used in illicit trade.

(tt) Making any express or implied statement or representation directed to consumers with respect to a tobacco product, in a label or labeling or through the media or advertising, that either conveys, or misleads or would mislead consumers into believing, that —

(1) the product is approved by the Food and Drug Administration;

(2) the Food and Drug Administration deems the product to be safe for use by consumers;

(3) the product is endorsed by the Food and Drug Administration for use by consumers; or

(4) the product is safe or less harmful by virtue of —

(A) its regulation or inspection by the Food and Drug Administration; or

(B) its compliance with regulatory requirements set by the Food and Drug Administration; including any such statement or representation rendering the product misbranded under section 903.

(uu) The operation of a facility that manufactures, processes, packs, or holds food for sale in the United States if the owner, operator, or agent in charge of such facility is not in compliance with section 418.

(vv) The failure to comply with the requirements under section 419.

(ww) The failure to comply with section 420.

(xx) The refusal or failure to follow an order under section 423.

(yy) The knowing and willful failure to comply with the notification requirement under section 417(h).

(zz) The importation or offering for importation of a food if the importer (as defined in section 805) does not have in place a foreign supplier verification program in compliance with such section 805.

(aaa) The failure to register in accordance with section 801(s).

(bbb) The failure to notify the Secretary in violation of section 568.

(ccc) —

(1) The resale of a compounded drug that is labeled "not for resale" in accordance with section 503B.

(2) With respect to a drug to be compounded pursuant to section 503A or 503B, the intentional falsification of a prescription, as applicable.

(3) The failure to report drugs or adverse events by an entity that is registered in accordance with subsection (b) of section 503B.

(ddd) **(1)** The manufacture or the introduction or delivery for introduction into interstate commerce of a rinse-off cosmetic that contains intentionally-added plastic microbeads.*

---

* Effective with respect to manufacture on July 1, 2017, and with respect to introduction or delivery for introduction into interstate commerce on July 1, 2018. Notwithstanding the foregoing, effective with respect to manufacture of a rinse-off cosmetic that is a nonprescription drug on July 1, 2018 and introduction or delivery for introduction into interstate commerce on July 1, 2019.

(2) In this paragraph

(A) the term "plastic microbead" means any solid plastic particle that is less than five millimeters in size and is intended to be used to exfoliate or cleanse the human body or any part thereof; and

(B) the term "rinse-off cosmetic" includes toothpaste.

Sec. 302. [332] Injunction Proceedings.

(a) The district courts of the United States and the United States courts of the Territories shall have jurisdiction, for cause shown to restrain violations of section 301, except paragraphs (h), (i), and (j).

(b) In case of violation of an injunction or restraining order issued under this section, which also constitutes a violation of this Act, trial shall be by the court, or, upon demand of the accused, by a jury.

Sec. 303. [333] Penalties.

(a) —

(1) Any person who violates a provision of section 301 shall be imprisoned for not more than one year or fined not more than $1,000, or both.

(2) Notwithstanding the provisions of paragraph (1) of this section, if any person commits such a violation after a conviction of him under this section has become final, or commits such a violation with the intent to defraud or mislead, such person shall be imprisoned for not more than three years or fined not more than $10,000 or both.

(b) —

(1) Notwithstanding subsection (a), any person who violates section 301(t) by —

(A) knowingly importing a drug in violation of section 801(d)(1),

(B) knowingly selling, purchasing, or trading a drug or drug sample or knowingly offering to sell, purchase, or trade a drug or drug sample, in violation of section 503(c)(1),

(C) knowingly selling, purchasing, or trading a coupon, knowingly offering to sell, purchase, or trade such a coupon, or knowingly counterfeiting such a coupon, in violation of section 503(c)(2), or

(D) knowingly distributing drugs in violation of section 503(e)(1) shall be imprisoned for not more than 10 years or fined not more than $250,000, or both.

(2) Any manufacturer or distributor who distributes drug samples by means other than the mail or common carrier whose representative, during the course of the representative's employment or association with that manufacturer or distributor, violated section 301(t) because of a violation of section 503(c)(1) or violated any State law prohibiting the sale, purchase, or trade of a drug sample subject to section 503(b) or the offer to sell, purchase, or trade such a drug sample shall, upon conviction of the representative for such violation, be subject to the following civil penalties:

(A) A civil penalty of not more than $50,000 for each of the first two such violations resulting in a conviction of any representative of the manufacturer or distributor in any 10-year period.

(B) A civil penalty of not more than $1,000,000 for each violation resulting in a conviction of any representative after the second conviction in any 10-year period.

For the purposes of this paragraph, multiple convictions of one or more persons arising out of the same event or transaction, or a related series of events or transactions, shall be considered as one violation.

(3) Any manufacturer or distributor who violates section 301(t) because of a failure to make a report required by section 503(d)(3)(E) shall be subject to a civil penalty of not more than $100,000.

(4) —

(A) If a manufacturer or distributor or any representative of such manufacturer or distributor provides information leading to the institution of a criminal proceeding against, and conviction of, any representative of that manufacturer or distributor for a violation of section 301(t) because of a sale, purchase, or trade or offer to purchase, sell, or trade a drug sample in violation of section 503(c)(1) or for a violation of State law prohibiting the sale, purchase, or trade or offer to sell, purchase, or trade a drug sample, the conviction of such representative shall not be considered as a violation for purposes of paragraph (2).

(B) If, in an action brought under paragraph (2) against a manufacturer or distributor relating to the conviction of a representative of such manufacturer or distributor for the sale, purchase, or trade of a drug or the offer to sell, purchase, or trade a drug, it is shown, by clear and convincing evidence —

(i) that the manufacturer or distributor conducted, before the institution of a criminal proceeding against such representative for the violation which resulted in such conviction, an investigation of events or transactions which would have led to the reporting of information leading to the institution of a criminal proceeding against, and conviction of, such representative for such purchase, sale, or trade or offer to purchase, sell, or trade, or

(ii) that, except in the case of the conviction of a representative employed in a supervisory function, despite diligent implementation by the manufacturer or distributor of an independent audit and security system designed to detect such a violation, the manufacturer or distributor could not reasonably have been expected to have detected such violation, e conviction of such representative shall not be considered as a conviction for purposes of paragraph (2).

(5) If a person provides information leading to the institution of a criminal proceeding against, and conviction of, a person for a violation of section 301(t) because of the sale, purchase, or trade of a drug sample or the offer to sell, purchase, or trade a drug sample in violation of section 503(c)(1), such person shall be entitled to one-half of the criminal fine imposed and collected for such violation but not more than $125,000.

(6) Notwithstanding subsection (a), any person who is a manufacturer or importer of a prescription drug under section 804(b) and knowingly fails to comply with a requirement of section 804(e) that is applicable to such manufacturer or importer, respectively, shall be imprisoned for not more than 10 years or fined not more than $250,000, or both.

(7) Notwithstanding subsection (a)(2), any person that knowingly and intentionally adulterates a drug such that the drug is adulterated under subsection (a)(1), (b), (c), or (d) of section 501 and has a reasonable probability of causing serious adverse health consequences or death to humans or animals shall be imprisoned for not more than 20 years or fined not more than $1,000,000, or both.

(8) Notwithstanding subsection (a), any person who violates section 301(i)(3) by knowingly making, selling or dispensing, or holding for sale or dispensing, a counterfeit drug shall be imprisoned for not more than 10 years or fined in accordance with title 18, United States Code, or both.

(c) No person shall be subject to the penalties of subsection (a)(1) of this section,

(1) for having received in interstate commerce any article and delivered it or proffered delivery of it, if such delivery or proffer was made in good faith, unless he refuses to furnish on request of an officer or employee duly designated by the Secretary the name and address of the person from whom he purchased or received such article and copies of all documents, if any there be, pertaining to the delivery of the article to him; or

(2) for having violated section 301(a) or (d), if he establishes a guaranty or undertaking signed by, and containing the name and address of, the person residing in the United States from whom he received in good faith the article, to the effect, in case of an alleged violation of section 301(a), that such article is not adulterated or misbranded, within the meaning of this Act, designating this Act, or to the effect, in case of an alleged violation of section 301(d), that such article is not an article which may not, under the provisions of section 404 or 505, be introduced into interstate commerce; or

(3) for having violated section 301(a), where the violation exists because the article is adulterated by reason of containing a color additive not from a batch certified in accordance with regulations promulgated by the Secretary under this Act, if such person establishes a guaranty or undertaking signed by, and containing the name and address of, the manufacturer of the color additive, to the effect that such color additive was from a batch certified in accordance with the applicable regulations promulgated by the Secretary under this Act; or

(4) for having violated section 301 (b), (c), or (k) by failure to comply with section 502(f) in respect to an article received in interstate commerce to which neither section 503(a) nor section 503(b)(1) is applicable, if the delivery or proffered delivery was made in good faith and the labeling at the time thereof contained the same directions for use and warning statements as were contained in the labeling at the time of such receipt of such article; or

(5) for having violated section 301(i)(2) if such person acted in good faith and had no reason to believe that use of the punch, die, plate, stone, or other thing involved would result in a drug being a counterfeit drug, or for having violated section 301(i)(3) if the person doing the act or causing it to be done acted in good faith and had no reason to believe that the drug was a counterfeit drug.

(d) No person shall be subject to the penalties of subsection (a)(1) of this section for a violation of section 301 involving misbranded food if the violation exists solely because the food is misbranded under section 403(a)(2) because of its advertising.

(e) —

(1) Except as provided in paragraph (2), whoever knowingly distributes, or possesses with intent to distribute, human growth hormone for any use in humans other than the treatment of a disease or other recognized medical condition, where such use has been authorized by the Secretary of Health and Human Services under section 505 and pursuant to the order of a physician, is guilty of an offense punishable by not more than 5 years in prison, such fines as are authorized by title 18, United States Code, or both.

(2) Whoever commits any offense set forth in paragraph (1) and such offense involves an individual under 18 years of age is punishable by not more than 10 years imprisonment, such fines as are authorized by title 18, United States Code, or both.

(3) Any conviction for a violation of paragraphs (1) and (2) of this subsection shall be considered a felony violation of the Controlled Substances Act for the purposes of forfeiture under section 413 of such Act.

(4) As used in this subsection the term "human growth hormone" means somatrem, somatropin, or an analogue of either of them.

(5) The Drug Enforcement Administration is authorized to investigate offenses punishable by this subsection.

(f) —

(1) —

(A) Except as provided in subparagraph (B), any person who violates a requirement of this Act which relates to devices shall be liable to the United States for a civil penalty in an amount not to exceed $15,000 for each such violation, and not to exceed $1,000,000 for all such violations adjudicated in a single proceeding. For purposes of the preceding sentence, a person accredited under paragraph (2) of section 704(g) who is substantially not in compliance with the standards of accreditation under such section, or who poses a threat to public health or fails to act in a manner that is consistent with the purposes of such section, shall be considered to have violated a requirement of this Act that relates to devices.

(B) Subparagraph (A) shall not apply —

(i) to any person who violates the requirements of section 519(a) or 520(f) unless such violation constitutes

(I) a significant or knowing departure from such requirements, or

(II) a risk to public health,

(ii) to any person who commits minor violations of section 519(e) or 519(g) (only with respect to correction reports) if such person demonstrates substantial compliance with such section, or

(iii) to violations of section 501(a)(2)(A) which involve one or more devices which are not defective.

(2) —

(A) Any person who introduces into interstate commerce or delivers for introduction into interstate commerce an article of food that is adulterated within the meaning of section 402(a)(2)(B) or any person who does not comply with a recall order under section 423 shall be subject to a civil money penalty of not more than $50,000 in the case of an individual and $250,000 in the case of any other person for such introduction or delivery, not to exceed $500,000 for all such violations adjudicated in a single proceeding.

(B) This paragraph shall not apply to any person who grew the article of food that is adulterated. If the Secretary assesses a civil penalty against any person under this paragraph, the Secretary may not use the criminal authorities under this section to sanction such person for the introduction or delivery for introduction into interstate commerce of the article of food that is adulterated. If the Secretary assesses a civil penalty against any person under this paragraph, the Secretary may not use the seizure authorities of section 304 or the injunction authorities of section 302 with respect to the article of food that is adulterated.

(C) In a hearing to assess a civil penalty under this paragraph, the presiding officer shall have the same authority with regard to compelling testimony or production of documents as a presiding officer has under section 408(g)(2)(B). The third sentence of paragraph (5)(A) shall not apply to any investigation under this paragraph.

(3) —

(A) Any person who violates section 301(jj) shall be subject to a civil monetary penalty of not more than $10,000 for all violations adjudicated in a single proceeding.

(B) If a violation of section 301(jj) is not corrected within the 30-day period following notification under section 402(j)(5)(C)(ii), the person shall, in addition to any penalty under subparagraph (A), be subject to a civil monetary penalty of not more than $10,000 for each day of the violation after such period until the violation is corrected.

(4) —

(A) Any responsible person (as such term is used in section 505–1) that violates a requirement of section 505(o), 505(p), or 505–1 shall be subject to a civil monetary penalty of—

(i) not more than $250,000 per violation, and not to exceed $1,000,000 for all such violations adjudicated in a single proceeding; or

(ii) in the case of a violation that continues after the Secretary provides written notice to the responsible person, the responsible person shall be subject to a civil monetary penalty of $250,000 for the first 30-day period (or any portion thereof) that the responsible person continues to be in violation, and such amount shall double for every 30-day period thereafter that the violation continues, not to exceed $1,000,000 for any 30-day period, and not to exceed $10,000,000 for all such violations adjudicated in a single proceeding.

(B) In determining the amount of a civil penalty under subparagraph (A)(ii), the Secretary shall take into consideration whether the responsible person is making efforts toward correcting the violation of the requirement of section 505(o), 505(p), or 505–1 for which the responsible person is subject to such civil penalty.

(C) In a hearing to assess a civil penalty under this paragraph, the presiding officer shall have the same authority with regard to compelling testimony or production of documents as a presiding officer has under section 408(g)(2)(B). The third sentence of paragraph (5)(A) shall not apply to any investigation under this paragraph.

(5) —

(A) A civil penalty under paragraph (1), (2), (3), (4), or (9) shall be assessed, or a no-tobacco-sale order may be imposed, by the Secretary by an order made on the record after opportunity for a hearing provided in accordance with this subparagraph and section 554 of title 5, United States Code. Before issuing such an order, the Secretary shall give written notice to the person to be assessed a civil penalty, or upon whom a no-tobacco-sale order is to be imposed, under such order of the Secretary's proposal to issue such order and provide such person an opportunity for a hearing on the order. In the course of any investigation, the Secretary may issue subpoenas requiring the attendance and testimony of witnesses and the production of evidence that relates to the matter under investigation.

(B) In determining the amount of a civil penalty, or the period to be covered by a no-tobacco-sale order, the Secretary shall take into account the nature, circumstances, extent, and gravity of the violation or violations and, with respect to the violator, ability to pay, effect on ability to continue to do business, any history of prior such violations, the degree of culpability, and such other matters as justice may require. A no-tobacco-sale order permanently prohibiting an individual retail outlet from selling tobacco products shall include provisions that allow the outlet, after a specified period of time, to request that the Secretary compromise, modify, or terminate the order.

(C) The Secretary may compromise, modify, or remit, with or without conditions, any civil penalty which may be assessed under paragraph (1), (2), (3), (4), or (9). The amount of such penalty, when finally determined, or the amount agreed upon in compromise, may be deducted from any sums owing by the United States to the person charged.

(D) The Secretary may compromise, modify, or terminate, with or without conditions, any no-tobacco-sale order.

(6) Any person who requested, in accordance with paragraph (5)(A), a hearing respecting the assessment of a civil penalty or the imposition of a no-tobacco-sale order and who is aggrieved by an order assessing a civil penalty or the imposition of a no-tobacco-sale order may file a petition for judicial review of such order with the United States Court of Appeals for the District of Columbia Circuit or for any other circuit in which such person resides or transacts business. Such a petition may only be filed within the 60-day period beginning on the date the order making such assessment was issued, or on which the no-tobacco-sale order was imposed, as the case may be.

(7) If any person fails to pay an assessment of a civil penalty —

(A) after the order making the assessment becomes final, and if such person does not file a petition for judicial review of the order in accordance with paragraph (6), or

(B) after a court in an action brought under paragraph (6) has entered a final judgment in favor of the Secretary,

the Attorney General shall recover the amount assessed (plus interest at currently prevailing rates from the date of the expiration of the 60-day period referred to in paragraph (6) or the date of such final judgment, as the case may be) in an action brought in any appropriate district court of the United States. In such an action, the validity, amount, and appropriateness of such penalty shall not be subject to review.

(8) If the Secretary finds that a person has committed repeated violations of restrictions promulgated under section 906(d) at a particular retail outlet then the Secretary may impose a no-tobacco-sale order on that person prohibiting the sale of tobacco products in that outlet. A no-tobacco-sale order may be imposed with a civil penalty under paragraph (1). Prior to the entry of a no-sale order under this paragraph, a person shall be entitled to a hearing pursuant to the procedures established through regulations of the Food and Drug Administration for assessing civil money penalties, including at a retailer's request a hearing by telephone, or at the nearest regional or field office of the Food and Drug Administration, or at a Federal, State, or county facility within 100 miles from the location of the retail outlet, if such a facility is available.

(g) —

(1) With respect to a person who is a holder of an approved application under section 505 for a drug subject to section 503(b) or under section 351 of the Public Health Service Act, any such person who disseminates or causes another party to disseminate a direct-to-consumer advertisement that is false or misleading shall be liable to the United States for a civil penalty in an amount not to exceed $250,000 for the first such violation in any 3-year period, and not to exceed $500,000 for each subsequent violation in any 3-year period. No other civil monetary penalties in this Act (including the civil penalty in section 303(f)(4)) shall apply to a violation regarding direct-to-consumer advertising. For purposes of this paragraph: (A) Repeated dissemination of the same or similar advertisement prior to the receipt of the written notice referred to in paragraph (2) for such advertisements shall be considered one violation. (B) On and after the date of the receipt of such a notice, all violations under this paragraph occurring in a single day shall be considered one violation. With respect to advertisements that appear in magazines or other publications that are published less frequently than daily, each issue date (whether weekly or monthly) shall be treated as a single day for the purpose of calculating the number of violations under this paragraph.

(2) A civil penalty under paragraph (1) shall be assessed by the Secretary by an order made on the record after providing written notice to the person to be assessed a civil penalty and an opportunity for a hearing in accordance with this paragraph and section 554 of title 5, United States Code. If upon receipt of the written notice, the person to be assessed a civil penalty objects and requests a hearing, then in the course of any investigation related to such hearing, the Secretary may issue subpoenas requiring the attendance and testimony of witnesses and the production of evidence that relates to the matter under investigation, including information pertaining to the factors described in paragraph (3).

(3) The Secretary, in determining the amount of the civil penalty under paragraph (1), shall take into account the nature, circumstances, extent, and gravity of the violation or violations, including the following factors:

(A) Whether the person submitted the advertisement or a similar advertisement for review under section 736A.

(B) Whether the person submitted the advertisement for review if required under section 503B.

(C) Whether, after submission of the advertisement as described in subparagraph (A) or (B), the person disseminated or caused another party to disseminate the advertisement before the end of the 45-day comment period.

(D) Whether the person incorporated any comments made by the Secretary with regard to the advertisement into the advertisement prior to its dissemination.

(E) Whether the person ceased distribution of the advertisement upon receipt of the written notice referred to in paragraph (2) for such advertisement.

(F) Whether the person had the advertisement reviewed by qualified medical, regulatory, and legal reviewers prior to its dissemination.

(G) Whether the violations were material.

(H) Whether the person who created the advertisement or caused the advertisement to be created acted in good faith.

(I) Whether the person who created the advertisement or caused the advertisement to be created has been assessed a civil penalty under this provision within the previous 1-year period.

(J) The scope and extent of any voluntary, subsequent remedial action by the person.

(K) Such other matters, as justice may require.

(4) —

(A) Subject to subparagraph (B), no person shall be required to pay a civil penalty under paragraph (1) if the person submitted the advertisement to the Secretary and disseminated or caused another party to disseminate such advertisement after incorporating each comment received from the Secretary.

(B) The Secretary may retract or modify any prior comments the Secretary has provided to an advertisement submitted to the Secretary based on new information or changed circumstances, so long as the Secretary provides written notice to the person of the new views of the Secretary on the advertisement and provides a reasonable time for modification or correction of the advertisement prior to seeking any civil penalty under paragraph (1).

(5) The Secretary may compromise, modify, or remit, with or without conditions, any civil penalty which may be assessed under paragraph (1). The amount of such penalty, when finally determined, or the amount charged upon in compromise, may be deducted from any sums owed by the United States to the person charged.

(6) Any person who requested, in accordance with paragraph (2), a hearing with respect to the assessment of a civil penalty and who is aggrieved by an order assessing a civil penalty, may file a petition for de novo judicial review of such order with the United States Court of Appeals for the District of Columbia Circuit or for any other circuit in which such person resides or transacts business. Such a petition may only be filed within the 60-day period beginning on the date the order making such assessments was issued.

(7) If any person fails to pay an assessment of a civil penalty under paragraph (1) —

(A) after the order making the assessment becomes final, and if such person does not file a petition for judicial review of the order in accordance with paragraph (6), or

(B) after a court in an action brought under paragraph (6) has entered a final judgment in favor of the Secretary, the Attorney General of the United States shall recover the amount assessed (plus interest at currently prevailing rates from the date of the expiration of the 60-day period referred to in paragraph (6) or the date of such final judgment, as the case may be) in an action brought in any appropriate district court of the United States. In such an action, the validity, amount, and appropriateness of such penalty shall not be subject to review.

Sec. 304. [334] Seizure.

(a) —

(1) Any article of food, drug, or cosmetic that is adulterated or misbranded when introduced into or while in interstate commerce or while held for sale (whether or not the first sale) after shipment in interstate commerce, or which may not, under the provisions of section 301(ll), 404, or 505, be introduced into interstate commerce, shall be liable to be proceeded against while in interstate commerce, or at any time thereafter, on libel of information and condemned in any district court of the United States or United States court of a Territory within the jurisdiction of which the article is found. No libel for condemnation shall be instituted under this Act, for any alleged misbranding if there is pending in any court a libel for condemnation proceeding under this Act based upon the same alleged misbranding, and not more than one such proceeding shall be instituted if no such proceeding is so pending, except that such limitations shall not apply

(A) when such misbranding has been the basis of a prior judgment in favor of the United States, in a criminal, injunction, or libel for condemnation proceeding under this Act, or

(B) when the Secretary has probable cause to believe from facts found, without hearing, by him or any officer or employee of the Department that the misbranded article is dangerous to health, or that the labeling of the misbranded article is fraudulent, or would be in a material respect misleading to the injury or damage of the purchaser or consumer.

In any case to where the number of libel for condemnation proceedings is limited as above provided the proceeding pending or instituted shall, on application of the claimant, seasonably made, be removed for trial to any district agreed upon by stipulation between the parties, or, in case of failure to so stipulate within a reasonable time, the claimant may apply to the court of the district in which the seizure has been made, and such court (after giving the United States attorney for such district reasonable notice and opportunity to be heard) shall by order, unless good cause to the contrary is shown, specify a district of reasonable proximity to the claimant's principal place of business to which the case shall be removed for trial.

(2) The following shall be liable to be proceeded against at any time on libel of information and condemned in any district court of the United States or United States court of a Territory within the jurisdiction of which they are found:

(A) Any drug that is a counterfeit drug,

(B) Any container of a counterfeit drug,

(C) Any punch, die, plate, stone, labeling, container, or other thing used or designed for use in making a counterfeit drug or drugs,

(D) Any adulterated or misbranded device, and

(E) Any adulterated or misbranded tobacco product.

(3) —

(A) Except as provided in subparagraph (B), no libel for condemnation may be instituted under paragraph (1) or (2) against any food which —

(i) is misbranded under section 403(a)(2) because of its advertising, and

(ii) is being held for sale to the ultimate consumer in an establishment other than an establishment owned or operated by a manufacturer, packer, or distributor of the food.

(B) A libel for condemnation may be instituted under paragraph (1) or (2) against a food described in subparagraph (A) if —

(i) —

(I) the food's advertising which resulted in the food being misbranded under section 403(a)(2) was disseminated in the establishment in which the food is being held for sale to the ultimate consumer,

(II) such advertising was disseminated by, or under the direction of, the owner or operator of such establishment, or

(III) all or part of the cost of such advertising was paid by such owner or operator; and

(ii) the owner or operator of such establishment used such advertising in the establishment to promote the sale of the food.

(b) The article, equipment, or other thing proceeded against shall be liable to seizure by process pursuant to the libel, and the procedure in cases under this section shall conform, as nearly as may be, to the procedure in admiralty; except that on demand of either party any issue of fact joined in any such case shall be tried by jury. When libel for condemnation proceedings under this section, involving the same claimant and the same issues of adulteration or misbranding, are pending in two or more jurisdictions, such pending proceedings, upon application of the claimant seasonably made to the court of one such jurisdiction, shall be consolidated for trial by order of such court, and tried in

(1) any district selected by the claimant where one of such proceedings is pending; or

(2) a district agreed upon by stipulation between the parties.

If no order for consolidation is so made within a reasonable time, the claimant may apply to the court of one such jurisdiction, and such court (after giving the United States attorney for such district reasonable notice and opportunity to be heard) shall by order, unless good cause to the contrary is shown, specify a district of reasonable proximity to the claimant's principal place of business, in which all such pending proceedings shall be consolidated for trial and tried. Such order of consolidation shall not apply so as to require the removal of any case the date for trial of which has been fixed. The court granting such order shall give prompt notification thereof to the other courts having jurisdiction of the cases covered thereby.

(c) The court at any time after seizure up to a reasonable time before trial shall by order allow any party to a condemnation proceeding, his attorney or agent, to obtain a representative sample of the article seized and a true copy of the analysis, if any, on which the proceeding is based and the identifying marks or numbers, if any, of the packages from which the samples analyzed were obtained.

(d) —

(1) Any food, drug, device, tobacco product, or cosmetic condemned under this section shall, after entry of the decree, be disposed of by destruction or sale as the court may, in accordance with the provisions of this section, direct and the proceeds thereof, if sold, less the legal costs and charges, shall be paid into the Treasury of the United States; but such article shall not be sold under such decree contrary to the provisions of this Act or the laws of the jurisdiction in which sold. After entry of the decree and upon the payment of the costs of such proceedings and the execution of a good and sufficient bond conditioned that such article shall not be sold or disposed of contrary to the provisions of this Act or the laws of any State or Territory in which sold, the court may by order direct that such article be delivered to the owner thereof to be destroyed or brought into compliance with the provisions of this Act under the supervision of an officer or employee duly designated by the Secretary, and the expenses of such supervision shall be paid by the person obtaining release of the article under bond. If the article was imported into the United States and the person seeking its release establishes

(A) that the adulteration, misbranding, or violation did not occur after the article was imported, and

(B) that he had no cause for believing that it was adulterated, misbranded, or in violation before it was released from customs custody, the court may permit the article to be delivered to the owner for exportation in lieu of destruction upon a showing by the owner that all of the conditions of section 801(e) can and will be met.

The provisions of this sentence shall not apply where condemnation is based upon violation of section 402(a)(1), (2), or (6), section 501(a)(3), section 502(j), or section 601 (a) or (d). Where such exportation is made to the original foreign supplier, then subparagraphs (A) and (B) of section 801(e)(1) and the preceding sentence shall not be applicable; and in all cases of exportation the bond shall be conditioned that the article shall not be sold or disposed of until the applicable conditions of section 801(e) have been met. Any person seeking to export an imported article pursuant to any of the provisions of this subsection shall establish that the article was intended for export at the time the article entered commerce. Any article condemned by reason of its being an article which may not, under section 404 or 505, be introduced into interstate commerce, shall be disposed of by destruction.

(2) The provisions of paragraph (1) of this subsection shall, to the extent deemed appropriate by the court, apply to any equipment or other thing which is not otherwise within the scope of such paragraph and which is referred to in paragraph (2) of subsection (a).

(3) Whenever in any proceeding under this section, involving paragraph (2) of subsection (a), the condemnation of any equipment or thing (other than a drug) is decreed, the court shall allow the claim of any claimant, to the extent of such claimant's interest, for remission or mitigation of such forfeiture if such claimant proves to the satisfaction of the court

(i) that he has not committed or caused to be committed any prohibited act referred to in such paragraph (2) and has no interest in any drug referred to therein,

(ii) that he has an interest in such equipment or other thing as owner or lienor or otherwise, acquired by him in good faith, and

(iii) that he at no time had any knowledge or reason to believe that such equipment or other thing was being or would be used in, or to facilitate, the violation of laws of the United States relating to counterfeit drugs.

(e) When a decree of condemnation is entered against the article, court costs and fees, and storage and other proper expenses, shall be awarded against the person, if any, intervening as claimant of the article.

(f) In the case of removal for trial of any case as provided by subsection (a) or (b) —

(1) The clerk of the court from which removal is made shall promptly transmit to the court in which the case is to be tried all records in the case necessary in order that such court may exercise jurisdiction.

(2) The court to which such case was removed shall have the powers and be subject to the duties for purposes of such case, which the court from which removal was made would have had, or to which such court would have been subject, if such case had not been removed.

(g) —

(1) If during an inspection conducted under section 704 of a facility or a vehicle, a device, drug, or tobacco product, which the officer or employee making the inspection has reason to believe is adulterated or misbranded is found in such facility or vehicle, such officer or employee may order the device, or drug, or tobacco product, detained (in accordance with regulations prescribed by the Secretary) for a reasonable period which may not exceed twenty days unless the Secretary determines that a period of detention greater than twenty days is required to institute an action under subsection (a) or section 302, in which case he may authorize a detention period of not to exceed thirty days. Regulations of the Secretary prescribed under this paragraph shall require that before a device may be ordered detained under this paragraph the Secretary or an officer or employee designated by the Secretary approve such order. A detention order under this paragraph may require the labeling or marking of a device, drug, or tobacco product, during the period of its detention for the purpose of identifying the device, drug, or tobacco product, as detained. Any person who would be entitled to claim a device, drug, or tobacco product, if it were seized under subsection (a) may appeal to the Secretary a detention of such device, drug, or tobacco product, under this paragraph. Within five days of the date an appeal of a detention is filed with the Secretary, the Secretary shall after affording opportunity for an informal hearing by order confirm the detention or revoke it.

(2) —

(A) Except as authorized by subparagraph (B), a device, drug, or tobacco product, subject to a detention order issued under paragraph (1) shall not be moved by any person from the place at which it is ordered detained until —

(i) released by the Secretary, or

(ii) the expiration of the detention period applicable to such order, whichever occurs first.

(B) A device or drug subject to a detention order under paragraph (1) may be moved —

(i) in accordance with regulations prescribed by the Secretary, and

(ii) if not in final form for shipment, at the discretion of the manufacturer of the device or drug for the purpose of completing the work required to put it in such form.

(h) Administrative Detention of Foods. —

(1) Detention Authority. —

(A) In General. — An officer or qualified employee of the Food and Drug Administration may order the detention, in accordance with this subsection, of any article of food that is found during an inspection, examination, or investigation under this Act conducted by such officer or qualified employee, if the officer or qualified employee has reason to believe that such article is adulterated or misbranded.

(B) Secretary's Approval. — An article of food may be ordered detained under subparagraph (A) only if the Secretary or an official designated by the Secretary approves the order. An official may not be so designated unless the official is the director of the district under this Act in which the article involved is located, or is an official senior to such director.

(2) Period of Detention. — An article of food may be detained under paragraph (1) for a reasonable period, not to exceed 20 days, unless a greater period, not to exceed 30 days, is necessary, to enable the Secretary to institute an action under subsection (a) or section 302. The Secretary shall by regulation provide for procedures for instituting such action on an expedited basis with respect to perishable foods.

(3) Security of Detained Article. — An order under paragraph (1) with respect to an article of food may require that such article be labeled or marked as detained, and shall require that the article be removed to a secure facility, as appropriate. An article subject to such an order shall not be transferred by any person from the place at which the article is ordered detained, or from the place to which the article is so removed, as the case may be, until released by the Secretary or until the expiration of the detention period applicable under such order, whichever occurs first. This subsection may not be construed as authorizing the delivery of the article pursuant to the execution of a bond while the article is subject to the order, and section 801(b) does not authorize the delivery of the article pursuant to the execution of a bond while the article is subject to the order.

(4) Appeal of Detention Order. —

(A) In General. — With respect to an article of food ordered detained under paragraph (1), any person who would be entitled to be a claimant for such article if the article were seized under subsection (a) may appeal the order to the Secretary. Within five days after such an appeal is filed, the Secretary, after providing opportunity for an informal hearing, shall confirm or terminate the order involved, and such confirmation by the Secretary shall be considered a final agency action for purposes of section 702 of title 5, United States Code. If during such five-day period the Secretary fails to provide such an opportunity, or to confirm or terminate such order, the order is deemed to be terminated.

(B) Effect of Instituting Court Action. — The process under subparagraph (A) for the appeal of an order under paragraph (1) terminates if the Secretary institutes an action under subsection (a) or section 302 regarding the article of food involved.

(i) Procedures for Promulgating Regulations. —

(1) In General. — In promulgating a regulation implementing this section, the Secretary shall —

(A) issue a notice of proposed rulemaking that includes the proposed regulation;

(B) provide a period of not less than 60 days for comments on the proposed regulation; and

(C) publish the final regulation not less than 30 days before the regulation's effective date.

(2) Restrictions. — Notwithstanding any other provision of Federal law, in implementing this section, the Secretary shall only promulgate regulations as described in paragraph (1).

Sec. 305. [335] Hearing Before Report of Criminal Violation.

Before any violation of this Act is reported by the Secretary to any United States attorney for institution of a criminal proceeding, the person against whom such proceeding is contemplated shall be given appropriate notice and an opportunity to present his views, either orally or in writing, with regard to such contemplated proceeding.

Sec. 306. [335a] Debarment, Temporary Denial of Approval, and Suspension.

(a) Mandatory Debarment; Certain Drug Applications. —

(1) Corporations, Partnerships, and Associations. — If the Secretary finds that a person other than an individual has been convicted, after the date of the enactment of this section, of a felony under Federal law for conduct relating to the development or approval, including the process for development or approval, of any abbreviated drug application, the Secretary shall debar such person from submitting, or assisting in the submission of, any such application.

(2) Individuals. — If the Secretary finds that an individual has been convicted of a felony under Federal law for conduct —

(A) relating to the development or approval, including the process for development or approval, of any drug product, or

(B) otherwise relating to the regulation of any drug product under this Act,

the Secretary shall debar such individual from providing services in any capacity to a person that has an approved or pending drug product application.

(b) Permissive Debarment; Certain Drug Applications; Food Imports. —

(1) In General. — The Secretary, on the Secretary's own initiative or in response to a petition, may, in accordance with paragraph (2), debar —

(A) a person other than an individual from submitting or assisting in the submission of any abbreviated drug application,

(B) an individual from providing services in any capacity to a person that has an approved or pending drug product application, or

(C) a person from importing an article of food or offering such an article for import into the United States.

(2) Persons Subject to Permissive Debarment; Certain Drug Applications. — The following persons are subject to debarment under subparagraph (A) or (B) of paragraph (1):

(A) Corporations, Partnerships, and Associations. — Any person other than an individual that the Secretary finds has been convicted —

(i) for conduct that —

(I) relates to the development or approval, including the process for the development or approval, of any abbreviated drug application; and

(II) is a felony under Federal law (if the person was convicted before the date of the enactment of this section, a misdemeanor under Federal law, or a felony under State law, or

(ii) of a conspiracy to commit, or aiding or abetting, a criminal offense described in clause (i) or a felony described in subsection (a)(1),

if the Secretary finds that the type of conduct which served as the basis for such conviction undermines the process for the regulation of drugs.

(B) Individuals. —

(i) Any individual whom the Secretary finds has been convicted of—

(I) a misdemeanor under Federal law or a felony under State law for conduct relating to the development or approval, including the process for development or approval, of any drug product or otherwise relating to the regulation of drug products under this Act, or

(II) a conspiracy to commit, or aiding or abetting, such criminal offense or a felony described in subsection (a)(2),

if the Secretary finds that the type of conduct which served as the basis for such conviction undermines the process for the regulation of drugs.

(ii) Any individual whom the Secretary finds has been convicted of—

(I) a felony which is not described in subsection (a)(2) or clause (i) of this subparagraph and which involves bribery, payment of illegal gratuities, fraud, perjury, false statement, racketeering, blackmail, extortion, falsification or destruction of records, or interference with, obstruction of an investigation into, or prosecution of, any criminal offense, or

(II) a conspiracy to commit, or aiding or abetting, such felony,

if the Secretary finds, on the basis of the conviction of such individual and other information, that such individual has demonstrated a pattern of conduct sufficient to find that there is reason to believe that such individual may violate requirements under this Act relating to drug products.

(iii) Any individual whom the Secretary finds materially participated in acts that were the basis for a conviction for an offense described in subsection (a) or in clause (i) or (ii) for which a conviction was obtained, if the Secretary finds, on the basis of such participation and other information, that such individual has demonstrated a pattern of conduct sufficient to find that there is reason to believe that such individual may violate requirements under this Act relating to drug products.

(iv) Any high managerial agent whom the Secretary finds—

(I) worked for, or worked as a consultant for, the same person as another individual during the period in which such other individual took actions for which a felony conviction was obtained and which resulted in the debarment under subsection (a)(2), or clause (i), of such other individual,

(II) had actual knowledge of the actions described in subclause (I) of such other individual, or took action to avoid such actual knowledge, or failed to take action for the purpose of avoiding such actual knowledge,

(III) knew that the actions described in subclause (I) were violative of law, and

(IV) did not report such actions, or did not cause such actions to be reported, to an officer, employee, or agent of the Department or to an appropriate law enforcement officer, or failed to take other appropriate action that would have ensured that the process for the regulation of drugs was not undermined, within a reasonable time after such agent first knew of such actions,

if the Secretary finds that the type of conduct which served as the basis for such other individual's conviction undermines the process for the regulation of drugs.

(3) Persons Subject to Permissive Debarment; Food Importation. — A person is subject to debarment under paragraph (1)(C) if—

(A) the person has been convicted of a felony for conduct relating to the importation into the United States of any food; or

(B) the person has engaged in a pattern of importing or offering for import adulterated food that presents a threat of serious adverse health consequences or death to humans or animals.

(4) Stay of Certain Orders. — An order of the Secretary under clause (iii) or (iv) of paragraph (2)(B) shall not take effect until 30 days after the order has been issued.

(c) Debarment Period and Considerations. —

(1) Effect of Debarment. — The Secretary —

(A) shall not accept or review (other than in connection with an audit under this section) any abbreviated drug application submitted by or with the assistance of a person debarred under subsection (a)(1) or (b)(2)(A) during the period such person is debarred,

(B) shall, during the period of a debarment under subsection (a)(2) or (b)(2)(B), debar an individual from providing services in any capacity to a person that has an approved or pending drug product application and shall not accept or review (other than in connection with an audit under this section) an abbreviated drug application from such individual, and

(C) shall, if the Secretary makes the finding described in paragraph (6) or (7) of section 307(a), assess a civil penalty in accordance with section 307.

(2) Debarment Periods. —

(A) In General. — The Secretary shall debar a person under subsection (a) or (b) for the following periods:

(i) The period of debarment of a person (other than an individual) under subsection (a)(1) shall not be less than 1 year or more than 10 years, but if an act leading to a subsequent debarment under subsection (a) occurs within 10 years after such person has been debarred under subsection (a)(1), the period of debarment shall be permanent.

(ii) The debarment of an individual under subsection (a)(2) shall be permanent.

(iii) The period of debarment of any person under paragraph (2) or (3) of subsection (b) shall not be more than 5 years.

The Secretary may determine whether debarment periods shall run concurrently or consecutively in the case of a person debarred for multiple offenses.

(B) Notification. — Upon a conviction for an offense described in subsection (a) or (b) or upon execution of an agreement with the United States to plead guilty to such an offense, the person involved may notify the Secretary that the person acquiesces to debarment and such person's debarment shall commence upon such notification.

(3) Considerations. — In determining the appropriateness and the period of a debarment of a person under subsection (b) and any period of debarment beyond the minimum specified in subparagraph (A)(i) of paragraph (2), the Secretary shall consider where applicable —

(A) the nature and seriousness of any offense involved,

(B) the nature and extent of management participation in any offense involved, whether corporate policies and practices encouraged the offense, including whether inadequate institutional controls contributed to the offense,

(C) the nature and extent of voluntary steps to mitigate the impact on the public of any offense involved, including the recall or the discontinuation of the distribution of suspect drugs, full cooperation with any investigations (including the extent of disclosure to appropriate authorities of all wrongdoing), the relinquishing of profits on drug approvals fraudulently obtained, and any other actions taken to substantially limit potential or actual adverse effects on the public health,

(D) whether the extent to which changes in ownership, management, or operations have corrected the causes of any offense involved and provide reasonable assurances that the offense will not occur in the future,

(E) whether the person to be debarred is able to present adequate evidence that current production of drugs subject to abbreviated drug applications and all pending abbreviated drug applications are free of fraud or material false statements, and

(F) prior convictions under this Act or under other Acts involving matters within the jurisdiction of the Food and Drug Administration.

(d) Termination of Debarment. —

(1) Application. — Any person that is debarred under subsection (a) (other than a person permanently debarred) or any person that is debarred under subsection (b) may apply to the Secretary for termination of the debarment under this subsection. Any information submitted to the Secretary under this paragraph does not constitute an amendment or supplement to pending or approved abbreviated drug applications.

(2) Deadline. — The Secretary shall grant or deny any application respecting a debarment which is submitted under paragraph (1) within 180 days of the date the application is submitted.

(3) Action by the Secretary. —

(A) Corporations. —

(i) Conviction Reversal. — If the conviction which served as the basis for the debarment of a person under subsection (a)(1) or paragraph (2)(A) or (3) of subsection (b) is reversed, the Secretary shall withdraw the order of debarment.

(ii) Application. — Upon application submitted under paragraph (1), the Secretary shall terminate the debarment of a person if the Secretary finds that —

(I) changes in ownership, management, or operations have fully corrected the causes of the offense involved and provide reasonable assurances that the offense will not occur in the future, and

(II) in applicable cases, sufficient audits, conducted by the Food and Drug Administration or by independent experts acceptable to the Food and Drug Administration, demonstrate that pending applications and the development of drugs being tested before the submission of an application are free of fraud or material false statements.

In the case of persons debarred under subsection (a)(1), such termination shall take effect no earlier than the expiration of one year from the date of the debarment.

(B) Individuals. —

(i) Conviction Reversal. — If the conviction which served as the basis for the debarment of an individual under subsection (a)(2) or clause (i), (ii), (iii), or (iv) of subsection (b)(2)(B) or subsection (b)(3) is reversed, the Secretary shall withdraw the order of debarment.

(ii) Application. — Upon application submitted under paragraph (1), the Secretary shall terminate the debarment of an individual who has been debarred under subsection (b)(2)(B) or subsection (b)(3) if such termination serves the interests of justice and adequately protects the integrity of the drug approval process or the food importation process, as the case may be.

(4) Special Termination. —

(A) Application. — Any person that is debarred under subsection (a)(1) (other than a person permanently debarred under subsection (c)(2)(A)(i)) or any individual who is debarred under subsection (a)(2) may apply to the Secretary for special termination of debarment under this subsection. Any information submitted to the Secretary under this subparagraph does not constitute an amendment or supplement to pending or approved abbreviated drug applications.

(B) Corporations. — Upon an application submitted under subparagraph (A), the Secretary may take the action described in subparagraph (D) if the Secretary, after an informal hearing, finds that —

(i) the person making the application under subparagraph (A) has demonstrated that the felony conviction which was the basis for such person's debarment involved the commission of an offense which was not authorized, requested, commanded, performed, or recklessly tolerated by the board of directors or by a high managerial agent acting on behalf of the person within the scope of the board's or agent's office or employment,

(ii) all individuals who were involved in the commission of the offense or who knew or should have known of the offense have been removed from employment involving the development or approval of any drug subject to section 505,

(iii) the person fully cooperated with all investigations and promptly disclosed all wrongdoing to the appropriate authorities, and

(iv) the person acted to mitigate any impact on the public of any offense involved, including the recall, or the discontinuation of the distribution, of any drug with respect to which the Secretary requested a recall or discontinuation of distribution due to concerns about the safety or efficacy of the drug.

(C) Individuals. — Upon an application submitted under subparagraph (A), the Secretary may take the action described in subparagraph (D) if the Secretary, after an informal hearing, finds that such individual has provided substantial assistance in the investigations or prosecutions of offenses which are described in subsection (a) or (b) or which relate to any matter under the jurisdiction of the Food and Drug Administration.

(D) Secretarial Action. — The action referred to in subparagraphs (B) and (C) is —

(i) in the case of a person other than an individual —

(I) terminating the debarment immediately, or

(II) limiting the period of debarment to less than one year, and

(ii) in the case of an individual, limiting the period of debarment to less than permanent but to no less than 1 year,

whichever best serves the interest of justice and protects the integrity of the drug approval process.

(e) Publication and List of Debarred Persons. — The Secretary shall publish in the Federal Register the name of any person debarred under subsection (a) or (b), the effective date of the debarment, and the period of the debarment. The Secretary shall also maintain and make available to the public a list, updated no less often than quarterly, of such persons, of the effective dates and minimum periods of such debarments, and of the termination of debarments.

(f) Temporary Denial of Approval. —

(1) In General. — The Secretary, on the Secretary's own initiative or in response to a petition, may, in accordance with paragraph (3), refuse by order, for the period prescribed by paragraph (2), to approve any abbreviated drug application submitted by any person —

(A) if such person is under an active Federal criminal investigation in connection with an action described in subparagraph (B),

(B) if the Secretary finds that such person —

(i) has bribed or attempted to bribe, has paid or attempted to pay an illegal gratuity, or has induced or attempted to induce another person to bribe or pay an illegal gratuity to any officer, employee, or agent of the Department of Health and Human Services or to any other Federal, State, or local official in connection with any abbreviated drug application, or has conspired to commit, or aided or abetted, such actions, or

(ii) has knowingly made or caused to be made a pattern or practice of false statements or misrepresentations with respect to material facts relating to any abbreviated drug application, or the production of any drug subject to an abbreviated drug application, to any officer, employee, or agent of the Department of Health and Human Services, or has conspired to commit, or aided or abetted, such actions, and

(C) if a significant question has been raised regarding —

(i) the integrity of the approval process with respect to such abbreviated drug application, or

(ii) the reliability of data in or concerning such person's abbreviated drug application.

Such an order may be modified or terminated at any time.

(2) Applicable Period. —

(A) In General. — Except as provided in subparagraph (B), a denial of approval of an application of a person under paragraph (1) shall be in effect for a period determined by the Secretary but not to exceed 18 months beginning on the date the Secretary finds that the conditions described in subparagraphs (A), (B), and (C) of paragraph (1) exist. The Secretary shall terminate such denial —

(i) if the investigation with respect to which the finding was made does not result in a criminal charge against such person, if criminal charges have been brought and the charges have been dismissed, or if a judgment of acquittal has been entered, or

(ii) if the Secretary determines that such finding was in error.

(B) Extension. — If, at the end of the period described in subparagraph (A), the Secretary determines that a person has been criminally charged for an action described in subparagraph (B) of paragraph (1), the Secretary may extend the period of denial of approval of an application for a period not to exceed 18 months. The Secretary shall terminate such extension if the charges have been dismissed, if a judgment of acquittal has been entered, or if the Secretary determines that the finding described in subparagraph (A) was in error.

(3) Informal Hearing. — Within 10 days of the date an order is issued under paragraph (1), the Secretary shall provide such person with an opportunity for an informal hearing, to be held within such 10 days, on the decision of the Secretary to refuse approval of an abbreviated drug application. Within 60 days of the date on which such hearing is held, the Secretary shall notify the person given such hearing whether the Secretary's refusal of approval will be continued, terminated, or otherwise modified. Such notification shall be final agency action.

(g) Suspension Authority. —

(1) In General. — If —

(A) the Secretary finds —

(i) that a person has engaged in conduct described in subparagraph (B) of subsection (f)(1) in connection with 2 or more drugs under abbreviated drug applications, or

(ii) that a person has engaged in flagrant and repeated, material violations of good manufacturing practice or good laboratory practice in connection with the development, manufacturing, or distribution of one or more drugs approved under an abbreviated drug application during a 2-year period, and —

(I) such violations may undermine the safety and efficacy of such drugs, and

(II) the causes of such violations have not been corrected within a reasonable period of time following notice of such violations by the Secretary, and

(B) such person is under an active investigation by a Federal authority in connection with a civil or criminal action involving conduct described in subparagraph (A),

the Secretary shall issue an order suspending the distribution of all drugs the development or approval of which was related to such conduct described in subparagraph (A) or suspending the distribution of all drugs approved under abbreviated drug applications of such person if the Secretary finds that such conduct may have affected the development or approval of a significant number of drugs which the Secretary is unable to identify. The Secretary shall exclude a drug from such order if the Secretary determines that such conduct was not likely to have influenced the safety or efficacy of such drug.

(2) Public Health Waiver. — The Secretary shall, on the Secretary's own initiative or in response to a petition, waive the suspension under paragraph (1) (involving an action described in paragraph (1)(A)(i)) with respect to any drug if the Secretary finds that such waiver is necessary to protect the public health because sufficient quantities of the drug would not otherwise be available. The Secretary shall act on any petition seeking action under this paragraph within 180 days of the date the petition is submitted to the Secretary.

(h) Termination of Suspension. — The Secretary shall withdraw an order of suspension of the distribution of a drug under subsection (g) if the person with respect to whom the order was issued demonstrates in a petition to the Secretary —

(1) —

(A) on the basis of an audit by the Food and Drug Administration or by experts acceptable to the Food and Drug Administration, or on the basis of other information, that the development, approval, manufacturing, and distribution of such drug is in substantial compliance with the applicable requirements of this Act, and

(B) changes in ownership, management, or operations —

(i) fully remedy the patterns or practices with respect to which the order was issued, and

(ii) provide reasonable assurances that such actions will not occur in the future, or **(2)** the initial determination was in error.

The Secretary shall act on a submission of a petition under this subsection within 180 days of the date of its submission and the Secretary may consider the petition concurrently with the suspension proceeding. Any information submitted to the Secretary under this subsection does not constitute an amendment or supplement to a pending or approved abbreviated drug application.

(i) Procedure. — The Secretary may not take any action under subsection (a), (b), (c), (d)(3), (g), or (h) with respect to any person unless the Secretary has issued an order for such action made on the record after opportunity for an agency hearing on disputed issues of material fact. In the course of any investigation or hearing under this subsection, the Secretary may administer oaths and affirmations, examine witnesses, receive evidence, and issue subpoenas requiring the attendance and testimony of witnesses and the production of evidence that relates to the matter under investigation.

(j) Judicial Review. —

(1) In General. — Except as provided in paragraph (2), any person that is the subject of an adverse decision under subsection (a), (b), (c), (d), (f), (g), or (h) may obtain a review of such decision by the United States Court of Appeals for the District of Columbia or for the circuit in which the person resides, by filing in such court (within 60 days following the date the person is notified of the Secretary's decision) a petition requesting that the decision be modified or set aside.

(2) Exception. — Any person that is the subject of an adverse decision under clause (iii) or (iv) of subsection (b)(2)(B) may obtain a review of such decision by the United States District Court for the District of Columbia or a district court of the United States for the district in which the person resides, by filing in such court (within 30 days following the date the person is notified of the Secretary's decision) a complaint requesting that the decision be modified or set aside. In such an action, the court shall determine the matter de novo.

(k) Certification. — Any application for approval of a drug product shall include —

(1) a certification that the applicant did not and will not use in any capacity the services of any person debarred under subsection (a) or (b), in connection with such application, and

(2) if such application is an abbreviated drug application, a list of all convictions, described in subsections (a) and (b) which occurred within the previous 5 years, of the applicant and affiliated persons responsible for the development or submission of such application.

(l) Applicability. —

(1) Conviction. — For purposes of this section, a person is considered to have been convicted of a criminal offense —

(A) when a judgment of conviction has been entered against the person by a Federal or State court, regardless of whether there is an appeal pending,

(B) when a plea of guilty or nolo contendere by the person has been accepted by a Federal or State court, or

(C) when the person has entered into participation in a first offender, deferred adjudication, or other similar arrangement or program where judgment of conviction has been withheld.

(2) Effective Dates. — Subsection (a), subparagraph (A) of subsection (b)(2), clauses (i) and (ii) of subsection (b)(2)(B), and subsection (b)(3)(A) shall not apply to a conviction which occurred more than 5 years before the initiation of an agency action proposed to be taken under subsection (a) or (b). Clauses (iii) and (iv) of subsection (b)(2)(B), subsection (b)(3)(B), and subsections (f) and (g) shall not apply to an act or action which occurred more than 5 years before the initiation of an agency action proposed to be taken under subsection (b), (f), or (g). Clause (iv) of subsection (b)(2)(B) shall not apply to an action which occurred before June 1, 1992. Subsection (k) shall not apply to applications submitted to the Secretary before June 1, 1992.

(m) Devices; Mandatory Debarment Regarding Third-Party Inspections and Reviews. —

(1) In General. — If the Secretary finds that a person has been convicted of a felony under section 301(gg), the Secretary shall debar such person from being accredited under section 523(b) or 704(g)(2) and from carrying out activities under an agreement described in section 803(b).

(2) Debarment Period. — The Secretary shall debar a person under paragraph (1) for the following periods:

(A) The period of debarment of a person (other than an individual) shall not be less than 1 year or more than 10 years, but if an act leading to a subsequent debarment under such paragraph occurs within 10 years after such person has been debarred under such paragraph, the period of debarment shall be permanent.

(B) The debarment of an individual shall be permanent.

(3) Termination of Debarment; Judicial Review; Other Matters. — Subsections (c)(3), (d), (e), (i), (j), and (l)(1) apply with respect to a person (other than an individual) or an individual who is debarred under paragraph (1) to the same extent and in the same manner as such subsections apply with respect to a person who is debarred under subsection (a)(1), or an individual who is debarred under subsection (a)(2), respectively.

Sec. 307. [335b] Civil Penalties.

(a) In General. — Any person that the Secretary finds —

(1) knowingly made or caused to be made, to any officer, employee, or agent of the Department of Health and Human Services, a false statement or misrepresentation of a material fact in connection with an abbreviated drug application,

(2) bribed or attempted to bribe or paid or attempted to pay an illegal gratuity to any officer, employee, or agent of the Department of Health and Human Services in connection with an abbreviated drug application,

(3) destroyed, altered, removed, or secreted, or procured the destruction, alteration, removal, or secretion of, any material document or other material evidence which was the property of or in the possession of the Department of Health and Human Services for the purpose of interfering with that Department's discharge of its responsibilities in connection with an abbreviated drug application,

(4) knowingly failed to disclose, to an officer or employee of the Department of Health and Human Services, a material fact which such person had an obligation to disclose relating to any drug subject to an abbreviated drug application,

(5) knowingly obstructed an investigation of the Department of Health and Human Services into any drug subject to an abbreviated drug application,

(6) is a person that has an approved or pending drug product application and has knowingly —

(A) employed or retained as a consultant or contractor, or

(B) otherwise used in any capacity the services of, a person who was debarred under section 306, or

(7) is an individual debarred under section 306 and, during the period of debarment, provided services in any capacity to a person that had an approved or pending drug product application,

shall be liable to the United States for a civil penalty for each such violation in an amount not to exceed $250,000 in the case of an individual and $1,000,000 in the case of any other person.

(b) Procedure. —

(1) In General. —

(A) Action by the Secretary. — A civil penalty under subsection (a) shall be assessed by the Secretary on a person by an order made on the record after an opportunity for an agency hearing on disputed issues of material fact and the amount of the penalty. In the course of any investigation or hearing under this subparagraph, the Secretary may administer oaths and affirmations, examine witnesses, receive evidence, and issue subpoenas requiring the attendance and testimony of witnesses and the production of evidence that relates to the matter under investigation.

(B) Action by the Attorney General. — In lieu of a proceeding under subparagraph (A), the Attorney General may, upon request of the Secretary, institute a civil action to recover a civil money penalty in the amount and for any of the acts set forth in subsection (a). Such an action may be instituted separately from or in connection with any other claim, civil or criminal, initiated by the Attorney General under this Act.

(2) Amount. — In determining the amount of a civil penalty under paragraph (1), the Secretary or the court shall take into account the nature, circumstances, extent, and gravity of the act subject to penalty, the person's ability to pay, the effect on the person's ability to continue to do business, any history of prior, similar acts, and such other matters as justice may require.

(3) Limitation on Actions. — No action may be initiated under this section —

(A) with respect to any act described in subsection (a) that occurred before the date of the enactment of this section, or

(B) more than 6 years after the date when facts material to the act are known or reasonably should have been known by the Secretary but in no event more than 10 years after the date the act took place.

(c) Judicial Review. — Any person that is the subject of an adverse decision under subsection (b)(1)(A) may obtain a review of such decision by the United States Court of Appeals for the District of Columbia or for the circuit in which the person resides, by filing in such court (within 60 days following the date the person is notified of the Secretary's decision) a petition requesting that the decision be modified or set aside.

(d) Recovery of Penalties. — The Attorney General may recover any civil penalty (plus interest at the currently prevailing rates from the date the penalty became final) assessed under subsection (b)(1)(A) in an action brought in the name of the United States. The amount of such penalty may be deducted, when the penalty has become final, from any sums then or later owing by the United States to the person against whom the penalty has been assessed. In an action brought under this subsection, the validity, amount, and appropriateness of the penalty shall not be subject to judicial review.

(e) Informants. — The Secretary may award to any individual (other than an officer or employee of the Federal Government or a person who materially participated in any conduct described in subsection (a)) who provides information leading to the imposition of a civil penalty under this section an amount not to exceed —

(1) $250,000, or

(2) one-half of the penalty so imposed and collected, whichever is less. The decision of the Secretary on such award shall not be reviewable.

Sec. 308. [335c] Authority to Withdraw Approval of Abbreviated Drug Applications.

(a) In General. — The Secretary —

(1) shall withdraw approval of an abbreviated drug application if the Secretary finds that the approval was obtained, expedited, or otherwise facilitated through bribery, payment of an illegal gratuity, or fraud or material false statement, and

(2) may withdraw approval of an abbreviated drug application if the Secretary finds that the applicant has repeatedly demonstrated a lack of ability to produce the drug for which the application was submitted in accordance with the formulations or manufacturing practice set forth in the abbreviated drug application and has introduced, or attempted to introduce, such adulterated or misbranded drug into commerce.

(b) Procedure. — The Secretary may not take any action under subsection (a) with respect to any person unless the Secretary has issued an order for such action made on the record after opportunity for an agency hearing on disputed issues of material fact. In the course of any investigation or hearing under this subsection, the Secretary may administer oaths and affirmations, examine witnesses, receive evidence, and issue subpoenas requiring the attendance and testimony of witnesses and the production of evidence that relates to the matter under investigation.

(c) Applicability. — Subsection (a) shall apply with respect to offenses or acts regardless of when such offenses or acts occurred.

(d) Judicial Review. — Any person that is the subject of an adverse decision under subsection (a) may obtain a review of such decision by the United States Court of Appeals for the District of Columbia or for the circuit in which the person abides, by filing in such court (within 60 days following the date the person is notified of the Secretary's decision) a petition requesting that the decision be modified or set aside.

Sec. 309. [336] Report of Minor Violations.

Nothing in this Act shall be construed as requiring the Secretary to report for prosecution, or for the institution of libel or injunction proceedings, minor violations of this Act whenever he believes that the public interest will be adequately served by a suitable written notice or warning.

Sec. 310. [337] Proceedings in Name of United States; Provision as to Subpoenas.

(a) Except as provided in subsection (b), all such proceedings for the enforcement, or to restrain violations, of this Act shall be by and in the name of the United States. Subpoenas for witnesses who are required to attend a court of the United States, in any district, may run into any other district in any proceeding under this section.

(b) —

(1) A State may bring in its own name and within its jurisdiction proceedings for the civil enforcement, or to restrain violations, of section 401, 403(b), 403(c), 403(d), 403(e), 403(f), 403(g), 403(h), 403(i), 403(k), 403(q), or 403(r) if the food that is the subject of the proceedings is located in the State.

(2) No proceeding may be commenced by a State under paragraph (1) —

(A) before 30 days after the State has given notice to the Secretary that the State intends to bring such proceeding,

(B) before 90 days after the State has given notice to the Secretary of such intent if the Secretary has, within such 30 days, commenced an informal or formal enforcement action pertaining to the food which would be the subject of such proceeding, or

(C) if the Secretary is diligently prosecuting a proceeding in court pertaining to such food, has settled such proceeding, or has settled the informal or formal enforcement action pertaining to such food.

In any court proceeding described in subparagraph (C), a State may intervene as a matter of right.

Sec. 311. [338] Extraterritorial Jurisdiction.

There is extraterritorial jurisdiction over any violation of this Act relating to any article regulated under this Act if such article was intended for import into the United States or if any act in furtherance of the violation was committed in the United States.

CHAPTER IV — FOOD

SEC. 401. [341] DEFINITIONS AND STANDARDS FOR FOOD.

Whenever in the judgment of the Secretary such action will promote honesty and fair dealing in the interest of consumers, he shall promulgate regulations fixing and establishing for any food, under its common or usual name so far as practicable, a reasonable definition and standard of identity, a reasonable standard of quality, or reasonable standards of fill of container. No definition and standard of identity and no standard of quality shall be established for fresh or dried fruits, fresh or dried vegetables, or butter, except that definitions and standards of identity may be established for avocados, cantaloupes, citrus fruits, and melons. In prescribing any standard of fill of container, the Secretary shall give due consideration to the natural shrinkage in storage and in transit of fresh natural food and to need for the necessary packing and protective material. In the prescribing of any standard of quality for any canned fruit or canned vegetable, consideration shall be given and due allowance made for the differing characteristics of the several varieties of such fruit or vegetable. In prescribing a definition and standard of identity for any food or class of food in which optional ingredients are permitted, the Secretary shall, for the purpose of promoting honesty and fair dealing in the interest of consumers, designate the optional ingredients which shall be named on the label. Any definition and standard of identity prescribed by the Secretary for avocados, cantaloupes, citrus fruits, or melons shall relate only to maturity and to the effects of freezing.

SEC. 402. [342] ADULTERATED FOOD.

A food shall be deemed to be adulterated —

(a) —

(1) If it bears or contains any poisonous or deleterious substance which may render it injurious to health; but in case the substance is not an added substance such food shall not be considered adulterated under this clause if the quantity of such substance in such food does not ordinarily render it injurious to health[; or]

(2) —

(A) if it bears or contains any added poisonous or added deleterious substance (other than a substance that is a pesticide chemical residue in or on a raw agricultural commodity or processed food, a food additive, a color additive, or a new animal drug) that is unsafe within the meaning of section 406; or

(B) if it bears or contains a pesticide chemical residue that is unsafe within the meaning of section 408(a); or

(C) if it is or if it bears or contains

(i) any food additive that is unsafe within the meaning of section 409; or

(ii) a new animal drug (or conversion product thereof) that is unsafe within the meaning of section 512; or

(3) if it consists in whole or in part of any filthy, putrid, or decomposed substance, or if it is otherwise unfit for food; or

(4) if it has been prepared, packed, or held under insanitary conditions whereby it may have become contaminated with filth, or whereby it may have been rendered injurious to health; or

(5) if it is, in whole or in part, the product of a diseased animal or of an animal which has died otherwise than by slaughter; or

(6) if its container is composed, in whole or in part, of any poisonous or deleterious substance which may render the contents injurious to health; or

(7) if it has been intentionally subjected to radiation, unless the use of the radiation was in conformity with a regulation or exemption in effect pursuant to section 409.

(b) —

(1) If any valuable constituent has been in whole or in part omitted or abstracted therefrom; or

(2) if any substance has been substituted wholly or in part therefor; or

(3) if damage or inferiority has been concealed in any manner; or

(4) if any substance has been added thereto or mixed or packed therewith so as to increase its bulk or weight, or reduce its quality or strength, or make it appear better or of greater value than it is.

(c) If it is, or it bears or contains, a color additive which is unsafe within the meaning of section 721(a).

(d) If it is confectionery, and —

(1) has partially or completely imbedded therein any nonnutritive object, except that this subparagraph shall not apply in the case of any nonnutritive object if, in the judgment of the Secretary as provided by regulations, such object is of practical functional value to the confectionery product and would not render the product injurious or hazardous to health;

(2) bears or contains any alcohol other than alcohol not in excess of one-half of 1 per centum by volume derived solely from the use of flavoring extracts, except that this clause shall not apply to confectionery which is introduced or delivered for introduction into, or received or held for sale in, interstate commerce if the sale of such confectionery is permitted under the laws of the State in which such confectionery is intended to be offered for sale; or

(3) bears or contains any nonnutritive substance, except that this subparagraph shall not apply to a safe nonnutritive substance which is in or on confectionery by reason of its use for some practical functional purpose in the manufacture, packaging, or storage of such confectionery if the use of the substance does not promote deception of the consumer or otherwise result in adulteration or misbranding in violation of any provision of this Act, except that the Secretary may, for the purpose of avoiding or resolving uncertainty as to the application of this subparagraph, issue regulations allowing or prohibiting the use of particular nonnutritive substances.

(e) If it is oleomargarine or margarine or butter and any of the raw material used therein consisted in whole or in part of any filthy, putrid, or decomposed substance, or such oleomargarine or margarine or butter is otherwise unfit for food.

(f) —

(1) If it is a dietary supplement or contains a dietary ingredient that —

(A) presents a significant or unreasonable risk of illness or injury under —

(i) conditions of use recommended or suggested in labeling, or

(ii) if no conditions of use are suggested or recommended in the labeling, under ordinary conditions of use;

(B) is a new dietary ingredient for which there is inadequate information to provide reasonable assurance that such ingredient does not present a significant or unreasonable risk of illness or injury;

(C) the Secretary declares to pose an imminent hazard to public health or safety, except that the authority to make such declaration shall not be delegated and the Secretary shall promptly after such a declaration initiate a proceeding in accordance with sections 554 and 556 of title 5, United States Code, to affirm or withdraw the declaration; or

(D) is or contains a dietary ingredient that renders it adulterated under paragraph (a)(1) under the conditions of use recommended or suggested in the labeling of such dietary supplement.

In any proceeding under this subparagraph, the United States shall bear the burden of proof on each element to show that a dietary supplement is adulterated. The court shall decide any issue under this paragraph on a de novo basis.

(2) Before the Secretary may report to a United States attorney a violation of paragraph (1)(A) for a civil proceeding, the person against whom such proceeding would be initiated shall be given appropriate notice and the opportunity to present views, orally and in writing, at least 10 days before such notice, with regard to such proceeding.

(g) —

(1) If it is a dietary supplement and it has been prepared, packed, or held under conditions that do not meet current good manufacturing practice regulations, including regulations requiring, when necessary, expiration date labeling, issued by the Secretary under subparagraph (2).

(2) The Secretary may by regulation prescribe good manufacturing practices for dietary supplements. Such regulations shall be modeled after current good manufacturing practice regulations for food and may not impose standards for which there is no current and generally available analytical methodology. No standard of current good manufacturing practice may be imposed unless such standard is included in a regulation promulgated after notice and opportunity for comment in accordance with chapter 5 of title 5, United States Code.

(h) If it is an article of food imported or offered for import into the United States and the article of food has previously been refused admission under section 801(a), unless the person reoffering the article affirmatively establishes, at the expense of the owner or consignee of the article, that the article complies with the applicable requirements of this Act, as determined by the Secretary.

(i) If it is transported or offered for transportation by a shipper, carrier by motor vehicle or rail vehicle, receiver, or any other person engaged in the transportation of food under conditions that are not in accordance with regulations promulgated under section 416.

Sec. 403. [343] Misbranded Food.

A food shall be deemed to be misbranded —

(a) If —

(1) its labeling is false or misleading in any particular, or

(2) in the case of a food to which section 411 applies, its advertising is false or misleading in a material respect or its labeling is in violation of section 411(b)(2).

(b) If it is offered for sale under the name of another food.

(c) If it is an imitation of another food, unless its label bears, in type of uniform size and prominence, the word "imitation" and, immediately thereafter, the name of the food imitated.

(d) If its container is so made, formed, or filled as to be misleading.

(e) If in package form unless it bears a label containing

(1) the name and place of business of the manufacturer, packer, or distributor; and

(2) an accurate statement of the quantity of the contents in terms of weight, measure, or numerical count,

except that under clause (2) of this paragraph reasonable variations shall be permitted, and exemptions as to small packages shall be established, by regulations prescribed by the Secretary.

(f) If any word, statement, or other information required by or under authority of this Act to appear on the label or labeling is not prominently placed thereon with such conspicuousness (as compared with other words, statements, designs, or devices, in the labeling) and in such terms as to render it likely to be read and understood by the ordinary individual under customary conditions of purchase and use.

(g) If it purports to be or is represented as a food for which a definition and standard of identity has been prescribed by regulations as provided by section 401, unless

(1) it conforms to such definition and standard, and

(2) its label bears the name of the food specified in the definition and standard, and, insofar as may be required by such regulations, the common names of optional ingredients (other than spices, flavoring, and coloring) present in such food.

(h) If it purports to be or is represented as —

(1) a food for which a standard of quality has been prescribed by regulations as provided by section 401, and its quality falls below such standard, unless its label bears, in such manner and form as such regulations specify, a statement that it falls below such standard;

(2) a food for which a standard or standards of fill of container have been prescribed by regulations as provided by section 401, and it falls below the standard of fill of container applicable thereto, unless its label bears, in such manner and form as such regulations specify, a statement that it falls below such standard; or

(3) a food that is pasteurized unless —

(A) such food has been subjected to a safe process or treatment that is prescribed as pasteurization for such food in a regulation promulgated under this Act; or

(B) —

(i) such food has been subjected to a safe process or treatment that —

(I) is reasonably certain to achieve destruction or elimination in the food of the most resistant micro-organisms of public health significance that are likely to occur in the food;

(II) is at least as protective of the public health as a process or treatment described in subparagraph (A);

(III) is effective for a period that is at least as long as the shelf life of the food when stored under normal and moderate abuse conditions; and

(IV) is the subject of a notification to the Secretary, including effectiveness data regarding the process or treatment; and

(ii) at least 120 days have passed after the date of receipt of such notification by the Secretary without the Secretary making a determination that the process or treatment involved has not been shown to meet the requirements of subclauses (I) through (III) of clause (i).

For purposes of paragraph (3), a determination by the Secretary that a process or treatment has not been shown to meet the requirements of subclauses (I) through (III) of subparagraph (B)(i) shall constitute final agency action under such subclauses.

(i) Unless its label bears

(1) the common or usual name of the food, if any there be, and

(2) in case it is fabricated from two or more ingredients, the common or usual name of each such ingredient and if the food purports to be a beverage containing vegetable or fruit juice, a statement with appropriate prominence on the information panel of the total percentage of such fruit or vegetable juice contained in the food;

except that spices, flavorings, and colors not required to be certified under section 721(c) unless sold as spices, flavorings, or such colors, may be designated as spices, flavorings, and colorings without naming each. To the extent that compliance with the requirements of clause (2) of this paragraph is impracticable, or results in deception or unfair competition, exemptions shall be established by regulations promulgated by the Secretary.

(j) If it purports to be or is represented for special dietary uses, unless its label bears such information concerning its vitamin, mineral, and other dietary properties as the Secretary determines to be, and by regulations prescribes as, necessary in order fully to inform purchasers as to its value for such uses.

(k) If it bears or contains any artificial flavoring, artificial coloring, or chemical preservative, unless it bears labeling stating that fact, except that to the extent that compliance with the requirements of this paragraph is impracticable, exemptions shall be established by regulations promulgated by the Secretary. The provisions of this paragraph and paragraphs (g) and (i) with respect to artificial coloring shall not apply in the case of butter, cheese, or ice cream. The provisions of this paragraph with respect to chemical preservatives shall not apply to a pesticide chemical when used in or on a raw agricultural commodity which is the produce of the soil.

(l) If it is a raw agricultural commodity which is the produce of the soil, bearing or containing a pesticide chemical applied after harvest, unless the shipping container of such commodity bears labeling which declares the presence of such chemical in or on such commodity and the common or usual name and the function of such chemical, except that no such declaration shall be required while such commodity, having been removed from the shipping container, is being held or displayed for sale at retail out of such container in accordance with the custom of the trade.

(m) If it is a color additive, unless its packaging and labeling are in conformity with such packaging and labeling requirements, applicable to such color additive, as may be contained in regulations issued under section 721.

(n) If its packaging or labeling is in violation of an applicable regulation issued pursuant to section 3 or 4 of the Poison Prevention Packaging Act of 1970.

(o) [Repealed.]

(p) [Repealed.]

(q) —

(1) Except as provided in subparagraphs (3), (4), and (5), if it is a food intended for human consumption and is offered for sale, unless its label or labeling bears nutrition information that provides —

(A) —

(i) the serving size which is an amount customarily consumed and which is expressed in a common household measure that is appropriate to the food, or

(ii) if the use of the food is not typically expressed in a serving size, the common household unit of measure that expresses the serving size of the food,

(B) the number of servings or other units of measure per container,

(C) the total number of calories —

(i) derived from any source, and

(ii) derived from the total fat,

in each serving size or other unit of measure of the food,

(D) the amount of the following nutrients: Total fat, saturated fat, cholesterol, sodium, total carbohydrates, complex carbohydrates, sugars, dietary fiber, and total protein contained in each serving size or other unit of measure,

(E) any vitamin, mineral, or other nutrient required to be placed on the label and labeling of food under this Act before October 1, 1990, if the Secretary determines that such information will assist consumers in maintaining healthy dietary practices.

The Secretary may by regulation require any information required to be placed on the label or labeling by this subparagraph or subparagraph (2)(A) to be highlighted on the label or labeling by larger type, bold type, or contrasting color if the Secretary determines that such highlighting will assist consumers in maintaining healthy dietary practices.

(2) —

(A) If the Secretary determines that a nutrient other than a nutrient required by subparagraph (1)(C), (1)(D), or (1)(E) should be included in the label or labeling of food subject to subparagraph (1) for purposes of providing information regarding the nutritional value of such food that will assist consumers in maintaining healthy dietary practices, the Secretary may by regulation require that information relating to such additional nutrient be included in the label or labeling of such food.

(B) If the Secretary determines that the information relating to a nutrient required by subparagraph (1)(C), (1)(D), or (1)(E) or clause (A) of this subparagraph to be included in the label or labeling of food is not necessary to assist consumers in maintaining healthy dietary practices, the Secretary may by regulation remove information relating to such nutrient from such requirement.

(3) For food that is received in bulk containers at a retail establishment, the Secretary may, by regulation, provide that the nutrition information required by subparagraphs (1) and (2) be displayed at the location in the retail establishment at which the food is offered for sale.

(4) —

(A) The Secretary shall provide for furnishing the nutrition information required by subparagraphs (1) and (2) with respect to raw agricultural commodities and raw fish by issuing voluntary nutrition guidelines, as provided by clause (B) or by issuing regulations that are mandatory as provided by clause (D).

(B) —

(i) Upon the expiration of 12 months after the date of the enactment of the Nutrition Labeling and Education Act of 1990 [November 8, 1991 — Ed.], the Secretary, after providing an opportunity for comment, shall issue guidelines for food retailers offering raw agricultural commodities or raw fish to provide nutrition information specified in subparagraphs (1) and (2). Such guidelines shall take into account the actions taken by food retailers during such 12-month period to provide to consumers nutrition information on raw agricultural commodities and raw fish. Such guidelines shall only apply —

(I) in the case of raw agricultural commodities, to the 20 varieties of vegetables most frequently consumed during a year and the 20 varieties of fruit most frequently consumed during a year, and

(II) to the 20 varieties of raw fish most frequently consumed during a year.

The vegetables, fruits, and raw fish to which such guidelines apply shall be determined by the Secretary by regulation and the Secretary may apply such guidelines regionally.

(ii) Upon the expiration of 12 months after the date of the enactment of the Nutrition Labeling and Education Act of 1990 [November 8, 1991 — Ed.], the Secretary shall issue a final regulation defining the circumstances that constitute substantial compliance by food retailers with the guidelines issued under subclause (i). The regulation shall provide that there is not substantial compliance if a significant number of retailers have failed to comply with the guidelines. The size of the retailers and the portion of the market served by retailers in compliance with the guidelines shall be considered in determining whether the substantial-compliance standard has been met.

(C) —

(i) Upon the expiration of 30 months after the date of the enactment of the Nutrition Labeling and Education Act of 1990 [May 8, 1993 — Ed.], the Secretary shall issue a report on actions taken by food retailers to provide consumers with nutrition information for raw agricultural commodities and raw fish under the guidelines issued under clause (A). Such report shall include a determination of whether there is substantial compliance with the guidelines.

(ii) If the Secretary finds that there is substantial compliance with the guidelines, the Secretary shall issue a report and make a determination of the type required in subclause (i) every two years.

(D) —

(i) If the Secretary determines that there is not substantial compliance with the guidelines issued under clause (A), the Secretary shall at the time such determination is made issue proposed regulations requiring that any person who offers raw agricultural commodities or raw fish to consumers provide, in a manner prescribed by regulations, the nutrition information required by subparagraphs (1) and (2). The Secretary shall issue final regulations imposing such requirements 6 months after issuing the proposed regulations. The final regulations shall become effective 6 months after the date of their promulgation.

(ii) Regulations issued under subclause (i) may require that the nutrition information required by subparagraphs (1) and (2) be provided for more than 20 varieties of vegetables, 20 varieties of fruit, and 20 varieties of fish most frequently consumed during a year if the Secretary finds that a larger number of such products are frequently consumed. Such regulations shall permit such information to be provided in a single location in each area in which raw agricultural commodities and raw fish are offered for sale. Such regulations may provide that information shall be expressed as an average or range per serving of the same type of raw agricultural commodity or raw fish. The Secretary shall develop and make available to the persons who offer such food to consumers the information required by subparagraphs (1) and (2).

(iii) Regulations issued under subclause (i) shall permit the required information to be provided in each area of an establishment in which raw agricultural commodities and raw fish are offered for sale. The regulations shall permit food retailers to display the required information by supplying copies of the information provided by the Secretary, by making the information available in brochure, notebook or leaflet form, or by posting a sign disclosing the information. Such regulations shall also permit presentation of the required information to be supplemented by a video, live demonstration, or other media which the Secretary approves.

(E) For purposes of this subparagraph, the term "fish" includes freshwater or marine fin fish, crustaceans, and mollusks, including shellfish, amphibians, and other forms of aquatic animal life.

(F) No person who offers raw agricultural commodities or raw fish to consumers may be prosecuted for minor violations of this subparagraph if there has been substantial compliance with the requirements of this paragraph.

(5) —

(A) Subparagraphs (1), (2), (3), and (4) shall not apply to food —

(i) except as provided in clause (H)(ii)(III), which is served in restaurants or other establishments in which food is served for immediate human consumption or which is sold for sale or use in such establishments,

(ii) except as provided in clause (H)(ii)(III), which is processed and prepared primarily in a retail establishment, which is ready for human consumption, which is of the type described in subclause (i), and which is offered for sale to consumers but not for immediate human consumption in such establishment and which is not offered for sale outside such establishment,

(iii) which is an infant formula subject to section 412,

(iv) which is a medical food as defined in section 5(b) of the Orphan Drug Act (21 U.S.C. 360ee(b)), or

(v) which is described in section 405(2).

(B) Subparagraphs (1) and (2) shall not apply to the label of a food if the Secretary determines by regulations that compliance with such subparagraphs is impracticable because the package of such food is too small to comply with the requirements of such subparagraphs and if the label of such food does not contain any nutrition information.

(C) If a food contains insignificant amounts, as determined by the Secretary, of all the nutrients required by subparagraphs (1) and (2) to be listed in the label or labeling of food, the requirements of such subparagraphs shall not apply to such food if the label, labeling, or advertising of such food does not make any claim with respect to the nutritional value of such food. If a food contains insignificant amounts, as determined by the Secretary, of more than one-half the nutrients required by subparagraphs (1) and (2) to be in the label or labeling of the food, the Secretary shall require the amounts of such nutrients to be stated in a simplified form prescribed by the Secretary.

(D) If a person offers food for sale and has annual gross sales made or business done in sales to consumers which is not more than $500,000 or has annual gross sales made or business done in sales of food to consumers which is not more than $50,000, the requirements of subparagraphs (1), (2), (3), and (4) shall not apply with respect to food sold by such person to consumers unless the label or labeling of food offered by such person provides nutrition information or makes a nutrition claim.

(E) —

(i) During the 12-month period for which an exemption from subparagraphs (1) and (2) is claimed pursuant to this subclause, the requirements of such subparagraphs shall not apply to any food product if—

(I) the labeling for such product does not provide nutrition information or make a claim subject to paragraph (r),

(II) the person who claims for such product an exemption from such subparagraphs employed fewer than an average of 100 full-time equivalent employees,

(III) such person provided the notice described in subclause (iii), and

(IV) in the case of a food product which was sold in the 12-month period preceding the period for which an exemption was claimed, fewer than 100,000 units of such product were sold in the United States during such preceding period, or in the case of a food product which was not sold in the 12-month period preceding the period for which such exemption is claimed, fewer than 100,000 units of such product are reasonably anticipated to be sold in the United States during the period for which such exemption is claimed.

(ii) During the 12-month period after the applicable date referred to in this sentence, the requirements of subparagraphs (1) and (2) shall not apply to any food product which was first introduced into interstate commerce before May 8, 1994, if the labeling for such product does not provide nutrition information or make a claim subject to paragraph (r), if such person provided the notice described in subclause (iii), and if—

(I) during the 12-month period preceding May 8, 1994, the person who claims for such product an exemption from such subparagraphs employed fewer than an average of 300 full-time equivalent employees and fewer than 600,000 units of such product were sold in the United States,

(II) during the 12-month period preceding May 8, 1995, the person who claims for such product an exemption from such subparagraphs employed fewer than an average of 300 full-time equivalent employees and fewer than 400,000 units of such product were sold in the United States, or

(III) during the 12-month period preceding May 8, 1996, the person who claims for such product an exemption from such subparagraphs employed fewer than an average of 200 full-time equivalent employees and fewer than 200,000 units of such product were sold in the United States.

(iii) The notice referred to in subclauses (i) and (ii) shall be given to the Secretary prior to the beginning of the period during which the exemption under subclause (i) or (ii) is to be in effect, shall state that the person claiming such exemption for a food product has complied with the applicable requirements of subclause (i) or (ii), and shall—

(I) state the average number of full-time equivalent employees such person employed during the 12 months preceding the date such person claims such exemption,

(II) state the approximate number of units the person claiming the exemption sold in the United States,

(III) if the exemption is claimed for a food product which was sold in the 12-month period preceding the period for which the exemption was claimed, state the approximate number of units of such product which were sold in the United States during such preceding period, and, if the exemption is claimed for a food product which was not sold in such preceding period, state the number of units of such product which such person reasonably anticipates will be sold in the United States during the period for which the exemption was claimed, and

(IV) contain such information as the Secretary may require to verify the information required by the preceding provisions of this subclause if the Secretary has questioned the validity of such information.

If a person is not an importer, has fewer than 10 full-time equivalent employees, and sells fewer than 10,000 units of any food product in any year, such person is not required to file a notice for such product under this subclause for such year.

(iv) In the case of a person who claimed an exemption under subclause (i) or (ii), if, during the period of such exemption, the number of full-time equivalent employees of such person exceeds the number in such subclause or if the number of food products sold in the United States exceeds the number in such subclause, such exemption shall extend to the expiration of 18 months after the date the number of full-time equivalent employees or food products sold exceeded the applicable number.

(v) For any food product first introduced into interstate commerce after May 8, 2002, the Secretary may by regulation lower the employee or units of food products requirement of subclause (i) if the Secretary determines that the cost of compliance with such lower requirement will not place an undue burden on persons subject to such lower requirement.

(vi) For purposes of subclauses (i), (ii), (iii), (iv), and (v) —

(I) the term "unit" means the packaging or, if there is no packaging, the form in which a food product is offered for sale to consumers,

(II) the term "food product" means food in any sized package which is manufactured by a single manufacturer or which bears the same brand name, which bears the same statement of identity, and which has similar preparation methods, and

(III) the term "person" in the case of a corporation includes all domestic and foreign affiliates of the corporation.

(F) A dietary supplement product (including a food to which section 411 applies) shall comply with the requirements of subparagraphs (1) and (2) in a manner which is appropriate for the product and which is specified in regulations of the Secretary which shall provide that —

(i) nutrition information shall first list those dietary ingredients that are present in the product in a significant amount and for which a recommendation for daily consumption has been established by the Secretary, except that a dietary ingredient shall not be required to be listed if it is not present in a significant amount, and shall list any other dietary ingredient present and identified as having no such recommendation;

(ii) the listing of dietary ingredients shall include the quantity of each such ingredient (or of a proprietary blend of such ingredients) per serving;

(iii) the listing of dietary ingredients may include the source of a dietary ingredient; and

(iv) the nutrition information shall immediately precede the ingredient information required under subclause (i), except that no ingredient identified pursuant to subclause (i) shall be required to be identified a second time.

(G) Subparagraphs (1), (2), (3), and (4) shall not apply to food which is sold by a food distributor if the food distributor principally sells food to restaurants or other establishments in which food is served for immediate human consumption and does not manufacture, process, or repackage the food it sells.

(H) Restaurants, Retail Food Establishments, and Vending Machines. —

(i) General Requirements for Restaurants and Similar Retail Food Establishments. — Except for food described in subclause (vii), in the case of food that is a standard menu item that is offered for sale in a restaurant or similar retail food establishment that is part of a chain with 20 or more locations doing business under the same name (regardless of the type of ownership of the locations) and offering for sale substantially the same menu items, the restaurant or similar retail food establishment shall disclose the information described in subclauses (ii) and (iii).

(ii) Information Required to be Disclosed by Restaurants and Retail Food Establishments. — Except as provided in subclause (vii), the restaurant or similar retail food establishment shall disclose in a clear and conspicuous manner —

(I) —

(aa) in a nutrient content disclosure statement adjacent to the name of the standard menu item, so as to be clearly associated with the standard menu item, on the menu listing the item for sale, the number of calories contained in the standard menu item, as usually prepared and offered for sale; and

(bb) a succinct statement concerning suggested daily caloric intake, as specified by the Secretary by regulation and posted prominently on the menu and designed to enable the public to understand, in the context of a total daily diet, the significance of the caloric information that is provided on the menu;

(II) —

(aa) in a nutrient content disclosure statement adjacent to the name of the standard menu item, so as to be clearly associated with the standard menu item, on the menu board, including a drive-through menu board, the number of calories contained in the standard menu item, as usually prepared and offered for sale; and

(bb) a succinct statement concerning suggested daily caloric intake, as specified by the Secretary by regulation and posted prominently on the menu board, designed to enable the public to understand, in the context of a total daily diet, the significance of the nutrition information that is provided on the menu board;

(III) in a written form, available on the premises of the restaurant or similar retail establishment and to the consumer upon request, the nutrition information required under clauses (C) and (D) of subparagraph (1); and

(IV) on the menu or menu board, a prominent, clear, and conspicuous statement regarding the availability of the information described in item (III).

(iii) Self-service Food and Food on Display. — Except as provided in subclause (vii), in the case of food sold at a salad bar, buffet line, cafeteria line, or similar self-service facility, and for self-service beverages or food that is on display and that is visible to customers, a restaurant or similar retail food establishment shall place adjacent to each food offered a sign that lists calories per displayed food item or per serving.

(iv) Reasonable Basis. — For the purposes of this clause, a restaurant or similar retail food establishment shall have a reasonable basis for its nutrient content disclosures, including nutrient databases, cookbooks, laboratory analyses, and other reasonable means, as described in section 101.10 of title 21, Code of Federal Regulations (or any successor regulation) or in a related guidance of the Food and Drug Administration.

(v) Menu Variability and Combination Meals. — The Secretary shall establish by regulation standards for determining and disclosing the nutrient content for standard menu items that come in different flavors, varieties, or combinations, but which are listed as a single menu item, such as soft drinks, ice cream, pizza, doughnuts, or children's combination meals, through means determined by the Secretary, including ranges, averages, or other methods.

(vi) Additional Information. — If the Secretary determines that a nutrient, other than a nutrient required under subclause (ii)(III), should be disclosed for the purpose of providing information to assist consumers in maintaining healthy dietary practices, the Secretary may require, by regulation, disclosure of such nutrient in the written form required under subclause (ii)(III).

(vii) Nonapplicability to Certain Food. —

(I) In General. — Subclauses (i) through (vi) do not apply to —

(aa) items that are not listed on a menu or menu board (such as condiments and other items placed on the table or counter for general use);

(bb) daily specials, temporary menu items appearing on the menu for less than 60 days per calendar year, or custom orders; or

(cc) such other food that is part of a customary market test appearing on the menu for less than 90 days, under terms and conditions established by the Secretary.

(II) Written Forms. — Subparagraph (5)(C) shall apply to any regulations promulgated under subclauses (ii)(III) and (vi).

(viii) Vending Machines. —

(I) In General. — In the case of an article of food sold from a vending machine that —

(aa) does not permit a prospective purchaser to examine the Nutrition Facts Panel before purchasing the article or does not otherwise provide visible nutrition information at the point of purchase; and

(bb) is operated by a person who is engaged in the business of owning or operating 20 or more vending machines, the vending machine operator shall provide a sign in close proximity to each article of food or the selection button that includes a clear and conspicuous statement disclosing the number of calories contained in the article.

(ix) Voluntary Provision of Nutrition Information. —

(I) In General. — An authorized official of any restaurant or similar retail food establishment or vending machine operator not subject to the requirements of this clause may elect to be subject to the requirements of such clause, by registering biannually the name and address of such restaurant or similar retail food establishment or vending machine operator with the Secretary, as specified by the Secretary by regulation.

(II) Registration. — Within 120 days of enactment of this clause, the Secretary shall publish a notice in the Federal Register specifying the terms and conditions for implementation of item (I), pending promulgation of regulations.

(III) Rule of Construction. — Nothing in this subclause shall be construed to authorize the Secretary to require an application, review, or licensing process for any entity to register with the Secretary, as described in such item.

(x) Regulations. —

(I) Proposed Regulation. — Not later than 1 year after the date of enactment of this clause, the Secretary shall promulgate proposed regulations to carry out this clause.

(II) Contents. — In promulgating regulations, the Secretary shall —

(aa) consider standardization of recipes and methods of preparation, reasonable variation in serving size and formulation of menu items, space on menus and menu boards, inadvertent human error, training of food service workers, variations in ingredients, and other factors, as the Secretary determines; and

(bb) specify the format and manner of the nutrient content disclosure requirements under this subclause.

(III) Reporting. — The Secretary shall submit to the Committee on Health, Education, Labor, and Pensions of the Senate and the Committee on Energy and Commerce of the House of Representatives a quarterly report that describes the Secretary's progress toward promulgating final regulations under this subparagraph.

(xi) Definition. — In this clause, the term "menu" or "menu board" means the primary writing of the restaurant or other similar retail food establishment from which a consumer makes an order selection.

(r) —

(1) Except as provided in clauses (A) through (C) of subparagraph (5), if it is a food intended for human consumption which is offered for sale and for which a claim is made in the label or labeling of the food which expressly or by implication —

(A) characterizes the level of any nutrient which is of the type required by paragraph (q)(1) or (q)(2) to be in the label or labeling of the food unless the claim is made in accordance with subparagraph (2), or

(B) characterizes the relationship of any nutrient which is of the type required by paragraph (q)(1) or (q)(2) to be in the label or labeling of the food to a disease or a health-related condition unless the claim is made in accordance with subparagraph (3) or (5)(D).

A statement of the type required by paragraph (q) that appears as part of the nutrition information required or permitted by such paragraph is not a claim which is subject to this paragraph and a claim subject to clause (A) is not subject to clause (B).

(2) —

(A) Except as provided in subparagraphs (4)(A)(ii) and (4)(A)(iii) and clauses (A) through (C) of subparagraph (5), a claim described in subparagraph (1)(A) —

(i) may be made only if the characterization of the level made in the claim uses terms which are defined in regulations of the Secretary,

(ii) may not state the absence of a nutrient unless —

(I) the nutrient is usually present in the food or in a food which substitutes for the food as defined by the Secretary by regulation, or

(II) the Secretary by regulation permits such a statement on the basis of a finding that such a statement would assist consumers in maintaining healthy dietary practices and the statement discloses that the nutrient is not usually present in the food,

(iii) may not be made with respect to the level of cholesterol in the food if the food contains, as determined by the Secretary by regulation, fat or saturated fat in an amount which increases to persons in the general population the risk of disease or a health related condition which is diet related unless —

(I) the Secretary finds by regulation that the level of cholesterol is substantially less than the level usually present in the food or in a food which substitutes for the food and which has a significant market share, or the Secretary by regulation permits a statement regarding the absence of cholesterol on the basis of a finding that cholesterol is not usually present in the food and that such a statement would assist consumers in maintaining healthy dietary practices and a requirement that the statement disclose that cholesterol is not usually present in the food, and

(II) the label or labeling of the food discloses the level of such fat or saturated fat in immediate proximity to such claim and with appropriate prominence which shall be no less than one-half the size of the claim with respect to the level of cholesterol,

(iv) may not be made with respect to the level of saturated fat in the food if the food contains cholesterol unless the label or labeling of the food discloses the level of cholesterol in the food in immediate proximity to such claim and with appropriate prominence which shall be no less than one-half the size of the claim with respect to the level of saturated fat,

(v) may not state that a food is high in dietary fiber unless the food is low in total fat as defined by the Secretary or the label or labeling discloses the level of total fat in the food in immediate proximity to such statement and with appropriate prominence which shall be no less than one-half the size of the claim with respect to the level of dietary fiber, and

(vi) may not be made if the Secretary by regulation prohibits the claim because the claim is misleading in light of the level of another nutrient in the food.

(B) If a claim described in subparagraph (1)(A) is made with respect to a nutrient in a food and the Secretary makes a determination that the food contains a nutrient at a level that increases to persons in the general population the risk of a disease or health-related condition that is diet related, the label or labeling of such food shall contain, prominently and in immediate proximity to such claim, the following statement: "See nutrition information for ______________ content." The blank shall identify the nutrient associated with the increased disease or health-related condition risk. In making the determination described in this clause, the Secretary shall take into account the significance of the food in the total daily diet.

(C) Subparagraph (2)(A) does not apply to a claim described in subparagraph (1)(A) and contained in the label or labeling of a food if such claim is contained in the brand name of such food and such brand name was in use on such food before October 25, 1989, unless the brand name contains a term defined by the Secretary under subparagraph (2)(A)(i). Such a claim is subject to paragraph (a).

(D) Subparagraph (2) does not apply to a claim described in subparagraph (1)(A) which uses the term "diet" and is contained in the label or labeling of a soft drink if

(i) such claim is contained in the brand name of such soft drink,

(ii) such brand name was in use on such soft drink before October 25, 1989, and

(iii) the use of the term "diet" was in conformity with section 105.66 of title 21 of the Code of Federal Regulations. Such a claim is subject to paragraph (a).

(E) Subclauses (i) through (v) of subparagraph (2)(A) do not apply to a statement in the label or labeling of food which describes the percentage of vitamins and minerals in the food in relation to the amount of such vitamins and minerals recommended for daily consumption by the Secretary.

(F) Subclause (i) clause (A) does not apply to a statement in the labeling of a dietary supplement that characterizes the percentage level of a dietary ingredient for which the Secretary has not established a reference daily intake, daily recommended value, or other recommendation for daily consumption.

(G) A claim of the type described in subparagraph (1)(A) for a nutrient, for which the Secretary has not promulgated a regulation under clause (A)(i), shall be authorized and may be made with respect to a food if—

(i) a scientific body of the United States Government with official responsibility for public health protection or research directly relating to human nutrition (such as the National Institutes of Health or the Centers for Disease Control and Prevention) or the National Academy of Sciences or any of its subdivisions has published an authoritative statement, which is currently in effect, which identifies the nutrient level to which the claim refers;

(ii) a person has submitted to the Secretary, at least 120 days (during which the Secretary may notify any person who is making a claim as authorized by clause (C) that such person has not submitted all the information required by such clause) before the first introduction into interstate commerce of the food with a label containing the claim,

(I) a notice of the claim, which shall include the exact words used in the claim and shall include a concise description of the basis upon which such person relied for determining that the requirements of subclause (i) have been satisfied,

(II) a copy of the statement referred to in subclause (i) upon which such person relied in making the claim, and

(III) a balanced representation of the scientific literature relating to the nutrient level to which the claim refers;

(iii) the claim and the food for which the claim is made are in compliance with clauses (A) and (B), and are otherwise in compliance with paragraph (a) and section 201(n); and

(iv) the claim is stated in a manner so that the claim is an accurate representation of the authoritative statement referred to in subclause (i) and so that the claim enables the public to comprehend the information provided in the claim and to understand the relative significance of such information in the context of a total daily diet.

For purposes of this clause, a statement shall be regarded as an authoritative statement of a scientific body described in subclause (i) only if the statement is published by the scientific body and shall not include a statement of an employee of the scientific body made in the individual capacity of the employee.

(H) A claim submitted under the requirements of clause (G) may be made until—

(i) such time as the Secretary issues a regulation—

(I) prohibiting or modifying the claim and the regulation has become effective, or

(II) finding that the requirements of clause (G) have not been met, including finding that the petitioner had not submitted all the information required by such clause; or

(ii) a district court of the United States in an enforcement proceeding under chapter III has determined that the requirements of clause (G) have not been met.

(3) —

(A) Except as provided in subparagraph (5), a claim described in subparagraph (1)(B) may only be made —

(i) if the claim meets the requirements of the regulations of the Secretary promulgated under clause (B), and

(ii) if the food for which the claim is made does not contain, as determined by the Secretary by regulation, any nutrient in an amount which increases to persons in the general population the risk of a disease or health-related condition which is diet related, taking into account the significance of the food in the total daily diet, except that the Secretary may by regulation permit such a claim based on a finding that such a claim would assist consumers in maintaining healthy dietary practices and based on a requirement that the label contain a disclosure of the type required by subparagraph (2)(B).

(B) —

(i) The Secretary shall promulgate regulations authorizing claims of the type described in subparagraph (1)(B) only if the Secretary determines, based on the totality of publicly available scientific evidence (including evidence from well-designed studies conducted in a manner which is consistent with generally recognized scientific procedures and principles), that there is significant scientific agreement, among experts qualified by scientific training and experience to evaluate such claims, that the claim is supported by such evidence.

(ii) A regulation described in subclause (i) shall describe—

(I) the relationship between a nutrient of the type required in the label or labeling of food by paragraph (q)(1) or (q)(2) and a disease or health-related condition, and

(II) the significance of each such nutrient in affecting such disease or health-related condition.

(iii) A regulation described in subclause (i) shall require such claim to be stated in a manner so that the claim is an accurate representation of the matters set out in subclause (ii) and so that the claim enables the public to comprehend the information provided in the claim and to understand the relative significance of such information in the context of a total daily diet.

(C) Notwithstanding the provisions of clauses (A)(i) and (B), a claim of the type described in subparagraph (1)(B) which is not authorized by the Secretary in a regulation promulgated in accordance with clause (B) shall be authorized and may be made with respect to a food if—

(i) a scientific body of the United States Government with official responsibility for public health protection or research directly relating to human nutrition (such as the National Institutes of Health or the Centers for Disease Control and Prevention) or the National Academy of Sciences or any of its subdivisions has published an authoritative statement, which is currently in effect, about the relationship between a nutrient and a disease or health-related condition to which the claim refers;

(ii) a person has submitted to the Secretary, at least 120 days (during which the Secretary may notify any person who is making a claim as authorized by clause (C) that such person has not submitted all the information required by such clause) before the first introduction into interstate commerce of the food with a label containing the claim,

(I) a notice of the claim, which shall include the exact words used in the claim and shall include a concise description of the basis upon which such person relied for determining that the requirements of subclause (i) have been satisfied,

(II) a copy of the statement referred to in subclause (i) upon which such person relied in making the claim, and

(III) a balanced representation of the scientific literature relating to the relationship between a nutrient and a disease or health-related condition to which the claim refers;

(iii) the claim and the food for which the claim is made are in compliance with clause (A)(ii) and are otherwise in compliance with paragraph (a) and section 201(n); and

(iv) the claim is stated in a manner so that the claim is an accurate representation of the authoritative statement referred to in subclause (i) and so that the claim enables the public to comprehend the information provided in the claim and to understand the relative significance of such information in the context of a total daily diet.

For purposes of this clause, a statement shall be regarded as an authoritative statement of a scientific body described in subclause (i) only if the statement is published by the scientific body and shall not include a statement of an employee of the scientific body made in the individual capacity of the employee.

(D) A claim submitted under the requirements of clause (C) may be made until —

(i) such time as the Secretary issues a regulation under the standard in clause (B)(i) —

(I) prohibiting or modifying the claim and the regulation has become effective, or

(II) finding that the requirements of clause (C) have not been met, including finding that the petitioner has not submitted all the information required by such clause; or

(ii) a district court of the United States in an enforcement proceeding under chapter III has determined that the requirements of clause (C) have not been met.

(4) —

(A) —

(i) Any person may petition the Secretary to issue a regulation under subparagraph (2)(A)(i) or (3)(B) relating to a claim described in subparagraph (1)(A) or (1)(B). Not later than 100 days after the petition is received by the Secretary, the Secretary shall issue a final decision denying the petition or file the petition for further action by the Secretary. If the Secretary does not act within such 100 days, the petition shall be deemed to be denied unless an extension is mutually agreed upon by the Secretary and the petitioner. If the Secretary denies the petition, or the petition is deemed to be denied, the petition shall not be made available to the public. If the Secretary files the petition, the Secretary shall deny the petition or issue a proposed regulation to take the action requested in the petition not later than 90 days after the date of such decision. If the Secretary does not act within such 90 days, the petition shall be deemed to be denied unless an extension is mutually agreed upon by the Secretary and the petitioner. If the Secretary issues a proposed regulation, the rulemaking shall be completed within 540 days of the date the petition is received by the Secretary. If the Secretary does not issue a regulation within such 540 days, the Secretary shall provide the Committee on Commerce of the House of Representatives and the Committee on Labor and Human Resources of the Senate the reasons action on the regulation did not occur within such 540 days.

(ii) Any person may petition the Secretary for permission to use in a claim described in subparagraph (1)(A) terms that are consistent with the terms defined by the Secretary under subparagraph (2)(A)(i). Within 90 days of the submission of such a petition, the Secretary shall issue a final decision denying the petition or granting such permission.

(iii) Any person may petition the Secretary for permission to use an implied claim described in subparagraph (1)(A) in a brand name. After publishing notice of an opportunity to comment on the petition in the Federal Register and making the petition available to the public, the Secretary shall grant the petition if the Secretary finds that such claim is not misleading and is consistent with terms defined by the Secretary under subparagraph (2)(A)(i). The Secretary shall grant or deny the petition within 100 days of the date it is submitted to the Secretary and the petition shall be considered granted if the Secretary does not act on it within such 100 days.

(B) A petition under clause (A)(i) respecting a claim described in subparagraph (1)(A) or (1)(B) shall include an explanation of the reasons why the claim meets the requirements of this paragraph and a summary of the scientific data which supports such reasons.

(C) If a petition for a regulation under subparagraph (3)(B) relies on a report from an authoritative scientific body of the United States, the Secretary shall consider such report and shall justify any decision rejecting the conclusions of such report.

(5) —

(A) This paragraph does not apply to infant formulas subject to section 412(h) and medical foods as defined in section 5(b) of the Orphan Drug Act.

(B) Subclauses (iii) through (v) of subparagraph (2)(A) and subparagraph (2)(B) do not apply to food which is served in restaurants or other establishments in which food is served for immediate human consumption or which is sold for sale or use in such establishments.

(C) A subparagraph (1)(A) claim made with respect to a food which claim is required by a standard of identity issued under section 401 shall not be subject to subparagraph (2)(A)(i) or (2)(B).

(D) A subparagraph (1)(B) claim made with respect to a dietary supplement of vitamins, minerals, herbs, or other similar nutritional substances shall not be subject to subparagraph (3) but shall be subject to a procedure and standard, respecting the validity of such claim, established by regulation of the Secretary.

(6) For purposes of paragraph (r)(1)(B), a statement for a dietary supplement may be made if —

(A) the statement claims a benefit related to a classical nutrient deficiency disease and discloses the prevalence of such disease in the United States, describes the role of a nutrient or dietary ingredient intended to affect the structure or function in humans, characterizes the documented mechanism by which a nutrient or dietary ingredient acts to maintain such structure or function, or describes general well-being from consumption of a nutrient or dietary ingredient,

(B) the manufacturer of the dietary supplement has substantiation that such statement is truthful and not misleading, and

(C) the statement contains, prominently displayed and in boldface type, the following: "This statement has not been evaluated by the Food and Drug Administration. This product is not intended to diagnose, treat, cure, or prevent any disease.".

A statement under this subparagraph may not claim to diagnose, mitigate, treat, cure, or prevent a specific disease or class of diseases. If the manufacturer of a dietary supplement proposes to make a statement described in the first sentence of this subparagraph in the labeling of the dietary supplement, the manufacturer shall notify the Secretary no later than 30 days after the first marketing of the dietary supplement with such statement that such a statement is being made.

(7) The Secretary may make proposed regulations issued under this paragraph effective upon publication pending consideration of public comment and publication of a final regulation if the Secretary determines that such action is necessary —

(A) to enable the Secretary to review and act promptly on petitions the Secretary determines provide for information necessary to —

(i) enable consumers to develop and maintain healthy dietary practices;

(ii) enable consumers to be informed promptly and effectively of important new knowledge regarding nutritional and health benefits of food; or

(iii) ensure that scientifically sound nutritional and health information is provided to consumers as soon as possible; or

(B) to enable the Secretary to act promptly to ban or modify a claim under this paragraph.

Such proposed regulations shall be deemed final agency action for purposes of judicial review.

(s) If —

(1) it is a dietary supplement; and

(2) —

(A) the label or labeling of the supplement fails to list —

(i) the name of each ingredient of the supplement that is described in section 201(ff); and

(ii) —

(I) the quantity of each such ingredient; or

(II) with respect to a proprietary blend of such ingredients, the total quantity of all ingredients in the blend;

(B) the label or labeling of the dietary supplement fails to identify the product by using the term "dietary supplement", which term may be modified with the name of such an ingredient;

(C) the supplement contains an ingredient described in section 201(ff)(1)(C), and the label or labeling of the supplement fails to identify any part of the plant from which the ingredient is derived;

(D) the supplement —

(i) is covered by the specifications of an official compendium;

(ii) is represented as conforming to the specifications of an official compendium; and

(iii) fails to so conform; or

(E) the supplement —

(i) is not covered by the specifications of an official compendium; and

(ii) —

(I) fails to have the identity and strength that the supplement is represented to have; or

(II) fails to meet the quality (including tablet or capsule disintegration), purity, or compositional specifications, based on validated assay or other appropriate methods, that the supplement is represented to meet.

A dietary supplement shall not be deemed misbranded solely because its label or labeling contains directions or conditions of use or warnings.

(t) If it purports to be or is represented as catfish, unless it is fish classified within the family Ictaluridae.

(u) If it purports to be or is represented as ginseng, unless it is an herb or herbal ingredient derived from a plant classified within the genus Panax.

(v) If —

(1) it fails to bear a label required by the Secretary under section 801(n)(1) (relating to food refused admission into the United States);

(2) the Secretary finds that the food presents a threat of serious adverse health consequences or death to humans or animals; and

(3) upon or after notifying the owner or consignee involved that the label is required under section 801, the Secretary informs the owner or consignee that the food presents such a threat.

(w) —

(1) If it is not a raw agricultural commodity and it is, or it contains an ingredient that bears or contains, a major food allergen, unless either —

(A) the word "Contains", followed by the name of the food source from which the major food allergen is derived, is printed immediately after or is adjacent to the list of ingredients (in a type size no smaller than the type size used in the list of ingredients) required under subsections (g) and (i); or

(B) the common or usual name of the major food allergen in the list of ingredients required under subsections (g) and (i) is followed in parentheses by the name of the food source from which the major food allergen is derived, except that the name of the food source is not required when —

(i) the common or usual name of the ingredient uses the name of the food source from which the major food allergen is derived; or

(ii) the name of the food source from which the major food allergen is derived appears elsewhere in the ingredient list, unless the name of the food source that appears elsewhere in the ingredient list appears as part of the name of a food ingredient that is not a major food allergen under section 201(qq)(2)(A) or (B).

(2) As used in this subsection, the term "name of the food source from which the major food allergen is derived" means the name described in section 201(qq)(1); provided that in the case of a tree nut, fish, or Crustacean shellfish, the term "name of the food source from which the major food allergen is derived" means the name of the specific type of nut or species of fish or Crustacean shellfish.

(3) The information required under this subsection may appear in labeling in lieu of appearing on the label only if the Secretary finds that such other labeling is sufficient to protect the public health. A finding by the

Secretary under this paragraph (including any change in an earlier finding under this paragraph) is effective upon publication in the Federal Register as a notice.

(4) Notwithstanding subsection (g), (i), or (k), or any other law, a flavoring, coloring, or incidental additive that is, or that bears or contains, a major food allergen shall be subject to the labeling requirements of this subsection.

(5) The Secretary may by regulation modify the requirements of subparagraph (A) or (B) of paragraph (1), or eliminate either the requirement of subparagraph (A) or the requirements of subparagraph (B) of paragraph (1), if the Secretary determines that the modification or elimination of the requirement of subparagraph (A) or the requirements of subparagraph (B) is necessary to protect the public health.

(6) —

(A) Any person may petition the Secretary to exempt a food ingredient described in section 201(qq)(2) from the allergen labeling requirements of this subsection.

(B) The Secretary shall approve or deny such petition within 180 days of receipt of the petition or the petition shall be deemed denied, unless an extension of time is mutually agreed upon by the Secretary and the petitioner.

(C) The burden shall be on the petitioner to provide scientific evidence (including the analytical method used to produce the evidence) that demonstrates that such food ingredient, as derived by the method specified in the petition, does not cause an allergic response that poses a risk to human health.

(D) A determination regarding a petition under this paragraph shall constitute final agency action.

(E) The Secretary shall promptly post to a public site all petitions received under this paragraph within 14 days of receipt and the Secretary shall promptly post the Secretary's response to each.

(7) —

(A) A person need not file a petition under paragraph (6) to exempt a food ingredient described in section 201(qq)(2) from the allergen labeling requirements of this subsection, if the person files with the Secretary a notification containing —

(i) scientific evidence (including the analytical method used) that demonstrates that the food ingredient (as derived by the method specified in the notification, where applicable) does not contain allergenic protein; or

(ii) a determination by the Secretary that the ingredient does not cause an allergic response that poses a risk to human health under a premarket approval or notification program under section 409.

(B) The food ingredient may be introduced or delivered for introduction into interstate commerce as a food ingredient that is not a major food allergen 90 days after the date of receipt of the notification by the Secretary, unless the Secretary determines within the 90-day period that the notification does not meet the requirements of this paragraph, or there is insufficient scientific evidence to determine that the food ingredient does not contain allergenic protein or does not cause an allergenic response that poses a risk to human health.

(C) The Secretary shall promptly post to a public site all notifications received under this subparagraph within 14 days of receipt and promptly post any objections thereto by the Secretary.

(x) Notwithstanding subsection (g), (i), or (k), or any other law, a spice, flavoring, coloring, or incidental additive that is, or that bears or contains, a food allergen (other than a major food allergen), as determined by the Secretary by regulation, shall be disclosed in a manner specified by the Secretary by regulation.

(y) If it is a dietary supplement that is marketed in the United States, unless the label of such dietary supplement includes a domestic address or domestic phone number through which the responsible person (as described in section 761) may receive a report of a serious adverse event with such dietary supplement.

Sec. 403A. [343-1] National Uniform Nutrition Labeling.

(a) Except as provided in subsection (b), no State or political subdivision of a State may directly or indirectly establish under any authority or continue in effect as to any food in interstate commerce —

(1) any requirement for a food which is the subject of a standard of identity established under section 401 that is not identical to such standard of identity or that is not identical to the requirement of section 403(g), except that this paragraph does not apply to a standard of identity of a State or political subdivision of a State for maple syrup that is of the type required by sections 401 and 403(g),

(2) any requirement for the labeling of food of the type required by section 403(c), 403(e), 403(i)(2), 403(w), or 403(x) that is not identical to the requirement of such section, except that this paragraph does not apply to a requirement of a State or political subdivision of a State that is of the type required by section 403(c) and that is applicable to maple syrup,

(3) any requirement for the labeling of food of the type required by section 403(b), 403(d), 403(f), 403(h), 403(i)(1), or 403(k) that is not identical to the requirement of such section, except that this paragraph does not apply to a requirement of a State or political subdivision of a State that is of the type required by section 403(h) (1) and that is applicable to maple syrup,

(4) any requirement for nutrition labeling of food that is not identical to the requirement of section 403(q), except that this paragraph does not apply to food that is offered for sale in a restaurant or similar retail food establishment that is not part of a chain with 20 or more locations doing business under the same name (regardless of the type of ownership of the locations) and offering for sale substantially the same menu items unless such restaurant or similar retail food establishment complies with the voluntary provision of nutrition information requirements under section 403(q)(5)(H)(ix), or

(5) any requirement respecting any claim of the type described in section 403(r)(1) made in the label or labeling of food that is not identical to the requirement of section 403(r), except a requirement respecting a claim made in the label or labeling of food which is exempt under section 403(r)(5)(B).

Paragraph (3) shall take effect in accordance with section 6(b) of the Nutrition Labeling and Education Act of 1990.

(b) Upon petition of a State or a political subdivision of a State, the Secretary may exempt from subsection (a), under such conditions as may be prescribed by regulation, any State or local requirement that —

(1) would not cause any food to be in violation of any applicable requirement under Federal law,

(2) would not unduly burden interstate commerce, and

(3) is designed to address a particular need for information which need is not met by the requirements of the sections referred to in subsection (a).

Sec. 403B. [343-2] Dietary Supplement Labeling Exemptions.

(a) In General. — A publication, including an article, a chapter in a book, or an official abstract of a peer-reviewed scientific publication that appears in an article and was prepared by the author or the editors of the publication, which is reprinted in its entirety, shall not be defined as labeling when used in connection with the sale of a dietary supplement to consumers when it —

(1) is not false or misleading;

(2) does not promote a particular manufacturer or brand of a dietary supplement;

(3) is displayed or presented, or is displayed or presented with other such items on the same subject matter, so as to present a balanced view of the available scientific information on a dietary supplement;

(4) if displayed in an establishment, is physically separate from the dietary supplements; and

(5) does not have appended to it any information by sticker or any other method.

(b) Application. — Subsection (a) shall not apply to or restrict a retailer or wholesaler of dietary supplements in any way whatsoever in the sale of books or other publications as a part of the business of such retailer or wholesaler.

(c) Burden of Proof. — In any proceeding brought under subsection (a), the burden of proof shall be on the United States to establish that an article or other such matter is false or misleading.

Sec. 403C. [343-3] Disclosure.

(a) No provision of section 201(n), 403(a), or 409 shall be construed to require on the label or labeling of a food a separate radiation disclosure statement that is more prominent than the declaration of ingredients required by section 403(i)(2).

(b) In this section, the term "radiation disclosure statement" means a written statement that discloses that a food has been intentionally subject to radiation.

Sec. 404. [344] Emergency Permit Control.

(a) Whenever the Secretary finds after investigation that the distribution in interstate commerce of any class of food may, by reason of contamination with micro-organisms during the manufacture, processing, or packing thereof in any locality, be injurious to health, and that such injurious nature cannot be adequately determined after such articles have entered interstate commerce, he then, and in such case only, shall promulgate regulations providing for the issuance, to manufacturers, processors, or packers of such class of food in such locality of permits to which shall be attached such conditions governing the manufacture, processing, or packaging of such class of food, for such temporary period of time, as may be necessary to protect the public health; and after the effective date of such regulations, and during such temporary period, no person shall introduce or deliver for introduction into interstate commerce any such food manufactured, processed, or packed by any such manufacturer, processor, or packer unless such manufacturer, processor, or packer holds a permit issued by the Secretary as provided by such regulations.

(b) The Secretary is authorized to suspend immediately upon notice any permit issued under authority of this section if it is found that any of the conditions of the permit have been violated. The holder of a permit so suspended shall be privileged at any time to apply for the reinstatement of such permit, and the Secretary shall, immediately after prompt hearing and an inspection of the establishment, reinstate such permit if it is found that adequate measures have been taken to comply with and maintain the conditions of the permit, as originally issued or as amended.

(c) Any officer or employee duly designated by the Secretary shall have access to any factory or establishment, the operator of which holds a permit from the Secretary, for the purpose of ascertaining whether or not the conditions of the permit are being complied with, and denial of access for such inspection shall be ground for suspension of the permit until such access is freely given by the operator.

Sec. 405. [345] Regulations Making Exemptions.

The Secretary shall promulgate regulations exempting from any labeling requirement of this Act

(1) small open containers of fresh fruits and fresh vegetables and

(2) food which is, in accordance with the practice of the trade, to be processed, labeled, or repacked in substantial quantities at establishments other than those where originally processed or packed, on condition that such food is not adulterated or misbranded under the provisions of this Act upon removal from such processing, labeling, or repacking establishment.

This section does not apply to the labeling requirements of sections 403(q) and 403(r).

Sec. 406. [346] Tolerances for Poisonous Ingredients in Food.

Any poisonous or deleterious substance added to any food, except where such substance is required in the production thereof or cannot be avoided by good manufacturing practice shall be deemed to be unsafe for purposes of the application of clause (2)(A) of section 402(a); but when such substance is so required or cannot be so avoided, the Secretary shall promulgate regulations limiting the quantity therein or thereon to such extent as he finds necessary for the protection of public health, and any quantity exceeding the limits so fixed shall also be deemed to be unsafe for purposes of the application of clause (2)(A) of section 402(a). While such a regulation is in effect limiting the quantity of any such substance in the case of any food, such food shall not, by reason of bearing or containing any added amount of such substance, be considered to be adulterated within the meaning of clause (1) of section 402(a). In determining the quantity of such added substance to be tolerated in or on different articles of food the Secretary shall take into account the extent to which the use of such substance is required or cannot be avoided in the production of each such article, and the other ways in which the consumer may be affected by the same or other poisonous or deleterious substances.

Sec. 407. [347] Oleomargarine or Margarine.

(a) Colored oleomargarine or colored margarine which is sold in the same State or Territory in which it is produced shall be subject in the same manner and to the same extent to the provisions of this Act as if it had been introduced in interstate commerce.

(b) No person shall sell, or offer for sale, colored oleomargarine or colored margarine unless —

(1) such oleomargarine or margarine is packaged,

(2) the net weight of the contents of any package sold in a retail establishment is one pound or less,

(3) there appears on the label of the package

(A) the word "oleomargarine" or "margarine" in type or lettering at least as large as any other type or lettering on such label, and

(B) a full and accurate statement of all the ingredients contained in such oleomargarine, or margarine, and

(4) each part of the contents of the package is contained in a wrapper which bears the word "oleomargarine" or "margarine" in type or lettering not smaller than 20-point type.

The requirements of this subsection shall be in addition to and not in lieu of any of the other requirements of this Act.

(c) No person shall possess in a form ready for serving colored oleomargarine or colored margarine at a public eating place unless a notice that oleomargarine or margarine is served is displayed prominently and conspicuously in such place and in such manner as to render it likely to be read and understood by the ordinary individual being served in such eating place or is printed or is otherwise set forth on the menu in type or lettering not smaller than that normally used to designate the serving of other food items. No person shall serve colored oleomargarine or colored margarine at a public eating place, whether or not any charge is made therefor, unless

(1) each separate serving bears or is accompanied by labeling identifying it as oleomargarine or margarine, or

(2) each separate serving thereof is triangular in shape.

(d) Colored oleomargarine or colored margarine when served with meals at a public eating place shall at the time of such service be exempt from the labeling requirements of section 403 (except (a) and 403 (f)) [probably should be "(except subsections (a) and (f))" — Ed.] if it complies with the requirements of subsection (b) of this section.

(e) For the purpose of this section colored oleomargarine or colored margarine is oleomargarine or margarine having a tint or shade containing more than one and six-tenths degrees of yellow, or of yellow and red collectively, but with an excess of yellow over red, measured in terms of Lovibond tintometer scale or its equivalent.

Sec. 408. [346a] Tolerances and Exemptions for Pesticide Chemical Residues.

(a) Requirement for Tolerance or Exemption. —

(1) General Rule. — Except as provided in paragraph (2) or (3), any pesticide chemical residue in or on a food shall be deemed unsafe for the purpose of section 402(a)(2)(B) unless —

(A) a tolerance for such pesticide chemical residue in or on such food is in effect under this section and the quantity of the residue is within the limits of the tolerance; or

(B) an exemption from the requirement of a tolerance is in effect under this section for the pesticide chemical residue.

For the purposes of this section, the term "food", when used as a noun without modification, shall mean a raw agricultural commodity or processed food.

(2) Processed Food. — Notwithstanding paragraph (1) —

(A) if a tolerance is in effect under this section for a pesticide chemical residue in or on a raw agricultural commodity, a pesticide chemical residue that is present in or on a processed food because the food is made from that raw agricultural commodity shall not be considered unsafe within the meaning of section 402(a)(2)(B) despite the lack of a tolerance for the pesticide chemical residue in or on the processed food if the pesticide chemical has been used in or on the raw agricultural commodity in conformity with a tolerance under this section, such residue in or on the raw agricultural commodity has been removed to the extent possible in good manufacturing practice, and the concentration of the pesticide chemical residue in the processed food is not greater than the tolerance prescribed for the pesticide chemical residue in the raw agricultural commodity; or

(B) if an exemption for the requirement for a tolerance is in effect under this section for a pesticide chemical residue in or on a raw agricultural commodity, a pesticide chemical residue that is present in or on a processed food because the food is made from that raw agricultural commodity shall not be considered unsafe within the meaning of section 402(a)(2)(B).

(3) Residues of Degradation Products. — If a pesticide chemical residue is present in or on a food because it is a metabolite or other degradation product of a precursor substance that itself is a pesticide chemical or pesticide chemical residue, such a residue shall not be considered to be unsafe within the meaning of section 402(a)(2)(B) despite the lack of a tolerance or exemption from the need for a tolerance for such residue in or on such food if —

(A) the Administrator has not determined that the degradation product is likely to pose any potential health risk from dietary exposure that is of a different type than, or of a greater significance than, any risk posed by dietary exposure to the precursor substance;

(B) either —

(i) a tolerance is in effect under this section for residues of the precursor substance in or on the food, and the combined level of residues of the degradation product and the precursor substance in or on the food is at or below the stoichiometrically equivalent level that would be permitted by the tolerance if the residue consisted only of the precursor substance rather than the degradation product; or

(ii) an exemption from the need for a tolerance is in effect under this section for residues of the precursor substance in or on the food; and

(C) the tolerance or exemption for residues of the precursor substance does not state that it applies only to particular named substances and does not state that it does not apply to residues of the degradation product.

(4) Effect of Tolerance or Exemption. — While a tolerance or exemption from the requirement for a tolerance is in effect under this section for a pesticide chemical residue with respect to any food, the food shall not by reason of bearing or containing any amount of such a residue be considered to be adulterated within the meaning of section 402(a)(1).

(b) Authority and Standard for Tolerance. —

(1) Authority. — The Administrator may issue regulations establishing, modifying, or revoking a tolerance for a pesticide chemical residue in or on a food —

(A) in response to a petition filed under subsection (d); or

(B) on the Administrator's own initiative under subsection (e).

As used in this section, the term "modify" shall not mean expanding the tolerance to cover additional foods.

(2) Standard. —

(A) General Rule. —

(i) Standard. — The Administrator may establish or leave in effect a tolerance for a pesticide chemical residue in or on a food only if the Administrator determines that the tolerance is safe. The Administrator shall modify or revoke a tolerance if the Administrator determines it is not safe.

(ii) Determination of Safety. — As used in this section, the term "safe", with respect to a tolerance for a pesticide chemical residue, means that the Administrator has determined that there is a reasonable certainty that no harm will result from aggregate exposure to the pesticide chemical residue, including all anticipated dietary exposures and all other exposures for which there is reliable information.

(iii) Rule of Construction. — With respect to a tolerance, a pesticide chemical residue meeting the standard under clause (i) is not an eligible pesticide chemical residue for purposes of subparagraph (B).

(B) Tolerances for Eligible Pesticide Chemical Residues. —

(i) Definition. — As used in this subparagraph, the term "eligible pesticide chemical residue" means a pesticide chemical residue as to which —

(I) the Administrator is not able to identify a level of exposure to the residue at which the residue will not cause or contribute to a known or anticipated harm to human health (referred to in this section as a "nonthreshold effect");

(II) the lifetime risk of experiencing the nonthreshold effect is appropriately assessed by quantitative risk assessment; and

(III) with regard to any known or anticipated harm to human health for which the Administrator is able to identify a level at which the residue will not cause such harm (referred to in this section as a "threshold effect"), the Administrator determines that the level of aggregate exposure is safe.

(ii) Determination of Tolerance. Notwithstanding subparagraph (A)(i), a tolerance for an eligible pesticide chemical residue may be left in effect or modified under this subparagraph if—

(I) at least one of the conditions described in clause (iii) is met; and

(II) both of the conditions described in clause (iv) are met.

(iii) Conditions Regarding Use. — For purposes of clause (ii), the conditions described in this clause with respect to a tolerance for an eligible pesticide chemical residue are the following:

(I) Use of the pesticide chemical that produces the residue protects consumers from adverse effects on health that would pose a greater risk than the dietary risk from the residue.

(II) Use of the pesticide chemical that produces the residue is necessary to avoid a significant disruption in domestic production of an adequate, wholesome, and economical food supply.

(iv) Conditions Regarding Risk. — For purposes of clause (ii), the conditions described in this clause with respect to a tolerance for an eligible pesticide chemical residue are the following:

(I) The yearly risk associated with the nonthreshold effect from aggregate exposure to the residue does not exceed 10 times the yearly risk that would be allowed under subparagraph (A) for such effect.

(II) The tolerance is limited so as to ensure that the risk over a lifetime associated with the nonthreshold effect from aggregate exposure to the residue is not greater than twice the lifetime risk that would be allowed under subparagraph (A) for such effect.

(v) Review. — Five years after the date on which the Administrator makes a determination to leave in effect or modify a tolerance under this subparagraph, and thereafter as the Administrator deems appropriate, the Administrator shall determine, after notice and opportunity for comment, whether it has been demonstrated to the Administrator that a condition described in clause (iii)(I) or clause (iii)(II) continues to exist with respect to the tolerance and that the yearly and lifetime risks from aggregate exposure to such residue continue to comply with the limits specified in clause (iv). If the Administrator determines by such date that such demonstration has not been made, the Administrator shall, not later than 180 days after the date of such determination, issue a regulation under subsection (e)(1) to modify or revoke the tolerance.

(vi) Infants and Children. — Any tolerance under this subparagraph shall meet the requirements of subparagraph (C).

(C) Exposure of Infants and Children. — In establishing, modifying, leaving in effect, or revoking a tolerance or exemption for a pesticide chemical residue, the Administrator —

(i) shall assess the risk of the pesticide chemical residue based on —

(I) available information about consumption patterns among infants and children that are likely to result in disproportionately high consumption of foods containing or bearing such residue among infants and children in comparison to the general population;

(II) available information concerning the special susceptibility of infants and children to the pesticide chemical residues, including neurological differences between infants and children and adults, and effects of in utero exposure to pesticide chemicals; and

(III) available information concerning the cumulative effects on infants and children of such residues and other substances that have a common mechanism of toxicity; and

(ii) shall —

(I) ensure that there is a reasonable certainty that no harm will result to infants and children from aggregate exposure to the pesticide chemical residue; and

(II) publish a specific determination regarding the safety of the pesticide chemical residue for infants and children.

The Secretary of Health and Human Services and the Secretary of Agriculture, in consultation with the Administrator, shall conduct surveys to document dietary exposure to pesticides among infants and children. In the case of threshold effects, for purposes of clause (ii)(I) an additional tenfold margin of safety for the pesticide chemical residue and other sources of exposure shall be applied for infants and children to take into account potential pre- and postnatal toxicity and completeness of the data with respect to exposure and toxicity to infants and children. Notwithstanding such requirement for an additional margin of safety, the Administrator may use a different margin of safety for the pesticide chemical residue only if, on the basis of reliable data, such margin will be safe for infants and children.

(D) Factors. — In establishing, modifying, leaving in effect, or revoking a tolerance or exemption for a pesticide chemical residue, the Administrator shall consider, among other relevant factors —

(i) the validity, completeness, and reliability of the available data from studies of the pesticide chemical and pesticide chemical residue;

(ii) the nature of any toxic effect shown to be caused by the pesticide chemical or pesticide chemical residue in such studies;

(iii) available information concerning the relationship of the results of such studies to human risk;

(iv) available information concerning the dietary consumption patterns of consumers (and major identifiable subgroups of consumers);

(v) available information concerning the cumulative effects of such residues and other substances that have a common mechanism of toxicity;

(vi) available information concerning the aggregate exposure levels of consumers (and major identifiable subgroups of consumers) to the pesticide chemical residue and to other related substances, including dietary exposure under the tolerance and all other tolerances in effect for the pesticide chemical residue, and exposure from other non-occupational sources;

(vii) available information concerning the variability of the sensitivities of major identifiable subgroups of consumers;

(viii) such information as the Administrator may require on whether the pesticide chemical may have an effect in humans that is similar to an effect produced by a naturally occurring estrogen or other endocrine effects; and

(ix) safety factors which in the opinion of experts qualified by scientific training and experience to evaluate the safety of food additives are generally recognized as appropriate for the use of animal experimentation data.

(E) Data and Information Regarding Anticipated and Actual Residue Levels. —

(i) Authority. — In establishing, modifying, leaving in effect, or revoking a tolerance for a pesticide chemical residue, the Administrator may consider available data and information on the anticipated residue levels of the pesticide chemical in or on food and the actual residue levels of the pesticide chemical that have been measured in food, including residue data collected by the Food and Drug Administration.

(ii) Requirement. — If the Administrator relies on anticipated or actual residue levels in establishing, modifying, or leaving in effect a tolerance, the Administrator shall pursuant to subsection (f)(1) require that data be provided five years after the date on which the tolerance is established, modified, or left in effect, and thereafter as the Administrator deems appropriate, demonstrating that such residue levels are not above the levels so relied on. If such data are not so provided, or if the data do not demonstrate that the residue levels are not above the levels so relied on, the Administrator shall, not later than 180 days after the date on which the data were required to be provided, issue a regulation under subsection (e)(1), or an order under subsection (f)(2), as appropriate, to modify or revoke the tolerance.

(F) Percent of Food Actually Treated. — In establishing, modifying, leaving in effect, or revoking a tolerance for a pesticide chemical residue, the Administrator may, when assessing chronic dietary risk, consider available data and information on the percent of food actually treated with the pesticide chemical (including aggregate pesticide use data collected by the Department of Agriculture) only if the Administrator —

(i) finds that the data are reliable and provide a valid basis to show what percentage of the food derived from such crop is likely to contain such pesticide chemical residue;

(ii) finds that the exposure estimate does not understate exposure for any significant subpopulation group;

(iii) finds that, if data are available on pesticide use and consumption of food in a particular area, the population in such area is not dietarily exposed to residues above those estimated by the Administrator; and

(iv) provides for the periodic reevaluation of the estimate of anticipated dietary exposure.

(3) Detection Methods. —

(A) General Rule. — A tolerance for a pesticide chemical residue in or on a food shall not be established or modified by the Administrator unless the Administrator determines, after consultation with the Secretary, that there is a practical method for detecting and measuring the levels of the pesticide chemical residue in or on the food.

(B) Detection Limit. — A tolerance for a pesticide chemical residue in or on a food shall not be established at or modified to a level lower than the limit of detection of the method for detecting and measuring the pesticide chemical residue specified by the Administrator under subparagraph (A).

(4) International Standards. — In establishing a tolerance for a pesticide chemical residue in or on a food, the Administrator shall determine whether a maximum residue level for the pesticide chemical has been established by the Codex Alimentarius Commission. If a Codex maximum residue level has been established for the pesticide chemical and the Administrator does not propose to adopt the Codex level, the Administrator shall publish for public comment a notice explaining the reasons for departing from the Codex level.

(c) Authority and Standard for Exemptions. —

(1) Authority. — The Administrator may issue a regulation establishing, modifying, or revoking an exemption from the requirement for a tolerance for a pesticide chemical residue in or on food —

(A) in response to a petition filed under subsection (d); or

(B) on the Administrator's initiative under subsection (e).

(2) Standard. —

(A) General Rule. —

(i) Standard. — The Administrator may establish or leave in effect an exemption from the requirement for a tolerance for a pesticide chemical residue in or on food only if the Administrator determines that the exemption is safe. The Administrator shall modify or revoke an exemption if the Administrator determines it is not safe.

(ii) Determination of Safety. — The term "safe", with respect to an exemption for a pesticide chemical residue, means that the Administrator has determined that there is a reasonable certainty that no harm will result from aggregate exposure to the pesticide chemical residue, including all anticipated dietary exposures and all other exposures for which there is reliable information.

(B) Factors. — In making a determination under this paragraph, the Administrator shall take into account, among other relevant considerations, the considerations set forth in subparagraphs (C) and (D) of subsection (b)(2).

(3) Limitation. — An exemption from the requirement for a tolerance for a pesticide chemical residue in or on food shall not be established or modified by the Administrator unless the Administrator determines, after consultation with the Secretary —

(A) that there is a practical method for detecting and measuring the levels of such pesticide chemical residue in or on food; or

(B) that there is no need for such a method, and states the reasons for such determination in issuing the regulation establishing or modifying the exemption.

(d) Petition for Tolerance or Exemption. —

(1) Petitions and Petitioners. — Any person may file with the Administrator a petition proposing the issuance of a regulation —

(A) establishing, modifying, or revoking a tolerance for a pesticide chemical residue in or on a food; or

(B) establishing, modifying, or revoking an exemption from the requirement of a tolerance for such a residue.

(2) Petition Contents. —

(A) Establishment. — A petition under paragraph (1) to establish a tolerance or exemption for a pesticide chemical residue shall be supported by such data and information as are specified in regulations issued by the Administrator, including —

(i) —

(I) an informative summary of the petition and of the data, information, and arguments submitted or cited in support of the petition; and

(II) a statement that the petitioner agrees that such summary or any information it contains may be published as a part of the notice of filing of the petition to be published under this subsection and as part of a proposed or final regulation issued under this section;

(ii) the name, chemical identity, and composition of the pesticide chemical residue and of the pesticide chemical that produces the residue;

(iii) data showing the recommended amount, frequency, method, and time of application of that pesticide chemical;

(iv) full reports of tests and investigations made with respect to the safety of the pesticide chemical, including full information as to the methods and controls used in conducting those tests and investigations;

(v) full reports of tests and investigations made with respect to the nature and amount of the pesticide chemical residue that is likely to remain in or on the food, including a description of the analytical methods used;

(vi) a practical method for detecting and measuring the levels of the pesticide chemical residue in or on the food, or for exemptions, a statement why such a method is not needed;

(vii) a proposed tolerance for the pesticide chemical residue, if a tolerance is proposed;

(viii) if the petition relates to a tolerance for a processed food, reports of investigations conducted using the processing method(s) used to produce that food;

(ix) such information as the Administrator may require to make the determination under subsection (b)(2)(C);

(x) such information as the Administrator may require on whether the pesticide chemical may have an effect in humans that is similar to an effect produced by a naturally occurring estrogen or other endocrine effects;

(xi) information regarding exposure to the pesticide chemical residue due to any tolerance or exemption already granted for such residue;

(xii) practical methods for removing any amount of the residue that would exceed any proposed tolerance; and

(xiii) such other data and information as the Administrator requires by regulation to support the petition.

If information or data required by this subparagraph is available to the Administrator, the person submitting the petition may cite the availability of the information or data in lieu of submitting it. The Administrator may require a petition to be accompanied by samples of the pesticide chemical with respect to which the petition is filed.

(B) Modification or Revocation. — The Administrator may by regulation establish the requirements for information and data to support a petition to modify or revoke a tolerance or to modify or revoke an exemption from the requirement for a tolerance.

(3) Notice. — A notice of the filing of a petition that the Administrator determines has met the requirements of paragraph (2) shall be published by the Administrator within 30 days after such determination. The notice shall announce the availability of a description of the analytical methods available to the Administrator for the detection and measurement of the pesticide chemical residue with respect to which the petition is filed or shall set forth the petitioner's statement of why such a method is not needed. The notice shall include the summary required by paragraph (2)(A)(i)(I).

(4) Actions by the Administrator. —

(A) In General. — The Administrator shall, after giving due consideration to a petition filed under paragraph (1) and any other information available to the Administrator —

(i) issue a final regulation (which may vary from that sought by the petition) establishing, modifying, or revoking a tolerance for the pesticide chemical residue or an exemption of the pesticide chemical residue from the requirement of a tolerance (which final regulation shall be issued without further notice and without further period for public comment);

(ii) issue a proposed regulation under subsection (e), and thereafter issue a final regulation under such subsection; or

(iii) issue an order denying the petition.

(B) Priorities. — The Administrator shall give priority to petitions for the establishment or modification of a tolerance or exemption for a pesticide chemical residue that appears to pose a significantly lower risk to human health from dietary exposure than pesticide chemical residues that have tolerances in effect for the same or similar uses.

(C) Expedited Review of Certain petitions. —

(i) Date Certain for Review. — If a person files a complete petition with the Administrator proposing the issuance of a regulation establishing a tolerance or exemption for a pesticide chemical residue that presents a lower risk to human health than a pesticide chemical residue for which a tolerance has been left in effect or modified under subsection (b)(2)(B), the Administrator shall complete action on such petition under this paragraph within 1 year.

(ii) Required Determinations. — If the Administrator issues a final regulation establishing a tolerance or exemption for a safer pesticide chemical residue under clause (i), the Administrator shall, not later than 180 days after the date on which the regulation is issued, determine whether a condition described in subclause (I) or (II) of subsection (b)(2)(B)(iii) continues to exist with respect to a tolerance that has been left in effect or modified under subsection (b)(2)(B). If such condition does not continue to exist, the Administrator shall, not later than 180 days after the date on which the determination under the preceding sentence is made, issue a regulation under subsection (e)(1) to modify or revoke the tolerance.

(e) Action on Administrator's Own Initiative. —

(1) General Rule. — The Administrator may issue a regulation —

(A) establishing, modifying, suspending under subsection (1)(3), or revoking a tolerance for a pesticide chemical or a pesticide chemical residue;

(B) establishing, modifying, suspending under subsection (1)(3), or revoking an exemption of a pesticide chemical residue from the requirement of a tolerance; or

(C) establishing general procedures and requirements to implement this section.

(2) Notice. — Before issuing a final regulation under paragraph (1), the Administrator shall issue a notice of proposed rulemaking and provide a period of not less than 60 days for public comment on the proposed regulation, except that a shorter period for comment may be provided if the Administrator for good cause finds that it would be in the public interest to do so and states the reasons for the finding in the notice of proposed rulemaking.

(f) Special Data Requirements. —

(1) Requiring Submission of Additional Data. — If the Administrator determines that additional data or information are reasonably required to support the continuation of a tolerance or exemption that is in effect under this section for a pesticide chemical residue on a food, the Administrator shall —

(A) issue a notice requiring the person holding the pesticide registrations associated with such tolerance or exemption to submit the data or information under section 3(c)(2)(B) of the Federal Insecticide, Fungicide, and Rodenticide Act;

(B) issue a rule requiring that testing be conducted on a substance or mixture under section 4 of the Toxic Substances Control Act; or

(C) publish in the Federal Register, after first providing notice and an opportunity for comment of not less than 60 days' duration, an order —

(i) requiring the submission to the Administrator by one or more interested persons of a notice identifying the person or persons who will submit the required data and information;

(ii) describing the type of data and information required to be submitted to the Administrator and stating why the data and information could not be obtained under the authority of section 3(c)(2)(B) of the Federal Insecticide, Fungicide, and Rodenticide Act or section 4 of the Toxic Substances Control Act;

(iii) describing the reports of the Administrator required to be prepared during and after the collection of the data and information;

(iv) requiring the submission to the Administrator of the data, information, and reports referred to in clauses (ii) and (iii); and

(v) establishing dates by which the submissions described in clauses (i) and (iv) must be made.

The Administrator may under subparagraph (C) revise any such order to correct an error. The Administrator may under this paragraph require data or information pertaining to whether the pesticide chemical may have an effect in humans that is similar to an effect produced by a naturally occurring estrogen or other endocrine effects.

(2) Noncompliance. — If a submission required by a notice issued in accordance with paragraph (1)(A), a rule issued under paragraph (1)(B), or an order issued under paragraph (1)(C) is not made by the time specified in such notice, rule, or order, the Administrator may by order published in the Federal Register modify or revoke the tolerance or exemption in question. In any review of such an order under subsection (g)(2), the only material issue shall be whether a submission required under paragraph (1) was not made by the time specified.

(g) Effective Date, Objections, Hearings, and Administrative Review. —

(1) Effective Date. — A regulation or order issued under subsection (d)(4), (e)(1), or (f)(2) shall take effect upon publication unless the regulation or order specifies otherwise. The Administrator may stay the effectiveness of the regulation or order if, after issuance of such regulation or order, objections are filed with respect to such regulation or order pursuant to paragraph (2).

(2) Further Proceedings. —

(A) Objections. — Within 60 days after a regulation or order is issued under subsection (d)(4), (e)(1)(A), (e)(1)(B), (f)(2), (n)(3), or (n)(5)(C), any person may file objections thereto with the Administrator, specifying with particularity the provisions of the regulation or order deemed objectionable and stating reasonable grounds therefor. If the regulation or order was issued in response to a petition under subsection (d)(1), a copy of each objection filed by a person other than the petitioner shall be served by the Administrator on the petitioner.

(B) Hearing. — An objection may include a request for a public evidentiary hearing upon the objection. The Administrator shall, upon the initiative of the Administrator or upon the request of an interested person and after due notice, hold a public evidentiary hearing if and to the extent the Administrator determines that such a public hearing is necessary to receive factual evidence relevant to material issues of fact raised by the objections. The presiding officer in such a hearing may authorize a party to obtain discovery from other persons and may upon a showing of good cause made by a party issue a subpoena to compel testimony or production of documents from any person. The presiding officer shall be governed by the Federal Rules of Civil Procedure in making any order for the protection of the witness or the content of documents produced and shall order the payment of reasonable fees and expenses as a condition to requiring testimony of the witness. On contest, such a subpoena may be enforced by a Federal district court.

(C) Final Decision. — As soon as practicable after receiving the arguments of the parties, the Administrator shall issue an order stating the action taken upon each such objection and setting forth any revision to the regulation or prior order that the Administrator has found to be warranted. If a hearing was held under subparagraph (B), such order and any revision to the regulation or prior order shall, with respect to questions of fact at issue in the hearing, be based only on substantial evidence of record at such hearing, and shall set forth in detail the findings of facts and the conclusions of law or policy upon which the order or regulation is based.

(h) Judicial Review. —

(1) Petition. — In a case of actual controversy as to the validity of any regulation issued under subsection (e)(1)(C), or any order issued under subsection (f)(1)(C) or (g)(2)(C), or any regulation that is the subject of such an order, any person who will be adversely affected by such order or regulation may obtain judicial review by filing in the United States Court of Appeals for the circuit wherein that person resides or has its principal place of business, or in the United States Court of Appeals for the District of Columbia Circuit, within 60 days after publication of such order or regulation, a petition praying that the order or regulation be set aside in whole or in part.

(2) Record and Jurisdiction. — A copy of the petition under paragraph (1) shall be forthwith transmitted by the clerk of the court to the Administrator, or any officer designated by the Administrator for that purpose, and thereupon the Administrator shall file in the court the record of the proceedings on which the Administrator based the order or regulation, as provided in section 2112 of title 28, United States Code. Upon the filing of such a petition, the court shall have exclusive jurisdiction to affirm or set aside the order or regulation complained of in whole or in part. As to orders issued following a public evidentiary hearing, the findings of the Administrator with respect to questions of fact shall be sustained only if supported by substantial evidence when considered on the record as a whole.

(3) Additional Evidence. — If a party applies to the court for leave to adduce additional evidence and shows to the satisfaction of the court that the additional evidence is material and that there were reasonable grounds for the failure to adduce the evidence in the proceeding before the Administrator, the court may order that the additional evidence (and evidence in rebuttal thereof) shall be taken before the Administrator in the manner and upon the terms and conditions the court deems proper. The Administrator may modify prior findings as to the facts by reason of the additional evidence so taken and may modify the order or regulation accordingly. The Administrator shall file with the court any such modified finding, order, or regulation.

(4) Final Judgment; Supreme Court Review. — The judgment of the court affirming or setting aside, in whole or in part, any regulation or any order and any regulation which is the subject of such an order shall be final, subject to review by the Supreme Court of the United States as provided in section 1254 of title 28 of the United States Code. The commencement of proceedings under this subsection shall not, unless specifically ordered by the court to the contrary, operate as a stay of a regulation or order.

(5) Application. — Any issue as to which review is or was obtainable under this subsection shall not be the subject of judicial review under any other provision of law.

(i) Confidentiality and Use of Data. —

(1) General Rule. — Data and information that are or have been submitted to the Administrator under this section or section 409 in support of a tolerance or an exemption from a tolerance shall be entitled to confidential treatment for reasons of business confidentiality and to exclusive use and data compensation to the same extent provided by sections 3 and 10 of the Federal Insecticide, Fungicide, and Rodenticide Act.

(2) Exceptions. —

(A) In General. — Data and information that are entitled to confidential treatment under paragraph (1) may be disclosed, under such security requirements as the Administrator may provide by regulation, to —

(i) employees of the United States authorized by the Administrator to examine such data and information in the carrying out of their official duties under this Act or other Federal statutes intended to protect the public health; or

(ii) contractors with the United States authorized by the Administrator to examine such data and information in the carrying out of contracts under this Act or such statutes.

(B) Congress. — This subsection does not authorize the withholding of data or information from either House of Congress or from, to the extent of matter within its jurisdiction, any committee or subcommittee of such committee or any joint committee of Congress or any subcommittee of such joint committee.

(3) Summaries. — Notwithstanding any provision of this subsection or other law, the Administrator may publish the informative summary required by subsection (d)(2)(A)(i) and may, in issuing a proposed or final regulation or order under this section, publish an informative summary of the data relating to the regulation or order.

(j) Status of Previously Issued Regulations. —

(1) Regulations Under Section 406. — Regulations affecting pesticide chemical residues in or on raw agricultural commodities promulgated, in accordance with section 701(e), under the authority of section 406(a) upon the basis of public hearings instituted before January 1, 1953, shall be deemed to be regulations issued under this section and shall be subject to modification or revocation under subsections (d) and (e), and shall be subject to review under subsection (q).

(2) Regulations Under Section 409. — Regulations that established tolerances for substances that are pesticide chemical residues in or on processed food, or that otherwise stated the conditions under which such pesticide chemicals could be safely used, and that were issued under section 409 on or before the date of the enactment of this paragraph, shall be deemed to be regulations issued under this section and shall be subject to modification or revocation under subsection (d) or (e), and shall be subject to review under subsection (q).

(3) Regulations Under Section 408. — Regulations that established tolerances or exemptions under this section that were issued on or before the date of the enactment of this paragraph shall remain in effect unless modified or revoked under subsection (d) or (e), and shall be subject to review under subsection (q).

(4) Certain Substances. — With respect to a substance that is not included in the definition of the term "pesticide chemical" under section 201(q)(1) but was so included on the day before the date of the enactment of the Antimicrobial Regulation Technical Corrections Act of 1998, the following applies as of such date of enactment:

(A) Notwithstanding paragraph (2), any regulation applying to the use of the substance that was in effect on the day before such date, and was on such day deemed in such paragraph to have been issued under this section, shall be considered to have been issued under section 409.

(B) Notwithstanding paragraph (3), any regulation applying to the use of the substance that was in effect on such day and was issued under this section (including any such regulation issued before the date of the enactment of the Food Quality Protection Act of 1996) is deemed to have been issued under section 409.

(k) Transitional Provision. — If, on the day before the date of the enactment of this subsection, a substance that is a pesticide chemical was, with respect to a particular pesticidal use of the substance and any resulting pesticide chemical residue in or on a particular food —

(1) regarded by the Administrator or the Secretary as generally recognized as safe for use within the meaning of the provisions of subsection (a) or section 201(s) as then in effect; or

(2) regarded by the Secretary as a substance described by section 201(s)(4);

such a pesticide chemical residue shall be regarded as exempt from the requirement for a tolerance, as of the date of enactment of this subsection. The Administrator shall by regulation indicate which substances are described by this subsection. Any exemption under this subsection may be modified or revoked as if it had been issued under subsection (c).

(l) Harmonization with Action Under Other Laws. —

(1) Coordination with FIFRA. — To the extent practicable and consistent with the review deadlines in subsection (q), in issuing a final rule under this subsection that suspends or revokes a tolerance or exemption for a pesticide chemical residue in or on food, the Administrator shall coordinate such action with any related necessary action under the Federal Insecticide, Fungicide, and Rodenticide Act.

(2) Revocation of Tolerance or Exemption Following Cancellation of Associated Registrations. — If the Administrator, acting under the Federal Insecticide, Fungicide, and Rodenticide Act, cancels the registration of each pesticide that contains a particular pesticide chemical and that is labeled for use on a particular food, or requires that the registration of each such pesticide be modified to prohibit its use in connection with the production, storage, or transportation of such food, due in whole or in part to dietary risks to humans posed by residues of that pesticide chemical on that food, the Administrator shall revoke any tolerance or exemption that allows the presence of the pesticide chemical, or any pesticide chemical residue that results from its use, in or on that food. Subsection (e) shall apply to actions taken under this paragraph. A revocation under this paragraph shall become effective not later than 180 days after —

(A) the date by which each such cancellation of a registration has become effective; or

(B) the date on which the use of the canceled pesticide becomes unlawful under the terms of the cancellation, whichever is later.

(3) Suspension of Tolerance or Exemption Following Suspension of Associated Registrations. —

(A) Suspension. — If the Administrator, acting under the Federal Insecticide, Fungicide, and Rodenticide Act, suspends the use of each registered pesticide that contains a particular pesticide chemical and that is labeled for use on a particular food, due in whole or in part to dietary risks to humans posed by residues of that pesticide chemical on that food, the Administrator shall suspend any tolerance or exemption that allows the presence of the pesticide chemical, or any pesticide chemical residue that results from its use, in or on that food. Subsection (e) shall apply to actions taken under this paragraph. A suspension under this paragraph shall become effective not later than 60 days after the date by which each such suspension of use has become effective.

(B) Effect of Suspension. — The suspension of a tolerance or exemption under subparagraph (A) shall be effective as long as the use of each associated registration of a pesticide is suspended under the Federal Insecticide, Fungicide, and Rodenticide Act. While a suspension of a tolerance or exemption is effective the tolerance or exemption shall not be considered to be in effect. If the suspension of use of the pesticide under that Act is terminated, leaving the registration of the pesticide for such use in effect under that Act, the Administrator shall rescind any associated suspension of tolerance or exemption.

(4) Tolerances for Unavoidable Residues. — In connection with action taken under paragraph (2) or (3), or with respect to pesticides whose registrations were suspended or canceled prior to the date of the enactment of this paragraph under the Federal Insecticide, Fungicide, and Rodenticide Act, if the Administrator determines that a residue of the canceled or suspended pesticide chemical will unavoidably persist in the environment and thereby be present in or on a food, the Administrator may establish a tolerance for the pesticide chemical residue. In establishing such a tolerance, the Administrator shall take into account both the factors set forth in subsection (b)(2) and the unavoidability of the residue. Subsection (e) shall apply to the establishment of such tolerance. The Administrator shall review any such tolerance periodically and modify it as necessary so that it allows no greater level of the pesticide chemical residue than is unavoidable.

(5) Pesticide Residues Resulting from Lawful Application of Pesticide. — Notwithstanding any other provision of this Act, if a tolerance or exemption for a pesticide chemical residue in or on a food has been revoked, suspended, or modified under this section, an article of that food shall not be deemed unsafe solely because of the presence of such pesticide chemical residue in or on such food if it is shown to the satisfaction of the Secretary that —

(A) the residue is present as the result of an application or use of a pesticide at a time and in a manner that was lawful under the Federal Insecticide, Fungicide, and Rodenticide Act; and

(B) the residue does not exceed a level that was authorized at the time of that application or use to be present on the food under a tolerance, exemption, food additive regulation, or other sanction then in effect under this Act;

unless, in the case of any tolerance or exemption revoked, suspended, or modified under this subsection or subsection (d) or (e), the Administrator has issued a determination that consumption of the legally treated food during the period of its likely availability in commerce will pose an unreasonable dietary risk.

(6) Tolerance for Use of Pesticides Under an Emergency Exemption. — If the Administrator grants an exemption under section 18 of the Federal Insecticide, Fungicide, and Rodenticide Act (7 U.S.C. 136p) for a pesticide chemical, the Administrator shall establish a tolerance or exemption from the requirement for a tolerance for the pesticide chemical residue. Such a tolerance or exemption from a tolerance shall have an expiration date. The Administrator may establish such a tolerance or exemption without providing notice or a period for comment on the tolerance or exemption. The Administrator shall promulgate regulations within 365 days after the date of the enactment of this paragraph governing the establishment of tolerances and exemptions under this paragraph. Such regulations shall be consistent with the safety standard under subsections (b)(2) and (c)(2) and with section 18 of the Federal Insecticide, Fungicide, and Rodenticide Act.

(m) Fees. —

(1) Amount. — The Administrator shall by regulation require the payment of such fees as will in the aggregate, in the judgment of the Administrator, be sufficient over a reasonable term to provide, equip, and maintain an adequate service for the performance of the Administrator's functions under this section. Under the regulations, the performance of the Administrator's services or other functions under this section, including —

(A) the acceptance for filing of a petition submitted under subsection (d);

(B) establishing, modifying, leaving in effect, or revoking a tolerance or establishing, modifying, leaving in effect, or revoking an exemption from the requirement for a tolerance under this section;

(C) the acceptance for filing of objections under subsection (g); or

(D) the certification and filing in court of a transcript of the proceedings and the record under subsection (h);

may be conditioned upon the payment of such fees. The regulations may further provide for waiver or refund of fees in whole or in part when in the judgment of the Administrator such a waiver or refund is equitable and not contrary to the purposes of this subsection.

(2) Deposit. — All fees collected under paragraph (1) shall be deposited in the Reregistration and Expedited Processing Fund created by section 4(k) of the Federal Insecticide, Fungicide, and Rodenticide Act. Such fees shall be available to the Administrator, without fiscal year limitation, for the performance of the Administrator's services or functions as specified in paragraph (1).

(n) National Uniformity of Tolerances. —

(1) Qualifying Pesticide Chemical Residue. — For purposes of this subsection, the term "qualifying pesticide chemical residue" means a pesticide chemical residue resulting from the use, in production, processing, or storage of a food, of a pesticide chemical that is an active ingredient and that —

(A) was first approved for such use in a registration of a pesticide issued under section 3(c)(5) of the Federal Insecticide, Fungicide, and Rodenticide Act on or after April 25, 1985, on the basis of data determined by the Administrator to meet all applicable requirements for data prescribed by regulations in effect under that Act on April 25, 1985; or

(B) was approved for such use in a reregistration eligibility determination issued under section 4(g) of that Act on or after the date of enactment of this subsection.

(2) Qualifying Federal Determination. — For purposes of this subsection, the term "qualifying Federal determination" means a tolerance or exemption from the requirement for a tolerance for a qualifying pesticide chemical residue that —

(A) is issued under this section after the date of the enactment of this subsection and determined by the Administrator to meet the standard under subsection (b)(2)(A) (in the case of a tolerance) or (c)(2) (in the case of an exemption); or

(B) —

(i) pursuant to subsection (j) is remaining in effect or is deemed to have been issued under this section, or is regarded under subsection (k) as exempt from the requirement for a tolerance; and

(ii) is determined by the Administrator to meet the standard under subsection (b)(2)(A) (in the case of a tolerance) or (c)(2) (in the case of an exemption).

(3) Limitation. — The Administrator may make the determination described in paragraph (2)(B)(ii) only by issuing a rule in accordance with the procedure set forth in subsection (d) or (e) and only if the Administrator issues a proposed rule and allows a period of not less than 30 days for comment on the proposed rule. Any such rule shall be reviewable in accordance with subsections (g) and (h).

(4) State Authority. — Except as provided in paragraphs (5), (6), and (8) no State or political subdivision may establish or enforce any regulatory limit on a qualifying pesticide chemical residue in or on any food if a qualifying Federal determination applies to the presence of such pesticide chemical residue in or on such food, unless such State regulatory limit is identical to such qualifying Federal determination. A State or political subdivision shall be deemed to establish or enforce a regulatory limit on a pesticide chemical residue in or on a food if it purports to prohibit or penalize the production, processing, shipping, or other handling of a food because it contains a pesticide residue (in excess of a prescribed limit).

(5) Petition Procedure. —

(A) In General. — Any State may petition the Administrator for authorization to establish in such State a regulatory limit on a qualifying pesticide chemical residue in or on any food that is not identical to the qualifying Federal determination applicable to such qualifying pesticide chemical residue.

(B) Petition Requirements. — Any petition under subparagraph (A) shall —

(i) satisfy any requirements prescribed, by rule, by the Administrator; and

(ii) be supported by scientific data about the pesticide chemical residue that is the subject of the petition or about chemically related pesticide chemical residues, data on the consumption within such State of food bearing the pesticide chemical residue, and data on exposure of humans within such State to the pesticide chemical residue.

(C) Authorization. — The Administrator may, by order, grant the authorization described in subparagraph

(A) if the Administrator determines that the proposed State regulatory limit —

(i) is justified by compelling local conditions; and

(ii) would not cause any food to be a violation of Federal law.

(D) Treatment. — In lieu of any action authorized under subparagraph (C), the Administrator may treat a petition under this paragraph as a petition under subsection (d) to modify or revoke a tolerance or an exemption. If the Administrator determines to treat a petition under this paragraph as a petition under subsection (d), the Administrator shall thereafter act on the petition pursuant to subsection (d).

(E) Review. — Any order of the Administrator granting or denying the authorization described in subparagraph (A) shall be subject to review in the manner described in subsections (g) and (h).

(6) Urgent Petition Procedure. — Any State petition to the Administrator pursuant to paragraph (5) that demonstrates that consumption of a food containing such pesticide residue level during the period of the food's likely availability in the State will pose a significant public health threat from acute exposure shall be considered an urgent petition. If an order by the Administrator to grant or deny the requested authorization in an urgent petition is not made within 30 days of receipt of the petition, the petitioning State may establish and enforce a temporary regulatory limit on a qualifying pesticide chemical residue in or on the food. The temporary regulatory limit shall be validated or terminated by the Administrator's final order on the petition.

(7) Residues from Lawful Application. — No State or political subdivision may enforce any regulatory limit on the level of a pesticide chemical residue that may appear in or on any food if, at the time of the application of the pesticide that resulted in such residue, the sale of such food with such residue level was lawful under this section and under the law of such State, unless the State demonstrates that consumption of the food containing such pesticide residue level during the period of the food's likely availability in the State will pose an unreasonable dietary risk to the health of persons within such State.

(8) Savings. — Nothing in this Act preempts the authority of any State or political subdivision to require that a food containing a pesticide chemical residue bear or be the subject of a warning or other statement relating to the presence of the pesticide chemical residue in or on such food.

(o) Consumer Right to Know. — Not later than 2 years after the date of the enactment of the Food Quality Protection Act of 1996 and annually thereafter, the Administrator shall, in consultation with the Secretary of Agriculture and the Secretary of Health and Human Services, publish in a format understandable to a lay person, and distribute to large retail grocers for public display (in a manner determined by the grocer), the following information, at a minimum:

(1) A discussion of the risks and benefits of pesticide chemical residues in or on food purchased by consumers.

(2) A listing of actions taken under subparagraph (B) of subsection (b)(2) that may result in pesticide chemical residues in or on food that present a yearly or lifetime risk above the risk allowed under subparagraph (A) of such subsection, and the food on which the pesticide chemicals producing the residues are used.

(3) Recommendations to consumers for reducing dietary exposure to pesticide chemical residues in a manner consistent with maintaining a healthy diet, including a list of food that may reasonably substitute for food listed under paragraph (2).

Nothing in this subsection shall prevent retail grocers from providing additional information.

(p) Estrogenic Substances Screening Program. —

(1) Development. — Not later than 2 years after the date of enactment of this section, the Administrator shall in consultation with the Secretary of Health and Human Services develop a screening program, using appropriate validated test systems and other scientifically relevant information, to determine whether certain substances may have an effect in humans that is similar to an effect produced by a naturally occurring estrogen, or such other endocrine effect as the Administrator may designate.

(2) Implementation. — Not later than 3 years after the date of enactment of this section, after obtaining public comment and review of the screening program described in paragraph (1) by the scientific advisory panel established under section 25(d) of the Federal Insecticide, Fungicide, and Rodenticide Act or the science advisory board established by section 8 of the Environmental Research, Development, and Demonstration [Authorization] Act of 1978 (42 U.S.C. 4365), the Administrator shall implement the program.

(3) Substances. — In carrying out the screening program described in paragraph (1), the Administrator —

(A) shall provide for the testing of all pesticide chemicals; and

(B) may provide for the testing of any other substance that may have an effect that is cumulative to an effect of a pesticide chemical if the Administrator determines that a substantial population may be exposed to such substance.

(4) Exemption. — Notwithstanding paragraph (3), the Administrator may, by order, exempt from the requirements of this section a biologic substance or other substance if the Administrator determines that the substance is anticipated not to produce any effect in humans similar to an effect produced by a naturally occurring estrogen.

(5) Collection of Information. —

(A) In General. — The Administrator shall issue an order to a registrant of a substance for which testing is required under this subsection, or to a person who manufactures or imports a substance for which testing is required under this subsection, to conduct testing in accordance with the screening program described in paragraph (1), and submit information obtained from the testing to the Administrator, within a reasonable time period that the Administrator determines is sufficient for the generation of the information.

(B) Procedures. — To the extent practicable the Administrator shall minimize duplicative testing of the same substance for the same endocrine effect, develop, as appropriate, procedures for fair and equitable sharing of test costs, and develop, as necessary, procedures for handling of confidential business information.

(C) Failure of Registrants to Submit Information. —

(i) Suspension. — If a registrant of a substance referred to in paragraph (3)(A) fails to comply with an order under subparagraph (A) of this paragraph, the Administrator shall issue a notice of intent to suspend the sale or distribution of the substance by the registrant. Any suspension proposed under this paragraph shall become final at the end of the 30-day period beginning on the date that the registrant receives the notice of intent to suspend, unless during that period a person adversely affected by the notice requests a hearing or the Administrator determines that the registrant has complied fully with this paragraph.

(ii) Hearing. — If a person requests a hearing under clause (i), the hearing shall be conducted in accordance with section 554 of title 5, United States Code. The only matter for resolution at the hearing shall be whether the registrant has failed to comply with an order under subparagraph (A) of this paragraph. A decision by the Administrator after completion of a hearing shall be considered to be a final agency action.

(iii) Termination of Suspensions. — The Administrator shall terminate a suspension under this subparagraph issued with respect to a registrant if the Administrator determines that the registrant has complied fully with this paragraph.

(D) Noncompliance by Other Persons. — Any person (other than a registrant) who fails to comply with an order under subparagraph (A) shall be liable for the same penalties and sanctions as are provided under section 16 of the Toxic Substances Control Act (15 U.S.C. 2601 and following) in the case of a violation referred to in that section. Such penalties and sanctions shall be assessed and imposed in the same manner as provided in such section 16.

(6) Agency Action. — In the case of any substance that is found, as a result of testing and evaluation under this section, to have an endocrine effect on humans, the Administrator shall, as appropriate, take action under such statutory authority as is available to the Administrator, including consideration under other sections of this Act, as is necessary to ensure the protection of public health.

(7) Report to Congress. — Not later than 4 years after the date of enactment of this section, the Administrator shall prepare and submit to Congress a report containing —

(A) the findings of the Administrator resulting from the screening program described in paragraph (1);

(B) recommendations for further testing needed to evaluate the impact on human health of the substances tested under the screening program; and

(C) recommendations for any further actions (including any action described in paragraph (6)) that the Administrator determines are appropriate based on the findings.

(q) Schedule for Review. —

(1) In General. — The Administrator shall review tolerances and exemptions for pesticide chemical residues in effect on the day before the date of the enactment of the Food Quality Protection Act of 1996, as expeditiously as practicable, assuring that —

(A) 33 percent of such tolerances and exemptions are reviewed within 3 years of the date of enactment of such Act;

(B) 66 percent of such tolerances and exemptions are reviewed within 6 years of the date of enactment of such Act; and

(C) 100 percent of such tolerances and exemptions are reviewed within 10 years of the date of enactment of such Act.

In conducting a review of a tolerance or exemption, the Administrator shall determine whether the tolerance or exemption meets the requirements of subsections (b)(2) or (c)(2) and shall, by the deadline for the review of the tolerance or exemption, issue a regulation under subsection (d)(4) or (e)(1) to modify or revoke the tolerance or exemption if the tolerance or exemption does not meet such requirements.

(2) Priorities. — In determining priorities for reviewing tolerances and exemptions under paragraph (1), the Administrator shall give priority to the review of the tolerances or exemptions that appear to pose the greatest risk to public health.

(3) Publication of Schedule. — Not later than 12 months after the date of the enactment of the Food Quality Protection Act of 1996, the Administrator shall publish a schedule for review of tolerances and exemptions established prior to the date of the enactment of the Food Quality Protection Act of 1996. The determination of priorities for the review of tolerances and exemptions pursuant to this subsection is not a rulemaking and shall not be subject to judicial review, except that failure to take final action pursuant to the schedule established by this paragraph shall be subject to judicial review.

(r) Temporary Tolerance or Exemption. — The Administrator may, upon the request of any person who has obtained an experimental permit for a pesticide chemical under the Federal Insecticide, Fungicide, and Rodenticide Act or upon the Administrator's own initiative, establish a temporary tolerance or exemption for the pesticide chemical residue for the uses covered by the permit. Subsections (b)(2), (c)(2), (d), and (e) shall apply to actions taken under this subsection.

(s) Savings Clause. — Nothing in this section shall be construed to amend or modify the provisions of the Toxic Substances Control Act or the Federal Insecticide, Fungicide, and Rodenticide Act.

Sec. 409. [348] Food Additives.

(a) Unsafe Food Additives. — A food additive shall, with respect to any particular use or intended use of such additives, be deemed to be unsafe for the purposes of the application of clause (2)(C) of section 402(a), unless —

(1) it and its use or intended use conform to the terms of an exemption which is in effect pursuant to subsection

(j) of an this section;

(2) there is in effect, and it and its use or intended use are in conformity with, a regulation issued under this section prescribing the conditions under which such additive may be safely used; or

(3) in the case of a food additive as defined in this Act that is a food contact substance, there is —

(A) in effect, and such substance and the use of such substance are in conformity with, a regulation issued under this section prescribing the conditions under which such additive may be safely used; or

(B) a notification submitted under subsection (h) that is effective.

While such a regulation relating to a food additive, or such a notification under subsection (h)(1) relating to a food additive that is a food contact substance, is in effect, and has not been revoked pursuant to subsection (i), a food shall not, by reason of bearing or containing such a food additive in accordance with the regulation or notification, be considered adulterated under section 402(a)(1).

(b) Petition to Establish Safety. —

(1) Any person may, with respect to any intended use of a food additive, file with the Secretary a petition proposing the issuance of a regulation prescribing the conditions under which such additive may be safely used.

(2) Such petition shall, in addition to any explanatory or supporting data, contain —

(A) the name and all pertinent information concerning such food additive, including, where available, its chemical identity and composition;

(B) a statement of the conditions of the proposed use of such additive, including all directions, recommendations, and suggestions proposed for the use of such additive, and including specimens of its proposed labeling;

(C) all relevant data bearing on the physical or other technical effect such additive is intended to produce, and the quantity of such additive required to produce such effect;

(D) a description of practicable methods for determining the quantity of such additive in or on food, and any substance formed in or on food, because of its use; and

(E) full reports of investigations made with respect to the safety for use of such additive, including full information as to the methods and controls used in conducting such investigations.

(3) Upon request of the Secretary, the petitioner shall furnish (or, if the petitioner is not the manufacturer of such additive, the petitioner shall have the manufacturer of such additive furnish, without disclosure to the petitioner), a full description of the methods used in, and the facilities and controls used for, the production of such additive.

(4) Upon request of the Secretary, the petitioner shall furnish samples of the food additive involved, or articles used as components thereof, and of the food in or on which the additive is proposed to be used.

(5) Notice of the regulation proposed by the petitioner shall be published in general terms by the Secretary within thirty days after filing.

(c) Action on the Petition. —

(1) The Secretary shall —

(A) by order establish a regulation (whether or not in accord with that proposed by the petitioner) prescribing, with respect to one or more proposed uses of the food additive involved, the conditions under which such additive may be safely used (including, but not limited to, specifications as to the particular food or classes of food in or on which such additive may be used, the maximum quantity which may be used or permitted to remain in or on such food, the manner in which such additive may be added to or used in or on such food, and any directions or other labeling or packaging requirements for such additive deemed necessary by him to assure the safety of such use), and shall notify the petitioner of such order and the reasons for such action; or

(B) by order deny the petition, and shall notify the petitioner of such order and of the reasons for such action.

(2) The order required by paragraph (1) (A) or (B) of this subsection shall be issued within ninety days after the date of filing of the petition, except that the Secretary may (prior to such ninetieth day), by written notice to the petitioner, extend such ninety-day period to such time (not more than one hundred and eighty days after the date of filing of the petition) as the Secretary deems necessary to enable him to study and investigate the petition.

(3) No such regulation shall issue if a fair evaluation of the data before the Secretary —

(A) fails to establish that the proposed use of the food additive, under the conditions of use to be specified in the regulation, will be safe: [p]rovided, [t]hat no additive shall be deemed to be safe if it is found to induce cancer when ingested by man or animal, or if it is found, after tests which are appropriate for the evaluation of the safety of food additives, to induce cancer in man or animal, except that this proviso shall not apply with respect to the use of a substance as an ingredient of feed for animals which are raised for food production, if the Secretary finds

(i) that, under the conditions of use and feeding specified in proposed labeling and reasonably certain to be followed in practice, such additive will not adversely affect the animals for which such feed is intended, and

(ii) that no residue of the additive will be found (by methods of examination prescribed or approved by the Secretary by regulations, which regulations shall not be subject to subsections (f) and (g)) in any edible portion of such animal after slaughter or in any food yielded by or derived from the living animal; or

(B) shows that the proposed use of the additive would promote deception of the consumer in violation of this Act or would otherwise result in adulteration or in misbranding of food within the meaning of this Act.

(4) If, in the judgment of the Secretary, based upon a fair evaluation of the data before him, a tolerance limitation is required in order to assure that the proposed use of an additive will be safe, the Secretary —

(A) shall not fix such tolerance limitation at a level higher than he finds to be reasonably required to accomplish the physical or other technical effect for which such additive is intended; and

(B) shall not establish a regulation for such proposed use if he finds upon a fair evaluation of the data before him that such data do not establish that such use would accomplish the intended physical or other technical effect.

(5) In determining, for the purposes of this section, whether a proposed use of a food additive is safe, the Secretary shall consider among other relevant factors —

(A) the probable consumption of the additive and of any substance formed in or on food because of the use of the additive;

(B) the cumulative effect of such additive in the diet of man or animals, taking into account any chemically or pharmacologically related substance or substances in such diet; and

(C) safety factors which in the opinion of experts qualified by scientific training and experience to evaluate the safety of food additives are generally recognized as appropriate for the use of animal experimentation data.

(d) Regulation Issued on Secretary's Initiative. — The Secretary may at any time, upon his own initiative, propose the issuance of a regulation prescribing, with respect to any particular use of a food additive, the conditions under which such additive may be safely used, and the reasons therefor. After the thirtieth day following publication of such a proposal, the Secretary may by order establish a regulation based upon the proposal.

(e) Publication and Effective Date of Orders. — Any order, including any regulation established by such order, issued under subsection (c) or (d) of this section, shall be published and shall be effective upon publication, but the Secretary may stay such effectiveness if, after issuance of such order, a hearing is sought with respect to such order pursuant to subsection (f).

(f) Objections and Public Hearing. —

(1) Within thirty days after publication of an order made pursuant to subsection (c) or (d) of this section, any person adversely affected by such an order may file objections thereto with the Secretary, specifying with particularity the provisions of the order deemed objectionable, stating reasonable grounds therefor, and requesting a public hearing upon such objections. The Secretary shall, after due notice, as promptly as possible hold such public hearing for the purpose of receiving evidence relevant and material to the issues raised by such objections. As soon as practicable after completion of the hearing, the Secretary shall by order act upon such objections and make such order public.

(2) Such order shall be based upon a fair evaluation of the entire record at such hearing, and shall include a statement setting forth in detail the findings and conclusions upon which the order is based.

(3) The Secretary shall specify in the order the date on which it shall take effect, except that it shall not be made to take effect prior to the ninetieth day after its publication, unless the Secretary finds that emergency conditions exist necessitating an earlier effective date, in which event the Secretary shall specify in the order his findings as to such conditions.

(g) Judicial Review. —

(1) In a case of actual controversy as to the validity of any order issued under subsection (f), including any order thereunder with respect to amendment or repeal of a regulation issued under this section, any person who will be adversely affected by such order may obtain judicial review by filing in the United States Court of Appeals for the circuit wherein such person resides or has his principal place of business, or in the United States Court of Appeals for the District of Columbia Circuit, within sixty days after the entry of such order, a petition praying that the order be set aside in whole or in part.

(2) A copy of such petition shall be forthwith transmitted by the clerk of the court to the Secretary, or any officer designated by him for that purpose, and thereupon the Secretary shall file in the court the record of the proceedings on which he based his order, as provided in section 2112 of title 28, United States Code. Upon the filing of such petition the court shall have jurisdiction, which upon the filing of the record with it shall be exclusive, to affirm or set aside the order complained of in whole or in part. Until the filing of the record the Secretary may modify or set aside his order. The findings of the Secretary with respect to questions of fact shall be sustained if based upon a fair evaluation of the entire record at such hearing.

(3) The court, on such judicial review, shall not sustain the order of the Secretary if he failed to comply with any requirement imposed on him by subsection (f)(2) of this section.

(4) If application is made to the court for leave to adduce additional evidence, the court may order such additional evidence to be taken before the Secretary and to be adduced upon the hearing in such manner and upon such terms and conditions as to the court may seem proper, if such evidence is material and there were reasonable grounds for failure to adduce such evidence in the proceedings below. The Secretary may modify his findings as to the facts and order by reason of the additional evidence so taken, and shall file with the court such modified findings and order.

(5) The judgment of the court affirming or setting aside, in whole or in part, any order under this section shall be final, subject to review by the Supreme Court of the United States upon certiorari or certification as provided in section 1254 of title 28 of the United States Code. The commencement of proceedings under this section shall not, unless specifically ordered by the court to the contrary, operate as a stay of an order.

(h) Notification Relating to a Food Contact Substance. —

(1) Subject to such regulations as may be promulgated under paragraph (3), a manufacturer or supplier of a food contact substance may, at least 120 days prior to the introduction or delivery for introduction into interstate commerce of the food contact substance, notify the Secretary of the identity and intended use of the food contact substance, and of the determination of the manufacturer or supplier that the intended use of such food contact substance is safe under the standard described in subsection (c)(3)(A). The notification shall contain the information that forms the basis of the determination and all information required to be submitted by regulations promulgated by the Secretary.

(2) —

(A) A notification submitted under paragraph (1) shall become effective 120 days after the date of receipt by the Secretary and the food contact substance may be introduced or delivered for introduction into interstate commerce, unless the Secretary makes a determination within the 120-day period that, based on the data and information before the Secretary, such use of the food contact substance has not been shown to be safe under the standard described in subsection (c)(3)(A), and informs the manufacturer or supplier of such determination.

(B) A decision by the Secretary to object to a notification shall constitute final agency action subject to judicial review.

(C) In this paragraph, the term "food contact substance" means the substance that is the subject of a notification submitted under paragraph (1), and does not include a similar or identical substance manufactured or prepared by a person other than the manufacturer identified in the notification.

(3) —

(A) The process in this subsection shall be utilized for authorizing the marketing of a food contact substance except where the Secretary determines that submission and review of a petition under subsection (b) is necessary to provide adequate assurance of safety, or where the Secretary and any manufacturer or supplier agree that such manufacturer or supplier may submit a petition under subsection (b).

(B) The Secretary is authorized to promulgate regulations to identify the circumstances in which a petition shall be filed under subsection (b), and shall consider criteria such as the probable consumption of such food contact substance and potential toxicity of the food contact substance in determining the circumstances in which a petition shall be filed under subsection (b).

(4) The Secretary shall keep confidential any information provided in a notification under paragraph (1) for 120 days after receipt by the Secretary of the notification. After the expiration of such 120 days, the information shall be available to any interested party except for any matter in the notification that is a trade secret or confidential commercial information.

(5) —

(A) —

(i) Except as provided in clause (ii), the notification program established under this subsection shall not operate in any fiscal year unless —

(I) an appropriation equal to or exceeding the applicable amount under clause (iv) is made for such fiscal year for carrying out such program in such fiscal year; and

(II) the Secretary certifies that the amount appropriated for such fiscal year for the Center for Food Safety and Applied Nutrition of the Food and Drug Administration (exclusive of the appropriation referred to in subclause (I)) equals or exceeds the amount appropriated for the Center for fiscal year 1997, excluding any amount appropriated for new programs.

(ii) The Secretary shall, not later than April 1, 1999, begin accepting and reviewing notifications submitted under the notification program established under this subsection if—

(I) an appropriation equal to or exceeding the applicable amount under clause (iii) is made for the last six months of fiscal year 1999 for carrying out such program during such period; and

(II) the Secretary certifies that the amount appropriated for such period for the Center for Food Safety and Applied Nutrition of the Food and Drug Administration (exclusive of the appropriation referred to in subclause (I)) equals or exceeds an amount equivalent to one-half the amount appropriated for the Center for fiscal year 1997, excluding any amount appropriated for new programs.

(iii) For the last six months of fiscal year 1999, the applicable amount under this clause is $1,500,000, or the amount specified in the budget request of the President for the six-month period involved for carrying out the notification program in fiscal year 1999, whichever is less.

(iv) For fiscal year 2000 and subsequent fiscal years, the applicable amount under this clause is $3,000,000, or the amount specified in the budget request of the President for the fiscal year involved for carrying out the notification program under this subsection, whichever is less.

(B) For purposes of carrying out the notification program under this subsection, there are authorized to be appropriated such sums as may be necessary for each of the fiscal years 1999 through fiscal year 2003, except that such authorization of appropriations is not effective for a fiscal year for any amount that is less than the applicable amount under clause (iii) or (iv) of subparagraph (A), whichever is applicable.

(C) Not later than April 1 of fiscal year 1998 and February 1 of each subsequent fiscal year, the Secretary shall submit a report to the Committees on Appropriations of the House of Representatives and the Senate, the Committee on Commerce of the House of Representatives, and the Committee on Labor and Human Resources of the Senate that provides an estimate of the Secretary of the costs of carrying out the notification program established under this subsection for the next fiscal year.

(6) In this section, the term "food contact substance" means any substance intended for use as a component of materials used in manufacturing, packing, packaging, transporting, or holding food if such use is not intended to have any technical effect in such food.

(i) Amendment or Repeal of Regulations. — The Secretary shall by regulation prescribe the procedure by which regulations under the foregoing provisions of this section may be amended or repealed, and such procedure shall conform to the procedure provided in this section for the promulgation of such regulations. The Secretary shall by regulation prescribe the procedure by which the Secretary may deem a notification under subsection (h) to no longer be effective.

(j) Exemptions for Investigational Use. — Without regard to subsections (b) to (i), inclusive, of this section, the Secretary shall by regulation provide for exempting from the requirements of this section any food additive, and any food bearing or containing such additive, intended solely for investigational use by qualified experts when in his opinion such exemption is consistent with the public health.

Sec. 410. [349] Bottled Drinking Water Standards.

(a) Except as provided in subsection (b), whenever the Administrator of the Environmental Protection Agency prescribes interim or revised national primary drinking water regulations under section 1412 of the Public Health Service Act, the Secretary shall consult with the Administrator and within 180 days after the promulgation of such drinking water regulations either promulgate amendments to regulations under this chapter applicable to bottled drinking water or publish in the Federal Register his reasons for not making such amendments.

(b) —

(1) Not later than 180 days before the effective date of a national primary drinking water regulation promulgated by the Administrator of the Environmental Protection Agency for a contaminant under section 1412 of the Safe Drinking Water Act (42 U.S.C. 300g-1), the Secretary shall promulgate a standard of quality regulation under this subsection for that contaminant in bottled water or make a finding that such a regulation is not necessary to protect the public health because the contaminant is contained in water in public water systems (as defined under section 1401(4) of such Act (42 U.S.C. 300f(4))) but not in water used for bottled drinking water. The effective date for any such standard of quality regulation shall be the same as the effective date for such national primary drinking water regulation, except for any standard of quality of regulation promulgated by the Secretary before the date of enactment of the Safe Drinking Water Act Amendments of 1996 for which (as of such date of enactment) an effective date had not been established. In the case of a standard of quality regulation to which such exception applies, the Secretary shall promulgate monitoring requirements for the contaminants covered by the regulation not later than 2 years after such date of enactment.

(2) A regulation issued by the Secretary as provided in this subsection shall include any monitoring requirements that the Secretary determines appropriate for bottled water.

(3) A regulation issued by the Secretary as provided in this subsection shall require the following:

(A) In the case of contaminants for which a maximum contaminant level is established in a national primary drinking water regulation under section 1412 of the Safe Drinking Water Act (42 U.S.C. 300g-1), the regulation under this subsection shall establish a maximum contaminant level for the contaminant in bottled water which is no less stringent than the maximum contaminant level provided in the national primary drinking water regulation.

(B) In the case of contaminants for which a treatment technique is established in a national primary drinking water regulation under section 1412 of the Safe Drinking Water Act (42 U.S.C. 300g-1), the regulation under this subsection shall require that bottled water be subject to requirements no less protective of the public health than those applicable to water provided by public water systems using the treatment technique required by the national primary drinking water regulation.

(4) —

(A) If the Secretary does not promulgate a regulation under this subsection within the period described in paragraph (1), the national primary drinking water regulation referred to in paragraph (1) shall be considered, as of the date on which the Secretary is required to establish a regulation under paragraph (1), as the regulation applicable under this subsection to bottled water.

(B) In the case of a national primary drinking water regulation that pursuant to subparagraph (A) is considered to be a standard of quality regulation, the Secretary shall, not later than the applicable date referred to in such subparagraph, publish in the Federal Register a notice —

(i) specifying the contents of such regulation, including monitoring requirements; and

(ii) providing that for purposes of this paragraph the effective date for such regulation is the same as the effective date for the regulation for purposes of the Safe Drinking Water Act (or, if the exception under paragraph (1) applies to the regulation, that the effective date for the regulation is not later than 2 years and 180 days after the date of enactment of the Safe Drinking Water Act Amendments of 1996).

Sec. 411. [350] Vitamins and Minerals.

(a) —

(1) Except as provided in paragraph (2) —

(A) the Secretary may not establish, under section 201(n), 401, or 403, maximum limits on the potency of any synthetic or natural vitamin or mineral within a food to which this section applies;

(B) the Secretary may not classify any natural or synthetic vitamin or mineral (or combination thereof) as a drug solely because it exceeds the level of potency which the Secretary determines is nutritionally rational or useful;

(C) the Secretary may not limit, under section 201(n), 401, or 403, the combination or number of any synthetic or natural —

(i) vitamin,

(ii) mineral, or

(iii) other ingredient of food,

within a food to which this section applies.

(2) Paragraph (1) shall not apply in the case of a vitamin, mineral, other ingredient of food, or food, which is represented for use by individuals in the treatment or management of specific diseases or disorders, by children, or by pregnant or lactating women. For purposes of this [paragraph], the term "children" means individuals who are under the age of twelve years.

(b) —

(1) A food to which this section applies shall not be deemed under section 403 to be misbranded solely because its label bears, in accordance with section 403(i)(2), all the ingredients in the food or its advertising contains references to ingredients in the food which are not vitamins or minerals.

(2) The labeling for any food to which this section applies may not list its ingredients which are not dietary supplement ingredients described in section 201(ff)

(i) except as a part of a list of all the ingredients of such food, and

(ii) unless such ingredients are listed in accordance with applicable regulations under section 403.

To the extent that compliance with clause (i) of this subparagraph is impracticable or results in deception or unfair competition, exemptions shall be established by regulations promulgated by the Secretary.

(c) —

(1) For purposes of this section, the term "food to which this section applies" means a food for humans which is a food for special dietary use —

(A) which is or contains any natural or synthetic vitamin or mineral, and

(B) which —

(i) is intended for ingestion in tablet, capsule, powder, softgel, gelcap, or liquid form, or

(ii) if not intended for ingestion in such a form, is not represented as conventional food and is not represented for use as a sole item of a meal or of the diet.

(2) For purposes of paragraph (1)(B)(i), a food shall be considered as intended for ingestion in liquid form only if it is formulated in a fluid carrier and it is intended for ingestion in daily quantities measured in drops or similar small units of measure.

(3) For purposes of paragraph (1) and of section 403 (j) insofar as that section is applicable to food to which this section applies, the term "special dietary use" as applied to food used by man means a particular use for which a food purports or is represented to be used, including but not limited to the following:

(A) Supplying a special dietary need that exists by reason of a physical, physiological, pathological, or other condition, including but not limited to the condition of disease, convalescence, pregnancy, lactation, infancy, allergic hypersensitivity to food, underweight, overweight, or the need to control the intake of sodium.

(B) Supplying a vitamin, mineral, or other ingredient for use by man to supplement his diet by increasing the total dietary intake.

(C) Supplying a special dietary need by reason of being a food for use as the sole item of the diet.

SEC. 412. [350a] REQUIREMENTS FOR INFANT FORMULAS.

(a) An infant formula, including an infant formula powder, shall be deemed to be adulterated if —

(1) such infant formula does not provide nutrients as required by subsection (i),

(2) such infant formula does not meet the quality factor requirements prescribed by the Secretary under subsection (b)(1), or

(3) the processing of such infant formula is not in compliance with the good manufacturing practices and the quality control procedures prescribed by the Secretary under subsection (b)(2).

(b) —

(1) The Secretary shall by regulation establish requirements for quality factors for infant formulas to the extent possible consistent with current scientific knowledge, including quality factor requirements for the nutrients required by subsection (i).

(2) —

(A) The Secretary shall by regulation establish good manufacturing practices for infant formulas, including quality control procedures that the Secretary determines are necessary to assure that an infant formula provides nutrients in accordance with this subsection and subsection (i) and is manufactured in a manner designed to prevent adulteration of the infant formula.

(B) The good manufacturing practices and quality control procedures prescribed by the Secretary under subparagraph (A) shall include requirements for —

(i) the testing, in accordance with paragraph (3) and by the manufacturer of an infant formula or an agent of such manufacturer, of each batch of infant formula for each nutrient required by subsection (i) before the distribution of such batch,

(ii) regularly scheduled testing, by the manufacturer of an infant formula or an agent of such manufacturer, of samples of infant formulas during the shelf life of such formulas to ensure that such formulas are in compliance with this section,

(iii) in-process controls including, where necessary, testing required by good manufacturing practices designed to prevent adulteration of each batch of infant formula, and

(iv) the conduct by the manufacturer of an infant formula or an agent of such manufacturer of regularly scheduled audits to determine that such manufacturer has complied with the regulations prescribed under subparagraph (A).

In prescribing requirements for audits under clause (iv), the Secretary shall provide that such audits be conducted by appropriately trained individuals who do not have any direct responsibility for the manufacture or production of infant formula.

(3) —

(A) At the final product stage, each batch of infant formula shall be tested for vitamin A, vitamin B1, vitamin C, and vitamin E to ensure that such infant formula is in compliance with the requirements of this subsection and subsection (i) relating to such vitamins.

(B) Each nutrient premix used in the manufacture of an infant formula shall be tested for each relied upon nutrient required by subsection (i) which is contained in such premix to ensure that such premix is in compliance with its specifications or certifications by a premix supplier.

(C) During the manufacturing process or at the final product stage and before distribution of an infant formula, an infant formula shall be tested for all nutrients required to be included in such formula by subsection (i) for which testing has not been conducted pursuant to subparagraph (A) or (B). Testing under this subparagraph shall be conducted to —

(i) ensure that each batch of such infant formula is in compliance with the requirements of subsection (i) relating to such nutrients, and

(ii) confirm that nutrients contained in any nutrient premix used in such infant formula are present in each batch of such infant formula in the proper concentration.

(D) If the Secretary adds a nutrient to the list of nutrients in the table in subsection (i), the Secretary shall by regulation require that the manufacturer of an infant formula test each batch of such formula for such new nutrient in accordance with subparagraph (A), (B), or (C).

(E) For purposes of this paragraph, the term "final product stage" means the point in the manufacturing process, before distribution of an infant formula, at which an infant formula is homogenous and is not subject to further degradation.

(4) —

(A) The Secretary shall by regulation establish requirements respecting the retention of records. Such requirements shall provide for —

(i) the retention of all records necessary to demonstrate compliance with the good manufacturing practices and quality control procedures prescribed by the Secretary under paragraph (2), including records containing the results of all testing required under paragraph (2)(B),

(ii) the retention of all certifications or guarantees of analysis by premix suppliers,

(iii) the retention by a premix supplier of all records necessary to confirm the accuracy of all premix certifications and guarantees of analysis,

(iv) the retention of —

(I) all records pertaining to the microbiological quality and purity of raw materials used in infant formula powder and in finished infant formula, and

(II) all records pertaining to food packaging materials which show that such materials do not cause an infant formula to be adulterated within the meaning of section 402(a)(2)(C) —

(v) the retention of all records of the results of regularly scheduled audits conducted pursuant to the requirements prescribed by the Secretary under paragraph (2)(B)(iv), and

(vi) the retention of all complaints and the maintenance of files with respect to, and the review of, complaints concerning infant formulas which may reveal the possible existence of a hazard to health.

(B) —

(i) Records required under subparagraph (A) with respect to an infant formula shall be retained for at least one year after the expiration of the shelf life of such infant formula. Except as provided in clause (ii), such records shall be made available to the Secretary for review and duplication upon request of the Secretary.

(ii) A manufacturer need only provide written assurances to the Secretary that the regularly scheduled audits required by paragraph (2)(B)(iv) are being conducted by the manufacturer, and need not make available to the Secretary the actual written reports of such audits.

(c) —

(1) No person shall introduce or deliver for introduction into interstate commerce any new infant formula unless —

(A) such person has, before introducing such new infant formula, or delivering such new infant formula for introduction, into interstate commerce, registered with the Secretary the name of such person, the place of business of such person, and all establishments at which such person intends to manufacture such new infant formula, and

(B) such person has at least 90 days before marketing such new infant formula, made the submission to the Secretary required by subsection (c)(1).

(2) For purposes of paragraph (1), the term "new infant formula" includes —

(A) an infant formula manufactured by a person which has not previously manufactured an infant formula, and

(B) an infant formula manufactured by a person which has previously manufactured infant formula and in which there is a major change, in processing or formulation, from a current or any previous formulation produced by such manufacturer.

For purposes of this paragraph, the term "major change" has the meaning given to such term in section 106.30(c)(2) of title 21, Code of Federal Regulations (as in effect on August 1, 1986), and guidelines issued thereunder.

(d) —

(1) A person shall, with respect to any infant formula subject to subsection (c), make a submission to the Secretary which shall include —

(A) the quantitative formulation of the infant formula,

(B) a description of any reformulation of the formula or change in processing of the infant formula,

(C) assurances that the infant formula will not be marketed unless it meets the requirements of subsections (b)(1) and (i), as demonstrated by the testing required under subsection (b)(3), and

(D) assurances that the processing of the infant formula complies with subsection (b)(2).

(2) After the first production of an infant formula subject to subsection (c), and before the introduction into interstate commerce of such formula, the manufacturer of such formula shall submit to the Secretary, in such form as may be prescribed by the Secretary, a written verification which summarizes test results and records demonstrating that such formula complies with the requirements of subsections (b)(1), (b)(2)(A), (b)(2)(B)(i), (b)(2)(B)(iii), (b)(3)(A), (b)(3)(C), and (i).

(3) If the manufacturer of an infant formula for commercial or charitable distribution for human consumption determines that a change in the formulation of the formula or a change in the processing of the formula may affect whether the formula is adulterated under subsection (a), the manufacturer shall, before the first processing of such formula, make the submission to the Secretary required by paragraph (1).

(e) —

(1) If the manufacturer of an infant formula has knowledge which reasonably supports the conclusion that an infant formula which has been processed by the manufacturer and which has left an establishment subject to the control of the manufacturer —

(A) may not provide the nutrients required by subsection (i), or

(B) may be otherwise adulterated or misbranded,

the manufacturer shall promptly notify the Secretary of such knowledge. If the Secretary determines that the infant formula presents a risk to human health, the manufacturer shall immediately take all actions necessary to recall shipments of such infant formula from all wholesale and retail establishments, consistent with recall regulations and guidelines issued by the Secretary.

(2) For purposes of paragraph (1), the term "knowledge" as applied to a manufacturer means

(A) the actual knowledge that the manufacturer had, or

(B) the knowledge which a reasonable person would have had under like circumstances or which would have been obtained upon the exercise of due care.

(f) —

(1) If a recall of infant formula is begun by a manufacturer, the recall shall be carried out in accordance with such requirements as the Secretary shall prescribe under paragraph (2) and —

(A) the Secretary shall, not later than the 15th day after the beginning of such recall and at least once every 15 days thereafter until the recall is terminated, review the actions taken under the recall to determine whether the recall meets the requirements prescribed under paragraph (2), and

(B) the manufacturer shall, not later than the 14th day after the beginning of such recall and at least once every 14 days thereafter until the recall is terminated, report to the Secretary the actions taken to implement the recall.

(2) The Secretary shall by regulation prescribe the scope and extent of recalls of infant formulas necessary and appropriate for the degree of risks to human health presented by the formula subject to the recall.

(3) The Secretary shall by regulation require each manufacturer of an infant formula who begins a recall of such formula because of a risk to human health to request each retail establishment at which such formula is sold or available for sale to post at the point of purchase of such formula a notice of such recall at such establishment for such time that the Secretary determines necessary to inform the public of such recall.

(g) —

(1) Each manufacturer of an infant formula shall make and retain such records respecting the distribution of the infant formula through any establishment owned or operated by such manufacturer as may be necessary to effect and monitor recalls of the formula. Such records shall be retained for at least one year after the expiration of the shelf life of the infant formula.

(2) To the extent that the Secretary determines that records are not being made or maintained in accordance with paragraph (1), the Secretary may by regulation prescribe the records required to be made under paragraph (1) and requirements respecting the retention of such records under such paragraph. Such regulations shall take effect on such date as the Secretary prescribes but not sooner than the 180th day after the date such regulations are promulgated. Such regulations shall apply only with respect to distributions of infant formulas made after such effective date.

(h) —

(1) Any infant formula which is represented and labeled for use by an infant —

(A) who has an inborn error of metabolism or a low birth weight, or

(B) who otherwise has an unusual medical or dietary problem,

is exempt from the requirements of subsections (a), (b), and (c). The manufacturer of an infant formula exempt under this paragraph shall, in the case of the exempt formula, be required to provide the notice required by subsection (e)(1) only with respect to adulteration or misbranding described in subsection (e)(1)(B) and to comply with the regulations prescribed by the Secretary under paragraph (2).

(2) The Secretary may by regulation establish terms and conditions for the exemption of an infant formula from the requirements of subsections (a), (b), and (c). An exemption of an infant formula under paragraph (1) may be withdrawn by the Secretary if such formula is not in compliance with applicable terms and conditions prescribed under this paragraph.

(i) —

(1) An infant formula shall contain nutrients in accordance with the table set out in this subsection or, if revised by the Secretary under paragraph (2), as so revised.

(2) The Secretary may by regulation —

(A) revise the list of nutrients in the table in this subsection, and

(B) revise the required level for any nutrient required by the table.

NUTRIENTS

Nutrient	Minimum	Maximum
Protein (gm)	1.8	4.5
Fat: (gm)	3.3	6.0
% cal	30.0	54.0
Essential fatty acids (linoleate):		
% cal	2.7	
mg	300.0	
Vitamins:		
A (IU)	250.0 (75μg)	750.0 (225μg)
D (IU)	40.0	100.0
K (μg)	4.0	
E (IU)	0.7 (with 0.7 IU/gm linoleic acid)	
C (ascorbic acid) (mg)	8.0	
B1 (thiamine) (μg)	40.0	
B2 (riboflavin) (μg)	60.0	
B6 (pyridoxine) (μg)	35.0 (with 15μg/gm of protein in formula)	
B12 (μg)	0.15	
Niacin (μg)	250.0	
Folic acid (μg)	4.0	
Pantothenic acid (μg)	300.0	
Biotin (μg)	1.5	
Choline (mg)	7.0	
Inositol (mg)	4.0	
Minerals:		
Calcium (mg)	50.0	
Phosphorus (mg)	25.0	
Magnesium (mg)	6.0	
Iron (mg)	0.15	
Iodine (μg)	5.0	
Zinc (mg)	0.5	
Copper (μg)	60.0	
Manganese (μg)	5.0	
Sodium (mg)	20.0	60.0
Potassium (mg)	80.0	200.0
Chloride (mg)	55.0	150.0

SEC. 413. [350b] NEW DIETARY INGREDIENTS.

(a) IN GENERAL. — A dietary supplement which contains a new dietary ingredient shall be deemed adulterated under section 402(f) unless it meets one of the following requirements:

(1) The dietary supplement contains only dietary ingredients which have been present in the food supply as an article used for food in a form in which the food has not been chemically altered.

(2) There is a history of use or other evidence of safety establishing that the dietary ingredient when used under the conditions recommended or suggested in the labeling of the dietary supplement will reasonably be expected to be safe and, at least 75 days before being introduced or delivered for introduction into interstate commerce, the manufacturer or distributor of the dietary ingredient or dietary supplement provides the Secretary with information, including any citation to published articles, which is the basis on which the manufacturer or distributor has concluded that a dietary supplement containing such dietary ingredient will reasonably be expected to be safe.

The Secretary shall keep confidential any information provided under paragraph (2) for 90 days following its receipt. After the expiration of such 90 days, the Secretary shall place such information on public display, except matters in the information which are trade secrets or otherwise confidential, commercial information.

(b) PETITION. — Any person may file with the Secretary a petition proposing the issuance of an order prescribing the conditions under which a new dietary ingredient under its intended conditions of use will reasonably be expected to be safe. The Secretary shall make a decision on such petition within 180 days of the date the petition is filed with the Secretary. For purposes of chapter 7 of title 5, United States Code, the decision of the Secretary shall be considered final agency action.

(c) Notification. —

(1) In General. — If the Secretary determines that the information in a new dietary ingredient notification submitted under this section for an article purported to be a new dietary ingredient is inadequate to establish that a dietary supplement containing such article will reasonably be expected to be safe because the article may be, or may contain, an anabolic steroid or an analogue of an anabolic steroid, the Secretary shall notify the Drug Enforcement Administration of such determination. Such notification by the Secretary shall include, at a minimum, the name of the dietary supplement or article, the name of the person or persons who marketed the product or made the submission of information regarding the article to the Secretary under this section, and any contact information for such person or persons that the Secretary has.

(2) Definitions. — For purposes of this subsection—

(A) the term "anabolic steroid" has the meaning given such term in section 102(41) of the Controlled Substances Act; and

(B) the term "analogue of an anabolic steroid" means a substance whose chemical structure is substantially similar to the chemical structure of an anabolic steroid.

(d) Definition. — For purposes of this section, the term "new dietary ingredient" means a dietary ingredient that was not marketed in the United States before October 15, 1994 and does not include any dietary ingredient which was marketed in the United States before October 15, 1994.

Sec. 414. [350c] Maintenance and Inspection of Records.

(a) Records Inspection. —

(1) Adulterated Food. — If the Secretary has a reasonable belief that an article of food, and any other article of food that the Secretary reasonably believes is likely to be affected in a similar manner, *is* adulterated and presents a threat of serious adverse health consequences or death to humans or animals, each person (excluding farms and restaurants) who manufactures, processes, packs, distributes, receives, holds, or imports such article shall, at the request of an officer or employee duly designated by the Secretary, permit such officer or employee, upon presentation of appropriate credentials and a written notice to such person, at reasonable times and within reasonable limits and in a reasonable manner, to have access to and copy all records relating to such article, and to any other article of food that the Secretary reasonably believes is likely to be affected in a similar manner, that are needed to assist the Secretary in determining whether the food is adulterated and presents a threat of serious adverse health consequences or death to humans or animals.

(2) Use or Exposure to Food of Concern. — If the Secretary believes that there is a reasonable probability that the use of or exposure to an article of food, and any other article of food that the Secretary reasonably believes is likely to be affected in a similar manner, will cause serious adverse health consequences or death to humans or animals, each person (excluding farms and restaurants) who manufactures, processes, packs, distributes, receives, holds, or imports such article shall, at the request of an officer or employee duly designated by the Secretary, permit such officer or employee, upon presentation of appropriate credentials and a written notice to such person, at reasonable times and within reasonable limits and in a reasonable manner, to have access to and copy all records relating to such article and to any other article of food that the Secretary reasonably believes is likely to be affected in a similar manner, that are needed to assist the Secretary in determining whether there is a reasonable probability that the use of or exposure to the food will cause serious adverse health consequences or death to humans or animals.

(3) Application. — The requirement under paragraphs (1) and (2) applies to all records relating to the manufacture, processing, packing, distribution, receipt, holding, or importation of such article maintained by or on behalf of such person in any format (including paper and electronic formats) and at any location.

(b) Regulations Concerning Recordkeeping. — The Secretary, in consultation and coordination, as appropriate, with other Federal departments and agencies with responsibilities for regulating food safety, may by regulation establish requirements regarding the establishment and maintenance, for not longer than two years, of records by persons (excluding farms and restaurants) who manufacture, process, pack, transport, distribute, receive, hold, or import food, which records are needed by the Secretary for inspection to allow the Secretary to identify the immediate previous sources and the immediate subsequent recipients of food, including its packaging, in order to address credible threats of serious adverse health consequences or death to humans or animals. The Secretary shall take into account the size of a business in promulgating regulations under this section.

(c) Protection of Sensitive Information. — The Secretary shall take appropriate measures to ensure that there are in effect effective procedures to prevent the unauthorized disclosure of any trade secret or confidential information that is obtained by the Secretary pursuant to this section.

(d) Limitations. — This section shall not be construed —

(1) to limit the authority of the Secretary to inspect records or to require establishment and maintenance of records under any other provision of this Act;

(2) to authorize the Secretary to impose any requirements with respect to a food to the extent that it is within the exclusive jurisdiction of the Secretary of Agriculture pursuant to the Federal Meat Inspection Act (21 U.S.C. 601 et seq.), the Poultry Products Inspection Act (21 U.S.C. 451 et seq.), or the Egg Products Inspection Act (21 U.S.C. 1031 et seq.);

(3) to have any legal effect on section 552 of title 5, United States Code, or section 1905 of title 18, United States Code; or

(4) to extend to recipes for food, financial data, pricing data, personnel data, research data, or sales data (other than shipment data regarding sales).

Sec. 415. [350d] Registration of Food Facilities.

(a) Registration. —

(1) In General. — The Secretary shall by regulation require that any facility engaged in manufacturing, processing, packing, or holding food for consumption in the United States be registered with the Secretary. To be registered —

(A) for a domestic facility, the owner, operator, or agent in charge of the facility shall submit a registration to the Secretary; and

(B) for a foreign facility, the owner, operator, or agent in charge of the facility shall submit a registration to the Secretary and shall include with the registration the name of the United States agent for the facility.

(2) Registration. — An entity (referred to in this section as the "registrant") shall submit a registration under paragraph (1) to the Secretary containing information necessary to notify the Secretary of the name and address of each facility at which, and all trade names under which, the registrant conducts business, the e-mail address for the contact person of the facility or, in the case of a foreign facility, the United States agent for the facility, and when determined necessary by the Secretary through guidance, the general food category (as identified under section 170.3 of title 21, Code of Federal Regulations, or any other food categories as determined appropriate by the Secretary, including by guidance) of any food manufactured, processed, packed, or held at such facility. The registration shall contain an assurance that the Secretary will be permitted to inspect such facility at the times and in the manner permitted by this Act. The registrant shall notify the Secretary in a timely manner of changes to such information.

(3) Biennial Registration Renewal. — During the period beginning on October 1 and ending on December 31 of each even-numbered year, a registrant that has submitted a registration under paragraph (1) shall submit to the Secretary a renewal registration containing the information described in paragraph (2). The Secretary shall provide for an abbreviated registration renewal process for any registrant that has not had any changes to such information since the registrant submitted the preceding registration or registration renewal for the facility involved.

(4) Procedure. — Upon receipt of a completed registration described in paragraph (1), the Secretary shall notify the registrant of the receipt of such registration and assign a registration number to each registered facility.

(5) List. — The Secretary shall compile and maintain an up-to-date list of facilities that are registered under this section. Such list and any registration documents submitted pursuant to this subsection shall not be subject to disclosure under section 552 of title 5, United States Code. Information derived from such list or registration documents shall not be subject to disclosure under section 552 of title 5, United States Code, to the extent that it discloses the identity or location of a specific registered person.

(b) Suspension of Registration. —

(1) In General. — If the Secretary determines that food manufactured, processed, packed, received, or held by a facility registered under this section has a reasonable probability of causing serious adverse health consequences or death to humans or animals, the Secretary may by order suspend the registration of a facility —

(A) that created, caused, or was otherwise responsible for such reasonable probability; or

(B) (i) that knew of, or had reason to know of, such reasonable probability; and

(ii) packed, received, or held such food.

(2) Hearing on Suspension. — The Secretary shall provide the registrant subject to an order under paragraph (1) with an opportunity for an informal hearing, to be held as soon as possible but not later than 2 business days after the issuance of the order or such other time period, as agreed upon by the Secretary and the registrant, on the actions required for reinstatement of registration and why the registration that is subject to suspension should be reinstated. The Secretary shall reinstate a registration if the Secretary determines, based on evidence presented, that adequate grounds do not exist to continue the suspension of the registration.

(3) Post-Hearing Corrective Action Plan; Vacating of Order. —

(A) Corrective Action Plan. — If, after providing opportunity for an informal hearing under paragraph (2), the Secretary determines that the suspension of registration remains necessary, the Secretary shall require the registrant to submit a corrective action plan to demonstrate how the registrant plans to correct the conditions found by the Secretary. The Secretary shall review such plan not later than 14 days after the submission of the corrective action plan or such other time period as determined by the Secretary.

(B) Vacating of Order. — Upon a determination by the Secretary that adequate grounds do not exist to continue the suspension actions required by the order, or that such actions should be modified, the Secretary shall promptly vacate the order and reinstate the registration of the facility subject to the order or modify the order, as appropriate.

(4) Effect of Suspension. — If the registration of a facility is suspended under this subsection, no person shall import or export food into the United States from such facility, offer to import or export food into the United States from such facility, or otherwise introduce food from such facility into interstate or intrastate commerce in the United States.

(5) Regulations. —

(A) In General. — The Secretary shall promulgate regulations to implement this subsection. The Secretary may promulgate such regulations on an interim final basis.

(B) Registration Requirement. — The Secretary may require that registration under this section be submitted in an electronic format. Such requirement may not take effect before the date that is 5 years after the date of enactment of the FDA Food Safety Modernization Act.

(6) Application Date. — Facilities shall be subject to the requirements of this subsection beginning on the earlier of—

(A) the date on which the Secretary issues regulations under paragraph (5); or

(B) 180 days after the date of enactment of the FDA Food Safety Modernization Act.

(7) No Delegation. — The authority conferred by this subsection to issue an order to suspend a registration or vacate an order of suspension shall not be delegated to any officer or employee other than the Commissioner.

(c) Facility. — For purposes of this section:

(1) The term "facility" includes any factory, warehouse, or establishment (including a factory, warehouse, or establishment of an importer) that manufactures, processes, packs, or holds food. Such term does not include farms; restaurants; other retail food establishments; nonprofit food establishments in which food is prepared for or served directly to the consumer; or fishing vessels (except such vessels engaged in processing as defined in section 123.3(k) of title 21, Code of Federal Regulations).

(2) The term "domestic facility" means a facility located in any of the States or Territories.

(3) —

(A) The term "foreign facility" means a facility that manufacturers, processes, packs, or holds food, but only if food from such facility is exported to the United States without further processing or packaging outside the United States.

(B) A food may not be considered to have undergone further processing or packaging for purposes of subparagraph (A) solely on the basis that labeling was added or that any similar activity of a de minimis nature was carried out with respect to the food.

(d) Rule of Construction. — Nothing in this section shall be construed to authorize the Secretary to require an application, review, or licensing process for a facility to be registered, except with respect to the reinstatement of a registration that is suspended under subsection (b).

Sec. 416. [350e] Sanitary Transportation Practices.

(a) Definitions. In this section:

(1) Bulk Vehicle. The term "bulk vehicle" includes a tank truck, hopper truck, rail tank car, hopper car, cargo tank, portable tank, freight container, or hopper bin, and any other vehicle in which food is shipped in bulk, with the food coming into direct contact with the vehicle.

(2) Transportation. The term "transportation" means any movement in commerce by motor vehicle or rail vehicle.

(b) Regulations. The Secretary shall by regulation require shippers, carriers by motor vehicle or rail vehicle, receivers, and other persons engaged in the transportation of food to use sanitary transportation practices prescribed by the Secretary to ensure that food is not transported under conditions that may render the food adulterated.

(c) Contents. The regulations under subsection (b) shall —

(1) prescribe such practices as the Secretary determines to be appropriate relating to —

(A) sanitation;

(B) packaging, isolation, and other protective measures;

(C) limitations on the use of vehicles;

(D) information to be disclosed —

(i) to a carrier by a person arranging for the transportation of food; and

(ii) to a manufacturer or other person that —

(I) arranges for the transportation of food by a carrier; or

(II) furnishes a tank vehicle or bulk vehicle for the transporting of food; and

(2) include —

(A) a list of nonfood products that the Secretary determines may, if shipped in a bulk vehicle, render adulterated food that is subsequently transported in the same vehicle; and

(B) a list of nonfood products that the Secretary determines may, if shipped in a motor vehicle or rail vehicle (other than a tank vehicle or bulk vehicle), render adulterated food that is simultaneously or subsequently transported in the same vehicle.

(d) Waivers.

(1) In General. The Secretary may waive any requirement under this section, with respect to any class of persons, vehicles, food, or no food products, if the Secretary determines that the waiver —

(A) will not result in the transportation of food under conditions that would be unsafe for human or animal health; and

(B) will not be contrary to the public interest.

(2) Publication. The Secretary shall publish in the Federal Register any waiver and the reasons for the waiver.

(e) Preemption.

(1) In General. A requirement of a State or political subdivision of a State that concerns the transportation of food is preempted if —

(A) complying with a requirement of the State or political subdivision and a requirement of this section, or a regulation prescribed under this section, is not possible; or

(B) the requirement of the State or political subdivision as applied or enforced is an obstacle to accomplishing and carrying out this section or a regulation prescribed under this section.

(2) Applicability. This subsection applies to transportation that occurs on or after the effective date of the regulations promulgated under subsection (b).

(f) Assistance of Other Agencies. The Secretary of Transportation, the Secretary of Agriculture, the Administrator of the Environmental Protection Agency, and the heads of other Federal agencies, as appropriate, shall provide assistance on request, to the extent resources are available, to the Secretary for the purposes of carrying out this section.

Sec. 417. [350f] Reportable Food Registry.

(a) Definitions. — In this section:

(1) Responsible Party. — The term "responsible party", with respect to an article of food, means a person that submits the registration under section 415(a) for a food facility that is required to register under section 415(a), at which such article of food is manufactured, processed, packed, or held.

(2) Reportable Food. — The term "reportable food" means an article of food (other than infant formula) for which there is a reasonable probability that the use of, or exposure to, such article of food will cause serious adverse health consequences or death to humans or animals.

(b) Establishment. —

(1) In General. — Not later than 1 year after the date of the enactment of this section, the Secretary shall establish within the Food and Drug Administration a Reportable Food Registry to which instances of reportable food may be submitted by the Food and Drug Administration after receipt of reports under subsection (d), via an electronic portal, from —

(A) Federal, State, and local public health officials; or

(B) responsible parties.

(2) Review by Secretary. — The Secretary shall promptly review and assess the information submitted under paragraph (1) for the purposes of identifying reportable food, submitting entries to the Reportable Food Registry, acting under subsection (c), and exercising other existing food safety authorities under this Act to protect the public health.

(c) Issuance of an Alert by the Secretary. —

(1) In General. — The Secretary shall issue, or cause to be issued, an alert or a notification with respect to a reportable food using information from the Reportable Food Registry as the Secretary deems necessary to protect the public health.

(2) Effect. — Paragraph (1) shall not affect the authority of the Secretary to issue an alert or a notification under any other provision of this Act.

(d) Reporting and Notification. —

(1) In General. — Except as provided in paragraph (2), as soon as practicable, but in no case later than 24 hours after a responsible party determines that an article of food is a reportable food, the responsible party shall —

(A) submit a report to the Food and Drug Administration through the electronic portal established under subsection (b) that includes the data elements described in subsection (e) (except the elements described in paragraphs (8), (9), and (10) of such subsection); and

(B) investigate the cause of the adulteration if the adulteration of the article of food may have originated with the responsible party.

(2) No Report Required. — A responsible party is not required to submit a report under paragraph (1) if —

(A) the adulteration originated with the responsible party;

(B) the responsible party detected the adulteration prior to any transfer to another person of such article of food; and

(C) the responsible party —

(i) corrected such adulteration; or

(ii) destroyed or caused the destruction of such article of food.

(3) Reports by Public Health Officials. — A Federal, State, or local public health official may submit a report about a reportable food to the Food and Drug Administration through the electronic portal established under subsection (b) that includes the data elements described in subsection (e) that the official is able to provide.

(4) Report Number. — The Secretary shall ensure that, upon submission of a report under paragraph (1) or (3), a unique number is issued through the electronic portal established under subsection (b) to the person submitting such report, by which the Secretary is able to link reports about the reportable food submitted and amended under this subsection and identify the supply chain for such reportable food.

(5) Review. — The Secretary shall promptly review a report submitted under paragraph (1) or (3).

(6) Response to Report Submitted by a Responsible party. — After consultation with the responsible party that submitted a report under paragraph (1), the Secretary may require such responsible party to perform, as soon as practicable, but in no case later than a time specified by the Secretary, 1 or more of the following:

(A) Amend the report submitted by the responsible party under paragraph (1) to include the data element described in subsection (e)(9).

(B) Provide a notification —

(i) to the immediate previous source of the article of food, if the Secretary deems necessary;

(ii) to the immediate subsequent recipient of the article of food, if the Secretary deems necessary; and

(iii) that includes —

(I) the data elements described in subsection (e) that the Secretary deems necessary;

(II) the actions described under paragraph (7) that the recipient of the notification shall perform, as required by the Secretary; and

(III) any other information that the Secretary may require.

(7) Subsequent Reports and Notifications. — Except as provided in paragraph (8), the Secretary may require a responsible party to perform, as soon as practicable, but in no case later than a time specified by the Secretary, after the responsible party receives a notification under subparagraph (C) or paragraph (6)(B), 1 or more of the following:

(A) Submit a report to the Food and Drug Administration through the electronic portal established under subsection (b) that includes those data elements described in subsection (e) and other information that the Secretary deems necessary.

(B) Investigate the cause of the adulteration if the adulteration of the article of food may have originated with the responsible party.

(C) Provide a notification —

(i) to the immediate previous source of the article of food, if the Secretary deems necessary;

(ii) to the immediate subsequent recipient of the article of food, if the Secretary deems necessary; and

(iii) that includes —

(I) the data elements described in subsection (e) that the Secretary deems necessary;

(II) the actions described under this paragraph that the recipient of the notification shall perform, as required by the Secretary; and

(III) any other information that the Secretary may require.

(8) Amended Report. — If a responsible party receives a notification under paragraph (6)(B) or paragraph (7)(C) with respect to an article of food after the responsible party has submitted a report to the Food and Drug Administration under paragraph (1) with respect to such article of food —

(A) the responsible party is not required to submit an additional report or make a notification under paragraph (7); and

(B) the responsible party shall amend the report submitted by the responsible party under paragraph (1) to include the data elements described in paragraph (9), and, with respect to both such notification and such report, paragraph (11) of subsection (e).

(e) Data Elements. — The data elements described in this subsection are the following:

(1) The registration numbers of the responsible party under section 415(a)(3).

(2) The date on which an article of food was determined to be a reportable food.

(3) A description of the article of food including the quantity or amount.

(4) The extent and nature of the adulteration.

(5) If the adulteration of the article of food may have originated with the responsible party, the results of the investigation required under paragraph (1)(B) or (7)(B) of subsection (d), as applicable and when known.

(6) The disposition of the article of food, when known.

(7) Product information typically found on packaging including product codes, use-by dates, and names of manufacturers, packers, or distributors sufficient to identify the article of food.

(8) Contact information for the responsible party.

(9) The contact information for parties directly linked in the supply chain and notified under paragraph (6)(B) or (7)(C) of subsection (d), as applicable.

(10) The information required by the Secretary to be included in a notification provided by the responsible party involved under paragraph (6)(B) or (7)(C) of subsection (d) or required in a report under subsection (d)(7)(A).

(11) The unique number described in subsection (d)(4).

(f) Critical Information. — Except with respect to fruits and vegetables that are raw agricultural commodities, not more than 18 months after the date of enactment of the FDA Food Safety Modernization Act, the Secretary may require a responsible party to submit to the Secretary consumer-oriented information regarding a reportable food, which shall include —

(1) a description of the article of food as provided in subsection (e)(3);

(2) as provided in subsection (e)(7), affected product identification codes, such as UPC, SKU, or lot or batch numbers sufficient for the consumer to identify the article of food;

(3) contact information for the responsible party as provided in subsection (e)(8); and

(4) any other information the Secretary determines is necessary to enable a consumer to accurately identify whether such consumer is in possession of the reportable food.

(g) Grocery Store Notification. —

(1) Action By Secretary. — The Secretary shall —

(A) prepare the critical information described under subsection (f) for a reportable food as a standardized one-page summary;

(B) publish such one-page summary on the Internet website of the Food and Drug Administration in a format that can be easily printed by a grocery store for purposes of consumer notification.

(2) Action by Grocery Store. — A notification described under paragraph (1)(B) shall include the date and time such summary was posted on the Internet website of the Food and Drug Administration.

(h) Consumer Notification. —

(1) In General. — If a grocery store sold a reportable food that is the subject of the posting and such establishment is part of chain of establishments with 15 or more physical locations, then such establishment shall, not later than 24 hours after a one page summary described in subsection (g) is published, prominently display such summary or the information from such summary via at least one of the methods identified under paragraph (2) and maintain the display for 14 days.

(2) List of Conspicuous Locations. — Not more than 1 year after the date of enactment of the FDA Food Safety Modernization Act, the Secretary shall develop and publish a list of acceptable conspicuous locations and manners, from which grocery stores shall select at least one, for providing the notification required in paragraph (1). Such list shall include —

(A) posting the notification at or near the register;

(B) providing the location of the reportable food;

(C) providing targeted recall information given to customers upon purchase of a food; and

(D) other such prominent and conspicuous locations and manners utilized by grocery stores as of the date of the enactment of the FDA Food Safety Modernization Act to provide notice of such recalls to consumers as considered appropriate by the Secretary.

(i) Coordination of Federal, State, and Local Efforts. —

(1) Department of Agriculture. — In implementing this section, the Secretary shall —

(A) share information and coordinate regulatory efforts with the Department of Agriculture; and

(B) if the Secretary receives a report submitted about a food within the jurisdiction of the Department of Agriculture, promptly provide such report to the Department of Agriculture.

(2) States and Localities. — In implementing this section, the Secretary shall work with the State and local public health officials to share information and coordinate regulatory efforts, in order to —

(A) help to ensure coverage of the safety of the food supply chain, including those food establishments regulated by the States and localities that are not required to register under section 415; and

(B) reduce duplicative regulatory efforts.

(j) Maintenance and Inspection of Records. — The responsible party shall maintain records related to each report received, notification made, and report submitted to the Food and Drug Administration under this section for 2 years. A responsible party shall, at the request of the Secretary, permit inspection of such records as provided for section 414.

(k) Request for Information. — Except as provided by section 415(a)(4), section 552 of title 5, United States Code, shall apply to any request for information regarding a record in the Reportable Food Registry.

(l) Safety Report. — A report or notification under subsection (d) shall be considered to be a safety report under section 756 and may be accompanied by a statement, which shall be part of any report released for public disclosure, that denies that the report or the notification constitutes an admission that the product involved caused or contributed to a death, serious injury, or serious illness.

(m) Admission. — A report or notification under this section shall not be considered an admission that the article of food involved is adulterated or caused or contributed to a death, serious injury, or serious illness.

(n) Homeland Security Notification. — If, after receiving a report under subsection (d), the Secretary believes such food may have been deliberately adulterated, the Secretary shall immediately notify the Secretary of Homeland Security. The Secretary shall make relevant information from the Reportable Food Registry available to the Secretary of Homeland Security.

Sec. 418. [350g] Hazard Analysis and Risk-Based Preventive Controls.

(a) In General. — The owner, operator, or agent in charge of a facility shall, in accordance with this section, evaluate the hazards that could affect food manufactured, processed, packed, or held by such facility, identify and implement preventive controls to significantly minimize or prevent the occurrence of such hazards and provide assurances that such food is not adulterated under section 402 or misbranded under section 403(w), monitor the performance of those controls, and maintain records of this monitoring as a matter of routine practice.

(b) Hazard Analysis — The owner, operator, or agent in charge of a facility shall —

(1) identify and evaluate known or reasonably foreseeable hazards that may be associated with the facility, including —

(A) biological, chemical, physical, and radiological hazards, natural toxins, pesticides, drug residues, decomposition, parasites, allergens, and unapproved food and color additives; and

(B) hazards that occur naturally, or may be unintentionally introduced; and

(2) identify and evaluate hazards that may be intentionally introduced, including by acts of terrorism; and

(3) develop a written analysis of the hazards.

(c) Preventive Controls. — The owner, operator, or agent in charge of a facility shall identify and implement preventive controls, including at critical control points, if any, to provide assurances that —

(1) hazards identified in the hazard analysis conducted under subsection (b)(1) will be significantly minimized or prevented;

(2) any hazards identified in the hazard analysis conducted under subsection (b)(2) will be significantly minimized or prevented and addressed, consistent with section 420, as applicable; and

(3) the food manufactured, processed, packed, or held by such facility will not be adulterated under section 402 or misbranded under section 403(w).

(d) Monitoring of Effectiveness. — The owner, operator, or agent in charge of a facility shall monitor the effectiveness of the preventive controls implemented under subsection (c) to provide assurances that the outcomes described in subsection (c) shall be achieved.

(e) Corrective Actions. — The owner, operator, or agent in charge of a facility shall establish procedures to ensure that, if the preventive controls implemented under subsection (c) are not properly implemented or are found to be ineffective —

(1) appropriate action is taken to reduce the likelihood of recurrence of the implementation failure;

(2) all affected food is evaluated for safety; and

(3) all affected food is prevented from entering into commerce if the owner, operator or agent in charge of such facility cannot ensure that the affected food is not adulterated under section 402 or misbranded under section 403(w).

(f) Verification. — The owner, operator, or agent in charge of a facility shall verify that —

(1) the preventive controls implemented under subsection (c) are adequate to control the hazards identified under subsection (b);

(2) the owner, operator, or agent is conducting monitoring in accordance with subsection (d);

(3) the owner, operator, or agent is making appropriate decisions about corrective actions taken under subsection (e);

(4) the preventive controls implemented under subsection (c) are effectively and significantly minimizing or preventing the occurrence of identified hazards, including through the use of environmental and product testing programs and other appropriate means; and

(5) there is documented, periodic reanalysis of the plan under subsection (i) to ensure that the plan is still relevant to the raw materials, conditions and processes in the facility, and new and emerging threats.

(g) Recordkeeping. — The owner, operator, or agent in charge of a facility shall maintain, for not less than 2 years, records documenting the monitoring of the preventive controls implemented under subsection (c), instances of nonconformance material to food safety, the results of testing and other appropriate means of verification under subsection (f)(4), instances when corrective actions were implemented, and the efficacy of preventive controls and corrective actions.

(h) Written Plan and Documentation. — The owner, operator, or agent in charge of a facility shall prepare a written plan that documents and describes the procedures used by the facility to comply with the requirements of this section, including analyzing the hazards under subsection (b) and identifying the preventive controls adopted under subsection (c) to address those hazards. Such written plan, together with the documentation described in subsection (g), shall be made promptly available to a duly authorized representative of the Secretary upon oral or written request.

(i) Requirement to Reanalyze. — The owner, operator, or agent in charge of a facility shall conduct a reanalysis under subsection (b) whenever a significant change is made in the activities conducted at a facility operated by such owner, operator, or agent if the change creates a reasonable potential for a new hazard or a significant increase in a previously identified hazard or not less frequently than once every 3 years, whichever is earlier. Such reanalysis shall be completed and additional preventive controls needed to address the hazard identified, if any, shall be implemented before the change in activities at the facility is operative. Such owner, operator, or agent shall revise the written plan required under subsection (h) if such a significant change is made or document the basis for the conclusion that no additional or revised preventive controls are needed. The Secretary may require a reanalysis under this section to respond to new hazards and developments in scientific understanding, including, as appropriate, results from the Department of Homeland Security biological, chemical, radiological, or other terrorism risk assessment.

(j) Exemption for Seafood, Juice, and Low-Acid Canned Food Facilities Subject to HACCP. —

(1) In General. — This section shall not apply to a facility if the owner, operator, or agent in charge of such facility is required to comply with, and is in compliance with, 1 of the following standards and regulations with respect to such facility:

(A) The Seafood Hazard Analysis Critical Control Points Program of the Food and Drug Administration.

(B) The Juice Hazard Analysis Critical Control Points Program of the Food and Drug Administration.

(C) The Thermally Processed Low-Acid Foods Packaged in Hermetically Sealed Containers standards of the Food and Drug Administration (or any successor standards).

(2) Applicability. — The exemption under paragraph (1)(C) shall apply only with respect to microbiological hazards that are regulated under the standards for Thermally Processed Low-Acid Foods Packaged in Hermetically Sealed Containers under part 113 of chapter 21, Code of Federal Regulations (or any successor regulations).

(k) Exception for Activities of Facilities Subject to Section 419. — This section shall not apply to activities of a facility that are subject to section 419.

(l) Modified Requirements for Qualified Facilities. —

(1) Qualified Facilities. —

(A) In General. — A facility is a qualified facility for purposes of this subsection if the facility meets the conditions under subparagraph (B) or (C).

(B) Very Small Business. — A facility is a qualified facility under this subparagraph —

(i) if the facility, including any subsidiary or affiliate of the facility, is, collectively, a very small business (as defined in the regulations promulgated under subsection (n)); and

(ii) in the case where the facility is a subsidiary or affiliate of an entity, if such subsidiaries or affiliates, are, collectively, a very small business (as so defined).

(C) Limited Annual Monetary Value of Sales. —

(i) In General. — A facility is a qualified facility under this subparagraph if clause (ii) applies —

(I) to the facility, including any subsidiary or affiliate of the facility, collectively; and

(II) to the subsidiaries or affiliates, collectively, of any entity of which the facility is a subsidiary or affiliate.

(ii) Average Annual Monetary Value. — This clause applies if —

(I) during the 3-year period preceding the applicable calendar year, the average annual monetary value of the food manufactured, processed, packed, or held at such facility (or the collective average annual monetary value of such food at any subsidiary or affiliate, as described in clause (i)) that is sold directly to qualified end-users during such period exceeded the average annual monetary value of the food manufactured, processed, packed, or held at such facility (or the collective average annual monetary value of such food at any subsidiary or affiliate, as so described) sold by such facility (or collectively by any such subsidiary or affiliate) to all other purchasers during such period; and

(II) the average annual monetary value of all food sold by such facility (or the collective average annual monetary value of such food sold by any subsidiary or affiliate, as described in clause (i) during such period was less than $500,000, adjusted for inflation.

(2) Exemption. — A qualified facility —

(A) shall not be subject to the requirements under subsections (a) through (i) and subsection (n) in an applicable calendar year; and

(B) shall submit to the Secretary —

(i) —

(I) documentation that demonstrates that the owner, operator, or agent in charge of the facility has identified potential hazards associated with the food being produced, is implementing preventive controls to address the hazards, and is monitoring the preventive controls to ensure that such controls are effective; or

(II) documentation (which may include licenses, inspection reports, certificates, permits, credentials, certification by an appropriate agency (such as a State department of agriculture), or other evidence of oversight), as specified by the Secretary, that the facility is in compliance with State, local, county, or other applicable non-Federal food safety law; and

(ii) documentation, as specified by the Secretary in a guidance document issued not later than 1 year after the date of enactment of this section, that the facility is a qualified facility under paragraph (1)(B) or (1)(C).

(3) Withdrawal; Rule of Construction —

(A) In General. — In the event of an active investigation of a foodborne illness outbreak that is directly linked to a qualified facility subject to an exemption under this subsection, or if the Secretary determines that it is necessary to protect the public health and prevent or mitigate a foodborne illness outbreak based on conduct or conditions associated with a qualified facility that are material to the safety of the food manufactured, processed, packed, or held at such facility, the Secretary may withdraw the exemption provided to such facility under this subsection.

(B) Rule of Construction. — Nothing in this subsection shall be construed to expand or limit the inspection authority of the Secretary.

(4) Definitions. — In this subsection:

(A) Affiliate. — The term "affiliate" means any facility that controls, is controlled by, or is under common control with another facility.

(B) Qualified End-User — The term "qualified end-user," with respect to a food, means —

(i) the consumer of the food; or

(ii) a restaurant or retail food establishment (as those terms are defined by the Secretary for purposes of section 415) that —

(I) is located —

(aa) in the same State as the qualified facility that sold the food to such restaurant or establishment; or

(bb) not more than 275 miles from such facility; and

(II) is purchasing the food for sale directly to consumers at such restaurant or retail food establishment.

(C) Consumer. — For purposes of subparagraph (B), the term "consumer" does not include a business.

(D) Subsidiary. — The term "subsidiary" means any company which is owned or controlled directly or indirectly by another company.

(5) Study. —

(A) In General. — The Secretary, in consultation with the Secretary of Agriculture, shall conduct a study of the food processing sector regulated by the Secretary to determine —

(i) the distribution of food production by type and size of operation, including monetary value of food sold;

(ii) the proportion of food produced by each type and size of operation;

(iii) the number and types of food facilities co-located on farms, including the number and proportion by commodity and by manufacturing or processing activity;

(iv) the incidence of foodborne illness originating from each size and type of operation and the type of food facilities for which no reported or known hazard exists; and

(v) the effect on foodborne illness risk associated with commingling, processing, transporting, and storing food and raw agricultural commodities, including differences in risk based on the scale and duration of such activities.

(B) Size. — The results of the study conducted under subparagraph (A) shall include the information necessary to enable the Secretary to define the terms "small business" and "very small business", for purposes of promulgating the regulation under subsection (n). In defining such terms, the Secretary shall include consideration of harvestable acres, income, the number of employees, and the volume of food harvested.

(C) Submission of Report. — Not later than 18 months after the date of enactment the FDA Food Safety Modernization Act, the Secretary shall submit to Congress a report that describes the results of the study conducted under subparagraph (A).

(6) No Preemption. — Nothing in this subsection preempts State, local, county, or other non-Federal law regarding the safe production of food. Compliance with this subsection shall not relieve any person from liability at common law or under State statutory law.

(7) Notification to Consumers. —

(A) In General. — A qualified facility that is exempt from the requirements under subsections (a) through (i) and subsection (n) and does not prepare documentation under paragraph (2)(B)(i)(I) shall—

(i) with respect to a food for which a food packaging label is required by the Secretary under any other provision of this Act, include prominently and conspicuously on such label the name and business address of the facility where the food was manufactured or processed; or

(ii) with respect to a food for which a food packaging label is not required by the Secretary under any other provisions of this Act, prominently and conspicuously display, at the point of purchase, the name and business address of the facility where the food was manufactured or processed, on a label, poster, sign, placard, or documents delivered contemporaneously with the food in the normal course of business, or, in the case of Internet sales, in an electronic notice.

(B) No Additional Label. — Subparagraph (A) does not provide authority to the Secretary to require a label that is in addition to any label required under any other provision of this Act.

(m) Authority with Respect to Certain Facilities. — The Secretary may, by regulation, exempt or modify the requirements for compliance under this section with respect to facilities that are solely engaged in the production of food for animals other than man, the storage of raw agricultural commodities (other than fruits and vegetables) intended for further distribution or processing, or the storage of packaged foods that are not exposed to the environment.

(n) Regulations. —

(1) In General. — Not later than 18 months after the date of enactment of the FDA Food Safety Modernization Act, the Secretary shall promulgate regulations —

(A) to establish science-based minimum standards for conducting a hazard analysis, documenting hazards, implementing preventive controls, and documenting the implementation of the preventive controls under this section; and

(B) to define, for purposes of this section, the terms "small business" and "very small business", taking into consideration the study described in subsection (l)(5).

(2) Coordination. — In promulgating the regulations under paragraph (1)(A), with regard to hazards that may be intentionally introduced, including by acts of terrorism, the Secretary shall coordinate with the Secretary of Homeland Security, as appropriate.

(3) Content. — The regulations promulgated under paragraph (1)(A) shall —

(A) provide sufficient flexibility to be practicable for all sizes and types of facilities, including small businesses such as a small food processing facility co-located on a farm;

(B) comply with chapter 35 of title 44, United States Code (commonly known as the "Paperwork Reduction Act"), with special attention to minimizing the burden (as defined in section 3502(2) of such Act) on the facility, and collection of information (as defined in section 3502(3) of such Act), associated with such regulations;

(C) acknowledge differences in risk and minimize, as appropriate, the number of separate standards that apply to separate foods; and

(D) not require a facility to hire a consultant or other third party to identify, implement, certify, or audit preventative controls, except in the case of negotiated enforcement resolutions that may require such a consultant or third party.

(4) Rule of Construction. — Nothing in this subsection shall be construed to provide the Secretary with the authority to prescribe specific technologies, practices, or critical controls for an individual facility.

(5) Review. — In promulgating the regulations under paragraph (1)(A), the Secretary shall review regulatory hazard analysis and preventive control programs in existence on the date of enactment of the FDA Food Safety Modernization Act, including the Grade 'A' Pasteurized Milk Ordinance to ensure that such regulations are consistent, to the extent practicable, with applicable domestic and internationally-recognized standards in existence on such date.

(o) Definitions. — For purposes of this section:

(1) Critical Control Point. — The term "critical control point" means a point, step, or procedure in a food process at which control can be applied and is essential to prevent or eliminate a food safety hazard or reduce such hazard to an acceptable level.

(2) Facility. — The term "facility" means a domestic facility or a foreign facility that is required to register under section 415.

(3) Preventive Controls. — The term "preventive controls" means those risk-based, reasonably appropriate procedures, practices, and processes that a person knowledgeable about the safe manufacturing, processing, packing, or holding of food would employ to significantly minimize or prevent the hazards identified under the hazard analysis conducted under subsection (b) and that are consistent with the current scientific understanding of safe food manufacturing, processing, packing, or holding at the time of the analysis. Those procedures, practices, and processes may include the following:

(A) Sanitation procedures for food contact surfaces and utensils and food-contact surfaces of equipment.

(B) Supervisor, manager, and employee hygiene training.

(C) An environmental monitoring program to verify the effectiveness of pathogen controls in processes where a food is exposed to a potential contaminant in the environment.

(D) A food allergen control program.

(E) A recall plan.

(F) Current Good Manufacturing Practices (CGMPS) under part 110 of title 21, Code of Federal Regulations (or any successor regulations).

(G) Supplier verification activities that relate to the safety of food.

Sec. 419. [350h] Standards for Produce Safety.

(a) Proposed Rulemaking. —

(1) In General. —

(A) Rulemaking. — Not later than 1 year after the date of enactment of the FDA Food Safety Modernization Act, the Secretary, in coordination with the Secretary of Agriculture and representatives of State departments of agriculture (including with regard to the national organic program established under the Organic Foods Production Act of 1990), and in consultation with the Secretary of Homeland Security, shall publish a notice of proposed rulemaking to establish science-based minimum standards for the safe production and harvesting of those types of fruits and vegetables, including specific mixes or categories of fruits and vegetables, that are raw agricultural commodities for which the Secretary has determined that such standards minimize the risk of serious adverse health consequences or death.

(B) Determination by Secretary. — With respect to small businesses and very small businesses (as such terms are defined in the regulation promulgated under subparagraph (A)) that produce and harvest those types of fruits and vegetables that are raw agricultural commodities that the Secretary has determined are low risk and do not present a risk of serious adverse health consequences or death, the Secretary may determine not to include production and harvesting of such fruits and vegetables in such rulemaking, or may modify the applicable requirements of regulations promulgated pursuant to this section.

(2) Public Input. — During the comment period on the notice of proposed rulemaking under paragraph (1), the Secretary shall conduct not less than 3 public meetings in diverse geographical areas of the United States to provide persons in different regions an opportunity to comment.

(3) Content. — The proposed rulemaking under paragraph (1) shall —

(A) provide sufficient flexibility to be applicable to various types of entities engaged in the production and harvesting of fruits and vegetables that are raw agricultural commodities, including small businesses and entities that sell directly to consumers, and be appropriate to the scale and diversity of the production and harvesting of such commodities;

(B) include, with respect to growing, harvesting, sorting, packing, and storage operations, science-based minimum standards related to soil amendments, hygiene, packaging, temperature controls, animals in the growing area, and water;

(C) consider hazards that occur naturally, may be unintentionally introduced, or may be intentionally introduced, including by acts of terrorism;

(D) take into consideration, consistent with ensuring enforceable public health protection, conservation and environmental practice standards and policies established by Federal natural resource conservation, wildlife conservation, and environmental agencies;

(E) in the case of production that is certified organic, not include any requirements that conflict with or duplicate the requirements of the national organic program established under the Organic Foods Production Act of 1990, while providing the same level of public health protection as the requirements under guidance documents, including guidance documents regarding action levels, and regulations under the FDA Food Safety Modernization Act; and

(F) define, for purposes of this section, the terms "small business" and "very small business."

(4) Prioritization. — The Secretary shall prioritize the implementation of the regulations under this section for specific fruits and vegetables that are raw agricultural commodities based on known risks which may include a history and severity of foodborne illness outbreaks.

(b) Final Regulation. —

(1) In General. — Not later than 1 year after the close of the comment period for the proposed rulemaking under subsection (a), the Secretary shall adopt a final regulation to provide for minimum science — based standards for those types of fruits and vegetables, including specific mixes or categories of fruits or vegetables, that are raw agricultural commodities, based on known safety risks, which may include a history of foodborne illness outbreaks.

(2) Final Regulation. — The final regulation shall —

(A) provide for coordination of education and enforcement activities by State and local officials, as designated by the Governors of the respective States or the appropriate elected State official as recognized by State statute; and

(B) include a description of the variance process under subsection (c) and the types of permissible variances the Secretary may grant.

(3) Flexibility for Small Businesses. — Notwithstanding paragraph (1) —

(A) the regulations promulgated under this section shall apply to a small business (as defined in the regulation promulgated under subsection (a)(1)) after the date that is 1 year after the effective date of the final regulation under paragraph (1); and

(B) the regulations promulgated under this section shall apply to a very small business (as defined in the regulation promulgated under subsection (a)(1)) after the date that is 2 years after the effective date of the final regulation under paragraph (1).

(c) Criteria. —

(1) In General. — The regulations adopted under subsection (b) shall —

(A) set forth those procedures, processes, and practices that the Secretary determines to minimize the risk of serious adverse health consequences or death, including procedures, processes, and practices that the Secretary determines to be reasonably necessary to prevent the introduction of known or reasonably foreseeable biological, chemical, and physical hazards, including hazards that occur naturally, may be unintentionally introduced, or may be intentionally introduced, including by acts of terrorism, into fruits and vegetables, including specific mixes or categories of fruits and vegetables, that are raw agricultural commodities and to provide reasonable assurances that the produce is not adulterated under section 402;

(B) provide sufficient flexibility to be practicable for all sizes and types of businesses, including small businesses such as a small food processing facility co-located on a farm;

(C) comply with chapter 35 of title 44, United States Code (commonly known as the "Paperwork Reduction Act"), with special attention to minimizing the burden (as defined in section 3502(2) of such Act) on the business, and collection of information (as defined in section 3502(3) of such Act), associated with such regulations;

(D) acknowledge differences in risk and minimize, as appropriate, the number of separate standards that apply to separate foods; and

(E) not require a business to hire a consultant or other third party to identify, implement, certify, compliance with these procedures, processes, and practices, except in the case of negotiated enforcement resolutions that may require such a consultant or third party; and

(F) permit States and foreign countries from which food is imported into the United States to request from the Secretary variances from the requirements of the regulations, subject to paragraph (2), where the State or foreign country determines that the variance is necessary in light of local growing conditions and that the procedures, processes, and practices to be followed under the variance are reasonably likely to ensure that the produce is not adulterated under section 402 and to provide the same level of public health protection as the requirements of the regulations adopted under subsection (b).

(2) Variances. —

(A) Requests for Variances. — A State or foreign country from which food is imported into the United States may in writing request a variance from the Secretary. Such request shall describe the variance requested and present information demonstrating that the variance does not increase the likelihood that the food for which the variance is requested will be adulterated under section 402, and that the variance provides the same level of public health protection as the requirements of the regulations adopted under subsection (b). The Secretary shall review such requests in a reasonable timeframe.

(B) Approval of Variances. — The Secretary may approve a variance in whole or in part, as appropriate, and may specify the scope of applicability of a variance to other similarly situated persons.

(C) Denial of Variances. — The Secretary may deny a variance request if the Secretary determines that such variance is not reasonably likely to ensure that the food is not adulterated under section 402 and is not reasonably likely to provide the same level of public health protection as the requirements of the regulation adopted under subsection (b). The Secretary shall notify the person requesting such variance of the reasons for the denial.

(D) Modification or Revocation of a Variance. — The Secretary, after notice and an opportunity for a hearing, may modify or revoke a variance if the Secretary determines that such variance is not reasonably likely to ensure that the food is not adulterated under section 402 and is not reasonably likely to provide the same level of public health protection as the requirements of the regulations adopted under subsection (b).

(d) Enforcement. — The Secretary may coordinate with the Secretary of Agriculture and, as appropriate, shall contract and coordinate with the agency or department designated by the Governor of each State to perform activities to ensure compliance with this section.

(e) Guidance. —

(1) In General. — Not later than 1 year after the date of enactment of the FDA Food Safety Modernization Act, the Secretary shall publish, after consultation with the Secretary of Agriculture, representatives of State departments of agriculture, farmer representatives, and various types of entities engaged in the production and harvesting or importing of fruits and vegetables that are raw agricultural commodities, including small businesses, updated good agricultural practices and guidance for the safe production and harvesting of specific types of fresh produce under this section.

(2) Public Meetings. — The Secretary shall conduct not fewer than 3 public meetings in diverse geographical areas of the United States as part of an effort to conduct education and outreach regarding the guidance described in paragraph (1) for persons in different regions who are involved in the production and harvesting of fruits and vegetables that are raw agricultural commodities, including persons that sell directly to consumers and farmer representatives, and for importers of fruits and vegetables that are raw agricultural commodities.

(3) Paperwork Reduction — The Secretary shall ensure that any updated guidance under this section will —

(A) provide sufficient flexibility to be practicable for all sizes and types of facilities, including small businesses such as a small food processing facility co-located on a farm; and

(B) acknowledge differences in risk and minimize, as appropriate, the number of separate standards that apply to separate foods.

(f) Exemption for Direct Farm Marketing. —

(1) In General. — A farm shall be exempt from the requirements under this section in a calendar year if —

(A) during the previous 3-year period, the average annual monetary value of the food sold by such farm directly to qualified end-users during such period exceeded the average annual monetary value of the food sold by such farm to all other buyers during such period; and

(B) the average annual monetary value of all food sold during such period was less than $500,000, adjusted for inflation.

(2) Notification to Consumers. —

(A) In General. — A farm that is exempt from the requirements under this section shall —

(i) with respect to a food for which a food packaging label is required by the Secretary under any other provision of this Act, include prominently and conspicuously on such label the name and business address of the farm where the produce was grown; or

(ii) with respect to a food for which a food packaging label is not required by the Secretary under any other provision of this Act, prominently and conspicuously display, at the point of purchase, the name and business address of the farm where the produce was grown, on a label, poster, sign, placard, or documents delivered contemporaneously with the food in the normal course of business, or, in the case of Internet sales, in an electronic notice.

(B) No Additional Label. — Subparagraph (A) does not provide authority to the Secretary to require a label that is in addition to any label required under any other provision of this Act.

(3) Withdrawal; Rule of Construction. —

(A) In General. — In the event of an active investigation of a foodborne illness outbreak that is directly linked to a farm subject to an exemption under this subsection, or if the Secretary determines that it is necessary to protect the public health and prevent or mitigate a foodborne illness outbreak based on conduct or conditions associated with a farm that are material to the safety of the food produced or harvested at such farm, the Secretary may withdraw the exemption provided to such farm under this subsection.

(B) Rule of Construction. — Nothing in this subsection shall be construed to expand or limit the inspection authority of the Secretary.

(4) Definitions. —

(A) Qualified End-User. — In this subsection, the term "qualified end-user", with respect to a food means —

(i) the consumer of the food; or

(ii) a restaurant or retail food establishment (as those terms are defined by the Secretary for purposes of section 415) that is located —

(I) in the same State as the farm that produced the food; or

(II) not more than 275 miles from such farm.

(B) Consumer. — For purposes of subparagraph (A), the term "consumer" does not include a business.

(5) No Preemption. — Nothing in this subsection preempts State, local, county, or other non-Federal law regarding the safe production, harvesting, holding, transportation, and sale of fresh fruits and vegetables. Compliance with this subsection shall not relieve any person from liability at common law or under State statutory law.

(6) Limitation of Effect. — Nothing in this subsection shall prevent the Secretary from exercising any authority granted in the other sections of this Act.

(g) Clarification. — This section shall not apply to produce that is produced by an individual for personal consumption.

(h) Exception for Activities of Facilities Subject to Section 418. — This section shall not apply to activities of a facility that are subject to section 418.

Sec. 420. [350i] Protection Against Intentional Adulteration.

(a) Determinations. —

(1) In General. — The Secretary shall —

(A) conduct a vulnerability assessment of the food system, including by consideration of the Department of Homeland Security biological, chemical, radiological, or other terrorism risk assessments;

(B) consider the best available understanding of uncertainties, risks, costs, and benefits associated with guarding against intentional adulteration of food at vulnerable points; and

(C) determine the types of science-based mitigation strategies or measures that are necessary to protect against the intentional adulteration of food.

(2) Limited Distribution. — In the interest of national security, the Secretary, in consultation with the Secretary of Homeland Security, may determine the time, manner, and form in which determinations made under paragraph (1) are made publicly available.

(b) Regulations. — Not later than 18 months after the date of enactment of the FDA Food Safety Modernization Act, the Secretary, in coordination with the Secretary of Homeland Security and in consultation with the Secretary of Agriculture, shall promulgate regulations to protect against the intentional adulteration of food subject to this Act. Such regulations shall —

(1) specify how a person shall assess whether the person is required to implement mitigation strategies or measures intended to protect against the intentional adulteration of food; and

(2) specify appropriate science-based mitigation strategies or measures to prepare and protect the food supply chain at specific vulnerable points, as appropriate.

(c) Applicability. — Regulations promulgated under subsection (b) shall apply only to food for which there is a high risk of intentional contamination, as determined by the Secretary, in consultation with the Secretary of Homeland Security, under subsection (a), that could cause serious adverse health consequences or death to humans or animals and shall include those foods —

(1) for which the Secretary has identified clear vulnerabilities (including short shelf-life or susceptibility to intentional contamination at critical control points); and

(2) in bulk or batch form, prior to being packaged for the final consumer.

(d) Exception. — This section shall not apply to farms, except for those that produce milk.

(e) Definition. — For purposes of this section, the term "farm" has the meaning given that term in section 1.227 of title 21, Code of Federal Regulations (or any successor regulation).

Sec. 421. [350j] Targeting of Inspection Resources for Domestic Facilities, Foreign Facilities, and Ports of Entry; Annual Report.

(a) Identification and Inspection of Facilities. —

(1) Identification. — The Secretary shall identify high-risk facilities and shall allocate resources to inspect facilities according to the known safety risks of the facilities, which shall be based on the following factors:

(A) The known safety risks of the food manufactured, processed, packed, or held at the facility.

(B) The compliance history of a facility, including with regard to food recalls, outbreaks of foodborne illness, and violations of food safety standards.

(C) The rigor and effectiveness of the facility's hazard analysis and risk-based preventive controls.

(D) Whether the food manufactured, processed, packed, or held at the facility meets the criteria for priority under section 801(h)(1).

(E) Whether the food or the facility that manufactured, processed, packed, or held such food has received a certification as described in section 801(q) or 806, as appropriate.

(F) Any other criteria deemed necessary and appropriate by the Secretary for purposes of allocating inspection resources.

(2) Inspections. —

(A) In General. — Beginning on the date of enactment of the FDA Food Safety Modernization Act, the Secretary shall increase the frequency of inspection of all facilities.

(B) Domestic High-Risk Facilities. — The Secretary shall increase the frequency of inspection of domestic facilities identified under paragraph (1) as high-risk facilities such that each such facility is inspected —

(i) not less often than once in the 5-year period following the date of enactment of the FDA Food Safety Modernization Act; and

(ii) not less often than once every 3 years thereafter.

(C) Domestic Non-High-Risk Facilities. — The Secretary shall ensure that each domestic facility that is not identified under paragraph (1) as a high-risk facility is inspected —

(i) not less often than once in the 7-year period following the date of enactment of the FDA Food Safety Modernization Act; and

(ii) not less often than once every 5 years thereafter.

(D) Foreign Facilities. —

(i) Year 1. — In the 1-year period following the date of enactment of the FDA Food Safety Modernization Act, the Secretary shall inspect not fewer than 600 foreign facilities.

(ii) Subsequent years. — In each of the 5 years following the 1-year period described in clause (i), the Secretary shall inspect not fewer than twice the number of foreign facilities inspected by the Secretary during the previous year.

(E) Reliance on Federal, State, or Local Inspections. — In meeting the inspection requirements under this subsection for domestic facilities, the Secretary may rely on inspections conducted by other Federal, State, or local agencies under interagency agreement, contract, memoranda of understanding, or other obligation.

(b) Identification and Inspection at Ports of Entry. — The Secretary, in consultation with the Secretary of Homeland Security, shall allocate resources to inspect any article of food imported into the United States according to the known safety risks of the article of food, which shall be based on the following factors:

(1) The known safety risks of the food imported.

(2) The known safety risks of the countries or regions of origin and countries through which such article of food is transported.

(3) The compliance history of the importer, including with regard to food recalls, outbreaks of foodborne illness, and violations of food safety standards.

(4) The rigor and effectiveness of the activities conducted by the importer of such article of food to satisfy the requirements of the foreign supplier verification program under section 805.

(5) Whether the food importer participates in the voluntary qualified importer program under section 806.

(6) Whether the food meets the criteria for priority under section 801(h)(1).

(7) Whether the food or the facility that manufactured, processed, packed, or held such food received a certification as described in section 801(q) or 806.

(8) Any other criteria deemed necessary and appropriate by the Secretary for purposes of allocating inspection resources.

(c) Interagency Agreements with Respect to Seafood. —

(1) In General. — The Secretary of Health and Human Services, the Secretary of Commerce, the Secretary of Homeland Security, the Chairman of the Federal Trade Commission, and the heads of other appropriate agencies may enter into such agreements as may be necessary or appropriate to improve seafood safety.

(2) Scope of Agreements. — The agreements under paragraph (1) may include —

(A) cooperative arrangements for examining and testing seafood imports that leverage the resources, capabilities, and authorities of each party to the agreement;

(B) coordination of inspections of foreign facilities to increase the percentage of imported seafood and seafood facilities inspected;

(C) standardization of data on seafood names, inspection records, and laboratory testing to improve interagency coordination;

(D) coordination to detect and investigate violations under applicable Federal law;

(E) a process, including the use or modification of existing processes, by which officers and employees of the National Oceanic and Atmospheric Administration may be duly designated by the Secretary to carry out seafood examinations and investigations under section 801 of this Act or section 203 of the Food Allergen Labeling and Consumer Protection Act of 2004;

(F) the sharing of information concerning observed non-compliance with United States food requirements domestically and in foreign nations and new regulatory decisions and policies that may affect the safety of food imported into the United States;

(G) conducting joint training on subjects that affect and strengthen seafood inspection effectiveness by Federal authorities; and

(H) outreach on Federal efforts to enhance seafood safety and compliance with Federal food safety requirements.

(d) Coordination. — The Secretary shall improve coordination and cooperation with the Secretary of Agriculture and the Secretary of Homeland Security to target food inspection resources.

(e) Facility. — For purposes of this section, the term "facility" means a domestic facility or a foreign facility that is required to register under section 415.

Sec. 422. [350k] Laboratory Accreditation for Analyses of Foods.

(a) Recognition of Laboratory Accreditation. —

(1) In General. — Not later than 2 years after the date of enactment of the FDA Food Safety Modernization Act, the Secretary shall —

(A) establish a program for the testing of food by accredited laboratories;

(B) establish a publicly available registry of accreditation bodies recognized by the Secretary and laboratories accredited by a recognized accreditation body, including the name of, contact information for, and other information deemed appropriate by the Secretary about such bodies and laboratories; and

(C) require, as a condition of recognition or accreditation, as appropriate, that recognized accreditation bodies and accredited laboratories report to the Secretary any changes that would affect the recognition of such accreditation body or the accreditation of such laboratory.

(2) Program Requirements. — The program established under paragraph (1)(A) shall provide for the recognition of laboratory accreditation bodies that meet criteria established by the Secretary for accreditation of laboratories, including independent private laboratories and laboratories run and operated by a Federal agency (including the Department of Commerce), State, or locality with a demonstrated capability to conduct 1 or more sampling and analytical testing methodologies for food.

(3) Increasing the Number of Qualified Laboratories. — The Secretary shall work with the laboratory accreditation bodies recognized under paragraph (1), as appropriate, to increase the number of qualified laboratories that are eligible to perform testing under subparagraph (b) beyond the number so qualified on the date of enactment of the FDA Food Safety Modernization Act.

(4) Limited Distribution. — In the interest of national security, the Secretary, in coordination with the Secretary of Homeland Security, may determine the time, manner, and form in which the registry established under paragraph (1)(B) is made publicly available.

(5) Foreign Laboratories. — Accreditation bodies recognized by the Secretary under paragraph (1) may accredit laboratories that operate outside the United States, so long as such laboratories meet the accreditation standards applicable to domestic laboratories accredited under this section.

(6) Model Laboratory Standards. — The Secretary shall develop model standards that a laboratory shall meet to be accredited by a recognized accreditation body for a specified sampling or analytical testing methodology and included in the registry provided for under paragraph (1). In developing the model standards, the Secretary shall consult existing standards for guidance. The model standards shall include —

(A) methods to ensure that —

(i) appropriate sampling, analytical procedures (including rapid analytical procedures), and commercially available techniques are followed and reports of analyses are certified as true and accurate;

(ii) internal quality systems are established and maintained;

(iii) procedures exist to evaluate and respond promptly to complaints regarding analyses and other activities for which the laboratory is accredited; and

(iv) individuals who conduct the sampling and analyses are qualified by training and experience to do so; and

(B) any other criteria determined appropriate by the Secretary.

(7) Review of Recognition. — To ensure compliance with the requirements of this section, the Secretary —

(A) shall periodically, and in no case less than once every 5 years, reevaluate accreditation bodies recognized under paragraph (1) and may accompany auditors from an accreditation body to assess whether the accreditation body meets the criteria for recognition; and

(B) shall promptly revoke the recognition of any accreditation body found not to be in compliance with the requirements of this section, specifying, as appropriate, any terms and conditions necessary for laboratories accredited by such body to continue to perform testing as described in this section.

(b) Testing Procedures. —

(1) In General. — Not later than 30 months after the date of enactment of the FDA Food Safety Modernization Act, food testing shall be conducted by Federal laboratories or non-Federal laboratories that have been accredited for the appropriate sampling or analytical testing methodology or methodologies by a recognized accreditation body on the registry established by the Secretary under subsection (a)(1)(B) whenever such testing is conducted —

(A) by or on behalf of an owner or consignee —

(i) in response to a specific testing requirement under this Act or implementing regulations, when applied to address an identified or suspected food safety problem; and

(ii) as required by the Secretary, as the Secretary deems appropriate, to address an identified or suspected food safety problem; or

(B) on behalf of an owner or consignee —

(i) in support of admission of an article of food under section 801(a); and

(ii) under an Import Alert that requires successful consecutive tests.

(2) Results of Testing. — The results of any such testing shall be sent directly to the Food and Drug Administration, except the Secretary may by regulation exempt test results from such submission requirement if the Secretary determines that such results do not contribute to the protection of public health. Test results required to be submitted may be submitted to the Food and Drug Administration through electronic means.

(3) Exception. — The Secretary may waive requirements under this subsection if —

(A) a new methodology or methodologies have been developed and validated but a laboratory has not yet been accredited to perform such methodology or methodologies; and

(B) the use of such methodology or methodologies are necessary to prevent, control, or mitigate a food emergency or foodborne illness outbreak.

(c) Review by Secretary. — If food sampling and testing performed by a laboratory run and operated by a State or locality that is accredited by a recognized accreditation body on the registry established by the Secretary under subsection (a) result in a State recalling a food, the Secretary shall review the sampling and testing results for the purpose of determining the need for a national recall or other compliance and enforcement activities.

(d) No Limit on Secretarial Authority. — Nothing in this section shall be construed to limit the ability of the Secretary to review and act upon information from food testing, including determining the sufficiency of such information and testing.

Sec. 423. [350l] Mandatory Recall Authority.

(a) Voluntary procedures. — If the Secretary determines, based on information gathered through the reportable food registry under section 417 or through any other means, that there is a reasonable probability that an article of food (other than infant formula) is adulterated under section 402 or misbranded under section 403(w) and the use of or exposure to such article will cause serious adverse health consequences or death to humans or animals, the Secretary shall provide the responsible party (as defined in section 417) with an opportunity to cease distribution and recall such article.

(b) Prehearing Order to Cease Distribution and Give Notice. —

(1) In General. — If the responsible party refuses to or does not voluntarily cease distribution or recall such article within the time and in the manner prescribed by the Secretary (if so prescribed), the Secretary may, by order require, as the Secretary deems necessary, such person to —

(A) immediately cease distribution of such article; and

(B) as applicable, immediately notify all persons —

(i) manufacturing, processing, packing, transporting, distributing, receiving, holding, or importing and selling such article; and

(ii) to which such article has been distributed, transported, or sold, to immediately cease distribution of such article.

(2) Required Additional Information. —

(A) In General. — If an article of food covered by a recall order issued under paragraph (1)(B) has been distributed to a warehouse-based third party logistics provider without providing such provider sufficient information to know or reasonably determine the precise identity of the article of food covered by a recall order that is in its possession, the notice provided by the responsible party subject to the order issued under paragraph (1)(B) shall include such information as is necessary for the warehouse-based third party logistics provider to identify the food.

(B) Rules of Construction. — Nothing in this paragraph shall be construed —

(i) to exempt a warehouse-based third party logistics provider from the requirements of this Act, including the requirements in this section and section 414; or

(ii) to exempt a warehouse-based third party logistics provider from being the subject of a mandatory recall order.

(3) Determination to Limit Areas Affected. — If the Secretary requires a responsible party to cease distribution under paragraph (1)(A) of an article of food identified in subsection (a), the Secretary may limit the size of the geographic area and the markets affected by such cessation if such limitation would not compromise the public health.

(c) Hearing on Order. — The Secretary shall provide the responsible party subject to an order under subsection (b) with an opportunity for an informal hearing, to be held as soon as possible, but not later than 2 days after the issuance of the order, on the actions required by the order and on why the article that is the subject of the order should not be recalled.

(d) Post-Hearing Recall Order and Modification of Order. —

(1) Amendment of Order. — If, after providing opportunity for an informal hearing under subsection (c), the Secretary determines that removal of the article from commerce is necessary, the Secretary shall, as appropriate —

(A) amend the order to require recall of such article or other appropriate action;

(B) specify a timetable in which the recall shall occur;

(C) require periodic reports to the Secretary describing the progress of the recall; and

(D) provide notice to consumers to whom such article was, or may have been, distributed.

(2) Vacating of Order. — If, after such hearing, the Secretary determines that adequate grounds do not exist to continue the actions required by the order, or that such actions should be modified, the Secretary shall vacate the order or modify the order.

(e) Rule Regarding Alcoholic Beverages. — The Secretary shall not initiate a mandatory recall or take any other action under this section with respect to any alcohol beverage until the Secretary has provided the Alcohol and Tobacco Tax and Trade Bureau with a reasonable opportunity to cease distribution and recall such article under the Alcohol and Tobacco Tax and Trade Bureau authority.

(f) Cooperation and Consultation. — The Secretary shall work with State and local public health officials in carrying out this section, as appropriate.

(g) Public Notification. — In conducting a recall under this section, the Secretary shall —

(1) ensure that a press release is published regarding the recall, as well as alerts and public notices, as appropriate, in order to provide notification —

(A) of the recall to consumers and retailers to whom such article was, or may have been, distributed; and

(B) that includes, at a minimum —

(i) the name of the article of food subject to the recall;

(ii) a description of the risk associated with such article; and

(iii) to the extent practicable, information for consumers about similar articles of food that are not affected by the recall;

(2) consult the policies of the Department of Agriculture regarding providing to the public a list of retail consignees receiving products involved in a Class I recall and shall consider providing such a list to the public, as determined appropriate by the Secretary; and

(3) if available, publish on the Internet Web site of the Food and Drug Administration an image of the article that is the subject of the press release described in (1).

(h) No Delegation. — The authority conferred by this section to order a recall or vacate a recall order shall not be delegated to any officer or employee other than the Commissioner.

(i) Effect. — Nothing in this section shall affect the authority of the Secretary to request or participate in a voluntary recall, or to issue an order to cease distribution or to recall under any other provision of this Act or under the Public Health Service Act.

(j) Coordinated Communication. —

(1) In General. — To assist in carrying out the requirements of this subsection, the Secretary shall establish an incident command operation or a similar operation within the Department of Health and Human Services that will operate not later than 24 hours after the initiation of a mandatory recall or the recall of an article of food for which the use of, or exposure to, such article will cause serious adverse health consequences or death to humans or animals.

(2) Requirements. — To reduce the potential for miscommunication during recalls or regarding investigations of a food borne illness outbreak associated with a food that is subject to a recall, each incident command operation or similar operation under paragraph (1) shall use regular staff and resources of the Department of Health and Human Services to —

(A) ensure timely and coordinated communication within the Department, including enhanced communication and coordination between different agencies and organizations within the Department;

(B) ensure timely and coordinated communication from the Department, including public statements, throughout the duration of the investigation and related foodborne illness outbreak;

(C) identify a single point of contact within the Department for public inquiries regarding any actions by the Secretary related to a recall;

(D) coordinate with Federal, State, local, and tribal authorities, as appropriate, that have responsibilities related to the recall of a food or a foodborne illness outbreak associated with a food that is subject to the recall, including notification of the Secretary of Agriculture and the Secretary of Education in the event such recalled food is a commodity intended for use in a child nutrition program (as identified in section 25(b) of the Richard B. Russell National School Lunch Act (42 U.S.C. 1769f(b)); and

(E) conclude operations at such time as the Secretary determines appropriate.

(3) Multiple Recalls. — The Secretary may establish multiple or concurrent incident command operations or similar operations in the event of multiple recalls or foodborne illness outbreaks necessitating such action by the Department of Health and Human Services.

Chapter V — Drugs and Devices

Subchapter A — Drugs and Devices

Sec. 501. [351] Adulterated Drugs and Devices.

A drug or device shall be deemed to be adulterated —

(a) —

(1) If it consists in whole or in part of any filthy, putrid, or decomposed substance; or

(2) —

(A) if it has been prepared, packed, or held under insanitary conditions whereby it may have been contaminated with filth, or whereby it may have been rendered injurious to health; or

(B) if it is a drug and the methods used in, or the facilities or controls used for, its manufacture, processing, packing or holding do not conform to or are not operated or administered in conformity with current good manufacturing practice to assure that such drug meets the requirements of this Act as to safety and has the identity and strength, and meets the quality and purity characteristics, which it purports or is represented to possess; or

(C) if it is a compounded positron emission tomography drug and the methods used in, or the facilities and controls used for, its compounding, processing, packing, or holding do not conform to or are not operated or administered in conformity with the positron emission tomography compounding standards and the official monographs of the United States Pharmacopeia to assure that such drug meets the requirements of this Act as to safety and has the identity and strength, and meets the quality and purity characteristics, that it purports or is represented to possess; or

(3) if its container is composed, in whole or in part, of any poisonous or deleterious substance which may render the contents injurious to health; or

(4) if —

(A) it bears or contains, for purposes of coloring only, a color additive which is unsafe within the meaning of section 721(a), or

(B) it is a color additive the intended use of which in or on drugs or devices is for purposes of coloring only and is unsafe within the meaning of section 721(a); or

(5) if it is a new animal drug which is unsafe within the meaning of section 512; or

(6) if it is an animal feed bearing or containing a new animal drug, and such animal feed is unsafe within the meaning of section 512.

(b) If it purports to be or is represented as a drug the name of which is recognized in an official compendium, and its strength differs from, or its quality or purity falls below, the standards set forth in such compendium. Such determination as to strength, quality, or purity shall be made in accordance with the tests or methods of assay set forth in such compendium, except that whenever tests or methods of assay have not been prescribed in such compendium, or such tests or methods of assay as are prescribed are, in the judgment of the Secretary, insufficient for the making of such determination, the Secretary shall bring such fact to the attention of the appropriate body charged with the revision of such compendium, and if such body fails within a reasonable time to prescribe tests or methods of assay which, in the judgment of the Secretary, are sufficient for purposes of this paragraph, then the Secretary shall promulgate regulations prescribing appropriate tests or methods of assay in accordance with which such determination as to strength, quality, or purity shall be made. No drug defined in an official compendium shall be deemed to be adulterated under this paragraph because it differs from the standard of strength, quality, or purity therefor set forth in such compendium, if its difference in strength, quality, or purity from such standards is plainly stated on its label. Whenever a drug is recognized in both the United States Pharmacopeia and the Homeopathic Pharmacopeia of the United States it shall be subject to the requirements of the United States Pharmacopeia unless it is labeled and offered for sale as a homeopathic drug, in which case it shall be subject to the provisions of the Homeopathic Pharmacopeia of the United States and not to those of the United States Pharmacopeia.

(c) If it is not subject to the provisions of paragraph (b) of this section and its strength differs from, or its purity or quality falls below, that which it purports or is represented to possess.

(d) If it is a drug and any substance has been

(1) mixed or packed therewith so as to reduce its quality or strength or

(2) substituted wholly or in part therefor.

(e) —

(1) If it is, or purports to be or is represented as, a device which is subject to a performance standard established under section 514, unless such device is in all respects in conformity with such standard.

(2) If it is declared to be, purports to be, or is represented as, a device that is in conformity with any standard recognized under section 514(c) unless such device is in all respects in conformity with such standard.

(f) —

(1) If it is a class III device —

(A) —

(i) which is required by an order issued under subsection (b) of section 515 to have an approval under such section of an application for premarket approval and which is not exempt from section 515 under section 520(g), and

(ii) —

(I) for which an application for premarket approval or a notice of completion of a product development protocol was not filed with the Secretary within the ninety-day period beginning on the date of the issuance of such order, or

(II) for which such an application was filed and approval of the application has been denied, suspended, or withdrawn, or such a notice was filed and has been declared not completed or the approval of the device under the protocol has been withdrawn;

(B) —

(i) which was classified under section 513(f) into class III, which under section 515(a) is required to have in effect an approved application for premarket approval, and which is not exempt from section 515 under section 520(g), and

(ii) which has an application which has been suspended or is otherwise not in effect; or

(C) which was classified under section 520(1) into class III, which under such section is required to have in effect an approved application under section 515, and which has an application which has been suspended or is otherwise not in effect.

(2) —

(A) In the case of a device classified under section 513(f) into class III and intended solely for investigational use, paragraph (1)(B) shall not apply with respect to such device during the period ending on the ninetieth day after the date of the promulgation of the regulations prescribing the procedures and conditions required by section 520(g)(2).

(B) In the case of a device subject to an order issued under subsection (b) of section 515, paragraph (1) shall not apply with respect to such device during the period ending —

(i) on the last day of the thirtieth calendar month beginning after the month in which the classification of the device in class III became effective under section 513, or

(ii) on the ninetieth day after the date of the issuance of such order,

whichever occurs later.

(3) In the case of a device with respect to which a regulation was promulgated under section 515(b) prior to the date of enactment of the Food and Drug Administration Safety and Innovation Act, a reference in this subsection to an order issued under section 515(b) shall be deemed to include such regulation.

(g) If it is a banned device.

(h) If it is a device and the methods used in, or the facilities or controls used for, its manufacture, packing, storage, or installation are not in conformity with applicable requirements under section 520(f)(1) or an applicable condition prescribed by an order under section 520(f)(2).

(i) If it is a device for which an exemption has been granted under section 520(g) for investigational use and the person who was granted such exemption or any investigator who uses such device under such exemption fails to comply with a requirement prescribed by or under such section.

(j) If it is a drug or device and it has been manufactured, processed, packed, or held in any factory, warehouse, or establishment and the owner, operator, or agent of such factory, warehouse, or establishment delays, denies, or limits an inspection, or refuses to permit entry or inspection.

For purposes of paragraph (a)(2)(B), the term "current good manufacturing practice" includes the implementation of oversight and controls over the manufacture of drugs to ensure quality, including managing the risk of an establishing the safety of raw materials, materials used in the manufacturing of drugs, and finished drug products.

Sec. 502. [352] Misbranded Drugs and Devices.

A drug or device shall be deemed to be misbranded —

(a) **(1)** If its labeling is false or misleading in any particular. Health care economic information provided to a payor, formulary committee, or other similar entity with knowledge and expertise in the area of health care economic analysis carrying out its responsibilities for the selection of drugs for coverage or reimbursement, shall not be considered to be false or misleading under this paragraph if the health care economic information relates to an indication approved under section 505 or under section 351(a) of the Public Health Service Act for such drug, is based on competent and reliable scientific evidence, and includes, where applicable, a conspicuous and prominent statement describing any material differences between the health care economic information and the labeling approved for the drug under section 505 or under section 351 of the Public Health Service Act. The requirements set forth in section 505(a) or in subsections (a) and (k) of section 351 of the Public Health Service Act shall not apply to health care economic information provided to such a payor, committee, or entity in accordance with this paragraph. Information that is relevant to the substantiation of the health care economic information presented pursuant to this paragraph shall be made available to the Secretary upon request.

(2) **(A)** For purposes of this paragraph, the term "health care economic information" means any analysis (including the clinical data, inputs, clinical or other assumptions, methods, results, and other components underlying or comprising the analysis) that identifies, measures, or describes the economic consequences, which may be based on the separate or aggregated clinical consequences of the represented health outcomes, of the use of a drug. Such analysis may be comparative to the use of another drug, to another health care intervention, or to no intervention.

(B) Such term does not include any analysis that relates only to an indication that is not approved under section 505 or under section 351 of the Public Health Service Act for such drug.

(b) If in a package form unless it bears a label containing

(1) the name and place of business of the manufacturer, packer, or distributor; and

(2) an accurate statement of the quantity of the contents in terms of weight, measure, or numerical count:

Provided, [t]hat under clause (2) of this paragraph reasonable variations shall be permitted, and exemptions as to small packages shall be established, by regulations prescribed by the Secretary.

(c) If any word, statement, or other information required by or under authority of this Act to appear on the label or labeling is not prominently placed thereon with such conspicuousness (as compared with other words, statements, designs, or devices, in the labeling) and in such terms as to render it likely to be read and understood by the ordinary individual under customary conditions of purchase and use.

(d) [Repealed.]

(e) —

(1) —

(A) If it is a drug, unless its label bears, to the exclusion of any other nonproprietary name (except the applicable systematic chemical name or the chemical formula) —

(i) the established name (as defined in subparagraph (3)) of the drug, if there is such a name;

(ii) the established name and quantity or, if determined to be appropriate by the Secretary, the proportion of each active ingredient, including the quantity, kind, and proportion of any alcohol, and also including whether active or not the established name and quantity or if determined to be appropriate by the Secretary, the proportion of any bromides, ether, chloroform, acetanilide, acetophenetidin, amidopyrine, antipyrine, atropine, hyoscine, hyoscyamine, arsenic, digitalis, digitalis glucosides, mercury, ouabain, strophanthin, strychnine, thyroid, or any derivative or preparation of any such substances, contained therein, except that the requirement for stating the quantity of the active ingredients, other than the quantity of those specifically named in this subclause, shall not apply to nonprescription drugs not intended for human use; and

(iii) the established name of each inactive ingredient listed in alphabetical order on the outside container of the retail package and, if determined to be appropriate by the Secretary, on the immediate container, as prescribed in regulation promulgated by the Secretary, except that nothing in this subclause shall be deemed to require that any trade secret be divulged, and except that the requirements of this subclause with respect to alphabetical order shall apply only to nonprescription drugs that are not also cosmetics and that this subclause shall not apply to nonprescription drugs not intended for human use.

(B) For any prescription drug the established name of such drug or ingredient, as the case may be, on such label (and on any labeling on which a name for such drug or ingredient is used) shall be printed prominently and in type at least half as large as that used thereon for any proprietary name or designation for such drug or ingredient, except that to the extent that compliance with the requirements of subclause (ii) or (iii) of clause (A) or this clause is impracticable, exemptions shall be established by regulations promulgated by the Secretary.

(2) If it is a device and it has an established name, unless its label bears, to the exclusion of any other nonproprietary name, its established name (as defined in subparagraph (4)) prominently printed in type at least half as large as that used thereon for any proprietary name or designation for such device, except that to the extent compliance with the requirements of this subparagraph is impracticable, exemptions shall be established by regulations promulgated by the Secretary.

(3) As used in subparagraph (1), the term "established name", with respect to a drug or ingredient thereof, means

(A) the applicable official name designated pursuant to section 508, or

(B) if there is no such name and such drug, or such ingredient, is an article recognized in an official compendium, then the official title thereof in such compendium, or

(C) if neither clause (A) nor clause (B) of this subparagraph applies, then the common or usual name, if any, of such drug or of such ingredient,

except that where clause (B) of this subparagraph applies to an article recognized in the United States Pharmacopeia and in the Homeopathic Pharmacopeia under different official titles, the official title used in the United States Pharmacopeia shall apply unless it is labeled and offered for sale as a homeopathic drug, in which case the official title used in the Homeopathic Pharmacopeia shall apply.

(4) As used in subparagraph (2), the term "established name" with respect to a device means

(A) the applicable official name of the device designated pursuant to section 508,

(B) if there is no such name and such device is an article recognized in an official compendium, then the official title thereof in such compendium, or

(C) if neither clause (A) nor clause (B) of this subparagraph applies, then any common or usual name of such device.

(f) Unless its labeling bears

(1) adequate directions for use; and

(2) such adequate warnings against use in those pathological conditions or by children where its use may be dangerous to health, or against unsafe dosage or methods or duration of administration or application, in such manner and form, as are necessary for the protection of users,

except that where any requirement of clause (1) of this paragraph, as applied to any drug or device, is not necessary for the protection of the public health, the Secretary shall promulgate regulations exempting such drug or device from such requirement. Required labeling for prescription devices intended for use in health care facilities or by a health care professional and required labeling for in vitro diagnostic devices intended for use by health care professionals or in blood establishments may be made available solely by electronic means, provided that the labeling complies with all applicable requirements of law, and that the manufacturer affords such users the opportunity to request the labeling in paper form, and after such request, promptly provides the requested information without additional cost.

(g) If it purports to be a drug the name of which is recognized in an official compendium, unless it is packaged and labeled as prescribed therein. The method of packing may be modified with the consent of the Secretary. Whenever a drug is recognized in both the United States Pharmacopeia and the Homeopathic Pharmacopeia of the United States, it shall be subject to the requirements of the United States Pharmacopeia with respect to packaging, and labeling unless it is labeled and offered for sale as a homeopathic drug, in which case it shall be subject to the provisions of the Homeopathic Pharmacopeia of the United States, and not to those of the United States Pharmacopeia, except that in the event of inconsistency between the requirements of this paragraph and those of paragraph (e) as to the name by which the drug or its ingredients shall be designated, the requirements of paragraph (e) shall prevail.

(h) If it has been found by the Secretary to be a drug liable to deterioration, unless it is packaged in such form and manner, and its label bears a statement of such precautions, as the Secretary shall by regulations require as necessary for the protection of the public health. No such regulation shall be established for any drug recognized in an official compendium until the Secretary shall have informed the appropriate body charged with the revision of such compendium of the need for such packaging or labeling requirements and such body shall have failed within a reasonable time to prescribe such requirements.

(i) —

> **(1)** If it is a drug and its container is so made, formed, or filled as to be misleading; or
>
> **(2)** if it is an imitation of another drug; or
>
> **(3)** if it is offered for sale under the name of another drug.

(j) If it is dangerous to health when used in the dosage or manner; or with the frequency or duration prescribed, recommended, or suggested in the labeling thereof.

(k) [Repealed.]

(l) [Repealed.]

(m) If it is a color additive the intended use of which is for the purpose of coloring only, unless its packaging and labeling are in conformity with such packaging and labeling requirements applicable to such color additive, as may be contained in regulations issued under section 721.

(n) In the case of any prescription drug distributed or offered for sale in any State, unless the manufacturer, packer, or distributor thereof includes in all advertisements and other descriptive printed matter issued or caused to be issued by the manufacturer, packer, or distributor with respect to that drug a true statement of—

> **(1)** the established name as defined in section 502(e), printed prominently and in type at least half as large as that used for any trade or brand name thereof,
>
> **(2)** the formula showing quantitatively each ingredient of such drug to the extent required for labels under section 502(e), and
>
> **(3)** such other information in brief summary relating to side effects, contraindications, and effectiveness as shall be required in regulations which shall be issued by the Secretary in accordance with section 701(a), and in the case of published direct-to-consumer advertisements the following statement printed in conspicuous text: 'You are encouraged to report negative side effects of prescription drugs to the FDA. Visit www.fda.gov/medwatch, or call 1-800-FDA-1088.', except that
>
> > **(A)** except in extraordinary circumstances, no regulation issued under this paragraph shall require prior approval by the Secretary of the content of any advertisement, and
> >
> > **(B)** no advertisement of a prescription drug, published after the effective date of regulations issued under this paragraph applicable to advertisements of prescription drugs, shall, with respect to the matters specified in this paragraph or covered by such regulations, be subject to the provisions of sections 12 through 17 of the Federal Trade Commission Act, as amended (15 U.S.C. 52-57).

This paragraph shall not be applicable to any printed matter which the Secretary determines to be labeling as defined in section 201(m) of this Act. Nothing in the Convention on Psychotropic Substances, signed at Vienna, Austria, on February 21, 1971, shall be construed to prevent drug price communications to consumers.

In the case of an advertisement for a drug subject to section 503(b)(1) presented directly to consumers in television or radio format and stating the name of the drug and its conditions of use, the major statement relating to side effects and contraindications shall be presented in a clear, conspicuous, and neutral manner.

(o) If it was manufactured, prepared, propagated, compounded, or processed in an establishment not duly registered under section 510, if it is a drug and was imported or offered for import by a commercial importer of drugs not duly registered under section 801(s), if it was not included in a list required by section 510(j), if a notice or other information respecting it was not provided as required by such section or section 510(k), or if it does not bear such symbols from the uniform system for identification of devices prescribed under section 510(e) as the Secretary by regulation requires.

(p) If it is a drug and its packaging or labeling is in violation of an applicable regulation issued pursuant to section 3 or 4 of the Poison Prevention Packaging Act of 1970.

(q) In the case of any restricted device distributed or offered for sale in any State, if

(1) its advertising is false or misleading in any particular, or

(2) it is sold, distributed, or used in violation of regulations prescribed under section 520(e).

(r) In the case of any restricted device distributed or offered for sale in any State, unless the manufacturer, packer, or distributor thereof includes in all advertisements and other descriptive printed matter issued or caused to be issued by the manufacturer, packer, or distributor with respect to that device —

(1) a true statement of the device's established name as defined in section 502(e), printed prominently and in type at least half as large as that used for any trade or brand name thereof, and

(2) a brief statement of the intended uses of the device and relevant warnings, precautions, side effects, and contraindications and, in the case of specific devices made subject to a finding by the Secretary after notice and opportunity for comment that such action is necessary to protect the public health, a full description of the components of such device or the formula showing quantitatively each ingredient of such device to the extent required in regulations which shall be issued by the Secretary after an opportunity for a hearing.

Except in extraordinary circumstances, no regulation issued under this paragraph shall require prior approval by the Secretary of the content of any advertisement and no advertisement of a restricted device, published after the effective date of this paragraph shall, with respect to the matters specified in this paragraph or covered by regulations issued hereunder, be subject to the provisions of sections 12 through 15 of the Federal Trade Commission Act (15 U.S.C. 52-55). This paragraph shall not be applicable to any printed matter which the Secretary determines to be labeling as defined in section 201(m).

(s) If it is a device subject to a performance standard established under section 514, unless it bears such labeling as may be prescribed in such performance standard.

(t) If it is a device and there was a failure or refusal

(1) to comply with any requirement prescribed under section 518 respecting the device,

(2) to furnish any material or information required by or under section 519 respecting the device, or

(3) to comply with a requirement under section 522.

(u) If it is a device, unless it, or an attachment thereto, prominently and conspicuously bears the name of the manufacturer of the device, a generally recognized abbreviation of such name, or a unique and generally recognized symbol identifying such manufacturer, except that the Secretary may waive any requirement under this paragraph for the device if the Secretary determines that compliance with the requirement is not feasible for the device or would compromise the provision of reasonable assurance of the safety or effectiveness of the device.

(v) If it is a reprocessed single-use device, unless all labeling of the device prominently and conspicuously bears the statement "Reprocessed device for single use. Reprocessed by–." The name of the manufacturer of the reprocessed device shall be placed in the space identifying the person responsible for reprocessing.

(w) If it is a new animal drug —

(1) that is conditionally approved under section 571 and its labeling does not conform with the approved application or section 571(f), or that is not conditionally approved under section 571 and its label bears the statement set forth in section 571(f)(1)(A); or

(2) that is indexed under section 572 and its labeling does not conform with the index listing under section 572(e) or 572(h), or that has not been indexed under section 572 and its label bears the statement set forth in section 572(h).

(x) If it is a nonprescription drug (as defined in section 760) that is marketed in the United States, unless the label of such drug includes a domestic address or domestic phone number through which the responsible person (as described in section 760) may receive a report of a serious adverse event (such as defined in section 760) with such drug.

(y) If it is a drug subject to an approved risk evaluation and mitigation strategy pursuant to section 505(p) and the responsible person (as such term is used in section 505–1) fails to comply with a requirement of such strategy provided for under subsection (d), (e), or (f) of section 505–1.

(z) If it is a drug, and the responsible person (as such term is used in section 505(o)) is in violation of a requirement established under paragraph (3) (relating to postmarket studies and clinical trials) or paragraph (4) (relating to labeling) of section 505(o) with respect to such drug.

(aa) If it is a drug, or an active pharmaceutical ingredient, and it was manufactured, prepared, propagated, compounded, or processed in a facility for which fees have not been paid as required by section 744A(a)(4) or for which identifying information required by section 744B(f) has not been submitted, or it contains an active pharmaceutical ingredient that was manufactured, prepared, propagated, compounded, or processed in such a facility.

(bb) If the advertising or promotion of a compounded drug is false or misleading in any particular.

(cc) If it is a drug and it fails to bear the product identifier as required by section 582.

(dd) If it is an antimicrobial drug, as defined in section 511A(f), and its labeling fails to conform with the requirements under section 511A(d).

Sec. 503. [353] Exemptions and Consideration for Certain Drugs, Devices, and Biological Products.

(a) The Secretary is hereby directed to promulgate regulations exempting from any labeling or packaging requirement of this Act drugs and devices which are, in accordance with the practice of the trade, to be processed, labeled, or repacked in substantial quantities at establishments other than those where originally processed or packed, on condition that such drugs and devices are not adulterated or misbranded, under the provisions of this Act upon removal from such processing, labeling, or repacking establishment.

(b) —

(1) A drug intended for use by man which —

(A) because of its toxicity or other potentiality for harmful effect, or the method of its use, or the collateral measures necessary to its use, is not safe for use except under the supervision of a practitioner licensed by law to administer such drug; or

(B) is limited by an approved application under section 505 to use under the professional supervision of a practitioner licensed by law to administer such drug;

shall be dispensed only

(i) upon a written prescription of a practitioner licensed by law to administer such drug, or

(ii) upon an oral prescription of such practitioner which is reduced promptly to writing and filed by the pharmacist, or

(iii) by refilling any such written or oral prescription if such refilling is authorized by the prescriber either in the original prescription or by oral order which is reduced promptly to writing and filed by the pharmacist.

The act of dispensing a drug contrary to the provisions of this paragraph shall be deemed to be an act which results in the drug being misbranded while held for sale.

(2) Any drug dispensed by filling or refilling a written or oral prescription of a practitioner licensed by law to administer such drug shall be exempt from the requirements of section 502, except paragraphs (a), (i) (2) and (3), (k), and (1), and the packaging requirements of paragraphs (g), (h), and (p), if the drug bears a label containing the name and address of the dispenser, the serial number and date of the prescription or of its filling, the name of the prescriber, and, if stated in the prescription, the name of the patient, and the directions for use and cautionary statements, if any, contained in such prescription. This exemption shall not apply to any drug dispensed in the course of the conduct of a business of dispensing drugs pursuant to diagnosis by mail, or to a drug dispensed in violation of paragraph (1) of this subsection.

(3) The Secretary may by regulation remove drugs subject to section 505 from the requirements of paragraph (1) of this subsection when such requirements are not necessary for the protection of the public health.

(4) —

(A) A drug that is subject to paragraph (1) shall be deemed to be misbranded if at any time prior to dispensing the label of the drug fails to bear, at a minimum, the symbol "Rx only".

(B) A drug to which paragraph (1) does not apply shall be deemed to be misbranded if at any time prior to dispensing the label of the drug bears the symbol described in subparagraph (A).

(5) Nothing in this subsection shall be construed to relieve any person from any requirement prescribed by or under authority of law with respect to drugs now included or which may hereafter be included within the classifications stated in section 3220 of the Internal Revenue Code (26 U.S.C. 3220), or to marihuana as defined in section 3238(b) of the Internal Revenue Code (26 U.S.C. 3238(b)).

(c) —

(1) No person may sell, purchase, or trade or offer to sell, purchase, or trade any drug sample. For purposes of this paragraph and subsection (d), the term "drug sample" means a unit of a drug, subject to subsection (b), which is not intended to be sold and is intended to promote the sale of the drug. Nothing in this paragraph shall subject an officer or executive of a drug manufacturer or distributor to criminal liability solely because of a sale, purchase, trade, or offer to sell, purchase, or trade in violation of this paragraph by other employees of the manufacturer or distributor.

(2) No person may sell, purchase, or trade, offer to sell, purchase, or trade, or counterfeit any coupon. For purposes of this paragraph, the term "coupon" means a form which may be redeemed, at no cost or at a reduced cost, for a drug which is prescribed in accordance with subsection (b).

(3) —

(A) No person may sell, purchase, or trade, or offer to sell, purchase, or trade, any drug —

(i) which is subject to subsection (b), and

(ii) —

(I) which was purchased by a public or private hospital or other health care entity, or

(II) which was donated or supplied at a reduced price to a charitable organization described in section 501(c)(3) of the Internal Revenue Code of 1954.

(B) Subparagraph (A) does not apply to —

(i) the purchase or other acquisition by a hospital or other health care entity which is a member of a group purchasing organization of a drug for its own use from the group purchasing organization or from other hospitals or health care entities which are members of such organization,

(ii) the sale, purchase, or trade of a drug or an offer to sell, purchase, or trade a drug by an organization described in subparagraph (A)(ii)(II) to a nonprofit affiliate of the organization to the extent otherwise permitted by law,

(iii) a sale, purchase, or trade of a drug or an offer to sell, purchase, or trade a drug among hospitals or other health care entities which are under common control,

(iv) a sale, purchase, or trade of a drug or an offer to sell, purchase, or trade a drug for emergency medical reasons, or

(v) a sale, purchase, or trade of a drug, an offer to sell, purchase, or trade a drug, or the dispensing of a drug pursuant to a prescription executed in accordance with subsection (b).

For purposes of this paragraph, the term "entity" does not include a wholesale distributor of drugs or a retail pharmacy licensed under State law and the term "emergency medical reasons" includes transfers of a drug between health care entities or from a health care entity to a retail pharmacy undertaken to alleviate temporary shortages of the drug arising from delays in or interruptions of regular distribution schedules.

(d) —

(1) Except as provided in paragraphs (2) and (3), no person may distribute any drug sample. For purposes of this subsection, the term "distribute" does not include the providing of a drug sample to a patient by a —

(A) practitioner licensed to prescribe such drug,

(B) health care professional acting at the direction and under the supervision of such a practitioner, or

(C) pharmacy of a hospital or of another health care entity that is acting at the direction of such a practitioner and that received such sample pursuant to paragraph (2) or (3).

(2) —

(A) The manufacturer or authorized distributor of record of a drug subject to subsection (b) may, in accordance with this paragraph, distribute drug samples by mail or common carrier to practitioners licensed to prescribe such drugs or, at the request of a licensed practitioner, to pharmacies of hospitals or other health care entities. Such a distribution of drug samples may only be made —

(i) in response to a written request for drug samples made on a form which meets the requirements of subparagraph (B), and

(ii) under a system which requires the recipient of the drug sample to execute a written receipt for the drug sample upon its delivery and the return of the receipt to the manufacturer or authorized distributor of record.

(B) A written request for a drug sample required by subparagraph (A)(i) shall contain —

(i) the name, address, professional designation, and signature of the practitioner making the request,

(ii) the identity of the drug sample requested and the quantity requested,

(iii) the name of the manufacturer of the drug sample requested, and

(iv) the date of the request.

(C) Each drug manufacturer or authorized distributor of record which makes distributions by mail or common carrier under this paragraph shall maintain, for a period of 3 years, the request forms submitted for such distributions and the receipts submitted for such distributions and shall maintain a record of distributions of drug samples which identifies the drugs distributed and the recipients of the distributions. Forms, receipts, and records required to be maintained under this subparagraph shall be made available by the drug manufacturer or authorized distributor of record to Federal and State officials engaged in the regulation of drugs and in the enforcement of laws applicable to drugs.

(3) The manufacturer or authorized distributor of record of a drug subject to subsection (b) may, by means other than mail or common carrier, distribute drug samples only if the manufacturer or authorized distributor of record makes the distributions in accordance with subparagraph (A) and carries out the activities described in subparagraphs (B) through (F) as follows:

(A) Drug samples may only be distributed —

(i) to practitioners licensed to prescribe such drugs if they make a written request for the drug samples, or

(ii) at the written request of such a licensed practitioner, to pharmacies of hospitals or other health care entities.

A written request for drug samples shall be made on a form which contains the practitioner's name, address, and professional designation, the identity of the drug sample requested, the quantity of drug samples requested, the name of the manufacturer or authorized distributor of record of the drug sample, the date of the request and signature of the practitioner making the request.

(B) Drug manufacturers or authorized distributors of record shall store drug samples under conditions that will maintain their stability, integrity, and effectiveness and will assure that the drug samples will be free of contamination, deterioration, and adulteration.

(C) Drug manufacturers or authorized distributors of record shall conduct, at least annually, a complete and accurate inventory of all drug samples in the possession of representatives of the manufacturer or authorized distributor of record. Drug manufacturers or authorized distributors of record shall maintain lists of the names and address of each of their representatives who distribute drug samples and of the sites where drug samples are stored. Drug manufacturers or authorized distributors of record shall maintain records for at least 3 years of all drug samples distributed, destroyed, or returned to the manufacturer or authorized distributor of record, of all inventories maintained under this subparagraph, of all thefts or significant losses of drug samples, and of all requests made under subparagraph (A) for drug samples. Records and lists maintained under this subparagraph shall be made available by the drug manufacturer or authorized distributor of record to the Secretary upon request.

(D) Drug manufacturers or authorized distributors of record shall notify the Secretary of any significant loss of drug samples and any known theft of drug samples.

(E) Drug manufacturers or authorized distributors of record shall report to the Secretary any conviction of their representatives for violations of subsection (c)(1) or a State law because of the sale, purchase, or trade of a drug sample or the offer to sell, purchase, or trade a drug sample.

(F) Drug manufacturers or authorized distributors of record shall provide to the Secretary the name and telephone number of the individual responsible for responding to a request for information respecting drug samples.

(4) In this subsection, the term "authorized distributors of record" means those distributors with whom a manufacturer has established an ongoing relationship to distribute such manufacturer's products.

(e) —

(1) Requirement. — Subject to section 583:

(A) In General. — No person may engage in wholesale distribution of a drug subject to subsection (b)(1) in any State unless such person —

(i)

(I) is licensed by the State from which the drug is distributed; or

(II) if the State from which the drug is distributed has not established a licensure requirement, is licensed by the Secretary; and

(ii) if the drug is distributed interstate, is licensed by the State into which the drug is distributed if the State into which the drug is distributed requires the licensure of a person that distributes drugs into the State.

(B) Standards. — Each Federal and State license described in subparagraph (A) shall meet the standards, terms, and conditions established by the Secretary under section 583.

(2) Reporting and Database. —

(A) Reporting. — Beginning January 1, 2015, any person who owns or operates an establishment that engages in wholesale distribution shall —

(i) report to the Secretary, on an annual basis pursuant to a schedule determined by the Secretary —

(I) each State by which the person is licensed and the appropriate identification number of each such license; and

(II) the name, address, and contact information of each facility at which, and all trade names under which, the person conducts business; and

(ii) report to the Secretary within a reasonable period of time and in a reasonable manner, as determined by the Secretary, any significant disciplinary actions, such as the revocation or suspension of a wholesale distributor license, taken by a State or the Federal Government during the reporting period against the wholesale distributor.

(B) Database. — Not later than January 1, 2015, the Secretary shall establish a database of authorized wholesale distributors. Such database shall —

(i) identify each authorized wholesale distributor by name, contact information, and each State where such wholesale distributor is appropriately licensed to engage in wholesale distribution;

(ii) be available to the public on the Internet Web site of the Food and Drug Administration; and

(iii) be regularly updated on a schedule determined by the Secretary.

(C) Coordination. — The Secretary shall establish a format and procedure for appropriate State officials to access the information provided pursuant to subparagraph (A) in a prompt and secure manner.

(D) Confidentiality. — Nothing in this paragraph shall be construed as authorizing the Secretary to disclose any information that is a trade secret or confidential information subject to section 552(b)(4) of title 5, United States Code, or section 1905 of title 18, United States Code.

(3) Costs. —

(A) Authorized Fees of Secretary. — If a State does not establish a licensing program for persons engaged in the wholesale distribution of a drug subject to subsection (b), the Secretary shall license a person engaged in wholesale distribution located in such State and may collect a reasonable fee in such amount necessary to reimburse the Secretary for costs associated with establishing and administering the licensure program and conducting periodic inspections under this section. The Secretary shall adjust fee rates as needed on an annual basis to generate only the amount of revenue needed to perform this service. Fees authorized under this paragraph shall be collected and available for obligation only to the extent and in the amount provided in advance in appropriations Acts. Such fees are authorized to remain available until expended. Such sums as may be necessary may be transferred from the Food and Drug Administration salaries and expenses appropriation account without fiscal year limitation to such appropriation account for salaries and expenses with such fiscal year limitation.

(B) State Licensing Fees. — Nothing in this Act shall prohibit States from collecting fees from wholesale distributors in connection with State licensing of such distributors.

(4) For the purposes of this subsection and subsection (d), the term "wholesale distribution" means the distribution of a drug subject to subsection (b) to a person other than a consumer or patient, or receipt of a drug subject to subsection (b) by a person other than the consumer or patient, but does not include —

(A) intracompany distribution of any drug between members of an affiliate or within a manufacturer;

(B) the distribution of a drug, or an offer to distribute a drug among hospitals or other health care entities which are under common control;

(C) the distribution of a drug or an offer to distribute a drug for emergency medical reasons, including a public health emergency declaration pursuant to section 319 of the Public Health Service Act, except that, for purposes of this paragraph, a drug shortage not caused by a public health emergency shall not constitute an emergency medical reason;

(D) the dispensing of a drug pursuant to a prescription executed in accordance with subsection (b)(1);

(E) the distribution of minimal quantities of drug by a licensed retail pharmacy to a licensed practitioner for office use;

(F) the distribution of a drug or an offer to distribute a drug by a charitable organization to a nonprofit affiliate of the organization to the extent otherwise permitted by law;

(G) the purchase or other acquisition by a dispenser, hospital, or other health care entity of a drug for use by such dispenser, hospital, or other health care entity;

(H) the distribution of a drug by the manufacturer of such drug;

(I) the receipt or transfer of a drug by an authorized third-party logistics provider provided that such third-party logistics provider does not take ownership of the drug;

(J) a common carrier that transports a drug, provided that the common carrier does not take ownership of the drug;

(K) the distribution of a drug, or an offer to distribute a drug by an authorized repackager that has taken ownership or possession of the drug and repacks it in accordance with section 582(e);

(L) salable drug returns when conducted by a dispenser;

(M) the distribution of a collection of finished medical devices, which may include a product or biological product, assembled in kit form strictly for the convenience of the purchaser or user (referred to in this subparagraph as a "medical convenience kit") if —

(i) the medical convenience kit is assembled in an establishment that is registered with the Food and Drug Administration as a device manufacturer in accordance with section 510(b)(2);

(ii) the medical convenience kit does not contain a controlled substance that appears in a schedule contained in the Comprehensive Drug Abuse Prevention and Control Act of 1970;

(iii) in the case of a medical convenience kit that includes a product, the person that manufacturers the kit, —

(I) purchased such product directly from the pharmaceutical manufacturer or from a wholesale distributor that purchased the product directly from the pharmaceutical manufacturer; and

(II) does not alter the primary container or label of the product as purchased from the manufacturer or wholesale distributor; and

(iv) in the case of a medical convenience kit that includes a product, the product is —

(I) an intravenous solution intended for the replenishment of fluids and electrolytes;

(II) a product intended to maintain the equilibrium of water and minerals in the body;

(III) a product intended for irrigation or reconstitution;

(IV) an anesthetic;

(V) an anticoagulant;

(VI) a vasopressor; or

(VII) a sympathomimetic;

(N) the distribution of an intravenous drug that, by its formulation, is intended for the replenishment of fluids and electrolytes (such as sodium, chloride, and potassium) or calories (such as dextrose and amino acids);

(O) the distribution of an intravenous drug used to maintain the equilibrium of water and minerals in the body, such as dialysis solutions;

(P) the distribution of a drug that is intended for irrigation, or sterile water, whether intended for such purposes or for injection;

(Q) the distribution of medical gas, as defined in section 575;

(R) facilitating the distribution of a product by providing solely administrative services, including processing of orders and payments; or

(S) the transfer of a product by a hospital or other health care entity, or by a wholesale distributor or manufacturer operating at the direction of the hospital or other health care entity, to a repackager described in section 581(16)(B) and registered under section 510 for the purpose of repackaging the drug for use by that hospital, or other health care entity and other health care entities that are under common control, if ownership of the drug remains with the hospital or other health care entity at all times.

(5) Third-party Logistics providers. — Notwithstanding paragraphs (1) through (4), each entity that meets the definition of a third-party logistics provider under section 581(22) shall obtain a license as a third-party logistics provider as described in section 584(a) and is not required to obtain a license as a wholesale distributor if the entity never assumes an ownership interest in the product it handles.

(6) Affiliate. — For purposes of this subsection, the term "affiliate" means a business entity that has a relationship with a second business entity if, directly or indirectly —

(A) one business entity controls, or has the power to control, the other business entity; or

(B) a third party controls, or has the power to control, both of the business entities.

(f) —

(1) —

(A) A drug intended for use by animals other than man other than a veterinary feed directive drug intended for use in animal feed or an animal feed bearing or containing a veterinary feed directive drug, which —

(i) because of its toxicity or other potentiality for harmful effect, or the method of its use, or the collateral measures necessary for its use, is not safe for animal use except under the professional supervision of a licensed veterinarian, or

(ii) is limited by an approved application under subsection (b) of section 512, a conditionally-approved application under section 571, or an index listing under section 572 to use under the professional supervision of a licensed veterinarian,

shall be dispensed only by or upon the lawful written or oral order of a licensed veterinarian in the course of the veterinarian's professional practice.

(B) For purposes of subparagraph (A), an order is lawful if the order —

(i) is a prescription or other order authorized by law,

(ii) is, if an oral order, promptly reduced to writing by the person lawfully filling the order, and filed by that person, and

(iii) is refilled only if authorized in the original order or in a subsequent oral order promptly reduced to writing by the person lawfully filling the order, and filed by that person.

(C) The act of dispensing a drug contrary to the provisions of this paragraph shall be deemed to be an act which results in the drug being misbranded while held for sale.

(2) Any drug when dispensed in accordance with paragraph (1) of this subsection —

(A) Shall be exempt from the requirements of section 502, except subsections (a), (g), (h), (i)(2), (i)(3), and (p) of such section, and

(B) shall be exempt from the packaging requirements of subsections (g), (h), and (p) of such section, if —

(i) when dispensed by a licensed veterinarian, the drug bears a label containing the name and address of the practitioner and any directions for use and cautionary statements specified by the practitioner, or

(ii) when dispensed by filling the lawful order of a licensed veterinarian, the drug bears a label containing the name and address of the dispenser, the serial number and date of the order or of its filing, the name of the licensed veterinarian, and the directions for use and cautionary statements, if any, contained in such order.

The preceding sentence shall not apply to any drug dispensed in the course of the conduct of a business of dispensing drugs pursuant to diagnosis by mail.

(3) The Secretary may by regulation exempt drugs for animals other than man subject to section 512, 571, or 572 from the requirements of paragraph (1) when such requirements are not necessary for the protection of the public health.

(4) A drug which is subject to paragraph (1) shall be deemed to be misbranded if at any time prior to dispensing its label fails to bear the statement "Caution: Federal law restricts this drug to use by or on the order of a licensed veterinarian.". A drug to which paragraph (1) does not apply shall be deemed to be misbranded if at any time prior to dispensing its label bears the statement specified in the preceding sentence.

(g)

(1) —

(A) The Secretary shall, in accordance with this subsection, assign a primary agency center to regulate products that constitute a combination of a drug, device, or biological product.

(B) The Secretary shall conduct the premarket review of any combination product under a single application, whenever appropriate.

(C) For purposes of this subsection, the term "primary mode of action" means the single mode of action of a combination product expected to make the greatest contribution to the overall intended therapeutic effects of the combination product.

(D) The Secretary shall determine the primary mode of action of the combination product. If the Secretary determines that the primary mode of action is that of—

(i) a drug (other than a biological product), the agency center charged with premarket review of drugs shall have primary jurisdiction;

(ii) a device, the agency center charged with premarket review of devices shall have primary jurisdiction; or

(iii) a biological product, the agency center charged with premarket review of biological products shall have primary jurisdiction.

(E) In determining the primary mode of action of a combination product, the Secretary shall not determine that the primary mode of action is that of a drug or biological product solely because the combination product has any chemical action within or on the human body.

(F) If a sponsor of a combination product disagrees with the determination under subparagraph (D)—

(i) such sponsor may request, and the Secretary shall provide, a substantive rationale to such sponsor that references scientific evidence provided by the sponsor and any other scientific evidence relied upon by the Secretary to support such determination; and

(ii) –

(I) the sponsor of the combination product may propose one or more studies (which may be nonclinical, clinical, or both) to establish the relevance, if any, of the chemical action in achieving the primary mode of action of such product;

(II) if the sponsor proposes any such studies, the Secretary and the sponsor of such product shall collaborate and seek to reach agreement, within a reasonable time of such proposal, not to exceed 90 calendar days, on the design of such studies; and

(III) if an agreement is reached under subclause (II) and the sponsor conducts one or more of such studies, the Secretary shall consider the data resulting from any such study when reevaluating the determination of the primary mode of action of such product, and unless and until such reevaluation has occurred and the Secretary issues a new determination, the determination of the Secretary under subparagraph (D) shall remain in effect.

(2) –

(A) –

(i) To establish clarity and certainty for the sponsor, the sponsor of a combination product may request a meeting on such combination product. If the Secretary concludes that a determination of the primary mode of action pursuant to paragraph (1)(D) is necessary, the sponsor may request such meeting only after the Secretary makes such determination. If the sponsor submits a written meeting request, the

Secretary shall, not later than 75 calendar days after receiving such request, meet with the sponsor of such combination product.

(ii) A meeting under clause (i) may—

(I) address the standards and requirements for market approval or clearance of the combination product;

(II) address other issues relevant to such combination product, such as requirements related to postmarket modification of such combination product and good manufacturing practices applicable to such combination product; and

(III) identify elements under subclauses (I) and (II) that may be more appropriate for discussion and agreement with the Secretary at a later date given that scientific or other information is not available, or agreement is otherwise not feasible regarding such elements, at the time a request for such meeting is made.

(iii) Any agreement under this subparagraph shall be in writing and made part of the administrative record by the Secretary.

(iv) Any such agreement shall remain in effect, except—

(I) upon the written agreement of the Secretary and the sponsor or applicant; or

(II) pursuant to a decision by the director of the reviewing division of the primary agency center, or a person more senior than such director, in consultation with consulting centers and the Office, as appropriate, that an issue essential to determining whether the standard for market clearance or other applicable standard under this Act or the Public Health Service Act applicable to the combination product has been identified since the agreement was reached, or that deviating from the agreement is otherwise justifiable based on scientific evidence, for public health reasons.

(3) For purposes of conducting the premarket review of a combination product that contains an approved constituent part described in paragraph (4), the Secretary may require that the sponsor of such combination product submit to the Secretary only data or information that the Secretary determines is necessary to meet the standard for clearance or approval, as applicable, under this Act or the Public Health Service Act, including any incremental risks and benefits posed by such combination product, using a risk-based approach and taking into account any prior finding of safety and effectiveness or substantial equivalence for the approved constituent part relied upon by the applicant in accordance with paragraph (5).

(4) For purposes of paragraph (3), an approved constituent part is—

(A) a drug constituent part of a combination product being reviewed in a single application or request under section 515, 510(k), or 513(f)(2) (submitted in accordance with paragraph (5)), that is an approved drug, provided such application or request complies with paragraph (5);

(B) a device constituent part approved under section 515 that is referenced by the sponsor and that is available for use by the Secretary under section 520(h)(4); or

(C) any constituent part that was previously approved, cleared, or classified under section 505, 510(k), 513(f)(2), or 515 of this Act for which the sponsor has a right of reference or any constituent part that is a nonprescription drug, as defined in section 760(a)(2).

(5) –

(A) If an application is submitted under section 515 or 510(k) or a request is submitted under section 513(f)(2), consistent with any determination made under paragraph (1)(D), for a combination product containing as a constituent part an approved drug—

(i) the application or request shall include the certification or statement described in section 505(b)(2); and

(ii) the applicant or requester shall provide notice as described in section 505(b)(3).

(B) For purposes of this paragraph and paragraph (4), the term 'approved drug' means an active ingredient—

(i) that was in an application previously approved under section 505(c);

(ii) where such application is relied upon by the applicant submitting the application or request described in subparagraph (A);

(iii) for which full reports of investigations that have been made to show whether such drug is safe for use and whether such drug is effective in use were not conducted by or for the applicant submitting the application or request described in subparagraph (A); and

(iv) for which the applicant submitting the application or request described in subparagraph (A) has not obtained a right of reference or use from the person by or for whom the investigations described in clause (iii) were conducted.

(C) The following provisions shall apply with respect to an application or request described in subparagraph (A) to the same extent and in the same manner as if such application or request were an application described in section 505(b)(2) that referenced the approved drug:

(i) Subparagraphs (A), (B), (C), and (D) of section 505(c)(3).

(ii) Clauses (ii), (iii), and (iv) of section 505(c)(3)(E).

(iii) Subsections (b) and (c) of section 505A.

(iv) Section 505E(a).

(v) Section 527(a).

(D) Notwithstanding any other provision of this subsection, an application or request for classification for a combination product described in subparagraph (A) shall be considered an application submitted under section 505(b)(2) for purposes of section 271(e)(2)(A) of title 35, United States Code.

(6) Nothing in this subsection shall be construed as prohibiting a sponsor from submitting separate applications for the constituent parts of a combination product, unless the Secretary determines that a single application is necessary.

(7) Nothing in this subsection shall prevent the Secretary from using any agency resources of the Food and Drug Administration necessary to ensure adequate review of the safety, effectiveness, or substantial equivalence of an article.

(8) —

(A) Not later than 60 days after the date of the enactment of this paragraph, the Secretary shall establish within the Office of the Commissioner of Food and Drugs an office to ensure the prompt assignment of combination products to agency centers, the timely and effective premarket review of such products, and consistent and appropriate postmarket regulation of like products subject to the same statutory requirements to the extent permitted by law. Additionally, the office shall, in determining whether a product is to be designated a combination product, consult with the component within the Office of the Commissioner of Food and Drugs that is responsible for such determinations. Such office (referred to in this paragraph as the "Office") shall have appropriate scientific and medical expertise, and shall be headed by a director.

(B) In carrying out this subsection, the Office shall, for each combination product, promptly assign an agency center with primary jurisdiction in accordance with paragraph (1) for the premarket review of such product.

(C) —

(i) In carrying out this subsection, the Office shall ensure timely and effective premarket review that involves more than one agency center by coordinating such reviews, overseeing the timeliness of such reviews, and overseeing the alignment of feedback regarding such reviews.

(ii) In order to ensure the timeliness and alignment of the premarket review of a combination product, the agency center with primary jurisdiction for the product, and the consulting agency center, shall be responsible to the Office with respect to the timeliness and alignment of the premarket review.

(iii) The Office shall ensure that, with respect to a combination product, a designated person or persons in the primary agency center is the primary point or points of contact for the sponsor of such combination product. The Office shall also coordinate communications to and from any consulting center involved in such premarket review, if requested by such primary agency center or any such consulting center. Agency communications and commitments, to the extent consistent with other provisions of law and the requirements of all affected agency centers, from the primary agency center shall be considered as communication from the Secretary on behalf of all agency centers involved in the review.

(iv) The Office shall, with respect to the premarket review of a combination product—

(I) ensure that any meeting between the Secretary and the sponsor of such product is attended by each agency center involved in the review, as appropriate;

(II) ensure that each consulting agency center has completed its premarket review and provided the results of such review to the primary agency center in a timely manner; and

(III) ensure that each consulting center follows the guidance described in clause (vi) and advises, as appropriate, on other relevant regulations, guidances, and policies.

(v) In seeking agency action with respect to a combination product, the sponsor of such product—

(I) shall identify the product as a combination product; and

(II) may request in writing the participation of representatives of the Office in meetings related to such combination product, or to have the Office otherwise engage on such regulatory matters concerning the combination product.

(vi) Not later than 4 years after the date of enactment of the 21st Century Cures Act [December 13, 2016 —Ed.], and after a public comment period of not less than 60 calendar days, the Secretary shall issue a final guidance that describes—

(I) the structured process for managing presubmission interactions with sponsors developing combination products;

(II) the best practices for ensuring that the feedback in such pre-submission interactions represents the Agency's best advice based on the information provided during such pre-submission interactions;

(III) the information that is required to be submitted with a meeting request under paragraph (2), how such meetings relate to other types of meetings in the Food and Drug Administration, and the form and content of any agreement reached through a meeting under such paragraph (2);

(D) In carrying out this subsection, the Office shall ensure the consistency and appropriateness of postmarket regulation of like products subject to the same statutory requirements to the extent permitted by law.

(E) —

(i) Any dispute regarding the timeliness of the premarket review of a combination product may be presented to the Office for resolution, unless the dispute is clearly premature.

(ii) During the review process, any dispute regarding the substance of the premarket review may be presented to the Commissioner of Food and Drugs after first being considered by the agency center with primary jurisdiction of the premarket review, under the scientific dispute resolution procedures for such center. The Commissioner of Food and Drugs shall consult with the Director of the Office in resolving the substantive dispute.

(F) The Secretary, acting through the Office, shall review each agreement, guidance, or practice of the Secretary that is specific to the assignment of combination products to agency centers and shall determine whether the agreement, guidance, or practice is consistent with the requirements of this subsection. In carrying out such review, the Secretary shall consult with stakeholders and the directors of the agency centers. After such consultation, the Secretary shall determine whether to continue in effect, modify, revise, or eliminate such agreement, guidance, or practice, and shall publish in the Federal Register a notice of the availability of such modified or revised agreement, guidance or practice. Nothing in this paragraph shall be construed as preventing the Secretary from following each agreement, guidance, or practice until continued, modified, revised, or eliminated.

(G) Not later than one year after the date of the enactment of this paragraph (except with respect to clause (iv), beginning not later than one year after the date of the enactment of the 21st Century Cures Act) and annually thereafter, the Secretary shall report to the appropriate committees of Congress on the activities and impact of the Office. The report shall include provisions —

(i) describing the numbers and types of combination products under review and the timeliness in days of such assignments, reviews, and dispute resolutions;

(ii) identifying the number of premarket reviews of such products that involved a consulting agency center;

(iii) describing improvements in the consistency of postmarket regulation of combination products; and

(iv) identifying the percentage of combination products for which a dispute resolution, with respect to premarket review, was requested by the combination product's sponsor.

(H) Nothing in this paragraph shall be construed to limit the regulatory authority of any agency center.

(9) As used in this subsection:

(A) The term "agency center" means a center or alternative organizational component of the Food and Drug Administration.

(B) The term "biological product" has the meaning given the term in section 351(i) of the Public Health Service Act (42 U.S.C. 262(i)).

(C) The term "market clearance" includes —

(i) approval of an application under section 505, 507, 515, or 520(g);

(ii) a finding of substantial equivalence under this subchapter;

(iii) approval of a biologics license application under subsection (a) of section 351 of the Public Health Service Act (42 U.S.C. 262); and

(iv) de novo classification under section 513(a)(1).

(D) The terms "premarket review" and "reviews" include all activities of the Food and Drug Administration conducted prior to approval or clearance of an application, notification, or request for classification submitted under section 505, 510(k), 513(f)(2), 515, or 520 of this Act or under section 351 of the Public Health Service Act, including with respect to investigational use of the product.

Sec. 503A. [353a] Pharmacy Compounding.

(a) In General. — Sections 501(a)(2)(B), 502(f)(1), and 505 shall not apply to a drug product if the drug product is compounded for an identified individual patient based on the receipt of a valid prescription order or a notation, approved by the prescribing practitioner, on the prescription order that a compounded product is necessary for the identified patient, if the drug product meets the requirements of this section, and if the compounding —

(1) is by —

(A) a licensed pharmacist in a State licensed pharmacy or a Federal facility, or

(B) a licensed physician,

on the prescription order for such individual patient made by a licensed physician or other licensed practitioner authorized by State law to prescribe drugs; or

(2) —

(A) is by a licensed pharmacist or licensed physician in limited quantities before the receipt of a valid prescription order for such individual patient; and

(B) is based on a history of the licensed pharmacist or licensed physician receiving valid prescription orders for the compounding of the drug product, which orders have been generated solely within an established relationship between —

(i) the licensed pharmacist or licensed physician; and

(ii) —

(I) such individual patient for whom the prescription order will be provided; or

(II) the physician or other licensed practitioner who will write such prescription order.

(b) Compounded Drug. —

(1) Licensed Pharmacist and Licensed Physician. — A drug product may be compounded under subsection (a) if the licensed pharmacist or licensed physician —

(A) compounds the drug product using bulk drug substances, as defined in regulations of the Secretary published at section 207.3(a)(4) of title 21 of the Code of Federal Regulations —

(i) that —

(I) comply with the standards of an applicable United States Pharmacopeia or National Formulary monograph, if a monograph exists, and the United States Pharmacopeia chapter on pharmacy compounding;

(II) if such a monograph does not exist, are drug substances that are components of drugs approved by the Secretary; or

(III) if such a monograph does not exist and the drug substance is not a component of a drug approved by the Secretary, that appear on a list developed by the Secretary through regulations issued by the Secretary under subsection (c);

(ii) that are manufactured by an establishment that is registered under section 510 (including a foreign establishment that is registered under section 510(i)); and

(iii) that are accompanied by valid certificates of analysis for each bulk drug substance;

(B) compounds the drug product using ingredients (other than bulk drug substances) that comply with the standards of an applicable United States Pharmacopeia or National Formulary monograph, if a monograph exists, and the United States Pharmacopeia chapter on pharmacy compounding;

(C) does not compound a drug product that appears on a list published by the Secretary in the Federal Register of drug products that have been withdrawn or removed from the market because such drug products or components of such drug products have been found to be unsafe or not effective; and

(D) does not compound regularly or in inordinate amounts (as defined by the Secretary) any drug products that are essentially copies of a commercially available drug product.

(2) Definition. — For purposes of paragraph (1)(D), the term "essentially a copy of a commercially available drug product" does not include a drug product in which there is a change, made for an identified individual patient, which produces for that patient a significant difference, as determined by the prescribing practitioner, between the compounded drug and the comparable commercially available drug product.

(3) Drug Product. — A drug product may be compounded under subsection (a) only if —

(A) such drug product is not a drug product identified by the Secretary by regulation as a drug product that presents demonstrable difficulties for compounding that reasonably demonstrate an adverse effect on the safety or effectiveness of that drug product; and

(B) such drug product is compounded in a State —

(i) that has entered into a memorandum of understanding with the Secretary which addresses the distribution of inordinate amounts of compounded drug products interstate and provides for appropriate investigation by a State agency of complaints relating to compounded drug products distributed outside such State; or

(ii) that has not entered into the memorandum of understanding described in clause (i) and the licensed pharmacist, licensed pharmacy, or licensed physician distributes (or causes to be distributed) compounded drug products out of the State in which they are compounded in quantities that do not exceed 5 percent of the total prescription orders dispensed or distributed by such pharmacy or physician.

The Secretary shall, in consultation with the National Association of Boards of Pharmacy, develop a standard memorandum of understanding for use by the States in complying with subparagraph (B)(i).

(c) Regulations. —

(1) In General. — The Secretary shall issue regulations to implement this section. Before issuing regulations to implement subsections (b)(1)(A)(i)(III), (b)(1)(C), or (b)(3)(A), the Secretary shall convene and consult an advisory committee on compounding unless the Secretary determines that the issuance of such regulations before consultation is necessary to protect the public health. The advisory committee shall include representatives from the National Association of Boards of Pharmacy, the United States Pharmacopeia, pharmacy, physician, and consumer organizations, and other experts selected by the Secretary.

(2) Limiting Compounding. — The Secretary, in consultation with the United States Pharmacopeia Convention, Incorporated, shall promulgate regulations identifying drug substances that may be used in compounding under subsection (b)(1)(A)(i)(III) for which a monograph does not exist or which are not components of drug products approved by the Secretary. The Secretary shall include in the regulation the criteria for such substances, which shall include historical use, reports in peer reviewed medical literature, or other criteria the Secretary may identify.

(d) Application. — This section shall not apply to —

(1) compounded positron emission tomography drugs as defined in section 201(ii); or

(2) radiopharmaceuticals.

(e) Definition. — As used in this section, the term "compounding" does not include mixing, reconstituting, or other such acts that are performed in accordance with directions contained in approved labeling provided by the product's manufacturer and other manufacturer directions consistent with that labeling.

Sec. 503B. [353b] Outsourcing Facilities.

(a) In General. — Sections 502(f)(1), 505, and 582 shall not apply to a drug compounded by or under the direct supervision of a licensed pharmacist in a facility that elects to register as an outsourcing facility if each of the following conditions is met:

(1) Registration and Reporting. — The drug is compounded in an outsourcing facility that is in compliance with the requirements of subsection (b).

(2) Bulk Drug Substances. — The drug is compounded in an outsourcing facility that does not compound using bulk drug substances (as defined in section 207.3(a)(4) of title 21, Code of Federal Regulations (or any successor regulation)), unless —

(A) —

(i) the bulk drug substance appears on a list established by the Secretary identifying bulk drug substances for which there is a clinical need, by —

(I) publishing a notice in the Federal Register proposing bulk drug substances to be included on the list, including the rationale for such proposal;

(II) providing a period of not less than 60 calendar days for comment on the notice; and

(III) publishing a notice in the Federal Register designating bulk drug substances for inclusion on the list; or

(ii) the drug compounded from such bulk drug substance appears on the drug shortage list in effect under section 506E at the time of compounding, distribution, and dispensing;

(B) if an applicable monograph exists under the United States Pharmacopeia, the National Formulary, or another compendium or pharmacopeia recognized by the Secretary for purposes of this paragraph, the bulk drug substances each comply with the monograph;

(C) the bulk drug substances are each manufactured by an establishment that is registered under section 510 (including a foreign establishment that is registered under section 510(i)); and

(D) the bulk drug substances are each accompanied by a valid certificate of analysis.

(3) Ingredients (Other Than Bulk Drug Substances). — If any ingredients (other than bulk drug substances) are used in compounding the drug, such ingredients comply with the standards of the applicable United States Pharmacopeia or National Formulary monograph, if such monograph exists, or of another compendium or pharmacopeia recognized by the Secretary for purposes of this paragraph if any.

(4) Drugs withdrawn or Removed Because Unsafe or Not Effective. — The drug does not appear on a list published by the Secretary of drugs that have been withdrawn or removed from the market because such drugs or components of such drugs have been found to be unsafe or not effective.

(5) Essentially a Copy of an Approved Drug. — The drug is not essentially a copy of one or more approved drugs.

(6) Drugs Presenting Demonstrable Difficulties for Compounding. — The drug —

(A) is not identified (directly or as part of a category of drugs) on a list published by the Secretary, through the process described in subsection (c), of drugs or categories of drugs that present demonstrable difficulties for compounding that are reasonably likely to lead to an adverse effect on the safety or effectiveness of the drug or category of drugs, taking into account the risks and benefits to patients; or

(B) is compounded in accordance with all applicable conditions identified on the list described in subparagraph (A) as conditions that are necessary to prevent the drug or category of drugs from presenting the demonstrable difficulties described in subparagraph (A).

(7) Elements to Assure Safe Use. — In the case of a drug that is compounded from a drug that is the subject of a risk evaluation and mitigation strategy approved with elements to assure safe use pursuant to section 505–1, or from a bulk drug substance that is a component of such drug, the outsourcing facility demonstrates to the Secretary prior to beginning compounding that such facility will utilize controls comparable to the controls applicable under the relevant risk evaluation and mitigation strategy.

(8) Prohibition on Wholesaling. — The drug will not be sold or transferred by an entity other than the outsourcing facility that compounded such drug. This paragraph does not prohibit administration of a drug in a health care setting or dispensing a drug pursuant to a prescription executed in accordance with section 503(b)(1).

(9) Fees. — The drug is compounded in an outsourcing facility that has paid all fees owed by such facility pursuant to section 744K.

(10) Labeling of Drugs. —

(A) Label. — The label of the drug includes —

(i) the statement 'This is a compounded drug.' or a reasonable comparable alternative statement (as specified by the Secretary) that prominently identifies the drug as a compounded drug;

(ii) the name, address, and phone number of the applicable outsourcing facility; and (iii) with respect to the drug —

(I) the lot or batch number;

(II) the established name of the drug;

(III) the dosage form and strength;

(IV) the statement of quantity or volume, as appropriate;

(V) the date that the drug was compounded;

(VI) the expiration date;

(VII) storage and handling instructions;

(VIII) the National Drug Code number, if available;

(IX) the statement 'Not for resale', and, if the drug is dispensed or distributed other than pursuant to a prescription for an individual identified patient, the statement 'Office Use Only'; and

(X) subject to subparagraph (B)(i), a list of active and inactive ingredients, identified by established name and the quantity or proportion of each ingredient.

(B) Container. — The container from which the individual units of the drug are removed for dispensing or for administration (such as a plastic bag containing individual product syringes) shall include —

(i) the information described under subparagraph (A)(iii)(X), if there is not space on the label for such information;

(ii) the following information to facilitate adverse event reporting: www.fda.gov/medwatch and 1–800–

FDA–1088 (or any successor Internet Web site or phone number); and

(iii) directions for use, including, as appropriate, dosage and administration.

(C) Additional Information. — The label and labeling of the drug shall include any other information as determined necessary and specified in regulations promulgated by the Secretary.

(11) Outsourcing Facility Requirement. — The drug is compounded in an outsourcing facility in which the compounding of drugs occurs only in accordance with this section.

(b) Registration of Outsourcing Facilities and Reporting of Drugs. —

(1) Registration of Outsourcing Facilities. —

(A) Annual Registration. — Upon electing and in order to become an outsourcing facility, and during the period beginning on October 1 and ending on December 31 of each year thereafter, a facility —

(i) shall register with the Secretary its name, place of business, and unique facility identifier (which shall conform to the requirements for the unique facility identifier established under section 510), and a point of contact email address; and

(ii) shall indicate whether the outsourcing facility intends to compound a drug that appears on the list in effect under section 506E during the subsequent calendar year.

(B) Availability of Registration for Inspection; List. —

(i) Registrations. — The Secretary shall make available for inspection, to any person so requesting, any registration filed pursuant to this paragraph.

(ii) List. — The Secretary shall make available on the public Internet Web site of the Food and Drug Administration a list of the name of each facility registered under this subsection as an outsourcing facility, the State in which each such facility is located, whether the facility compounds from bulk drug substances, and whether any such compounding from bulk drug substances is for sterile or nonsterile drugs.

(2) Drug Reporting by Outsourcing Facilities. —

(A) In General. — Upon initially registering as an outsourcing facility, once during the month of June of each year, and once during the month of December of each year, each outsourcing facility that registers with the Secretary under paragraph (1) shall submit to the Secretary a report—

(i) identifying the drugs compounded by such outsourcing facility during the previous 6-month period; and

(ii) with respect to each drug identified under clause (i), providing the active ingredient, the source of such active ingredient, the National Drug Code number of the source drug or bulk active ingredient if available, the strength of the active ingredient per unit, the dosage form and route of administration, the package description, the number of individual units produced, and the National Drug Code number of the final product, if assigned.

(B) Form. — Each report under subparagraph (A) shall be prepared in such form and manner as the Secretary may prescribe by regulation or guidance.

(C) Confidentiality. — Reports submitted under this paragraph shall be exempt from inspection under paragraph (1)(B)(i), unless the Secretary finds that such an exemption would be inconsistent with the protection of the public health.

(3) Electronic Registration and Reporting. — Registrations and drug reporting under this subsection (including the submission of updated information) shall be submitted to the Secretary by electronic means unless the Secretary grants a request for waiver of such requirement because use of electronic means is not reasonable for the person requesting waiver.

(4) Risk-Based Inspection Frequency. —

(A) In General. — Outsourcing facilities —

(i) shall be subject to inspection pursuant to section 704; and

(ii) shall not be eligible for the exemption under section 704(a)(2)(A).

(B) Risk-Based Schedule. — The Secretary, acting through one or more officers or employees duly designated by the Secretary, shall inspect outsourcing facilities in accordance with a risk-based schedule established by the Secretary.

(C) Risk Factors. — In establishing the risk-based schedule, the Secretary shall inspect outsourcing facilities according to the known safety risks of such outsourcing facilities, which shall be based on the following factors:

(i) The compliance history of the outsourcing facility.

(ii) The record, history, and nature of recalls linked to the outsourcing facility.

(iii) The inherent risk of the drugs compounded at the outsourcing facility.

(iv) The inspection frequency and history of the outsourcing facility, including whether the outsourcing facility has been inspected pursuant to section 704 within the last 4 years.

(v) Whether the outsourcing facility has registered under this paragraph as an entity that intends to compound a drug that appears on the list in effect under section 506E.

(vi) Any other criteria deemed necessary and appropriate by the Secretary for purposes of allocating inspection resources.

(5) Adverse Event Reporting. — Outsourcing facilities shall submit adverse event reports to the Secretary in accordance with the content and format requirements established through guidance or regulation under section 310.305 of title 21, Code of Federal Regulations (or any successor regulations).

(c) Regulations. —

(1) In General. — The Secretary shall implement the list described in subsection (a)(6) through regulations.

(2) Advisory Committee On Compounding. — Before issuing regulations to implement subsection (a)(6), the Secretary shall convene and consult an advisory committee on compounding. The advisory committee shall include representatives from the National Association of Boards of Pharmacy, the United States Pharmacopeia, pharmacists with current experience and expertise in compounding, physicians with background and knowledge in compounding, and patient and public health advocacy organizations.

(3) Interim List. —

(A) In General. — Before the effective date of the regulations finalized to implement subsection (a)(6), the Secretary may designate drugs, categories of drugs, or conditions as described such subsection by —

(i) publishing a notice of such substances, drugs, categories of drugs, or conditions proposed for designation, including the rationale for such designation, in the Federal Register;

(ii) providing a period of not less than 60 calendar days for comment on the notice; and

(iii) publishing a notice in the Federal Register designating such drugs, categories of drugs, or conditions.

(B) Sunset of Notice. — Any notice provided under subparagraph (A) shall not be effective after the earlier of —

(i) the date that is 5 years after the date of enactment of the Compounding Quality Act; or **(ii)** the effective date of the final regulations issued to implement subsection (a)(6).

(4) Updates. — The Secretary shall review, and update as necessary, the regulations containing the lists of drugs, categories of drugs, or conditions described in subsection (a)(6) regularly, but not less than once every 4 years. Nothing in the previous sentence prohibits submissions to the Secretary, before or during any 4-year period described in such sentence, requesting updates to such lists.

(d) Definitions. — In this section:

(1) The term "compounding" includes the combining, admixing, mixing, diluting, pooling, reconstituting, or otherwise altering of a drug or bulk drug substance to create a drug.

(2) The term "essentially a copy of an approved drug" means —

(A) a drug that is identical or nearly identical to an approved drug, or a marketed drug not subject to section 503(b) and not subject to approval in an application submitted under section 505, unless, in the case of an approved drug, the drug appears on the drug shortage list in effect under section 506E at the time of compounding, distribution, and dispensing; or

(B) a drug, a component of which is a bulk drug substance that is a component of an approved drug or a marketed drug that is not subject to section 503(b) and not subject to approval in an application submitted under section 505, unless there is a change that produces for an individual patient a clinical difference, as determined by the prescribing practitioner, between the compounded drug and the comparable approved drug.

(3) The term "approved drug" means a drug that is approved under section 505 and does not appear on the list described in subsection (a)(4) of drugs that have been withdrawn or removed from the market because such drugs or components of such drugs have been found to be unsafe or not effective.

(4) —

(A) The term "outsourcing facility" means a facility at one geographic location or address that—

(i) is engaged in the compounding of sterile drugs;

(ii) has elected to register as an outsourcing facility; and

(iii) complies with all of the requirements of this section.

(B) An outsourcing facility is not required to be a licensed pharmacy.

(C) An outsourcing facility may or may not obtain prescriptions for identified individual patients.

(5) The term "sterile drug" means a drug that is intended for parenteral administration, an ophthalmic or oral inhalation drug in aqueous format, or a drug that is required to be sterile under Federal or State law.

(d) Obligation to Pay Fees. — Payment of the fee under section 744K, as described in subsection (a)(9), shall not relieve an outsourcing facility that is licensed as a pharmacy in any State that requires pharmacy licensing fees of its obligation to pay such State fees.-

Sec. 503C. [353c] Prereview of Television Advertisements.

(a) In General. — The Secretary may require the submission of any television advertisement for a drug (including any script, story board, rough, or a completed video production of the television advertisement) to the Secretary for review under this section not later than 45 days before dissemination of the television advertisement.

(b) Review. — In conducting a review of a television advertisement under this section, the Secretary may make recommendations with respect to information included in the label of the drug —

(1) on changes that are —

(A) necessary to protect the consumer good and wellbeing; or

(B) consistent with prescribing information for the product under review; and

(2) if appropriate and if information exists, on statements for inclusion in the advertisement to address the specific efficacy of the drug as it relates to specific population groups, including elderly populations, children, and racial and ethnic minorities.

(c) No Authority to Require Changes. — Except as provided by subsection (e), this section does not authorize the Secretary to make or direct changes in any material submitted pursuant to subsection (a).

(d) Elderly Populations, Children, Racially And Ethnically Diverse Communities. — In formulating recommendations under subsection (b), the Secretary shall take into consideration the impact of the advertised drug on elderly populations, children, and racially and ethnically diverse communities.

(e) Specific Disclosures. —

(1) Serious Risk; Safety Protocol. — In conducting a review of a television advertisement under this section, if the Secretary determines that the advertisement would be false or misleading without a specific disclosure about a serious risk listed in the labeling of the drug involved, the Secretary may require inclusion of such disclosure in the advertisement.

(2) Date of Approval. — In conducting a review of a television advertisement under this section, the Secretary may require the advertisement to include, for a period not to exceed 2 years from the date of the approval of the drug under section 505 or section 351 of the Public Health Service Act, a specific disclosure of such date of approval if the Secretary determines that the advertisement would otherwise be false or misleading.

(f) Rule of Construction. — Nothing in this section may be construed as having any effect on requirements under section 502(n) or on the authority of the Secretary under section 314.550, 314.640, 601.45, or 601.94 of title 21, Code of Federal Regulations (or successor regulations).

Sec. 504. [354] Veterinary Feed Directive Drugs.

(a) —

(1) A drug intended for use in or on animal feed which is limited by an approved application filed pursuant to section 512(b), a conditionally-approved application filed pursuant to section 571, or an index listing pursuant to section 572 to use under the professional supervision of a licensed veterinarian is a veterinary feed directive drug. Any animal feed bearing or containing a veterinary feed directive drug shall be fed to animals only by or upon a lawful veterinary feed directive issued by a licensed veterinarian in the course of the veterinarian's professional practice. When labeled, distributed, held, and used in accordance with this section, a veterinary feed directive drug and any animal feed bearing or containing a veterinary feed directive drug shall be exempt from section 502(f).

(2) A veterinary feed directive is lawful if it —

(A) contains such information as the Secretary may by general regulation or by order require; and

(B) is in compliance with the conditions and indications for use of the drug set forth in the notice published pursuant to section 512(i), or the index listing pursuant to section 572(e).

(3) —

(A) Any persons involved in the distribution or use of animal feed bearing or containing a veterinary feed directive drug and the licensed veterinarian issuing the veterinary feed directive shall maintain a copy of the veterinary feed directive applicable to each such feed, except in the case of a person distributing such feed to another person for further distribution. Such person distributing the feed shall maintain a written acknowledgment from the person to whom the feed is shipped stating that that person shall not ship or move such feed to an animal production facility without a veterinary feed directive or ship such feed to another person for further distribution unless that person has provided the same written acknowledgment to its immediate supplier.

(B) Every person required under subparagraph (A) to maintain records, and every person in charge or custody thereof, shall, upon request of an officer or employee designated by the Secretary, permit such officer or employee at all reasonable times to have access to and copy and verify such records.

(C) Any person who distributes animal feed bearing or containing a veterinary feed directive drug shall upon first engaging in such distribution notify the Secretary of that person's name and place of business. The failure to provide such notification shall be deemed to be an act which results in the drug being misbranded.

(b) A veterinary feed directive drug and any feed bearing or containing a veterinary feed directive drug shall be deemed to be misbranded if their labeling fails to bear such cautionary statement and such other information as the Secretary may by general regulation or by order prescribe, or their advertising fails to conform to the conditions and indications for use published pursuant to section 512(i), or the index listing pursuant to section 572(e) or fails to contain the general cautionary statement prescribed by the Secretary.

(c) Neither a drug subject to this section, nor animal feed bearing or containing such a drug, shall be deemed to be a prescription article under any Federal or State law.

Sec. 505. [355] New Drugs.

(a) No person shall introduce or deliver for introduction into interstate commerce any new drug, unless an approval of an application filed pursuant to subsection (b) or (j) is effective with respect to such drug.

(b) —

(1) Any person may file with the Secretary an application with respect to any drug subject to the provisions of subsection (a). Such persons shall submit to the Secretary as a part of the application

(A) full reports of investigations which have been made to show whether or not such drug is safe for use and whether such drug is effective in use;

(B) a full list of the articles used as components of such drug;

(C) a full statement of the composition of such drug;

(D) a full description of the methods used in, and the facilities and controls used for, the manufacture, processing, and packing of such drug;

(E) such samples of such drug and of the articles used as components thereof as the Secretary may require;

(F) specimens of the labeling proposed to be used for such drug, and

(G) any assessments required under section 505B.

The applicant shall file with the application the patent number and the expiration date of any patent which claims the drug for which the applicant submitted the application or which claims a method of using such drug and with respect to which a claim of patent infringement could reasonably be asserted if a person not licensed by the owner engaged in the manufacture, use, or sale of the drug. If an application is filed under this subsection for a drug and a patent which claims such drug or a method of using such drug is issued after the filing date but before approval of the application, the applicant shall amend the application to include the information required by the preceding sentence. Upon approval of the application, the Secretary shall publish information submitted under the two preceding sentences. The Secretary shall, in consultation with the Director of the National Institutes of Health and with representatives of the drug manufacturing industry, review and develop guidance, as appropriate, on the inclusion of women and minorities in clinical trials required by clause (A).

(2) An application submitted under paragraph (1) for a drug for which the investigations described in clause (A) of such paragraph and relied upon by the applicant for approval of the application were not conducted by or for the applicant and for which the applicant has not obtained a right of reference or use from the person by or for whom the investigations were conducted shall also include —

(A) a certification, in the opinion of the applicant and to the best of his knowledge, with respect to each patent which claims the drug for which such investigations were conducted or which claims a use for such drug for which the applicant is seeking approval under this subsection and for which information is required to be filed under paragraph (1) or subsection (c) —

(i) that such patent information has not been filed,

(ii) that such patent has expired,

(iii) of the date on which such patent will expire, or

(iv) that such patent is invalid or will not be infringed by the manufacture, use, or sale of the new drug for which the application is submitted; and

(B) if with respect to the drug for which investigations described in paragraph (1)(A) were conducted information was filed under paragraph (1) or subsection (c) for a method of use patent which does not claim a use for which the applicant is seeking approval under this subsection, a statement that the method of use patent does not claim such a use.

(3) Notice of Opinion That Patent Is Invalid or Will Not Be Infringed. —

(A) Agreement to Give Notice. — An applicant that makes a certification described in paragraph (2)(A)(iv) shall include in the application a statement that the applicant will give notice as required by this paragraph.

(B) Timing of Notice. — An applicant that makes a certification described in paragraph (2)(A)(iv) shall give notice as required under this paragraph —

(i) if the certification is in the application, not later than 20 days after the date of the postmark on the notice with which the Secretary informs the applicant that the application has been filed; or

(ii) if the certification is in an amendment or supplement to the application, at the time at which the applicant submits the amendment or supplement, regardless of whether the applicant has already given notice with respect to another such certification contained in the application or in an amendment or supplement to the application.

(C) Recipients of Notice. — An applicant required under this paragraph to give notice shall give notice to —

(i) each owner of the patent that is the subject of the certification (or a representative of the owner designated to receive such a notice); and

(ii) the holder of the approved application under this subsection for the drug that is claimed by the patent or a use of which is claimed by the patent (or a representative of the holder designated to receive such a notice).

(D) Contents of Notice. — A notice required under this paragraph shall —

(i) state that an application that contains data from bioavailability or bioequivalence studies has been submitted under this subsection for the drug with respect to which the certification is made to obtain approval to engage in the commercial manufacture, use, or sale of the drug before the expiration of the patent referred to in the certification; and

(ii) include a detailed statement of the factual and legal basis of the opinion of the applicant that the patent is invalid or will not be infringed.

(4) —

(A) An applicant may not amend or supplement an application referred to in paragraph (2) to seek approval of a drug that is a different drug than the drug identified in the application as submitted to the Secretary.

(B) With respect to the drug for which such an application is submitted, nothing in this subsection or subsection (c)(3) prohibits an applicant from amending or supplementing the application to seek approval of a different strength.

(5) —

(A) The Secretary shall issue guidance for the individuals who review applications submitted under paragraph (1) or under section 351 of the Public Health Service Act, which shall relate to promptness in conducting the review, technical excellence, lack of bias and conflict of interest, and knowledge of regulatory and scientific standards, and which shall apply equally to all individuals who review such applications.

(B) The Secretary shall meet with a sponsor of an investigation or an applicant for approval for a drug under this subsection or section 351 of the Public Health Service Act if the sponsor or applicant makes a reasonable written request for a meeting for the purpose of reaching agreement on the design and size— (i) of clinical trials intended to form the primary basis of an effectiveness claim; or (ii) in the case where human efficacy studies are not ethical or feasible, of animal and any associated clinical trials which, in combination, are intended to form the primary basis of an effectiveness claim; or (iii) with respect to an application for approval of a biological product under section 351(k) of the Public Health Service Act, of any necessary clinical study or studies. The sponsor or applicant shall provide information necessary for discussion and agreement on the design and size of the clinical trials. Minutes of any such meeting shall be prepared by the Secretary and made available to the sponsor or applicant upon request.

(C) Any agreement regarding the parameters of the design and size of clinical trials of a new drug under this paragraph that is reached between the Secretary and a sponsor or applicant shall be reduced to writing and made part of the administrative record by the Secretary. Such agreement shall not be changed after the testing begins, except —

(i) with the written agreement of the sponsor or applicant; or

(ii) pursuant to a decision, made in accordance with subparagraph (D) by the director of the reviewing division, that a substantial scientific issue essential to determining the safety or effectiveness of the drug has been identified after the testing has begun.

(D) A decision under subparagraph (C)(ii) by the director shall be in writing and the Secretary shall provide to the sponsor or applicant an opportunity for a meeting at which the director and the sponsor or applicant will be present and at which the director will document the scientific issue involved.

(E) The written decisions of the reviewing division shall be binding upon, and may not directly or indirectly be changed by, the field or compliance division personnel unless such field or compliance division personnel demonstrate to the reviewing division why such decision should be modified.

(F) No action by the reviewing division may be delayed because of the unavailability of information from or action by field personnel unless the reviewing division determines that a delay is necessary to assure the marketing of a safe and effective drug.

(G) For purposes of this paragraph, the reviewing division is the division responsible for the review of an application for approval of a drug under this subsection or section 351 of the Public Health Service Act (including all scientific and medical matters, chemistry, manufacturing, and controls).

(6) An application submitted under this subsection shall be accompanied by the certification required under section 402(j)(5)(B) of the Public Health Service Act. Such certification shall not be considered an element of such application.

(c) —

(1) Within one hundred and eighty days after the filing of an application under subsection (b), or such additional period as may be agreed upon by the Secretary and the applicant, the Secretary shall either —

(A) Approve the application if he then finds that none of the grounds for denying approval specified in subsection (d) applies, or

(B) Give the applicant notice of an opportunity for a hearing before the Secretary under subsection (d) on the question whether such application is approvable. If the applicant elects to accept the opportunity for hearing by written request within thirty days after such notice, such hearing shall commence not more than ninety days after the expiration of such thirty days unless the Secretary and the applicant otherwise agree. Any such hearing shall thereafter be conducted on an expedited basis and the Secretary's order thereon shall be issued within ninety days after the date fixed by the Secretary for filing final briefs.

(2) If the patent information described in subsection (b) could not be filed with the submission of an application under subsection (b) because the application was filed before the patent information was required under subsection (b) or a patent was issued after the application was approved under such subsection, the holder of an approved application shall file with the Secretary, the patent number and the expiration date of any patent which claims the drug for which the application was submitted or which claims a method of using such drug and with respect to which a claim of patent infringement could reasonably be asserted if a person not licensed by the owner engaged in the manufacture, use, or sale of the drug. If the holder of an approved application could not file patent information under subsection (b) because it was not required at the time the application was approved, the holder shall file such information under this subsection not later than thirty days after the date of the enactment of this sentence [September 24, 1984 — Ed.], and if the holder of an approved application could not file patent information under subsection (b) because no patent had been issued when an application was filed or approved, the holder shall file such information under this subsection not later than thirty days after the date the patent involved is issued. Upon the submission of patent information under this subsection, the Secretary shall publish it.

(3) The approval of an application filed under subsection (b) which contains a certification required by paragraph (2) of such subsection shall be made effective on the last applicable date determined by applying the following to each certification made under subsection (b)(2)(A):

(A) If the applicant only made a certification described in clause (i) or (ii) of subsection (b)(2)(A) or in both such clauses, the approval may be made effective immediately.

(B) If the applicant made a certification described in clause (iii) of subsection (b)(2)(A), the approval may be made effective on the date certified under clause (iii).

(C) If the applicant made a certification described in clause (iv) of subsection (b)(2)(A), the approval shall be made effective immediately unless, before the expiration of 45 days after the date on which the notice described in subsection (b)(3) is received, an action is brought for infringement of the patent that is the subject of the certification and for which information was submitted to the Secretary under paragraph (2) or subsection (b)(1) before the date on which the application (excluding an amendment or supplement to the application) was submitted. If such an action is brought before the expiration of such days, the approval may be made effective upon the expiration of the thirty-month period beginning on the date of the receipt of the notice provided under subsection (b)(3) or such shorter or longer period as the court may order because either party to the action failed to reasonably cooperate in expediting the action, except that —

(i) if before the expiration of such period the district court decides that the patent is invalid or not infringed (including any substantive determination that there is no cause of action for patent infringement or invalidity), the approval shall be made effective on —

(I) the date on which the court enters judgment reflecting the decision; or

(II) the date of a settlement order or consent decree signed and entered by the court stating that the patent that is the subject of the certification is invalid or not infringed;

(ii) if before the expiration of such period the district court decides that the patent has been infringed —

(I) if the judgment of the district court is appealed, the approval shall be made effective on —

(aa) the date on which the court of appeals decides that the patent is invalid or not infringed (including any substantive determination that there is no cause of action for patent infringement or invalidity); or

(bb) the date of a settlement order or consent decree signed and entered by the court of appeals stating that the patent that is the subject of the certification is invalid or not infringed; or

(II) if the judgment of the district court is not appealed or is affirmed, the approval shall be made effective on the date specified by the district court in a court order under section 271(e)(4)(A) of title 35, United States Code;

(iii) if before the expiration of such period the court grants a preliminary injunction prohibiting the applicant from engaging in the commercial manufacture or sale of the drug until the court decides the issues of patent validity and infringement and if the court decides that such patent is invalid or not infringed, the approval shall be made effective as provided in clause (i); or

(iv) if before the expiration of such period the court grants a preliminary injunction prohibiting the applicant from engaging in the commercial manufacture or sale of the drug until the court decides the issues of patent validity and infringement and if the court decides that such patent has been infringed, the approval shall be made effective as provided in clause (ii).

In such an action, each of the parties shall reasonably cooperate in expediting the action.

(D) Civil Action to Obtain Patent Certainty. —

(i) Declaratory Judgment Absent Infringement Action. —

(I) In General. — No action may be brought under section 2201 of title 28, United States Code, by an applicant referred to in subsection (b)(2) for a declaratory judgment with respect to a patent which is the subject of the certification referred to in subparagraph (C) unless —

(aa) the 45-day period referred to in such subparagraph has expired;

(bb) neither the owner of such patent nor the holder of the approved application under subsection (b) for the drug that is claimed by the patent or a use of which is claimed by the patent brought a civil action against the applicant for infringement of the patent before the expiration of such period; and

(cc) in any case in which the notice provided under paragraph (2)(B) [probably should be "subsection (b)(3)" — Ed.] relates to noninfringement, the notice was accompanied by a document described in subclause (III).

(II) Filing of Civil Action. — If the conditions described in items (aa), (bb), and as applicable, (cc) of subclause (I) have been met, the applicant referred to in such subclause may, in accordance with section

2201 of title 28, United States Code, bring a civil action under such section against the owner or holder referred to in such subclause (but not against any owner or holder that has brought such a civil action against the applicant, unless that civil action was dismissed without prejudice) for a declaratory judgment that the patent is invalid or will not be infringed by the drug for which the applicant seeks approval, except that such civil action may be brought for a declaratory judgment that the patent will not be infringed only in a case in which the condition described in subclause (I)(cc) is applicable. A civil action referred to in this subclause shall be brought in the judicial district where the defendant has its principal place of business or a regular and established place of business.

(III) Offer of Confidential Access to Application. — For purposes of subclause (I)(cc), the document described in this subclause is a document providing an offer of confidential access to the application that is in the custody of the applicant referred to in subsection (b)(2) for the purpose of determining whether an action referred to in subparagraph (C) should be brought. The document providing the offer of confidential access shall contain such restrictions as to persons entitled to access, and on the use and disposition of any information accessed, as would apply had a protective order been entered for the purpose of protecting trade secrets and other confidential business information. A request for access to an application under an offer of confidential access shall be considered acceptance of the offer of confidential access with the restrictions as to persons entitled to access, and on the use and disposition of any information accessed, contained in the offer of confidential access, and those restrictions and other terms of the offer of confidential access shall be considered terms of an enforceable contract. Any person provided an offer of confidential access shall review the application for the sole and limited purpose of evaluating possible infringement of the patent that is the subject of the certification under subsection (b)(2)(A)(iv) and for no other purpose, and may not disclose information of no relevance to any issue of patent infringement to any person other than a person provided an offer of confidential access. Further, the application may be redacted by the applicant to remove any information of no relevance to any issue of patent infringement.

(ii) Counterclaim to Infringement Action. —

(I) In General. — If an owner of the patent or the holder of the approved application under subsection (b) for the drug that is claimed by the patent or a use of which is claimed by the patent brings a patent infringement action against the applicant, the applicant may assert a counterclaim seeking an order requiring the holder to correct or delete the patent information submitted by the holder under subsection (b) or this subsection on the ground that the patent does not claim either—

(aa) the drug for which the application was approved; or

(bb) an approved method of using the drug.

(II) No Independent Cause of Action. — Subclause (I) does not authorize the assertion of a claim described in subclause (I) in any civil action or proceeding other than a counterclaim described in subclause (I).

(iii) No Damages. — An applicant shall not be entitled to damages in a civil action under clause (i) or a counterclaim under clause (ii).

(E) —

(i) If an application (other than an abbreviated new drug application) submitted under subsection (b) for a drug, no active ingredient (including any ester or salt of the active ingredient) of which has been approved in any other application under subsection (b), was approved during the period beginning January 1, 1982, and ending on the date of the enactment of this subsection, the Secretary may not make the approval of another application for a drug for which the investigations described in clause (A) of subsection (b)(1) and relied upon by the applicant for approval of the application were not conducted by or for the applicant and for which the applicant has not obtained a right of reference or use from the person by or for whom the investigations were conducted effective before the expiration of ten years from the date of the approval of the application previously approved under subsection (b).

(ii) If an application submitted under subsection (b) for a drug, no active ingredient (including any ester or salt of the active ingredient) of which has been approved in any other application under subsection (b), is approved after the date of the enactment of this clause, no application which refers to the drug for which the subsection (b) application was submitted and for which the investigations described in clause (A) of subsection (b)(1) and relied upon by the applicant for approval of the application were not conducted by or for the applicant and for which the applicant has not obtained a right of reference or use from the person by or for whom the investigations were conducted may be submitted under subsection (b) before the expiration of five years from the date of the approval of the application under subsection (b), except that such an application may be submitted under subsection (b) after the expiration of four years from the date of the approval of the subsection (b) application if it contains a certification of patent invalidity or noninfringement described in clause (iv) of subsection (b)(2)(A). The approval of such an application shall be made effective in accordance with this paragraph except that, if an action for patent infringement is commenced during the one-year period beginning forty-eight months after the date of the approval of the subsection (b) application, the thirty-month period referred to in subparagraph (C) shall be extended by such amount of time (if any) which is required for seven and one-half years to have elapsed from the date of approval of the subsection (b) application.

(iii) If an application submitted under subsection (b) for a drug, which includes an active ingredient (including any ester or salt of the active ingredient) that has been approved in another application approved under subsection (b), is approved after the date of the enactment of this clause, and if such application contains reports of new clinical investigations (other than bioavailability studies) essential to the approval of the application and conducted or sponsored by the applicant, the Secretary may not make the approval of an application submitted under subsection (b) for the conditions of approval of such drug in the approved subsection (b) application effective before the expiration of three years from the date of the approval of the application under subsection (b) if the investigations described in clause (A) of subsection (b)(1) and relied upon by the applicant for approval of the application were not conducted by or for the applicant and if the applicant has not obtained a right of reference or use from the person by or for whom the investigations were conducted.

(iv) If a supplement to an application approved under subsection (b) is approved after the date of the enactment of this clause, and the supplement contains reports of new clinical investigations (other than bioavailability studies) essential to the approval of the supplement and conducted or sponsored by the person submitting the supplement, the Secretary may not make the approval of an application submitted under subsection (b) for a change approved in the supplement effective before the expiration of three years from the date of the approval of the supplement under subsection (b) if the investigations described in clause (A) of subsection (b)(1) and relied upon by the applicant for approval of the application were not conducted by or for the applicant and if the applicant has not obtained a right of reference or use from the person by or for whom the investigations were conducted.

(v) If an application (or supplement to an application) submitted under subsection (b) for a drug, which includes an active ingredient (including any ester or salt of the active ingredient) that has been approved in another application under subsection (b), was approved during the period beginning January 1, 1982, and ending on the date of the enactment of this clause, the Secretary may not make the approval of an application submitted under this subsection and for which the investigations described in clause (A) of subsection (b)(1) and relied upon by the applicant for approval of the application were not conducted by or for the applicant and for which the applicant has not obtained a right of reference or use from the person by or for whom the investigations were conducted and which refers to the drug for which the subsection (b) application was submitted effective before the expiration of two years from the date of enactment of this clause.

(4) A drug manufactured in a pilot or other small facility may be used to demonstrate the safety and effectiveness of the drug and to obtain approval for the drug prior to manufacture of the drug in a larger facility, unless the Secretary makes a determination that a full scale production facility is necessary to ensure the safety or effectiveness of the drug.

(5) (A) The Secretary may rely upon qualified data summaries to support the approval of a supplemental application, with respect to a qualified indication for a drug, submitted under subsection (b), if such supplemental application complies with subparagraph (B).

(B) A supplemental application is eligible for review as described in subparagraph (A) only if—

(i) there is existing data available and acceptable to the Secretary demonstrating the safety of the drug; and

(ii) all data used to develop the qualified data summaries are submitted to the Secretary as part of the supplemental application.

(C) The Secretary shall post on the Internet website of the Food and Drug Administration and update annually—

(i) the number of applications reviewed solely under subparagraph (A) or section 351(a)(2)(E) of the Public Health Service Act;

(ii) the average time for completion of review under subparagraph (A) or section 351(a)(2)(E) of the Public Health Service Act;

(iii) the average time for review of supplemental applications where the Secretary did not use review flexibility under subparagraph (A) or section 351(a)(2)(E) of the Public Health Service Act; and

(iv) the number of applications reviewed under subparagraph (A) or section 351(a)(2)(E) of the Public Health Service Act for which the Secretary made use of full data sets in addition to the qualified data summary.

(D) In this paragraph—

(i) the term "qualified indication" means an in dication for a drug that the Secretary determines to be appropriate for summary level review under this paragraph; and

(ii) the term "qualified data summary" means a summary of clinical data that demonstrates the safety and effectiveness of a drug with respect to a qualified indication.

(d) If the Secretary finds, after due notice to the applicant in accordance with subsection (c) and giving him an opportunity for a hearing, in accordance with said subsection, that

(1) the investigations, reports of which are required to be submitted to the Secretary pursuant to subsection (b), do not include adequate tests by all methods reasonably applicable to show whether or not such drug is safe for use under the conditions prescribed, recommended, or suggested in the proposed labeling thereof;

(2) the results of such tests show that such drug is unsafe for use under such conditions or do not show that such drug is safe for use under such conditions;

(3) the methods used in, and the facilities and controls used for, the manufacture, processing, and packing of such drug are inadequate to preserve its identity, strength, quality, and purity;

(4) upon the basis of the information submitted to him as part of the application, or upon the basis of any other information before him with respect to such drug, he has insufficient information to determine whether such drug is safe for use under such conditions; or

(5) evaluated on the basis of the information submitted to him as part of the application and any other information before him with respect to such drug, there is a lack of substantial evidence that the drug will have the effect it purports or is represented to have under the conditions of use prescribed, recommended, or suggested in the proposed labeling thereof; or

(6) the application failed to contain the patent information prescribed by subsection (b); or

(7) based on a fair evaluation of all material facts, such labeling is false or misleading in any particular; he shall issue an order refusing to approve the application. If, after such notice and opportunity for hearing, the Secretary finds that clauses (1) through (6) do not apply, he shall issue an order approving the application. As used in this subsection and subsection (e), the term "substantial evidence" means evidence consisting of adequate and well-controlled investigations, including clinical investigations, by experts qualified by scientific training and experience to evaluate the effectiveness of the drug involved, on the basis of which it could fairly and responsibly be concluded by such experts that the drug will have the effect it purports or is represented to have under the conditions of use prescribed, recommended, or suggested in the labeling or proposed labeling thereof. If the Secretary determines, based on relevant science, that data from one adequate and well-controlled clinical investigation and confirmatory evidence (obtained prior to or after such investigation) are sufficient to establish effectiveness, the Secretary may consider such data and evidence to constitute substantial evidence for purposes of the preceding sentence. The Secretary shall implement a structured risk-benefit assessment framework in the new drug approval process to facilitate the balanced consideration of benefits and risks, a consistent and systematic approach to the discussion and regulatory decisionmaking, and the communication of the benefits and risks of new drugs. Nothing in the preceding sentence shall alter the criteria for evaluating an application for marketing approval of a drug.

(e) The Secretary shall, after due notice and opportunity for hearing to the applicant, withdraw approval of an application with respect to any drug under this section if the Secretary finds

(1) that clinical or other experience, tests, or other scientific data show that such drug is unsafe for use under the conditions of use upon the basis of which the application was approved;

(2) that new evidence of clinical experience, not contained in such application or not available to the Secretary until after such application was approved, or tests by new methods, or tests by methods not deemed reasonably applicable when such application was approved, evaluated together with the evidence available to the Secretary when the application was approved, shows that such drug is not shown to be safe for use under the conditions of use upon the basis of which the application was approved; or

(3) on the basis of new information before him with respect to such drug, evaluated together with the evidence available to him when the application was approved, that there is a lack of substantial evidence that the drug will have the effect it purports or is represented to have under the conditions of use prescribed, recommended, or suggested in the labeling thereof; or

(4) the patent information prescribed by subsection (c) was not filed within thirty days after the receipt of written notice from the Secretary specifying the failure to file such information; or

(5) that the application contains any untrue statement of a material fact:

Provided, [t]hat if the Secretary (or in his absence the officer acting as Secretary) finds that there is an imminent hazard to the public health, he may suspend the approval of such application immediately, and give the applicant prompt notice of his action and afford the applicant the opportunity for an expedited hearing under this subsection; but the authority conferred by this proviso to suspend the approval of an application shall not be delegated. The

Secretary may also, after due notice and opportunity for hearing to the applicant, withdraw the approval of an application submitted under subsection (b) or (j) with respect to any drug under this section if the Secretary finds

(A) that the applicant has failed to establish a system for maintaining required records, or has repeatedly or deliberately failed to maintain such records or to make required reports, in accordance with a regulation or order under subsection (k) or to comply with the notice requirements of section 510(k)(2), or the applicant has refused to permit access to, or copying or verification of, such records as required by paragraph (2) of such subsection; or

(B) that on the basis of new information before him, evaluated together with the evidence before him when the application was approved, the methods used in, or the facilities and controls used for, the manufacture, processing, and packing of such drug are inadequate to assure and preserve its identity, strength, quality, and purity and were not made adequate within a reasonable time after receipt of written notice from the Secretary specifying the matter complained of; or

(C) that on the basis of new information before him, evaluated together with the evidence before him when the application was approved, the labeling of such drug, based on a fair evaluation of all material facts, is false or misleading in any particular and was not corrected within a reasonable time after receipt of written notice from the Secretary specifying the matter complained of.

Any order under this subsection shall state the findings upon which it is based.

The Secretary may withdraw the approval of an application submitted under this section, or suspend the approval of such an application, as provided under this subsection, without first ordering the applicant to submit an assessment of the approved risk evaluation and mitigation strategy for the drug under section 505–1(g)(2)(D).

(f) Whenever the Secretary finds that the facts so require, he shall revoke any previous order under subsection (d) or (e) refusing, withdrawing, or suspending approval of an application and shall approve such application or reinstate such approval, as may be appropriate.

(g) Orders of the Secretary issued under this section shall be served

(1) in person by any officer or employee of the Department designated by the Secretary or

(2) by mailing the order by registered mail or by certified mail addressed to the applicant or respondent at his last-known address in the records of the Secretary.

(h) An appeal may be taken by the applicant from an order of the Secretary refusing or withdrawing approval of an application under this section. Such appeal shall be taken by filing in the United States court of appeals for the circuit wherein such applicant resides or has his principal place of business, or in the United States Court of Appeals for the District of Columbia Circuit, within sixty days after the entry of such order, a written petition praying that the order of the Secretary be set aside. A copy of such petition shall be forthwith transmitted by the clerk of the court to the Secretary, or any officer designated by him for that purpose, and thereupon the Secretary shall certify and file in the court the record upon which the order complained of was entered, as provided in section 2112 of title 28, United States Code. Upon the filing of such petition such court shall have exclusive jurisdiction to affirm or set aside such order, except that until the filing of the record the Secretary may modify or set aside his order. No objection to the order of the Secretary shall be considered by the court unless such objection shall have been urged before the Secretary or unless there were reasonable grounds for failure so to do. The finding of the Secretary as to the facts, if supported by substantial evidence, shall be conclusive. If any person shall apply to the court for leave to adduce additional evidence, and shall show to the satisfaction of the court that such additional evidence is material and that there were reasonable grounds for failure to adduce such evidence in the proceeding before the Secretary, the court may order such additional evidence to be taken before the Secretary and to be adduced upon the hearing in such manner and upon such terms and conditions as to the court may seem proper. The Secretary may modify his findings as to the facts by reason of the additional evidence so taken, and he shall file with the court such modified findings which, if supported by substantial evidence, shall be conclusive, and his recommendation, if any, for the setting aside of the original order. The judgment of the court affirming or setting aside any such order of the Secretary shall be final, subject to review by the Supreme Court of the United States upon certiorari or certification as provided in section 1254 of title 28 of the United States Code. The commencement of proceedings under this subsection shall not, unless specifically ordered by the court to the contrary, operate as a stay of the Secretary's order.

(i) —

(1) The Secretary shall promulgate regulations for exempting from the operation of the foregoing subsections of this section drugs intended solely for investigational use by experts qualified by scientific training and experience to investigate the safety and effectiveness of drugs. Such regulations may, within the discretion of the Secretary, among other conditions relating to the protection of the public health, provide for conditioning such exemption upon —

(A) the submission to the Secretary, before any clinical testing of a new drug is undertaken, of reports, by the manufacturer or the sponsor of the investigation of such drug, of preclinical tests (including tests on animals) of such drug adequate to justify the proposed clinical testing;

(B) the manufacturer or the sponsor of the investigation of a new drug proposed to be distributed to investigators for clinical testing obtaining a signed agreement from each of such investigators that patients to whom the drug is administered will be under his personal supervision, or under the supervision of investigators responsible to him, and that he will not supply such drug to any other investigator, or to clinics, for administration to human beings;

(C) the establishment and maintenance of such records, and the making of such reports to the Secretary, by the manufacturer or the sponsor of the investigation of such drug, of data (including but not limited to analytical reports by investigators) obtained as the result of such investigational use of such drug, as the Secretary finds will enable him to evaluate the safety and effectiveness of such drug in the event of the filing of an application pursuant to subsection (b); and

(D) the submission to the Secretary by the manufacturer or the sponsor of the investigation of a new drug of a statement of intent regarding whether the manufacturer or sponsor has plans for assessing pediatric safety and efficacy.

(2) Subject to paragraph (3), a clinical investigation of a new drug may begin 30 days after the Secretary has received from the manufacturer or sponsor of the investigation a submission containing such information about the drug and the clinical investigation, including —

(A) information on design of the investigation and adequate reports of basic information, certified by the applicant to be accurate reports, necessary to assess the safety of the drug for use in clinical investigation; and

(B) adequate information on the chemistry and manufacturing of the drug, controls available for the drug, and primary data tabulations from animal or human studies.

(3) —

(A) At any time, the Secretary may prohibit the sponsor of an investigation from conducting the investigation (referred to in this paragraph as a "clinical hold") if the Secretary makes a determination described in subparagraph (B). The Secretary shall specify the basis for the clinical hold, including the specific information available to the Secretary which served as the basis for such clinical hold, and confirm such determination in writing.

(B) For purposes of subparagraph (A), a determination described in this subparagraph with respect to a clinical hold is that —

(i) the drug involved represents an unreasonable risk to the safety of the persons who are the subjects of the clinical investigation, taking into account the qualifications of the clinical investigators, information about the drug, the design of the clinical investigation, the condition for which the drug is to be investigated, and the health status of the subjects involved; or

(ii) the clinical hold should be issued for such other reasons as the Secretary may by regulation establish (including reasons established by regulation before the date of the enactment of the Food and Drug Administration Modernization Act of 1997 [November 21, 1997 — Ed.]).

(C) Any written request to the Secretary from the sponsor of an investigation that a clinical hold be removed shall receive a decision, in writing and specifying the reasons therefor, within 30 days after receipt of such request. Any such request shall include sufficient information to support the removal of such clinical hold.

(4) Regulations under paragraph (1) shall provide that such exemption shall be conditioned upon the manufacturer, or the sponsor of the investigation, requiring that experts using such drugs for investigational purposes certify to such manufacturer or sponsor that they will inform any human beings to whom such drugs, or any controls used in connection therewith, are being administered, or their representatives, that such drugs are being used for investigational purposes and will obtain the consent of such human beings or their representatives, except where it is not feasible, it is contrary to the best interests of such human beings, or the proposed clinical testing poses no more than minimal risk to such human beings and includes appropriate safeguards as prescribed to protect the rights, safety, and welfare of such human beings. Nothing in this subsection shall be construed to require any clinical investigator to submit directly to the Secretary reports on the investigational use of drugs. The Secretary shall update such regulations to require inclusion in the informed consent documents and process a statement that clinical trial information for such clinical investigation has been or will be submitted for inclusion in the registry data bank pursuant to subsection (j) of section 402 of the Public Health Service Act.

(j) —

(1) Any person may file with the Secretary an abbreviated application for the approval of a new drug.

(2) —

(A) An abbreviated application for a new drug shall contain —

(i) information to show that the conditions of use prescribed, recommended, or suggested in the labeling proposed for the new drug have been previously approved for a drug listed under paragraph (7) (hereinafter in this subsection referred to as a "listed drug");

(ii) —

(I) if the listed drug referred to in clause (i) has only one active ingredient, information to show that the active ingredient of the new drug is the same as that of the listed drug;

(II) if the listed drug referred to in clause (i) has more than one active ingredient, information to show that the active ingredients of the new drug are the same as those of the listed drug, or

(III) if the listed drug referred to in clause (i) has more than one active ingredient and if one of the active ingredients of the new drug is different and the application is filed pursuant to the approval of a petition filed under subparagraph (C), information to show that the other active ingredients of the new drug are the same as the active ingredients of the listed drug, information to show that the different active ingredient is an active ingredient of a listed drug or of a drug which does not meet the requirements of section 201(p), and such other information respecting the different active ingredient with respect to which the petition was filed as the Secretary may require;

(iii) information to show that the route of administration, the dosage form, and the strength of the new drug are the same as those of the listed drug referred to in clause (i) or, if the route of administration, the dosage form, or the strength of the new drug is different and the application is filed pursuant to the approval of a petition filed under subparagraph (C), such information respecting the route of administration, dosage form, or strength with respect to which the petition was filed as the Secretary may require;

(iv) information to show that the new drug is bioequivalent to the listed drug referred to in clause (i), except that if the application is filed pursuant to the approval of a petition filed under subparagraph (C), information to show that the active ingredients of the new drug are of the same pharmacological or therapeutic class as those of the listed drug referred to in clause (i) and the new drug can be expected to have the same therapeutic effect as the listed drug when administered to patients for a condition of use referred to in clause (i);

(v) information to show that the labeling proposed for the new drug is the same as the labeling approved for the listed drug referred to in clause (i) except for changes required because of differences approved under a petition filed under subparagraph (C) or because the new drug and the listed drug are produced or distributed by different manufacturers;

(vi) the items specified in clauses (B) through (F) of subsection (b)(1);

(vii) a certification, in the opinion of the applicant and to the best of his knowledge, with respect to each patent which claims the listed drug referred to in clause (i) or which claims a use for such listed drug for which the applicant is seeking approval under this subsection and for which information is required to be filed under subsection (b) or (c) —

(I) that such patent information has not been filed,

(II) that such patent has expired,

(III) of the date on which such patent will expire, or

(IV) that such patent is invalid or will not be infringed by the manufacture, use, or sale of the new drug for which the application is submitted; and

(viii) if with respect to the listed drug referred to in clause (i) information was filed under subsection (b) or (c) for a method of use patent which does not claim a use for which the applicant is seeking approval under this subsection, a statement that the method of use patent does not claim such a use.

The Secretary may not require that an abbreviated application contain information in addition to that required by clauses (i) through (viii).

(B) Notice of Opinion That Patent Is Invalid or Will Not Be Infringed. —

(i) Agreement To Give Notice. — An applicant that makes a certification described in subparagraph (A)(vii)(IV) shall include in the application a statement that the applicant will give notice as required by this subparagraph.

(ii) Timing of Notice. — An applicant that makes a certification described in subparagraph (A)(vii)(IV) shall give notice as required under this subparagraph —

(I) if the certification is in the application, not later than 20 days after the date of the postmark on the notice with which the Secretary informs the applicant that the application has been filed; or

(II) if the certification is in an amendment or supplement to the application, at the time at which the applicant submits the amendment or supplement, regardless of whether the applicant has already given notice with respect to another such certification contained in the application or in an amendment or supplement to the application.

(iii) Recipients of Notice. — An applicant required under this subparagraph to give notice shall give notice to —

(I) each owner of the patent that is the subject of the certification (or a representative of the owner designated to receive such a notice); and

(II) the holder of the approved application under subsection (b) for the drug that is claimed by the patent or a use of which is claimed by the patent (or a representative of the holder designated to receive such a notice).

(iv) Contents of Notice. — A notice required under this subparagraph shall —

(I) state that an application that contains data from bioavailability or bioequivalence studies has been submitted under this subsection for the drug with respect to which the certification is made to obtain approval to engage in the commercial manufacture, use, or sale of the drug before the expiration of the patent referred to in the certification; and

(II) include a detailed statement of the factual and legal basis of the opinion of the applicant that the patent is invalid or will not be infringed.

(C) If a person wants to submit an abbreviated application for a new drug which has a different active ingredient or whose route of administration, dosage form, or strength differ from that of a listed drug, such person shall submit a petition to the Secretary seeking permission to file such an application. The Secretary shall approve or disapprove a petition submitted under this subparagraph within ninety days of the date the petition is submitted. The Secretary shall approve such a petition unless the Secretary finds —

(i) that investigations must be conducted to show the safety and effectiveness of the drug or of any of its active ingredients, the route of administration, the dosage form, or strength which differ from the listed drug; or

(ii) that any drug with a different active ingredient may not be adequately evaluated for approval as safe and effective on the basis of the information required to be submitted in an abbreviated application.

(D) —

(i) An applicant may not amend or supplement an application to seek approval of a drug referring to a different listed drug from the listed drug identified in the application as submitted to the Secretary.

(ii) With respect to the drug for which an application is submitted, nothing in this subsection prohibits an applicant from amending or supplementing the application to seek approval of a different strength.

(iii) Within 60 days after the date of the enactment of the Medicare Prescription Drug, Improvement, and Modernization Act of 2003 [December 8, 2003 — Ed.], the Secretary shall issue guidance defining the term "listed drug" for purposes of this subparagraph.

(3) —

(A) The Secretary shall issue guidance for the individuals who review applications submitted under paragraph (1), which shall relate to promptness in conducting the review, technical excellence, lack of bias and conflict of interest, and knowledge of regulatory and scientific standards, and which shall apply equally to all individuals who review such applications.

(B) The Secretary shall meet with a sponsor of an investigation or an applicant for approval for a drug under this subsection if the sponsor or applicant makes a reasonable written request for a meeting for the purpose of reaching agreement on the design and size of bioavailability and bioequivalence studies needed for approval of such application. The sponsor or applicant shall provide information necessary for discussion and agreement on the design and size of such studies. Minutes of any such meeting shall be prepared by the Secretary and made available to the sponsor or applicant.

(C) Any agreement regarding the parameters of design and size of bioavailability and bioequivalence studies of a drug under this paragraph that is reached between the Secretary and a sponsor or applicant shall be reduced to writing and made part of the administrative record by the Secretary. Such agreement shall not be changed after the testing begins, except —

(i) with the written agreement of the sponsor or applicant; or

(ii) pursuant to a decision, made in accordance with subparagraph (D) by the director of the reviewing division, that a substantial scientific issue essential to determining the safety or effectiveness of the drug has been identified after the testing has begun.

(D) A decision under subparagraph (C)(ii) by the director shall be in writing and the Secretary shall provide to the sponsor or applicant an opportunity for a meeting at which the director and the sponsor or applicant will be present and at which the director will document the scientific issue involved.

(E) The written decisions of the reviewing division shall be binding upon, and may not directly or indirectly be changed by, the field or compliance office personnel unless such field or compliance office personnel demonstrate to the reviewing division why such decision should be modified.

(F) No action by the reviewing division may be delayed because of the unavailability of information from or action by field personnel unless the reviewing division determines that a delay is necessary to assure the marketing of a safe and effective drug.

(G) For purposes of this paragraph, the reviewing division is the division responsible for the review of an application for approval of a drug under this subsection (including scientific matters, chemistry, manufacturing, and controls).

(4) Subject to paragraph (5), the Secretary shall approve an application for a drug unless the Secretary finds —

(A) the methods used in, or the facilities and controls used for, the manufacture, processing, and packing of the drug are inadequate to assure and preserve its identity, strength, quality, and purity;

(B) information submitted with the application is insufficient to show that each of the proposed conditions of use have been previously approved for the listed drug referred to in the application;

(C) —

(i) if the listed drug has only one active ingredient, information submitted with the application is insufficient to show that the active ingredient is the same as that of the listed drug;

(ii) if the listed drug has more than one active ingredient, information submitted with the application is insufficient to show that the active ingredients are the same as the active ingredients of the listed drug, or

(iii) if the listed drug has more than one active ingredient and if the application is for a drug which has an active ingredient different from the listed drug, information submitted with the application is insufficient to show —

(I) that the other active ingredients are the same as the active ingredients of the listed drug, or

(II) that the different active ingredient is an active ingredient of a listed drug or a drug which does not meet the requirements of section 201(p),

or no petition to file an application for the drug with the different ingredient was approved under paragraph (2)(C);

(D) —

(i) if the application is for a drug whose route of administration, dosage form, or strength of the drug is the same as the route of administration, dosage form, or strength of the listed drug referred to in the application, information submitted in the application is insufficient to show that the route of administration, dosage form, or strength is the same as that of the listed drug, or

(ii) if the application is for a drug whose route of administration, dosage form, or strength of the drug is different from that of the listed drug referred to in the application, no petition to file an application for the drug with the different route of administration, dosage form, or strength was approved under paragraph (2)(C);

(E) if the application was filed pursuant to the approval of a petition under paragraph (2)(C), the application did not contain the information required by the Secretary respecting the active ingredient, route of administration, dosage form, or strength which is not the same;

(F) information submitted in the application is insufficient to show that the drug is bioequivalent to the listed drug referred to in the application or, if the application was filed pursuant to a petition approved under paragraph (2)(C), information submitted in the application is insufficient to show that the active ingredients of the new drug are of the same pharmacological or therapeutic class as those of the listed drug referred to in paragraph (2)(A)(i) and that the new drug can be expected to have the same therapeutic effect as the listed drug when administered to patients for a condition of use referred to in such paragraph;

(G) information submitted in the application is insufficient to show that the labeling proposed for the drug is the same as the labeling approved for the listed drug referred to in the application except for changes required because of differences approved under a petition filed under paragraph (2)(C) or because the drug and the listed drug are produced or distributed by different manufacturers;

(H) information submitted in the application or any other information available to the Secretary shows that

(i) the inactive ingredients of the drug are unsafe for use under the conditions prescribed, recommended, or suggested in the labeling proposed for the drug, or

(ii) the composition of the drug is unsafe under such conditions because of the type or quantity of inactive ingredients included or the manner in which the inactive ingredients are included;

(I) the approval under subsection (c) of the listed drug referred to in the application under this subsection has been withdrawn or suspended for grounds described in the first sentence of subsection (e), the Secretary has published a notice of opportunity for hearing to withdraw approval of the listed drug under subsection (c) for grounds described in the first sentence of subsection (e), the approval under this subsection of the listed drug referred to in the application under this subsection has been withdrawn or suspended under paragraph (6), or the Secretary has determined that the listed drug has been withdrawn from sale for safety or effectiveness reasons;

(J) the application does not meet any other requirement of paragraph (2)(A); or

(K) the application contains an untrue statement of material fact.

(5) —

(A) Within one hundred and eighty days of the initial receipt of an application under paragraph (2) or within such additional period as may be agreed upon by the Secretary and the applicant, the Secretary shall approve or disapprove the application.

(B) The approval of an application submitted under paragraph (2) shall be made effective on the last applicable date determined by applying the following to each certification made under paragraph (2)(A)(vii):

(i) If the applicant only made a certification described in subclause (I) or (II) of paragraph (2)(A)(vii) or in both such subclauses, the approval may be made effective immediately.

(ii) If the applicant made a certification described in subclause (III) of paragraph (2)(A)(vii), the approval may be made effective on the date certified under subclause (III).

(iii) If the applicant made a certification described in subclause (IV) of paragraph (2)(A)(vii), the approval shall be made effective immediately unless, before the expiration of 45 days after the date on which the notice described in paragraph (2)(B) is received, an action is brought for infringement of the patent that is the subject of the certification and for which information was submitted to the Secretary under subsection (b)(1) or (c)(2) before the date on which the application (excluding an amendment or supplement to the application), which the Secretary later determines to be substantially complete, was submitted. If such an action is brought before the expiration of such days, the approval shall be made effective upon the expiration of the thirty-month period beginning on the date of the receipt of the notice provided under paragraph (2)(B)(i) or such shorter or longer period as the court may order because either party to the action failed to reasonably cooperate in expediting the action, except that —

(I) if before the expiration of such period the district court decides that the patent is invalid or not infringed (including any substantive determination that there is no cause of action for patent infringement or invalidity), the approval shall be made effective on —

(aa) the date on which the court enters judgment reflecting the decision; or

(bb) the date of a settlement order or consent decree signed and entered by the court stating that the patent that is the subject of the certification is invalid or not infringed;

(II) if before the expiration of such period the district court decides that the patent has been infringed —

(aa) if the judgment of the district court is appealed, the approval shall be made effective on —

(AA) the date on which the court of appeals decides that the patent is invalid or not infringed (including any substantive determination that there is no cause of action for patent infringement or invalidity); or

(BB) the date of a settlement order or consent decree signed and entered by the court of appeals stating that the patent that is the subject of the certification is invalid or not infringed; or

(bb) if the judgment of the district court is not appealed or is affirmed, the approval shall be made effective on the date specified by the district court in a court order under section 271(e)(4)(A) of title 35, United States Code;

(III) if before the expiration of such period the court grants a preliminary injunction prohibiting the applicant from engaging in the commercial manufacture or sale of the drug until the court decides the issues of patent validity and infringement and if the court decides that such patent is invalid or not infringed, the approval shall be made effective as provided in subclause (I); or

(IV) if before the expiration of such period the court grants a preliminary injunction prohibiting the applicant from engaging in the commercial manufacture or sale of the drug until the court decides the issues of patent validity and infringement and if the court decides that such patent has been infringed, the approval shall be made effective as provided in subclause (II).

In such an action, each of the parties shall reasonably cooperate in expediting the action.

(iv) 180-day exclusivity period. —

(I) Effectiveness of Application. — Subject to subparagraph (D), if the application contains a certification described in paragraph (2)(A)(vii)(IV) and is for a drug for which a first applicant has submitted an application containing such a certification, the application shall be made effective on the date that is 180 days after the date of the first commercial marketing of the drug (including the commercial marketing of the listed drug) by any first applicant.

(II) Definitions. — In this paragraph:

(aa) 180-Day Exclusivity Period. — The term "180-day exclusivity period" means the 180-day period ending on the day before the date on which an application submitted by an applicant other than a first applicant could become effective under this clause.

(bb) First Applicant. — As used in this subsection, the term "first applicant" means an applicant that, on the first day on which a substantially complete application containing a certification described in paragraph (2)(A)(vii)(IV) is submitted for approval of a drug, submits a substantially complete application that contains and lawfully maintains a certification described in paragraph (2)(A)(vii)(IV) for the drug.

(cc) Substantially Complete Application. — As used in this subsection, the term "substantially complete application" means an application under this subsection that on its face is sufficiently complete to permit a substantive review and contains all the information required by paragraph (2)(A).

(dd) Tentative Approval. —

(AA) In General. — The term "tentative approval" means notification to an applicant by the Secretary that an application under this subsection meets the requirements of paragraph (2)(A), but cannot receive effective approval because the application does not meet the requirements of this subparagraph, there is a period of exclusivity for the listed drug under subparagraph (F) or section 505A, or there is a 7-year period of exclusivity for the listed drug under section 527.

(BB) Limitation. — A drug that is granted tentative approval by the Secretary is not an approved drug and shall not have an effective approval until the Secretary issues an approval after any necessary additional review of the application.

(v) 180-Day Exclusivity Period for Competitive Generic Therapies. —

(I) Effectiveness of Application. — Subject to subparagraph (D)(iv), if the application is for a drug that is the same as a competitive generic therapy for which any first approved applicant has commenced commercial marketing, the application shall be made effective on the date that is 180 days after the date of the first commercial marketing of the competitive generic therapy (including the commercial marketing of the listed drug) by any first approved applicant.

(II) Limitation. — The exclusivity period under subclause (I) shall not apply with respect to a competitive generic therapy that has previously received an exclusivity period under subclause (I).

(III) Definitions. — In this clause and subparagraph (D)(iv):

(aa) The term 'competitive generic therapy' means a drug —

(AA) that is designated as a competitive generic therapy under section 506H; and

(BB) for which there are no unexpired patents or exclusivities on the list of products described in section 505(j)(7)(A) at the time of submission.

(bb) The term 'first approved applicant' means any applicant that has submitted an application that —

(AA) is for a competitive generic therapy that is approved on the first day on which any application for such competitive generic therapy is approved;

(BB) is not eligible for a 180-day exclusivity period under clause (iv) for the drug that is the subject of the application for the competitive generic therapy; and

(CC) is not for a drug for which all drug versions have forfeited eligibility for a 180-day exclusivity period under clause (iv) pursuant to subparagraph (D).

(C) Civil Action to Obtain Patent Certainty. —

(i) Declaratory Judgment Absent Infringement Action. —

(I) In General. — No action may be brought under section 2201 of title 28, United States Code, by an applicant under paragraph (2) for a declaratory judgment with respect to a patent which is the subject of the certification referred to in subparagraph (B)(iii) unless —

(aa) the 45-day period referred to in such subparagraph has expired;

(bb) neither the owner of such patent nor the holder of the approved application under subsection (b) for the drug that is claimed by the patent or a use of which is claimed by the patent brought a civil action against the applicant for infringement of the patent before the expiration of such period; and

(cc) in any case in which the notice provided under paragraph (2)(B) relates to noninfringement, the notice was accompanied by a document described in subclause (III).

(II) Filing of Civil Action. — If the conditions described in items (aa), (bb), and as applicable, (cc) of subclause (I) have been met, the applicant referred to in such subclause may, in accordance with section 2201 of title 28, United States Code, bring a civil action under such section against the owner or holder referred to in such subclause (but not against any owner or holder that has brought such a civil action against the applicant, unless that civil action was dismissed without prejudice) for a declaratory judgment that the patent is invalid or will not be infringed by the drug for which the applicant seeks approval, except that such civil action may be brought for a declaratory judgment that the patent will not be infringed only in a case in which the condition described in subclause (I)(cc) is applicable. A civil action referred to in this subclause shall be brought in the judicial district where the defendant has its principal place of business or a regular and established place of business.

(III) Offer of Confidential Access to Application. — For purposes of subclause (I)(cc), the document described in this subclause is a document providing an offer of confidential access to the application that is in the custody of the applicant under paragraph (2) for the purpose of determining whether an action referred to in subparagraph (B)(iii) should be brought. The document providing the offer of confidential access shall contain such restrictions as to persons entitled to access, and on the use and disposition of any information accessed, as would apply had a protective order been entered for the purpose of protecting trade secrets and other confidential business information. A request for access to an application under an offer of confidential access shall be considered acceptance of the offer of confidential access with the restrictions as to persons entitled to access, and on the use and disposition of any information accessed, contained in the offer of confidential access, and those restrictions and other terms of the offer of confidential access shall be considered terms of an enforceable contract. Any person provided an offer of confidential access shall review the application for the sole and limited purpose of evaluating possible infringement of the patent that is the subject of the certification under paragraph (2)(A)(vii)(IV) and for no other purpose, and may not disclose information of no relevance to any issue of patent infringement to any person other than a person provided an offer of confidential access. Further, the application may be redacted by the applicant to remove any information of no relevance to any issue of patent infringement.

(ii) Counterclaim to Infringement Action. —

(I) In General. — If an owner of the patent or the holder of the approved application under subsection (b) for the drug that is claimed by the patent or a use of which is claimed by the patent brings a patent infringement action against the applicant, the applicant may assert a counterclaim seeking an order requiring the holder to correct or delete the patent information submitted by the holder under subsection (b) or (c) on the ground that the patent does not claim either —

(aa) the drug for which the application was approved; or

(bb) an approved method of using the drug.

(II) No Independent Cause of Action. — Subclause (I) does not authorize the assertion of a claim described in subclause (I) in any civil action or proceeding other than a counterclaim described in subclause (I).

(iii) No Damages. — An applicant shall not be entitled to damages in a civil action under clause (i) or a counterclaim under clause (ii).

(D) Forfeiture of 180-Day Exclusivity Period. —

(i) Definition of Forfeiture Event. — In this subparagraph, the term "forfeiture event", with respect to an application under this subsection, means the occurrence of any of the following:

(I) Failure to Market. — The first applicant fails to market the drug by the later of —

(aa) the earlier of the date that is —

(AA) 75 days after the date on which the approval of the application of the first applicant is made effective under subparagraph (B)(iii); or

(BB) 30 months after the date of submission of the application of the first applicant; or

(bb) with respect to the first applicant or any other applicant (which other applicant has received tentative approval), the date that is 75 days after the date as of which, as to each of the patents with respect to which the first applicant submitted and lawfully maintained a certification qualifying the first applicant for the 180-day exclusivity period under subparagraph (B)(iv), at least 1 of the following has occurred:

(AA) In an infringement action brought against that applicant with respect to the patent or in a declaratory judgment action brought by that applicant with respect to the patent, a court enters a final decision from which no appeal (other than a petition to the Supreme Court for a writ of certiorari) has been or can be taken that the patent is invalid or not infringed.

(BB) In an infringement action or a declaratory judgment action described in subitem (AA), a court signs a settlement order or consent decree that enters a final judgment that includes a finding that the patent is invalid or not infringed.

(CC) The patent information submitted under subsection (b) or (c) is withdrawn by the holder of the application approved under subsection (b).

(II) Withdrawal of Application. — The first applicant withdraws the application or the Secretary considers the application to have been withdrawn as a result of a determination by the Secretary that the application does not meet the requirements for approval under paragraph (4).

(III) Amendment of Certification. — The first applicant amends or withdraws the certification for all of the patents with respect to which that applicant submitted a certification qualifying the applicant for the 180-day exclusivity period.

(IV) Failure to Obtain Tentative Approval. — The first applicant fails to obtain tentative approval of the application within 30 months after the date on which the application is filed, unless the failure is caused by a change in or a review of the requirements for approval of the application imposed after the date on which the application is filed.

(V) Agreement with Another Applicant, the Listed Drug Application Holder, or a Patent Owner. — The first applicant enters into an agreement with another applicant under this subsection for the drug, the holder of the application for the listed drug, or an owner of the patent that is the subject of the certification under paragraph (2)(A)(vii)(IV), the Federal Trade Commission or the Attorney General files a complaint, and there is a final decision of the Federal Trade Commission or the court with regard to the complaint from which no appeal (other than a petition to the Supreme Court for a writ of certiorari) has been or can be taken that the agreement has violated the antitrust laws (as defined in section 1 of the Clayton Act (15 U.S.C. 12), except that the term includes section 5 of the Federal Trade Commission Act (15 U.S.C. 45) to the extent that that section applies to unfair methods of competition).

(VI) Expiration of All Patents. — All of the patents as to which the applicant submitted a certification qualifying it for the 180-day exclusivity period have expired.

(ii) Forfeiture. — The 180-day exclusivity period described in subparagraph (B)(iv) shall be forfeited by a first applicant if a forfeiture event occurs with respect to that first applicant.

(iii) Subsequent Applicant. — If all first applicants forfeit the 180-day exclusivity period under clause (ii) —

(I) approval of any application containing a certification described in paragraph (2)(A)(vii)(IV) shall be made effective in accordance with subparagraph (B)(iii); and

(II) no applicant shall be eligible for a 180-day exclusivity period.

(iv) Special Forfeiture Rule for Competitive Generic Therapy. — The 180-day exclusivity period described in subparagraph (B)(v) shall be forfeited by a first approved applicant if the applicant fails to market the competitive generic therapy within 75 days after the date on which the approval of the first approved applicant's application for the competitive generic therapy is made effective.

(E) If the Secretary decides to disapprove an application, the Secretary shall give the applicant notice of an opportunity for a hearing before the Secretary on the question of whether such application is approvable. If the applicant elects to accept the opportunity for hearing by written request within thirty days after such notice, such hearing shall commence not more than ninety days after the expiration of such thirty days unless the Secretary and the applicant otherwise agree. Any such hearing shall thereafter be conducted on an expedited basis and the Secretary's order thereon shall be issued within ninety days after the date fixed by the Secretary for filing final briefs.

(F) —

(i) If an application (other than an abbreviated new drug application) submitted under subsection (b) for a drug, no active ingredient (including any ester or salt of the active ingredient) of which has been approved in any other application under subsection (b), was approved during the period beginning January 1, 1982, and ending on the date of the enactment of this subsection, the Secretary may not make the approval of an application submitted under this subsection which refers to the drug for which the subsection (b) application was submitted effective before the expiration of ten years from the date of the approval of the application under subsection (b).

(ii) If an application submitted under subsection (b) for a drug, no active ingredient (including any ester or salt of the active ingredient) of which has been approved in any other application under subsection (b), is approved after the date of the enactment of this subsection, no application may be submitted under this subsection which refers to the drug for which the subsection (b) application was submitted before the expiration of five years from the date of the approval of the application under subsection (b), except that such an application may be submitted under this subsection after the expiration of four years from the date of the approval of the subsection (b) application if it contains a certification of patent invalidity or noninfringement described in subclause (IV) of paragraph (2)(A)(vii). The approval of such an application shall be made effective in accordance with subparagraph (B) except that, if an action for patent infringement is commenced during the one-year period beginning forty-eight months after the date of the approval of the subsection (b) application, the thirty-month period referred to in subparagraph (B)(iii) shall be extended by such amount of time (if any) which is required for seven and one-half years to have elapsed from the date of approval of the subsection (b) application.

(iii) If an application submitted under subsection (b) for a drug, which includes an active ingredient (including any ester or salt of the active ingredient) that has been approved in another application approved under subsection (b), is approved after the date of the enactment of this subsection, and if such application contains reports of new clinical investigations (other than bioavailability studies) essential to the approval of the application and conducted or sponsored by the applicant, the Secretary may not make the approval of an application submitted under this subsection for the conditions of approval of such drug in the subsection (b) application effective before the expiration of three years from the date of the approval of the application under subsection (b) for such drug.

(iv) If a supplement to an application approved under subsection (b) is approved after the date of the enactment of this subsection, and the supplement contains reports of new clinical investigations (other than bioavailability studies) essential to the approval of the supplement and conducted or sponsored by the person submitting the supplement, the Secretary may not make the approval of an application submitted under this subsection for a change approved in the supplement effective before the expiration of three years from the date of the approval of the supplement under subsection (b).

(v) If an application (or supplement to an application) submitted under subsection (b) for a drug, which includes an active ingredient (including any ester or salt of the active ingredient) that has been approved in another application under subsection (b), was approved during the period beginning January 1, 1982, and ending on the date of the enactment of this subsection, the Secretary may not make the approval of an application submitted under this subsection which refers to the drug for which the subsection (b) application was submitted or which refers to a change approved in a supplement to the subsection (b) application effective before the expiration of two years from the date of enactment of this subsection.

(6) If a drug approved under this subsection refers in its approved application to a drug the approval of which was withdrawn or suspended for grounds described in the first sentence of subsection (e) or was withdrawn or suspended under this paragraph or which, as determined by the Secretary, has been withdrawn from sale for safety or effectiveness reasons, the approval of the drug under this subsection shall be withdrawn or suspended —

(A) for the same period as the withdrawal or suspension under subsection (e) or this paragraph, or

(B) if the listed drug has been withdrawn from sale, for the period of withdrawal from sale or, if earlier, the period ending on the date the Secretary determines that the withdrawal from sale is not for safety or effectiveness reasons.

(7) —

(A) —

(i) Within sixty days of the date of the enactment of this subsection, the Secretary shall publish and make available to the public —

(I) a list in alphabetical order of the official and proprietary name of each drug which has been approved for safety and effectiveness under subsection (c) before the date of the enactment of this subsection;

(II) the date of approval if the drug is approved after 1981 and the number of the application which was approved; and

(III) whether in vitro or in vivo bioequivalence studies, or both such studies, are required for applications filed under this subsection which will refer to the drug published.

(ii) Every thirty days after the publication of the first list under clause (i) the Secretary shall revise the list to include each drug which has been approved for safety and effectiveness under subsection (c) or approved under this subsection during the thirty-day period.

(iii) When patent information submitted under subsection (b) or (c) respecting a drug included on the list is to be published by the Secretary, the Secretary shall, in revisions made under clause (ii), include such information for such drug.

(B) A drug approved for safety and effectiveness under subsection (c) or approved under this subsection shall, for purposes of this subsection, be considered to have been published under subparagraph (A) on the date of its approval or the date of enactment, whichever is later.

(C) If the approval of a drug was withdrawn or suspended for grounds described in the first sentence of subsection (e) or was withdrawn or suspended under paragraph (6) or if the Secretary determines that a drug has been withdrawn from sale for safety or effectiveness reasons, it may not be published in the list under subparagraph (A) or, if the withdrawal or suspension occurred after its publication in such list, it shall be immediately removed from such list —

(i) for the same period as the withdrawal or suspension under subsection (e) or paragraph (6), or

(ii) if the listed drug has been withdrawn from sale, for the period of withdrawal from sale or, if earlier, the period ending on the date the Secretary determines that the withdrawal from sale is not for safety or effectiveness reasons.

A notice of the removal shall be published in the Federal Register.

(8) For purposes of this subsection:

(A) —

(i) The term "bioavailability" means the rate and extent to which the active ingredient or therapeutic ingredient is absorbed from a drug and becomes available at the site of drug action.

(ii) For a drug that is not intended to be absorbed into the bloodstream, the Secretary may assess bioavailability by scientifically valid measurements intended to reflect the rate and extent to which the active ingredient or therapeutic ingredient becomes available at the site of drug action.

(B) A drug shall be considered to be bioequivalent to a listed drug if —

(i) the rate and extent of absorption of the drug do not show a significant difference from the rate and extent of absorption of the listed drug when administered at the same molar dose of the therapeutic ingredient under similar experimental conditions in either a single dose or multiple doses; or

(ii) the extent of absorption of the drug does not show a significant difference from the extent of absorption of the listed drug when administered at the same molar dose of the therapeutic ingredient under similar experimental conditions in either a single dose or multiple doses and the difference from the listed drug in the rate of absorption of the drug is intentional, is reflected in its proposed labeling, is not essential to the attainment of effective body drug concentrations on chronic use, and is considered medically insignificant for the drug.

(C) For a drug that is not intended to be absorbed into the bloodstream, the Secretary may establish alternative, scientifically valid methods to show bioequivalence if the alternative methods are expected to detect a significant difference between the drug and the listed drug in safety and therapeutic effect.

(9) The Secretary shall, with respect to each application submitted under this subsection, maintain a record of—

(A) the name of the applicant,

(B) the name of the drug covered by the application,

(C) the name of each person to whom the review of the chemistry of the application was assigned and the date of such assignment, and

(D) the name of each person to whom the bioequivalence review for such application was assigned and the date of such assignment.

The information the Secretary is required to maintain under this paragraph with respect to an application submitted under this subsection shall be made available to the public after the approval of such application.

(10) —

(A) If the proposed labeling of a drug that is the subject of an application under this subsection differs from the listed drug due to a labeling revision described under clause (i), the drug that is the subject of such application shall, notwithstanding any other provision of this Act, be eligible for approval and shall not be considered misbranded under section 502 if—

(i) the application is otherwise eligible for approval under this subsection but for expiration of patent, an exclusivity period, or of a delay in approval described in paragraph (5)(B)(iii), and a revision to the labeling of the listed drug has been approved by the Secretary within 60 days of such expiration;

(ii) the labeling revision described under clause (i) does not include a change to the 'Warnings' section of the labeling;

(iii) the sponsor of the application under this subsection agrees to submit revised labeling of the drug that is the subject of such application not later than 60 days after the notification of any changes to such labeling required by the Secretary; and

(iv) such application otherwise meets the applicable requirements for approval under this subsection.

(B) If, after a labeling revision described in subparagraph (A)(i), the Secretary determines that the continued presence in interstate commerce of the labeling of the listed drug (as in effect before the revision described in subparagraph (A)(i)) adversely impacts the safe use of the drug, no application under this subsection shall be eligible for approval with such labeling.

(11) —

(A) Subject to subparagraph (B), the Secretary shall prioritize the review of, and act within 8 months of the date of the submission of, an original abbreviated new drug application submitted for review under this subsection that is for a drug—

(i) for which there are not more than 3 approved drug products listed under paragraph (7) and for which there are no blocking patents and exclusivities; or

(ii) that has been included on the list under section 506E.

(B) To qualify for priority review under this paragraph, not later than 60 days prior to the submission of an application described in subparagraph (A) or that the Secretary may prioritize pursuant to subparagraph (D), the applicant shall provide complete, accurate information regarding facilities involved in manufacturing processes and testing of the drug that is the subject of the application, including facilities in corresponding Type II active pharmaceutical ingredients drug master files referenced in an application and sites or organizations involved in bioequivalence and clinical studies used to support the application, to enable the Secretary to make a determination regarding whether an inspection of a facility is necessary. Such information shall include the relevant (as determined by the Secretary) sections of such application, which shall be unchanged relative to the date of the submission of such application, except to the extent that a change is made to such information to exclude a facility that was not used to generate data to meet any application requirements for such submission and that is not the only facility intended to conduct one or more unit operations in commercial production. Information provided by an applicant under this subparagraph shall not be considered the submission of an application under this subsection.

(C) The Secretary may expedite an inspection or reinspection under section 704 of an establishment that proposes to manufacture a drug described in subparagraph (A).

(D) Nothing in this paragraph shall prevent the Secretary from prioritizing the review of other applications as the Secretary determines appropriate.

(12) The Secretary shall publish on the internet website of the Food and Drug Administration, and update at least once every 6 months, a list of all drugs approved under subsection (c) for which all patents and periods of exclusivity under this Act have expired and for which no application has been approved under this subsection.

(13) Upon the request of an applicant regarding one or more specified pending applications under this subsection, the Secretary shall, as appropriate, provide review status updates indicating the categorical status of the applications by each relevant review discipline.

(k) —

(1) In the case of any drug for which an approval of an application filed under subsection (b) or (j) is in effect, the applicant shall establish and maintain such records, and make such reports to the Secretary, of data relating to clinical experience and other data or information, received or otherwise obtained by such applicant with respect to such drug, as the Secretary may by general regulation, or by order with respect to such application, prescribe on the basis of a finding that such records and reports are necessary in order to enable the Secretary to determine, or facilitate a determination, whether there is or may be ground for invoking subsection (e) of this section. Regulations and orders issued under this subsection and under subsection (i) shall have due regard for the professional ethics of the medical profession and the interests of patients and shall provide, where the Secretary deems it to be appropriate, for the examination, upon request, by the persons to whom such regulations or orders are applicable, of similar information received or otherwise obtained by the Secretary.

(2) Every person required under this section to maintain records, and every person in charge or custody thereof, shall, upon request of an officer or employee designated by the Secretary, permit such officer or employee at all reasonable times to have access to and copy and verify such records.

(3) Active Postmarket Risk Identification. —

(A) Definition. — In this paragraph, the term "data" refers to information with respect to a drug approved under this section or under section 351 of the Public Health Service Act, including claims data, patient survey data, standardized analytic files that allow for the pooling and analysis of data from disparate data environments, and any other data deemed appropriate by the Secretary.

(B) Development of Postmarket Risk Identification and Analysis Methods. — The Secretary shall, not later than 2 years after the date of the enactment of the Food and Drug Administration Amendments Act of 2007, in collaboration with public, academic, and private entities —

(i) develop methods to obtain access to disparate data sources including the data sources specified in subparagraph (C);

(ii) develop validated methods for the establishment of a postmarket risk identification and analysis system to link and analyze safety data from multiple sources, with the goals of including, in aggregate —

(I) at least 25,000,000 patients by July 1, 2010; and

(II) at least 100,000,000 patients by July 1, 2012; and

(iii) convene a committee of experts, including individuals who are recognized in the field of protecting data privacy and security, to make recommendations to the Secretary on the development of tools and methods for the ethical and scientific uses for, and communication of, postmarketing data specified under subparagraph (C), including recommendations on the development of effective research methods for the study of drug safety questions.

(C) Establishment of the Postmarket Risk Identification and Analysis System. —

(i) In General. — The Secretary shall, not later than 1 year after the development of the risk identification and analysis methods under subparagraph (B), establish and maintain procedures —

(I) for risk identification and analysis based on electronic health data, in compliance with the regulations promulgated under section 264(c) of the Health Insurance Portability and Accountability Act of 1996, and in a manner that does not disclose individually identifiable health information in violation of paragraph (4)(B);

(II) for the reporting (in a standardized form) of data on all serious adverse drug experiences (as defined in section 505–1(b)) submitted to the Secretary under paragraph (1), and those adverse events submitted by patients, providers, and drug sponsors, when appropriate;

(III) to provide for active adverse event surveillance using the following data sources, as available:

(aa) Federal health-related electronic data (such as data from the Medicare program and the health systems of the Department of Veterans Affairs);

(bb) private sector health-related electronic data (such as pharmaceutical purchase data and health insurance claims data); and

(cc) other data as the Secretary deems necessary to create a robust system to identify adverse events and potential drug safety signals;

(IV) to identify certain trends and patterns with respect to data accessed by the system;

(V) to provide regular reports to the Secretary concerning adverse event trends, adverse event patterns, incidence and prevalence of adverse events, and other information the Secretary determines appropriate, which may include data on comparative national adverse event trends; and

(VI) to enable the program to export data in a form appropriate for further aggregation, statistical analysis, and reporting.

(ii) Timeliness of Reporting. — The procedures established under clause (i) shall ensure that such data are accessed, analyzed, and reported in a timely, routine, and systematic manner, taking into consideration the need for data completeness, coding, cleansing, and standardized analysis and transmission.

(iii) Private Sector Resources. — To ensure the establishment of the active postmarket risk identification and analysis system under this subsection not later than 1 year after the development of the risk identification and analysis methods under subparagraph (B), as required under clause (i), the Secretary may, on a temporary or permanent basis, implement systems or products developed by private entities.

(iv) Complementary Approaches. — To the extent the active postmarket risk identification and analysis system under this subsection is not sufficient to gather data and information relevant to a priority drug safety question, the Secretary shall develop, support, and participate in complementary approaches to gather and analyze such data and information, including —

(I) approaches that are complementary with respect to assessing the safety of use of a drug in domestic populations not included, or underrepresented, in the trials used to approve the drug (such as older people, people with comorbidities, pregnant women, or children); and

(II) existing approaches such as the Vaccine Adverse Event Reporting System and the Vaccine Safety Datalink or successor databases.

(v) Authority for Contracts. — The Secretary may enter into contracts with public and private entities to fulfill the requirements of this subparagraph.

(4) Advanced Analysis of Drug Safety Data. —

(A) Purpose. — The Secretary shall establish collaborations with public, academic, and private entities, which may include the Centers for Education and Research on Therapeutics under section 912 of the Public Health Service Act, to provide for advanced analysis of drug safety data described in paragraph (3)(C) and other information that is publicly available or is provided by the Secretary, in order to —

(i) improve the quality and efficiency of postmarket drug safety risk-benefit analysis;

(ii) provide the Secretary with routine access to outside expertise to study advanced drug safety questions; and

(iii) enhance the ability of the Secretary to make timely assessments based on drug safety data.

(B) Privacy. — Such analysis shall not disclose individually identifiable health information when presenting such drug safety signals and trends or when responding to inquiries regarding such drug safety signals and trends.

(C) Public Process for Priority Questions. — At least biannually, the Secretary shall seek recommendations from the Drug Safety and Risk Management Advisory Committee (or any successor committee) and from other advisory committees, as appropriate, to the Food and Drug Administration on —

(i) priority drug safety questions; and

(ii) mechanisms for answering such questions, including through —

(I) active risk identification under paragraph (3); and

(II) when such risk identification is not sufficient, postapproval studies and clinical trials under subsection (o)(3).

(D) Procedures for the Development of Drug Safety Collaborations. —

(i) In General. — Not later than 180 days after the date of the establishment of the active postmarket risk identification and analysis system under this subsection, the Secretary shall establish and implement procedures under which the Secretary may routinely contract with one or more qualified entities to —

(I) classify, analyze, or aggregate data described in paragraph (3)(C) and information that is publicly available or is provided by the Secretary;

(II) allow for prompt investigation of priority drug safety questions, including —

(aa) unresolved safety questions for drugs or classes of drugs; and

(bb) for a newly-approved drugs, safety signals from clinical trials used to approve the drug and other preapproval trials; rare, serious drug side effects; and the safety of use in domestic populations not included, or underrepresented, in the trials used to approve the drug (such as older people, people with comorbidities, pregnant women, or children);

(III) perform advanced research and analysis on identified drug safety risks;

(IV) focus postapproval studies and clinical trials under subsection (o)(3) more effectively on cases for which reports under paragraph (1) and other safety signal detection is not sufficient to resolve whether there is an elevated risk of a serious adverse event associated with the use of a drug; and

(V) carry out other activities as the Secretary deems necessary to carry out the purposes of this paragraph.

(ii) Request for Specific Methodology. — The procedures described in clause (i) shall permit the Secretary to request that a specific methodology be used by the qualified entity. The qualified entity shall work with the Secretary to finalize the methodology to be used.

(E) Use of Analyses. — The Secretary shall provide the analyses described in this paragraph, including the methods and results of such analyses, about a drug to the sponsor or sponsors of such drug.

(F) Qualified Entities. —

(i) In General. — The Secretary shall enter into contracts with a sufficient number of qualified entities to develop and provide information to the Secretary in a timely manner.

(ii) Qualification. — The Secretary shall enter into a contract with an entity under clause (i) only if the Secretary determines that the entity has a significant presence in the United States and has one or more of the following qualifications:

(I) The research, statistical, epidemiologic, or clinical capability and expertise to conduct and complete the activities under this paragraph, including the capability and expertise to provide the Secretary de-identified data consistent with the requirements of this subsection.

(II) An information technology infrastructure in place to support electronic data and operational standards to provide security for such data.

(III) Experience with, and expertise on, the development of drug safety and effectiveness research using electronic population data.

(IV) An understanding of drug development or risk/benefit balancing in a clinical setting.

(V) Other expertise which the Secretary deems necessary to fulfill the activities under this paragraph.

(G) Contract Requirements. — Each contract with a qualified entity under subparagraph (F)(i) shall contain the following requirements:

(i) Ensuring Privacy. — The qualified entity shall ensure that the entity will not use data under this subsection in a manner that —

(I) violates the regulations promulgated under section 264(c) of the Health Insurance Portability and Accountability Act of 1996;

(II) violates sections 552 or 552a of title 5, United States Code, with regard to the privacy of individually-identifiable beneficiary health information; or

(III) discloses individually identifiable health information when presenting drug safety signals and trends or when responding to inquiries regarding drug safety signals and trends.

Nothing in this clause prohibits lawful disclosure for other purposes.

(ii) Component of Another Organization. — If a qualified entity is a component of another organization —

(I) the qualified entity shall establish appropriate security measures to maintain the confidentiality and privacy of such data; and

(II) the entity shall not make an unauthorized disclosure of such data to the other components of the organization in breach of such confidentiality and privacy requirement.

(iii) Termination or Nonrenewal. — If a contract with a qualified entity under this subparagraph is terminated or not renewed, the following requirements shall apply:

(I) Confidentiality And privacy protections. — The entity shall continue to comply with the confidentiality and privacy requirements under this paragraph with respect to all data disclosed to the entity.

(II) Disposition of Data. — The entity shall return any data disclosed to such entity under this subsection to which it would not otherwise have access or, if returning the data is not practicable, destroy the data.

(H) Competitive Procedures. — The Secretary shall use competitive procedures (as defined in section 4(5) of the Federal Procurement Policy Act) to enter into contracts under subparagraph (G).

(I) Review of Contract in the Event of a Merger or Acquisition. — The Secretary shall review the contract with a qualified entity under this paragraph in the event of a merger or acquisition of the entity in order to ensure that the requirements under this paragraph will continue to be met.

(J) Coordination. — In carrying out this paragraph, the Secretary shall provide for appropriate communications to the public, scientific, public health, and medical communities, and other key stakeholders, and to the extent practicable shall coordinate with the activities of private entities, professional associations, or other entities that may have sources of drug safety data.

(5) The Secretary shall —

(A) conduct regular (Per Sec. 3075 of the 21st Century Cures Act) screenings of the Adverse Event Reporting System database and post a quarterly report on the Adverse Event Reporting System Web site of any new safety information or potential signal of a serious risk identified by Adverse Event Reporting System within the last quarter; and

(B) on an annual basis, review the entire backlog of postmarket safety commitments to determine which commitments require revision or should be eliminated, report to the Congress on these determinations, and assign start dates and estimated completion dates for such commitments; and

(C) make available on the Internet website of the Food and Drug Administration—

(i) guidelines, developed with input from experts qualified by scientific training and experience to evaluate the safety and effectiveness of drugs, that detail best practices for drug safety surveillance using the Adverse Event Reporting System; and

(ii) criteria for public posting of adverse event signals.

(l) —

(1) Safety and effectiveness data and information which has been submitted in an application under subsection (b) for a drug and which has not previously been disclosed to the public shall be made available to the public, upon request, unless extraordinary circumstances are shown —

(A) if no work is being or will be undertaken to have the application approved,

(B) if the Secretary has determined that the application is not approvable and all legal appeals have been exhausted,

(C) if approval of the application under subsection (c) is withdrawn and all legal appeals have been exhausted,

(D) if the Secretary has determined that such drug is not a new drug, or

(E) upon the effective date of the approval of the first application under subsection (j) which refers to such drug or upon the date upon which the approval of an application under subsection (j) which refers to such drug could be made effective if such an application had been submitted.

(2) Action Package for Approval. —

(A) Action Package. — The Secretary shall publish the action package for approval of an application under subsection (b) or section 351 of the Public Health Service Act on the Internet Web site of the Food and Drug Administration —

(i) not later than 30 days after the date of approval of such application for a drug no active ingredient (including any ester or salt of the active ingredient) of which has been approved in any other application under this section or section 351 of the Public Health Service Act; and

(ii) not later than 30 days after the third request for such action package for approval received under section 552 of title 5, United States Code, for any other drug.

(B) Immediate Publication of Summary Review. — Notwithstanding subparagraph (A), the Secretary shall publish, on the Internet Web site of the Food and Drug Administration, the materials described in subparagraph (C)(iv) not later than 48 hours after the date of approval of the drug, except where such materials require redaction by the Secretary.

(C) Contents. — An action package for approval of an application under subparagraph (A) shall be dated and shall include the following:

(i) Documents generated by the Food and Drug Administration related to review of the application.

(ii) Documents pertaining to the format and content of the application generated during drug development.

(iii) Labeling submitted by the applicant.

(iv) A summary review that documents conclusions from all reviewing disciplines about the drug, noting any critical issues and disagreements with the applicant and within the review team and how they were resolved, recommendations for action, and an explanation of any nonconcurrence with review conclusions.

(v) The Division Director and Office Director's decision document which includes —

(I) a brief statement of concurrence with the summary review;

(II) a separate review or addendum to the review if disagreeing with the summary review; and

(III) a separate review or addendum to the review to add further analysis.

(vi) Identification by name of each officer or employee of the Food and Drug Administration who—

(I) participated in the decision to approve the application; and

(II) consents to have his or her name included in the package.

(D) Review. — A scientific review of an application is considered the work of the reviewer and shall not be altered by management or the reviewer once final.

(E) Confidential Information. — This paragraph does not authorize the disclosure of any trade secret, confidential commercial or financial information, or other matter listed in section 552(b) of Title 5, United States Code.

(m) For purposes of this section, the term "patent" means a patent issued by the United States Patent and Trademark Office.

(n) —

(1) For the purpose of providing expert scientific advice and recommendations to the Secretary regarding a clinical investigation of a drug or the approval for marketing of a drug under section 505 or section 351 of the Public Health Service Act, the Secretary shall establish panels of experts or use panels of experts established before the date of enactment of the Food and Drug Administration Modernization Act of 1997 [November 21, 1997 — Ed.], or both.

(2) The Secretary may delegate the appointment and oversight authority granted under section 1004 to a director of a center or successor entity within the Food and Drug Administration.

(3) The Secretary shall make appointments to each panel established under paragraph (1) so that each panel shall consist of —

(A) members who are qualified by training and experience to evaluate the safety and effectiveness of the drugs to be referred to the panel and who, to the extent feasible, possess skill and experience in the development, manufacture, or utilization of such drugs;

(B) members with diverse expertise in such fields as clinical and administrative medicine, pharmacy, pharmacology, pharmacoeconomics, biological and physical sciences, and other related professions;

(C) a representative of consumer interests, and a representative of interests of the drug manufacturing industry not directly affected by the matter to be brought before the panel; and

(D) two or more members who are specialists or have other expertise in the particular disease or condition for which the drug under review is proposed to be indicated.

Scientific, trade, and consumer organizations shall be afforded an opportunity to nominate individuals for appointment to the panels. No individual who is in the regular full-time employ of the United States and engaged in the administration of thisAct may be a voting member of any panel. The Secretary shall designate one of the members of each panel to serve as chairman thereof.

(4) The Secretary shall, as appropriate, provide education and training to each new panel member before such member participates in a panel's activities, including education regarding requirements under this Act and related regulations of the Secretary, and the administrative processes and procedures related to panel meetings.

(5) Panel members (other than officers or employees of the United States), while attending meetings or conferences of a panel or otherwise engaged in its business, shall be entitled to receive compensation for each day so engaged, including traveltime, at rates to be fixed by the Secretary, but not to exceed the daily equivalent of the rate in effect for positions classified above grade Gs-15 of the General Schedule. While serving away from their homes or regular places of business, panel members may be allowed travel expenses (including per diem in lieu of subsistence) as authorized by section 5703 of title 5, United States Code, for persons in the Government service employed intermittently.

(6) The Secretary shall ensure that scientific advisory panels meet regularly and at appropriate intervals so that any matter to be reviewed by such a panel can be presented to the panel not more than 60 days after the matter is ready for such review. Meetings of the panel may be held using electronic communication to convene the meetings.

(7) Within 90 days after a scientific advisory panel makes recommendations on any matter under its review, the Food and Drug Administration official responsible for the matter shall review the conclusions and recommendations of the panel, and notify the affected persons of the final decision on the matter, or of the reasons that no such decision has been reached. Each such final decision shall be documented including the rationale for the decision.

(o) Postmarket Studies and Clinical Trials; Labeling. —

(1) In General. — A responsible person may not introduce or deliver for introduction into interstate commerce the new drug involved if the person is in violation of a requirement established under paragraph (3) or (4) with respect to the drug.

(2) Definitions. — For purposes of this subsection:

(A) Responsible Person. — The term "responsible person" means a person who —

(i) has submitted to the Secretary a covered application that is pending; or

(ii) is the holder of an approved covered application.

(B) Covered Application. — The term "covered application" means —

(i) an application under subsection (b) for a drug that is subject to section 503(b); and

(ii) an application under section 351 of the Public Health Service Act.

(C) New Safety Information; Serious Risk. — The terms "new safety information", "serious risk", and "signal of a serious risk" have the meanings given such terms in section 505–1(b).

(3) Studies and Clinical Trials. —

(A) In General. — For any or all of the purposes specified in subparagraph (B), the Secretary may, subject to subparagraph (D), require a responsible person for a drug to conduct a postapproval study or studies of the drug, or a postapproval clinical trial or trials of the drug, on the basis of scientific data deemed appropriate by the Secretary, including information regarding chemically-related or pharmacologically-related drugs.

(B) Purposes of Study or Clinical Trial. — The purposes referred to in this subparagraph with respect to a postapproval study or postapproval clinical trial are the following:

(i) To assess a known serious risk related to the use of the drug involved.

(ii) To assess signals of serious risk related to the use of the drug.

(iii) To identify an unexpected serious risk when available data indicates the potential for a serious risk.

(C) Establishment of Requirement After Approval of Covered Application. — The Secretary may require a postapproval study or studies or postapproval clinical trial or trials for a drug for which an approved covered application is in effect as of the date on which the Secretary seeks to establish such requirement only if the Secretary becomes aware of new safety information.

(D) Determination by Secretary. —

(i) Postapproval Studies. — The Secretary may not require the responsible person to conduct a study under this paragraph, unless the Secretary makes a determination that the reports under subsection (k)(1) and the active postmarket risk identification and analysis system as available under subsection (k)(3) will not be sufficient to meet the purposes set forth in subparagraph (B).

(ii) Postapparoval Clinical Trials. — The Secretary may not require the responsible person to conduct a clinical trial under this paragraph, unless the Secretary makes a determination that a postapproval study or studies will not be sufficient to meet the purposes set forth in subparagraph (B).

(E) Notification; Timetables; Periodic Reports. —

(i) Notification. — The Secretary shall notify the responsible person regarding a requirement under this paragraph to conduct a postapproval study or clinical trial by the target dates for communication of feedback from the review team to the responsible person regarding proposed labeling and postmarketing study commitments as set forth in the letters described in section 101(c) of the Food and Drug Administration Amendments Act of 2007.

(ii) Timetable; Periodic Reports. — For each study or clinical trial required to be conducted under this paragraph, the Secretary shall require that the responsible person submit a timetable for completion of the study or clinical trial. With respect to each study required to be conducted under this paragraph or otherwise undertaken by the responsible person to investigate a safety issue, the Secretary shall require the responsible person to periodically report to the Secretary on the status of such study including whether any difficulties in completing the study have been encountered. With respect to each clinical trial required to be conducted under this paragraph or otherwise undertaken by the responsible person to investigate a safety issue, the Secretary shall require the responsible person to periodically report to the Secretary on the status of such clinical trial including whether enrollment has begun, the number of participants enrolled, the expected completion date, whether any difficulties completing the clinical trial have been encountered, and registration information with respect to the requirements under section 402(j) of the Public Health Service Act. If the responsible person fails to comply with such timetable or violates any other requirement of this subparagraph, the responsible person shall be considered in violation of this subsection, unless the responsible person demonstrates good cause for such noncompliance or such other violation. The Secretary shall determine what constitutes good cause under the preceding sentence.

(F) Dispute Resolution. — The responsible person may appeal a requirement to conduct a study or clinical trial under this paragraph using dispute resolution procedures established by the Secretary in regulation and guidance.

(4) Safety Labeling Changes Requested By Secretary. —

(A) New Safety Information. — If the Secretary becomes aware of new safety information that the Secretary believes should be included in the labeling of the drug, the Secretary shall promptly notify the responsible person or, if the same drug approved under section 505(b) is not currently marketed, the holder of an approved application under 505(j).

(B) Response to Notification. — Following notification pursuant to subparagraph (A), the responsible person or the holder of the approved application under section 505(j) shall within 30 days —

(i) submit a supplement proposing changes to the approved labeling to reflect the new safety information, including changes to boxed warnings, contraindications, warnings, precautions, or adverse reactions; or

(ii) notify the Secretary that the responsible person or the holder of the approved application under section 505(j) does not believe a labeling change is warranted and submit a statement detailing the reasons why such a change is not warranted.

(C) Review. — Upon receipt of such supplement, the Secretary shall promptly review and act upon such supplement. If the Secretary disagrees with the proposed changes in the supplement or with the statement setting forth the reasons why no labeling change is necessary, the Secretary shall initiate discussions to reach agreement on whether the labeling for the drug should be modified to reflect the new safety information, and if so, the contents of such labeling changes.

(D) Discussions. — Such discussions shall not extend for more than 30 days after the response to the notification under subparagraph (B), unless the Secretary determines an extension of such discussion period is warranted.

(E) Order. — Within 15 days of the conclusion of the discussions under subparagraph (D), the Secretary may issue an order directing the responsible person or the holder of the approved application under section 505(j) to make such a labeling change as the Secretary deems appropriate to address the new safety information. Within 15 days of such an order, the responsible person or the holder of the approved application under section 505(j) shall submit a supplement containing the labeling change.

(F) Dispute Resolution. — Within 5 days of receiving an order under subparagraph (E), the responsible person or the holder of the approved application under section 505(j) may appeal using dispute resolution procedures established by the Secretary in regulation and guidance.

(G) Violation. — If the responsible person or the holder of the approved application under section 505(j) has not submitted a supplement within 15 days of the date of such order under subparagraph (E), and there is no appeal or dispute resolution proceeding pending, the responsible person or holder shall be considered to be in violation of this subsection. If at the conclusion of any dispute resolution procedures the Secretary determines that a supplement must be submitted and such a supplement is not submitted within 15 days of the date of that determination, the responsible person or holder shall be in violation of this subsection.

(H) Public Health Threat. — Notwithstanding subparagraphs (A) through (F), if the Secretary concludes that such a labeling change is necessary to protect the public health, the Secretary may accelerate the timelines in such subparagraphs.

(I) Rule of Construction. — This paragraph shall not be construed to affect the responsibility of the responsible person or the holder of the approved application under section 505(j) to maintain its label in accordance with existing requirements, including subpart B of part 201 and sections 314.70 and 601.12 of title 21, Code of Federal Regulations (or any successor regulations).

(5) Non-Delegation. — Determinations by the Secretary under this subsection for a drug shall be made by individuals at or above the level of individuals empowered to approve a drug (such as division directors within the Center for Drug Evaluation and Research).

(p) Risk Evaluation and Mitigation Strategy. —

(1) In General. — A person may not introduce or deliver for introduction into interstate commerce a new drug if —

(A)(i) the application for such drug is approved under subsection (b) or (j) and is subject to section 503(b); or

(ii) the application for such drug is approved under section 351 of the Public Health Service Act; and

(B) a risk evaluation and mitigation strategy is required under section 505–1 with respect to the drug and the person fails to maintain compliance with the requirements of the approved strategy or with other requirements under section 505–1, including requirements regarding assessments of approved strategies.

(2) Certain Postmarket Studies. — The failure to conduct a postmarket study under section 506, subpart H of part 314, or subpart E of part 601 of title 21, Code of Federal Regulations (or any successor regulations), is deemed to be a violation of paragraph (1).

(q) Petitions and Civil Actions Regarding Approval of Certain Applications. —

(1) In General. —

(A) Determination. — The Secretary shall not delay approval of a pending application submitted under subsection (b)(2) or (j) of this section or section 351(k) of the Public Health Service Act because of any request to take any form of action relating to the application, either before or during consideration of the request, unless —

(i) the request is in writing and is a petition submitted to the Secretary pursuant to section 10.30 or 10.35 of title 21, Code of Federal Regulations (or any successor regulations); and

(ii) the Secretary determines, upon reviewing the petition, that a delay is necessary to protect the public health.

(B) Notification. — If the Secretary determines under subparagraph (A) that a delay is necessary with respect to an application, the Secretary shall provide to the applicant, not later than 30 days after making such determination, the following information:

(i) Notification of the fact that a determination under subparagraph (A) has been made.

(ii) If applicable, any clarification or additional data that the applicant should submit to the docket on the petition to allow the Secretary to review the petition promptly.

(iii) A brief summary of the specific substantive issues raised in the petition which form the basis of the determination.

(C) Format. — The information described in subparagraph (B) shall be conveyed via either, at the discretion of the Secretary —

(i) a document; or

(ii) a meeting with the applicant involved.

(D) Public Disclosure. — Any information conveyed by the Secretary under subparagraph (C) shall be considered part of the application and shall be subject to the disclosure requirements applicable to information in such application.

(E) Denial Based on Intent to Delay. — If the Secretary determines that a petition or a supplement to the petition was submitted with the primary purpose of delaying the approval of an application and the petition does not on its face raise valid scientific or regulatory issues, the Secretary may deny the petition at any point based on such determination. The Secretary may issue guidance to describe the factors that will be used to determine under this subparagraph whether a petition is submitted with the primary purpose of delaying the approval of an application.

(F) Final Agency Action. — The Secretary shall take final agency action on a petition not later than 150 days after the date on which the petition is submitted. The Secretary shall not extend such period for any reason, including —

(i) any determination made under subparagraph (A);

(ii) the submission of comments relating to the petition or supplemental information supplied by the petitioner; or

(iii) the consent of the petitioner.

(G) Extension of 30-Month Period. — If the filing of an application resulted in first-applicant status under subsection (j)(5)(D)(i)(IV) and approval of the application was delayed because of a petition, the 30-month period under such subsection is deemed to be extended by a period of time equal to the period beginning on the date on which the Secretary received the petition and ending on the date of final agency action on the petition (inclusive of such beginning and ending dates), without regard to whether the Secretary grants, in whole or in part, or denies, in whole or in part, the petition.

(H) Certification. — The Secretary shall not consider a petition for review unless the party submitting such petition does so in written form and the subject document is signed and contains the following certification: 'I certify that, to my best knowledge and belief: (a) this petition includes all information and views upon which the petition relies; (b) this petition includes representative data and/ or information known to the petitioner which are unfavorable to the petition; and (c) I have taken reasonable steps to ensure that any representative data and/or information which are unfavorable to the petition were disclosed to me. I further certify that the information upon which I have based the action requested herein first became known to the party on whose behalf this petition is submitted on or about the following date: —. If I received or expect to receive payments, including cash and other forms of consideration, to file this information or its contents, I received or expect to receive those payments from the following persons or organizations: — . I verify under penalty of perjury that the foregoing is true and correct as of the date of the submission of this petition.', with the date on which such information first became known to such party and the names of such persons or organizations inserted in the first and second blank space, respectively.

(I) Verification. — The Secretary shall not accept for review any supplemental information or comments on a petition unless the party submitting such information or comments does so in written form and the subject document is signed and contains the following verification: 'I certify that, to my best knowledge and belief: (a) I have not intentionally delayed submission of this document or its contents; and (b) the information upon which I have based the action requested herein first became known to me on or about ________________. If I received or expect to receive payments, including cash and other forms of consideration, to file this information or its contents, I received or expect to receive those payments from the following persons or organizations:__________________. I verify under penalty of perjury that the foregoing is true and correct as of the date of the submission of this petition.', with the date on which such information first became known to the party and the names of such persons or organizations inserted in the first and second blank space, respectively.

(2) Exhaustion of Administrative Remedies. —

(A) Final Agency Action within 150 Days. — The Secretary shall be considered to have taken final agency action on a petition if—

(i) during the 150-day period referred to in paragraph (1)(F), the Secretary makes a final decision within the meaning of section 10.45(d) of title 21, Code of Federal Regulations (or any successor regulation); or

(ii) such period expires without the Secretary having made such a final decision.

(B) Dismissal of Certain Civil Actions. — If a civil action is filed against the Secretary with respect to any issue raised in the petition before the Secretary has taken final agency action on the petition within the meaning of subparagraph (A), the court shall dismiss without prejudice the action for failure to exhaust administrative remedies.

(C) Administrative Record. — For purposes of judicial review related to the approval of an application for which a petition under paragraph (1) was submitted, the administrative record regarding any issue raised by the petition shall include —

(i) the petition filed under paragraph (1) and any supplements and comments thereto:

(ii) the Secretary's response to such petition, if issued; and

(iii) other information, as designated by the Secretary, related to the Secretary's determinations regarding the issues raised in such petition, as long as the information was considered by the agency no later than the date of final agency action as defined under subparagraph (2)(A), and regardless of whether the Secretary responded to the petition at or before the approval of the application at issue in the petition.

(3) Annual Report on Delays in Approvals Per Petitions. — The Secretary shall annually submit to the Congress a report that specifies —

(A) the number of applications that were approved during the preceding 12-month period;

(B) the number of such applications whose effective dates were delayed by petitions referred to in paragraph (1) during such period;

(C) the number of days by which such applications were so delayed; and

(D) the number of such petitions that were submitted during such period.

(4) Exceptions. —

(A) This subsection does not apply to —

(i) a petition that relates solely to the timing of the approval of an application pursuant to subsection (j)(5)(B)(iv); or

(ii) a petition that is made by the sponsor of an application and that seeks only to have the Secretary take or refrain from taking any form of action with respect to that application.

(B) Paragraph (2) does not apply to a petition addressing issues concerning an application submitted pursuant to section 351(k) of the Public Health Service Act.

(5) Definitions. —

(A) Application. — For purposes of this subsection, the term "application" means an application submitted under subsection (b)(2) or (j) of this section or section 351(k) of the Public Health Service Act.

(B) Petition. — For purposes of this subsection, other than paragraph (1)(A)(i), the term "petition" means a request described in paragraph (1)(A)(i).

(r) Postmarket Drug Safety Information for Patients and Providers. —

(1) Establishment. — Not later than 1 year after the date of the enactment of the Food and Drug Administration Amendment Act of 2007, the Secretary shall improve the transparency of information about drugs and allow patients and health care providers better access to information about drugs by developing and maintaining an Internet Web site that —

(A) provides links to drug safety information listed in paragraph (2) for prescription drugs that are approved under this section or licensed under section 351 of the Public Health Service Act; and

(B) improves communication of drug safety information to patients and providers.

(2) Internet Web site. — The Secretary shall carry out paragraph (1) by —

(A) developing and maintaining a accessible, consolidated Internet Web site with easily searchable drug safety information, including the information found on United States Government Internet Web sites, such as the United States National Library of Medicine's Daily Med and Medline Plus Web sites, in addition to other such Web sites maintained by the Secretary;

(B) ensuring that the information provided on the Internet Web site is comprehensive and includes, when available and appropriate —

(i) patient labeling and patient packaging inserts;

(ii) a link to a list of each drug, whether approved under this section or licensed under such section 351, for which a Medication Guide, as provided for under part 208 of title 21, Code of Federal Regulations (or any successor regulations), is required;

(iii) a link to the registry and results data bank provided for under subsections (i) and (j) of section 402 of the Public Health Services Act;

(iv) the most recent safety information and alerts issued by the Food and Drug Administration for drugs approved by the Secretary under this section, such as product recalls, warning letters, and import alerts;

(v) publicly available information about implemented RiskMAPs and risk evaluation and mitigation strategies under subsection (o);

(vi) guidance documents and regulations related to drug safety; and

(vii) other material determined appropriate by the Secretary;

(C) providing access to summaries of the assessed and aggregated data collected from the active surveillance infrastructure under subsection (k)(3) to provide information of known and serious side-effects for drugs approved under this section or licensed under such section 351;

(D) preparing and making publicly available on the Internet website established under paragraph (1) best practices for drug safety surveillance activities for drugs approved under this section or section 351 of the Public Health Service Act;

(E) enabling patients, providers, and drug sponsors to submit adverse event reports through the Internet Web site;

(F) providing educational materials for patients and providers about the appropriate means of disposing of expired, damaged, or unusable medications; and

(G) supporting initiatives that the Secretary determines to be useful to fulfill the purposes of the Internet Web site.

(3) Posting of Drug Labeling. — The Secretary shall post on the Internet Web site established under paragraph (1) the approved professional labeling and any required patient labeling of a drug approved under this section or licensed under such section 351 not later than 21 days after the date the drug is approved or licensed, including in a supplemental application with respect to a labeling change.

(4) Private Sector Resources. — To ensure development of the Internet Web site by the date described in paragraph (1), the Secretary may, on a temporary or permanent basis, implement systems or products developed by private entities.

(5) Authority for Contracts. — The Secretary may enter into contracts with public and private entities to fulfill the requirements of this subsection.

(6) Review. — The Advisory Committee on Risk Communication under section 567 shall, on a regular basis, perform a comprehensive review and evaluation of the types of risk communication information provided on the Internet Web site established under paragraph (1) and, through other means, shall identify, clarify, and define the purposes and types of information available to facilitate the efficient flow of information to patients and providers, and shall recommend ways for the Food and Drug Administration to work with outside entities to help facilitate the dispensing of risk communication information to patients and providers.

(s) Referral to Advisory Committee. — Prior to the approval of a drug no active ingredient (including any ester or salt of the active ingredient) of which has been approved in any other application under this section or section 351 of the Public Health Service Act, the Secretary shall —

(1) refer such drug to a Food and Drug Administration advisory committee for review at a meeting of such advisory committee; or

(2) if the Secretary does not refer such a drug to a Food and Drug Administration advisory committee prior to the approval of the drug, provide in the action letter on the application for the drug a summary of the reasons why the Secretary did not refer the drug to an advisory committee prior to approval.

(t) Database for Authorized Generic Drugs. —

(1) In General. —

(A) Publication. — The Commissioner shall —

(i) not later than 9 months after the date of the enactment of the Food and Drug Administration Amendments Act of 2007, publish a complete list on the Internet Web site of the Food and Drug Administration of all authorized generic drugs (including drug trade name, brand company manufacturer, and the date the authorized generic drug entered the market); and

(ii) update the list quarterly to include each authorized generic drug included in an annual report submitted to the Secretary by the sponsor of a listed drug during the preceding 3-month period.

(B) Notification. — The Commissioner shall notify relevant Federal agencies, including the Centers for Medicare & Medicaid Services and the Federal Trade Commission, when the Commissioner first publishes the information described in subparagraph (A) that the information has been published and that the information will be updated quarterly.

(2) Inclusion. — The Commissioner shall include in the list described in paragraph (1) each authorized generic drug included in an annual report submitted to the Secretary by the sponsor of a listed drug after January 1, 1999.

(3) Authorized Generic Drug. — In this section, the term "authorized generic drug" means a listed drug (as that term is used in subsection (j)) that —

(A) has been approved under subsection (c); and

(B) is marketed, sold, or distributed directly or indirectly to retail class of trade under a different labeling, packaging (other than repackaging as the listed drug in blister packs, unit doses, or similar packaging for use in institutions), product code, labeler code, trade name, or trademark than the listed drug.

(u) Certain Drugs Containing Single Enantiomers. —

(1) In General. — For purposes of subsections (c)(3)(E)(ii) and (j)(5)(F)(ii), if an application is submitted under subsection (b) for a non-racemic drug containing as an active ingredient (including any ester or salt of the active ingredient) a single enantiomer that is contained in a racemic drug approved in another application under subsection (b), the applicant may, in the application for such non-racemic drug, elect to have the single enantiomer not be considered the same active ingredient as that contained in the approved racemic drug, if —

(A) —

(i) the single enantiomer has not been previously approved except in the approved racemic drug; and

(ii) the application submitted under subsection (b) for such non-racemic drug —

(I) includes full reports of new clinical investigations (other than bioavailability studies) — (aa) necessary for the approval of the application under subsections (c) and (d); and (bb) conducted or sponsored by the applicant; and

(II) does not rely on any clinical investigations that are part of an application submitted under subsection (b) for approval of the approved racemic drug; and

(B) the application submitted under subsection (b) for such non-racemic drug is not submitted for approval of a condition of use —

(i) in a therapeutic category in which the approved racemic drug has been approved; or

(ii) for which any other enantiomer of the racemic drug has been approved.

(2) Limitation. —

(A) No Approval in Certain Therapeutic Categories. — Until the date that is 10 years after the date of approval of a non-racemic drug described in paragraph (1) and with respect to which the applicant has made the election provided for by such paragraph, the Secretary shall not approve such non-racemic drug for any condition of use in the therapeutic category in which the racemic drug has been approved.

(B) Labeling. — If applicable, the labeling of a nonracemic drug described in paragraph (1) and with respect to which the applicant has made the election provided for by such paragraph shall include a statement that the non-racemic drug is not approved, and has not been shown to be safe and effective, for any condition of use of the racemic drug.

(3) Definition. —

(A) In General. — For purposes of this subsection, the term "therapeutic category" means a therapeutic category identified in the list developed by the United States Pharmacopeia pursuant to section 1860D–4(b)(3)(C)(ii) of the Social Security Act and as in effect on the date of the enactment of this subsection.

(B) Publication By Secretary. — The Secretary shall publish the list described in subparagraph (A) and may amend such list by regulation.

(4) Availability. — The election referred to in paragraph (1) may be made only in an application that is submitted to the Secretary after the date of the enactment of this subsection and before October 1, ~~2017.~~ <u>2022.</u>

(v) Antibiotic Drugs Submitted Before November 21, 1997. —

(1) Antibiotic Drugs Approved Before November 21, 1997. —

(A) In General. — Notwithstanding any provision of the Food and Drug Administration Modernization Act of 1997 or any other provision of law, a sponsor of a drug that is the subject of an application described in subparagraph (B)(i) shall be eligible for, with respect to the drug, the 3-year exclusivity period referred to under clauses (iii) and (iv) of subsection (c)(3)(E) and under clauses (iii) and (iv) of subsection (j)(5)(F), subject to the requirements of such clauses, as applicable.

(B) Application; Antibiotic Drug Described. —

(i) Application. — An application described in this clause is an application for marketing submitted under this section after the date of the enactment of this subsection in which the drug that is the subject of the application contains an antibiotic drug described in clause (ii).

(ii) Antibiotic Drug. — An antibiotic drug described in this clause is an antibiotic drug that was the subject of an application approved by the Secretary under section 507 of this Act (as in effect before November 21, 1997).

(2) Antibiotic Drugs Submitted Before November 21, 1997, But Not Approved. —

(A) In General. — Notwithstanding any provision of the Food and Drug Administration Modernization Act of 1997 or any other provision of law, a sponsor of a drug that is the subject of an application described in subparagraph (B)(i) may elect to be eligible for, with respect to the drug —

(i) —

(I) the 3-year exclusivity period referred to under clauses (iii) and (iv) of subsection (c)(3)(E) and under clauses (iii) and (iv) of subsection (j)(5)(F), subject to the requirements of such clauses, as applicable; and

(II) the 5-year exclusivity period referred to under clause (ii) of subsection (c)(3)(E) and under clause (ii) of subsection (j)(5)(F), subject to the requirements of such clauses, as applicable; or

(ii) a patent term extension under section 156 of title 35, United States Code, subject to the requirements of such section.

(B) Application; Antibiotic Drug Described. —

(i) Application. — An application described in this clause is an application for marketing submitted under this section after the date of the enactment of this subsection in which the drug that is the subject of the application contains an antibiotic drug described in clause (ii).

(ii) Antibiotic Drug. — An antibiotic drug described in this clause is an antibiotic drug that was the subject of 1 or more applications received by the Secretary under section 507 of this Act (as in effect before November 21, 1997), none of which was approved by the Secretary under such section.

(3) Limitations. —

(A) Exclusivities and Extensions. — Paragraphs (1)(A) and (2)(A) shall not be construed to entitle a drug that is the subject of an approved application described in subparagraphs (1)(B)(i) or (2)(B)(i), as applicable, to any market exclusivities or patent extensions other than those exclusivities or extensions described in paragraph (1)(A) or (2)(A).

(B) Conditions of Use. — Paragraphs (1)(A) and (2)(A)(i) shall not apply to any condition of use for which the drug referred to in subparagraph (1)(B)(i) or (2)(B)(i), as applicable, was approved before the date of the enactment of this subsection.

(4) Application of Certain Provisions. — Notwithstanding section 125, or any other provision, of the Food and Drug Administration Modernization Act of 1997, or any other provision of law, and subject to the limitations in paragraphs (1), (2), and (3), the provisions of the Drug Price Competition and Patent Term Restoration Act of 1984 shall apply to any drug subject to paragraph (1) or any drug with respect to which an election is made under paragraph (2)(A).

(w) Deadline for Determination on Certain Petitions. — The Secretary shall issue a final, substantive determination on a petition submitted pursuant to subsection (b) of section 314.161 of title 21, Code of Federal Regulations (or any successor regulations), no later than 270 days after the date the petition is submitted.

(x) Date of Approval in the Case of Recommended Controls Under the CSA. —

(1) In General. — In the case of an application under subsection (b) with respect to a drug for which the Secretary provides notice to the sponsor that the Secretary intends to issue a scientific and medical evaluation and recommend controls under the Controlled Substances Act, approval of such application shall not take effect until the interim final rule controlling the drug is issued in accordance with section 201(j) of the Controlled Substances Act.

(2) Date of Approval. — For purposes of this section, with respect to an application described in paragraph (1), the term "date of approval" shall mean the later of —

(A) the date an application under subsection (b) is approved under subsection (c); or

(B) the date of issuance of the interim final rule controlling the drug.

(y) Contrast Agents Intended for Use with Applicable Medical Imaging Devices. —

(1) In General.—The sponsor of a contrast agent for which an application has been approved under this section may submit a supplement to the application seeking approval for a new use following the authorization of a premarket submission for an applicable medical imaging device for that use with the contrast agent pursuant to section 520(p)(1).

(2) REVIEW OF SUPPLEMENT.—In reviewing a supplement submitted under this subsection, the agency center charged with the premarket review of drugs may—

(A) consult with the center charged with the premarket review of devices; and

(B) review information and data submitted to the Secretary by the sponsor of an applicable medical imaging device pursuant to section 515, 510(k), or 513(f)(2) so long as the sponsor of such applicable medical imaging device has provided to the sponsor of the contrast agent a right of reference.

(3) DEFINITIONS.—For purposes of this subsection—

(A) the term 'new use' means a use of a contrast agent that is described in the approved labeling of an applicable medical imaging device described in section 520(p), but that is not described in the approved labeling of the contrast agent; and

(B) the terms 'applicable medical imaging device' and 'contrast agent' have the meanings given such terms in section 520(p).

SEC. 505–1. [355-1] RISK EVALUATION AND MITIGATION STRATEGIES.

(a) SUBMISSION OF PROPOSED STRATEGY. —

(1) INITIAL APPROVAL. — If the Secretary, in consultation with the office responsible for reviewing the drug and the office responsible for postapproval safety with respect to the drug, determines that a risk evaluation and mitigation strategy is necessary to ensure that the benefits of the drug outweigh the risks of the drug, and informs the person who submits such application of such determination, then such person shall submit to the Secretary as part of such application a proposed risk evaluation and mitigation strategy. In making such a determination, the Secretary shall consider the following factors:

(A) The estimated size of the population likely to use the drug involved.

(B) The seriousness of the disease or condition that is to be treated with the drug.

(C) The expected benefit of the drug with respect to such disease or condition.

(D) The expected or actual duration of treatment with the drug.

(E) The seriousness of any known or potential adverse events that may be related to the drug and the background incidence of such events in the population likely to use the drug.

(F) Whether the drug is a new molecular entity.

(2) POSTAPPROVAL REQUIREMENT. —

(A) IN GENERAL. — If the Secretary has approved a covered application (including an application approved before the effective date of this section) and did not when approving the application require a risk evaluation and mitigation strategy under paragraph (1), the Secretary, in consultation with the offices described in paragraph (1), may subsequently require such a strategy for the drug involved (including when acting on a supplemental application seeking approval of a new indication for use of the drug) if the Secretary becomes aware of new safety information and makes a determination that such a strategy is necessary to ensure that the benefits of the drug outweigh the risks of the drug.

(B) SUBMISSION OF PROPOSED STRATEGY. — Not later than 120 days after the Secretary notifies the holder of an approved covered application that the Secretary has made a determination under subparagraph (A) with respect to the drug involved, or within such other reasonable time as the Secretary requires to protect the public health, the holder shall submit to the Secretary a proposed risk evaluation and mitigation strategy.

(3) ABBREVIATED NEW DRUG APPLICATIONS. — The applicability of this section to an application under section 505(j) is subject to subsection (i).

(4) NON-DELEGATION. — Determinations by the Secretary under this subsection for a drug shall be made by individuals at or above the level of individuals empowered to approve a drug (such as division directors within the Center for Drug Evaluation and Research).

(b) DEFINITIONS. — For purposes of this section:

(1) ADVERSE DRUG EXPERIENCE. — The term "adverse drug experience" means any adverse event associated with the use of a drug in humans, whether or not considered drug related, including —

(A) an adverse event occurring in the course of the use of the drug in professional practice;

(B) an adverse event occurring from an overdose of the drug, whether accidental or intentional;

(C) an adverse event occurring from abuse of the drug;

(D) an adverse event occurring from withdrawal of the drug; and

(E) any failure of expected pharmacological action of the drug.

(2) Covered Application. — The term "covered application" means an application referred to in section 505(p)(1)(A).

(3) New Safety Information. — The term "new safety information", with respect to a drug, means information derived from a clinical trial, an adverse event report, a postapproval study (including a study under section 505(o)(3)), or peer reviewed biomedical literature; data derived from the postmarket risk identification and analysis system under section 505(k); or other scientific data deemed appropriate by the Secretary about —

(A) a serious risk or an unexpected serious risk associated with use of the drug that the Secretary has become aware of (that may be based on a new analysis of existing information) since the drug was approved, since the risk evaluation and mitigation strategy was required, or since the last assessment of the approved risk evaluation and mitigation strategy for the drug; or

(B) the effectiveness of the approved risk evaluation and mitigation strategy for the drug obtained since the last assessment of such strategy.

(4) Serious Adverse Drug Experience. —

The term "serious adverse drug experience" is an adverse drug experience that —

(A) results in —

(i) death;

(ii) an adverse drug experience that places the patient at immediate risk of death from the adverse drug experience as it occurred (not including an adverse drug experience that might have caused death had it occurred in a more severe form);

(iii) inpatient hospitalization or prolongation of existing hospitalization;

(iv) a persistent or significant incapacity or substantial disruption of the ability to conduct normal life functions; or

(v) a congenital anomaly or birth defect; or

(B) based on appropriate medical judgment, may jeopardize the patient and may require a medical or surgical intervention to prevent an outcome described under subparagraph (A).

(5) Serious Risk. — The term "serious risk" means a risk of a serious adverse drug experience.

(6) Signal of a Serious Risk. — The term "signal of a serious risk" means information related to a serious adverse drug experience associated with use of a drug and derived from—

(A) a clinical trial;

(B) adverse event reports;

(C) a postapproval study, including a study under section 505(o)(3);

(D) peer-reviewed biomedical literature;

(E) data derived from the postmarket risk identification and analysis system under section 505(k)(4); or

(F) other scientific data deemed appropriate by the Secretary.

(7) Responsible Person. — The term "responsible person" means the person submitting a covered application or the holder of the approved such application.

(8) Unexpected Serious Risk. — The term "unexpected serious risk" means a serious adverse drug experience that is not listed in the labeling of a drug, or that may be symptomatically and pathophysiologically related to an adverse drug experience identified in the labeling, but differs from such adverse drug experience because of greater severity, specificity, or prevalence.

(c) Contents. — A proposed risk evaluation and mitigation strategy under subsection (a) shall —

(1) include the timetable required under subsection (d); and

(2) to the extent required by the Secretary, in consultation with the office responsible for reviewing the drug and the office responsible for postapproval safety with respect to the drug, include additional elements described in subsections (e) and (f).

(d) Minimal Strategy. — For purposes of subsection (c)(1), the risk evaluation and mitigation strategy for a drug shall require a timetable for submission of assessments of the strategy that —

(1) includes an assessment, by the date that is 18 months after the strategy is initially approved;

(2) includes an assessment by the date that is 3 years after the strategy is initially approved;

(3) includes an assessment in the seventh year after the strategy is so approved; and

(4) subject to paragraphs (1), (2), and (3) —

(A) is at a frequency specified in the strategy;

(B) is increased or reduced in frequency as necessary as provided for in subsection (g)(4)(A); and

(C) is eliminated after the 3-year period described in paragraph (1) if the Secretary determines that serious risks of the drug have been adequately identified and assessed and are being adequately managed.

(e) Additional Potential Elements of Strategy. —

(1) In General. — The Secretary, in consultation with the offices described in subsection (c)(2), may under such subsection require that the risk evaluation and mitigation strategy for a drug include 1 or more of the additional elements described in this subsection if the Secretary makes the determination required with respect to each element involved.

(2) Medication Guide; Patient Package Insert. — The risk evaluation and mitigation strategy for a drug may require that, as applicable, the responsible person develop for distribution to each patient when the drug is dispensed —

(A) a Medication Guide, as provided for under part 208 of title 21, Code of Federal Regulations (or any successor regulations); and

(B) a patient package insert, if the Secretary determines that such insert may help mitigate a serious risk of the drug.

(3) Communication Plan. — The risk evaluation and mitigation strategy for a drug may require that the responsible person conduct a communication plan to health care providers, if, with respect to such drug, the Secretary determines that such plan may support implementation of an element of the strategy (including under this paragraph). Such plan may include —

(A) sending letters to health care providers;

(B) disseminating information about the elements of the risk evaluation and mitigation strategy to encourage implementation by health care providers of components that apply to such health care providers, or to explain certain safety protocols (such as medical monitoring by periodic laboratory tests); ~~or~~

(C) disseminating information to health care providers through professional societies about any serious risks of the drug and any protocol to assure safe use~~.~~; or

(D) disseminating information to health care providers about drug formulations or properties, including information about the limitations or patient care implications of such formulations or properties, and how such formulations or properties may be related to serious adverse drug events associated with use of the drug.

(f) Providing Safe Access for Patients to Drugs with Known Serious Risks that Would Otherwise be Unavailable. —

(1) Allowing Safe Access to Drugs with Known Serious Risks. — The Secretary, in consultation with the offices described in subsection (c)(2), may require that the risk evaluation and mitigation strategy for a drug include such elements as are necessary to assure safe use of the drug, because of its inherent toxicity or potential harmfulness, if the Secretary determines that —

(A) the drug, which has been shown to be effective, but is associated with a serious adverse drug experience, can be approved only if, or would be withdrawn unless, such elements are required as part of such strategy to mitigate a specific serious risk listed in the labeling of the drug; and

(B) for a drug initially approved without elements to assure safe use, other elements under subsections (c), (d), and (e) are not sufficient to mitigate such serious risk.

(2) Assuring Access and Minimizing Burden. —

Such elements to assure safe use under paragraph (1) shall —

(A) be commensurate with the specific serious risk listed in the labeling of the drug;

(B) within 30 days of the date on which any element under paragraph (1) is imposed, be posted publicly by the Secretary with an explanation of how such elements will mitigate the observed safety risk;

(C) considering such risk, not be unduly burdensome on patient access to the drug, considering in particular —

(i) patients with serious or life-threatening diseases or conditions; and

(ii) patients who have difficulty accessing health care (such as patients in rural or medically underserved areas); and

(D) to the extent practicable, so as to minimize the burden on the health care delivery system —

(i) conform with elements to assure safe use for other drugs with similar, serious risks; and

(ii) be designed to be compatible with established distribution, procurement, and dispensing systems for drugs.

(3) Elements to Assure Safe Use. — The elements to assure safe use under paragraph (1) shall include 1 or more goals to mitigate a specific serious risk listed in the labeling of the drug and, to mitigate such risk, may require that —

(A) health care providers who prescribe the drug have particular training or experience, or are specially certified (the opportunity to obtain such training or certification with respect to the drug shall be available to any willing provider from a frontier area in a widely available training or certification method (including an on-line course or via mail) as approved by the Secretary at reasonable cost to the provider);

(B) pharmacies, practitioners, or health care settings that dispense the drug are specially certified (the opportunity to obtain such certification shall be available to any willing provider from a frontier area);

(C) the drug be dispensed to patients only in certain health care settings, such as hospitals;

(D) the drug be dispensed to patients with evidence or other documentation of safe-use conditions, such as laboratory test results;

(E) each patient using the drug be subject to certain monitoring; or

(F) each patient using the drug be enrolled in a registry.

(4) Implementation System. — The elements to assure safe use under paragraph (1) that are described in subparagraphs (B), (C), and (D) of paragraph (3) may include a system through which the applicant is able to take reasonable steps to —

(A) monitor and evaluate implementation of such elements by health care providers, pharmacists, and other parties in the health care system who are responsible for implementing such elements; and

(B) work to improve implementation of such elements by such persons.

(5) Evaluation of Elements to Assure Safe Use. — The Secretary, through the Drug Safety and Risk Management Advisory Committee (or successor committee) or other advisory committee of the Food and Drug Administration, shall —

(A) seek input from patients, physicians, pharmacists, and other health care providers about how elements to assure safe use under this subsection for 1 or more drugs may be standardized so as not to be —

(i) unduly burdensome on patient access to the drug; and

(ii) to the extent practicable, minimize the burden on the health care delivery system;

(B) periodically evaluate, for 1 or more drugs, the elements to assure safe use of such drug to assess whether the elements —

(i) assure safe use of the drug;

(ii) are not unduly burdensome on patient access to the drug; and

(iii) to the extent practicable, minimize the burden on the health care delivery system; and

(C) considering such input and evaluations —

(i) issue or modify agency guidance about how to implement the requirements of this subsection; and

(ii) modify elements under this subsection for 1 or more drugs as appropriate.

(6) Additional Mechanisms to Assure Access. — The mechanisms under section 561 to provide for expanded access for patients with serious or life-threatening diseases or conditions may be used to provide access for patients with a serious or life-threatening disease or condition, the treatment of which is not an approved use for the drug, to a drug that is subject to elements to assure safe use under this subsection. The Secretary shall promulgate regulations for how a physician may provide the drug under the mechanisms of section 561.

(7) Limitation. — No holder of an approved covered application shall use any element to assure safe use required by the Secretary under this subsection to block or delay approval of an application under section 505(b) (2) or (j) or to prevent application of such element under subsection (i)(1)(B) to a drug that is the subject of an abbreviated new drug application.

(g) Assessment and Modification of Approved Strategy. —

(1) Voluntary Assessments. — After the approval of a risk evaluation and mitigation strategy under subsection (a), the responsible person involved may, subject to paragraph (2), submit to the Secretary an assessment of the approved strategy for the drug involved at any time.

(2) Required Assessments. — A responsible person shall submit an assessment of the approved risk evaluation and mitigation strategy for a drug —

(A) when submitting a supplemental application for a new indication for use under section 505(b) or under section 351 of the Public Health Service Act, unless the drug is not subject to section 503(b) and the risk evaluation and mitigation strategy for the drug includes only the timetable under subsection (d);

(B) when required by the strategy, as provided for in such timetable under subsection (d);

(C) within a time period to be determined by the Secretary, if the Secretary, in consultation with the offices described in subsection (c)(2), determines that an assessment is needed to evaluate whether the approved strategy should be modified to —

(i) ensure the benefits of the drug outweigh the risks of the drug; or

(ii) to minimize the burden on the health care delivery system of complying with the strategy.

(3) Requirements for Assessments. — An assessment under paragraph (1) or (2) of an approved risk evaluation and mitigation strategy for a drug shall include, with respect to each goal included in the strategy, an assessment of the extent to which the approved strategy, including each element of the strategy, is meeting the goal or whether 1 or more such goals or such elements should be modified.

(4) Modification. —

(A) On Initiative of Responsible Person. — After the approval of a risk evaluation and mitigation strategy by the Secretary, the responsible person may, at any time, submit to the Secretary a proposal to modify the approved strategy. Such proposal may propose the addition, modification, or removal of any goal or element of the approved strategy and shall include an adequate rationale to support such proposed addition, modification, or removal of any goal or element of the strategy.

(B) On Initiative of Secretary — After the approval of a risk evaluation and mitigation strategy by the Secretary, the Secretary may, at any time, require a responsible person to submit a proposed modification to the strategy within 120 days or within such reasonable time as the Secretary specifies, if the Secretary, in consultation with the offices described in subsection (c)(2), determines that 1 or more goals or elements should be added, modified, or removed from the approved strategy to —

(i) ensure the benefits of the drug outweigh the risks of the drug; or

(ii) minimize the burden on the health care delivery system of complying with the strategy.

(h) Review of Proposed Strategies; Review of Assessments and Modifications of Approved Strategies. —

(1) In General. — The Secretary, in consultation with the offices described in subsection (c)(2), shall promptly review each proposed risk evaluation and mitigation strategy for a drug submitted under subsection (a) and each assessment of and proposed modification to an approved risk evaluation and mitigation strategy for a drug submitted under subsection (g), and, if necessary, promptly initiate discussions with the responsible person about such proposed strategy, assessment, or modification.

(2) Action. —

(A) In General. —

(i) Timeframe. — Unless the dispute resolution process described under paragraph (3) or (4) applies, and, except as provided in clause (ii) or clause (iii) below, the Secretary, in consultation with the offices described in subsection (c)(2), shall review and act on the proposed risk evaluation and mitigation strategy for a drug or any proposed modification to any required strategy within 180 days of receipt of the proposed strategy or modification.

(ii) Minor Modifications. — The Secretary shall review and act on a proposed minor modification, as defined by the Secretary in guidance, within 60 days of receipt of such modification.

(iii) REMS Modification Due to Safety Labeling Changes. — Not later than 60 days after the Secretary receives a proposed modification to an approved risk evaluation and mitigation strategy to conform the strategy to approved safety labeling changes, including safety labeling changes initiated by the responsible person in accordance with FDA regulatory requirements, or to a safety labeling change that the Secretary has directed the holder of the application to make pursuant to section 505(o)(4), the Secretary shall review and act on such proposed modification to the approved strategy.

(iv) Guidance. — The Secretary shall establish, through guidance, that responsible persons may implement certain modifications to an approved risk evaluation and mitigation strategy following notification to the Secretary.

(B) Inaction. — An approved risk evaluation and mitigation strategy shall remain in effect until the Secretary acts, if the Secretary fails to act as provided under subparagraph (A).

(C) Public Availability. — Upon acting on a proposed risk evaluation and mitigation strategy or proposed modification to a risk evaluation and mitigation strategy under subparagraph (A), the Secretary shall make publicly available an action letter describing the actions taken by the Secretary under such subparagraph (A).

(3) Dispute Resolution at Initial Approval. — If a proposed risk evaluation and mitigation strategy is submitted under subsection (a)(1) in an application for initial approval of a drug and there is a dispute about the strategy, the responsible person shall use the major dispute resolution procedures as set forth in the letters described in section 101(c) of the Food and Drug Administration Amendments Act of 2007.

(4) Dispute Resolution in All Other Cases. —

(A) Request for Review. —

(i) In General. — The responsible person may, after the sponsor is required to make a submission under subsection (a)(2) or (g), request in writing that a dispute about the strategy be reviewed by the Drug Safety Oversight Board under subsection (j), except that the determination of the Secretary to require a risk evaluation and mitigation strategy is not subject to review under this paragraph. The preceding sentence does not prohibit review under this paragraph of the particular elements of such a strategy.

(ii) Scheduling. — Upon receipt of a request under clause (i), the Secretary shall schedule the dispute involved for review under subparagraph (B) and, not later than 5 business days of scheduling the dispute for review, shall publish by posting on the Internet or otherwise a notice that the dispute will be reviewed by the Drug Safety Oversight Board.

(B) Scheduling Review. — If a responsible person requests review under subparagraph (A), the Secretary —

(i) shall schedule the dispute for review at 1 of the next 2 regular meetings of the Drug Safety Oversight Board, whichever meeting date is more practicable; or

(ii) may convene a special meeting of the Drug Safety Oversight Board to review the matter more promptly, including to meet an action deadline on an application (including a supplemental application).

(C) Agreement After Discussion or Administrative Appeals. —

(i) Further Discussion or Administrative Appeals. — A request for review under subparagraph (A) shall not preclude further discussions to reach agreement on the risk evaluation and mitigation strategy, and such a request shall not preclude the use of administrative appeals within the Food and Drug Administration to reach agreement on the strategy, including appeals as described in the letters described in section 101(c) of the Food and Drug Administration Amendments Act of 2007 for procedural or scientific matters involving the review of human drug applications and supplemental applications that cannot be resolved at the divisional level. At the time a review has been scheduled under subparagraph (B) and notice of such review has been posted, the responsible person shall either withdraw the request under subparagraph (A) or terminate the use of such administrative appeals.

(ii) Agreement Terminates Dispute Resolution. — At any time before a decision and order is issued under subparagraph (G), the Secretary (in consultation with the offices described in subsection (c)(2)) and the responsible person may reach an agreement on the risk evaluation and mitigation strategy through further discussion or administrative appeals, terminating the dispute resolution process, and the Secretary shall issue an action letter or order, as appropriate, that describes the strategy.

(D) Meeting of the Board. — At a meeting of the Drug Safety Oversight Board described in subparagraph (B), the Board shall —

(i) hear from both parties via written or oral presentation; and

(ii) review the dispute.

(E) Record of Proceedings. — The Secretary shall ensure that the proceedings of any such meeting are recorded, transcribed, and made public within 90 days of the meeting. The Secretary shall redact the transcript to protect any trade secrets and other information that is exempted from disclosure under section 552 of title 5, United States Code, or section 552a of title 5, United States Code.

(F) Recommendation of the Board. — Not later than 5 days after any such meeting, the Drug Safety Oversight Board shall provide a written recommendation on resolving the dispute to the Secretary. Not later than 5 days after the Board provides such written recommendation to the Secretary, the Secretary shall make the recommendation available to the public.

(G) Action by the Secretary. —

(i) Action Letter. — With respect to a proposal or assessment referred to in paragraph (1), the Secretary shall issue an action letter that resolves the dispute not later than the later of —

(I) the action deadline for the action letter on the application; or

(II) 7 days after receiving the recommendation of the Drug Safety Oversight Board.

(ii) Order. — With respect to an assessment of an approved risk evaluation and mitigation strategy under subsection (g)(1) or under any of subparagraphs (B) through (D) of subsection (g)(2), the Secretary shall issue an order, which shall be made public, that resolves the dispute not later than 7 days after receiving the recommendation of the Drug Safety Oversight Board.

(H) Inaction. — An approved risk evaluation and mitigation strategy shall remain in effect until the Secretary acts, if the Secretary fails to act as provided for under subparagraph (G).

(I) Effect on Action Deadline. — With respect to a proposal or assessment referred to in paragraph (1), the Secretary shall be considered to have met the action deadline for the action letter on the application if the responsible person requests the dispute resolution process described in this paragraph and if the Secretary has complied with the timing requirements of scheduling review by the Drug Safety Oversight Board, providing a written recommendation, and issuing an action letter under subparagraphs (B), (F), and (G), respectively.

(J) Disqualification. — No individual who is an employee of the Food and Drug Administration and who reviews a drug or who participated in an administrative appeal under subparagraph (C)(i) with respect to such drug may serve on the Drug Safety Oversight Board at a meeting under subparagraph (D) to review a dispute about the risk evaluation and mitigation strategy for such drug.

(K) Additional Expertise. — The Drug Safety Oversight Board may add members with relevant expertise from the Food and Drug Administration, including the Office of Pediatrics, the Office of Women's Health, or the Office of Rare Diseases, or from other Federal public health or health care agencies, for a meeting under subparagraph (D) of the Drug Safety Oversight Board.

(5) Use of Advisory Committees. — The Secretary may convene a meeting of 1 or more advisory committees of the Food and Drug Administration to —

(A) review a concern about the safety of a drug or class of drugs, including before an assessment of the risk evaluation and mitigation strategy or strategies of such drug or drugs is required to be submitted under subparagraphs (B) or (C) of subsection (g)(2);

(B) review the risk evaluation and mitigation strategy or strategies of a drug or group of drugs; or

(C) review a dispute under paragraph (3) or (4).

(6) Process for Addressing Drug Class Effects. —

(A) In General. — When a concern about a serious risk of a drug may be related to the pharmacological class of the drug, the Secretary, in consultation with the offices described in subsection (c)(2), may defer assessments of the approved risk evaluation and mitigation strategies for such drugs until the Secretary has convened 1 or more public meetings to consider possible responses to such concern.

(B) Notice. — If the Secretary defers an assessment under subparagraph (A), the Secretary shall —

(i) give notice of the deferral to the holder of the approved covered application not later than 5 days after the deferral;

(ii) publish the deferral in the Federal Register; and

(iii) give notice to the public of any public meetings to be convened under subparagraph (A), including a description of the deferral.

(C) Public Meetings. — Such public meetings may include —

(i) 1 or more meetings of the responsible person for such drugs;

(ii) 1 or more meetings of 1 or more advisory committees of the Food and Drug Administration, as provided for under paragraph (6); or

(iii) 1 or more workshops of scientific experts and other stakeholders.

(D) Action. — After considering the discussions from any meetings under subparagraph (A), the Secretary may —

(i) announce in the Federal Register a planned regulatory action, including a modification to each risk evaluation and mitigation strategy, for drugs in the pharmacological class;

(ii) seek public comment about such action; and

(iii) after seeking such comment, issue an order addressing such regulatory action.

(7) International Coordination. — The Secretary, in consultation with the offices described in subsection (c)(2), may coordinate the timetable for submission of assessments under subsection (d), or a study or clinical trial under section 505(o)(3), with efforts to identify and assess the serious risks of such drug by the marketing authorities of other countries whose drug approval and risk management processes the Secretary deems comparable to the drug approval and risk management processes of the United States. If the Secretary takes action to coordinate such timetable, the Secretary shall give notice to the responsible person.

(8) Effect. — Use of the processes described in paragraphs (6) and (7) shall not be the sole source of delay of action on an application or a supplement to an application for a drug.

(i) Abbreviated New Drug Applications. —

(1) In General. — A drug that is the subject of an abbreviated new drug application under section 505(j) is subject to only the following elements of the risk evaluation and mitigation strategy required under subsection (a) for the applicable listed drug:

(A) A Medication Guide or patient package insert, if required under subsection (e) for the applicable listed drug.

(B) Elements to assure safe use, if required under subsection (f) for the listed drug. A drug that is the subject of an abbreviated new drug application and the listed drug shall use a single, shared system under subsection (f). The Secretary may waive the requirement under the preceding sentence for a drug that is the subject of an abbreviated new drug application, and permit the applicant to use a different, comparable aspect of the elements to assure safe use, if the Secretary determines that —

(i) the burden of creating a single, shared system outweighs the benefit of a single, system, taking into consideration the impact on health care providers, patients, the applicant for the abbreviated new drug application, and the holder of the reference drug product; or

(ii) an aspect of the elements to assure safe use for the applicable listed drug is claimed by a patent that has not expired or is a method or process that, as a trade secret, is entitled to protection, and the applicant for the abbreviated new drug application certifies that it has sought a license for use of an aspect of the elements to assure safe use for the applicable listed drug and that it was unable to obtain a license.

A certification under clause (ii) shall include a description of the efforts made by the applicant for the abbreviated new drug application to obtain a license. In a case described in clause (ii), the Secretary may seek to negotiate a voluntary agreement with the owner of the patent, method, or process for a license under which the applicant for such abbreviated new drug application may use an aspect of the elements to assure safe use, if required under subsection (f) for the applicable listed drug, that is claimed by a patent that has not expired or is a method or process that as a trade secret is entitled to protection.

(2) Action by the Secretary. — For an applicable listed drug for which a drug is approved under section 505(j), the Secretary —

(A) shall undertake any communication plan to health care providers required under subsection (e)(3) for the applicable listed drug; and

(B) shall inform the responsible person for the drug that is so approved if the risk evaluation and mitigation strategy for the applicable listed drug is modified.

(j) Drug Safety Oversight Board. —

(1) In General. — There is established a Drug Safety Oversight Board.

(2) Composition; Meetings. — The Drug Safety Oversight Board shall —

(A) be composed of scientists and health care practitioners appointed by the Secretary, each of whom is an employee of the Federal Government;

(B) include representatives from offices throughout the Food and Drug Administration, including the offices responsible for postapproval safety of drugs;

(C) include at least 1 representative each from the National Institutes of Health and the Department of Health and Human Services (other than the Food and Drug Administration);

(D) include such representatives as the Secretary shall designate from other appropriate agencies that wish to provide representatives; and

(E) meet at least monthly to provide oversight and advice to the Secretary on the management of important drug safety issues.

(k) Waiver in Public Health Emergencies.—The Secretary may waive any requirement of this section with respect to a qualified countermeasure (as defined in section 319F-1(a)(2) of the Public Health Service Act) to which a requirement under this section has been applied, if the Secretary determines that such waiver is required to mitigate the effects of, or reduce the severity of, the circumstances under which—

(1) a determination described in subparagraph (A), (B), or (C) of section 564(b)(1) has been made by the Secretary of Homeland Security, the Secretary of Defense, or the Secretary, respectively; or

(2) the identification of a material threat described in subparagraph (D) of section 564(b)(1) has been made pursuant to section 319F-2 of the Public Health Service Act.

Sec. 505A. [355a] Pediatric Studies of Drugs.

(a) Definitions. — As used in this section, the term "pediatric studies" or "studies" means at least one clinical investigation (that, at the Secretary's discretion, may include pharmacokinetic studies) in pediatric age groups (including neonates in appropriate cases) in which a drug is anticipated to be used, and, at the discretion of the Secretary, may include preclinical studies.

(b) Market Exclusivity for New Drugs. —

(1) In General. — Except as provided in paragraph (2), if, prior to approval of an application that is submitted under section 505(b)(1), the Secretary determines that information relating to the use of a new drug in the pediatric population may produce health benefits in that population, the Secretary makes a written request for pediatric studies (which shall include a timeframe for completing such studies), the applicant agrees to the request, such studies are completed using appropriate formulations for each age group for which the study is requested within any such timeframe, and the reports thereof are submitted and accepted in accordance with subsection ~~(d)(3)~~ (d)(4) —

(A) —

(i) —

(I) the period referred to in subsection (c)(3)(E)(ii) of section 505, and in subsection (j)(5)(F)(ii) of such section, is deemed to be five years and six months rather than five years, and the references in subsections (c)(3)(E)(ii) and (j)(5)(F)(ii) of such section to four years, to forty-eight months, and to seven and one-half years are deemed to be four and one-half years, fifty-four months, and eight years, respectively; or

(II) the period referred to in clauses (iii) and (iv) of subsection (c)(3)(E) of such section, and in clauses (iii) and (iv) of subsection (j)(5)(F) of such section, is deemed to be three years and six months rather than three years; and

(ii) if the drug is designated under section 526 for a rare disease or condition, the period referred to in section 527(a) is deemed to be seven years and six months rather than seven years; and

(B) —

(i) if the drug is the subject of—

(I) a listed patent for which a certification has been submitted under subsection (b)(2)(A)(ii) or (j)(2)(A)(vii)(II) of section 505 and for which pediatric studies were submitted prior to the expiration of the patent (including any patent extensions); or

(II) a listed patent for which a certification has been submitted under subsections (b)(2)(A)(iii) or (j)(2)(A)(vii)(III) of section 505,

the period during which an application may not be approved under section 505(c)(3) or section 505(j)(5)(B) shall be extended by a period of six months after the date the patent expires (including any patent extensions); or

(ii) if the drug is the subject of a listed patent for which a certification has been submitted under subsection (b)(2)(A)(iv) or (j)(2)(A)(vii)(IV) of section 505, and in the patent infringement litigation resulting from the certification the court determines that the patent is valid and would be infringed, the period during which an application may not be approved under section 505(c)(3) or section 505(j)(5)(B) shall be extended by a period of six months after the date the patent expires (including any patent extensions).

(2) Exception. — The Secretary shall not extend the period referred to in paragraph (1)(A) or (1)(B) if the determination made under subsection (d)(3) is made later than 9 months prior to the expiration of such period.

(c) Market Exclusivity for Already-Marketed Drugs. —

(1) In General. — Except as provided in paragraph (2), if the Secretary determines that information relating to the use of an approved drug in the pediatric population may produce health benefits in that population and makes a written request to the holder of an approved application under section 505(b)(1) for pediatric studies (which shall include a timeframe for completing such studies), the holder agrees to the request, such studies are completed using appropriate formulations for each age group for which the study is requested within any such timeframe, and the reports thereof are submitted and accepted in accordance with subsection ~~(d)(3)~~ (d)(4) —

(A) —

(i) —

(I) the period referred to in subsection (c)(3)(E)(ii) of section 505, and in subsection (j)(5)(F)(ii) of such section, is deemed to be five years and six months rather than five years, and the references in subsections (c)(3)(E)(ii) and (j)(5)(F)(ii) of such section to four years, to forty-eight months, and to seven and one-half years are deemed to be four and one-half years, fifty-four months, and eight years, respectively; or

(II) the period referred to in clauses (iii) and (iv) of subsection (c)(3)(D) of such section, and in clauses (iii) and (iv) of subsection (j)(5)(F) of such section, is deemed to be three years and six months rather than three years; and

(ii) if the drug is designated under section 526 for a rare disease or condition, the period referred to in section 527(a) is deemed to be seven years and six months rather than seven years; and

(B) —

(i) if the drug is the subject of—

(I) a listed patent for which a certification has been submitted under subsection (b)(2)(A)(ii) or (j)(2)(A)(vii)(II) of section 505 and for which pediatric studies were submitted prior to the expiration of the patent (including any patent extensions); or

(II) a listed patent for which a certification has been submitted under subsection (b)(2)(A)(iii) or (j)(2)(A)(vii)(III) of section 505, the period during which an application may not be approved under section 505(c)(3) or section 505(j) (5)(B)(ii) shall be extended by a period of six months after the date the patent expires (including any patent extensions); or

(ii) if the drug is the subject of a listed patent for which a certification has been submitted under subsection (b)(2)(A)(iv) or (j)(2)(A)(vii)(IV) of section 505, and in the patent infringement litigation resulting from the certification the court determines that the patent is valid and would be infringed, the period during which an application may not be approved under section 505(c)(3) or section 505(j)(5)

(B) shall be extended by a period of six months after the date the patent expires (including any patent extensions).

(2) Exception. — The Secretary shall not extend the period referred to in paragraph (1)(A) or (1)(B) if the determination made under subsection ~~(d)(3)~~ (d)(4) is made later than 9 months prior to the expiration of such period.

(d) Conduct of Pediatric Studies. —

(1) Request for Studies. —

(A) In General. — The Secretary may, after consultation with the sponsor of an application for an investigational new drug under section 505(i), the sponsor of an application for a new drug under section 505(b)(1), or the holder of an approved application for a drug under section 505(b)(1), issue to the sponsor or holder a written request for the conduct of pediatric studies for such drug. In issuing such request, the Secretary shall take into account adequate representation of children of ethnic and racial minorities. Such request to conduct pediatric studies shall be in writing and shall include a timeframe for such studies and a request to the sponsor or holder to propose pediatric labeling resulting from such studies. If a request under this subparagraph does not request studies in neonates, such request shall include a statement describing the rationale for not requesting studies in neonates.

(B) Single Written Request. — A single written request —

(i) may relate to more than one use of a drug; and

(ii) may include uses that are both approved and unapproved.

(2) Written Request for Pediatric Studies. —

(A) Request and Response. —

(i) In General. — If the Secretary makes a written request for pediatric studies (including neonates, as appropriate) under subsection (b) or (c), the applicant or holder, not later than 180 days after receiving the written request, shall respond to the Secretary as to the intention of the applicant or holder to act on the request by —

(I) indicating when the pediatric studies will be initiated, if the applicant or holder agrees to the request; or

(II) indicating that the applicant or holder does not agree to the request and stating the reasons for declining the request.

(ii) Disagree with Request. — If, on or after the date of the enactment of the Best Pharmaceuticals for Children Act of 2007, the applicant or holder does not agree to the request on the grounds that it is not possible to develop the appropriate pediatric formulation, the applicant or holder shall submit to the Secretary the reasons such pediatric formulation cannot be developed.

(B) Adverse Event Reports. — An applicant or holder that, on or after the date of the enactment of the Best Pharmaceuticals for Children Act of 2007, agrees to the request for such studies shall provide the Secretary, at the same time as the submission of the reports of such studies, with all postmarket adverse event reports regarding the drug that is the subject of such studies and are available prior to submission of such reports.

(3) Action on Submissions. — The Secretary shall review and act upon a submission by a sponsor or holder of a proposed pediatric study request or a proposed amendment to a written request for pediatric studies within 120 calendar days of the submission.

~~(3)~~ **(4) Meeting the Studies Requirement.** — Not later than 180 days after the submission of the reports of the studies, the Secretary shall accept or reject such reports and so notify the sponsor or holder. The Secretary's only responsibility in accepting or rejecting the reports shall be to determine, within the 180-day period, whether the studies fairly respond to the written request, have been conducted in accordance with commonly accepted scientific principles and protocols, and have been reported in accordance with the requirements of the Secretary for filing.

~~(4)~~ (5) Effect of Subsection. — Nothing in this subsection alters or amends section 301(j) of this Act or section 552 of title 5 or section 1905 of title 18, United States Code.

~~(5)~~ (6) Consultation.—With respect to a drug that is a qualified countermeasure (as defined in section 319F-1 of the Public Health Service Act), a security countermeasure (as defined in section 319F-2 of the Public Health Service Act), or a qualified pandemic or epidemic product (as defined in section 319F- 3 of the Public Health Service Act), the Secretary shall solicit input from the Assistant Secretary for Preparedness and Response regarding the need for and, from the Director of the Biomedical Advanced Research and Development Authority regarding the conduct of, pediatric studies under this section.

(e) Notice of Determinations on Studies Requirement. —

(1) In General. — The Secretary shall publish a notice of any determination, made on or after the date of the enactment of the Best Pharmaceuticals for Children Act of 2007, that the requirements of subsection (d) have been met and that submissions and approvals under subsection (b)(2) or (j) of section 505 for a drug will be subject to the provisions of this section. Such notice shall be published not later than 30 days after the date of the Secretary's determination regarding market exclusivity and shall include a copy of the written request made under subsection (b) or (c).

(2) Identification of Certain Drugs. — The Secretary shall publish a notice identifying any drug for which, on or after the date of the enactment of the Best Pharmaceuticals for Children Act of 2007, a pediatric formulation was developed, studied, and found to be safe and effective in the pediatric population (or specified subpopulation) if the pediatric formulation for such drug is not introduced onto the market within one year after the date that the Secretary publishes the notice described in paragraph (1). Such notice identifying such drug shall be published not later than 30 days after the date of the expiration of such one year period.

(f) Internal Review of Written Requests and Pediatric Studies. —

(1) Internal Review. — The Secretary shall utilize the internal review committee established under section 505C to review all written requests issued on or after the date of the enactment of the Best Pharmaceuticals for Children Act of 2007, in accordance with paragraph (2).

(2) Review of Written Requests. — The committee referred to in paragraph (1) shall review all written requests issued pursuant to this section prior to being issued.

(3) Review of Pediatric Studies. — The committee referred to in paragraph (1) may review studies conducted pursuant to this section to make a recommendation to the Secretary whether to accept or reject such reports under subsection ~~(d)(3)~~ (d)(4).

(4) Activity by Committee. — The committee referred to in paragraph (1) may operate using appropriate members of such committee and need not convene all members of the committee.

(5) Documentation of Committee Action. — For each drug, the committee referred to in paragraph (1) shall document, for each activity described in paragraph (2) or (3), which members of the committee participated in such activity.

(6) Tracking Pediatric Studies and Labeling Changes. — The Secretary, in consultation with the committee referred to in paragraph (1), shall track and make available to the public, in an easily accessible manner, including through posting on the Web site of the Food and Drug Administration —

(A) the number of studies conducted under this section and under section 409I of the Public Health Service Act;

(B) the specific drugs and drug uses, including labeled and off-labeled indications, studied under such sections;

(C) the types of studies conducted under such sections, including trial design, the number of pediatric patients studied, and the number of centers and countries involved;

(D) the number of pediatric formulations developed and the number of pediatric formulations not developed and the reasons such formulations were not developed;

(E) the labeling changes made as a result of studies conducted under such sections;

(F) an annual summary of labeling changes made as a result of studies conducted under such sections for distribution pursuant to subsection (k)(2); and

(G) information regarding reports submitted on or after the date of the enactment of the Best Pharmaceuticals for Children Act of 2007.

(7) Informing Internal Review Committee. — The Secretary shall provide to the committee referred to in paragraph (1) any response issued to an applicant or holder with respect to a proposed pediatric study request.

(g) Limitations. — Notwithstanding subsection (c)(2), a drug to which the six-month period under subsection (b) or (c) has already been applied —

(1) may receive an additional six-month period under subsection (c)(1)(A)(i)(II) for a supplemental application if all other requirements under this section are satisfied, except that such drug may not receive any additional such period under subsection (c)(1)(B); and

(2) may not receive any additional such period under subsection (c)(1)(A)(ii).

(h) Relationship to Pediatric Research Requirements. — Exclusivity under this section shall only be granted for the completion of a study or studies that are the subject of a written request and for which reports are submitted and accepted in accordance with subsection ~~(d)(3)~~ (d)(4). Written requests under this section may consist of a study or studies required under section 505B.

(i) Labeling Changes. —

(1) Priority Status for Pediatric Applications and Supplements. — Any application or supplement to an application under section 505 proposing a labeling change as a result of any pediatric study conducted pursuant to this section —

(A) shall be considered to be a priority application or supplement; and

(B) shall be subject to the performance goals established by the Commissioner for priority drugs.

(2) Dispute Resolution. —

(A) Request for Labeling Change and Failure to Agree. — If, on or after the date of the enactment of the Best Pharmaceuticals for Children Act of 2007, the Commissioner determines that the sponsor and the Commissioner have been unable to reach agreement on appropriate changes to the labeling for the drug that is the subject of the application, not later than 180 days after the date of submission of the application —

(i) the Commissioner shall request that the sponsor of the application make any labeling change that the Commissioner determines to be appropriate; and

(ii) if the sponsor of the application does not agree within 30 days after the Commissioner's request to Commissioner, the Commissioner shall refer the matter to the Pediatric Advisory Committee.

(B) Action by the Pediatric Advisory Committee. — Not later than 90 days after receiving a referral under subparagraph (A)(ii), the Pediatric Advisory Committee shall —

(i) review the pediatric study reports; and

(ii) make a recommendation to the Commissioner concerning appropriate labeling changes, if any.

(C) Consideration of Recommendations. — The Commissioner shall consider the recommendations of the Pediatric Advisory Committee and, if appropriate, not later than 30 days after receiving the recommendation, make a request to the sponsor of the application to make any labeling change that the Commissioner determines to be appropriate.

(D) Misbranding. — If the sponsor of the application, within 30 days after receiving a request under subparagraph (C), does not agree to make a labeling change requested by the Commissioner, the Commissioner may deem the drug that is the subject of the application to be misbranded.

(E) No Effect on Authority. — Nothing in this subsection limits the authority of the United States to bring an enforcement action under this Act when a drug lacks appropriate pediatric labeling. Neither course of action (the Pediatric Advisory Committee process or an enforcement action referred to in the preceding sentence) shall preclude, delay, or serve as the basis to stay the other course of action.

(j) Other Labeling Changes. — If, on or after the date of the enactment of the Best Pharmaceuticals for Children Act of 2007, the Secretary determines that a pediatric study conducted under this section does or does not demonstrate that the drug that is the subject of the study is safe and effective, including whether such study results are inconclusive, in pediatric populations or subpopulations, the Secretary shall order the labeling of such product to include information about the results of the study and a statement of the Secretary's determination.

(k) Dissemination of Pediatric Information. —

(1) In General. — Not later than 210 days after the date of submission of a report on a pediatric study under this section, the Secretary shall make available to the public the medical, statistical, and clinical pharmacology reviews of pediatric studies conducted under subsection (b) or (c).

(2) Dissemination of Information Regarding Labeling Changes. — Beginning on the date of the enactment of the Best Pharmaceuticals for Children Act of 2007, the Secretary shall include as a requirement of a written request that the sponsors of the studies that result in labeling changes that are reflected in the annual summary developed pursuant to subsection (f)(6)(F) distribute, at least annually (or more frequently if the Secretary determines that it would be beneficial to the public health), such information to physicians and other health care providers.

(3) Effect of Subsection. — Nothing in this subsection alters or amends section 301(j) of this Act or section 552 of title 5 or section 1905 of title 18, United States Code.

(l) Adverse Event Reporting. —

(1) Reporting in First 18-Month Period. — Beginning on the date of the enactment of the Best Pharmaceuticals for Children Act of 2007, during the 18-month period beginning on the date a labeling change is approved pursuant to subsection (i), the Secretary shall ensure that all adverse event reports that have been received for such drug (regardless of when such report was received) are referred to the Office of Pediatric Therapeutics established under section 6 of the Best Pharmaceuticals for Children Act (Public Law 107–109). In considering the reports, the Director of such Office shall provide for the review of the reports by the Pediatric Advisory Committee, including obtaining any recommendations of such Committee regarding whether the Secretary should take action under this Act in response to such reports.

(2) Reporting in Subsequent Periods. — Following the 18-month period described in paragraph (1), the Secretary shall, as appropriate, refer to the Office of Pediatric Therapeutics all pediatric adverse event reports for a drug for which a pediatric study was conducted under this section. In considering such reports, the Director of such Office may provide for the review of such reports by the Pediatric Advisory Committee, including obtaining any recommendation of such Committee regarding whether the Secretary should take action in response to such reports.

(3) Preservation of Authority. — Nothing in this subsection shall prohibit the Office of Pediatric Therapeutics from providing for the review of adverse event reports by the Pediatric Advisory Committee prior to the 18-month period referred to in paragraph (1), if such review is necessary to ensure safe use of a drug in a pediatric population.

(4) Effect. — The requirements of this subsection shall supplement, not supplant, other review of such adverse event reports by the Secretary.

(m) Clarification of Interaction of Market Exclusivity Under This Section and Market Exclusivity Awarded to an Applicant for Approval of a Drug Under Section 505(j). — If a 180-day period under section 505(j)(5)(B)(iv) overlaps with a 6-month exclusivity period under this section, so that the applicant for approval of a drug under section 505(j) entitled to the 180-day period under that section loses a portion of the 180-day period to which the applicant is entitled for the drug, the 180-day period shall be extended from —

(1) the date on which the 180-day period would have expired by the number of days of the overlap, if the 180-day period would, but for the application of this subsection, expire after the 6-month exclusivity period; or

(2) the date on which the 6-month exclusivity period expires, by the number of days of the overlap if the 180-day period would, but for the application of this subsection, expire during the six-month exclusivity period.

(n) Referral if Pediatric Studies Not Submitted. —

(1) In General. — Beginning on the date of the enactment of the Best Pharmaceuticals for Children Act of 2007, if pediatric studies of a drug have not been submitted by the date specified in the written request issued or if the applicant or holder does not agree to the request under subsection (d) and if the Secretary, through the committee established under section 505C, determines that there is a continuing need for information relating to the use of the drug in the pediatric population (including neonates, as appropriate), the Secretary shall carry out the following:

(A) For a drug for which a listed patent has not expired, or for which a period of exclusivity eligible for extension under subsection (b)(1) or (c)(1) of this section or under subsection (m)(2) or (m)(3) of section 351 of the Public Health Service Act has not ended, make a determination regarding whether an assessment shall be required to be submitted under section 505B(b).

(B) For a drug that has no unexpired listed patents and for which no unexpired periods of exclusivity eligible for extension under subsection (b)(1) or (c)(1) of this section or under subsection (m)(2) or (m)(3) of section

351 of the Public Health Service Act apply, the Secretary shall refer the drug for inclusion on the list established under section 409I of the Public Health Service Act for the conduct of studies.

(C) For a drug that is a qualified countermeasure (as defined in section 319F-1 of the Public Health Service Act), a security countermeasure (as defined in section 319F-2 of the Public Health Service Act), or a qualified pandemic or epidemic product (as defined in section 319F-3 of such Act), in addition to any action with respect to such drug under subparagraph (A) or (B), the Secretary shall notify the Assistant Secretary for Preparedness and Response and the Director of the Biomedical Advanced Research and Development Authority of all pediatric studies in the written request issued by the Commissioner of Food and Drugs.

(2) PUBLIC NOTICE. — The Secretary shall give the public notice of a decision under paragraph (1)(A) not to require an assessment under section 505B and the basis for such decision.

(3) EFFECT OF SUBSECTION. — Nothing in this subsection alters or amends section 301(j) of this Act or section 552 of title 5 or section 1905 of title 18, United States Code.

(o) PROMPT APPROVAL OF DRUGS ~~UNDER SECTION 505(J)~~ WHEN PEDIATRIC INFORMATION IS ADDED TO LABELING. —

(1) GENERAL RULE. — A drug for which an application has been submitted or approved under ~~section 505(j)~~ subsection (b)(2) or (j) of section 505 shall not be considered ineligible for approval under that section or misbranded under section 502 on the basis that the labeling of the drug omits a pediatric indication or any other aspect of labeling pertaining to pediatric use when the omitted indication or other aspect is protected by patent or by exclusivity under clause (iii) or (iv) of section 505(j)(5)(F), clause (iii) or (iv) of section 505(c)(3)(E), or section 527(a), or by an extension of such exclusivity under this section or section 505E.

(2) LABELING. — Notwithstanding clauses (iii) and (iv) of section 505(j)(5)(F), clauses (iii) and (iv) of section 505(c)(3)(E), or section 527, the Secretary may require that the labeling of a drug approved ~~under section 505(j)~~ pursuant to an application submitted under subsection (b)(2) or (j) of section 505 that omits a pediatric indication or other aspect of labeling as described in paragraph (1) include —

(A) a statement that, because of marketing exclusivity for a manufacturer—

(i) the drug is not labeled for pediatric use; or

(ii) in the case of a drug for which there is an additional pediatric use not referred to in paragraph (1), the drug is not labeled for the pediatric use under paragraph (1); and

(B) a statement of any appropriate pediatric contraindications, warnings, precautions, or other information that the Secretary considers necessary to assure safe use.

(3) PRESERVATION OF PEDIATRIC EXCLUSIVITY AND OTHER PROVISIONS. — This subsection does not affect —

(A) the availability or scope of exclusivity under ~~this section;~~ —

(i) this section;

(ii) section 505 for pediatric formulations; or

(iii) section 527;

(B) the availability or scope of ~~exclusivity under section 505 for pediatric formulations;~~ an extension to any such exclusivity, including an extension under this section or section 505E;

(C) the question of the eligibility for approval ~~of any application under section 505(j) that omits any other conditions of approval entitled to exclusivity under clause (iii) or (iv) of section 505(j)(5)(F); or~~ under section 505 of any application described in subsection (b)(2) or (j) of such section that omits any other aspect of labeling protected by exclusivity under —

(i) clause (iii) or (iv) of section 505(j)(5)(F);

(ii) clause (iii) or (iv) of section 505(c)(3)(E); or

(iii) section 527(a); or

(D) except as expressly provided in paragraphs (1) and (2), the operation of section 505.

SEC.___. [355b] ADVERSE-EVENT REPORTING.

(a) Not later than one year after January 4, 2002, the Secretary of Health and Human Services shall promulgate a final rule requiring that the labeling of each drug for which an application is approved under section 505 of this Act (regardless of the date on which approved) include the toll-free number maintained by the Secretary for the purpose of receiving reports of adverse events regarding drugs and a statement that such number is to be used for reporting purposes only, not to receive medical advice. With respect to the final rule:

(1) The rule shall provide for the implementation of such labeling requirement in a manner that the Secretary considers to be most likely to reach the broadest consumer audience.

(2) In promulgating the rule, the Secretary shall seek to minimize the cost of the rule on the pharmacy profession.

(3) The rule shall take effect not later than 60 days after the date on which the rule is promulgated.

(b) —

(1) During the one year beginning on the date on which a drug receives a period of market exclusivity under section 505Aof this Act, any report of an adverse event regarding the drug that the Secretary of Health and Human Services receives shall be referred to the Office of Pediatric Therapeutics established under 21 U.S.C. 393a. In considering the report, the Director of such Office shall provide for the review of the report by the Pediatric Advisory Committee, including obtaining any recommendations of such subcommittee regarding whether the Secretary should take action under the Federal Food, Drug, and Cosmetic Act in response to the report.

(2) Paragraph (1) may not be construed as restricting the authority of the Secretary of Health and Human Services to continue carrying out the activities described in such paragraph regarding a drug after the one-year period described in such paragraph regarding the drug has expired.

Sec. 505B. [355c] Research into Pediatric Uses for Drugs and Biological Products.

(a) New Drugs and Biological Products. —

(1) In General. — ~~A person that submits, on or after the date of the enactment of the Pediatric Research Equity Act of 2007, an application (or supplement to an application) for a drug —~~

(A) General Requirements. — Except with respect to an application for which subparagraph (B) applies, a person that submits, on or after the date of the enactment of the Pediatric Research Equity Act of 2007, an application (or supplement to an application) for a drug —

~~(A)~~ **(i)** under section 505 for a new active ingredient, new indication, new dosage form, new dosing regimen, or new route of administration~~, or~~ ; or

~~(B)~~ **(ii)** under section 351 of the Public Health Service Act (42 U.S.C. 262) for a new active ingredient, new indication, new dosage form, new dosing regimen, or new route of administration,

shall submit with the application the assessments described in paragraph (2).

(B) Certain Molecularly Targeted Cancer Indications. — A person that submits, on or after the date that is 3 years after the date of enactment of the FDA Reauthorization Act of 2017, an original application for a new active ingredient under section 505 of this Act or section 351 of the Public Health Service Act, shall submit with the application reports on the investigation described in paragraph (3) if the drug or biological product that is the subject of the application is —

(i) intended for the treatment of an adult cancer; and

(ii) directed at a molecular target that the Secretary determines to be substantially relevant to the growth or progression of a pediatric cancer.

(2) Assessments. —

(A) In General. — The assessments referred to in paragraph ~~(1)~~ (1)(A) shall contain data, gathered using appropriate formulations for each age group for which the assessment is required, that are adequate —

(i) to assess the safety and effectiveness of the drug or the biological product for the claimed indications in all relevant pediatric subpopulations; and

(ii) to support dosing and administration for each pediatric subpopulation for which the drug or the biological product is safe and effective.

(B) Similar Course of Disease or Similar Effect of Drug or Biological Product. —

(i) In General. — If the course of the disease and the effects of the drug are sufficiently similar in adults and pediatric patients, the Secretary may conclude that pediatric effectiveness can be extrapolated from adequate and well-controlled studies in adults, usually supplemented with other information obtained in pediatric patients, such as pharmacokinetic studies.

(ii) Extrapolation Between Age Groups. — A study may not be needed in each pediatric age group if data from one age group can be extrapolated to another age group.

(iii) Information on Extrapolation. — A brief documentation of the scientific data supporting the conclusion under clauses (i) and (ii) shall be included in any pertinent reviews for the application under section 505 of this Act or section 351 of the Public Health Service Act (42 U.S.C. 262).

(3) Molecularly Targeted Pediatric Cancer Investigation. —

(A) In General. — With respect to a drug or biological product described in paragraph (1)(B), the investigation described in this paragraph is a molecularly targeted pediatric cancer investigation, which shall be designed to yield clinically meaningful pediatric study data, gathered using appropriate formulations for each age group for which the study is required, regarding dosing, safety, and preliminary efficacy to inform potential pediatric labeling.

(B) Extrapolation of Data. — Paragraph (2)(B) shall apply to investigations described in this paragraph to the same extent and in the same manner as paragraph (2)(B) applies with respect to the assessments required under paragraph (1)(A).

(C) Deferrals and Waivers. — Deferrals and waivers under paragraphs (4) and (5) shall apply to investigations described in this paragraph to the same extent and in the same manner as such deferrals and waivers apply with respect to the assessments under paragraph (2)(B).

~~(3)~~ (4) Deferral. —

(A) In General. — On the initiative of the Secretary or at the request of the applicant, the Secretary may defer submission of some or all assessments required under ~~paragraph (1)~~ paragraph (1)(A) or reports on the investigation required under paragraph (1)(B) until a specified date after approval of the drug or issuance of the license for a biological product if —

(i) the Secretary finds that —

(I) the drug or biological product is ready for approval for use in adults before pediatric studies are complete;

(II) pediatric studies should be delayed until additional safety or effectiveness data have been collected; or

(III) there is another appropriate reason for deferral; and

(ii) the applicant submits to the Secretary —

(I) certification of the grounds for deferring the ~~assessments~~ assessments or reports on the investigation;

(II) a pediatric study plan as described in subsection (e);

(III) evidence that the studies are being conducted or will be conducted with due diligence and at the earliest possible time; and

(IV) a timeline for the completion of such studies.

(B) Deferral Extension. —

(i) In General. — On the initiative of the Secretary or at the request of the applicant, the Secretary may grant an extension of a deferral approved under subparagraph (A) for submission of some or all assessments required under ~~paragraph (1)~~ paragraph (1)(A) or reports on the investigation required under paragraph (1)(B) if —

(I) the Secretary determines that the conditions described in subclause (II) or (III) of subparagraph (A)(i) continue to be met; and

(II) the applicant submits a new timeline under subparagraph (A)(ii)(IV) and any significant updates to the information required under subparagraph (A)(ii).

(ii) Timing And Information. — If the deferral extension under this subparagraph is requested by the applicant, the applicant shall submit the deferral extension request containing the information described in this subparagraph not less than 90 days prior to the date that the deferral would expire. The Secretary shall respond to such request not later than 45 days after the receipt of such letter. If the Secretary grants such an extension, the specified date shall be the extended date. The sponsor of the required assessment under ~~paragraph (1)~~ paragraph (1)(A) or reports on the investigation under paragraph (1)(B) shall not be issued a letter described in subsection (d) unless the specified or extended date of submission for such required studies has passed or if the request for an extension is pending. For a deferral that has expired prior to the date of enactment of the Food and Drug Administration Safety and Innovation Act or that will expire prior to 270 days after the date of enactment of such Act, a deferral extension shall be requested by an applicant not later than 180 days after the date of enactment of such Act. The Secretary shall respond to any such request as soon as practicable, but not later than 1 year after the date of enactment of such Act. Nothing in this clause shall prevent the Secretary from updating the status of a study or studies publicly if components of such study or studies are late or delayed.

(C) Annual Review. —

(i) In General. — On an annual basis following the approval of a deferral under subparagraph (A), the applicant shall submit to the Secretary the following information:

(I) Information detailing the progress made in conducting pediatric studies.

(II) If no progress has been made in conducting such studies, evidence and documentation that such studies will be conducted with due diligence and at the earliest possible time.

(III) Projected completion date for pediatric studies.

(IV) The reason or reasons why a deferral or deferral extension continues to be necessary.

(ii) Public Availability. — Not later than 90 days after the submission to the Secretary of the information submitted through the annual review under clause (i), the Secretary shall make available to the public in an easily accessible manner, including through the Internet Web site of the Food and Drug Administration —

(I) such information;

(II) the name of the applicant for the product subject to the ~~assessment~~ assessment or investigation;

(III) the date on which the product was approved; and

(IV) the date of each deferral or deferral extension under this paragraph for the product.

~~(4)~~ (5) **Waivers.** —

(A) Full Waiver. — On the initiative of the Secretary or at the request of an applicant, the Secretary shall grant a full waiver, as appropriate, of the requirement to submit ~~assessments~~ assessments or reports on the investigation for a drug or biological product under this subsection if the applicant certifies and the Secretary finds that —

(i) necessary studies are impossible or highly impracticable (because, for example, the number of patients is so small or the patients are geographically dispersed);

(ii) there is evidence strongly suggesting that the drug or biological product would be ineffective or unsafe in all pediatric age groups; or

(iii) the drug or biological product —

(I) does not represent a meaningful therapeutic benefit over existing therapies for pediatric patients; and

(II) is not likely to be used in a substantial number of pediatric patients.

(B) Partial Waiver. — On the initiative of the Secretary or at the request of an applicant, the Secretary shall grant a partial waiver, as appropriate, of the requirement to submit ~~assessments~~ assessments or reports on the investigation for a drug or biological product under this subsection with respect to a specific pediatric age group if the applicant certifies and the Secretary finds that —

(i) necessary studies are impossible or highly impracticable (because, for example, the number of patients in that age group is so small or patients in that age group are geographically dispersed);

(ii) there is evidence strongly suggesting that the drug or biological product would be ineffective or unsafe in that age group;

(iii) the drug or biological product —

(I) does not represent a meaningful therapeutic benefit over existing therapies for pediatric patients in that age group; and

(II) is not likely to be used by a substantial number of pediatric patients in that age group; or

(iv) the applicant can demonstrate that reasonable attempts to produce a pediatric formulation necessary for that age group have failed.

(C) Pediatric Formulation Not Possible. — If a partial waiver is granted on the ground that it is not possible to develop a pediatric formulation, the waiver shall cover only the pediatric groups requiring that formulation. An applicant seeking such a partial waiver shall submit to the Secretary documentation detailing why a pediatric formulation cannot be developed and, if the waiver is granted, the applicant's submission shall promptly be made available to the public in an easily accessible manner, including through posting on the Web site of the Food and Drug Administration.

(D) Labeling Requirement. — If the Secretary grants a full or partial waiver because there is evidence that a drug or biological product would be ineffective or unsafe in pediatric populations, the information shall be included in the labeling for the drug or biological product.

(b) Marketed Drugs and Biological Products. —

(1) In General. — The Secretary may (by order in the form of a letter) require the sponsor or holder of an approved application for a drug under section 505 or the holder of a license for a biological product under section 351 of the Public Health Service Act to submit by a specified date the assessments described in subsection (a)(2), if the Secretary finds that —

(A) —

(i) the drug or biological product is used for a substantial number of pediatric patients for the labeled indications; and

(ii) adequate pediatric labeling could confer a benefit on pediatric patients;

(B) there is reason to believe that the drug or biological product would represent a meaningful therapeutic benefit over existing therapies for pediatric patients for 1 or more of the claimed indications; or

(C) the absence of adequate pediatric labeling could pose a risk to pediatric patients.

(2) Waivers. —

(A) Full Waiver. — At the request of an applicant, the Secretary shall grant a full waiver, as appropriate, of the requirement to submit assessments under this subsection if the applicant certifies and the Secretary finds that —

(i) necessary studies are impossible or highly impracticable (because, for example, the number of patients in that age group is so small or patients in that age group are geographically dispersed); or

(ii) there is evidence strongly suggesting that the drug or biological product would be ineffective or unsafe in all pediatric age groups.

(B) Partial Waiver. — At the request of an applicant, the Secretary shall grant a partial waiver, as appropriate, of the requirement to submit assessments under this subsection with respect to a specific pediatric age group if the applicant certifies and the Secretary finds that —

(i) necessary studies are impossible or highly impracticable (because, for example, the number of patients in that age group is so small or patients in that age group are geographically dispersed);

(ii) there is evidence strongly suggesting that the drug or biological product would be ineffective or unsafe in that age group;

(iii) —

(I) the drug or biological product —

(aa) does not represent a meaningful therapeutic benefit over existing therapies for pediatric patients in that age group; and

(bb) is not likely to be used in a substantial number of pediatric patients in that age group; and

(II) the absence of adequate labeling could not pose significant risks to pediatric patients; or

(iv) the applicant can demonstrate that reasonable attempts to produce a pediatric formulation necessary for that age group have failed.

(C) Pediatric Formulation Not Possible. — If a waiver is granted on the ground that it is not possible to develop a pediatric formulation, the waiver shall cover only the pediatric groups requiring that formulation. An applicant seeking either a full or partial waiver shall submit to the Secretary documentation detailing why a pediatric formulation cannot be developed and, if the waiver is granted, the applicant's submission shall promptly be made available to the public in an easily accessible manner, including through posting on the Web site of the Food and Drug Administration.

(D) Labeling Requirement. — If the Secretary grants a full or partial waiver because there is evidence that a drug or biological product would be ineffective or unsafe in pediatric populations, the information shall be included in the labeling for the drug or biological product.

(3) Effect of Subsection. — Nothing in this subsection alters or amends section 301(j) of this Act or section 552 of title 5 or section 1905 of title 18, United States Code.

(c) Meaningful Therapeutic Benefit. — For the purposes of paragraph (4)(A)(iii)(I) and (4)(B)(iii)(I) of subsection (a) and paragraphs (1)(B) and (2)(B)(iii)(I)(aa) of subsection (b), a drug or biological product shall be considered to represent a meaningful therapeutic benefit over existing therapies if the Secretary determines that—

(1) if approved, the drug or biological product could represent an improvement in the treatment, diagnosis, or prevention of a disease, compared with marketed products adequately labeled for that use in the relevant pediatric population; or

(2) the drug or biological product is in a class of products or for an indication for which there is a need for additional options.

(d) Submission of ~~Assessments~~ Assessments and Reports on the Investigation. — If a person fails to submit a required assessment described in subsection ~~(a)(2)~~ (a)(2) or the investigation described in subsection (a)(3), fails to meet the applicable requirements in subsection ~~(a)(3)~~ (a)(4), or fails to submit a request for approval of a pediatric formulation described in subsection (a) or (b), in accordance with applicable provisions of subsections (a) and (b), the following shall apply:

(1) Beginning 270 days after the date of enactment of the Food and Drug Administration Safety and Innovation Act, the Secretary shall issue a noncompliance letter to such person informing them of such failure to submit or meet the requirements of the applicable subsection. Such letter shall require the person to respond in writing within 45 calendar says of issuance of such letter. Such response may include the person's request for a deferral extension if applicable. Such letter and the person's written response to such letter shall be made publicly available on the Internet Web site of the Food and Drug Administration 60 calendar days after issuance, with redactions for any trade secrets and confidential commercial information. If the Secretary determines that the letter was issued in error, the requirements of this paragraph shall not apply. The Secretary shall inform the Pediatric Advisory Committee of letters issued under this paragraph and responses to such letters.

(2) The drug or biological product that is the subject of an assessment described in subsection ~~(a)(2)~~ (a)(2) or the investigation described in subsection (a)(3), applicable requirements in subsection ~~(a)(3)~~ (a)(4), or request for approval of a pediatric formulation, may be considered misbranded solely because of that failure and subject to relevant enforcement action (except that the drug or biological product shall not be subject to action under section 303), but such failure shall not be the basis for a proceeding —

(A) to withdraw approval for a drug under section 505(e); or

(B) to revoke the license for a biological product under section 351 of the Public Health Service Act.

(e) Pediatric Study Plans. —

(1) In General. — An applicant subject to subsection (a) shall submit to the Secretary an initial pediatric study plan prior to the submission of the assessments described under subsection ~~(a)(2)~~ (a)(2) or the investigation described in subsection (a)(3).

(2) Timing; Content; ~~Meeting~~ Meetings. —

(A) Timing. — An applicant shall submit the initial pediatric study plan under paragraph (1) —

(i) before the date on which the applicant submits the assessments under subsection ~~(a)(2)~~ (a)(2) or the investigation described in subsection (a)(3); and

(ii) not later than —

(I) 60 calendar days after the date of the end-of-Phase 2 meeting (as such term is used in section 312.47 of title 21, Code of Federal Regulations, or successor regulations); or

(II) such other time as may be agreed upon between the Secretary and the applicant.

Nothing in this section shall preclude the Secretary from accepting the submission of an initial pediatric study plan earlier than the date otherwise applicable under this subparagraph.

(B) CONTENT OF INITIAL PEDIATRIC STUDY PLAN. — The initial pediatric study plan shall include —

(i) an outline of the pediatric study or studies that the applicant plans to conduct (including, to the extent practicable study objectives and design, age groups, relevant endpoints, and statistical approach);

(ii) any request for a deferral, partial waiver, or waiver under this section, if applicable, along with any supporting information; and

(iii) other information specified in the regulations promulgated under paragraph (7).

(C) ~~MEETING~~ MEETINGS. — The Secretary —

(i) shall meet with the applicant ~~to discuss the initial pediatric study plan as soon as practicable, but not later than 90 calendar days after the receipt of such plan under subparagraph (A);~~ —

(I) if requested by the applicant with respect to a drug or biological product that is intended to treat a serious or life-threatening disease or condition, to discuss preparation of the initial pediatric study plan, not later than the end-of-Phase 1 meeting (as such term is used in section 312.82(b) of title 21, Code of Federal Regulations, or successor regulations) or within 30 calendar days of receipt of such request, whichever is later;

(II) to discuss the initial pediatric study plan as soon as practicable, but not later than 90 calendar days after the receipt of such plan under subparagraph (A); and

(III) to discuss the bases for the deferral under subsection (a)(4) or a full or partial waiver under subsection (a)(5);

(ii) may determine that a written response to the initial pediatric study plan is sufficient to communicate comments on the initial pediatric study plan, and that no meeting under clause (i)(II) is necessary; and

(iii) if the Secretary determines that no meeting under clause (i)(II) is necessary, shall so notify the applicant and provide written comments of the Secretary as soon as practicable, but not later than 90 calendar days after the receipt of the initial pediatric study plan.

(3) AGREED INITIAL PEDIATRIC STUDY PLAN. — Not later than 90 calendar days following the meeting under paragraph ~~(2)(C)(i)~~ (2)(C)(i)(II) or the receipt of a written response from the Secretary under paragraph (2)(C)(iii), the applicant shall document agreement on the initial pediatric study plan in a submission to the Secretary marked "Agreed Initial Pediatric Study Plan", and the Secretary shall confirm such agreement to the applicant in writing not later than 30 calendar days of receipt of such agreed initial pediatric study plan.

(4) DEFERRAL AND WAIVER. — If the agreed initial pediatric study plan contains a request from the applicant for a deferral, partial waiver, or waiver under this section, the written confirmation under paragraph (3) shall include a recommendation from the Secretary as to whether such request meets the standards under paragraphs (3) or (4) of subsection (a).

(5) AMENDMENTS TO THE AGREED INITIAL PEDIATRIC STUDY PLAN. — At the initiative of the Secretary or the applicant, the agreed initial pediatric study plan may be amended at any time. The requirements of paragraph (2)(C) shall apply to any such proposed amendment in the same manner and to the same extent as such requirements apply to an initial pediatric study plan under paragraph (1). The requirements of paragraphs (3) and (4) shall apply to any agreement resulting from such proposed amendment in the same manner and to the same extent as such requirements apply to an agreed initial pediatric study plan.

(6) INTERNAL COMMITTEE. — The Secretary shall consult the internal committee under section 505C on the review of the initial pediatric study plan, agreed initial pediatric study plan, and any significant amendments to such plans.

(7) REQUIRED RULEMAKING. — Not later than 1 year after the date of enactment of the Food and Drug Administration Safety and Innovation Act, the Secretary shall promulgate proposed regulations and issue guidance to implement the provisions of this subsection.

(f) REVIEW OF PEDIATRIC STUDY PLANS, ASSESSMENTS, DEFERRALS, DEFERRAL EXTENSIONS, AND WAIVERS. —

(1) Review. — Beginning not later than 30 days after the date of the enactment of the Pediatric Research Equity Act of 2007, the Secretary shall utilize the internal committee established under section 505C to provide consultation to reviewing divisions on initial pediatric study plans, agreed initial pediatric study plans and any significant amendments to such plans, and assessments prior to approval of an application or supplement for which a pediatric assessment is required under this section and all deferral, deferral extension, and waiver requests granted pursuant to this section.

(2) Activity by Committee. — The committee referred to in paragraph (1) may operate using appropriate members of such committee and need not convene all members of the committee.

(3) Documentation of Committee Action. — For each drug or biological product, the committee referred to in paragraph (1) shall document, for each activity described in paragraph (4) or (5), which members of the committee participated in such activity.

(4) Review of Pediatric Study Plans, Assessments, Deferrals, Deferral Extensions, and Waivers. — Consultation on initial pediatric study plans, agreed initial pediatric study plans, and assessments by the committee referred to in paragraph (1) pursuant to this section shall occur prior to approval of an application or supplement for which a pediatric assessment is required under this section. The committee shall review all requests for deferrals, deferral extensions, and waivers from the requirement to submit a pediatric assessment granted under this section and shall provide recommendations as needed to reviewing divisions, including with respect to whether such a supplement, when submitted, shall be considered for priority review.

(5) Retrospective Review of Pediatric Assessments, Deferrals, and Waivers. — Not later than 1 year after the date of the enactment of the Pediatric Research Equity Act of 2007, the committee referred to in paragraph (1) shall conduct a retrospective review and analysis of a representative sample of assessments submitted and deferrals and waivers approved under this section since the enactment of the Pediatric Research Equity Act of 2003. Such review shall include an analysis of the quality and consistency of pediatric information in pediatric assessments and the appropriateness of waivers and deferrals granted. Based on such review, the Secretary shall issue recommendations to the review divisions for improvements and initiate guidance to industry related to the scope of pediatric studies required under this section.

(6) Tracking of Assessments and Labeling Changes. — The Secretary, in consultation with the committee referred to in paragraph (1), shall track and make available to the public in an easily accessible manner, including through posting on the Web site of the Food and Drug Administration —

(A) the number of assessments conducted under this section;

(B) the specific drugs and biological products and their uses assessed under this section;

(C) the types of assessments conducted under this section, including trial design, the number of pediatric patients studied, and the number of centers and countries involved;

(D) aggregated on an annual basis —

(i) the total number of deferrals and deferral extensions requested and granted under this section and, if granted, the reasons for each such deferral or deferral extension;

(ii) the timeline for completion of the assessments;

(iii) the number of assessments completed and pending; and

(iv) the number of postmarket noncompliance letters issued pursuant to subsection (d), and the recipients of such letters;

(E) the number of waivers requested and granted under this section and, if granted, the reasons for the waivers;

(F) the number of pediatric formulations developed and the number of pediatric formulations not developed and the reasons any such formulation was not developed;

(G) the labeling changes made as a result of assessments conducted under this section;

(H) an annual summary of labeling changes made as a result of assessments conducted under this section for distribution pursuant to subsection (h)(2);

(I) an annual summary of information submitted pursuant to subsection (a)(3)(B); and

(J) the number of times the committee referred to in paragraph (1) made a recommendation to the Secretary under paragraph (4) regarding priority review, the number of times the Secretary followed or did not follow such a recommendation, and, if not followed, the reasons why such a recommendation was not followed.

(g) Labeling Changes. —

(1) **Dispute Resolution.** —

(A) **Request for Labeling Change and Failure to Agree.** — If, on or after the date of the enactment of the Pediatric Research Equity Act of 2007, the Commissioner determines that a sponsor and the Commissioner have been unable to reach agreement on appropriate changes to the labeling for the drug that is the subject of the application or supplement, not later than 180 days after the date of the submission of the application or supplement that receives a priority review or 330 days after the date of the submission of an application or supplement that receives a standard review —

(i) the Commissioner shall request that the sponsor of the application make any labeling change that the Commissioner determines to be appropriate; and

(ii) if the sponsor does not agree within 30 days after the Commissioner's request to make a labeling change requested by the Commissioner, the Commissioner shall refer the matter to the Pediatric Advisory Committee.

(B) **Action by the Pediatric Advisory Committee.** — Not later than 90 days after receiving a referral under subparagraph (A)(ii), the Pediatric Advisory Committee shall—

(i) review the pediatric study reports; and

(ii) make a recommendation to the Commissioner concerning appropriate labeling changes, if any.

(C) **Consideration of Recommendations.** — The Commissioner shall consider the recommendations of the Pediatric Advisory Committee and, if appropriate, not later than 30 days after receiving the recommendation, make a request to the sponsor of the application or supplement to make any labeling changes that the Commissioner determines to be appropriate.

(D) **Misbranding.** — If the sponsor of the application or supplement, within 30 days after receiving a request under subparagraph (C), does not agree to make a labeling change requested by the Commissioner, the Commissioner may deem the drug that is the subject of the application or supplement to be misbranded.

(E) **No Effect on Authority.** — Nothing in this subsection limits the authority of the United States to bring an enforcement action under this Act when a drug lacks appropriate pediatric labeling. Neither course of action (the Pediatric Advisory Committee process or an enforcement action referred to in the preceding sentence) shall preclude, delay, or serve as the basis to stay the other course of action.

(2) **Other Labeling Changes.** — If, on or after the date of the enactment of the Pediatric Research Equity Act of 2007, the Secretary makes a determination that a pediatric assessment conducted under this section does or does not demonstrate that the drug that is the subject of such assessment is safe and effective in pediatric populations or subpopulations, including whether such assessment results are inconclusive, the Secretary shall order the labeling of such product to include information about the results of the assessment and a statement of the Secretary's determination.

(h) **Dissemination of Pediatric Information.** —

(1) **In General.** — Not later than 210 days after the date of submission of an application (or supplement to an application) that contains a pediatric assessment under this section, if the application (or supplement) receives a priority review, or not later than 330 days after the date of submission of an application (or supplement to an application) that contains a pediatric assessment under this section, if the application (or supplement) receives a standard review, the Secretary shall make available to the public in an easily accessible manner the medical, statistical, and clinical pharmacology reviews of such pediatric assessments, and shall post such assessments on the Web site of the Food and Drug Administration.

(2) **Dissemination of Information Regarding Labeling Changes.** — Beginning on the date of the enactment of the Pediatric Research Equity Act of 2007, the Secretary shall require that the sponsors of the assessments that result in labeling changes that are reflected in the annual summary developed pursuant to subsection (f)(6) (H) distribute such information to physicians and other health care providers.

(3) **Effect of Subsection.** — Nothing in this subsection shall alter or amend section 301(j) of this Act or section 552 of title 5 or section 1905 of title 18, United States Code.

(i) **Adverse Event Reporting.** —

(1) **Reporting in First 18-Month Period.** — Beginning on the date of the enactment of the Pediatric Research Equity Act of 2007, during the 18-month period beginning on the date a labeling change is made pursuant to subsection (g), the Secretary shall ensure that all adverse event reports that have been received for such drug (regardless of when such report was received) are referred to the Office of Pediatric Therapeutics. In considering

such reports, the Director of such Office shall provide for the review of such reports by the Pediatric Advisory Committee, including obtaining any recommendations of such committee regarding whether the Secretary should take action under this Act in response to such reports.

(2) Reporting in Subsequent Periods. — Following the 18-month period described in paragraph (1), the Secretary shall, as appropriate, refer to the Office of Pediatric Therapeutics all pediatric adverse event reports for a drug for which a pediatric study was conducted under this section. In considering such reports, the Director of such Office may provide for the review of such reports by the Pediatric Advisory Committee, including obtaining any recommendation of such Committee regarding whether the Secretary should take action in response to such reports.

(3) Preservation of Authority. — Nothing in this subsection shall prohibit the Office of Pediatric Therapeutics from providing for the review of adverse event reports by the Pediatric Advisory Committee prior to the 18-month period referred to in paragraph (1), if such review is necessary to ensure safe use of a drug in a pediatric population.

(4) Effect. — The requirements of this subsection shall supplement, not supplant, other review of such adverse event reports by the Secretary.

(j) Scope of Authority. — Nothing in this section provides to the Secretary any authority to require a pediatric assessment of any drug or biological product, or any assessment regarding other populations or uses of a drug or biological product, other than the pediatric assessments described in this section.

~~(k) Orphan Drugs. — Unless the Secretary requires otherwise by regulation, this section does not apply to any drug for an indication for which orphan designation has been granted under section 526.~~

(k) Relation to Orphan Drugs. —

(1) In General; Exemption for Orphan Indications. — Unless the Secretary requires otherwise by regulation and except as provided in paragraph (2), this section does not apply to any drug or biological product for an indication for which orphan designation has been granted under section 526.

(2) Applicability Despite Orphan Designation of Certain Indications. — This section shall apply with respect to a drug or biological product for which an indication has been granted orphan designation under 526 if the investigation described in subsection (a)(3) applies to the drug or biological product as described in subsection (a)(1)(B).

(l) New Active Ingredient. —

(1) Non-Interchangeable Biosimilar Biological Product. — A biological product that is biosimilar to a reference product under section 351 of the Public Health Service Act, and that the Secretary has not determined to meet the standards described in subsection (k)(4) of such section for interchangeability with the reference product, shall be considered to have a new active ingredient under this section.

(2) Interchangeable Biosimilar Biological Product. — A biological product that is interchangeable with a reference product under section 351 of the Public Health Service Act shall not be considered to have a new active ingredient under this section.

(m) List of Primary Molecular Targets. —

(1) In General. — Within one year of the date of enactment of the FDA Reauthorization Act of 2017, the Secretary shall establish and update regularly, and shall publish on the internet website of the Food and Drug Administration —

(A) a list of molecular targets considered, on the basis of data the Secretary determines to be adequate, to be substantially relevant to the growth and progression of a pediatric cancer, and that may trigger the requirements under this section; and

(B) a list of molecular targets of new cancer drugs and biological products in development for which pediatric cancer study requirements under this section will be automatically waived.

(2) Consultation. — In establishing the lists described in paragraph (1), the Secretary shall consult the National Cancer Institute, members of the internal committee under section 505C, and the Pediatric Oncology Subcommittee of the Oncologic Drugs Advisory Committee, and shall take into account comments from the meeting under subsection (c).

(3) Rule of Construction. — Nothing in paragraph (1) shall be construed —

(A) to require the inclusion of a molecular target on the list published under such paragraph as a condition for triggering the requirements under subsection (a)(1)(B) with respect to a drug or biological product directed at such molecular target; or

(B) to authorize the disclosure of confidential commercial information, as prohibited under section 301(j) of this Act or section 1905 of title 18, United States Code.

Sec. 505B-1. [355c-1] Report.

(a) In General — Not later than four years after the date of enactment of this Act* and every five years thereafter, the Secretary shall prepare and submit to the Committee on Health, education, Labor, and Pensions of the Senate and the Committee on Energy and Commerce of the House of Representatives, and make publicly available, including through posting on the Internet Web site of the Food and Drug Administration, a report on the implementation of sections 505A and 505B of the Federal Food, Drug, and Cosmetic Act (21 U.S.C. 355a, 355c).

(b) Contents. — Each report under subsection (a) shall include —

(1) an assessment of the effectiveness of sections 505A and 505B of the Federal Food, Drug, and Cosmetic Act in improving information about pediatric uses for approved drugs and biological products, including the number and type of labeling changes made since the date of enactment of this Act and the importance of such uses in the improvement of the health of children;

(2) the number of required studies under such section 505B that have not been met the initial deadline provided under such section 50B, including —

(A) the number of deferrals and deferral extensions granted and the reasons such extensions were granted;

(B) the number of waivers and partial waivers granted; and

(C) the number of letters issued under subsection (d) of such section 505B;

(3) an assessment of the timeliness and effectiveness of pediatric study planning since the date of enactment of this Act, including the number of initial pediatric study plans not submitted in accordance with the requirements of subsection (e) of such section 505B and any resulting rulemaking;

(4) the number of written requests issued, accepted, and declined under such section 505A since the date of enactment of this Act, and a listing of any important gaps in pediatric information as a result of such declined requests;

(5) a description and current status of referrals made under subsection (n) of such section 505A;

(6) an assessment of the effectiveness of studying biological products in pediatric populations under such sections 505A and 505B and section 409I of the Public Health Service Act (42 U.S.C. 284m);

(7)(A) the efforts made by the Secretary to increase the number of studies conducted in the neonatal population (including efforts made to encourage the conduct of appropriate studies in neonates by companies with products that have sufficient safety and other information to make the conduct of the studies ethical and safe); and

(B) the results of such efforts;

(8)(A) the number and importance of drugs and biological products for children with cancer that are being tested as a result of the programs under such sections 505A and 505B and under section 409I of the Public Health Service Act; and

(B) any recommendations for modifications to such programs that would lead to new and better therapies for children with cancer, including a detailed rationale for each recommendation;

(9) any recommendations for modification to such programs that would improve pediatric drug research and increase pediatric labeling of drugs and biological products;

(10) an assessment of the successes of and limitations to studying drugs for rare diseases under such sections 505A and 505B; ~~and~~

~~**(11)** an assessment of the Secretary's efforts to address the suggestions and options described in any prior report issued by the Comptroller General, Institute of Medicine, or the Secretary, and any subsequent reports, including recommendations therein, regarding the topics addressed in the reports under this section, including with respect to —~~

* "Act" as referenced here refers to the Food and Drug Administration Safety and Innovation Act (FDASIA).

~~(A) improving public access to information from pediatric studies conducted under sections 505A and 505B; and~~

~~(B) improving the timeliness of pediatric studies and pediatric study planning under such sections 505A and 505B.~~

(11) an assessment of the impact of the amendments to such section 505B made by the FDA Reauthorization Act of 2017 on pediatric research and labeling of drugs and biological products and pediatric labeling of molecularly targeted drugs and biological products for the treatment of cancer;

(12) an assessment of the efforts of the Secretary to implement the plan developed under section 505C-1 of the Federal Food, Drug, and Cosmetic Act, regarding earlier submission of pediatric studies under sections 505A and 505B of such Act and section 351(m) of the Public Health Service Act, including —

(A) the average length of time after the approval of an application under section 505(b)(1) of the Federal Food, Drug, and Cosmetic Act (21 U.S.C. 355(b)(1)) or section 351(a) of the Public Health Service Act (42 U.S.C. 262(a)) before studies conducted pursuant to such section 505A, 505B, or section 351(m) are completed, submitted, and incorporated into labeling;

(B) the average length of time after the receipt of a proposed pediatric study request before the Secretary responds to such request;

(C) the average length of time after the submission of a proposed pediatric study request before the Secretary issues a written request for such studies;

(D) the number of written requests issued for each investigational new drug or biological product prior to the submission of an application under section 505(b)(1) of the Federal Food, Drug, and Cosmetic Act or section 351(a) of the Public Health Service Act; and

(E) the average number, and range of numbers, of amendments to written requests issued, and the time the Secretary requires to review and act on proposed amendments to written requests;

(13) a list of sponsors of applications or holders of approved applications who received exclusivity under such section 505A or such section 351(m) after receiving a letter issued under such section 505B(d)(1) for any drug or biological product before the studies referred to in such letter were completed and submitted;

(14) a list of assessments and investigations required under such section 505B;

(15) how many requests under such section 505A for molecular targeted cancer drugs, as defined by subsection (a)(1)(B) of such section 505B, approved prior to 3 years after the date of enactment of the FDA Reauthorization Act of 2017, have been issued by the Food and Drug Administration, and how many such requests have been completed; and

(16) the Secretary's assessment of the overall impact of the amendments made by section 504 of the FDA Reauthorization Act of 2017 on the conduct and effectiveness of pediatric cancer research and the orphan drug program, as well any subsequent recommendations.

(c) Stakeholder Comment. — At least 180 days prior to the submission of each report under subsection (a), the Secretary shall consult with representatives of patient groups (including pediatric patient groups), consumer groups, regulated industry, academia, and other interested parties to obtain any recommendations or information relevant to the report including suggestions for modifications that would improve pediatric drug research and pediatric labeling of drugs and biological products.

Sec. 505C. [355d] Internal Committee for Review of Pediatric Plans, Assessments, Deferrals, Deferral Extensions, and Waivers.

The Secretary shall establish an internal committee within the Food and Drug Administration to carry out the activities as described in sections 505A(f) and 505B(f). Such internal committee shall include employees of the Food and Drug Administration, with expertise in pediatrics (including representation from the Office of Pediatric Therapeutics), biopharmacology, statistics, chemistry, legal issues, pediatric ethics, neonatology, and the appropriate expertise pertaining to the pediatric product under review, such as expertise in child and adolescent ~~psychiatry,~~ psychiatry or pediatric rare diseases, and other individuals designated by the Secretary.

Sec. 505D. [355e] Pharmaceutical Security.

(a) In General. — The Secretary shall develop standards and identify and validate effective technologies for the purpose of securing the drug supply chain against counterfeit, diverted, subpotent, substandard, adulterated, misbranded, or expired drugs.

(b) Standards Development. —

(1) In General. — The Secretary shall, in consultation with the agencies specified in paragraph (4), manufacturers, distributors, pharmacies, and other supply chain stakeholders, prioritize and develop standards for the identification, validation, authentication, and tracking and tracing of prescription drugs.

(2) Standardized Numeral Identifier. — Not later than 30 months after the date of the enactment of the Food and Drug Administration Amendments Act of 2007, the Secretary shall develop a standardized numerical identifier (which, to the extent practicable, shall be harmonized with international consensus standards for such an identifier) to be applied to a prescription drug at the point of manufacturing and repackaging (in which case the numerical identifier shall be linked to the numerical identifier applied at the point of manufacturing) at the package or pallet level, sufficient to facilitate the identification, validation, authentication, and tracking and tracing of the prescription drug.

(3) Promising Technologies. — The standards developed under this subsection shall address promising technologies, which may include —

(A) radio frequency identification technology;

(B) nanotechnology;

(C) encryption technologies; and

(D) other track-and-trace or authentication technologies.

(4) Interagency Collaboration. — In carrying out this subsection, the Secretary shall consult with Federal health and security agencies, including —

(A) the Department of Justice;

(B) the Department of Homeland Security;

(C) the Department of Commerce; and

(D) other appropriate Federal and State agencies.

(c) Inspection And Enforcement. —

(1) In General. — The Secretary shall expand and enhance the resources and facilities of agency components of the Food and Drug Administration involved with regulatory and criminal enforcement of this Act to secure the drug supply chain against counterfeit, diverted, subpotent, substandard, adulterated, misbranded, or expired drugs including biological products and active pharmaceutical ingredients from domestic and foreign sources.

(2) Activities. — The Secretary shall undertake enhanced and joint enforcement activities with other Federal and State agencies, and establish regional capacities for the validation of prescription drugs and the inspection of the prescription drug supply chain.

(d) Definition. — In this section, the term "prescription drug" means a drug subject to section 503(b)(1).

Sec. 505E. [355f] Extension of Exclusivity Period for New Qualified Infectious Disease Products.

(a) Extension. — If the Secretary approves an application pursuant to section 505 for a drug that has been designated as a qualified infectious disease product under subsection (d), the 4- and 5-year periods described in subsections (c)(3)(E)(ii) and (j)(5)(F)(ii) of section 505, the 3-year periods described in clauses (iii) and (iv) of subsection (c)(3)(A) and clauses (iii) and (iv) of subsection (j)(5)(F) of section 505, or the 7-year period described in section 527, as applicable, shall be extended by 5 years.

(b) Relation to Pediatric Exclusivity. — Any extension under subsection (a) of a period shall be in addition to any extension of the period under section 505A with respect to the drug.

(c) Limitations. — Subsection (a) does not apply to the approval of —

(1) a supplement to an application under section 505(b) for any qualified infectious disease product for which an extension described in subsection (a) is in effect or has expired;

(2) a subsequent application filed with respect to a product approved under section 505 for a change that results in a new indication, route of administration, dosing schedule, dosage form, delivery system, delivery device, or strength; or

(3) a product that does not meet the definition of a qualified infectious disease product under subsection (g) based upon its approved uses.

(d) Designation. —

(1) In General. — The manufacturer or sponsor of a drug may request the Secretary to designate a drug as a qualified infectious disease product at any time before the submission of an application under section 505(b) for such drug. The Secretary shall, not later than 60 days after the submission of such a request, determine whether the drug is a qualified infectious disease product.

(2) Limitation. — Except as provided in paragraph (3), a designation under this subsection shall not be withdrawn for any reason, including modification to the list of qualifying pathogens under subsection (f)(2)(C).

(3) Revocation of Designation. — The Secretary may revoke a designation of a drug as a qualified infectious disease product if the Secretary finds that the request for such designation contained an untrue statement of material fact.

(e) Regulations. —

(1) In General. — Not later than 2 years after the date of enactment of the Food and Drug Administration Safety and Innovation Act, the Secretary shall adopt final regulations implementing this section, including developing the list of qualifying pathogens described in subsection (f).

(2) Procedure. — In promulgating a regulation implementing this section, the Secretary shall —

(A) issue a notice of proposed rulemaking that includes the proposed regulation;

(B) provide a period of not less than 60 days for comments on the proposed regulation; and

(C) publish the final regulation not less than 30 days before the effective date of the regulation.

(3) Restrictions. — Notwithstanding any other provision of law, the Secretary shall promulgate regulations implementing this section only as described in paragraph (2), except that the Secretary may issue interim guidance for sponsors seeking designation under subsection (d) prior to the promulgation of such regulations.

(4) Designation Prior to Regulations. — The Secretary shall designate drugs as qualified infection disease products under subsection (d) prior to the promulgation of regulations under this subsection, if such drugs meet the definition of a qualified infection disease product described in subsection (g).

(f) Qualifying Pathogen. —

(1) Definition. — In this section, the term "qualifying pathogen" means a pathogen identified and listed by the Secretary under paragraph (2) that has the potential to pose a serious threat to public health, such as —

(A) resistant gram positive pathogens, including methicillin-resistant Staphylococcus aureus, vancomycin-resistant Staphylococcus aureus, and vancomycin-resistant enterococcus;

(B) multi-drug resistant gram negative bacteria, including Acinetobacter, Klebsiella, Pseudomonas, and E. coli species;

(C) multi-drug resistant tuberculosis; and

(D) Clostridium difficile.

(2) List of Qualifying Pathogens. —

(A) In General. — The Secretary shall establish and maintain a list of qualifying pathogens, and shall make public the methodology for developing such list.

(B) Considerations. — In establishing and maintaining the list of pathogens described in this section, the Secretary shall —

(i) consider —

(I) the impact on the public health due to drug-resistant organisms in humans;

(II) the rate of growth of drug-resistant organisms in humans;

(III) the increase in resistance rates in humans; and

(IV) the morbidity and mortality in humans; and

(ii) consult with experts in infectious diseases and antibiotic resistance, including the Centers for Disease Control and Prevention, the Food and Drug Administration, medical professionals, and the clinical research community.

(C) Review. — Every 5 years, or more often as needed, the Secretary shall review, provide modifications to, and publish the list of qualifying pathogens under subparagraph (A) and shall by regulation revise the list as necessary, in accordance with subsection (e).

(g) Qualified Infectious Disease Product. — The term "qualified infectious disease product" means an antibacterial or antifungal drug for human use intended to treat serious or life-threatening infections, including those caused by —

(1) an antibacterial or antifungal resistant pathogen, including novel or emerging infectious pathogens; or

(2) qualifying pathogens listed by the Secretary under subsection (f).

Sec. 505F. [355g] Utilizing Real World Evidence.

(a) In General.—The Secretary shall establish a program to evaluate the potential use of real world evidence—

(1) to help to support the approval of a new indication for a drug approved under section 505(e); and

(2) to help to support or satisfy postapproval study requirements.

(b) Real World Evidence Defined.—In this section, the term "real world evidence" means data regarding the usage, or the potential benefits or risks, of a drug derived from sources other than ~~randomized~~ traditional clinical trials.

(c) Program Framework.—

(1) In General.—Not later than 2 years after the date of enactment of the 21st Century Cures Act [December 13, 2016 —Ed.], the Secretary shall establish a draft framework for implementation of the program under this section.

(2) Contents of Framework.—The framework shall include information describing—

(A) the sources of real world evidence, including ongoing safety surveillance, observational studies, registries, claims, and patient-centered outcomes research activities;

(B) the gaps in data collection activities;

(C) the standards and methodologies for collection and analysis of real world evidence; and

(D) the priority areas, remaining challenges, and potential pilot opportunities that the program established under this section will address.

(3) Consultation.—

(A) In General.—In developing the program framework under this subsection, the Secretary shall consult with regulated industry, academia, medical professional organizations, representatives of patient advocacy organizations, consumer organizations, disease research foundations, and other interested parties.

(B) Process.—The consultation under subparagraph (A) may be carried out through approaches such as—

(i) a public-private partnership with the entities described in such subparagraph in which the Secretary may participate;

(ii) a contract, grant, or other arrangement, as the Secretary determines appropriate, with such a partnership or an independent research organization; or

(iii) public workshops with the entities described in such subparagraph.

(d) Program Implementation.—The Secretary shall, not later than ~~2~~ 3 years after the date of enactment of the 21st Century Cures Act [December 13, 2016 —Ed.] and in accordance with the framework established under subsection (c), implement the program to evaluate the potential use of real world evidence.

(e) Guidance for Industry.—The Secretary shall—

(1) utilize the program established under subsection (a), its activities, and any subsequent pilots or written reports, to inform a guidance for industry on—

(A) the circumstances under which sponsors of drugs and the Secretary may rely on real world evidence for the purposes described in paragraphs (1) and (2) of subsection (a); and

(B) the appropriate standards and methodologies for collection and analysis of real world evidence submitted for such purposes;

(2) not later than 5 years after the date of enactment of the 21st Century Cures Act [December 13, 2016 —Ed.], issue draft guidance for industry as described in paragraph (1); and

(3) not later than 18 months after the close of the public comment period for the draft guidance described in paragraph (2), issue revised draft guidance or final guidance.

(f) Rule of Construction.—

(1) In General.—Subject to paragraph (2), nothing in this section prohibits the Secretary from using real world evidence for purposes not specified in this section, provided the Secretary determines that sufficient basis exists for any such nonspecified use.

(2) Standards of Evidence and Secretary's Authority.—This section shall not be construed to alter—

(A) the standards of evidence under—

(i) subsection (c) or (d) of section 505, including the substantial evidence standard in such subsection (d); or

(ii) section 351(a) of the Public Health Service Act; or

(B) the Secretary's authority to require postapproval studies or clinical trials, or the standards of evidence under which studies or trials are evaluated.

Sec. 506. [356] Fast Track Products.

(a) Designation of a Drug as a Breakthrough Therapy. —

(1) In General. — The Secretary shall, at the request of the sponsor of a drug, expedite the development and review of such drug if the drug is intended, alone or in combination with 1 or more other drugs, to treat a serious or life-threatening disease or condition and preliminary clinical evidence indicates that the drug may demonstrate substantial improvement over existing therapies on 1 or more clinically significant endpoints, such as substantial treatment effects observed early in clinical development. (In this section, such a drug is referred to as a "breakthrough therapy".)

(2) Request for Designation. — The sponsor of a drug may request the Secretary to designate the drug as a breakthrough therapy. A request for the designation may be made concurrently with, or at any time after, the submission of an application for the investigation of the drug under section 505(i) or section 351(a)(3) of the Public Health Service Act.

(3) Designation. —

(A) In General. — Not later than 60 calendar days after the receipt of a request under paragraph (2), the Secretary shall determine whether the drug that is the subject of the request meets the criteria described in paragraph (1). If the Secretary finds that the drug meets the criteria, the Secretary shall designate the drug as a breakthrough therapy and shall take such actions as are appropriate to expedite the development and review of the application for approval of such drug.

(B) Actions. — The actions to expedite the development and review of an application under subparagraph (A) may include, as appropriate —

(i) holding meetings with the sponsor and the review team throughout the development of the drug;

(ii) providing timely advice to, and interactive communication with, the sponsor regarding the development of the drug to ensure that the development program to gather the nonclinical and clinical data necessary for approval is as efficient as practicable;

(iii) involving senior managers and experienced review staff, as appropriate, in a collaborative, cross-disciplinary review;

(iv) assigning a cross-disciplinary project lead for the Food and Drug Administration review team to facilitate an efficient review of the development program and to serve as a scientific liaison between the review team and the sponsor; and

(v) taking steps to ensure that the design of the clinical trials is as efficient as practicable, when scientifically appropriate, such as by minimizing the number of patients exposed to a potentially less efficacious treatment.

(b) Designation of Drug as a Fast Track Product. —

(1) In General. — The Secretary shall, at the request of the sponsor of a new drug, facilitate the development and expedite the review of such drug if it is intended, whether alone or in combination with one or more other drugs, for the treatment of a serious or life-threatening condition, and it demonstrates the potential to address unmet medical needs for such a disease or condition, or if the Secretary designates the drug as a qualified infectious disease product under section 505E(d). (In this section, such a drug is referred to as a "fast track product".)

(2) Request for Designation. — The sponsor of a new drug may request the Secretary to designate the drug as a fast track product. A request for the designation may be made concurrently with, or at any time after, submission of an application for the investigation of the drug under section 505(i) or section 351(a)(3) of the Public Health Service Act.

(3) Designation. — Within 60 calendar days after the receipt of a request under paragraph (2), the Secretary shall determine whether the drug that is the subject of the request meets the criteria described in paragraph (1). If the Secretary finds that the drug meets the criteria, the Secretary shall designate the drug as a fast track product and shall take such actions as are appropriate to expedite the development and review of the application for approval of such product.

(c) Accelerated Approval of a Drug for a Serious or Life-Threatening Disease or Condition, Including a Fast Track Product. —

(1) In General. —

(A) Accelerated Approval. — The Secretary may approve an application for approval of a product for a serious or life-threatening disease or condition, including a fast track product, under section 505(c) or section 351(a) of the Public Health Service Act upon a determination that the product has an effect on a surrogate endpoint that is reasonably likely to predict clinical benefit, or on a clinical endpoint that can be measured earlier than irreversible morbidity or mortality, that is reasonably likely to predict an effect on irreversible morbidity or mortality or other clinical benefit, taking into account the severity, rarity, or prevalence of the condition and the availability or lack of alternative treatments. The approval described in the preceding sentence is referred to in this section as 'accelerated approval'.

(B) Evidence. — The evidence to support that an endpoint is reasonably likely to predict clinical benefit under subparagraph (A) may include epidemiological, pathophysiological, therapeutic, pharmacologic, or other evidence developed using biomarkers, for example, or other scientific methods or tools.

(2) Limitation. — Approval of a product under this subsection may be subject to 1 or both of the following requirements:

(A) That the sponsor conduct appropriate postapproval studies to verify and describe the predicted effect on irreversible morbidity or mortality or other clinical benefit.

(B) That the sponsor submit copies of all promotional materials related to the product during the preapproval review period and, following approval and for such period thereafter as the Secretary determines to be appropriate, at least 30 days prior to dissemination of the materials.

(3) Expedited Withdrawal of Approval. — The Secretary may withdraw approval of a product approved under accelerated approval using expedited procedures (as prescribed by the Secretary in regulations which shall include an opportunity for an informal hearing) if —

(A) the sponsor fails to conduct any required post-approval study of the drug with due diligence;

(B) a study required to verify and describe the predicted effect on irreversible morbidity or mortality or other clinical benefit of the product fails to verify and describe such effect or benefit;

(C) other evidence demonstrates that the product is not safe or effective under the conditions of use; or

(D) the sponsor disseminates false or misleading promotional materials with respect to the product.

(d) Review of Incomplete Applications for Approval of a Fast Track Product. —

(1) In General. — If the Secretary determines, after preliminary evaluation of clinical data submitted by the sponsor, that a fast track product may be effective, the Secretary shall evaluate for filing, and may commence review of portions of, an application for the approval of the product before the sponsor submits a complete application. The Secretary shall commence such review only if the applicant —

(A) provides a schedule for submission of information necessary to make the application complete; and

(B) pays any fee that may be required under section 736.

(2) Exception. — Any time period for review of human drug applications that has been agreed to by the Secretary and that has been set forth in goals identified in letters of the Secretary (relating to the use of fees collected under section 736 to expedite the drug development process and the review of human drug applications) shall not apply to an application submitted under paragraph (1) until the date on which the application is complete.

(e) Construction. —

(1) Purpose. — The amendments made by the Food and Drug Administration Safety and Innovation Act and the 21st Century Cures Act to this section are intended to encourage the Secretary to utilize innovative and flexible approaches to the assessment of products under accelerated approval for treatments for patients with serious or life-threatening diseases or conditions and unmet medical needs.

(2) Construction. — Nothing in this section shall be construed to alter the standards of evidence under subsection (c) or (d) of section 505 (including the substantial evidence standard in section 505(d) of this Act or under section 351(a) of the Public Health Service Act). Such sections and standards of evidence apply to the review and approval of products under this section, including whether a product is safe and effective. Nothing in this section alters the ability of the Secretary to rely on evidence that does not come from adequate and well-controlled investigations for the purpose of determining whether an endpoint is reasonably likely to predict clinical benefit as described in subsection (b)(1)(B).

(f) Awareness Efforts. — The Secretary shall —

(1) develop and disseminate to physicians, patient organizations, pharmaceutical and biotechnology companies, and other appropriate persons a description of the provisions of this section applicable to breakthrough therapies, accelerated approval, and fast track products; and

(2) establish a program to encourage the development of surrogate and clinical endpoints, including biomarkers, and other scientific methods and tools that can assist the Secretary in determining whether the evidence submitted in an application is reasonably likely to predict clinical benefit for serious or life-threatening conditions for which significant unmet medical needs exist.

(g) Regenerative Advanced Therapy.—

(1) In General.—The Secretary, at the request of the sponsor of a drug, shall facilitate an efficient development program for, and expedite review of, such drug if the drug qualifies as a regenerative advanced therapy under the criteria described in paragraph (2).

(2) Criteria.—A drug is eligible for designation as a regenerative advanced therapy under this subsection if—

(A) the drug is a regenerative medicine therapy (as defined in paragraph (8));

(B) the drug is intended to treat, modify, reverse, or cure a serious or life-threatening disease or condition; and

(C) preliminary clinical evidence indicates that the drug has the potential to address unmet medical needs for such a disease or condition.

(3) Request for Designation.—The sponsor of a drug may request the Secretary to designate the drug as a regenerative advanced therapy concurrently with, or at any time after, submission of an application for the investigation of the drug under section 505(i) of this Act or section 351(a)(3) of the Public Health Service Act.

(4) Designation.—Not later than 60 calendar days after the receipt of a request under paragraph (3), the Secretary shall determine whether the drug that is the subject of the request meets the criteria described in paragraph (2). If the Secretary determines that the drug meets the criteria, the Secretary shall designate the drug as a regenerative advanced therapy and shall take such actions as are appropriate under paragraph (1). If the Secretary determines that a drug does not meet the criteria for such designation, the Secretary shall include with the determination a written description of the rationale for such determination.

(5) Actions.—The sponsor of a regenerative advanced therapy shall be eligible for the actions to expedite development and review of such therapy under subsection (a)(3)(B), including early interactions to discuss any potential surrogate or intermediate endpoint to be used to support the accelerated approval of an application for the product under subsection (c).

(6) Access to Expedited Approval Pathways.—An application for a regenerative advanced therapy under section 505(b)(1) of this Act or section 351(a) of the Public Health Service Act may be—

(A) eligible for priority review, as described in the Manual of Policies and Procedures of the Food and Drug Administration and goals identified in the letters described in section 101(b) of the Prescription Drug User Fee Amendments of 2012; and

(B) eligible for accelerated approval under subsection (c), as agreed upon pursuant to subsection (a)(3)(B), through, as appropriate—

(i) surrogate or intermediate endpoints reasonably likely to predict long-term clinical benefit; or

(ii) reliance upon data obtained from a meaningful number of sites, including through expansion to additional sites, as appropriate.

(7) Postapproval Requirements.—The sponsor of a regenerative advanced therapy that is granted accelerated approval and is subject to the postapproval requirements under subsetction (c) may, as appropriate, fulfill such requirements, as the Secretary may require, through—

(A) the submission of clinical evidence, clinical studies, patient registries, or other sources of real world evidence, such as electronic health records;

(B) the collection of larger confirmatory data sets, as agreed upon pursuant to subsection (a)(3)(B); or

(C) postapproval monitoring of all patients treated with such therapy prior to approval of the therapy.

(8) Definition.—For purposes of this section, the term "regenerative medicine therapy" includes cell therapy, therapeutic tissue engineering products, human cell and tissue products, and combination products using any such therapies or products, except for those regulated solely under section 361 of the Public Health Service Act and part 1271 of title 21, Code of Federal Regulations.

(h) Limited Population Pathway for Antibacterial and Antifungal Drugs.—

(1) In General.— The Secretary may approve an antibacterial or antifungal drug, alone or in combination with one or more other drugs, as a limited population drug pursuant to this subsection only if—

(A) the drug is intended to treat a serious or life-threatening infection in a limited population of patients with unmet needs;

(B) the standards for approval under section 505(c) and (d), or the standards for licensure under section 351 of the Public Health Service Act, as applicable, are met; and

(C) the Secretary receives a written request from the sponsor to approve the drug as a limited population drug pursuant to this subsection.

(2) Benefit-Risk Consideration.—The Secretary's determination of safety and effectiveness of an antibacterial or antifungal drug shall reflect the benefit-risk profile of such drug in the intended limited population, taking into account the severity, rarity, or prevalence of the infection the drug is intended to treat and the availability or lack of alternative treatment in such limited population. Such drug may be approved under this subsection notwithstanding a lack of evidence to fully establish a favorable benefit-risk profile in a population that is broader than the intended limited population.

(3) Additional Requirements.—A drug approved under this subsection shall be subject to the following requirements, in addition to any other applicable requirements of this Act:

(A) Labeling.—To indicate that the safety and effectiveness of a drug approved under this subsection has been demonstrated only with respect to a limited population—

(i) all labeling and advertising of an antibacterial or antifungal drug approved under this subsection shall contain the statement "Limited Population" in a prominent manner and adjacent to, and not more prominent than—

(I) the proprietary name of such drug, if any; or

(II) if there is no proprietary name, the established name of the drug, if any, as defined in section 503(e)(3), or, in the case of a drug that is a biological product, the proper name, as defined by regulation; and

(ii) the prescribing information for the drug required by section 201.57 of title 21, Code of Federal Regulations (or any successor regulation) shall also include the following statement: "This drug is indicated for use in a limited and specific population of patients."

(B) Promotional Material.—The sponsor of an antibacterial or antifungal drug subject to this subsection shall submit to the Secretary copies of all promotional materials related to such drug at least 30 calendar days prior to dissemination of the materials.

(4) Other Programs.—A sponsor of a drug that seeks approval of a drug under this subsection may also seek designation or approval, as applicable, of such drug under other applicable sections or subsections of this Act or the Public Health Service Act.

(5) Guidance.—Not later than 18 months after the date of enactment of the 21st Century Cures Act [December 13, 2016 —Ed.], the Secretary shall issue draft guidance describing criteria, processes, and other general considerations for demonstrating the safety and effectiveness of limited population antibacterial and antifungal drugs. The Secretary shall publish final guidance within 18 months of the close of the public comment period on such draft guidance. The Secretary may approve antibacterial and antifungal drugs under this subsection prior to issuing guidance under this paragraph.

(6) Advice.—The Secretary shall provide prompt advice to the sponsor of a drug for which the sponsor seeks approval under this subsection to enable the sponsor to plan a development program to obtain the necessary data for such approval, and to conduct any additional studies that would be required to gain approval of such drug for use in a broader population.

(7) Termination of Limitations.—If, after approval of a drug under this subsection, the Secretary approves a broader indication for such drug under section 505(b) or section 351(a) of the Public Health Service Act, the Secretary may remove any postmarketing conditions, including requirements with respect to labeling and review of promotional materials under paragraph (3), applicable to the approval of the drug under this subsection.

(8) Rules of Construction.—Nothing in this subsection shall be construed to alter the authority of the Secretary to approve drugs pursuant to this Act or section 351 of the Public Health Service Act, including the standards of evidence and applicable conditions for approval under such Acts, the standards of approval of a drug under such Acts, or to alter the authority of the Secretary to monitor drugs pursuant to such Acts.

(9) Reporting and Accountability.—

(A) Biennial Reporting.—The Secretary shall report to Congress not less often than once every 2 years on the number of requests for approval, and the number of approvals, of an antibacterial or antifungal drug under this subsection.

(B) GAO Report.—Not later than December 2021, the Comptroller General of the United States shall submit to the Committee on Energy and Commerce of the House of Representatives and the Committee on Health, Education, Labor and Pensions of the Senate a report on the coordination of activities required under section 319E of the Public Health Service Act. Such report shall include a review of such activities, and the extent to which the use of the pathway established under this subsection has streamlined premarket approval for antibacterial or antifungal drugs for limited populations, if such pathway has functioned as intended, if such pathway has helped provide for safe and effective treatment for patients, if such premarket approval would be appropriate for other categories of drugs, and if the authorities under this subsection have affected antibacterial or antifungal resistance.

Sec.___. [356-1] Accelerated Approval of Priority Countermeasures.

(a) The Secretary of Health and Human Services may designate a priority countermeasure as a fast-track product pursuant to section 506 or as a device granted review priority pursuant to section 515(d)(5). Such a designation may be made prior to the submission of—

(1) a request for designation by the sponsor or applicant; or

(2) an application for the investigation of the drug under section 505(i) or section 351(a)(3) of the Public Health Service Act.

Nothing in this subsection shall be construed to prohibit a sponsor or applicant from declining such a designation.

(b) A drug for which approval is sought under section 505(b) or section 351 of the Public Health Service Act on the basis of evidence of effectiveness that is derived from animal studies pursuant to section 123 may be designated as a fast track product for purposes of this section.

(c) A priority countermeasure that is a drug or biological product shall be considered a priority drug or biological product for purposes of performance goals for priority drugs or biological products agreed to by the Commissioner of Food and Drugs.

(d) For purposes of this title:

(1) The term "priority countermeasure" has the meaning given such term in section 247d-6(h)(4) of Title 42.

(2) The term "priority drugs or biological products" means a drug or biological product that is the subject of a drug or biologics application referred to in section 101(4) of the Food and Drug Administration Modernization Act of 1997.

Sec. 506A. [356a] Manufacturing Changes.

(a) In General. — With respect to a drug for which there is in effect an approved application under section 505 or 512 or a license under section 351 of the Public Health Service Act, a change from the manufacturing process approved pursuant to such application or license may be made, and the drug as made with the change may be distributed, if —

(1) the holder of the approved application or license (referred to in this section as a "holder") has validated the effects of the change in accordance with subsection (b); and

(2) —

(A) in the case of a major manufacturing change, the holder has complied with the requirements of subsection (c); or

(B) in the case of a change that is not a major manufacturing change, the holder complies with the applicable requirements of subsection (d).

(b) Validation of Effects of Changes. — For purposes of subsection (a)(1), a drug made with a manufacturing change (whether a major manufacturing change or otherwise) may be distributed only if, before distribution of the drug as so made, the holder involved validates the effects of the change on the identity, strength, quality, purity, and potency of the drug as the identity, strength, quality, purity, and potency may relate to the safety or effectiveness of the drug.

(c) Major Manufacturing Changes. —

(1) Requirement of Supplemental Application. — For purposes of subsection (a)(2)(A), a drug made with a major manufacturing change may be distributed only if, before the distribution of the drug as so made, the holder involved submits to the Secretary a supplemental application for such change and the Secretary approves the application. The application shall contain such information as the Secretary determines to be appropriate, and shall include the information developed under subsection (b) by the holder in validating the effects of the change.

(2) Changes Qualifying as Major Changes. — For purposes of subsection (a)(2)(A), a major manufacturing change is a manufacturing change that is determined by the Secretary to have substantial potential to adversely affect the identity, strength, quality, purity, or potency of the drug as they may relate to the safety or effectiveness of a drug. Such a change includes a change that —

(A) is made in the qualitative or quantitative formulation of the drug involved or in the specifications in the approved application or license referred to in subsection (a) for the drug (unless exempted by the Secretary by regulation or guidance from the requirements of this subsection);

(B) is determined by the Secretary by regulation or guidance to require completion of an appropriate clinical study demonstrating equivalence of the drug to the drug as manufactured without the change; or

(C) is another type of change determined by the Secretary by regulation or guidance to have a substantial potential to adversely affect the safety or effectiveness of the drug.

(d) Other Manufacturing Changes. —

(1) In General. — For purposes of subsection (a)(2)(B), the Secretary may regulate drugs made with manufacturing changes that are not major manufacturing changes as follows:

(A) The Secretary may in accordance with paragraph (2) authorize holders to distribute such drugs without submitting a supplemental application for such changes.

(B) The Secretary may in accordance with paragraph (3) require that, prior to the distribution of such drugs, holders submit to the Secretary supplemental applications for such changes.

(C) The Secretary may establish categories of such changes and designate categories to which subparagraph (A) applies and categories to which subparagraph (B) applies.

(2) Changes Not Requiring Supplemental Application. —

(A) Submission of Report. — A holder making a manufacturing change to which paragraph (1)(A) applies shall submit to the Secretary a report on the change, which shall contain such information as the Secretary determines to be appropriate, and which shall include the information developed under subsection (b) by the holder in validating the effects of the change. The report shall be submitted by such date as the Secretary may specify.

(B) Authority Regarding Annual Reports. — In the case of a holder that during a single year makes more than one manufacturing change to which paragraph (1)(A) applies, the Secretary may in carrying out subparagraph (A) authorize the holder to comply with such subparagraph by submitting a single report for the year that provides the information required in such subparagraph for all the changes made by the holder during the year.

(3) Changes Requiring Supplemental Application. —

(A) Submission of Supplemental Application. — The supplemental application required under paragraph (1)(B) for a manufacturing change shall contain such information as the Secretary determines to be appropriate, which shall include the information developed under subsection (b) by the holder in validating the effects of the change.

(B) Authority for Distribution. — In the case of a manufacturing change to which paragraph (1)(B) applies:

(i) The holder involved may commence distribution of the drug involved 30 days after the Secretary receives the supplemental application under such paragraph, unless the Secretary notifies the holder within such 30-day period that prior approval of the application is required before distribution may be commenced.

(ii) The Secretary may designate a category of such changes for the purpose of providing that, in the case of a change that is in such category, the holder involved may commence distribution of the drug involved upon the receipt by the Secretary of a supplemental application for the change.

(iii) If the Secretary disapproves the supplemental application, the Secretary may order the manufacturer to cease the distribution of the drugs that have been made with the manufacturing change.

Sec. 506B. [356b] Reports of Postmarketing Studies.

(a) Submission —

(1) In General. — A sponsor of a drug that has entered into an agreement with the Secretary to conduct a postmarketing study of the drug shall submit to the Secretary, within 1 year after the approval of such drug and annually thereafter until the study is completed or terminated, a report of the progress of the study or the reasons for the failure of the sponsor to conduct the study. The report shall be submitted in such form as is prescribed by the Secretary in regulations issued by the Secretary.

(2) Agreements Prior to Effective Date. — Any agreements entered into between the Secretary and a sponsor of a drug, prior to the date of enactment of the Food and Drug Administration Modernization Act of 1997 [November 21, 1997 — Ed.], to conduct a postmarketing study of a drug shall be subject to the requirements of paragraph (1). An initial report for such an agreement shall be submitted within 6 months after the date of the issuance of the regulations under paragraph (1).

(b) Consideration of Information as Public Information. — Any information pertaining to a report described in subsection (a) shall be considered to be public information to the extent that the information is necessary —

(1) to identify the sponsor; and

(2) to establish the status of a study described in subsection (a) and the reasons, if any, for any failure to carry out the study.

(c) Status of Studies and Reports. — The Secretary shall annually develop and publish in the Federal Register a report that provides information on the status of the postmarketing studies —

(1) that sponsors have entered into agreements to conduct; and

(2) for which reports have been submitted under subsection (a)(1).

(d) Disclosure. — If a sponsor fails to complete an agreed upon study required by this section by its original or otherwise negotiated deadline, the Secretary shall publish a statement on the Internet site of the Food and Drug Administration stating that the study was not completed and, if the reasons for such failure to complete the study were not satisfactory to the Secretary, a statement that such reasons were not satisfactory to the Secretary.

(e) Notification. — With respect to studies of the type required under section 506(c)(2)(A) or under section 314.510 or 601.41 of title 21, Code of Federal Regulations, as each of such sections was in effect on the day before the effective date [October 1, 2002 — Ed.] of this subsection, the Secretary may require that a sponsor who, for reasons not satisfactory to the Secretary, fails to complete by its deadline a study under any of such sections of such type for a drug or biological product (including such a study conducted after such effective date) notify practitioners who prescribe such drug or biological product of the failure to complete such study and the questions of clinical benefit, and, where appropriate, questions of safety, that remain unanswered as a result of the failure to complete such study. Nothing in this subsection shall be construed as altering the requirements of the types of studies required under section 506(c)(2)(A) or under section 314.510 or 601.41 of title 21, Code of Federal Regulations, as so in effect, or as prohibiting the Secretary from modifying such sections of title 21 of such Code to provide for studies in addition to those of such type.

Sec. 506C. [356c] Discontinuance or Interruption in the Production of Life-Saving Drugs.

(a) In General. — A manufacturer of a drug —

(1) that is —

(A) life-supporting;

(B) life-sustaining; or

(C) intended for use in the prevention or treatment of a debilitating disease or condition, including any such drug used in emergency medical care or during surgery; and

(2) that is not a radio pharmaceutical drug product or any other product as designated by the Secretary,

shall notify the Secretary, in accordance with subsection (b), of a permanent discontinuance in the manufacture of the drug or an interruption of the manufacture of the drug that is likely to lead to a meaningful disruption in the supply of that drug in the United States, and the reasons for such discontinuance or interruption.

(b) Timing. — A notice required under subsection (a) shall be submitted to the Secretary —

(1) at least 6 months prior to the date of the discontinuance or interruption; or

(2) if compliance with paragraph (1) is not possible, as soon as practicable.

(c) Distribution. — To the maximum extent practicable, the Secretary shall distribute, through such means as the Secretary deems appropriate, information on the discontinuance or interruption of the manufacture of the drugs described in subsection (a) to appropriate organizations, including physician, health provider, and patient organizations, as described in section 506E.

(d) Confidentiality. — Nothing in this section shall be construed as authorizing the Secretary to disclose any information that is a trade secret or confidential information subject to section 552(b)(4) of title 5, United States Code, or section 1905 of title 18, United States Code.

(e) Coordination with Attorney General. — Not later than 30 days after the receipt of a notification described in subsection (a), the Secretary shall —

(1) determine whether the notification pertains to a controlled substance subject to a production quota under section 306 of the Controlled Substances Act; and

(2) if necessary, as determined by the Secretary —

(A) notify the Attorney General that the Secretary has received such a notification;

(B) request that the Attorney General increase the aggregate and individual production quotas under section 306 of the Controlled Substances Act applicable to such controlled substance and any ingredient therein to a level the Secretary deems necessary to address a shortage of a controlled substance based on the best available market data; and

(C) if the Attorney General determines that the level requested is not necessary to address a shortage of a controlled substance, the Attorney General shall provide to the Secretary a written response detailing the basis for the Attorney General's determination.

The Secretary shall make the written response provided under subparagraph (C) available to the public on the Internet Web site of the Food and Drug Administration.

(f) Failure to Meet Requirements. — If a person fails to submit information required under subsection (a) in accordance with subsection (b) —

(1) the Secretary shall issue a letter to such person information such person of such failure;

(2) not later than 30 calendar days after the issuance of the letter under paragraph (1), the person who receives such letter shall submit to the Secretary a written response to such letter setting forth the basis for noncompliance and providing information required under subsection (a); and

(3) not later than 45 calendar days after the issuance of a letter under paragraph (1), the Secretary shall make such letter and any response to such letter under paragraph (2) available to the public on the Internet Web site of the Food and Drug Administration, with appropriate redactions made to protect information described in subsection (d), except that, if the Secretary determines that the letter under paragraph (1) was issued in error or, after review of such response, the person had a reasonable basis for not notifying as required under subsection (a), the requirements of this paragraph shall not apply.

(g) Expedited Inspections and Reviews. — If, based on notifications described in subsection (a) or any other relevant information, the Secretary concludes that there is, or is likely to be, a drug shortage of a drug described in subsection (a), the Secretary may —

(1) expedite the review of a supplement to a new drug application submitted under section 505(b), an abbreviated new drug application submitted under section 505(j), or a supplement to such an application submitted under section 505(j), that could help mitigate or prevent such shortage; or

(2) expedite an inspection or reinspection of an establishment that could help mitigate or prevent such drug shortage.

(h) Definitions. — For purposes of this section —

(1) the term "drug" —

(A) means a drug (as defined in section 201(g)) that is intended for human use and that is subject to section 503(b)(1); and

(B) does not include biological products (as defined in section 351 of the Public Health Service Act), unless otherwise provided by the Secretary in the regulations promulgated under subsection (i);

(2) the term "drug shortage" or "shortage", with respect to a drug, means a period of time when the demand or projected demand for the drug within the United States exceeds the supply of the drug; and

(3) the term "meaningful disruption" —

(A) means a change in production that is reasonably likely to lead to a reduction in the supply of a drug by a manufacturer that is more than negligible and affects the ability of the manufacturer to fill orders or meet expected demand for its product; and

(B) does not include interruptions in manufacturing due to matters such as routine maintenance or insignificant changes in manufacturing so long as the manufacturer expects to resume operations in a short period of time.

(i) Regulations. —

(1) In General. — Not later than 18 months after the date of enactment of the Food and Drug Administration Safety and Innovation Act, the Secretary shall adopt a final regulation implementing this section.

(2) Contents. — Such regulations shall define, for purposes of this section, the terms "life-supporting", "life-sustaining", and "intended for use in the prevention or treatment of a debilitating disease or condition".

(3) Inclusion of Biological Products. —

(A) In General. — The Secretary may by regulation apply this section to biological products (as defined in section 351 of the Public Health Service Act), including plasma products derived from human plasma protein and their recombinant analogs, if the Secretary determines such inclusion would benefit the public health. Such regulation shall take into account any supply reporting programs and shall aim to reduce duplicative notification.

(B) Rule for Vaccines. — If the Secretary applies this section to vaccines pursuant to subparagraph (A), the Secretary shall —

(i) consider whether the notification requirement under subsection (a) may be satisfied by submitting a notification to the Centers for Disease Control and Prevention under the vaccine shortage notification program of such Centers; and

(ii) explain the determination made by the Secretary under clause (i) in the regulation.

(4) Procedure. — In promulgating a regulation implementing this section, the Secretary shall —

(A) issue a notice of proposed rulemaking that includes the proposed regulation;

(B) provide a period of not less than 60 days for comments on the proposed regulation; and

(C) publish the final regulation not less than 30 days before the regulation's effective date.

(5) Restrictions. — Notwithstanding any other provision of Federal law, in implementing this section, the Secretary shall only promulgate regulations as described in paragraph (4).

Sec. 506C-1. [356c-1] Annual Reporting on Drug Shortages.

(a) Annual Reports to Congress. — Not later than March 31 of each calendar year, the Secretary shall submit to the Committee on Energy and Commerce of the House of Representatives and the Committee on Health, Education, Labor, and Pensions of the Senate a report, with respect to the preceding calendar year, on drug shortages that —

(1) Specifies the number of manufacturers that submitted a notification to the Secretary under section 506C(a) during such calendar year;

(2) describes the communication between the field investigators of the Food and Drug Administration and the staff of the Center for Drug Evaluation and Research's Office of Compliance and Drug Shortage Program, including the Food and Drug Administration's procedures for enabling and ensuring such communication;

(3) —

(A) lists the major actions taken by the Secretary to prevent or mitigate the drug shortages described in paragraph (7);

(B) in the list under subparagraph (A), includes —

(i) the number of applications and supplements for which the Secretary expedited review under section 506C(g)(1) during such calendar year; and

(ii) the number of establishment inspections or reinspections that the Secretary expedited under section 506C(g)(2) during such calendar year;

(4) describes the coordination between the Food and Drug Administration and the Drug Enforcement Administration on efforts to prevent or alleviate drug shortages;

(5) identifies the number of and describes the instances in which the Food and Drug Administration exercised regulatory flexibility and discretion to prevent or alleviate a drug shortage;

(6) lists the names of manufacturers that were issued letters under section 506C(f); and

(7) specifies the number of drug shortages occurring during such calendar year, as identified by the Secretary.

(b) Trend Analysis. — The Secretary is authorized to retain a third party to conduct a study, if the Secretary believes such a study would help clarify the causes, trends, or solutions related to drug shortages.

(c) Definition. — In this section, the term "drug shortage" or "shortage" has the meaning given such term in section 506C.

Sec. 506D. [356d] Coordination; Task Force and Strategic Plan.

(a) Task Force and Strategic Plan. —

(1) In General. —

(A) Task Force. — As soon as practicable after the date of enactment of the Food and Drug Administration Safety and Innovation Act, the Secretary shall establish a task force to develop and implement a strategic plan for enhancing the Secretary's response to preventing and mitigating drug shortages.

(B) Strategic Plan. — The strategic plan described in subparagraph (A) shall include —

(i) plans for enhanced interagency and intra-agency coordination, communication, and decisionmaking;

(ii) plans for ensuring that drug shortages are considered when the Secretary initiates a regulatory action that could precipitate a drug shortage or exacerbate an existing drug shortage;

(iii) plans for effective communication with outside stakeholders, including who the Secretary should alert about potential or actual drug shortages, how the communication should occur, and what types of information should be shared;

(iv) plans for considering the impact of drug shortages on research and clinical trials; and

(v) an examination of whether to establish a "qualified manufacturing partner program", as described in subparagraph (C).

(C) Description of Program. — In conducting the examination of a "qualified manufacturing partner program" under subparagraph (B)(v), the Secretary —

(i) shall take into account that —

(I) a "qualified manufacturer", for purposes of such program, would need to have the capability and capacity to supply products determined or anticipated to be in shortage; and

(II) in examining the capability and capacity to supply products in shortage, the "qualified manufacturer" could have a site that manufactures a drug listed under section 506E or have the capacity to produce drugs in response to a shortage within a rapid timeframe; and

(ii) shall examine whether incentives are necessary to encourage the participation of "qualified manufacturers" in such a program.

(D) Consultation. — In carrying out this paragraph, the task force shall ensure consultation with the appropriate offices within the Food and Drug Administration, including the Office of the Commissioner, the Center for Drug Evaluation and Research, the Office of Regulatory Affairs, and employees within the Department of Health and Human Services with expertise regarding drug shortages. The Secretary shall engage external stakeholders and experts as appropriate.

(2) Timing. — Not later than 1 year after the date of enactment of the Food and Drug Administration Safety and Innovation Act, the task force shall —

(A) publish the strategic plan described in paragraph (1); and

(B) submit such plan to Congress.

(b) Communication. — The Secretary shall ensure that, prior to any enforcement action or issuance of a warning letter that the Secretary determines could reasonably be anticipated to lead to a meaningful disruption in the supply in the United States of a drug described under section 506C(a), there is a communication with the appropriate office of the Food and Drug Administration with expertise regarding drug shortages regarding whether the action or letter could cause, or exacerbate, a shortage of the drug.

(c) Action. — If the Secretary determines, after the communication described in subsection (b), that an enforcement action or a warning letter could reasonably cause or exacerbate a shortage of a drug described under section 506C(a), then the Secretary shall evaluate the risks associated with the impact of such shortage upon patients and those risks associated with the violation involved before taking such action or issuing such letter, unless there is imminent risk of serious adverse health consequences or death to humans.

(d) Reporting by Other Entities. — The Secretary shall identify or establish a mechanism by which health care providers and other third-party organizations may report to the Secretary evidence of a drug shortage.

(e) Review and Construction. — No determination, finding, action, or omission of the Secretary under this section shall —

(1) be subject to judicial review; or

(2) be construed to establish a defense to an enforcement action by the Secretary.

(f) Sunset. — Subsections (a), (b), (c), and (e) shall cease to be effective on the date that is 5 years after the date of enactment of the Food and Drug Administration Safety and Innovation Act.

Sec. 506E. [356e] Drug Shortage List.

(a) Establishment. — The Secretary shall maintain an up-to-date list of drugs that are determined by the Secretary to be in shortage in the United States.

(b) Contents. — For each drug on such list, the Secretary shall include the following information:

(1) The name of the drug in shortage, including the National Drug Code number for such drug.

(2) The name of each manufacturer of such drug.

(3) The reason for the shortage, as determined by the Secretary, selecting from the following categories:

(A) Requirements related to complying with good manufacturing practices.

(B) Regulatory delay.

(C) Shortage of an active ingredient.

(D) Shortage of an inactive ingredient component.

(E) Discontinuance of the manufacture of the drug.

(F) Delay in shipping of the drug.

(G) Demand increase for the drug.

(4) The estimated duration of the shortage as determined by the Secretary.

(c) Public Availability. —

(1) In General. — Subject to paragraphs (2) and (3), the Secretary shall make the information in such list publicly available.

(2) Trade Secrets and Confidential Information. — Nothing in this section alters or amends section 1905 of title 18, United States Code, or section 552(b)(4) of title 5 of such Code.

(3) Public Health Exception. — The Secretary may choose not to make information collected under this section publicly available under paragraph (1) or section 506C(c) if the Secretary determines that disclosure of such information would adversely affect the public health (such as by increasing the possibility of hoarding or other disruption of the availability of drug products to patients).

Sec. 506F. [356f] Hospital Repackaging of Drugs in Shortage.

(a) Definitions. — In this section:

(1) Drug. — The term "drug" excludes any controlled substance (as such term is defined in section 102 of the Controlled Substances Act).

(2) Health System. — The term "health system" means a collection of hospitals that are owned and operated by the same entity and that share access to databases with drug order information for their patients.

(3) Repackage. — For the purposes of this section only, the term "repackage", with respect to a drug, means to divide the volume of a drug into smaller amounts in order to —

(A) extend the supply of a drug in response to the placement of the drug on a drug shortage list under section 506(E); and

(B) facilitate access to the drug by hospitals within the same health system.

(b) Exclusion from Registration. — Notwithstanding any other provision of this Act, a hospital shall not be considered an establishment for which registration is required under section 510 solely because it repackages a drug and transfers it to another hospital within the same health system in accordance with the conditions in subsection (c) —

(1) during any period in which the drug is listed on the drug shortage list under section 506E; or

(2) during the 60-day period following any period described in paragraph (1).

(c) Conditions. — Subsection (b) shall only apply to a hospital, with respect to the repackaging of a drug for transfer to another hospital within the same health system, if the following conditions are met:

(1) Drug for Intrasystem Use Only. — In no case may a drug that has been repackaged in accordance with this section be sold or otherwise distributed by the health system or a hospital within the system to an entity or individual that is not a hospital within such health system.

(2) Compliance with State Rules. — Repackaging of a drug under this section shall be done in compliance with applicable State requirements of each State in which the drug is repackaged and received.

(d) Termination. — This section shall not apply on or after the date on which the Secretary issues final guidance that clarifies the policy of the Food and Drug Administration regarding hospital pharmacies repackaging and safely transferring repackaged drugs to other hospitals within the same health system during a drug shortage.

Sec. 506G. [356g] Standards for Regenerative Medicine and Regenerative Advanced Therapies.

(a) In General.—Not later than 2 years after the date of enactment of the 21st Century Cures Act [December 13, 2016 —Ed.], the Secretary, in consultation with the National Institute of Standards and Technology and stakeholders (including regenerative medicine and advanced therapies manufacturers and clinical trial sponsors, contract manufacturers, academic institutions, practicing clinicians, regenerative medicine and advanced therapies industry organizations, and standard setting organizations), shall facilitate an effort to coordinate and prioritize the development of standards and consensus definition of terms, through a public process, to support, through regulatory predictability, the development, evaluation, and review of regenerative medicine therapies and regenerative advanced therapies, including with respect to the manufacturing processes and controls of such products.

(b) Activities.—

(1) In General.—In carrying out this section, the Secretary shall continue to—

(A) identify opportunities to help advance the development of regenerative medicine therapies and regenerative advanced therapies;

(B) identify opportunities for the development of laboratory regulatory science research and documentary standards that the Secretary determines would help support the development, evaluation, and review of regenerative medicine therapies and regenerative advanced therapies through regulatory predictability; and

(C) work with stakeholders, such as those described in subsection (a), as appropriate, in the development of such standards.

(2) Regulations and Guidance.— Not later than 1 year after the development of standards as described in subsection (a), the Secretary shall review relevant regulations and guidance and, through a public process, update such regulations and guidance as the Secretary determines appropriate.

(c) Definitions.—For purposes of this section, the terms "regenerative medicine therapy" and "regenerative advanced therapy" have the meanings given such terms in section 506(g).

Sec. 506H. [356h] Competitive Generic Therapies.

(a) In General. — The Secretary may, at the request of an applicant of a drug that is designated as a competitive generic therapy pursuant to subsection (b), expedite the development and review of an abbreviated new drug application under section 505(j) for such drug.

(b) Designation Process. —

(1) Request. — The applicant may request the Secretary to designate the drug as a competitive generic therapy.

(2) Timing. — A request under paragraph (1) may be made concurrently with, or at any time prior to, the submission of an abbreviated new drug application for the drug under section 505(j).

(3) Criteria. — A drug is eligible for designation as a competitive generic therapy under this section if the Secretary determines that there is inadequate generic competition.

(4) Designation. — Not later than 60 calendar days after the receipt of a request under paragraph (1), the Secretary may —

(A) determine whether the drug that is the subject of the request meets the criteria described in paragraph (3); and

(B) if the Secretary finds that the drug meets such criteria, designate the drug as a competitive generic therapy.

(c) Actions. — In expediting the development and review of an application under subsection (a), the Secretary may, as requested by the applicant, take actions including the following:

(1) Hold meetings with the applicant and the review team throughout the development of the drug prior to submission of the application for such drug under section 505(j).

(2) Provide timely advice to, and interactive communication with, the applicant regarding the development of the drug to ensure that the development program to gather the data necessary for approval is as efficient as practicable.

(3) Involve senior managers and experienced review staff, as appropriate, in a collaborative, coordinated review of such application, including with respect to drug-device combination products and other complex products.

(4) Assign a cross-disciplinary project lead —

(A) to facilitate an efficient review of the development program and application, including manufacturing inspections; and

(B) to serve as a scientific liaison between the review team and the applicant.

(d) Reporting Requirement. — Not later than one year after the date of the approval of an application under section 505(j) with respect to a drug for which the development and review is expedited under this section ,the sponsor of such drug shall report to the Secretary on whether the drug has been marketed in interstate commerce since the date of such approval.

(e) Definitions. — In this section:

(1) The term 'generic drug' means a drug that is approved pursuant to section 505(j).

(2) The term 'inadequate generic competition' means, with respect to a drug, there is not more than one approved drug on the list of drugs described in section 505(j)(7)(A) (not including drugs on the discontinued section of such list) that is —

(A) the reference listed drug; or

(B) a generic drug with the same reference listed drug as the drug for which designation as a competitive generic therapy is sought.

(3) The term 'reference listed drug' means the listed drug (as such term is used in section 505(j)) for the drug involved.

Sec. 506I. [356i] Prompt Reports of Marketing Status.

(a) Notification of Withdrawal. — The holder of an application approved under subsection (c) or (j) of section 505 shall notify the Secretary in writing 180 days prior to withdrawing the approved drug from sale, or if 180 days is not practicable as soon as practicable but not later than the date of withdrawal. The holder shall include with such notice the—

(1) National Drug Code;

(2) identity of the drug by established name and by proprietary name, if any;

(3) new drug application number or abbreviated application number;

(4) strength of the drug;

(5) date on which the drug is expected to no longer be available for sale; and

(6) reason for withdrawal of the drug.

(b) Notification of Drug Not Available for Sale.—The holder of an application approved under subsection (c) or (j) shall notify the Secretary in writing within 180 calendar days of the date of approval of the drug if the drug will not be available for sale within 180 calendar days of such date of approval. The holder shall include with such notice the—

(1) identity of the drug by established name and by proprietary name, if any;

(2) new drug application number or abbreviated application number;

(3) strength of the drug;

(4) date on which the drug will be available for sale, if known; and

(5) reason for not marketing the drug after approval.

(c) Additional One-Time Report.—Within 180 days of the date of enactment of this section, all holders of applications approved under subsection (c) or (j) of section 505 shall review the information in the list published under subsection 505(j)(7)(A) and shall notify the Secretary in writing that—

(1) all of the application holder's drugs in the active section of the list published under subsection 505(j)(7)(A) are available for sale; or

(2) one or more of the application holder's drugs in the active section of the list published under subsection 505(j)(7)(A) have been withdrawn from sale or have never been available for sale, and include with such notice the information required pursuant to subsection (a) or (b), as applicable.

(d) Failure to Meet Requirements.—If a holder of an approved application fails to submit the information required under subsection (a), (b), or (c), the Secretary may move the application holder's drugs from the active section of the list published under subsection 505(j)(7)(A) to the discontinued section of the list, except that the Secretary shall remove from the list in accordance with subsection 505(j)(7)(C) drugs the Secretary determines have been withdrawn from sale for reasons of safety of effectiveness.

(e) Updates.—The Secretary shall update the list published under subsection 505(j)(7)(A) based on the information provided under subsections (a), (b), and (c) by moving drugs that are not available for sale from the active section to the discontinued section of the list, except that drugs the Secretary determines have been withdrawn from sale for reasons of safety or effectiveness shall be removed from the list in accordance with subsection 505(j)(7)(C). The Secretary shall make monthly updates to the list based on the information provided pursuant to subsections (a) and (b), and shall update the list based on the information provided under subsection (c) as soon as practicable.

(f) Limitation on Use of Notices.—Any notice submitted under this section shall not be made public by the Secretary and shall be used solely for the purpose of the updates described in subsection (e).

Sec. 507. [357] Qualification of Drug Development Tools.

(a) Process for Qualification.—

(1) In General.—The Secretary shall establish a process for the qualification of drug development tools for a proposed context of use under which—

(A)(i) a requestor initiates such process by submitting a letter of intent to the Secretary; and

(ii) the Secretary accepts or declines to accept such letter of intent;

(B)(i) if the Secretary accepts the letter of intent, a requestor submits a qualification plan to the Secretary; and

(ii) the Secretary accepts or declines to accept the qualification plan; and

(C)(i) if the Secretary accepts the qualification plan, the requestor submits to the Secretary a full qualification package;

(ii) the Secretary determines whether to accept such qualification package for review; and

(iii) if the Secretary accepts such qualification package for review, the Secretary conducts such review in accordance with this section.

(2) Acceptance and Review of Submissions.—

(A) In General.—Subparagraphs (B), (C), and (D) shall apply with respect to the treatment of a letter of intent, a qualification plan, or a full qualification package submitted under paragraph (1) (referred to in this paragraph as "qualification submissions").

(B) Acceptance Factors; Nonacceptance.—The Secretary shall determine whether to accept a qualification submission based on factors which may include the scientific merit of the qualification submission. A determination not to accept a submission under paragraph (1) shall not be construed as a final determination by the Secretary under this section regarding the qualification of a drug development tool for its proposed context of use.

(C) Prioritization of Qualification Review.—The Secretary may prioritize the review of a full qualification package submitted under paragraph (1) with respect to a drug development tool, based on factors determined appropriate by the Secretary, including—

(i) as applicable, the severity, rarity, or prevalence of the disease or condition targeted by the drug development tool and the availability or lack of alternative treatments for such disease or condition; and

(ii) the identification, by the Secretary or by biomedical research consortia and other expert stakeholders, of such a drug development tool and its proposed context of use as a public health priority.

(D) Engagement of External Experts.—The Secretary may, for purposes of the review of qualification submissions, through the use of cooperative agreements, grants, or other appropriate mechanisms, consult with biomedical research consortia and may consider the recommendations of such consortia with respect to the review of any qualification plan submitted under paragraph (1) or the review of any full qualification package under paragraph (3).

(3) Review of Full Qualification Package.—The Secretary shall—

(A) conduct a comprehensive review of a full qualification package accepted under paragraph (1)(C); and

(B) determine whether the drug development tool at issue is qualified for its proposed context of use.

(4) Qualification.— The Secretary shall determine whether a drug development tool is qualified for a proposed context of use based on the scientific merit of a full qualification package reviewed under paragraph (3).

(b) Effect of Qualification.—

(1) In General.— A drug development tool determined to be qualified under subsection (a)(4) for a proposed context of use specified by the requestor may be used by any person in such context of use for the purposes described in paragraph (2).

(2) Use of a Drug Development Tool.— Subject to paragraph (3), a drug development tool qualified under this section may be used for—

(A) supporting or obtaining approval or licensure (as applicable) of a drug or biological product (including in accordance with section 506(c)) under section 505 of this Act or section 351 of the Public Health Service Act; or

(B) supporting the investigational use of a drug or biological product under section 505(i) of this Act or section 351(a)(3) of the Public Health Service Act.

(3) Rescission or Modification.—

(A) In General.— The Secretary may rescind or modify a determination under this section to qualify a drug development tool if the Secretary determines that the drug development tool is not appropriate for the proposed context of use specified by the requestor. Such a determination may be based on new information that calls into question the basis for such qualification.

(B) Meeting for Review.— If the Secretary rescinds or modifies under subparagraph (A) a determination to qualify a drug development tool, the requestor involved shall, on request, be granted a meeting with the Secretary to discuss the basis of the Secretary's decision to rescind or modify the determination before the effective date of the rescission or modification.

(c) Transparency.—

(1) In General.—Subject to paragraph (3), the Secretary shall make publicly available, and update on at least a biannual basis, on the Internet website of the Food and Drug Administration the following:

(A) Information with respect to each qualification submission under the qualification process under subsection (a), including—

(i) the stage of the review process applicable to the submission,

(ii) the date of the most recent change in stage status;

(iii) whether external scientific experts were utilized in the development of a qualification plan or the review of a full qualification package; and

(iv) submissions from requestors under the qualification process under subsection (a), including any data and evidence contained in such submissions, and any updates to such submissions.

(B) The Secretary's formal written determinations in response to such qualification submissions.

(C) Any rescissions or modifications under subsection (b)(3) of a determination to qualify a drug development tool.

(D) Summary reviews that document conclusions and recommendations for determinations to qualify drug development tools under subsection (a).

(E) A comprehensive list of—

(i) all drug development tools qualified under subsection (a); and

(ii) all surrogate endpoints which were the basis of approval or licensure (as applicable) of a drug or biological product (including in accordance with section 506(c)) under section 505 of this Act or section 351 of the Public Health Service Act.

(2) Relation to Trade Secrets Act.—Information made publicly available by the Secretary under paragraph (1) shall be considered a disclosure authorized by law for purposes of section 1905 of title 18, United States Code.

(3) **Applicability.**—Nothing in this section shall be construed as authorizing the Secretary to disclose any information contained in an application submitted under section 505 of this Act or section 351 of the Public Health Service Act that is confidential commercial or trade secret information subject to section 552(b)(4) of title 5, United States Code, or section 1905 of title 18, United States Code.

(d) **Rule of Construction.**—Nothing in this section shall be construed—

(1) to alter the standards of evidence under subsection (c) or (d) of section 505, including the substantial evidence standard in such subsection (d), or under section 351 of the Public Health Service Act (as applicable); or

(2) to limit the authority of the Secretary to approve or license products under this Act or the Public Health Service Act, as applicable (as in effect before the date of the enactment of the 21st Century Cures Act).

(e) **Definitions.**—In this section:

(1) **Biomarker.**—The term "biomarker"—

(A) means a characteristic (such as a physiologic, pathologic, or anatomic characteristic or measurement) that is objectively measured and evaluated as an indicator of normal biologic processes, pathologic processes, or biological responses to a therapeutic intervention; and

(B) includes a surrogate endpoint.

(2) **Biomedical Research Consortia.**—The term "biomedical research consortia" means collaborative groups that may take the form of public-private partnerships and may include government agencies, institutions of higher education (as defined in section 101(a) of the Higher Education Act of 1965), patient advocacy groups, industry representatives, clinical and scientific experts, and other relevant entities and individuals.

(3) **Clinical Outcome Assessment.**—The term "clinical outcome assessment" means—

(A) a measurement of a patient's symptoms, overall mental state, or the effects of a disease or condition on how the patient functions; and

(B) includes a patient-reported outcome.

(4) **Context of Use.**—The term "context of use" means, with respect to a drug development tool, the circumstances under which the drug development tool is to be used in drug development and regulatory review.

(5) **Drug Development Tool.**—The term "drug development tool" includes—

(A) a biomarker;

(B) a clinical outcome assessment; and

(C) any other method, material, or measure that the Secretary determines aids drug development and regulatory review for purposes of this section.

(6) **Patient-Reported Outcome.**—The term "patient-reported outcome" means a measurement based on a report from a patient regarding the status of the patient's health condition without amendment or interpretation of the patient's report by a clinician or any other person.

(7) **Qualification.**—The terms "qualification" and "qualified" mean a determination by the Secretary that a drug development tool and its proposed context of use can be relied upon to have a specific interpretation and application in drug development and regulatory review under this Act.

(8) **Requestor.**—The term "requestor" means an entity or entities, including a drug sponsor or a biomedical research consortia, seeking to qualify a drug development tool for a proposed context of use under this section.

(9) **Surrogate Endpoint.**—The term "surrogate endpoint" means a marker, such as a laboratory measurement, radiographic image, physical sign, or other measure, that is not itself a direct measurement of clinical benefit, and—

(A) is known to predict clinical benefit and could be used to support traditional approval of a drug or biological product; or

(B) is reasonably likely to predict clinical benefit and could be used to support the accelerated approval of a drug or biological product in accordance with section 506(c).

Sec. 508. [358] Authority to Designate Official Names.

(a) The Secretary may designate an official name for any drug or device if he determines that such action is necessary or desirable in the interest of usefulness and simplicity. Any official name designated under this section for any drug or device shall be the only official name of that drug or device used in any official compendium published after such name has been prescribed or for any other purpose of this Act. In no event, however, shall the Secretary establish an official name so as to infringe a valid trademark.

(b) Within a reasonable time after the effective date of this section, and at such other times as he may deem necessary, the Secretary shall cause a review to be made of the official names by which drugs are identified in the official United States Pharmacopeia, the official Homeopathic Pharmacopeia of the United States, and the official National Formulary, and all supplements thereto, and at such times as he may deem necessary shall cause a review to be made of the official names by which devices are identified in any official compendium (and all supplements thereto) to determine whether revision of any of those names is necessary or desirable in the interest of usefulness and simplicity.

(c) Whenever he determines after any such review that

(1) any such official name is unduly complex or is not useful for any other reason,

(2) two or more official names have been applied to a single drug or device, or to two or more drugs which are identical in chemical structure and pharmacological action and which are substantially identical in strength, quality, and purity, or to two or more devices which are substantially equivalent in design and purpose or

(3) no official name has been applied to a medically useful drug or device,

he shall transmit in writing to the compiler of each official compendium in which that drug or drugs or device are identified and recognized his request for the recommendation of a single official name for such drug or drugs or device which will have usefulness and simplicity. Whenever such a single official name has been recommended within one hundred and eighty days after such request, or the Secretary determines that any name so recommended is not useful for any reason, he shall designate a single official name for such drug or drugs or device. Whenever he determines that the name so recommended is useful, he shall designate that name as the official name of such drug or drugs or device. Such designation shall be made as a regulation upon public notice and in accordance with the procedure set forth in section 553 of title 5, United States Code.

(d) After such review, and at such other times as the Secretary may determine to be necessary or desirable, the Secretary shall cause to be compiled, published, and publicly distributed a list which shall list all revised official names of drugs or devices designated under this section and shall contain such descriptive and explanatory matter as the Secretary may determine to be required for the effective use of those names.

(e) Upon a request in writing by any compiler of any official compendium that the Secretary exercise the authority granted to him under section 508(a), he shall upon public notice and in accordance with the procedure set forth in section 553 of title 5, United States Code designate the official name of the drug or device for which the request is made.

Sec. 509. [359] Nonapplicability to Cosmetics.

This chapter, as amended by the Drug Amendments of 1962, shall not apply to any cosmetic unless such cosmetic is also a drug or device or component thereof.

Sec. 510. [360] Registration of Producers of Drugs and Devices.

(a) As used in this section —

(1) the term "manufacture, preparation, propagation, compounding, or processing" shall include repackaging or otherwise changing the container, wrapper, or labeling of any drug package or device package in furtherance of the distribution of the drug or device from the original place of manufacture to the person who makes final delivery or sale to the ultimate consumer or user; and

(2) the term "name" shall include in the case of a partnership the name of each partner and, in the case of a corporation, the name of each corporate officer and director, and the State of incorporation.

(b) —

(1) During the period beginning on October 1 and ending on December 31 of each year, every person who owns or operates any establishment in any State engaged in the manufacture, preparation, propagation, compounding, or processing of a drug or drugs shall register with the Secretary the name of such person, places of business of such person, all such establishments, the unique facility identifier of each such establishment, and a point of contact e-mail address.

(2) During the period beginning on October 1 and ending on December 31 of each year, every person who owns or operates any establishment in any State engaged in the manufacture, preparation, propagation, compounding, or processing of a device or devices shall register with the Secretary his name, places of business, and all such establishments.

(3) The Secretary shall specify the unique facility identifier system that shall be used by registrants under paragraph (1). The requirement to include a unique facility identifier in a registration under paragraph (1) shall not apply until the date that the identifier system is specified by the Secretary under the preceding sentence.

(c) Every person upon first engaging in the manufacture, preparation, propagation, compounding, or processing of a drug or drugs or a device or devices in any establishment which he owns or operates in any State shall immediately register with the Secretary —

(1) with respect to drugs, the information described under subsection (b)(1); and

(2) with respect to devices, the information described under subsection (b)(2).

(d) Every person duly registered in accordance with the foregoing subsections of this section shall immediately register with the Secretary any additional establishment which he owns or operates in any State and in which he begins the manufacture, preparation, propagation, compounding, or processing of a drug or drugs or a device or devices.

(e) The Secretary may assign a registration number to any person or any establishment registered in accordance with this section. The Secretary may also assign a listing number to each drug or class of drugs listed under subsection (j). Any number assigned pursuant to the preceding sentence shall be the same as that assigned pursuant to the National Drug Code. The Secretary may by regulation prescribe a uniform system for the identification of devices intended for human use and may require that persons who are required to list such devices pursuant to subsection (j) shall list such devices in accordance with such system.

(f) The Secretary shall make available for inspection, to any person so requesting, any registration filed pursuant to this section; except that any list submitted pursuant to paragraph (3) of subsection (j) and the information accompanying any list or notice filed under paragraph (1) or (2) of that subsection shall be exempt from such inspection unless the Secretary finds that such an exemption would be inconsistent with protection of the public health.

(g) The foregoing subsections of this section shall not apply to —

(1) pharmacies which maintain establishments in conformance with any applicable local laws regulating the practice of pharmacy and medicine and which are regularly engaged in dispensing prescription drugs or devices, upon prescriptions of practitioners licensed to administer such drugs or devices to patients under the care of such practitioners in the course of their professional practice, and which do not manufacture, prepare, propagate, compound, or process drugs or devices for sale other than in the regular course of their business of dispensing or selling drugs or devices at retail;

(2) practitioners licensed by law to prescribe or administer drugs or devices and who manufacture, prepare, propagate, compound, or process drugs or devices solely for use in the course of their professional practice;

(3) persons who manufacture, prepare, propagate, compound, or process drugs or devices solely for use in research, teaching, or chemical analysis and not for sale;

(4) any distributor who acts as a wholesale distributor of devices, and who does not manufacture, repackage, process, or relabel a device; or

(5) such other classes of persons as the Secretary may by regulation exempt from the application of this section upon a finding that registration by such classes of persons in accordance with this section is not necessary for the protection of the public health.

In this subsection, the term "wholesale distributor" means any person (other than the manufacturer or the initial importer) who distributes a device from the original place of manufacture to the person who makes the final delivery or sale of the device to the ultimate consumer or user.

(h) Inspections. —

(1) In General. — Every establishment that is required to be registered with the Secretary under this section shall be subject to inspection pursuant to section 704.

~~**(2) Biennial Inspections for Devices.** — Every establishment described in paragraph (1), in any State, that is engaged in the manufacture, propagation, compounding, or processing of a device or devices classified in class II or III shall be so inspected by one or more officers or employees duly designated by the Secretary, or by persons accredited to conduct inspections under section 704(g), at least once in the 2-year period beginning~~

~~with the date of registration of such establishment pursuant to this section and at least once in every successive 2-year period thereafter.~~

(2) Risk-Based Schedule for Devices. —

(A) In General. — The Secretary, acting through one or more officers or employees duly designated by the Secretary, shall inspect establishments described in paragraph (1) that are engaged in the manufacture, propagation, compounding, or processing of a device or devices (referred to in this subsection as 'device establishments') in accordance with a risk-based schedule established by the Secretary.

(B) Factors and Considerations. — In establishing the risk-based schedule under subparagraph (A), the Secretary shall —

(i) apply, to the extent applicable for device establishments, the factors identified in paragraph (4); and

(ii) consider the participation of the device establishment, as applicable, in international device audit programs in which the United States participates or the United States recognizes for purposes of inspecting device establishments.

(3) Risk-Based Schedule for Drugs. — The Secretary, acting through one or more officers or employees duly designated by the Secretary, shall inspect establishments described in paragraph (1) that are engaged in the manufacture, preparation, propagation, compounding, or processing of a drug or drugs (referred to in this subsection as "drug establishments") in accordance with a risk-based schedule established by the Secretary.

(4) Risk Factors. — In establishing a risk-based schedule under paragraph (2) or (3), the Secretary shall inspect establishments according to the known safety risks of such establishments, which shall be based on the following factors:

(A) The compliance history of the establishment.

(B) The record, history, and nature of the recalls linked to the establishment.

(C) The inherent risk of the drug or device manufactured, prepared, propagated, compounded, or processed at the establishment.

(D) The inspection frequency and history of the establishment, including whether the establishment has been inspected pursuant to section 704 within the last 4 years.

(E) Whether the establishment has been inspected by a foreign government or an agency of a foreign government recognized under section 809.

(F) Any other criteria deemed necessary and appropriate by the Secretary for the purposes of allocating inspection resources.

(5) Effect of Status. — In determining the risk associated with an establishment for purposes of establishing a risk-based schedule under paragraph (3), the Secretary shall not consider whether the drugs manufactured, prepared, propagated, compounded, or processed by such establishment are drugs described in section 503(b).

(6) Annual Report on Inspections of Establishments. — Beginning in 2014, not later than ~~February 1~~ May 1 of each year, the Secretary shall make available on the Internet Web site of the Food and Drug Administration a report regarding —

(A) —

(i) the number of domestic and foreign establishments registered pursuant to this section in the previous calendar year; and

(ii) the number of such domestic establishments and the number of such foreign establishments that the Secretary inspected in the previous calendar year;

(B) with respect to establishments that manufacture, prepare, propagate, compound, or process an active ingredient of a drug or a finished drug product, the number of each such type of establishment; and

(C) the percentage of the budget of the Food and Drug Administration used to fund the inspections described under subparagraph (A).

(i) —

(1) Every person who owns or operates any establishment within any foreign country engaged in the manufacture, preparation, propagation, compounding, or processing of a drug or device that is imported or offered for import into the United States shall, through electronic means in accordance with the criteria of the Secretary —

(A) upon first engaging in any such activity, immediately submit a registration to the Secretary that includes —

(i) with respect to drugs, the name and place of business of such person, all such establishments, the unique facility identifier of each such establishment, a point of contact e-mail address, the name of the United States agent of each such establishment, the name of each importer of such drug in the United States that is known to the establishment, and the name of each person who imports or offers for import such drug to the United States for purposes of importation; and

(ii) with respect to devices, the name and place of business of the establishment, the name of the United States agent for the establishment, the name of each importer of such device in the United States that is known to the establishment, and the name of each person who imports or offers for import such device to the United States for purposes of importation; and

(B) each establishment subject to the requirements of subparagraph (A) shall thereafter register with the Secretary during the period beginning on October 1 and ending on December 31 of each year.

(2) The establishment shall also provide the information required by subsection (j).

(3) The Secretary is authorized to enter into cooperative arrangements with officials of foreign countries to ensure that adequate and effective means are available for purposes of determining, from time to time, whether drugs or devices manufactured, prepared, propagated, compounded, or processed by an establishment described in paragraph (1), if imported or offered for import into the United States, shall be refused admission on any of the grounds set forth in section 810(a).

(4) The Secretary shall specify the unique facility identifier system that shall be used by registrants under paragraph (1) with respect to drugs. The requirement to include a unique facility identifier in a registration under paragraph (1) with respect to drugs shall not apply until the date that the identifier system is specified by the Secretary under the preceding sentence.

(j) —

(1) Every person who registers with the Secretary under subsection (b), (c), (d), or (i) shall, at the time of registration under any such subsection, file with the Secretary a list of all drugs and a list of all devices and a brief statement of the basis for believing that each device included in the list is a device rather than a drug (with each drug and device in each list listed by its established name (as defined in section 502(e)) and by any proprietary name) which are being manufactured, prepared, propagated, compounded, or processed by him for commercial distribution and which he has not included in any list of drugs or devices filed by him with the Secretary under this paragraph or paragraph (2) before such time of registration. Such list shall be prepared in such form and manner as the Secretary may prescribe and shall be accompanied by —

(A) in the case of a drug contained in the applicable list and subject to section 505 or 512, or a device intended for human use contained in the applicable list with respect to which a performance standard has been established under section 514 or which is subject to section 515, a reference to the authority for the marketing of such drug or device and a copy of all labeling for such drug or device;

(B) in the case of any other drug or device contained in an applicable list —

(i) which drug is subject to section 503(b)(1), or which device is a restricted device, a copy of all labeling for such drug or device, a representative sampling of advertisements for such drug or device, and, upon request made by the Secretary for good cause, a copy of all advertisements for a particular drug product or device, or

(ii) which drug is not subject to section 503(b)(1) or which device is not a restricted device, the label and package insert for such drug or device and a representative sampling of any other labeling for such drug or device;

(C) in the case of any drug contained in an applicable list which is described in subparagraph (B), a quantitative listing of its active ingredient or ingredients, except that with respect to a particular drug product the Secretary may require the submission of a quantitative listing of all ingredients if he finds that such submission is necessary to carry out the purposes of this Act;

(D) if the registrant filing a list has determined that a particular drug product or device contained in such list is not subject to section 505 or 512, or the particular device contained in such list is not subject to a performance standard established under section 514 or to section 515 or is not a restricted device, a brief statement of the basis upon which the registrant made such determination if the Secretary requests such a statement with respect to that particular drug product or device; and

(E) in the case of a drug contained in the applicable list, the name and place of business of each manufacturer of an excipient of the listed drug with which the person listing the drug conducts business, including all establishments used in the production of such excipient, the unique facility identifier of each such establishment, and a point of contact e-mail address for each such excipient manufacturer.

(2) Each person who registers with the Secretary under this section shall report to the Secretary, with regard to drugs once during the month of June of each year and once during the month of December of each year, and with regard to devices once each year during the period beginning on October 1 and ending on December 31, the following information:

(A) A list of each drug or device introduced by the registrant for commercial distribution which has not been included in any list previously filed by him with the Secretary under this subparagraph or paragraph (1) of this subsection. A list under this subparagraph shall list a drug or device by its established name (as defined in section 502(e)) and by any proprietary name it may have and shall be accompanied by the other information required by paragraph (1).

(B) If since the date the registrant last made a report under this paragraph (or if he has not made a report under this paragraph, since the effective date of this subsection [February 1, 1973 — Ed.]) he has discontinued the manufacture, preparation, propagation, compounding, or processing for commercial distribution of a drug or device included in a list filed by him under subparagraph (A) or paragraph (1); notice of such discontinuance, the date of such discontinuance, and the identity (by established name (as defined in section 502(e)) and by any proprietary name) of such drug or device.

(C) If since the date the registrant reported pursuant to subparagraph (B) a notice of discontinuance he has resumed the manufacture, preparation, propagation, compounding, or processing for commercial distribution of the drug or device with respect to which such notice of discontinuance was reported; notice of such resumption, the date of such resumption, the identity of such drug or device (by established name (as defined in section 502(e)) and by any proprietary name), and the other information required by paragraph (1), unless the registrant has previously reported such resumption to the Secretary pursuant to this subparagraph.

(D) Any material change in any information previously submitted pursuant to this paragraph or paragraph (1).

(3) The Secretary may also require each registrant under this section to submit a list of each drug product which

(A) the registrant is manufacturing, preparing, propagating, compounding, or processing for commercial distribution, and

(B) contains a particular ingredient.

The Secretary may not require the submission of such a list unless he has made a finding that the submission of such a list is necessary to carry out the purposes of this Act.

(4) The Secretary shall require persons subject to this subsection to use, for the purposes of this subsection, the unique facility identifier systems specified under subsections (b)(3) and (i)(4) with respect to drugs. Such requirement shall not apply until the date that the facility identifier system under subsection (b)(3) or (i)(4), as applicable, is specified by the Secretary.

(k) Each person who is required to register under this section and who proposes to begin the introduction or delivery for introduction into interstate commerce for commercial distribution of a device intended for human use shall, at least ninety days before making such introduction or delivery, report to the Secretary or person who is accredited under section 523(a) (in such form and manner as the Secretary shall by regulation prescribe) —

(1) the class in which the device is classified under section 513 or if such person determines that the device is not classified under such section, a statement of that determination and the basis for such person's determination that the device is or is not so classified, and

(2) action taken by such person to comply with requirements under section 514 or 515 which are applicable to the device.

A notification submitted under this subsection that contains clinical trial data for an applicable device clinical trial (as defined in section 402(j)(1) of the Public Health Service Act) shall be accompanied by the certification required under section 402(j)(5)(B) of such Act. Such certification shall not be considered an element of such notification.

(l)(1) A report under subsection (k) is not required for a device intended for human use that is exempted from the requirements of this subsection under subsection (m) or is within a type that has been classified into class I under section 513. The exception established in the preceding sentence does not apply to any class I device that is intended for a use which is of substantial importance in preventing impairment of human health, or to any class I device that presents a potential unreasonable risk of illness or injury.

(2) Not later than 120 calendar days after the date of enactment of the 21st Century Cures Act [December 13, 2016 —Ed.] and at least once every 5 years thereafter, as the Secretary determines appropriate, the Secretary shall identify, through publication in the Federal Register, any type of class I device that the Secretary determines no longer requires a report under subsection (k) to provide reasonable assurance of safety and effectiveness. Upon such publication—

(A) each type of class I device so identified shall be exempt from the requirement for a report under subsection (k); and

(B) the classification regulation applicable to each such type of device shall be deemed amended to incorporate such exemption.

(m)—

(1) The Secretary shall—

(A) not later than 90 days after the date of enactment of the 21st Century Cures Act [December 13, 2016 —Ed.] and at least once every 5 years thereafter, as the Secretary determines appropriate—

(i) publish in the Federal Register a notice that contains a list of each type of class II device that the Secretary determines no longer requires a report under subsection (k) to provide reasonable assurance of safety and effectiveness; and

(ii) provide a period of not less than 60 calendar days for public comment beginning on the date of the publication of such notice; and

(B) not later than 210 calendar days after the date of enactment of the 21st Century Cures Act [December 13, 2016 —Ed.], publish in the Federal Register a list representing the Secretary's final determination with respect to the devices contained in the list published under subparagraph (A).

(2) Beginning on the date that is 1 calendar day after the date of publication of the final list under paragraph (1)(B), the Secretary may exempt a class II device from the requirement to submit a report under subsection (k), upon the Secretary's own initiative or a petition of an interested person, if the Secretary determines that such report is not necessary to assure the safety and effectiveness of the device. The Secretary shall publish in the Federal Register notice of the intent of the Secretary to exempt the device, or of the petition, and provide a 60-calendar-day period for public comment. Within 120 days after the issuance of the notice in the Federal Register, the Secretary shall publish an order in the Federal Register, that sets forth the final determination of the Secretary regarding the exemption of the device that was the subject of the notice. If the Secretary fails to respond to a petition within 180 days of receiving it, the petition shall be deemed to be granted.

(3) Upon publication of the final list under paragraph (1)(B)—

(A) each type of class II device so listed shall be exempt from the requirement for a report under subsection (k); and

(B) the classification regulation applicable to each such type of device shall be deemed amended to incorporate such exemption.

(n)—

(1) The Secretary shall review the report required in subsection (k) and make a determination under section 513(f)(1) not later than 90 days after receiving the report.

(2) —

(A) Not later than 18 months after the date of enactment of this paragraph, the Secretary shall submit to the Committee on Energy and Commerce of the House of Representatives and the Committee on Health, Education, Labor, and Pensions of the Senate a report regarding when a premarket notification under subsection (k) should be submitted for a modification or change to a legally marketed device. The report shall include the Secretary's interpretation of the following terms: "could significantly affect the safety or effectiveness of the device," "a significant change or modification in design, material, chemical composition, energy source, or manufacturing process", and "major change or modification in the intended use of the device". The report also shall discuss possible processes for industry to use to determine whether a new submission under subsection (k) is required and shall analyze how to leverage existing quality systems requirements to reduce premarket burden, facilitate continual device improvement, and provide reasonable assurance of safety and effectiveness of modified devices. In developing such report, the Secretary shall consider the input of interested stakeholders.

(B) The Secretary shall withdraw the Food and Drug Administration draft guidance entitled "Guidance for Industry and **FDA** Staff — 510(k) Device Modifications: Deciding When to Submit a 510(k) for a Change to an Existing Device", dated July 27, 2011, and shall not use this draft guidance as part of, or for the basis of, any premarket review or any compliance or enforcement decisions or actions. The Secretary shall not issue —

(i) any draft guidance or proposed regulation that addresses when to submit a premarket notification submission for changes and modifications made to a manufacturer's previously cleared device before the receipt by the Committee on Energy and Commerce of the House of Representatives and the Committee on Health, Education, Labor, and Pensions of the Senate of the report required in subparagraph (A); and

(ii) any final guidance or regulation on that topic for one year after the date of receipt of such report by the Committee on Energy and Commerce of the House of Representatives and the Committee on Health, Education, Labor, and Pensions of the Senate.

(C) The Food and Drug Administration guidance entitled "Deciding When to Submit a 510(k) for a Change to an Existing Device", dated January 10, 1997, shall be in effect until the subsequent issuance of guidance or promulgation, if appropriate, of a regulation described in subparagraph (B), and the Secretary shall interpret such guidance in a manner that is consistent with the manner in which the Secretary has interpreted such guidance since 1997.

(o) —

(1) With respect to reprocessed single-use devices for which reports are required under subsection (k):

(A) The Secretary shall identify such devices or types of devices for which reports under such subsection must, in order to ensure that the device is substantially equivalent to a predicate device, include validation data, the types of which shall be specified by the Secretary, regarding cleaning and sterilization, and functional performance demonstrating that the single-use device will remain substantially equivalent to its predicate device after the maximum number of times the device is reprocessed as intended by the person submitting the premarket notification. Within six months after enactment of this subsection, the Secretary shall publish in the Federal Register a list of the types so identified, and shall revise the list as appropriate. Reports under subsection (k) for devices or types of devices within a type included on the list are, upon publication of the list, required to include such validation data.

(B) In the case of each report under subsection (k) that was submitted to the Secretary before the publication of the initial list under subparagraph (A), or any revision thereof, and was for a device or type of device included on such list, the person who submitted the report under subsection (k) shall submit validation data as described in subparagraph (A) to the Secretary not later than nine months after the publication of the list. During such nine-month period, the Secretary may not take any action under this Act against such device solely on the basis that the validation data for the device have not been submitted to the Secretary. After the submission of the validation data to the Secretary, the Secretary may not determine that the device is misbranded under section 502(o) or adulterated under section 501(f)(1)(B), or take action against the device under section 301(p) for failure to provide any information required by subsection (k) until

(i) the review is terminated by withdrawal of the submission of the report under subsection (k);

(ii) the Secretary finds the data to be acceptable and issues a letter; or

(iii) the Secretary determines that the device is not substantially equivalent to a predicate device.

Upon a determination that a device is not substantially equivalent to a predicate device, or if such submission is withdrawn, the device can no longer be legally marketed.

(C) In the case of a report under subsection (k) for a device identified under subparagraph (A) that is of a type for which the Secretary has not previously received a report under such subsection, the Secretary may, in advance of revising the list under subparagraph (A) to include such type, require that the report include the validation data specified in subparagraph (A).

(D) Section 502(o) applies with respect to the failure of a report under subsection (k) to include validation data required under subparagraph (A).

(2) With respect to critical or semi-critical reprocessed single-use devices that, under subsection (l) or (m), are exempt from the requirement of submitting reports under subsection (k):

(A) The Secretary shall identify such devices or types of devices for which such exemptions should be terminated in order to provide a reasonable assurance of the safety and effectiveness of the devices. The Secretary shall publish in the Federal Register a list of the devices or types of devices so identified, and shall revise the list as appropriate. The exemption for each device or type included on the list is terminated upon the publication of the list. For each report under subsection (k) submitted pursuant to this subparagraph the Secretary shall require the validation data described in paragraph (1)(A).

(B) For each device or type of device included on the list under subparagraph (A), a report under subsection (k) shall be submitted to the Secretary not later than 15 months after the publication of the initial list, or a revision of the list, whichever terminates the exemption for the device. During such 15-month period, the Secretary may not take any action under this Act against such device solely on the basis that such report has not been submitted to the Secretary. After the submission of the report to the Secretary the Secretary may not determine that the device is misbranded under section 502(o) or adulterated under section 501(f)(1)(B), or take action against the device under section 301(p) for failure to provide any information required by subsection (k) until

(i) the review is terminated by withdrawal of the submission;

(ii) the Secretary determines by order that the device is substantially equivalent to a predicate device; or

(iii) the Secretary determines by order that the device is not substantially equivalent to a predicate device. Upon a determination that a device is not substantially equivalent to a predicate device, the device can no longer be legally marketed.

(C) In the case of semi-critical devices, the initial list under subparagraph (A) shall be published not later than 18 months after the effective date of this subsection. In the case of critical devices, the initial list under such subparagraph shall be published not later than six months after such effective date.

(D) Section 502(o) applies with respect to the failure to submit a report under subsection (k) that is required pursuant to subparagraph (A), including a failure of the report to include validation data required in such subparagraph.

(E) The termination under subparagraph (A) of an exemption under subsection (l) or (m) for a critical or semi-critical reprocessed single-use device does not terminate the exemption under subsection (l) or (m) for the original device.

(p) Electronic Registration and Listing. —

(1) In General. — Registrations and listings under this section (including the submission of updated information) shall be submitted to the Secretary by electronic means unless the Secretary grants a request for waiver of such requirement because use of electronic means is not reasonable for the person requesting such waiver.

(2) Electronic Database. — Not later than 2 years after the Secretary specifies a unique facility identifier system under subsections (b) and (i), the Secretary shall maintain an electronic database, which shall not be subject to inspection under subsection (f), populated with the information submitted as described under paragraph (1) that —

(A) enables personnel of the Food and Drug Administration to search the database by any field of information submitted in a registration described under paragraph (1), or combination of such fields; and

(B) uses the unique facility identifier system to link with other relevant databases within the Food and Drug Administration, including the database for submission of information under 801(r).

(3) Risk-Based Information and Coordination. — The Secretary shall ensure the accuracy and coordination of relevant Food and Drug Administration databases in order to identify and inform risk-based inspections under section 510(h).

(q) Reusable Medical Devices. —

(1) In General. — Not later than 180 days after the date of enactment of the 21st Century Cures Act [December 13, 2016 —Ed.], the Secretary shall identify and publish a list of reusable device types for which reports under subsection (k) are required to include—

(A) instructions for use, which have been validated in a manner specified by the Secretary; and

(B) validation data, the types of which shall be specified by the Secretary;

regarding cleaning, disinfection, and sterilization, and for which a substantial equivalence determination may be based.

(2) Revision of the List. — The Secretary shall revise the list under paragraph (2), as the Secretary determines appropriate, with notice in the Federal Register.

(3) Content of Reports. — Reports under subsection (k) that are submitted after the publication of the list described in paragraph (1), for devices or types of devices included on such list, shall include such instructions for use and validation data.

Sec. 511. [360a] Clinical Trial Guidance for Antibiotic Drugs.

(a) In General. — Not later than 1 year after the date of the enactment of this section, the Secretary shall issue guidance for the conduct of clinical trials with respect to antibiotic drugs, including antimicrobials to treat acute bacterial sinusitis, acute bacterial otitis media, and acute bacterial exacerbation of chronic bronchitis. Such guidance shall indicate the appropriate models and valid surrogate markers.

(b) Review. — Not later than 5 years after the date of the enactment of this section, the secretary shall review and update the guidance described under subsection (a) to reflect developments in scientific and medical information and technology.

Sec. 511A. [360a-2] Susceptibility Test Interpretive Criteria for Microorganisms.

(a) Purpose; Identification of Criteria.—

(1) Purpose.— The purpose of this section is to clarify the Secretary's authority to—

(A) efficiently update susceptibility test interpretive criteria for antimicrobial drugs when necessary for public health, due to, among other things, the constant evolution of microorganisms that leads to the development of resistance to drugs that have been effective in decreasing morbidity and mortality for patients, which warrants unique management of antimicrobial drugs that is inappropriate for most other drugs in order to delay or prevent the development of further resistance to existing therapies;

(B) provide for public notice of the availability of recognized interpretive criteria and interpretive criteria standards; and

(C) clear under section 510(k), classify under section 513(f)(2), or approve under section 515, antimicrobial susceptibility testing devices utilizing updated, recognized susceptibility test interpretive criteria to characterize the in vitro susceptibility of particular bacteria, fungi, or other microorganisms, as applicable, to antimicrobial drugs.

(2) Identification of Criteria.—The Secretary shall identify appropriate susceptibility test interpretive criteria with respect to antimicrobial drugs—

(A) if such criteria are available on the date of approval of the drug under section 505 of this Act or licensure of the drug under section 351 of the Public Health Service Act (as applicable), upon such approval or licensure; or

(B) if such criteria are unavailable on such date, on the date on which such criteria are available for such drug.

(3) Bases for Initial Identification.—The Secretary shall identify appropriate susceptibility test interpretive criteria under paragraph (2), based on the Secretary's review of, to the extent available and relevant—

(A) preclinical and clinical data, including pharmacokinetic, pharmacodynamic, and epidemiological data;

(B) the relationship of susceptibility test interpretive criteria to morbidity and mortality associated with the disease or condition for which such drug is used; and

(C) such other evidence and information as the Secretary considers appropriate.

(b) Susceptibility Test Interpretive Criteria Website.—

(1) In General.— Not later than 1 year after the date of the enactment of the 21st Century Cures Act, the Secretary shall establish, and maintain thereafter, on the website of the Food and Drug Administration, a dedicated website that contains a list of any appropriate new or updated susceptibility test interpretive criteria standards and interpretive criteria in accordance with paragraph (2) (referred to in this section as the "Interpretive Criteria Website").

(2) Listing of Susceptibility Test Interpretive Criteria Standards and Interpretive Criteria.—

(A) In General.— The list described in paragraph (1) shall consist of any new or updated susceptibility test interpretive criteria standards that are—

(i) established by a nationally or internationally recognized standard development organization that—

(I) establishes and maintains procedures to address potential conflicts of interest and ensure transparent decisionmaking;

(II) holds open meetings to ensure that there is an opportunity for public input by interested parties, and establishes and maintains processes to ensure that such input is considered in decisionmaking; and

(III) permits its standards to be made publicly available, through the National Library of Medicine or another similar source acceptable to the Secretary; and

(ii) recognized in whole, or in part, by the Secretary under subsection (c).

(B) Other List.—The Interpretive Criteria Website shall, in addition to the list described in subparagraph (A), include a list of interpretive criteria, if any, that the Secretary has determined to be appropriate with respect to legally marketed antimicrobial drugs, where—

(i) the Secretary does not recognize, in whole or in part, an interpretive criteria standard described under subparagraph (A) otherwise applicable to such a drug;

(ii) the Secretary withdraws under subsection (c)(1)(A) recognition of a standard, in whole or in part, otherwise applicable to such a drug;

(iii) the Secretary approves an application under section 505 of this Act or section 351 of the Public Health Service Act, as applicable, with respect to marketing of such a drug for which there are no relevant interpretive criteria included in a standard recognized by the Secretary under subsection (c); or

(iv) because the characteristics of such a drug differ from other drugs with the same active ingredient, the interpretive criteria with respect to such drug—

(I) differ from otherwise applicable interpretive criteria included in a standard listed under subparagraph (A) or interpretive criteria otherwise listed under this subparagraph; and

(II) are determined by the Secretary to be appropriate for the drug.

(C) Required Statements.—The Interpretive Criteria Website shall include statements conveying—

(i) that the website provides information about the in vitro susceptibility of bacteria, fungi, or other microorganisms, as applicable to a certain drug (or drugs);

(ii) that—

(I) the safety and efficacy of such drugs in treating clinical infections due to such bacteria, fungi, or other microorganisms, as applicable, may or may not have been established in adequate and well-controlled clinical trials in order for the susceptibility information described in clause (i) to be included on the website; and

(II) the clinical significance of such susceptibility information in such instances is unknown;

(iii) that the approved product labeling for specific drugs provides the uses for which the Secretary has approved the product; and

(iv) any other information that the Secretary determines appropriate to adequately convey the meaning of the data supporting the recognition or listing of susceptibility test interpretive criteria standards or susceptibility test interpretive criteria included on the website.

(3) Notice.—Not later than the date on which the Interpretive Criteria Website is established, the Secretary shall publish a notice of that establishment in the Federal Register.

(4) Inapplicability of Misbranding Provision.—The inclusion in the approved labeling of an antimicrobial drug of a reference or hyperlink to the Interpretive Criteria Website, in and of itself, shall not cause the drug to be misbranded in violation of section 502.

(5) Trade Secrets and Confidential Information.—Nothing in this section shall be construed as authorizing the Secretary to disclose any information that is a trade secret or confidential information subject to section 552(b)(4) of title 5, United States Code.

(c) Recognition of Susceptibility Test Interpretive Criteria.—

(1) Evaluation and Publication.—

(A) In General.—Beginning on the date of the establishment of the Interpretive Criteria Website, and at least every 6 months thereafter, the Secretary shall—

(i) evaluate any appropriate new or updated susceptibility test interpretive criteria standards established by a nationally or internationally recognized standard development organization described in subsection (b)(2)(A)(i); and

(ii) publish on the public website of the Food and Drug Administration a notice—

(I) withdrawing recognition of any different susceptibility test interpretive criteria standard, in whole or in part;

(II) recognizing the new or updated standards;

(III) recognizing one or more parts of the new or updated interpretive criteria specified in such a standard and declining to recognize the remainder of such standard; and

(IV) making any necessary updates to the lists under subsection (b)(2).

(B) Upon Approval of a Drug.—Upon the approval of an initial or supplemental application for an antimicrobial drug under section 505 of this Act or section 351 of the Public Health Service Act, as applicable, where such approval is based on susceptibility test interpre- tive criteria which differ from those contained in a standard recognized, or from those otherwise listed, by the Secretary pursuant to this subsection, or for which there are no relevant interpretive criteria standards recognized, or interpretive criteria otherwise listed, by the Secretary pursuant to this subsection, the Secretary shall update the lists under subparagraphs (A) and (B) of subsection (b)(2) to include the susceptibility test interpretive criteria upon which such approval was based.

(2) Bases for Updating Interpretive Criteria Standards.— In evaluating new or updated susceptibility test interpretive criteria standards under paragraph (1)(A), the Secretary may consider—

(A) the Secretary's determination that such a standard is not applicable to a particular drug because the characteristics of the drug differ from other drugs with the same active ingredient;

(B) information provided by interested third parties, including public comment on the annual compilation of notices published under paragraph (3);

(C) any bases used to identify susceptibility test interpretive criteria under subsection (a)(2); and

(D) such other information or factors as the Secretary determines appropriate.

(3) Annual Compilation of Notices.—Each year, the Secretary shall compile the notices published under paragraph (1)(A) and publish such compilation in the Federal Register and provide for public comment. If the Secretary receives comments, the Secretary shall review such comments and, if the Secretary determines appropriate, update pursuant to this subsection susceptibility test interpretive criteria standards or criteria—

(A) recognized by the Secretary under this subsection; or

(B) otherwise listed on the Interpretive Criteria Website under subsection (b)(2).

(4) Relation to Section 514(C).—Any susceptibility test interpretive standard recognized under this subsection or any criteria otherwise listed under subsection (b)(2)(B) shall be deemed to be recognized as a standard by the Secretary under section 514(c)(1).

(5) Voluntary Use of Interpretive Criteria.—Nothing in this section prohibits a person from seeking approval or clearance of a drug or device, or changes to the drug or the device, on the basis of susceptibility test interpretive criteria which differ from those contained in a standard recognized, or from those otherwise listed, by the Secretary pursuant to subsection (b)(2).

(d) Antimicrobial Drug Labeling.—

(1) Drugs Marketed Prior to Establishment of Interpretive Criteria Website.—

(A) In General.—With respect to an antimicrobial drug lawfully introduced or delivered for introduction into interstate commerce for commercial distribution before the establishment of the Interpretive Criteria Website, a holder of an approved application under section 505 of this Act or section 351 of the Public Health Service Act, as applicable, for each such drug, not later than 1 year after establishment of the Interpretive Criteria

Website described in subsection (b)(1), shall remove susceptibility test interpretive criteria, if any, and related information from the approved drug labeling and replace it with a reference to the Interpretive Criteria Website.

(B) Labeling Changes.—The labeling changes required by this section shall be considered a minor change under section 314.70 of title 21, Code of Federal Regulations (or any successor regulations) that may be implemented through documentation in the next applicable annual report.

(2) Drugs Marketed Subsequent to Establishment of Interpretive Criteria Website.—With respect to antimicrobial drugs approved on or after the date of the establishment of the Interpretive Criteria Website described in subsection (b)(1), the labeling for such a drug shall include, in lieu of susceptibility test interpretive criteria and related information, a reference to such Website.

(e) Special Condition for Marketing of Antimicrobial Susceptibility Testing Devices.—

(1) In General.— Notwithstanding sections 501, 502, 505, 510, 513, and 515, if the conditions specified in paragraph (2) are met (in addition to other applicable provisions under this chapter) with respect to an antimicrobial susceptibility testing device described in subsection (f)(1), the Secretary may authorize the marketing of such device for a use described in such subsection.

(2) Conditions Applicable to Antimicrobial Susceptibility Testing Devices.—The conditions specified in this paragraph are the following:

(A) The device is used to make a determination of susceptibility using susceptibility test interpretive criteria that are—

(i) included in a standard recognized by the Secretary under subsection (c); or

(ii) otherwise listed on the Interpretive Criteria Website under subsection (b)(2).

(B) The labeling of such device includes statements conveying—

(i) that the device provides information about the in vitro susceptibility of bacteria, fungi, or other microorganisms, as applicable to antimicrobial drugs;

(ii) that—

(I) the safety and efficacy of such drugs in treating clinical infections due to such bacteria, fungi, or other microorganisms, as applicable, may or may not have been established in adequate and well-controlled clinical trials in order for the device to report the susceptibility of such bacteria, fungi, or other microorganisms, as applicable, to such drugs; and

(II) the clinical significance of such susceptibility information in those instances is unknown;

(iii) that the approved labeling for drugs tested using such a device provides the uses for which the Secretary has approved such drugs; and

(iv) any other information the Secretary determines appropriate to adequately convey the meaning of the data supporting the recognition or listing of susceptibility test interpretive criteria standards or susceptibility test interpretive criteria described in subparagraph (A).

(C) The antimicrobial susceptibility testing device meets all other requirements to be cleared under section 510(k), classified under section 513(f)(2), or approved under section 515.

(f) Definitions.—In this section:

(1) The term "antimicrobial susceptibility testing device" means a device that utilizes susceptibility test interpretive criteria to determine and report the in vitro susceptibility of certain microorganisms to a drug (or drugs).

(2) The term "qualified infectious disease product" means a qualified infectious disease product designated under section 505E(d).

(3) The term "susceptibility test interpretive criteria" means—

(A) one or more specific numerical values which characterize the susceptibility of bacteria or other microorganisms to the drug tested; and

(B) related categorizations of such susceptibility, including categorization of the drug as susceptible, intermediate, resistant, or such other term as the Secretary determines appropriate.

(4) –

(A) The term "antimicrobial drug" means, subject to subparagraph (B), a systemic antibacterial or antifungal drug that—

(i) is intended for human use in the treatment of a disease or condition caused by a bacterium or fungus;

(ii) may include a qualified infectious disease product designated under section 505E(d); and

(iii) is subject to section 503(b)(1).

(B) If provided by the Secretary through regulations, such term may include—

(i) drugs other than systemic antibacterial and antifungal drugs; and

(ii) biological products (as such term is defined in section 351 of the Public Health Service Act) to the extent such products exhibit antimicrobial activity.

(5) The term "interpretive criteria standard" means a compilation of susceptibility test interpretive criteria developed by a standard development organization that meets the criteria set forth in subsection (b)(2)(A)(i).

(g) Rule of Construction.—nothing in this section shall be construed to—

(1) alter the standards of evidence under subsection (c) or (d) of section 505 (including the substantial evidence standard under section 505(d)) or under section 351 of the Public Health Service Act (as applicable); or

(2) with respect to clearing devices under section 510(k), classifying devices under section 513(f)(2), or approving devices under section 515—

(A) apply with respect to any drug, device, or biological product, in any context other than an antimicrobial drug and an antimicrobial susceptibility testing device that uses susceptibility test interpretive criteria to characterize and report the susceptibility of certain bacteria, fungi, or other microorganisms, as applicable, to such drug to reflect patient morbidity and mortality in accordance with this section; or

(B) unless specifically stated, have any effect on authorities provided under other sections of this Act, including any regulations issued under such sections.

Sec. 512. [360b] New Animal Drugs.

(a) —

(1) A new animal drug shall, with respect to any particular use or intended use of such drug, be deemed unsafe for purposes of section 501(a)(5) and section 402(a)(2)(C)(ii) unless —

(A) there is in effect an approval of an application filed pursuant to subsection (b) with respect to such use or intended use of such drug, and such drug, its labeling, and such use conform to such approved application;

(B) there is in effect a conditional approval of an application filed pursuant to section 571 with respect to such use or intended use of such drug, and such drug, its labeling, and such use conform to such conditionally approved application; or

(C) there is in effect an index listing pursuant to section 572 with respect to such use or intended use of such drug in a minor species, and such drug, its labeling, and such use conform to such index listing.

A new animal drug shall also be deemed unsafe for such purposes in the event of removal from the establishment of a manufacturer, packer, or distributor of such drug for use in the manufacture of animal feed in any State unless at the time of such removal such manufacturer, packer, or distributor has an unrevoked written statement from the consignee of such drug, or notice from the Secretary, to the effect that, with respect to the use of such drug in animal feed, such consignee

(i) holds a license issued under subsection (m) and has in its possession current approved labeling for such drug in animal feed; or

(ii) will, if the consignee is not a user of the drug, ship such drug only to a holder of a license issued under subsection (m).

(2) An animal feed bearing or containing a new animal drug shall, with respect to any particular use or intended use of such animal feed be deemed unsafe for purposes of section 501(a)(6) unless —

(A) there is in effect —

(i) an approval of an application filed pursuant to subsection (b) with respect to such drug, as used in such animal feed, and such animal feed and its labeling, distribution, holding, and use conform to such approved application;

(ii) a conditional approval of an application filed pursuant to section 571 with respect to such drug, as used in such animal feed, and such animal feed and its labeling, distribution, holding, and use conform to such conditionally approved application; or

(iii) an index listing pursuant to section 572 with respect to such drug, as used in such animal feed, and such animal feed and its labeling, distribution, holding, and use conform to such index listing; and

(B) such animal feed is manufactured at a site for which there is in effect a license issued pursuant to subsection (m)(1) to manufacture such animal feed.

(3) A new animal drug or an animal feed bearing or containing a new animal drug shall not be deemed unsafe for the purposes of section 501(a)(5) or (6) if such article is for investigational use and conforms to the terms of an exemption in effect with respect thereto under section 512(j).

(4) —

(A) Except as provided in subparagraph (B), if an approval of an application filed under subsection (b) is in effect with respect to a particular use or intended use of a new animal drug, the drug shall not be deemed unsafe for the purposes of paragraph (1) and shall be exempt from the requirements of section 502(f) with respect to a different use or intended use of the drug, other than a use in or on animal feed, if such use or intended use —

(i) is by or on the lawful written or oral order of a licensed veterinarian within the context of a veterinarian-client-patient relationship, as defined by the Secretary; and

(ii) is in compliance with regulations promulgated by the Secretary that establish the conditions for such different use or intended use.

The regulations promulgated by the Secretary under clause (ii) may prohibit particular uses of an animal drug and shall not permit such different use of an animal drug if the labeling of another animal drug that contains the same active ingredient and which is in the same dosage form and concentration provides for such different use.

(B) If the Secretary finds that there is a reasonable probability that a use of an animal drug authorized under subparagraph (A) may present a risk to the public health, the Secretary may —

(i) establish a safe level for a residue of an animal drug when it is used for such different use authorized by subparagraph (A); and

(ii) require the development of a practical, analytical method for the detection of residues of such drug above the safe level established under clause (i).

The use of an animal drug that results in residues exceeding a safe level established under clause (i) shall be considered an unsafe use of such drug under paragraph (1). Safe levels may be established under clause (i) either by regulation or order.

(C) The Secretary may by general regulation provide access to the records of veterinarians to ascertain any use or intended use authorized under subparagraph (A) that the Secretary has determined may present a risk to the public health.

(D) If the Secretary finds, after affording an opportunity for public comment, that a use of an animal drug authorized under subparagraph (A) presents a risk to the public health or that an analytical method required under subparagraph (B) has not been developed and submitted to the Secretary, the Secretary may, by order, prohibit any such use.

(5) If the approval of an application filed under section 505 is in effect, the drug under such application shall not be deemed unsafe for purposes of paragraph (1) and shall be exempt from the requirements of section 502(f) with respect to a use or intended use of the drug in animals if such use or intended use —

(A) is by or on the lawful written or oral order of a licensed veterinarian within the context of a veterinarian-client-patient relationship, as defined by the Secretary; and

(B) is in compliance with regulations promulgated by the Secretary that establish the conditions for the use or intended use of the drug in animals.

(6) For purposes of section 402(a)(2)(D) [probably should read "402(a)(2)(C)(ii)" — Ed.] a use or intended use of a new animal drug shall not be deemed unsafe under this section if the Secretary establishes a tolerance for such drug and any edible portion of any animal imported into the United States does not contain residues exceeding such tolerance. In establishing such tolerance, the Secretary shall rely on data sufficient to demonstrate that a proposed tolerance is safe based on similar food safety criteria used by the Secretary to establish tolerances for applications for new animal drugs filed under subsection (b)(1). The Secretary may consider and rely on data submitted by the drug manufacturer, including data submitted to appropriate regulatory authorities in any country where the new animal drug is lawfully used or data available from a relevant international organization, to the extent such data are not inconsistent with the criteria used by the Secretary to establish a tolerance for applications for new animal drugs filed under subsection (b)(1). For purposes of this paragraph, "relevant international organization" means the Codex Alimenterius Commission or other international organization deemed appropriate by the Secretary. The Secretary may, under procedures specified by regulation, revoke a tolerance established under this paragraph if information demonstrates that the use of the new animal drug under actual use conditions results in food being imported into the United States with residues exceeding the tolerance or if scientific evidence shows the tolerance to be unsafe.

(b) —

(1) Any person may file with the Secretary an application with respect to any intended use or uses of a new animal drug. Such person shall submit to the Secretary as a part of the application

(A) full reports of investigations which have been made to show whether or not such drug is safe and effective for use;

(B) a full list of the articles used as components of such drug;

(C) a full statement of the composition of such drug;

(D) a full description of the methods used in, and the facilities and controls used for, the manufacture, processing, and packing of such drug;

(E) such samples of such drug and of the articles used as components thereof, of any animal feed for use in or on which such drug is intended, and of the edible portions or products (before or after slaughter) of animals to which such drug (directly or in or on animal feed) is intended to be administered, as the Secretary may require;

(F) specimens of the labeling proposed to be used for such drug, or in case such drug is intended for use in animal feed, proposed labeling appropriate for such use, and specimens of the labeling for the drug to be manufactured, packed, or distributed by the applicant;

(G) a description of practicable methods for determining the quantity, if any, of such drug in or on food, and any substance formed in or on food, because of its use; and

(H) the proposed tolerance or withdrawal period or other use restrictions for such drug if any tolerance or withdrawal period or other use restrictions are required in order to assure that the proposed use of such drug will be safe.

The applicant shall file with the application the patent number and the expiration date of any patent which claims the new animal drug for which the applicant filed the application or which claims a method of using such drug and with respect to which a claim of patent infringement could reasonably be asserted if a person not licensed by the owner engaged in the manufacture, use, or sale of the drug. If an application is filed under this subsection for a drug and a patent which claims such drug or a method of using such drug is issued after the filing date but before approval of the application, the applicant shall amend the application to include the information required by the preceding sentence. Upon approval of the application, the Secretary shall publish information submitted under the two preceding sentences.

(2) Any person may file with the Secretary an abbreviated application for the approval of a new animal drug. An abbreviated application shall contain the information required by subsection (n).

(3) Any person intending to file an application under paragraph (1), section 571, or a request for an investigational exemption under subsection (j) shall be entitled to one or more conferences prior to such submission to reach an agreement acceptable to the Secretary establishing a submission or an investigational requirement, which may include a requirement for a field investigation. A decision establishing a submission or an investigational requirement shall bind the Secretary and the applicant or requester unless

(A) the Secretary and the applicant or requester mutually agree to modify the requirement, or

(B) the Secretary by written order determines that a substantiated scientific requirement essential to the determination of safety or effectiveness of the animal drug involved has appeared after the conference.

No later than 25 calendar days after each such conference, the Secretary shall provide a written order setting forth a scientific justification specific to the animal drug and intended uses under consideration if the agreement referred to in the first sentence requires more than one field investigation as being essential to provide substantial evidence of effectiveness for the intended uses of the drug. Nothing in this paragraph shall be construed as compelling the Secretary to require a field investigation.

(c) —

(1) Within one hundred and eighty days after the filing of an application pursuant to subsection (b), or such additional period as may be agreed upon by the Secretary and the applicant, the Secretary shall either

(A) issue an order approving the application if he then finds that none of the grounds for denying approval specified in subsection (d) applies, or

(B) give the applicant notice of an opportunity for a hearing before the Secretary under subsection (d) on the question whether such application is approvable. If the applicant elects to accept the opportunity for a hearing by written request within thirty days after such notice, such hearing shall commence not more than ninety days after the expiration of such thirty days unless the Secretary and the applicant otherwise agree. Any such hearing shall thereafter be conducted on an expedited basis and the Secretary's order thereon shall be issued within ninety days after the date fixed by the Secretary for filing final briefs.

(2) —

(A) Subject to subparagraph (C), the Secretary shall approve an abbreviated application for a drug unless the Secretary finds —

(i) the methods used in, or the facilities and controls used for, the manufacture, processing, and packing of the drug are inadequate to assure and preserve its identity, strength, quality, and purity;

(ii) the conditions of use prescribed, recommended, or suggested in the proposed labeling are not reasonably certain to be followed in practice or, except as provided in subparagraph (B), information submitted with the application is insufficient to show that each of the proposed conditions of use or similar limitations (whether in the labeling or published pursuant to subsection (i)) have been previously approved for the approved new animal drug referred to in the application;

(iii) information submitted with the application is insufficient to show that the active ingredients are the same as those of the approved new animal drug referred to in the application;

(iv) —

(I) if the application is for a drug whose active ingredients, route of administration, dosage form, strength, or use with other animal drugs in animal feed is the same as the active ingredients, route of administration, dosage form, strength, or use with other animal drugs in animal feed of the approved new animal drug referred to in the application, information submitted in the application is insufficient to show that the active ingredients, route of administration, dosage form, strength, or use with other animal drugs in animal feed is the same as that of the approved new animal drug, or

(II) if the application is for a drug whose active ingredients, route of administration, dosage form, strength, or use with other animal drugs in animal feed is different from that of the approved new animal drug referred to in the application, no petition to file an application for the drug with the different active ingredients, route of administration, dosage form, strength, or use with other animal drugs in animal feed was approved under subsection (n)(3);

(v) if the application was filed pursuant to the approval of a petition under subsection (n)(3), the application did not contain the information required by the Secretary respecting the active ingredients, route of administration, dosage form, strength, or use with other animal drugs in animal feed which is not the same;

(vi) information submitted in the application is insufficient to show that the drug is bioequivalent to the approved new animal drug referred to in the application, or if the application is filed under a petition approved pursuant to subsection (n)(3), information submitted in the application is insufficient to show that the active ingredients of the new animal drug are of the same pharmacological or therapeutic class as the pharmacological or therapeutic class of the approved new animal drug and that the new animal drug can be expected to have the same therapeutic effect as the approved new animal drug when used in accordance with the labeling;

(vii) information submitted in the application is insufficient to show that the labeling proposed for the drug is the same as the labeling approved for the approved new animal drug referred to in the application except for changes required because of differences approved under a petition filed under subsection (n)(3), because of a different withdrawal period, or because the drug and the approved new animal drug are produced or distributed by different manufacturers;

(viii) information submitted in the application or any other information available to the Secretary shows that

(I) the inactive ingredients of the drug are unsafe for use under the conditions prescribed, recommended, or suggested in the labeling proposed for the drug,

(II) the composition of the drug is unsafe under such conditions because of the type or quantity of inactive ingredients included or the manner in which the inactive ingredients are included, or

(III) in the case of a drug for food producing animals, the inactive ingredients of the drug or its composition may be unsafe with respect to human food safety;

(ix) the approval under subsection (b)(1) of the approved new animal drug referred to in the application filed under subsection (b)(2) has been withdrawn or suspended for grounds described in paragraph (1) of subsection (e), the Secretary has published a notice of a hearing to withdraw approval of the approved new animal drug for such grounds, the approval under this paragraph of the new animal drug for which the application under subsection (b)(2) was filed has been withdrawn or suspended under subparagraph (G) for such grounds, or the Secretary has determined that the approved new animal drug has been withdrawn from sale for safety or effectiveness reasons;

(x) the application does not meet any other requirement of subsection (n); or

(xi) the application contains an untrue statement of material fact.

(B) If the Secretary finds that a new animal drug for which an application is submitted under subsection (b)(2) is bioequivalent to the approved new animal drug referred to in such application and that residues of the new animal drug are consistent with the tolerances established for such approved new animal drug but at a withdrawal period which is different than the withdrawal period approved for such approved new animal drug, the Secretary may establish, on the basis of information submitted, such different withdrawal period as the withdrawal period for the new animal drug for purposes of the approval of such application for such drug.

(C) Within 180 days of the initial receipt of an application under subsection (b)(2) or within such additional period as may be agreed upon by the Secretary and the applicant, the Secretary shall approve or disapprove the application.

(D) The approval of an application filed under subsection (b)(2) shall be made effective on the last applicable date determined under the following:

(i) If the applicant only made a certification described in clause (i) or (ii) of subsection (n)(1)(G) or in both such clauses, the approval may be made effective immediately.

(ii) If the applicant made a certification described in clause (iii) of subsection (n)(1)(G), the approval may be made effective on the date certified under clause (iii).

(iii) If the applicant made a certification described in clause (iv) of subsection (n)(1)(G), the approval shall be made effective immediately unless an action is brought for infringement of a patent which is the subject of the certification before the expiration of 45 days from the date the notice provided under subsection (n)(2)(B)(i) is received. If such an action is brought before the expiration of such days, the approval shall be made effective upon the expiration of the 30 month period beginning on the date of the receipt of the notice provided under subsection (n)(2)(B) or such shorter or longer period as the court may order because either party to the action failed to reasonably cooperate in expediting the action, except that if before the expiration of such period —

(I) the court decides that such patent is invalid or not infringed, the approval shall be made effective on the date of the court decision,

(II) the court decides that such patent has been infringed, the approval shall be made effective on such date as the court orders under section 271(e)(4)(A) of title 35, United States Code, or

(III) the court grants a preliminary injunction prohibiting the applicant from engaging in the commercial manufacture or sale of the drug until the court decides the issues of patent validity and infringement and if the court decides that such patent is invalid or not infringed, the approval shall be made effective on the date of such court decision.

In such an action, each of the parties shall reasonably cooperate in expediting the action. Until the expiration of 45 days from the date the notice made under subsection (n)(2)(B) is received, no action may be brought under section 2201 of title 28, United States Code, for a declaratory judgment with respect to the patent. Any action brought under section 2201 shall be brought in the judicial district where the defendant has its principal place of business or a regular and established place of business.

(iv) If the application contains a certification described in clause (iv) of subsection (n)(1)(G) and is for a drug for which a previous application has been filed under this subsection containing such a certification, the application shall be made effective not earlier than 180 days after —

(I) the date the Secretary receives notice from the applicant under the previous application of the first commercial marketing of the drug under the previous application, or

(II) the date of a decision of a court in an action described in subclause (III) [probably should be "clause (iii)(III)" — Ed.] holding the patent which is the subject of the certification to be invalid or not infringed,

whichever is earlier.

(E) If the Secretary decides to disapprove an application, the Secretary shall give the applicant notice of an opportunity for a hearing before the Secretary on the question of whether such application is approvable. If the applicant elects to accept the opportunity for hearing by written request within 30 days after such notice, such hearing shall commence not more than 90 days after the expiration of such 30 days unless the Secretary and the applicant otherwise agree. Any such hearing shall thereafter be conducted on an expedited basis and the Secretary's order thereon shall be issued within 90 days after the date fixed by the Secretary for filing final briefs.

(F) —

(i) If an application submitted under subsection (b)(1) for a drug, no active ingredient (including any ester or salt of the active ingredient) of which has been approved in any other application under subsection (b)(1), is approved after the date of the enactment of this paragraph, no application may be submitted under subsection (b)(2) which refers to the drug for which the subsection (b)(1) application was submitted before the expiration of 5 years from the date of the approval of the application under subsection (b)(1), except that such an application may be submitted under subsection (b)(2) after the expiration of 4 years from the date of the approval of the subsection (b)(1) application if it contains a certification of patent invalidity or noninfringement described in clause (iv) of subsection (n)(1)(G). The approval of such an application shall be made effective in accordance with subparagraph (B) except that, if an action for patent infringement is commenced during the one-year period beginning 48 months after the date of the approval of the subsection (b) application, the 30 month period referred to in subparagraph (D)(iii) shall be extended by such amount of time (if any) which is required for seven and one-half years to have elapsed from the date of approval of the subsection (b) application.

(ii) If an application submitted under subsection (b)(1) for a drug, which includes an active ingredient (including any ester or salt of the active ingredient) that has been approved in another application approved under such subsection, is approved after the date of enactment of this paragraph, and if such application contains substantial evidence of the effectiveness of the drug involved, any studies of animal safety, or, in the case of food producing animals, human food safety studies (other than bioequivalence studies or residue depletion studies, except residue depletion studies for minor uses or minor species) required for the approval of the application and conducted or sponsored by the applicant, the Secretary may not make the approval of an application submitted under subsection (b)(2) for the conditions of approval of such drug in the subsection (b)(1) application effective before the expiration of 3 years from the date of the approval of the application under subsection (b)(1) for such drug.

(iii) If a supplement to an application approved under subsection (b)(1) is approved after the date of enactment of this paragraph, and the supplement contains substantial evidence of the effectiveness of the drug involved, any studies of animal safety, or, in the case of food producing animals, human food safety studies (other than bioequivalence studies or residue depletion studies, except residue depletion studies for minor uses or minor species) required for the approval of the supplement and conducted or sponsored by the person submitting the supplement, the Secretary may not make the approval of an application submitted under subsection (b)(2) for a change approved in the supplement effective before the expiration of 3 years from the date of the approval of the supplement.

(iv) An applicant under subsection (b)(1) who comes within the provisions of clause (i) of this subparagraph as a result of an application which seeks approval for a use solely in non-food producing animals, may elect, within 10 days of receiving such approval, to waive clause (i) of this subparagraph, in which event the limitation on approval of applications submitted under subsection (b)(2) set forth in clause (ii) of this subparagraph shall be applicable to the subsection (b)(1) application.

(v) If an application (including any supplement to a new animal drug application) submitted under subsection (b)(1) for a new animal drug for a food-producing animal use, which includes an active ingredient (including any ester or salt of the active ingredient) which has been the subject of a waiver under clause (iv) is approved after the date of enactment of this paragraph [November 16, 1998 — Ed.], and if the application contains substantial evidence of the effectiveness of the drug involved, any studies of animal safety, or human food safety studies (other than bioequivalence studies or residue depletion studies, except residue depletion studies for minor uses or minor species) required for the new approval of the application and conducted or sponsored by the applicant, the Secretary may not make the approval of an application (including any supplement to such application) submitted under subsection (b)(2) for the new conditions of approval of such drug in the subsection (b)(1) application effective before the expiration of five years from the date of approval of the application under subsection (b)(1) for such drug. The provisions of this paragraph shall apply only to the first approval for a food- producing animal use for the same applicant after the waiver under clause (iv).

(G) If an approved application submitted under subsection (b)(2) for a new animal drug refers to a drug the approval of which was withdrawn or suspended for grounds described in paragraph (1) or (2) of subsection (e) or was withdrawn or suspended under this subparagraph or which, as determined by the Secretary, has been withdrawn from sale for safety or effectiveness reasons, the approval of the drug under this paragraph shall be withdrawn or suspended —

(i) for the same period as the withdrawal or suspension under subsection (e) or this subparagraph, or

(ii) if the approved new animal drug has been withdrawn from sale, for the period of withdrawal from sale or, if earlier, the period ending on the date the Secretary determines that the withdrawal from sale is not for safety or effectiveness reasons.

(H) For purposes of this paragraph:

(i) The term "bioequivalence" means the rate and extent to which the active ingredient or therapeutic ingredient is absorbed from a new animal drug and becomes available at the site of drug action.

(ii) A new animal drug shall be considered to be bioequivalent to the approved new animal drug referred to in its application under subsection (n) if —

(I) the rate and extent of absorption of the drug do not show a significant difference from the rate and extent of absorption of the approved new animal drug referred to in the application when administered at the same dose of the active ingredient under similar experimental conditions in either a single dose or multiple doses;

(II) the extent of absorption of the drug does not show a significant difference from the extent of absorption of the approved new animal drug referred to in the application when administered at the same dose of the active ingredient under similar experimental conditions in either single dose or multiple doses and the difference from the approved new animal drug in the rate of absorption of the drug is intentional, is reflected in its proposed labeling, is not essential to the attainment of effective drug concentrations in use, and is considered scientifically insignificant for the drug in attaining the intended purposes of its use and preserving human food safety; or

(III) in any case in which the Secretary determines that the measurement of the rate and extent of absorption or excretion of the new animal drug in biological fluids is inappropriate or impractical, an appropriate acute pharmacological effects test or other test of the new animal drug and, when deemed scientifically necessary, of the approved new animal drug referred to in the application in the species to be tested or in an appropriate animal model does not show a significant difference between the new animal drug and such approved new animal drug when administered at the same dose under similar experimental conditions.

If the approved new animal drug referred to in the application for a new animal drug under subsection (n) is approved for use in more than one animal species, the bioequivalency information described in subclauses (I), (II), and (III) shall be obtained for one species, or if the Secretary deems appropriate based on scientific principles, shall be obtained for more than one species. The Secretary may prescribe the dose to be used in determining bioequivalency under subclause (I), (II), or (III). To assure that the residues of the new animal drug will be consistent with the established tolerances for the approved new animal drug referred to in the application under subsection (b)(2) upon the expiration of the withdrawal period contained in the application for the new animal drug, the Secretary shall require bioequivalency data or residue depletion studies of the new animal drug or such other data or studies as the Secretary considers appropriate based on scientific principles. If the Secretary requires one or more residue studies under the preceding sentence, the Secretary may not require that the assay methodology used to determine the withdrawal period of the new animal drug be more rigorous than the methodology used to determine the withdrawal period for the approved new animal drug referred to in the application. If such studies are required and if the approved new animal drug, referred to in the application for the new animal drug for which such studies are required, is approved for use in more than one animal species, such studies shall be conducted for one species, or if the Secretary deems appropriate based on scientific principles, shall be conducted for more than one species.

(3) If the patent information described in subsection (b)(1) could not be filed with the submission of an application under subsection (b)(1) because the application was filed before the patent information was required under subsection (b)(1) or a patent was issued after the application was approved under such subsection, the holder of an approved application shall file with the Secretary the patent number and the expiration date of any patent which claims the new animal drug for which the application was filed or which claims a method of using such drug and with respect to which a claim of patent infringement could reasonably be asserted if a person not licensed by the owner engaged in the manufacture, use, or sale of the drug. If the holder of an approved application could not file patent information under subsection (b)(1) because it was not required at the time the application was approved, the holder shall file such information under this subsection not later than 30 days after the date of the enactment of this sentence [November 16, 1988 — Ed.], and if the holder of an approved application could not file patent information under subsection (b)(1) because no patent had been issued when an application was filed or approved, the holder shall file such information under this subsection not later than 30 days after the date the patent involved is issued. Upon the submission of patent information under this subsection, the Secretary shall publish it.

(4) A drug manufactured in a pilot or other small facility may be used to demonstrate the safety and effectiveness of the drug and to obtain approval for the drug prior to manufacture of the drug in a larger facility, unless the Secretary makes a determination that a full scale production facility is necessary to ensure the safety or effectiveness of the drug.

(d) —

(1) If the Secretary finds, after due notice to the applicant in accordance with subsection (c) and giving him an opportunity for a hearing, in accordance with said subsection, that —

(A) the investigations, reports of which are required to be submitted to the Secretary pursuant to subsection (b), do not include adequate tests by all methods reasonably applicable to show whether or not such drug is safe for use under the conditions prescribed, recommended, or suggested in the proposed labeling thereof;

(B) the results of such tests show that such drug is unsafe for use under such conditions or do not show that such drug is safe for use under such conditions;

(C) the methods used in, and the facilities and controls used for, the manufacture, processing, and packing of such drug are inadequate to preserve its identity, strength, quality, and purity;

(D) upon the basis of the information submitted to him as part of the application, or upon the basis of any other information before him with respect to such drug, he has insufficient information to determine whether such drug is safe for use under such conditions;

(E) evaluated on the basis of the information submitted to him as part of the application and any other information before him with respect to such drug, there is a lack of substantial evidence that the drug will have the effect it purports or is represented to have under the conditions of use prescribed, recommended, or suggested in the proposed labeling thereof;

(F) upon the basis of information submitted to the Secretary as part of the application or any other information before the Secretary with respect to such drug, any use prescribed, recommended, or suggested in labeling proposed for such drug will result in a residue of such drug in excess of a tolerance found by the Secretary to be safe for such drug;

(G) the application failed to contain the patent information prescribed by subsection (b)(1);

(H) based on a fair evaluation of all material facts, such labeling is false or misleading in any particular; or

(I) such drug induces cancer when ingested by man or animal or, after tests which are appropriate for the evaluation of the safety of such drug, induces cancer in man or animal, except that the foregoing provisions of this subparagraph shall not apply with respect to such drug if the Secretary finds that, under the conditions of use specified in proposed labeling and reasonably certain to be followed in practice

(i) such drug will not adversely affect the animals for which it is intended, and

(ii) no residue of such drug will be found (by methods of examination prescribed or approved by the Secretary by regulations, which regulations shall not be subject to subsections (c), (d), and (h)), in any edible portion of such animals after slaughter or in any food yielded by or derived from the living animals;

he shall issue an order refusing to approve the application. If, after such notice and opportunity for hearing, the Secretary finds that subparagraphs (A) through (I) do not apply, he shall issue an order approving the application.

(2) In determining whether such drug is safe for use under the conditions prescribed, recommended, or suggested in the proposed labeling thereof, the Secretary shall consider, among other relevant factors,

(A) the probable consumption of such drug and of any substance formed in or on food because of the use of such drug,

(B) the cumulative effect on man or animal of such drug, taking into account any chemically or pharmacologically related substance,

(C) safety factors which in the opinion of experts, qualified by scientific training and experience to evaluate the safety of such drugs, are appropriate for the use of animal experimentation data, and

(D) whether the conditions of use prescribed, recommended, or suggested in the proposed labeling are reasonably certain to be followed in practice.

Any order issued under this subsection refusing to approve an application shall state the findings upon which it is based.

(3) As used in this section, the term "substantial evidence" means evidence consisting of one or more adequate and well controlled investigations, such as —

(A) a study in a target species;

(B) a study in laboratory animals;

(C) any field investigation that may be required under this section and that meets the requirements of subsection (b)(3) if a presubmission conference is requested by the applicant;

(D) a bioequivalence study; or

(E) an in vitro study;

by experts qualified by scientific training and experience to evaluate the effectiveness of the drug involved, on the basis of which it could fairly and reasonably be concluded by such experts that the drug will have the effect it purports or is represented to have under the conditions of use prescribed, recommended, or suggested in the labeling or proposed labeling thereof.

(4) In a case in which an animal drug contains more than one active ingredient, or the labeling of the drug prescribes, recommends, or suggests use of the drug in combination with one or more other animal drugs, and the active ingredients or drugs intended for use in the combination have previously been separately approved pursuant to an application submitted under section 512(b)(1) [probably should be "subsection (b)(1) — Ed.] for particular uses and conditions of use for which they are intended for use in the combination —

(A) the Secretary shall not issue an order under paragraph (1)(A), (1)(B), or (1)(D) refusing to approve the application for such combination on human food safety grounds unless the Secretary finds that the application fails to establish that —

(i) none of the active ingredients or drugs intended for use in the combination, respectively, at the longest withdrawal time of any of the active ingredients or drugs in the combination, respectively, exceeds its established tolerance; or

(ii) none of the active ingredients or drugs in the combination interferes with the methods of analysis for another of the active ingredients or drugs in the combination, respectively;

(B) the Secretary shall not issue an order under paragraph (1)(A), (1)(B), or (1)(D) refusing to approve the application for such combination on target animal safety grounds unless the Secretary finds that —

(i) —

(I) there is a substantiated scientific issue, specific to one or more of the active ingredients or animal drugs in the combination, that cannot adequately be evaluated based on information contained in the application for the combination (including any investigations, studies, or tests for which the applicant has a right of reference or use from the person by or for whom the investigations, studies, or tests were conducted); or

(II) there is a scientific issue raised by target animal observations contained in studies submitted to the Secretary as part of the application; and

(ii) based on the Secretary's evaluation of the information contained in the application with respect to the issues identified in clauses (i) (I) and (II), paragraph (1) (A), (B), or (D) apply;

(C) except in the case of a combination that contains a nontopical antibacterial ingredient or animal drug, the Secretary shall not issue an order under paragraph (1)(E) refusing to approve an application for a combination animal drug intended for use other than in animal feed or drinking water unless the Secretary finds that the application fails to demonstrate that —

(i) there is substantial evidence that any active ingredient or animal drug intended only for the same use as another active ingredient or animal drug in the combination makes a contribution to labeled effectiveness;

(ii) each active ingredient or animal drug intended for at least one use that is different from all other active ingredients or animal drugs used in the combination provides appropriate concurrent use for the intended target population; or

(iii) where based on scientific information the Secretary has reason to believe the active ingredients or animal drugs may be physically incompatible or have disparate dosing regimens, such active ingredients or animal drugs are physically compatible or do not have disparate dosing regimens; and

(D) the Secretary shall not issue an order under paragraph (1)(E) refusing to approve an application for a combination animal drug intended for use in animal feed or drinking water unless the Secretary finds that the application fails to demonstrate that —

(i) there is substantial evidence that any active ingredient or animal drug intended only for the same use as another active ingredient or animal drug in the combination makes a contribution to the labeled effectiveness;

(ii) each of the active ingredients or animal drugs intended for at least one use that is different from all other active ingredients or animal drugs used in the combination provides appropriate concurrent use for the intended target population;

(iii) where a combination contains more than one nontopical antibacterial ingredient or animal drug, there is substantial evidence that each of the nontopical antibacterial ingredients or animal drugs makes a contribution to the labeled effectiveness, except that for purposes of this clause, antibacterial ingredient or animal drug does not include the ionophore or arsenical classes of animal drugs; or

(iv) where based on scientific information the Secretary has reason to believe the active ingredients or animal drugs intended for use in drinking water may be physically incompatible, such active ingredients or animal drugs intended for use in drinking water are physically compatible.

(5) In reviewing an application that proposes a change to add an intended use for a minor use or a minor species to an approved new animal drug application, the Secretary shall reevaluate only the relevant information in the approved application to determine whether the application for the minor use or minor species can be approved. A decision to approve the application for the minor use or minor species is not, implicitly or explicitly, a reaffirmation of the approval of the original application.

(e) —

(1) The Secretary shall, after due notice and opportunity for hearing to the applicant, issue an order withdrawing approval of an application filed pursuant to subsection (b) with respect to any new animal drug if the Secretary finds —

(A) that experience or scientific data show that such drug is unsafe for use under the conditions of use upon the basis of which the application was approved or the condition of use authorized under subsection (a)(4) (A);

(B) that new evidence not contained in such application or not available to the Secretary until after such application was approved, or tests by new methods, or tests by methods not deemed reasonably applicable when such application was approved, evaluated together with the evidence available to the Secretary when the application was approved, shows that such drug is not shown to be safe for use under the conditions of use upon the basis of which the application was approved or that subparagraph (I) of paragraph (1) of subsection (d) applies to such drug;

(C) on the basis of new information before him with respect to such drug, evaluated together with the evidence available to him when the application was approved, that there is a lack of substantial evidence that such drug will have the effect it purports or is represented to have under the conditions of use prescribed, recommended, or suggested in the labeling thereof;

(D) the patent information prescribed by subsection (c)(3) was not filed within 30 days after the receipt of written notice from the Secretary specifying the failure to file such information;

(E) that the application contains any untrue statement of a material fact; or

(F) that the applicant has made any changes from the standpoint of safety or effectiveness beyond the variations provided for in the application unless he has supplemented the application by filing with the Secretary adequate information respecting all such changes and unless there is in effect an approval of the supplemental application. The supplemental application shall be treated in the same manner as the original application.

If the Secretary (or in his absence the officer acting as Secretary) finds that there is an imminent hazard to the health of man or of the animals for which such drug is intended, he may suspend the approval of such application immediately, and give the applicant prompt notice of his action and afford the applicant the opportunity for an expedited hearing under this subsection; but the authority conferred by this sentence to suspend the approval of an application shall not be delegated.

(2) The Secretary may also, after due notice and opportunity for hearing to the applicant, issue an order withdrawing the approval of an application with respect to any new animal drug under this section if the Secretary finds —

(A) that the applicant has failed to establish a system for maintaining required records, or has repeatedly or deliberately failed to maintain such records or to make required reports in accordance with a regulation or order under subsection (1), or the applicant has refused to permit access to, or copying or verification of, such records as required by paragraph (2) of such subsection;

(B) that on the basis of new information before him, evaluated together with the evidence before him when the application was approved, the methods used in, or the facilities and controls used for, the manufacture, processing, and packing of such drug are inadequate to assure and preserve its identity, strength, quality, and purity and were not made adequate within a reasonable time after receipt of written notice from the Secretary specifying the matter complained of; or

(C) that on the basis of new information before him, evaluated together with the evidence before him when the application was approved, the labeling of such drug, based on a fair evaluation of all material facts, is false or misleading in any particular and was not corrected within a reasonable time after receipt of written notice from the Secretary specifying the matter complained of.

(3) Any order under this subsection shall state the findings upon which it is based.

(f) Whenever the Secretary finds that the facts so require, he shall revoke any previous order under subsection (d), (e), or (m) or section 571 (c), (d), or (e), refusing, withdrawing, or suspending approval of an application and shall approve such application or reinstate such approval, as may be appropriate.

(g) Orders of the Secretary issued under this section, or section 571 (other than orders issuing, amending, or repealing regulations) shall be served

(1) in person by any officer or employee of the department designated by the Secretary or

(2) by mailing the order by registered mail or by certified mail addressed to the applicant or respondent at his last known address in the records of the Secretary.

(h) An appeal may be taken by the applicant from an order of the Secretary refusing or withdrawing approval of an application filed under subsection (b) or (m) of this section. The provisions of subsection (h) of section 505 of this Act shall govern any such appeal.

(i) When a new animal drug application filed pursuant to subsection (b) or section 571 is approved, the Secretary shall by notice, which upon publication shall be effective as a regulation, publish in the Federal Register the name and address of the applicant and the conditions and indications of use of the new animal drug covered by such application, including any tolerance and withdrawal period or other use restrictions and, if such new animal drug is intended for use in animal feed, appropriate purposes and conditions of use (including special labeling requirements and any requirement that an animal feed bearing or containing the new animal drug be limited to use under the professional supervision of a licensed veterinarian) applicable to any animal feed for use in which such drug is approved, and such other information, upon the basis of which such application was approved, as the Secretary deems necessary to assure the safe and effective use of such drug. Upon withdrawal of approval of such new animal drug application or upon its suspension or upon failure to renew a conditional approval under section 571, the Secretary shall forthwith revoke or suspend, as the case may be, the regulation published pursuant to this subsection (i) insofar as it is based on the approval of such application.

(j) To the extent consistent with the public health, the Secretary shall promulgate regulations for exempting from the operation of this section new animal drugs, and animal feeds bearing or containing new animal drugs, intended solely for investigational use by experts qualified by scientific training and experience to investigate the safety and effectiveness of animal drugs. Such regulations may, in the discretion of the Secretary, among other conditions relating to the protection of the public health, provide for conditioning such exemption upon the establishment and maintenance of such records, and the making of such reports to the Secretary, by the manufacturer or the sponsor of the investigation of such article, of data (including but not limited to analytical reports by investigators) obtained as a result of such investigational use of such article, as the Secretary finds will enable him to evaluate the safety and effectiveness of such article in the event of the filing of an application pursuant to this section. Such regulations, among other things, shall set forth the conditions (if any) upon which animals treated with such articles, and any products of such animals (before or after slaughter), may be marketed for food use.

(k) While approval of an application for a new animal drug is effective, a food shall not, by reason of bearing or containing such drug or any substance formed in or on the food because of its use in accordance with such application (including the conditions and indications of use prescribed pursuant to subsection (i)), be considered adulterated within the meaning of clause (1) of section 402(a).

(l) —

(1) In the case of any new animal drug for which an approval of an application filed pursuant to subsection (b) or section 571 is in effect, the applicant shall establish and maintain such records, and make such reports to the Secretary, of data relating to experience, including experience with uses authorized under subsection (a)(4)(A), and other data or information, received or otherwise obtained by such applicant with respect to such drug, or with respect to animal feeds bearing or containing such drug, as the Secretary may by general regulation, or by order with respect to such application, prescribe on the basis of a finding that such records and reports are necessary in order to enable the Secretary to determine, or facilitate determination, whether there is or may be ground for invoking subsection (e) or subsection (m)(4) of this section. Such regulation or order shall provide, where the Secretary deems it to be appropriate, for the examination, upon request, by the persons to whom such regulation or order is applicable, of similar information received or otherwise obtained by the Secretary.

(2) Every person required under this subsection to maintain records, and every person in charge or custody thereof, shall, upon request of an officer or employee designated by the Secretary, permit such officer or employee at all reasonable times to have access to and copy and verify such records.

(m) —

(1) Any person may file with the Secretary an application for a license to manufacture animal feeds bearing or containing new animal drugs. Such person shall submit to the Secretary as part of the application

(A) a full statement of the business name and address of the specific facility at which the manufacturing is to take place and the facility's registration number,

(B) the name and signature of the responsible individual or individuals for that facility,

(C) a certification that the animal feeds bearing or containing new animal drugs are manufactured and labeled in accordance with the applicable regulations published pursuant to subsection (i) or for indexed new animal drugs in accordance with the index listing published pursuant to section 572(e)(2) and the labeling requirements set forth in section 572(h), and

(D) a certification that the methods used in, and the facilities and controls used for, manufacturing, processing, packaging, and holding such animal feeds are in conformity with current good manufacturing practice as described in section 501(a)(2)(B).

(2) Within 90 days after the filing of an application pursuant to paragraph (1), or such additional period as may be agreed upon by the Secretary and the applicant, the Secretary shall

(A) issue an order approving the application if the Secretary then finds that none of the grounds for denying approval specified in paragraph (3) applies, or

(B) give the applicant notice of an opportunity for a hearing before the Secretary under paragraph (3) on the question whether such application is approvable. The procedure governing such a hearing shall be the procedure set forth in the last two sentences of subsection (c)(1).

(3) If the Secretary, after due notice to the applicant in accordance with paragraph (2) and giving the applicant an opportunity for a hearing in accordance with such paragraph, finds, on the basis of information submitted to the Secretary as part of the application, on the basis of a preapproval inspection, or on the basis of any other information before the Secretary —

(A) that the application is incomplete, false, or misleading in any particular;

(B) that the methods used in, and the facilities and controls used for, the manufacture, processing, and packing of such animal feed are inadequate to preserve the identity, strength, quality, and purity of the new animal drug therein; or

(C) that the facility manufactures animal feeds bearing or containing new animal drugs in a manner that does not accord with the specifications for manufacture or labels animal feeds bearing or containing new animal drugs in a manner that does not accord with the conditions or indications of use that are published pursuant to subsection (i) or an index listing pursuant to section 572(e),

the Secretary shall issue an order refusing to approve the application. If, after such notice and opportunity for hearing, the Secretary finds that subparagraphs (A) through (C) do not apply, the Secretary shall issue an order approving the application. An order under this subsection approving an application for a license to manufacture animal feeds bearing or containing new animal drugs shall permit a facility to manufacture only those animal feeds bearing or containing new animal drugs for which there are in effect regulations pursuant to subsection (i) or an index listing pursuant to section 572(e) relating to the use of such drugs in or on such animal feed.

(4) —

(A) The Secretary shall, after due notice and opportunity for hearing to the applicant, revoke a license to manufacture animal feeds bearing or containing new animal drugs under this subsection if the Secretary finds —

(i) that the application for such license contains any untrue statement of a material fact; or

(ii) that the applicant has made changes that would cause the application to contain any untrue statements of material fact or that would affect the safety or effectiveness of the animal feeds manufactured at the facility unless the applicant has supplemented the application by filing with the Secretary adequate information respecting all such changes and unless there is in effect an approval of the supplemental application.

If the Secretary (or in the Secretary's absence the officer acting as the Secretary) finds that there is an imminent hazard to the health of humans or of the animals for which such animal feed is intended, the Secretary may suspend the license immediately, and give the applicant prompt notice of the action and afford the applicant the opportunity for an expedited hearing under this subsection; but the authority conferred by this sentence shall not be delegated.

(B) The Secretary may also, after due notice and opportunity for hearing to the applicant, revoke a license to manufacture animal feed under this subsection if the Secretary finds —

(i) that the applicant has failed to establish a system for maintaining required records, or has repeatedly or deliberately failed to maintain such records or to make required reports in accordance with a regulation or order under paragraph (5)(A) of this subsection or section 504(a)(3)(A), or the applicant has refused to permit access to, or copying or verification of, such records as required by subparagraph (B) of such paragraph or section 504(a)(3)(B);

(ii) that on the basis of new information before the Secretary, evaluated together with the evidence before the Secretary when such license was issued, the methods used in, or the facilities and controls used for, the manufacture, processing, packing, and holding of such animal feed are inadequate to assure and preserve the identity, strength, quality, and purity of the new animal drug therein, and were not made adequate within a reasonable time after receipt of written notice from the Secretary, specifying the matter complained of;

(iii) that on the basis of new information before the Secretary, evaluated together with the evidence before the Secretary when such license was issued, the labeling of any animal feeds, based on a fair evaluation of all material facts, is false or misleading in any particular and was not corrected within a reasonable time after receipt of written notice from the Secretary specifying the matter complained of; or

(iv) that on the basis of new information before the Secretary, evaluated together with the evidence before the Secretary when such license was issued, the facility has manufactured, processed, packed, or held animal feed bearing or containing a new animal drug adulterated under section 501(a)(6) and the facility did not discontinue the manufacture, processing, packing, or holding of such animal feed within a reasonable time after receipt of written notice from the Secretary specifying the matter complained of.

(C) The Secretary may also revoke a license to manufacture animal feeds under this subsection if an applicant gives notice to the Secretary of intention to discontinue the manufacture of all animal feed covered under this subsection and waives an opportunity for a hearing on the matter.

(D) Any order under this paragraph shall state the findings upon which it is based.

(5) When a license to manufacture animal feeds bearing or containing new animal drugs has been issued —

(A) the applicant shall establish and maintain such records, and make such reports to the Secretary, or (at the option of the Secretary) to the appropriate person or persons holding an approved application filed under subsection (b), as the Secretary may by general regulation, or by order with respect to such application, prescribe on the basis of a finding that such records and reports are necessary in order to enable the Secretary to determine, or facilitate a determination, whether there is or may be ground for invoking subsection (e) or paragraph (4); and

(B) every person required under this subsection to maintain records, and every person in charge or custody thereof, shall, upon request of an officer or employee designated by the Secretary, permit such officer or employee at all reasonable times to have access to and copy and verify such records.

(6) To the extent consistent with the public health, the Secretary may promulgate regulations for exempting from the operation of this subsection facilities that manufacture, process, pack, or hold animal feeds bearing or containing new animal drugs.

(n) —

(1) An abbreviated application for a new animal drug shall contain —

(A) —

(i) except as provided in clause (ii), information to show that the conditions of use or similar limitations (whether in the labeling or published pursuant to subsection (i)) prescribed, recommended, or suggested in the labeling proposed for the new animal drug have been previously approved for a new animal drug listed under paragraph (4) (hereinafter in this subsection referred to as an "approved new animal drug"), and

(ii) information to show that the withdrawal period at which residues of the new animal drug will be consistent with the tolerances established for the approved new animal drug is the same as the withdrawal period previously established for the approved new animal drug or, if the withdrawal period is proposed to be different, information showing that the residues of the new animal drug at the proposed different withdrawal period will be consistent with the tolerances established for the approved new animal drug;

(B) —

(i) information to show that the active ingredients of the new animal drug are the same as those of the approved new animal drug, and

(ii) if the approved new animal drug has more than one active ingredient, and if one of the active ingredients of the new animal drug is different from one of the active ingredients of the approved new animal drug and the application is filed pursuant to the approval of a petition filed under paragraph (3)

—

(I) information to show that the other active ingredients of the new animal drug are the same as the active ingredients of the approved new animal drug,

(II) information to show either that the different active ingredient is an active ingredient of another approved new animal drug or of an animal drug which does not meet the requirements of section 201(v), and

(III) such other information respecting the different active ingredients as the Secretary may require;

(C) —

(i) if the approved new animal drug is permitted to be used with one or more animal drugs in animal feed, information to show that the proposed uses of the new animal drug with other animal drugs in animal feed are the same as the uses of the approved new animal drug, and

(ii) if the approved new animal drug is permitted to be used with one or more other animal drugs in animal feed, and one of the other animal drugs proposed for use with the new animal drug in animal feed is different from one of the other animal drugs permitted to be used in animal feed with the approved new animal drug, and the application is filed pursuant to the approval of a petition filed under paragraph (3) —

(I) information to show either that the different animal drug proposed for use with the approved new animal drug in animal feed is an approved new animal drug permitted to be used in animal feed or does not meet the requirements of section 201(v) when used with another animal drug in animal feed,

(II) information to show that other animal drugs proposed for use with the new animal drug in animal feed are the same as the other animal drugs permitted to be used with the approved new animal drug, and

(III) such other information respecting the different animal drug or combination with respect to which the petition was filed as the Secretary may require,

(D) information to show that the route of administration, the dosage form, and the strength of the new animal drug are the same as those of the approved new animal drug or, if the route of administration, the dosage form, or the strength of the new animal drug is different and the application is filed pursuant to the approval of a petition filed under paragraph (3), such information respecting the route of administration, dosage form, or strength with respect to which the petition was filed as the Secretary may require;

(E) information to show that the new animal drug is bioequivalent to the approved new animal drug, except that if the application is filed pursuant to the approval of a petition filed under paragraph (3) for the purposes described in subparagraph (B) or (C), information to show that the active ingredients of the new animal drug are of the same pharmacological or therapeutic class as the pharmacological or therapeutic class of the approved new animal drug and that the new animal drug can be expected to have the same therapeutic effect as the approved new animal drug when used in accordance with the labeling;

(F) information to show that the labeling proposed for the new animal drug is the same as the labeling approved for the approved new animal drug except for changes required because of differences approved under a petition filed under paragraph (3), because of a different withdrawal period, or because the new animal drug and the approved new animal drug are produced or distributed by different manufacturers;

(G) the items specified in clauses (B) through (F) of subsection (b)(1);

(H) a certification, in the opinion of the applicant and to the best of his knowledge, with respect to each patent which claims the approved new animal drug or which claims a use for such approved new animal drug for which the applicant is seeking approval under this subsection and for which information is required to be filed under subsection (b)(1) or (c)(3) —

(i) that such patent information has not been filed,

(ii) that such patent has expired,

(iii) of the date on which such patent will expire, or

(iv) that such patent is invalid or will not be infringed by the manufacture, use, or sale of the new animal drug for which the application is filed; and

(I) if with respect to the approved new animal drug information was filed under subsection (b)(1) or (c)(3) for a method of use patent which does not claim a use for which the applicant is seeking approval of an application under subsection (c)(2), a statement that the method of use patent does not claim such a use.

The Secretary may not require that an abbreviated application contain information in addition to that required by subparagraphs (A) through (I).

(2) —

(A) An applicant who makes a certification described in paragraph (1)(G)(iv) shall include in the application a statement that the applicant will give the notice required by subparagraph (B) to —

(i) each owner of the patent which is the subject of the certification or the representative of such owner designated to receive such notice, and

(ii) the holder of the approved application under subsection (c)(1) for the drug which is claimed by the patent or a use of which is claimed by the patent or the representative of such holder designated to receive such notice.

(B) The notice referred to in subparagraph (A) shall state that an application, which contains data from bioequivalence studies, has been filed under this subsection for the drug with respect to which the certification is made to obtain approval to engage in the commercial manufacture, use, or sale of such drug before the expiration of the patent referred to in the certification. Such notice shall include a detailed statement of the factual and legal basis of the applicant's opinion that the patent is not valid or will not be infringed.

(C) If an application is amended to include a certification described in paragraph (1)(G)(iv), the notice required by subparagraph (B) shall be given when the amended application is filed.

(3) If a person wants to submit an abbreviated application for a new animal drug —

(A) whose active ingredients, route of administration, dosage form, or strength differ from that of an approved new animal drug, or

(B) whose use with other animal drugs in animal feed differs from that of an approved new animal drug,

such person shall submit a petition to the Secretary seeking permission to file such an application. The Secretary shall approve a petition for a new animal drug unless the Secretary finds that —

(C) investigations must be conducted to show the safety and effectiveness, in animals to be treated with the drug, of the active ingredients, route of administration, dosage form, strength, or use with other animal drugs in animal feed which differ from the approved new animal drug, or

(D) investigations must be conducted to show the safety for human consumption of any residues in food resulting from the proposed active ingredients, route of administration, dosage form, strength, or use with other animal drugs in animal feed for the new animal drug which is different from the active ingredients, route of administration, dosage form, strength, or use with other animal drugs in animal feed of the approved new animal drug.

The Secretary shall approve or disapprove a petition submitted under this paragraph within 90 days of the date the petition is submitted.

(4) —

(A) —

(i) Within 60 days of the date of the enactment of this subsection, the Secretary shall publish and make available to the public a list in alphabetical order of the official and proprietary name of each new animal drug which has been approved for safety and effectiveness before the date of the enactment of this subsection.

(ii) Every 30 days after the publication of the first list under clause (i) the Secretary shall revise the list to include each new animal drug which has been approved for safety and effectiveness under subsection (c) during the 30 day period.

(iii) When patent information submitted under subsection (b)(1) or (c)(3) respecting a new animal drug included on the list is to be published by the Secretary, the Secretary shall, in revisions made under clause (ii), include such information for such drug.

(B) A new animal drug approved for safety and effectiveness before the date of the enactment of this subsection or approved for safety and effectiveness under subsection (c) shall, for purposes of this subsection, be considered to have been published under subparagraph (A) on the date of its approval or the date of enactment, whichever is later.

(C) If the approval of a new animal drug was withdrawn or suspended under subsection (c)(2)(G) or for grounds described in subsection (e) or if the Secretary determines that a drug has been withdrawn from sale for safety or effectiveness reasons, it may not be published in the list under subparagraph (A) or, if the withdrawal or suspension occurred after its publication in such list, it shall be immediately removed from such list —

(i) for the same period as the withdrawal or suspension under subsection (c)(2)(G) or (e), or

(ii) if the listed drug has been withdrawn from sale, for the period of withdrawal from sale or, if earlier, the period ending on the date the Secretary determines that the withdrawal from sale is not for safety or effectiveness reasons.

A notice of the removal shall be published in the Federal Register.

(5) If an application contains the information required by clauses (A), (G), and (H) of subsection (b)(1) and such information —

(A) is relied on by the applicant for the approval of the application, and

(B) is not information derived either from investigations, studies, or tests conducted by or for the applicant or for which the applicant had obtained a right of reference or use from the person by or for whom the investigations, studies, or tests were conducted,

such application shall be considered to be an application filed under subsection (b)(2).

(o) For purposes of this section, the term "patent" means a patent issued by the United States Patent and Trademark Office.

(p) —

(1) Safety and effectiveness data and information which has been submitted in an application filed under subsection (b)(1) or section 571(a) for a drug and which has not previously been disclosed to the public shall be made available to the public, upon request, unless extraordinary circumstances are shown —

(A) if no work is being or will be undertaken to have the application approved,

(B) if the Secretary has determined that the application is not approvable and all legal appeals have been exhausted,

(C) if approval of the application under subsection (c) is withdrawn and all legal appeals have been exhausted,

(D) if the Secretary has determined that such drug is not a new drug, or

(E) upon the effective date of the approval of the first application filed under subsection (b)(2) which refers to such drug or upon the date upon which the approval of an application filed under subsection (b)(2) which refers to such drug could be made effective if such an application had been filed.

(2) Any request for data and information pursuant to paragraph (1) shall include a verified statement by the person making the request that any data or information received under such paragraph shall not be disclosed by such person to any other person —

(A) for the purpose of, or as part of a plan, scheme, or device for, obtaining the right to make, use, or market, or making, using, or marketing, outside the United States, the drug identified in the application filed under subsection (b)(1) or section 571(a), and

(B) without obtaining from any person to whom the data and information are disclosed an identical verified statement, a copy of which is to be provided by such person to the Secretary, which meets the requirements of this paragraph.

(q) Date of Approval in the Case of Recommended Controls Under the CSA

(1) In General. — In the case of an application under subsection (b) with respect to a drug for which the Secretary provides notice to the sponsor that the Secretary intends to issue a scientific and medical evaluation and recommend controls under the Controlled Substances Act, approval of such application shall not take effect until the interim final rule controlling the drug is issued in accordance with section 201(j) of the Controlled Substances Act.

(2) Date of Approval. — For purposes of this section, with respect to an application described in paragraph (1), the term "date of approval" shall mean the later of—

(A) the date an application under subsection (b) is approved under subsection (c); or

(B) the date of issuance of the interim final rule controlling the drug.

Sec. 513. [360c] Classification of Devices Intended for Human Use.

(a) Device Classes. —

(1) There are established the following classes of devices intended for human use:

(A) Class I, General Controls. —

(i) A device for which the controls authorized by or under section 501, 502, 510, 516, 518, 519, or 520 or any combination of such sections are sufficient to provide reasonable assurance of the safety and effectiveness of the device.

(ii) A device for which insufficient information exists to determine that the controls referred to in clause

(iii) are sufficient to provide reasonable assurance of the safety and effectiveness of the device or to establish special controls to provide such assurance, but because it —

(I) is not purported or represented to be for a use in supporting or sustaining human life or for a use which is of substantial importance in preventing impairment of human health, and

(II) does not present a potential unreasonable risk of illness or injury, is to be regulated by the controls referred to in clause (i).

(B) Class II, Special Controls. — A device which cannot be classified as a class I device because the general controls by themselves are insufficient to provide reasonable assurance of the safety and effectiveness of the device, and for which there is sufficient information to establish special controls to provide such assurance, including the promulgation of performance standards, postmarket surveillance, patient registries, development and dissemination of guidelines (including guidelines for the submission of clinical data in premarket notification submissions in accordance with section 510(k)), recommendations, and other appropriate actions as the Secretary deems necessary to provide such assurance. For a device that is purported or represented to be for a use in supporting or sustaining human life, the Secretary shall examine and identify the special controls, if any, that are necessary to provide adequate assurance of safety and effectiveness and describe how such controls provide such assurance.

(C) Class III, Premarket Approval. — A device which because —

(i) it

(I) cannot be classified as a class I device because insufficient information exists to determine that the application of general controls are sufficient to provide reasonable assurance of the safety and effectiveness of the device, and

(II) cannot be classified as a class II device because insufficient information exists to determine that the special controls described in subparagraph (B) would provide reasonable assurance of its safety and effectiveness, and

(ii) —

(I) is purported or represented to be for a use in supporting or sustaining human life or for a use which is of substantial importance in preventing impairment of human health, or

(II) presents a potential unreasonable risk of illness or injury, is to be subject, in accordance with section 515, to premarket approval to provide reasonable assurance of its safety and effectiveness.

If there is not sufficient information to establish a performance standard for a device to provide reasonable assurance of its safety and effectiveness, the Secretary may conduct such activities as may be necessary to develop or obtain such information.

(2) For purposes of this section and sections 514 and 515, the safety and effectiveness of a device are to be determined —

(A) with respect to the persons for whose use the device is represented or intended,

(B) with respect to the conditions of use prescribed, recommended, or suggested in the labeling of the device, and

(C) weighing any probable benefit to health from the use of the device against any probable risk of injury or illness from such use.

(3) —

(A) Except as authorized by subparagraph (B), the effectiveness of a device is, for purposes of this section and sections 514 and 515, to be determined, in accordance with regulations promulgated by the Secretary, on the basis of well-controlled investigations, including 1 or more clinical investigations where appropriate, by experts qualified by training and experience to evaluate the effectiveness of the device, from which investigations it can fairly and responsibly be concluded by qualified experts that the device will have the effect it purports or is represented to have under the conditions of use prescribed, recommended, or suggested in the labeling of the device.

(B) If the Secretary determines that there exists valid scientific evidence (other than evidence derived from investigations described in subparagraph (A)) —

(i) which is sufficient to determine the effectiveness of a device, and

(ii) from which it can fairly and responsibly be concluded by qualified experts that the device will have the effect it purports or is represented to have under the conditions of use prescribed, recommended, or suggested in the labeling of the device,

then, for purposes of this section and sections 514 and 515, the Secretary may authorize the effectiveness of the device to be determined on the basis of such evidence.

(C) In making a determination of a reasonable assurance of the effectiveness of a device for which an application under section 515 has been submitted, the Secretary shall consider whether the extent of data that otherwise would be required for approval of the application with respect to effectiveness can be reduced through reliance on postmarket controls.

(D) —

(i) The Secretary, upon the written request of any person intending to submit an application under section 515, shall meet with such person to determine the type of valid scientific evidence (within the meaning of subparagraphs (A) and (B)) that will be necessary to demonstrate for purposes of approval of an application the effectiveness of a device for the conditions of use proposed by such person. The written request shall include a detailed description of the device, a detailed description of the proposed conditions of use of the device, a proposed plan for determining whether there is a reasonable assurance of effectiveness, and, if available, information regarding the expected performance from the device. Within 30 days after such meeting, the Secretary shall specify in writing the type of valid scientific evidence that will provide a reasonable assurance that a device is effective under the conditions of use proposed by such person.

(ii) Any clinical data, including one or more well-controlled investigations, specified in writing by the Secretary for demonstrating a reasonable assurance of device effectiveness shall be specified as a result of a determination by the Secretary that such data are necessary to establish device effectiveness. The Secretary shall consider, in consultation with the applicant, the least burdensome appropriate means of evaluating device effectiveness that would have a reasonable likelihood of resulting in approval.

(iii) For purposes of clause (ii), the term "necessary" means the minimum required information that would support a determination by the Secretary that an application provides reasonable assurance of the effectiveness of the device.

(iv) Nothing in this subparagraph shall alter the criteria for evaluating an application for premarket approval of a device.

(v) The determination of the Secretary with respect to the specification of valid scientific evidence under clauses (i) and (ii) shall be binding upon the Secretary, unless such determination by the Secretary could be contrary to the public health.

(b) Classification; Classification Panels. —

(1) For purposes of —

(A) determining which devices intended for human use should be subject to the requirements of general controls, performance standards, or premarket approval, and

(B) providing notice to the manufacturers and importers of such devices to enable them to prepare for the application of such requirements to devices manufactured or imported by them,

the Secretary shall classify all such devices (other than devices classified by subsection (f)) into the classes established by subsection (a). For the purpose of securing recommendations with respect to the classification of devices, the Secretary shall establish panels of experts or use panels of experts established before the date of the enactment of this section, or both. Section 14 of the Federal Advisory Committee Act shall not apply to the duration of a panel established under this paragraph.

(2) The Secretary shall appoint to each panel established under paragraph (1) persons who are qualified by training and experience to evaluate the safety and effectiveness of the devices to be referred to the panel and who, to the extent feasible, possess skill in the use of, or experience in the development, manufacture, or utilization of, such devices. The Secretary shall make appointments to each panel so that each panel shall consist of members with adequately diversified expertise in such fields as clinical and administrative medicine, engineering, biological and physical sciences, and other related professions. In addition, each panel shall include as nonvoting members a representative of consumer interests and a representative of interests of the device manufacturing industry. Scientific, trade, and consumer organizations shall be afforded an opportunity to nominate individuals for appointment to the panels. No individual who is in the regular full-time employ of the United States and engaged in the administration of this Act may be a member of any panel. The Secretary shall designate one of the members of each panel to serve as chairman thereof.

(3) Panel members (other than officers or employees of the United States), while attending meetings or conferences of a panel or otherwise engaged in its business, shall be entitled to receive compensation at rates to be fixed by the Secretary, but not at rates exceeding the daily equivalent of the rate in effect for grade GS–18 of the General Schedule, for each day so engaged, including traveltime; and while so serving away from their homes or regular places of business each member may be allowed travel expenses (including per diem in lieu of subsistence) as authorized by section 5703 of title 5, United States Code, for persons in the Government service employed intermittently.

(4) The Secretary shall furnish each panel with adequate clerical and other necessary assistance.

(5)

(A) Classification panels covering each type of device shall be scheduled to meet at such times as may be appropriate for the Secretary to meet applicable statutory deadlines.

(B) When a device is specifically the subject of a review by a classification panel, the Secretary shall—

(i) ensure that adequate expertise is represented on the classification panel to assess—

(I) the disease or condition which the device is intended to cure, treat, mitigate, prevent, or diagnose; and

(II) the technology of the device; and

(ii) provide an opportunity for the person whose device is specifically the subject of a panel review to provide recommendations on the expertise needed among the voting members of the panel.

(C) For the purposes of subparagraph (B)(i), the term "adequate expertise" means that the membership of the classification panel includes—

(i) two or more voting members, with a speciality or other expertise clinically relevant to the device under review; and

(ii) at least one voting member who is knowledgeable about the technology of the device.

(D) The Secretary shall provide an annual opportunity for patients, representatives of patients, and sponsors of ~~medical device submissions~~ medical devices that may be specifically the subject of a review by a classification panel to provide recommendations for individuals with appropriate expertise to fill voting member positions on classification panels.

(6) —

(A) Any person whose device is specifically the subject of review by a classification panel shall have,

(i) the same access to data and information submitted to a classification panel (except for data and information that are not available for public disclosure under section 552 of title 5, United States Code) as the Secretary;

(ii) the opportunity to submit, for review by a classification panel, information that is based on the data or information provided in the application submitted under section 515 by the person, which information shall be submitted to the Secretary for prompt transmittal to the classification panel; and

(iii) the same opportunity as the Secretary to participate in meetings of the panel, including, subject to the discretion of the panel chairperson, by designating a representative who will be provided a time during the panel meeting to address the panel for the purpose of correcting misstatements of fact or providing clarifying information, and permitting the person or representative to call on experts within the person's organization to address such specific issues in the time provided.

(B)

(i) Any meeting of a classification panel with respect to the review of a device shall—

(I) provide adequate time for initial presentations by the person whose device is specifically the subject of such review and by the Secretary; and

(II) encourage free and open participation by all interested persons.

(ii) Following the initial presentations described in clause (i), the panel may—

(I) Pose questions to a designated representative described in subparagraph (A)(iii); and

(II) consider the responses to such questions in the panel's review of the device.

(7) After receiving from a classification panel the conclusions and recommendations of the panel on a matter that the panel has reviewed, the Secretary shall review the conclusions and recommendations, shall make a final decision on the matter in accordance with section 515(d)(2), and shall notify the affected persons of the decision in writing and, if the decision differs from the conclusions and recommendations of the panel, shall include the reasons for the difference.

(8) A classification panel under this subsection shall not be subject to the annual chartering and annual report requirements of the Federal Advisory Committee Act.

~~(9) The Secretary shall classify an accessory under this section based on the intended use of the accessory, notwithstanding the classification of any other device with which such accessory is intended to be used.~~

(c) Classification Panel Organization and Operation. —

(1) The Secretary shall organize the panels according to the various fields of clinical medicine and fundamental sciences in which devices intended for human use are used. The Secretary shall refer a device to be classified under this section to an appropriate panel established or authorized to be used under subsection (b) for its review and for its recommendation respecting the classification of the device. The Secretary shall by regulation prescribe the procedure to be followed by the panels in making their reviews and recommendations. In making their reviews of devices, the panels, to the maximum extent practicable, shall provide an opportunity for interested persons to submit data and views on the classification of the devices.

(2) —

(A) Upon completion of a panel's review of a device referred to it under paragraph (1), the panel shall, subject to subparagraphs (B) and (C), submit to the Secretary its recommendation for the classification of the device. Any such recommendation shall

(i) contain

(I) a summary of the reasons for the recommendation,

(II) a summary of the data upon which the recommendation is based, and

(III) an identification of the risks to health (if any) presented by the device with respect to which the recommendation is made, and

(ii) to the extent practicable, include a recommendation for the assignment of a priority for the application of the requirements of section 514 or 515 to a device recommended to be classified in class II or class III.

(B) A recommendation of a panel for the classification of a device in class I shall include a recommendation as to whether the device should be exempted from the requirements of section 510, 519, or 520(f).

(C) In the case of a device which has been referred under paragraph (1) to a panel, and which —

(i) is intended to be implanted in the human body or is purported or represented to be for a use in supporting or sustaining human life, and

(ii) —

(I) has been introduced or delivered for introduction into interstate commerce for commercial distribution before the date of enactment of this section, or

(II) is within a type of device which was so introduced or delivered before such date and is substantially equivalent to another device within that type,

such panel shall recommend to the Secretary that the device be classified in class III unless the panel determines that classification of the device in such class is not necessary to provide reasonable assurance of its safety and effectiveness. If a panel does not recommend that such a device be classified in class III, it shall in its recommendation to the Secretary for the classification of the device set forth the reasons for not recommending classification of the device in such class.

(3) The panels shall submit to the Secretary within one year of the date funds are first appropriated for the implementation of this section their recommendations respecting all devices of a type introduced or delivered for introduction into interstate commerce for commercial distribution before the date of the enactment of this section.

(d) CLASSIFICATION. —

(1) Upon receipt of a recommendation from a panel respecting a device, the Secretary shall publish in the Federal Register the panel's recommendation and a proposed regulation classifying such device and shall provide interested persons an opportunity to submit comments on such recommendation and the proposed regulation. After reviewing such comments, the Secretary shall, subject to paragraph (2), by regulation classify such device.

(2) —

(A) A regulation under paragraph (1) classifying a device in class I shall prescribe which, if any, of the requirements of section 510, 519 or 520(f) shall not apply to the device. A regulation which makes a requirement of section 510, 519, or 520(f) inapplicable to a device shall be accompanied by a statement of the reasons of the Secretary for making such requirement inapplicable.

(B) A device described in subsection (c)(2)(C) shall be classified in class III unless the Secretary determines that classification of the device in such class is not necessary to provide reasonable assurance of its safety and effectiveness. A proposed regulation under paragraph (1) classifying such a device in a class other than class III shall be accompanied by a full statement of the reasons of the Secretary (and supporting documentation and data) for not classifying such device in such class and an identification of the risks to health (if any) presented by such device.

(3) In the case of devices classified in class II and devices classified under this subsection in class III and described in section 515(b)(1) the Secretary may establish priorities which, in his discretion, shall be used in applying sections 514 and 515, as appropriate, to such devices.

(e) Classification Changes. —

(1) —

(A) —

(i) Based on new information respecting a device, the Secretary may, upon the initiative of the Secretary or upon petition of an interested person, change the classification of such device, and revoke, on account of the change in classification, any regulation or requirement in effect under section 514 or 515 with respect to such device, by administrative order published in the Federal Register following publication of a proposed reclassification order in the Federal Register, a meeting of a device classification panel described in subsection (b), and consideration of comments to a public docket, notwithstanding subchapter II of chapter 5 of title 5, United States Code. The proposed reclassification order published in the Federal Register shall set forth the proposed reclassification, and a substantive summary of the valid scientific evidence concerning the proposed reclassification, including —

(I) the public health benefit of the use of the device, and the nature and, if known, incidence of the risk of the device;

(II) in the case of a reclassification from class II to class III, why general controls pursuant to subsection (a)(1)(A) and special controls pursuant to subsection (a)(1)(B) together are not sufficient to provide a reasonable assurance of safety and effectiveness for such device; and

(III) in the case of reclassification from class III to class II, why general controls pursuant to subsection (a)(1)(A) and special controls pursuant to subsection (a)(1)(B) together are sufficient to provide a reasonable assurance of safety and effectiveness for such device.

(ii) An order under this subsection changing the classification of a device from Class III to class II may provide that such reclassification shall not take effect until the effective date of a performance standard established under section 514 for such device.

(B) Authority to issue such administrative order shall not be delegated below the Director of the Center for Devices and Radiological Health, acting in consultation with the Commissioner.

(2) By an order issued under paragraph (1), the Secretary may change the classification of a device from class III —

(A) to class II if the Secretary determines that special controls would provide reasonable assurance of the safety and effectiveness of the device and that general controls would not provide reasonable assurance of the safety and effectiveness of the device, or

(B) to class I if the Secretary determines that general controls would provide reasonable assurance of the safety and effectiveness of the device.

(f) Initial Classification and Reclassification of Certain Devices. —

(1) Any device intended for human use which was not introduced or delivered for introduction into interstate commerce for commercial distribution before the date of the enactment of this section is classified in class III unless —

(A) the device —

(i) is within a type of device

(I) which was introduced or delivered for introduction into interstate commerce for commercial distribution before such date and which is to be classified pursuant to subsection (b), or

(II) which was not so introduced or delivered before such date and has been classified in class I or II, and

(ii) is substantially equivalent to another device within such type;

(B) the Secretary in response to a petition submitted under paragraph (3) has classified such device in class I or II; or

(C) the device is classified pursuant to a request submitted under paragraph (2).

A device classified in class III under this paragraph shall be classified in that class until the effective date of an order of the Secretary under paragraph (2) or (3) classifying the device in class I or II.

(2) —

(A) —

(i) Any person who submits a report under section 510(k) for a type of device that has not been previously classified under this Act, and that is classified into class III under paragraph (1), may request, after receiving written notice of such a classification, the Secretary to classify the device.

(ii) In lieu of submitting a report under section 510(k) and submitting a request for classification under clause (i) for a device, if a person determines there is no legally marketed device upon which to base a determination of substantial equivalence (as defined in subsection (i)), a person may submit a request under this clause for the Secretary to classify the device.

(iii) Upon receipt of a request under clause (i) or (ii), the Secretary shall classify the device subject to the request under the criteria set forth in subparagraphs (A) through (C) of subsection (a)(1) within 120 days.

(iv) Notwithstanding clause (iii), the Secretary may decline to undertake a classification request submitted under clause (ii) if the Secretary identifies a legally marketed device that could provide a reasonable basis for review of substantial equivalence under paragraph (1), or when the Secretary determines that the device submitted is not of low to moderate risk or that general controls would be inadequate to control the risks and special controls to mitigate the risks cannot be developed.

(v) The person submitting the request for classification under this subparagraph may recommend to the Secretary a classification for the device and shall, if recommending classification in class II, include in the request an initial draft proposal for applicable special controls, as described in subsection (a)(1)(B), that are necessary, in conjunction with general controls, to provide reasonable assurance of safety and effectiveness and a description of how the special controls provide such assurance. Any such request shall describe the device and provide detailed information an reasons for the recommended classification.

(B) —

(i) The Secretary shall by written order classify the device involved. Such classification shall be the initial classification of the device for purposes of paragraph (1) and any device classified under this paragraph shall be a predicate device for determining substantial equivalence under paragraph (1).

(ii) A device that remains in Class III under this subparagraph shall be deemed to be adulterated within the meaning of section 501(f)(1)(B) until approved under section 515 or exempted from such approval under section 520(g).

(C) Within 30 days after the issuance of an order classifying a device under this paragraph, the Secretary shall publish a notice in the Federal Register announcing such classification.

(3) —

(A) The Secretary may initiate the reclassification of a device classified into class III under paragraph (1) of this subsection or the manufacturer or importer of a device classified under paragraph (1) may petition the Secretary (in such form and manner as he shall prescribe) for the issuance of an order classifying the device in class I or class II. Within thirty days of the filing of such a petition, the Secretary shall notify the petitioner of any deficiencies in the petition which prevent the Secretary from making a decision on the petition.

(B) —

(i) Upon determining that a petition does not contain any deficiency which prevents the Secretary from making a decision on the petition, the Secretary may for good cause shown refer the petition to an appropriate panel established or authorized to be used under subsection (b). A panel to which such a petition has been referred shall not later than ninety days after the referral of the petition make a recommendation to the Secretary respecting approval or denial of the petition. Any such recommendation shall contain

(I) a summary of the reasons for the recommendation,

(II) a summary of the data upon which the recommendation is based, and

(III) an identification of the risks to health (if any) presented by the device with respect to which the petition was filed.

In the case of a petition for a device which is intended to be implanted in the human body or which is purported or represented to be for a use in supporting or sustaining human life, the panel shall recommend that the petition be denied unless the panel determines that the classification in class III of the device is not necessary to provide reasonable assurance of its safety and effectiveness. If the panel recommends that such petition be approved, it shall in its recommendation to the Secretary set forth its reasons for such recommendation.

(ii) The requirements of paragraphs (1) and (2) of subsection (c) (relating to opportunities for submission of data and views and recommendations respecting priorities and exemptions from sections 510, 519, and 520(f)) shall apply with respect to consideration by panels of petitions submitted under subparagraph (A).

(C) —

(i) Within ninety days from the date the Secretary receives the recommendation of a panel respecting a petition (but not later than 210 days after the filing of such petition) the Secretary shall by order deny or approve the petition. If the Secretary approves the petition, the Secretary shall order the classification of the device into class I or class II in accordance with the criteria prescribed by subsection (a)(1)(A) or (a)(1)(B). In the case of a petition for a device which is intended to be implanted in the human body or which is purported or represented to be for a use in supporting or sustaining human life, the Secretary shall deny the petition unless the Secretary determines that the classification in class III of the device is not necessary to provide reasonable assurance of its safety and effectiveness. An order approving such petition shall be accompanied by a full statement of the reasons of the Secretary (and supporting documentation and data) for approving the petition and an identification of the risks to health (if any) presented by the device to which such order applies.

(ii) The requirements of paragraphs (1) and (2)(A) of subsection (d) (relating to publication of recommendations, opportunity for submission of comments, and exemption from sections 510, 519 and 520(f)) shall apply with respect to action by the Secretary on petitions submitted under subparagraph (A).

(4) If a manufacturer reports to the Secretary under section 510(k) that a device is substantially equivalent to another device —

(A) which the Secretary has classified as a class III device under subsection (b),

(B) which was introduced or delivered for introduction into interstate commerce for commercial distribution before December 1, 1990, and

(C) for which no final regulation requiring premarket approval has been promulgated under section 515(b), the manufacturer shall certify to the Secretary that the manufacturer has conducted a reasonable search of all information known or otherwise available to the manufacturer respecting such other device and has included in the report under section 510(k) a summary of and a citation to all adverse safety and effectiveness data respecting such other device and respecting the device for which the section 510(k) report is being made and which has not been submitted to the Secretary under section 519. The Secretary may require the manufacturer to submit the adverse safety and effectiveness data described in the report.

(5) The Secretary may not withhold a determination of the initial classification of a device under paragraph (1) because of a failure to comply with any provision of this Act unrelated to a substantial equivalence decision, including a finding that the facility in which the device is manufactured is not in compliance with good manufacturing requirements as set forth in regulations of the Secretary under section 520(f) (other than a finding that there is a substantial likelihood that the failure to comply with such regulations will potentially present a serious risk to human health).

(6) —

(A) Subject to the succeeding subparagraphs of this paragraph, the Secretary shall, by written order, classify an accessory under this section based on the risks of the accessory when used as intended and the level of regulatory controls necessary to provide a reasonable assurance of safety and effectiveness of the accessory, notwithstanding the classification of any other device with which such accessory is intended to be used.

(B) The classification of any accessory distinct from another device by regulation or written order issued prior to December 13, 2016, shall continue to apply unless and until the accessory is reclassified by the Secretary, notwithstanding the classification of any other device with which such accessory is intended to be used. Nothing in this paragraph shall preclude the Secretary's authority to initiate the classification of an accessory through regulation or written order, as appropriate.

(C) —

(i) In the case of a device intended to be used with an accessory, where the accessory has been included in an application for premarket approval of such device under section 515 or a report under section 510(k) for clearance of such device and the Secretary has not classified such accessory distinctly from another device in accordance with subparagraph (A), the person filing the application or report (as applicable) at the time such application or report is filed —

(I) may include a written request for the proper classification of the accessory pursuant to subparagraph (A);

(II) shall include in any such request such information as may be necessary for the Secretary to evaluate, based on the least burdensome approach, the appropriate class for the accessory under subsection (a); and

(III) shall, if the request under subclause (I) is requesting classification of the accessory in class II, include in the application an initial draft proposal for special controls, if special controls would be required pursuant to subsection (a)(1)(B).

(ii) The Secretary's response under section 515(d) or section 510(n) (as applicable) to an application or report described in clause (i) shall also contain the Secretary's granting or denial of the request for classification of the accessory involved.

(iii) The Secretary's evaluation of an accessory under clause (i) shall constitute an order establishing a new classification for such accessory for the specified intended use or uses of such accessory and for any accessory with the same intended use or uses as such accessory.

(D) For accessories that have been granted marketing authorization as part of a submission for another device with which the accessory involved is intended to be used, through an application for such other device under section 515(c), a report under section 510(k), or a request for classification under paragraph (2) of this subsection, the following shall apply:

(i) Not later than the date that is one year after the date of enactment of the FDA Reauthorization Act of 2017 and at least once every 5 years thereafter, and as the Secretary otherwise determines appropriate, pursuant to this paragraph, the Secretary shall publish in the Federal Register a notice proposing a list of such accessories that the Secretary determines may be suitable for a distinct classification in class I and the proposed regulations for such classifications. In developing such list, the Secretary shall consider recommendations from sponsors of device submissions and other stakeholders for accessories to be included on such list. The notices shall provide for a period of not less than 60 calendar days for public comment. Within 180 days after the end of the comment period, the Secretary shall publish in the Federal Register a final action classifying such suitable accessories into class I.

(ii) A manufacturer or importer of an accessory that has been granted such marketing authorization may submit to the Secretary a written request for the appropriate classification of the accessory based on the risks and appropriate level of regulatory controls as described in subparagraph (A), and shall, if the request is requesting classification of the accessory in class II, include in the submission an initial draft proposal for special controls, if special controls would be required pursuant to subsection (a)(1)(B). Such request shall include such information as may be necessary for the Secretary to evaluate, based on the least burdensome approach, the appropriate class for the accessory under subsection (a). The Secretary shall provide an opportunity for a manufacturer or importer to meet with appropriate personnel of the Food and Drug Administration to discuss the appropriate classification of such accessory prior to submitting a written request under this clause for classification of the accessory.

(iii) The Secretary shall respond to a request made under clause (ii) not later than 85 calendar days after receiving such request by issuing a written order classifying the accessory or denying the request. If the Secretary does not agree with the recommendation for classification submitted by the manufacturer or importer, the response shall include a detailed description and justification for such determination. Within 30 calendar days after granting such a request, the Secretary shall publish a notice in the Federal Register announcing such response.

(E) Nothing in this paragraph may be construed as precluding a manufacturer of an accessory of a new type from using the classification process described in subsection (f)(2) to obtain classification of such accessory in accordance with the criteria and requirements set forth in that subsection.

(g) Information. — Within sixty days of the receipt of a written request of any person for information respecting the class in which a device has been classified or the requirements applicable to a device under this Act, the Secretary shall provide such person a written statement of the classification (if any) of such device and the requirements of this Act applicable to the device.

(h) Definitions. — For purposes of this section and sections 501, 510, 514, 515, 516, 519, and 520 —

(1) a reference to "general controls" is a reference to the controls authorized by or under sections 501, 502, 510, 516, 518, 519, and 520,

(2) a reference to "class I," "class II," or "class III" is a reference to a class of medical devices described in subparagraph (A), (B), or (C) of subsection (a)(1), and

(3) a reference to a "panel under section 513" is a reference to a panel established or authorized to be used under this section.

(i) Substantial Equivalence. —

(1) —

(A) For purposes of determinations of substantial equivalence under subsection (f) and section 520(1), the term "substantially equivalent" or "substantial equivalence" means, with respect to a device being compared to a predicate device, that the device has the same intended use as the predicate device and that the Secretary by order has found that the device —

(i) has the same technological characteristics as the predicate device, or

(ii) —

(I) has different technological characteristics and the information submitted that the device is substantially equivalent to the predicate device contains information, including appropriate clinical or scientific data if deemed necessary by the Secretary or a person accredited under section 523, that demonstrates that the device is as safe and effective as a legally marketed device, and

(II) does not raise different questions of safety and effectiveness than the predicate device.

(B) For purposes of subparagraph (A), the term "different technological characteristics" means, with respect to a device being compared to a predicate device, that there is a significant change in the materials, design, energy source, or other features of the device from those of the predicate device.

(C) To facilitate reviews of reports submitted to the Secretary under section 510(k), the Secretary shall consider the extent to which reliance on postmarket controls may expedite the classification of devices under subsection (f)(1) of this section.

(D) —

(i) Whenever the Secretary requests information to demonstrate that devices with differing technological characteristics are substantially equivalent, the Secretary shall only request information that is necessary to making substantial equivalence determinations. In making such request, the Secretary shall consider the least burdensome means of demonstrating substantial equivalence and request information accordingly.

(ii) For purposes of clause (i), the term "necessary" means the minimum required information that would support a determination of substantial equivalence between a new device and a predicate device.

(iii) Nothing in this subparagraph shall alter the standard for determining substantial equivalence between a new device and a predicate device.

(E) —

(i) Any determination by the Secretary of the intended use of a device shall be based upon the proposed labeling submitted in a report for the device under section 510(k). However, when determining that a device can be found substantially equivalent to a legally marketed device, the director of the organizational unit responsible for regulating devices (in this subparagraph referred to as the "Director") may require a statement in labeling that provides appropriate information regarding a use of the device not identified in the proposed labeling if, after providing an opportunity for consultation with the person who submitted such report, the Director determines and states in writing —

(I) that there is a reasonable likelihood that the device will be used for an intended use not identified in the proposed labeling for the device; and

(II) that such use could cause harm.

(ii) Such determination shall —

(I) be provided to the person who submitted the report within 10 days from the date of the notification of the Director's concerns regarding the proposed labeling;

(II) specify the limitations on the use of the device not included in the proposed labeling; and

(III) find the device substantially equivalent if the requirements of subparagraph (A) are met and if the labeling for such device conforms to the limitations specified in subclause (II).

(iii) The responsibilities of the Director under this subparagraph may not be delegated.

(iv) [Repealed.]

(F) Not later than 270 days after the date of the enactment of the Food and Drug Administration Modernization Act of 1997 [November 21, 1997 — Ed.], the Secretary shall issue guidance specifying the general principles that the Secretary will consider in determining when a specific intended use of a device is not reasonably included within a general use of such device for purposes of a determination of substantial equivalence under subsection (f) or section 520(l).

(2) A device may not be found to be substantially equivalent to a predicate device that has been removed from the market at the initiative of the Secretary or that has been determined to be misbranded or adulterated by a judicial order.

(3) —

(A) As part of a submission under section 510(k) respecting a device, the person required to file a premarket notification under such section shall provide an adequate summary of any information respecting safety and effectiveness or state that such information will be made available upon request by any person.

(B) Any summary under subparagraph (A) respecting a device shall contain detailed information regarding data concerning adverse health effects and shall be made available to the public by the Secretary within 30 days of the issuance of a determination that such device is substantially equivalent to another device.

(j) Training and Oversight of Least Burdensome Requirements. —

(1) The Secretary shall—

(A) ensure that each employee of the Food and Drug Administration who is involved in the review of premarket submissions, including supervisors, receives training regarding the meaning and implementation of the least burdensome requirements under subsections (a)(3)(D) and (i)(1)(D) of this section and section 515(c)(5); and

(B) periodically assess the implementation of the least burdensome requirements, including the employee training under subparagraph (A), to ensure that the least burdensome requirements are fully and consistently applied.

(2) Not later than 18 months after the date of enactment of the 21st Century Cures Act [December 13, 2016 —Ed.], the ombudsman for any organizational unit of the Food and Drug Administration responsible for the premarket review of devices shall—

(A) conduct an audit of the training described in paragraph (1)(A), including the effectiveness of such training in implementing the least burdensome requirements;

(B) include in such audit interviews of persons who are representatives of the device industry regarding their experiences in the device premarket review process, including with respect to the application of the least burdensome concepts to premarket review and decision-making;

(C) include in such audit a list of the measurement tools the Secretary uses to assess the implementation of the least burdensome requirements, including under paragraph (1)(B) and section 517A(a)(3), and may also provide feedback on the effectiveness of such tools in the implementation of the least burdensome requirements;

(D) summarize the findings of such audit in a final audit report; and

(E) within 30 calendar days of completion of such final audit report, make such final audit report available—

(i) to the Committee on Health, Education, Labor, and Pensions of the Senate and the Committee on Energy and Commerce of the House of Representatives; and

(ii) on the Internet website of the Food and Drug Administration.

Sec. 514. [360d] Performance Standards.

(a) Provisions of Standards. —

(1) The special controls required by section 513(a)(1)(B) shall include performance standards for a class II device if the Secretary determines that a performance standard is necessary to provide reasonable assurance of the safety and effectiveness of the device. A class III device may also be considered a class II device for purposes of establishing a standard for the device under subsection (b) if the device has been reclassified as a class II device under an administrative order under section 513(e) (or a regulation promulgated under such section prior to the date of enactment of the Food and Drug Administration Safety and Innovation Act) but such order (or regulation) provides that the reclassification is not to take effect until the effective date of such a standard for the device.

(2) A performance standard established under subsection (b) for a device —

(A) shall include provisions to provide reasonable assurance of its safe and effective performance;

(B) shall, where necessary to provide reasonable assurance of its safe and effective performance, include —

(i) provisions respecting the construction, components, ingredients, and properties of the device and its compatibility with power systems and connections to such systems,

(ii) provisions for the testing (on a sample basis or, if necessary, on an individual basis) of the device or, if it is determined that no other more practicable means are available to the Secretary to assure the conformity of the device to the standard, provisions for the testing (on a sample basis or, if necessary, on an individual basis) by the Secretary or by another person at the direction of the Secretary,

(iii) provisions for the measurement of the performance characteristics of the device,

(iv) provisions requiring that the results of each or of certain of the tests of the device required to be made under clause (ii) show that the device is in conformity with the portions of the standard for which the test or tests were required, and

(v) a provision requiring that the sale and distribution of the device be restricted but only to the extent that the sale and distribution of a device may be restricted under a regulation under section 520(e); and

(C) shall, where appropriate, require the use and prescribe the form and content of labeling for the proper installation, maintenance, operation, and use of the device.

(3) The Secretary shall provide for periodic evaluation of performance standards established under subsection (b) to determine if such standards should be changed to reflect new medical, scientific, or other technological data.

(4) In carrying out his duties under this subsection and subsection (b), the Secretary shall, to the maximum extent practicable —

(A) use personnel, facilities, and other technical support available in other Federal agencies,

(B) consult with other Federal agencies concerned with standard-setting and other nationally or internationally recognized standard-setting entities, and

(C) invite appropriate participation, through joint or other conferences, workshops, or other means, by informed persons representative of scientific, professional, industry, or consumer organizations who in his judgment can make a significant contribution.

(b) Establishment of a Standard. —

(1) —

(A) The Secretary shall publish in the Federal Register a notice of proposed rulemaking for the establishment, amendment, or revocation of any performance standard for a device.

(B) A notice of proposed rulemaking for the establishment or amendment of a performance standard for a device shall —

(i) set forth a finding with supporting justification that the performance standard is appropriate and necessary to provide reasonable assurance of the safety and effectiveness of the device,

(ii) set forth proposed findings with respect to the risk of illness or injury that the performance standard is intended to reduce or eliminate,

(iii) invite interested persons to submit to the Secretary, within 30 days of the publication of the notice, requests for changes in the classification of the device pursuant to section 513(e) based on new information relevant to the classification, and

(iv) invite interested persons to submit an existing performance standard for the device, including a draft or proposed performance standard, for consideration by the Secretary.

(C) A notice of proposed rulemaking for the revocation of a performance standard shall set forth a finding with supporting justification that the performance standard is no longer necessary to provide reasonable assurance of the safety and effectiveness of a device.

(D) The Secretary shall provide for a comment period of not less than 60 days.

(2) If, after publication of a notice in accordance with paragraph (1), the Secretary receives a request for a change in the classification of the device, the Secretary shall, within 60 days of the publication of the notice, after consultation with the appropriate panel under section 513, either deny the request or give notice of an intent to initiate such change under section 513(e).

(3) —

(A) After the expiration of the period for comment on a notice of proposed rulemaking published under paragraph (1) respecting a performance standard and after consideration of such comments and any report from an advisory committee under paragraph (5), the Secretary shall

(i) promulgate a regulation establishing a performance standard and publish in the Federal Register findings on the matters referred to in paragraph (1), or

(ii) publish a notice terminating the proceeding for the development of the standard together with the reasons for such termination.

If a notice of termination is published, the Secretary shall (unless such notice is issued because the device is a banned device under section 516) initiate a proceeding under section 513(e) to reclassify the device subject to the proceeding terminated by such notice.

(B) A regulation establishing a performance standard shall set forth the date or dates upon which the standard shall take effect, but no such regulation may take effect before one year after the date of its publication unless

(i) the Secretary determines that an earlier effective date is necessary for the protection of the public health and safety, or

(ii) such standard has been established for a device which, effective upon the effective date of the standard, has been reclassified from class III to class II.

Such date or dates shall be established so as to minimize, consistent with the public health and safety, economic loss to, and disruption or dislocation of, domestic and international trade.

(4) —

(A) The Secretary, upon his own initiative or upon petition of an interested person may by regulation, promulgated in accordance with the requirements of paragraphs (1), (2), and (3)(B) of this subsection, amend or revoke a performance standard.

(B) The Secretary may declare a proposed amendment of a performance standard to be effective on and after its publication in the Federal Register and until the effective date of any final action taken on such amendment if he determines that making it so effective is in the public interest. A proposed amendment of a performance standard made so effective under the preceding sentence may not prohibit, during the period in which it is so effective, the introduction or delivery for introduction into interstate commerce of a device which conforms to such standard without the change or changes provided by such proposed amendment.

(5) —

(A) The Secretary —

(i) may on his own initiative refer a proposed regulation for the establishment, amendment, or revocation of a performance standard, or

(ii) shall, upon the request of an interested person which demonstrates good cause for referral and which is made before the expiration of the period for submission of comments on such proposed regulation refer such proposed regulation, to an advisory committee of experts, established pursuant to subparagraph (B) for a report and recommendation with respect to any matter involved in the proposed regulation which requires the exercise of scientific judgment.

If a proposed regulation is referred under this subparagraph to an advisory committee, the Secretary shall provide the advisory committee with the data and information on which such proposed regulation is based. The advisory committee shall, within sixty days of the referral of a proposed regulation and after independent study of the data and information furnished to it by the Secretary and other data and information before it, submit to the Secretary a report and recommendation respecting such regulation, together with all underlying data and information and a statement of the reason or basis for the recommendation. A copy of such report and recommendation shall be made public by the Secretary.

(B) The Secretary shall establish advisory committees (which may not be panels under section 513) to receive referrals under subparagraph (A). The Secretary shall appoint as members of any such advisory committee persons qualified in the subject matter to be referred to the committee and of appropriately diversified professional background, except that the Secretary may not appoint to such a committee any individual who is in the regular full-time employ of the United States and engaged in the administration of this Act. Each such committee shall include as nonvoting members a representative of consumer interests and a representative of interests of the device manufacturing industry. Members of an advisory committee who are not officers or employees of the United States, while attending conferences or meetings of their committee or otherwise serving at the request of the Secretary, shall be entitled to receive compensation at rates to be fixed by the Secretary, which rates may not exceed the daily equivalent of the rate in effect for grade Gs–18 of the General Schedule, for each day (including traveltime) they are so engaged; and while so serving away from their homes or regular places of business each member may be allowed travel expenses, including per diem in lieu of subsistence, as authorized by section 5703 of title 5 of the United States Code for persons in the Government service employed intermittently. The Secretary shall designate one of the members of each advisory committee to serve as chairman thereof. The Secretary shall furnish each advisory committee with clerical and other assistance, and shall by regulation prescribe the procedures to be followed by each such committee in acting on referrals made under subparagraph (A).

(c) Recognition of a Standard. —

(1) —

(A) In addition to establishing a performance standard under this section, the Secretary shall, by publication in the Federal Register (or, with respect to a susceptibility test interpretive criteria standard under section 511A, by posting on the Interpretive Criteria Website in accordance with such section), recognize all or part of an appropriate standard established by a nationally or internationally recognized standard development organization for which a person may submit a declaration of conformity in order to meet a premarket submission requirement or other requirement under this Act to which such standard is applicable.

(B) If a person elects to use a standard recognized by the secretary under subparagraph (A) to meet the requirements described in such subparagraph, the person shall provide a declaration of conformity to the Secretary that certifies that the device is in conformity with such standard. A person may elect to use the data, or information, other than data required by a standard recognized under subparagraph (A) to meet any requirement regarding devices under this Act.

(C)

(i) Any person may submit a request for recognition under subparagraph (A) of all or part of an appropriate standard established by a nationally or internationally recognized standard organization.

(ii) Not later than 60 calendar days after the Secretary receives such a request, the Secretary shall—

(I) make a determination to recognize all, part, or none of the standard that is the subject of the request; and

(II) issue to the person who submitted such request a response in writing that states the Secretary's rationale for that determination, including the scientific, technical, regulatory, or other basis for such determination.

(iii) The Secretary shall make a response issued under clause (ii)(II) publicly available, in such a manner as the Secretary determines appropriate.

(iv) The Secretary shall take such actions as may be necessary to implement all or part of a standard recognized under clause (ii)(I), in accordance with subparagraph (A).

(D) The Secretary shall make publicly available, in such manner as the Secretary determines appropriate, the rationale for recognition under subparagraph (A) of all, part, or none of a standard, including the scientific, technical, regulatory, or other basis for the decision regarding such recognition.

(2) The Secretary may withdraw such recognition of a standard through publication of a notice in the Federal Register if the Secretary determines that the standard is no longer appropriate for meeting a requirement regarding devices under this Act.

(3) —

(A) Subject to subparagraph (B), the Secretary shall accept a declaration of conformity that a device is in conformity with a standard recognized under paragraph (1) unless the Secretary finds —

(i) that the data or information submitted to support such declaration does not demonstrate that the device is in conformity with the standard identified in the declaration of conformity; or

(ii) that the standard identified in the declaration of conformity is not applicable to the particular device under review.

(B) The Secretary may request, at any time, the data or information relied on by the person to make a declaration of conformity with respect to a standard recognized under paragraph (1).

(C) A person making a declaration of conformity with respect to a standard recognized under paragraph (1) shall maintain the data and information demonstrating conformity of the device to the standard for a period of two years after the date of the classification or approval of the device by the Secretary or a period equal to the expected design life of the device, whichever is longer.

(4) The Secretary shall provide to all employees of the Food and Drug Administration who review premarket submissions for devices periodic training on the concept and use of recognized standards for purposes of meeting a premarket submission requirement or other applicable requirement under this Act, including standards relevant to an employee's area of device review.

(d) Pilot Accreditation Scheme for Conformity Assessment.—

(1) In General.—The Secretary shall establish a pilot program under which—

(A) testing laboratories may be accredited, by accreditation bodies meeting criteria specified by the Secretary, to assess the conformance of a device with certain standards recognized under this section; and

(B) subject to paragraph (2), determinations by testing laboratories so accredited that a device conforms with such standard or standards shall be accepted by the Secretary for purposes of demonstrating such conformity under this section unless the Secretary finds that a particular such determination shall not be so accepted.

(2) Secretarial Review of Accredited Laboratory Determinations. — The Secretary may —

(A) review determinations by testing laboratories accredited pursuant to this subsection, including by conducting periodic audits of such determinations or processes of accredited bodies or testing laboratories and, following such review, taking additional measures under this Act, such as suspension or withdrawal of accreditation of such testing laboratory under paragraph (1)(A) or requesting additional information with respect to such device, as the Secretary determines appropriate; and

(B) if the Secretary becomes aware of information materially bearing on safety or effectiveness of a device assessed for conformity by a testing laboratory so accredited, take such additional measures under this Act as the Secretary determines appropriate, such as suspension or withdrawal of accreditation of such testing laboratory under paragraph (1)(A), or requesting additional information with regard to such device.

(3) Implementation and Reporting. —

(A) Public Meeting. — The Secretary shall publish in the Federal Register a notice of a public meeting to be held no later than September 30, 2018, to discuss and obtain input and recommendations from stakeholders regarding the goals and scope of, and a suitable framework and procedures and requirements for, the pilot program under this subsection.

(B) Pilot Program Guidance. — The Secretary shall —

(i) not later than September 30, 2019, issue draft guidance regarding the goals and implementation of the pilot program under this subsection; and

(ii) not later than September 30, 2021, issue final guidance with respect to the implementation of such program.

(C) Pilot Program Initiation.—Not later than September 30, 2020, the Secretary shall initiate the pilot program under this subsection.

(D) Report.—The Secretary shall make available on the internet website of the Food and Drug Administration an annual report on the progress of the pilot program under this subsection.

(4) Sunset.—As of October 1, 2022—

(A) the authority for accreditation bodies to accredit testing laboratories pursuant to paragraph (1)(A) shall cease to have force or effect;

(B) the Secretary—

(i) may not accept a determination pursuant to paragraph (1)(B) made by a testing laboratory after such date; and

(ii) may accept such a determination made prior to such date;

(C) except for purposes of accepting a determination described in subparagraph (B)(ii), the Secretary shall not continue to recognize the accreditation of testing laboratories accredited under paragraph (1)(A); and

(D) the Secretary may take actions in accordance with paragraph (2) with respect to the determinations made prior to such date and recognition of the accreditation of testing laboratories pursuant to determinations made prior to such date.

Sec. 515. [360e] Premarket Approval.

(a) General Requirement. — A class III device —

(1) which is subject to an order issued under subsection (b) (or a regulation promulgated under such subsection prior to the date of enactment of the Food and Drug Administration Safety and Innovation Act); or

(2) which is a class III device because of section 513(f),

is required to have, unless exempt under section 520(g), an approval under this section of an application for premarket approval or, as applicable, an approval under subsection (c)(2) of a report seeking premarket approval.

(b) Order to Require premarket Approval. —

(1) In the case of a class III device which —

(A) was introduced or delivered for introduction into interstate commerce for commercial distribution before the date of enactment of this section; or

(B) is

(i) of a type so introduced or delivered, and

(ii) is substantially equivalent to another device within that type;

the Secretary shall by administrative order following publication of a proposed order in the Federal Register, a meeting of a device classification panel described in section 513(b), and consideration of comments from all affected stakeholders, including patients, payors, and providers, notwithstanding subchapter II of chapter 5 of title 5, United States Code, require that such device have an approval under this section of an application for premarket approval. Authority to issue such administrative order shall not be delegated below the Director of the Center for Devices and Radiological Health, acting in consultation with the Commissioner.

(2) A proposed order required under paragraph (1) shall contain —

(A) the proposed order;

(B) proposed findings with respect to the degree of risk of illness or injury designed to be eliminated or reduced by requiring the device to have an approved application for premarket approval and the benefit to the public from use of the device;

(C) opportunity for the submission of comments on the proposed order and the proposed findings; and

(D) opportunity to request a change in the classification of the device based on new information relevant to the classification of the device.

(3) After the expiration of the period for comment on a proposed order and proposed findings published under paragraph (2), consideration of comments submitted on such proposed order and findings and a meeting of a device classification panel described in section 513(b), the Secretary shall

(A) issue an administrative order under paragraph (1) and publish in the Federal Register findings on the matters referred to in paragraph (2)(B), or

(B) publish a notice terminating the proceeding for the issuance of the administrative order together with the reasons for such termination. If a notice of termination is published, the Secretary shall (unless such notice is issued because the device is a banned device under section 516) initiate a proceeding under section 513(e) to reclassify the device subject to the proceeding terminated by such notice.

(c) Application for Premarket Approval. —

(1) Any person may file with the Secretary an application for premarket approval for a class III device. Such an application for a device shall contain —

(A) full reports of all information, published or known to or which should reasonably be known to the applicant, concerning investigations which have been made to show whether or not such device is safe and effective;

(B) a full statement of the components, ingredients, and properties and of the principle or principles of operation, of such device;

(C) a full description of the methods used in, and the facilities and controls used for, the manufacture, processing, and, when relevant, packing and installation of, such device;

(D) an identifying reference to any performance standard under section 514 which would be applicable to any aspect of such device if it were a class II device, and either adequate information to show that such aspect of such device fully meets such performance standard or adequate information to justify any deviation from such standard;

(E) such samples of such device and of components thereof as the Secretary may reasonably require, except that where the submission of such samples is impracticable or unduly burdensome, the requirement of this subparagraph may be met by the submission of complete information concerning the location of one or more such devices readily available for examination and testing;

(F) specimens of the labeling proposed to be used for such device;

(G) the certification required under section 402(j)(5)(B) of the Public Health Service Act (which shall not be considered an element of such application); and

(H) such other information relevant to the subject matter of the application as the Secretary, with the concurrence of the appropriate panel under section 513, may require.

(2) —

(A) Any person may file with the Secretary a report seeking premarket approval for a class III device referred to in subsection (a) that is a reprocessed single-use device. Such a report shall contain the following:

(i) The device name, including both the trade or proprietary name and the common or usual name.

(ii) The establishment registration number of the owner or operator submitting the report.

(iii) Actions taken to comply with performance standards under section 514.

(iv) Proposed labels, labeling, and advertising sufficient to describe the device, its intended use, and directions for use.

(v) Full reports of all information, published or known to or which should be reasonably known to the applicant, concerning investigations which have been made to show whether or not the device is safe or effective.

(vi) A description of the device's components, ingredients, and properties.

(vii) A full description of the methods used in, and the facilities and controls used for, the reprocessing and packing of the device.

(viii) Such samples of the device that the Secretary may reasonably require.

(ix) A financial certification or disclosure statement or both, as required by part 54 of title 21, Code of Federal Regulations.

(x) A statement that the applicant believes to the best of the applicant's knowledge that all data and information submitted to the Secretary are truthful and accurate and that no material fact has been omitted in the report.

(xi) Any additional data and information, including information of the type required in paragraph (1) for an application under such paragraph, that the Secretary determines is necessary to determine whether there is reasonable assurance of safety and effectiveness for the reprocessed device.

(xii) Validation data described in section 510(o)(1)(A) that demonstrates that the reasonable assurance of the safety or effectiveness of the device will remain after the maximum number of times the device is reprocessed as intended by the person submitting such report.

(B) In the case of a class III device referred to in subsection (a) that is a reprocessed single-use device:

(i) Subparagraph (A) of this paragraph applies in lieu of paragraph (1).

(ii) Subject to clause (i), the provisions of this section apply to a report under subparagraph (A) to the same extent and in the same manner as such provisions apply to an application under paragraph (1).

(iii) Each reference in other sections of this Act to an application under this section, other than such a reference in section 737 or 738, shall be considered to be a reference to a report under subparagraph (A).

(iv) Each reference in other sections of this Act to a device for which an application under this section has been approved, or has been denied, suspended, or withdrawn, other than such a reference in section 737 or 738, shall be considered to be a reference to a device for which a report under subparagraph (A) has been approved, or has been denied, suspended, or withdrawn, respectively.

(3) Upon receipt of an application meeting the requirements set forth in paragraph (1), the Secretary —

(A) may on the Secretary's own initiative, or

(B) shall, upon the request of an applicant unless the Secretary finds that the information in the application which would be reviewed by a panel substantially duplicates information which has previously been reviewed by a panel appointed under section 513,

refer such application to the appropriate panel under section 513 for study and for submission (within such period as he may establish) of a report and recommendation respecting approval of the application, together with all underlying data and the reasons or basis for the recommendation. Where appropriate, the Secretary shall ensure that such panel includes, or consults with, one or more pediatric experts.

(4) —

(A) Prior to the submission of an application under this subsection, the Secretary shall accept and review any portion of the application that the applicant and the Secretary agree is complete, ready, and appropriate for review, except that such requirement does not apply, and the Secretary has discretion whether to accept and review such portion, during any period in which, under section ~~738(h)~~ 738(g), the Secretary does not have the authority to collect fees under section 738(a).

(B) Each portion of a submission reviewed under subparagraph (A) and found acceptable by the Secretary shall not be further reviewed after receipt of an application that satisfies the requirements of paragraph (1), unless a significant issue of safety or effectiveness provides the Secretary reason to review such accepted portion.

(C) Whenever the Secretary determines that a portion of a submission under subparagraph (A) is unacceptable, the Secretary shall, in writing, provide to the applicant a description of any deficiencies in such portion and identify the information that is required to correct these deficiencies, unless the applicant is no longer pursuing the application and such application shall include the certification required under section 402(j)(5)(B) of the Public Health Service Act (which shall not be considered an element of such application).

(5) —

(A) In requesting additional information with respect to an application under this section, the Secretary shall consider the least burdensome appropriate means necessary to demonstrate a reasonable assurance of device safety and effectiveness.

(B) For purposes of subparagraph (A), the term "necessary" means the minimum required information that would support a determination by the Secretary that an application provides a reasonable assurance of the safety and effectiveness of the device.

(C) For purposes of this paragraph, the Secretary shall consider the role of postmarket information in determining the least burdensome means of demonstrating a reasonable assurance of device safety and effectiveness.

(D) Nothing in this paragraph alters the standards for premarket approval of a device.

(d) Action on an Application for Premarket Approval. —

(1) —

(A) As promptly as possible, but in no event later than one hundred and eighty days after the receipt of an application under subsection (c) (except as provided in section 520(1)(3)(D)(ii) or unless, in accordance with subparagraph (B)(i), an additional period as agreed upon by the Secretary and the applicant), the Secretary, after considering the report and recommendation submitted under paragraph (2) of such subsection, shall —

(i) issue an order approving the application if he finds that none of the grounds for denying approval specified in paragraph (2) of this subsection applies; or

(ii) deny approval of the application if he finds (and sets forth the basis for such finding as part of or accompanying such denial) that one or more grounds for denial specified in paragraph (2) of this subsection apply.

In making the determination whether to approve or deny the application, the Secretary shall rely on the conditions of use included in the proposed labeling as the basis for determining whether or not there is a reasonable assurance of safety and effectiveness, if the proposed labeling is neither false nor misleading. In determining whether or not such labeling is false or misleading, the Secretary shall fairly evaluate all material facts pertinent to the proposed labeling.

(B) —

(i) The Secretary may not enter into an agreement to extend the period in which to take action with respect to an application submitted for a device subject to a regulation promulgated under subsection (b) unless he finds that the continued availability of the device is necessary for the public health.

(ii) An order approving an application for a device may require as a condition to such approval that the sale and distribution of the device be restricted but only to the extent that the sale and distribution of a device may be restricted under a regulation under section 520(e).

(iii) The Secretary shall accept and review statistically valid and reliable data and any other information from investigations conducted under the authority of regulations required by section 520(g) to make a determination of whether there is a reasonable assurance of safety and effectiveness of a device subject to a pending application under this section if —

(I) the data or information is derived from investigations of an earlier version of the device, the device has been modified during or after the investigation (but prior to submission of an application under subsection (c)) and such a modification of the device does not constitute a significant change in the design or in the basic principles of operation of the device that would invalidate the data or information; or

(II) the data or information relates to a device approved under this section, is available for use under this Act, and is relevant to the design and intended use of the device for which the application is pending.

(2) The Secretary shall deny approval of an application for a device if, upon the basis of the information submitted to the Secretary as part of the application and any other information before him with respect to such device, the Secretary finds that —

(A) there is a lack of a showing of reasonable assurance that such device is safe under the conditions of use prescribed, recommended, or suggested in the proposed labeling thereof;

(B) there is a lack of a showing of reasonable assurance that the device is effective under the conditions of use prescribed, recommended, or suggested in the proposed labeling thereof;

(C) the methods used in, or the facilities or controls used for, the manufacture, processing, packing, or installation of such device do not conform to the requirements of section 520(f);

(D) based on a fair evaluation of all material facts, the proposed labeling is false or misleading in any particular; or

(E) such device is not shown to conform in all respects to a performance standard in effect under section 514 compliance with which is a condition to approval of the application and there is a lack of adequate information to justify the deviation from such standard.

Any denial of an application shall, insofar as the Secretary determines to be practicable, be accompanied by a statement informing the applicant of the measures required to place such application in approvable form (which measures may include further research by the applicant in accordance with one or more protocols prescribed by the Secretary).

(3) —

(A) —

(i) The Secretary shall, upon the written request of an applicant, meet with the applicant, not later than 100 days after the receipt of an application that has been filed as complete under subsection (c), to discuss the review status of the application.

(ii) The Secretary shall, in writing and prior to the meeting, provide to the applicant a description of any deficiencies in the application that, at that point, have been identified by the Secretary based on an interim review of the entire application and identify the information that is required to correct those deficiencies.

(iii) The Secretary shall notify the applicant promptly of —

(I) any additional deficiency identified in the application, or

(II) any additional information required to achieve completion of the review and final action on the application,

that was not described as a deficiency in the written description provided by the Secretary under clause (ii).

(B) The Secretary and the applicant may, by mutual consent, establish a different schedule for a meeting required under this paragraph.

(4) An applicant whose application has been denied approval may, by petition filed on or before the thirtieth day after the date upon which he receives notice of such denial, obtain review thereof in accordance with either paragraph (1) or (2) of subsection (g), and any interested person may obtain review, in accordance with paragraph (1) or (2) of subsection (g), of an order of the Secretary approving an application.

(5) —

(A) —

(i) A supplemental application shall be required for any change to a device subject to an approved application under this subsection that affects safety or effectiveness, unless such change is a modification in a manufacturing procedure or method of manufacturing and the holder of the approved application submits a written notice to the Secretary that describes in detail the change, summarizes the data or information supporting the change, and informs the Secretary that the change has been made under the requirements of section 520(f).

(ii) The holder of an approved application who submits a notice under clause (i) with respect to a manufacturing change of a device may distribute the device 30 days after the date on which the

Secretary receives the notice, unless the Secretary within such 30-day period notifies the holder that the notice is not adequate and describes such further information or action that is required for acceptance of such change. If the Secretary notifies the holder that a supplemental application is required, the Secretary shall review the supplement within 135 days after the receipt of the supplement. The time used by the Secretary to review the notice of the manufacturing change shall be deducted from the 135-day review period if the notice meets appropriate content requirements for premarket approval supplements.

(B) —

(i) Subject to clause (ii), in reviewing a supplement to an approved application, for an incremental change to the design of a device that affects safety or effectiveness, the Secretary shall approve such supplement if—

(I) nonclinical data demonstrate that the design modification creates the intended additional capacity, function, or performance of the device; and

(II) clinical data from the approved application and any supplement to the approved application provide a reasonable assurance of safety and effectiveness for the changed device.

(ii) The Secretary may require, when necessary, additional clinical data to evaluate the design modification of the device to provide a reasonable assurance of safety and effectiveness.

(e) Withdrawal and Temporary Suspension of Approval of Application. —

(1) The Secretary shall, upon obtaining, where appropriate, advice on scientific matters from a panel or panels under section 513, and after due notice and opportunity for informal hearing to the holder of an approved application for a device, issue an order withdrawing approval of the application if the Secretary finds—

(A) that such device is unsafe or ineffective under the conditions of use prescribed, recommended, or suggested in the labeling thereof;

(B) on the basis of new information before him with respect to such device, evaluated together with the evidence available to him when the application was approved, that there is a lack of a showing of reasonable assurance that the device is safe or effective under the conditions of use prescribed, recommended, or suggested in the labeling thereof;

(C) that the application contained or was accompanied by an untrue statement of a material fact;

(D) that the applicant

(i) has failed to establish a system for maintaining records, or has repeatedly or deliberately failed to maintain records or to make reports, required by an applicable regulation under section 519(a),

(ii) has refused to permit access to, or copying or verification of, such records as required by section 704, or

(iii) has not complied with the requirements of section 510;

(E) on the basis of new information before him with respect to such device, evaluated together with the evidence before him when the application was approved, that the methods used in, or the facilities and controls used for, the manufacture, processing, packing, or installation of such device do not conform with the requirements of section 520(f) and were not brought into conformity with such requirements within a reasonable time after receipt of written notice from the Secretary of nonconformity;

(F) on the basis of new information before him, evaluated together with the evidence before him when the application was approved, that the labeling of such device, based on a fair evaluation of all material facts, is false or misleading in any particular and was not corrected within a reasonable time after receipt of written notice from the Secretary of such fact; or

(G) on the basis of new information before him, evaluated together with the evidence before him when the application was approved, that such device is not shown to conform in all respects to a performance standard which is in effect under section 514 compliance with which was a condition to approval of the application and that there is a lack of adequate information to justify the deviation from such standard.

(2) The holder of an application subject to an order issued under paragraph (1) withdrawing approval of the application may, by petition filed on or before the thirtieth day after the date upon which he receives notice of such withdrawal, obtain review thereof in accordance with either paragraph (1) or (2) of subsection (g).

(3) If, after providing an opportunity for an informal hearing, the Secretary determines there is reasonable probability that the continuation of distribution of a device under an approved application would cause serious, adverse health consequences or death, the Secretary shall by order temporarily suspend the approval of the application approved under this section. If the Secretary issues such an order, the Secretary shall proceed expeditiously under paragraph (1) to withdraw such application.

(f) Product Development Protocol. —

(1) In the case of a class III device which is required to have an approval of an application submitted under subsection (c), such device shall be considered as having such an approval if a notice of completion of testing conducted in accordance with a product development protocol approved under paragraph (4) has been declared completed under paragraph (6).

(2) Any person may submit to the Secretary a proposed product development protocol with respect to a device. Such a protocol shall be accompanied by data supporting it. If, within thirty days of the receipt of such a protocol, the Secretary determines that it appears to be appropriate to apply the requirements of this subsection to the device with respect to which the protocol is submitted, the Secretary —

(A) may, at the initiative of the Secretary, refer the proposed protocol to the appropriate panel under section 513 for its recommendation respecting approval of the protocol; or

(B) shall so refer such protocol upon the request of the submitter, unless the Secretary finds that the proposed protocol and accompanying data which would be reviewed by such panel substantially duplicate a product development protocol and accompanying data which have previously been reviewed by such a panel.

(3) A proposed product development protocol for a device may be approved only if —

(A) the Secretary determines that it is appropriate to apply the requirements of this subsection to the device in lieu of the requirement of approval of an application submitted under subsection (c); and

(B) the Secretary determines that the proposed protocol provides —

(i) a description of the device and the changes which may be made in the device,

(ii) a description of the preclinical trials (if any) of the device and a specification of

(I) the results from such trials to be required before the commencement of clinical trials of the device, and

(II) any permissible variations in preclinical trials and the results therefrom,

(iii) a description of the clinical trials (if any) of the device and a specification of

(I) the results from such trials to be required before the filing of a notice of completion of the requirements of the protocol, and

(II) any permissible variations in such trials and the results therefrom,

(iv) a description of the methods to be used in, and the facilities and controls to be used for, the manufacture, processing, and when relevant, packing and installation of the device,

(v) an identifying reference to any performance standard under section 514 to be applicable to any aspect of such device,

(vi) if appropriate, specimens of the labeling proposed to be used for such device,

(vii) such other information relevant to the subject matter of the protocol as the Secretary, with the concurrence of the appropriate panel or panels under section 513, may require, and

(viii) a requirement for submission of progress reports and, when completed, records of the trials conducted under the protocol which records are adequate to show compliance with the protocol.

(4) The Secretary shall approve or disapprove a proposed product development protocol submitted under paragraph (2) within one hundred and twenty days of its receipt unless an additional period is agreed upon by the Secretary and the person who submitted the protocol. Approval of a protocol or denial of approval of a protocol is final agency action subject to judicial review under chapter 7 of title 5, United States Code.

(5) At any time after a product development protocol for a device has been approved pursuant to paragraph (4), the person for whom the protocol was approved may submit a notice of completion—

(A) stating

(i) his determination that the requirements of the protocol have been fulfilled and that, to the best of his knowledge, there is no reason bearing on safety or effectiveness why the notice of completion should not become effective, and

(ii) the data and other information upon which such determination was made, and

(B) setting forth the results of the trials required by the protocol and all the information required by subsection (c)(1).

(6) —

(A) The Secretary may, after providing the person who has an approved protocol an opportunity for an informal hearing and at any time prior to receipt of notice of completion of such protocol, issue a final order to revoke such protocol if he finds that—

(i) such person has failed substantially to comply with the requirements of the protocol,

(ii) the results of the trials obtained under the protocol differ so substantially from the results required by the protocol that further trials cannot be justified, or

(iii) the results of the trials conducted under the protocol or available new information do not demonstrate that the device tested under the protocol does not present an unreasonable risk to health and safety.

(B) After the receipt of a notice of completion of an approved protocol the Secretary shall, within the ninety-day period beginning on the date such notice is received, by order either declare the protocol completed or declare it not completed. An order declaring a protocol not completed may take effect only after the Secretary has provided the person who has the protocol opportunity for an informal hearing on the order. Such an order may be issued only if the Secretary finds —

(i) such person has failed substantially to comply with the requirements of the protocol,

(ii) the results of the trials obtained under the protocol differ substantially from the results required by the protocol, or

(iii) there is a lack of a showing of reasonable assurance of the safety and effectiveness of the device under the conditions of use prescribed, recommended, or suggested in the proposed labeling thereof.

(C) A final order issued under subparagraph (A) or (B) shall be in writing and shall contain the reasons to support the conclusions thereof.

(7) At any time after a notice of completion has become effective the Secretary may issue an order (after due notice and opportunity for an informal hearing to the person for whom the notice is effective) revoking the approval of a device provided by a notice of completion which has become effective as provided in subparagraph (B) if he finds that any of the grounds listed in subparagraphs (A) through (G) of subsection (e)(1) of this section apply. Each reference in such subparagraphs to an application shall be considered for purposes of this paragraph as a reference to a protocol and the notice of completion of such protocol, and each reference to the time when an application was approved shall be considered for purposes of this paragraph as a reference to the time when a notice of completion took effect.

(8) A person who has an approved protocol subject to an order issued under paragraph (6)(A) revoking such protocol, a person who has an approved protocol with respect to which an order under paragraph (6)(B) was issued declaring that the protocol had not been completed, or a person subject to an order issued under paragraph (7) revoking the approval of a device may, by petition filed on or before the thirtieth day after the date upon which he receives notice of such order, obtain review thereof in accordance with either paragraph (1) or (2) of subsection (g).

(g) Review. —

(1) Upon petition for review of —

(A) an order under subsection (d) approving or denying approval of an application or an order under subsection (e) withdrawing approval of an application, or

(B) an order under subsection (f)(6)(A) revoking an approved protocol, under subsection (f)(6)(B) declaring that an approved protocol has not been completed, or under subsection (f)(7) revoking the approval of a device, the Secretary shall, unless he finds the petition to be without good cause or unless a petition for review of such order has been submitted under paragraph (2), hold a hearing, in accordance with section 554 of title 5 of the United States Code, on the order. The panel or panels which considered the application, protocol, or device subject to such order shall designate a member to appear and testify at any such hearing upon request of the Secretary, the petitioner, or the officer conducting the hearing, but this requirement does not preclude any other member of the panel or panels from appearing and testifying at any such hearing. Upon completion of such hearing and after considering the record established in such hearing, the Secretary shall issue an order either affirming the order subject to the hearing or reversing such order and, as appropriate, approving or denying approval of the application, reinstating the application's approval, approving the protocol, or placing in effect a notice of completion.

(2) —

(A) Upon petition for review of—

(i) an order under subsection (d) approving or denying approval of an application or an order under subsection (e) withdrawing approval of an application, or

(ii) an order under subsection (f)(6)(A) revoking an approved protocol, under subsection (f)(6)(B) declaring that an approved protocol has not been completed, or under subsection (f)(7) revoking the approval of a device,

the Secretary shall refer the application or protocol subject to the order and the basis for the order to an advisory committee of experts established pursuant to subparagraph (B) for a report and recommendation with respect to the order. The advisory committee shall, after independent study of the data and information furnished to it by the Secretary and other data and information before it, submit to the Secretary a report and recommendation, together with all underlying data and information and a statement of the reasons or basis for the recommendation. A copy of such report shall be promptly supplied by the Secretary to any person who petitioned for such referral to the advisory committee.

(B) The Secretary shall establish advisory committees (which may not be panels under section 513) to receive referrals under subparagraph (A). The Secretary shall appoint as members of any such advisory committee persons qualified in the subject matter to be referred to the committee and of appropriately diversified professional backgrounds, except that the Secretary may not appoint to such a committee any individual who is in the regular full-time employ of the United States and engaged in the administration of this Act. Members of an advisory committee (other than officers or employees of the United States), while attending conferences or meetings of their committee or otherwise serving at the request of the Secretary, shall be entitled to receive compensation at rates to be fixed by the Secretary which rates may not exceed the daily equivalent for grade Gs–18 of the General Schedule for each day (including traveltime) they are so engaged; and while so serving away from their homes or regular places of business each member may be allowed travel expenses, including per diem in lieu of subsistence, as authorized by section 5703 of title 5 of the United States Code for persons in the Government service employed intermittently. The Secretary shall designate the chairman of an advisory committee from its members. The Secretary shall furnish each advisory committee with clerical and other assistance, and shall by regulation prescribe the procedures to be followed by each such committee in acting on referrals made under subparagraph (A).

(C) The Secretary shall make public the report and recommendation made by an advisory committee with respect to an application and shall by order, stating the reasons therefor, either affirm the order referred to the advisory committee or reverse such order and, if appropriate, approve or deny approval of the application, reinstate the application's approval, approve the protocol, or place in effect a notice of completion.

(h) Service of Orders. — Orders of the Secretary under this section shall be served

(1) in person by any officer or employee of the department designated by the Secretary, or

(2) by mailing the order by registered mail or certified mail addressed to the applicant at his last known address in the records of the Secretary.

(i) Revision. —

(1) Before December 1, 1995, the Secretary shall by order require manufacturers of devices, which were introduced or delivered for introduction into interstate commerce for commercial distribution before May 28, 1976, and which are subject to revision of classification under paragraph (2), to submit to the Secretary a summary of and citation to any information known or otherwise available to the manufacturer respecting such devices, including adverse safety or effectiveness information which has not been submitted under section 519. The Secretary may require the manufacturer to submit the adverse safety or effectiveness data for which a summary and citation were submitted, if such data are available to the manufacturer.

(2) After the issuance of an order under paragraph (1) but before the date that is 2 years after the date of enactment of the Food and Drug Administration Safety and Innovation Act, the Secretary shall issue an administrative order following publication of a proposed order in the Federal Register, a meeting of a device classification panel described in section 513(b), and consideration of comments from all affected stakeholders, including patients, payors, and providers, notwithstanding subchapter II of chapter 5 of title 5, United States Code, for each device —

(A) which the Secretary has classified as a class III device, and

(B) for which no administrative order has been issued under subsection (b) (or no regulation has been promulgated under such subsection prior to the date of enactment of the Food and Drug Administration Safety and Innovation Act),

revising the classification of the device so that the device is classified into class I or class II, unless the administrative order issued under this paragraph requires the device to remain in class III. In determining whether to revise the classification of a device or to require a device to remain in class III, the Secretary shall apply the criteria set forth in section 513(a).

(3) The Secretary shall, as promptly as is reasonably achievable, but not later than 12 months after the effective date of the order requiring a device to remain in class III, establish a schedule for the issuance of an administrative order under subsection (b) for each device which is subject to the order requiring the device to remain in class III.

Sec. 515A. [360e-1] Pediatric Uses of Devices.

(a) New Devices. —

(1) In General. — A person that submits to the Secretary an application under section 520(m), or an application (or supplement to an application) or a product development protocol under section 515, shall include in the application or protocol the information described in paragraph (2).

(2) Required Information. — The application or protocol described in paragraph (1) shall include, with respect to the device for which approval is sought and if readily available —

(A) a description of any pediatric subpopulations that suffer from the disease or condition that the device is intended to treat, diagnose, or cure; and

(B) the number of affected pediatric patients.

(3) Annual Report. — Not later than 18 months after the date of the enactment of this section, and annually thereafter, the Secretary shall submit to the Committee on Health, Education, Labor, and Pensions of the Senate and the Committee on Energy and Commerce of the House of Representatives a report that includes —

(A) the number of devices approved in the year preceding the year in which the report is submitted, for which there is a pediatric subpopulation that suffers from the disease or condition that the device is intended to treat, diagnose, or cure;

(B) any information, based on a review of data available to the Secretary, regarding devices used in pediatric patients but not labeled for such use for which the Secretary determines that approved pediatric labeling could confer a benefit to pediatric patients;

(C) the number of pediatric devices that receive a humanitarian use exemption under section 520(m);

~~**(B)**~~ **(D)** the number of devices approved in the year preceding the year in which the report is submitted, labeled for use in pediatric patients;

~~**(C)**~~ **(E)** the number of pediatric devices approved in the year preceding the year in which the report is submitted, exempted from a fee pursuant to section 738(a)(2)(B)(v); ~~and~~

~~**(D)**~~ **(F)** the review time for each device described in subparagraphs (A), ~~(B), and (C)~~ (C), (D), and (E);

(G) the number of devices for which the Secretary relied on data with respect to adults to support a determination of a reasonable assurance of safety and effectiveness in pediatric patients;

(H) the number of devices for which the Secretary relied on data from one pediatric subpopulation to support a determination of a reasonable assurance of safety and effectiveness in another pediatric subpopulation.

For the items described in this paragraph, such report shall disaggregate the number of devices by pediatric subpopulation.

(b) Determination of Pediatric Effectiveness Based on Similar Course of Disease or Condition or Similar Effect of Device on Adults. —

(1) In General. — If the course of the disease or condition and the effects of the device are sufficiently similar in adults and pediatric patients, the Secretary may conclude that adult data may be used to support a determination of a reasonable assurance of effectiveness in pediatric populations, as appropriate.

(2) Extrapolation Between Subpopulations. — A study may not be needed in each pediatric subpopulation if data from one subpopulation can be extrapolated to another subpopulation.

(c) Pediatric Subpopulation. — For purposes of this section, the term "pediatric subpopulation" has the meaning given the term in section 520(m)(6)(E)(ii).

Sec. 515B. [360e-3] Breakthrough Devices.

(a) Purpose. —The purpose of this section is to encourage the Secretary, and provide the Secretary with sufficient authority, to apply efficient and flexible approaches to expedite the development of, and prioritize the Food and Drug Administration's review of, devices that represent breakthrough technologies.

(b) Establishment of Program. —The Secretary shall establish a program to expedite the development of, and provide for the priority review for, devices, as determined by the Secretary—

(1) That provide for more effective treatment or diagnosis of life-threatening or irreversiably debilitating human disease or conditions; and

(2)

(A) that represent breakthrough technologies;

(B) for which no approved or cleared alternatives exist;

(C) that offer significant advantages over existing approved or cleared alternatives, including the potential, compared to existing approved alternatives, to reduce or eliminate the need for hospitalization, improve patient quality of life, facilitate patients' ability to manage their own care (such as through self-directed personal assistance), or establish long-term clinical efficiencies; or

(D) the availability of which is in the best interest of patients.

(c) Request for Designation. —A sponsor of a device may request that the Secretary designate such device for expedited development and priority review under this section. Any such request for designation may be made at any time prior to the submission of an application under section 515(c), a notification under section 510(k), or a petition for classification under section 513(f)(2).

(d) Designation Process. —

(1) In General. —Not later than 60 calendar days after the receipt of a request under subsection (c), the Secretary shall determine whether the device that is the subject of the request meets the criteria described in subsection (b). If the Secretary determines that the device meets the criteria, the Secretary shall designate the device for expedited development and priority review.

(2) Review. —Review of a request under subsection (c) shall be undertaken by a team that is composed of experienced staff and senior managers of the Food and Drug Administration.

(3) Withdrawal. —The Secretary may not withdraw a designation granted under this section on the basis of the criteria under subsection (b) no longer applying because of the subsequent clearance or approval of another device that—

(A) was designated under this section; or

(B) was given priority review under section 515(d)(5), as in effect prior to the date of enactment of the 21st Century Cures Act [December 13, 2016 —Ed.].

(e) Expedited Development and Priority Review. —

(1) Actions. —For purposes of expediting the development and review of devices designated under subsection (d) the Secretary shall—

(A) assign a team of staff, including a team leader with appropriate subject matter expertise and experience, for each device for which a request is submitted under subsection (c);

(B) provide for oversight of the team by senior agency personnel to facilitate the efficient development of the device and the efficient review of any submission described in subsection (c) for the device;

(C) adopt an efficient process for timely dispute resolution;

(D) provide for interactive and timely communication with the sponsor of the device during the development program and review process;

(E) expedite the Secretary's review of manufacturing and quality systems compliance, as applicable;

(F) disclose to the sponsor, not less than 5 business days in advance, the topics of any consultation the Secretary intends to undertake with external experts or an advisory committee concerning the sponsor's device and provide the sponsor the opportunity to recommend such external experts;

(G) provide for advisory committee input, as the Secretary determines appropriate (including the response to the request of the sponsor) for applications submitted under section 515(c); and

(H) assign staff to be available within a reasonable time to address questions by institutional review committees concerning the conditions and clinical testing requirements applicable to the investigational use of the device pursuant to an exemption under section 520(g).

(2) Additional Actions. —In addition to the actions described in paragraph (1), for purposes of expediting the development and review of devices designated under subsection (d), the Secretary, in collaboration with the device sponsor, may, as appropriate—

(A) coordinate with the sponsor regarding early agreement on a data development plan;

(B) take steps to ensure the design of clinical trials is as efficient and flexible as practicable, when scientifically appropriate;

(C) facilitate, when scientifically appropriate, expedited and efficient development and review of the device through utilization of timely postmarket data collection with regard to application for approval under section 515(c); and

(D) agree in writing to clinical protocols that the Secretary will consider binding on the Secretary and the sponsor, subject to—

(i) changes to such protocols agreed to in writing by the sponsor and the Secretary; or

(ii) a decision, made by the director of the office responsible for reviewing the device submission, that a substantial scientific issue essential to determining the safety or effectiveness of such device exists, provided that such decision is in writing, and is made only after the Secretary provides to the device sponsor or applicant an opportunity for a meeting at which the director and the sponsor or applicant are present and at which the director documents the substantial scientific issue.

(f) Priority Review Guidance. —

(1) Content. —Not later than 1 year after the date of enactment of the 21st Century Cures Act [December 13, 2016 —Ed.], the Secretary shall issue guidance on the implementation of this section. Such guidance shall—

(A) set forth the process by which a person may seek a designation under subsection (d);

(B) provide a template for requests under subsection (c);

(C) identify the criteria the Secretary will use in evaluating a request for designation under this section; and

(D) identify the criteria and processes the Secretary will use to assign a team of staff, including team leaders, to review devices designated for expedited development and priority review, including any training required for such personnel to ensure effective and efficient review.

(2) Process. —Prior to finalizing the guidance under paragraph (1), the Secretary shall seek public comment on ~~a proposed guidance.~~ a draft version of that guidance.

(g) Rule of Construction. —Nothing in this section shall be construed to affect —

(1) the criteria and standards for evaluating an application pursuant to section 515(c), a report and request for classification under section 513(f)(2), or a report under section 510(k), including the recognition of valid scientific evidence as described in section 513(a)(3)(B) and consideration and application of the least burdensome means of evaluating device effectiveness or demonstrating substantial equivalence between devices with differing technological characteristics, as applicable;

(2) the authority of the Secretary with respect to clinical holds under section 520(g)(8)(A);

(3) the authority of the Secretary to act on an application pursuant to section 515(d) before completion of an establishment inspection, as the Secretary determines appropriate; or

(4) the authority of the Secretary with respect to postmarket surveillance under sections 519(h) and 522.

Sec. 516. [360f] Banned Devices.

(a) General Rule. — Whenever the Secretary finds, on the basis of all available data and information, that —

(1) a device intended for human use presents substantial deception or an unreasonable and substantial risk of illness or injury; and

(2) in the case of substantial deception or an unreasonable and substantial risk of illness or injury which the Secretary determined could be corrected or eliminated by labeling or change in labeling and with respect to which the Secretary provided written notice to the manufacturer specifying the deception or risk of illness or injury, the labeling or change in labeling to correct the deception or eliminate or reduce such risk, and the period within which such labeling or change in labeling was to be done, such labeling or change in labeling was not done within such period;

he may initiate a proceeding to promulgate a regulation to make such device a banned device.

(b) Special Effective Date. — The Secretary may declare a proposed regulation under subsection (a) to be effective upon its publication in the Federal Register and until the effective date of any final action taken respecting such regulation if

(1) he determines, on the basis of all available data and information, that the deception or risk of illness or injury associated with the use of the device which is subject to the regulation presents an unreasonable, direct, and substantial danger to the health of individuals, and

(2) before the date of the publication of such regulation, the Secretary notifies the manufacturer of such device that such regulation is to be made so effective. If the Secretary makes a proposed regulation so effective, he shall, as expeditiously as possible, give interested persons prompt notice of his action under this subsection, provide reasonable opportunity for an informal hearing on the proposed regulation, and either affirm, modify, or revoke such proposed regulation

Sec. 517. [360g] Judicial Review.

(a) Application of Section. — Not later than thirty days after —

(1) the promulgation of a regulation under section 513 classifying a device in class I, an administrative order changing the classification of a device to class I, or an order under subsection (f)(2) of such section reclassifying a device or denying a petition for reclassification of a device,

(2) the promulgation of a regulation under section 514 establishing, amending, or revoking a performance standard for a device,

(3) the issuance of an order under section 514(b)(2) or 515(b)(2)(B) denying a request for reclassification of a device,

(4) the promulgation of a regulation under paragraph (3) of section 515(b) requiring a device to have an approval of a premarket application, a regulation under paragraph (4) of that section amending or revoking a regulation under paragraph (3), or an order pursuant to section 515(g)(1) or 515(g)(2)(C),

(5) the promulgation of a regulation under section 516 (other than a proposed regulation made effective under subsection (b) of such section upon the regulation's publication) making a device a banned device,

(6) the issuance of an order under section 520(f)(2),

(7) an order under section 520(g)(4) disapproving an application for an exemption of a device for investigational use or an order under section 520(g)(5) withdrawing such an exemption for a device,

(8) an order pursuant to section 513(i), or

(9) a regulation under section 515(i)(2) or 520(1)(5)(B),

any person adversely affected by such regulation or order may file a petition with the United States Court of Appeals for the District of Columbia or for the circuit wherein such person resides or has his principal place of business for judicial review of such regulation or order. A copy of the petition shall be transmitted by the clerk of the court to the Secretary or other officer designated by him for that purpose. The Secretary shall file in the court the record of the proceedings on which the Secretary based his regulation or order as provided in section 2112 of title 28, United States Code. For purposes of this section, the term "record" means all notices and other matter published in the Federal Register with respect to the regulation or order reviewed, all information submitted to the Secretary with respect to such regulation or order, proceedings of any panel or advisory committee with respect to such regulation or order, any hearing held with respect to such regulation or order, and any other information identified by the Secretary, in the administrative proceeding held with respect to such regulation or order, as being relevant to such regulation or order.

(b) Additional Data, Views, and Arguments. — If the petitioner applies to the court for leave to adduce additional data, views, or arguments respecting the regulation or order being reviewed and shows to the satisfaction of the court that such additional data, views, or arguments are material and that there were reasonable grounds for the petitioner's failure to adduce such data, views, or arguments in the proceedings before the Secretary, the court may order the Secretary to provide additional opportunity for the oral presentation of data, views, or arguments and for written submissions. The Secretary may modify his findings, or make new findings by reason of the additional data, views, or arguments so taken and shall file with the court such modified or new findings, and his recommendation, if any, for the modification or setting aside of the regulation or order being reviewed, with the return of such additional data, views, or arguments.

(c) Standard for Review. — Upon the filing of the petition under subsection (a) of this section for judicial review of a regulation or order, the court shall have jurisdiction to review the regulation or order in accordance with chapter 7 of title 5, United States Code, and to grant appropriate relief, including interim relief, as provided in such chapter. A regulation described in paragraph (2) or (5) of subsection (a) and an order issued after the review provided by section 515(g) shall not be affirmed if it is found to be unsupported by substantial evidence on the record taken as a whole.

(d) Finality of Judgments. — The judgment of the court affirming or setting aside, in whole or in part, any regulation or order shall be final, subject to review by the Supreme Court of the United States upon certiorari or certification, as provided in section 1254 of title 28 of the United States Code.

(e) Other Remedies. — The remedies provided for in this section shall be in addition to and not in lieu of any other remedies provided by law.

(f) Statement of Reasons. — To facilitate judicial review under this section or under any other provision of law of a regulation or order issued under section 513, 514, 515, 516, 518, 519, 520, or 521 each such regulation or order shall contain a statement of the reasons for its issuance and the basis, in the record of the proceedings held in connection with its issuance, for its issuance.

Sec. 517A. [360g-1] Agency Documentation and Review of Significant Decisions Regarding Devices.

(a) Documentation of Rationale for Significant Decisions. —

(1) In General. — The Secretary shall provide a substantive summary of the scientific and regulatory rationale for any significant decision of the Center for Devices and Radiological Health regarding submission or review of a report under section 510(k), an application under section 515, a request for designation under section 515C, or an application for an exemption under section 520(g), including documentation of significant controversies or differences of opinion and the resolution of such controversies or differences of opinion.

(2) Provision of Documentation. — Upon request, the Secretary shall furnish such substantive summary to the person who is seeking to submit, or who has submitted, such report or application.

(3) Application of Least Burdensome Requirements. — The substantive summary required under this subsection shall include a brief statement regarding how the least burdensome requirements were considered and applied consistent with section 513(i)(1)(D), section 513(a)(3)(D), and section 515(c)(5), as applicable.

(b) Review of Significant Decisions. —

(1) Request for Supervisory Review of Significant Decision. — Any person may request a supervisory review of the significant decision described in subsection (a)(1). Such review may be conducted at the next supervisory level or higher above the individual who made the significant decision

(2) Submission of Request. — A person requesting a supervisory review under paragraph (1) shall submit such request to the Secretary not later than 30 days after such decision and shall indicate in the request whether such person seeks an in-person meeting or a teleconference review.

(3) Timeframe. —

(A) In General. — Except as provided in subparagraph (B), the Secretary shall schedule an in-person or teleconference review, if so requested, not later than 30 days after such request is made. The Secretary shall issue a decision to the person requesting a review under this subsection not later than 45 days after the request is made under paragraph (1), or, in the case of a person who requests an in-person meeting or teleconference, 30 days after such meeting or teleconference.

(B) Exception. — Subparagraph (A) shall not apply in cases that are referred to experts outside of the Food and Drug Administration.

Sec. 518. [360h] Notification and Other Remedies.

(a) Notification. — If the Secretary determines that —

(1) a device intended for human use which is introduced or delivered for introduction into interstate commerce for commercial distribution presents an unreasonable risk of substantial harm to the public health, and

(2) notification under this subsection is necessary to eliminate the unreasonable risk of such harm and no more practicable means is available under the provisions of this Act (other than this section) to eliminate such risk,

the Secretary may issue such order as may be necessary to assure that adequate notification is provided in an appropriate form, by the persons and means best suited under the circumstances involved, to all health professionals who prescribe or use the device and to any other person (including manufacturers, importers, distributors, retailers, and device users) who should properly receive such notification in order to eliminate such risk. An order under this subsection shall require that the individuals subject to the risk with respect to which the order is to be issued be included in the persons to be notified of the risk unless the Secretary determines that notice to such individuals would present a greater danger to the health of such individuals than no such notification. If the Secretary makes such a determination with respect to such individuals, the order shall require that the health professionals who prescribe or use the device provide for the notification of the individuals whom the health professionals treated with the device of the risk presented by the device and of any action which may be taken by or on behalf of such individuals to eliminate or reduce such risk. Before issuing an order under this subsection, the Secretary shall consult with the persons who are to give notice under the order.

(b) Repair, Replacement, or Refund. —

(1) —

(A) If, after affording opportunity for an informal hearing, the Secretary determines that —

(i) a device intended for human use which is introduced or delivered for introduction into interstate commerce for commercial distribution presents an unreasonable risk of substantial harm to the public health.

(ii) there are reasonable grounds to believe that the device was not properly designed or manufactured with reference to the state of the art as it existed at the time of its design or manufacture,

(iii) there are reasonable grounds to believe that the unreasonable risk was not caused by failure of a person other than a manufacturer, importer, distributor, or retailer of the device to exercise due care in the installation, maintenance, repair, or use of the device, and

(iv) the notification authorized by subsection (a) would not by itself be sufficient to eliminate the unreasonable risk and action described in paragraph (2) of this subsection is necessary to eliminate such risk,

the Secretary may order the manufacturer, importer, or any distributor of such device, or any combination of such persons, to submit to him within a reasonable time a plan for taking one or more of the actions described in paragraph (2). An order issued under the preceding sentence which is directed to more than one person shall specify which person may decide which action shall be taken under such plan and the person specified shall be the person who the Secretary determines bears the principal, ultimate financial responsibility for action taken under the plan unless the Secretary cannot determine who bears such responsibility or the Secretary determines that the protection of the public health requires that such decision be made by a person (including a device user or health professional) other than the person he determines bears such responsibility.

(B) The Secretary shall approve a plan submitted pursuant to an order issued under subparagraph (A) unless he determines (after affording opportunity for an informal hearing) that the action or actions to be taken under the plan or the manner in which such action or actions are to be taken under the plan will not assure that the unreasonable risk with respect to which such order was issued will be eliminated. If the Secretary disapproves a plan, he shall order a revised plan to be submitted to him within a reasonable time. If the Secretary determines (after affording opportunity for an informal hearing) that the revised plan is unsatisfactory or if no revised plan or no initial plan has been submitted to the Secretary within the prescribed time, the Secretary shall

(i) prescribe a plan to be carried out by the person or persons to whom the order issued under subparagraph (A) was directed, or

(ii) after affording an opportunity for an informal hearing, by order prescribe a plan to be carried out by a person who is a manufacturer, importer, distributor, or retailer of the device with respect to which the order was issued but to whom the order under subparagraph (A) was not directed.

(2) The actions which may be taken under a plan submitted under an order issued under paragraph (1) are as follows:

(A) To repair the device so that it does not present the unreasonable risk of substantial harm with respect to which the order under paragraph (1) was issued.

(B) To replace the device with a like or equivalent device which is in conformity with all applicable requirements of this Act.

(C) To refund the purchase price of the device (less a reasonable allowance for use if such device has been in the possession of the device user for one year or more —

(i) at the time of notification ordered under subsection (a), or

(ii) at the time the device user receives actual notice of the unreasonable risk with respect to which the order was issued under paragraph (1), whichever first occurs).

(3) No charge shall be made to any person (other than a manufacturer, importer, distributor or retailer) for availing himself of any remedy, described in paragraph (2) and provided under an order issued under paragraph (1), and the person subject to the order shall reimburse each person (other than a manufacturer, importer, distributor, or retailer) who is entitled to such a remedy for any reasonable and foreseeable expenses actually incurred by such person in availing himself of such remedy.

(c) Reimbursement. — An order issued under subsection (b) with respect to a device may require any person who is a manufacturer, importer, distributor, or retailer of the device to reimburse any other person who is a manufacturer, importer, distributor, or retailer of such device for such other person's expenses actually incurred in connection with carrying out the order if the Secretary determines such reimbursement is required for the protection of the public health. Any such requirement shall not affect any rights or obligations under any contract to which the person receiving reimbursement or the person making such reimbursement is a party.

(d) Effect on Other Liability. — Compliance with an order issued under this section shall not relieve any person from liability under Federal or State law. In awarding damages for economic loss in an action brought for the enforcement of any such liability, the value to the plaintiff in such action of any remedy provided him under such order shall be taken into account.

(e) Recall Authority. —

(1) If the Secretary finds that there is a reasonable probability that a device intended for human use would cause serious, adverse health consequences or death, the Secretary shall issue an order requiring the appropriate person (including the manufacturers, importers, distributors, or retailers of the device) —

(A) to immediately cease distribution of such device, and

(B) to immediately notify health professionals and device user facilities of the order and to instruct such professionals and facilities to cease use of such device.

The order shall provide the person subject to the order with an opportunity for an informal hearing, to be held not later than 10 days after the date of the issuance of the order, on the actions required by the order and on whether the order should be amended to require a recall of such device. If, after providing an opportunity for such a hearing, the Secretary determines that inadequate grounds exist to support the actions required by the order, the Secretary shall vacate the order.

(2) —

(A) If, after providing an opportunity for an informal hearing under paragraph (1), the Secretary determines that the order should be amended to include a recall of the device with respect to which the order was issued, the Secretary shall, except as provided in subparagraphs (B) and (C), amend the order to require a recall. The Secretary shall specify a timetable in which the device recall will occur and shall require periodic reports to the Secretary describing the progress of the recall.

(B) An amended order under subparagraph (A) —

(i) shall —

(I) not include recall of a device from individuals, and

(II) not include recall of a device from device user facilities if the Secretary determines that the risk of recalling such device from the facilities presents a greater health risk than the health risk of not recalling the device from use, and

(ii) shall provide for notice to individuals subject to the risks associated with the use of such device.

In providing the notice required by clause (ii), the Secretary may use the assistance of health professionals who prescribed or used such a device for individuals. If a significant number of such individuals cannot be identified, the Secretary shall notify such individuals pursuant to section 705(b).

(3) The remedy provided by this subsection shall be in addition to remedies provided by subsections (a), (b), and (c).

SEC. 518A. [360h-1] PROGRAM TO IMPROVE THE DEVICE RECALL SYSTEM.

(a) IN GENERAL. — The Secretary shall —

(1) establish a program to routinely and systematically assess information relating to device recalls and use such information to proactively identify strategies for mitigating health risks presented by defective or unsafe devices;

(2) clarify procedures for conducting device recall audit checks to improve the ability of investigators to perform those checks in a consistent manner;

(3) develop detailed criteria for assessing whether a person performing a device recall has performed an effective correction or action plan for the recall; and

(4) document the basis for each termination by the Food and Drug Administration of a device recall.

(b) ASSESSMENT CONTENT. — The program established under subsection (a)(1) shall, at a minimum, identify —

(1) trends in the number and types of device recalls;

(2) devices that are most frequently the subject of a recall; and

(3) underlying causes of device recalls.

(c) DEFINITION. — In this section, the term "recall" means —

(1) the removal from the market of a device pursuant to an order of the Secretary under subsection (b) or (e) of section 518; or

(2) the correction or removal from the market of a device at the initiative of the manufacturer or importer of the device that is required to be reported to the Secretary under section 519(g).

SEC. 519. [360i] RECORDS AND REPORTS ON DEVICES.

(a) GENERAL RULE. — Every person who is a manufacturer or importer of a device intended for human use shall establish and maintain such records, make such reports, and provide such information, as the Secretary may by regulation reasonably require to assure that such device is not adulterated or misbranded and to otherwise assure its safety and effectiveness. Regulations prescribed under the preceding sentence —

(1) shall require a device manufacturer or importer to report to the Secretary whenever the manufacturer or importer receives or otherwise becomes aware of information that reasonably suggests that one of its marketed devices —

(A) may have caused or contributed to a death or serious injury, or

(B) has malfunctioned and that such device or a similar device marketed by the manufacturer or importer would be likely to cause or contribute to a death or serious injury if the malfunction were to recur, which report under this subparagraph—

(i) shall be submitted in accordance with part 803 of title 21, Code of Federal Regulations (or successor regulations), unless the Secretary grants an exemption or variance from, or an alternative to, a requirement under such regulations pursuant to section 803.19 of such part, if the device involved is—

(I) a class III device;

(II) a class II device that is permanently implantable, is life supporting, or is life sustaining; or

(III) a type of device which the Secretary has, by notice published in the Federal Register or letter to the person who is the manufacturer or importer of the device, indicated should be subject to such part 803 in order to protect the public health;

(ii) shall, if the device is not subject to clause (i), be submitted in accordance with criteria established by the Secretary for reports made pursuant to this clause, which criteria shall require the reports to be in summary form and made on a quarterly basis; or

(iii) shall, if the device is imported into the United States and for which part 803 of title 21, Code of Federal Regulations (or successor regulations) requires an importer to submit a report to the manufacturer, be submitted by the importer to the manufacturer in accordance with part 803 of title 21, Code of Federal Regulations (or successor regulations)

(2) shall define the term "serious injury" to mean an injury that —

(A) is life threatening,

(B) results in permanent impairment of a body function or permanent damage to a body structure, or

(C) necessitates medical or surgical intervention to preclude permanent impairment of a body function or permanent damage to a body structure;

(3) shall require reporting of other significant adverse device experiences as determined by the Secretary to be necessary to be reported;

(4) shall not impose requirements unduly burdensome to a device manufacturer or importer taking into account his cost of complying with such requirements and the need for the protection of the public health and the implementation of this Act;

(5) which prescribe the procedure for making requests for reports or information shall require that each request made under such regulations for submission of a report or information to the Secretary state the reason or purpose for such request and identify to the fullest extent practicable such report or information;

(6) which require submission of a report or information to the Secretary shall state the reason or purpose for the submission of such report or information and identify to the fullest extent practicable such report or information;

(7) may not require that the identity of any patient be disclosed in records, reports, or information required under this subsection unless required for the medical welfare of an individual, to determine the safety or effectiveness of a device, or to verify a record, report, or information submitted under this Act; and

(8) may not require a manufacturer or importer of a class I device to —

(A) maintain for such a device records respecting information not in the possession of the manufacturer or importer, or

(B) to submit for such a device to the Secretary any report or information —

(i) not in the possession of the manufacturer or importer, or

(ii) on a periodic basis,

unless such report or information is necessary to determine if the device should be reclassified or if the device is adulterated or misbranded.

In prescribing such regulations, the Secretary shall have due regard for the professional ethics of the medical profession and the interests of patients. The prohibitions of paragraph (7) of this subsection continue to apply to records, reports, and information concerning any individual who has been a patient, irrespective of whether or not he ceases to be a patient. The Secretary shall by regulation require distributors to keep records and make such records available to the Secretary upon request. Paragraphs (4) and (8) apply to distributors to the same extent and in the same manner as such paragraphs apply to manufacturers and importers.

(b) User Reports. —

(1) —

(A) Whenever a device user facility receives or otherwise becomes aware of information that reasonably suggests that a device has or may have caused or contributed to the death of a patient of the facility, the facility shall, as soon as practicable but not later than 10 working days after becoming aware of the information, report the information to the Secretary and, if the identity of the manufacturer is known, to the manufacturer of the device. In the case of deaths, the Secretary may by regulation prescribe a shorter period for the reporting of such information.

(B) Whenever a device user facility receives or otherwise becomes aware of —

(i) information that reasonably suggests that a device has or may have caused or contributed to the serious illness of, or serious injury to, a patient of the facility, or

(ii) other significant adverse device experiences as determined by the Secretary by regulation to be necessary to be reported,

the facility shall, as soon as practicable but not later than 10 working days after becoming aware of the information, report the information to the manufacturer of the device or to the Secretary if the identity of the manufacturer is not known.

(C) Each device user facility shall submit to the Secretary on an annual basis a summary of the reports made under subparagraphs (A) and (B). Such summary shall be submitted on January 1 of each year. The summary shall be in such form and contain such information from such reports as the Secretary may require and shall include —

(i) sufficient information to identify the facility which made the reports for which the summary is submitted,

(ii) in the case of any product which was the subject of a report, the product name, serial number, and model number,

(iii) the name and the address of the manufacturer of such device, and

(iv) a brief description of the event reported to the manufacturer.

(D) For purposes of subparagraphs (A), (B), and (C), a device user facility shall be treated as having received or otherwise become aware of information with respect to a device of that facility when medical personnel who are employed by or otherwise formally affiliated with the facility receive or otherwise become aware of information with respect to that device in the course of their duties.

(2) The Secretary may not disclose the identity of a device user facility which makes a report under paragraph (1) except in connection with —

(A) an action brought to enforce section 301(q), or

(B) a communication to a manufacturer of a device which is the subject of a report under paragraph (1).

This paragraph does not prohibit the Secretary from disclosing the identity of a device user facility making a report under paragraph (1) or any information in such a report to employees of the Department of Health and Human Services, to the Department of Justice, or to the duly authorized committees and subcommittees of the Congress.

(3) No report made under paragraph (1) by —

(A) a device user facility,

(B) an individual who is employed by or otherwise formally affiliated with such a facility, or

(C) a physician who is not required to make such a report,

shall be admissible into evidence or otherwise used in any civil action involving private parties unless the facility, individual, or physician who made the report had knowledge of the falsity of the information contained in the report.

(4) A report made under paragraph (1) does not affect any obligation of a manufacturer who receives the report to file a report as required under subsection (a).

(5) With respect to device user facilities:

(A) The Secretary shall by regulation plan and implement a program under which the Secretary limits user reporting under paragraphs (1) through (4) to a subset of other user facilities that constitutes a representative profile of user reports for device deaths and serious illnesses or serious injuries.

(B) During the period of planning the program under subparagraph (A), paragraphs (1) through (4) continue to apply.

(C) During the period in which the Secretary is providing for a transition to the full implementation of the program, paragraphs (1) through (4) apply except to the extent that the Secretary determines otherwise.

(D) On and after the date on which the program is fully implemented, paragraphs (1) through (4) do not apply to a user facility unless the facility is included in the subset referred to in subparagraph (A).

(E) Not later than 2 years after the date of the enactment of the Food and Drug Administration Modernization Act of 1997 [November 21, 1997 —Ed.], the Secretary shall submit to the Committee on Commerce of the House of Representatives, and to the Committee on Labor and Human Resources of the Senate, a report describing the plan developed by the Secretary under subparagraph (A) and the progress that has been made toward the implementation of the plan.

(6) For purposes of this subsection:

(A) The term "device user facility" means a hospital, ambulatory surgical facility, nursing home, or outpatient treatment facility which is not a physician's office. The Secretary may by regulation include an outpatient diagnostic facility which is not a physician's office in such term.

(B) The terms "serious illness" and "serious injury" mean illness or injury, respectively, that —

(i) is life threatening,

(ii) results in permanent impairment of a body function or permanent damage to a body structure, or

(iii) necessitates medical or surgical intervention to preclude permanent impairment of a body function or permanent damage to a body structure.

(c) Persons Exempt. — Subsection (a) shall not apply to —

(1) any practitioner who is licensed by law to prescribe or administer devices intended for use in humans and who manufactures or imports devices solely for use in the course of his professional practice;

(2) any person who manufactures or imports devices intended for use in humans solely for such person's use in research or teaching and not for sale (including any person who uses a device under an exemption granted under section 520(g)); and

(3) any other class of persons as the Secretary may by regulation exempt from subsection (a) upon a finding that compliance with the requirements of such subsection by such class with respect to a device is not necessary to

(A) assure that a device is not adulterated or misbranded or

(B) otherwise to assure its safety and effectiveness.

(d) [Repealed.]

(e) Device Tracking. —

(1) The Secretary may by order require a manufacturer to adopt a method of tracking a class II or class III device —

(A) the failure of which would be reasonably likely to have serious adverse health consequences; or

(B) which is —

(i) intended to be implanted in the human body for more than one year, or

(ii) a life sustaining or life supporting device used outside a device user facility.

(2) Any patient receiving a device subject to tracking under paragraph (1) may refuse to release, or refuse permission to release, the patient's name, address, social security number, or other identifying information for the purpose of tracking.

(f) Unique Device Identification System. — Not later than December 31, 2012, the Secretary shall issue proposed regulations establishing a unique device identification system for medical devices requiring the label of devices to bear a unique identifier, unless the Secretary requires an alternative placement or provides an exception for a particular device or type of device. The unique identifier shall adequately identify the device through distribution and use, and may include information on the lot or serial number. The Secretary shall finalize the proposed regulations not later than 6 months after the close of the comment period and shall implement the final regulations with respect to devices that are implantable, life-saving, or life sustaining not later than 2 years after the regulations are finalized, taking into account patient access to medical devices and therapies.

(g) Reports of Removals and Corrections. —

(1) Except as provided in paragraph (2), the Secretary shall by regulation require a manufacturer or importer of a device to report promptly to the Secretary any correction or removal of a device undertaken by such manufacturer or importer if the removal or correction was undertaken —

(A) to reduce a risk to health posed by the device, or

(B) to remedy a violation of this Act caused by the device which may present a risk to health.

A manufacturer or importer of a device who undertakes a correction or removal of a device which is not required to be reported under this paragraph shall keep a record of such correction or removal.

(2) No report of the corrective action or removal of a device may be required under paragraph (1) if a report of the corrective action or removal is required and has been submitted under subsection (a).

(3) For purposes of paragraphs (1) and (2), the terms "correction" and "removal" do not include routine servicing.

(h) Inclusion of Devices in the Postmarket Risk Identification and Analysis System. —

(1) In General. —

(A) Application to Devices. — The Secretary shall amend the procedures established and maintained under clauses (i), (ii), (iii), and (v) of section 505(k)(3)(C) in order to expand the postmarket risk identification and analysis system established under such section to include and apply to devices.

(B) Exception. — Subclause (II) of clause (i) of section 505(k)(3)(C) shall not apply to devices.

(C) Clarification. — With respect to devices, the private sector health-related electronic data provided under section 505(k)(3)(C)(i)(III)(bb) may include medical device utilization data, health insurance claims data, and procedure and device registries.

(2) Data. — In expanding the system as described in paragraph (1)(A), the Secretary shall use relevant data with respect to devices cleared under section 510(k) or approved under section 515, including claims data, patient survey data, and any other data deemed appropriate by the Secretary.

(3) Stakeholder Input. — To help ensure effective implementation of the system as described in paragraph (1) with respect to devices, the Secretary shall engage outside stakeholders in development of the system, and gather information from outside stakeholders regarding the content of an effective sentinel program, through a public hearing, advisory committee meeting, maintenance of a public docket, or other similar public measures.

(4) Voluntary Surveys. — Chapter 35 of title 44, United States Code, shall not apply to the collection of voluntary information from health care providers, such as voluntary surveys or questionnaires, initiated by the Secretary for purposes of postmarket risk identification, mitigation, and analysis for devices.

(i) Postmarket Pilot. —

(1) In General. — In order to provide timely and reliable information on the safety and effectiveness of devices approved under section 515, cleared under section 510(k), or classified under section 513(f)(2), including responses to adverse events and malfunctions, and to advance the objectives of part 803 of title 21, Code of Federal Regulations (or successor regulations), and advance the objectives of, and evaluate innovative new methods of compliance with, this section and section 522, the Secretary shall, within one year of the date of enactment of the FDA Reauthorization Act of 2017, initiate one or more pilot projects for voluntary participation by a manufacturer or manufacturers of a device or device type, or continue existing projects, in accordance with paragraph (3), that —

(A) are designed to efficiently generate reliable and timely safety and active surveillance data for use by the Secretary or manufacturers of the devices that are involved in the pilot project;

(B) inform the development of methods, systems, data criteria, and programs that could be used to support safety and active surveillance activities for devices included or not included in such project;

(C) may be designed and conducted in coordination with a comprehensive system for evaluating medical device technology that operates under a governing board with appropriate representation of stakeholders, including patient groups and device manufacturers;

(D) use electronic health data including claims data, patient survey data, or any other data, as the Secretary determines appropriate; and

(E) prioritize devices and device types that meet one or more of the following criteria:

(i) Devices and device types for which the collection and analysis of real world evidence regarding a device's safety and effectiveness is likely to advance public health.

(ii) Devices and device types that are widely used.

(iii) Devices and device types, the failure of which has significant health consequences.

(iv) Devices and device types for which the Secretary —

(I) has received public recommendations in accordance with paragraph (2)(B); and

(II) has determined to meet one or more of the criteria under clause (i), (ii), or (iii) and is appropriate for such a pilot project.

(2) Participation. — The Secretary shall establish the conditions and processes —

(A) under which a manufacturer of a device may voluntarily participate in a pilot project described in paragraph (1); and

(B) for facilitating public recommendations for devices to be prioritized under such a pilot project, including requirements for the data necessary to support such a recommendation.

(3) Continuation of Ongoing Projects. — The Secretary may continue or expand projects, with respect to providing timely and reliable information on the safety and effectiveness of devices approved under section 515, cleared under section 510(k), or classified under section 513(f)(2), that are being carried out as of the date of the enactment of the FDA Reauthorization Act of 2017. The Secretary shall, beginning on such date of enactment, take such steps as may be necessary —

(A) to ensure such projects meet the requirements of subparagraphs (A) through (E) of paragraph (1); and

(B) to increase the voluntary participation in such projects of manufacturers of devices and facilitate public recommendations for any devices prioritized under such a project.

(4) Implementation. —

(A) Contracting Authority. — The Secretary may carry out a pilot project meeting the criteria specified in subparagraphs (A) through (E) of paragraph (1) or a project continued or expanded under paragraph (3) by entering into contracts, cooperative agreements, grants, or other appropriate agreements with public or private entities that have a significant presence in the United States and meet the following conditions:

(i) If such an entity is a component of another organization, the entity and the organization have established an agreement under which appropriate security measures are implemented to maintain the confidentiality and privacy of the data described in paragraph (1)(D) and such agreement ensures that the entity will not make an unauthorized disclosure of such data to the other components of the organization in breach of requirements with respect to confidentiality and privacy of such data established under such security measures.

(ii) In the case of the termination or nonrenewal of such a contract, cooperative agreement, grant, or other appropriate agreement, the entity or entities involved shall comply with each of the following:

(I) The entity or entities shall continue to comply with the requirements with respect to confidentiality and privacy referred to in clause (i) with respect to all data disclosed to the entity under such an agreement.

(II) The entity or entities shall return any data disclosed to such entity pursuant to this subsection and to which it would not otherwise have access or, if returning such data is not practicable, destroy the data.

(iii) The entity or entities shall have one or more qualifications with respect to—

(I) research, statistical, epidemiologic, or clinical capability and expertise to conduct and complete the activities under this subsection, including the capability and expertise to provide the Secretary access to de-identified data consistent with the requirements of this subsection;

(II) an information technology infrastructure to support electronic data and operational standards to provide security for such data, as appropriate;

(III) experience with, and expertise on, the development of research on, and surveillance of, device safety and effectiveness using electronic health data; or

(IV) such other expertise which the Secretary determines necessary to carry out such a project.

(B) Review of Contract in the Event of a Merger or Acquisition. — The Secretary shall review any contract, cooperative agreement, grant, or other appropriate agreement entered into under this paragraph with an entity meeting the conditions specified in subparagraph (A) in the event of a merger or acquisition of the entity in order to ensure that the requirements specified in this subsection will continue to be met.

(5) Compliance with Requirements for Records or Reports on Devices. — The participation of a manufacturer in pilot projects under this subsection or a project continued or expanded under paragraph (3) shall not affect the eligibility of such manufacturer to participate in any quarterly reporting program with respect to devices carried out under this section 519 or section 522. The Secretary may determine that, for a specified time period to be determined by the Secretary, a manufacturer's participation in a pilot project under this subsection or a project continued or expanded under paragraph (3) may meet the applicable requirements of this section or section 522, if—

(A) the project has demonstrated success in capturing relevant adverse event information; and

(B) the Secretary has established procedures for making adverse event and safety information collected from such project public, to the extent possible.

(6) Privacy Requirements. — With respect to the disclosure of any health information collected through a project conducted under this subsection —

(A) individually identifiable health information so collected shall not be disclosed when presenting any information from such project; and

(B) any such disclosure shall be made in compliance with regulations issued pursuant to section 264(c) of the Health Insurance Portability and Accountability Act of 1996 (42 U.S.C. 1320d–2 note) and sections 552 and 552a of title 5, United States Code.

(7) Limitations. — No pilot project under this subsection, or in coordination with the comprehensive system described in paragraph (1)(C), may allow for an entity participating in such project, other than the Secretary, to make determinations of safety or effectiveness, or substantial equivalence, for purposes of this Act.

(8) Other Projects Required to Comply. — Paragraphs (1)(B), (4)(A)(i), (4)(A)(ii), (5), (6), and (7) shall apply with respect to any pilot project undertaken in coordination with the comprehensive system described in paragraph (1)(C) that relates to the use of real world evidence for devices in the same manner and to the same extent as such paragraphs apply with respect to pilot projects conducted under this subsection.

(9) Report to Congress. — Not later than 18 months after the date of enactment of this Act, and annually thereafter, the Secretary shall submit to the Committee on Energy and Commerce of the House of Representatives and the Committee on Health, Education, Labor and Pensions of the Senate a report containing a description of the pilot projects being conducted under this subsection and projects continued or expanded pursuant to paragraph (3), including for each such project—

(A) how the project is being implemented in accordance with paragraph (4), including how such project is being implemented through a contract, cooperative agreement, grant, or other appropriate agreement, if applicable;

(B) the number of manufacturers that have agreed to participate in such project;

(C) the data sources used to conduct such project;

(D) the devices or device categories involved in such project;

(E) the number of patients involved in such project; and

(F) the findings of the project in relation to device safety, including adverse events, malfunctions, and other safety information.

(10) Sunset. — The Secretary may not carry out a pilot project initiated by the Secretary under this subsection after October 1, 2022.

Sec. 520. [360j] General Provisions Respecting Control of Devices Intended for Human Use.

(a) General Rule. — Any requirement authorized by or under section 501, 502, 510, or 519 applicable to a device intended for human use shall apply to such device until the applicability of the requirement to the device has been changed by action taken under section 513, 514, or 515 or under subsection (g) of this section, and any requirement established by or under section 501, 502, 510, or 519 which is inconsistent with a requirement imposed on such device under section 514 or 515 or under subsection (g) of this section shall not apply to such device.

(b) Custom Devices. —

(1) In General. — The requirements of sections 514 and 515 shall not apply to a device that —

(A) is created or modified in order to comply with the order of an individual physician or dentist (or any other specially qualified person designated under regulations promulgated by the Secretary after an opportunity for an oral hearing);

(B) in order to comply with an order described in subparagraph (A), necessarily deviates from an otherwise applicable performance standard under section 514 or requirement under section 515;

(C) is not generally available in the United States in finished form through labeling or advertising by the manufacturer, importer, or distributor for commercial distribution;

(D) is designed to treat a unique pathology or physiological condition that no other device is domestically available to treat;

(E) —

(i) is intended to meet the special needs of such physician or dentist (or other specially qualified person so designated) in the course of the professional practice of such physician or dentist (or other specially qualified person so designated); or

(ii) is intended for use by an individual patient named in such order of such physician or dentist (or other specially qualified person so designated);

(F) is assembled from components or manufactured and finished on a case-by-case basis to accommodate the unique needs of individuals described in clause (i) or (ii) of subparagraph (E); and

(G) may have common, standardized design characteristics, chemical and material compositions, and manufacturing processes as commercially distributed devices.

(2) Limitations. — Paragraph (1) shall apply to a device only if —

(A) such device is for the purpose of treating a sufficiently rare condition, such that conducting clinical investigations on such device would be impractical;

(B) production of such device under paragraph (1) is limited to no more than 5 units per year of a particular device type, provided that such replication otherwise complies with this section; and

(C) the manufacturer of such device notifies the Secretary on an annual basis, in a manner prescribed by the Secretary, of the manufacture of such device.

(3) Guidance. — Not later than 2 years after the date of enactment of this section, the Secretary shall issue final guidance on replication of multiple devices described in paragraph (2)(B).

(c) Trade Secrets. — Any information reported to or otherwise obtained by the Secretary or his representative under section 513, 514, 515, 516, 518, 519, or 704 or under subsection (f) or (g) of this section which is exempt from disclosure pursuant to subsection (a) of section 552 of title 5, United States Code, by reason of subsection (b)(4) of such section shall be considered confidential and shall not be disclosed and may not be used by the Secretary as the basis for the reclassification of a device from class III to class II or class I or as the basis for the establishment or amendment of a performance standard under section 514 for a device reclassified from class III to class II, except

(1) in accordance with subsection (h), and

(2) that such information may be disclosed to other officers or employees concerned with carrying out this Act or when relevant in any proceeding under this Act (other than section 513 or 514 thereof).

(d) Notices And Findings. — Each notice of proposed rulemaking under section 513, 514, 515, 516, 518, or 519, or under this section, any other notice which is published in the Federal Register with respect to any other action taken under any such section and which states the reasons for such action, and each publication of findings required to be made in connection with rulemaking under any such section shall set forth —

(1) the manner in which interested persons may examine data and other information on which the notice or findings is based, and

(2) the period within which interested persons may present their comments on the notice or findings (including the need therefor) orally or in writing, which period shall be at least sixty days but may not exceed ninety days unless the time is extended by the Secretary by a notice published in the Federal Register stating good cause therefor.

(e) Restricted Devices. —

(1) The Secretary may by regulation require that a device be restricted to sale, distribution, or use —

(A) only upon the written or oral authorization of a practitioner licensed by law to administer or use such device, or

(B) upon such other conditions as the Secretary may prescribe in such regulation,

if, because of its potentiality for harmful effect or the collateral measures necessary to its use, the Secretary determines that there cannot otherwise be reasonable assurance of its safety and effectiveness. No condition prescribed under subparagraph (B) may restrict the use of a device to persons with specific training or experience in its use or to persons for use in certain facilities unless the Secretary determines that such a restriction is required for the safe and effective use of the device. No such condition may exclude a person from using a device solely because the person does not have the training or experience to make him eligible for certification by a certifying board recognized by the American Board of Medical Specialties or has not been certified by such a Board. A device subject to a regulation under this subsection is a restricted device.

(2) The label of a restricted device shall bear such appropriate statements of the restrictions required by a regulation under paragraph (1) as the Secretary may in such regulation prescribe.

(f) Good Manufacturing Practice Requirements. —

(1) —

(A) The Secretary may, in accordance with subparagraph (B), prescribe regulations requiring that the methods used in, and the facilities and controls used for, the manufacture, pre-production design validation (including a process to assess the performance of a device but not including an evaluation of the safety or effectiveness of a device), packing, storage, and installation of a device conform to current good manufacturing practice, as prescribed in such regulations, to assure that the device will be safe and effective and otherwise in compliance with this Act.

(B) Before the Secretary may promulgate any regulation under subparagraph (A) he shall —

(i) afford the advisory committee established under paragraph (3) an opportunity to submit recommendations to him with respect to the regulation proposed to be promulgated;

(ii) afford opportunity for an oral hearing; and

(iii) ensure that such regulation conforms, to the extent practicable, with internationally recognized standards defining quality systems, or parts of the standards, for medical devices.

The Secretary shall provide the advisory committee a reasonable time to make its recommendation with respect to proposed regulations under subparagraph (A).

(2) —

(A) Any person subject to any requirement prescribed by regulations under paragraph (1) may petition the Secretary for an exemption or variance from such requirement. Such a petition shall be submitted to the Secretary in such form and manner as he shall prescribe and shall —

(i) in the case of a petition for an exemption from a requirement, set forth the basis for the petitioner's determination that compliance with the requirement is not required to assure that the device will be safe and effective and otherwise in compliance with this Act,

(ii) in the case of a petition for a variance from a requirement, set forth the methods proposed to be used in, and the facilities and controls proposed to be used for, the manufacture, packing, storage, and installation of the device in lieu of the methods, facilities, and controls prescribed by the requirement, and

(iii) contain such other information as the Secretary shall prescribe.

(B) The Secretary may refer to the advisory committee established under paragraph (3) any petition submitted under subparagraph (A). The advisory committee shall report its recommendations to the Secretary with respect to a petition referred to it within sixty days of the date of the petition's referral. Within sixty days after —

(i) the date the petition was submitted to the Secretary under subparagraph (A), or

(ii) if the petition was referred to an advisory committee, the expiration of the sixty-day period beginning on the date the petition was referred to the advisory committee,

whichever occurs later, the Secretary shall by order either deny the petition or approve it.

(C) The Secretary may approve —

(i) a petition for an exemption for a device from a requirement if he determines that compliance with such requirement is not required to assure that the device will be safe and effective and otherwise in compliance with this Act, and

(ii) a petition for a variance for a device from a requirement if he determines that the methods to be used in, and the facilities and controls to be used for, the manufacture, packing, storage, and installation of the device in lieu of the methods, controls, and facilities prescribed by the requirement are sufficient to assure that the device will be safe and effective and otherwise in compliance with this Act.

An order of the Secretary approving a petition for a variance shall prescribe such conditions respecting the methods used in, and the facilities and controls used for, the manufacture, packing, storage, and installation of the device to be granted the variance under the petition as may be necessary to assure that the device will be safe and effective and otherwise in compliance with this Act.

(D) After the issuance of an order under subparagraph (B) respecting a petition, the petitioner shall have an opportunity for an informal hearing on such order.

(3) The Secretary shall establish an advisory committee for the purpose of advising and making recommendations to him with respect to regulations proposed to be promulgated under paragraph (1)(A) and the approval or disapproval of petitions submitted under paragraph (2). The advisory committee shall be composed of nine members as follows:

(A) Three of the members shall be appointed from persons who are officers or employees of any State or local government or of the Federal Government.

(B) Two of the members shall be appointed from persons who are representative of interests of the device manufacturing industry; two of the members shall be appointed from persons who are representative of the interests of physicians and other health professionals; and two of the members shall be representative of the interests of the general public.

Members of the advisory committee who are not officers or employees of the United States, while attending conferences or meetings of the committee or otherwise engaged in its business, shall be entitled to receive compensation at rates to be fixed by the Secretary, which rates may not exceed the daily equivalent of the rate in effect for grade GS–18 of the General Schedule, for each day (including traveltime) they are so engaged; and while so serving away from their homes or regular places of business each member may be allowed travel expenses, including per diem in lieu of subsistence, as authorized by section 5703 of title 5 of the United States Code for persons in the Government service employed intermittently. The Secretary shall designate one of the members of the advisory committee to serve as its chairman. The Secretary shall furnish the advisory committee with clerical and other assistance. Section 14 of the Federal Advisory Committee Act shall not apply with respect to the duration of the advisory committee established under this paragraph.

(g) Exemption for Devices for Investigational Use. —

(1) It is the purpose of this subsection to encourage to the extent consistent with the protection of the public health and safety and with ethical standards, the discovery and development of useful devices intended for human use and to that end to maintain optimum freedom for scientific investigators in their pursuit of that purpose.

(2) —

(A) The Secretary shall, within the one hundred and twenty-day period beginning on the date of the enactment of this section, by regulation prescribe procedures and conditions under which devices intended for human use may upon application be granted an exemption from the requirements of section 502, 510, 514, 515, 516, 519, or 721 or subsection (e) or (f) of this section or from any combination of such requirements to permit the investigational use of such devices by experts qualified by scientific training and experience to investigate the safety and effectiveness of such devices.

(B) The conditions prescribed pursuant to subparagraph (A) shall include the following:

(i) A requirement that an application be submitted to the Secretary before an exemption may be granted and that the application be submitted in such form and manner as the Secretary shall specify.

(ii) A requirement that the person applying for an exemption for a device assure the establishment and maintenance of such records, and the making of such reports to the Secretary of safety or effectiveness data obtained as a result of the investigational use of the device during the exemption, as the Secretary determines will enable him to assure compliance with such conditions, review the progress of the investigation, and evaluate the safety and effectiveness of the device.

(iii) Such other requirements as the Secretary may determine to be necessary for the protection of the public health and safety.

(C) Procedures and conditions prescribed pursuant to subparagraph (A) for an exemption may appropriately vary depending on

(i) the scope and duration of clinical testing to be conducted under such exemption,

(ii) the number of human subjects that are to be involved in such testing,

(iii) the need to permit changes to be made in the device subject to the exemption during testing conducted in accordance with a clinical testing plan required under paragraph (3)(A), and

(iv) whether the clinical testing of such device is for the purpose of developing data to obtain approval for the commercial distribution of such device.

(3) Procedures and conditions prescribed pursuant to paragraph (2)(A) shall require, as a condition to the exemption of any device to be the subject of testing involving human subjects, that the person applying for the exemption —

(A) submit a plan for any proposed clinical testing of the device and a report of prior investigations of the device (including, where appropriate, tests on animals) adequate to justify the proposed clinical testing —

(i) to the institutional review committee established in accordance with regulations of the Secretary to supervise clinical testing of devices in the facilities where the proposed clinical testing is to be conducted, or

(ii) to the Secretary, if —

(I) no such committee exists, or

(II) the Secretary finds that the process of review by such committee is inadequate (whether or not the plan for such testing has been approved by such committee),

for review for adequacy to justify the commencement of such testing; and, unless the plan and report are submitted to the Secretary, submit to the Secretary a summary of the plan and a report of prior investigations of the device (including, where appropriate, tests on animals);

(B) promptly notify the Secretary (under such circumstances and in such manner as the Secretary prescribes) of approval by an institutional review committee of any clinical testing plan submitted to it in accordance with subparagraph (A);

(C) in the case of a device to be distributed to investigators for testing, obtain signed agreements from each of such investigators that any testing of the device involving human subjects will be under such investigator's supervision and in accordance with subparagraph (D) and submit such agreements to the Secretary; and

(D) assure that informed consent will be obtained from each human subject (or his representative) of proposed clinical testing involving such device, except where, subject to such conditions as the Secretary may prescribe—

(i) the proposed clinical testing poses no more than minimal risk to the human subject and includes appropriate safeguards to protect the rights, safety, and welfare of the human subject; or

(ii) the investigator conducting or supervising the proposed clinical testing of the device determines in writing that there exists a life threatening situation involving the human subject of such testing which necessitates the use of such device and it is not feasible to obtain informed consent from the subject and there is not sufficient time to obtain such consent from his representative.

The determination required by subparagraph (D)(ii) shall be concurred in by a licensed physician who is not involved in the testing of the human subject with respect to which such determination is made unless immediate use of the device is required to save the life of the human subject of such testing and there is not sufficient time to obtain such concurrence.

(4) —

(A) An application, submitted in accordance with the procedures prescribed by regulations under paragraph (2), for an exemption for a device (other than an exemption from section 516) shall be deemed approved on the thirtieth day after the submission of the application to the Secretary unless on or before such day the Secretary by order disapproves the application and notifies the applicant of the disapproval of the application.

(B) The Secretary may disapprove an application only if he finds that the investigation with respect to which the application is submitted does not conform to procedures and conditions prescribed under regulations under paragraph (2). Such a notification shall contain the order of disapproval and a complete statement of the reasons for the Secretary's disapproval of the application and afford the applicant opportunity for an informal hearing on the disapproval order.

(C) Consistent with paragraph (1), the Secretary shall not disapprove an application under this subsection because the Secretary determines that —

(i) the investigation may not support a substantial equivalence or de novo classification determination or approval of the device;

(ii) the investigation may not meet a requirement, including a data requirement, relating to the approval or clearance of a device; or

(iii) an additional or different investigation may be necessary to support clearance or approval of the device.

(5) The Secretary may by order withdraw an exemption granted under this subsection for a device if the Secretary determines that the conditions applicable to the device under this subsection for such exemption are not met. Such an order may be issued only after opportunity for an informal hearing, except that such an order may be issued before the provision of an opportunity for an informal hearing if the Secretary determines that the continuation of testing under the exemption with respect to which the order is to be issued will result in an unreasonable risk to the public health.

(6) —

(A) Not later than 1 year after the date of the enactment of the Food and Drug Administration Modernization Act of 1997 [November 21, 1997 — Ed.], the Secretary shall by regulation establish, with respect to a device for which an exemption under this subsection is in effect, procedures and conditions that, without requiring an additional approval of an application for an exemption or the approval of a supplement to such an application, permit —

(i) developmental changes in the device (including manufacturing changes) that do not constitute a significant change in design or in basic principles of operation and that are made in response to information gathered during the course of an investigation; and

(ii) changes or modifications to clinical protocols that do not affect —

(I) the validity of the data or information resulting from the completion of an approved protocol, or the relationship of likely patient risk to benefit relied upon to approve a protocol;

(II) the scientific soundness of an investigational plan submitted under paragraph (3)(A); or

(III) the rights, safety, or welfare of the human subjects involved in the investigation.

(B) Regulations under subparagraph (A) shall provide that a change or modification described in such subparagraph may be made if —

(i) the sponsor of the investigation determines, on the basis of credible information (as defined by the Secretary) that the applicable conditions under subparagraph (A) are met; and

(ii) the sponsor submits to the Secretary, not later than 5 days after making the change or modification, a notice of the change or modification.

(7) —

(A) In the case of a person intending to investigate the safety or effectiveness of a class III device or any implantable device, the Secretary shall ensure that the person has an opportunity, prior to submitting an application to the Secretary or to an institutional review committee, to submit to the Secretary, for review, an investigational plan (including a clinical protocol). If the applicant submits a written request for a meeting with the Secretary regarding such review, the Secretary shall, not later than 30 days after receiving the request, meet with the applicant for the purpose of reaching agreement regarding the investigational plan (including a clinical protocol). The written request shall include a detailed description of the device, a detailed description of the proposed conditions of use of the device, a proposed plan (including a clinical protocol) for determining whether there is a reasonable assurance of effectiveness, and, if available, information regarding the expected performance from the device.

(B) Any agreement regarding the parameters of an investigational plan (including a clinical protocol) that is reached between the Secretary and a sponsor or applicant shall be reduced to writing and made part of the administrative record by the Secretary. Any such agreement shall not be changed, except —

(i) with the written agreement of the sponsor or applicant; or

(ii) pursuant to a decision, made in accordance with subparagraph (C) by the director of the office in which the device involved is reviewed, that a substantial scientific issue essential to determining the safety and effectiveness of the device has been identified.

(C) A decision under paragraph (B)(ii) by the director shall be in writing, and may be made only after the Secretary has provided to the sponsor or applicant an opportunity for a meeting at which the director and the sponsor or applicant are present and at which the director documents the scientific issue involved.

(8)

(A) At any time, the Secretary may prohibit the sponsor of an investigation from conducting the investigation (referred to in this paragraph as a "clinical hold") if the Secretary makes a determination described in subparagraph (B). The Secretary shall specify the basis for the clinical hold, including the specific information available to the Secretary which served as the basis for such clinical hold, and confirm such determination in writing.

(B) For purposes of subparagraph (A), a determination described in this subparagraph with respect to a clinical hold is a determination that —

(i) the device involved represents an unreasonable risk to the safety of the persons who are the subjects of the clinical investigation, taking into account the qualifications of the clinical investigators, information about the device, the design of the clinical investigation, the condition for which the device is to be investigated, and the health status of the subjects involved; or

(ii) the clinical hold should be issued for such other reasons as the Secretary may by regulation establish.

(C) Any written request to the Secretary from the sponsor of an investigation that a clinical hold be removed shall receive a decision, in writing and specifying the reasons therefor, within 30 days after receipt of such request. Any such request shall include sufficient information to support the removal of such clinical hold.

(h) Release of Safety and Effectiveness Information. —

(1) The Secretary shall promulgate regulations under which a detailed summary of information respecting the safety and effectiveness of a device which information was submitted to the Secretary and which was the basis for —

(A) an order under section 515(d)(1)(A) approving an application for premarket approval for the device or denying approval of such an application or an order under section 515(e) withdrawing approval of such an application for the device,

(B) an order under section 515(f)(6)(A) revoking an approved protocol for the device, an order under section 515(f)(6)(B) declaring a protocol for the device completed or not completed, or an order under section 515(f)(7) revoking the approval of the device, or

(C) an order approving an application under subsection (g) for an exemption for the device from section 516 or an order disapproving, or withdrawing approval of, an application for an exemption under such subsection for the device, shall be made available to the public upon issuance of the order. Summaries of information made available pursuant to this paragraph respecting a device shall include information respecting any adverse effects on health of the device.

(2) The Secretary shall promulgate regulations under which each advisory committee established under section 515(g)(2)(B) shall make available to the public a detailed summary of information respecting the safety and effectiveness of a device which information was submitted to the advisory committee and which was the basis for its recommendation to the Secretary made pursuant to section 515(g)(2)(A). A summary of information upon which such a recommendation is based shall be made available pursuant to this paragraph only after the issuance of the order with respect to which the recommendation was made and each summary shall include information respecting any adverse effect on health of the device subject to such order.

(3) Except as provided in paragraph (4), any information respecting a device which is made available pursuant to paragraph (1) or (2) of this subsection

(A) may not be used to establish the safety or effectiveness of another device for purposes of this Act by any person other than the person who submitted the information so made available, and

(B) shall be made available subject to subsection (c) of this section.

(4) —

(A) Subject to subparagraph (C), any information contained in an application for premarket approval filed with the Secretary pursuant to section 515(c) (including information from clinical and pre-clinical tests or studies that demonstrate the safety and effectiveness of a device, but excluding descriptions of methods of manufacture and product composition and other trade secrets) shall be available, 6 years after the application has been approved by the Secretary, for use by the Secretary in —

(i) approving another device;

(ii) determining whether a product development protocol has been completed, under section 515 for another device;

(iii) establishing a performance standard or special control under this Act; or

(iv) classifying or reclassifying another device under section 513 and subsection (l)(2).

(B) The publicly available detailed summaries of information respecting the safety and effectiveness of devices required by paragraph (1)(A) shall be available for use by the Secretary as the evidentiary basis for the regulatory action described in subparagraph (A).

(C) No information contained in an application for premarket approval filed with the Secretary pursuant to section 515(c) may be used to approve or clear any application submitted under section 515 or 510(k) or to classify a product under section 513(f)(2) for a combination product containing as a constituent part an approved drug (as defined in section 503(g)(5)(B)) unless—

(i) the application includes the certification or statement referenced in section 503(g)(5)(A);

(ii) the applicant provides notice as described in section 503(g)(5)(A); and

(iii) the Secretary's approval of such application is subject to the provisions in section 503(g)(5)(C).

(i) Proceedings of Advisory Panels and Committees. — Each panel under section 513 and each advisory committee established under section 514(b)(5)(B) or 515(g) or under subsection (f) of this section shall make and maintain a transcript of any proceeding of the panel or committee. Each such panel and committee shall delete from any transcript made pursuant to this subsection information which under subsection (c) of this section is to be considered confidential.

(j) Traceability Requirements. — Except as provided in section 519(e), no regulation under this Act may impose on a type or class of device requirements for the traceability of such type or class of device unless such requirements are necessary to assure the protection of the public health.

(k) Research and Development. — The Secretary may enter into contracts for research, testing, and demonstrations respecting devices and may obtain devices for research, testing, and demonstration purposes without regard to sections 3648 and 3709 of the Revised Statutes (31 U.S.C. 529, 41 U.S.C. 5).

(l) Transitional Provisions for Devices Considered as New Drugs. —

(1) Any device intended for human use —

(A) for which on the date of enactment of the Medical Device Amendments of 1976 [May 28, 1976 — Ed.] (hereinafter in this subsection referred to as the "enactment date") an approval of an application submitted under section 505(b) was in effect;

(B) for which such an application was filed on or before the enactment date and with respect to which application no order of approval or refusing to approve had been issued on such date under subsection (c) or (d) of such section;

(C) for which on the enactment date an exemption under subsection (i) of such section was in effect;

(D) which is within a type of device described in subparagraph (A), (B), or (C) and is substantially equivalent to another device within that type;

(E) which the Secretary in a notice published in the Federal Register before the enactment date has declared to be a new drug subject to section 505; or

(F) with respect to which on the enactment date an action is pending in a United States court under section 302, 303, or 304 for an alleged violation of a provision of section 301 which enforces a requirement of section 505 or for an alleged violation of section 505(a),

is classified in class III unless the Secretary in response to a petition submitted under paragraph (2) has classified such device in class I or II.

(2) The Secretary may initiate the reclassification of a device classified into class III under paragraph (1) of this subsection or the manufacturer or importer of a device classified under paragraph (1) may petition the Secretary (in such form and manner as he shall prescribe) for the issuance of an order classifying the device in class I or class II. Within thirty days of the filing of such a petition, the Secretary shall notify the petitioner of any deficiencies in the petition which prevent the Secretary from making a decision on the petition. Except as provided in paragraph (3)(D)(ii), within one hundred and eighty days after the filing of a petition under this paragraph, the Secretary shall, after consultation with the appropriate panel under section 513, by order either deny the petition or order the classification, in accordance with the criteria prescribed by section 513(a)(1)(A) or 513(a)(1)(B), of the device in class I or class II.

(3) —

(A) In the case of a device which is described in paragraph (1)(A) and which is in class III —

(i) such device shall on the enactment date be considered a device with an approved application under section 515, and

(ii) the requirements applicable to such device before the enactment date under section 505 shall continue to apply to such device until changed by the Secretary as authorized by this Act.

(B) In the case of a device which is described in paragraph (1)(B) and which is in class III, an application for such device shall be considered as having been filed under section 515 on the enactment date. The period in which the Secretary shall act on such application in accordance with section 515(d)(1) shall be one hundred and eighty days from the enactment date (or such greater period as the Secretary and the applicant may agree upon after the Secretary has made the finding required by section 515(d)(1)(B)(i)) less the number of days in the period beginning on the date an application for such device was filed under section 505 and ending on the enactment date. After the expiration of such period such device is required, unless exempt under subsection (g), to have in effect an approved application under section 515.

(C) A device which is described in paragraph (1)(C) and which is in class III shall be considered a new drug until the expiration of the ninety-day period beginning on the date of the promulgation of regulations under subsection (g) of this section. After the expiration of such period such device is required, unless exempt under subsection (g), to have in effect an approved application under section 515.

(D) —

(i) Except as provided in clauses (ii) and (iii), a device which is described in subparagraph (D), (E), or (F) of paragraph (1) and which is in class III is required, unless exempt under subsection (g) of this section, to have on and after sixty days after the enactment date in effect an approved application under section 515.

(ii) If —

(I) a petition is filed under paragraph (2) for a device described in subparagraph (D), (E), or (F) of paragraph (1), or

(II) an application for premarket approval is filed under section 515 for such a device,

within the sixty-day period beginning on the enactment date (or within such greater period as the Secretary, after making the finding required under section 515(d)(1)(B), and the petitioner or applicant may agree upon), the Secretary shall act on such petition or application in accordance with paragraph (2) or section 515 except that the period within which the Secretary must act on the petition or application shall be within the one hundred and twenty-day period beginning on the date the petition or application is filed. If such a petition or application is filed within such sixty-day (or greater) period, clause (i) of this subparagraph shall not apply to such device before the expiration of such one hundred and twenty- day period, or if such petition is denied or such application is denied approval, before the date of such denial, whichever occurs first.

(iii) In the case of a device which is described in subparagraph (E) of paragraph (1), which the Secretary in a notice published in the Federal Register after March 31, 1976, declared to be a new drug subject to section 505, and which is in class III —

(I) the device shall, after eighteen months after the enactment date, have in effect an approved application under section 515 unless exempt under subsection (g) of this section, and

(II) the Secretary may, during the period beginning one hundred and eighty days after the enactment date and ending eighteen months after such date, restrict the use of the device to investigational use by experts qualified by scientific training and experience to investigate the safety and effectiveness of such device, and to investigational use in accordance with the requirements applicable under regulations under subsection (g) of this section to investigational use of devices granted an exemption under such subsection.

If the requirements under subsection (g) of this section are made applicable to the investigational use of such a device, they shall be made applicable in such a manner that the device shall be made reasonably available to physicians meeting appropriate qualifications prescribed by the Secretary.

(4) [Repealed.]

(5) —

(A) Before December 1, 1991, the Secretary shall by order require manufacturers of devices described in paragraph (1), which are subject to revision of classification under subparagraph (B), to submit to the Secretary a summary of and citation to any information known or otherwise available to the manufacturers respecting the devices, including adverse safety or effectiveness information which has not been submitted under section 519. The Secretary may require a manufacturer to submit the adverse safety or effectiveness data for which a summary and citation were submitted, if such data are available to the manufacturer.

(B) Except as provided in subparagraph (C), after the issuance of an order under subparagraph (A) but before December 1, 1992, the Secretary shall publish a regulation in the Federal Register for each device which is classified in class III under paragraph (1) revising the classification of the device so that the device is classified into class I or class II, unless the regulation requires the device to remain in class III. In determining whether to revise the classification of a device or to require a device to remain in class III, the Secretary shall apply the criteria set forth in section 513(a). Before the publication of a regulation requiring a device to remain in class III or revising its classification, the Secretary shall publish a proposed regulation respecting the classification of a device under this subparagraph and provide an opportunity for the submission of comments on any such regulation. No regulation under this subparagraph requiring a device to remain in class III or revising its classification may take effect before the expiration of 90 days from the date of the publication in the Federal Register of the proposed regulation.

(C) The Secretary may by notice published in the Federal Register extend the period prescribed by subparagraph (B) for a device for an additional period not to exceed 1 year.

(m) Humanitarian Device Exemption. —

(1) To the extent consistent with the protection of the public health and safety and with ethical standards, it is the purpose of this subsection to encourage the discovery and use of devices intended to benefit patients in the treatment and diagnosis of diseases or conditions that affect not more than 8,000 individuals in the United States.

(2) The Secretary may grant a request for an exemption from the effectiveness requirements of sections 514 and 515 for a device for which the Secretary finds that —

(A) the device is designed to treat or diagnose a disease or condition that affects not more than 8,000 individuals in the United States,

(B) the device would not be available to a person with a disease or condition referred to in subparagraph (A) unless the Secretary grants such an exemption and there is no comparable device, other than under this exemption, available to treat or diagnose such disease or condition, and

(C) the device will not expose patients to an unreasonable or significant risk of illness or injury and the probable benefit to health from the use of the device outweighs the risk of injury or illness from its use, taking into account the probable risks and benefits of currently available device or alternative forms of treatment.

The request shall be in the form of an application submitted to the Secretary and such application shall include the certification required under section 402(i)(5)(B) of the Public Health Services Act (which shall not be considered an element of such application. Not later than 75 days after the date of the receipt of the application, the Secretary shall issue an order approving or denying the application.

(3) Except as provided in paragraph (6), no person granted an exemption under paragraph (2) with respect to a device may sell the device for an amount that exceeds the costs of research and development, fabrication, and distribution of the device.

(4) Devices granted an exemption under paragraph (2) may only be used —

(A) in facilities in which clinical testing of devices is supervised by an institutional review committee established in accordance with the regulations of the Secretary; and

(B) if, before the use of a device, an institutional review committee or an appropriate local committee approves the use in the treatment or diagnosis of a disease or condition referred to in paragraph (2)(A), unless a physician determines in an emergency situation that approval from an institutional review committee or an appropriate local committee can not be obtained in time to prevent serious harm or death to a patient.

In a case described in subparagraph (B) in which a physician uses a device without an approval from an institutional review committee or an appropriate local committee, the physician shall, after the use of the device, notify the chairperson of the institutional review committee or an appropriate local committee of such use. Such notification shall include the identification of the patient involved, the date on which the device was used, and the reason for the use.

(5) The Secretary may require a person granted an exemption under paragraph (2) to demonstrate continued compliance with the requirements of this subsection if the Secretary believes such demonstration to be necessary to protect the public health, if the Secretary has reason to believe that the requirements of paragraph (6) are no longer met, or if the Secretary has reason to believe that the criteria for the exemption are no longer met. If the person granted an exemption under paragraph (2) fails to demonstrate continued compliance with the requirements of this subsection, the Secretary may suspend or withdraw the exemption from the effectiveness requirements of sections 514 and 515 for a humanitarian device only after providing notice and an opportunity for an informal hearing.

(6) —

(A) Except as provided in subparagraph (D), the prohibition in paragraph (3) shall not apply with respect to a person granted an exemption under paragraph (2) if each of the following conditions apply:

(i) The device with respect to which the exemption is granted —

(I) is intended for the treatment or diagnosis of a disease or condition that occurs in pediatric patients or in a pediatric subpopulation, and such device is labeled for use in pediatric patients or in a pediatric subpopulation in which the disease or condition occurs; or

(II) is intended for the treatment or diagnosis of a disease or condition that does not occur in pediatric patients or that occurs in pediatric patients in such numbers that the development of the device for such patients is impossible, highly impracticable, or unsafe.

(ii) During any calendar year, the number of such devices distributed during that year under each exemption granted under this subsection does not exceed the annual distribution number for such device. In this paragraph, the term "annual distribution number" means the number of such devices reasonably needed to treat, diagnose, or cure a population of 8,000 individuals in the United States. The Secretary shall determine the annual distribution number when the Secretary grants such exemption.

(iii) Such person immediately notifies the Secretary if the number of such devices distributed during any calendar year exceeds the annual distribution number referred to in clause (ii).

(iv) The request for such exemption is submitted on or before October 1, 2022.

(B) The Secretary may inspect the records relating to the number of devices distributed during any calendar year of a person granted an exemption under paragraph (2) for which the prohibition in paragraph (3) does not apply.

(C) A person may petition the Secretary to modify the annual distribution number determined by the Secretary under subparagraph (A)(ii) with respect to a device if additional information arises, and the Secretary may modify such annual distribution number.

(D) If a person notifies the Secretary, or the Secretary determines through an inspection under subparagraph (B), that the number of devices distributed during any calendar year exceeds the annual distribution number, as required under subparagraph (A)(iii), and modified under subparagraph (C), if applicable, then the prohibition in paragraph (3) shall apply with respect to such person for such device for any sales of such device after such notification.

(E) —

(i) In this subsection, the term "pediatric patients" means patients who are 21 years of age or younger at the time of the diagnosis or treatment.

(ii) In this subsection, the term "pediatric subpopulation" means 1 of the following populations:

(I) Neonates.

(II) Infants.

(III) Children.

(IV) Adolescents.

(7) The Secretary shall refer any report of an adverse event regarding a device described in paragraph (6)(A)(i) (I) for which the prohibition under paragraph (3) does not apply pursuant to paragraph (6)(A) that the Secretary receives to the Office of Pediatric Therapeutics, established under section 6 of the Best Pharmaceuticals for Children Act (Public Law 107–109). In considering the report, the Director of the Office of Pediatric Therapeutics, in consultation with experts in the Center for Devices and Radiological Health, shall provide for periodic review of the report by the Pediatric Advisory Committee, including obtaining any recommendations of such committee regarding whether the Secretary should take action under this Act in response to the report.

(8) The Secretary, acting through the Office of Pediatric Therapeutics and the Center for Devices and Radiological Health, shall provide for an annual review by the Pediatric Advisory Committee of all devices described in paragraph (6)(A)(i)(I) to ensure that the exemption under paragraph (2) remains appropriate for the pediatric populations for which it is granted.

(n) Regulation of Contact Lenses as Devices.

(1) All contact lenses shall be deemed to be devices under section 201(h).

(2) Paragraph (1) shall not be construed as bearing on or being relevant to the questions of whether any product other than a contact lens is a device as defined by section 201(h) or a drug as defined by section 201(g).

(o) Regulation of Medical and Certain Decisions Support Software—

(1) The term device, as defined in section 201(j), shall not include a software function that is intended—

(A) for administrative support of a health care facility, including the processing and maintenance of financial records, claims or billing information, appointment schedules, business analytics, information about patient populations, admissions, practice and inventory management, analysis of historical claims data to predict future utilization or cost-effectiveness, determination of health benefit eligibility, population health management, and laboratory workflow;

(B) for maintaining or encouraging a healthy lifestyle and is unrelated to the diagnosis, cure, mitigation, prevention, or treatment of a disease or condition;

(C) to serve as electronic patient reocrds, including patient-provided information, to the extent that such records are intended to transfer, store, convert formats, or display the equivalent of a paper medical chart, so long as—

(i) such records were created, stored, transferred, or reviewed by health care professionals, or by individuals working under supervision of such professionals;

(ii) such records are part of health information technology that is certified under section 3001(c)(5) of the Public Health Service Act; and

(iii) such function is not intended to interpret or analyze patient records, including medical image data, for the purpose of the diagnosis, cure, mitigation, prevention, or treatment of a disease or condition;

(D) For transferring, storing, converting formats, or displaying clinical laboratory test or other device data and results, findings by a health care professional with respect to such data and results, general information about such findings, and general background information about such laboratory test or other device, unless such function is intended to interpret or analyze clinical laboratory test or other device data, results, and findings; or

(E) Unless the function is intended to acquire, process, or analyze a medical image or a signal from an in vitro diagnostic device or a pattern or signal from a signal acquisition system, for the purpose of—

(i) displaying, analyzing, or printing medical information about a patient or other medical information (such as peer-reviewed clinical studies and clinical practice guidelines);

(ii) supporting or providing recommendations to a health care professional about prevention, diagnosis, or treatment of a disease or condition; and

(iii) enabling such health care professional to independently review the basis for such recommendation that such software presents so that it is not the intent that such health care professional rely primarily on any of such recommendations to make a clinical diagnosis or treatment decision regarding an individual patient.

(2) In the case of a product with multiple functions that contains—

(A) at least one software function that meets the criteria under paragraph (1) or that otherwise does not meet the definition of device under section 201(h); and

(B) at least one function that does not meet the criteria under paragraph (1) and that otherwise meets the definition of a device under section 201(h),

the Secretary shall not regulate the software function of such product described in subparagraph (A) as a device. Notwithstanding the preceding sentence, when assessing the safety and effectiveness of the device function or functions of such product described in subparagraph (B), the Secretary may assess the impact of the software function or functions described in subparagraph (A) have on such device function or functions.

(3)

(A) Notwithstanding paragraph (1), a software function described in subparagraph (C), (D), or (E) of paragraph (1) shall not be excluded from the definition of a device under section 201(h) if—

(i) the Secretary makes a finding that use of such software function would be reasonably likely to have serious adverse health consequences; and

(ii) the software function has been identified in a final order issued by the Secretary under subparagraph (B).

(B) Subparagraph (A) shall apply only if the Secretary—

(i) publishes a notification and proposed order in the Federal Register;

(ii) includes in such notification the Secretary's finding, including the rationale and identification of the evidence on which such finding was based, as described in subparagraph (A)(i); and

(iii) provides for a period of not less than 30 calendar days for public comment before issuing a final order or withdrawing such proposed order.

(C) In making a finding under subparagraph (A)(i) with respect to a software function, the Secretary shall consider—

(i) the likelihood and severity of patient harm if the software function were not to perform as intended;

(ii) the extent to which the software function is intended to support the clinical judgment of a health care professional;

(iii) whether there is a reasonable opportunity for a health care professional to review the basis of the information or treatment recommendation provided by the software function; and

(iv) the intended user and user environment, such as whether a health care professional will use a software function of a type described in subparagraph (E) of paragraph (1).

(4) Nothing in this subsection shall be construed as limiting the authority of the Secretary to—

(A) exercise enforcement discretion as to any device subject to regulation under this Act;

(B) regulate software used in the manufacture and transfusion of blood and blood components to assist in the prevention of disease in humans; or

(C) regulate software as a device under this Act if such software meets the criteria under section 513(a)(1)(C).

(p) Diagnostic Imaging Devices Intended for Use with Contrast Agents. —

(1) In General.—The Secretary may, subject to the succeeding provisions of this subsection, approve an application (or a supplement to such an application) submitted under section 515 with respect to an applicable medical imaging device, or, in the case of an applicable medical imaging device for which a notification is submitted under section 510(k), may make a substantial equivalence determination with respect to an applicable medical imaging device, or may grant a request submitted under section 513(f)(2) for an applicable medical imaging device, if such application, notification, or request involves the use of a contrast agent that is not —

(A) in a concentration, rate of administration, or route of administration that is different from those described in the approved labeling of the contrast agent, except that the Secretary may approve such application, make such substantial equivalence determination, or grant such request if the Secretary determines that such differences in concentration, rate of administration, or route of administration exist but do not adversely affect the safety and effectiveness of the contrast agent when used with the device;

(B) in a region, organ, or system of the body that is different from those described in the approved labeling of the contrast agent, except that the Secretary may approve such application, make such substantial equivalence determination, or grant such request if the Secretary determines that such differences in region, organ, or system of the body exist but do not adversely affect the safety and effectiveness of the contrast agent when used with the device;

(C) in a patient population that is different from those described in the approved labeling of the contrast agent, except that the Secretary may approve such application, make such substantial equivalence determination, or grant such request if the Secretary determines such differences in patient population exist but do not adversely affect the safety and effectiveness of the contrast agent when used with the device; or

(D) in an imaging modality that is different from those described in the approved labeling of the contrast agent.

(2) Premarket Review. — The agency center charged with premarket review of devices shall have primary jurisdiction with respect to the review of an application, notification, or request described in paragraph (1). In conducting such review, such agency center may —

(A) consult with the agency center charged with the premarket review of drugs or biological products; and

(B) review information and data provided to the Secretary by the sponsor of a contrast agent in an application submitted under section 505 of this Act or section 351 of the Public Health Service Act, so long as the sponsor of such contrast agent has provided to the sponsor of the applicable medical imaging device that is the subject of such review a right of reference and the application is submitted in accordance with this subsection.

(3) Applicable Requirements. — An application submitted under section 515, a notification submitted under section 510(k), or a request submitted under section 513(f)(2), as described in paragraph (1), with respect to an applicable medical imaging device shall be subject to the requirements of such respective section. Such application, notification, or request shall only be subject to the requirements of this Act applicable to devices.

(4) Definitions. — For purposes of this subsection —

(A) the term 'applicable medical imaging device' means a device intended to be used in conjunction with a contrast agent (or class of contrast agents) for an imaging use that is not described in the approved labeling of such contrast agent (or the approved labeling of any contrast agent in the same class as such contrast agent); and

(B) the term 'contrast agent' means a drug that is approved under section 505 or licensed under section 351 of the Public Health Service Act, is intended for use in conjunction with an applicable medical imaging device, and —

(i) is a diagnostic radiopharmaceutical, as defined in section 315.2 and 601.31 of title 21, Code of Federal Regulations (or any successor regulations); or

(ii) is a diagnostic agent that improves the visualization of structure or function within the body by increasing the relative difference in signal intensity within the target tissue, structure, or fluid.

(q) Regulation of Over-the-Counter Hearing Aids. —

(1) Definition. —

(A) In General. — In this subsection, the term 'over-the-counter hearing aid' means a device that—

(i) uses the same fundamental scientific technology as air conduction hearing aids (as defined in section 874.3300 of title 21, Code of Federal Regulations) (or any successor regulation) or wireless air conduction hearing aids (as defined in section 874.3305 of title 21, Code of Federal Regulations) (or any successor regulation);

(ii) is intended to be used by adults age 18 and older to compensate for perceived mild to moderate hearing impairment;

(iii) through tools, tests, or software, allows the user to control the over-the-counter hearing aid and customize it to the user's hearing needs;

(iv) may —

(I) use wireless technology; or

(II) include tests for self-assessment of hearing loss; and

(v) is available over-the-counter, without the supervision, prescription, or other order, involvement, or intervention of a licensed person, to consumers through in-person transactions, by mail, or online.

(B) Exception. — Such term does not include a personal sound amplification product intended to amplify sound for nonhearing impaired consumers in situations including hunting and bird-watching.

(2) Regulation. — An over-the-counter hearing aid shall be subject to the regulations promulgated in accordance with section 709(b) of the FDA Reauthorization Act of 2017 and shall be exempt from sections 801.420 and 801.421 of title 21, Code of Federal Regulations (or any successor regulations).

Sec. 521. [360k] State and Local Requirements Respecting Devices.

(a) General Rule. — Except as provided in subsection (b), no State or political subdivision of a State may establish or continue in effect with respect to a device intended for human use any requirement —

(1) which is different from, or in addition to, any requirement applicable under this Act to the device, and

(2) which relates to the safety or effectiveness of the device or to any other matter included in a requirement applicable to the device under this Act.

(b) Exempt Requirements. — Upon application of a State or a political subdivision thereof, the Secretary may, by regulation promulgated after notice and opportunity for an oral hearing, exempt from subsection (a), under such conditions as may be prescribed in such regulation, a requirement of such State or political subdivision applicable to a device intended for human use if —

(1) the requirement is more stringent than a requirement under this Act which would be applicable to the device if an exemption were not in effect under this subsection; or

(2) the requirement —

(A) is required by compelling local conditions, and

(B) compliance with the requirement would not cause the device to be in violation of any applicable requirement under this Act.

Sec. 522. [360l] Postmarket Surveillance.

(a) Postmarket Surveillance. —

(1) In General . —

(A) Conduct. —The Secretary may by order, at the time of approval or clearance of a device or at any time thereafter, require a manufacturer to conduct postmarket surveillance for any device of the manufacturer that is a class II or class III device —

(i) the failure of which would be reasonably likely to have serious adverse health consequences;

(ii) that is expected to have significant use in pediatric populations; or

(iii) that is intended to be—

(I) implanted in the human body for more than 1 year; or

(II) a life-sustaining or life-supporting device used outside a device user facility.

(B) Condition. — The Secretary may order a postmarket surveillance under subparagraph (A) as a condition to approval or clearance of a device described in subparagraph (A)(ii).

(2) Rule of Construction. —

The provisions of paragraph (1) shall have no effect on authorities otherwise provided under the Act or regulations issued under this Act.

(b) Surveillance Approval. —

(1) In General. — Each manufacturer required to conduct a surveillance of a device shall, within 30 days of receiving an order from the Secretary prescribing that the manufacturer is required under this section to conduct such surveillance, submit, for the approval of the Secretary, a plan for the required surveillance. The Secretary, within 60 days of the receipt of such plan, shall determine if the person designated to conduct the surveillance has appropriate qualifications and experience to undertake such surveillance and if the plan will result in the collection of useful data that can reveal unforeseen adverse events or other information necessary to protect the public health. The manufacturer shall commence surveillance under this section not later than 15 months after the day on which the Secretary issues an order under this section. Except as provided in paragraph (2), the Secretary, in consultation with the manufacturer, may by order require a prospective surveillance period of up to 36 months. Except as provided in paragraph (2), any determination by the Secretary that a longer period is necessary shall be made by mutual agreement between the Secretary and the manufacturer or, if no agreement can be reached, after the completion of a dispute resolution process as described in section 562.

(2) Longer Surveillance for Pediatric Devices. — The Secretary may by order require a prospective surveillance period of more than 36 months with respect to a device that is expected to have significant use in pediatric populations if such period of more than 36 months is necessary in order to assess the impact of the device on growth and development, or the effects of growth, development, activity level, or other factors on the safety or efficacy of the device.

(c) Dispute Resolution. — A manufacturer may request review under section 562 of any order or condition requiring postmarket surveillance under this section. During the pendency of such review, the device subject to such a postmarket surveillance order or condition shall not, because of noncompliance with such order or condition, be deemed in violation of section 301(q)(1)(C), adulterated under section 501(f)(1), misbranded under section 502(t)(3), or in violation of, as applicable, section 510(k) or section 515, unless deemed necessary to protect the public health.

Sec. 523. [360m] Accredited Persons.

(a) In General. —

(1) Review and Classification of Devices. — Not later than 1 year after the date of enactment of the Food and Drug Administration Modernization Act of 1997 [November 21, 1997 — Ed.], the Secretary shall, subject to paragraph (3), accredit persons for the purpose of reviewing reports submitted under section 510(k) and making recommendations to the Secretary regarding the initial classification of devices under section 513(f)(1).

(2) Requirements Regarding Review. —

(A) In General. — In making a recommendation to the Secretary under paragraph (1), an accredited person shall notify the Secretary in writing of the reasons for the recommendation.

(B) Time Period for Review. — Not later than 30 days after the date on which the Secretary is notified under subparagraph (A) by an accredited person with respect to a recommendation of an initial classification of a device, the Secretary shall make a determination with respect to the initial classification.

(C) Special Rule. — The Secretary may change the initial classification under section 513(f)(1) that is recommended under paragraph (1) by an accredited person, and in such case shall provide to such person, and the person who submitted the report under section 510(k) for the device, a statement explaining in detail the reasons for the change.

(3) Certain Devices. —

(A) In General. — An accredited person may not be used to perform a review of —

(i) a class III device;

~~**(ii)** a class II device which is intended to be permanently implantable or life sustaining or life supporting; or~~

~~**(iii)** a class II device which requires clinical data in the report submitted under section 510(k) for the device, except that the number of class II devices to which the Secretary applies this clause for a year, less the number of such reports to which clauses (i) and (ii) apply, may not exceed 6 percent of the number that is equal to the total number of reports submitted to the Secretary under such section for such year less the number of such reports to which such clauses apply for such year.~~

(ii) a device classified under section 513(f)(2) or designated under section 515C(d);

(iii) a device that is intended to be permanently implantable, life sustaining, or life supporting, unless otherwise determined by the Secretary in accordance with subparagraph (B)(i)(II) and listed as eligible for review under subparagraph (B)(iii); or

(iv) a device that is of a type, or subset of a type, listed as not eligible for review under subparagraph (B)(iii).

~~**(B) Adjustment.** — In determining for a year the ratio described in subparagraph (A)(iii), the Secretary shall not include in the numerator class III devices that the Secretary reclassified into class II, and the Secretary shall include in the denominator class II devices for which reports under section 510(k) were not required to be submitted by reason of the operation of section 510(m).~~

(B) Designation for Review. — The Secretary shall —

(i) issue draft guidance on the factors the Secretary will use in determining whether a class I or class II device type, or subset of such device types, is eligible for review by an accredited person, including—

(I) the risk of the device type, or subset of such device type; and

(II) whether the device type, or subset of such device type, is permanently implantable, life sustaining, or life supporting, and whether there is a detailed public health justification for permitting the review by an accredited person of such device type or subset;

(ii) not later than 24 months after the date on which the Secretary issues such draft guidance, finalize such guidance; and

(iii) beginning on the date such guidance is finalized, designate and post on the internet website of the Food and Drug Administration, an updated list of class I and class II device types, or subsets of such device types, and the Secretary's determination with respect to whether each such device type, or subset of a device type, is eligible or not eligible for review by an accredited person under this section based on the factors described in clause (i).

(C) Interim Rule. — Until the date on which the updated list is designated and posted in accordance with subparagraph (B)(iii), the list in effect on the date of enactment the Medical Device User Fee Amendments of 2017 shall be in effect.

(b) Accreditation. —

(1) Programs. — The Secretary shall provide for such accreditation through programs administered by the Food and Drug Administration, other government agencies, or by other qualified nongovernment organizations.

(2) Accreditation. —

(A) In General. — Not later than 180 days after the date of the enactment of the Food and Drug Administration Modernization Act of 1997 [November 21, 1997 — Ed.], the Secretary shall establish and publish in the Federal Register criteria to accredit or deny accreditation to persons who request to perform the duties specified in subsection (a). The Secretary shall respond to a request for accreditation within 60 days of the receipt of the request. The accreditation of such person shall specify the particular activities under subsection (a) for which such person is accredited.

(B) Withdrawal of Accreditation. — The Secretary may suspend or withdraw accreditation of any person accredited under this paragraph, after providing notice and an opportunity for an informal hearing, when such person is substantially not in compliance with the requirements of this section or poses a threat to public health or fails to act in a manner that is consistent with the purposes of this section.

(C) Performance Auditing. — To ensure that persons accredited under this section will continue to meet the standards of accreditation, the Secretary shall —

(i) make onsite visits on a periodic basis to each accredited person to audit the performance of such person; and

(ii) take such additional measures as the Secretary determines to be appropriate.

~~**(D) Annual Report.** — The Secretary shall include in the annual report required under section 1003(g) the names of all accredited persons and the particular activities under subsection (a) for which each such person is accredited and the name of each accredited person whose accreditation has been withdrawn during the year.~~

~~**(E)**~~ **(D) Periodic Reaccreditation.** —

(i) Period. — Subject to suspension or withdrawal under subparagraph (B), any accreditation under this section shall be valid for a period of 3 years after its issuance.

(ii) Response to Reaccreditation Request. — Upon the submission of a request by an accredited person for reaccreditation under this section, the Secretary shall approve or deny such request not later than 60 days after receipt of the request.

(iii) Criteria. — Not later than 120 days after the date of enactment of this subparagraph, the Secretary shall establish and publish in the Federal Register criteria to reaccredit or deny reaccreditation to persons under this section. The reaccreditation of persons under this section shall specify the particular activities under subsection (a), and the devices, for which such persons are reaccredited.

(3) Qualifications. — An accredited person shall, at a minimum, meet the following requirements:

(A) Such person may not be an employee of the Federal Government.

(B) Such person shall be an independent organization which is not owned or controlled by a manufacturer, supplier, or vendor of devices and which has no organizational, material, or financial affiliation with such a manufacturer, supplier, or vendor.

(C) Such person shall be a legally constituted entity permitted to conduct the activities for which it seeks accreditation.

(D) Such person shall not engage in the design, manufacture, promotion, or sale of devices.

(E) The operations of such person shall be in accordance with generally accepted professional and ethical business practices ~~and shall agree in writing that as a minimum it will:~~.

(F) Such person shall agree, at minimum, to include in its request for accreditation a commitment to, at the time of accreditation, and at any time it is performing any review pursuant to this section —

(i) certify that reported information accurately reflects data reviewed;

(ii) limit work to that for which competence and capacity are available;

(iii) treat information received, records, reports, and recommendations as proprietary information;

(iv) promptly respond and attempt to resolve complaints regarding its activities for which it is accredited; and

(v) protect against the use, in carrying out subsection (a) with respect to a device, of any officer or employee of the person who has a financial conflict of interest regarding the device, and annually make available to the public disclosures of the extent to which the person, and the officers and employees of the person, have maintained compliance with requirements under this clause relating to financial conflicts of interest.

(4) Selection of Accredited Persons. — The Secretary shall provide each person who chooses to use an accredited person to receive a section 510(k) report a panel of at least two or more accredited persons from which the regulated person may select one for a specific regulatory function.

(5) Compensation of Accredited Persons. — Compensation for an accredited person shall be determined by agreement between the accredited person and the person who engages the services of the accredited person, and shall be paid by the person who engages such services.

(c) Duration. — The authority provided by this section terminates October 1, ~~2017~~ 2022.

Subchapter B — Drugs for Rare Diseases or Conditions

Sec. 524. [360n] Priority Review to Encourage Treatments for Tropical Diseases.

(a) Definitions. — In this section:

(1) Priority Review. — The term "priority review", with respect to a human drug application as defined in section 735(1), means review and action by the Secretary on such application not later than 6 months after receipt by the Secretary of such application, as described in the Manual of Policies and Procedures of the Food and Drug Administration and goals identified in the letters described in section 101(c) of the Food and Drug Administration Amendments Act of 2007.

(2) Priority Review Voucher. — The term "priority review voucher" means a voucher issued by the Secretary to the sponsor of a tropical disease product application that entitles the holder of such voucher to priority review of a single human drug application submitted under section 505(b)(1) or section 351 of the Public Health Service Act after the date of approval of the tropical disease product application.

(3) Tropical Disease. — The term "tropical disease" means any of the following:

(A) Tuberculosis.

(B) Malaria.

(C) Blinding trachoma.

(D) Buruli Ulcer.

(E) Cholera.

(F) Dengue/dengue haemorrhagic fever.

(G) Dracunculiasis (guinea-worm disease).

(H) Fascioliasis.

(I) Human African trypanosomiasis.

(J) Leishmaniasis.

(K) Leprosy.

(L) Lymphatic filariasis.

(M) Onchocerciasis.

(N) Schistosomiasis.

(O) Soil transmitted helmithiasis.

(P) Yaws.

(Q) Filovirus Diseases

(R) Zika Virus Disease

(S) Any other infectious disease for which there is no significant market in developed nations and that disproportionately affects poor and marginalized populations, designated by order of the Secretary.

(4) Tropical Disease Product Application. — The term "tropical disease product application" means an application that —

(A) is a human drug application as defined in section 735(1) —

(i) for prevention or treatment of a tropical disease; ~~and~~

(ii) the Secretary deems eligible for priority review;

(iii) that contains reports of one or more new clinical investigations (other than bioavailability studies) that are essential to the approval of the application and conducted or sponsored by the sponsor of such application; and

(iv) that contains an attestation from the sponsor of the application that such reports were not submitted as part of an application for marketing approval or licensure by a regulatory authority in India, Brazil, Thailand, or any country that is a member of the Pharmaceutical Inspection Convention or the Pharmaceutical Inspection Cooperation Scheme prior to September 27, 2007.

(B) is approved after the date of the enactment of the Food and Drug Administration Amendments Act of 2007, by the Secretary for use in the prevention, detection, or treatment of a tropical disease; and

(C) is for a human drug, no active ingredient (including any ester or salt of the active ingredient) of which has been approved in any other application under section 505(b)(1) or section 351 of the Public Health Service Act.

(b) Priority Review Voucher. —

(1) In General. — The Secretary shall award a priority review voucher to the sponsor of a tropical disease product application upon approval by the Secretary of such tropical disease product application.

(2) Transferability. — The sponsor of a tropical disease product that receives a priority review voucher under this section may transfer (including by sale) the entitlement to such voucher to a sponsor of a human drug for which an application under section 505(b)(1) or section 351 of the Public Health Service Act will be submitted after the date of the approval of the tropical disease product application. There is no limit on the number of times a priority review voucher may be transferred before such voucher is used.

(3) Limitation. —

(A) No Award for Prior Approved Application. — A sponsor of a tropical disease product may not receive a priority review voucher under this section if the tropical disease product application was submitted to the Secretary prior to the date of the enactment of this section.

(B) One-Year Waiting Period. — The Secretary shall issue a priority review voucher to the sponsor of a tropical disease product no earlier than the date that is 1 year after the date of the enactment of the Food and Drug Administration Amendments Act of 2007.

(4) Notification. — The sponsor of a human drug application shall notify the Secretary not later than 365 days prior to submission of the human drug application that is the subject of a priority review voucher of an intent to submit the human drug application, including the date on which the sponsor intends to submit the application. Such notification shall be a legally binding commitment to pay for the user fee to be assessed in accordance with this section.

(c) Priority Review User Fee. —

(1) In General. — The Secretary shall establish a user fee program under which a sponsor of a human drug application that is the subject of a priority review voucher shall pay to the Secretary a fee determined under paragraph (2). Such fee shall be in addition to any fee required to be submitted by the sponsor under chapter VII.

(2) Fee Amount. — The amount of the priority review user fee shall be determined each fiscal year by the Secretary and based on the average cost incurred by the agency in the review of a human drug application subject to priority review in the previous fiscal year.

(3) Annual Fee Setting. — The Secretary shall establish, before the beginning of each fiscal year beginning after September 30, 2007, for that fiscal year, the amount of the priority review user fee.

(4) Payment. —

(A) In General. — The priority review user fee required by this subsection shall be due upon the submission of a human drug application under section 505(b)(1) or section 351 of the Public Health Service Act for which the priority review voucher is used.

(B) Complete Application. — An application described under subparagraph (A) for which the sponsor requests the use of a priority review voucher shall be considered incomplete if the fee required by this subsection and all other applicable user fees are not paid in accordance with the Secretary's procedures for paying such fees.

(C) No Waivers, Exemptions, Reductions, or Refunds. — The Secretary may not grant a waiver, exemption, reduction, or refund of any fees due and payable under this section.

(5) Offsetting Collections. — Fees collected pursuant to this subsection for any fiscal year—

(A) shall be deposited and credited as offsetting collections to the account providing appropriations to the Food and Drug Administration; and

(B) shall not be collected for any fiscal year except to the extent provided in advance in appropriation Acts.

Sec. 524A. [360n-1] Priority Review for Qualified Infectious Disease Products.

(a) In General.—If the Secretary designates a drug under section 505E(d) as a qualified infectious disease product, then the Secretary shall give priority review to the first application submitted for approval for such drug under section 505(b).

(b) Construction.—Nothing in this section shall prohibit the Secretary from giving priority review to a human drug application or efficacy supplement submitted for approval under section 505(b) that otherwise meets the criteria for the Secretary to grant priority review.

Sec. 525. [360aa] Recommendations for Investigations of Drugs for Rare Diseases or Conditions.

(a) The sponsor of a drug for a disease or condition which is rare in the States may request the Secretary to provide written recommendations for the nonclinical and clinical investigations which must be conducted with the drug before —

(1) it may be approved for such disease or condition under section 505, or

(2) if the drug is a biological product, it may be licensed for such disease or condition under section 351 of the Public Health Service Act.

If the Secretary has reason to believe that a drug for which a request is made under this section is a drug for a disease or condition which is rare in the States, the Secretary shall provide the person making the request written recommendations for the nonclinical and clinical investigations which the Secretary believes, on the basis of information available to the Secretary at the time of the request under this section, would be necessary for approval of such drug for such disease or condition under section 505 or licensing of such drug for such disease or condition under section 351 of the Public Health Service Act.

(b) The Secretary shall by regulation promulgate procedures for the implementation of subsection (a).

Sec. 526. [360bb] Designation of Drugs for Rare Diseases or Conditions.

(a) —

(1) The manufacturer or the sponsor of a drug may request the Secretary to designate the drug as a drug for a rare disease or condition. A request for designation of a drug shall be made before the submission of an application under section 505(b) for the drug, or the submission of an application for licensing of the drug under section 351 of the Public Health Service Act. If the Secretary finds that a drug for which a request is submitted under this subsection is being or will be investigated for a rare disease or condition and —

(A) if an application for such drug is approved under section 505, or

(B) if a license for such drug is issued under section 351 of the Public Health Service Act,
the approval, certification, or license would be for use for such disease or condition, the Secretary shall designate the drug as a drug for such disease or condition. A request for a designation of a drug under this subsection shall contain the consent of the applicant to notice being given by the Secretary under subsection (b) respecting the designation of the drug.

(2) For purposes of paragraph (1), the term "rare disease or condition" means any disease or condition which

(A) affects less than 200,000 persons in the United States, or

(B) affects more than 200,000 in the United States and for which there is no reasonable expectation that the cost of developing and making available in the United States a drug for such disease or condition will be recovered from sales in the United States of such drug. Determinations under the preceding sentence with respect to any drug shall be made on the basis of the facts and circumstances as of the date the request for designation of the drug under this subsection is made.

(b) A designation of a drug under subsection (a) shall be subject to the condition that —

(1) if an application was approved for the drug under section 505(b) or a license was issued for the drug under section 351 of the Public Health Service Act, the manufacturer of the drug will notify the Secretary of any discontinuance of the production of the drug at least one year before discontinuance, and

(2) if an application has not been approved for the drug under section 505(b) or a license has not been issued for the drug under section 351 of the Public Health Service Act and if preclinical investigations or investigations under section 505(i) are being conducted with the drug, the manufacturer or sponsor of the drug will notify the

Secretary of any decision to discontinue active pursuit of approval of an application under section 505(b) or approval of a license under section 351 of the Public Health Service Act.

(c) Notice respecting the designation of a drug under subsection (a) shall be made available to the public.

(d) The Secretary shall by regulation promulgate procedures for the implementation of subsection (a).

Sec. 527. [360cc] Protection for Drugs for Rare Diseases or Conditions.

(a) Except as provided in subsection (b) of this section, if the Secretary —

(1) approves an application filed pursuant to section 505, or

(2) issues a license under section 351 of the Public Health Service Act

for a drug designated under section 526 for a rare disease or condition, the Secretary may not approve another application under section 505 or issue another license under section 351 of the Public Health Service Act for ~~such drug for such disease or condition~~ the same drug for the same disease or condition for a person who is not the holder of such approved application or of such license until the expiration of seven years from the date of the approval of the approved application or the issuance of the license. Section 505(c)(2) does not apply to the refusal to approve an application under the preceding sentence.

(b) ~~If an application filed pursuant to section 505 is approved for a drug designated under section 526 for a rare disease or condition, or if a license is issued under section 351 of the Public Health Service Act for such a drug, the Secretary may, during the seven-year period beginning on the date of the application approval, or of the issuance of the license, approve another application under section 505 or issue a license under section 351 of the Public Health Service Act, for such drug for such disease or condition for a person who is not the holder of such approved application or of such license if —~~ During the 7-year period described in subsection (a) for an approved application under section 505 or license under section 351 of the Public Health Service Act, the Secretary may approve an application or issue a license for a drug that is otherwise the same, as determined by the Secretary, as the already approved drug for the same rare disease or condition if

(1) the Secretary finds, after providing the holder ~~notice and opportunity for the submission of views, that in such period the holder of the approved application or of the license cannot assure~~ of exclusive approval or licensure notice and opportunity for the submission of views, that during such period the holder of the exclusive approval or licensure cannot ensure the availability of sufficient quantities of the drug to meet the needs of persons with the disease or condition for which the drug was designated; or

(2) ~~such~~ the holder provides the Secretary in writing the consent of such holder for the approval of other applications, or the issuance of other licenses before the expiration of such seven-year period.

(c) Condition of Clinical Superiority. —

(1) In General.—If a sponsor of a drug that is designated under section 526 and is otherwise the same, as determined by the Secretary, as an already approved or licensed drug is seeking exclusive approval or exclusive licensure described in subsection (a) for the same rare disease or condition as the already approved drug, the Secretary shall require such sponsor, as a condition of such exclusive approval or licensure, to demonstrate that such drug is clinically superior to any already approved or licensed drug that is the same drug.

(2) Definition.—For purposes of paragraph (1), the term 'clinically superior' with respect to a drug means that the drug provides a significant therapeutic advantage over and above an already approved or licensed drug in terms of greater efficacy, greater safety, or by providing a major contribution to patient care.

(d) Regulations.—The Secretary may promulgate regulations for the implementation of subsection (c). Beginning on the date of enactment of the FDA Reauthorization Act of 2017, until such time as the Secretary promulgates regulations in accordance with this subsection, the Secretary may apply any definitions set forth in regulations that were promulgated prior to such date of enactment, to the extent such definitions are not inconsistent with the terms of this section, as amended by such Act.

(e) Demonstration of Clinical Superiority Standard. — To assist sponsors in demonstrating clinical superiority as described in subsection (c), the Secretary —

(1) upon the designation of any drug under section 526, shall notify the sponsor of such drug in writing of the basis for the designation, including, as applicable, any plausible hypothesis offered by the sponsor and relied upon by the Secretary that the drug is clinically superior to a previously approved drug; and

(2) upon granting exclusive approval or licensure under subsection (a) on the basis of a demonstration of clinical superiority as described in subsection (c), shall publish a summary of the clinical superiority findings.

Sec. 528. [360dd] Open Protocols for Investigations of Drugs for Rare Diseases or Conditions.

If a drug is designated under section 526 as a drug for a rare disease or condition and if notice of a claimed exemption under section 505(i) or regulations issued thereunder is filed for such drug, the Secretary shall encourage the sponsor of such drug to design protocols for clinical investigations of the drug which may be conducted under the exemption to permit the addition to the investigations of persons with the disease or condition who need the drug to treat the disease or condition and who cannot be satisfactorily treated by available alternative drugs.

Sec.___. [360ee] Grants and Contracts for Development of Drugs for Rare Diseases and Conditions.

(a) The Secretary may make grants to and enter into contracts with public and private entities and individuals to assist in

(1) defraying the costs of developing drugs for rare diseases or conditions, including qualified testing expenses,

(2) defraying the costs of developing medical devices for rare diseases or conditions, and

(3) defraying the costs of developing medical foods for rare diseases or conditions.

(b) For purposes of subsection (a):

(1) The term "qualified testing" means —

(A) human clinical testing —

(i) which is carried out under an exemption for a drug for a rare disease or condition under 505(i) (or regulations issued under such section); and

(ii) which occurs before the date on which an application with respect to such drug is submitted under section 505(b) or under section 351 of the Public Health Service Act;

(B) preclinical testing involving a drug for a rare disease or condition which occurs after the date such drug is designated under section 526 and before the date on which an application with respect to such drug is submitted under section 505(b) or under section 351 of the Public Health Service Act; and

(C) prospectively planned and designed observational studies and other analyses conducted to assist in the understanding of the natural history of a rare disease or condition and in the development of a therapy, including studies and analyses to—

(i) develop or validate a drug development tool related to a rare disease or condition; or

(ii) understand the full spectrum of the disease manifestations, including describing genotypic and phenotypic variability and identifying and defining distinct subpopulations affected by a rare disease or condition.

(2) The term "rare disease or condition" means

(1) in the case of a drug, any disease or condition which

(A) affects less than 200,000 persons in the United States, or

(B) affects more than 200,000 in the United States and for which there is no reasonable expectation that the cost of developing and making available in the United States a drug for such disease or condition will be recovered from sales in the United States of such drug,

(2) in the case of a medical device, any disease or condition that occurs so infrequently in the United States that there is no reasonable expectation that a medical device for such disease or condition will be developed without assistance under subsection (a), and

(3) in the case of a medical food, any disease or condition that occurs so infrequently in the United States that there is no reasonable expectation that a medical food for such disease or condition will be developed without assistance under subsection (a). Determinations under the preceding sentence with respect to any drug shall be made on the basis of the facts and circumstances as of the date the request for designation of the drug under section 526 is made.

(3) The term "medical food" means a food which is formulated to be consumed or administered enterally under the supervision of a physician and which is intended for the specific dietary management of a disease or condition for which distinctive nutritional requirements, based on recognized scientific principles, are established by medical evaluation.

(c) Authorization of Appropriations. — For grants and contracts under subsection (a), there is authorized to be appropriated $30,000,000 for each of fiscal years ~~2013 through 2017.~~ 2018 through 2022.

Sec. 529. [360ff] Priority Review to Encourage Treatments for Rare Pediatric Diseases.

(a) Definitions. — In this section:

(1) Priority Review. — The term "priority review", with respect to a human drug application as defined in section 735(1), means review and action by the Secretary on such application not later than 6 months after receipt by the Secretary of such application, as described in the Manual of Policies and Procedures of the Food and Drug Administration and goals identified in the letters described in section 101(b) of the Prescription Drug User Fee Amendments of 2012.

(2) Priority Review Voucher. — The term "priority review voucher" means a voucher issued by the Secretary to the sponsor of a rare pediatric disease product application that entitles the holder of such voucher to priority review of a single human drug application submitted under section 505(b)(1) or section 351(a) of the Public Health Service Act after the date of approval of the rare pediatric disease product application.

(3) Rare Pediatric Disease. — The term "rare pediatric disease" means a disease that meets each of the following criteria:

(A) The disease is a serious or life-threatening disease in which the serious or life-threatening manifestations primarily affect individuals aged from birth to 18 years, including age groups often called neonates, infants, children, and adolescents.

(B) The disease is a rare disease or condition, within the meaning of section 526.

(4) Rare Pediatric Disease Product Application. — The term "rare pediatric disease product application" means a human drug application, as defined in section 735(1), that —

(A) is for a drug or biological product —

(i) that is for the prevention or treatment of a rare pediatric disease; and

(ii) that contains no active ingredient (including any ester or salt of the active ingredient) that has been previously approved in any other application under section 505(b)(1), 505(b)(2), or 505(j) of this Act or section 351(a) or 351(k) of the Public Health Service Act;

(B) is submitted under section 505(b)(1) of this Act or section 351(a) of the Public Health Service Act;

(C) the Secretary deems eligible for priority review;

(D) that relies on clinical data derived from studies examining a pediatric population and dosages of the drug intended for that population;

(E) that does not seek approval for an adult indication in the original rare pediatric disease product application; and

(F) is approved after the date of enactment of the Advancing Hope Act of 2016 [September 30, 2016 –Ed.].

(b) Priority Review Voucher. —

(1) In General. — The Secretary shall award a priority review voucher to the sponsor of a rare pediatric disease product application upon approval by the Secretary of such rare pediatric disease product application.

(2) Transferability. —

(A) In General. — The sponsor of a rare pediatric disease product application that receives a priority review voucher under this section may transfer (including by sale) the entitlement to such voucher. There is no limit on the number of times a priority voucher may be transferred before such voucher is used.

(B) Notification of Transfer — Each person to whom a voucher is transferred shall notify the Secretary of such change in ownership of the voucher not later than 30 days after such transfer.

(3) Limitation. — A sponsor of a rare pediatric disease product application may not receive a priority review voucher under this section if the rare pediatric disease product application was submitted to the Secretary prior to the date that is 90 days after the date of enactment of the Prescription Drug User Fee Amendments of 2012.

(4) Notification. —

(A) Sponsor of Rare Pediatric Disease Product.

(i) In General. — Beginning on the date that is 90 days after the date of enactment of the Advancing Hope Act of 2016 [September 30, 2016 –Ed.], the sponsor of a rare pediatric disease product application that intends to request a priority voucher under this section shall notify the Secretary of such intent upon submission of the rare pediatric disease product application that is the basis of the request for a priority review voucher.

(ii) Applications Submitted but Not Yet Approved. — The sponsor of a rare pediatric disease product application that was submitted and that has not been approved as of the date of enactment of the Advancing Hope Act of 2016 [September 30, 2016 –Ed.] shall be considered eligible for a priority review voucher if—

(I) such sponsor has submitted such rare pediatric disease application—

(aa) on or after the date that is 90 days after the date of enactment of the Prescription Drug User Fee Amendments of 2012; and

(bb) on or before the date of enactment of the Advancing Hope Act of 2016 [September 30, 2016 –Ed.]; and

(II) such application otherwise meets the criteria for a priority review voucher under this section.

(B) Sponsor of a Drug Application Using a Priority Review Voucher—

(i) In General. — The sponsor of a human drug application shall notify the Secretary not later than 90 days prior to submission of the human drug application that is the subject of a priority review voucher of an intent to submit the human drug application, including the date on which the sponsor intends to submit the application. Such notification shall be a legally binding commitment to pay the user fee to be assessed in accordance with this section.

(ii) Transfer After Notice. — The sponsor of a human drug application that provides notification of the intent of such sponsor to use the voucher for the human drug application under clause (i) may transfer the voucher after such notification is provided, if such sponsor has not yet submitted the human drug application described in the notification.

(5) Termination of Authority. — The Secretary may not award any priority review vouchers under paragraph (1) after September 30, 2020, unless the rare pediatric disease product application—

(A) is for a drug that, not later than September 30, 2020, is designated under subsection (d) as a drug for a rare pediatric disease; and

(B) is, not later than September 30, 2022, approved under section 505(b)(1) of this Act or section 351(a) of the Public Health Service Act.

(c) Priority Review User Fee. —

(1) In General. — The Secretary shall establish a user fee program under which a sponsor of a human drug application that is the subject of a priority review voucher shall pay to the Secretary a fee determined under paragraph (2). Such fee shall be In addition to any fee required to be submitted by the sponsor under chapter VII.

(2) Fee Amount. — The amount of the priority review user fee shall be determined each fiscal year by the Secretary, based on the difference between —

(A) the average cost incurred by the Food and Drug Administration in the review of a human drug application subject to priority review in the previous fiscal year; and

(B) the average cost incurred by the Food and Drug Administration in the review of a human drug application that is not subject to priority review in the previous fiscal year.

(3) Annual Fee Setting. — The Secretary shall establish, before the beginning of each fiscal year beginning after September 30, 2012, the amount of the priority review user fee for that fiscal year.

(4) Payment. —

(A) In General. — The priority review user fee required by this subsection shall be due upon the notification by a sponsor of the intent of such sponsor to use the voucher, as specified in subsection (b)(4)(A). All other user fees associated with the human drug application shall be due as required by the Secretary or under applicable law.

(B) Complete Application. — An application described under subparagraph (A) for which the sponsor requests the use of a priority review voucher shall be considered incomplete if the fee required by this subsection and all other applicable user fees are not paid in accordance with the Secretary's procedures for paying such fees.

(C) No Waivers, Exemptions, Reductions, or Refunds. — The Secretary may not grant a waiver, exemption, reduction, or refund of any fees due and payable under this section.

(5) Offsetting Collections. — Fees collected pursuant to this subsection for any fiscal year —

(A) shall be deposited and credited as off-setting collections to the account providing appropriations to the Food and Drug Administration; and

(B) shall not be collected for any fiscal year except to the extent provided in advance in appropriations Acts.

(d) Designation Process. —

(1) In General. — Upon the request of the manufacturer or the sponsor of a new drug, the Secretary may designate —

(A) the new drug as a drug for a rare pediatric disease; and

(B) the application for the new drug as a rare pediatric disease product application.

(2) Request for Designation. — The request for a designation under paragraph (1) shall be made at the same time a request for designation of orphan disease status under section 526 or fast-track designation under section 506 is made. Requesting designation under this subsection is not a prerequisite to receiving a priority review voucher under this section.

(3) Determination by Secretary. — Not later than 60 days after a request is submitted under paragraph (1), the Secretary shall determine whether —

(A) the disease or condition that is the subject of such request is a rare pediatric disease; and

(B) the application for the new drug is a rare pediatric disease product application.

(e) Marketing of Rare Pediatric Disease Products. —

(1) Revocation. — The Secretary may revoke any priority review voucher awarded under subsection (b) if the rare pediatric disease product for which such voucher was awarded is not marketed in the United States within the 365-day period beginning on the date of the approval of such drug under section 505 of this Act or section 351 of the Public Health Service Act.

(2) Postapproval Production Report. — The sponsor of an approved rare pediatric disease product shall submit a report to the Secretary not later than 5 years after the approval of the applicable rare pediatric disease product application. Such report shall provide the following information, with respect to each of the first 4 years after approval of such product:

(A) The estimated population in the United States suffering from the rare pediatric disease.

(B) The estimated demand in the United States for such rare pediatric disease product.

(C) The actual amount of such rare pediatric disease product distributed in the United States.

(f) Notice and Report. —

(1) Notice of Issuance of Voucher and Approval of Products Under Voucher. — The Secretary shall publish a notice in the Federal Register and on the Internet Web site of the Food and Drug Administration not later than 30 days after the occurrence of each of the following:

(A) The Secretary issues a priority review voucher under this section.

(B) The Secretary approves a drug pursuant to an application submitted under section 505(b) of this Act or section 351(a) of the Public Health Service Act for which the sponsor of the application used a priority review voucher under this section.

(2) Notification. — If, after the last day of the 1-year period that begins on the date that the Secretary awards the third rare pediatric disease priority voucher under this section, a sponsor of an application submitted under section 505(b) of this Act or section 351(a) of the Public Health Service Act for a drug uses a priority review voucher under this section for such application, the Secretary shall submit to the Committee on Energy and Commerce of the House of Representatives and the Committee on Health, Education, Labor, and Pensions of the Senate a document —

(A) notifying such Committees of the use of such voucher; and

(B) identifying the drug for which such priority review voucher is used.

(g) Eligibility for Other Programs. — Nothing in this section precludes a sponsor who seeks a priority review voucher under this section from participating in any other incentive program, including under this Act.

(h) Relation to Other Provisions. — The provisions of this section shall supplement, not supplant, any other provisions of this Act or the Public Health Service Act that encourage the development of drugs for tropical diseases and rare pediatric diseases.

(i) GAO Study and Report. —

(1) Study. —

(A) In General. — Beginning on the date that the Secretary awards the third rare pediatric disease priority voucher under this section, the Comptroller General of the United States shall conduct a study of the effectiveness of awarding rare pediatric disease priority vouchers under this section in the development of human drug products that treat or prevent such diseases.

(B) Contents of Study. — In conducting the study under subparagraph (A), the Comptroller General shall examine the following:

(i) The indications for which each rare disease product for which a priority review voucher was awarded was approved under section 505 or section 351 of the Public Health Service Act.

(ii) Whether, and to what extent, an unmet need related to the treatment or prevention of a rare pediatric disease was met through the approval of such rare disease product.

(iii) The value of the priority review voucher if transferred.

(iv) Identification of each drug for which a priority review voucher was used.

(v) The length of the period of time between the date on which a priority review voucher was awarded and the date on which it was used.

(2) Report. — Not later than 1 year after the date under paragraph (1)(A), the Comptroller General shall submit to the Committee on Energy and Commerce of the House of Representatives and the Committee on Health, Education, Labor, and Pensions of the Senate, a report containing the results of the study under paragraph (1).

Sec. 529A. [360gg] Targeted Drugs for Rare Diseases.

(a) Purpose.—The purpose of this section, through the approach provided for in subsection (b), is to—

(1) Facilitate the development, review, and approval of genetically targeted drugs and variant protein targeted drugs to address an unmet medical need in one or more patient subgroups, including subgroups of patients with different mutations of a gene, with respect to rare diseases or conditions that are serious or life-threatening; and

(2) maximize the use of scientific tools or methods, including surrogate endpoints and other biomarkers, for such purposes.

(b) Leveraging of Data from Previously Approved Drug Application or Applications.—The Secretary may, consistent with applicable standards for approval under this Act or section 351(a) of the Public Health Service Act, allow the sponsor of an application under section 505(b)(1) of this Act or section 351(a) of the Public Health Service Act for a genetically targeted drug or a variant protein targeted drug to rely upon data and information—

(1) previously developed by the same sponsor (or another sponsor that has provided the sponsor with a contractual right of reference to such data and information); and

(2) submitted by a sponsor described in paragraph (1) in support of one or more previously approved applications that were submitted under section 505(b)(1) of this Act or section 351(a) of the Public Health Service Act,

for a drug that incorporates or utilizes the same or similar genetically targeted technology as the drug or drugs that are the subject of an application or applications described in paragraph (2) or for a variant protein targeted drug that is the same or incorporates or utilizes the same variant protein targeted drug, as the drug or drugs that are the subject of an application or applications described in paragraph (2).

(c) Definitions.—For purposes of this section—

(1) the term "genetically targeted drug" means a drug that—

(A) is the subject of an application under section 505(b)(1) of this Act or section 351(a) of the Public Health Service Act for the treatment of a rare disease or condition (as such term is defined in section 526) that is serious or life-threatening;

(B) may result in the modulation (including suppression, up-regulation, or activation) of the function of a gene or its associated gene product; and

(C) incorporates or utilizes a genetically targeted technology;

(2) the term "genetically targeted technology" means a technology comprising non-replicating nucleic acid or analogous compounds with a common or similar chemistry that is intended to treat one or more patient subgroups, including subgroups of patients with different mutations of a gene, with the same disease or condition, including a disease or condition due to other variants in the same gene; and

(3) the term "variant protein targeted drug" means a drug that—

(A) is the subject of an application under section 505(b)(1) of this Act for the treatment of a rare disease or condition (as such term is defined in section 526) that is serious or life-threatening;

(B) modulates the function of a product of a mutated gene where such mutation is responsible in whole or in part for a given disease or condition; and

(C) is intended to treat one or more patient subgroups, including subgroups of patients with different mutations of a gene, with the same disease or condition.

(d) Rule of Construction.—Nothing in this section shall be construed to—

(1) alter the authority of the Secretary to approve drugs pursuant to this Act or section 351 of the Public Health Service Act (as authorized prior to the date of enactment of the 21st Century Cures Act [December 13, 2016 — Ed.]), including the standards of evidence, and applicable conditions, for approval under such applicable Act; or

(2) confer any new rights, beyond those authorized under this Act or the Public Health Service Act prior to enactment of this section, with respect to the permissibility of a sponsor referencing information contained in another application submitted under section 505(b)(1) of this Act or section 351(a) of the Public Health Service Act.

Subchapter C — Electronic Product Radiation Control

Sec. 531. [360hh] Definitions.

As used in this subchapter —

(1) the term "electronic product radiation" means —

(A) any ionizing or non-ionizing electromagnetic or particulate radiation, or

(B) any sonic, infrasonic, or ultrasonic wave, which is emitted from an electronic product as the result of the operation of an electronic circuit in such product;

(2) the term "electronic product" means

(A) any manufactured or assembled product which, when in operation,

(i) contains or acts as part of an electronic circuit and

(ii) emits (or in the absence of effective shielding or other controls would emit) electronic product radiation, or

(B) any manufactured or assembled article which is intended for use as a component, part, or accessory of a product described in clause (A) and which when in operation emits (or in the absence of effective shielding or other controls would emit) such radiation;

(3) the term "manufacturer" means any person engaged in the business of manufacturing, assembling, or importing of electronic products;

(4) the term "commerce" means

(A) commerce between any place in any State and any place outside thereof; and

(B) commerce wholly within the District of Columbia; and

(5) the term "State" includes the District of Columbia, the Commonwealth of Puerto Rico, the Northern Mariana Islands, the Virgin Islands, Guam, and American Samoa.

Sec. 532. [360ii] Electronic Product Radiation Control Program.

(a) The Secretary shall establish and carry out an electronic product radiation control program designed to protect the public health and safety from electronic product radiation. As a part of such program, he shall —

(1) pursuant to section 534, develop and administer performance standards for electronic products;

(2) plan, conduct, coordinate, and support research, development, training, and operational activities to minimize the emissions of and the exposure of people to, unnecessary electronic product radiation;

(3) maintain liaison with and receive information from other Federal and State departments and agencies with related interests, professional organizations, industry, industry and labor associations, and other organizations on present and future potential electronic product radiation;

(4) study and evaluate emissions of, and conditions of exposure to, electronic product radiation and intense magnetic fields;

(5) develop, test, and evaluate the effectiveness of procedures and techniques for minimizing exposure to electronic product radiation; and

(6) consult and maintain liaison with the Secretary of Commerce, the Secretary of Defense, the Secretary of Labor, the Atomic Energy Commission, and other appropriate Federal departments and agencies on

(A) techniques, equipment, and programs for testing and evaluating electronic product radiation, and

(B) the development of performance standards pursuant to section 534 to control such radiation emissions.

(b) In carrying out the purposes of subsection (a), the Secretary is authorized to —

(1) —

(A) collect and make available, through publications and other appropriate means, the results of, and other information concerning, research and studies relating to the nature and extent of the hazards and control of electronic product radiation; and

(B) make such recommendations relating to such hazards and control as he considers appropriate;

(2) make grants to public and private agencies, organizations, and institutions, and to individuals for the purposes stated in paragraphs (2), (4), and (5) of subsection (a) of this section;

(3) contract with public or private agencies, institutions, and organizations, and with individuals, without regard to section 3324 of title 31, United States Code, and section 3709 of the Revised Statutes of the United States (41 U.S.C. 5); and

(4) procure (by negotiation or otherwise) electronic products for research and testing purposes, and sell or otherwise dispose of such products.

(c) —

(1) Each recipient of assistance under this subchapter pursuant to grants or contracts entered into under other than competitive bidding procedures shall keep such records as the Secretary shall prescribe, including records which fully disclose the amount and disposition by such recipient of the proceeds of such assistance, the total cost of the project or undertaking in connection with which such assistance is given or used, and the amount of that portion of the cost of the project or undertaking supplied by other sources, and such other records as will facilitate an effective audit.

(2) The Secretary and the Comptroller General of the United States, or any of their duly authorized representatives, shall have access for the purpose of audit and examination to any books, documents, papers, and records of the recipient that are pertinent to the grants or contracts entered into under this subchapter under other than competitive bidding procedures.

Sec. 533. [360jj] Studies by the Secretary.

(a) The Secretary shall conduct the following studies, and shall make a report or reports of the results of such studies to the Congress on or before January 1, 1970, and from time to time thereafter as he may find necessary, together with such recommendations for legislation as he may deem appropriate:

(1) A study of present State and Federal control of health hazards from electronic product radiation and other types of ionizing radiation, which study shall include, but not be limited to —

(A) control of health hazards from radioactive materials other than materials regulated under the Atomic Energy Act of 1954;

(B) any gaps and inconsistencies in present controls;

(C) the need for controlling the sale of certain used electronic products, particularly antiquated X-ray equipment, without upgrading such products to meet the standards for new products or separate standards for used products;

(D) measures to assure consistent and effective control of the aforementioned health hazards;

(E) measures to strengthen radiological health programs of State governments; and

(F) the feasibility of authorizing the Secretary to enter into arrangements with individual States or groups of States to define their respective functions and responsibilities for the control of electronic product radiation and other ionizing radiation;

(2) A study to determine the necessity for the development of standards for the use of nonmedical electronic products for commercial and industrial purposes; and

(3) A study of the development of practicable procedures for the detection and measurement of electronic product radiation which may be emitted from electronic products manufactured or imported prior to the effective date of any applicable standard established pursuant to this subchapter.

(b) In carrying out these studies, the Secretary shall invite the participation of other Federal departments and agencies having related responsibilities and interests, State governments — particularly those of States which regulate radioactive materials under section 274 of the Atomic Energy Act of 1954, as amended, and interested professional, labor, and industrial organizations. Upon request from congressional committees interested in these studies, the Secretary shall keep these committees currently informed as to the progress of the studies and shall permit the committees to send observers to meetings of the study groups.

(c) The Secretary or his designee shall organize the studies and the participation of the invited participants as he deems best. Any dissent from the findings and recommendations of the Secretary shall be included in the report if so requested by the dissenter.

Sec. 534. [360kk] Performance Standards for Electronic Products.

(a) —

(1) The Secretary shall by regulation prescribe performance standards for electronic products to control the emission of electronic product radiation from such products if he determines that such standards are necessary for the protection of the public health and safety. Such standards may include provisions for the testing of such products and the measurement of their electronic product radiation emissions, may require the attachment of warning signs and labels, and may require the provision of instructions for the installation, operation, and use of such products. Such standards may be prescribed from time to time whenever such determinations are made, but the first of such standards shall be prescribed prior to January 1, 1970. In the development of such standards, the Secretary shall consult with Federal and State departments and agencies having related responsibilities or interests and with appropriate professional organizations and interested persons, including representatives of industries and labor organizations which would be affected by such standards, and shall give consideration to —

(A) the latest available scientific and medical data in the field of electronic product radiation;

(B) the standards currently recommended by

(i) other Federal agencies having responsibilities relating to the control and measurement of electronic product radiation, and

(ii) public or private groups having an expertise in the field of electronic product radiation;

(C) the reasonableness and technical feasibility of such standards as applied to a particular electronic product;

(D) the adaptability of such standards to the need for uniformity and reliability of testing and measuring procedures and equipment; and

(E) in the case of a component, or accessory described in paragraph (2)(B) of section 531, the performance of such article in the manufactured or assembled product for which it is designed.

(2) The Secretary may prescribe different and individual performance standards, to the extent appropriate and feasible, for different electronic products so as to recognize their different operating characteristics and uses.

(3) The performance standards prescribed under this section shall not apply to any electronic product which is intended solely for export if

(A) such product and the outside of any shipping container used in the export of such product are labeled or tagged to show that such product is intended for export, and

(B) such product meets all the applicable requirements of the country to which such product is intended for export.

(4) The Secretary may by regulation amend or revoke any performance standard prescribed under this section.

(5) The Secretary may exempt from the provisions of this section any electronic product intended for use by departments or agencies of the United States provided such department or agency has prescribed procurement specifications governing emissions of electronic product radiation and provided further that such product is of a type used solely or predominantly by departments or agencies of the United States.

(b) The provisions of subchapter II of chapter 5 of title 5 of the United States Code (relating to the administrative procedure for rulemaking), and of chapter 7 of such title (relating to judicial review), shall apply with respect to any regulation prescribing, amending, or revoking any standard prescribed under this section.

(c) Each regulation prescribing, amending, or revoking a standard shall specify the date on which it shall take effect which, in the case of any regulation prescribing, or amending any standard, may not be sooner than one year or not later than two years after the date on which such regulation is issued, unless the Secretary finds, for good cause shown, that an earlier or later effective date is in the public interest and publishes in the Federal Register his reason for such finding, in which case such earlier or later date shall apply.

(d) —

(1) In a case of actual controversy as to the validity of any regulation issued under this section prescribing, amending, or revoking a performance standard, any person who will be adversely affected by such regulation when it is effective may at any time prior to the sixtieth day after such regulation is issued file a petition with the United States court of appeals for the circuit wherein such person resides or has his principal place of business, for a judicial review of such regulation. A copy of the petition shall be forthwith transmitted by the clerk of the court to the Secretary or other officer designated by him for that purpose. The Secretary thereupon shall file in the court the record of the proceedings on which the Secretary based the regulation, as provided in section 2112 of title 28 of the United States Code.

(2) If the petitioner applies to the court for leave to adduce additional evidence, and shows to the satisfaction of the court that such additional evidence is material and that there were reasonable grounds for the failure to adduce such evidence in the proceeding before the Secretary, the court may order such additional evidence (and evidence in rebuttal thereof) to be taken before the Secretary, and to be adduced upon the hearing, in such manner and upon such terms and conditions as to the court may seem proper. The Secretary may modify his findings, or make new findings, by reason of the additional evidence so taken, and he shall file such modified or new findings, and his recommendations, if any, for the modification or setting aside of his original regulation, with the return of such additional evidence.

(3) Upon the filing of the petition referred to in paragraph (1) of this subsection, the court shall have jurisdiction to review the regulation in accordance with chapter 7 of title 5 of the United States Code and to grant appropriate relief as provided in such chapter.

(4) The judgment of the court affirming or setting aside, in whole or in part, any such regulation of the Secretary shall be final, subject to review by the Supreme Court of the United States upon certiorari or certification as provided in section 1254 of title 28 of the United States Code.

(5) Any action instituted under this subsection shall survive, notwithstanding any change in the person occupying the office of Secretary or any vacancy in such office.

(6) The remedies provided for in this subsection shall be in addition to and not in substitution for any other remedies provided by law.

(e) A certified copy of the transcript of the record and administrative proceedings under this section shall be furnished by the Secretary to any interested party at his request, and payment of the costs thereof, and shall be admissible in any criminal, exclusion of imports, or other proceeding arising under or in respect of this subchapter, irrespective of whether proceedings with respect to the regulation have previously been initiated or become final under this section.

(f) —

(1) —

(A) The Secretary shall establish a Technical Electronic Product Radiation Safety Standards Committee (hereafter in this subchapter referred to as the "Committee") which he shall consult before prescribing any standard under this section. The Committee shall be appointed by the Secretary, after consultation with public and private agencies concerned with the technical aspect of electronic product radiation safety, and shall be composed of fifteen members each of whom shall be technically qualified by training and experience in one or more fields of science or engineering applicable to electronic product radiation safety, as follows:

(i) Five members shall be selected from governmental agencies, including State and Federal Governments;

(ii) Five members shall be selected from the affected industries after consultation with industry representatives; and

(iii) Five members shall be selected from the general public, of which at least one shall be a representative of organized labor.

(B) The Committee may propose electronic product radiation safety standards to the Secretary for his consideration. All proceedings of the Committee shall be recorded and the record of each such proceeding shall be available for public inspection.

(2) Payments to members of the Committee who are not officers or employees of the United States pursuant to subsection (c) of section 208 of the Public Health Service Act shall not render members of the Committee officers or employees of the United States for any purpose.

(g) The Secretary shall review and evaluate on a continuing basis testing programs carried out by industry to assure the adequacy of safeguards against hazardous electronic product radiation and to assure that electronic products comply with standards prescribed under this section.

(h) Every manufacturer of an electronic product to which is applicable a standard in effect under this section shall furnish to the distributor or dealer at the time of delivery of such product, in the form of a label or tag permanently affixed to such product or in such manner as approved by the Secretary, the certification that such product conforms to all applicable standards under this section. Such certification shall be based upon a test, in accordance with such standard, of the individual article to which it is attached or upon a testing program which is in accord with good manufacturing practice and which has not been disapproved by the Secretary (in such manner as he shall prescribe by regulation) on the grounds that it does not assure the adequacy of safeguards against hazardous electronic product radiation or that it does not assure that electronic products comply with the standards prescribed under this section.

Sec. 535. [360ll] Notification of Defects in, and Repair or Replacement of, Electronic Products.

(a) —

(1) Every manufacturer of electronic products, who discovers that an electronic product produced, assembled, or imported by him has a defect which relates to the safety of use of such product by reason of the emission of electronic product radiation, or that an electronic product produced, assembled, or imported by him on or after the effective date of an applicable standard prescribed pursuant to section 534 fails to comply with such standard, shall immediately notify the Secretary of such defect or failure to comply if such product has left the place of manufacture and shall (except as authorized by paragraph (2)) with reasonable promptness furnish notification of such defect or failure to the persons (where known to the manufacturer) specified in subsection (b) of this section.

(2) If, in the opinion of such manufacturer, the defect or failure to comply is not such as to create a significant risk of injury, including genetic injury, to any person, he may, at the time of giving notice to the Secretary of such defect or failure to comply, apply to the Secretary for an exemption from the requirement of notice to the persons specified in subsection (b). If such application states reasonable grounds for such exemption, the Secretary shall afford such manufacturer an opportunity to present his views and evidence in support of the application, the burden of proof being on the manufacturer. If, after such presentation, the Secretary is satisfied that such defect or failure to comply is not such as to create a significant risk of injury, including genetic injury, to any person, he shall exempt such manufacturer from the requirement of notice to the persons specified in subsection (b) of this section and from the requirements of repair or replacement imposed by subsection (f) of this section.

(b) The notification (other than to the Secretary) required by paragraph (1) of subsection (a) of this section shall be accomplished —

(1) by certified mail to the first purchaser of such product for purposes other than resale, and to any subsequent transferee of such product; and

(2) by certified mail or other more expeditious means to the dealers or distributors of such manufacturer to whom such product was delivered.

(c) The notifications required by paragraph (1) of subsection (a) of this section shall contain a clear description of such defect or failure to comply with an applicable standard, an evaluation of the hazard reasonably related to such defect or failure to comply, and a statement of the measures to be taken to repair such defect. In the case of a notification to a person referred to in subsection (b) of this section, the notification shall also advise the person of his rights under subsection (f) of this section.

(d) Every manufacturer of electronic products shall furnish to the Secretary a true or representative copy of all notices, bulletins, and other communications to the dealers or distributors of such manufacturer or to purchasers (or subsequent transferees) of electronic products of such manufacturer regarding any such defect in such product or any such failure to comply with a standard applicable to such product. The Secretary shall disclose to the public so much of the information contained in such notice or other information obtained under section 537 as he deems will assist in carrying out the purposes of this subchapter, but he shall not disclose any information which contains or relates to a trade secret or other matter referred to in section 1905 of title 18 of the United States Code unless he determines that it is necessary to carry out the purposes of this subchapter.

(e) If through testing, inspection, investigation, or research carried out pursuant to this subchapter, or examination of reports submitted pursuant to section 537, or otherwise, the Secretary determines that any electronic product —

(1) does not comply with an applicable standard prescribed pursuant to section 534; or

(2) contains a defect which relates to the safety of use of such product by reason of the emission of electronic product radiation;

he shall immediately notify the manufacturer of such product of such defect or failure to comply. The notice shall contain the findings of the Secretary and shall include all information upon which the findings are based. The Secretary shall afford such manufacturer an opportunity to present his views and evidence in support thereof, to establish that there is no failure of compliance or that the alleged defect does not exist or does not relate to safety of use of the product by reason of the emission of such radiation hazard. If after such presentation by the manufacturer the Secretary determines that such product does not comply with an applicable standard prescribed pursuant to section 534, or that it contains a defect which relates to the safety of use of such product by reason of the emission of electronic product radiation, the Secretary shall direct the manufacturer to furnish the notification specified in subsection (c) of this section to the persons specified in paragraphs (1) and (2) of subsection (b) of this section (where known to the manufacturer), unless the manufacturer has applied for an exemption from the requirement of such notification on the ground specified in paragraph (2) of subsection (a) and the Secretary is satisfied that such noncompliance or defect is not such as to create a significant risk of injury, including genetic injury, to any person.

(f) If any electronic product is found under subsection (a) or (e) to fail to comply with an applicable standard prescribed under this subchapter or to have a defect which relates to the safety of use of such product, and the notification specified in subsection (c) is required to be furnished on account of such failure or defect, the manufacturer of such product shall

(1) without charge, bring such product into conformity with such standard or remedy such defect and provide reimbursement for any expenses for transportation of such product incurred in connection with having such product brought into conformity or having such defect remedied,

(2) replace such product with a like or equivalent product which complies with each applicable standard prescribed under this subchapter and which has no defect relating to the safety of its use, or

(3) make a refund of the cost of such product.

The manufacturer shall take the action required by this subsection in such manner, and with respect to such persons, as the Secretary by regulations shall prescribe.

(g) This section shall not apply to any electronic product that was manufactured before the date of the enactment of this subchapter [October 18, 1968 — Ed.].

Sec. 536. [360mm] Imports.

(a) Any electronic product offered for importation into the United States which fails to comply with an applicable standard prescribed under this subchapter, or to which is not affixed a certification in the form of a label or tag in conformity with section 534(h) shall be refused admission into the United States. The Secretary of the Treasury shall deliver to the Secretary of Health and Human Services, upon the latter's request, samples of electronic products which are being imported or offered for import into the United States, giving notice thereof to the owner or consignee, who may have a hearing before the Secretary of Health and Human Services. If it appears from an examination of such samples or otherwise that any electronic product fails to comply with applicable standards prescribed pursuant to section 534, then, unless subsection (b) of this section applies and is complied with,

(1) such electronic product shall be refused admission, and

(2) the Secretary of the Treasury shall cause the destruction of such electronic product unless such article is exported, under regulations prescribed by the Secretary of the Treasury, within 90 days after the date of notice of refusal of admission or within such additional time as may be permitted by such regulations.

(b) If it appears to the Secretary of Health and Human Services that any electronic product refused admission pursuant to subsection (a) of this section can be brought into compliance with applicable standards prescribed pursuant to section 534, final determination as to admission of such electronic product may be deferred upon filing of timely written application by the owner or consignee and the execution by him of a good and sufficient bond providing for the payment of such liquidated damages in the event of default as the Secretary of Health and Human Services may by regulation prescribe. If such application is filed and such bond is executed the Secretary of Health and Human Services may, in accordance with rules prescribed by him, permit the applicant to perform such operations with respect to such electronic product as may be specified in the notice of permission.

(c) All expenses (including travel, per diem or subsistence, and salaries of officers or employees of the United States) in connection with the destruction provided for in subsection (a) of this section and the supervision of operations provided for in subsection (b) of this section, and all expenses in connection with the storage, cartage, or labor with respect to any electronic product refused admission pursuant to subsection (a) of this section, shall be paid by the owner or consignee, and, in event of default, shall constitute a lien against any future importations made by such owner or consignee.

(d) It shall be the duty of every manufacturer offering an electronic product for importation into the United States to designate in writing an agent upon whom service of all administrative and judicial processes, notices, orders, decisions, and requirements may be made for and on behalf of said manufacturer, and to file such designation with the Secretary, which designation may from time to time be changed by like writing, similarly filed. Service of all administrative and judicial processes, notices, orders, decisions, and requirements may be made upon said manufacturer by service upon such designated agent at his office or usual place of residence with like effect as if made personally upon said manufacturer, and in default of such designation of such agent, service of process, notice, order, requirement, or decision in any proceeding before the Secretary or in any judicial proceeding for enforcement of this subchapter or any standards prescribed pursuant to this subchapter may be made by posting such process, notice, order, requirement, or decision in the Office of the Secretary or in a place designated by him by regulation.

Sec. 537. [360nn] Inspection and Reports.

(a) If the Secretary finds for good cause that the methods, tests, or programs related to electronic product radiation safety in a particular factory, warehouse, or establishment in which electronic products are manufactured or held, may not be adequate or reliable, officers or employees duly designated by the Secretary, upon presenting appropriate credentials and a written notice to the owner, operator, or agent in charge, are thereafter authorized

(1) to enter, at reasonable times, any area in such factory, warehouse, or establishment in which the manufacturer's tests (or testing programs) required by section 534(h) are carried out, and

(2) to inspect, at reasonable times and within reasonable limits and in a reasonable manner, the facilities and procedures within such area which are related to electronic product radiation safety. Each such inspection shall be commenced and completed with reasonable promptness.

In addition to other grounds upon which good cause may be found for purposes of this subsection, good cause will be considered to exist in any case where the manufacturer has introduced into commerce any electronic product which does not comply with an applicable standard prescribed under this subchapter and with respect to which no exemption from the notification requirements has been granted by the Secretary under section 535(a)(2) or 535(e).

(b) Every manufacturer of electronic products shall establish and maintain such records (including testing records), make such reports, and provide such information, as the Secretary may reasonably require to enable him to determine whether such manufacturer has acted or is acting in compliance with this subchapter and standards prescribed pursuant to this subchapter and shall, upon request of an officer or employee duly designated by the Secretary, permit such officer or employee to inspect appropriate books, papers, records, and documents relevant to determining whether such manufacturer has acted or is acting in compliance with standards prescribed pursuant to this subchapter.

(c) Every manufacturer of electronic products shall provide to the Secretary such performance data and other technical data related to safety as may be required to carry out the purposes of this subchapter. The Secretary is authorized to require the manufacturer to give such notification of such performance and technical data at the time of original purchase to the ultimate purchaser of the electronic product, as he determines necessary to carry out the purposes of this subchapter after consulting with the affected industry.

(d) Accident and investigation reports made under this subchapter by any officer, employee, or agent of the Secretary shall be available for use in any civil, criminal, or other judicial proceeding arising out of such accident. Any such officer, employee, or agent may be required to testify in such proceedings as to the fact developed in such investigations. Any such report shall be made available to the public in a manner which need not identify individuals. All reports on research projects, demonstration projects, and other related activities shall be public information.

(e) The Secretary or his representative shall not disclose any information reported to or otherwise obtained by him, pursuant to subsection (a) or (b) of this section, which concerns any information which contains or relates to a trade secret or other matter referred to in section 1905 of title 18 of the United States Code, except that such information may be disclosed to other officers or employees of the Department and of other agencies concerned with carrying out this subchapter or when relevant in any proceeding under this subchapter. Nothing in this section shall authorize the withholding of information by the Secretary, or by any officers or employees under his control, from the duly authorized committees of the Congress.

(f) The Secretary may by regulation

(1) require dealers and distributors of electronic products, to which there are applicable standards prescribed under this subchapter and the retail prices of which is not less than $50, to furnish manufacturers of such products such information as may be necessary to identify and locate, for purposes of section 535, the first purchasers of such products for purposes other than resale, and

(2) require manufacturers to preserve such information. Any regulation establishing a requirement pursuant to clause (1) of the preceding sentence shall

(A) authorize such dealers and distributors to elect, in lieu of immediately furnishing such information to the manufacturer, to hold and preserve such information until advised by the manufacturer or Secretary that such information is needed by the manufacturer for purposes of section 535, and

(B) provide that the dealer or distributor shall, upon making such election, give prompt notice of such election (together with information identifying the notifier and the product) to the manufacturer and shall, when advised by the manufacturer or Secretary, of the need therefor for the purposes of section 535, immediately furnish the manufacturer with the required information.

If a dealer or distributor discontinues the dealing in or distribution of electronic products, he shall turn the information over to the manufacturer. Any manufacturer receiving information pursuant to this subsection concerning first purchasers of products for purposes other than resale shall treat it as confidential and may use it only if necessary for the purpose of notifying persons pursuant to section 535(a).

Sec. 538. [360oo] Prohibited Acts.

(a) It shall be unlawful —

(1) for any manufacturer to introduce, or to deliver for introduction, into commerce, or to import into the United States, any electronic product which does not comply with an applicable standard prescribed pursuant to section 534;

(2) for any person to fail to furnish any notification or other material or information required by section 535 or 537; or to fail to comply with the requirements of section 535(f);

(3) for any person to fail or to refuse to establish or maintain records required by this subchapter or to permit access by the Secretary or any of his duly authorized representatives to, or the copying of, such records, or to permit entry or inspection, as required by or pursuant to section 537;

(4) for any person to fail or to refuse to make any report required pursuant to section 537(b) or to furnish or preserve any information required pursuant to section 537(f); or

(5) for any person

(A) to fail to issue a certification as required by section 534(h), or

(B) to issue such a certification when such certification is not based upon a test or testing program meeting the requirements of section 534(h) or when the issuer, in the exercise of due care, would have reason to know that such certification is false or misleading in a material respect.

(b) The Secretary may exempt any electronic product, or class thereof, from all or part of subsection (a), upon such conditions as he may find necessary to protect the public health or welfare, for the purpose of research, investigations, studies, demonstrations, or training, or for reasons of national security.

Sec. 539. [360pp] Enforcement.

(a) The district courts of the United States shall have jurisdiction, for cause shown, to restrain violations of section 538 and to restrain dealers and distributors of electronic products from selling or otherwise disposing of electronic products which do not conform to an applicable standard prescribed pursuant to section 534 except when such products are disposed of by returning them to the distributor or manufacturer from whom they were obtained. The district courts of the United States shall also have jurisdiction in accordance with section 1355 of title 28 of the United States Code to enforce the provisions of subsection (b) of this section.

(b) —

(1) Any person who violates section 538 shall be subject to a civil penalty of not more than $1,000. For purposes of this subsection, any such violation shall with respect to each electronic product involved, or with respect to each act or omission made unlawful by section 538, constitute a separate violation, except that the maximum civil penalty imposed on any person under this subsection for any related series of violations shall not exceed $300,000.

(2) Any such civil penalty may on application be remitted or mitigated by the Secretary. In determining the amount of such penalty, or whether it should be remitted or mitigated and in what amount, the appropriateness of such penalty to the size of the business of the person charged and the gravity of the violation shall be considered. The amount of such penalty, when finally determined, may be deducted from any sums owing by the United States to the person charged.

(c) Actions under subsections (a) and (b) of this section may be brought in the district court of the United States for the district wherein any act or omission or transaction constituting the violation occurred, or in such court for the district where the defendant is found or transacts business, and process in such cases may be served in any other district of which the defendant is an inhabitant or wherever the defendant may be found.

(d) Nothing in this subchapter shall be construed as requiring the Secretary to report for the institution of proceedings minor violations of this subchapter whenever he believes that the public interest will be adequately served by a suitable written notice or warning.

(e) Except as provided in the first sentence of section 542, compliance with this subchapter or any regulations issued thereunder shall not relieve any person from liability at common law or under statutory law.

(f) The remedies provided for in this subchapter shall be in addition to and not in substitution for any other remedies provided by law.

Sec. 540. [360qq]. [Repealed.]

Sec. 541. [360rr] Federal-State Cooperation.

The Secretary is authorized

(1) to accept from State and local authorities engaged in activities related to health or safety or consumer protection, on a reimbursable basis or otherwise, any assistance in the administration and enforcement of this subchapter which he may request and which they may be able and willing to provide and, if so agreed, may pay in advance or otherwise for the reasonable cost of such assistance, and

(2) he may, for the purpose of conducting examinations, investigations, and inspections, commission any officer or employee of any such authority as an officer of the Department.

Sec. 542. [360ss] Effect on State Standards.

Whenever any standard prescribed pursuant to section 534 with respect to an aspect of performance of an electronic product is in effect, no State or political subdivision of a State shall have any authority either to establish, or to continue in effect, any standard which is applicable to the same aspect of performance of such product and which is not identical to the Federal standard. Nothing in this subchapter shall be construed to prevent the Federal Government or the government of any State or political subdivision thereof from establishing a requirement with respect to emission of radiation from electronic products procured for its own use if such requirement imposes a more restrictive standard than that required to comply with the otherwise applicable Federal standard.

Subchapter D — Dissemination of Treatment Information

Sec. 551. [360aaa] Requirements for Dissemination of Treatment Information on Drugs or Devices.

(a) In General. — Notwithstanding sections 301(d), 502(f), and 505, and section 351 of the Public Health Service Act (42 U.S.C. 262), a manufacturer may disseminate to —

(1) a health care practitioner;

(2) a pharmacy benefit manager;

(3) a health insurance issuer;

(4) a group health plan; or

(5) a Federal or State governmental agency;

written information concerning the safety, effectiveness, or benefit of a use not described in the approved labeling of a drug or device if the manufacturer meets the requirements of subsection (b).

(b) Specific Requirements. — A manufacturer may disseminate information under subsection (a) on a new use only if —

(1) —

(A) in the case of a drug, there is in effect for the drug an application filed under subsection (b) or (j) of section 505 or a biologics license issued under section 351 of the Public Health Service Act; or

(B) in the case of a device, the device is being commercially distributed in accordance with a regulation under subsection (d) or (e) of section 513, an order under subsection (f) of such section, or the approval of an application under section 515;

(2) the information meets the requirements of section 552;

(3) the information to be disseminated is not derived from clinical research conducted by another manufacturer or if it was derived from research conducted by another manufacturer, the manufacturer disseminating the information has the permission of such other manufacturer to make the dissemination;

(4) the manufacturer has, 60 days before such dissemination, submitted to the Secretary —

(A) a copy of the information to be disseminated; and

(B) any clinical trial information the manufacturer has relating to the safety or effectiveness of the new use, any reports of clinical experience pertinent to the safety of the new use, and a summary of such information;

(5) the manufacturer has complied with the requirements of section 554 (relating to a supplemental application for such use);

(6) the manufacturer includes along with the information to be disseminated under this subsection —

(A) a prominently displayed statement that discloses —

(i) that the information concerns a use of a drug or device that has not been approved or cleared by the Food and Drug Administration;

(ii) if applicable, that the information is being disseminated at the expense of the manufacturer;

(iii) if applicable, the name of any authors of the information who are employees of, consultants to, or have received compensation from, the manufacturer, or who have a significant financial interest in the manufacturer;

(iv) the official labeling for the drug or device and all updates with respect to the labeling;

(v) if applicable, a statement that there are products or treatments that have been approved or cleared for the use that is the subject of the information being disseminated pursuant to subsection (a)(1); and

(vi) the identification of any person that has provided funding for the conduct of a study relating to the new use of a drug or device for which such information is being disseminated; and

(B) a bibliography of other articles from a scientific reference publication or scientific or medical journal that have been previously published about the use of the drug or device covered by the information disseminated (unless the information already includes such bibliography).

(c) Additional Information. — If the Secretary determines, after providing notice of such determination and an opportunity for a meeting with respect to such determination, that the information submitted by a manufacturer under subsection (b)(3)(B), with respect to the use of a drug or device for which the manufacturer intends to disseminate information, fails to provide data, analyses, or other written matter that is objective and balanced, the Secretary may require the manufacturer to disseminate —

(1) additional objective and scientifically sound information that pertains to the safety or effectiveness of the use and is necessary to provide objectivity and balance, including any information that the manufacturer has submitted to the Secretary, or, where appropriate, a summary of such information or any other information that the Secretary has authority to make available to the public; and

(2) an objective statement of the Secretary, based on data or other scientifically sound information available to the Secretary, that bears on the safety or effectiveness of the new use of the drug or device.

Sec. 552. [360aaa-1] Information Authorized to Be Disseminated.

(a) Authorized Information. — A manufacturer may disseminate information under section 551 on a new use only if the information —

(1) is in the form of an unabridged —

(A) reprint or copy of an article, peer-reviewed by experts qualified by scientific training or experience to evaluate the safety or effectiveness of the drug or device involved, which was published in a scientific or medical journal (as defined in section 556(5)), which is about a clinical investigation with respect to the drug or device, and which would be considered to be scientifically sound by such experts; or

(B) reference publication, described in subsection (b), that includes information about a clinical investigation with respect to the drug or device that would be considered to be scientifically sound by experts qualified by scientific training or experience to evaluate the safety or effectiveness of the drug or device that is the subject of such a clinical investigation; and

(2) is not false or misleading and would not pose a significant risk to the public health.

(b) Reference Publication. — A reference publication referred to in subsection (a)(1)(B) is a publication that —

(1) has not been written, edited, excerpted, or published specifically for, or at the request of, a manufacturer of a drug or device;

(2) has not been edited or significantly influenced by a such a manufacturer;

(3) is not solely distributed through such a manufacturer but is generally available in bookstores or other distribution channels where medical textbooks are sold;

(4) does not focus on any particular drug or device of a manufacturer that disseminates information under section 551 and does not have a primary focus on new uses of drugs or devices that are marketed or under investigation by a manufacturer supporting the dissemination of information; and

(5) presents materials that are not false or misleading.

Sec. 553. [360aaa-2] Establishment of List of Articles and Publications Disseminated and List of Providers That Received Articles and Reference Publications.

(a) In General. — A manufacturer may disseminate information under section 551 on a new use only if the manufacturer prepares and submits to the Secretary biannually —

(1) a list containing the titles of the articles and reference publications relating to the new use of drugs or devices that were disseminated by the manufacturer to a person described in section 551(a) for the 6-month period preceding the date on which the manufacturer submits the list to the Secretary; and

(2) a list that identifies the categories of providers (as described in section 551(a)) that received the articles and reference publications for the 6-month period described in paragraph (1).

(b) Records. — A manufacturer that disseminates information under section 551 shall keep records that may be used by the manufacturer when, pursuant to section 555, such manufacturer is required to take corrective action and shall be made available to the Secretary, upon request, for purposes of ensuring or taking corrective action pursuant to such section. Such records, at the Secretary's discretion, may identify the recipient of information provided pursuant to section 551 or the categories of such recipients.

Sec. 554. [360aaa-3] Requirement Regarding Submission of Supplemental Application for New Use; Exemption from Requirement.

(a) In General. — A manufacturer may disseminate information under section 551 on a new use only if —

(1) —

(A) the manufacturer has submitted to the Secretary a supplemental application for such use; or

(B) the manufacturer meets the condition described in subsection (b) or (c) (relating to a certification that the manufacturer will submit such an application); or

(2) there is in effect for the manufacturer an exemption under subsection (d) from the requirement of paragraph (1).

(b) Certification on Supplemental Application; Condition in Case of Completed Studies. — For purposes of subsection (a)(1)(B), a manufacturer may disseminate information on a new use if the manufacturer has submitted to the Secretary an application containing a certification that —

(1) the studies needed for the submission of a supplemental application for the new use have been completed; and

(2) the supplemental application will be submitted to the Secretary not later than 6 months after the date of the initial dissemination of information under section 551.

(c) Certification on Supplemental Application; Condition in Case of Planned Studies. —

(1) In General. — For purposes of subsection (a)(1)(B), a manufacturer may disseminate information on a new use if —

(A) the manufacturer has submitted to the Secretary an application containing —

(i) a proposed protocol and schedule for conducting the studies needed for the submission of a supplemental application for the new use; and

(ii) a certification that the supplemental application will be submitted to the Secretary not later than 36 months after the date of the initial dissemination of information under section 551 (or, as applicable, not later than such date as the Secretary may specify pursuant to an extension under paragraph (3)); and

(B) the Secretary has determined that the proposed protocol is adequate and that the schedule for completing such studies is reasonable.

(2) Progress Reports on Studies. — A manufacturer that submits to the Secretary an application under paragraph (1) shall submit to the Secretary periodic reports describing the status of the studies involved.

(3) Extension of Time Regarding Planned Studies. — The period of 36 months authorized in paragraph (1)(A)(ii) for the completion of studies may be extended by the Secretary if —

(A) the Secretary determines that the studies needed to submit such an application cannot be completed and submitted within 36 months; or

(B) the manufacturer involved submits to the Secretary a written request for the extension and the Secretary determines that the manufacturer has acted with due diligence to conduct the studies in a timely manner, except that an extension under this subparagraph may not be provided for more than 24 additional months.

(d) Exemption from Requirement of Supplemental Application. —

(1) In General. — For purposes of subsection (a)(2), a manufacturer may disseminate information on a new use if —

(A) the manufacturer has submitted to the Secretary an application for an exemption from meeting the requirement of subsection (a)(1); and

(B) —

(i) the Secretary has approved the application in accordance with paragraph (2); or

(ii) the application is deemed under paragraph (3)(A) to have been approved (unless such approval is terminated pursuant to paragraph (3)(B)).

(2) Conditions for Approval. — The Secretary may approve an application under paragraph (1) for an exemption if the Secretary makes a determination described in subparagraph (A) or (B), as follows:

(A) The Secretary makes a determination that, for reasons defined by the Secretary, it would be economically prohibitive with respect to such drug or device for the manufacturer to incur the costs necessary for the submission of a supplemental application. In making such determination, the Secretary shall consider (in addition to any other considerations the Secretary finds appropriate) —

(i) the lack of the availability under law of any period during which the manufacturer would have exclusive marketing rights with respect to the new use involved; and

(ii) the size of the population expected to benefit from approval of the supplemental application.

(B) The Secretary makes a determination that, for reasons defined by the Secretary, it would be unethical to conduct the studies necessary for the supplemental application. In making such determination, the Secretary shall consider (in addition to any other considerations the Secretary finds appropriate) whether the new use involved is the standard of medical care for a health condition.

(3) Time for Consideration of Application; Deemed Approval. —

(A) In General. — The Secretary shall approve or deny an application under paragraph (1) for an exemption not later than 60 days after the receipt of the application. If the Secretary does not comply with the preceding sentence the application is deemed to be approved.

(B) Termination of Deemed Approval. — If pursuant to a deemed approval under subparagraph (A) a manufacturer disseminates written information under section 551 on a new use, the Secretary may at any time terminate such approval and under section 555(b)(3) order the manufacturer to cease disseminating the information.

(e) Requirements Regarding Applications. — Applications under this section shall be submitted in the form and manner prescribed by the Secretary.

Sec. 555. [360aaa-4] Corrective Actions; Cessation of Dissemination.

(a) Post Dissemination Data Regarding Safety and Effectiveness. —

(1) Corrective Actions. — With respect to data received by the Secretary after the dissemination of information under section 551 by a manufacturer has begun (whether received pursuant to paragraph (2) or otherwise), if the Secretary determines that the data indicate that the new use involved may not be effective or may present a significant risk to public health, the Secretary shall, after consultation with the manufacturer, take such action regarding the dissemination of the information as the Secretary determines to be appropriate for the protection of the public health, which may include ordering that the manufacturer cease the dissemination of the information.

(2) Responsibilities of Manufacturers to Submit Data. — After a manufacturer disseminates information under section 551, the manufacturer shall submit to the Secretary a notification of any additional knowledge of the manufacturer on clinical research or other data that relate to the safety or effectiveness of the new use involved. If the manufacturer is in possession of the data, the notification shall include the data. The Secretary shall by regulation establish the scope of the responsibilities of manufacturers under this paragraph, including such limits on the responsibilities as the Secretary determines to be appropriate.

(b) Cessation of Dissemination. —

(1) Failure of Manufacturer to Comply with Requirements. — The Secretary may order a manufacturer to cease the dissemination of information pursuant to section 551 if the Secretary determines that the information being disseminated does not comply with the requirements established in this subchapter. Such an order may be issued only after the Secretary has provided notice to the manufacturer of the intent of the Secretary to issue the order and (unless paragraph (2)(B) applies) has provided an opportunity for a meeting with respect to such intent. If the failure of the manufacturer constitutes a minor violation of this subchapter, the Secretary shall delay issuing the order and provide to the manufacturer an opportunity to correct the violation.

(2) Supplemental Applications. — The Secretary may order a manufacturer to cease the dissemination of information pursuant to section 551 if —

(A) in the case of a manufacturer that has submitted a supplemental application for a new use pursuant to section 554(a)(1), the Secretary determines that the supplemental application does not contain adequate information for approval of the new use for which the application was submitted;

(B) in the case of a manufacturer that has submitted a certification under section 554(b), the manufacturer has not, within the 6-month period involved, submitted the supplemental application referred to in the certification; or

(C) in the case of a manufacturer that has submitted a certification under section 554(c) but has not yet submitted the supplemental application referred to in the certification, the Secretary determines, after an informal hearing, that the manufacturer is not acting with due diligence to complete the studies involved.

(3) Termination of Deemed Approval of Exemption Regarding Supplemental Applications. — If under section 554(d)(3) the Secretary terminates a deemed approval of an exemption, the Secretary may order the manufacturer involved to cease disseminating the information. A manufacturer shall comply with an order under the preceding sentence not later than 60 days after the receipt of the order.

(c) Corrective Actions by Manufacturers. —

(1) In General. — In any case in which under this section the Secretary orders a manufacturer to cease disseminating information, the Secretary may order the manufacturer to take action to correct the information that has been disseminated, except as provided in paragraph (2).

(2) Termination of Deemed Approval of Exemption Regarding Supplemental Applications. — In the case of an order under subsection (b)(3) to cease disseminating information, the Secretary may not order the manufacturer involved to take action to correct the information that has been disseminated unless the Secretary determines that the new use described in the information would pose a significant risk to the public health.

Sec. 556. [360aaa-5] Definitions.

For purposes of this subchapter:

(1) The term "health care practitioner" means a physician, or other individual who is a provider of health care, who is licensed under the law of a State to prescribe drugs or devices.

(2) The terms "health insurance issuer" and "group health plan" have the meaning given such terms under section 2791 of the Public Health Service Act.

(3) The term "manufacturer" means a person who manufactures a drug or device, or who is licensed by such person to distribute or market the drug or device.

(4) The term "new use" —

(A) with respect to a drug, means a use that is not included in the labeling of the approved drug; and

(B) with respect to a device, means a use that is not included in the labeling for the approved or cleared device.

(5) The term "scientific or medical journal" means a scientific or medical publication —

(A) that is published by an organization —

(i) that has an editorial board;

(ii) that utilizes experts, who have demonstrated expertise in the subject of an article under review by the organization and who are independent of the organization, to review and objectively select, reject, or provide comments about proposed articles; and

(iii) that has a publicly stated policy, to which the organization adheres, of full disclosure of any conflict of interest or biases for all authors or contributors involved with the journal or organization;

(B) whose articles are peer-reviewed and published in accordance with the regular peer-review procedures of the organization;

(C) that is generally recognized to be of national scope and reputation;

(D) that is indexed in the Index Medicus of the National Library of Medicine of the National Institutes of Health; and

(E) that is not in the form of a special supplement that has been funded in whole or in part by one or more manufacturers.

Sec. 557. [360aaa-6] Rules of Construction.

(a) Unsolicited Request. — Nothing in section 551 shall be construed as prohibiting a manufacturer from disseminating information in response to an unsolicited request from a health care practitioner.

(b) Dissemination of Information on Drugs or Devices Not Evidence of Intended Use. — Notwithstanding subsection (a), (f), or (o) of section 502, or any other provision of law, the dissemination of information relating to a new use of a drug or device, in accordance with section 551, shall not be construed by the Secretary as evidence of a new intended use of the drug or device that is different from the intended use of the drug or device set forth in the official labeling of the drug or device. Such dissemination shall not be considered by the Secretary as labeling, adulteration, or misbranding of the drug or device.

(c) Patent Protection. — Nothing in section 551 shall affect patent rights in any manner.

(d) Authorization for Dissemination of Articles and Fees for Reprints of Articles. — Nothing in section 551 shall be construed as prohibiting an entity that publishes a scientific journal (as defined in section 556(5)) from requiring authorization from the entity to disseminate an article published by such entity or charging fees for the purchase of reprints of published articles from such entity.

Subchapter E — General Provisions Relating to Drugs and Devices

Sec. 561. [360bbb] Expanded Access to Unapproved Therapies and Diagnostics.

(a) Emergency Situations. — The Secretary may, under appropriate conditions determined by the Secretary, authorize the shipment of investigational drugs or investigational devices for the diagnosis, monitoring, or treatment of a serious disease or condition in emergency situations.

(b) Individual Patient Access to Investigational Products Intended for Serious Diseases. — Any person, acting through a physician licensed in accordance with State law, may request from a manufacturer or distributor, and any manufacturer or distributor may, after complying with the provisions of this subsection, provide to such physician an investigational drug or investigational device for the diagnosis, monitoring, or treatment of a serious disease or condition if—

(1) the licensed physician determines that the person has no comparable or satisfactory alternative therapy available to diagnose, monitor, or treat the disease or condition involved, and that the probable risk to the person from the investigational drug or investigational device is not greater than the probable risk from the disease or condition;

(2) the Secretary determines that there is sufficient evidence of safety and effectiveness to support the use of the investigational drug or investigational device in the case described in paragraph (1);

(3) the Secretary determines that provision of the investigational drug or investigational device will not interfere with the initiation, conduct, or completion of clinical investigations to support marketing approval; and

(4) the sponsor, or clinical investigator, of the investigational drug or investigational device submits to the Secretary a clinical protocol consistent with the provisions of section 505(i) or 520(g), including any regulations promulgated under section 505(i) or 520(g), describing the use of the investigational drug or investigational device in a single patient or a small group of patients.

(c) Treatment Investigational New Drug Applications and Treatment Investigational Device Exemptions. — Upon submission by a sponsor or a physician of a protocol intended to provide widespread access to an investigational drug or investigational device for eligible patients (referred to in this subsection as an "expanded access protocol"), the Secretary shall permit such investigational drug or investigational device to be made available for expanded access under a treatment investigational new drug application or treatment investigational device exemption if the Secretary determines that—

(1) under the treatment investigational new drug application or treatment investigational device exemption, the investigational drug or investigational device is intended for use in the diagnosis, monitoring, or treatment of a serious or immediately life-threatening disease or condition;

(2) there is no comparable or satisfactory alternative therapy available to diagnose, monitor, or treat that stage of disease or condition in the population of patients to which the investigational drug or investigational device is intended to be administered;

(3) —

(A) the investigational drug or investigational device is under investigation in a controlled clinical trial for the use described in paragraph (1) under an investigational drug application in effect under section 505(i) or investigational device exemption in effect under section 520(g); or

(B) all clinical trials necessary for approval of that use of the investigational drug or investigational device have been completed;

(4) the sponsor of the controlled clinical trials is actively pursuing marketing approval of the investigational drug or investigational device for the use described in paragraph (1) with due diligence;

(5) in the case of an investigational drug or investigational device described in paragraph (3)(A), the provision of the investigational drug or investigational device will not interfere with the enrollment of patients in ongoing clinical investigations under section 505(i) or 520(g);

(6) in the case of serious diseases, there is sufficient evidence of safety and effectiveness to support the use described in paragraph (1); and

(7) in the case of immediately life-threatening diseases, the available scientific evidence, taken as a whole, provides a reasonable basis to conclude that the investigational drug or investigational device may be effective for its intended use and would not expose patients to an unreasonable and significant risk of illness or injury.

A protocol submitted under this subsection shall be subject to the provisions of section 505(i) or 520(g), including regulations promulgated under section 505(i) or 520(g). The Secretary may inform national, State, and local medical associations and societies, voluntary health associations, and other appropriate persons about the availability of an investigational drug or investigational device under expanded access protocols submitted under this subsection. The information provided by the Secretary, in accordance with the preceding sentence, shall be the same type of information that is required by section 402(j)(3) of the Public Health Service Act.

(d) Termination. — The Secretary may, at any time with respect to a sponsor, physician, manufacturer, or distributor described in this section, terminate expanded access provided under this section for an investigational drug or investigational device if the requirements under this section are no longer met.

(e) Definitions. — In this section, the terms "investigational drug", "investigational device", "treatment investigational new drug application", and "treatment investigational device exemption" shall have the meanings given the terms in regulations prescribed by the Secretary.

Sec. 561A. [360bbb-0] Expanded Access Policy Required for Investigational Drugs.

(a) In General.—The manufacturer or distributor of one or more investigational drugs for the diagnosis, monitoring, or treatment of one or more serious diseases or conditions shall make available the policy of the manufacturer or distributor on evaluating and responding to requests submitted under section 561(b) for provision of such a drug.

(b) Public Availability of Expanded Access Policy.—The policies under subsection (a) shall be made public and readily available, such as by posting such policies on a publicly available Internet website. Such policies may be generally applicable to all investigational drugs of such manufacturer or distributor.

(c) Content of Policy.—A policy described in subsection (a) shall include—

(1) contact information for the manufacturer or distributor to facilitate communication about requests described in subsection (a);

(2) procedures for making such requests;

(3) the general criteria the manufacturer or distributor will use to evaluate such requests for individual patients, and for responses to such requests;

(4) the length of time the manufacturer or distributor anticipates will be necessary to acknowledge receipt of such requests; and

(5) a hyperlink or other reference to the clinical trial record containing information about the expanded access for such drug that is required under section 402(j)(2)(A)(ii)(II)(gg) of the Public Health Service Act.

(d) No Guarantee of Access.—The posting of policies by manufacturers and distributors under subsection (a) shall not serve as a guarantee of access to any specific investigational drug by any individual patient.

(e) Revised Policy.—Nothing in this section shall prevent a manufacturer or distributor from revising a policy required under this section at any time.

(f) Application.—This section shall apply to a manufacturer or distributor with respect to an investigational drug beginning on the ~~later~~ earlier of—

~~(1) the date that is 60 calendar days after the date of enactment of the 21st Century Cures Act [December 13, 2016 — Ed.]; or~~

~~(2)~~ (1) the first initiation of a phase 2 or phase 3 study (as such terms are defined in section 312.21(b) and (c) of title 21, Code of Federal Regulations (or any successor regulations)) with respect to such investigational drug~~.~~; or

(2) as applicable, 15 days after the drug receives a designation as a breakthrough therapy, fast track product, or regenerative advanced therapy under subsection (a), (b), or (g), respectively, of section 506.

Sec. 562. [360bbb-1] Dispute Resolution.

If, regarding an obligation concerning drugs or devices under this Act or section 351 of the Public Health Service Act, there is a scientific controversy between the Secretary and a person who is a sponsor, applicant, or manufacturer and no specific provision of the Act involved, including a regulation promulgated under such Act, provides a right of review of the matter in controversy, the Secretary shall, by regulation, establish a procedure under which such sponsor, applicant, or manufacturer may request a review of such controversy, including a review by an appropriate scientific advisory panel described in section 505(n) or an advisory committee described in section 515(g)(2)(B). Any such review shall take place in a timely manner. The Secretary shall promulgate such regulations within 1 year after the date of the enactment of the Food and Drug Administration Modernization Act of 1997 [November 21, 1997 — Ed.].

Sec. 563. [360bbb-2] Classification of Products.

(a) Request. — A person who submits an application or submission (including a petition, notification, and any other similar form of request) under this Act for a product, may submit a request to the Secretary respecting the classification of the product as a drug, biological product, device, or a combination product subject to section 503(g) or respecting the component of the Food and Drug Administration that will regulate the product. In submitting the request, the person shall recommend a classification for the product, or a component to regulate the product, as appropriate.

(b) Statement. — Not later than 60 days after the receipt of the request described in subsection (a), the Secretary shall determine the classification of the product under subsection (a), or the component of the Food and Drug Administration that will regulate the product, and shall provide to the person a written statement that identifies such classification or such component, and the reasons for such determination. The Secretary may not modify such statement except with the written consent of the person, or for public health reasons based on scientific evidence.

(c) Inaction of Secretary. — If the Secretary does not provide the statement within the 60-day period described in subsection (b), the recommendation made by the person under subsection (a) shall be considered to be a final determination by the Secretary of such classification of the product, or the component of the Food and Drug Administration that will regulate the product, as applicable, and may not be modified by the Secretary except with the written consent of the person, or for public health reasons based on scientific evidence.

Sec. 564. [360bbb-3] Authorization for Medical Products for Use in Emergencies.

(a) In General. —

(1) Emergency Uses. — Notwithstanding any provision of this Act and section 351 of the Public Health Service Act, and subject to the provisions of this section, the Secretary may authorize the introduction into interstate commerce, during the effective period of a declaration under subsection (b), of a drug, device, or biological product intended for use in an actual or potential emergency (referred to in this section as an "emergency use").

(2) Approval Status of Product. — An authorization under paragraph (1) may authorize an emergency use of a product that —

(A) is not approved, licensed, or cleared for commercial distribution under section 505, 510(k), or 515 of this Act or section 351 of the Public Health Service Act (referred to in this section as an "unapproved product"); or

(B) is approved, licensed, or cleared under such a provision, but which use is not under such provision an approved, licensed, or cleared use of the product (referred to in this section as an "unapproved use of an approved product").

(3) Relation to Other Uses. — An emergency use authorized under paragraph (1) for a product is in addition to any other use that is authorized for the product under a section of this Act or the Public Health Service Act referred to in paragraph (2)(A).

(4) Definitions. — For purposes of this section:

(A) The term "biological product" has the meaning given such term in section 351 of the Public Health Service Act.

(B) The term "emergency use" has the meaning indicated for such term in paragraph (1).

(C) The term "product" means a drug, device, or biological product.

(D) The term "unapproved product" has the meaning indicated for such term in paragraph (2)(A).

(E) The term "unapproved use of an approved product" has the meaning indicated for such term in paragraph (2)(B).

(b) Declaration of Emergency or Threat Justifying Emergency Authorized Use. —

(1) In General. — The Secretary may make a declaration that the circumstances exist justifying the authorization under this subsection for a product on the basis of —

(A) a determination by the Secretary of Homeland Security that there is a domestic emergency, or a significant potential for a domestic emergency, involving a heightened risk of attack with a biological, chemical, radiological, or nuclear agent or agents;

(B) a determination by the Secretary of Defense that there is a military emergency, or a significant potential for a military emergency, involving a heightened risk to United States military forces of attack with a biological, chemical, radiological, or nuclear agent or agents;

(C) a determination by the Secretary that there is a public health emergency, or a significant potential for a public health emergency, that affects, or has a significant potential to affect, national security or the health and security of United States citizens living abroad, and that involves a biological, chemical, radiological, or nuclear agent or agents, or a disease or condition that may be attributable to such agent or agents; or

(D) the identification of a material threat pursuant to section 319F-2 of the Public Health Service Act sufficient to affect national security or the health and security of United States citizens living abroad.

(2) Termination of Declaration. —

(A) In General. — A declaration under this subsection shall terminate upon the earlier of —

(i) a determination by the Secretary, in consultation as appropriate with the Secretary of Homeland Security or the Secretary of Defense, that the circumstances described in paragraph (1) have ceased to exist; or

(ii) a change in the approval status of the product such that the circumstances described in subsection (a)(2) have ceased to exist.

(B) Disposition of Product. — If an authorization under this section with respect to an unapproved product ceases to be effective as a result of a termination under subparagraph (A) of this paragraph, the Secretary shall consult with the manufacturer of such product with respect to the appropriate disposition of the product.

(3) Advance Notice of Termination. — The Secretary shall provide advance notice that a declaration under this subsection will be terminated. The period of advance notice shall be a period reasonably determined to provide —

(A) in the case of an unapproved product, a sufficient period for disposition of the product, including the return of such product (except such quantities of product as are necessary to provide for continued use consistent with subsection (f)(2)) to the manufacturer (in the case of a manufacturer that chooses to have such product returned); and

(B) in the case of an unapproved use of an approved product, a sufficient period for the disposition of any labeling, or any information under subsection (e)(2)(B)(ii), as the case may be, that was provided with respect to the emergency use involved.

(4) Publication.—The Secretary shall promptly publish in the Federal Register each declaration, determination, and advance notice of termination under this subsection.

(5) Explanation by Secretary.— If an authorization under this section with respect to an unapproved product or an unapproved use of an approved product has been in effect for more than 1 year, the Secretary shall provide in writing to the sponsor of such product an explanation of the scientific, regulatory, or other obstacles to approval, licensure, or clearance of such product or use, including specific actions to be taken by the Secretary and the sponsor to overcome such obstacles.

(c) Criteria for Issuance of Authorization. — The Secretary may issue an authorization under this section with respect to the emergency use of a product only if, after consultation with the Assistant Secretary for Preparedness and Response, the Director of the National Institutes of Health, and the Director of the Centers for Disease Control and Prevention (to the extent feasible and appropriate given the applicable circumstances described in subsection (b)(1)), the Secretary concludes —

(1) that an agent referred to in a declaration under subsection (b) can cause a serious or life-threatening disease or condition;

(2) that, based on the totality of scientific evidence available to the Secretary, including data from adequate and well-controlled clinical trials, if available, it is reasonable to believe that —

(A) the product may be effective in diagnosing, treating, or preventing —

(i) such disease or condition; or

(ii) a serious or life-threatening disease or condition caused by a product authorized under this section, approved or cleared under this Act, or licensed under section 351 of the Public Health Service Act, for diagnosing, treating, or preventing such a disease or condition caused by such an agent; and

(B) the known and potential benefits of the product, when used to diagnose, prevent, or treat such disease or condition, outweigh the known and potential risks of the product, taking into consideration the material threat posed by the agent or agents identified in a declaration under subsection (b)(1)(D), if applicable;

(3) that there is no adequate, approved, and available alternative to the product for diagnosing, preventing, or treating such disease or condition; and

(4) that such other criteria as the Secretary may by regulation prescribe are satisfied.

(d) Scope of Authorization. — An authorization of a product under this section shall state —

(1) each disease or condition that the product may be used to diagnose, prevent, or treat within the scope of the authorization;

(2) the Secretary's conclusions, made under subsection (c)(2)(B), that the known and potential benefits of the product, when used to diagnose, prevent, or treat such disease or condition, outweigh the known and potential risks of the product; and

(3) the Secretary's conclusions, made under subsection (c), concerning the safety and potential effectiveness of the product in diagnosing, preventing, or treating such diseases or conditions, including, to the extent practicable given the circumstances of the emergency, an assessment of the available scientific evidence.

(e) Conditions of Authorization. —

(1) Unapproved Product. —

(A) Required Conditions. — With respect to the emergency use of an unapproved product, the Secretary, to the extent practicable given the applicable circumstances described in subsection (b)(1), shall, for a person who carries out any activity for which the authorization is issued, establish such conditions on an authorization under this section as the Secretary finds necessary or appropriate to protect the public health, including the following:

(i) Appropriate conditions designed to ensure that health care professionals administering the product are informed —

(I) that the Secretary has authorized the emergency use of the product;

(II) of the significant known and potential benefits and risks of the emergency use of the product, and of the extent to which such benefits and risks are unknown; and

(III) of the alternatives to the product that are available, and of their benefits and risks.

(ii) Appropriate conditions designed to ensure that individuals to whom the product is administered are informed —

(I) that the Secretary has authorized the emergency use of the product;

(II) of the significant known and potential benefits and risks of such use, and of the extent to which such benefits and risks are unknown; and

(III) of the option to accept or refuse administration of the product, of the consequences, if any, of refusing administration of the product, and of the alternatives to the product that are available and of their benefits and risks.

(iii) Appropriate conditions for the monitoring and reporting of adverse events associated with the emergency use of the product.

(iv) For manufacturers of the product, appropriate conditions concerning recordkeeping and reporting, including records access by the Secretary, with respect to the emergency use of the product.

(B) Authority for Additional Conditions. — With respect to the emergency use of an unapproved product, the Secretary may, for a person who carries out any activity for which the authorization is issued, establish such conditions on an authorization under this section as the Secretary finds necessary or appropriate to protect the public health, including the following:

(i) Appropriate conditions on which entities may distribute the product with respect to the emergency use of the product (including limitation to distribution by government entities), and on how distribution is to be performed.

(ii) Appropriate conditions on who may administer the product with respect to the emergency use of the product, and on the categories of individuals to whom, and the circumstances under which, the product may be administered with respect to such use.

(iii) Appropriate conditions with respect to collection and analysis of information concerning the safety and effectiveness of the product with respect to the use of such product during the period when the authorization is in effect and a reasonable time following such period.

(iv) For persons other than manufacturers of the product, appropriate conditions concerning recordkeeping and reporting, including records access by the Secretary, with respect to the emergency use of the product.

(2) Unapproved Use. — With respect to the emergency use of a product that is an unapproved use of an approved product:

(A) For a person who carries out any activity for which the authorization is issued, the Secretary shall, to the extent practicable given the applicable circumstances described in subsection (b)(1), establish conditions described in clauses (i) and (ii) of paragraph (1)(A), and may establish conditions described in clauses (iii) and (iv) of such paragraph or in paragraph (1)(B).

(B) —

(i) If the authorization under this section regarding the emergency use authorizes a change in the labeling of the product, but the manufacturer of the product chooses not to make such change, such authorization may not authorize distributors of the product or any other person to alter or obscure the labeling provided by the manufacturer, except as provided in section 564A with respect to authorized changes to the product expiration date.

(ii) In the circumstances described in clause (i), for a person who does not manufacture the product and who chooses to act under this clause, an authorization under this section regarding the emergency use shall, to the extent practicable given the circumstances of the emergency, authorize such person to provide appropriate information with respect to such product in addition to the labeling provided by the manufacturer, subject to compliance with clause (i). While the authorization under this section is effective, such additional information shall not be considered labeling for purposes of section 502.

(C) In establishing conditions under this paragraph with respect to the distribution and administration of the product for the unapproved use, the Secretary shall not impose conditions that would restrict distribution or administration of the product when distributed or administered for the approved use.

(3) Good Manufacturing Practice; Prescription. — With respect to the emergency use of a product for which an authorization under this section is issued (whether an unapproved product or an unapproved use of an approved product), the Secretary may waive or limit, to the extent appropriate given the applicable circumstances described in subsection (b)(1)—

(A) requirements regarding current good manufacturing practice otherwise applicable to the manufacture, processing, packing, or holding of products subject to regulation under this Act, including such requirements established under section 501 or 520(f)(1), and including relevant conditions prescribed with respect to the product by an order under section 520(f)(2);

(B) requirements established under section 503(b); and

(C) requirements established under section 520(e).

(4) Advertising. — The Secretary may establish conditions on advertisements and other promotional descriptive printed matter that relate to the emergency use of a product for which an authorization under this section is issued (whether an unapproved product or an unapproved use of an approved product), including, as appropriate —

(A) with respect to drugs and biological products, requirements applicable to prescription drugs pursuant to section 502(n); or

(B) with respect to devices, requirements applicable to restricted devices pursuant to section 502(r).

(f) Duration of Authorization. —

(1) In General. — Except as provided in paragraph (2), an authorization under this section shall be effective until the earlier of the termination of the declaration under subsection (b) or a revocation under subsection (g).

(2) Continued Use After End of Effective Period. — Notwithstanding the termination of the declaration under subsection (b) or a revocation under subsection (g), an authorization shall continue to be effective to provide for continued use of an unapproved product with respect to a patient to whom it was administered during the period described by paragraph (1), to the extent found necessary by such patient's attending physician.

(g) Review and Revocation of Authorization. —

(1) Review. — The Secretary shall periodically review the circumstances and the appropriateness of an authorization under this section. As part of such review, the Secretary shall regularly review the progress made with respect to the approval, licensure, or clearance of—

(A) an unapproved product for which an authorization was issued under this section; or

(B) an unapproved use of an approved product for which an authorization was issued under this section.

(2) Revision and Revocation. — The Secretary may revise or revoke an authorization under this section if—

(A) the circumstances described under subsection (b)(1) no longer exist;

(B) the criteria under subsection (c) for issuance of such authorization are no longer met; or

(C) other circumstances make such revision or revocation appropriate to protect the public health or safety.

(h) Publication; Confidential Information. —

(1) Publication. — The Secretary shall promptly publish in the Federal Register a notice of each authorization, and each termination or revocation of an authorization under this section, and an explanation of the reasons therefor (which may include a summary of data or information that has been submitted to the Secretary in an application under section 505(i) or section 520(g), even if such summary may indirectly reveal the existence of such application). The Secretary shall make any revisions to an authorization under this section available on the internet Web site of the Food and Drug Administration.

(2) Confidential Information. — Nothing in this section alters or amends section 1905 of title 18, United States Code, or section 552(b)(4) of title 5 of such Code.

(i) Actions Committed to Agency Discretion. — Actions under the authority of this section by the Secretary, by the Secretary of Defense, or by the Secretary of Homeland Security are committed to agency discretion.

(j) Rules of Construction. — The following applies with respect to this section:

(1) Nothing in this section impairs the authority of the President as Commander in Chief of the Armed Forces of the United States under article II, section 2 of the United States Constitution.

(2) Nothing in this section impairs the authority of the Secretary of Defense with respect to the Department of Defense, including the armed forces, under other provisions of Federal law.

(3) Nothing in this section (including any exercise of authority by a manufacturer under subsection (e)(2)) impairs the authority of the United States to use or manage quantities of a product that are owned or controlled by the United States (including quantities in the stockpile maintained under section 319F-2 of the Public Health Service Act).

(4) Nothing in this section shall be construed as authorizing a delay in the review or other consideration by the Secretary of any application or submission pending before the Food and Drug Administration for a product for which an authorization under this section is issued.

(k) Relation to Other Provisions. — If a product is the subject of an authorization under this section, the use of such product within the scope of the authorization shall not be considered to constitute a clinical investigation for purposes of section 505(i), section 520(g), or any other provision of this Act or section 351 of the Public Health Service Act.

(l) Option to Carry Out Authorized Activities. — Nothing in this section provides the Secretary any authority to require any person to carry out any activity that becomes lawful pursuant to an authorization under this section, and no person is required to inform the Secretary that the person will not be carrying out such activity, except that a manufacturer of a sole-source unapproved product authorized for emergency use shall report to the Secretary within a reasonable period of time after the issuance by the Secretary of such authorization if such manufacturer does not intend to carry out any activity under the authorization. This section only has legal effect on a person who carries out an activity for which an authorization under this section is issued. This section does not modify or affect activities carried out pursuant to other provisions of this Act or section 351 of the Public Health Service Act. Nothing in this subsection may be construed as restricting the Secretary from imposing conditions on persons who carry out any activity pursuant to an authorization under this section.

(m) Categorization of Laboratory Tests Associated with Devices Subject to Authorization.—

(1) In General.—In issuing an authorization under this section with respect to a device, the Secretary may, subject to the provisions of this section, determine that a laboratory examination or procedure associated with such device shall be deemed, for purposes of section 353 of the Public Health Service Act, to be in a particular category of examinations and procedures (including the category described by subsection (d)(3) of such section) if, based on the totality of scientific evidence available to the Secretary—

(A) such categorization would be beneficial to protecting the public health; and

(B) the known and potential benefits of such categorization under the circumstances of the authorization outweigh the known and potential risks of the categorization.

(2) Conditions of Determination.—The Secretary may establish appropriate conditions on the performance of the examination or procedure pursuant to such determination.

(3) Effective Period.—A determination under this subsection shall be effective for purposes of section 353 of the Public Health Service Act notwithstanding any other provision of that section during the effective period of the relevant declaration under subsection (b).

Sec. 564A. [360bbb-3a] Emergency Use of Medical Products.

(a) Definitions.—In this section:

(1) Eligible Product.—The term "eligible product" means a product that—

(A) is approved or cleared under this chapter or licensed under section 351 of the Public Health Service Act;

(B) **(i)** is intended for use to prevent, diagnose, or treat a disease or condition involving a biological, chemical, radiological, or nuclear agent or agents; or

(ii) is intended for use to prevent, diagnose, or treat a serious or life-threatening disease or condition caused by a product described in clause (i); and

(C) is intended for use during the circumstances under which—

(i) a determination described in subparagraph (A), (B), or (C) of section 564(b)(1) has been made by the Secretary of Homeland Security, the Secretary of Defense, or the Secretary, respectively; or

(ii) the identification of a material threat described in subparagraph (D) of section 564(b)(1) has been made pursuant to section 319F-2 of the Public Health Service Act.

(2) Product.—The term "product" means a drug, device, or biological product.

(b) Expiration Dating.—

(1) In General.—The Secretary may extend the expiration date and authorize the introduction or delivery for introduction into interstate commerce of an eligible product after the expiration date provided by the manufacturer if—

(A) the expiration date extension is intended to support the United States ability to protect—

(i) the public health; or

(ii) military preparedness and effectiveness; and

(B) the expiration date extension is supported by an appropriate scientific evaluation that is conducted or accepted by the Secretary.

(2) Requirements and Conditions.—Any extension of an expiration date under paragraph (1) shall, as part of the extension, identify—

(A) each specific lot, batch, or other unit of the product for which extended expiration is authorized;

(B) the duration of the extension; and

(C) any other requirements or conditions as the Secretary may deem appropriate for the protection of the public health, which may include requirements for, or conditions on, product sampling, storage, packaging or repackaging, transport, labeling, notice to product recipients, recordkeeping, periodic testing or retesting, or product disposition.

(3) Effect.—Notwithstanding any other provision of this Act or the Public Health Service Act, an eligible product shall not be considered an unapproved product (as defined in section 564(a)(2)(A)) and shall not be deemed adulterated or misbranded under this Act because, with respect to such product, the Secretary has, under paragraph (1), extended the expiration date and authorized the introduction or delivery for introduction into interstate commerce of such product after the expiration date provided by the manufacturer.

(4) Expiration Date.—For purposes of this subsection, the term "expiration date" means the date established through appropriate stability testing required by the regulations issued by the Secretary to ensure that the product meets applicable standards of identity, strength, quality, and purity at the time of use.

(c) Current Good Manufacturing Practice.—

(1) In General.—The Secretary may, when the circumstances of a domestic, military, or public health emergency or material threat described in subsection (a)(1)(C) so warrant, authorize, with respect to an eligible product, deviations from current good manufacturing practice requirements otherwise applicable to the manufacture, processing, packing, or holding of products subject to regulation under this Act, including requirements under section 501 or 520(f)(1) or applicable conditions prescribed with respect to the eligible product by an order under section 520(f)(2).

(2) Effect.—Notwithstanding any other provision of this Act or the Public Health Service Act, an eligible product shall not be considered an unapproved product (as defined in section 564(a)(2)(A)) and shall not be deemed adulterated or misbranded under this Act because, with respect to such product, the Secretary has authorized deviations from current good manufacturing practices under paragraph (1).

(d) Emergency Dispensing.—The requirements of sections 503(b) and 520(e) shall not apply to an eligible product, and the product shall not be considered an unapproved product (as defined in section 564(a)(2)(A)) and shall not be deemed adulterated or misbranded under this Act because it is dispensed without an individual prescription, if—

(1) the product is dispensed during the circumstances described in subsection (a)(1)(C); and

(2) such dispensing without an individual prescription occurs—

(A) as permitted under the law of the State in which the product is dispensed; or

(B) in accordance with an order issued by the Secretary, for the purposes and duration of the circumstances described in subsection (a)(1)(C).

(e) Emergency Use Instructions.—

(1) In General.—The Secretary, acting through an appropriate official within the Department of Health and Human Services, may create and issue emergency use instructions to inform health care providers or individuals to whom an eligible product is to be administered concerning such product's approved, licensed, or cleared conditions of use.

(2) Effect.—Notwithstanding any other provisions of this Act or the Public Health Service Act, a product shall not be considered an unapproved product and shall not be deemed adulterated or misbranded under this Act because of the issuance of emergency use instructions under paragraph (1) with respect to such product or the introduction or delivery for introduction of such product into interstate commerce accompanied by such instructions—

(A) during an emergency response to an actual emergency that is the basis for a determination described in subsection (a)(1)(C)(i); or

(B) by a government entity (including a Federal, State, local, or tribal government entity), or a person acting on behalf of such a government entity, in preparation for an emergency response.

Sec. 564B. [360bbb-3b] Products Held for Emergency Use.

It is not a violation of any section of this Act or of the Public Health Service Act for a government entity (including a Federal, State, local, or tribal government entity), or a person acting on behalf of such a government entity, to introduce into interstate commerce a product (as defined in section 564(a)(4)) intended for emergency use, if that product—

(1) is intended to be held and not used; and

(2) is held and not used, unless and until that product—

(A) is approved, cleared, or licensed under section 505, 510(k), or 515 of this Act or section 351 of the Public Health Service Act;

(B) is authorized for investigational use under section 505 or 520 of this Act or section 351 of the Public Health Service Act; or

(C) is authorized for use under section 564.

Sec. 565. [360bbb-4] Countermeasure Development, Review, and Technical Assistance.

(a) Definitions.—In this section—

(1) the term "countermeasure" means a qualified countermeasure, a security countermeasure, and a qualified pandemic or epidemic product;

(2) the term "qualified countermeasure" has the meaning given such term in section 247d–6a of title 42;

(3) the term "security countermeasure" has the meaning given such term in section 247d–6b of title 42; and

(4) the term "qualified pandemic or epidemic product" means a product that meets the definition given such term in section 247d–6d of title 42 and—

(A) that has been identified by the Department of Health and Human Services or the Department of Defense as receiving funding directly related to addressing chemical, biological, radiological, or nuclear threats, including pandemic influenza; or

(B) is included under this paragraph pursuant to a determination by the Secretary.

(b) General Duties.— In order to accelerate the development, stockpiling, approval, licensure, and clearance of qualified countermeasures, security countermeasures, and qualified pandemic or epidemic products, the Secretary, in consultation with the Assistant Secretary for Preparedness and Response, shall—

(1) ensure the appropriate involvement of Food and Drug Administration personnel in interagency activities related to countermeasure advanced research and development, consistent with sections 319F, 319F-1, 319F-2, 319F-3, 319L, and 2811 of the Public Health Service Act;

(2) ensure the appropriate involvement and consultation of Food and Drug Administration personnel in any flexible manufacturing activities carried out under section 319L of the Public Health Service Act, including with respect to meeting regulatory requirements set forth in this Act;

(3) promote countermeasure expertise within the Food and Drug Administration by—

(A) ensuring that Food and Drug Administration personnel involved in reviewing countermeasures for approval, licensure, or clearance are informed by the Assistant Secretary for Preparedness and Response on the material threat assessment conducted under section 319F-2 of the Public Health Service Act for the agent or agents for which the countermeasure under review is intended;

(B) training Food and Drug Administration personnel regarding review of countermeasures for approval, licensure, or clearance;

(C) holding public meetings at least twice annually to encourage the exchange of scientific ideas; and

(D) establishing protocols to ensure that countermeasure reviewers have sufficient training or experience with countermeasures;

(4) maintain teams, composed of Food and Drug Administration personnel with expertise on countermeasures, including specific countermeasures, populations with special clinical needs (including children and pregnant women that may use countermeasures, as applicable and appropriate), classes or groups of countermeasures, or other countermeasure-related technologies and capabilities, that shall—

(A) consult with countermeasure experts, including countermeasure sponsors and applicants, to identify and help resolve scientific issues related to the approval, licensure, or clearance of countermeasures, through workshops or public meetings; and

(B) improve and advance the science relating to the development of new tools, standards, and approaches to assessing and evaluating countermeasures—

(i) in order to inform the process for countermeasure approval, clearance, and licensure; and

(ii) with respect to the development of countermeasures for populations with special clinical needs, including children and pregnant women, in order to meet the needs of such populations, as necessary and appropriate; and

(5) establish within the Food and Drug Administration a team of experts on manufacturing and regulatory activities (including compliance with current Good Manufacturing Practice) to provide both off-site and on-site technical assistance to the manufacturers of qualified countermeasures (as defined in section 247d–6a of title 42), security countermeasures (as defined in section 247d–6b of title 42), or vaccines, at the request of such a manufacturer and at the discretion of the Secretary, if the Secretary determines that a shortage or potential shortage may occur in the United States in the supply of such vaccines or countermeasures and that the provision of such assistance would be beneficial in helping alleviate or avert such shortage.

(c) Final Guidance on Development of Animal Models.—

(1) In General.—Not later than 1 year after March 13, 2013, the Secretary shall provide final guidance to industry regarding the development of animal models to support approval, clearance, or licensure of countermeasures referred to in subsection (a) when human efficacy studies are not ethical or feasible.

(2) Authority to Extend Deadline.—The Secretary may extend the deadline for providing final guidance under paragraph (1) by not more than 6 months upon submission by the Secretary of a report on the status of such guidance to the Committee on Energy and Commerce of the House of Representatives and the Committee on Health, Education, Labor, and Pensions of the Senate.

(d) Development and Animal Modeling Procedures.—

(1) Availability of Animal Model Meetings.—To facilitate the timely development of animal models and support the development, stockpiling, licensure, approval, and clearance of countermeasures, the Secretary shall, not later than 180 days after March 13, 2013, establish a procedure by which a sponsor or applicant that is developing a countermeasure for which human efficacy studies are not ethical or practicable, and that has an approved investigational new drug application or investigational device exemption, may request and receive—

(A) a meeting to discuss proposed animal model development activities; and

(B) a meeting prior to initiating pivotal animal studies.

(2) Pediatric Models.—To facilitate the development and selection of animal models that could translate to pediatric studies, any meeting conducted under paragraph (1) shall include discussion of animal models for pediatric populations, as appropriate.

(e) Review and Approval of Countermeasures.—

(1) Material Threat.—When evaluating an application or submission for approval, licensure, or clearance of a countermeasure, the Secretary shall take into account the material threat posed by the chemical, biological, radiological, or nuclear agent or agents identified under section 319F-2 of the Public Health Service Act for which the countermeasure under review is intended.

(2) Review Expertise.—When practicable and appropriate, teams of Food and Drug Administration personnel reviewing applications or submissions described under paragraph (1) shall include a reviewer with sufficient training or experience with countermeasures pursuant to the protocols established under subsection (b)(3)(D).

(f) Regulatory Management Plan.—

(1) Definition.—In this subsection, the term "eligible countermeasure" means—

(A) a security countermeasure with respect to which the Secretary has entered into a procurement contract under section 319F-2(c) of the Public Health Service Act; or

(B) a countermeasure with respect to which the Biomedical Advanced Research and Development Authority has provided funding under section 319L of the Public Health Service Act for advanced research and development.

(2) Regulatory Management Plan Process.—The Secretary, in consultation with the Assistant Secretary for Preparedness and Response and the Director of the Biomedical Advanced Research and Development Authority, shall establish a formal process for obtaining scientific feedback and interactions regarding the development and regulatory review of eligible countermeasures by facilitating the development of written regulatory management plans in accordance with this subsection.

(3) Submission of Request and Proposed Plan by Sponsor or Applicant.—

(A) In General.—A sponsor or applicant of an eligible countermeasure may initiate the process described under paragraph (2) upon submission of a written request to the Secretary. Such request shall include a proposed regulatory management plan.

(B) Timing of Submission.—A sponsor or applicant may submit a written request under subparagraph (A) after the eligible countermeasure has an investigational new drug or investigational device exemption in effect.

(C) Response by Secretary.—The Secretary shall direct the Food and Drug Administration, upon submission of a written request by a sponsor or applicant under subparagraph (A), to work with the sponsor or applicant to agree on a regulatory management plan within a reasonable time not to exceed 90 days. If the Secretary determines that no plan can be agreed upon, the Secretary shall provide to the sponsor or applicant, in writing, the scientific or regulatory rationale why such agreement cannot be reached.

(4) Plan.—The content of a regulatory management plan agreed to by the Secretary and a sponsor or applicant shall include—

(A) an agreement between the Secretary and the sponsor or applicant regarding developmental milestones that will trigger responses by the Secretary as described in subparagraph (B);

(B) performance targets and goals for timely and appropriate responses by the Secretary to the triggers described under subparagraph (A), including meetings between the Secretary and the sponsor or applicant, written feedback, decisions by the Secretary, and other activities carried out as part of the development and review process; and

(C) an agreement on how the plan shall be modified, if needed.

(5) Milestones and Performance Targets.—The developmental milestones described in paragraph (4)(A) and the performance targets and goals described in paragraph (4)(B) shall include—

(A) feedback from the Secretary regarding the data required to support the approval, clearance, or licensure of the eligible countermeasure involved;

(B) feedback from the Secretary regarding the data necessary to inform any authorization under section 360bbb–3 of this title;

(C) feedback from the Secretary regarding the data necessary to support the positioning and delivery of the eligible countermeasure, including to the Strategic National Stockpile;

(D) feedback from the Secretary regarding the data necessary to support the submission of protocols for review under section 505(b)(5)(B);

(E) feedback from the Secretary regarding any gaps in scientific knowledge that will need resolution prior to approval, licensure, or clearance of the eligible countermeasure and plans for conducting the necessary scientific research;

(F) identification of the population for which the countermeasure sponsor or applicant seeks approval, licensure, or clearance and the population for which desired labeling would not be appropriate, if known; and

(G) as necessary and appropriate, and to the extent practicable, a plan for demonstrating safety and effectiveness in pediatric populations, and for developing pediatric dosing, formulation, and administration with respect to the eligible countermeasure, provided that such plan would not delay authorization under section 564, approval, licensure, or clearance for adults.

(6) Prioritization.—

(A) Plans for Security Countermeasures.—The Secretary shall establish regulatory management plans for all security countermeasures for which a request is submitted under paragraph (3)(A).

(B) Plans for Other Eligible Countermeasures.—The Secretary shall determine whether resources are available to establish regulatory management plans for eligible countermeasures that are not security countermeasures. If resources are available to establish regulatory management plans for eligible countermeasures that are not security countermeasures, and if resources are not available to establish regulatory management plans for all eligible countermeasures for which requests have been submitted, the Director of the Biomedical Advanced Research and Development Authority, in consultation with the Commissioner, shall prioritize which eligible countermeasures may receive regulatory management plans.

(g) Annual Report.—Not later than 180 days after March 13, 2013, and annually thereafter, the Secretary shall make publicly available on the Web site of the Food and Drug Administration a report that details the countermeasure development and review activities of the Food and Drug Administration, including—

(1) with respect to the development of new tools, standards, and approaches to assess and evaluate countermeasures—

(A) the identification of the priorities of the Food and Drug Administration and the progress made on such priorities; and

(B) the identification of scientific gaps that impede the development, approval, licensure, or clearance of countermeasures for populations with special clinical needs, including children and pregnant women, and the progress made on resolving these challenges;

(2) with respect to countermeasures for which a regulatory management plan has been agreed upon under subsection (f), the extent to which the performance targets and goals set forth in subsection (f)(4)(B) and the regulatory management plan have been met, including, for each such countermeasure

(A) whether the regulatory management plan was completed within the required timeframe, and the length of time taken to complete such plan;

(B) whether the Secretary adhered to the timely and appropriate response times set forth in such plan; and

(C) explanations for any failure to meet such performance targets and goals;

(3) the number of regulatory teams established pursuant to subsection (b)(4), the number of products, classes of products, or technologies assigned to each such team, and the number of, type of, and any progress made as a result of consultations carried out under subsection (b)(4)(A);

(4) an estimate of resources obligated to countermeasure development and regulatory assessment, including—

(A) Center-specific objectives and accomplishments; and

(B) the number of full-time equivalent employees of the Food and Drug Administration who directly support the review of countermeasures;

(5) the number of countermeasure applications and submissions submitted, the number of countermeasures approved, licensed, or cleared, the status of remaining submitted applications and submissions, and the number of each type of authorization issued pursuant to section 564;

(6) the number of written requests for a regulatory management plan submitted under subsection (f)(3)(A), the number of regulatory management plans developed, and the number of such plans developed for security countermeasures; and

(7) the number, type, and frequency of meetings between the Food and Drug Administration and—

(A) sponsors of a countermeasure as defined in subsection (a); or

(B) another agency engaged in development or management of portfolios for such countermeasures, including the Centers for Disease Control and Prevention, the Biomedical Advanced Research and Development Authority, the National Institutes of Health, and the appropriate agencies of the Department of Defense.

Sec. 565A. [360bbb-4a] Priority Review to Encourage Treatments for Agents that Present National Security Threats.

(a) Definitions.—In this section:

(1) Human Drug Application.—The term "human drug application" has the meaning given such term in section 735(1).

(2) Priority Review.—The term "priority review," with respect to a human drug application, means review and action by the Secretary on such application not later than 6 months after receipt by the Secretary of such application, as described in the Manual of Policies and Procedures in the Food and Drug Administration and goals identified in the letters described in section 101(b) of the Food and Drug Administration Safety and Innovation Act.

(3) Priority Review Voucher.—The term "priority review voucher" means a voucher issued by the Secretary to the sponsor of a material threat medical countermeasure application that entitles the holder of such voucher to priority review of a single human drug application submitted under section 505(b)(1) or section 351(a) of the Public Health Service Act after the date of approval of the material threat medical countermeasure application.

(4) Material Threat Medical Countermeasure Application.—The term "material threat medical countermeasure application" means an application that—

(A) is a human drug application for a drug intended for use—

(i) to prevent, or treat harm from a biological, chemical, radiological, or nuclear agent identified as a material threat under section 319F-2(c)(2)(A)(ii) of the Public Health Service Act; or

(ii) to mitigate, prevent, or treat harm from a condition that may result in adverse health consequences or death and may be caused by administering a drug, or biological product against such agent; and

(B) the Secretary determines eligible for priority review;

(C) is approved after the date of enactment of the 21st Century Cures Act [December 13, 2016 —Ed.]; and

(D) is for a human drug, no active ingredient (including any ester or salt of the active ingredient) of which has been approved in any other application under section 505(b)(1) or section 351(a) of the Public Health Service Act.

(b) Priority Review Voucher.—

(1) In General.—The Secretary shall award a priority review voucher to the sponsor of a material threat medical countermeasure application upon approval by the Secretary of such material threat medical countermeasure application.

(2) Transferability.—The sponsor of a material threat medical countermeasure application that receives a priority review voucher under this section may transfer (including by sale) the entitlement to such voucher to a sponsor of a human drug for which an application under section 505(b)(1) or section 351(a) of the Public Health Service Act will be submitted after the date of the approval of the material threat medical countermeasure application. There is no limit on the number of times a priority review voucher may be transferred before such voucher is used.

(3) Notification.—

(A) In General.—The sponsor of a human drug application shall notify the Secretary not later than 90 calendar days prior to submission of the human drug application that is the subject of a priority review voucher of an intent to submit the human drug application, including the date on which the sponsor intends to submit the application. Such notification shall be a legally binding commitment to pay for the user fee to be assessed in accordance with this section.

(B) Transfer After Notice.—The sponsor of a human drug application that provides notification of the intent of such sponsor to use the voucher for the human drug application under subparagraph (A) may transfer the voucher after such notification is provided, if such sponsor has not yet submitted the human drug application described in the notification.

(c) Priority Review User Fee.—

(1) In General.—The Secretary shall establish a user fee program under which a sponsor of a human drug application that is the subject of a priority review voucher shall pay to the Secretary a fee determined under paragraph (2). Such fee shall be in addition to any fee required to be submitted by the sponsor under chapter VII.

(2) Fee Amount.—The amount of the priority review user fee shall be determined each fiscal year by the Secretary and based on the average cost incurred by the agency in the review of a human drug application subject to priority review in the previous fiscal year.

(3) Annual Fee Setting.—The Secretary shall establish, before the beginning of each fiscal year beginning after September 30, 2016, for that fiscal year, the amount of the priority review user fee.

(4) Payment.—

(A) In General.—The priority review user fee required by this subsection shall be due upon the submission of a human drug application under section 505(b)(1) or section 351(a) of the Public Health Service Act for which the priority review voucher is used.

(B) Complete Application.—An application described under subparagraph (A) for which the sponsor requests the use of a priority review voucher shall be considered incomplete if the fee required by this subsection and all other applicable user fees are not paid in accordance with the Secretary's procedures for paying such fees.

(C) No Waivers, Exemptions, Reductions, or Refunds.—The Secretary may not grant a waiver, exemption, reduction, or refund of any fees due and payable under this section.

(5) Offsetting Collections.—Fees collected pursuant to this subsection for any fiscal year—

(A) shall be deposited and credited as off-setting collections to the account providing appropriations to the Food and Drug Administration; and

(6) shall not be collected for any fiscal year except to the extent provided in advance in appropriation Acts.

(d) Notice of Issuance of Voucher and Approval of Products Under Voucher.—The Secretary shall publish a notice in the Federal Register and on the Internet website of the Food and Drug Administration not later than 30 calendar days after the occurrence of each of the following:

(1) The Secretary issues a priority review voucher under this section.

(2) The Secretary approves a drug pursuant to an application submitted under section 505(b) of this Act or section 351(a) of the Public Health Service Act for which the sponsor of the application used a priority review voucher issued under this section.

(e) Eligibility for Other Programs.—Nothing in this section precludes a sponsor who seeks a priority review voucher under this section from participating in any other incentive program, including under this Act, except that no sponsor of a material threat medical countermeasure application may receive more than one priority review voucher issued under any section of this Act with respect to such drug.

(f) Relation to Other Provisions.—The provisions of this section shall supplement, not supplant, any other provisions of this Act or the Public Health Service Act that encourage the development of medical countermeasures.

(g) Sunset.—The Secretary may not award any priority review vouchers under subsection (b) after October 1, 2023.

Sec. 566. [360bbb-5] Critical Path Public-Private Partnerships.

(a) Establishment. —The Secretary, acting through the Commissioner of Food and Drugs, may enter into collaborative agreements, to be known as Critical Path Public-Private Partnerships, with one or more eligible entities to implement the Critical Path Initiative of the Food and Drug Administration by developing innovative, collaborative projects in research, education, and outreach for the purpose of fostering medical product innovation, enabling the acceleration of medical product development, manufacturing, and translational therapeutics, and enhancing medical product safety.

(b) Eligible Entity. — In this section, the term "eligible entity" means an entity that meets each of the following:

(1) The entity is —

(A) an institution of higher education (as such term is defined in section 101 of the Higher Education Act of 1965) or a consortium of such institutions; or

(B) an organization described in section 501(c)(3) of the Internal Revenue Code of 1986 and exempt from tax under section 501(a) of such Code.

(2) The entity has experienced personnel and clinical and other technical expertise in the biomedical sciences, which may include graduate training programs in areas relevant to priorities of the Critical Path Initiative.

(3) The entity demonstrates to the Secretary's satisfaction that the entity is capable of —

(A) developing and critically evaluating tools, methods, and processes —

(i) to increase efficiency, predictability, and productivity of medical product development; and

(ii) to more accurately identify the benefits and risks of new and existing medical products;

(B) establishing partnerships, consortia, and collaborations with health care practitioners and other providers of health care goods or services; pharmacists; pharmacy benefit managers and purchasers; health maintenance organizations and other managed health care organizations; health care insurers; government agencies; patients and consumers; manufacturers of prescription drugs, biological products, diagnostic technologies, and devices; and academic scientists; and

(C) securing funding for the projects of a Critical Path Public-Private Partnership from Federal and nonfederal governmental sources, foundations, and private individuals.

(c) Funding. — The Secretary may not enter into a collaborative agreement under subsection (a) unless the eligible entity involved provides an assurance that the entity will not accept funding for a Critical Path Public-Private Partnership project from any organization that manufactures or distributes products regulated by the Food and Drug Administration unless the entity provides assurances in its agreement with the Food and Drug Administration that the results of the Critical Path Public-Private Partnership project will not be influenced by any source of funding.

(d) Annual Report. — Not later than 18 months after the date of the enactment of this section, and annually thereafter, the Secretary, in collaboration with the parties to each Critical Path Public-Private Partnership, shall submit a report to the Committee on Health, Education, Labor, and Pensions of the Senate and the Committee on Energy and Commerce of the House of Representatives —

(1) reviewing the operations and activities of the Partnerships in the previous year; and

(2) addressing such other issues relating to this section as the Secretary determines to be appropriate.

(e) Definition. — In this section, the term "medical product" includes a drug, a biological product as defined in section 351 of the Public Health Service Act, a device, and any combination of such products.

(f) Authorization of Appropriations. — To carry out this section, there is authorized to be appropriated $6,000,000 for each of fiscal years ~~2013 through 2017.~~ <u>2018 through 2022.</u>

Sec. 567. [360bbb-6] Risk Communication.

(a) Advisory Committee on Risk Communication. —

(1) In General. — The Secretary shall establish an advisory committee to be known as the "Advisory Committee on Risk Communication" (referred to in this section as the "Committee").

(2) Duties of Committee. — The Committee shall advise the Commissioner on methods to effectively communicate risks associated with the products regulated by the Food and Drug Administration.

(3) Members. — The Secretary shall ensure that the Committee is composed of experts on risk communication, experts on the risks described in subsection (b), and representatives of patient, consumer, and health professional organizations.

(4) Permanence of Committee. — Section 14 of the Federal Advisory Committee Act shall not apply to the Committee established under this subsection.

(b) Partnerships for Risk Communication. —

(1) In General. — The Secretary shall partner with professional medical societies, medical schools, academic medical centers, and other stakeholders to develop robust and multi-faceted systems for communication to health care providers about emerging postmarket drug risks.

(2) Partnerships. — The systems developed under paragraph (1) shall —

(A) account for the diversity among physicians in terms of practice, willingness to adopt technology, and medical specialty; and

(B) include the use of existing communication channels, including electronic communications, in place at the Food and Drug Administration.

SEC. 568. [360bbb-7] NOTIFICATION.

(a) NOTIFICATION TO SECRETARY. — With respect to a drug, the Secretary may require notification to the Secretary by a regulated person if the regulated person knows —

(1) that the use of such drug in the United States may result in serious injury or death;

(2) of a significant loss or known theft of such drug intended for use in the United States; or

(3) that —

(A) such drug has been or is being counterfeited; and

(B) —

(i) the counterfeit product is in commerce in the United States or could be reasonably expected to be introduced into commerce in the United States; or

(ii) such drug has been or is being imported into the United States or may reasonably be expected to be offered for import into the United States.

(b) MANNER OF NOTIFICATION. — Notification under this section shall be made in such manner and by such means as the Secretary may specify by regulation or guidance.

(c) SAVINGS CLAUSE. — Nothing in this section shall be construed as limiting any other authority of the Secretary to require notifications related to a drug under any other provision of this Act or the Public Health Service Act.

(d) DEFINITION. — In this section, the term "regulated person" means —

(1) a person who is required to register under section 510 or 801(s);

(2) a wholesale distributor of a drug product; or

(3) any other person that distributes drugs except a person that distributes drugs exclusively for retail sale.

SEC. 569. [360bbb-8] CONSULTATION WITH EXTERNAL EXPERTS ON RARE DISEASES, TARGETED THERAPIES, AND GENETIC TARGETING OF TREATMENTS.

(a) IN GENERAL. — For the purpose of promoting the efficiency of and informing the review by the Food and Drug Administration of new drugs and biological products for rare diseases and drugs and biological products that are genetically targeted, the following shall apply:

(1) CONSULTATION WITH STAKEHOLDERS. — Consistent with sections X.C and IX.E.4 of the PDUFA Reauthorization Performance Goals and Procedures Fiscal Years 2013 through 2017, as referenced in the letters described in section 101(b) of the Prescription Drug User Fee Amendments of 2012, the Secretary shall ensure that opportunities exist, at a time the Secretary determines appropriate, for consultations with stakeholders on the topics described in subsection (b).

(2) CONSULTATION WITH EXTERNAL EXPERTS. —

(A) IN GENERAL. — The Secretary shall develop and maintain a list of external experts who, because of their special expertise, are qualified to provide advice on rare disease issues, including topics described in subsection (cb). The Secretary may, when appropriate to address a specific regulatory question, consult such external experts on issues related to the review of new drugs and biological products for rare diseases and drugs and biological products that are genetically targeted, including the topics described in subsection (b), when such consultation is necessary because the Secretary lacks the specific scientific, medical, or technical expertise necessary for the performance of the Secretary's regulatory responsibilities and the necessary expertise can be provided by the external experts.

(B) EXTERNAL EXPERTS. — For purposes of subparagraph (A), external experts are individuals who possess scientific or medical training that the Secretary lacks with respect to one or more rare diseases.

(b) TOPICS FOR CONSULTATION. — Topics for consultation pursuant to this section may include —

(1) rare diseases;

(2) the severity of rare diseases;

(3) the unmet medical need associated with rare diseases;

(4) the willingness and ability of individuals with a rare disease to participate in clinical trials;

(5) an assessment of the benefits and risks of therapies to treat rare diseases;

(6) the general design of clinical trials for rare disease populations and subpopulations; and

(7) the demographics and the clinical description of patient populations.

(c) Classification as Special Government Employees. — The external experts who are consulted under this section may be considered special government employees, as defined under section 202 of title 18, United States Code.

(d) Protection of Confidential Information and Trade Secrets. —

(1) Rule of Construction. — Nothing in this section shall be construed to alter the protection offered by laws, regulations, and policies governing disclosure of confidential commercial or trade secret information, and any other information exempt from disclosure pursuant to section 552(b) of title 5, United States Code, as such provisions would be applied to consultation with individuals and organizations prior to the date of enactment of this section.

(2) Consent Required for Disclosure. — The Secretary shall not disclose confidential commercial or trade secret information to an expert consulted under this section without the written consent of the sponsor unless the expert is a special government employee (as defined under section 202 of title 18, United States Code) or the disclosure is otherwise authorized by law.

(e) Other Consultation. — Nothing in this section shall be construed to limit the ability of the Secretary to consult with individuals and organization as authorized prior to the date of enactment of this section.

(f) No Right or Obligation. —

(1) No Right to Consultation. — Nothing in this section shall be construed to create a legal right for a consultation on any matter or require the Secretary to meet with any particular expert or stakeholder.

(2) No Altering of Goals. — Nothing in this section shall be construed to alter agreed upon goals and procedures identified in the letters described in section 101(b) of the Prescription Drug User Fee Amendments of 2012.

(3) No Change to Number of Review Cycles. — Nothing in this section is intended to increase the number of review cycles as in effect before the date of enactment of this section.

(g) No Delay in Product Review. —

(1) In General. — Prior to a consultation with an external expert, as described in this section, relating to an investigational new drug application under section 505(i), a new drug application under section 505(b), or a biologics license application under section 351 of the Public Health Service Act, the Director of the Center for Drug Evaluation and Research or the Director of the Center for Biologics Evaluation and Research (or appropriate Division Director), as appropriate, shall determine that —

(A) such consultation will —

(i) facilitate the Secretary's ability to complete the Secretary's review; and

(ii) address outstanding deficiencies in the application; or

(B) the sponsor authorized such consultation.

(2) Limitation. — The requirements of this subsection shall apply only in instances where the consultation is undertaken solely under the authority of this section. The requirements of this subsection shall not apply to any consultation initiated under any other authority.

Sec. 569A. [360bbb-8a] Optimizing Global Clinical Trials.

(a) In General. — The Secretary shall —

(1) work with other regulatory authorities of similar standing, medical research companies, and international organizations to foster and encourage uniform, scientifically driven clinical trial standards with respect to medical products around the world; and

(2) enhance the commitment to provide consistent parallel scientific advice to manufacturers seeking simultaneous global development of new medical products in order to —

(A) enhance medical product development;

(B) facilitate the use of foreign data; and

(C) minimize the need to conduct duplicative clinical studies, preclinical studies, or non-clinical studies.

(b) Medical Product. — In this section, the term "medical product" means a drug, as defined in subsection (g) of section 201, a device, as defined in subsection (h) of such section, or a biological product, as defined in section 351(i) of the Public Health Service Act.

(c) Savings Clause. — Nothing in this section shall alter the criteria for evaluating the safety or effectiveness of a medical product under this Act or under the Public Health Service Act.

Sec. 569B. [360bbb-8b] Use of Clinical Investigation Data from Outside the United States.

(a) In General. — In determining whether to approve, license, or clear a drug, biological product, or device pursuant to an application submitted under this chapter, the Secretary shall accept data from clinical investigations conducted outside of the United States, including the European Union, if the applicant demonstrates that such data are adequate under applicable standards to support approval, licensure, or clearance of the drug, biological product, or device in the United States.

(b) Notice to Sponsor. — If the Secretary finds under subsection (a) that the data from clinical investigations conducted outside the United States, including in the European Union, are inadequate for the purpose of making a determination on approval, clearance, or licensure of a drug, biological product, or device pursuant to an application submitted under this chapter, the Secretary shall provide written notice to the sponsor of the application of such finding and include the rationale for such finding.

Sec. 569C. [360bbb-8c] Patient Participation in Medical Product Discussion.

(a) Patient Engagement in Drugs and Devices —

(1) In General.— The Secretary shall develop and implement strategies to solicit the views of patients during the medical product development process and consider the perspectives of patients during regulatory discussions, including by —

(A) Fostering participation of a patient representative who may serve as a special government employee in appropriate agency meetings with medical product sponsors and investigators; and

(B) exploring means to provide for identification of patient representatives who do not have any, or have minimal, financial interests in the medical products industry.

(2) Protection of Proprietary Information. — Nothing in this section shall be construed to alter the protections offered by laws, regulations, or policies governing disclosure of confidential commercial or trade secret information and any other information exempt from disclosure pursuant to section 552(b) of title 5, United States Code, as such laws, regulations, or policies would apply to consultation with individuals and organizations prior to the date of enactment of this section.

(3) Other Consultation. — Nothing in this section shall be construed to limit the ability of the Secretary to consult with individuals and organizations as authorized prior to the date of enactment of this section.

(4) No Right or Obligation. — Nothing in this section shall be construed to create a legal right for a consultation on any matter or require the Secretary to meet with any particular expert or stakeholder. Nothing in this section shall be construed to alter agreed upon goals and procedures identified in the letters described in section 101(b) of the Prescription Drug User Fee Amendments of 2012. Nothing in this section is intended to increase the number of review cycles as in effect before the date of enactment of this section.

(5) Financial Interest. — In this section, the term "financial interest" means a financial interest under section 208(a) of title 18, United States Code.

(b) Statement of Patient Experience. —

(1) In General.—Following the approval of an application that was submitted under section 505(b) of this Act or section 351(a) of the Public Health Service Act at least 180 days after the date of enactment of the 21st Century Cures Act [December 13, 2016 —Ed.], the Secretary shall make public a brief statement regarding the patient experience data and related information, if any, submitted and reviewed as part of such application.

(2) Data and Information.—The data and information referred to in paragraph (1) are—

(A) patient experience data;

(B) information on patient-focused drug development tools; and

(C) other relevant information, as determined by the Secretary.

(c) Patient Experience Data.—For purposes of this section, the term "patient experience data" includes data that—

(1) are collected by any persons (including patients, family members and caregivers of patients, patient advocacy organizations, disease research foundations, researchers, and drug manufacturers); and

(2) are intended to provide information about patients' experiences with a disease or condition, including—

(A) ~~the impact of such disease or condition, or a related therapy,~~ impact (including physical and psychosocial impacts) of such disease or condition, or a related therapy or clinical investigation on patients' lives; and

(B) patient preferences with respect to treatment of such disease or condition.

Subchapter F — New Animal Drugs for Minor Use and Minor Species

Sec. 571. [360ccc] Conditional Approval of New Animal Drugs for Minor Use and Minor Species.

(a) —

(1) Except as provided in paragraph (3) of this section, any person may file with the Secretary an application for conditional approval of a new animal drug intended for a minor use or a minor species. Such an application may not be a supplement to an application approved under section 512. Such application must comply in all respects with the provisions of section 512 of this Act except sections 512(a)(4), 512(b)(2), 512(c)(1), 512(c)(2), 512(c)(3), 512(d)(1), 512(e), 512(h), and 512(n) unless otherwise stated in this section, and any additional provisions of this section. New animal drugs are subject to application of the same safety standards that would be applied to such drugs under section 512(d) (including, for antimicrobial new animal drugs, with respect to antimicrobial resistance).

(2) The applicant shall submit to the Secretary as part of an application for the conditional approval of a new animal drug —

(A) all information necessary to meet the requirements of section 512(b)(1) except section 512(b)(1)(A);

(B) full reports of investigations which have been made to show whether or not such drug is safe under section 512(d) (including, for an antimicrobial new animal drug, with respect to antimicrobial resistance) and there is a reasonable expectation of effectiveness for use;

(C) data for establishing a conditional dose;

(D) projections of expected need and the justification for that expectation based on the best information available;

(E) information regarding the quantity of drug expected to be distributed on an annual basis to meet the expected need; and

(F) a commitment that the applicant will conduct additional investigations to meet the requirements for the full demonstration of effectiveness under section 512(d)(1)(E) within 5 years.

(3) A person may not file an application under paragraph (1) if —

(A) the application seeks conditional approval of a new animal drug that is contained in, or is a product of, a transgenic animal.

(B) the person has previously filed an application for conditional approval under paragraph (1) for the same drug in the same dosage form for the same intended use whether or not subsequently conditionally approved by the Secretary under subsection (b), or

(C) the person obtained the application, or data or other information contained therein, directly or indirectly from the person who filed for conditional approval under paragraph (1) for the same drug in the same dosage form for the same intended use whether or not subsequently conditionally approved by the Secretary under subsection (b).

(b) Within 180 days after the filing of an application pursuant to subsection (a), or such additional period as may be agreed upon by the Secretary and the applicant, the Secretary shall either —

(1) issue an order, effective for one year, conditionally approving the application if the Secretary finds that none of the grounds for denying conditional approval, specified in subsection (c) applies and publish a Federal Register notice of the conditional approval, or

(2) give the applicant notice of an opportunity for an informal hearing on the question whether such application can be conditionally approved.

(c) If the Secretary finds, after giving the applicant notice and an opportunity for an informal hearing, that—

(1) any of the provisions of section 512(d)(1) (A) through (D) or (F) through (I) are applicable;

(2) the information submitted to the Secretary as part of the application and any other information before the Secretary with respect to such drug, is insufficient to show that there is a reasonable expectation that the drug will have the effect it purports or is represented to have under the conditions of use prescribed, recommended, or suggested in the proposed labeling thereof; or

(3) another person has received approval under section 512 for the same drug in the same dosage form for the same intended use, and that person is able to assure the availability of sufficient quantities of the drug to meet the needs for which the drug is intended;

the Secretary shall issue an order refusing to conditionally approve the application. If, after such notice and opportunity for an informal hearing, the Secretary finds that paragraphs (1) through (3) do not apply, the Secretary shall issue an order conditionally approving the application effective for one year and publish a Federal Register notice of the conditional approval. Any order issued under this subsection refusing to conditionally approve an application shall state the findings upon which it is based.

(d) A conditional approval under this section is effective for a 1-year period and is thereafter renewable by the Secretary annually for up to 4 additional 1-year terms. A conditional approval shall be in effect for no more than 5 years from the date of approval under subsection (b)(1) or (c) of this section unless extended as provided for in subsection (h) of this section. The following shall also apply:

(1) No later than 90 days from the end of the 1-year period for which the original or renewed conditional approval is effective, the applicant may submit a request to renew a conditional approval for an additional 1-year term.

(2) A conditional approval shall be deemed renewed at the end of the 1-year period, or at the end of a 90-day extension that the Secretary may, at the Secretary's discretion, grant by letter in order to complete review of the renewal request, unless the Secretary determines before the expiration of the 1-year period or the 90-day extension that—

(A) the applicant failed to submit a timely renewal request;

(B) the request fails to contain sufficient information to show that—

(i) the applicant is making sufficient progress toward meeting approval requirements under section 512(d)(1) (E), and is likely to be able to fulfill those requirements and obtain an approval under section 512 before the expiration of the 5-year maximum term of the conditional approval;

(ii) the quantity of the drug that has been distributed is consistent with the conditionally approved intended use and conditions of use, unless there is adequate explanation that ensures that the drug is only used for its intended purpose; or

(iii) the same drug in the same dosage form for the same intended use has not received approval under section 512, or if such a drug has been approved, that the holder of the approved application is unable to assure the availability of sufficient quantities of the drug to meet the needs for which the drug is intended; or

(C) any of the provisions of section 512(e)(1) (A) through (B) or (D) through (F) are applicable.

(3) If the Secretary determines before the end of the 1-year period or the 90-day extension, if granted, that a conditional approval should not be renewed, the Secretary shall issue an order refusing to renew the conditional approval, and such conditional approval shall be deemed withdrawn and no longer in effect. The Secretary shall thereafter provide an opportunity for an informal hearing to the applicant on the issue whether the conditional approval shall be reinstated.

(4)—

(A) In the case of an application under subsection (a) with respect to a drug for which the Secretary provides notice to the sponsor that the Secretary intends to issue a scientific and medical evaluation and recommend controls under the Controlled Substances Act, conditional approval of such application shall not take effect until the interim final rule controlling the drug is issued in accordance with section 201(j) of the Controlled Substances Act.

(B) For purposes of this section, with respect to an application described in subparagraph (A), the term "date of approval" shall mean the later of—

(i) the date an application under subsection (a) is conditionally approved under subsection (b); or

(ii) the date of issuance of the interim final rule controlling the drug.

(e) —

(1) The Secretary shall issue an order withdrawing conditional approval of an application filed pursuant to subsection (a) if the Secretary finds that another person has received approval under section 512 for the same drug in the same dosage form for the same intended use and that person is able to assure the availability of sufficient quantities of the drug to meet the needs for which the drug is intended.

(2) The Secretary shall, after due notice and opportunity for an informal hearing to the applicant, issue an order withdrawing conditional approval of an application filed pursuant to subsection (a) if the Secretary finds that —

(A) any of the provisions of section 512(e)(1) (A) through (B) or (D) through (F) are applicable; or

(B) on the basis of new information before the Secretary with respect to such drug, evaluated together with the evidence available to the Secretary when the application was conditionally approved, that there is not a reasonable expectation that such drug will have the effect it purports or is represented to have under the conditions of use prescribed, recommended, or suggested in the labeling thereof.

(3) The Secretary may also, after due notice and opportunity for an informal hearing to the applicant, issue an order withdrawing conditional approval of an application filed pursuant to subsection (a) if the Secretary finds that any of the provisions of section 512(e)(2) are applicable.

(f) —

(1) The label and labeling of a new animal drug with a conditional approval under this section shall —

(A) bear the statement, "conditionally approved by FDA pending a full demonstration of effectiveness under application number"; and

(B) contain such other information as prescribed by the Secretary.

(2) An intended use that is the subject of a conditional approval under this section shall not be included in the same product label with any intended use approved under section 512.

(g) A conditionally approved new animal drug application may not be amended or supplemented to add indications for use.

(h) 180 days prior to the termination date established under subsection (d) of this section, an applicant shall have submitted all the information necessary to support a complete new animal drug application in accordance with section 512(b)(1) or the conditional approval issued under this section is no longer in effect. Following review of this information, the Secretary shall either —

(1) issue an order approving the application under section 512(c) if the Secretary finds that none of the grounds for denying approval specified in section 512(d)(1) applies, or

(2) give the applicant an opportunity for a hearing before the Secretary under section 512(d) on the question whether such application can be approved.

Upon issuance of an order approving the application, product labeling and administrative records of approval shall be modified accordingly. If the Secretary has not issued an order under section 512(c) approving such application prior to the termination date established under subsection (d) of this section, the conditional approval issued under this section is no longer in effect unless the Secretary grants an extension of an additional 180-day period so that the Secretary can complete review of the application. The decision to grant an extension is committed to the discretion of the Secretary and not subject to judicial review.

(i) The decision of the Secretary under subsection (c), (d), or (e) of this section refusing or withdrawing conditional approval of an application shall constitute final agency action subject to judicial review.

(j) In this section and section 572, the term "transgenic animal" means an animal whose genome contains a nucleotide sequence that has been intentionally modified in vitro, and the progeny of such an animal; Provided that the term "transgenic animal" does not include an animal of which the nucleotide sequence of the genome has been modified solely by selective breeding.

Sec. 572. [360ccc-1] Index of Legally Marketed Unapproved New Animal Drugs for Minor Species.

(a) —

(1) The Secretary shall establish an index limited to —

(A) new animal drugs intended for use in a minor species for which there is a reasonable certainty that the animal or edible products from the animal will not be consumed by humans or food-producing animals; and

(B) new animal drugs intended for use only in a hatchery, tank, pond, or other similar contained man-made structure in an early, non-food life stage of a food-producing minor species, where safety for humans is demonstrated in accordance with the standard of section 512(d) (including, for an antimicrobial new animal drug, with respect to antimicrobial resistance).

(2) The index shall not include a new animal drug that is contained in or a product of a transgenic animal.

(b) Any person intending to file a request under this section shall be entitled to one or more conferences to discuss the requirements for indexing a new animal drug.

(c) —

(1) Any person may submit a request to the Secretary for a determination whether a new animal drug may be eligible for inclusion in the index. Such a request shall include —

(A) information regarding the need for the new animal drug, the species for which the new animal drug is intended, the proposed intended use and conditions of use, and anticipated annual distribution;

(B) information to support the conclusion that the proposed use meets the conditions of subparagraph (A) or (B) of subsection (a)(1) of this section;

(C) information regarding the components and composition of the new animal drug;

(D) a description of the methods used in, and the facilities and controls used for, the manufacture, processing, and packing of such new animal drug;

(E) an environmental assessment that meets the requirements of the National Environmental Policy Act of 1969, as amended, and as defined in 21 CFR Part 25, as it appears on the date of enactment of this provision [August 2, 2004 — Ed.] and amended thereafter or information to support a categorical exclusion from the requirement to prepare an environmental assessment;

(F) information sufficient to support the conclusion that the proposed use of the new animal drug is safe under section 512(d) with respect to individuals exposed to the new animal drug through its manufacture or use; and

(G) such other information as the Secretary may deem necessary to make this eligibility determination.

(2) Within 90 days after the submission of a request for a determination of eligibility for indexing based on subsection (a)(1)(A) of this section, or 180 days for a request submitted based on subsection (a)(1)(B) of this section, the Secretary shall grant or deny the request, and notify the person who requested such determination of the Secretary's decision. The Secretary shall grant the request if the Secretary finds that —

(A) the same drug in the same dosage form for the same intended use is not approved or conditionally approved;

(B) the proposed use of the drug meets the conditions of subparagraph (A) or (B) of subsection (a)(1), as appropriate;

(C) the person requesting the determination has established appropriate specifications for the manufacture and control of the new animal drug and has demonstrated an understanding of the requirements of current good manufacturing practices;

(D) the new animal drug will not significantly affect the human environment; and

(E) the new animal drug is safe with respect to individuals exposed to the new animal drug through its manufacture or use.

If the Secretary denies the request, the Secretary shall thereafter provide due notice and an opportunity for an informal conference. A decision of the Secretary to deny an eligibility request following an informal conference shall constitute final agency action subject to judicial review.

(d) —

(1) With respect to a new animal drug for which the Secretary has made a determination of eligibility under subsection (c), the person who made such a request may ask that the Secretary add the new animal drug to the index established under subsection (a). The request for addition to the index shall include —

(A) a copy of the Secretary's determination of eligibility issued under subsection (c);

(B) a written report that meets the requirements in subsection (d)(2) of this section;

(C) a proposed index entry;

(D) facsimile labeling;

(E) anticipated annual distribution of the new animal drug;

(F) a written commitment to manufacture the new animal drug and animal feeds bearing or containing such new animal drug according to current good manufacturing practices;

(G) a written commitment to label, distribute, and promote the new animal drug only in accordance with the index entry;

(H) upon specific request of the Secretary, information submitted to the expert panel described in paragraph (3); and

(I) any additional requirements that the Secretary may prescribe by general regulation or specific order.

(2) The report required in paragraph (1) shall —

(A) be authored by a qualified expert panel;

(B) include an evaluation of all available target animal safety and effectiveness information, including anecdotal information;

(C) state the expert panel's opinion regarding whether the benefits of using the new animal drug for the proposed use in a minor species outweigh its risks to the target animal, taking into account the harm being caused by the absence of an approved or conditionally approved new animal drug for the minor species in question;

(D) include information from which labeling can be written; and

(E) include a recommendation regarding whether the new animal drug should be limited to use under the professional supervision of a licensed veterinarian.

(3) A qualified expert panel, as used in this section, is a panel that —

(A) is composed of experts qualified by scientific training and experience to evaluate the target animal safety and effectiveness of the new animal drug under consideration;

(B) operates external to FDA; and

(C) is not subject to the Federal Advisory Committee Act, 5 U.S.C. App. 2.

The Secretary shall define the criteria for selection of a qualified expert panel and the procedures for the operation of the panel by regulation.

(4) Within 180 days after the receipt of a request for listing a new animal drug in the index, the Secretary shall grant or deny the request. The Secretary shall grant the request if the request for indexing continues to meet the eligibility criteria in subsection (a) and the Secretary finds, on the basis of the report of the qualified expert panel and other information available to the Secretary, that the benefits of using the new animal drug for the proposed use in a minor species outweigh its risks to the target animal, taking into account the harm caused by the absence of an approved or conditionally-approved new animal drug for the minor species in question. If the Secretary denies the request, the Secretary shall thereafter provide due notice and the opportunity for an informal conference. The decision of the Secretary following an informal conference shall constitute final agency action subject to judicial review.

(e) —

(1) The index established under subsection (a) shall include the following information for each listed drug —

(A) the name and address of the person who holds the index listing;

(B) the name of the drug and the intended use and conditions of use for which it is being indexed;

(C) product labeling; and

(D) conditions and any limitations that the Secretary deems necessary regarding use of the drug.

(2) The Secretary shall publish the index, and revise it periodically.

(3) The Secretary may establish by regulation a process for reporting changes in the conditions of manufacturing or labeling of indexed products.

(f) —

(1) If the Secretary finds, after due notice to the person who requested the index listing and an opportunity for an informal conference, that —

(A) the expert panel failed to meet the requirements as set forth by the Secretary by regulation;

(B) on the basis of new information before the Secretary, evaluated together with the evidence available to the Secretary when the new animal drug was listed in the index, the benefits of using the new animal drug for the indexed use do not outweigh its risks to the target animal;

(C) the conditions of subsection (c)(2) of this section are no longer satisfied;

(D) the manufacture of the new animal drug is not in accordance with current good manufacturing practices;

(E) the labeling, distribution, or promotion of the new animal drug is not in accordance with the index entry;

(F) the conditions and limitations of use associated with the index listing have not been followed; or

(G) the request for indexing contains any untrue statement of material fact,

the Secretary shall remove the new animal drug from the index. The decision of the Secretary following an informal conference shall constitute final agency action subject to judicial review.

(2) If the Secretary finds that there is a reasonable probability that the use of the drug would present a risk to the health of humans or other animals, the Secretary may —

(A) suspend the listing of such drug immediately;

(B) give the person listed in the index prompt notice of the Secretary's action; and

(C) afford that person the opportunity for an informal conference.

The decision of the Secretary following an informal conference shall constitute final agency action subject to judicial review.

(g) For purposes of indexing new animal drugs under this section, to the extent consistent with the public health, the Secretary shall promulgate regulations for exempting from the operation of section 512 minor species new animal drugs and animal feeds bearing or containing new animal drugs intended solely for investigational use by experts qualified by scientific training and experience to investigate the safety and effectiveness of minor species animal drugs. Such regulations may, at the discretion of the Secretary, among other conditions relating to the protection of the public health, provide for conditioning such exemption upon the establishment and maintenance of such records, and the making of such reports to the Secretary, by the manufacturer or the sponsor of the investigation of such article, of data (including but not limited to analytical reports by investigators) obtained as a result of such investigational use of such article, as the Secretary finds will enable the Secretary to evaluate the safety and effectiveness of such article in the event of the filing of a request for an index listing pursuant to this section.

(h) The labeling of a new animal drug that is the subject of an index listing shall state, prominently and conspicuously —

(1) "NOT APPROVED BY FDA. — Legally marketed as an FDA indexed product. Extra-label use is prohibited.";

(2) except in the case of new animal drugs indexed for use in an early life stage of a food-producing animal, "This product is not to be used in animals intended for use as food for humans or other animals."; and

(3) such other information as may be prescribed by the Secretary in the index listing.

(i) —

(1) In the case of any new animal drug for which an index listing pursuant to subsection (a) is in effect, the person who has an index listing shall establish and maintain such records, and make such reports to the Secretary, of data relating to experience, and other data or information, received or otherwise obtained by such person with respect to such drug, or with respect to animal feeds bearing or containing such drug, as the Secretary may by general regulation, or by order with respect to such listing, prescribe on the basis of a finding that such records and reports are necessary in order to enable the Secretary to determine, or facilitate a determination, whether there is or may be ground for invoking subsection (f). Such regulation or order shall provide, where the Secretary deems it to be appropriate, for the examination, upon request, by the persons to whom such regulation or order is applicable, of similar information received or otherwise obtained by the Secretary.

(2) Every person required under this subsection to maintain records, and every person in charge or custody thereof, shall, upon request of an officer or employee designated by the Secretary, permit such officer or employee at all reasonable times to have access to and copy and verify such records.

(j) —

(1) Safety and effectiveness data and information which has been submitted in support of a request for a new animal drug to be indexed under this section and which has not been previously disclosed to the public shall be made available to the public, upon request, unless extraordinary circumstances are shown —

(A) if no work is being or will be undertaken to have the drug indexed in accordance with the request,

(B) if the Secretary has determined that such drug cannot be indexed and all legal appeals have been exhausted,

(C) if the indexing of such drug is terminated and all legal appeals have been exhausted, or

(D) if the Secretary has determined that such drug is not a new animal drug.

(2) Any request for data and information pursuant to paragraph (1) shall include a verified statement by the person making the request that any data or information received under such paragraph shall not be disclosed by such person to any other person —

(A) for the purpose of, or as part of a plan, scheme, or device for, obtaining the right to make, use, or market, or making, using, or marketing, outside the United States, the drug identified in the request for indexing; and

(B) without obtaining from any person to whom the data and information are disclosed an identical verified statement, a copy of which is to be provided by such person to the Secretary, which meets the requirements of this paragraph.

(k) In the case of a request under subsection (d) to add a drug to the index under subsection (a) with respect to a drug for which the Sectetary provides notice to the person filing the request that the Secretary intends to issue a scientific and medical evaluation and recommend controls under the Controlled Substances Act, a determination to grant the request to add such drug to the index shall not take effect until the interim final rule controlling the drug is issued in accordance with section 201(j) of the Controlled Substances Act.

Sec. 573. [360ccc-2] Designated New Animal Drugs for Minor Use or Minor Species.

(a) Designation. —

(1) The manufacturer or the sponsor of a new animal drug for a minor use or use in a minor species may request that the Secretary declare that drug a "designated new animal drug". A request for designation of a new animal drug shall be made before the submission of an application under section 512(b) or section 571 for the new animal drug.

(2) The Secretary may declare a new animal drug a "designated new animal drug" if —

(A) it is intended for a minor use or use in a minor species; and

(B) the same drug in the same dosage form for the same intended use is not approved under section 512 or 571 or designated under this section at the time the request is made.

(3) Regarding the termination of a designation —

(A) the sponsor of a new animal drug shall notify the Secretary of any decision to discontinue active pursuit of approval under section 512 or 571 of an application for a designated new animal drug. The Secretary shall terminate the designation upon such notification;

(B) the Secretary may also terminate designation if the Secretary independently determines that the sponsor is not actively pursuing approval under section 512 or 571 with due diligence;

(C) the sponsor of an approved designated new animal drug shall notify the Secretary of any discontinuance of the manufacture of such new animal drug at least one year before discontinuance. The Secretary shall terminate the designation upon such notification; and

(D) the designation shall terminate upon the expiration of any applicable exclusivity period under subsection (c).

(4) Notice respecting the designation or termination of designation of a new animal drug shall be made available to the public.

(b) Grants and Contracts for Development of Designated New Animal Drugs. —

(1) The Secretary may make grants to and enter into contracts with public and private entities and individuals to assist in defraying the costs of qualified safety and effectiveness testing expenses and manufacturing expenses incurred in connection with the development of designated new animal drugs.

(2) For purposes of paragraph (1) of this section —

(A) The term "qualified safety and effectiveness testing" means testing —

(i) which occurs after the date such new animal drug is designated under this section and before the date on which an application with respect to such drug is submitted under section 512; and

(ii) which is carried out under an investigational exemption under section 512(j).

(B) The term "manufacturing expenses" means expenses incurred in developing processes and procedures associated with manufacture of the designated new animal drug which occur after the new animal drug is designated under this section and before the date on which an application with respect to such new animal drug is submitted under section 512 or 571.

(c) Exclusivity for Designated New Animal Drugs. —

(1) Except as provided in subsection (c)(2), if the Secretary approves or conditionally approves an application for a designated new animal drug, the Secretary may not approve or conditionally approve another application submitted for such new animal drug with the same intended use as the designated new animal drug for another applicant before the expiration of seven years from the date of approval or conditional approval of the application.

(2) If an application filed pursuant to section 512 or section 571 is approved for a designated new animal drug, the Secretary may, during the 7-year exclusivity period beginning on the date of the application approval or conditional approval, approve or conditionally approve another application under section 512 or section 571 for such drug for such minor use or minor species for another applicant if —

(A) the Secretary finds, after providing the holder of such an approved application notice and opportunity for the submission of views, that in the granted exclusivity period the holder of the approved application cannot assure the availability of sufficient quantities of the drug to meet the needs for which the drug was designated; or

(B) such holder provides written consent to the Secretary for the approval or conditional approval of other applications before the expiration of such exclusivity period.

(3) For purposes of determining the 7-year period of exclusivity under paragraph (1) for a drug for which the Secretary intends to issue a scientific and medical evaluation and recommend controls under the Controlled Substances Act, the drug shall not be considered approved or conditionally approved until the date that the interim final rule controlling the drug is issued in accordance with section 201(j) of the Controlled Substances Act.

Subchapter G — Medical Gases

Sec. 575. [360ddd] Definitions.

In this subchapter:

(1) the term "designated medical gas" means any of the following:

(A) Oxygen that meets the standards set forth in an official compendium.

(B) Nitrogen that meets the standards set forth in an official compendium.

(C) Nitrous oxide that meets the standards set forth in an official compendium.

(D) Carbon dioxide that meets the standards set forth in an official compendium.

(E) Helium that meets the standards set forth in an official compendium.

(F) Carbon monoxide that meets the standards set forth in an official compendium.

(G) Medical air that meets the standards set forth in an official compendium.

(H) Any other medical gas deemed appropriate by the Secretary, after taking into account any investigational new drug application or investigational new animal drug application for the same medical gas submitted in accordance with regulations applicable to such applications in title 21 of the Code of Federal Regulations, unless any period of exclusivity for a new drug under section 505(c)(3)(E)(ii) or section 505(j)(5)(F)(ii), or the extension of any such period under section 505A, or any period of exclusivity for a new animal drug under section 512(c)(2)(F), applicable to such medical gas has not expired.

(2) the term "medical gas" means a drug that —

(A) is manufactured or stored In a liquefied, nonliquefied, or cryogenic state; and

(B) is administered as a gas.

SEC. 576. [360ddd-1] REGULATION OF MEDICAL GASES.

(a) CERTIFICATION OF DESIGNATED MEDICAL GASES. —

(1) SUBMISSION. — Beginning 180 days after the date of enactment of this section, any person who seeks to initially introduce or deliver for introduction a designated medical gas into interstate commerce may file with the Secretary a request for certification of a medical gas as a designated medical gas. Any such request shall contain the following information:

(A) A description of the medical gas.

(B) The name and address of the sponsor.

(C) The name and address of the facility or facilities where the medical gas is or will be manufactured.

(D) Any other information deemed appropriate by the Secretary to determine whether the medical gas is a designated medical gas.

(2) GRANT OF CERTIFICATION. — The certification requested under paragraph (1) is deemed to be granted unless, within 60 days of the filing of such request, the Secretary finds that —

(A) the medical gas subject to the certification is not a designated medical gas;

(B) the request does not contain the information required under paragraph (1) or otherwise lacks sufficient information to permit the Secretary to determine that the medical gas is a designated medical gas; or

(C) denying the request is necessary to protect the public health.

(3) EFFECT OF CERTIFICATION. —

(A) IN GENERAL. —

(i) APPROVED USES. — A designated medical gas for which a certification is granted under paragraph (2) is deemed, alone or in combination, as medically appropriate, with another designated medical gas or gases for which a certification or certifications have been granted, to have in effect an approved application under section 505 or 512, subject to all applicable postapproval requirements, for the following indications for use:

(I) In the case of oxygen, the treatment or prevention of hypoxemia or hypoxia.

(II) In the case of nitrogen, use in hypoxic challenge testing.

(III) In the case of nitrous oxide, analgesia.

(IV) In the case of carbon dioxide, use in extracorporeal membrane oxygenation therapy or respiratory stimulation.

(V) In the case of helium, the treatment of upper airway obstruction or increased airway resistance.

(VI) In the case of medical air, to reduce the risk of hyperoxia.

(VII) In the case of carbon monoxide, use in lung diffusion testing.

(VIII) Any other indication for use for a designated medical gas or combination of designated medical gases deemed appropriate by the Secretary, unless any period of exclusivity for a new drug under clause (iii) or (iv) of section 505(c)(3)(E), clause (iii) or (iv) of section 505(j)(5)(F), or section 527, or the extension of any such period under section 505A, applicable to such indication for use for such gas or combination of gases has not expired.

(ii) LABELING. — the requirements of sections 503(b)(4) and 502(f) are deemed to have been met for a designated medical gas if the labeling on the final use container for such medical gas bears —

(I) the information required by section 503(b)(4);

(II) a warning statement concerning the use of the medical gas as determined by the Secretary by regulation; and

(III) appropriate directions and warnings concerning storage and handling.

(B) Inapplicability of Exclusivity Provisions. —

(i) No Exclusivity for a Certified Medical Gas. — No designated medical gas deemed under subparagraph (A)(i) to have in effect an approved application is eligible for any period of exclusivity for a new drug under section 505(c), 505(j), or 527, or the extension of any such period under section 505A, on the basis of such deemed approval.

(ii) Effect on Certification. — No period of exclusivity under section 505(c), 505(j), or section 527, or the extension of any such period under section 505A, with respect to an application for a drug product, shall prohibit, limit, or otherwise affect the submission, grant, or effect of a certification under this section, except as provided in subsection (a)(3)(A)(i)(VIII) and section 575(1)(H).

(4) Withdrawal, Suspension, or Revocation of Approval. —

(A) Withdrawal, Suspension of Approval. — Nothing in this subchapter limits the Secretary's authority to withdraw or suspend approval of a drug product, including a designated medical gas deemed under this section to have in effect an approved application under section 505 or section 512 of this Act.

(B) Revocation of Certification. — The Secretary may revoke the grant of a certification under paragraph (2) if the Secretary determines that the request for certification contains any material omission or falsification.

(b) Prescription Requirement. —

(1) In General. — A designated medical gas shall be subject to the requirements of section 503(b)(1) unless the Secretary exercises the authority provided in section 503(b)(3) to remove such medical gas from the requirements of section 503(b)(1), the gas is approved for use without a prescription pursuant to an application under section 505 or 512, or the use in question is authorized pursuant to another provision of this Act relating to use of medical products in emergencies.

(2) Oxygen. —

(A) No Prescription Required for Certain Uses. — Notwithstanding paragraph (1), oxygen may be provided without a prescription for the following uses:

(i) For use in the event of depressurization or other environmental oxygen deficiency.

(ii) For oxygen deficiency or for use in emergency resuscitation, when administered by properly trained personnel.

(B) Labeling. — For oxygen provided pursuant to subparagraph (A), the requirements of section 503(b)(4) shall be deemed to have been met if its labeling bears a warning that the oxygen can be used for emergency use only and for all other medical applications a prescription is required.

Sec. 577. [360ddd-2] Inapplicability of Drug Fees to Designated Medical Gases.

A designated medical gas, alone or in combination with another designated gas or gases (as medically appropriate) deemed under section 576 to have in effect an approved application shall not be assessed fees under section 736(a) or 740(a) on the basis of such deemed approval.

Subchapter H — Pharmaceutical Distribution Supply Chain

Sec. 581. [360eee] Definitions.

In this subchapter:

(1) Affiliate. — The term "affiliate" means a business entity that has a relationship with a second business entity if, directly or indirectly —

(A) one business entity controls, or has the power to control, the other business entity; or

(B) a third party controls, or has the power to control, both of the business entities.

(2) Authorized. — The term "authorized" means —

(A) in the case of a manufacturer or repackager, having a valid registration in accordance with section 510;

(B) in the case of a wholesale distributor, having a valid license under State law or section 583, in accordance with section 582(a)(6), and complying with the licensure reporting requirements under section 503(e), as amended by the Drug Supply Chain Security Act;

(C) in the case of a third-party logistics provider, having a valid license under State law or section 584(a)(1), in accordance with section 582(a)(7), and complying with the licensure reporting requirements under section 584(b); and

(D) in the case of a dispenser, having a valid license under State law.

(3) Dispenser. — The term "dispenser" —

(A) means a retail pharmacy, hospital pharmacy, a group of chain pharmacies under common ownership and control that do not act as a wholesale distributor, or any other person authorized by law to dispense or administer prescription drugs, and the affiliated warehouses or distribution centers of such entities under common ownership and control that do not act as a wholesale distributor; and

(B) does not include a person who dispenses only products to be used in animals in accordance with section 512(a)(5).

(4) Disposition. — The term "disposition", with respect to a product within the possession or control of an entity, means the removal of such product from the pharmaceutical distribution supply chain, which may include disposal or return of the product for disposal or other appropriate handling and other actions, such as retaining a sample of the product for further additional physical examination or laboratory analysis of the product by a manufacturer or regulatory or law enforcement agency.

(5) Distribute or Distribution. — The term "distribute" or "distribution" means the sale, purchase, trade, delivery, handling, storage, or receipt of a product, and does not include the dispensing of a product pursuant to a prescription executed in accordance with section 503(b)(1) or the dispensing of a product approved under section 512(b).

(6) Exclusive Distributor. — The term "exclusive distributor" means the wholesale distributor that directly purchased the product from the manufacturer and is the sole distributor of that manufacturer's product to a subsequent repackager, wholesale distributor, or dispenser.

(7) Homogeneous Case. — The term "homogeneous case" means a sealed case containing only product that has a single National Drug Code number belonging to a single lot.

(8) Illegitimate Product. — The term "illegitimate product" means a product for which credible evidence shows that the product —

(A) is counterfeit, diverted, or stolen;

(B) is intentionally adulterated such that the product would result in serious adverse health consequences or death to humans;

(C) is the subject of a fraudulent transaction; or

(D) appears otherwise unfit for distribution such that the product would be reasonably likely to result in serious adverse health consequences or death to humans.

(9) Licensed. — The term "licensed" means —

(A) in the case of a wholesale distributor, having a valid license in accordance with section 503(e) or section 582(a)(6), as applicable;

(B) in the case of a third-party logistics provider, having a valid license in accordance with section 584(a) or section 582(a)(7), as applicable; and

(C) in the case of a dispenser, having a valid license under State law.

(10) Manufacturer. — The term "manufacturer" means, with respect to a product —

(A) a person that holds an application approved under section 505 or a license issued under section 351 of the Public Health Service Act for such product, or if such product is not the subject of an approved application or license, the person who manufactured the product;

(B) a co-licensed partner of the person described in subparagraph (A) that obtains the product directly from a person described in this subparagraph or subparagraph (A) or (C); or

(C) an affiliate of a person described in subparagraph (A) or (B) that receives the product directly from a person described in this subparagraph or subparagraph (A) or (B).

(11) Package. —

(A) In General. — The term "package" means the smallest individual saleable unit of product for distribution by a manufacturer or repackager that is intended by the manufacturer for ultimate sale to the dispenser of such product.

(B) Individual Saleable Unit. — For purposes of this paragraph, an "individual saleable unit" is the smallest container of product introduced into commerce by the manufacturer or repackager that is intended by the manufacturer or repackager for individual sale to a dispenser.

(12) Prescription Drug. — The term "prescription drug" means a drug for human use subject to section 503(b)(1).

(13) Product. — The term "product" means a prescription drug in a finished dosage form for administration to a patient without substantial further manufacturing (such as capsules, tablets, and lyophilized products before reconstitution), but for purposes of section 582, does not include blood or blood components intended for transfusion, radioactive drugs or radioactive biological products (as defined in section 600.3(ee) of title 21, Code of Federal Regulations) that are regulated by the Nuclear Regulatory Commission or by a State pursuant to an agreement with such Commission under section 274 of the Atomic Energy Act of 1954 (42 U.S.C. 2021), imaging drugs, an intravenous product described in clause (xiv), (xv), or (xvi) of paragraph (24)(B), any medical gas (as defined in section 575), homeopathic drugs marketed in accordance with applicable guidance under this Act, or a drug compounded in compliance with section 503A or 503B.

(14) Product Identifier. — The term "product identifier" means a standardized graphic that includes, in both human-readable form and on a machine-readable data carrier that conforms to the standards developed by a widely recognized international standards development organization, the standardized numerical identifier, lot number, and expiration date of the product.

(15) Quarantine. — The term "quarantine" means the storage or identification of a product, to prevent distribution or transfer of the product, in a physically separate area clearly identified for such use or through other procedures.

(16) Repackager. — The term "repackager" means a person who owns or operates an establishment that repacks and relabels a product or package for —

(A) further sale; or

(B) distribution without a further transaction.

(17) Return. — The term "return" means providing product to the authorized immediate trading partner from which such product was purchased or received, or to a returns processor or reverse logistics provider for handling of such product.

(18) Returns Processor or Reverse Logistics Provider. — The term "returns processor" or "reverse logistics provider" means a person who owns or operates an establishment that dispositions or otherwise processes saleable or nonsaleable product received from an authorized trading partner such that the product may be processed for credit to the purchaser, manufacturer, or seller or disposed of for no further distribution.

(19) Specific Patient Need. — The term "specific patient need" refers to the transfer of a product from one pharmacy to another to fill a prescription for an identified patient. Such term does not include the transfer of a product from one pharmacy to another for the purpose of increasing or replenishing stock in anticipation of a potential need.

(20) Standardized Numerical Identifier. — The term "standardized numerical identifier" means a set of numbers or characters used to uniquely identify each package or homogenous case that is composed of the National Drug Code that corresponds to the specific product (including the particular package configuration) combined with a unique alphanumeric serial number of up to 20 characters.

(21) Suspect Product. — The term "suspect product" means a product for which there is reason to believe that such product —

(A) is potentially counterfeit, diverted, or stolen;

(B) is potentially intentionally adulterated such that the product would result in serious adverse health consequences or death to humans;

(C) is potentially the subject of a fraudulent transaction; or

(D) appears otherwise unfit for distribution such that the product would result in serious adverse health consequences or death to humans.

(22) Third-Party Logistics Provider. — The term "third-party logistics provider" means an entity that provides or coordinates warehousing, or other logistics services of a product in interstate commerce on behalf of a manufacturer, wholesale distributor, or dispenser of a product, but does not take ownership of the product, nor have responsibility to direct the sale or disposition of the product.

(23) Trading Partner. — The term "trading partner" means —

(A) a manufacturer, repackager, wholesale distributor, or dispenser from whom a manufacturer, repackager, wholesale distributor, or dispenser accepts direct ownership of a product or to whom a manufacturer, repackager, wholesale distributor, or dispenser transfers direct ownership of a product; or

(B) a third-party logistics provider from whom a manufacturer, repackager, wholesale distributor, or dispenser accepts direct possession of a product or to whom a manufacturer, repackager, wholesale distributor, or dispenser transfers direct possession of a product.

(24) Transaction. —

(A) In General. — The term "transaction" means the transfer of product between persons in which a change of ownership occurs.

(B) **Exemptions.** — The term "transaction" does not include —

(i) intracompany distribution of any product between members of an affiliate or within a manufacturer;

(ii) the distribution of a product among hospitals or other health care entities that are under common control;

(iii) the distribution of a product for emergency medical reasons including a public health emergency declaration pursuant to section 319 of the Public Health Service Act, except that a drug shortage not caused by a public health emergency shall not constitute an emergency medical reason;

(iv) the dispensing of a product pursuant to a prescription executed in accordance with section 503(b) (1);

(v) the distribution of product samples by a manufacturer or a licensed wholesale distributor in accordance with section 503(d);

(vi) the distribution of blood or blood components intended for transfusion;

(vii) the distribution of minimal quantities of product by a licensed retail pharmacy to a licensed practitioner for office use;

(viii) the sale, purchase, or trade of a drug or an offer to sell, purchase, or trade a drug by a charitable organization described in section 501(c)(3) of the Internal Revenue Code of 1986 to a nonprofit affiliate of the organization to the extent otherwise permitted by law;

(ix) the distribution of a product pursuant to the sale or merger of a pharmacy or pharmacies or a wholesale distributor or wholesale distributors, except that any records required to be maintained for the product shall be transferred to the new owner of the pharmacy or pharmacies or wholesale distributor or wholesale distributors;

(x) the dispensing of a product approved under section 512(c);

(xi) products transferred to or from any facility that is licensed by the Nuclear Regulatory Commission or by a State pursuant to an agreement with such Commission under section 274 of the Atomic Energy Act of 1954 (42 U.S.C. 2021);

(xii) a combination product that is not subject to approval under section 505 or licensure under section 351 of the Public Health Service Act, and that is —

(I) a product comprised of a device and 1 or more other regulated components (such as a drug/ device, biologic/device, or drug/device/biologic) that are physically, chemically, or otherwise combined or mixed and produced as a single entity;

(II) 2 or more separate products packaged together in a single package or as a unit and comprised of a drug and device or device and biological product; or

(III) 2 or more finished medical devices plus one or more drug or biological products that are packaged together in what is referred to as a 'medical convenience kit' as described in clause (xiii);

(xiii) the distribution of a collection of finished medical devices, which may include a product or biological product, assembled in kit form strictly for the convenience of the purchaser or user (referred to in this clause as a "medical convenience kit") if—

(I) the medical convenience kit is assembled in an establishment that is registered with the Food and Drug Administration as a device manufacturer in accordance with section 510(b)(2);

(II) the medical convenience kit does not contain a controlled substance that appears in a schedule contained in the Comprehensive Drug Abuse Prevention and Control Act of 1970;

(III) in the case of a medical convenience kit that includes a product, the person that manufacturers the kit —

(aa) purchased such product directly from the pharmaceutical manufacturer or from a wholesale distributor that purchased the product directly from the pharmaceutical manufacturer; and

(bb) does not alter the primary container or label of the product as purchased from the manufacturer or wholesale distributor; and

(IV) in the case of a medical convenience kit that includes a product, the product is —

(aa) an intravenous solution intended for the replenishment of fluids and electrolytes;

(bb) a product intended to maintain the equilibrium of water and minerals in the body;

(cc) a product intended for irrigation or reconstitution;

(dd) an anesthetic;

(ee) an anticoagulant;

(ff) a vasopressor; or

(gg) a sympathomimetic;

(xiv) the distribution of an intravenous product that, by its formulation, is intended for the replenishment of fluids and electrolytes (such as sodium, chloride, and potassium) or calories (such as dextrose and amino acids);

(xv) the distribution of an intravenous product used to maintain the equilibrium of water and minerals in the body, such as dialysis solutions;

(xvi) the distribution of a product that is intended for irrigation, or sterile water, whether intended for such purposes or for injection;

(xvii) the distribution of a medical gas (as defined in section 575); or

(xviii) the distribution or sale of any licensed product under section 351 of the Public Health Service Act that meets the definition of a device under section 201(h).

(25) Transaction History. — The term "transaction history" means a statement in paper or electronic form, including the transaction information for each prior transaction going back to the manufacturer of the product.

(26) Transaction Information. — The term "transaction information" means —

(A) the proprietary or established name or names of the product;

(B) the strength and dosage form of the product;

(C) the National Drug Code number of the product;

(D) the container size;

(E) the number of containers;

(F) the lot number of the product;

(G) the date of the transaction;

(H) the date of the shipment, if more than 24 hours after the date of the transaction;

(I) the business name and address of the person from whom ownership is being transferred; and

(J) the business name and address of the person to whom ownership is being transferred.

(27) Transaction Statement. — The "transaction statement" is a statement, in paper or electronic form, that the entity transferring ownership in a transaction —

(A) is authorized as required under the Drug Supply Chain Security Act;

(B) received the product from a person that is authorized as required under the Drug Supply Chain Security Act;

(C) received transaction information and a transaction statement from the prior owner of the product, as required under section 582;

(D) did not knowingly ship a suspect or illegitimate product;

(E) had systems and processes in place to comply with verification requirements under section 582;

(F) did not knowingly provide false transaction information; and

(G) did not knowingly alter the transaction history.

(28) Verification or Verify. — The term "verification" or "verify" means determining whether the product identifier affixed to, or imprinted upon, a package or homogeneous case corresponds to the standardized numerical identifier or lot number and expiration date assigned to the product by the manufacturer or the repackager, as applicable in accordance with section 582.

(29) Wholesale Distributor. — The term "wholesale distributor" means a person (other than a manufacturer, a manufacturer's co-licensed partner, a third-party logistics provider, or repackager) engaged in wholesale distribution (as defined in section 503(e)(4), as amended by the Drug Supply Chain Security Act).

Sec. 582. [360eee-1] Requirements.

(a) In General. —

(1) Other Activities. — Each manufacturer, repackager, wholesale distributor, and dispenser shall comply with the requirements set forth in this section with respect to the role of such manufacturer, repackager, wholesale distributor, or dispenser in a transaction involving product. If an entity meets the definition of more than one of the entities listed in the preceding sentence, such entity shall comply with all applicable requirements in this section, but shall not be required to duplicate requirements.

(2) Initial Standards. —

(A) In General. — The Secretary shall, in consultation with other appropriate Federal officials, manufacturers, repackagers, wholesale distributors, dispensers, and other pharmaceutical distribution supply chain stakeholders, issue a draft guidance document that establishes standards for the interoperable exchange of transaction information, transaction history, and transaction statements, in paper or electronic format, for compliance with this subsection and subsections (b), (c), (d), and (e). In establishing such standards, the Secretary shall consider the feasibility of establishing standardized documentation to be used by members of the pharmaceutical distribution supply chain to convey the transaction information, transaction history, and transaction statement to the subsequent purchaser of a product and to facilitate the exchange of lot level data. The standards established under this paragraph shall take into consideration the standards established under section 505D and shall comply with a form and format developed by a widely recognized international standards development organization.

(B) Public Input. — Prior to issuing the draft guidance under subparagraph (A), the Secretary shall gather comments and information from stakeholders and maintain such comments and information in a public docket for at least 60 days prior to issuing such guidance.

(C) Publication. — The Secretary shall publish the standards established under subparagraph (A) not later than 1 year after the date of enactment of the Drug Supply Chain Security Act.

(3) Waivers, Exceptions, and Exemptions. —

(A) In General. — Not later than 2 years after the date of enactment of the Drug Supply Chain Security Act, the Secretary shall, by guidance —

(i) establish a process by which an authorized manufacturer, repackager, wholesale distributor, or dispenser may request a waiver from any of the requirements set forth in this section, which the Secretary may grant if the Secretary determines that such requirements would result in an undue economic hardship or for emergency medical reasons, including a public health emergency declaration pursuant to section 319 of the Public Health Service Act;

(ii) establish a process by which the Secretary determines exceptions, and a process through which a manufacturer or repackager may request such an exception, to the requirements relating to product, identifiers if a product is packaged in a container too small or otherwise unable to accommodate a label with sufficient, space to bear the information required for compliance with this section; and

(iii) establish a process by which the Secretary may determine other products or transactions that shall be exempt from the requirements of this section.

(B) Content. — The guidance issued under subparagraph (A) shall include a process for the biennial review and renewal of such waivers, exceptions, and exemptions, as applicable.

(C) Process. — In issuing the guidance under this paragraph, the Secretary shall provide an effective date that is not later than 180 days prior to the date on which manufacturers are required to affix or imprint a product identifier to each package and homogenous case of product intended to be introduced in a transaction into commerce consistent with this section.

(4) Self-Executing Requirements. — Except where otherwise specified, the requirements of this section may be enforced without further regulations or guidance from the Secretary.

(5) Grandfathering Product. —

(A) Product Identifier. — Not, later than 2 years after the date of enactment of the Drug Supply Chain Security Act, the Secretary shall finalize guidance specifying whether and under what circumstances product that is not labeled with a product identifier and that is in the pharmaceutical distribution supply chain at the time of the effective date of the requirements of this section shall be exempted from the requirements of this section.

(B) Tracing. — For a product that entered the pharmaceutical distribution supply chain prior to January 1, 2015 —

(i) authorized trading partners shall be exempt from providing transaction information as required under subsections (b)(1)(A)(i), (c)(1)(A)(ii), (d)(1)(A)(ii), and (e)(1)(A)(ii);

(ii) transaction history required under this section shall begin with the owner of such product on such date; and

(iii) the owners of such product on such date shall be exempt from asserting receipt of transaction information and transaction statement from the prior owner as required under this section.

(6) Wholesale Distributor Licenses. — Notwithstanding section 581(9)(A), until the effective date of the wholesale distributor licensing regulations under section 583, the term "licensed" or "authorized", as it relates to a wholesale distributor with respect to prescription drugs, shall mean a wholesale distributor with a valid license under State law.

(7) Third-Party Logistics Provider Licenses. — Until the effective date of the third-party logistics provider licensing regulations under section 584, a third-party logistics provider shall be considered "licensed" under section 581(9)(B) unless the Secretary has made a finding that the third-party logistics provider does not utilize good handling and distribution practices and publishes notice thereof.

(8) Label Changes. — Changes made to package labels solely to incorporate the product identifier may be submitted to the Secretary in the annual report of an establishment, in accordance with section 314.70(d) of chapter 21, Code of Federal Regulations (or any successor regulation).

(9) Product Identifiers. — With respect to any requirement relating to product identifiers under this subchapter —

(A) unless the Secretary allows, through guidance, the use of other technologies for data instead of or in addition to the technologies described in clauses (i) and (ii), the applicable data —

(i) shall be included in a 2-dimensional data matrix barcode when affixed to, or imprinted upon, a package; and

(ii) shall be included in a linear or 2-dimensional data matrix barcode when affixed to, or imprinted upon, a homogeneous case; and

(B) verification of the product identifier may occur by using human-readable or machine-readable methods.

(b) Manufacturer Requirements. —

(1) Product Tracing. —

(A) In General. — Beginning not later than January 1, 2015, a manufacturer shall —

(i) prior to, or at the time of, each transaction in which such manufacturer transfers ownership of a product, provide the subsequent owner with transaction history, transaction information, and a transaction statement, in a single document in an paper or electronic format; and

(ii) capture the transaction information (including lot level information), transaction history, and transaction statement for each transaction and maintain such information, history, and statement for not less than 6 years after the date of the transaction.

(B) Requests for Information. — Upon a request, by the Secretary or other appropriate Federal or State official, in the event of a recall or for the purpose of investigating a suspect product or an illegitimate product, a manufacturer shall, not later than 1 business day, and not, to exceed 48 hours, after receiving the request, or in other such reasonable time as determined by the Secretary, based on the circumstances of the request, provide the applicable transaction information, transaction history, and transaction statement for the product.

(C) Electronic Format. —

(i) In General. — Beginning not later than 4 years after the date of enactment of the Drug Supply Chain Security Act, except as provided under clause (ii), a manufacturer shall provide the transaction information, transaction history, and transaction statement required under subparagraph (A)(i) in electronic format.

(ii) Exception. — A manufacturer may continue to provide the transaction information, transaction history, and transaction statement required under subparagraph (A)(i) in a paper format to a licensed health care practitioner authorized to prescribe medication under State law or other licensed individual under the supervision or direction of such a practitioner who dispenses product in the usual course of professional practice.

(2) Product Identifier. —

(A) In General. — Beginning not later than 4 years after the date of enactment of the Drug Supply Chain Security Act, a manufacturer shall affix or imprint a product identifier to each package and homogenous case of a product, intended to be introduced in a transaction into commerce. Such manufacturer shall maintain the product identifier information for such product for not less than 6 years after the date of the transaction.

(B) Exception. — A package that is required to have a standardized numerical identifier is not required to have a unique device identifier.

(3) Authorized Trading Partners. — Beginning not later than January 1, 2015, the trading partners of a manufacturer may be only authorized trading partners.

(4) Verification. — Beginning not later than January 1, 2015, a manufacturer shall have systems in place to enable the manufacturer to comply with the following requirements:

(A) Suspect Product. —

(i) In General. — Upon making a determination that a product in the possession or control of the manufacturer is a suspect product, or upon receiving a request for verification from the Secretary that has made a determination that a product within the possession or control of a manufacturer is a suspect product, a manufacturer shall —

(I) quarantine such product within the possession or control of the manufacturer from product intended for distribution until such product is cleared or dispositioned; and

(II) promptly conduct an investigation in coordination with trading partners, as applicable, to determine whether the product is an illegitimate product, which shall include validating any applicable transaction history and transaction information in the possession of the manufacturer and otherwise investigating to determine whether the product is an illegitimate product, and, beginning 4 years after the date of enactment of the Drug Supply Chain Security Act, verifying the product at the package level, including the standardized numerical identifier.

(ii) Cleared Product. — If the manufacturer makes the determination that a suspect product is not an illegitimate product, the manufacturer shall promptly notify the Secretary, if applicable, of such determination and such product may be further distributed.

(iii) Records. — A manufacturer shall keep records of the investigation of a suspect product for not less than 6 years after the conclusion of the investigation.

(B) Illegitimate Product. —

(i) In General. — Upon determining that a product in the possession or control of a manufacturer is an illegitimate product, the manufacturer shall, in a manner consistent with the systems and processes of such manufacturer —

(I) quarantine such product within the possession or control of the manufacturer from product intended for distribution until such product is dispositioned;

(II) disposition the illegitimate product within the possession or control of the manufacturer;

(III) take reasonable and appropriate steps to assist, a trading partner to disposition an illegitimate product not in the possession or control of the manufacturer; and

(IV) retain a sample of the product for further physical examination or laboratory analysis of the product by the manufacturer or Secretary (or other appropriate Federal or State official) upon request by the Secretary (or other appropriate Federal or State official), as necessary and appropriate.

(ii) Making a Notification.

(I) Illegitimate Product. — Upon determining that a product in the possession or control of the manufacturer is an illegitimate product, the manufacturer shall notify the Secretary and all immediate trading partners that the manufacturer has reason to believe may have received such illegitimate product of such determination not later than 24 hours after making such determination.

(II) High Risk of Illegitimacy. — Amanufacturer shall notify the Secretary and immediate trading partners that the manufacturer has reason to believe may have in the trading partner's possession a product manufactured by, or purported to be a product manufactured by, the manufacturer not later than 24 hours after determining or being notified by the Secretary or a trading partner that there is a high risk that such product is an illegitimate product. For purposes of this subclause, a 'high risk' may include a specific high risk that could increase the likelihood that illegitimate product will enter the pharmaceutical distribution supply chain and other high risks as determined by the Secretary in guidance pursuant to subsection (h).

(iii) Responding to a Notification. — Upon the receipt of a notification from the Secretary or a trading partner that a determination has been made that a product is an illegitimate product, a manufacturer shall identify all illegitimate product subject to such notification that is in the possession or control of the manufacturer, including any product that is subsequently received, and shall perform the activities described in subparagraph (A).

(iv) Terminating a Notification. — Upon making a determination, in consultation with the Secretary, that a notification is no longer necessary, a manufacturer shall promptly notify immediate trading partners that the manufacturer notified pursuant to clause (ii) that such notification has been terminated.

(v) Records. — A manufacturer shall keep records of the disposition of an illegitimate product for not less than 6 years after the conclusion of the disposition.

(C) Requests for Verification. — Beginning 4 years after the date of enactment of the Drug Supply Chain Security Act, upon receiving a request for verification from an authorized repackager, wholesale distributor, or dispenser that is in possession or control of a product such person believes to be manufactured by such manufacturer, a manufacturer shall, not later than 24 hours after receiving the request for verification or in other such reasonable time as determined by the Secretary, based on the circumstances of the request, notify the person making the request whether the product identifier, including the standardized numerical identifier, that is the subject of the request corresponds to the product identifier affixed or imprinted by the manufacturer. If a manufacturer responding to a request for verification identifies a product identifier that does not correspond to that affixed or imprinted by the manufacturer, the manufacturer shall treat such product as suspect product and conduct an investigation as described in subparagraph (A). If the manufacturer has reason to believe the product is an illegitimate product, the manufacturer shall advise the person making the request of such belief at the time such manufacturer responds to the request for verification.

(D) Electronic Database. — A manufacturer may satisfy the requirements of this paragraph by developing a secure electronic database or utilizing a secure electronic database developed or operated by another entity. The owner of such database shall establish the requirements and processes to respond to requests and may provide for data access to other members of the pharmaceutical distribution supply chain, as appropriate.

The development and operation of such a database shall not relieve a manufacturer of the requirement under this paragraph to respond to a request for verification submitted by means other than a secure electronic database.

(E) Saleable Returned Product. — Beginning 4 years after the date of enactment of the Drug Supply Chain Security Act (except as provided pursuant to subsection (a)(5)), upon receipt of a returned product that, the manufacturer intends to further distribute, before further distributing such product, the manufacturer shall verify the product identifier, including the standardized numerical identifier, for each sealed homogeneous case of such product or, if such product is not, in a sealed homogeneous case, verify the product identifier, including the standardized numerical identifier, on each package.

(F) Nonsaleable Returned Product. — A manufacturer may return a nonsaleable product to the manufacturer or repackager, to the wholesale distributor from whom such product was purchased, or to a person acting on behalf of such a person, including a returns processor, without providing the information described in paragraph (l)(A)(i).

(c) Wholesale Distributor Requirements. —

(1) Product Tracing. —

(A) In General. — Beginning not later than January 1, 2015, the following requirements shall apply to wholesale distributors:

(i) A wholesale distributor shall not accept ownership of a product unless the previous owner prior to, or at the time of, the transaction provides the transaction history, transaction information, and a transaction statement for the product, as applicable under this subparagraph.

(ii)

(I)

(aa) If the wholesale distributor purchased a product directly from the manufacturer, the exclusive distributor of the manufacturer, or a repackager that purchased directly from the manufacturer, then prior to, or at the time of, each transaction in which the wholesale distributor transfers ownership of a product, the wholesale distributor shall provide to the subsequent purchaser —

(AA) a transaction statement, which shall state that such wholesale distributor, or a member of the affiliate of such wholesale distributor, purchased the product directly from the manufacturer, exclusive distributor of the manufacturer, or repackager that purchased the product directly from the manufacturer; and

(BB) subject to subclause (II), the transaction history and transaction information.

(bb) The wholesale distributor shall provide the transaction history, transaction information, and transaction statement under item (aa) —

(AA) if provided to a dispenser, on a single document in a paper or electronic format; and

(BB) if provided to a wholesale distributor, through any combination of self-generated paper, electronic data, or manufacturer-provided information on the product package.

(II) For purposes of transactions described in subclause (I), transaction history and transaction information shall not be required to include the lot number of the product, the initial transaction date, or the initial shipment date from the manufacturer (as defined in subparagraphs (F), (G), and (H) of section 581(26)).

(iii) If the wholesale distributor did not purchase a product directly from the manufacturer, the exclusive distributor of the manufacturer, or a repackager that purchased directly from the manufacturer, as described in clause (ii), then prior to, or at the time of, each transaction or subsequent transaction, the wholesale distributor shall provide to the subsequent purchaser a transaction statement, transaction history, and transaction information, in a paper or electronic format that complies with the guidance document issued under subsection (a)(2).

(iv) For the purposes of clause (iii), the transaction history supplied shall begin only with the wholesale distributor described in clause (ii)(I), but the wholesale distributor described in clause (iii) shall inform the subsequent purchaser that such wholesale distributor received a direct purchase statement from a wholesale distributor described in clause (ii)(I).

(v) A wholesale distributor shall —

(I) capture the transaction information (including lot level information) consistent with the requirements of this section, transaction history, and transaction statement for each transaction described in clauses (i), (ii), and (iii) and maintain such information, history, and statement for not less than 6 years after the date of the transaction; and

(II) maintain the confidentiality of the transaction information (including any lot level information consistent with the requirements of this section), transaction history, and transaction statement for a product in a manner that prohibits disclosure to any person other than the Secretary or other appropriate Federal or State official, except to comply with clauses (ii) and (iii), and, as applicable, pursuant to an agreement under subparagraph (D).

(B) Returns. —

(i) Saleable Returns. — Notwithstanding subparagraph (A)(i), the following shall apply:

(I) Requirements. — Until the date that is 6 years after the date of enactment of the Drug Supply Chain Security Act (except as provided pursuant to subsection (a)(5)), a wholesale distributor may accept returned product from a dispenser or repackager pursuant to the terms and conditions of any agreement between the parties, and, notwithstanding subparagraph (A)(ii), may distribute such returned product without providing the transaction history. For transactions subsequent to the return, the transaction history of such product shall begin with the wholesale distributor that accepted the returned product, consistent with the requirements of this subsection.

(II) Enhanced Requirements. — Beginning 6 years after the date of enactment of the Drug Supply Chain Security Act (except, as provided pursuant, to subsection (a)(5)), a wholesale distributor may accept returned product from a dispenser or repackager only if the wholesale distributor can associate returned product with the transaction information and transaction statement associated with that product. For all transactions after such date, the transaction history, as applicable, of such product shall begin with the wholesale distributor that accepted and verified the returned product. For purposes of this subparagraph, the transaction information and transaction history, as applicable, need not include transaction dates if it is not reasonably practicable to obtain such dates.

(ii) Nonsaleable Returns. — A wholesale distributor may return a non-saleable product to the manufacturer or repackager, to the wholesale distributor from whom such product, was purchased, or to a person acting on behalf of such a person, including a returns processor, without providing the information required under sub-paragraph (A)(i).

(C) Requests for Information. — Upon a request by the Secretary or other appropriate Federal or State official, in the event, of a recall or for the purpose of investigating a suspect product or an illegitimate product, a wholesale distributor shall, not later than 1 business day, and not to exceed 48 hours, after receiving the request, or in other such reasonable time as determined by the Secretary, based on the circumstances of the request provide the applicable transaction information, transaction history, and transaction statement for the product.

(D) Trading Partner Agreements. — Beginning 6 years after the date of enactment of the Drug Supply Chain Security Act, a wholesale distributor may disclose the transaction information, including lot level information, transaction history, or transaction statement of a product to the subsequent purchaser of the product, pursuant to a written agreement between such wholesale distributor and such subsequent purchaser. Nothing in this subparagraph shall be construed to limit the applicability of subparagraphs (A) through (C).

(2) Product Identifier. — Beginning 6 years after the date of enactment of the Drug Supply Chain Security Act, a wholesale distributor may engage in transactions involving a product only if such product is encoded with a product identifier (except as provided pursuant to subsection (a)(5)).

(3) Authorized Trading Partners. — Beginning not later than January 1, 2015, the trading partners of a wholesale distributor may be only authorized trading partners.

(4) Verification. — Beginning not later than January 1, 2015, a wholesale distributor shall have systems in place to enable the wholesale distributor to comply with the following requirements:

(A) Suspect Product. —

(i) In General. — Upon making a determination that a product in the possession or control of a wholesale distributor is a suspect product, or upon receiving a request for verification from the Secretary that has made a determination that a product within the possession or control of a wholesale distributor is a suspect product, a wholesale distributor shall —

(I) quarantine such product within the possession or control of the wholesale distributor from product intended for distribution until such product is cleared or dispositioned; and

(II) promptly conduct an investigation in coordination with trading partners, as applicable, to determine whether the product is an illegitimate product, which shall include validating any applicable transaction history and transaction information in the possession of the wholesale distributor and otherwise investigating to determine whether the product is an illegitimate product, and, beginning 6 years after the date of enactment of the Drug Supply Chain Security Act (except as provided pursuant to subsection (a)(5)), verifying the product at the package level, including the standardized numerical identifier.

(ii) Cleared Product. — If the wholesale distributor determines that a suspect product is not an illegitimate product, the wholesale distributor shall promptly notify the Secretary, if applicable, of such determination and such product may be further distributed.

(iii) Records. — A wholesale distributor shall keep records of the investigation of a suspect product for not less than 6 years after the conclusion of the investigation.

(B) Illegitimate Product. —

(i) In General. — Upon determining, in coordination with the manufacturer, that a product in the possession or control of a wholesale distributor is an illegitimate product, the wholesale distributor shall, in a manner that is consistent with the systems and processes of such wholesale distributor —

(I) quarantine such product within the possession or control of the wholesale distributor from product intended for distribution until such product is dispositioned;

(II) disposition the illegitimate product within the possession or control of the wholesale distributor;

(III) take reasonable and appropriate steps to assist a trading partner to disposition an illegitimate product not in the possession or control of the wholesale distributor; and

(IV) retain a sample of the product for further physical examination or laboratory analysis of the product by the manufacturer or Secretary (or other appropriate Federal or State official) upon request by the manufacturer or Secretary (or other appropriate Federal or State official), as necessary and appropriate.

(ii) Making a Notification. — Upon determining that a product in the possession or control of the wholesale distributor is an illegitimate product, the wholesale distributor shall notify the Secretary and all immediate trading partners that the wholesale distributor has reason to believe may have received such illegitimate product of such determination not later than 24 hours after making such determination.

(iii) Responding to a Notification. — Upon the receipt of a notification from the Secretary or a trading partner that a determination has been made that a product is an illegitimate product, a wholesale distributor shall identify all illegitimate product subject to such notification that is in the possession or control of the wholesale distributor, including any product that is subsequently received, and shall perform the activities described in subparagraph (A).

(iv) Terminating a Notification. — Upon making a determination, in consultation with the Secretary, that a notification is no longer necessary, a wholesale distributor shall promptly notify immediate trading partners that the wholesale distributor notified pursuant to clause (ii) that such notification has been terminated.

(v) Records. — A wholesale distributor shall keep records of the disposition of an illegitimate product for not less than 6 years after the conclusion of the disposition.

(C) Electronic Database. — A wholesale distributor may satisfy the requirements of this paragraph by developing a secure electronic database or utilizing a secure electronic database developed or operated by another entity. The owner of such database shall establish the requirements and processes to respond to requests and may provide for data access to other members of the pharmaceutical distribution supply chain, as appropriate. The development and operation of such a database shall not relieve a wholesale distributor of the requirement under this paragraph to respond to a verification request submitted by means other than a secure electronic database.

(D) Verification of Saleable Returned Product. — Beginning 6 years after the date of enactment of the Drug Supply Chain Security Act, upon receipt of a returned product that the wholesale distributor intends to further distribute, before further distributing such product, the wholesale distributor shall verify the product identifier, including the standardized numerical identifier, for each sealed homogeneous case of such product or, if such product is not in a sealed homogeneous case, verify the product identifier, including the standardized numerical identifier, on each package.

(d) Dispenser Requirements. —

(1) Product Tracing. —

(A) In General. — Beginning July 1, 2015, a dispenser —

(i) shall not accept ownership of a product, unless the previous owner prior to, or at the time of, the transaction, provides transaction history, transaction information, and a transaction statement;

(ii) prior to, or at the time of, each transaction in which the dispenser transfers ownership of a product (but not including dispensing to a patient, or returns) shall provide the subsequent owner with transaction history, transaction information, and a transaction statement for the product, except that the requirements of this clause shall not apply to sales by a dispenser to another dispenser to fulfill a specific patient need; and

(iii) shall capture transaction information (including lot level information, if provided), transaction history, and transaction statements, as necessary to investigate a suspect, product, and maintain such information, history, and statements for not less than 6 years after the transaction.

(B) Agreements with Third Parties. — A dispenser may enter into a written agreement with a third party, including an authorized wholesale distributor, under which the third party confidentially maintains the transaction information, transaction history, and transaction statements required to be maintained under this subsection on behalf of the dispenser. If a dispenser enters into such an agreement, the dispenser shall maintain a copy of the written agreement and shall not be relieved of the obligations of the dispenser under this subsection.

(C) Returns. —

(i) Saleable Returns. — A dispenser may return product to the trading partner from which the dispenser obtained the product without providing the information required under subparagraph (A).

(ii) Nonsaleable Returns. — A dispenser may return a nonsaleable product to the manufacturer or repackager, to the wholesale distributor from whom such product was purchased, to a returns processor, or to a person acting on behalf of such a person without providing the information required under subparagraph (A).

(D) Requests for Information. — Upon a request by the Secretary or other appropriate Federal or State official, in the event of a recall or for the purpose of investigating a suspect or an illegitimate product, a dispenser shall, not later than 2 business days after receiving the request or in another such reasonable time as determined by the Secretary, based on the circumstances of the request, provide the applicable transaction information, transaction statement, and transaction history which the dispenser received from the previous owner, which shall not include the lot number of the product, the initial transaction date, or the initial shipment date from the manufacturer unless such information was included in the transaction information, transaction statement, and transaction history provided by the manufacturer or wholesale distributor to the dispenser. The dispenser may respond to the request by providing the applicable information in either paper or electronic format. Until the date that is 4 years after the date of enactment of the Drug Supply Chain Security Act, the Secretary or other appropriate Federal or State official shall grant a dispenser additional time, as necessary, only with respect to a request to provide lot level information described in subparagraph (F) of section 581(26) that was provided to the dispenser in paper format, limit the request time period to the 6 months preceding the request or other relevant date, and, in the event of a recall, the Secretary, or other appropriate Federal or State official may request information only if such recall involves a serious adverse health consequence or death to humans.

(2) Product Identifier. — Beginning not later than 7 years after the date of enactment of the Drug Supply Chain Security Act, a dispenser may engage in transactions involving a product only if such product is encoded with a product identifier (except as provided pursuant, to subsection (a)(5)).

(3) Authorized Trading Partners. — Beginning not later than January 1, 2015, the trading partners of a dispenser may be only authorized trading partners.

(4) Verification. — Beginning not later than January 1, 2015, a dispenser shall have systems in place to enable the dispenser to comply with the following requirements:

(A) Suspect Product. —

(i) In General. — Upon making a determination that a product in the possession or control of the dispenser is a suspect product, or upon receiving a request for verification from the Secretary that has made a determination that a product within the possession or control of a dispenser is a suspect product, a dispenser shall —

(I) quarantine such product within the possession or control of the dispenser from product intended for distribution until such product is cleared or dispositioned; and

(II) promptly conduct an investigation in coordination with trading partners, as applicable, to determine whether the product is an illegitimate product.

(ii) Investigation. — An investigation conducted under clause (i)(II) shall include —

(I) beginning 7 years after the date of enactment of the Drug Supply Chain Security Act, verifying whether the lot number of a suspect product corresponds with the lot number for such product;

(II) beginning 7 years after the date of enactment of such Act, verifying that the product identifier, including the standardized numerical identifier, of at least 3 packages or 10 percent of such suspect product, whichever is greater, or all packages, if there are fewer than 3, corresponds with the product identifier for such product;

(III) validating any applicable transaction history and transaction information in the possession of the dispenser; and

(IV) otherwise investigating to determine whether the product is an illegitimate product.

(iii) Cleared Product. — If the dispenser makes the determination that a suspect product is not an illegitimate product, the dispenser shall promptly notify the Secretary, if applicable, of such determination and such product may be further distributed or dispensed.

(iv) Records. — A dispenser shall keep records of the investigation of a suspect product for not less than 6 years after the conclusion of the investigation.

(B) Illegitimate Product. —

(i) In General. — Upon determining, in coordination with the manufacturer, that a product in the possession or control of a dispenser is an illegitimate product, the dispenser shall —

(I) disposition the illegitimate product within the possession or control of the dispenser;

(II) take reasonable and appropriate steps to assist a trading partner to disposition an illegitimate product not in the possession or control of the dispenser; and

(III) retain a sample of the product for further physical examination or laboratory analysis of the product by the manufacturer or Secretary (or other appropriate Federal or State official) upon request by the manufacturer or Secretary (or other appropriate Federal or State official), as necessary and appropriate.

(ii) Making A Notification. — Upon determining that a product, in the possession or control of the dispenser is an illegitimate product, the dispenser shall notify the Secretary and all immediate trading partners that the dispenser has reason to believe may have received such illegitimate product of such determination not later than 24 hours after making such determination.

(iii) Responding to a Notification. — Upon the receipt of a notification from the Secretary or a trading partner that a determination has been made that a product is an illegitimate product, a dispenser shall identify all illegitimate product subject to such notification that is in the possession or control of the dispenser, including any product that is subsequently received, and shall perform the activities described in subparagraph (A).

(iv) Terminating a Notification. — Upon making a determination, in consultation with the Secretary, that a notification is no longer necessary, a dispenser shall promptly notify immediate trading partners that the dispenser notified pursuant to clause (ii) that such notification has been terminated.

(v) Records. — A dispenser shall keep records of the disposition of an illegitimate product for not less than 6 years after the conclusion of the disposition.

(C) Electronic Database. — A dispenser may satisfy the requirements of this paragraph by developing a secure electronic database or utilizing a secure electronic database developed or operated by another entity.

(5) Exception. — Notwithstanding any other provision of law, the requirements under paragraphs (1) and (4) shall not apply to licensed health care practitioners authorized to prescribe or administer medication under State law or other licensed individuals under the supervision or direction of such practitioners who dispense or administer product in the usual course of professional practice.

(e) Repackager Requirements. —

(1) Product Tracing. —

(A) In General. — Beginning not later than January 1, 2015, a repackager described in section 581(16)(A) shall —

(i) not accept ownership of a product unless the previous owner, prior to, or at the time of, the transaction, provides transaction history, transaction information, and a transaction statement for the product;

(ii) prior to, or at the time of, each transaction in which the repackager transfers ownership of a product, provide the subsequent, owner with transaction history, transaction information, and a transaction statement, for the product; and

(iii) capture the transaction information (including lot level information), transaction history, and transaction statement for each transaction described in clauses (i) and (ii) and maintain such information, history, and statement, for not less than 6 years after the transaction.

(B) Returns. —

(i) Nonsaleable Product. — A re-packager described in section 581(16)(A) may return a nonsaleable product to the manufacturer or repackager, or to the wholesale distributor from whom such product was purchased, or to a person acting on behalf of such a person, including a returns processor, without providing the information required under subparagraph (A)(ii).

(ii) Saleable Or Nonsaleable Product. — A repackager described in section 581(16)(B) may return a saleable or nonsaleable product to the manufacturer, repackager, or to the wholesale distributor from whom such product, was received without, providing the information required under subparagraph (A)(ii) on behalf of the hospital or other health care entity that took ownership of such product pursuant to the terms and conditions of any agreement between such repackager and the entity that owns the product.

(C) Requests for Information. — Upon a request by the Secretary or other appropriate Federal or State official, in the event of a recall or for the purpose of investigating a suspect product or an illegitimate product, a repackager described in section 581(16)(A) shall, not later than 1 business day, and not to exceed 48 hours, after receiving the request or in other such reasonable time as determined by the Secretary, provide the applicable transaction information, transaction history, and transaction statement for the product.

(2) Product Identifier. —

(A) In General. — Beginning not later than 5 years after the date of enactment of the Drug Supply Chain Security Act, a repackager described in section 581(16)(A) —

(i) shall affix or imprint a product identifier to each package and homogenous ease of product intended to be introduced in a transaction in commerce;

(ii) shall maintain the product identifier information for such product for not less than 6 years after the date of the transaction;

(iii) may engage in transactions involving a product only if such product is encoded with a product identifier (except as provided pursuant to subsection (a)(5)); and

(iv) shall maintain records for not less than 6 years to allow the repackager to associate the product identifier the repackager affixes or imprints with the product identifier assigned by the original manufacturer of the product.

(B) Exception. — A package that is required to have a standardized numerical identifier is not required to have a unique device identifier.

(3) Authorized Trading Partners. — Beginning January 1, 2015, the trading partners of a repackager described in section 581(16) may be only authorized trading partners.

(4) Verification. — Beginning not later than January 1, 2015, a repackager described in section 581(16)(A) shall have systems in place to enable the repackager to comply with the following requirements:

(A) Suspect product. —

(i) In General. — Upon making a determination that a product in the possession or control of the repackager is a suspect product, or upon receiving a request for verification from the Secretary that has made a determination that a product within the possession or control of a repackager is a suspect product, a repackager shall —

(I) quarantine such product within the possession or control of the repackager from product intended for distribution until such product is cleared or dispositioned; and

(II) promptly conduct an investigation in coordination with trading partners, as applicable, to determine whether the product is an illegitimate product, which shall include validating any applicable transaction history and transaction information in the possession of the repackager and otherwise investigating to determine whether the product is an illegitimate product, and, beginning 5 years after the date of enactment of the Drug Supply Chain Security Act, (except as provided pursuant to subsection (a)(5)), verifying the product at the package level, including the standardized numerical identifier.

(ii) Cleared Product. — If the repackager makes the determination that a suspect product is not an illegitimate product, the repackager shall promptly notify the Secretary, if applicable, of such determination and such product may be further distributed.

(iii) Records. — A repackager shall keep records of the investigation of a suspect product for not less than 6 years after the conclusion of the investigation.

(B) Illegitimate Product. —

(i) In General. — Upon determining, in coordination with the manufacturer, that a product in the possession or control of a repackager is an illegitimate product, the repackager shall, in a manner that is consistent with the systems and processes of such repackager —

(I) quarantine such product within the possession or control of the repackager from product intended for distribution until such product is dispositioned;

(II) disposition the illegitimate product within the possession or control of the repackager;

(III) take reasonable and appropriate steps to assist a trading partner to disposition an illegitimate product not in the possession or control of the repackager; and

(IV) retain a sample of the product for further physical examination or laboratory analysis of the product by the manufacturer or Secretary (or other appropriate Federal or State official) upon request by the manufacturer or Secretary (or other appropriate Federal or State official), as necessary and appropriate.

(ii) Making a Notification. — Upon determining that a product in the possession or control of the repackager is an illegitimate product, the repackager shall notify the Secretary and all immediate trading partners that the repackager has reason to believe may have received the illegitimate product of such determination not later than 24 hours after making such determination.

(iii) Responding to a Notification. — Upon the receipt of a notification from the Secretary or a trading partner, a repackager shall identify all illegitimate product subject to such notification that is in the possession or control of the repackager, including any product that is subsequently received, and shall perform the activities described in subparagraph (A).

(iv) Terminating a Notification. — Upon making a determination, in consultation with the Secretary, that a notification is no longer necessary, a repackager shall promptly notify immediate trading partners that the repackager notified pursuant to clause (ii) that such notification has been terminated.

(v) Records. — A repackager shall keep records of the disposition of an illegitimate product for not less than 6 years after the conclusion of the disposition.

(C) Requests for Verification. — Beginning 5 years after the date of enactment of the Drug Supply Chain Security Act, upon receiving a request for verification from an authorized manufacturer, wholesale distributor, or dispenser that is in possession or control of a product they believe to be repackaged by such repackager, a repackager shall, not, later than 24 hours after receiving the verification request or in other such reasonable time as determined by the Secretary, based on the circumstances of the request, notify the person making the request whether the product identifier, including the standardized numerical identifier, that is the subject of the request corresponds to the product identifier affixed or imprinted by the repackager. If a repackager responding to a verification request identifies a product identifier that does not correspond to that affixed or imprinted by the repackager, the repackager shall treat such product as suspect product and conduct an investigation as described in subparagraph (A). If the repackager has reason to believe the product is an illegitimate product, the repackager shall advise the person making the request of such belief at the time such repackager responds to the verification request.

(D) Electronic Database. — A repackager may satisfy the requirements of paragraph (4) by developing a secure electronic database or utilizing a secure electronic database developed or operated by another entity. The owner of such database shall establish the requirements and processes to respond to requests and may provide for data access to other members of the pharmaceutical distribution supply chain, as appropriate. The development and operation of such a database shall not relieve a repackager of the requirement under subparagraph (C) to respond to a verification request submitted by means other than a secure electronic database.

(E) Verification of Saleable Returned Product. — Beginning 5 years after the date of enactment of the Drug Supply Chain Security Act, upon receipt of a returned product that the repackager intends to further distribute, before further distributing such product, the repackager shall verify the product identifier for each sealed homogeneous case of such product or, if such product is not in a sealed homogeneous case, verify the product identifier on each package.

(f) Drop Shipments. —

(1) In General. — A wholesale distributor that does not physically handle or store product shall be exempt from the provisions of this section, except the notification requirements under clauses (ii), (iii), and (iv) of subsection (c)(4)(B), provided that the manufacturer, repackager, or other wholesale distributor that distributes the product to the dispenser by means of a drop shipment for such wholesale distributor includes on the transaction information and transaction history to the dispenser the contact information of such wholesale distributor and provides the transaction information, transaction history, and transaction statement directly to the dispenser.

(2) Clarification. — For purposes of this subsection, providing administrative services, including processing of orders and payments, shall not by itself, be construed as being involved in the handling, distribution, or storage of a product.

(g) Enhanced Drug Distribution Security. —

(1) In General. — On the date that is 10 years after the date of enactment of the Drug Supply Chain Security Act, the following interoperable, electronic tracing of product at the package level requirements shall go into effect:

(A) The transaction information and the transaction statements as required under this section shall be exchanged in a secure, interoperable, electronic manner in accordance with the standards established under the guidance issued pursuant to paragraphs (3) and (4) of subsection (h), including any revision of such guidance issued in accordance with paragraph (5) of such subsection.

(B) The transaction information required under this section shall include the product identifier at the package level for each package included in the transaction.

(C) Systems and processes for verification of product at the package level, including the standardized numerical identifier, shall be required in accordance with the standards established under the guidance issued pursuant to subsection (a)(2) and the guidances issued pursuant to paragraphs (2), (3), and (4) of subsection (h), including any revision of such guidances issued in accordance with paragraph (5) of such subsection, which may include the use of aggregation and inference as necessary.

(D) The systems and processes necessary to promptly respond with the transaction information and transaction statement for a product upon a request by the Secretary (or other appropriate Federal or State official) in the event of a recall or for the purposes of investigating a suspect product or an illegitimate product shall be required.

(E) The systems and processes necessary to promptly facilitate gathering the information necessary to produce the transaction information for each transaction going back to the manufacturer, as applicable, shall be required —

(i) in the event of a request by the Secretary (or other appropriate Federal or State official), on account of a recall or for the purposes of investigating a suspect product or an illegitimate product; or

(ii) in the event of a request by an authorized trading partner, in a secure manner that ensures the protection of confidential commercial information and trade secrets, for purposes of investigating a suspect product or assisting the Secretary (or other appropriate Federal or State official) with a request described in clause (i).

(F) Each person accepting a saleable return shall have systems and processes in place to allow acceptance of such product and may accept saleable returns only if such person can associate the saleable return product with the transaction information and transaction statement associated with that product.

(2) Compliance. —

(A) Information Maintenance Agreement. — A dispenser may enter into a written agreement with a third party, including an authorized wholesale distributor, under which the third party shall confidentially maintain any information and statements required to be maintained under this section. If a dispenser enters into such an agreement, the dispenser shall maintain a copy of the written agreement and shall not be relieved of the obligations of the dispenser under this subsection.

(B) Alternate Methods. — The Secretary, taking into consideration the assessment conducted under paragraph (3), shall provide for alternative methods of compliance with any of the requirements set forth in paragraph (1), including —

(i) establishing timelines for compliance by small businesses (including small business dispensers with 25 or fewer full-time employees) with such requirements, in order to ensure that such requirements do not impose undue economic hardship for small businesses, including small business dispensers for whom the criteria set forth in the assessment, under paragraph (3) is not met, if the Secretary determines that such requirements under paragraph (1) would result in undue economic hardship; and

(ii) establishing a process by which a dispenser may request a waiver from any of the requirements set forth in paragraph (1) if the Secretary determines that such requirements would result in an undue economic hardship, which shall include a process for the biennial review and renewal of any such waiver.

(3) Assessment. —

(A) In General. — Not later than the date that is 18 months after the Secretary issues the final guidance required under subsection (h), the Secretary shall enter into a contract with a private, independent consulting firm with expertise to conduct a technology and software assessment that looks at the feasibility of dispensers with 25 or fewer full-time employees conducting interoperable, electronic tracing of products at the package level. Such assessment shall be completed not later than 81/2 years after the date of enactment of the Drug Supply Chain Security Act.

(B) Condition. — As a condition of the award of the contract under subparagraph (A), the private, independent consulting firm shall agree to consult with dispensers with 25 or fewer full-time employees when conducting the assessment under such subparagraph.

(C) Content. — The assessment under subparagraph (A) shall assess whether —

(i) the necessary software and hardware is readily accessible to such dispensers;

(ii) the necessary software and hardware is prohibitively expensive to obtain, install, and maintain for such dispensers; and

(iii) the necessary hardware and software can be integrated into business practices, such as interoperability with wholesale distributors, for such dispensers.

(D) Publication. — The Secretary shall —

(i) publish the statement of work for the assessment under subparagraph (A) for public comment prior to beginning the assessment;

(ii) publish the final assessment for public comment not later than 30 calendar days after receiving such assessment; and

(iii) hold a public meeting not later than 180 calendar days after receiving the final assessment at which public stakeholders may present their views on the assessment.

(4) Procedure. — Notwithstanding section 553 of title 5, United States Code, the Secretary, in promulgating any regulation pursuant to this section, shall —

(A) provide appropriate flexibility by —

(i) not requiring the adoption of specific business systems for the maintenance and transmission of data;

(ii) prescribing alternative methods of compliance for any of the requirements set forth in paragraph (1) or set forth in regulations implementing such requirements, including —

(I) timelines for small businesses to comply with the requirements set forth in the regulations in order to ensure that such requirements do not impose undue economic hardship for small businesses (including small business dispensers for whom the criteria set forth in the assessment under paragraph (3) is not met), if the Secretary determines that such requirements would result in undue economic hardship; and

(II) the establishment of a process by which a dispenser may request a waiver from any of the requirements set forth in such regulations if the Secretary determines that such requirements would result in an undue economic hardship; and

(iii) taking into consideration —

(I) the results of pilot projects, including pilot projects pursuant to this section and private sector pilot projects, including those involving the use of aggregation and inference;

(II) the public meetings held and related guidance documents issued under this section;

(III) the public health benefits of any additional regulations in comparison to the cost of compliance with such requirements, including on entities of varying sizes and capabilities;

(IV) the diversity of the pharmaceutical distribution supply chain by providing appropriate flexibility for each sector, including both large and small businesses; and

(V) the assessment pursuant to paragraph (3) with respect to small business dispensers, including related public comment and the public meeting, and requirements under this section;

(B) issue a notice of proposed rulemaking that includes a copy of the proposed regulation;

(C) provide a period of not less than 60 days for comments on the proposed regulation; and

(D) publish in the Federal Register the final regulation not less than 2 years prior to the effective date of the regulation.

(h) Guidance Documents. —

(1) In General. — For the purposes of facilitating the successful and efficient adoption of secure, interoperable product tracing at the package level in order to enhance drug distribution security and further protect the public health, the Secretary shall issue the guidance documents as provided for in this subsection.

(2) Suspect and Illegitimate Product. —

(A) In General. — Not later than 180 days after the date of enactment of the Drug Supply Chain Security Act, the Secretary shall issue a guidance document to aid trading partners in the identification of a suspect product and notification termination. Such guidance document shall —

(i) identify specific scenarios that could significantly increase the risk of a suspect product entering the pharmaceutical distribution supply chain;

(ii) provide recommendation on how trading partners may identify such product and make a determination on whether the product is a suspect product as soon as practicable; and

(iii) set forth the process by which manufacturers, repackagers, wholesale distributors, and dispensers shall terminate notifications in consultation with the Secretary regarding illegitimate product pursuant to subsections (b)(4)(B), (c)(4)(B), (d)(4)(B), and (e)(4)(B).

(B) Revised Guidance. — If the Secretary revises the guidance issued under subparagraph (A), the Secretary shall follow the procedure set forth in paragraph (5).

(3) Unit Level Tracing. —

(A) In General. — In order to enhance drug distribution security at the package level, not later than 18 months after conducting a public meeting on the system attributes necessary to enable secure tracing of product at the package level, including allowing for the use of verification, inference, and aggregation, as necessary, the Secretary shall issue a final guidance document that outlines and makes recommendations with respect to the system attributes necessary to enable secure tracing at the package level as required under the requirements established under subsection (g). Such guidance document shall —

(i) define the circumstances under which the sectors within the pharmaceutical distribution supply chain may, in the most, efficient, manner practicable, infer the contents of a case, pallet, tote, or other aggregate of individual packages or containers of product, from a product identifier associated with the case, pallet, tote, or other aggregate, without opening each case, pallet, tote, or other aggregate or otherwise individually scanning each package;

(ii) identify methods and processes to enhance secure tracing of product at the package level, such as secure processes to facilitate the use of inference, enhanced verification activities, the use of aggregation and inference, processes that utilize the product identifiers to enhance tracing of product at the package level, including the standardized numerical identifier, or package security features; and ensure the protection of confidential commercial information and trade secrets.

(B) Procedure. — In issuing the guidance under subparagraph (A), and in revising such guidance, if applicable, the Secretary shall follow the procedure set forth in paragraph (5).

(4) Standards for Interoperable Data Exchange. —

(A) In General. — In order to enhance secure tracing of a product at the package level, the Secretary, not later than 18 months after conducting a public meeting on the interoperable standards necessary to enhance the security of the pharmaceutical distribution supply chain, shall update the guidance issued pursuant to subsection (a)(2), as necessary and appropriate, and finalize such guidance document so that the guidance document —

(i) identifies and makes recommendations with respect to the standards necessary for adoption in order to support the secure, interoperable electronic data exchange among the pharmaceutical distribution supply chain that comply with a form and format developed by a widely recognized international standards development organization;

(ii) takes into consideration standards established pursuant to subsection (a)(2) and section 505D;

(iii) facilitates the creation of a uniform process or methodology for product tracing; and

(iv) ensures the protection of confidential commercial information and trade secrets.

(B) Procedure. — In issuing the guidance under subparagraph (A), and in revising such guidance, if applicable, the Secretary shall follow the procedure set forth in paragraph (5).

(5) Procedure. — In issuing or revising any guidance issued pursuant to this subsection or subsection (g), except the initial guidance issued under paragraph (2)(A), the Secretary shall —

(A) publish a notice in the Federal Register for a period not less than 30 days announcing that the draft or revised draft guidance is available;

(B) post the draft guidance document on the Internet Web site of the Food and Drug Administration and make such draft guidance document available in hard copy;

(C) provide an opportunity for comment and review and take into consideration any comments received;

(D) revise the draft guidance, as appropriate;

(E) publish a notice in the Federal Register for a period not less than 30 days announcing that the final guidance or final revised guidance is available;

(F) post the final guidance document on the Internet Web site of the Food and Drug Administration and make such final guidance document available in hard copy; and

(G) provide for an effective date of not earlier than 1 year after such guidance becomes final.

(i) Public Meetings. —

(1) In General. — The Secretary shall hold not less than 5 public meetings to enhance the safety and security of the pharmaceutical distribution supply chain and provide for comment. The Secretary may hold the first such public meeting not earlier than 1 year after the date of enactment of the Drug Supply Chain Security Act. In carrying out the public meetings described in this paragraph, the Secretary shall —

(A) prioritize topics necessary to inform the issuance of the guidance described in paragraphs (3) and (4) of subsection (h); and

(B) take all measures reasonable and practicable to ensure the protection of confidential commercial information and trade secrets.

(2) Content. — Each of the following topics shall be addressed in at least one of the public meetings described in paragraph (1):

(A) An assessment of the steps taken under subsections (b) through (e) to build capacity for a unit-level system, including the impact of the requirements of such subsections on —

(i) the ability of the health care system collectively to maintain patient access to medicines;

(ii) the scalability of such requirements, including as it relates to product lines; and

(iii) the capability of different sectors and subsectors, including both large and small businesses, to affix and utilize the product identifier.

(B) The system attributes necessary to support the requirements set forth under subsection (g), including the standards necessary for adoption in order to support the secure, interoperable electronic data exchange among sectors within the pharmaceutical distribution supply chain.

(C) Best practices in each of the different sectors within the pharmaceutical distribution supply chain to implement the requirements of this section.

(D) The costs and benefits of the implementation of this section, including the impact on each pharmaceutical distribution supply chain sector and on public health.

(E) Whether electronic tracing requirements, including tracing of product at the package level, are feasible, cost effective, and needed to protect the public health.

(F) The systems and processes needed to utilize the product identifiers to enhance tracing of product at the package level, including allowing for verification, aggregation, and inference, as necessary.

(G) The technical capabilities and legal authorities, if any, needed to establish an interoperable, electronic system that provides for tracing of product at the package level.

(H) The impact that such additional requirements would have on patient safety, the drug supply, cost and regulatory burden, and timely patient access to prescription drugs.

(I) Other topics, as determined appropriate by the Secretary.

(j) Pilot Projects. —

(1) In General. — The Secretary shall establish 1 or more pilot projects, in coordination with authorized manufacturers, repackagers, wholesale distributors, and dispensers, to explore and evaluate methods to enhance the safety and security of the pharmaceutical distribution supply chain. Such projects shall build upon efforts, in existence as of the date of enactment of the Drug Supply Chain Security Act, to enhance the safety and security of the pharmaceutical distribution supply chain, take into consideration any pilot projects conducted prior to such date of enactment, including any pilot projects that use aggregation and inference, and inform the draft and final guidance under paragraphs (3) and (4) of subsection (h).

(2) Content. —

(A) In General. — The Secretary shall ensure that the pilot projects under paragraph (1) reflect the diversity of the pharmaceutical distribution supply chain and that the pilot projects, when taken as a whole, include participants representative of every sector, including both large and small businesses.

(B) Project Design. — The pilot projects under paragraph (1) shall be designed to —

(i) utilize the product identifier for tracing of a product, which may include verification of the product identifier of a product, including the use of aggregation and inference;

(ii) improve the technical capabilities of each sector and subsector to comply with systems and processes needed to utilize the product identifiers to enhance tracing of a product;

(iii) identify system attributes that are necessary to implement the requirements established under this section; and

(iv) complete other activities as determined by the Secretary.

(k) Sunset. — The following requirements shall have no force or effect beginning on the date that is 10 years after the date of enactment of the Drug Supply Chain Security Act:

(1) The provision and receipt of transaction history under this section.

(2) The requirements set forth for returns under subsections (b)(4)(E), (c)(1)(B)(i), (d)(1)(C)(i), and (e)(4)(E).

(3) The requirements set forth under subparagraphs (A)(v)(II) and (D) of subsection (c)(1), as applied to lot level information only.

(l) Rule of Construction. — The requirements set forth in subsections (g)(4), (i), and (j) shall not be construed as a condition, prohibition, or precedent for precluding or delaying the provisions becoming effective pursuant to subsection (g).

(m) Requests for Information. — On the date that is 10 years after the date of enactment of the Drug Supply Chain Security Act, the timeline for responses to requests for information from the Secretary, or other appropriate Federal or State official, as applicable, under subsections (b)(1)(B), (e)(1)(C), and (e)(1)(C) shall be not later than 24 hours after receiving the request from the Secretary or other appropriate Federal or State official, as applicable, or in such other reasonable time as determined by the Secretary based on the circumstances of the request."

Sec. 583. [360eee-2] National Standards for Prescription Drug Wholesale Distributors.

(a) In General. — The Secretary shall, not later than 2 years after the date of enactment of the Drug Supply Chain Security Act, establish by regulation standards for the licensing of persons under section 503(e)(1) (as amended by the Drug Supply Chain Security Act), including the revocation, reissuance, and renewal of such license.

(b) Content. — For the purpose of ensuring uniformity with respect to standards set forth in this section, the standards established under subsection (a) shall apply to all State and Federal licenses described under section 503(e) (1) (as amended by the Drug Supply Chain Security Act) and shall include standards for the following:

(1) The storage and handling of prescription drugs, including facility requirements.

(2) The establishment and maintenance of records of the distributions of such drugs.

(3) The furnishing of a bond or other equivalent means of security, as follows:

(A)

(i) For the issuance or renewal of a wholesale distributor license, an applicant that, is not a government owned and operated wholesale distributor shall submit a surety bond of $100,000 or other equivalent means of security acceptable to the State.

(ii) For purposes of clause (i), the State or other applicable authority may accept a surety bond in the amount, of $25,000 if the annual gross receipts of the previous tax year for the wholesaler is $10,000,000 or less.

(B) If a wholesale distributor can provide evidence that it possesses the required bond in a State, the requirement for a bond in another State shall be waived.

(4) Mandatory background cheeks and fingerprinting of facility managers or designated representatives.

(5) The establishment and implementation of qualifications for key personnel.

(6) The mandatory physical inspection of any facility to be used in wholesale distribution within a reasonable time frame from the initial application of the facility and to be conducted by the licensing authority or by the State, consistent with subsection (c).

(7) In accordance with subsection (d), the prohibition of certain persons from receiving or maintaining licensure for wholesale distribution.

(c) Inspections. — To satisfy the inspection requirement under subsection (b)(6), the Federal or State licensing authority may conduct the inspection or may accept an inspection by the State in which the facility is located, or by a third-party accreditation or inspection service approved by the Secretary or the State licensing such wholesale distributor.

(d) Prohibited Persons. — The standards established under subsection (a) shall include requirements to prohibit a person from receiving or maintaining licensure for wholesale distribution if the person —

(1) has been convicted of any felony for conduct relating to wholesale distribution, any felony violation of subsection (i) or (k) of section 301, or any felony violation of section 1365 of title 18, United States Code, relating to product tampering; or

(2) has engaged in a pattern of violating the requirements of this section, or State requirements for licensure, that presents a threat of serious adverse health consequences or death to humans.

(e) Requirements. — The Secretary, in promulgating any regulation pursuant to this section, shall, notwithstanding section 553 of title 5, United States Code —

(1) issue a notice of proposed rulemaking that includes a copy of the proposed regulation;

(2) provide a period of not less than 60 days for comments on the proposed regulation; and

(3) provide that the final regulation take effect on the date that is 2 years after the date such final regulation is published.

Sec. 584. [360eee-3] National Standards for Third-Party Logistics Providers.

(a) Requirements. — No third-party logistics provider in any State may conduct activities in any State unless each facility of such third-party logistics provider —

(1)

(A) is licensed by the State from which the drug is distributed by the third-party logistics provider, in accordance with the regulations promulgated under subsection (d); or

(B) if the State from which the drug distributed by the third-party logistics provider has not established a licensure requirement, is licensed by the Secretary, in accordance with the regulations promulgated under subsection (d); and

(2) if the drug is distributed interstate, is licensed by the State into which the drug is distributed by the third-party logistics provider if such State licenses third-party logistics providers that distribute drugs into the State and the third-party logistics provider is not licensed by the Secretary as described in paragraph (1)(B).

(b) Reporting. — Beginning 1 year after the date of enactment of the Drug Supply Chain Security Act, a facility of a third-party logistics provider shall report to the Secretary, on an annual basis pursuant to a schedule determined by the Secretary —

(1) the State by which the facility is licensed and the appropriate identification number of such license; and

(2) the name and address of the facility and all trade names under which such facility conducts business.

(c) Costs. —

(1) Authorized Fees of Secretary. — If a State does not establish a licensing program for a third-party logistics provider, the Secretary shall license the third-party logistics provider located in such State and may collect a reasonable fee in such amount necessary to reimburse the Secretary for costs associated with establishing and administering the licensure program and conducting periodic inspections under this section. The Secretary shall adjust fee rates as needed on an annual basis to generate only the amount of revenue needed to perform this service. Fees authorized under this paragraph shall be collected and available for obligation only to the extent and in the amount provided in advance in appropriations Acts. Such fees are authorized to remain available until expended. Such sums as may be necessary may be transferred from the Food and Drug Administration salaries and expenses appropriation account without fiscal year limitation to such appropriation account for salaries and expenses with such fiscal year limitation.

(2) State Licensing Fees. —

(A) State Established Program. — Nothing in this Act shall prohibit a State that has established a program to license a third-party logistics provider from collecting fees from a third-party logistics provider for such a license.

(B) No State Established Program. — A State that does not establish a program to license a third-party logistics provider in accordance with this section shall be prohibited from collecting a State licensing fee from a third-party logistics provider.

(d) Regulations. —

(1) In General. — Not later than 2 years after the date of enactment of the Drug Supply Chain Security Act, the Secretary shall issue regulations regarding the standards for licensing under subsection (a), including the revocation and reissuance of such license, to third-party logistics providers under this section.

(2) Content. — Such regulations shall —

(A) establish a process by which a third party accreditation program approved by the Secretary shall, upon request by a third-party logistics provider, issue a license to each third-party logistics provider that meets the requirements set forth in this section;

(B) establish a process by which the Secretary shall issue a license to each third-party logistics provider that meets the requirements set forth in this section if the Secretary is not able to approve a third-party accreditation program because no such program meets the Secretary's requirements necessary for approval of such a third-party accreditation program;

(C) require that the entity complies with storage practices, as determined by the Secretary for such facility, including —

(i) maintaining access to warehouse space of suitable size to facilitate safe operations, including a suitable area to quarantine suspect product;

(ii) maintaining adequate security; and

(iii) having written policies and procedures to —

(I) address receipt, security, storage, inventory, shipment, and distribution of a product;

(II) identify, record, and report confirmed losses or thefts in the United States;

(III) correct errors and inaccuracies in inventories;

(IV) provide support for manufacturer recalls;

(V) prepare for, protect against, and address any reasonably foreseeable crisis that affects security or operation at the facility, such as a strike, fire, or flood;

(VI) ensure that any expired product is segregated from other products and returned to the manufacturer or repackager or destroyed;

(VII) maintain the capability to trace the receipt and outbound distribution of a product, and supplies and records of inventory; and

(VIII) quarantine or destroy a suspect product if directed to do so by the respective manufacturer, wholesale distributor, dispenser, or an authorized government agency;

(D) provide for periodic inspection by the licensing authority, as determined by the Secretary, of such facility warehouse space to ensure compliance with this section;

(E) prohibit a facility from having as a manager or designated representative anyone convicted of any felony violation of subsection (i) or (k) of section 301 or any violation of section 1365 of title 18, United States Code relating to product tampering;

(F) provide for mandatory background checks of a facility manager or a designated representative of such manager;

(G) require a third-party logistics provider to provide the applicable licensing authority, upon a request, by such authority, a list of all product manufacturers, wholesale distributors, and dispensers for whom the third-party logistics provider provides services at such facility; and

(H) include procedures under which any third-party logistics provider license —

(i) expires on the date that is 3 years after issuance of the license; and

(ii) may be renewed for additional 3-year periods.

(3) Procedure. — In promulgating the regulations under this subsection, the Secretary shall, notwithstanding section 553 of title 5, United States Code —

(A) issue a notice of proposed rulemaking that includes a copy of the proposed regulation;

(B) provide a period of not less than 60 days for comments on the proposed regulation; and

(C) provide that the final regulation takes effect, upon the expiration of 1 year after the date that such final regulation is issued.

(e) Validity. — A license issued under this section shall remain valid as long as such third-party logistics provider remains licensed consistent with this section. If the Secretary finds that the third-party accreditation program demonstrates that all applicable requirements for licensure under this section are met, the Secretary shall issue a license under this section to a third-party logistics provider receiving accreditation, pursuant to subsection (d)(2)(A).

Sec. 585. [360eee-4] Uniform National Policy.

(a) Product Tracing and Other Requirements. — Beginning on the date of enactment of the Drug Supply Chain Security Act, no State or political subdivision of a State may establish or continue in effect any requirements for tracing products through the distribution system (including any requirements with respect to statements of distribution history, transaction history, transaction information, or transaction statement of a product as such product changes ownership in the supply chain, or verification, investigation, disposition, notification, or recordkeeping relating to such systems, including paper or electronic pedigree systems or for tracking and tracing drugs throughout the distribution system) which are inconsistent with, more stringent than, or in addition to, any requirements applicable under section 503(e) (as amended by such Act) or this subchapter (or regulations issued thereunder), or which are inconsistent with —

(1) any waiver, exception, or exemption pursuant to section 581 or 582; or

(2) any restrictions specified in section 582.

(b) Wholesale Distributor and Third-Party Logistics Provider Standards. —

(1) In General. — Beginning on the date of enactment of the Drug Supply Chain Security Act, no State or political subdivision of a State may establish or continue any standards, requirements, or regulations with respect to wholesale prescription drug distributor or third-party logistics provider licensure that are inconsistent with, less stringent than, directly related to, or covered by the standards and requirements applicable under section 503(e) (as amended by such Act), in the case of a wholesale distributor, or section 584, in the case of a third-party logistics provider.

(2) State Regulation of Third-Party Logistics Providers. — No State shall regulate third-party logistics providers as wholesale distributors.

(3) Administration Fees. — Notwithstanding paragraph (1), a State may administer fee collections for effectuating the wholesale drug distributor and third-party logistics provider licensure requirements under sections 503(e) (as amended by the Drug Supply Chain Security Act), 583, and 584.

(4) Enforcement, Suspension, and Revocation. — Notwithstanding paragraph (1), a State —

(A) may take administrative action, including fines, to enforce a requirement promulgated by the State in accordance with section 503(e) (as amended by the Drug Supply Chain Security Act) or this subchapter;

(B) may provide for the suspension or revocation of licenses issued by the State for violations of the laws of such State;

(C) upon conviction of violations of Federal, State, or local drug laws or regulations, may provide for fines, imprisonment, or civil penalties; and

(D) may regulate activities of licensed entities in a manner that is consistent with product tracing requirements under section 582.

(c) Exception. — Nothing in this section shall be construed to preempt State requirements related to the distribution of prescription drugs if such requirements are not related to product tracing as described in subsection (a) or wholesale distributor and third-party logistics provider licensure as described in subsection (b) applicable under section 503(e) (as amended by the Drug Supply Chain Security Act) or this subchapter (or regulations issued thereunder).

SUBCHAPTER I—NONPRESCRIPTION SUNSCREEN AND OTHER ACTIVE INGREDIENTS

SEC. 586. [360fff] DEFINITIONS.

In this subchapter—

(1) the term "Advisory Committee" means the Nonprescription Drug Advisory Committee of the Food and Drug Administration or any successor to such Committee;

(2) the term "final sunscreen order" means an order published by the Secretary in the Federal Register containing information stating that a nonprescription sunscreen active ingredient or combination of nonprescription sunscreen active ingredients—

(A) is GRASE and is not misbranded if marketed in accordance with such order; or

(B) is not GRASE and is misbranded;

(3) the term "GRASE" means generally recognized, among experts qualified by scientific training and experience to evaluate the safety and effectiveness of drugs, as safe and effective for use under the conditions prescribed, recommended, or suggested in the labeling of a drug as described in section 201(p);

(4) the term "GRASE determination" means, with respect to a nonprescription active ingredient or a combination of nonprescription active ingredients, a determination of whether such ingredient or combination of ingredients is GRASE;

(5) the term "nonprescription" means not subject to section 503(b)(1);

(6) the term "pending request" means each request with respect to a nonprescription sunscreen active ingredient submitted under section 330.14 of title 21, Code of Federal Regulations (as in effect on November 26, 2014) for consideration for inclusion in the over-the-counter drug monograph system—

(A) that was determined to be eligible for such review by publication of a notice of eligibility in the Federal Register prior to November 26, 2014; and

(B) for which safety and effectiveness data have been submitted to the Secretary prior to November 26, 2014;

(7) the term "proposed sunscreen order" means an order containing a tentative determination published by the Secretary in the Federal Register containing information proposing that a nonprescription sunscreen active ingredient or combination of nonprescription sunscreen active ingredients—

(A) is GRASE and is not misbranded if marketed in accordance with such order;

(B) is not GRASE and is misbranded; or

(C) is not GRASE and is misbranded because the data are insufficient to classify such ingredient or combination of ingredients as GRASE and not misbranded and additional information is necessary to allow the Secretary to determine otherwise;

(8) the term "sponsor" means the person that submitted—

(A) a request under section 586A;

(B) a pending request; or

(C) any other application subject to this subchapter;

(9) the term "sunscreen" means a drug containing one or more sunscreen active ingredients; and

(10) the term "sunscreen active ingredient" means an active ingredient that is intended for application to the skin of humans for purposes of absorbing, reflecting, or scattering ultraviolet radiation.

SEC. 586A. [360fff-1] SUBMISSION OF REQUESTS.

Any person may submit a request to the Secretary for a determination of whether a nonprescription sunscreen active ingredient or a combination of non prescription sunscreen active ingredients, for use under specified conditions, to be prescribed, recommended, or suggested in the labeling thereof (including dosage form, dosage strength, and route of administration) is GRASE and should be included in part 352 of title 21, Code of Federal Regulations (or any successor regulations) concerning nonprescription sunscreen.

Sec. 586B. [360fff-2] Eligibility Determinations; Data Submission; Filing.

(a) Eligibility Determinations.—

(1) In General.—Not later than 60 calendar days after the date of receipt of a request under section 586A, the Secretary shall—

(A) determine, in accordance with paragraph (2), whether the request is eligible for further review under subsection (b) and section 586C;

(B) notify the sponsor of the determination of the Secretary; and

(C) make such determination publicly available in accordance with paragraph (3) and subsection (b)(1).

(2) Criteria for Eligibility.—

(A) In General.—To be eligible for review under subsection (b) and section 586C, a request shall be for a nonprescription sunscreen active ingredient or combination of nonprescription sunscreen active ingredients, for use under specified conditions, to be prescribed, recommended, or suggested in the labeling thereof, that—

(i) is not included in part 352 of title 21, Code of Federal Regulations (or any successor regulations) concerning nonprescription sunscreen; and

(ii) has been used to a material extent and for a material time under such conditions, as described in section 201(p)(2).

(B) Establishment of Time and Extent—A sponsor shall include in a request under section 586A the information required under section 330.14 of title 21, Code of Federal Regulations (or any successor regulations) to meet the standard described in subparagraph (A)(ii).

(3) Public Availability.—

(A) Redactions for Confidential Information.— If a nonprescription sunscreen active ingredient or combination of nonprescription sunscreen active ingredients is determined under paragraph (1)(A) to be eligible for further review, the Secretary shall make the request publicly available, with redactions for information that is treated as confidential under section 552(b) of title 5, United States Code, section 1905 of title 18, United States Code, or section 301(j) of this Act.

(B) Identification of Confidential Information By Sponsor.—At the time that a request is made under section 586A, the sponsor of such request shall identify any information that such sponsor considers to he confidential information described in subparagraph (A).

(C) Confidentiality During Eligibility Review.— The information contained in a request under section 586A shall remain confidential during the Secretary's consideration under this section of whether the request is eligible for further review consistent with section 330.14 of title 21, Code of Federal Regulations (or any successor regulations).

(B) Data Submission and Filing of Requests.—

(1) In General.—In the case of a request under section 586A that is determined to be eligible under subsection (a) for further review under this section and section 586C, the Secretary shall, in notifying the public under subsection (a)(1)(C) of such eligibility determination, post the eligibility determination on the Internet website of the Food and Drug Administration, invite the sponsor of such request and any other interested party to submit comments, and provide a period of not less than 45 calendar days for comments in support of or otherwise relating to a GRASE determination, including published and unpublished data and other information related to the safety and efficacy of such request.

(2) Filing Determination.—Not later than 60 calendar days after the submission of data and other information described in paragraph (1) by the sponsor, the Secretary shall determine whether the data and other information submitted by the sponsor under this section are sufficiently complete, including being formatted in a manner that enables the Secretary to determine the completeness of such data and information, to enable the Secretary to conduct a substantive review under section 586C with respect to such request. Not later than 60 calendar days after the submission of data and other information described in paragraph (1) by the sponsor, if the Secretary determines—

(A) that such data and other information are sufficiently complete, the Secretary shall—

(i) issue a written notification to the sponsor of the determination to file such request, and make such notification publicly available; and

(ii) file such request made under section 586A; or

(B) that such data and other information are not sufficiently complete, the Secretary shall issue a written notification to the sponsor of the determination to refuse to file the request, which shall include the reasons for the refusal, including why such data and other information are not sufficiently complete, and make such notification publicly available.

(3) Refusal to File a Request.—

(A) Request for Meetings; Submission of Data and Other Information.—If the Secretary refuses to file a request made under section 586A, the sponsor may—

(i) within 30 calendar days of receipt of written notification of such refusal, request, in writing, a meeting with the Secretary regarding the filing determination; and

(ii) submit additional data or other information.

(B) Meetings —

(i) In General.—If a sponsor seeks a meeting under subparagraph (A)(i), the Secretary shall convene the meeting within 30 calendar days of the request for such meeting.

(ii) After Meeting.—Following any meeting held under clause (i)—

(I) the Secretary may file the request within 60 calendar days;

(II) the sponsor may submit additional data or other information; or

(III) if the sponsor elects, within 120 calendar days, to have the Secretary file the request (with or without amendments to correct any purported deficiencies to the request)—

(aa) the Secretary shall file the request over protest, not later than 30 calendar days after the sponsor makes such election;

(bb) at the time of filing, the Secretary shall provide written notification of such filing to the sponsor; and

(cc) the Secretary shall make such notification publicly available.

(iii) Requests Filed Over Protest.—The Secretary shall not require the sponsor to resubmit a copy of the request for purposes of filing a request filed over protest, as described in clause (ii)(III).

(C) Submissions of Additional Data or Other Information.—Within 60 calendar days of any submission of additional data or other information under subparagraph (A)(ii) or (B)(ii)(II), the Secretary shall reconsider the previous determination made under paragraph (2) with respect to the applicable request and make a new determination in accordance with paragraph (2).

(4) Public Availability.—

(A) Redactions for Confidential Information.—After the period of confidentiality described in subsection (a)(3)(C), the Secretary shall make data and other information submitted in connection with a request under section 586A publicly available, with redactions for information that is treated as confidential under section 552(b) of title 5, United States Code, section 1905 of title 18, United States Code, or section 301(j) of this Act.

(B) Identification of Confidential Information by Sponsor.—A person submitting information under this section shall identify at the time of such submission the portions of such information that the person considers to be confidential information described in subparagraph (A).

Sec. 586C. [360fff-3] GRASE Determination.

(a) Review of New Request.—

(1) Proposed Sunscreen Order.—In the case of a request under section 586A, not later than 300 calendar days after the date on which such request is filed under subsection (b)(2)(A) or (b)(3)(B)(ii)(III) of section 586B, the Secretary—

(A) may convene a meeting of the Advisory Committee to review such request; and

(B) shall complete the review of such request and issue a proposed sunscreen order with respect to such request.

(2) Proposed Sunscreen Order by Commissioner.—If the Secretary does not issue a proposed sunscreen order under paragraph (1)(B) within such 300-day period, the sponsor of such request may notify the Office of the Commissioner of such request and request review by the Office of the Commissioner. If such sponsor so notifies the Office of the Commissioner, the Commissioner shall, not later than 60 calendar days after the date of notification under this paragraph, issue a proposed sunscreen order with respect to such request.

(3) Public Comment Period.—A proposed sunscreen order issued under paragraph (1)(B) or (2) with respect to a request shall provide for a period of 45 calendar days for public comment.

(4) Meeting.—A sponsor may request, in writing, a meeting with respect to a proposed sunscreen order issued under this subsection and described in subparagraph (B) or (C) of section 586(7), not later than 30 calendar days after the Secretary issues such order. The Secretary shall convene a meeting with such sponsor not later than 45 calendar days after such request for a meeting.

(5) Final Sunscreen Order.—With respect to a proposed sunscreen order under paragraph (1)(B) or (2)—

(A) the Secretary shall issue a final sunscreen order—

(i) in the case of a proposed sunscreen order described in subparagraph (A) or (B) of section 586(7), not later than 90 calendar days after the end of the public comment period under paragraph (3); or

(ii) in the case of a proposed sunscreen order described in subparagraph (C) of section 586(7), not later than 210 calendar days after the date on which the sponsor submits the additional information requested pursuant to such proposed sunscreen order; or

(B) if the Secretary does not issue such final sunscreen order within such 90- or 210-calendar-day period, as applicable, the sponsor of such request may notify the Office of the Commissioner of such request and request review by the Office of the Commissioner.

(6) Final Sunscreen Order by Commissioner.—The Commissioner shall issue a final sunscreen order with respect to a proposed sunscreen order subject to paragraph (5)(B) not later than 60 calendar days after the date of notification under such paragraph.

(b) Review of Pending Requests.—

(1) In General.—The review of a pending request shall be carried out by the Secretary in accordance with this subsection.

(2) Inapplicability of Sections 586A and 586B.—Sections 586A and 586B shall not apply with respect to any pending request.

(3) Feedback Letters as Proposed Sunscreen Order.— Notwithstanding the requirements of section 586(7), a letter issued pursuant to section 330.14(g) of title 21, Code of Federal Regulations before November 26, 2014, with respect to a pending request, shall be deemed to be a proposed sunscreen order and displayed on the Internet website of the Food and Drug Administration. Notification of the availability of such letter shall be published in the Federal Register not later than 45 calendar days after November 26, 2014.

(4) Proposed Sunscreen Order.—In the case of a pending request for which the Secretary has not issued a letter pursuant to section 330.14(g) of title 21, Code of Federal Regulations before November 26, 2014, the Secretary shall complete review of such request and, not later than 90 calendar days after November 26, 2014, issue a proposed sunscreen order with respect to such request.

(5) Proposed Sunscreen Order by Commissioner.—If the Secretary does not issue a proposed sunscreen order under paragraph (4), or the Secretary does not publish a notification of the availability of a letter under paragraph (3), as applicable, the sponsor of such request may notify the Office of the Commissioner of such request and request review by the Office of the Commissioner. The Commissioner shall, not later than 60 calendar days after the date of notification under this paragraph, issue a proposed order with respect to such request.

(6) Public Comment Period.—A proposed sunscreen order issued under paragraph (4) or (5), or a notification of the availability of a letter under paragraph (3), with respect to a pending request shall provide for a period of 45 calendar days for public comment.

(7) Meeting.—A sponsor may request, in writing, a meeting with respect to a proposed sunscreen order issued under this subsection, including a letter deemed to be a proposed sunscreen order under paragraph (3), not later than 30 calendar days after the Secretary issues such order or the date upon which such feedback letter is deemed to be a proposed sunscreen order, as applicable. The Secretary shall convene a meeting with such sponsor not later than 45 calendar days after the date of such request for a meeting.

(8) Advisory Committee.—In the case of a proposed sunscreen order under paragraph (3), (4), or (5), an Advisory Committee meeting may be convened for the purpose of reviewing and providing recommendations regarding the pending request.

(9) Final Sunscreen Order.—In the case of a proposed sunscreen order under paragraph (3), (4), or (5)—

(A) the Secretary shall issue a final sunscreen order with respect to the request—

(i) in the case of a proposed sunscreen order described in subparagraph (A) or (B) of section 586(7), not later than 90 calendar days after the end of the public comment period under paragraph (6); or

(ii) in the case of a proposed sunscreen order described in subparagraph (C) of section 586(7)—

(I) if the Advisory Committee is not convened under paragraph (8), not later than 210 calendar days after the date on which the sponsor submits the additional information requested pursuant to such proposed sunscreen order, which shall include a rationale for not convening such Advisory Committee; or

(II) if the Advisory Committee is convened under paragraph (8), not later than 270 calendar days after the date on which the sponsor submits such additional information; or

(B) if the Secretary does not issue such final sunscreen order within such 90-, 210-, or 270-calendar-day period, as applicable, the sponsor of such request may notify the Office of the Commissioner about such request and request review by the Office of the Commissioner.

(10) Final Sunscreen order by Commissioner.—The Commissioner shall issue a final sunscreen order with respect to a proposed sunscreen order subject to paragraph (9)(B) not later than 60 calendar days after the date of notification under such paragraph.

(c) Advisory Committee.—The Secretary shall not be required to—

(1) convene the Advisory Committee—

(A) more than once with respect to any request under section 586A or any pending request; or

(B) more than twice in any calendar year with respect to the review under this section; or

(2) submit more than a total of 3 requests under section 586A or pending requests to the Advisory Committee per meeting.

(d) No Delegation.—Any responsibility vested in the Commissioner by subsection (a)(2), (a)(6), (b)(5), or (b)(10) shall not be delegated.

(e) Effect of Final Sunscreen Order.—

(1) In General. —

(A) Sunscreen Active Ingredients Determined to Be GRASE.—Upon issuance of a final sunscreen order determining that a nonprescription sunscreen active ingredient or combination of nonprescription sunscreen active ingredients is GRASE and is not misbranded, a sunscreen containing such ingredient or combination of ingredients shall be permitted to be introduced or delivered into interstate commerce for use under the conditions described in such final sunscreen order, in accordance with all requirements applicable to drugs not subject to section 503(b)(1), for so long as such final sunscreen order remains in effect.

(B) Sunscreen Active Ingredients Determined Not to Be GRASE.—Upon issuance of a final sunscreen order determining that a nonprescription sunscreen active ingredient or combination of nonprescription sunscreen active ingredients is not GRASE and is misbranded, a sunscreen containing such ingredient or combination of ingredients shall not be introduced or delivered into interstate commerce, for use under the conditions described in such final sunscreen order, unless an application is approved pursuant to section 505 with respect to a sunscreen containing such ingredient or combination of ingredients, or unless conditions are later established under which such ingredient or combination of ingredients is later determined to be GRASE and not misbranded under the over-the-counter drug monograph system.

(2) Amendments to Final Sunscreen Orders.—

(A) Amendments at Initiative of Secretary.—In the event that information relevant to a nonprescription sunscreen active ingredient or combination of nonprescription sunscreen active ingredients becomes available to the Secretary after issuance of a final sunscreen order, the Secretary may amend such final sunscreen order by issuing a new proposed sunscreen order under subsection (a)(1) and following the procedures set forth in this section.

(B) Petition to Amend Final Order.—Any interested person may petition the Secretary to amend a final sunscreen order under section 10.30, title 21 Code of Federal Regulations (or any successor regulations). If the Secretary grants any petition under such section, the Secretary shall initiate the process for amending a final sunscreen order by issuing a new proposed sunscreen order under subsection (a)(1) and following the procedures set forth in this section.

(C) Applicability of Final Orders.—Once the Secretary issues a new proposed sunscreen order to amend a final sunscreen order under subparagraph (A) or (B), such final sunscreen order shall remain in effect and paragraph (3) shall not apply to such final sunscreen order until the Secretary has issued a new final sunscreen order or has determined not to amend the final sunscreen order.

(3) Inclusion of Ingredients that are Subjects of Final Orders in the Sunscreen Monograph.—

(A) Amending Regulations.—

(i) Requirement.—At any time that the Secretary proposes to amend part 352 of title 21, Code of Federal Regulations (or any successor regulations) concerning nonprescription sunscreen, including pursuant to section 586E, except as provided in clause (iv), the Secretary shall include in such part 352 (or any successor regulations) any nonprescription sunscreen active ingredient or combination of nonprescription sunscreen active ingredients that is the subject of an effective final sunscreen order of the type described in section 586(2)(A) and issued since the time that the Secretary last amended such regulations. Such regulation shall set forth conditions of use under which each such ingredient or combination of ingredients is GRASE and not misbranded. If these conditions differ from, or are in addition to, those previously set forth in the applicable final sunscreen order, the Secretary shall provide notice and opportunity for comment on such conditions in the rulemaking, and the applicable final sunscreen order shall continue in effect until the effective date of a final regulation, as set forth in clause (iii).

(ii) Inclusion of Orders.—In proposing to amend the regulations as described in clause (i), the Secretary shall include in the proposed regulations a list of final sunscreen orders that shall cease to be effective on the effective date of a resulting final regulation. Such list shall include all final sunscreen orders of the type described in section 586(2)(A) that are in effect on the date that such regulations are proposed, with the exception that such list shall not include any final sunscreen orders that, on the date that the regulations are proposed, the Secretary is in the process of amending under paragraph (2).

(iii) Orders no Longer Effective.—Any final sunscreen order included by the Secretary in a list described in clause (ii) and in a list included in resulting final regulations shall cease to be effective on the date that such final regulations including such order in such list become effective.

(iv) Ingredients Not GRASE.—If, notwithstanding a final sunscreen order stating that a nonprescription sunscreen active ingredient or combination of nonprescription sunscreen active ingredients is GRASE and is not misbranded if marketed in accordance with such order, while amending the regulations as described in clause (i), the Secretary concludes that such ingredient or combination of ingredients is no longer GRASE for use in nonprescription sunscreen, the Secretary shall, at the discretion of the Secretary, either initiate the process for amending the final sunscreen order set forth in paragraph (2) of this subsection or include in a proposed regulation an explanation and information supporting the determination of the Secretary that such ingredient or combination of ingredients is no longer GRASE for use in nonprescription sunscreen.

(B) Procedure for Updating Regulations.—After the Secretary amends and finalizes the regulations under part 352 of title 21, Code of Federal Regulations under section 586E and such regulations become effective, the Secretary may use direct final rulemaking to include in such regulations any nonprescription sunscreen active ingredients that are the subject of effective final sunscreen orders.

Sec. 586D. [360fff-4] Guidance; Other Provisions.

(a) Guidance.—

(1) In General.—

(A) Draft Guidance.—Not later than 1 year after November 26, 2014, the Secretary shall issue draft guidance on the implementation of, and compliance with, the requirements with respect to sunscreen under this subchapter, including guidance on—

(i) the format and content of information submitted by a sponsor in support of a request under section 586A or a pending request;

(ii) the data required to meet the safety and efficacy standard for determining whether a nonprescription sunscreen active ingredient or combination of nonprescription sunscreen active ingredients is GRASE and is not misbranded;

(iii) the process by which a request under section 586A or a pending request is withdrawn; and

(iv) the process by which the Secretary will carry out section 586C(c), including with respect to how the Secretary will address the total number of requests received under section 586A and pending requests.

(B) Final Guidance.—The Secretary shall finalize the guidance described in subparagraph (A) not later than 2 years after November 26, 2014.

(C) Inapplicability of Paperwork Reduction Act.— Chapter 35 of title 44, United States Code shall not apply to collections of information made for purposes of' guidance under this subsection.

(2) Submissions Pending Issuance of Final Guidance.— Irrespective of whether final guidance under paragraph (1) has been issued—

(A) persons may, beginning on November 26, 2014, make submissions under this subchapter; and

(B) the Secretary shall review and act upon such submissions in accordance with this subchapter.

(b) Rules of Construction.—

(1) Currently Marketed Sunscreens.—Nothing in this subchapter shall be construed to affect the marketing of sunscreens that are marketed in interstate commerce on or before November 26, 2014, except as otherwise provided in this subchapter.

(2) Ensuring Safety and Effectiveness.—Nothing in this subchapter shall be construed to alter the authority of the Secretary with respect to prohibiting the marketing of a sunscreen that is not safe and effective or is misbranded, or with respect to imposing restrictions on the marketing of a sunscreen to ensure safety and effectiveness, except as otherwise provided in this subchapter, including section 586C(e).

(3) Other Drugs.—Except as otherwise provided in section 586F, nothing in this subchapter shall be construed to affect the authority of the Secretary under this Act or the Public Health Service Act (42 U.S.C. 201 et seq.) with respect to a drug other than a nonprescription sunscreen.

(4) Effect on Drugs Otherwise Approved.—Nothing in this subchapter shall affect the marketing of a drug approved under section 505 of this Act or section 351 of the Public Health Service Act.

(c) Timelines.—The timelines for the processes and procedures under paragraphs (1), (2), (5), and (6) of section 586C(a) shall not apply to any requests submitted to the Secretary under section 586A after the date that is 6 years after November 26, 2014.

Sec. 586E. [360fff-5] Sunscreen Monograph.

(a) In General.—Not later than 5 years after November 26, 2014, the Secretary shall amend and finalize regulations under part 352 of title 21, Code of Federal Regulations concerning nonprescription sunscreen that are effective not later than 5 years after such date of enactment. The Secretary shall publish such regulations not less than 30 calendar days before the effective date of such regulations.

(b) Reports.—If the regulations promulgated under subsection (a) do not include provisions related to the effectiveness of various sun protection factor levels, and do not address all dosage forms known to the Secretary to be used in sunscreens marketed in the United States without a new drug approval under section 505, the Secretary shall submit a report to the Committee on Health, Education, Labor, and Pensions of the Senate and the Committee on Energy and Commerce of the House of Representatives on the rationale for such provisions not being included in such regulations, and a plan and timeline to compile any information necessary to address such provisions through final regulations.

Sec. 586F. [360fff-6] Non-Sunscreen Time and Extent Applications.

(a) Pending Time and Extent Applications .—

(1) In General.—

(A) Request for Framework for Review.—If, prior to November 26, 2014, an application was submitted pursuant to section 330.14 of title 21, Code of Federal Regulations for a GRASE determination for a drug other than a nonprescription sunscreen active ingredient or combination of nonprescription sunscreen active ingredients and such drug was found to be eligible to be considered for inclusion in the over-the-counter drug monograph system pursuant to section 330.14 of title 21, Code of Federal Regulations, the sponsor of such application may request that the Secretary provide a framework under paragraph (2) for the review of such application.

(B) Request Requirements.—A request for a framework for review of an application made under subparagraph (A) shall be made within 180 calendar days of November 26, 2014 and shall include the preference of such sponsor as to whether such application is reviewed by the Secretary in accordance with—

(i) the processes and procedures set forth for pending requests under section 586C(b), except that specific timelines shall be determined in accordance with other applicable requirements under this section;

(ii) the processes and procedures set forth under part 330 of title 21, Code of Federal Regulations (or any successor regulations);

(iii) an initial filing determination under the processes and procedures described in section 586B(b) and the processes and procedures set forth for pending requests under section 586C(b), except that specific timelines shall be determined in accordance with other applicable requirements under this section; or

(iv) an initial filing determination under the processes and procedures described in section 586B(b) and the processes and procedures set forth under part 330 of title 21, Code of Federal Regulations (or any successor regulations).

(C) No Request.—If a sponsor described in subparagraph (A) does not make such request within 180 calendar days of November 26, 2014, such application shall be reviewed by the Secretary in accordance with the timelines of the applicable regulations when such regulations are finalized under subsection (b).

(2) Framework.—Not later than 1 year after November 26, 2014, the Secretary shall provide, in writing, a framework to each sponsor that submitted a request under paragraph (1). Such framework shall set forth the various timelines, in calendar days, with respect to the processes and procedures for review under clauses (i), (ii), (iii), and (iv) of paragraph (1)(B) and—

(A) such timelines shall account for the considerations under paragraph (5); and

(B) the timelines for the various processes and procedures shall not be shorter than the timelines set forth for pending requests under sections 586B(b) and 586C(b), as applicable.

(3) Governing Processes and Procedures for Review.—

(A) Election.—Not later than 60 calendar days after the Secretary provides a framework to a sponsor under paragraph (2), such sponsor may provide an election to the Secretary regarding the processes and procedures for review under clause (i), (ii), (iii), or (iv) of paragraph (1)(B). If such sponsor makes such election, the Secretary shall review the application that is the subject of such election pursuant to the processes and procedures elected by such sponsor and the applicable timelines in calendar days set forth under such framework, which the Secretary shall confirm in writing to the sponsor not later than the date upon which the Secretary provides a report under paragraph (4). If such sponsor does not make such election, such application shall be reviewed by the Secretary in accordance with the timelines of the applicable regulations when such regulations are finalized under subsection (b).

(B) Different Processes and Procedures.—At any time during review of an application, the Secretary may review such application under different processes and procedures under clause (i), (ii), (iii), or (iv) of paragraph (1)(B) than the processes and procedures the sponsor elected in accordance with subparagraph (A), so long as the Secretary proposes, in writing, the change and the sponsor agrees, in writing, to such change,

(C) Inclusion of Ingredients in Monographs.—If the sponsor elects to use the processes and procedures for review in accordance with clause (i) or (iii) of paragraph (1)(B), the Secretary may incorporate any resulting final order into a regulation addressing the conditions under which other drugs in the same therapeutic category are GRASE and not misbranded, including through direct final rulemaking, and the final order so incorporated shall cease to be effective on the effective date of the final regulation that addresses such drug.

(4) Letter Regarding Pending Applications.—Not later than 18 months after November 26, 2014, the Secretary shall report to the Committee on Health, Education, Labor, and Pensions of the Senate and the Committee on Energy and Commerce of the House of Representatives, in writing, regarding all pending applications subject to paragraph (1). In such letter, the Secretary shall provide a report on the review of such applications, including the timelines, in calendar days, for the review and GRASE determination for each application. Such timelines shall account for the considerations under paragraph (5).

(5) Timelines.—The timelines in calendar days established by the Secretary pursuant to this subsection—

(A) may vary based on the content, complexity, and format of the application submitted to the Secretary; and

(B) shall—

(i) reflect the public health priorities of the Food and Drug Administration, including the potential public health benefits posed by the inclusion of additional drugs in the over-the-counter drug monograph system;

(ii) take into consideration the resources available to the Secretary for carrying out such priorities and the processes and procedures described in paragraphs (1)(B) and (2); and

(iii) be reasonable, taking into consideration the requirements described in clauses (i) and (ii).

(b) New Time and Extent Applications.—

(1) In General.—Not later than 18 months after November 26, 2014, the Secretary shall issue proposed regulations establishing timelines for the review of applications for GRASE determinations for drugs other than nonprescription sunscreen active ingredients or combinations of nonprescription sunscreen active ingredients that are submitted to the Secretary after November 26, 2014, under section 330.14 of title 21, Code of Federal Regulations (or any successor regulations), and that are found to be eligible to be considered for inclusion in the over-the-counter drug monograph system pursuant to section 330.14 of title 21, Code of Federal Regulations (or any successor regulations), or that are subject to this subsection pursuant to paragraph (1) or (3) of subsection (a), as applicable, providing—

(A) timely and efficient completion of evaluations of applications under section 330.14 of title 21, Code of Federal Regulations (or any successor regulations) for drugs other than sunscreens; and

(B) timely and efficient completion of the review of the safety and effectiveness submissions pursuant to such applications, including establishing—

(i) reasonable timelines, in calendar days, for the applicable proposed and final regulations for applications of various content, complexity, and format, and timelines for internal procedures related to such processes; and

(ii) measurable metrics for tracking the extent to which the timelines set forth in the regulations are met.

(2) Timelines.—The timelines in calendar days established in the regulations under paragraph (1)—

(A) may vary based on the content, complexity, and format of the application submitted to the Secretary; and

(B) shall—

(i) reflect the public health priorities of the Food and Drug Administration, including the potential public health benefits posed by the inclusion of additional drugs in the over-the-counter drug monograph system;

(ii) take into consideration the resources available to the Secretary for carrying out such priorities and the processes and procedures described in paragraph (1); and

(iii) be reasonable, taking into consideration the requirements described in clauses (i) and (ii).

(3) Procedure.—In promulgating regulations under this subsection, the Secretary shall issue a notice of proposed rulemaking that includes a copy of the proposed regulation, provide a period of not less than 60 calendar days for comments on the proposed regulation, and publish the final regulation not less than 30 calendar days before the effective date of the regulation.

(4) Restrictions.—Notwithstanding any other provision of law, the Secretary shall promulgate regulations implementing this section only as described in paragraphs (1), (2), and (3).

(5) Final Regulations.—The Secretary shall finalize the regulations under this section not later than 27 months after November 26, 2014.

Sec. 586G. [360fff-7] Report.

(a) In General.—

(1) In General.—Not later than 18 months after November 26, 2014, and on the dates that are 2 and 4 years thereafter, the Secretary shall issue a report to the Committee on Health, Education, Labor, and Pensions of the Senate and the Committee on Energy and Commerce of the House of Representatives describing actions taken under this subchapter.

(2) Contents.—The reports under this subsection shall include—

(A) a review of the progress made in issuing GRASE determinations for pending requests, including the number of pending requests—

(i) reviewed and the decision times for each request, measured from the date of the original request for an eligibility determination submitted by the sponsor;

(ii) resulting in a determination that the nonprescription sunscreen active ingredient or combination of nonprescription sunscreen active ingredients is GRASE and is not misbranded;

(iii) resulting in a determination that the nonprescription sunscreen active ingredient or combination of nonprescription sunscreen active ingredients is not GRASE and is misbranded and the reasons for such determinations; and

(iv) for which a determination has not been made, and an explanation for the delay, a description of the current status of each such request, and the length of time each such request has been pending, measured from the date of original request for an eligibility determination by the sponsor;

(B) a review of the progress made in issuing GRASE determinations for requests not included in the reporting under subparagraph (A), including the number of such requests—

(i) reviewed and the decision times for each request;

(ii) resulting in a determination that the nonprescription sunscreen active ingredient, combination of nonprescription sunscreen active ingredients, or other ingredient is GRASE and is not misbranded;

(iii) resulting in a determination that the nonprescription sunscreen active ingredient, combination of nonprescription sunscreen active ingredients, or other ingredient is not GRASE and is misbranded and the reasons for such determinations; and

(iv) for which a determination has not been made, and an explanation for the delay, a description of the current status of each such request, and the length of time each such request has been pending, measured from the date of original request for an eligibility determination by the sponsor;

(C) an annual accounting (including information from years prior to the date of November 26, 2014 where such information is available) of the total number of requests submitted, pending, or completed under this subchapter, including whether such requests were the subject of an advisory committee convened by the Secretary;

(D) a description of the staffing and resources relating to the costs associated with the review and decisionmaking pertaining to requests under this subchapter;

(E) a review of the progress made in meeting the deadlines with respect to processing requests under this subchapter; and

(F) to the extent the Secretary determines appropriate, recommendations for process improvements in the handling of requests under this subchapter, including the advisory committee review process.

(b) Method.—The Secretary shall publish the reports under subsection (a) in the manner the Secretary determines to be the most effective for efficiently disseminating the report, including publication of the report on the Internet website of the Food and Drug Administration.

Chapter VI — Cosmetics

Sec. 601. [361] Adulterated Cosmetics. — A cosmetic shall be deemed to be adulterated —

(a) If it bears or contains any poisonous or deleterious substance which may render it injurious to users under the conditions of use prescribed in the labeling thereof, or, under such conditions of use as are customary or usual, except that this provision shall not apply to coal-tar hair dye, the label of which bears the following legend conspicuously displayed thereon: "Caution — This product contains ingredients which may cause skin irritation on certain individuals and a preliminary test according to accompanying directions should first be made. This product must not be used for dyeing the eyelashes or eyebrows; to do so may cause blindness.", and the labeling of which bears adequate directions for such preliminary testing. For the purposes of this paragraph and paragraph (e) the term "hair dye" shall not include eyelash dyes or eyebrow dyes.

(b) If it consists in whole or in part of any filthy, putrid, or decomposed substance.

(c) If it has been prepared, packed, or held under unsanitary conditions whereby it may have become contaminated with filth, or whereby it may have been rendered injurious to health.

(d) If its container is composed, in whole or in part, of any poisonous or deleterious substance which may render the contents injurious to health.

(e) If it is not a hair dye and it is, or it bears or contains, a color additive which is unsafe within the meaning of section 721(a).

Sec. 602. [362] Misbranded Cosmetics. — A cosmetic shall be deemed to be misbranded —

(a) If its labeling is false or misleading in any particular.

(b) If in package form unless it bears a label containing

(1) the name and place of business of the manufacturer, packer, or distributor; and

(2) an accurate statement of the quantity of the contents in terms of weight, measure, or numerical count:

Provided, [t]hat under clause (2) of this paragraph reasonable variations shall be permitted, and exemptions as to small packages shall be established, by regulations prescribed by the Secretary.

(c) If any word, statement, or other information required by or under authority of this Act to appear on the label or labeling is not prominently placed thereon with such conspicuousness (as compared with other words, statements, designs, or devices in the labeling) and in such terms as to render it likely to be read and understood by the ordinary individual under customary conditions of purchase and use.

(d) If its container is so made, formed, or filled as to be misleading.

(e) If it is a color additive, unless its packaging and labeling are in conformity with such packaging and labeling requirements, applicable to such color additive, as may be contained in regulations issued under section 721. This paragraph shall not apply to packages of color additives which, with respect to their use for cosmetics, are marketed and intended for use only in or on hair dyes (as defined in the last sentence of section 601(a)).

(f) If its packaging or labeling is in violation of an applicable regulation issued pursuant to section 3 or 4 of the Poison Prevention Packaging Act of 1970.

Sec. 603. [363] Regulations Making Exemptions.

The Secretary shall promulgate regulations exempting from any labeling requirement of this Act cosmetics which are, in accordance with the practice of the trade, to be processed, labeled, or repacked in substantial quantities at establishments other than those where originally processed or packed, on condition that such cosmetics are not adulterated or misbranded under the provisions of this Act upon removal from such processing, labeling, or repacking establishment.

Chapter VII — General Authority

Subchapter A — General Administrative Provisions

Sec. 701. [371] Regulations and Hearings.

(a) The authority to promulgate regulations for the efficient enforcement of this Act, except as otherwise provided in this section, is hereby vested in the Secretary.

(b) The Secretary of the Treasury and the Secretary of Health and Human Services shall jointly prescribe regulations for the efficient enforcement of the provisions of section 801, except as otherwise provided therein. Such regulations shall be promulgated in such manner and take effect at such time, after due notice, as the Secretary of Health and Human Services shall determine.

(c) Hearings authorized or required by this Act shall be conducted by the Secretary or such officer or employee as he may designate for the purpose.

(d) The definitions and standards of identity promulgated in accordance with the provisions of this Act shall be effective for the purposes of the enforcement of this Act, notwithstanding such definitions and standards as may be contained in other laws of the United States and regulations promulgated thereunder.

(e) —

(1) Any action for the issuance, amendment, or repeal of any regulation under section 403(j), 404(a), 406, 501(b), or 502 (d) or (h) of this Act, and any action for the amendment or repeal of any definition and standard of identity under section 401 of this Act for any dairy product (including products regulated under parts 131, 133 and 135 of title 21, Code of Federal Regulations) shall be begun by a proposal made

(A) by the Secretary on his own initiative, or

(B) by petition of any interested persons, showing reasonable grounds therefor, filed with the Secretary.

The Secretary shall publish such proposal and shall afford all interested persons an opportunity to present their views thereon, orally or in writing. As soon as practicable thereafter, the Secretary shall by order act upon such proposal and shall make such order public. Except as provided in paragraph (2), the order shall become effective at such time as may be specified therein, but not prior to the day following the last day on which objections may be filed under such paragraph.

(2) On or before the thirtieth day after the date on which an order entered under paragraph (1) is made public, any person who will be adversely affected by such order if placed in effect may file objections thereto with the Secretary, specifying with particularity the provisions of the order deemed objectionable, stating the grounds therefor, and requesting a public hearing upon such objections. Until final action upon such objections is taken by the Secretary under paragraph (3), the filing of such objections shall operate to stay the effectiveness of those provisions of the order to which the objections are made. As soon as practicable after the time for filing objections has expired the Secretary shall publish a notice in the Federal Register specifying those parts of the order which have been stayed by the filing of objections and, if no objections have been filed, stating that fact.

(3) As soon as practicable after such request for a public hearing, the Secretary, after due notice, shall hold such a public hearing for the purpose of receiving evidence relevant and material to the issues raised by such objections. At the hearing, any interested person may be heard in person or by representative. As soon as practicable after completion of the hearing, the Secretary shall by order act upon such objections and make such order public. Such order shall be based only on substantial evidence of record at such hearing and shall set forth, as part of the order, detailed findings of fact on which the order is based. The Secretary shall specify in the order the date on which it shall take effect, except that it shall not be made to take effect prior to the ninetieth day after its publication unless the Secretary finds that emergency conditions exist necessitating an earlier effective date, in which event the Secretary shall specify in the order his findings as to such conditions.

(f) —

(1) In a case of actual controversy as to the validity of any order under subsection (e), any person who will be adversely affected by such order if placed in effect may at any time prior to the ninetieth day after such order is issued file a petition with the Circuit Court of Appeals of the United States for the circuit wherein such person resides or has his principal place of business, for a judicial review of such order. A copy of the petition shall be forthwith transmitted by the clerk of the court to the Secretary or other officer designated by him for that purpose. The Secretary thereupon shall file in the court the record of the proceedings on which the Secretary based his order, as provided in section 2112 of title 28, United States Code.

(2) If the petitioner applies to the court for leave to adduce additional evidence, and shows to the satisfaction of the court that such additional evidence is material and that there were reasonable grounds for the failure to adduce such evidence in the proceeding before the Secretary the court may order such additional evidence (and evidence in rebuttal thereof) to be taken before the Secretary, and to be adduced upon the hearing, in such manner and upon such terms and conditions as to the court may seem proper. The Secretary may modify his findings as to the facts, or make new findings, by reason of the additional evidence, so taken, and he shall file such modified or new findings, and his recommendation, if any, for the modification or setting aside of his original order, with the return of such additional evidence.

(3) Upon the filing of the petition referred to in paragraph (1) of this subsection, the court shall have jurisdiction to affirm the order, or to set it aside in whole or in part, temporarily or permanently. If the order of the Secretary refuses to issue, amend, or repeal a regulation and such order is not in accordance with law the court shall by its judgment order the Secretary to take action with respect to such regulation, in accordance with law. The findings of the Secretary as to the facts, if supported by substantial evidence, shall be conclusive.

(4) The judgment of the court affirming or setting aside, in whole or in part, any such order of the Secretary shall be final, subject to review by the Supreme Court of the United States upon certiorari or certification as provided in section 1254 of title 28, United States Code.

(5) Any action instituted under this subsection shall survive notwithstanding any change in the person occupying the office of Secretary or any vacancy in such office.

(6) The remedies provided for in this subsection shall be in addition to and not in substitution for any other remedies provided by law.

(g) A certified copy of the transcript of the record and proceedings under subsection (e) shall be furnished by the Secretary to any interested party at his request, and payment of the costs thereof, and shall be admissible in any criminal libel for condemnation, exclusion of imports, or other proceeding arising under or in respect of this Act, irrespective of whether proceedings with respect to the order have previously been instituted or become final under subsection (f).

(h) —

(1) —

(A) The Secretary shall develop guidance documents with public participation and ensure that information identifying the existence of such documents and the documents themselves are made available to the public both in written form and, as feasible, through electronic means. Such documents shall not create or confer any rights for or on any person, although they present the views of the Secretary on matters under the jurisdiction of the Food and Drug Administration.

(B) Although guidance documents shall not be binding on the Secretary, the Secretary shall ensure that employees of the Food and Drug Administration do not deviate from such guidances without appropriate justification and supervisory concurrence. The Secretary shall provide training to employees in how to develop and use guidance documents and shall monitor the development and issuance of such documents.

(C) —

(i) For guidance documents that set forth initial interpretations of a statute or regulation, changes in interpretation or policy that are of more than a minor nature, complex scientific issues, or highly controversial issues, the Secretary shall ensure public participation prior to implementation of guidance documents, unless the Secretary determines that such prior public participation is not feasible or appropriate. In such cases, the Secretary shall provide for public comment upon implementation and take such comment into account.

(ii) With respect to devices, if a notice to industry guidance letter, a notice to industry advisory letter, or any similar notice sets forth initial interpretations of a regulation or policy or sets forth changes in interpretation or policy, such notices shall be treated as a guidance document for purposes of this subparagraph.

(D) For guidance documents that set forth existing practices or minor changes in policy, the Secretary shall provide for public comment upon implementation.

(2) In developing guidance documents, the Secretary shall ensure uniform nomenclature for such documents and uniform internal procedures for approval of such documents. The Secretary shall ensure that guidance documents and revisions of such documents are properly dated and indicate the nonbinding nature of the documents. The Secretary shall periodically review all guidance documents, and, where appropriate, revise such documents.

(3) The Secretary, acting through the Commissioner, shall maintain electronically and update and publish periodically in the Federal Register a list of guidance documents. All such documents shall be made available to the public.

(4) The Secretary shall ensure that an effective appeals mechanism is in place to address complaints that the Food and Drug Administration is not developing and using guidance documents in accordance with this subsection.

(5) Not later than July 1, 2000, the Secretary after evaluating the effectiveness of the Good Guidance Practices document, published in the Federal Register at 62 Fed. Reg. 8961, shall promulgate a regulation consistent with this subsection specifying the policies and procedures of the Food and Drug Administration for the development, issuance, and use of guidance documents.

Sec. 702. [372] Examinations and Investigations.

(a) —

(1) —

(A) The Secretary is authorized to conduct examinations and investigations for the purposes of this Act through officers and employees of the Department or through any health, food, or drug officer or employee of any State, Territory, or political subdivision thereof, duly commissioned by the Secretary as an officer of the Department.

(B) —

(i) For a tobacco product, to the extent feasible, the Secretary shall contract with the States in accordance with this paragraph to carry out inspections of retailers within that State in connection with the enforcement of this Act.

(ii) The Secretary shall not enter into any contract under clause (i) with the government of any of the several States to exercise enforcement authority under this Act on Indian country without the express written consent of the Indian tribe involved.

(2) —

(A) In addition to the authority established in paragraph (1), the Secretary, pursuant to a memorandum of understanding between the Secretary and the head of another Federal department or agency, is authorized to conduct examinations and investigations for the purposes of this Act through the officers and employees of such other department or agency, subject to subparagraph (B). Such a memorandum shall include provisions to ensure adequate training of such officers and employees to conduct the examinations and investigations. The memorandum of understanding shall contain provisions regarding reimbursement. Such provisions may, at the sole discretion of the head of the other department or agency, require reimbursement, in whole or in part, from the Secretary for the examinations or investigations performed under this section by the officers or employees of the other department or agency.

(B) A memorandum of understanding under subparagraph (A) between the Secretary and another Federal department or agency is effective only in the case of examinations or inspections at facilities or other locations that are jointly regulated by the Secretary and such department or agency.

(C) For any fiscal year in which the Secretary and the head of another Federal department or agency carries out one or more examinations or inspections under a memorandum of understanding under subparagraph (A), the Secretary and the head of such department or agency shall with respect to their respective departments or agencies submit to the committees of jurisdiction (authorizing and appropriating) in the House of Representatives and the Senate a report that provides, for such year —

(i) the number of officers or employees that carried out one or more programs, projects, or activities under such memorandum;

(ii) the number of additional articles that were inspected or examined as a result of such memorandum; and

(iii) the number of additional examinations or investigations that were carried out pursuant to such memorandum.

(3) In the case of food packed in the Commonwealth of Puerto Rico or a Territory the Secretary shall attempt to make inspection of such food at the first point of entry within the United States when, in his opinion and with due regard to the enforcement of all the provisions of this Act, the facilities at his disposal will permit of such inspection.

(4) For the purposes of this subsection, the term "United States" means the States and the District of Columbia.

(b) Where a sample of a food, drug, or cosmetic is collected for analysis under this Act the Secretary shall, upon request, provide a part of such official sample for examination or analysis by any person named on the label of the article, or the owner thereof, or his attorney or agent; except that the Secretary is authorized, by regulations, to make such reasonable exceptions from, and impose such reasonable terms and conditions relating to, the operation of this subsection as he finds necessary for the proper administration of the provisions of this Act.

(c) For purposes of enforcement of this Act, records of any department or independent establishment in the executive branch of the Government shall be open to inspection by any official of the Department duly authorized by the Secretary to make such inspection.

(d) The Secretary is authorized and directed, upon request from the Under Secretary of Commerce for Intellectual Property and Director of the United States Patent and Trademark Office, to furnish full and complete information with respect to such questions relating to drugs as the Director may submit concerning any patent application. The Secretary is further authorized, upon receipt of any such request, to conduct or cause to be conducted, such research as may be required.

(e) Any officer or employee of the Department designated by the Secretary to conduct examinations, investigations, or inspections under this Act relating to counterfeit drugs may, when so authorized by the Secretary —

(1) carry firearms;

(2) execute and serve search warrants and arrest warrants;

(3) execute seizure by process issued pursuant to libel under section 304;

(4) make arrests without warrant for offenses under this Act with respect to such drugs if the offense is committed in his presence or, in the case of a felony, if he has probable cause to believe that the person so arrested has committed, or is committing, such offense; and

(5) make, prior to the institution of libel proceedings under section 304(a)(2), seizures of drugs or containers or of equipment, punches, dies, plates, stones, labeling, or other things, if they are, or he has reasonable grounds to believe that they are, subject to seizure and condemnation under such section 304(a)(2). In the event of seizure pursuant to this paragraph (5) [probably should be "this paragraph" — Ed.], libel proceedings under section 304(a)(2) shall be instituted promptly and the property seized be placed under the jurisdiction of the court.

SEC. 703. [373] RECORDS OF INTERSTATE SHIPMENT.

For the purpose of enforcing the provisions of this Act, carriers engaged in interstate commerce, and persons receiving food, drugs, devices, tobacco products, or cosmetics in interstate commerce or holding such articles so received, shall, upon the request of an officer or employee duly designated by the Secretary, permit such officer or employee, at reasonable times, to have access to and to copy all records showing the movement in interstate commerce of any food, drug, device, tobacco product, or cosmetic, or the holding thereof during or after such movement, and the quantity, shipper, and consignee thereof; and it shall be unlawful for any such carrier or person to fail to permit such access to and copying of any such record so requested when such request is accompanied by a statement in writing specifying the nature or kind of food, drug, device, tobacco product, or cosmetic to which such request relates, except that evidence obtained under this section, or any evidence which is directly or indirectly derived from such evidence, shall not be used in a criminal prosecution of the person from whom obtained, and except that carriers shall not be subject to the other provisions of this Act by reason of their receipt, carriage, holding, or delivery of food, drugs, devices, tobacco products, or cosmetics in the usual course of business as carriers.

Sec. 704. [374] Factory Inspection.

(a) —

(1) For purposes of enforcement of this Act, officers or employees duly designated by the Secretary, upon presenting appropriate credentials and a written notice to the owner, operator, or agent in charge, are authorized

(A) to enter, at reasonable times, any factory, warehouse, or establishment in which food, drugs, devices, tobacco products, or cosmetics are manufactured, processed, packed, or held, for introduction in interstate commerce or after such introduction, or to enter any vehicle, being used to transport or hold such food, drugs, devices, tobacco products, or cosmetics in interstate commerce; and

(B) to inspect, at reasonable times and within reasonable limits and in a reasonable manner, such factory, warehouse, establishment, or vehicle and all pertinent equipment, finished and unfinished materials, containers, and labeling therein.

In the case of any person (excluding farms and restaurants) who manufactures, processes, packs, transports, distributes, holds, or imports foods, the inspection shall extend to all records and other information described in section 414, when the standard for records inspection under paragraph (1) or (2) of section 414(a) applies, subject to the limitations established in section 414(d). In the case of any factory, warehouse, establishment, or consulting laboratory in which prescription drugs, nonprescription drugs intended for human use, restricted devices or tobacco products, are manufactured, processed, packed, or held, inspection shall extend to all things therein (including records, files, papers, processes, controls, and facilities) bearing on whether prescription drugs, nonprescription drugs intended for human use, restricted devices or tobacco products, which are adulterated or misbranded within the meaning of this Act, or which may not be manufactured, introduced into interstate commerce, or sold, or offered for sale by reason of any provision of this Act, have been or are being manufactured, processed, packed, transported, or held in any such place, or otherwise bearing on violation of this Act. No inspection authorized by the preceding sentence or by paragraph (3) shall extend to financial data, sales data other than shipment data, pricing data, personnel data (other than data as to qualification of technical and professional personnel performing functions subject to this Act), and research data (other than data relating to new drugs, antibiotic drugs, devices, and tobacco products and subject to reporting and inspection under regulations lawfully issued pursuant to section 505(i) or (k), section 519, section 520(g), or chapter IX and data relating to other drugs, devices, or tobacco products which in the case of a new drug would be subject to reporting or inspection under lawful regulations issued pursuant to section 505(j)). A separate notice shall be given for each such inspection, but a notice shall not be required for each entry made during the period covered by the inspection. Each such inspection shall be commenced and completed with reasonable promptness.

(2) The provisions of the third sentence of paragraph (1) shall not apply to —

(A) pharmacies which maintain establishments in conformance with any applicable local laws regulating the practice of pharmacy and medicine and which are regularly engaged in dispensing prescription drugs or devices, upon prescriptions of practitioners licensed to administer such drugs or devices to patients under the care of such practitioners in the course of their professional practice, and which do not, either through a subsidiary or otherwise, manufacture, prepare, propagate, compound, or process drugs or devices for sale other than in the regular course of their business of dispensing or selling drugs or devices at retail;

(B) practitioners licensed by law to prescribe or administer drugs, or prescribe or use devices, as the case may be, and who manufacture, prepare, propagate, compound, or process drugs, or manufacture or process devices solely for use in the course of their professional practice;

(C) persons who manufacture, prepare, propagate, compound, or process drugs, or manufacture or process devices solely for use in research, teaching, or chemical analysis and not for sale;

(D) such other classes of persons as the Secretary may by regulation exempt from the application of this section upon a finding that inspection as applied to such classes of persons in accordance with this section is not necessary for the protection of the public health.

(3) An officer or employee making an inspection under paragraph (1) for purposes of enforcing the requirements of section 412 applicable to infant formulas shall be permitted, at all reasonable times, to have access to and to copy and verify any records —

(A) bearing on whether the infant formula manufactured or held in the facility inspected meets the requirements of section 412, or

(B) under section 412.

(4) —

(A) Any records or other information that the Secretary may inspect under this section from a person that owns or operates an establishment that is engaged in the manufacture, preparation, propagation, compounding, or processing of a drug shall, upon the request of the Secretary, be provided to the Secretary by such person, in advance of or in lieu of an inspection, within a reasonable timeframe, within reasonable limits, and in a reasonable manner, and in either electronic or physical form, at the expense of such person. The Secretary's request shall include a sufficient description of the records requested.

(B) Upon receipt of the records requested under subparagraph (A), the Secretary shall provide to the person confirmation on receipt.

(C) Nothing in this paragraph supplants the authority of the Secretary to conduct inspections otherwise permitted under this Act in order to ensure compliance with this Act.

(b) Upon completion of any such inspection of a factory, warehouse, consulting laboratory, or other establishment, and prior to leaving the premises, the officer or employee making the inspection shall give to the owner, operator, or agent in charge a report in writing setting forth any conditions or practices observed by him which, in his judgment, indicate that any food, drug, device, tobacco product, or cosmetic in such establishment

(1) consists in whole or in part of any filthy, putrid, or decomposed substance, or

(2) has been prepared, packed, or held under unsanitary conditions whereby it may have become contaminated with filth, or whereby it may have been rendered injurious to health.

A copy of such report shall be sent promptly to the Secretary.

(c) If the officer or employee making any such inspection of a factory, warehouse, or other establishment has obtained any sample in the course of the inspection, upon completion of the inspection and prior to leaving the premises he shall give to the owner, operator, or agent in charge a receipt describing the samples obtained.

(d) Whenever in the course of any such inspection of a factory or other establishment where food is manufactured, processed, or packed, the officer or employee making the inspection obtains a sample of any such food, and an analysis is made of such sample for the purpose of ascertaining whether such food consists in whole or in part of any filthy, putrid, or decomposed substance, or is otherwise unfit for food, a copy of the results of such analysis shall be furnished promptly to the owner, operator, or agent in charge.

(e) Every person required under section 519 or 520(g) to maintain records and every person who is in charge or custody of such records shall, upon request of an officer or employee designated by the Secretary, permit such officer or employee at all reasonable times to have access to, and to copy and verify, such records.

(f) —

(1) An accredited person described in paragraph (3) shall maintain records documenting the training qualifications of the person and the employees of the person, the procedures used by the person for handling confidential information, the compensation arrangements made by the person, and the procedures used by the person to identify and avoid conflicts of interest. Upon the request of an officer or employee designated by the Secretary, the person shall permit the officer or employee, at all reasonable times, to have access to, to copy, and to verify, the records.

(2) Within 15 days after the receipt of a written request from the Secretary to an accredited person described in paragraph (3) for copies of records described in paragraph (1), the person shall produce the copies of the records at the place designated by the Secretary.

(3) For purposes of paragraphs (1) and (2), an accredited person described in this paragraph is a person who —

(A) is accredited under subsection (g); or

(B) is accredited under section 523.

(g) —

(1) The Secretary shall, subject to the provisions of this subsection, accredit persons for the purpose of conducting inspections of establishments that manufacture, prepare, propagate, compound, or process class II or class III devices, which inspections are required under section 510(h) or are inspections of such establishments required to register under section 510(i). The owner or operator of such an establishment that is eligible under paragraph (6) may, from the list published under paragraph (4), select an accredited person to conduct such inspections.

(2) The Secretary shall publish in the Federal Register criteria to accredit or deny accreditation to persons who request to perform the duties specified in paragraph (1). Thereafter, the Secretary shall inform those requesting accreditation, within 60 days after the receipt of such request, whether the request for accreditation is adequate for review, and the Secretary shall promptly act on the request for accreditation. Any resulting accreditation shall state that such person is accredited to conduct inspections at device establishments identified in paragraph (1). The accreditation of such person shall specify the particular activities under this subsection for which such person is accredited.

(3) An accredited person shall, at a minimum, meet the following requirements:

(A) Such person may not be an employee of the Federal Government.

(B) Such person shall be an independent organization which is not owned or controlled by a manufacturer, supplier, or vendor of articles regulated under this Act and which has no organizational, material, or financial affiliation (including a consultative affiliation) with such a manufacturer, supplier, or vendor.

(C) Such person shall be a legally constituted entity permitted to conduct the activities for which it seeks accreditation.

(D) Such person shall not engage in the design, manufacture, promotion, or sale of articles regulated under this Act.

(E) The operations of such person shall be in accordance with generally accepted professional and ethical business practices, and such person shall agree in writing that at a minimum the person will —

(i) certify that reported information accurately reflects data reviewed, inspection observations made, other matters that relate to or may influence compliance with this Act, and recommendations made during an inspection or at an inspection's closing meeting;

(ii) limit work to that for which competence and capacity are available;

(iii) treat information received, records, reports, and recommendations as confidential commercial or financial information or trade secret information, except such information may be made available to the Secretary;

(iv) promptly respond and attempt to resolve complaints regarding its activities for which it is accredited; and

(v) protect against the use, in carrying out paragraph (1), of any officer or employee of the accredited person who has a financial conflict of interest regarding any product regulated under this Act, and annually make available to the public disclosures of the extent to which the accredited person, and the officers and employees of the person, have maintained compliance with requirements under this clause relating to financial conflicts of interest.

(F) Such person shall notify the Secretary of any withdrawal, suspension, restriction, or expiration of certificate of conformance with the quality systems standard referred to in paragraph (7) for any device establishment that such person inspects under this subsection not later than 30 days after such withdrawal, suspension, restriction, or expiration.

(G) Such person may conduct audits to establish conformance with the quality systems standard referred to in paragraph (7).

(4) The Secretary shall publish on the Internet site of the Food and Drug Administration a list of persons who are accredited under paragraph (2). Such list shall be updated to ensure that the identity of each accredited person, and the particular activities for which the person is accredited, is known to the public. The updating of such list shall be no later than one month after the accreditation of a person under this subsection or the suspension or withdrawal of accreditation, or the modification of the particular activities for which the person is accredited.

(5) —

(A) To ensure that persons accredited under this subsection continue to meet the standards of accreditation, the Secretary shall

(i) audit the performance of such persons on a periodic basis through the review of inspection reports and inspections by persons designated by the Secretary to evaluate the compliance status of a device establishment and the performance of accredited persons, and

(ii) take such additional measures as the Secretary determines to be appropriate.

(B) The Secretary may withdraw accreditation of any person accredited under paragraph (2), after providing notice and an opportunity for an informal hearing, when such person is substantially not in compliance with the standards of accreditation, poses a threat to public health, fails to act in a manner that is consistent with the purposes of this subsection, or where the Secretary determines that there is a financial conflict of interest in the relationship between the accredited person and the owner or operator of a device establishment that the accredited person has inspected under this subsection. The Secretary may suspend the accreditation of such person during the pendency of the process under the preceding sentence.

(6) —

(A) Subject to subparagraphs (B) and (C), a device establishment is eligible for inspections by persons accredited under paragraph (2) if the following conditions are met:

(i) The Secretary classified the results of the most recent inspection of the establishment as "no action indicated" or "voluntary action indicated".

(ii) With respect to inspections of the establishment to be conducted by an accredited person, the owner or operator of the establishment submits to the Secretary a notice that

(I) provides the date of the last inspection of the establishment by the Secretary and the classification of that inspection;

(II) states the intention of the owner or operator to use an accredited person to conduct inspections of the establishment;

(III) identifies the particular accredited person the owner or operator intends to select to conduct such inspections; and

(IV) includes a certification that, with respect to the devices that are manufactured, prepared, propagated, compounded, or processed in the establishment —

(aa) at least 1 of such devices is marketed in the United States; and

(bb) at least 1 of such devices is marketed, or is intended to be marketed, in 1 or more foreign countries, 1 of which countries certifies, accredits, or otherwise recognizes the person accredited under paragraph (2) and identified under subclause (III) as a person authorized to conduct inspections of device establishments.

(B) —

(i) Except with respect to the requirement of subparagraph (A)(i), a device establishment is deemed to have clearance to participate in the program and to use the accredited person identified in the notice under subparagraph (A)(ii) for inspections of the establishment unless the Secretary, not later than 30 days after receiving such notice, issues a response that —

(I) denies clearance to participate as provided under subparagraph (C); or

(II) makes a request under clause (ii).

(ii) The Secretary may request from the owner or operator of a device establishment in response to the notice under subparagraph (A)(ii) with respect to the establishment, or from the particular accredited person identified in such notice —

(I) compliance data for the establishment in accordance with clause (iii)(I); or

(II) information concerning the relationship between the owner or operator of the establishment and the accredited person identified in such notice in accordance with clause (iii)(II).

The owner or operator of the establishment, or such accredited person, as the case may be, shall respond to such a request not later than 60 days after receiving such request.

(iii) —

(I) The compliance data to be submitted by the owner or operator of a device establishment in response to a request under clause (ii)(I) are data describing whether the quality controls of the establishment have been sufficient for ensuring consistent compliance with current good manufacturing practice within the meaning of section 501(h) and with other applicable provisions of this Act. Such data shall include complete reports of inspectional findings regarding good manufacturing practice or other quality control audits that, during the preceding 2-year period, were conducted at the establishment by persons other than the owner or operator of the establishment, together with all other compliance data the Secretary deems necessary. Data under the preceding sentence shall demonstrate to the Secretary whether the establishment has facilitated consistent compliance by promptly correcting any compliance problems identified in such inspections.

(II) A request to an accredited person under clause (ii)(II) may not seek any information that is not required to be maintained by such person in records under subsection (f)(1).

(iv) A device establishment is deemed to have clearance to participate in the program and to use the accredited person identified in the notice under subparagraph (A)(ii) for inspections of the establishment unless the Secretary, not later than 60 days after receiving the information requested under clause (ii), issues a response that denies clearance to participate as provided under subparagraph (C).

(C) —

(i) The Secretary may deny clearance to a device establishment if the Secretary has evidence that the certification under subparagraph (A)(ii)(IV) is untrue and the Secretary provides to the owner or operator of the establishment a statement summarizing such evidence.

(ii) The Secretary may deny clearance to a device establishment if the Secretary determines that the establishment has failed to demonstrate consistent compliance for purposes of subparagraph (B)(iii)(I) and the Secretary provides to the owner or operator of the establishment a statement of the reasons for such determination.

(iii) —

(I) The Secretary may reject the selection of the accredited person identified in the notice under subparagraph (A)(ii) if the Secretary provides to the owner or operator of the establishment a statement of the reasons for such rejection. Reasons for the rejection may include that the establishment or the accredited person, as the case may be, has failed to fully respond to the request, or that the Secretary has concerns regarding the relationship between the establishment and such accredited person.

(II) If the Secretary rejects the selection of an accredited person by the owner or operator of a device establishment, the owner or operator may make an additional selection of an accredited person by submitting to the Secretary a notice that identifies the additional selection. Clauses (i) and (ii) of subparagraph (B), and subclause (I) of this clause, apply to the selection of an accredited person through a notice under the preceding sentence in the same manner and to the same extent as such provisions apply to a selection of an accredited person through a notice under subparagraph (A)(ii).

(iv) In the case of a device establishment that is denied clearance under clause (i) or (ii) or with respect to which the selection of the accredited person is rejected under clause (iii), the Secretary shall designate a person to review the statement of reasons, or statement summarizing such evidence, as the case may be, of the Secretary under such clause if, during the 30-day period beginning on the date on which the owner or operator of the establishment receives such statement, the owner or operator requests the review. The review shall commence not later than 30 days after the owner or operator requests the review, unless the Secretary and the owner or operator otherwise agree.

(7) —

(A) Persons accredited under paragraph (2) to conduct inspections shall record in writing their inspection observations and shall present the observations to the device establishment's designated representative and describe each observation. Additionally, such accredited person shall prepare an inspection report in a form and manner designated by the Secretary to conduct inspections, taking into consideration the goals of international harmonization of quality systems standards. Any official classification of the inspection shall be determined by the Secretary.

(B) At a minimum, an inspection report under subparagraph (A) shall identify the persons responsible for good manufacturing practice compliance at the inspected device establishment, the dates of the inspection, the scope of the inspection, and shall describe in detail each observation identified by the accredited person, identify other matters that relate to or may influence compliance with this Act, and describe any recommendations during the inspection or at the inspection's closing meeting.

(C) An inspection report under subparagraph (A) shall be sent to the Secretary and to the designated representative of the inspected device establishment at the same time, but under no circumstances later than three weeks after the last day of the inspection. The report to the Secretary shall be accompanied by all written inspection observations previously provided to the designated representative of the establishment.

(D) Any statement or representation made by an employee or agent of a device establishment to a person accredited under paragraph (2) to conduct inspections shall be subject to section 1001 of title 18, United States Code.

(E) If at any time during an inspection by an accredited person the accredited person discovers a condition that could cause or contribute to an unreasonable risk to the public health, the accredited person shall immediately notify the Secretary of the identification of the device establishment subject to inspection and such condition.

(F) For the purpose of setting risk-based inspectional priorities, the Secretary shall accept voluntary submissions of reports of audits assessing conformance with appropriate quality systems standards set by the International Organization for Standardization (ISO) and identified by the Secretary in public notice. If the owner or operator of an establishment elects to submit audit reports under this subparagraph, the owner or operator shall submit all such audit reports with respect to the establishment during the preceding 2-year periods.

(8) Compensation for an accredited person shall be determined by agreement between the accredited person and the person who engages the services of the accredited person, and shall be paid by the person who engages such services.

(9) Nothing in this subsection affects the authority of the Secretary to inspect any device establishment pursuant to this Act.

(10) —

(A) For fiscal year 2005 and each subsequent fiscal year, no device establishment may be inspected during the fiscal year involved by a person accredited under paragraph (2) if—

(i) of the amounts appropriated for salaries and expenses of the Food and Drug Administration for the preceding fiscal year (referred to in this subparagraph as the "first prior fiscal year"), the amount obligated by the Secretary for inspections of device establishments by the Secretary was less than the adjusted base amount applicable to such first prior fiscal year; and

(ii) of the amounts appropriated for salaries and expenses of the Food and Drug Administration for the fiscal year preceding the first prior fiscal year (referred to in this subparagraph as the "second prior fiscal year"), the amount obligated by the Secretary for inspections of device establishments by the Secretary was less than the adjusted base amount applicable to such second prior fiscal year.

(B) —

(i) Subject to clause (ii), the Comptroller General of the United States shall determine the amount that was obligated by the Secretary for fiscal year 2002 for compliance activities of the Food and Drug Administration with respect to devices (referred to in this subparagraph as the "compliance budget"), and of such amount, the amount that was obligated for inspections by the Secretary of device establishments (referred to in this subparagraph as the "inspection budget").

(ii) For purposes of determinations under clause (i), the Comptroller General shall not include in the compliance budget or the inspection budget any amounts obligated for inspections of device establishments conducted as part of the process of reviewing applications under section 515.

(iii) Not later than March 31, 2003, the Comptroller General shall complete the determinations required in this subparagraph and submit to the Secretary and the Congress a report describing the findings made through such determinations.

(C) For purposes of this paragraph:

(i) The term "base amount" means the inspection budget determined under subparagraph (B) for fiscal year 2002.

(ii) The term "adjusted base amount", in the case of applicability to fiscal year 2003, means an amount equal to the base amount increased by 5 percent.

(iii) The term "adjusted base amount", with respect to applicability to fiscal year 2004 or any subsequent fiscal year, means the adjusted base amount applicable to the preceding year increased by 5 percent.

(11) The authority provided by this subsection terminates on October 1, ~~2017~~ 2022.

(12) No later than four years after the enactment of this subsection the Comptroller General shall report to the Committee on Energy and Commerce of the House of Representatives and the Committee on Health, Education, Labor and Pensions of the Senate —

(A) the number of inspections conducted by accredited persons pursuant to this subsection and the number of inspections conducted by Federal employees pursuant to section 510(h) and of device establishments required to register under section 510(i);

(B) the number of persons who sought accreditation under this subsection, as well as the number of persons who were accredited under this subsection;

(C) the reasons why persons who sought accreditation, but were denied accreditation, were denied;

(D) the number of audits conducted by the Secretary of accredited persons, the quality of inspections conducted by accredited persons, whether accredited persons are meeting their obligations under this Act, and whether the number of audits conducted is sufficient to permit these assessments;

(E) whether this subsection is achieving the goal of ensuring more information about device establishment compliance is being presented to the Secretary, and whether that information is of a quality consistent with information obtained by the Secretary pursuant to inspections conducted by Federal employees;

(F) whether this subsection is advancing efforts to allow device establishments to rely upon third-party inspections for purposes of compliance with the laws of foreign governments; and

(G) whether the Congress should continue, modify, or terminate the program under this subsection.

(13) The Secretary shall include in the annual report required under section 1003(g) the names of all accredited persons and the particular activities under this subsection for which each such person is accredited and the name of each accredited person whose accreditation has been withdrawn during the year.

(14) Notwithstanding any provision of this subsection, this subsection does not have any legal effect on any agreement described in section 803(b) between the Secretary and a foreign country.

(15) —

(A) Notwithstanding any other provision of this subsection, the Secretary may recognize auditing organizations that are recognized by organizations established by governments to facilitate international harmonization for purposes of conducting inspections of —

(i) establishments that manufacture, prepare, propagate, compound, or process devices (other than types of devices licensed under section 351 of the Public Health Service Act), as required under section 510(h); or

(ii) establishments required to register pursuant to section 510(i).

(B) Nothing in this paragraph affects —

(i) the authority of the Secretary to inspect any device establishment pursuant to this Act; or

(ii) the authority of the Secretary to determine the official classification of an inspection.

(h) —

(1) In the case of inspections other than for-cause inspections, the Secretary shall review processes and standards applicable to inspections of domestic and foreign device establishments in effect as of the date of the enactment of this subsection, and update such processes and standards through the adoption of uniform processes and standards applicable to such inspections. Such uniform processes and standards shall provide for —

(A) exceptions to such processes and standards, as appropriate;

(B) announcing the inspection of the establishment within a reasonable time before such inspection occurs, including by providing to the owner, operator, or agent in charge of the establishment a notification regarding the type and nature of the inspection;

(C) a reasonable estimate of the timeframe for the inspection, an opportunity for advance communications between the officers or employees carrying out the inspection under subsection (a)(1) and the owner, operator, or agent in charge of the establishment concerning appropriate working hours during the inspection, and, to the extent feasible, advance notice of some records that will be requested; and

(D) regular communications during the inspection with the owner, operator, or agent in charge of the establishment regarding inspection status, which may be recorded by either party with advance notice and mutual consent.

(2) —

(A) The Secretary shall, with respect to a request described in subparagraph (B), provide nonbinding feedback with respect to such request not later than 45 days after the Secretary receives such request.

(B) A request described in this subparagraph is a request for feedback —

(i) that is made by the owner, operator, or agent in charge of such establishment in a timely manner; and

(ii) with respect to actions proposed to be taken by a device establishment in a response to a report received by such establishment pursuant to subsection (b) that involve a public health priority, that implicate systemic or major actions, or relate to emerging safety issues (as determined by the Secretary).

(3) Nothing in this subsection affects the authority of the Secretary to conduct inspections otherwise permitted under this Act in order to ensure compliance with this Act.

Sec. 705. [375] Publicity.

(a) The Secretary shall cause to be published from time to time reports summarizing all judgments, decrees, and court orders which have been rendered under this Act, including the nature of the charge and the disposition thereof.

(b) The Secretary may also cause to be disseminated information regarding food, drugs, devices, tobacco products, or cosmetics in situations involving, in the opinion of the Secretary, imminent danger to health, or gross deception of the consumer. Nothing in this section shall be construed to prohibit the Secretary from collecting, reporting, and illustrating the results of the investigations of the Department.

Sec. 706. [376] Seafood Inspection.

The Secretary, upon application of any packer of any seafood for shipment or sale within the jurisdiction of this Act, may, at his discretion, designate inspectors to examine and inspect such food and the production, packing, and labeling thereof. If on such examination and inspection compliance is found with the provisions of this Act and regulations promulgated thereunder, the applicant shall be authorized or required to mark the food as provided by regulation to show such compliance. Services under this section shall be rendered only upon payment by the applicant of fees fixed by regulation in such amounts as may be necessary to provide, equip, and maintain an adequate and efficient inspection service. Receipts from such fees shall be covered into the Treasury and shall be available to the Secretary for expenditures incurred in carrying out the purposes of this section, including expenditures for salaries of additional inspectors when necessary to supplement the number of inspectors for whose salaries Congress has appropriated. The Secretary is hereby authorized to promulgate regulations governing the sanitary and other conditions under which the service herein provided shall be granted and maintained and for otherwise carrying out the purposes of this section. Any person who forges, counterfeits, simulates, or falsely represents, or without proper authority uses any mark, stamp, tag, label, or other identification devices authorized or required by the provisions of this section or regulations thereunder, shall be guilty of a misdemeanor, and shall on conviction thereof be subject to imprisonment for not more than one year or a fine of not less than $1,000 nor more than $5,000 or both such imprisonment and fine.

Sec. 707. [378] Advertising of Certain Foods.

(a) —

(1) Except as provided in subsection (c), before the Secretary may initiate any action under chapter III —

(A) with respect to any food which the Secretary determines is misbranded under section 403(a)(2) because of its advertising, or

(B) with respect to a food's advertising which the Secretary determines causes the food to be so misbranded, the Secretary shall, in accordance with paragraph (2), notify in writing the Federal Trade Commission of the action the Secretary proposes to take respecting such food or advertising.

(2) The notice required by paragraph (1) shall —

(A) contain

(i) a description of the action the Secretary proposes to take and of the advertising which the Secretary has determined causes a food to be misbranded,

(ii) a statement of the reasons for the Secretary's determination that such advertising has caused such food to be misbranded, and

(B) be accompanied by the records, documents, and other written materials which the Secretary determines supports his determination that such food is misbranded because of such advertising.

(b) —

(1) If the Secretary notifies the Federal Trade Commission under subsection (a) of action proposed to be taken under chapter III with respect to a food or food advertising and the Commission notifies the Secretary in writing, within the 30-day period beginning on the date of the receipt of such notice, that —

(A) it has initiated under the Federal Trade Commission Act an investigation of such advertising to determine if it is prohibited by such Act or any order or rule under such Act,

(B) it has commenced (or intends to commence) a civil action under section 5, 13, or 19 with respect to such advertising or the Attorney General has commenced (or intends to commence) a civil action under section 5 with respect to such advertising,

(C) it has issued and served (or intends to issue and serve) a complaint under section 5(b) of such Act respecting such advertising, or

(D) pursuant to section 16(b) of such Act it has made a certification to the Attorney General respecting such advertising,

the Secretary may not, except as provided by paragraph (2), initiate the action described in the Secretary's notice to the Federal Trade Commission.

(2) If, before the expiration of the 60-day period beginning on the date the Secretary receives a notice described in paragraph (1) from the Federal Trade Commission in response to a notice of the Secretary under subsection (a) —

(A) the Commission or the Attorney General does not commence a civil action described in subparagraph (B) of paragraph (1) of this subsection respecting the advertising described in the Secretary's notice,

(B) the Commission does not issue and serve a complaint described in subparagraph (C) of such paragraph respecting such advertising, or

(C) the Commission does not (as described in subparagraph (D) of such paragraph) make a certification to the Attorney General respecting such advertising, or, if the Commission does make such a certification to the Attorney General respecting such advertising, the Attorney General, before the expiration of such period, does not cause appropriate criminal proceedings to be brought against such advertising, the Secretary may, after the expiration of such period, initiate the action described in the notice to the Commission pursuant to subsection (a). The Commission shall promptly notify the Secretary of the commencement by the Commission of such a civil action, the issuance and service by it of such a complaint, or the causing by the Attorney General of criminal proceedings to be brought against such advertising.

(c) The requirements of subsections (a) and (b) do not apply with respect to action under chapter III with respect to any food or food advertising if the Secretary determines that such action is required to eliminate an imminent hazard to health.

(d) For the purpose of avoiding unnecessary duplication, the Secretary shall coordinate any action taken under chapter III because of advertising which the Secretary determines causes a food to be misbranded with any action of the Federal Trade Commission under the Federal Trade Commission Act with respect to such advertising.

Sec. 708. [379] Confidential Information.

(a) Contractors. — The Secretary may provide any information which is exempt from disclosure pursuant to subsection (a) of section 552 of title 5, United States Code, by reason of subsection (b)(4) of such section to a person other than an officer or employee of the Department if the Secretary determines such other person requires the information in connection with an activity which is undertaken under contract with the Secretary, which relates to the administration of this Act, and with respect to which the Secretary (or an officer or employee of the Department) is not prohibited from using such information. The Secretary shall require as a condition to the provision of information under this section that the person receiving it take such security precautions respecting the information as the Secretary may by regulation prescribe.

(b) Ability to Receive and Protect Confidential Information Obtained from Foreign Governments. —

(1) In General. — The Secretary shall not be required to disclose under section 552 of title 5, United States Code (commonly referred to as the "Freedom of Information Act"), or any other provision of law, any information relating to drugs obtained from a foreign government agency, if —

(A) the information concerns the inspection of a facility, is part of an investigation, alerts the United States to the potential need for an investigation, or concerns a drug that has a reasonable probability of causing serious adverse health consequences or death to humans or animals;

(B) the information is provided or made available to the United States Government voluntarily on the condition that it not be released to the public; and

(C) the information is covered by, and subject to, a written agreement between the Secretary and the foreign government.

(2) Time Limitations. — The written agreement described in paragraph (1)(C) shall specify the time period for which paragraph (1) shall apply to the voluntarily disclosed information. Paragraph (1) shall not apply with respect to such information after the date specified in such agreement, but all other applicable legal protections, including the provisions of section 552 of title 5, United States Code, and section 319L(e)(1) of the Public Health Service Act, as applicable, shall continue to apply to such information. If no date is specified in the written agreement, paragraph (1) shall not apply with respect to such information for a period of more than 36 months.

(3) Disclosures not Affected. — Nothing in this section authorizes any official to withhold, or to authorize the withholding of, information from Congress or information required to be disclosed pursuant to an order of a court of the United States.

(4) Relation to Other Law. — For purposes of section 552 of title 5, United States Code, this subsection shall be considered a statute described in subsection (b)(3)(B) of such section 552.

(c) Authority to Enter Into Memoranda of Understanding for Purposes of Information Exchange. — The Secretary may enter into written agreements to provide information referenced in section 301(j) to foreign governments subject to the following criteria:

(1) Certification. — The Secretary may enter into a written agreement to provide information under this subsection to a foreign government only if the Secretary has certified such government as having the authority and demonstrated ability to protect trade secret information from disclosure. Responsibility for this certification shall not be delegated to any officer or employee other than the Commissioner of Food and Drugs.

(2) Written Agreement. — The written agreement to provide information to the foreign government under this subsection shall include a commitment by the foreign government to protect information exchanged under this subsection from disclosure unless and until the sponsor gives written permission for disclosure or the Secretary makes a declaration of a public health emergency pursuant to section 319 of the Public Health Service Act that is relevant to the information.

(3) Information Exchange. — The Secretary may provide to a foreign government that has been certified under paragraph (1) and that has executed a written agreement under paragraph (2) information referenced in section 301(j) in only the following circumstances:

(A) Information concerning the inspection of a facility may be provided to a foreign government if —

(i) the Secretary reasonably believes, or the written agreement described in paragraph (2) establishes, that the government has authority to otherwise obtain such information; and

(ii) the written agreement executed under paragraph (2) limits the recipient's use of the information to the recipient's civil regulatory purposes.

(B) Information not described in subparagraph (A) may be provided as part of an investigation, or to alert the foreign government to the potential need for an investigation, if the Secretary has reasonable grounds to believe that a drug has a reasonable probability of causing serious adverse health consequences or death to humans or animals.

(4) Effect of Subsection. — Nothing in this subsection affects the ability of the Secretary to enter into any written agreement authorized by other provisions of law to share confidential information.

Sec. 709. [379a] Presumption.

In any action to enforce the requirements of this Act respecting a device, tobacco product, food, drug, or cosmetic the connection with interstate commerce required for jurisdiction in such action shall be presumed to exist.

Sec. 710. [379b] Consolidated Administrative and Laboratory Facility.

(a) Authority. — The Secretary, in consultation with the Administrator of the General Services Administration, shall enter into contracts for the design, construction, and operation of a consolidated Food and Drug Administration administrative and laboratory facility.

(b) Awarding of Contract. — The Secretary shall solicit contract proposals under subsection (a) from interested parties. In awarding contracts under such subsection, the Secretary shall review such proposals and give priority to those alternatives that are the most cost effective for the Federal Government and that allow for the use of donated land, federally owned property, or lease-purchase arrangements. A contract under this subsection shall not be entered into unless such contract results in a net cost savings to the Federal Government over the duration of the contract, as compared to the Government purchase price including borrowing by the Secretary of the Treasury.

(c) Donations. — In carrying out this section, the Secretary shall have the power, in connection with real property, buildings, and facilities, to accept on behalf of the Food and Drug Administration gifts or donations of services or property, real or personal, as the Secretary determines to be necessary.

(d) Authorization of Appropriations. — There are authorized to be appropriated to carry out this section $100,000,000 for fiscal year 1991, and such sums as may be necessary for each of the subsequent fiscal years, to remain available until expended.

Sec. 711. [379d] Automation of Food and Drug Administration.

(a) In General. — The Secretary, acting through the Commissioner of Food and Drugs, shall automate appropriate activities of the Food and Drug Administration to ensure timely review of activities regulated under this Act.

(b) Authorization of Appropriations. — There are authorized to be appropriated each fiscal year such sums as are necessary to carry out this section.

Sec. 712. [379d-1] Conflicts of Interest.

(a) Definitions. — For purposes of this section:

(1) Advisory Committee. — The term "advisory committee" means an advisory committee under the Federal Advisory Committee Act that provides advice or recommendations to the Secretary regarding activities of the Food and Drug Administration.

(2) Financial Interest. — The term "financial interest" means a financial interest under section 208(a) of title 18, United States Code.

(b) Recruitment for Advisory Committees. —

(1) In General. — The Secretary shall —

(A) develop and implement strategies on effective outreach to potential members of advisory committees at universities, colleges, other academic research centers, professional and medical societies, and patient and consumer groups;

(B) seek input from professional medical and scientific societies to determine the most effective informational and recruitment activities;

(C) at least every 180 days, request referrals for potential members of advisory committees from a variety of stakeholders, including —

(i) product developers, patient groups, and disease advocacy organizations; and

(ii) relevant —

(I) professional societies;

(II) medical societies;

(III) academic organizations; and

(IV) governmental organizations; and

(D) in carrying out subparagraphs (A) and (B), take into account the levels of activity (including the numbers of annual meetings) and the numbers of vacancies of the advisory committees.

(2) Recruitment Activities. — The recruitment activities under paragraph (1) may include—

(A) advertising the process for becoming an advisory committee member at medical and scientific society conferences;

(B) making widely available, including by using existing electronic communications channels, the contact information for the Food and Drug Administration point of contact regarding advisory committee nominations; and

(C) developing a method through which an entity receiving funding from the National Institutes of Health, the Agency for Healthcare Research and Quality, the Centers for Disease Control and Prevention, or the Veterans Health Administration can identify a person who the Food and Drug Administration can contact regarding the nomination of individuals to serve on advisory committees.

(3) Expertise. — In carrying out this subsection, the Secretary shall seek to ensure that the Secretary has access to the most current expert advice.

(c) Disclosure of Determinations and Certifications. — Notwithstanding section 107(a)(2) of the Ethics in Government Act of 1978, the following shall apply:

(1) 15 or More Days in Advance. — As soon as practicable, but (except as provided in paragraph (2)) not later than 15 days prior to a meeting of an advisory committee to which a written determination as referred to in section 208(b)(1) of title 18, United States Code, a written certification as referred to in section 208(b)(3) of such title, or a waiver as referred to in paragraph (2)(b) applies, the Secretary shall disclose (other than information exempted from disclosure under section 552 or section 552a of title 5, United States Code (popularly known as the Freedom of Information Act and the Privacy Act of 1974, respectively)) on the Internet Web site of the Food and Drug Administration—

(A) the type, nature, and magnitude of the financial interests of the advisory committee member to which such determination or certification applies; and

(B) the reasons of the Secretary for such determination or certification, including, as appropriate, the public health interest in having the expertise of the member with respect to the particular matter before the advisory committee.

(2) Less Than 30 Days in Advance. — In the case of a financial interest that becomes known to the Secretary less than 30 days prior to a meeting of an advisory committee to which a written determination as referred to in section 208(b)(1) of title 18, United States Code, or a written certification as referred to in section 208(b)(3) of such title applies, the Secretary shall disclose (other than information exempted from disclosure under section 552 or 552a of title 5, United States Code) on the Internet Web site of the Food and Drug Administration, the information described in subparagraphs (A) and (B) as soon as practicable after the Secretary makes such determination or certification, but in no case later than the date of such meeting.

(d) Public Record. — The Secretary shall ensure that the public record and transcript of each meeting of an advisory committee includes the disclosure required under subsection (c)(3) (other than information exempted from disclosure under section 552 of title 5, United States Code, and section 552a of title 5, United States Code).

(e) Annual Report. —

(1) In General. — Not later than February 1 of each year, the Secretary shall submit to the Committee on Appropriations and the Committee on Health, Education, Labor, and Pensions of the Senate, and the Committee on Appropriations and the Committee on Energy and Commerce of the House of Representatives a report that describes—

(A) with respect to the fiscal year that ended on September 30 of the previous year, the number of persons nominated for participation at meetings for each advisory committee, the number of persons so nominated, and willing to serve, the number of vacancies on each advisory committee, the number of persons contacted for service as members on each advisory committee meeting for each advisory committee who did not participate because of the potential for such participation to constitute a disqualifying financial interest under section 208 of title 18, United States Code;

(B) with respect to such year, the number of persons contacted for service as members for each advisory committee meeting for each advisory committee who did not participate because of reasons other than the potential for such participation to constitute a disqualifying financial interest under section 208 of title 18, United States Code;

(C) with respect to such year, the number of members attending meetings for each advisory committee; and

(D) with respect to such year, the aggregate number of disclosures required under subsection (d) and the percentage of individuals to whom such disclosures did not apply who served on such committee.

(2) Public Availability — Not later than 30 days after submitting any report under paragraph (1) to the committees specified in such paragraph, the Secretary shall make each such report available to the public.

(f) Periodic Review of Guidance. — Not less than once every 5 years, the Secretary shall —

(1) review guidance of the Food and Drug Administration with respect to advisory committees regarding disclosure of conflicts of interest and the application of section 208 of title 18, United States Code; and

(2) update such guidance as necessary to ensure that the Food and Drug Administration receives appropriate access to needed scientific expertise, with due consideration of the requirements of such section 208.

(g) Guidance on Reported Disclosed Financial Interest or Involvement. — The Secretary shall issue guidance that describes how the Secretary reviews the financial interests and involvement of advisory committee members that are disclosed under subsection (c) but that the Secretary determines not to meet the definition of a disqualifying interest under section 208 of title 18, United States Code for the purposes of participating in a particular matter.

Sec. 713. [379d-2] Policy on the Review and Clearance of Scientific Articles Published by FDA Employees.

(a) Definition. — In this section, the term "article" means a paper, poster, abstract, book, book chapter, or other published writing.

(b) Policies. — The Secretary, through the Commissioner of Food and Drugs, shall establish and make publicly available clear written policies to implement this section and govern the timely submission, review, clearance, and disclaimer requirements for articles.

(c) Timing of Submission for Review. — If an officer or employee, including a Staff Fellow and a contractor who performs staff work, of the Food and Drug Administration is directed by the policies established under subsection (b) to submit an article to the supervisor of such officer or employee, or to some other official of the Food and Drug Administration, for review and clearance before such officer or employee may seek to publish or present such an article at a conference, such officer or employee shall submit such article for such review and clearance not less than 30 days before submitting the article for publication or presentation.

(d) Timing for Review and Clearance. — The supervisor or other reviewing official shall review such article and provide written clearance, or written clearance on the condition of specified changes being made, to such officer or employee not later than 30 days after such officer or employee submitted such article for review.

(e) Non-Timely Review. — If, 31 days after such submission under subsection (c), the supervisor or other reviewing official has not cleared or has not reviewed such article and provided written clearance, such officer or employee may consider such article not to have been cleared and may submit the article for publication or presentation with an appropriate disclaimer as specified in the policies established under subsection (b).

(f) Effect. — Nothing in this section shall be construed as affecting any restrictions on such publication or presentation provided by other provisions of law.

Sec. 714. [379d-3] Streamlined Hiring Authority.

(a) In General. — In addition to any other personnel authorities under other provisions of law, the Secretary may, without regard to the provisions of title 5, United States Code, governing appointments in the competitive service, appoint employees to positions in the Food and Drug Administration to perform, administer, or support activities described in subsection (b), if the Secretary determines that such appointments are needed to achieve the objectives specified in subsection (c).

(b) Activities Described. — The activities described in this subsection are —

(1) activities under this Act related to the process for the review of device applications (as defined in section 737~~(8)~~(9)); and

(2) activities under this Act related to human generic drug activities (as defined in section 744A).

(c) Objectives Specified. — The objectives specified in this subsection are —

(1) with respect to the activities under subsection (b)(1), the goals referred to in section 738A(a)(1); and

(2) with respect to the activities under subsection (b)(2), the goals referred to in section 744C(a).

(d) Internal Controls. — The Secretary shall institute appropriate internal controls for appointments under this section.

(e) Sunset. — The authority to appoint employees under this section shall terminate on the date that is 3 years after the date of enactment of this section.

Sec. 714A. [379d-3a] Hiring Authority for Scientific, Technical, and Professional Personnel.

(a) In General.—The Secretary may, notwithstanding title 5, United States Code, governing appointments in the competitive service, appoint outstanding and qualified candidates to scientific, technical, or professional positions that support the development, review, and regulation of medical products. Such positions shall be within the competitive service.

(b) Compensation.—

(1) In General.—Notwithstanding any other provision of law, including any requirement with respect to General Schedule pay rates under sub-chapter III of chapter 53 of title 5, United States Code, and consistent with the requirements of paragraph (2), the Commissioner of Food and Drugs may determine and set—

(A) the annual rate of pay of any individual appointed under subsection (a); and

(B) for purposes of retaining qualified employees, the annual rate of pay for any qualified scientific, technical, or professional personnel appointed to a position described in sub- section (a) before the date of enactment of the 21st Century Cures Act [December 13, 2016 —Ed.].

(2) Limitation.—The annual rate of pay established pursuant to paragraph (1) may not exceed the amount of annual compensation (excluding expenses) specified in section 102 of title 3, United States Code.

(3) Public Availability.—The annual rate of pay provided to an individual in accordance with this section shall be publicly available information.

(c) Rule of Construction.—The Authorities under this section shall not be construed to affect the authority provided under section 714.

(d) Report on Workforce Planning.—

(1) In General.—Not later than 18 months after the date of enactment of the 21st Century Cures Act [December 13, 2016 —Ed.], the Secretary shall submit a report on workforce planning to the Committee on Health, Education, Labor, and Pensions of the Senate and the Committee on Energy and Commerce of the House of Representatives that examines the extent to which the Food and Drug Administration has a critical need for qualified individuals for scientific, technical, or professional positions, including—

(A) an analysis of the workforce needs at the Food and Drug Administration and the Secretary's strategic plan for addressing such needs, including through use of the authority under this section; and

(B) a recruitment and retention plan for hiring qualified scientific, technical, and professional candidates, which may include the use of—

(i) recruitment through nongovernmental recruitment or placement agencies;

(ii) recruitment through academic institutions;

(iii) recruitment or hiring bonuses, if applicable;

(iv) recruitment using targeted direct hiring authorities; and

(v) retention of qualified scientific, technical, and professional employees using the authority under this section, or other applicable authorities of the Secretary.

(2) Recommendations.—The report under paragraph (1) may include the recommendations of the Commissioner of Food and Drugs that would help the Food and Drug Administration to better recruit and retain qualified individuals for scientific, technical, or professional positions at the agency.

Sec. 715. [379d-4] Reporting Requirements.

(a) Generic Drugs. — Beginning with fiscal year 2013 and ending after fiscal year 2017, not later than 120 days after the end of each fiscal year for which fees are collected under part 7 of subchapter C, the Secretary shall prepare and submit to the Committee on Health, Education, Labor, and Pensions of the Senate and the Committee on Energy and Commerce of the House of Representatives a report concerning, for all applications for approval of a generic drug under section 505(j), amendments to such applications, and prior approval supplements with respect to such applications filed in the previous fiscal year —

(1) the number of such applications that met the goals identified for purposes of part 7 of subchapter C, in the letters from the Secretary of Health and Human Services to the Chairman of the Committee on Health, Education, Labor, and Pensions of the Senate and the Chairman of the Committee on Energy and Commerce of the House of Representatives, as set forth in the Congressional Record;

(2) the average total time to decision by the Secretary for applications for approval of a generic drug under section 505(j), amendments to such applications, and prior approval supplements with respect to such applications filed in the previous fiscal year, including the number of calendar days spent during the review by the Food and Drug Administration and the number of calendar days spent by the sponsor responding to a complete response letter.

(3) the total number of applications under section 505(j), amendments to such applications, and prior approval supplements with respect to such applications that were pending with the Secretary for more than 10 months on the date of enactment of the Food and Drug Administration Safety and Innovation Act; and

(4) the number of applications described in paragraph (3) on which the Food and Drug Administration took final regulatory action in the previous fiscal year.

(b) Biosimilar Biological Products. —

(1) In General. — Beginning with fiscal year 2014, not later than 120 days after the end of each fiscal year for which fees are collected under part 8 of subchapter C, the Secretary shall prepare and submit to the Committee on Health, Education, Labor, and Pensions of the Senate and the Committee on Energy and Commerce of the House of Representatives a report concerning —

(A) the number of applications for approval filed under section 351(k) of the Public Health Service Act; and

(B) the percentage of applications described in subparagraph (A) that were approved by the Secretary.

(2) Additional Information. — As part of the performance report described in paragraph (1), the Secretary shall include an explanation of how the Food and Drug Administration is managing the biological product review program to ensure that the user fees collected under part 2 are not used to review an application under section 351(k) of the Public Health Service Act.

Subchapter B — Colors

Sec. 721. [379e] Listing and Certification of Color Additives for Foods, Drugs, and Cosmetics.

(a) When Color Additives Deemed Unsafe. — A color additive shall, with respect to any particular use (for which it is being used or intended to be used or is represented as suitable) in or on food or drugs or devices or cosmetics be deemed unsafe for the purposes of the application of section 402(c), section 501(a)(4), or section 601(e), as the case may be unless —

(1) —

(A) there is in effect, and such additive and such use are in conformity with, a regulation issued under subsection (b) of this section listing such additive for such use, including any provision of such regulation prescribing the conditions under which such additive may be safely used, and

(B) such additive either

(i) is from a batch certified, in accordance with regulations issued pursuant to subsection (c), for such use, or

(ii) has, with respect to such use, been exempted by the Secretary from the requirement of certification; or

(2) such additive and such use thereof conform to the terms of an exemption which is in effect pursuant to subsection (f) of this section.

While there are in effect regulations under subsections (b) and (c) of this section relating to a color additive or an exemption pursuant to subsection (f) with respect to such additive, an article shall not, by reason of bearing or containing such additive in all respects in accordance with such regulations or such exemption, be considered adulterated within the meaning of clause (1) of section 402(a) if such article is a food, or within the meaning of section 601(a) if such article is a cosmetic other than a hair dye (as defined in the last sentence of section 601(a)). A color additive for use in or on a device shall be subject to this section only if the color additive comes in direct contact with the body of man or other animals for a significant period of time. The Secretary may by regulation designate the uses of color additives in or on devices which are subject to this section.

(b) Listing of Colors.

(1) The Secretary shall, by regulation, provide for separately listing color additives for use in or on food, color additives for use in or on drugs or devices, and color additives for use in or on cosmetics, if and to the extent that such additives are suitable and safe for any such use when employed in accordance with such regulations.

(2) —

(A) Such regulations may list any color additive for use generally in or on food, or in or on drugs or devices, or in or on cosmetics, if the Secretary finds that such additive is suitable and may safely be employed for such general use.

(B) If the data before the Secretary do not establish that the additive satisfies the requirements for listing such additive on the applicable list pursuant to subparagraph (A) of this paragraph, or if the proposal is for listing such additive for a more limited use or uses, such regulations may list such additive only for any more limited use or uses for which it is suitable and may safely be employed.

(3) Such regulations shall, to the extent deemed necessary by the Secretary to assure the safety of the use or uses for which a particular color additive is listed, prescribe the conditions under which such additive may be safely employed for such use or uses (including, but not limited to, specifications, hereafter in this section referred to as tolerance limitations, as to the maximum quantity or quantities which may be used or permitted to remain in or on the article or articles in or on which it is used; specifications as to the manner in which such additive may be added to or used in or on such article or articles; and directions or other labeling or packaging requirements for such additive).

(4) The Secretary shall not list a color additive under this section for a proposed use unless the data before him establish that such use, under the conditions of use specified in the regulations, will be safe: Provided, however, That a color additive shall be deemed to be suitable and safe for the purpose of listing under this subsection for use generally in or on food, while there is in effect a published finding of the Secretary declaring such substance exempt from the term "food additive" because of its being generally recognized by qualified experts as safe for its intended use, as provided in section 201(s).

(5) —

(A) In determining, for the purposes of this section, whether a proposed use of a color additive is safe, the Secretary shall consider, among other relevant factors—

(i) the probable consumption of, or other relevant exposure from, the additive and of any substance formed in or on food, drugs or devices, or cosmetics because of the use of the additive;

(ii) the cumulative effect, if any, of such additive in the diet of man or animals, taking into account the same or any chemically or pharmacologically related substance or substances in such diet;

(iii) safety factors which, in the opinion of experts qualified by scientific training and experience to evaluate the safety of color additives for the use or uses for which the additive is proposed to be listed, are generally recognized as appropriate for the use of animal experimentation data; and

(iv) the availability of any needed practicable methods of analysis for determining the identity and quantity of

(I) the pure dye and all intermediates and other impurities contained in such color additive,

(II) such additive in or on any article of food, drug or devices, or cosmetic, and

(III) any substance formed in or on such article because of the use of such additive.

(B) A color additive

(i) shall be deemed unsafe, and shall not be listed, for any use which will or may result in ingestion of all or part of such additive, if the additive is found by the Secretary to induce cancer when ingested by man or animal, or if it is found by the Secretary, after tests which are appropriate for the evaluation of the safety of additives for use in food, to induce cancer in man or animal, and

(ii) shall be deemed unsafe, and shall not be listed, for any use which will not result in ingestion of any part of such additive, if, after tests which are appropriate for the evaluation of the safety of additives for such use, or after other relevant exposure of man or animal to such additive, it is found by the Secretary to induce cancer in man or animal:

Provided, [t]hat clause (i) of this subparagraph (B) shall not apply with respect to the use of a color additive as an ingredient of feed for animals which are raised for food production, if the Secretary finds that, under the conditions of use and feeding specified in proposed labeling and reasonably certain to be followed in practice, such additive will not adversely affect the animals for which such feed is intended, and that no residue of the additive will be found (by methods of examination prescribed or approved by the Secretary by regulations, which regulations shall not be subject to subsection (d)) in any edible portion of such animals after slaughter or in any food yielded by or derived from the living animal.

(C) —

(i) In any proceeding for the issuance, amendment, or repeal of a regulation listing a color additive, whether commenced by a proposal of the Secretary on his own initiative or by a proposal contained in a petition, the petitioner, or any other person who will be adversely affected by such proposal or by the Secretary's order issued in accordance with paragraph (1) of section 701(e) if placed in effect, may request, within the time specified in this subparagraph, that the petition or order thereon, or the Secretary's proposal, be referred to an advisory committee for a report and recommendations with respect to any matter arising under subparagraph (B) of this paragraph, which is involved in such proposal or order and which requires the exercise of scientific judgment. Upon such request, or if the Secretary within such time deems such a referral necessary, the Secretary shall forthwith appoint an advisory committee under subparagraph (D) of this paragraph and shall refer to it, together with all the data before him, such matter arising under subparagraph (B) for study thereof and for a report and recommendations on such matter. A person who has filed a petition or who has requested the referral of a matter to an advisory committee pursuant to this subparagraph (C) as well as representatives of the Department, shall have the right to consult with such advisory committee in connection with the matter referred to it. The request for referral under this subparagraph, or the Secretary's referral on his own initiative, may be made at any time before, or within thirty days after, publication of an order of the Secretary acting upon the petition or proposal.

(ii) Within sixty days after the date of such referral, or within an additional thirty days if the committee deems such additional time necessary, the committee shall, after independent study of the data furnished to it by the Secretary and other data before it, certify to the Secretary a report and recommendations, together with all underlying data and a statement of the reasons or basis for the recommendations. A copy of the foregoing shall be promptly supplied by the Secretary to any person who has filed a petition, or who has requested such referral to the advisory committee. Within thirty days after such certification, and after giving due consideration to all data then before him, including such report, recommendation, underlying data, and statement, and to any prior order issued by him in connection with such matter, the Secretary shall by order confirm or modify any order therefore issued or, if no such prior order has been issued, shall by order act upon the petition or other proposal.

(iii) Where —

(I) by reason of subparagraph (B) of this paragraph, the Secretary has initiated a proposal to remove from listing a color additive previously listed pursuant to this section; and

(II) a request has been made for referral of such proposal to an advisory committee;

the Secretary may not act by order on such proposal until the advisory committee has made a report and recommendations to him under clause (ii) of this subparagraph and he has considered such recommendations, unless the Secretary finds that emergency conditions exist necessitating the issuance of an order notwithstanding this clause.

(D) The advisory committee referred to in subparagraph (C) of this paragraph shall be composed of experts selected by the National Academy of Sciences, qualified in the subject matter referred to the committee and of adequately diversified professional background, except that in the event of the inability or refusal of the National Academy of Sciences to act, the Secretary shall select the members of the committee. The size of the committee shall be determined by the Secretary. Members of any advisory committee established under this Act, while attending conferences or meetings of their committees or otherwise serving at the request of the Secretary, shall be entitled to receive compensation at rates to be fixed by the Secretary but at rates not exceeding the daily equivalent of the rate specified at the time of such service for grade GS-18 of the General Schedule, including traveltime; and while away from their homes or regular places of business they may be allowed travel expenses, including per diem in lieu of subsistence, as authorized by section 5703 of title 5 of the United States Code for persons in the Government service employed intermittently. The members shall not be subject to any other provisions of law regarding the appointment and compensation of employees of the United States. The Secretary shall furnish the committee with adequate clerical and other assistance, and shall by rules and regulations prescribe the procedure to be followed by the committee.

(6) The Secretary shall not list a color additive under this subsection for a proposed use if the data before him show that such proposed use would promote deception of the consumer in violation of this Act or would otherwise result in misbranding or adulteration within the meaning of this Act.

(7) If, in the judgment of the Secretary, a tolerance limitation is required in order to assure that a proposed use of a color additive will be safe, the Secretary —

(A) shall not list the additive for such use if he finds that the data before him do not establish that such additive, if used within a safe tolerance limitation, would achieve the intended physical or other technical effect; and

(B) shall not fix such tolerance limitation at a level higher than he finds to be reasonably required to accomplish the intended physical or other technical effect.

(8) If, having regard to the aggregate quantity of color additive likely to be consumed in the diet or to be applied to the human body, the Secretary finds that the data before him fail to show that it would be safe and otherwise permissible to list a color additive (or pharmacologically related color additives) of all uses proposed therefor and at the levels of concentration proposed, the Secretary shall, in determining for which use or uses such additive (or such related additives) shall be or remain listed, or how the aggregate allowable safe tolerance for such additive or additives shall be allocated by him among the uses under consideration, take into account, among other relevant factors (and subject to the paramount criterion of safety),

(A) the relative marketability of the articles involved as affected by the proposed uses of the color additive (or of such related additives) in or on such articles, and the relative dependence of the industries concerned on such uses;

(B) the relative aggregate amounts of such color additive which he estimates would be consumed in the diet or applied to the human body by reason of the various uses and levels of concentration proposed; and

(C) the availability, if any, of other color additives suitable and safe for one or more of the uses proposed.

(c) Certification of Colors. — The Secretary shall further, by regulation, provide

(1) for the certification, with safe diluents or without diluents, of batches of color additives listed pursuant to subsection (b) and conforming to the requirements for such additives established by regulations under such subsection and this subsection, and

(2) for exemption from the requirement of certification in the case of any such additive, or any listing or use thereof, for which he finds such requirement not to be necessary in the interest of the protection of the public health:

Provided, [t]hat, with respect to any use in or on food for which a listed color additive is deemed to be safe by reason of the proviso to paragraph (4) of subsection (b), the requirement of certification shall be deemed not to be necessary in the interest of public health protection.

(d) Procedure for Issuance, Amendment, or Repeal of Regulations. — The provisions of section 701 (e), (f), and (g) of this Act shall, subject to the provisions of subparagraph (C) of subsection (b)(5) of this section, apply to and in all respects govern proceedings for the issuance, amendment, or repeal of regulations under subsection (b) or (c) of this section (including judicial review of the Secretary's action in such proceedings) and the admissibility of transcripts of the record of such proceedings in other proceedings, except that —

(1) if the proceeding is commenced by the filing of a petition, notice of the proposal made by the petition shall be published in general terms by the Secretary within thirty days after such filing, and the Secretary's order (required by paragraph (1) of section 701(e)) acting upon such proposal shall, in the absence of prior referral (or request for referral) to an advisory committee, be issued within ninety days after the date of such filing, except that the Secretary may (prior to such ninetieth day) by written notice to the petitioner, extend such ninety-day period to such time (not more than one hundred and eighty days after the date of filing of the petition) as the Secretary deems necessary to enable him to study and investigate the petition;

(2) any report, recommendations, underlying data, and reasons certified to the Secretary by an advisory committee appointed pursuant to subparagraph (D) of subsection (b)(5) of this section, shall be made a part of the record of any hearing if relevant and material, subject to the provisions of section 7(c) of the Administrative Procedure Act (5 U.S.C. 1006(c)). The advisory committee shall designate a member to appear and testify at any such hearing with respect to the report and recommendations of such committee upon request of the Secretary, the petitioner, or the officer conducting the hearing, but this shall not preclude any other member of the advisory committee from appearing and testifying at such hearing;

(3) the Secretary's order after public hearing (acting upon objections filed to an order made prior to hearings) shall be subject to the requirements of section 409(f)(2); and

(4) the scope of judicial review of such order shall be in accordance with the fourth sentence of paragraph (2), and with the provisions of paragraph (3), of section 409(g).

(e) Fees. — The admitting to listing and certification of color additives, in accordance with regulations prescribed under this Act, shall be performed only upon payment of such fees, which shall be specified in such regulations, as may be necessary to provide, maintain, and equip an adequate service for such purposes.

(f) Exemptions. — The Secretary shall by regulations (issued without regard to subsection (d)) provide for exempting from the requirements of this section any color additive or any specific type of use thereof, and any article of food, drug or device, or cosmetic bearing or containing such additive, intended solely for investigational use by qualified experts when in his opinion such exemption is consistent with the public health.

Subchapter C — Fees

Part 1 — Freedom of Information Fees

Sec. 731. [379f] Recovery and Retention of Fees for Freedom of Information Requests.

(a) In General. — The Secretary, acting through the Commissioner of Food and Drugs, may —

(1) set and charge fees, in accordance with section 552(a)(4)(A) of title 5, United States Code, to recover all reasonable costs incurred in processing requests made under section 552 of title 5, United States Code, for records obtained or created under this Act or any other Federal law for which responsibility for administration has been delegated to the Commissioner by the Secretary;

(2) retain all fees charged for such requests; and

(3) establish an accounting system and procedures to control receipts and expenditures of fees received under this section.

(b) Use of Fees. — The Secretary and the Commissioner of Food and Drugs shall not use fees received under this section for any purpose other than funding the processing of requests described in subsection (a)(1). Such fees shall not be used to reduce the amount of funds made to carry out other provisions of this Act.

(c) Waiver of Fees. — Nothing in this section shall supersede the right of a requester to obtain a waiver of fees pursuant to section 552(a)(4)(A) of title 5, United States Code.

Part 2 — Fees Relating to Drugs

Sec. 735. [379g] Definitions.*

For purposes of this part:

(1) The term "human drug application" means an application for —

(A) approval of a new drug submitted under section 505(b), or

(B) licensure of a biological product under subsection (a) of section 351 of the Public Health Service Act.

* Ceases to be effective October 1, ~~2017~~ 2022.

Such term does not include a supplement to such an application, does not include an application with respect to whole blood or a blood component for transfusion, does not include an application with respect to a bovine blood product for topical application licensed before September 1, 1992, an allergenic extract product, or an in vitro diagnostic biologic product licensed under section 351 of the Public Health Service Act, does not include an application with respect to a large volume parenteral drug product approved before September 1, 1992, does not include an application for a licensure of a biological product for further manufacturing use only, and does not include an application or supplement submitted by a State or Federal Government entity for a drug that is not distributed commercially. Such term does include an application for licensure, as described in subparagraph (B), of a large volume biological product intended for single dose injection for intravenous use or infusion.

(2) The term "supplement" means a request to the Secretary to approve a change in a human drug application which has been approved.

(3) The term "prescription drug product" means a specific strength or potency of a drug in final dosage form —

(A) for which a human drug application has been approved,

(B) which may be dispensed only under prescription pursuant to section 503(b), and

(C) which is on the list of products described in section 505(j)(7)(A) (not including the discontinued section of such list) or is on a list created and maintained by the Secretary of products approved under human drug applications under section 351 of the Public Health Service Act (not including the discontinued section of such list).

Such term does not include whole blood or a blood component for transfusion, does not include a bovine blood product for topical application licensed before September 1, 1992, an allergenic extract product, or an in vitro diagnostic biologic product licensed under section 351 of the Public Health Service Act. Such term does not include a biological product that is licensed for further manufacturing use only, and does not include a drug that is not distributed commercially and is the subject of an application or supplement submitted by a State or Federal Government entity. Such term does include a large volume biological product intended for single dose injection for intravenous use or infusion.

(4) The term "final dosage form" means, with respect to a prescription drug product, a finished dosage form which is approved for administration to a patient without substantial further manufacturing (such as capsules, tablets, or lypholized products before reconstitution).

(5) The term "prescription drug establishment" means a foreign or domestic place of business which is at one general physical location consisting of one or more buildings all of which are within five miles of each other and at which one or more prescription drug products are manufactured in final dosage form.

(6) The term "process for the review of human drug applications" means the following activities of the Secretary with respect to the review of human drug applications and supplements:

(A) The activities necessary for the review of human drug applications and supplements.

(B) The issuance of action letters which approve human drug applications or which set forth in detail the specific deficiencies in such applications and, where appropriate, the actions necessary to place such applications in condition for approval.

(C) The inspection of prescription drug establishments and other facilities undertaken as part of the Secretary's review of pending human drug applications and supplements.

(D) Activities necessary for the review of applications for licensure of establishments subject to section 351 of the Public Health Service Act and for the release of lots of biologics under such section.

(E) Monitoring of research conducted in connection with the review of human drug applications.

(F) Postmarket safety activities with respect to drugs approved under human drug applications or supplements, including the following activities:

(i) Collecting, developing, and reviewing safety information on approved drugs, including adverse event reports.

(ii) Developing and using improved adverse-event data-collection systems, including information technology systems.

(iii) Developing and using improved analytical tools to assess potential safety problems, including access to external data bases.

(iv) Implementing and enforcing section 505(o) (relating to postapproval studies and clinical trials and labeling changes) and section 505(p) (relating to risk evaluation and mitigation strategies).

(v) Carrying out section 505(k)(5) (relating to adverse event reports and postmarket safety activities).

(7) The term "costs of resources allocated for the process for the review of human drug applications" means the expenses in connection with the process for the review of human drug applications for —

(A) officers and employees of the Food and Drug Administration, contractors of the Food and Drug Administration, advisory committees, and costs related to such officers, employees, and committees and to contracts with such contractors,

(B) management of information, and the acquisition, maintenance, and repair of computer resources,

(C) leasing, maintenance, renovation, and repair of facilities and acquisition, maintenance, and repair of fixtures, furniture, scientific equipment, and other necessary materials and supplies, and

(D) collecting fees under section 736 and accounting for resources allocated for the review of human drug applications and supplements.

(8) The term "adjustment factor" applicable to a fiscal year is the Consumer Price Index for all urban consumers (all items; United States city average) for October of the preceding fiscal year divided by such Index for October 1996.

(9) The term "person" includes an affiliate thereof.

(10) The term "active", with respect to a commercial investigational new drug application, means such an application to which information was submitted during the relevant period.

(11) The term "affiliate" means a business entity that has a relationship with a second business entity if, directly or indirectly —

(A) one business entity controls, or has the power to control, the other business entity; or

(B) a third party controls, or has the power to control, both of the business entities.

Sec. 736. [379h] Authority to Assess and Use Drug Fees.*

(a) Types of Fees. — Beginning in fiscal year ~~2013~~ 2018, the Secretary shall assess and collect fees in accordance with this section as follows:

(1) Human Drug Application ~~and Supplement~~ Fee. —

(A) In General. — Each person that submits, on or after September 1, 1992, a human drug application ~~or a supplement~~ shall be subject to a fee as follows:

(i) A fee established under subsection (c)~~(4)~~(5) for a human drug application for which clinical data (other than bioavailability or bioequivalence studies) with respect to safety or effectiveness are required for approval.

(ii) ~~A fee established under subsection (c)(4) for a human drug application for which clinical data with respect to safety or effectiveness are not required or a supplement for which clinical data (other than bioavailability or bioequivalence studies) with respect to safety or effectiveness are required.~~ A fee established under subsection (c)(5) for a human drug application for which clinical data (other than bioavailability or bioequivalence studies) with respect to safety or effectiveness are not required for approval. Such fee shall be half of the amount of the fee established under clause (i).

(B) Payment. — The fee required by subparagraph (A) shall be due upon submission of the application ~~or supplement~~.

(C) Exception for Previously Filed Application ~~or Supplement~~. — If a human drug application ~~or supplement~~ was submitted by a person that paid the fee for such application ~~or supplement~~, was accepted for filing, and was not approved or was withdrawn (without a waiver), the submission of a human drug application ~~or a supplement~~ for the same product by the same person (or the person's licensee, assignee, or successor) shall not be subject to a fee under subparagraph (A).

* Ceases to be effective October 1, ~~2017~~ 2022.

(D) Refund of Fee if Application Refused for Filing or Withdrawn Before Filing. — The Secretary shall refund 75 percent of the fee paid under subparagraph (B) for any application ~~or supplement~~ which is refused for filing or withdrawn without a waiver before filing.

(E) Fees for Applications Previously Refused for Filing or Withdrawn Before Filing. —A human drug application ~~or supplement~~ that was submitted but was refused for filing, or was withdrawn before being accepted or refused for filing, shall be subject to the full fee under subparagraph (A) upon being resubmitted or filed over protest, unless the fee is waived or reduced under subsection (d).

(F) Exception for Designated Orphan Drug ~~or Indication~~. —A human drug application for a prescription drug product that has been designated as a drug for a rare disease or condition pursuant to section 526 shall not be subject to a fee under subparagraph (A), unless the human drug application includes an indication for other than a rare disease or condition. ~~A supplement proposing to include a new indication for a rare disease or condition in a human drug application shall not be subject to a fee under subparagraph (A), if the drug has been designated pursuant to section 526 as a drug for a rare disease or condition with regard to the indication proposed in such supplement.~~

(G) Refund of Fee if Application Withdrawn. — If an application ~~or supplement~~ is withdrawn after the application ~~or supplement~~ was filed, the Secretary may refund the fee or a portion of the fee if no substantial work was performed on the application ~~or supplement~~ after the application ~~or supplement~~ was filed. The Secretary shall have the sole discretion to refund a fee or a portion of the fee under this subparagraph. A determination by the Secretary concerning a refund under this paragraph shall not be reviewable.

~~**(2) Prescription Drug Establishment Fee.** —~~

~~**(A) In General.** — Except as provided in subparagraphs (B) and (C), each person that —~~

~~(i) is named as the applicant in a human drug application; and~~

~~(ii) after September 1, 1992, had pending before the Secretary a human drug application or supplement, shall be assessed an annual fee established under subsection (c)(54) for each prescription drug establishment listed in its approved human drug application as an establishment that manufactures the prescription drug product named in the application. The annual establishment fee shall be assessed in each fiscal year in which the prescription drug product named in the application is assessed a fee under paragraph (3) unless the prescription drug establishment listed in the application does not engage in the manufacture of the prescription drug product during the fiscal year. The establishment fee shall be due on the later of the first business day on or after October 1 of each fiscal year or the first business day after the enactment of an appropriations Act providing for the collection and obligation of fees for such fiscal year under this section. Each such establishment shall be assessed only one fee per establishment, notwithstanding the number of prescription drug products manufactured at the establishment. In the event an establishment is listed in a human drug application by more than one applicant, the establishment fee for the fiscal year shall be divided equally and assessed among the applicants whose prescription drug products are manufactured by the establishment during the fiscal year and assessed product fees under paragraph (3).~~

~~**(B) Exception.** — If, during the fiscal year, an applicant initiates or causes to be initiated the manufacture of a prescription drug product at an establishment listed in its human drug application —~~

~~(i) that did not manufacture the product in the previous fiscal year; and~~

~~(ii) for which the full establishment fee has been assessed in the fiscal year at a time before manufacture of the prescription drug product was begun;~~

~~the applicant will not be assessed a share of the establishment fee for the fiscal year in which the manufacture of the product began.~~

~~**(C) Special Rules for Positron Emission Tomography Drugs.** —~~

~~**(i) In General.** — Except as provided in clause (ii), each person who is named as the applicant in an approved human drug application for a positron emission tomography drug shall be subject under subparagraph (A) to one-sixth of an annual establishment fee with respect to each such establishment identified in the application as producing positron emission tomography drugs under the approved application.~~

~~**(ii) Exception from Annual Establishment Fee.** — Each person who is named as the applicant in an application described in clause (i) shall not be assessed an annual establishment fee for a fiscal year~~

~~if the person certifies to the Secretary, at a time specified by the Secretary and using procedures specified by the Secretary, that —~~

~~**(I)** the person is a not-for-profit medical center that has only 1 establishment for the production of positron emission tomography drugs; and~~

~~**(II)** at least 95 percent of the total number of doses of each positron emission tomography drug produced by such establishment during such fiscal year will be used within the medical center.~~

~~**(iii) Definition.** — For purposes of this subparagraph, the term "positron emission tomography drug" has the meaning given to the term "compounded positron emission tomography drug" in section 201(ii), except that paragraph (1)(B) of such section shall not apply.~~

~~**(3) Prescription Drug Product Fee.**~~ <u>**(2) Prescription Drug Program Fee.**</u> —

(A) In General. — Except as provided in ~~subparagraph (B)~~ <u>subparagraphs (B) and (C)</u>, each person who is named as the applicant in a human drug application, and who, after September 1, 1992, had pending before the Secretary a human drug application or supplement, shall pay ~~for each such prescription drug product~~ the ~~annual fee~~ <u>annual prescription drug program fee</u> established under subsection ~~(c)(4).~~ <u>(c)(5) for each prescription drug product that is identified in such a human drug application approved as of October 1 of such fiscal year.</u> Such fee shall be due on the later of the first business day on or after October 1 of each fiscal year or the first business day after the enactment of an appropriations Act providing for the collection and obligation of fees for such fiscal year under this section. Such fee shall be paid only once for each product for a fiscal year in which the fee is payable.

(B) ~~**Exception**~~ <u>**Exception for Certain Prescription Drug Products.**</u> — ~~A prescription drug product shall not be assessed a fee~~ <u>A prescription drug program fee shall not be assessed for a prescription drug product</u> under subparagraph (A) if such product is

(i) identified on the list compiled under section 505(j)(7) with a potency described in terms of per 100 mL;

(ii) the same product as another product that —

(I) was approved under an application filed under section 505(b) or 505(j); and

(II) is not in the list of discontinued products compiled under section 505(j)(7);

(iii) the same product as another product that was approved under an abbreviated application filed under section 507 (as in effect on the day before the date of enactment of the Food and Drug Administration Modernization Act of 1997 [November 21, 1997 — Ed.]); or

(iv) the same product as another product that was approved under an abbreviated new drug application pursuant to regulations in effect prior to the implementation of the Drug Price Competition and Patent Term Restoration Act of 1984.

<u>**(C) Limitation.** — A person who is named as the applicant in an approved human drug application shall not be assessed more than 5 prescription drug program fees for a fiscal year for prescription drug products identified in such approved human drug application.</u>

(b) Fee Revenue Amounts. —

(1) In General. — For each of the fiscal years ~~2013 through 2017~~ <u>2018 through 2022</u>, fees under subsection (a) shall, except as provided in subsections (c), (d), (f), and (g), be established to generate a total revenue amount under such subsection that is equal to the sum of —

~~**(A)** $693,099,000; and~~

~~**(B)** the dollar amount equal to the inflation adjustment for fiscal year 2013 (as determined under paragraph (3)(A)); and~~

~~**(C)** the dollar amount equal to the workload adjustment for fiscal year 2013 (as determined under paragraph (3)(B)).~~

~~**(2) Types of Fees.** — Of the total revenue amount determined for a fiscal year under paragraph (1) —~~

~~**(B)** one-third shall be derived from fees under subsection (a)(1) (relating to human drug applications and supplements);~~

~~**(C)** one-third shall be derived from fees under subsection (a)(2) (relating to prescription drug establishments); and~~

~~**(D)** one-third shall be derived from fees under subsection (a)(3) (relating to prescription drug products).~~

~~**(3) Fiscal year 2013 Inflation and workload Adjustments.** — For purposes of paragraph (1), the dollar amount of the inflation and workload adjustments for fiscal year 2013 shall be determined as follows:~~

~~**(A) Inflation Adjustment.** — The inflation adjustment for fiscal year 2013 shall be the sum of—~~

~~**(i)** $652,709,000 multiplied by the result of an inflation adjustment calculation determined using the methodology described in subsection (c)(1)(B); and~~

~~**(ii)** $652,709,000 multiplied by the result of an inflation adjustment calculation determined using the methodology described in subsection (c)(1)(C).~~

~~**(B) Workload Adjustment.** — Subject to subparagraph (C), the workload adjustment for fiscal 2013 shall be—~~

~~**(i)** $652,709,000 plus the amount of the inflation adjustment calculated under subparagraph (A); multiplied by~~

~~**(ii)** the amount (if any) by which a percentage workload adjustment for fiscal year 2013, as determined using the methodology described in subsection (c)(2)(A), would exceed the percentage workload adjustment (as so determined) for fiscal year 2012, if both such adjustment percentages were calculated using the 5-year base period consisting of fiscal years 2003 through 2007.~~

~~**(C) Limitation.** — Under no circumstances shall the adjustment under subparagraph (B) result in fee revenues for fiscal year 2013 that are less than the sum of the amount under paragraph (1)(A) and the amount under paragraph (1)(B).~~

(A) the annual base revenue for the fiscal year (as determined under paragraph (3));

(B) the dollar amount equal to the inflation adjustment for the fiscal year (as determined under subsection (c)(1));

(C) the dollar amount equal to the capacity planning adjustment for the fiscal year (as determined under subsection (c)(2));

(D) the dollar amount equal to the operating reserve adjustment for the fiscal year, if applicable (as determined under subsection (c)(3));

(E) the dollar amount equal to the additional direct cost adjustment for the fiscal year (as determined under subsection (c)(4)); and

(F) additional dollar amounts for each fiscal year as follows:

(i) $20,077,793 for fiscal year 2018.

(ii) $21,317,472 for fiscal year 2019.

(iii) $16,953,329 for fiscal year 2020.

(iv) $5,426,896 for fiscal year 2021.

(v) $2,769,609 for fiscal year 2022.

(2) Types of Fees. — Of the total revenue amount determined for a fiscal year under paragraph (1)—

(A) 20 percent shall be derived from human drug application fees under subsection (a)(1); and

(B) 80 percent shall be derived from prescription drug program fees under subsection (a)(2).

(3) Annual Base Revenue. — For purposes of paragraph (1), the dollar amount of the annual base revenue for a fiscal year shall be—

(A) for fiscal year 2018, $878,590,000; and

(B) for fiscal years 2019 through 2022, the dollar amount of the total revenue amount established under paragraph (1) for the previous fiscal year, not including any adjustments made under subsection (c)(3) or (c)(4).

~~**(c)**~~ **Adjustments.** —

~~**(1)** Inflation Adjustment. — For fiscal year 2014 and subsequent fiscal years, the revenues established in subsection (b) shall be adjusted by the Secretary by notice, published in the Federal Register, for a fiscal year by the amount equal to the sum of—~~

~~**(A)** one;~~

~~(B) the average annual percent change in the cost, per full-time equivalent position of the Food and Drug Administration, of all personnel compensation and benefits paid with respect to such positions for the first 3 years of the preceding 4 fiscal years, multiplied by the proportion of personnel compensation and benefits costs to total costs of the process for the review of human drug applications (as defined in section 735(6)) for the first 3 years of the preceding 4 fiscal years, and~~

~~(C) the average annual percent change that occurred in the Consumer Price Index for urban consumers (Washington-Baltimore, DC-MD-VA-WV; Not Seasonally Adjusted; All Items; Annual Index) for the first 3 years of the preceding 4 years of available data multiplied by the proportion of all costs other than personnel compensation and benefits costs to total costs of the process for the review of human drug applications (as defined in section 735(6)) for the first 3 years of the preceding 4 fiscal years.~~

~~The adjustment made each fiscal year under this paragraph shall be added on a compounded basis to the sum of all adjustments made each fiscal year after fiscal year 2013 under this paragraph.~~

~~(2) Workload Adjustment. — For fiscal year 2014 and subsequent fiscal years, after the fee revenues established in subsection (b) are adjusted for a fiscal year for inflation in accordance with paragraph (1), the fee revenues shall be adjusted further for such fiscal year to reflect changes in the workload of the Secretary for the process for the review of human drug applications. With respect to such adjustment:~~

~~(A) The adjustment shall be determined by the Secretary based on a weighted average of the change in the total number of human drug applications (adjusted for changes in review activities, as described in the notice that the Secretary is required to publish in the Federal Register under this subparagraph), efficacy supplements, and manufacturing supplements submitted to the Secretary, and the change in the total number of active commercial investigational new drug applications (adjusted for changes in review activities, as so described) during the most recent 12-month period for which data on such submissions is available. The Secretary shall publish in the Federal Register the fee revenues and fees resulting from the adjustment and the supporting methodologies.~~

~~(B) Under no circumstances shall the adjustment result in fee revenues for a fiscal year that are less than the sum of the amount under subsection (b)(1)(A) and the amount under subsection (b)(1)(B), as adjusted for inflation under paragraph (1).~~

~~(C) The Secretary shall contract with an independent accounting or consulting firm to periodically review the adequacy of the adjustment and publish the results of those reviews. The first review shall be conducted and published by the end of fiscal year 2013 (to examine the performance of the adjustment since fiscal year 2009), and the second review shall be conducted and published by the end of fiscal year 2015 (to examine the continued performance of the adjustment). The reports shall evaluate whether the adjustment reasonably represents actual changes in workload volume and complexity and present options to discontinue, retain, or modify any elements of the adjustment. The reports shall be published for public comment. After review of the reports and receipt of public comments, the Secretary shall, if warranted, adopt appropriate changes to the methodology. If the Secretary adopts changes to the methodology based on the first report, the changes shall be effective for the first fiscal year for which fees are set after the Secretary adopts such changes and each subsequent fiscal year.~~

~~(3) Final Year Adjustment. — For fiscal year 2017, the Secretary may, in addition to adjustments under this paragraph and paragraphs (1) and (2), further increase the fee revenues and fees established in subsection (b) if such an adjustment is necessary to provide for not more than 3 months of operating reserves of carryover user fees for the process for the review of human drug applications for the first 3 months of fiscal year 2018. If such an adjustment is necessary, the rationale for the amount of the increase shall be contained in the annual notice establishing fee revenues and fees for fiscal year 2017. If the Secretary has carryover balances for such process in excess of 3 months of such operating reserves, the adjustment under this paragraph shall not be made.~~

~~(4) Annual Fee Setting. — The Secretary shall, not later than 60 days before the start of each fiscal year that begins after September 30, 2012, establish, for the next fiscal year, application, product, and establishment fees under subsection (a), based on the revenue amounts established under subsection (b) and the adjustments provided under this subsection.~~

~~(5) Limit. — The total amount of fees charged, as adjusted under this subsection, for a fiscal year may not exceed the total costs for such fiscal year for the resources allocated for the process for the review of human drug applications.~~

(c) Adjustments; Annual Fee Setting. —

(1) Inflation Adjustment. —

(A) In General. — For purposes of subsection (b)(1)(B), the dollar amount of the inflation adjustment to the annual base revenue for each fiscal year shall be equal to the product of—

(i) such annual base revenue for the fiscal year under subsection (b)(1)(A); and

(ii) the inflation adjustment percentage under subparagraph (B).

(B) Inflation Adjustment Percentage. — The inflation adjustment percentage under this subparagraph for a fiscal year is equal to the sum of—

(i) the average annual percent change in the cost, per full-time equivalent position of the Food and Drug Administration, of all personnel compensation and benefits paid with respect to such positions for the first 3 years of the preceding 4 fiscal years, multiplied by the proportion of personnel compensation and benefits costs to total costs of the process for the review of human drug applications (as defined in section 735(6)) for the first 3 years of the preceding 4 fiscal years; and

(ii) the average annual percent change that occurred in the Consumer Price Index for urban consumers (Washington-Baltimore, DC-MD-VA-WV; Not Seasonally Adjusted; All items; Annual Index) for the first 3 years of the preceding 4 years of available data multiplied by the proportion of all costs other than personnel compensation and benefits costs to total costs of the process for the review of human drug applications (as defined in section 735(6)) for the first 3 years of the preceding 4 fiscal years.

(2) Capacity Planning Adjustment. —

(A) In General. — For each fiscal year, after the annual base revenue established in subsection (b)(1)(A) is adjusted for inflation in accordance with paragraph (1), such revenue shall be adjusted further for such fiscal year, in accordance with this paragraph, to reflect changes in the resource capacity needs of the Secretary for the process for the review of human drug applications.

(B) Interim Methodology. —

(i) In General. — Until the capacity planning methodology described in subparagraph (C) is effective, the adjustment under this paragraph for a fiscal year shall be based on the product of—

(I) the annual base revenue for such year, as adjusted for inflation under paragraph (1); and

(II) the adjustment percentage under clause (ii).

(ii) Adjustment Percentage. — The adjustment percentage under this clause for a fiscal year is the weighted change in the 3-year average ending in the most recent year for which data are available, over the 3-year average ending in the previous year, for—

(I) the total number of human drug applications, efficacy supplements, and manufacturing supplements submitted to the Secretary;

(II) the total number of active commercial investigational new drug applications; and

(III) the total number of formal meetings scheduled by the Secretary, and written responses issued by the Secretary in lieu of such formal meetings, as identified in section I.H of the letters described in section 101(b) of the Prescription Drug User Fee Amendments of 2017.

(C) Capacity Planning Methodology. —

(i) Development; Evaluation and Report. — The Secretary shall obtain, through a contract with an independent accounting or consulting firm, a report evaluating options and recommendations for a new methodology to accurately assess changes in the resource and capacity needs of the process for the review of human drug applications. The capacity planning methodological options and recommendations presented in such report shall utilize and be informed by personnel time reporting data as an input. The report shall be published for public comment no later than the end of fiscal year 2020.

(ii) Establishment and Implementation. — After review of the report described in clause (i) and any public comments thereon, the Secretary shall establish a capacity planning methodology for purposes of this paragraph, which shall—

(I) replace the interim methodology under subparagraph (B);

(II) incorporate such approaches and attributes as the Secretary determines appropriate; and

(III) be effective beginning with the first fiscal year for which fees are set after such capacity planning methodology is established.

(D) Limitation. — Under no circumstances shall an adjustment under this paragraph result in fee revenue for a fiscal year that is less than the sum of the amounts under subsections (b)(1)(A) (the annual base revenue for the fiscal year) and (b)(1)(B) (the dollar amount of the inflation adjustment for the fiscal year).

(E) Publication in Federal Register. — The Secretary shall publish in the Federal Register notice under paragraph (5) of the fee revenue and fees resulting from the adjustment and the methodologies under this paragraph.

(3) Operating Reserve Adjustment. —

(A) Increase. — For fiscal year 2018 and subsequent fiscal years, the Secretary may, in addition to adjustments under paragraphs (1) and (2), further increase the fee revenue and fees if such an adjustment is necessary to provide for not more than 14 weeks of operating reserves of carryover user fees for the process for the review of human drug applications.

(B) Decrease. — If the Secretary has carryover balances for such process in excess of 14 weeks of such operating reserves, the Secretary shall decrease such fee revenue and fees to provide for not more than 14 weeks of such operating reserves.

(C) Notice of Rationale. — If an adjustment under subparagraph (A) or (B) is made, the rationale for the amount of the increase or decrease (as applicable) in fee revenue and fees shall be contained in the annual Federal Register notice under paragraph (5) establishing fee revenue and fees for the fiscal year involved.

(4) Additional Direct Cost Adjustment. —

(A) In General. — The Secretary shall, in addition to adjustments under paragraphs (1), (2), and (3), further increase the fee revenue and fees—

(i) for fiscal year 2018, by $8,730,000; and

(ii) for fiscal year 2019 and subsequent fiscal years, by the amount determined under subparagraph (B).

(B) Amount. — The amount determined under this subparagraph is—

(i) $8,730,000, multiplied by (ii) the Consumer Price Index for urban consumers (Washington-Baltimore, DC-MD-VA-WV; Not Seasonally Adjusted; All Items; Annual Index) for the most recent year of available data, divided by such Index for 2016.

(5) Annual Fee Setting. — The Secretary shall, not later than 60 days before the start of each fiscal year that begins after September 30, 2017—

(A) establish, for each such fiscal year, human drug application fees and prescription drug program fees under subsection (a), based on the revenue amounts established under subsection (b) and the adjustments provided under this subsection; and

(B) publish such fee revenue and fees in the Federal Register.

(6) Limit. — The total amount of fees charged, as adjusted under this subsection, for a fiscal year may not exceed the total costs for such fiscal year for the resources allocated for the process for the review of human drug applications.

(d) Fee Waiver or Reduction. —

(1) In general. — The Secretary shall grant to a person who is named as the applicant in a human drug application a waiver from or a reduction of one or more fees assessed to that person under subsection (a) where the Secretary finds that —

(A) such waiver or reduction is necessary to protect the public health,

(B) the assessment of the fee would present a significant barrier to innovation because of limited resources available to such person or other circumstances~~,~~ or,

~~**(C)** the fees to be paid by such person will exceed the anticipated present and future costs incurred by the Secretary in conducting the process for the review of human drug applications for such person, or~~

~~**(D)**~~ **(C)** the applicant involved is a small business submitting its first human drug application to the Secretary for review.

(2) Considerations. — In determining whether to grant a waiver or reduction of a fee under paragraph (1), the Secretary shall consider only the circumstances and assets of the applicant involved and any affiliate of the applicant.

~~**(3) Use of Standard Costs.** — In making the finding in paragraph (1)(C), the Secretary may use standard costs.~~

~~(4)~~ (3) **Rules Relating to Small Businesses.** —

(A) Definition. — In paragraph (1)~~(D)~~(C), the term "small business" means an entity that has fewer than 500 employees, including employees of affiliates, and that does not have a drug product that has been approved under a human drug application and introduced or delivered for introduction into interstate commerce.

(B) Waiver of Application Fee. — The Secretary shall waive under paragraph (1)~~(D)~~(C) the application fee for the first human drug application that a small business or its affiliate submits to the Secretary for review. After a small business or its affiliate is granted such a waiver, the small business or its affiliate shall pay ~~(i)~~ application fees for all subsequent human drug applications submitted to the Secretary for review in the same manner as an entity that does not qualify as a small business~~; and~~.

~~(ii) all supplement fees for all supplements to human drug applications submitted to the Secretary for review in the same manner as an entity that does not qualify as a small business.~~

(e) Effect of Failure to Pay Fees. — A human drug application or supplement submitted by a person subject to fees under subsection (a) shall be considered incomplete and shall not be accepted for filing by the Secretary until ~~all~~ all such fees owed by such person have been paid.

(f) Limitations. —

(1) In General. — Fees under subsection (a) shall be refunded for a fiscal year beginning after fiscal year 1997 unless appropriations for salaries and expenses of the Food and Drug Administration for such fiscal year (excluding the amount of fees appropriated for such fiscal year) are equal to or greater than the amount of appropriations for the salaries and expenses of the Food and Drug Administration for the fiscal year 1997 (excluding the amount of fees appropriated for such fiscal year) multiplied by the adjustment factor applicable to the fiscal year involved.

(2) Authority. — If the Secretary does not assess fees under subsection (a) during any portion of a fiscal year because of paragraph (1) and if at a later date in such fiscal year the Secretary may assess such fees, the Secretary may assess and collect such fees, without any modification in the rate, for human drug applications and ~~supplements, prescription drug establishments, and prescription drug products~~ prescription drug program fees at any time in such fiscal year notwithstanding the provisions of subsection (a) relating to the date fees are to be paid.

(3) Limitation. — Beginning on October 1, 2023, the authorities under section 735(7)(C) shall include only expenditures for leasing and necessary scientific equipment.

(g) Crediting and Availability of Fees. —

(1) In General. — Subject to paragraph (2)(C), fees authorized under subsection (a) shall be collected and available for obligation only to the extent and in the amount provided in advance in appropriations Acts. Such fees are authorized to remain available until expended. Such sums as may be necessary may be transferred from the Food and Drug Administration salaries and expenses appropriation account without fiscal year limitation to such appropriation account for salaries and expenses with such fiscal year limitation. The sums transferred shall be available solely for the process for the review of human drug applications.

(2) Collections and Appropriation Acts. —

(A) In General. — The fees authorized by this section —

(i) subject to subparagraph (C), shall be collected and available in each fiscal year in an amount not to exceed the amount specified in appropriation Acts, or otherwise made available for obligation, for such fiscal year, and

(ii) shall be available to defray increases in the costs of the resources allocated for the process for the review of human drug applications (including increases in such costs for an additional number of full-time equivalent positions in the Department of Health and Human Services to be engaged in such process) over such costs, excluding costs paid from fees collected under this section, for fiscal year 1997 multiplied by the adjustment factor.

(B) Compliance. — The Secretary shall be considered to have met the requirements of subparagraph (A)

(ii) in any fiscal year if the costs funded by appropriations and allocated for the process for the review of human drug applications —

(i) are not more than 3 percent below the level specified in subparagraph (A)(ii); or

(ii) —

(I) are more than 3 percent below the level specified in subparagraph (A)(ii), and fees assessed for the fiscal year following the subsequent fiscal year are decreased by the amount in excess of 3 percent by which such costs fell below the level specified in such subparagraph; and

(II) such costs are not more than 5 percent below the level specified in such subparagraph.

(C) Provision for Early Payments. — Payment of fees authorized under this section for a fiscal year, prior to the due date for such fees, may be accepted by the Secretary in accordance with authority provided in advance in a prior year appropriations Act.

(3) Authorization of Appropriations. — For each of the fiscal years ~~2013 through 2017~~ 2018 through 2022, there is authorized to be appropriated for fees under this section an amount equal to the total revenue amount determined under subsection (b) for the fiscal year, as adjusted or otherwise affected under subsection (c) ~~and paragraph (4) of this subsection~~.

~~**(4) Offset.** — If the sum of the cumulative amount of fees collected under this section for the fiscal years 2013 through 2015 and the amount of fees estimated to be collected under this section for fiscal year 2016 exceeds the cumulative amount appropriated under paragraph (3) for the fiscal years 2013 through 2016, the excess shall be credited to the appropriation account of the Food and Drug Administration as provided in paragraph (1), and shall be subtracted from the amount of fees that would otherwise be authorized to be collected under this section pursuant to appropriation Acts for fiscal year 2017.~~

(h) Collection of Unpaid Fees. — In any case where the Secretary does not receive payment of a fee assessed under subsection (a) within 30 days after it is due, such fee shall be treated as a claim of the United States Government subject to subchapter II of chapter 37 of title 31, United States Code.

(i) Written Requests for Waivers, Reductions, and Refunds. — To qualify for consideration for a waiver or reduction under subsection (d), or for a refund of any fee collected in accordance with subsection (a), a person shall submit to the Secretary a written request for such waiver, reduction, or refund not later than 180 days after such fee is due.

(j) Construction. — This section may not be construed to require that the number of full-time equivalent positions in the Department of Health and Human Services, for officers, employers, and advisory committees not engaged in the process of the review of human drug applications, be reduced to offset the number of officers, employees, and advisory committees so engaged.

(k) Orphan Drugs. —

(1) Exemption. — A drug designated under section 526 for a rare disease or condition and approved under section 505 or under section 351 of the Public Health Service Act shall be exempt from ~~product and establishment~~ prescription drug program fees under this section, if the drug meets all of the following conditions:

(A) The drug meets the public health requirements contained in this Act as such requirements are applied to requests for waivers for ~~product and establishment~~ prescription drug program fees.

(B) The drug is owned or licensed and is marketed by a company that had less than $50,000,000 in gross worldwide revenue during the previous year.

(2) Evidence of Qualification. — An exemption under paragraph (1) applies with respect to a drug only if the applicant involved submits a certification that its gross annual revenues did not exceed $50,000,000 for the preceding 12 months before the exemption was requested.

Sec. 736A. [379h-1] Fees Relating to Advisory Review of Prescription Drug Television Advertising.*

(a) Types of Direct-to-Consumer Television Advertisement Review Fees. — Beginning in fiscal year 2008, the Secretary shall assess and collect fees in accordance with this section as follows:

(1) Advisory Review Fee. —

(A) In General. — With respect to a proposed direct-to-consumer television advertisement (referred to in this section as a "DTC advertisement"), each person that on or after October 1, 2007, submits such an advertisement for advisory review by the Secretary prior to its initial public dissemination shall, except as provided in subparagraph (B), be subject to a fee established under subsection (c)(3).

* Ceasesd to be effective October 1, 2012.

(B) Exception for Required Submissions. — A DTC advertisement that is required to be submitted to the Secretary prior to initial public dissemination is not subject to a fee under subparagraph (A) unless the sponsor designates the submission as a submission for advisory review.

(C) Notice to Secretary of Number of Advertisements. — Not later than June 1 of each fiscal year, the Secretary shall publish a notice in the Federal Register requesting any person to notify the Secretary within 30 days of the number of DTC advertisements the person intends to submit for advisory review in the next fiscal year. Notwithstanding the preceding sentence, for fiscal year 2008, the Secretary shall publish such a notice in the Federal Register not later than 30 days after the date of the enactment of the Food and Drug Administration Amendments Act of 2007.

(D) Payment. —

(i) In General. — The fee required by subparagraph (A) (referred to in this section as "an advisory review fee") shall be due not later than October 1 of the fiscal year in which the DTC advertisement involved is intended to be submitted for advisory review, subject to subparagraph (F)(i). Notwithstanding the preceding sentence, the advisory review fee for any DTC advertisement that is intended to be submitted for advisory review during fiscal year 2008 shall be due not later than 120 days after the date of the enactment of the Food and Drug Administration Amendments of 2007 or an earlier date as specified by the Secretary.

(ii) Effect of Submission. — Notification of the Secretary under subparagraph (C) of the number of DTC advertisements a person intends to submit for advisory review is a legally binding commitment by that person to pay the annual advisory review fee for that number of submissions on or before October 1 of the fiscal year in which the advertisement is intended to be submitted. Notwithstanding the preceding sentence, the commitment shall be a legally binding commitment by that person to pay the annual advisory review fee for that number of submissions for fiscal year 2008 by the date specified in clause (i).

(iii) Notice Regarding Carryover Submissions. — In making a notification under subparagraph (C), the person involved shall in addition notify the Secretary if under subparagraph (F)(i) the person intends to submit a DTC advertisement for which the advisory review fee has already been paid. If the person does not so notify the Secretary, each DTC advertisement submitted by the person for advisory review in the fiscal year involved shall be subject to the advisory review fee.

(E) Modification of Advisory Review Fee. —

(i) Late Payment. — If a person has submitted a notification under subparagraph (C) with respect to a fiscal year and has not paid all advisory review fees due under subparagraph (D) not later than November 1 of such fiscal year (or, in the case of such a notification submitted with respect to fiscal year 2008, not later than 150 days after the date of the enactment of the Food and Drug Administration Amendments Act of 2007 or an earlier date specified by the Secretary), the fees shall be regarded as late and an increase in the amount of fees applies in accordance with this clause, notwithstanding any other provision of this section. For such person, all advisory review fees for such fiscal year shall be due and payable 20 days before any direct-to-consumer advertisement is submitted to the Secretary foradvisory review, and each such fee shall be equal to 150 percent of the fee that otherwise would have applied pursuant to subsection (c)(3).

(ii) Exceeding Identified Number of Submissions. — If a person submits a number of DTC advertisements for advisory review in a fiscal year that exceeds the number identified by the person under subparagraph (C), an increase in the amount of fees applies under this clause for each submission in excess of such number, notwithstanding any other provision of this section. For each such DTC advertisement, the advisory review fee shall be due and payable 20 days before the advertisement is submitted to the Secretary, and the fee shall be equal to 150 percent of the fee that otherwise would have applied pursuant to subsection (c)(3).

(F) Limits. —

(i) Submissions. — For each advisory review fee paid by a person for a fiscal year, the person is entitled to acceptance for advisory review by the Secretary of one DTC advertisement and acceptance of one resubmission for advisory review of the same advertisement. The advertisement shall be submitted for review in the fiscal year for which the fee was assessed, except that a person may carry over not more than one paid advisory review submission to the next fiscal year. Resubmissions may be submitted without regard to the fiscal year of the initial advisory review submission.

(ii) No Refunds. — Except as provided by subsections (d)(4) and (f), fees paid under this section shall not be refunded.

(iii) No Waivers, Exemptions, or Reductions. — The Secretary shall not grant a waiver, exemption, or reduction of any fees due or payable under this section.

(iv) Right to Advisory Review Not Transferable. — The right to an advisory review under this paragraph is not transferable, except to a successor in interest.

(2) Operating Reserve Fee. —

(A) In General. — Each person that on or after October 1, 2007, is assessed an advisory review fee under paragraph (1) shall be subject to fee established under subsection (d)(2) (referred to in this section as an "operating reserve fee") for the first fiscal year in which an advisory review fee is assessed to such person. The person is not subject to an operating reserve fee for any other fiscal year.

(B) Payment. — Except as provided in subparagraph (C), the operating reserve fee shall be due no later than—

(i) October 1 of the first fiscal year in which the person is required to pay an advisory review fee under paragraph (1); or

(ii) for fiscal year 2008, 120 days after the date of the enactment of the Food and Drug Administration AmendmentsAct of 2007 or an earlier date specified by the Secretary.

(C) Late Notice of Submission. — If, in the first fiscal year of a person's participation in the program under this section, that person submits any DTC advertisements for advisory review that are in excess of the number identified by that person in response to the Federal Register notice described in subsection (a)(1)(C), that person shall pay an operating reserve fee for each of those advisory reviews equal to the advisory review fee for each submission established under paragraph (1)(E)(ii). Fees required by this subparagraph shall be in addition to any fees required by subparagraph (A). Fees under this subparagraph shall be due 20 days before any DTC advertisement is submitted by such person to the Secretary for advisory review.

(D) Late Payment. —

(i) In General. — Notwithstanding subparagraph (B), and subject to clause (ii), an operating reserve fee shall be regarded as late if the person required to pay the fee has not paid the complete operating reserve fee by—

(I) for fiscal year 2008, 150 days after the date of the enactment of the Food and Drug Administration Amendments Act of 2007 or an earlier date specified by the Secretary; or

(II) in any subsequent year, November 1.

(ii) Complete Payment. — The complete operating reserve fee shall be due and payable 20 days before any DTC advertisement is submitted by such person to the Secretary for advisory review.

(iii) Amount. — Notwithstanding any other provision of this section, an operating reserve fee that is regarded as late under this subparagraph shall be equal to 150 percent of the operating reserve fee that otherwise would have applied pursuant to subsection (d).

(b) Advisory Review Fee Revenue Amounts. —

Fees under subsection (a)(1) shall be established to generate revenue amounts of $6,250,000 for each of fiscal years 2008 through 2012, as adjusted pursuant to subsections (c) and (g)(4).

(c) Adjustments. —

(1) Inflation Adjustment. — Beginning with fiscal year 2009, the revenues established in subsection (b) shall be adjusted by the Secretary by notice, published in the Federal Register, for a fiscal year to reflect the greater of—

(A) the total percentage change that occurred in the Consumer Price Index for all urban consumers (all items; U.S. city average), for the 12-month period ending June 30 preceding the fiscal year for which fees are being established;

(B) the total percentage change for the previous fiscal year in basic pay under the General Schedule in accordance with section 5332 of title 5, United States Code, as adjusted by any locality-based comparability payment pursuant to section 5304 of such title for Federal employees stationed in the District of Columbia; or

(C) the average annual change in the cost, per fulltime equivalent position of the Food and Drug Administration, of all personnel compensation and benefits paid with respect to such positions for the first 5 fiscal years of the previous 6 fiscal years.

The adjustment made each fiscal year by this subsection shall be added on a compounded basis to the sum of all adjustments made each fiscal year after fiscal year 2008 under this subsection.

(2) Workload Adjustment. — Beginning with fiscal year 2009, after the fee revenues established in subsection (b) are adjusted for a fiscal year for inflation in accordance with paragraph (1), the fee revenues shall be adjusted further for such fiscal year to reflect changes in the workload of the Secretary with respect to the submission of DTC advertisements for advisory review prior to initial dissemination. With respect to such adjustment:

(A) The adjustment shall be determined by the Secretary based upon the number of DTC advertisements identified pursuant to subsection (a)(1)(C) for the upcoming fiscal year, excluding allowable previously paid carry over submissions. The adjustment shall be determined by multiplying the number of such advertisements projected for that fiscal year that exceeds 150 by $27,600 (adjusted each year beginning with fiscal year 2009 for inflation in accordance with paragraph (1)). The Secretary shall publish in the Federal Register the fee revenues and fees resulting from the adjustment and the supporting methodologies.

(B) Under no circumstances shall the adjustment result in fee revenues for a fiscal year that are less than the fee revenues established for the prior fiscal year.

(3) Annual Fee Setting for Advisory Review —

(A) In General. — Not later than August 1 of each fiscal year (or, with respect to fiscal year 2008, not later than 90 days after the date of the enactment of the Food and Drug Administration Amendments Act of 2007), the Secretary shall establish for the next fiscal year the DTC advertisement advisory review fee under subsection (a)(1), based on the revenue amounts established under subsection (b), the adjustments provided under paragraphs (1) and (2), and the number of DTC advertisements identified pursuant to subsection (a)(1)(C), excluding allowable previously- paid carry over submissions. The annual advisory review fee shall be established by dividing the fee revenue for a fiscal year (as adjusted pursuant to this subsection) by the number of DTC advertisements so identified, excluding allowable previously-paid carry over submissions under subsection (a)(1)(F)(i).

(B) Fiscal Year 2008 Fee Limit. — Notwithstanding subsection (b) and the adjustments pursuant to this subsection, the fee established under subparagraph (A) for fiscal year 2008 may not be more than $83,000 per submission for advisory review.

(C) Annual Fee Limit. — Notwithstanding subsection (b) and the adjustments pursuant to this subsection, the fee established under subparagraph (A) for a fiscal year after fiscal year 2008 may not be more than 50 percent more than the fee established for the prior fiscal year.

(D) Limit. — The total amount of fees obligated for a fiscal year may not exceed the total costs for such fiscal year for the resources allocated for the process for the advisory review of prescription drug advertising.

(d) Operating Reserves. —

(1) In General. — The Secretary shall establish in the Food and Drug Administration salaries and expenses appropriation account without fiscal year limitation a Direct-to-Consumer Advisory Review Operating Reserve, of at least $6,250,000 in fiscal year 2008, to continue the program under this section in the event the fees collected in any subsequent fiscal year pursuant to subsection (a)(1) do not generate the fee revenue amount established for that fiscal year.

(2) Fee Setting. — The Secretary shall establish the operating reserve fee under subsection (a)(2)(A) for each person required to pay the fee by multiplying the number of DTC advertisements identified by that person pursuant to subsection (a)(1)(C) by the advisory review fee established pursuant to subsection (c)(3) for that fiscal year, except that in no case shall the operating reserve fee assessed be less than the operating reserve fee assessed if the person had first participated in the program under this section in fiscal year 2008.

(3) Use of Operating Reserve. — The Secretary may use funds from the reserves only to the extent necessary in any fiscal year to make up the difference between the fee revenue amount established for that fiscal year under subsections (b) and (c) and the amount of fees actually collected for that fiscal year pursuant to subsection (a)(1), or to pay costs of ending the program under this section if it is terminated pursuant to subsection (f) or not reauthorized beyond fiscal year 2012.

(4) Refund of Operating Reserves. — Within 120 days after the end of fiscal year 2012, or if the program under this section ends early pursuant to subsection (f), the Secretary, after setting aside sufficient operating reserve amounts to terminate the program under this section, shall refund all amounts remaining in the operating reserve on a pro rata basis to each person that paid an operating reserve fee assessment. In no event shall the refund to any person exceed the total amount of operating reserve fees paid by such person pursuant to subsection (a)(2).

(e) Effect of Failure to Pay Fees. — Notwithstanding any other requirement, a submission for advisory review of a DTC advertisement submitted by a person subject to fees under subsection (a) shall be considered incomplete and shall not be accepted for review by the Secretary until all fees owed by such person under this section have been paid.

(f) Effect of Inadequate Funding of Program. —

(1) Initial Funding. — If on November 1, 2007, or 120 days after the date of the enactment of the Food and Drug Administration Amendments Act of 2007, whichever is later, the Secretary has not received at least $11,250,000 in advisory review fees and operating reserve fees combined, the program under this section shall not commence and all collected fees shall be refunded.

(2) Later Fiscal Years. — Beginning in fiscal year 2009, if, on November 1 of the fiscal year, the combination of the operating reserves, annual fee revenues from that fiscal year, and unobligated fee revenues from prior fiscal years falls below $9,000,000, adjusted for inflation (as described in subsection (c)(1)), the program under this section shall terminate, and the Secretary shall notify all participants, retain any money from the unused advisory review fees and the operating reserves needed to terminate the program, and refund the remainder of the unused fees and operating reserves. To the extent required to terminate the program, the Secretary shall first use unobligated advisory review fee revenues from prior fiscal years, then the operating reserves, and finally, unused advisory review fees from the relevant fiscal year.

(g) Crediting and Availability of Fees. —

(1) In General. — Fees authorized under subsection (a) shall be collected and available for obligation only to the extent and in the amount provided in advance in appropriations Acts. Such fees are authorized to remain available until expended. Such sums as may be necessary may be transferred from the Food and Drug Administration salaries and expenses appropriation account without fiscal year limitation to such appropriation account for salaries and expenses with such fiscal year limitation. The sums transferred shall be available solely for the process for the advisory review of prescription drug advertising.

(2) Collections and Appropriation Acts. —

(A) In General. — The fees authorized by this section —

(i) shall be retained in each fiscal year in an amount not to exceed the amount specified in appropriation Acts, or otherwise made available for obligation for such fiscal year; and

(ii) shall be available for obligation only if the amounts appropriated as budget authority for such fiscal year are sufficient to support a number of fulltime equivalent review employees that is not fewer than the number of such employees supported in fiscal year 2007.

(B) Review Employees. — For purposes of subparagraph (A)(ii), the term "full-time equivalent review employees" means the total combined number of full-time equivalent employees in—

(i) the Center for Drug Evaluation and Research, Division of Drug Marketing, Advertising, and Communications, Food and Drug Administration; and

(ii) the Center for Biologics Evaluation and Research, Advertising and Promotional Labeling Branch, Food and Drug Administration.

(3) Authorization of Appropriations. — For each of the fiscal years 2008 through 2012, there is authorized to be appropriated for fees under this section an amount equal to the total revenue amount determined under subsection (b) for the fiscal year, as adjusted pursuant to subsection (c) and paragraph (4) of this subsection, plus amounts collected for the reserve fund under subsection (d).

(4) Offset. — Any amount of fees collected for a fiscal year under this section that exceeds the amount of fees specified in appropriation Acts for such fiscal year shall be credited to the appropriation account of the Food and Drug Administration as provided in paragraph (1), and shall be subtracted from the amount of fees that would otherwise be collected under this section pursuant to appropriation Acts for a subsequent fiscal year.

(h) Definitions. — For purposes of this section:

(1) The term "advisory review" means reviewing and providing advisory comments on DTC advertisements regarding compliance of a proposed advertisement with the requirements of this Act prior to its initial public dissemination.

(2) The term "advisory review fee" has the meaning indicated for such term in subsection (a)(1)(D).

(3) The term "carry over submission" means a submission for an advisory review for which a fee was paid in one fiscal year that is submitted for review in the following fiscal year.

(4) The term "direct-to-consumer television advertisement" means an advertisement for a prescription drug product (as defined in section 735(3)) intended to be displayed on any television channel for less than 3 minutes.

(5) The term "DTC advertisement" has the meaning indicated for such term in subsection (a)(1)(A).

(6) The term "operating reserve fee" has the meaning indicated for such term in subsection (a)(2)(A).

(7) The term "person" includes an individual, partnership, corporation, and association, and any affiliate thereof or successor in interest.

(8) The term "process for the advisory review of prescription drug advertising" means the activities necessary to review and provide advisory comments on DTC advertisements prior to public dissemination and, to the extent the Secretary has additional staff resources available under the program under this section that are not necessary for the advisory review of DTC advertisements, the activities necessary to review and provide advisory comments on other proposed advertisements and promotional material prior to public dissemination.

(9) The term "resources allocated for the process for the advisory review of prescription drug advertising" means the expenses incurred in connection with the process for the advisory review of prescription drug advertising for —

(A) officers and employees of the Food and Drug Administration, contractors of the Food and Drug Administration, advisory committees, and costs related to such officers, employees, and committees, and to contracts with such contractors;

(B) management of information, and the acquisition, maintenance, and repair of computer resources;

(C) leasing, maintenance, renovation, and repair of facilities and acquisition, maintenance, and repair of fixtures, furniture, scientific equipment, and other necessary materials and supplies;

(D) collection of fees under this section and accounting for resources allocated for the advisory review of prescription drug advertising; and

(E) terminating the program under this section pursuant to subsection (f)(2) if that becomes necessary.

(10) The term "resubmission" means a subsequent submission for advisory review of a direct-to-consumer television advertisement that has been revised in response to the Secretary's comments on an original submission. A resubmission may not introduce significant new concepts or creative themes into the television advertisement.

(11) The term "submission for advisory review" means an original submission of a direct-to-consumer television advertisement for which the sponsor voluntarily requests advisory comments before the advertisement is publicly disseminated.

Sec. 736B. [379h-2] Reauthorization; Reporting Requirements.[*]

(a) Performance Report. —

(1) In General. — Beginning with fiscal year ~~2013~~ 2018, not later than 120 days after the end of each fiscal year for which fees are collected under this part, the Secretary shall prepare and submit to the Committee on Energy and Commerce of the House of Representatives and the Committee on Health, Education, Labor, and Pensions of the Senate a report concerning —

(A) the progress of the Food and Drug Administration in achieving the goals identified in the letters described in section 101(b) of the Prescription Drug User Fee Amendments of ~~2012~~ 2017 during such fiscal year and the future plans of the Food and Drug Administration for meeting the goals, including the status of the independent assessment described in such letters; and

* Ceases to be effective January 31, 2018.

(B) the progress of the Center for Drug Evaluation and Research and the Center for Biologics Evaluation and Research in achieving the goals, and future plans for meeting the goals, including, for each review division —

(i) the number of original standard new drug applications and biologics license applications filed per fiscal year for each review division;

(ii) the number of original priority new drug applications and biologics license applications filed per fiscal year for each review division;

(iii) the number of standard efficacy supplements filed per fiscal year for each review division;

(iv) the number of priority efficacy supplements filed per fiscal year for each review division;

(v) the number of applications filed for review under accelerated approval per fiscal year for each review division;

(vi) the number of applications filed for review as fast track products per fiscal year for each review division;

(vii) the number of applications filed for orphan-designated products per fiscal year for each review division; and

(viii) the number of breakthrough designations for a fiscal year for each review division.

(2) Inclusion. — The report under this subsection for a fiscal year shall include information on all previous cohorts for which the Secretary has not given a complete response on all human drug applications and supplements in the cohort.

(3) Real Time Reporting. —

(A) In General. — Not later than 30 calendar days after the end of the second quarter of fiscal year 2018, and not later than 30 calendar days after the end of each quarter of each fiscal year thereafter, the Secretary shall post the data described in subparagraph (B) on the internet website of the Food and Drug Administration for such quarter and on a cumulative basis for such fiscal year, and may remove duplicative data from the annual performance report under this subsection.

(B) Data. — The Secretary shall post the following data in accordance with subparagraph (A):

(i) The number and titles of draft and final guidance on topics related to the process for the review of human drug applications, and whether such guidances were issued as required by statute or pursuant to a commitment under the letters described in section 101(b) of the Prescription Drug User Fee Amendments of 2017.

(ii) The number and titles of public meetings held on topics related to the process for the review of human drug applications, and whether such meetings were required by statute or pursuant to a commitment under the letters described in section 101(b) of the Prescription Drug User Fee Amendments of 2017.

(iii) The number of new drug applications and biological licensing applications approved.

(iv) The number of new drug applications and biological licensing applications filed.

(4) Rationale for PDUFA Program Changes. — Beginning with fiscal year 2020, the Secretary shall include in the annual report under paragraph (1) —

(A) data, analysis, and discussion of the changes in the number of full-time equivalents hired as agreed upon in the letters described in section 101(b) of the Prescription Drug User Fee Amendments of 2017 and the number of full time equivalents funded by budget authority at the Food and Drug Administration by each division within the Center for Drug Evaluation and Research, the Center for Biologics Evaluation and Research, the Office of Regulatory Affairs, and the Office of the Commissioner;

(B) data, analysis, and discussion of the changes in the fee revenue amounts and costs for the process for the review of human drugs, including identifying drivers of such changes; and

(C) for each of the Center for Drug Evaluation and Research, the Center for Biologics Evaluation and Research, the Office of Regulatory Affairs, and the Office of the Commissioner, the number of employees for whom time reporting is required and the number of employees for whom time reporting is not required.

(5) Analysis. — For each fiscal year, the Secretary shall include in the report under paragraph (1) an analysis of the following:

(A) The difference between the aggregate number of human drug applications filed and the aggregate number of approvals, accounting for —

(i) such applications filed during one fiscal year for which a decision is not scheduled to be made until the following fiscal year;

(ii) the aggregate number of applications for each fiscal year that did not meet the goals identified in the letters described in section 101(b) of the Prescription Drug User Fee Amendments of 2017 for the applicable fiscal year.

(B) Relevant data to determine whether the Center for Drug Evaluation and Research and the Center for Biologics Evaluation and Research have met performance enhancement goals identified in the letters described in section 101(b) of the Prescription Drug User Fee Amendments of 2017 for the applicable fiscal year.

(C) The most common causes and trends of external or other circumstances affecting the ability of the Center for Drug Evaluation and Research, the Center for Biologics Evaluation and Research, Office of Regulatory Affairs, and the Food and Drug Administration to meet the review time and performance enhancement goals identified in the letters described in section 101(b) of the Prescription Drug User Fee Amendments of 2017.

(b) Fiscal Report. — Beginning with fiscal year ~~2013~~ 2018, not later than 120 days after the end of each fiscal year for which fees are collected under this part, the Secretary shall prepare and submit to the Committee on Energy and Commerce of the House of Representatives and the Committee on Health, Education, Labor, and Pensions of the Senate a report on the implementation of the authority for such fees during such fiscal year and the use, by the Food and Drug Administration, of the fees collected for such fiscal year.

(c) Corrective Action Report. — Beginning with fiscal year 2018, for each fiscal year for which fees are collected under this part, the Secretary shall prepare and submit a corrective action report to the Committee on Energy and Commerce and the Committee on Appropriations of the House of Representatives and the Committee on Health, Education, Labor, and Pensions and the Committee on Appropriations of the Senate. The report shall include the following information, as applicable:

(1) Goals Met. — For each fiscal year, if the Secretary determines, based on the analysis under subsection (a)(5), that each of the goals identified in the letters described in section 101(b) of the Prescription Drug User Fee Amendments of 2017 for the applicable fiscal year have been met, the corrective action report shall include recommendations on ways in which the Secretary can improve and streamline the human drug application review process.

(2) Goals Missed. — For any of the goals identified in the letters described in section 101(b) of the Prescription Drug User Fee Amendments of 2017 for the applicable fiscal year that the Secretary determines to not have been met, the corrective action report shall include—

(A) a detailed justification for such determination and a description, as applicable, of the types of circumstances and trends under which human drug applications that missed the review goal time were approved during the first cycle review, or application review goals were missed; and

(B) with respect to performance enhancement goals that were not achieved, a description of efforts the Food and Drug Administration has put in place for the fiscal year in which the report is submitted to improve the ability of such agency to meet each such goal for the such fiscal year.

(d) Enhanced Communication. —

(1) Communications with Congress. — Each fiscal year, as applicable and requested, representatives from the Centers with expertise in the review of human drugs shall meet with representatives from the Committee on Health, Education, Labor, and Pensions of the Senate and the Committee on Energy and Commerce of the House of Representatives to report on the contents described in the reports under this section.

(2) Participation in Congressional Hearing. — Each fiscal year, as applicable and requested, representatives from the Food and Drug Administration shall participate in a public hearing before the Committee on Health, Education, Labor, and Pensions of the Senate and the Committee on Energy and Commerce of the House of Representatives, to report on the contents described in the reports under this section. Such hearing shall occur not later than 120 days after the end of each fiscal year for which fees are collected under this part.

~~(c)~~ (e) Public Availability. — The Secretary shall make the reports required under subsections (a) and (b) available to the public on the Internet Web site of the Food and Drug Administration.

~~(d)~~ (f) Reauthorization. —

(1) Consultation. — In developing recommendations to present to the Congress with respect to the goals, and plans for meeting the goals, for the process for the review of human drug applications for the first 5 fiscal years after fiscal year ~~2017~~ 2022, and for the reauthorization of this part for such fiscal years, the Secretary shall consult with —

(A) the Committee on Energy and Commerce of the House of Representatives;

(B) the Committee on Health, Education, Labor, and Pensions of the Senate;

(C) scientific and academic experts;

(D) health care professionals;

(E) representatives of patient and consumer advocacy groups; and

(F) the regulated industry.

(2) Prior Public Input. — Prior to beginning negotiations with the regulated industry on the reauthorization of this part, the Secretary shall —

(A) publish a notice in the Federal Register requesting public input on the reauthorization;

(B) hold a public meeting at which the public may present its views on the reauthorization, including specific suggestions for changes to the goals referred to in subsection (a);

(C) provide a period of 30 days after the public meeting to obtain written comments from the public suggesting changes to this part; and

(D) publish the comments on the Food and Drug Administration's Internet Web site.

(3) Periodic Consultation. — Not less frequently than once every month during negotiations with the regulated industry, the Secretary shall hold discussions with representatives of patient and consumer advocacy groups to continue discussions of their views on the reauthorization and their suggestions for changes to this part as expressed under paragraph (2).

(4) Public Review of Recommendations. — After negotiations with the regulated industry, the Secretary shall—

(A) present the recommendations developed under paragraph (1) to the Congressional committees specified in such paragraph;

(B) publish such recommendations in the Federal Register;

(C) provide for a period of 30 days for the public to provide written comments on such recommendations;

(D) hold a meeting at which the public may present its views on such recommendations; and

(E) after consideration of such public views and comments, revise such recommendations as necessary.

(5) Transmittal of Recommendations. — Not later than January 15, 2017, the Secretary shall transmit to the Congress the revised recommendations under paragraph (4), a summary of the views and comments received under such paragraph, and any changes made to the recommendations in response to such views and comments.

(6) Minutes of Negotiation Meetings. —

(A) Public Availability. — Before presenting the recommendations developed under paragraphs (1) through (5) to the Congress, the Secretary shall make publicly available, on the public Web site of the Food and Drug Administration, minutes of all negotiation meetings conducted under this subsection between the Food and Drug Administration and the regulated industry.

(B) Content. — The minutes described under subparagraph (A) shall summarize any substantive proposal made by any party to the negotiations as well as significant controversies or differences of opinion during the negotiations and their resolution.

Part 3 — Fees Relating to Devices

Sec. 737. [379i] Definitions.*

For purposes of this part:

(1) The term "premarket application" means —

* Ceases to be effective October 1, ~~2017~~ 2022.

(A) an application for approval of a device submitted under section 515(c) or section 351 of the Public Health Service Act; or

(B) a product development protocol described in section 515(f).

Such term does not include a supplement, a premarket report, or a premarket notification submission.

(2) The term "premarket report" means a report submitted under section 515(c)(2).

(3) The term "premarket notification submission" means a report submitted under section 510(k).

(4) —

(A) The term "supplement", with respect to a panel-track supplement, a 180-day supplement, a real-time supplement, or an efficacy supplement, means a request to the Secretary to approve a change in a device for which —

(i) an application or report has been approved under section 515(d), or an application has been approved under section 351 of the Public Health Service Act; or

(ii) a notice of completion has become effective under section 515(f).

(B) The term "panel-track supplement" means a supplement to an approved premarket application or premarket report under section 515 that requests a significant change in design or performance of the device, or a new indication for use of the device, and for which substantial clinical data are necessary to provide a reasonable assurance of safety and effectiveness.

(C) The term "180-day supplement" means a supplement to an approved premarket application or premarket report under section 515 that is not a paneltrack supplement and requests a significant change in components, materials, design, specification, software, color additives, or labeling.

(D) The term "real-time supplement" means a supplement to an approved premarket application or premarket report under section 515 that requests a minor change to the device, such as a minor change to the design of the device, software, sterilization, or labeling, and for which the applicant has requested and the agency has granted a meeting or similar forum to jointly review and determine the status of the supplement.

(E) The term "efficacy supplement" means a supplement to an approved premarket application under section 351 of the Public Health Service Act that requires substantive clinical data.

(5) The term "30-day notice" means a notice under section 515(d)(5) that is limited to a request to make modifications to manufacturing procedures or methods of manufacture affecting the safety and effectiveness of the device.

(6) The term "request for classification information" means a request made under section 513(g) for information respecting the class in which a device has been classified or the requirements applicable to a device.

(7) The term "annual fee", for periodic reporting concerning a class III device, means the annual fee associated with periodic reports required by a premarket application approval order.

(8) The term "de novo classification request" means a request made under section 513(f)(2)(A) with respect to the classification of a device.

~~**(8)**~~ **(9)** The term "process for the review of device applications" means the following activities of the Secretary with respect to the review of premarket applications, premarket reports, supplements, and premarket notification submissions:

(A) The activities necessary for the review of premarket applications, premarket reports, supplements, and premarket notification submissions.

(B) The issuance of action letters that allow the marketing of devices or which set forth in detail the specific deficiencies in such applications, reports, supplements, or submissions and, where appropriate, the actions necessary to place them in condition for approval.

(C) The inspection of manufacturing establishments and other facilities undertaken as part of the Secretary's review of pending premarket applications, premarket reports, and supplements.

(D) Monitoring of research conducted in connection with the review of such applications, reports, supplements, and submissions.

(E) Review of device applications subject to section 351 of the Public Health Service Act for an investigational new drug application under section 505(i) or for an investigational device exemption under section 520(g) and activities conducted in anticipation of the submission of such applications under section 505(i) or 520(g).

(F) The development of guidance, policy documents, or regulations to improve the process for the review of premarket applications, premarket reports, supplements, and premarket notification submissions.

(G) The development of voluntary test methods, consensus standards, or mandatory performance standards under section 514 in connection with the review of such applications, reports, supplements, or submissions and related activities.

(H) The provision of technical assistance to device manufacturers in connection with the submission of such applications, reports, supplements, or submissions.

(I) Any activity undertaken under section 513 or 515(i) in connection with the initial classification or reclassification of a device or under section 515(b) in connection with any requirement for approval of a device.

(J) Evaluation of postmarket studies required as a condition of an approval of a premarket application or premarket report under section 515 or a premarket application under section 351 of the Public Health Service Act.

(K) Compiling, developing, and reviewing information on relevant devices to identify safety and effectiveness issues for devices subject to premarket applications, premarket reports, supplements, or premarket notification submissions.

~~**(9)**~~ **(10)** The term "costs of resources allocated for the process for the review of device applications" means the expenses in connection with the process for the review of device applications for —

(A) officers and employees of the Food and Drug Administration, contractors of the Food and Drug Administration, advisory committees, and costs related to such officers, employees, and committees and to contracts with such contractors;

(B) management of information, and the acquisition, maintenance, and repair of computer resources;

(C) leasing, maintenance, renovation, and repair of facilities and acquisition, maintenance, and repair of fixtures, furniture, scientific equipment, and other necessary materials and supplies; and

(D) collecting fees and accounting for resources allocated for the review of premarket applications, premarket reports, supplements, ~~and submissions~~ submissions, and de novo classification requests.

~~**(10)**~~ **(11)** The term "adjustment factor" applicable to a fiscal year is the Consumer Price Index for all urban consumers (all items; United States city average) for October of the preceding fiscal year divided by such Index for October ~~2011~~ 2016.

~~**(11)**~~ **(12)** The term "person" includes an affiliate thereof.

~~**(12)**~~ **(13)** The term "affiliate" means a business entity that has a relationship with a second business entity (whether domestic or international) if, directly or indirectly —

(A) one business entity controls, or has the power to control, the other business entity; or

(B) a third party controls, or has power to control, both of the business entities.

~~**(13)**~~ **(14)** The term "establishment subject to a registration fee" means an establishment that is registered (or is required to register) with the Secretary under section 510 because such establishment is engaged in the manufacture, preparation, propagation, compounding, or processing of a device.

Sec. 738. [379j] Authority to Assess and Use Device Fees.*

(a) Types of Fees. —

(1) In General. — Beginning in fiscal year ~~2013~~ 2018, the Secretary shall assess and collect fees in accordance with this section.

(2) Premarket Application, Premarket Report, Supplement, and Submission Fee, and Annual Fee for Periodic Reporting Concerning a Class III Device. —

(A) In General. — Except as provided in subparagraph (B) and subsections ~~(d), (e), and (f),~~ (d) and (e), each person who submits any of the following, on or after October 1, ~~2012~~ 2017, shall be subject to a fee established under subsection (c) for the fiscal year involved in accordance with the following:

* Ceases to be effective October 1, ~~2017~~ 2022.

(i) A premarket application.

(ii) For a premarket report, a fee equal to the fee that applies under clause (i).

(iii) For a panel track supplement, a fee equal to 75 percent of the fee that applies under clause (i).

(iv) For a 180-day supplement, a fee equal to 15 percent of the fee that applies under clause (i).

(v) For a real-time supplement, a fee equal to 7 percent of the fee that applies under clause (i).

(vi) For a 30-day notice, a fee equal to 1.6 percent of the fee that applies under clause (i).

(vii) For an efficacy supplement, a fee equal to the fee that applies under clause (i).

(viii) For a premarket notification submission, a fee equal to ~~2~~ <u>3.4</u> percent of the fee that applies under clause (i).

(ix) For a request for classification information, a fee equal to 1.35 percent of the fee that applies under clause (i).

(x) For periodic reporting concerning a class III device, an annual fee equal to 3.5 percent of the fee that applies under clause (i).

<u>**(xi)** For a de novo classification request, a fee equal to 30 percent of the fee that applies under clause (i).</u>

(B) Exceptions. —

(i) Humanitarian Device Exemption. — An application under section 520(m) is not subject to any fee under subparagraph (A).

(ii) Further Manufacturing Use. — No fee shall be required under subparagraph (A) for the submission of a premarket application under section 351 of the Public Health Service Act for a product licensed for further manufacturing use only.

(iii) State or Federal Government Sponsors. — No fee shall be required under subparagraph (A) for a premarket application, premarket report, supplement, or premarket notification submission submitted by a State or Federal Government entity unless the device involved is to be distributed commercially.

(iv) Premarket Notifications by Third Parties. — No fee shall be required under subparagraph (A) for a premarket notification submission reviewed by an accredited person pursuant to section 523.

(v) Pediatric Conditions of Use. —

(I) In General. — No fee shall be required under subparagraph (A) for a premarket application, premarket report, ~~or premarket notification submission~~ <u>premarket notification submission, or de novo classification request</u> if the proposed conditions of use for the device involved are solely for a pediatric population. No fee shall be required under such subparagraph for a supplement if the sole purpose of the supplement is to propose conditions of use for a pediatric population.

(II) Subsequent Proposal of Adult Conditions of Use. — In the case of a person who submits a premarket application or premarket report for which, under subclause (I), a fee under subparagraph (A) is not required, any supplement to such application that proposes conditions of use for any adult population is subject to the fee that applies under such subparagraph for a premarket application.

(C) Payment. — The fee required by subparagraph (A) shall be due upon submission of the premarket application, premarket report, supplement, premarket notification submission, 30-day notice, request for classification information, or periodic reporting concerning a class III device. Applicants submitting portions of applications pursuant to section 515(c)(4) shall pay such fees upon submission of the first portion of such applications.

(D) Refunds. —

(i) Application Refused for Filing. — The Secretary shall refund 75 percent of the fee paid under subparagraph (A) for any application, report, or supplement that is refused for filing.

(ii) Application Withdrawn Before Filing. — The Secretary shall refund 75 percent of the fee paid under subparagraph (A) for any application, report, or supplement that is withdrawn prior to the filing decision of the Secretary.

(iii) Application Withdrawn Before First Action. — After receipt of a request for a refund of the fee paid under subparagraph (A) for a premarket application, premarket report, or supplement that is withdrawn after filing but before a first action, the Secretary may return some or all of the fee. The amount of refund, if any, shall be based on the level of effort already expended on the review of such application, report, or supplement.

(iv) Modular Applications Withdrawn Before First Action. — The Secretary shall refund 75 percent of the application fee paid for an application submitted under section 515(c)(4) that is withdrawn before a second portion is submitted and before a first action on the first portion.

(v) Later Withdrawn Modular Applications. — If an application submitted under section 515(c)(4) is withdrawn after a second or subsequent portion is submitted but before any first action, the Secretary may return a portion of the fee. The amount of refund, if any, shall be based on the level of effort already expended on the review of the portions submitted.

(vi) Sole Discretion to Refund. — The Secretary shall have sole discretion to refund a fee or portion of the fee under clause (iii) or (v). A determination by the Secretary concerning a refund under clause (iii) or (v) shall not be reviewable.

(3) Annual Establishment Registration Fee. —

(A) In General. — Except as provided in subparagraph (B)~~ and subsection (f),~~ , each establishment subject to a registration fee shall be subject to a fee for each initial or annual registration under section 510 beginning with its registration for fiscal year 2008.

(B) Exception. — No fee shall be required under subparagraph (A) for an establishment operated by a State or Federal governmental entity or an Indian tribe (as defined in the Indian Self Determination and Educational Assistance Act), unless a device manufactured by the establishment is to be distributed commercially.

(C) Payment. — The fee required under subparagraph (A) shall be due once each fiscal year, upon the later of —

(i) the initial or annual registration (as applicable) of the establishment under section 510; or

(ii) the first business day after the date of enactment of an appropriations Act providing for the collection and obligation of fees for such year under this section.

~~**(b) Fee Amounts.**~~ —

~~**(1) In General.** — Subject to subsections (c), (d), (e), (f), and (i), for each of fiscal years 2013 through 2017, fees under subsection (a) shall be derived from the base fee amounts specified in paragraph (2), to generate the total revenue amounts specified in paragraph (3).~~

~~**(2) Base Fee Amounts Specified.** — For purposes of paragraph (1), the base fee amounts specified in this paragraph are as follows:~~

~~Fee Type~~	~~Fiscal Year 2013~~	~~Fiscal Year 2014~~	~~Fiscal Year 2015~~	~~Fiscal Year 2016~~	~~Fiscal Year 2017~~
~~Premarket Application~~	~~$248,000~~	~~$252,960~~	~~$258,019~~	~~$263,180~~	~~$268,443~~
~~Establishment Registration~~	~~$2,575~~	~~$3,200~~	~~$3,750~~	~~$3,872~~	~~$3,872~~

~~**(3) Total Revenue Amounts Specified.** — For purposes of paragraph (1), the total revenue amounts specified in this paragraph are as follows:~~

~~**(A)** $97,722,301 for fiscal year 2013.~~

~~**(B)** $112,580,497 for fiscal year 2014.~~

~~**(C)** $125,767,107 for fiscal year 2015.~~

~~**(D)** $129,339,949 for fiscal year 2016.~~

~~**(E)** $130,184,348 for fiscal year 2017.~~

(b) Fee Amounts. —

(1) In General. — Subject to subsections (c), (d), (e), and (h), for each of fiscal years 2018 through 2022, fees under subsection (a) shall be derived from the base fee amounts specified in paragraph (2), to generate the total revenue amounts specified in paragraph (3).

(2) Base Fee Amounts Specified. — For purposes of paragraph (1), the base fee amounts specified in this paragraph are as follows:

Fee Type	Fiscal Year 2018	Fiscal Year 2019	Fiscal Year 2020	Fiscal Year 2021	Fiscal Year 2022
Premarket Application	$294,000	$300,000	$310,000	$328,000	$329,000
Establishment Registration	$4,375	$4,548	$4,760	$4,975	$4,978

(3) Total Revenue Amounts Specified. — For purposes of paragraph (1), the total revenue amounts specified in this paragraph are as follows:

(A) $183,280,756 for fiscal year 2018.

(B) $190,654,875 for fiscal year 2019.

(C) $200,132,014 for fiscal year 2020.

(D) $211,748,789 for fiscal year 2021.

(E) $213,687,660 for fiscal year 2022.

(c) Annual Fee Setting; Adjustments. —

(1) In General. — The Secretary shall, 60 days before the start of each fiscal year after September 30, ~~2012~~ 2017, establish fees under subsection (a), based on amounts specified under subsection (b) and the adjustments provided under this subsection, and publish such fees, and the rationale for any adjustments to such fees, in the Federal Register.

(2) Inflation Adjustments. —

(A) Adjustment to Total Revenue Amounts. — For fiscal year ~~2014~~ 2018 and each subsequent fiscal year, the Secretary shall adjust the total revenue amount specified in subsection (b)(3) for such fiscal year by multiplying such amount by the applicable inflation adjustment under subparagraph (B) for such year.

(B) Applicable Inflation Adjustment to Total Revenue Amounts. — The applicable inflation adjustment for ~~a fiscal year is~~ fiscal year 2018 and each subsequent year is the product of—

(i) ~~for fiscal year 2014,~~ the base inflation adjustment under subparagraph (C) for such fiscal year; and

(ii) ~~for fiscal year 2015 and each subsequent fiscal year,~~ the product ~~of —~~ of the base inflation adjustment under subparagraph (C) for each of the fiscal years preceding such fiscal year, beginning with fiscal year 2016.

~~(I) the base inflation adjustment under subparagraph (C) for such fiscal year; and~~

~~(II) the product of the base inflation adjustment under subparagraph (C) for each of the fiscal years preceding such fiscal year, beginning with fiscal year 2014.~~

(C) Base Inflation Adjustment ~~to Total Revenue Amounts~~. —

(i) In General. — Subject to further adjustment under clause (ii), the base inflation adjustment for a fiscal year is the sum of one plus—

(I) the average annual percent change in the cost, per full-time equivalent position of the Food and Drug Administration, of all personnel compensation and benefits paid with respect to such positions for the first 3 years of the preceding 4 fiscal years, multiplied by 0.60; and

(II) the average annual percent change that occurred in the Consumer Price Index for urban consumers (Washington-Baltimore, DC-MD-VA-WV; Not Seasonally Adjusted; All items; Annual Index) for the first 3 years of the preceding 4 years of available data multiplied by 0.40.

(ii) Limitations. — For purposes of subparagraph (B), if the base inflation adjustment for a fiscal year under clause (i)—

(I) is less than 1, such adjustment shall be considered to be equal to 1; or

(II) is greater than 1.04, such adjustment shall be considered to be equal to 1.04.

(D) Adjustment to Base Fee Amounts. — ~~For each of fiscal years 2014 through 2017, the base fee amounts specified in subsection (b)(2) shall be adjusted as needed, on a uniform proportionate basis, to generate the total revenue amounts under subsection (b)(3), as adjusted for inflation under subparagraph (A)~~. For each of fiscal years 2018 through 2022, the Secretary shall—

(i) adjust the base fee amounts specified in subsection (b)(2) for such fiscal year by multiplying such amounts by the applicable inflation adjustment under subparagraph (B) for such year; and

(ii) if the Secretary determines necessary, increase (in addition to the adjustment under clause (i)) such base fee amounts, on a uniform proportionate basis, to generate the total revenue amounts under subsection (b)(3), as adjusted for inflation under subparagraph (A).

(3) Volume-Based Adjustments to Establishment Registration Base Fees. — For each of fiscal years ~~2014 through 2017~~ 2018 through 2022, after the base fee amounts specified in subsection (b)(2) are adjusted under paragraph (2)(D), the base establishment registration fee amounts specified in such subsection shall be ~~further adjusted~~ increased, as the Secretary estimates is necessary in order for total fee collections for such fiscal year to generate the total revenue amounts, as adjusted under paragraph (2).

(4) Limit. The total amount of fees charged, as adjusted under this subsection, for a fiscal year may not exceed the total costs for such fiscal year for the resources allocated for the process for the review of device applications.

(5) Supplement.

(A) In General. The Secretary may use unobligated carryover balances from fees collected in previous fiscal years to ensure that sufficient fee revenues are available in that fiscal year, so long as the Secretary maintains unobligated carryover balances of not less than 1 month of operating reserves for the first month of the next fiscal year.

(B) Notice to Congress. Not later than 14 days before the Secretary anticipates the use of funds described in subparagraph (A), the Secretary shall provide notice to the Committee on Health, Education, Labor, and Pensions and the Committee on Appropriations of the Senate and the Committee on Energy and Commerce and the Committee on Appropriations of the House of Representatives.

(d) Small Businesses; Fee Waiver and Fee Reduction Regarding Premarket Approval Fees. —

(1) In General. The Secretary shall grant a waiver of the fee required under subsection (a) for one premarket application, or one premarket report, where the Secretary finds that the applicant involved is a small business submitting its first premarket application to the Secretary, or its first premarket report, respectively, for review. For the purposes of this paragraph, the term "small business" means an entity that reported $30,000,000 or less of gross receipts or sales in its most resent Federal income tax return for a taxable year, including such returns of all of its affiliates.

In addition, for subsequent premarket applications, premarket reports, and supplements where the Secretary finds that the applicant involved is a small business, the fees specified in clauses (i) through ~~(v) and clauses (vii, (ix), and (x)~~ (vii) and clauses (ix), (x), and (xi) of subsection (a)(2)(A) may be paid at a reduced rate in accordance with paragraph (2)(C).

(2) Rules Relating to Premarket Approval Fees. —

(A) Definition. For purposes of this paragraph, the term "small business" means an entity that reported $100,000,000 or less of gross receipts or sales in its most recent Federal income tax return for a taxable year, including such returns of all of its affiliates.

(B) Evidence of Qualification.

(i) In General. — An applicant shall pay the higher fees established by the Secretary each year unless the applicant submits evidence that it qualifies for a waiver of the fee or the lower fee rate.

(ii) Firms Submitting Tax Returns to the United States Internal Revenue Service. — The applicant shall support its claim that it meets the definition under subparagraph (A) by submission of a copy of its most recent Federal income tax return for a taxable year, and a copy of such returns of its affiliates, which show an amount of gross sales or receipts that is less than the maximum established in subparagraph (A). The applicant, and each of such affiliates, shall certify that the information provided is a true and accurate copy of the actual tax forms they submitted to the Internal Revenue Service. If no tax forms are submitted for any affiliate, the applicant shall certify that the applicant has no affiliates.

(iii) Firms Not Submitting Tax Returns to the United States Internal Revenue Service. — In the case of an applicant that has not previously submitted a Federal income tax return, the applicant and each of its affiliates shall demonstrate that it meets the definition under subparagraph (A) by submission of a signed certification, in such form as the Secretary may direct through a notice published in the Federal Register, that the applicant or affiliate meets the criteria for a small business and a certification, in English, from the national taxing authority of the country in which the applicant or, if applicable, affiliate is headquartered. The certification from such taxing authority shall bear the official seal of such taxing authority and shall provide the applicant's or affiliate's gross receipts or sales for the most recent year in both the local currency of such country and in United States dollars, the exchange rate used in converting such local currency to dollars, and the dates during which these receipts or sales were collected. The applicant shall also submit a statement signed by the head of the applicant's firm or by its chief financial officer that the applicant has submitted certifications for all of its affiliates, or that the applicant has no affiliates.

(C) Reduced Fees. — Where the Secretary finds that the applicant involved meets the definition under subparagraph (A), the fees established under subsection (c)(1) may be paid at a reduced rate of—

(i) 25 percent of the fee established under such subsection for a premarket application, a premarket report, a supplement, ~~or~~ periodic reporting concerning a class III device~~; and~~, or a de novo classification request; and

(ii) 50 percent of the fee established under such subsection for a 30-day notice or a request for classification information.

(e) Small Businesses; Fee Reduction Regarding Premarket Notification Submissions. —

(1) In General. — For fiscal year 2008 and each subsequent fiscal year, where the Secretary finds that the applicant involved is a small business, the fee specified in subsection (a)(2)(A)(viii) may be paid at a reduced rate in accordance with paragraph (2)(C).

(2) Rules Relating to Premarket Notification Submissions. —

(A) Definition. — For purposes of this subsection, the term "small business" means an entity that reported $100,000,000 or less of gross receipts or sales in its most recent Federal income tax return for a taxable year, including such returns of all of its affiliates.

(B) Evidence of Qualification. —

(i) In General. — An applicant shall pay the higher fees established by the Secretary each year unless the applicant submits evidence that it qualifies for the lower fee rate.

(ii) Firms Submitting Tax Returns to the United States Internal Revenue Service. — The applicant shall support its claim that it meets the definition under subparagraph (A) by submission of a copy of its most recent Federal income tax return for a taxable year, and a copy of such returns of its affiliates, which show an amount of gross sales or receipts that is less than the maximum established in subparagraph (A). The applicant, and each of such affiliates, shall certify that the information provided is a true and accurate copy of the actual tax forms they submitted to the Internal Revenue Service. If no tax forms are submitted for any affiliate, the applicant shall certify that the applicant has no affiliates.

(iii) Firms Not Submitting Tax Returns to the United States Internal Revenue Service. — In the case of an applicant that has not previously submitted a Federal income tax return, the applicant and each of its affiliates shall demonstrate that it meets the definition under subparagraph (A) by submission of a signed certification, in such form as the Secretary may direct through a notice published in the Federal Register, that the applicant or affiliate meets the criteria for a small business and a certification, in English, from the national taxing authority of the country in which the applicant or, if applicable, affiliate is headquartered. The certification from such taxing authority shall bear the official seal of such taxing authority and shall provide the applicant's or affiliate's gross receipts or sales for the most recent year in both the local currency of such country and in United States dollars, the exchange rate used in converting such local currency to dollars, and the dates during which these receipts or sales were collected. The applicant shall also submit a statement signed by the head of the applicant's firm or by its chief financial officer that the applicant has submitted certifications for all of its affiliates, or that the applicant has no affiliates.

(C) Reduced Fees. — For fiscal year 2008 and each subsequent fiscal year, where the Secretary finds that the applicant involved meets the definition under subparagraph (A), the fee for a premarket notification submission may be paid at ~~50~~ 25 percent of the fee that applies under subsection (a)(2)(A)(viii), and as established under subsection (c)(1).

(D) Request for Reduction. — An applicant seeking a fee reduction under this subsection shall submit supporting information to the Secretary at least 60 days before the fee is required pursuant to subsection (a). The decision of the Secretary regarding whether an entity qualifies for such a reduction is not reviewable.

~~**(f) Fee Waiver or Reduction.** —~~

~~**(1) In General.** — The Secretary may, at the Secretary's sole discretion, grant a waiver or reduction of fees under subsection (a)(2) or (a)(3) if the Secretary finds that such waiver or reduction is in the interest of public health.~~

~~**(2) Limitation.** — The sum of all fee waivers or reductions granted by the Secretary in any fiscal year under paragraph (1) shall not exceed 2 percent of the total fee revenue amounts established for such year under subsection (c).~~

~~**(3) Duration.** — The authority provided by this subsection terminates October 1, 2017.~~

~~(g)~~ (f) Effect of Failure to Pay Fees. —

(1) No Acceptance of Submissions. — A premarket application, premarket report, supplement, premarket notification submission, 30-day notice, request for classification information, ~~or~~ periodic reporting concerning a class III device, or de novo classification request submitted by a person subject to fees under subsections (a)(2) and (a)(3) shall be considered incomplete and shall not be accepted by the Secretary until ~~all fees~~ all such fees owed by such person have been paid.

(2) No Registration. — Registration information submitted under section 510 by an establishment subject to a registration fee shall be considered incomplete and shall not be accepted by the Secretary until the registration fee under subsection (a)(3) owed for the establishment has been paid. Until the fee is paid and the registration is complete, the establishment is deemed to have failed to register in accordance with section 510.

~~(h)~~ (g) Conditions. —

(1) Performance Goals; Termination of Program. — With respect to the amount that, under the salaries and expenses account of the Food and Drug Administration, is appropriated for a fiscal year for devices and radiological products, fees may not be assessed under subsection (a) for the fiscal year, and the Secretary is not expected to meet any performance goals identified for the fiscal year, if—

(A) the amount so appropriated for the fiscal year, excluding the amount of fees appropriated for the fiscal year, is more than 1 percent less than ~~$280,587,000~~ $320,825,000 multiplied by the adjustment factor applicable to such fiscal year; or

(B) fees were not assessed under subsection (a) for the previous fiscal year.

(2) Authority. — If the Secretary does not assess fees under subsection (a) during any portion of a fiscal year because of paragraph (1) and if at a later date in such fiscal year the Secretary may assess such fees, the Secretary may assess and collect such fees, without any modification in the rate for premarket applications, supplements, premarket reports, premarket notification submissions, 30-day notices, requests for classification information, periodic reporting concerning a class III device, and establishment registrations at any time in such fiscal year, notwithstanding the provisions of subsection (a) relating to the date fees are to be paid.

(3) Limitation. — Beginning on October 1, 2023, the authorities under section 737(9)(C) shall include only leasing and necessary scientific equipment.

~~(i)~~ (h) Crediting and Availability of Fees. —

(1) In General. — Subject to paragraph (2)(C), fees authorized under subsection (a) shall be collected and available for obligation only to the extent and in the amount provided in advance in appropriation Acts. Such fees are authorized to be appropriated to remain available until expended. Such sums as may be necessary may be transferred from the Food and Drug Administration salaries and expenses appropriation account without fiscal year limitation to such appropriation account for salaries and expenses with such fiscal year limitation. The sums transferred shall be available solely for the process for the review of device applications.

(2) Collections and Appropriation Acts. —

(A) In General. — The fees authorized by this section —

(i) subject to subparagraph (C), shall be collected and available in each fiscal year in an amount not to exceed the amount specified in appropriation Acts, or otherwise made available for obligation, for such fiscal year, and

(ii) shall only be available to defray increases in the costs of the resources allocated for the process for the review of device applications (including increases in such costs for an additional number of full-time equivalent positions in the Department of Health and Human Services to be engaged in such process) over such costs, excluding costs paid from fees collected under this section, for fiscal year 2009 multiplied by the adjustment factor.

(B) Compliance. —

(i) In General. — The Secretary shall be considered to have met the requirements of subparagraph (A)(ii) in any fiscal year if the costs funded by appropriations and allocated for the process for the review of device applications —

(I) are not more than 3 percent below the level specified in subparagraph (A)(ii); or

(II) —

(aa) are more than 3 percent below the level specified in subparagraph (A)(ii), and fees assessed for a subsequent fiscal year are decreased by the amount in excess of 3 percent by which such costs fell below the level specified in such subparagraph; and

(bb) such costs are not more than 5 percent below the level specified in such subparagraph.

(ii) More Than 5 Percent. — To the extent such costs are more than 5 percent below the specified level in subparagraph (A)(ii), fees may not be collected under this section for that fiscal year.

(C) Provision for Early Payments. — Payment of fees authorized under this section for a fiscal year, prior to the due date for such fees, may be accepted by the Secretary in accordance with authority provided in advance in a prior year appropriations Act.

(3) Authorizations of Appropriations. — For each of the fiscal years ~~2013 through 2017~~ 2018 through 2022, there is authorized to be appropriated for fees under this section an amount equal to the total revenue amount specified under subsection (b)(3) for the fiscal year, as adjusted under subsection (c) ~~and, for fiscal year 2017 only, as further adjusted under paragraph (4).~~ .

~~**(4) Offset.** — If the cumulative amount of fees collected during fiscal years 2013, 2014, and 2015, added to the amount estimated to be collected for fiscal year 2016, which estimate shall be based upon the amount of fees received by the Secretary through June 30, 2016, exceeds the cumulative amount appropriated pursuant to paragraph (3) for these four fiscal years, the excess shall be credited to the appropriation account of the Food and Drug Administration as provided in paragraph (1), and shall be subtracted from the amount of fees that would otherwise be authorized to be collected under this section pursuant to appropriation Acts for fiscal year 2017.~~

~~**(j)**~~ **(i) Collection of Unpaid Fees.** — In any case where the Secretary does not receive payment of a fee assessed under subsection (a) within 30 days after it is due, such fee shall be treated as a claim of the United States Government subject to subchapter II of chapter 37 of title 31, United States Code.

~~**(k)**~~ **(j) Written Requests for Refunds.** — To qualify for consideration for a refund under subsection (a)(2)(D), a person shall submit to the Secretary a written request for such refund not later than 180 days after such fee is due.

~~**(l)**~~ **(k) Construction.** — This section may not be construed to require that the number of full-time equivalent positions in the Department of Health and Human Services, for officers, employees, and advisory committees not engaged in the process of the review of device applications, be reduced to offset the number of officers, employees, and advisory committees so engaged.

SEC. 738A. [379j-1] REAUTHORIZATION; REPORTING REQUIREMENTS.*

(a) REPORTS. —

(1) PERFORMANCE REPORT. —

(A) ~~**IN GENERAL. —** Beginning~~

(i) GENERAL REQUIREMENTS — Beginning with fiscal year ~~2013~~ 2018, for each fiscal year for which fees are collected under this part, the Secretary shall prepare and submit to the Committee on Health, Education, Labor, and Pensions of the Senate and the Committee on Energy and Commerce of the House of Representatives annual reports concerning the progress of the Food and Drug Administration in achieving the goals identified in the letters described in section 201(b) of the Medical Device User Fee Amendments of ~~2012~~ 2017 during such fiscal year and the future plans of the Food and Drug Administration for meeting the goals.

(ii) ADDITIONAL INFORMATION.—Beginning with fiscal year 2018, the annual report under this subparagraph shall include the progress of the Center for Devices and Radiological Health in achieving the goals, and future plans for meeting the goals, including—

(I) the number of premarket applications filed under section 515 per fiscal year for each review division;

(II) the number of reports submitted under section 510(k) per fiscal year for each review division; and

(III) the number of expedited development and priority review designations under section 515C per fiscal year.

(iii) REAL TIME REPORTING.—

(I) IN GENERAL.—Not later than 30 calendar days after the end of the second quarter of fiscal year 2018, and not later than 30 calendar days after the end of each quarter of each fiscal year thereafter, the Secretary shall post the data described in subclause (II) on the internet website of the Food and Drug Administration for such quarter and on a cumulative basis for such fiscal year, and may remove duplicative data from the annual report under this subparagraph.

(II) DATA.—The Secretary shall post the following data in accordance with subclause (I):

(aa) The number and titles of draft and final guidance on topics related to the process for the review of devices, and whether such guidances were issued as required by statute or pursuant to the letters described in section 201(b) of the Medical Device User Fee Amendments of 2017; and

(bb) The number and titles of public meetings held on topics related to the process for the review of devices, and if such meetings were required by statute or pursuant to a commitment under the letters described in section 201(b) of the Medical Device User Fee Amendments of 2017.

(iv) RATIONALE FOR MDUFA PROGRAM CHANGES. — Beginning with fiscal year 2020, the Secretary shall include in the annual report under paragraph (1)—

(I) data, analysis, and discussion of the changes in the number of full-time equivalents hired as agreed upon in the letters described in section 201(b) of the Medical Device User Fee Amendments of 2017 and the number of full time equivalents funded by budget authority at the Food and Drug Administration by each division within the Center for Devices and Radiological Health, the Center for Biologics Evaluation and Research, the Office of Regulatory Affairs, and the Office of the Commissioner;

(II) data, analysis, and discussion of the changes in the fee revenue amounts and costs for the process for the review of devices, including identifying drivers of such changes; and

(III) for each of the Center for Devices and Radiological Health, the Center for Biologics Evaluation and Research, the Office of Regulatory Affairs, and the Office of the Commissioner, the number of employees for whom time reporting is required and the number of employees for whom time reporting is not required.

* Ceases to be effective January 31, 2018.

(v) ANALYSIS.—For each fiscal year, the Secretary shall include in the report under clause (i) an analysis of the following:

(I) The difference between the aggregate number of premarket applications filed under section 515 and aggregate reports submitted under section 510(k) and the aggregate number of major deficiency letters, not approvable letters, and denials for such applications issued by the agency, accounting for—

(aa) the number of applications filed and reports submitted during one fiscal year for which a decision is not scheduled to be made until the following fiscal year; and

(bb) the aggregate number of applications for each fiscal year that did not meet the goals as identified by the letters described in section 201(b) of the Medical Device User Fee Amendments of 2017 for the applicable fiscal year.

(II) Relevant data to determine whether the Center for Devices and Radiological Health has met performance enhancement goals identified by the letters described in section 201(b) of the Medical Device User Fee Amendments of 2017 for the applicable fiscal year.

(III) The most common causes and trends for external or other circumstances affecting the ability of the Center for Devices and Radiological Health, the Office of Regulatory Affairs, or the Food and Drug Administration to meet review time and performance enhancement goals identified by the letters described in section 201(b) of the Medical Device User Fee Amendments of 2017.

(B) PUBLICATION. — With regard to information to be reported by the Food and Drug Administration to industry on a quarterly and annual basis pursuant to the letters described in section 201(b) of the Medical Device User Fee Amendments Act of ~~2012~~ 2017, the Secretary shall make such information publicly available on the Internet Web site of the Food and Drug Administration not later than 60 days after the end of each quarter or 120 days after the end of each fiscal year, respectively, to which such information applies. This information shall include the status of the independent assessment identified in the letters described in such section 201(b).

(C) UPDATES. — The Secretary shall include in each report under subparagraph (A) information on all previous cohorts for which the Secretary has not given a complete response on all device premarket applications and reports, supplements, and premarket notifications in the cohort.

(2) CORRECTIVE ACTION REPORT. — Beginning with fiscal year 2018, for each fiscal year for which fees are collected under this part, the Secretary shall prepare and submit a corrective action report to the Committee on Energy and Commerce and the Committee on Appropriations of the House of Representatives and the Committee on Health, Education, Labor, and Pensions and the Committee on Appropriations of the Senate. The report shall include the following information, as applicable:

(A) GOALS MET. — For each fiscal year, if the Secretary determines, based on the analysis under paragraph (1)(A)(iv), that each of the goals identified by the letters described in section 201(b) of the Medical Device User Fee Amendments of 2017 for the applicable fiscal year have been met, the corrective action report shall include recommendations on ways in which the Secretary can improve and streamline the medical device application review process.

(B) GOALS MISSED. — For each of the goals identified by the letters described in section 201(b) of the Medical Device User Fee Amendments of 2017 for the applicable fiscal year that the Secretary determines to not have been met, the corrective action report shall include—

(i) a justification for such determination;

(ii) a description of the types of circumstances, in the aggregate, under which applications or reports submitted under section 515 or notifications submitted under section 510(k) missed the review goal times but were approved during the first cycle review, as applicable;

(iii) a summary and any trends with regard to the circumstances for which a review goal was missed; and

(iv) the performance enhancement goals that were not achieved during the previous fiscal year and a description of efforts the Food and Drug Administration has put in place for the fiscal year in which the report is submitted to improve the ability of such agency to meet each such goal for the such fiscal year.

(3) Enhanced Communication.—

(A) Communications with Congress. — Each fiscal year, as applicable and requested, representatives from the Centers with expertise in the review of devices shall meet with representatives from the Committee on Health, Education, Labor, and Pensions of the Senate and the Committee on Energy and Commerce of the House of Representatives to report on the contents described in the reports under this section.

(B) Participation in Congressional Hearing. — Each fiscal year, as applicable and requested, representatives from the Food and Drug Administration shall participate in a public hearing before the Committee on Health, Education, Labor, and Pensions of the Senate and the Committee on Energy and Commerce of the House of Representatives, to report on the contents described in the reports under this section. Such hearing shall occur not later than 120 days after the end of each fiscal year for which fees are collected under this part.

~~(2)~~ (4) Fiscal Report. — For fiscal years ~~2013 through 2017~~ 2018 through 2022, not later than 120 days after the end of each fiscal year during which fees are collected under this part, the Secretary shall prepare and submit to the Committee on Health, Education, Labor, and Pensions of the Senate and the Committee on Energy and Commerce of the House of Representatives, a report on the implementation of the authority for such fees during such fiscal year and the use, by the Food and Drug Administration, of the fees collected during such fiscal year for which the report is made.

~~(3)~~ (5) Public Availability. — The Secretary shall make the reports required under paragraphs (1) and (2) available to the public on the Internet Web site of the Food and Drug Administration.

(b) Reauthorization. —

(1) Consultation. — In developing recommendations to present to Congress with respect to the goals, and plans for meeting the goals, for the process for the review of device applications for the first 5 fiscal years after fiscal year ~~2017~~ 2022, and for the reauthorization of this part for such fiscal years, the Secretary shall consult with—

(A) the Committee on Energy and Commerce of the House of Representatives;

(B) the Committee on Health, Education, Labor, and Pensions of the Senate;

(C) scientific and academic experts;

(D) health care professionals;

(E) representatives of patient and consumer advocacy groups; and

(F) the regulated industry.

(2) Prior Public Input. — Prior to beginning negotiations with the regulated industry on the reauthorization of this part, the Secretary shall—

(A) publish a notice in the Federal Register requesting public input on the reauthorization;

(B) hold a public meeting at which the public may present its views on the reauthorization, including specific suggestions for changes to the goals referred to in subsection (a)(1);

(C) provide a period of 30 days after the public meeting to obtain written comments from the public suggesting changes to this part; and

(D) publish the comments on the Food and Drug Administration's Internet Web site.

(3) Periodic Consultation. — Not less frequently than once every month during negotiations with the regulated industry, the Secretary shall hold discussions with representatives of patient and consumer advocacy groups to continue discussions of their views on the reauthorization and their suggestions for changes to this part as expressed under paragraph (2).

(4) Public Review of Recommendations. — After negotiations with the regulated industry, the Secretary shall—

(A) present the recommendations developed under paragraph (1) to the Congressional committees specified in such paragraph;

(B) publish such recommendations in the Federal Register;

(C) provide for a period of 30 days for the public to provide written comments on such recommendations;

(D) hold a meeting at which the public may present its views on such recommendations; and

(E) after consideration of such public views and comments, revise such recommendations as necessary.

(5) Transmittal of Recommendations. — Not later than January 15, ~~2017,~~ 2022, the Secretary shall transmit to Congress the revised recommendations under paragraph (4), a summary of the views and comments received under such paragraph, and any changes made to the recommendations in response to such views and comments.

(6) Minutes of Negotiation Meetings. —

(A) Public Availability. — Before presenting the recommendations developed under paragraphs (1) through (5) to the Congress, the Secretary shall make publicly available, on the public Web site of the Food and Drug Administration, minutes of all negotiation meetings conducted under this subsection between the Food and Drug Administration and the regulated industry.

(B) Content. — The minutes described under subparagraph (A) shall summarize any substantive proposal made by any party to the negotiations as well as significant controversies or differences of opinion during the negotiations and their resolution.

Part 4 — Fees Relating to Animal Drugs

Sec. 739. [379j-11] Definitions.

For purposes of this part:

(1) The term "animal drug application" means an application for approval of any new animal drug submitted under section 512(b)(1). Such term does not include either a new animal drug application submitted under section 512(b)(2) or a supplemental animal drug application.

(2) The term "supplemental animal drug application" means —

(A) a request to the Secretary to approve a change in an animal drug application which has been approved; or

(B) a request to the Secretary to approve a change to an application approved under section 512(c)(2) for which data with respect to safety or effectiveness are required.

(3) The term "animal drug product" means each specific strength or potency of a particular active ingredient or ingredients in final dosage form marketed by a particular manufacturer or distributor, which is uniquely identified by the labeler code and product code portions of the national drug code, and for which an animal drug application or a supplemental animal drug application has been approved.

(4) The term "animal drug establishment" means a foreign or domestic place of business which is at one general physical location consisting of one or more buildings all of which are within 5 miles of each other, at which one or more animal drug products are manufactured in final dosage form.

(5) The term "investigational animal drug submission" means —

(A) the filing of a claim for an investigational exemption under section 512(j) for a new animal drug intended to be the subject of an animal drug application or a supplemental animal drug application,; or

(B) the submission of information for the purpose of enabling the Secretary to evaluate the safety or effectiveness of an animal drug application or supplemental animal drug application in the event of their filing.

(6) The term "animal drug sponsor" means either an applicant named in an animal drug application that has not been withdrawn by the applicant and for which approval has not been withdrawn by the Secretary, or a person who has submitted an investigational animal drug submission that has not been terminated or otherwise rendered inactive by the Secretary.

(7) The term "final dosage form" means, with respect to an animal drug product, a finished dosage form which is approved for administration to an animal without substantial further manufacturing. Such term includes animal drug products intended for mixing in animal feeds.

(8) The term "process for the review of animal drug applications" means the following activities of the Secretary with respect to the review of animal drug applications, supplemental animal drug applications, and investigational animal drug submissions:

(A) The activities necessary for the review of animal drug applications, supplemental animal drug applications, and investigational animal drug submissions.

(B) The issuance of action letters which approve animal drug applications or supplemental animal drug applications or which set forth in detail the specific deficiencies in animal drug applications, supplemental animal drug applications, or investigational animal drug submissions and, where appropriate, the actions necessary to place such applications, supplements or submissions in condition for approval.

(C) The inspection of animal drug establishments and other facilities undertaken as part of the Secretary's review of pending animal drug applications, supplemental animal drug applications, and investigational animal drug submissions.

(D) Monitoring of research conducted in connection with the review of animal drug applications, supplemental animal drug applications, and investigational animal drug submissions.

(E) The development of regulations and policy related to the review of animal drug applications, supplemental animal drug applications, and investigational animal drug submissions.

(F) Development of standards for products subject to review.

(G) Meetings between the agency and the animal drug sponsor.

(H) Review of advertising and labeling prior to approval of an animal drug application or supplemental animal drug application, but not after such application has been approved.

(9) The term "costs of resources allocated for the process for the review of animal drug applications" means the expenses in connection with the process for the review of animal drug applications for —

(A) officers and employees of the Food and Drug Administration, contractors of the Food and Drug Administration, advisory committees consulted with respect to the review of specific animal drug applications, supplemental animal drug applications, or investigational animal drug submissions, and costs related to such officers, employees, committees, and contractors, including costs for travel, education, and recruitment and other personnel activities,;

(B) management of information, and the acquisition, maintenance, and repair of computer resources,;

(C) leasing, maintenance, renovation, and repair of facilities and acquisition, maintenance, and repair of fixtures, furniture, scientific equipment, and other necessary materials and supplies,; and

(D) collecting fees under section 740 and accounting for resources allocated for the review of animal drug applications, supplemental animal drug applications, and investigational animal drug submissions.

(10) The term "adjustment factor" applicable to a fiscal year refers to the formula set forth in section 735(8) with the base or comparator month being October 2002.

(11) The term "person" includes an affiliate thereof.

(12) The term "affiliate" refers to the definition set forth in section735(11).

SEC. 740. [379j-12] AUTHORITY TO ASSESS AND USE ANIMAL DRUG FEES.*

(a) TYPES OF FEES. — Beginning in fiscal year 2004, the Secretary shall assess and collect fees in accordance with this section as follows:

(1) ANIMAL DRUG APPLICATION AND SUPPLEMENT FEE. —

(A) IN GENERAL. — Each person that submits, on or after September 1, 2003, an animal drug application or a supplemental animal drug application shall be subject to a fee as follows:

(i) A fee established in subsection (c) for an animal drug application, except an animal drug application subject to the criteria set forth in section 512(d)(4).

(ii) A fee established in subsection (c), in an amount that is equal to 50 percent of the amount of the fee under clause (i), for —

(I) a supplemental animal drug application for which safety or effectiveness data are required; and

(II) an animal drug application subject to the criteria set forth in section 512(d)(4).

(B) PAYMENT. — The fee required by subparagraph (A) shall be due upon submission of the animal drug application or supplemental animal drug application.

* Ceases to be effective October 1, 2018.

(C) Exception for Previously Filed Application or Supplement. — If an animal drug application or a supplemental animal drug application was submitted by a person that paid the fee for such application or supplement, was accepted for filing, and was not approved or was withdrawn (without a waiver or refund), the submission of an animal drug application or a supplemental animal drug application for the same product by the same person (or the person's licensee, assignee, or successor) shall not be subject to a fee under subparagraph (A).

(D) Refund of Fee if Application Refused for Filing. — The Secretary shall refund 75 percent of the fee paid under subparagraph (B) for any animal drug application or supplemental animal drug application which is refused for filing.

(E) Refund of Fee if Application Withdrawn. — If an animal drug application or a supplemental animal drug application is withdrawn after the application or supplement was filed, the Secretary may refund the fee or portion of the fee paid under subparagraph (B) if no substantial work was performed on the application or supplement after the application or supplement was filed. The Secretary shall have the sole discretion to refund the fee under this paragraph. A determination by the Secretary concerning a refund under this paragraph shall not be reviewable.

(2) Animal Drug Product Fee.

(A) In General. — Each person —

(i) who is named as the applicant in an animal drug application or supplemental animal drug application for an animal drug product which has been submitted for listing under section 510 and

(ii) who, after September 1, 2003, had pending before the Secretary an animal drug application or supplemental animal drug application,;

shall pay for each such animal drug product the annual fee established in subsection (c).

(B) Payment; Fee Due Date. — Such fee shall be payable for the fiscal year in which the animal drug product is first submitted for listing under section 510, or is submitted for relisting under section 510 if the animal drug product has been withdrawn from listing and relisted. After such fee is paid for that fiscal year, such fee shall be due each subsequent fiscal year that the product remains listed, upon the later of —

(i) the first business day after the date of enactment of an appropriations Act providing for the collection and obligation of fees for such fiscal year under this section; or

(ii) January 31 of each year.

(C) Limitation. Such fee shall be paid only once for each animal drug product for a fiscal year in which the fee is payable.

(3) Animal Drug Establishment Fee. —

(A) In General. — Each person —

(i) who owns or operates, directly or through an affiliate, an animal drug establishment;

(ii) who is named as the applicant in an animal drug application or supplemental animal drug application for an animal drug product which has been submitted for listing under section 510; and

(iii) who, after September 1, 2003, had pending before the Secretary an animal drug application or supplemental animal drug application,

shall be assessed an annual establishment fee as established in subsection (c) for each animal drug establishment listed in its approved animal drug application as an establishment that manufactures the animal drug product named in the application.

(B) Payment; Fee Due Date. — The annual establishment fee shall be assessed in each fiscal year in which the animal drug product named in the application is assessed a fee under paragraph (2) unless the animal drug establishment listed in the application does not engage in the manufacture of the animal drug product during the fiscal year. The fee under this paragraph for a fiscal year shall be due upon the later of —

(i) the first business day after the date of enactment of an appropriations Act providing for the collection and obligation of fees for such fiscal year under this section; or

(ii) January 31 of each year.

(C) Limitation. —

(i) In General. — An establishment shall be assessed only one fee per fiscal year under this section~~, subject to clause (ii).~~

(ii) Certain Manufacturers. — If a single establishment manufactures both animal drug products and prescription drug products, as defined in section 735(3), such establishment shall be assessed both the animal drug establishment fee and the prescription drug establishment fee, as set forth in section 736(a)(2), within a single fiscal year.

(4) Animal Drug Sponsor Fee. —

(A) In General. — Each person —

(i) who meets the definition of an animal drug sponsor within a fiscal year; and

(ii) who, after September 1, 2003, had pending before the Secretary an animal drug application, a supplemental animal drug application, or an investigational animal drug submission,

shall be assessed an annual sponsor fee as established under subsection (c).

(B) Payment; Fee Due Date. — The fee under this paragraph for a fiscal year shall be due upon the later of —

(i) the first business day after the date of enactment of an appropriations Act providing for the collection and obligation of fees for such fiscal year under this section; or

(ii) January 31 of each year.

(C) Limitation. —Each animal drug sponsor shall pay only one such fee each fiscal year.

(b) Fee Revenue Amounts. —

(1) In General. — Subject to subsections (c), (d), (f), and (g) of this section —

(A) for fiscal year 2014, the fees required under subsection (a) shall be established to generate a total revenue amount of $23,600,000; and

(B) for each of fiscal years 2015 through 2018, the fees required under subsection (a) shall be established to generate a total revenue amount of $21,600,000.

(2) Types of Fees. — Of the total revenue amount determined for a fiscal year under paragraph (1) —

(A) 20 percent shall be derived from fees under subsection (a)(1) (relating to animal drug applications and supplements);

(B) 27 percent shall be derived from fees under subsection (a)(2) (relating to animal drug products);

(C) 26 percent shall be derived from fees under subsection (a)(3) (relating to animal drug establishments); and

(D) 27 percent shall be derived from fees under subsection (a)(4) (relating to animal drug sponsors).

(c) Annual Fee Setting; Adjustments. —

(1) Annual Fee Setting. — The Secretary shall establish, 60 days before the start of each fiscal year beginning after September 30, 2003, for that fiscal year, animal drug application fees, supplemental animal drug application fees, animal drug sponsor fees, animal drug establishment fees, and animal drug product fees based on the revenue amounts established under subsection (b) and the adjustments provided under this subsection.

(2) Inflation Adjustment. — For fiscal year 2015 and subsequent fiscal years, the revenue amounts established in subsection (b) shall be adjusted by the Secretary by notice, published in the Federal Register, for a fiscal year, by an amount equal to the sum of —

(A) one;

(B) the average annual percent change in the cost, per full-time equivalent position of the Food and Drug Administration, of all personnel compensation and benefits paid with respect to such positions for the first 3 of the preceding 4 fiscal years for which data are available, multiplied by the average proportion of personnel compensation and benefits costs to total Food and Drug Administration costs for the first 3 years of the preceding 4 fiscal years for which data are available; and

(C) the average annual percent change that occurred in the Consumer Price Index for urban consumers (Washington-Baltimore, DC–MD–VA–WV; not seasonally adjusted; all items less food and energy; annual index) for the first 3 years of the preceding 4 years for which data are available multiplied by the average proportion of all costs other than personnel compensation and benefits costs to total Food and Drug Administration costs for the first 3 years of the preceding 4 fiscal years for which data are available.

(3) Workload Adjustment. — For fiscal year 2015 and subsequent fiscal years, after the revenue amounts established in subsection (b) are adjusted for inflation in accordance with paragraph (2), the revenue amounts shall be further adjusted for such fiscal year to reflect changes in the workload of the Secretary for the process for the review of animal drug applications. With respect to such adjustment:

(A) such adjustment shall be determined by the Secretary based on a weighted average of the change in the total number of animal drug applications, supplemental animal drug applications for which data with respect to safety or effectiveness are required, manufacturing supplemental animal drug applications, investigational animal drug study submissions, and investigational animal drug protocol submissions submitted to the Secretary;

(B) the Secretary shall publish in the Federal Register the fees resulting from such adjustment and the supporting methodologies; and

(C) under no circumstances shall such adjustment result in fee revenues for a fiscal year that are less than the fee revenues for that fiscal year established in subsection (b) of this section, as adjusted for inflation under paragraph (2).

(4) Final Year Adjustment. — For fiscal year 2018, the Secretary may, in addition to other adjustments under this subsection, further increase the fees under this section, if such an adjustment is necessary, to provide for up to 3 months of operating reserves of carryover user fees for the process for the review of animal drug applications for the first 3 months of fiscal year 2019. If the Food and Drug Administration has carryover balances for the process for the review of animal drug applications in excess of 3 months of such operating reserves, then this adjustment will not be made. If this adjustment is necessary, then the rationale for the amount of the increase shall be contained in the annual notice setting fees for fiscal year 2018.

(5) Limit. — The total amount of fees charged, as adjusted under this subsection, for a fiscal year may not exceed the total costs for such fiscal year for the resources allocated for the process for the review of animal drug applications.

(d) Fee Waiver or Reduction. —

(1) In General. — The Secretary shall grant a waiver from or a reduction of one or more fees assessed under subsection (a) of this section where the Secretary finds that —

(A) the assessment of the fee would present a significant barrier to innovation because of limited resources available to such person or other circumstances,;

(B) the fees to be paid by such person will exceed the anticipated present and future costs incurred by the Secretary in conducting the process for the review of animal drug applications for such person,;

(C) the animal drug application or supplemental animal drug application is intended solely to provide for use of the animal drug in —

(i) a Type B medicated feed (as defined in section 558.3(b)(3) of title 21, Code of Federal Regulations (or any successor regulation)) intended for use in the manufacture of Type C free-choice medicated feeds,; or

(ii) a Type C free-choice medicated feed (as defined in section 558.3(b)(4) of title 21, Code of Federal Regulations (or any successor regulation));

(D) the animal drug application or supplemental animal drug application is intended solely to provide for a minor use or minor species indication,; or

(E) the sponsor involved is a small business submitting its first animal drug application to the Secretary for review.

(2) Use of Standard Costs. — In making the finding in paragraph (1)(B), the Secretary may use standard costs.

(3) Rules for Small Businesses. —

(A) Definition. — In paragraph (1)(E), the term "small business" means an entity that has fewer than 500 employees, including employees of affiliates.

(B) Waiver of Application Fee. — The Secretary shall waive under paragraph (1)(E) the application fee for the first animal drug application that a small business or its affiliate submits to the Secretary for review. After a small business or its affiliate is granted such a waiver, the small business or its affiliate shall pay application fees for all subsequent animal drug applications and supplemental animal drug applications for which safety or effectiveness data are required in the same manner as an entity that does not qualify as a small business.

(C) Certification. — The Secretary shall require any person who applies for a waiver under paragraph (1)(E) to certify their qualification for the waiver. The Secretary shall periodically publish in the Federal Register a list of persons making such certifications.

(e) Effect of Failure to Pay Fees. — An animal drug application or supplemental animal drug application submitted by a person subject to fees under subsection (a) of this section shall be considered incomplete and shall not be accepted for filing by the Secretary until all fees owed by such person have been paid. An investigational animal drug submission under section 379j-11(5)(B) of this title that is submitted by a person subject to fees under subsection (a) of this section shall be considered incomplete and shall not be accepted for review by the Secretary until all fees owed by such person have been paid. The Secretary may discontinue review of any animal drug application, supplemental animal drug application or investigational animal drug submission from a person if such person has not submitted for payment all fees owed under this section by 30 days after the date upon which they are due.

(f) Assessment of Fees. —

(1) Limitation. — Fees may not be assessed under subsection (a) of this section for a fiscal year beginning after fiscal year 2003 unless appropriations for salaries and expenses of the Food and Drug Administration for such fiscal year (excluding the amount of fees appropriated for such fiscal year) are equal to or greater than the amount of appropriations for the salaries and expenses of the Food and Drug Administration for the fiscal year 2003 (excluding the amount of fees appropriated for such fiscal year) multiplied by the adjustment factor applicable to the fiscal year involved.

(2) Authority. — If the Secretary does not assess fees under subsection (a) of this section during any portion of a fiscal year because of paragraph (1) and if at a later date in such fiscal year the Secretary may assess such fees, the Secretary may assess and collect such fees, without any modification in the rate, for animal drug applications, supplemental animal drug applications, investigational animal drug submissions, animal drug sponsors, animal drug establishments and animal drug products at any time in such fiscal year notwithstanding the provisions of subsection (a) relating to the date fees are to be paid.

(g) Crediting and Availability of Fees. —

(1) In General. — Subject to paragraph 2(C), fees authorized under subsection (a) of this section shall be collected and available for obligation only to the extent and in the amount provided in advance in appropriations Acts. Such fees are authorized to be appropriated to remain available until expended. Such sums as may be necessary may be transferred from the Food and Drug Administration salaries and expenses appropriation account without fiscal year limitation to such appropriation account for salary and expenses with such fiscal year limitation. The sums transferred shall be available solely for the process for the review of animal drug applications.

(2) Collections and Appropriation Acts. —

(A) In General. — The fees authorized by this section —

(i) subject to paragraph (C), shall be collected and available in each fiscal year in an amount not to exceed the amount specified in appropriation Acts, or otherwise made available for obligation for such fiscal year, and

(ii) shall be available to defray increases in the costs of the resources allocated for the process for the review of animal drug applications (including increases in such costs for an additional number of full-time equivalent positions in the Department of Health and Human Services to be engaged in such process) over such costs, excluding costs paid from fees collected under this section, for fiscal year 2003 multiplied by the adjustment factor.

(B) Compliance. — The Secretary shall be considered to have met the requirements of subparagraph (A)(ii) in any fiscal year if the costs funded by appropriations and allocated for the process for the review of animal drug applications —

(i) are not more than 3 percent below the level specified in subparagraph (A)(ii); or

(ii) —

(I) are more than 3 percent below the level specified in subparagraph (A)(ii), and fees assessed for the fiscal year following the subsequent fiscal year are decreased by the amount in excess of 3 percent by which such costs fell below the level specified in subparagraph (A)(ii); and

(II) such costs are not more than 5 percent below the level specified in subparagraph (A)(ii).

(C) Provision for Early Payments. — Payment of fees authorized under this section for a fiscal year, prior to the due date for such fees, may be accepted by the Secretary in accordance with authority provided in advance in a prior year appropriations Act.

(3) Authorization of Appropriations. — For each of the fiscal years 2014 through 2018, there is authorized to be appropriated for fees under this section an amount equal to the total revenue amount determined under subsection (b) for the fiscal year, as adjusted or otherwise affected under subsection (c) and paragraph (4).

(4) Offset of Overcollections; Recovery of Collection Shortfalls. —

(A) Offset of Overcollections. — If the sum of the cumulative amount of fees collected under this section for fiscal years 2014 through 2016 and the amount of fees estimated to be collected under this section for fiscal year 2017 (including any increased fee collections attributable to subparagraph (B)), exceeds the cumulative amount appropriated pursuant to paragraph (3) for the fiscal years 2014 through 2017, the excess amount shall be credited to the appropriation account of the Food and Drug Administration as provided in paragraph (1), and shall be subtracted from the amount of fees that would otherwise be authorized to be collected under this section pursuant to appropriation Acts for fiscal year 2018.

(B) Recovery of Collection Shortfalls.—

(i) Fiscal Year 2016. — For fiscal year 2016, the amount of fees otherwise authorized to be collected under this section shall be increased by the amount, if any, by which the amount collected under this section and appropriated for fiscal year 2014 falls below the amount of fees authorized for fiscal year 2014 under paragraph (3).

(ii) Fiscal Year 2017. — For fiscal year 2017, the amount of fees otherwise authorized to be collected under this section shall be increased by the amount, if any, by which the amount collected under this section and appropriated for fiscal year 2015 falls below the amount of fees authorized for fiscal year 2015 under paragraph (3).

(iii) Fiscal Year 2018. — For fiscal year 2018, the amount of fees otherwise authorized to be collected under this section (including any reduction in the authorized amount under subparagraph (A)), shall be increased by the cumulative amount, if any, by which the amount collected under this section and appropriated for fiscal years 2016 and 2017 (including estimated collections for fiscal year 2017) falls below the cumulative amount of fees authorized under paragraph (3) for fiscal years 2016 and 2017.

(h) Collection of Unpaid Fees. — In any case where the Secretary does not receive payment of a fee assessed under subsection (a) within 30 days after it is due, such fee shall be treated as a claim of the United States Government subject to subchapter II of chapter 37 of title 31, United States Code.

(i) Written Requests for Waivers, Reductions, and Refunds. — To qualify for consideration for a waiver or reduction under subsection (d), or for a refund of any fee collected in accordance with subsection (a), a person shall submit to the Secretary a written request for such waiver, reduction, or refund not later than 180 days after such fee is due.

(j) Construction. — This section may not be construed to require that the number of full-time equivalent positions in the Department of Health and Human Services, for officers, employees, and advisory committees not engaged in the process of the review of animal drug applications, be reduced to offset the number of officers, employees, and advisory committees so engaged.

(k) Abbreviated New Animal Drug Applications. — The Secretary shall —

(1) to the extent practicable, segregate the review of abbreviated new animal drug applications from the process for the review of animal drug applications,; and

(2) adopt other administrative procedures to ensure that review times of abbreviated new animal drug applications do not increase from their current level due to activities under the user fee program.

Sec. 740A. [379j-13] Reauthorization; Reporting Requirements.

(a) Performance Report. — Beginning with fiscal year 2014, not later than 120 days after the end of each fiscal year during which fees are collected under this part, the Secretary shall prepare and submit to the Committee on Health, Education, Labor, and Pensions of the Senate and the Committee on Energy and Commerce of the House of Representatives a report concerning the progress of the Food and Drug Administration in achieving the goals identified in the letters described in section 101(b) of the Animal Drug User Fee Amendments of 2013 toward expediting the animal drug development process and the review of the new and supplemental animal drug applications and investigational animal drug submissions during such fiscal year, the future plans of the Food and Drug Administration for meeting the goals, the review times for abbreviated new animal drug applications, and the administrative procedures adopted by the Food and Drug Administration to ensure that review times for abbreviated new animal drug applications are not increased from their current level due to activities under the user fee program.

(b) Fiscal Report. — Beginning with fiscal year 2014, not later than 120 days after the end of each fiscal year during which fees are collected under this part, the Secretary shall prepare and submit to the Committee on Health, Education, Labor, and Pensions of the Senate and the Committee on Energy and Commerce of the House of Representatives a report on the implementation of the authority for such fees during such fiscal year and the use, by the Food and Drug Administration, of the fees collected during such fiscal year for which the report is made.

(c) Public Availability. — The Secretary shall make the reports required under subsections (a) and (b) available to the public on the Internet Web site of the Food and Drug Administration.

(d) Reauthorization. —

(1) Consultation. — In developing recommendations to present to the Congress with respect to the goals, and plans for meeting the goals, for the process for the review of animal drug applications for the first 5 fiscal years after fiscal year 2018, and for the reauthorization of this part for such fiscal years, the Secretary shall consult with —

(A) the Committee on Health, Education, Labor, and Pensions of the Senate;

(B) the Committee on Energy and Commerce of the House of Representatives;

(C) scientific and academic experts;

(D) veterinary professionals;

(E) representatives of patient and consumer advocacy groups; and

(F) the regulated industry.

(2) Prior Public Input. — Prior to beginning negotiations with the regulated industry on the reauthorization of this part, the Secretary shall —

(A) publish a notice in the Federal Register requesting public input on the reauthorization;

(B) hold a public meeting at which the public may present its views on the reauthorization, including specific suggestions for changes to the goals referred to in subsection (a);

(C) provide a period of 30 days after the public meeting to obtain written comments from the public suggesting changes to this part; and

(D) publish the comments on the Food and Drug Administration's Internet Web site.

(3) Periodic Consultation. — Not less frequently than once every 4 months during negotiations with the regulated industry, the Secretary shall hold discussions with representatives of veterinary, patient, and consumer advocacy groups to continue discussions of their views on the reauthorization and their suggestions for changes to this part as expressed under paragraph (2).

(4) Public Review of Recommendations. — After negotiations with the regulated industry, the Secretary shall —

(A) present the recommendations developed under paragraph (1) to the Congressional committees specified in such paragraph;

(B) publish such recommendations in the Federal Register;

(C) provide for a period of 30 days for the public to provide written comments on such recommendations;

(D) hold a meeting at which the public may present its views on such recommendations; and

(E) after consideration of such public views and comments, revise such recommendations as necessary.

(5) Transmittal of Recommendations. — Not later than January 15, 2018, the Secretary shall transmit to Congress the revised recommendations under paragraph (4) a summary of the views and comments received under such paragraph, and any changes made to the recommendations in response to such views and comments.

(6) Minutes of Negotiation Meetings. —

(A) Public Availability. — Before presenting the recommendations developed under paragraphs (1) through (5) to Congress, the Secretary shall make publicly available, on the Internet Web site of the Food and Drug Administration, minutes of all negotiation meetings conducted under this subsection between the Food and Drug Administration and the regulated industry.

(B) Content. — The minutes described under subparagraph (A) shall summarize any substantive proposal made by any party to the negotiations as well as significant controversies or differences of opinion during the negotiations and their resolution.

Part 5 — Fees Relating to Generic Animal Drugs*

Sec. 741. [379j-21] Authority to Assess and Use Generic New Animal Drug Fees

(a) Types of Fees. — Beginning with respect to fiscal year 2009, the Secretary shall assess and collect fees in accordance with this section as follows:

(1) Abbreviated Application Fee. —

(A) In General. — Each person that submits, on or after July 1, 2008, an abbreviated application for a generic new animal drug shall be subject to a fee as established in subsection (c) for such an application.

(B) Payment. — The fee required by subparagraph (A) shall be due upon submission of the abbreviated application.

(C) Exceptions. —

(i) Previously Filed Application. — If an abbreviated application was submitted by a person that paid the fee for such application, was accepted for filing, and was not approved or was withdrawn (without a waiver or refund), the submission of an abbreviated application for the same product by the same person (or the person's licensee, assignee, or successor) shall not be subject to a fee under subparagraph (A).

(ii) Certain Abbreviated Applications Involving Combination Animal Drugs. — An abbreviated application which is subject to the criteria in section 512(d)(4) and submitted on or after October 1, 2013 shall be subject to a fee equal to 50 percent of the amount of the abbreviated application fee established in subsection (c).

(D) Refund of Fee if Application Refused for Filing. — The Secretary shall refund 75 percent of the fee paid under subparagraph (B) for any abbreviated application which is refused for filing.

(E) Refund of Fee if Application Withdrawn. — If an abbreviated application is withdrawn after the application was filed, the Secretary may refund the fee or portion of the fee paid under subparagraph (B) if no substantial work was performed on the application after the application was filed. The Secretary shall have the sole discretion to refund the fee under this subparagraph. A determination by the Secretary concerning a refund under this subparagraph shall not be reviewable.

(2) Generic New Animal Drug Product Fee. —

(A) In General. —Each Person —

(i) who is named as the applicant in an abbreviated application or supplemental abbreviated application for a generic new animal drug product which has been submitted for listing under section 510; and

(ii) who, after September 1, 2008, had pending before the Secretary an abbreviated application or supplemental abbreviated application,

shall pay for each such generic new animal drug product the annual fee established in subsection (c).

* Edits in this section reflect amendments made by the Animal Generic Drug User Fee Amendments of 2013, as well as by the Animal Generic Drug User Fee Act of 2008, which were not incorporated into previous versions of this book. Ceases to be effective October 1, 2018.

(B) Payment; Fee Due Date. — Such fee shall be payable for the fiscal year in which the generic new animal drug product is first submitted for listing under section 510, or is submitted for relisting under section 510 if the generic new animal drug product has been withdrawn from listing and relisted. After such fee is paid for that fiscal year, such fee shall be due each subsequent fiscal year that the product remains listed, upon the later of—

(i) the first business day after the date of enactment of an appropriations Act providing for the collection and obligation of fees for such fiscal year under this section; or

(ii) January 31 of each year.

(C) Limitation. — Such fee shall be paid only once for each generic new animal drug product for a fiscal year in which the fee is payable.

(3) Generic New Animal Drug Sponsor Fee. —

(A) In General. — Each person —

(i) who meets the definition of a generic new animal drug sponsor within a fiscal year; and

(ii) who, after September 1, 2008, had pending before the Secretary an abbreviated application, a supplemental abbreviated application, or an investigational submission,

shall be assessed an annual generic new animal drug sponsor fee as established under subsection (c).

(B) Payment; Fee Due Date. — Such fee shall be due each fiscal year upon the later of—

(i) the first business day after the date of enactment of an appropriations Act providing for the collection and obligation of fees for such fiscal year under this section; or

(ii) January 31 of each year.

(C) Amount of Fee. — Each generic new animal drug sponsor shall pay only 1 such fee each fiscal year, as follows:

(i) 100 percent of the amount of the generic new animal drug sponsor fee published for that fiscal year under subsection (c) for an applicant with more than 6 approved abbreviated applications.

(ii) 75 percent of the amount of the generic new animal drug sponsor fee published for that fiscal year under subsection (c) for an applicant with more than 1 and fewer than 7 approved abbreviated applications.

(iii) 50 percent of the amount of the generic new animal drug sponsor fee published for that fiscal year under subsection (c) for an applicant with 1 or fewer approved abbreviated applications.

(b) Fee Amounts. — Subject to subsections (c), (d), (f), and (g), the fees required under subsection (a) shall be established to generate fee revenue amounts as follows:

(1) Total Fee Revenues for Application Fees. — The total fee revenues to be collected in abbreviated application fees under subsection (a)(1) shall be $1,832,000 for fiscal year 2014, $1,736,000 for fiscal year 2015, $1,857,000 for fiscal year 2016, $1,984,000 for fiscal year 2017, and $2,117,000 for fiscal year 2018.

(2) Total Fee Revenues for Product Fees. — The total fee revenues to be collected in generic new animal drug product fees under subsection (a)(2) shall be $2,748,000 for fiscal year 2014, $2,604,000 for fiscal year 2015, $2,786,000 for fiscal year 2016, $2,976,000 for fiscal year 2017, and $3,175,000 for fiscal year 2018.

(3) Total Fee Revenues for Sponsor Fees. — The total fee revenues to be collected in generic new animal drug sponsor fees under subsection (a)(3) shall be $2,748,000 for fiscal year 2014, $2,604,000 for fiscal year 2015, $2,786,000 for fiscal year 2016, $2,976,000 for fiscal year 2017, and $3,175,000 for fiscal year 2018.

(c) Annual Fee Setting; Adjustments. —

(1) Annual Fee Setting. — The Secretary shall establish, 60 days before the start of each fiscal year beginning after September 30, 2008, for that fiscal year, abbreviated application fees, generic new animal drug sponsor fees, and generic new animal drug product fees, based on the revenue amounts established under subsection (b) and the adjustments provided under this subsection.

(2) Workload Adjustment. — The fee revenues shall be adjusted each fiscal year after fiscal year 2014 to reflect changes in review workload. With respect to such adjustment:

(A) This adjustment shall be determined by the Secretary based on a weighted average of the change in the total number of abbreviated applications for generic new animal drugs, manufacturing supplemental abbreviated applications for generic new animal drugs, investigational generic new animal drug study submissions, and investigational generic new animal drug protocol submissions submitted to the Secretary. The Secretary shall publish in the Federal Register the fees resulting from this adjustment and the supporting methodologies.

(B) Under no circumstances shall this workload adjustment result in fee revenues for a fiscal year that are less than the fee revenues for that fiscal year established in subsection (b).

(3) Final Year Adjustment. — For fiscal year 2018, the Secretary may, in addition to other adjustments under this subsection, further increase the fees under this section, if such an adjustment is necessary, to provide for up to 3 months of operating reserves of carryover user fees for the process for the review of abbreviated applications for generic new animal drugs for the first 3 months of fiscal year 2019. If the Food and Drug Administration has carryover balances for the process for the review of abbreviated applications for generic new animal drugs in excess of 3 months of such operating reserves, then this adjustment shall not be made. If this adjustment is necessary, then the rationale for the amount of the increase shall be contained in the annual notice setting fees for fiscal year 2018.

(4) Limit. — The total amount of fees charged, as adjusted under this subsection, for a fiscal year may not exceed the total costs for such fiscal year for the resources allocated for the process for the review of abbreviated applications for generic new animal drugs.

(d) Fee Waiver or Reduction. — The Secretary shall grant a waiver from or a reduction of 1 or more fees assessed under subsection (a) where the Secretary finds that the generic new animal drug is intended solely to provide for a minor use or minor species indication.

(e) Effect of Failure to Pay Fees. — An abbreviated application for a generic new animal drug submitted by a person subject to fees under subsection (a) shall be considered incomplete and shall not be accepted for filing by the Secretary until all fees owed by such person have been paid. An investigational submission for a generic new animal drug that is submitted by a person subject to fees under subsection (a) shall be considered incomplete and shall not be accepted for review by the Secretary until all fees owed by such person have been paid. The Secretary may discontinue review of any abbreviated application for a generic new animal drug, supplemental abbreviated application for a generic new animal drug, or investigational submission for a generic new animal drug from a person if such person has not submitted for payment all fees owed under this section by 30 days after the date upon which they are due.

(f) Assessment of Fees. —

(1) Limitation. — Fees may not be assessed under subsection (a) for a fiscal year beginning after fiscal year 2008 unless appropriations for salaries and expenses of the Food and Drug Administration for such fiscal year (excluding the amount of fees appropriated for such fiscal year) are equal to or greater than the amount of appropriations for the salaries and expenses of the Food and Drug Administration for the fiscal year 2003 (excluding the amount of fees appropriated for such fiscal year) multiplied by the adjustment factor applicable to the fiscal year involved.

(2) Authority. — If the Secretary does not assess fees under subsection (a) during any portion of a fiscal year because of paragraph (1) and if at a later date in such fiscal year the Secretary may assess such fees, the Secretary may assess and collect such fees, without any modification in the rate, for abbreviated applications, generic new animal drug sponsors, and generic new animal drug products at any time in such fiscal year notwithstanding the provisions of subsection (a) relating to the date fees are to be paid.

(g) Crediting and Availability of Fees. —

(1) In General. — Subject to paragraph (2)(C), fees authorized under subsection (a) shall be collected and available for obligation only to the extent and in the amount provided in advance in appropriations Acts. Such fees are authorized to be appropriated to remain available until expended. Such sums as may be necessary may be transferred from the Food and Drug Administration salaries and expenses appropriation account without fiscal year limitation to such appropriation account for salary and expenses with such fiscal year limitation. The sums transferred shall be available solely for the process for the review of abbreviated applications for generic new animal drugs.

(2) Collections and Appropriation Acts. —

(A) In General. — The fees authorized by this section —

(i) subject to subparagraph (C), shall be collected and available in each fiscal year in an amount not to exceed the amount specified in appropriation Acts, or otherwise made available for obligation for such fiscal year; and

(ii) shall be available to defray increases in the costs of the resources allocated for the process for the review of abbreviated applications for generic new animal drugs (including increases in such costs for an additional number of full-time equivalent positions in the Department of Health and Human Services to be engaged in such process) over such costs, excluding costs paid from fees collected under this section, for fiscal year 2008 multiplied by the adjustment factor.

(B) Compliance. — The Secretary shall be considered to have met the requirements of subparagraph (A)(ii) in any fiscal year if the costs funded by appropriations and allocated for the process for the review of abbreviated applications for generic new animal drugs —

(i) are not more than 3 percent below the level specified in subparagraph (A)(ii); or

(ii) —

(I) are more than 3 percent below the level specified in subparagraph (A)(ii), and fees assessed for the fiscal year following the subsequent fiscal year are decreased by the amount in excess of 3 percent by which such costs fell below the level specified in subparagraph (A)(ii); and

(II) such costs are not more than 5 percent below the level specified in subparagraph (A)(ii).

(C) Provision for Early Payments. — Payment of fees authorized under this section for a fiscal year, prior to the due date for such fees, may be accepted by the Secretary in accordance with authority provided in advance in a prior year appropriations Act.

(3) Authorization of Appropriations. — There are authorized to be appropriated for fees under this section —

(A) $7,328,000 for fiscal year 2014;

(B) $6,944,000 for fiscal year 2015;

(C) $7,429,000 for fiscal year 2016;

(D) $7,936,000 for fiscal year 2017; and

(E) $8,467,000 for fiscal year 2018;

as adjusted to reflect adjustments in the total fee revenues made under this section and changes in the total amounts collected by abbreviated application fees, generic new animal drug sponsor fees, and generic new animal drug product fees.

(4) Offset. — If the sum of the cumulative amount of fees collected under this section for the fiscal years 2014 through 2016 and the amount of fees estimated to be collected under this section for fiscal year 2017 exceeds the cumulative amount appropriated under paragraph (3) for the fiscal years 2014 through 2017, the excess amount shall be credited to the appropriation account of the Food and Drug Administration as provided in paragraph (1), and shall be subtracted from the amount of fees that would otherwise be authorized to be collected under this section pursuant to appropriation Acts for fiscal year 2018.

(h) Collection of Unpaid Fees. — In any case where the Secretary does not receive payment of a fee assessed under subsection (a) within 30 days after it is due, such fee shall be treated as a claim of the United States Government subject to subchapter II of chapter 37 of title 31, United States Code.

(i) Written Requests for Waivers, Reductions, and Refunds. — To qualify for consideration for a waiver or reduction under subsection (d), or for a refund of any fee collected in accordance with subsection (a), a person shall submit to the Secretary a written request for such waiver, reduction, or refund not later than 180 days after such fee is due.

(j) Construction. — This section may not be construed to require that the number of full-time equivalent positions in the Department of Health and Human Services, for officers, employees, and advisory committees not engaged in the process of the review of abbreviated applications for generic new animal drugs, be reduced to offset the number of officers, employees, and advisory committees so engaged.

(k) Definitions. — In this section and section 742:

(1) Abbreviated Application for a Generic New Animal Drug. — The terms "abbreviated application for a generic new animal drug" and "abbreviated application" mean an abbreviated application for the approval of any generic new animal drug submitted under section 512(b)(2). Such term does not include a supplemental abbreviated application for a generic new animal drug.

(2) Adjustment Factor. — The term "adjustment factor" applicable to a fiscal year is the Consumer Price Index for all urban consumers (all items; United States city average) for October of the preceding fiscal year divided by —

(A) for purposes of subsection (f)(1), such Index for October 2002; and

(B) for purposes of subsection (g)(2)(A)(ii), such Index for October 2007.

(3) Costs of Resources Allocated for the Process for the Review of Abbreviated Applications for Generic New Animal Drugs. — The term "costs of resources allocated for the process for the review of abbreviated applications for generic new animal drugs" means the expenses in connection with the process for the review of abbreviated applications for generic new animal drugs for —

(A) officers and employees of the Food and Drug Administration, contractors of the Food and Drug Administration, advisory committees consulted with respect to the review of specific abbreviated applications, supplemental abbreviated applications, or investigational submissions, and costs related to such officers, employees, committees, and contractors, including costs for travel, education, and recruitment and other personnel activities;

(B) management of information, and the acquisition, maintenance, and repair of computer resources;

(C) leasing, maintenance, renovation, and repair of facilities and acquisition, maintenance, and repair of fixtures, furniture, scientific equipment, and other necessary materials and supplies; and

(D) collecting fees under this section and accounting for resources allocated for the review of abbreviated applications, supplemental abbreviated applications, and investigational submissions.

(4) Final Dosage Form. — The term "final dosage form" means, with respect to a generic new animal drug product, a finished dosage form which is approved for administration to an animal without substantial further manufacturing. Such term includes generic new animal drug products intended for mixing in animal feeds.

(5) Generic New Animal Drug. — The term "generic new animal drug" means a new animal drug that is the subject of an abbreviated application.

(6) Generic New Animal Drug Product. — The term "generic new animal drug product" means each specific strength or potency of a particular active ingredient or ingredients in final dosage form marketed by a particular manufacturer or distributor, which is uniquely identified by the labeler code and product code portions of the national drug code, and for which an abbreviated application for a generic new animal drug or a supplemental abbreviated application has been approved.

(7) Generic New Animal Drug Sponsor. — The term "generic new animal drug sponsor" means either an applicant named in an abbreviated application for a generic new animal drug that has not been withdrawn by the applicant and for which approval has not been withdrawn by the Secretary, or a person who has submitted an investigational submission for a generic new animal drug that has not been terminated or otherwise rendered inactive by the Secretary.

(8) Investigational Submission for a Generic New Animal Drug. — The terms "investigational submission for a generic new animal drug" and "investigational submission" mean —

(A) the filing of a claim for an investigational exemption under section 512(j) for a generic new animal drug intended to be the subject of an abbreviated application or a supplemental abbreviated application; or

(B) the submission of information for the purpose of enabling the Secretary to evaluate the safety or effectiveness of a generic new animal drug in the event of the filing of an abbreviated application or supplemental abbreviated application for such drug.

(9) Person. —The term "person" includes an affiliate thereof (as such term is defined in section 735(11)).

(10) Process for the Review of Abbreviated Applications for Generic New Animal Drugs. — The term "process for the review of abbreviated applications for generic new animal drugs" means the following activities of the Secretary with respect to the review of abbreviated applications, supplemental abbreviated applications, and investigational submissions:

(A) The activities necessary for the review of abbreviated applications, supplemental abbreviated applications, and investigational submissions.

(B) The issuance of action letters which approve abbreviated applications or supplemental abbreviated applications or which set forth in detail the specific deficiencies in abbreviated applications, supplemental abbreviated applications, or investigational submissions and, where appropriate, the actions necessary to place such applications, supplemental applications, or submissions in condition for approval.

(C) The inspection of generic new animal drug establishments and other facilities undertaken as part of the Secretary's review of pending abbreviated applications, supplemental abbreviated applications, and investigational submissions.

(D) Monitoring of research conducted in connection with the review of abbreviated applications, supplemental abbreviated applications, and investigational submissions.

(E) The development of regulations and policy related to the review of abbreviated applications, supplemental abbreviated applications, and investigational submissions.

(F) Development of standards for products subject to review.

(G) Meetings between the agency and the generic new animal drug sponsor.

(H) Review of advertising and labeling prior to approval of an abbreviated application or supplemental abbreviated application, but not after such application has been approved.

(11) Supplemental Abbreviated Application for Generic New Animal Drug. — The terms "supplemental abbreviated application for a generic new animal drug" and "supplemental abbreviated application" mean a request to the Secretary to approve a change in an approved abbreviated application.

Sec. 742. [379j-22] Reauthorization; Reporting Requirements.*

(a) Performance Reports. — Beginning with fiscal year 2014, not later than 120 days after the end of each fiscal year during which fees are collected under this part, the Secretary shall prepare and submit to the Committee on Health, Education, Labor, and Pensions of the Senate, and the Committee on Energy and Commerce of the House of Representatives a report concerning the progress of the Food and Drug Administration in achieving the goals identified in the letters described in section 201(b) of the Animal Generic Drug User Fee Amendments of 2013 toward expediting the generic new animal drug development process and the review of abbreviated applications for generic new animal drugs, supplemental abbreviated applications for generic new animal drugs, and investigational submissions for generic new animal drugs during such fiscal year.

(b) Fiscal Report. — Beginning with fiscal year 2014, not later than 120 days after the end of each fiscal year during which fees are collected under this part, the Secretary shall prepare and submit to Committee on Health, Education, Labor, and Pensions of the Senate and the Committee on Energy and Commerce of the House of Representatives a report on the implementation of the authority for such fees during such fiscal year and the use, by the Food and Drug Administration, of the fees collected during such fiscal year for which the report is made.

(c) Public Availability. — The Secretary shall make the reports required under subsections (a) and (b) available to the public on the Internet Web site of the Food and Drug Administration.

(d) Reauthorization. —

(1) Consultation. — In developing recommendations to present to Congress with respect to the goals, and plans for meeting the goals, for the process for the review of abbreviated applications for generic new animal drugs for the first 5 fiscal years after fiscal year 2018, and for the reauthorization of this part for such fiscal years, the Secretary shall consult with—

(A) the Committee on Energy and Commerce of the House of Representatives;

(B) the Committee on Health, Education, Labor, and Pensions of the Senate;

(C) scientific and academic experts;

(D) veterinary professionals;

(E) representatives of patient and consumer advocacy groups; and

(F) the regulated industry.

(2) Prior Public Input. — Prior to beginning negotiations with the regulated industry on the reauthorization of this part, the Secretary shall—

(A) publish a notice in the Federal Register requesting public input on the reauthorization;

* Edits in this section reflect amendments made by the Animal Generic Drug User Fee Amendments of 2013, as well as by the Animal Generic Drug User Fee Act of 2008, which were not incorporated into previous versions of this book. This section ceases to be effective January 31, 2019.

(B) hold a public meeting at which the public may present its views on the reauthorization, including specific suggestions for changes to the goals referred to in subsection (a);

(C) provide a period of 30 days after the public meeting to obtain written comments from the public suggesting changes to this part; and

(D) publish the comments on the Food and Drug Administration's Internet Web site.

(3) Periodic Consultation. — Not less frequently than once every 4 months during negotiations with the regulated industry, the Secretary shall hold discussions with representatives of veterinary, patient, and consumer advocacy groups to continue discussions of their views on the reauthorization and their suggestions for changes to this part as expressed under paragraph (2).

(4) Public Review of Recommendations. — After negotiations with the regulated industry, the Secretary shall—

(A) present the recommendations developed under paragraph (1) to the congressional committees specified in such paragraph;

(B) publish such recommendations in the Federal Register;

(C) provide for a period of 30 days for the public to provide written comments on such recommendations;

(D) hold a meeting at which the public may present its views on such recommendations; and

(E) after consideration of such public views and comments, revise such recommendations as necessary.

(5) Transmittal of Recommendations. — Not later than January 15, 2018, the Secretary shall transmit to Congress the revised recommendations under paragraph (4), a summary of the views and comments received under such paragraph, and any changes made to the recommendations in response to such views and comments.

(6) Minutes of Negotiation Meetings. —

(A) Public Availability. — Before presenting the recommendations developed under paragraphs (1) through (5) to Congress, the Secretary shall make publicly available, on the Internet Web site of the Food and Drug Administration, minutes of all negotiation meetings conducted under this subsection between the Food and Drug Administration and the regulated industry.

(B) Content. — The minutes described under subparagraph (A) shall summarize any substantive proposal made by any party to the negotiations as well as significant controversies or differences of opinion during the negotiations and their resolution.

Part 6 — Fees Related to Food

Sec. 743. [379j-31] Authority to Collect and Use Fees.

(a) In General —

(1) Purpose and Authority. — For fiscal year 2010 and each subsequent fiscal year, the Secretary shall, in accordance with this section, assess and collect fees from—

(A) the responsible party for each domestic facility (as defined in section 415(b)) and the United States agent for each foreign facility subject to a reinspection in such fiscal year, to cover reinspection-related costs for such year;

(B) the responsible party for a domestic facility (as defined in section 415(b)) and an importer who does not comply with a recall order under section 423 or under section 412(f) in such fiscal year, to cover food recall activities associated with such order performed by the Secretary, including technical assistance, follow-up effectiveness checks, and public notifications, for such year;

(C) each importer participating in the voluntary qualified importer program under section 806 in such year, to cover the administrative costs of such program for such year; and

(D) each importer subject to a reinspection in such fiscal year, to cover reinspection-related costs for such year.

(2) Definitions. — For purposes of this section—

(A) the term "reinspection" means—

(i) with respect to domestic facilities (as defined in section 415(b)), 1 or more inspections conducted under section 704 subsequent to an inspection conducted under such provision which identified noncompliance materially related to a food safety requirement of this Act, specifically to determine whether compliance has been achieved to the Secretary's satisfaction; and

(ii) with respect to importers, 1 or more examinations conducted under section 801 subsequent to an examination conducted under such provision which identified noncompliance materially related to a food safety requirement of this Act, specifically to determine whether compliance has been achieved to the Secretary's satisfaction;

(B) the term "reinspection-related costs" means all expenses, including administrative expenses, incurred in connection with—

(i) arranging, conducting, and evaluating the results of reinspections; and

(ii) assessing and collecting reinspection fees under this section; and

(C) the term "responsible party" has the meaning given such term in section 417(a)(1).

(b) Establishment of Fees. —

(1) In General. — Subject to subsections (c) and (d), the Secretary shall establish the fees to be collected under this section for each fiscal year specified in subsection (a)(1), based on the methodology described under paragraph (2), and shall publish such fees in a Federal Register notice not later than 60 days before the start of each such year.

(2) Fee Methodology. —

(A) Fees. — Fees amounts established for collection—

(i) under subparagraph (A) of subsection (a)(1) for a fiscal year shall be based on the Secretary's estimate of 100 percent of the costs of the reinspection-related activities (including by type or level of reinspection activity, as the Secretary determines applicable) described in such subparagraph (A) for such year;

(ii) under subparagraph (B) of subsection (a)(1) for a fiscal year shall be based on the Secretary's estimate of 100 percent of the costs of the activities described in such subparagraph (B) for such year;

(iii) under subparagraph (C) of subsection (a)(1) for a fiscal year shall be based on the Secretary's estimate of 100 percent of the costs of the activities described in such subparagraph (C) for such year; and

(iv) under subparagraph (D) of subsection (a)(1) for a fiscal year shall be based on the Secretary's estimate of 100 percent of the costs of the activities described in such subparagraph (D) for such year.

(B) Other Considerations. —

(i) Voluntary Qualified Importer Program. — In establishing the fee amounts under subparagraph (A)(iii) for a fiscal year, the Secretary shall provide for the number of importers who have submitted to the Secretary a notice under section 806(c) informing the Secretary of the intent of such importer to participate in the program under section 806 in such fiscal year.

(I) [Not enacted.]

(II) Recoupment. — In establishing the fee amounts under subparagraph (A)(iii) for the first 5 fiscal years after the date of enactment of this section, the Secretary shall include in such fee a reasonable surcharge that provides a recoupment of the costs expended by the Secretary to establish and implement the first year of the program under section 806.

(ii) Crediting of Fees. — In establishing the fee amounts under subparagraph (A) for a fiscal year, the Secretary shall provide for the crediting of fees from the previous year to the next year if the Secretary overestimated the amount of fees needed to carry out such activities, and consider the need to account for any adjustment of fees and such other factors as the Secretary determines appropriate.

(iii) Published Guidelines. — Not later than 180 days after the date of enactment of the FDA Food Safety Modernization Act, the Secretary shall publish in the Federal Register a proposed set of guidelines in consideration of the burden of fee amounts on small business. Such consideration may include reduced fee amounts for small businesses. The Secretary shall provide for a period of public comment on such guidelines. The Secretary shall adjust the fee schedule for small businesses subject to such fees only through notice and comment rulemaking.

(3) Use of Fees. — The Secretary shall make all of the fees collected pursuant to clause (i), (ii), (iii), and (iv) of paragraph (2)(A) available solely to pay for the costs referred to in such clause (i), (ii), (iii), and (iv) of paragraph (2)(A), respectively.

(c) Limitations. —

(1) In General. — Fees under subsection (a) shall be refunded for a fiscal year beginning after fiscal year 2010 unless the amount of the total appropriations for food safety activities at the Food and Drug Administration for such fiscal year (excluding the amount of fees appropriated for such fiscal year) is equal to or greater than the amount of appropriations for food safety activities at the Food and Drug Administration for fiscal year 2009 (excluding the amount of fees appropriated for such fiscal year), multiplied by the adjustment factor under paragraph (3).

(2) Authority. — If—

(A) the Secretary does not assess fees under subsection (a) for a portion of a fiscal year because paragraph (1) applies; and

(B) at a later date in such fiscal year, such paragraph (1) ceases to apply,

the Secretary may assess and collect such fees under subsection (a), without any modification to the rate of such fees, notwithstanding the provisions of subsection (a) relating to the date fees are to be paid.

(3) Adjustment Factor. —

(A) In General.— The adjustment factor described in paragraph (1) shall be the total percentage change that occurred in the Consumer Price Index for all urban consumers (all items; United States city average) for the 12-month period ending June 30 preceding the fiscal year, but in no case shall such adjustment factor be negative.

(B) Compounded Basis. — The adjustment under subparagraph (A) made each fiscal year shall be added on a compounded basis to the sum of all adjustments made each fiscal year after fiscal year 2009.

(4) Limitation on Amount of Certificates. —

(A) In General. — Notwithstanding any other provision of this section and subject to subparagraph (B), the Secretary may not collect fees in a fiscal year such that the amount collected—

(i) under subparagraph (B) of subsection (a)(1) exceeds $20,000,000; and

(ii) under subparagraphs (A) and (D) of subsection (a)(1) exceeds $25,000,000 combined.

(B) Exception. — If a domestic facility (as defined in section 415(b)) or an importer becomes subject to a fee described in subparagraph (A), (B), or (D) of subsection (a)(1) after the maximum amount of fees has been collected by the Secretary under subparagraph (A), the Secretary may collect a fee from such facility or importer.

(d) Crediting and Availability of Fees. — Fees authorized under subsection (a) shall be collected and available for obligation only to the extent and in the amount provided in appropriations Acts. Such fees are authorized to remain available until expended. Such sums as may be necessary may be transferred from the Food and Drug Administration salaries and expenses account without fiscal year limitation to such appropriation account for salaries and expenses with such fiscal year limitation. The sums transferred shall be available solely for the purpose of paying the operating expenses of the Food and Drug Administration employees and contractors performing activities associated with these food safety fees.

(e) Collection of Fees. —

(1) In General. — The Secretary shall specify in the Federal Register notice described in subsection (b)(1) the time and manner in which fees assessed under this section shall be collected.

(2) Collection of Unpaid Fees. — In any case where the Secretary does not receive payment of a fee assessed under this section within 30 days after it is due, such fee shall be treated as a claim of the United States Government subject to provisions of subchapter II of chapter 37 of title 31, United States Code.

(f) Annual Report to Congress. — Not later than 120 days after each fiscal year for which fees are assessed under this section, the Secretary shall submit a report to the Committee on Health, Education, Labor, and Pensions of the Senate and the Committee on Energy and Commerce of the House of Representatives, to include a description of fees assessed and collected for each such year and a summary description of the entities paying such fees and the types of business in which such entities engage.

(g) Authorization of Appropriations. — For fiscal year 2010 and each fiscal year thereafter, there is authorized to be appropriated for fees under this section an amount equal to the total revenue amount determined under subsection (b) for the fiscal year, as adjusted or otherwise affected under the other provisions of this section.

Part 7 — Fees Relating to Generic Drugs

Sec. 744A. [379j-41] Definitions.*

For purposes of this part:

(1) The term "abbreviated new drug application" —

(A) means an application submitted under section 505(j), an abbreviated application submitted under section 507 (as in effect on the day before the date of enactment of the Food and Drug Administration Modernization Act of 1997), or an abbreviated new drug application submitted pursuant to regulations in effect prior to the implementation of the Drug Price Competition and Patent Term Restoration Act of 1984; and

(B) does not include an ~~application for a positron emission tomography drug.~~ application—

(i) for a positron emission tomography drug; or

(ii) submitted by a State or Federal governmental entity for a drug that is not distributed commercially.

(2) The term "active pharmaceutical ingredient" means —

(A) a substance, or a mixture when the substance is unstable or cannot be transported on its own, intended —

(i) to be used as a component of a drug; and

(ii) to furnish pharmacological activity or other direct effect In the diagnosis, cure, mitigation, treatment, or prevention of disease, or to affect the structure or any function of the human body; or

(B) a substance intended for final crystallization, purification, or salt formation, or any combination of those activities, to become a substance or mixture described in subparagraph (A).

(3) The term "adjustment factor" means a factor applicable to a fiscal year that is the Consumer Price Index for all urban consumers (all items; United States city average) for October of the preceding fiscal year divided by such Index for October 2011.

(4) The term "affiliate" means a business entity that has a relationship with a second business entity if, directly or indirectly —

(A) one business entity controls, or has the power to control, the other business entity; or

(B) a third party controls, or has power to control, both of the business entities.

(5) The term "contract manufacturing organization facility" means a manufacturing facility of a finished dosage form of a drug approved pursuant to an abbreviated new drug application, where such manufacturing facility is not identified in an approved abbreviated new drug application held by the owner of such facility or an affiliate of such owner or facility.

~~(5)~~ (6) —

(A) The term "facility" —

(i) means a business or other entity —

(I) under one management, either direct or indirect; and

(II) at one geographic location or address engaged in manufacturing or processing an active pharmaceutical ingredient or a finished dosage form; and

(ii) does not include a business or other entity whose only manufacturing or processing activities are one or more of the following: repackaging, relabeling, or testing.

(B) For purposes of subparagraph (A), separate buildings within close proximity are considered to be at one geographic location or address if the activities in them are —

* Ceases to be effective October 1, ~~2017~~ 2022.

(i) closely related to the same business enterprise;

(ii) under the supervision of the same local management; and

(iii) capable of being inspected by the Food and Drug Administration during a single inspection.

(C) If a business or other entity would meet the definition of a facility under this paragraph but for being under multiple management, the business or other entity is deemed to constitute multiple facilities, one per management entity, for purposes of this paragraph.

~~(6)~~ (7) The term "finished dosage form" means —

(A) a drug product in the form in which it will be administered to a patient, such as a tablet, capsule, solution, or topical application;

(B) a drug product in a form in which reconstitution is necessary prior to administration to a patient, such as oral suspensions or lyophilized powers; or

(C) any combination of an active pharmaceutical ingredient with another component of a drug product for purposes of production of a drug product described in subparagraph (A) or (B).

~~(7)~~ (8) The term "generic drug submission" means an abbreviated new drug application, an amendment to an abbreviated new drug application, or a prior approval supplement to an abbreviated new drug application.

~~(8)~~ (9) The term "human generic drug activities" means the following activities of the Secretary associated with generic drugs and inspection of facilities associated with generic drugs:

(A) The activities necessary for the review of generic drug submissions, including review of drug master files referenced in such submissions.

(B) The issuance of —

(i) approval letters which approve abbreviated new drug applications or supplements to such applications; or

(ii) complete response letters which set forth in detail the specific deficiencies in such applications and, where appropriate, the actions necessary to place such applications in condition for approval.

(C) The issuance of letters related to Type II active pharmaceutical drug master files which —

(i) set forth in detail the specific deficiencies in such submissions, and where appropriate, the actions necessary to resolve those deficiencies; or

(ii) document that no deficiencies need to be addressed.

(D) Inspections related to generic drugs.

(E) Monitoring of research conducted in connection with the review of generic drug submissions and drug master files.

(F) Postmarket safety activities with respect to drugs approved under abbreviated new drug applications or supplements, including the following activities:

(i) Collecting, developing, and reviewing safety information on approved drugs, including adverse event reports.

(ii) Developing and using improved adverse-event data-collection systems, including information technology systems.

(iii) Developing and using improved analytical tools to assess potential safety problems, including access to external data bases.

(iv) Implementing and enforcing section 505(o) (relating to postapproval studies and clinical trials and labeling changes) and section 505(p) (relating to risk evaluation and mitigation strategies) insofar as those activities relate to abbreviated new drug applications.

(v) Carrying out section 505(k)(5) (relating to adverse-event reports and postmarket safety activities).

(G) Regulatory science activities related to generic drugs.

~~(9)~~ (10) The term "positron emission tomography drug" has the meaning given to the term "compounded positron emission tomography drug" in section 201(ii), except that paragraph (1)(B) of such section shall not apply.

~~(10)~~ (11) The term "prior approval supplement" means a request to the Secretary to approve a change in the drug substance, drug product, production process, quality controls, equipment, or facilities covered by an approved abbreviated new drug application when that change has a substantial potential to have an adverse effect on the identity, strength, quality, purity, or potency of the drug product as these factors may relate to the safety or effectiveness of the drug product.

~~(11)~~ (12) The term "resources allocated for human generic drug activities" means the expenses for—

(A) officers and employees of the Food and Drug Administration, contractors of the Food and Drug Administration, advisory committees, and costs related to such officers and employees and to contracts with such contractors;

(B) management of information, and the acquisition, maintenance, and repair of computer resources;

(C) leasing, maintenance, renovation, and repair of facilities and acquisition, maintenance, and repair of fixtures, furniture, scientific equipment, and other necessary materials and supplies; and

(D) collecting fees under subsection (a) and accounting for resources allocated for the review of abbreviated new drug applications and supplements and inspection related to generic drugs.

~~(12)~~ (13) The term "Type II active pharmaceutical ingredient drug master file" means a submission of information to the Secretary by a person that intends to authorize the Food and Drug Administration to reference the information to support approval of a generic drug submission without the submitter having to disclose the information to the generic drug submission applicant.

Sec. 744B. [379j-42] Authority to Assess and Use Human Generic Drug Fees.[*]

(a) Types of Fees. — Beginning in fiscal year ~~2013~~ 2018, the Secretary shall assess and collect fees in accordance with this section as follows;

(1) One-Time Backlog Fee for Abbreviated New Drug Applications Pending on October 1, 2012. —

(A) In General. — Each person that owns an abbreviated new drug application that is pending on October 1, 2012, and that has not received a tentative approval prior to that date, shall be subject to a fee for each such application, as calculated under subparagraph (B).

(B) Method of Fee Amount Calculation. — The amount of each one-time backlog fee shall be calculated by dividing $50,000,000 by the total number of abbreviated new drug applications pending on October 1, 2012, that have not received a tentative approval as of that date.

(C) Notice. — Not later than October 31, 2012, the Secretary shall publish in the Federal Register a notice announcing the amount of the fee required by subparagraph (A).

(D) Fee Due Date — The fee required by subparagraph (A) shall be due no later than 30 calendar days after the date of the publication of the notice specified in subparagraph (C).

(E) Sunset.— This paragraph shall cease to be effective October 1, 2022.

(2) Drug Master File Fee. —

(A) In General. — Each person that owns a Type II active pharmaceutical ingredient drug master file that is referenced on or after October 1, 2012, in a generic drug submission by any initial letter of authorization shall be subject to a drug master file fee.

(B) One-Time Payment. — If a person has paid a drug master file fee for a Type II active pharmaceutical ingredient drug master file, the person shall not be required to pay a subsequent drug master file fee when that Type II active pharmaceutical ingredient drug master file is subsequently referenced in generic drug submissions.

(C) Notice. — Not later than 60 days before the start of each of fiscal years 2018 through 2022, the Secretary shall publish in the Federal Register the amount of the drug master file fee established by this paragraph for such fiscal year.

~~(i) Fiscal Year 2013. — Not later than October 31, 2012, the Secretary shall publish in the Federal Register a notice announcing the amount of the drug master file fee for fiscal year 2013.~~

[*] Ceases to be effective October 1, ~~2017~~ 2022.

~~**(ii)** Fiscal Years 2014 through 2017. — Not later than 60 days before the start of each of fiscal years 2014 through 2017, the Secretary shall publish in the Federal Register the amount of the drug master file fee established by this paragraph for such fiscal year.~~

(D) Availability for Reference. —

(i) In General. — Subject to subsection (g)(2)(C), for a generic drug submission to reference a Type II active pharmaceutical ingredient drug master file, the drug master file must be deemed available for reference by the Secretary.

(ii) Conditions. — A drug master file shall be deemed available for reference by the Secretary if —

(I) the person that owns a Type II active pharmaceutical ingredient drug master file has paid the fee required under subparagraph (A) within 20 calendar days after the applicable due date under subparagraph (E); and

(II) the drug master file has not failed an initial completeness assessment by the Secretary, in accordance with criteria to be published by the Secretary.

(iii) List. — The Secretary shall make publicly available on the Internet Web site of the Food and Drug Administration a list of the drug master file numbers that correspond to drug master files that have successfully undergone an initial completeness assessment, in accordance with criteria to be published by the Secretary, and are available for reference.

(E) Fee Due Date. —

(i) In General. — Subject to clause (ii), a drug master file fee shall be due ~~no later than the date on which the first generic drug submission is submitted that references the associated Type II active pharmaceutical ingredient drug master file.~~ <u>on the earlier of—</u>

<u>**(I)** the date on which the first generic drug submission is submitted that references the associated Type II active pharmaceutical ingredient drug master file; or</u>

<u>**(II)** the date on which the drug master file holder requests the initial completeness assessment.</u>

(ii) Limitation. — No fee shall be due under subparagraph (A) for a fiscal year until the later of —

(I) 30 calendar days after publication of the notice provided for in ~~clause (i) or (ii) of~~ subparagraph (C)~~, as applicable~~; or

(II) 30 calendar days after the date of enactment of an appropriations Act providing for the collection and obligation of fees under this section.

(3) Abbreviated New Drug Application ~~and Prior Approval Supplement~~ Filing Fee. —

(A) In General. — Each applicant that submits, on or after October 1, 2012, an abbreviated new drug application ~~or a prior approval supplement to an abbreviated new drug application~~ shall be subject to a fee for each such submission in the amount established under subsection (d).

(B) Notice. — <u>Not later than 60 days before the start of each of fiscal years 2018 through 2022, the Secretary shall publish in the Federal Register the amount of the fees under subparagraph (A) for such fiscal year.</u>

~~**(i) Fiscal Year 2013.** — Not later than October 31, 2012, the Secretary shall publish in the Federal Register a notice announcing the amount of the fees under subparagraph (A) for fiscal year 2013.~~

~~**(ii) Fiscal Years 2014 Through 2017.** — Not later than 60 days before the start of each of fiscal years 2014 through 2017, the Secretary shall publish in the Federal Register the amount of the fees under subparagraph (A) for such fiscal year.~~

(C) Fee Due Date. — <u>The fees required by subparagraphs (A) and (F) shall be due no later than the date of submission of the abbreviated new drug application or prior approval supplement for which such fee applies.</u>

~~**(i) In General.** — Except as provided in clause (ii), the fees required by subparagraphs (A) and (F) shall be due no later than the date of submission of the abbreviated new drug application or prior approval supplement for which such fee applies.~~

~~**(ii) Special Rule for 2013.** — For fiscal year 2013, such fees shall be due on the later of —~~

~~**(I)** the date on which the fee is due under clause (i);~~

~~**(II)** 30 calendar days after publication of the notice referred to in subparagraph (B)(i); or~~

~~(III) if an appropriations Act is not enacted providing for the collection and obligation of fees under this section by the date of submission of the application or prior approval supplement for which the fees under subparagraphs (A) and (F) apply, 30 calendar days after the date that such an appropriations Act is enacted.~~

(D) Refund of Fee if Abbreviated New Drug Application is Not Considered to Have Been Received, is Withdrawn Prior to Being Received, or is No Longer Received. — ~~The Secretary shall refund 75% of the fee paid under subparagraph (A) for any abbreviated new drug application or prior approval supplement to an abbreviated new drug application that the Secretary considers not to have been received within the meaning of section 505(j)(5)(A) for a cause other than failure to pay fees.~~

(i) Applications Not Considered to have Been Received and Applications Withdrawn Prior to Being Received.— The Secretary shall refund 75 percent of the fee paid under subparagraph (A) for any abbreviated new drug application that the Secretary considers not to have been received within the meaning of section 505(j)(5)(A) for a cause other than failure to pay fees, or that has been withdrawn prior to being received within the meaning of section 505(j)(5)(A).

(ii) Applications No Longer Received.— The Secretary shall refund 100 percent of the fee paid under subparagraph (A) for any abbreviated new drug application if the Secretary initially receives the application under section 505(j)(5)(A) and subsequently determines that an exclusivity period for a listed drug should have prevented the Secretary from receiving such application, such that the abbreviated new drug application is no longer received within the meaning of section 505(j)(5)(A).

(E) Fee for an Application the Secretary Considers Not to Have Been Received, or That Has Been Withdrawn. — An abbreviated new drug application ~~or prior approval supplement~~ that was submitted on or after October 1, 2012, and that the Secretary considers not to have been received, or that has been withdrawn, shall, upon resubmission of the application or a subsequent new submission following the applicant's withdrawal of the application, be subject to a full fee under subparagraph (A).

(F) Additional Fee for Active Pharmaceutical Ingredient Information Not Includeed by Reference to Type II Active Pharmaceutical Ingredient Drug Master File. — An applicant that submits a generic drug submission on or after October 1, ~~2012~~ 2017, shall pay a fee, in the amount determined under subsection (d)~~(3)~~(2), in addition to the fee required under subparagraph (A), if—

(i) such submission contains information concerning the manufacture of an active pharmaceutical ingredient at a facility by means other than reference by a letter of authorization to a Type II active pharmaceutical drug master file; and

(ii) a fee in the amount equal to the drug master file fee established in paragraph (2) has not been previously paid with respect to such information.

(4) Generic Drug Facility Fee and Active Pharmaceutical Ingredient Facility Fee. —

(A) In General. — Facilities identified~~, or intended to be identified, in at least one generic drug submission that is pending or~~ in at least one generic drug submission that is approved to produce a finished dosage form of a human generic drug or an active pharmaceutical ingredient contained in a human generic drug shall be subject to fees as follows:

(i) Generic Drug Facility. — Each person that owns a facility which is identified ~~or intended to be identified in at least one generic drug submission that is pending or~~ in at least one generic drug submission that is approved to produce one or more finished dosage forms of a human generic drug shall be assessed an annual fee for each such facility.

(ii) Active Pharmaceutical Ingredient Facility. — Each person that owns a facility which ~~produces, or which is pending review to produce, one or more active pharmaceutical ingredients identified, or intended to be identified, in at least one generic drug submission that is pending or approved or in a Type II active pharmaceutical ingredient drug master file referenced in such a~~ is identified in at least one generic drug submission in which the facility is approved to produce one or more active pharmaceutical ingredients or in a Type II active pharmaceutical ingredient drug master file referenced in at least one such generic drug submission, shall be assessed an annual fee for each such facility.

(iii) Facilities Producing Both Active Pharmaceutical Ingredients and Finished Dosage Forms. — Each person that owns a facility identified~~, or intended to be identified, in at least one generic drug submission that is pending or~~ in at least one generic drug submission that is approved to produce both one or more finished dosage forms subject to clause (i) and one or more active pharmaceutical ingredients subject to clause (ii) shall be subject ~~to fees under both such clauses~~ only to the fee attributable to the manufacture of the finished dosage forms for that facility.

(B) Amount. — The amount of fees established under subparagraph (A) shall be established under subsection (d).

~~**(C) Notice.** —~~

~~**(i) Fiscal Year 2013.** — For fiscal year 2013, the Secretary shall publish in the Federal Register a notice announcing the amount of the fees provided for in subparagraph (A) within the timeframe specified in subsection (d)(1)(B).~~

~~**(ii) Fiscal Years 2014 Through 2017.** — Within the timeframe specified in subsection (d)(2), the Secretary shall publish in the Federal Register the amount of the fees under subparagraph (A) for such fiscal year.~~

~~**(D) Fee Due Date.** —~~

~~**(i) Fiscal Year 2013.** — For fiscal year 2013, the fees under subparagraph (A) shall be due on the later of —~~

~~**(I)** not later than 45 days after the publication of the notice under subparagraph (B); or~~

~~**(II)** if an appropriations Act is not enacted providing for the collection and obligation of fees under this section by the date of the publication of such notice, 30 days after the date that such an appropriations Act is enacted.~~

~~**(ii) Fiscal Years 2014 Through 2017.** — For each of fiscal years 2014 though 2017, the fees under subparagraph (A) for such fiscal year shall be due on the later of —~~

~~**(I)** the first business day on or after October 1 of each such year; or~~

~~**(II)** the first business day after the enactment of an appropriations Act providing for the collection and obligation of fees under this section for such year.~~

(C) Notice. — Within the timeframe specified in subsection (d)(1), the Secretary shall publish in the Federal Register the amount of the fees under subparagraph (A) for such fiscal year.

(D) Fee Due Date. — For each of fiscal years 2018 through 2022, the fees under subparagraph (A) for such fiscal year shall be due on the later of —

(i) the first business day on or after October 1 of each such year; or

(ii) the first business day after the enactment of an appropriations Act providing for the collection and obligation of fees for such year under this section for such year.

(5) Generic Drug Applicant Program Fee. —

(A) In General. — A generic drug applicant program fee shall be assessed annually as described in subsection (b)(2)(E).

(B) Amount. — The amount of fees established under subparagraph (A) shall be established under subsection (d).

(C) Notice. — Within the timeframe specified in subsection (d)(1), the Secretary shall publish in the Federal Register the amount of the fees under subparagraph (A) for such fiscal year.

(D) Fee Due Date. — For each of fiscal years 2018 through 2022, the fees under subparagraph (A) for such fiscal year shall be due on the later of —

(i) the first business day on or after October 1 of each such fiscal year; or

(ii) the first business day after the date of enactment of an appropriations Act providing for the collection and obligation of fees for such fiscal year under this section for such fiscal year.

~~(5)~~ **(6) Date of Submission.** — For purposes of this Act, a generic drug submission or Type II pharmaceutical master file is deemed to be "submitted" to the Food and Drug Administration —

(A) if it is submitted via a Food and Drug Administration electronic gateway, on the day when transmission to that electronic gateway is completed, except that submission or master file that arrives on a weekend, Federal holiday, or day when the Food and Drug Administration office that will review that submission is not otherwise open for business shall be deemed to be submitted on the next day when that office is open for business; or

(B) If it is submitted in physical media form, on the day it arrives at the appropriate designated document room of the Food and Drug Administration.

(b) Fee Revenue Amounts. —

(1) In General. —

(A) Fiscal Year ~~2013~~ 2018. — For fiscal year ~~2013~~ 2018, fees under subsection (a) shall be established to generate a total estimated revenue amount under such subsection of ~~$299,000,000.~~ $493,600,000. ~~Of that amount —~~

~~(i) $50,000,000 shall be generated by the one-time backlog fee for generic drug applications pending on October 1, 2012, established in subsection (a)(1); and~~

~~(ii) $249,000,000 shall be generated by the fees under paragraphs (2) through (4) of subsection (a).~~

(B) Fiscal Years ~~2014~~ 2019 Through ~~2017~~ 2022. — For each of the fiscal years ~~2014 through 2017~~ 2019 through 2022, fees under paragraphs (2) through ~~(4)~~ (5) of subsection (a) shall be established to generate a total estimated revenue amount under such subsection that is equal to ~~$299,000,000~~ $493,600,000, as adjusted pursuant to subsection (c).

(2) Types of Fees. — In establishing fees under ~~paragraph (1) to generate the revenue amounts specified in paragraph (1)(A)(ii) for fiscal year 2013 and paragraph (1)(B) for each of fiscal years 2014 through 2017,~~ such paragraph for a fiscal year, such fees shall be derived from the fees under paragraphs (2) through ~~(4)~~ (5) of subsection (a) as follows:

(A) ~~Six~~ Five percent shall be derived from fees under subsection (a)(2) (relating to drug master files).

(B) ~~Twenty-four percent shall be derived from fees under subsection (a)(3) (relating to abbreviated new drug applications and supplements). The amount of a fee for a prior approval supplement shall be half the amount of the fee for an abbreviated new drug application.~~ Thirty-three percent shall be derived from fees under subsection (a)(3) (relating to abbreviated new drug applications).

(C) ~~Fifty-six percent shall be derived from fees under subsection (a)(4)(A)(i) (relating to generic drug facilities). The amount of the fee for a facility located outside the United States and its territories and possessions shall be not less than $15,000 and not more than $30,000 higher than the amount of the fee for a facility located in the United States and its territories and possessions, as determined by the Secretary on the basis of data concerning the difference in cost between inspections of facilities located in the United States, including its territories and possessions, and those located outside of the United States and its territories and possessions.~~ Twenty percent shall be derived from fees under subsection (a)(4)(A)(i) (relating to generic drug facilities). The amount of the fee for a contract manufacturing organization facility shall be equal to one-third the amount of the fee for a facility that is not a contract manufacturing organization facility. The amount of the fee for a facility located outside the United States and its territories and possessions shall be $15,000 higher than the amount of the fee for a facility located in the United States and its territories and possessions.

(D) ~~Fourteen~~ Seven percent shall be derived from fees under subsection (a)(4)(A)(ii) (relating to active pharmaceutical ingredient facilities). The amount of the fee for a facility located outside the United States and its territories and possessions shall be ~~not less than $15,000 and not more than $30,000~~ $15,000 higher than the amount of the fee for a facility located in the United States, including its territories and possessions, ~~as determined by the Secretary on the basis of data concerning the difference in cost between inspections of facilities located in the United States and its territories and possessions and those located outside of the United States and its territories and possessions.~~

(E)(i) Thirty-five percent shall be derived from fees under subsection (a)(5) (relating to generic drug applicant program fees). For purposes of this subparagraph, if a person has affiliates, a single program fee shall be assessed with respect to that person, including its affiliates, and may be paid by that person or any one of its affiliates. The Secretary shall determine the fees as follows:

(I) If a person (including its affiliates) owns at least one but not more than 5 approved abbreviated new drug applications on the due date for the fee under this subsection, the person (including its affiliates) shall be assessed a small business generic drug applicant program fee equal to one-tenth of the large size operation generic drug applicant program fee.

(II) If a person (including its affiliates) owns at least 6 but not more than 19 approved abbreviated new drug applications on the due date for the fee under this subsection, the person (including its affiliates) shall be assessed a medium size operation generic drug applicant program fee equal to two-fifths of the large size operation generic drug applicant program fee.

(III) If a person (including its affiliates) owns 20 or more approved abbreviated new drug applications on the due date for the fee under this subsection, the person (including its affiliates) shall be assessed a large size operation generic drug applicant program fee.

(ii) For purposes of this subparagraph, an abbreviated new drug application shall be deemed not to be approved if the applicant has submitted a written request for withdrawal of approval of such abbreviated new drug application by April 1 of the previous fiscal year.

(c) Adjustments. —

(1) Inflation Adjustment. — For fiscal year ~~2014~~ 2019 and subsequent fiscal years, the revenues established in subsection (b) shall be adjusted by the Secretary by notice, published in the Federal Register, for a fiscal year, to equal the product of the total revenues established in such notice for the prior fiscal year multiplied by an amount equal to the sum of —

(A) one;

(B) the average annual percent change in the cost, per full-time equivalent position of the Food and Drug Administration, of all personnel compensation and benefits paid with respect to such positions for the first 3 years of the preceding 4 fiscal years multiplied by the proportion of personnel compensation and benefits costs to total costs of human generic drug activities for the first 3 years of the preceding 4 fiscal years; and

(C) the average annual percent change that occurred in the Consumer Price Index for urban consumers (Washington-Baltimore, DC-MD-VA-WV; Not Seasonally Adjusted; All items; Annual Index) for the first 3 years of the preceding 4 years of available data multiplied by the proportion of all costs other than personnel compensation and benefits costs to total costs of human generic drug activities for the first 3 years of the preceding 4 fiscal years.

~~The adjustment made each fiscal year under this subsection shall be added on a compounded basis to the sum of all adjustments made each fiscal year after fiscal year 2013 under this subsection.~~

(2) Final Year Adjustment. — For fiscal year ~~2017~~ 2022, the Secretary may, in addition to adjustments under paragraph (1), further increase the fee revenues and fees established in subsection (b) if such an adjustment is necessary to provide for not more than 3 months of operating reserves of carryover user fees for human generic drug activities for the first 3 months of fiscal year ~~2018~~ 2023. ~~Such fees may only be used in fiscal year 2018.~~ If such an adjustment is necessary, the rationale for the amount of the increase shall be contained in the annual notice establishing fee revenues and fees for fiscal year ~~2017~~ 2022. If the Secretary has carryover balances for such activities in excess of 3 months of such operating reserves, the adjustment under this subparagraph shall not be made.

(d) Annual Fee Setting. —

~~**(1) Fiscal Year 2013.** — For fiscal year 2013—~~

~~**(A)** the Secretary shall establish, by October 31, 2012, the one-time generic drug backlog fee for generic drug applications pending on October 1, 2012, the drug master file fee, the abbreviated new drug application fee, and the prior approval supplement fee under subsection (a), based on the revenue amounts established under subsection (b); and~~

~~**(B)** the Secretary shall establish, not later than 45 days after the date to comply with the requirement for identification of facilities in subsection (f)(2), the generic drug facility fee and active pharmaceutical ingredient facility fee under subsection (a) based on the revenue amounts established under subsection (b).~~

~~**(2)**~~ **(1) Fiscal Years** ~~**2014**~~ **2018 Through** ~~**2017**~~ **2022.** — Not more than 60 days before the first day of each of fiscal years ~~2014 through 2017~~ 2018 through 2022, the Secretary shall establish the ~~drug master file fee, the abbreviated new drug application fee, and the prior approval supplement fee, the generic drug facility fee, and the active pharmaceutical ingredient facility fee under subsection (a) for such fiscal year,~~ fees described in paragraphs (2) through (5) of subsection (a), based on the revenue amounts established under subsection (b) and the adjustments provided under subsection (c).

~~(3)~~ (2) Fee for Active Pharmaceutical Ingredient Information Not Included by Reference to Type II Active Pharmaceutical Ingredient Drug Master File. — In establishing the ~~fees under paragraphs (1) and (2)~~ fee under paragraph (1), the amount of the fee under subsection (a)(3)(F) shall be determined by multiplying —

(A) the sum of —

(i) the total number of such active pharmaceutical ingredients in such submission; and

(ii) for each such ingredient that is manufactured at more than one such facility, the total number of such additional facilities; and

(B) the amount equal to the drug master file fee established in subsection (a)(2) for such submission.

(e) ~~Limit~~ Limitations. — ~~The total amount~~

(1) In General. — The total amount of fees charged, as adjusted under subsection (c), for a fiscal year may not exceed the total costs for such fiscal year for the resources allocated for human generic drug activities.

(2) Leasing and Necessary Equipment. — Beginning on October 1, 2023, the authorities under section 744A(11)(C) shall include only leasing and necessary scientific equipment.

(f) Identification of Facilities. —

~~**(1) Publication of Notice; Deadline for Compliance.** — Not later than October 1, 2012, the Secretary shall publish in the Federal Register a notice requiring each person that owns a facility described in subsection (a)(4)(A), or a site or organization required to be identified by paragraph (4), to submit to the Secretary information on the identity of each such facility, site, or organization. The notice required by this paragraph shall specify the type of information to be submitted and the means and format for submission of such information.~~

~~(2)~~ (1) Required Submission of Facility Identification. — Each person that owns a facility described in subsection (a)(4)(A) or a site or organization required to be identified by paragraph ~~(4)~~ (3) shall submit to the Secretary the information required under this subsection each year. Such information ~~shall—~~ shall, for each fiscal year, be submitted, updated, or reconfirmed on or before June 1 of the previous fiscal year.

~~**(A)** for fiscal year 2013, be submitted not later than 60 days after the publication of the notice under paragraph (1); and~~

~~**(B)** for each subsequent fiscal year, be submitted, updated, or reconfirmed on or before June 1 of the previous year.~~

~~(3)~~ (2) ~~Contents of Notice~~ Information Required to be Submitted. — At a minimum, the submission required by paragraph ~~(2)~~ (1) shall include for each such facility —

(A) identification of a facility identified ~~or intended to be identified~~ in an approved or pending generic drug submission;

(B) whether the facility manufactures active pharmaceutical ingredients or finished dosage forms, or both;

(C) whether or not the facility is located within the United States and its territories and possessions;

(D) whether the facility manufactures positron emission tomography drugs solely, or in addition to other drugs; ~~and~~

(E) whether the facility manufactures drugs that are not generic drugs~~.~~; and

(F) whether the facility is a contract manufacturing organization facility.

~~(4)~~ (3) Certain Sites and Organizations. —

(A) In General. — Any person that owns or operates a site or organization described in subparagraph (B) shall submit to the Secretary information concerning the ownership, name, and address of the site or organization.

(B) Sites and Organizations. — A site or organization is described in this subparagraph if it is identified in a generic drug submission and is —

(i) a site in which a bioanalytical study is conducted;

(ii) a clinical research organization;

(iii) a contract analytical testing site; or

(iv) a contract repackager site.

(C) Notice. — The Secretary may, by notice published in the Federal Register, specify the means and format for submission of the information under subparagraph (A) and may specify, as necessary for purposes of this section, any additional information to be submitted.

(D) Inspection Authority. — The Secretary's inspection authority under section 704(a)(1) shall extend to all such sites and organizations.

(g) Effect of Failure to Pay Fees. —

(1) Generic Drug Backlog Fee. — Failure to pay the fee under subsection (a)(1) shall result in the Secretary placing the person that owns the abbreviated new drug application subject to that fee on a publicly available arrears list, such that no new abbreviated new drug applications or supplements submitted on or after October 1, 2012, from that person, or any affiliate of that person, will be received within the meaning of section 505(j)(5)(A) until such outstanding fee is paid. This paragraph shall cease to be effective on October 1, 2022.

(2) Drug Master File Fee. —

(A) Failure to pay the fee under subsection (a)(2) within 20 calendar days after the applicable due date under subparagraph (E) of such subsection (as described in subsection (a)(2)(D)(ii)(I)) shall result in the Type II active pharmaceutical ingredient drug master file not being deemed available for reference.

(B) —

(i) Any generic drug submission submitted on or after October 1, 2012, that references, by a letter of authorization, a Type II active pharmaceutical ingredient drug master file that has not been deemed available for reference shall not be received within the meaning of section 505(j)(5)(A) unless the condition specified in clause (ii) is met.

(ii) The condition specified in this clause is that the fee established under subsection (a)(2) has been paid within 20 calendar days of the Secretary providing the notification to the sponsor of the abbreviated new drug application or supplement of the failure of the owner of the Type II active pharmaceutical ingredient drug master file to pay the drug master file fee as specified in paragraph(C).

(C) —

(i) If an abbreviated new drug application or supplement to an abbreviated new drug application references a Type II active pharmaceutical ingredient drug master file for which a fee under subsection (a)(2)(A) has not been paid by the applicable date under subsection (a)(2)(E), the Secretary shall notify the sponsor of the abbreviated new drug application or supplement of the failure of the owner of the Type II active pharmaceutical ingredient drug master file to pay the applicable fee.

(ii) If such fee is not paid within 20 calendar days of the Secretary providing the notification, the abbreviated new drug application or supplement to an abbreviated new drug application shall not be received within the meaning ~~of~~ of section 505(j)(5)(A).

(3) Abbreviated New Drug Application Fee and Prior Approval Supplement Fee. — Failure to pay a fee under subparagraph (A) or (F) of subsection (a)(3) within 20 calendar days of the applicable due date under subparagraph (C) of such subsection shall result in the abbreviated new drug application or the prior approval supplement to an abbreviated new drug application not being received within the meaning of section 505(j)(5)(A) until such outstanding fee is paid.

(4) Generic Drug Facility Fee and Active Pharmaceutical Ingredient Facility Fee. —

(A) In General. — Failure to pay the fee under subsection (a)(4) within 20 calendar days of the due date as specified in subparagraph (D) of such subsection shall result in the following:

(i) The Secretary shall place the facility on a publicly available arrears list, such that no new abbreviated new drug application or supplement submitted on or after October 1, 2012, from the person that is responsible for paying such fee, or any affiliate of that person, will be received within the meaning of section 505(j)(5) (A).

(ii) Any new generic drug submission submitted on or after October 1, 2012, that references such a facility shall not be received, within the meaning of section 505(j)(5)(A) if the outstanding facility fee is not paid within 20 calendar days of the Secretary providing the notification to the sponsor of the failure of the owner of the facility to pay the facility fee under subsection (a)(4)(C).

(iii) All drugs or active pharmaceutical ingredients manufactured in such a facility or containing an ingredient manufactured in such a facility shall be deemed misbranded under section 502(aa).

(B) Application of Penalties. — The penalties under this paragraph shall apply until the fee established by subsection (a)(4) is paid or the facility is removed from all generic drug submissions that refer to the facility.

(C) Nonreceival for Nonpayment. —

(i) Notice. — If an abbreviated new drug application or supplement to an abbreviated new drug application submitted on or after October 1, 2012, references a facility for which a facility fee has not been paid by the applicable date under subsection (a)(4)(C), the Secretary shall notify the sponsor of the generic drug submission of the failure of the owner of the facility to pay the facility fee.

(ii) Nonreceival. — If the facility fee is not paid within 20 calendar days of the Secretary providing the notification under clause (i), the abbreviated new drug application or supplement to an abbreviated new drug application shall not be received within the meaning of section 505(j)(5)(A).

(5) Generic Drug Applicant Program Fee. —

(A) In General. — A person who fails to pay a fee as required under subsection (a)(5) by the date that is 20 calendar days after the due date, as specified in subparagraph (D) of such subsection, shall be subject to the following:

(i) The Secretary shall place the person on a publicly available arrears list.

(ii) Any abbreviated new drug application submitted by the generic drug applicant or an affiliate of such applicant shall not be received, within the meaning of section 505(j)(5)(A).

(iii) All drugs marketed pursuant to any abbreviated new drug application held by such applicant or an affiliate of such applicant shall be deemed misbranded under section 502(aa).

(B) Application of Penalties. — The penalties under subparagraph (A) shall apply until the fee required under subsection (a)(5) is paid.

(h) Limitations. —

(1) In General. — Fees under subsection (a) shall be refunded for a fiscal year beginning after fiscal year 2012, unless appropriations for salaries and expenses of the Food and Drug Administration for such fiscal year (excluding the amount of fees appropriated for such fiscal year) are equal to or greater than the amount of appropriations for the salaries and expenses of the Food and Drug Administration for fiscal year 2009 (excluding the amount of fees appropriated for such fiscal year) multiplied by the adjustment factor (as defined in Section 744A) applicable to the fiscal year involved.

(2) Authority. — If the Secretary does not assess fees under subsection (a) during any portion of a fiscal year and if at a later date in such fiscal year the Secretary may assess such fees, the Secretary may assess and collect such fees, without any modification in the rate~~, for Type II active pharmaceutical ingredient drug master files, abbreviated new drug applications and prior approval supplements, and generic drug facilities and active pharmaceutical ingredient facilities~~ at any time in such fiscal year notwithstanding the provisions of subsection (a) relating to the date fees are to be paid.

(i) Crediting and Availability of Fees. —

(1) In General. — Fees authorized under subsection (a) shall be collected and available for obligation only to the extent and in the amount provided in advance in appropriations Acts, subject to paragraph (2). Such fees are authorized to remain available until expended. Such sums as may be necessary may be transferred from the Food and Drug Administration salaries and expenses appropriation account without fiscal year limitation to such appropriation account for salaries and expenses with such fiscal year limitation. The sums transferred shall be available solely for human generic drug activities.

(2) Collections and Appropriation Acts. —

(A) In General. — The fees authorized by this section —

(i) subject to ~~subparagraphs (C) and (D)~~ subparagraph (C), shall be collected and available in each fiscal year in an amount not to exceed the amount specified in appropriations Acts, or otherwise made available for obligation for such fiscal year; and

(ii) shall be available for a fiscal year beginning after fiscal year 2012 to defray the costs of human generic drug activities (including such costs for an additional number of full-time equivalent positions in the Department of Health and Human Services to be engaged in such activities), only if the Secretary allocates for such purpose an amount for such fiscal year (excluding amounts from fees collected under this section) no less than $97,000,000 multiplied by the adjustment factor defined in section 744A(3) applicable to the fiscal year involved.

(B) Compliance. — The Secretary shall be considered to have met the requirements of subparagraph (A)(ii) in any fiscal year if the costs funded by appropriations and allocated for human generic activities are not more than 10 percent below the level specified in such subparagraph.

~~(C) Fee Collection During First Program Year. — Until the date of enactment of an Act making appropriations through September 30, 2013 for the salaries and expenses account of the Food and Drug Administration, fees authorized by this section for fiscal year 2013, may be collected and shall be credited to such account and remain available until expended.~~

~~(D)~~ (C) Provision for Early Payments ~~in Subsequent Years~~. — Payment of fees authorized under this section for a fiscal year ~~(after fiscal year 2013)~~, prior to the due date for such fees, may be accepted by the Secretary in accordance with authority provided in advance in a prior year appropriations Act.

(3) Authorization of Appropriations. — For each of the fiscal years ~~2013 through 2017~~ 2018 through 2022, there is authorized to be appropriated for fees under this section an amount equivalent to the total revenue amount determined under subsection (b) for the fiscal year, as adjusted under subsection (c), if applicable, or as otherwise affected under paragraph (2) of this subsection.

(j) Collection of Unpaid Fees. — In any case where the Secretary does not receive payment of a fee assessed under subsection (a) within 30 calendar days after it is due, such fee shall be treated as a claim of the United States Government subject to subchapter II of chapter 37 of title 31, United States Code.

(k) Construction. — This section may not be construed to require that the number of full-time equivalent positions in the Department of Health and Human Services, for officers, employees, and advisory committees not engaged in human generic drug activities, be reduced to offset the number of officers, employees, and advisory committees so engaged.

(l) Positron Emission Tomography Drugs. —

(1) Exemption from Fees. — Submission of an application for a positron emission tomography drug or active pharmaceutical ingredient for a positron emission tomography drug shall not require the payment of any fee under this section. Facilities that solely produce positron emission tomography drugs shall not be required to pay a facility fee as established in subsection (a)(4).

(2) Identification Requirement. — Facilities that produce positron emission tomography drugs or active pharmaceutical ingredients of such drugs are required to be identified pursuant to subsection (f).

(m) Disputes Concerning Fees. — To qualify for the return of a fee claimed to have been paid in error under this section, a person shall submit to the Secretary a written request justifying such return within 180 calendar days after such fee was paid.

(n) Substantially Complete Applications. — An abbreviated new drug application that is not considered to be received within the meaning of section 505(j)(5)(A) because of failure to pay an applicable fee under this provision within the time period specified in subsection (g) shall be deemed not to have been "substantially complete" on the date of its submission within the meaning of section 505(j)(5)(B)(iv)(II)(cc). An abbreviated new drug application that is not substantially complete on the date of its submission solely because of failure to pay an applicable fee under the preceding sentence shall be deemed substantially complete and received within the meaning of section 505(j)(5)(A) as of the date such applicable fee is received.

(o) Information on Abbreviated New Drug Applications Owned by Applicants and Their Affiliates. —

(1) In General. — By April 1 of each year, each person that owns an abbreviated new drug application, or a designated affiliate of such person, shall submit, on behalf of the person and the affiliates of such person, to the Secretary a list of —

(A) all approved abbreviated new drug applications owned by such person; and

(B) if any affiliate of such person also owns an abbreviated new drug application, all affiliates that own any such abbreviated new drug application and all approved abbreviated new drug applications owned by any such affiliate.

(2) Format and Method. — The Secretary shall specify in guidance the format and method for submission of lists under this subsection.

SEC. 744C. [379j-43] REAUTHORIZATION; REPORTING REQUIREMENTS.*

(a) PERFORMANCE REPORT. —

(1) GENERAL REQUIREMENTS. — Beginning with fiscal year ~~2013~~ 2018, not later than 120 days after the end of each fiscal year for which fees are collected under this part, the Secretary shall prepare and submit to the Committee on Energy and Commerce of the House of Representatives and the Committee on Health, Education, Labor, and Pensions of the Senate a report concerning the progress of the Food and Drug Administration in achieving the goals identified in the letters described in section 301(b) of the Generic Drug User Fee Amendments of ~~2012~~ 2017 during such fiscal year and the future plans of the Food and Drug Administration for meeting the goals.

(2) REAL TIME REPORTING. —

(A) IN GENERAL. — Not later than 30 calendar days after the end of the second quarter of fiscal year 2018, and not later than 30 calendar days after the end of each quarter of each fiscal year thereafter, the Secretary shall post the data described in subparagraph (B) on the internet website of the Food and Drug Administration, and may remove duplicative data from the annual report under this subsection.

(B) DATA. — The Secretary shall post the following data in accordance with subparagraph (A):

(i) The number and titles of draft and final guidance on topics related to human generic drug activities and whether such guidances were issued as required by statute or pursuant to a commitment under the letters described in section 301(b) of the Generic Drug User Fee Amendments of 2017.

(ii) The number and titles of public meetings held on topics related to human generic drug activities and whether such meetings were required by statute or pursuant to a commitment under the letters described in section 301(b) of the Generic Drug User Fee Amendments of 2017.

(3) RATIONALE FOR GDUFA PROGRAM CHANGES. — Beginning with fiscal year 2020, the Secretary shall include in the annual report under paragraph (1) —

(A) data, analysis, and discussion of the changes in the number of full-time equivalents hired as agreed upon in the letters described in section 301(b) of the Generic Drug User Fee Amendments of 2017 and the number of full time equivalents funded by budget authority at the Food and Drug Administration by each division within the Center for Drug Evaluation and Research, the Center for Biologics Evaluation and Research, the Office of Regulatory Affairs, and the Office of the Commissioner;

(B) data, analysis, and discussion of the changes in the fee revenue amounts and costs for human generic drug activities, including identifying drivers of such changes; and

(C) for each of the Center for Drug Evaluation and Research, the Center for Biologics Evaluation and Research, the Office of Regulatory Affairs, and the Office of the Commissioner, the number of employees for whom time reporting is required and the number of employees for whom time reporting is not required.

(4) ANALYSIS. — For each fiscal year, the Secretary shall include in the report an analysis of the following:

(A) The difference between the aggregate number of abbreviated new drug applications filed and the aggregate number of approvals or aggregate number of complete response letters issued by the agency, accounting for —

(i) such applications filed during one fiscal year for which a decision is not scheduled to be made until the following fiscal year; and

(ii) the aggregate number of applications for each fiscal year that did not meet the goals identified by the letters described in section 301(b) of the Generic Drug User Fee Amendments of 2017 for the applicable fiscal year.

(B) Relevant data to determine whether the Food and Drug Administration has met the performance enhancement goals identified by the letters described in section 301(b) of the Generic Drug User Fee Amendments of 2017 for the applicable fiscal year.

(C) The most common causes and trends for external or other circumstances that affected the ability of the Secretary to meet review time and performance enhancement goals identified by the letters described in section 301(b) of the Generic Drug User Fee Amendments of 2017.

(b) FISCAL REPORT. — Beginning with fiscal year ~~2013~~ 2018, not later than 120 days after the end of each fiscal year for which fees are collected under this part, the Secretary shall prepare and submit to the Committee on Energy and Commerce of the House of Representatives and the Committee on Health, Education, Labor, and Pensions of the

* Ceases to be effective January 31, 2018.

Senate a report on the implementation of the authority for such fees during such fiscal year and the use, by the Food and Drug Administration, of the fees collected for such fiscal year.

(c) Corrective Action Report. — Beginning with fiscal year 2018, for each fiscal year for which fees are collected under this part, the Secretary shall prepare and submit a corrective action report to the Committee on Energy and Commerce and the Committee on Appropriations of the House of Representatives and the Committee on Health, Education, Labor, and Pensions and the Committee on Appropriations of the Senate. The report shall include the following information, as applicable:

(1) Goals Met. — For each fiscal year, if the Secretary determines, based on the analysis under subsection (a)(4), that each of the goals identified by the letters described in section 301(b) of the Generic Drug User Fee Amendments of 2017 for the applicable fiscal year have been met, the corrective action report shall include recommendations on ways in which the Secretary can improve and streamline the abbreviated new drug application review process.

(2) Goals Missed. — For each of the goals identified by the letters described in section 301(b) of the Generic Drug User Fee Amendments of 2017 for the applicable fiscal year that the Secretary determines to not have been met, the corrective action report shall include —

(A) a detailed justification for such determination and a description, as applicable, of the types of circumstances and trends under which abbreviated new drug applications missed the review goal times but were approved during the first cycle review, or review goals were missed; and

(B) with respect to performance enhancement goals that were not achieved, a detailed description of efforts the Food and Drug Administration has put in place for the fiscal year in which the report is submitted to improve the ability of such agency to meet each such goal for the such fiscal year.

(d) Enhanced Communication. —

(1) Communications with Congress. — Each fiscal year, as applicable and requested, representatives from the Centers with expertise in the review of human drugs shall meet with representatives from the Committee on Health, Education, Labor, and Pensions of the Senate and the Committee on Energy and Commerce of the House of Representatives to report on the contents described in the reports under this section.

(2) Participation in Congressional Hearing. — Each fiscal year, as applicable and requested, representatives from the Food and Drug Administration shall participate in a public hearing before the Committee on Health, Education, Labor, and Pensions of the Senate and the Committee on Energy and Commerce of the House of Representatives, to report on the contents described in the reports under this section. Such hearing shall occur not later than 120 days after the end of each fiscal year for which fees are collected under this part.

~~(c)~~ (e) Public Availability. — The Secretary shall make the reports required under subsections (a) and (b) available to the public on the Internet Web site of the Food and Drug Administration.

~~(d)~~ (f) Reauthorization. —

(1) Consultation. — In developing recommendations to present to the Congress with respect to the goals, and plans for meeting the goals, for human generic drug activities for the first 5 fiscal years after the fiscal year ~~2017~~ 2022, and for the reauthorization of this part for such fiscal years, the Secretary shall consult with —

(A) the Committee on Energy and Commerce of the House of Representatives;

(B) the Committee on Health, Education, Labor, and Pensions of the Senate;

(C) scientific and academic experts;

(D) health care professionals;

(E) representatives of patient and consumer advocacy groups; and

(F) the generic drug industry.

(2) Prior Public Input. — Prior to beginning negotiations with the generic drug industry on the reauthorization of this part, the Secretary shall —

(A) publish a notice in the Federal Register requesting public input on the reauthorization;

(B) hold a public meeting at which the public may present its views on the reauthorization, including specific suggestions for changes to the goals referred to in subsection (a);

(C) provide a period of 30 days after the public meeting to obtain written comments from the public suggesting changes to this part; and

(D) publish the comments on the Food and Drug Administration's Internet Web site.

(3) Periodic Consultation. — Not less frequently than once every month during negotiations with the generic drug industry, the Secretary shall hold discussions with representatives of patient and consumer advocacy groups to continue discussions of their views on the reauthorization and their suggestions for changes to this part as expressed under paragraph (2).

(4) Public Review of Recommendations. — After negotiations with the generic drug industry, the Secretary shall —

(A) present the recommendations developed under paragraph (1) to the congressional committees specified in such paragraph;

(B) publish such recommendations in the Federal Register;

(C) provide for a period of 30 days for the public to provide written comments on such recommendations;

(D) hold a meeting at which the public may present its views on such recommendations; and

(E) after consideration of such public views and comments, revise such recommendations as necessary.

(5) Transmittal of Recommendations. — Not later than January 15, ~~2017~~ 2022, the Secretary shall transmit to the Congress the revised recommendations under paragraph (4), a summary of the views and comments received under such paragraph, and any changes made to the recommendations in response to such views and comments.

(6) Minutes of Negotiation Meetings. —

(A) Public Availability. — Before presenting the recommendations developed under paragraphs (1) through (5) to the Congress, the Secretary shall make publicly available, on the Internet Web site of the Food and Drug Administration, minutes of all negotiation meetings conducted under this subsection between the Food and Drug Administration and the generic drug industry.

(B) Content. — The minutes described under subparagraph (A) shall summarize any substantive proposal made by any party to the negotiations as well as significant controversies or differences of opinion during the negotiations and their resolution.

Part 8 — Fees Relating to Biosimilar Biological Products

Sec. 744G. [379j-51] Definitions.*

For purposes of this part:

(1) The term "adjustment factor" applicable to a fiscal year that is the Consumer Price Index for ~~all urban consumers (Washington-Baltimore, DC–MD–VA–WV; Not Seasonally Adjusted; All items) of the preceding fiscal year divided by such Index for September 2011.~~ urban consumers (Washington-Baltimore, DC–MD–VA–WV; Not Seasonally Adjusted; All items) for October of the preceding fiscal year divided by such Index for October 2011.

(2) The term "affiliate" means a business entity that has a relationship with a second business entity if, directly or indirectly —

(A) one business entity controls, or has the power to control, the other business entity; or

(B) a third party controls, or has the power to control, both of the business entities.

(3) The term "biosimilar biological product" ~~means a product~~ means a specific strength of a biological product in final dosage form for which a biosimilar biological product application has been approved.

(4) —

(A) Subject to subparagraph (B), the term "biosimilar biological product application" means an application for licensure of a biological product under section 351(k) of the Public Health Service Act.

(B) Such term does not include —

* Ceases to be effective October 1, ~~2017~~ 2022.

(i) a supplement to such an application;

(ii) an application filed under section 351(k) of the Public Health Service Act that cites as the reference product a bovine blood product for topical application licensed before September 1, 1992, or a large volume parenteral drug product approved before such date;

(iii) an application filed under section 351(k) of the Public Health Service Act with respect to —

(I) whole blood or a blood component for transfusion;

(II) an allergenic extract product;

(III) an in vitro diagnostic biological product; or

(IV) a biological product for further manufacturing use only; or

(iv) an application for licensure under section 351(k) of the Public Health Service Act that is submitted by a State or Federal Government entity for a product that is not distributed commercially.

(5) The term "biosimilar biological product development meeting" means any meeting, other than a biosimilar initial advisory meeting, regarding the content of a development program, including a proposed design for, or data from, a study intended to support a biosimilar biological product application.

(6) The term "biosimilar biological product development program" means the program under this part for expediting the process for the review of submissions in connection with biosimilar biological product development.

(7) —

(A) The term "biosimilar biological product establishment" means a foreign or domestic place of business —

(i) that is at one general physical location consisting of one or more buildings, all of which are within 5 miles of each other; and

(ii) at which one or more biosimilar biological products are manufactured in final dosage form.

(B) For purposes of subparagraph (A)(ii), the term "manufactured" does not include packaging.

(8) The term "biosimilar initial advisory meeting" —

(A) means a meeting, if requested, that is limited to —

(i) a general discussion regarding whether licensure under section 351(k) of the Public Health Service Act may be feasible for a particular product; and

(ii) if so, general advice on the expected content of the development program; and

(B) does not include any meeting that involves substantive review of summary data or full study reports.

(9) The term "costs of resources allocated for the process for the review of biosimilar biological product applications" means the expenses in connection with the process for the review of biosimilar biological product applications for —

(A) officers and employees of the Food and Drug Administration, contractors of the Food and Drug Administration, advisory committees, and costs related to such officers employees and committees and to contracts with such contractors;

(B) management of information, and the acquisition, maintenance, and repair of computer resources;

(C) leasing, maintenance, renovation, and repair of facilities and acquisition, maintenance, and repair of fixtures, furniture, scientific equipment, and other necessary materials and supplies; and

(D) collecting fees under section 744H and accounting for resources allocated for the review of submissions in connection with biosimilar biological product development, biosimilar biological product applications, and supplements.

(10) The term "final dosage form" means, with respect to a biosimilar biological product, a finished dosage form which is approved for administration to a patient without substantial further manufacturing (such as lyophilized products before reconstitution).

(11) The term "financial hold" —

(A) means an order issued by the Secretary to prohibit the sponsor of a clinical investigation from continuing the investigation if the Secretary determines that the investigation is intended to support a biosimilar biological product application and the sponsor has failed to pay any fee for the product required under subparagraph (A), (B), or (D) of section 744H(a)(1); and

(B) does not mean that any of the bases for a "clinical hold" under section 505(i)(3) have been determined by the Secretary to exist concerning the investigation.

(12) The term "person" includes an affiliate of such person.

(13) The term "process for the review of biosimilar biological product applications" means the following activities of the Secretary with respect to the review of submissions in connection with biosimilar biological product development, biosimilar biological product applications, and supplements:

(A) The activities necessary for the review of submissions in connection with biosimilar biological product development, biosimilar biological product applications, and supplements.

(B) Actions related to submissions in connection with biosimilar biological product development, the issuance of action letters which approve biosimilar biological product applications or which set forth in detail the specific deficiencies in such applications, and where appropriate, the actions necessary to place such applications in condition for approval.

(C) The inspection of biosimilar biological product establishments and other facilities undertaken as part of the Secretary's review of pending biosimilar biological product applications and supplements.

(D) Activities necessary for the release of lots of biosimilar biological products under section 351(k) of the Public Health Service Act.

(E) Monitoring of research conducted in connection with the review of biosimilar biological product applications.

(F) Postmarket safety activities with respect to biologics approved under biosimilar biological product applications or supplements, including the following activities:

(i) Collecting, developing, and reviewing safety information on biosimilar biological products, including adverse-event reports.

(ii) Developing and using improved adverse-event data-collection systems, including information technology systems.

(iii) Developing and using improved analytical tools to assess potential safety problems, including access to external data bases.

(iv) Implementing and enforcing section 505(o) (relating to postapproval studies and clinical trials and labeling changes) and section 505(p) (relating to risk evaluation and mitigation strategies).

(v) Carrying out section 505(k)(5) (relating to adverse-event reports and postmarket safety activities).

(14) The term "supplement" means a request to the Secretary to approve a change in a biosimilar biological product application which has been approved, including a supplement requesting that the Secretary determine that the biosimilar biological product meets the standards for interchangeability described in section 351(k)(4) of the Public Health ServiceAct.

SEC. 744H. [379j-52] AUTHORITY TO ASSESS AND USE BIOSIMILAR BIOLOGICAL PRODUCT FEES.*

(a) TYPES OF FEES. — Beginning in fiscal year ~~2013~~ 2018, the Secretary shall assess and collect fees in accordance with this section as follows:

(1) ~~BIOSIMILAR~~ BIOSIMILAR BIOLOGICAL PRODUCT DEVELOPMENT PROGRAM FEES. —

(A) INITIAL BIOSIMILAR BIOLOGICAL PRODUCT DEVELOPMENT FEE. —

(i) IN GENERAL. — Each person that submits to the Secretary a meeting request described under clause (ii) or a clinical protocol for an investigational new drug protocol described under clause (iii) shall pay for the product named in the meeting request or the investigational new drug application the initial biosimilar biological product development fee established under subsection ~~(b)(1)(A)~~ (c)(5).

(ii) MEETING REQUEST. — The meeting request described in this clause is a request for a biosimilar biological product development meeting for a product.

* Ceases to be effective October 1, ~~2017~~ 2022.

(iii) Clinical Protocol for IND. — A clinical protocol for an investigational new drug protocol described in this clause is a clinical protocol consistent with the provisions of section 505(i), including any regulations promulgated under section 505(i), (referred to in this section as "investigational new drug application") describing an investigation that the Secretary determines is intended to support a biosimilar biological product application for a product.

(iv) Due Date. — The initial biosimilar biological product development fee shall be due by the earlier of the following:

(I) Not later than 5 days after the Secretary grants a request for a biosimilar biological product development meeting.

(II) The date of submission of an investigational new drug application describing an investigation that the Secretary determines is intended to support a biosimilar biological product application.

(v) Transition Rule. — Each person that has submitted an investigational new drug application prior to the date of enactment of the Biosimilar User Fee Act of 2012 shall pay the initial biosimilar biological product development fee by the earlier of the following:

(I) Not later than 60 days after the date of the enactment of the Biosimilars User Fee Act of 2012, if the Secretary determines that the investigational new drug application describes an investigation that is intended to support of biosimilar biological product application.

(II) Not later than 5 days after the Secretary grants a request for a biosimilar biological product development meeting.

(B) Annual Biosimilar Biological Product Development Fee. —

(i) In General. — A person that pays an initial biosimilar biological product development fee for a product shall pay for such product, beginning in the fiscal year following the fiscal year in which the initial biosimilar biological product development fee was paid, an annual fee established under subsection ~~(b)(1)(B)~~ (c)(5) for the biosimilar biological product development program for biosimilar biological product development (referred to in this section as "annual biosimilar biological product development fee").

(ii) Due Date. — The annual biosimilar biological product development ~~program~~ fee for each fiscal year will be due on the later of —

(I) the first business day on or after October 1 of each such year; or

(II) the first business day after the enactment of an appropriations Act providing for the collection and obligation of fees for such year under this section.

(iii) Exception. — The annual biosimilar ~~development program~~ biological product development fee for each fiscal year will be due on the date specified in clause (ii), unless the person has —

(I) submitted a marketing application for the biological product that was accepted for filing; or

(II) discontinued participation in the biosimilar biological product development program for the product under subparagraph (C).

(iv) Refund.— If a person submits a marketing application for a biosimilar biological product before October 1 of a fiscal year and such application is accepted for filing on or before October 1 of such fiscal year, the person may request a refund equal to the annual biosimilar biological product development fee paid by the person for the product for such fiscal year. To qualify for consideration for a refund under this clause, a person shall submit to the Secretary a written request for such refund not later than 180 days after the marketing application is accepted for filing.

(C) Discontinuation of Fee Obligation. — A person may discontinue participation in the biosimilar biological product development program ~~for a product effective October 1 of a fiscal year by,~~ for a product, effective October 1 of a fiscal year, by, not later than August 1 of the preceding fiscal year —

(i) if no investigational new drug application concerning the product has been submitted, submitting to the Secretary a written declaration that the person has no present intention of further developing the product as a biosimilar biological product; or

(ii) if an investigational new drug application concerning the product has been submitted, withdrawing the investigational new drug application in accordance with part 312 of title 21, Code of Federal Regulations (or any successor regulations).

(D) Reactivation Fee. —

(i) In General. — A person that has discontinued participation in the biosimilar biological product development program for a product under subparagraph (C) shall if the person seeks to resume participation in such program pay a fee (referred to in this section as "reactivation fee") by the earlier of the following:

(I) Not later than 5 days after the Secretary grants a request by such person for a biosimilar biological product development meeting for the product (after the date on which such participation was discontinued).

(II) Upon the date of submission (after the date on which such participation was discontinued) by such person of an investigational new drug application describing an investigation that the Secretary determines is intended to support a biosimilar biological product application for that product.

(ii) Application of Annual Fee. — A person that pays a reactivation fee for a product shall pay for such product, beginning in the next fiscal year, the annual biosimilar biological product development fee under subparagraph (B).

(E) Effect of Failure to Pay ~~Biosimilar Development Program~~ Fees. —

(i) No Biosimilar Biological Product Development Meetings. — If a person has failed to pay an initial or annual biosimilar biological product development fee as required under subparagraph (A) or (B), or a reactivation fee as required under subparagraph (D), the Secretary shall not provide a biosimilar biological product development meeting relating to the product for which fees are owed.

(ii) No Receipt of Investigational New Drug Applications. — Except in extraordinary circumstances, the Secretary shall not consider an investigational new drug application to have been received under section 505(i)(2) if—

(I) the Secretary determines that the investigation is intended to support a biosimilar biological product application; and

(II) the sponsor has failed to pay an initial or annual biosimilar biological product development fee for the product as required under subparagraph (A) or (B), or a reactivation fee as required under subparagraph (D).

(iii) Financial Hold. — Notwithstanding section 505(i)(2), except in extraordinary circumstances, the Secretary shall prohibit the sponsor of a clinical investigation from continuing the investigation if—

(I) the Secretary determines that the investigation is intended to support a biosimilar biological product application; and

(II) the sponsor has failed to pay an initial or annual biosimilar biological product development fee for the product as required under subparagraph (A) or (B), or a reactivation fee for the product as required under subparagraph (D).

(iv) No Acceptance of Biosimilar Biological Product Applications or Supplements. — If a person has failed to pay an initial or annual biosimilar biological product development fee as required under subparagraph (A) or (B), or a reactivation fee as required under subparagraph (D), any biosimilar biological product application or supplement submitted by that person shall be considered incomplete and shall not be accepted for filing by the Secretary until all such fees owed by such person have been paid.

(F) Limits Regarding ~~Biosimilar Development Program~~ Fees. —

(i) ~~No~~ Refunds. — ~~The~~ Except as provided in subparagraph (B)(iv), the Secretary shall not refund any initial or annual biosimilar biological product development fee paid under subparagraph (A) or (B), or any reactivation fee paid under subparagraph (D).

(ii) No Waivers, Exemptions, or Reductions. — The Secretary shall not grant a waiver, exemption, or reduction of any initial or annual biosimilar biological product development fee due or payable under subparagraph (A) or (B), or any reactivation fee due or payable under subparagraph (D).

(2) Biosimilar Biological Product Application ~~and Supplement~~ Fee. —

~~(A) In general. — Each person that submits, on or after October 1, 2012, a biosimilar biological product application or a supplement shall be subject to the following fees:~~

~~(i) A fee for a biosimilar biological product application that is equal to —~~

~~(I) the amount of the fee established under subsection (b)(1)(D) for a biosimilar biological product application for which clinical data (other than comparative bioavailability studies) with respect to safety or effectiveness are required for approval; minus~~

~~(II) the cumulative amount of fees paid, if any, under subparagraphs (A), (B), and (D) of paragraph (1) for the product that is the subject of the application.~~

~~(ii) A fee for a biosimilar biological product application for which clinical data (other than comparative bioavailability studies) with respect to safety or effectiveness are not required, that is equal to —~~

~~(I) half of the amount of the fee established under subsection (b)(1)(D) for a biosimilar biological product application; minus~~

~~(II) the cumulative amount of fees paid, if any, under subparagraphs (A), (B), and (D) of paragraph (1) for that product.~~

~~(iii) A fee for a supplement for which clinical data (other than comparative bioavailability studies) with respect to safety or effectiveness are required, that is equal to half of the amount of the fee established under subsection (b)(1)(D) for a biosimilar biological product application.~~

~~(B) Reduction in Fees. — Notwithstanding section 404 of the Biosimilar User Fee Act of 2012, any person who pays a fee under subparagraph (A), (B), or (D) of paragraph (1) for a product before October 1, 2017, but submits a biosimilar biological product application for that product after such date, shall be entitled to the reduction of any biosimilar biological product application fees that may be assessed at the time when such biosimilar biological product application is submitted, by the cumulative amount of fees paid under subparagraphs (A), (B), and (D) of paragraph (1) for that product.~~

(A) In General. —Each person that submits, on or after October 1, 2017, a biosimilar biological product application shall be subject to the following fees:

(i) A fee established under subsection (c)(5) for a biosimilar biological product application for which clinical data (other than comparative bioavailability studies) with respect to safety or effectiveness are required for approval.

(ii) A fee established under subsection (c)(5) for a biosimilar biological product application for which clinical data (other than comparative bioavailability studies) with respect to safety or effectiveness are not required for approval. Such fee shall be equal to half of the amount of the fee described in clause (i).

(B) Rule of Applicability; Treatment of Certain Previously Paid Fees. — Any person who pays a fee under subparagraph (A), (B), or (D) of paragraph (1) for a product before October 1, 2017, but submits a biosimilar biological product application for that product after such date, shall —

(i) be subject to any biosimilar biological product application fees that may be assessed at the time when such biosimilar biological product application is submitted; and

(ii) be entitled to no reduction of such application fees based on the amount of fees paid for that product before October 1, 2017, under such subparagraph (A), (B), or (D).

(C) Payment Due Date. — Any fee required by subparagraph (A) shall be due upon submission of the application ~~or supplement~~ for which such fee applies.

(D) Exception for Previously Filed Application ~~or Supplement~~. — If a biosimilar biological product application ~~or supplement~~ was submitted by a person that paid the fee for such application ~~or supplement~~, was accepted for filing, and was not approved or was withdrawn (without a waiver), the submission of a biosimilar biological product application ~~or supplement~~ for the same product by the same person (or the person's licensee, assignee, or successor) shall not be subject to a fee under subparagraph (A).

(E) Refund of Application Fee if Application Refused for Filing or Withdrawn Before Filing. — The Secretary shall refund 75 percent of the fee paid under this paragraph for any application ~~or supplement~~ which is refused for filing or withdrawn without a waiver before filing.

(F) Fees for Applications Previously Refused for Filing or Withdrawn Before Filing. — A biosimilar biological product application ~~or supplement~~ that was submitted but was refused for filing, or was withdrawn before being accepted or refused for filing, shall be subject to the full fee under subparagraph (A) upon being resubmitted or filed over protest, unless the fee in waived under subsection ~~(c)~~ (d).

(3) Biosimilar Biological Product ~~Establishment~~ Program Fee. —

~~(A) In General. — Except as provided in subparagraph (E), each person that is named as the applicant in a biosimilar biological product application shall be assessed an annual fee established under subsection (b)(1)(E) for each biosimilar biological product establishment that is listed in the approved biosimilar biological product application as an establishment that manufactures the biosimilar biological product named in such application.~~

~~(B) Assessment in Fiscal Years. — The establishment fee shall be assessed in each fiscal year for which the biosimilar biological product named in the application is assessed a fee under paragraph (4) unless the biosimilar biological product establishment listed in the application does not engage in the manufacture of the biosimilar biological product during such fiscal year.~~

~~(C) Due Date. — The establishment fee for a fiscal year shall be due on the later of —~~

~~(i) the first business day on or after October 1 of such fiscal year; or~~

~~(ii) the first business day after the enactment of an appropriations Act providing for the collection and obligation of fees for such fiscal year under this section.~~

~~(D) Application to Establishment. —~~

~~(i) Each biosimilar biological product establishment shall be assessed only one fee per biosimilar biological product establishment, notwithstanding the number of biosimilar biological products manufactured at the establishment, subject to clause (ii).~~

~~(ii) In the event an establishment is listed in a biosimilar biological product application by more than one applicant, the establishment fee for the fiscal year shall be divided equally and assessed among the applicants whose biosimilar biological products are manufactured by the establishment during the fiscal year and assessed biosimilar biological product fees under paragraph (4).~~

~~(E) Exception for New Products. — If, during the fiscal year, an applicant initiates or causes to be initiated the manufacture of a biosimilar biological product at an establishment listed in its biosimilar biological product application —~~

~~(i) that did not manufacture the biosimilar biological product in the previous fiscal year; and~~

~~(ii) for which the full biosimilar biological product establishment fee has been assessed in the fiscal year at a time before manufacture of the biosimilar biological product was begun,~~

~~the applicant shall not be assessed a share of the biosimilar biological product establishment fee for the fiscal year in which the manufacture of the product began.~~

(A) In General. — Each person who is named as the applicant in a biosimilar biological product application shall pay the annual biosimilar biological product program fee established for a fiscal year under subsection (c)(5) for each biosimilar biological product that —

(i) is identified in such a biosimilar biological product application approved as of October 1 of such fiscal year; and

(ii) as of October 1 of such fiscal year, does not appear on a list, developed and maintained by the Secretary, of discontinued biosimilar biological products.

(B) Due Date. — The biosimilar biological product program fee for a fiscal year shall be due on the later of —

(i) the first business day on or after October 1 of each such year; or

(ii) the first business day after the enactment of an appropriations Act providing for the collection and obligation of fees for such year under this section.

(C) One Fee Per Product Per Year. — The biosimilar biological product program fee shall be paid only once for each product for each fiscal year.

(D) Limitation. — A person who is named as the applicant in a biosimilar biological product application shall not be assessed more than 5 biosimilar biological product program fees for a fiscal year for biosimilar biological products identified in such biosimilar biological product application.

(4) Biosimilar Biological Product Fee. —

(A) In General. — Each person who is named as the applicant in a biosimilar biological product application shall pay for each such biosimilar biological product the annual fee established under section ~~(b)(1)(F)~~ (c)(5).

(B) Due Date. — The biosimilar biological product fee for a fiscal year shall be due on the later of —

(i) the first business day on or after October 1 of each such year; or

(ii) the first business day after the enactment of an appropriations Act providing for the collection and obligation of fees for such year under this section.

(C) One Fee Per Product Per Year. — The biosimilar biological product fee shall be paid only once for each product for each fiscal year.

~~**(b) Fee Setting and Amounts.** —~~

~~**(1) In General.** — Subject to paragraph (2), the Secretary shall, 60 days before the start of each fiscal year that begins after September 30, 2012, establish, for the next fiscal year, the fees under subsection (a). Except as provided in subsection (c), such fees shall be in the following amounts:~~

~~**(A) Initial Biosimilar Biological Product Development Fee.** — The initial biosimilar biological product development fee under subsection (a)(1)(A) for a fiscal year shall be equal to 10 percent of the amount established under section 736(c)(4) for a human drug application described in section 736(a)(1)(A)(i) for that fiscal year.~~

~~**(B) Annual Biosimilar Biological Product Development Fee.** — The annual biosimilar biological product development fee under subsection (a)(1)(B) for a fiscal year shall be equal to 10 percent of the amount established under section 736(c)(4) for a human drug application described in section 736(a)(1)(A)(i) for that fiscal year.~~

~~**(C) Reactivation Fee.** — The reactivation fee under subsection (a)(1)(D) for a fiscal year shall be equal to 20 percent of the amount of the fee established under section 736(c)(4) for a human drug application described in section 736(a)(1)(A)(i) for that fiscal year.~~

~~**(D) Biosimilar Biological Product Application Fee.** — The biosimilar biological product application fee under subsection (a)(2) for a fiscal year shall be equal to the amount established under section 736(c)(4) for a human drug application described in section 736(a)(1)(A)(i) for that fiscal year.~~

~~**(E) Biosimilar Biological Product Establishment Fee.** — The biosimilar biological product establishment fee under subsection (a)(3) for a fiscal year shall be equal to the amount established under section 736(c)(4) for a prescription drug establishment for that fiscal year.~~

~~**(F) Biosimilar Biological Product Fee.** — The biosimilar biological product fee under subsection (a)(4) for a fiscal year shall be equal to the amount established under section 736(c)(4) for a prescription drug product for that fiscal year.~~

~~**(2) Limit.** — The total amount of fees charged for a fiscal year under this section may not exceed the total amount for such fiscal year of the costs of resources allocated for the process for the review of biosimilar biological product applications.~~

(b) Fee Revenue Amounts. —

(1) Fiscal Year 2018. — For fiscal year 2018, fees under subsection (a) shall be established to generate a total revenue amount equal to the sum of —

(A) $45,000,000; and

(B) the dollar amount equal to the fiscal year 2018 adjustment (as determined under subsection (c)(4)).

(2) Subsequent Fiscal Years. — For each of the fiscal years 2019 through 2022, fees under subsection (a) shall, except as provided in subsection (c), be established to generate a total revenue amount equal to the sum of —

(A) the annual base revenue for the fiscal year (as determined under paragraph (4));

(B) the dollar amount equal to the inflation adjustment for the fiscal year (as determined under subsection (c)(1));

(C) the dollar amount equal to the capacity planning adjustment for the fiscal year (as determined under subsection (c)(2)); and

(D) the dollar amount equal to the operating reserve adjustment for the fiscal year, if applicable (as determined under subsection (c)(3)).

(3) ALLOCATION OF REVENUE AMOUNT AMONG FEES; LIMITATIONS ON FEE AMOUNTS. —

(A) ALLOCATION. — The Secretary shall determine the percentage of the total revenue amount for a fiscal year to be derived from, respectively —

(i) initial and annual biosimilar biological product development fees and reactivation fees under subsection (a)(1);

(ii) biosimilar biological product application fees under subsection (a)(2); and

(iii) biosimilar biological product program fees under subsection (a)(3).

(B) LIMITATIONS ON FEE AMOUNTS. — Until the first fiscal year for which the capacity planning adjustment under subsection (c)(2) is effective, the amount of any fee under subsection (a) for a fiscal year after fiscal year 2018 shall not exceed 125 percent of the amount of such fee for fiscal year 2018.

(C) BIOSIMILAR BIOLOGICAL PRODUCT DEVELOPMENT FEES. — The initial biosimilar biological product development fee under subsection (a)(1)(A) for a fiscal year shall be equal to the annual biosimilar biological product development fee under subsection (a)(1)(B) for that fiscal year.

(D) REACTIVATION FEE. — The reactivation fee under subsection (a)(1)(D) for a fiscal year shall be equal to twice the amount of the annual biosimilar biological product development fee under subsection (a)(1)(B) for that fiscal year.

(4) ANNUAL BASE REVENUE. — For purposes of paragraph (2), the dollar amount of the annual base revenue for a fiscal year shall be the dollar amount of the total revenue amount for the previous fiscal year, excluding any adjustments to such revenue amount under subsection (c)(3).

(c) ADJUSTMENTS; ANNUAL FEE SETTING. —

(1) INFLATION ADJUSTMENT. —

(A) IN GENERAL. — For purposes of subsection (b)(2)(B), the dollar amount of the inflation adjustment to the annual base revenue for each fiscal year shall be equal to the product of —

(i) such annual base revenue for the fiscal year under subsection (b); and

(ii) the inflation adjustment percentage under subparagraph (B).

(B) INFLATION ADJUSTMENT PERCENTAGE. — The inflation adjustment percentage under this subparagraph for a fiscal year is equal to the sum of —

(i) the average annual percent change in the cost, per full-time equivalent position of the Food and Drug Administration, of all personnel compensation and benefits paid with respect to such positions for the first 3 years of the preceding 4 fiscal years, multiplied by the proportion of personnel compensation and benefits costs to total costs of the process for the review of biosimilar biological product applications (as defined in section 744G(13)) for the first 3 years of the preceding 4 fiscal years; and

(ii) the average annual percent change that occurred in the Consumer Price Index for urban consumers (Washington-Baltimore, DC-MD-VA-WV; Not Seasonally Adjusted; All items; Annual Index) for the first 3 years of the preceding 4 years of available data multiplied by the proportion of all costs other than personnel compensation and benefits costs to total costs of the process for the review of biosimilar biological product applications (as defined in section 744G(13)) for the first 3 years of the preceding 4 fiscal years.

(2) CAPACITY PLANNING ADJUSTMENT. —

(A) IN GENERAL. — Beginning with the fiscal year described in subparagraph (B)(ii)(II), the Secretary shall, in addition to the adjustment under paragraph (1), further increase the fee revenue and fees under this section for a fiscal year to reflect changes in the resource capacity needs of the Secretary for the process for the review of biosimilar biological product applications.

(B) CAPACITY PLANNING METHODOLOGY. —

(i) DEVELOPMENT; EVALUATION AND REPORT. — The Secretary shall obtain, through a contract with an independent accounting or consulting firm, a report evaluating options and recommendations for a new methodology to accurately assess changes in the resource and capacity needs of the process for the review of biosimilar biological product applications. The capacity planning methodological options and recommendations presented in such report shall utilize and be informed by personnel time reporting data as an input. The report shall be published for public comment not later than September 30, 2020.

(ii) Establishment and Implementation. — After review of the report described in clause (i) and receipt and review of public comments thereon, the Secretary shall establish a capacity planning methodology for purposes of this paragraph, which shall —

(I) incorporate such approaches and attributes as the Secretary determines appropriate; and

(II) be effective beginning with the first fiscal year for which fees are set after such capacity planning methodology is established.

(C) Limitation. — Under no circumstances shall an adjustment under this paragraph result in fee revenue for a fiscal year that is less than the sum of the amounts under subsections (b)(2)(A) (the annual base revenue for the fiscal year) and (b)(2)(B) (the dollar amount of the inflation adjustment for the fiscal year).

(D) Publication in Federal Register. — The Secretary shall publish in the Federal Register notice under paragraph (5) the fee revenue and fees resulting from the adjustment and the methodologies under this paragraph.

(3) Operating Reserve Adjustment. —

(A) Interim Application; Fee Reduction. — Until the first fiscal year for which the capacity planning adjustment under paragraph (2) is effective, the Secretary may, in addition to the adjustment under paragraph (1), reduce the fee revenue and fees under this section for a fiscal year as the Secretary determines appropriate for long-term financial planning purposes.

(B) General Application and Methodology. — Beginning with the first fiscal year for which the capacity planning adjustment under paragraph (2) is effective, the Secretary may, in addition to the adjustments under paragraphs (1) and (2) —

(i) reduce the fee revenue and fees under this section as the Secretary determines appropriate for long-term financial planning purposes; or

(ii) increase the fee revenue and fees under this section if such an adjustment is necessary to provide for not more than 21 weeks of operating reserves of carryover user fees for the process for the review of biosimilar biological product applications.

(C) Federal Register Notice. — If an adjustment under subparagraph (A) or (B) is made, the rationale for the amount of the increase or decrease (as applicable) in fee revenue and fees shall be contained in the annual Federal Register notice under paragraph (5)(B) establishing fee revenue and fees for the fiscal year involved.

(4) Fiscal Year 2018 Adjustment. —

(A) In General. — For fiscal year 2018, the Secretary shall adjust the fee revenue and fees under this section in such amount (if any) as needed to reflect an updated assessment of the workload for the process for the review of biosimilar biological product applications.

(B) Methodology. — The Secretary shall publish under paragraph (5)(B) a description of the methodology used to calculate the fiscal year 2018 adjustment under this paragraph in the Federal Register notice establishing fee revenue and fees for fiscal year 2018.

(C) Limitation. — No adjustment under this paragraph shall result in an increase in fee revenue and fees under this section in excess of $9,000,000.

(5) Annual Fee Setting. — For fiscal year 2018 and each subsequent fiscal year, the Secretary shall, not later than 60 days before the start of each such fiscal year —

(A) establish, for the fiscal year, initial and annual biosimilar biological product development fees and reactivation fees under subsection (a)(1), biosimilar biological product application fees under subsection (a)(2), and biosimilar biological product program fees under subsection (a)(3), based on the revenue amounts established under subsection (b) and the adjustments provided under this subsection; and

(B) publish such fee revenue and fees in the Federal Register.

(6) Limit. — The total amount of fees assessed for a fiscal year under this section may not exceed the total costs for such fiscal year for the resources allocated for the process for the review of biosimilar biological product applications.

~~(c)~~ (d) Application Fee Waiver for Small Business. —

(1) Waiver of Application Fee. — The Secretary shall grant to a person who is named in a biosimilar biological product application a waiver from the application fee assessed to that person under subsection (a)(2)(A) for the first biosimilar biological product application that a small business or its affiliate submits to the Secretary for review. After a small business or its affiliate is granted such a waiver, the small business or its affiliate ~~shall pay — (A) application fees~~ shall pay application fees for all subsequent biosimilar biological product applications submitted to the Secretary for review in the same manner as an entity that is not a small business~~; and~~ .

~~(B) all supplement fees for all supplements to biosimilar biological product applications submitted to the Secretary for review in the same manner as an entity that is not a small business.~~

(2) Considerations. — In determining whether to grant a waiver of a fee under paragraph (1), the Secretary shall consider only the circumstances and assets of the applicant involved and any affiliate of the applicant.

(3) Small Business Defined. — In this subsection, the term "small business" means an entity that has fewer than 500 employees, including employees of affiliates, and does not have a drug product that has been approved under a human drug application (as defined in section 735) or a biosimilar biological product application (as defined in section 744G(4)) and introduced or delivered for introduction into interstate commerce.

~~(d)~~ (e) Effect of Failure to Pay Fees. — A biosimilar biological product application or supplement submitted by a person subject to fees under subsection (a) shall be considered incomplete and shall not be accepted for filing by the Secretary until ~~all fees~~ all such fees owed by such person have been paid.

~~(e)~~ (f) Crediting and Availability of Fees. —

(1) In General. — Subject to paragraph (2), fees authorized under subsection (a) shall be collected and available for obligation only to the extent and in the amount provided in advance in appropriations Acts. Such fees are authorized to remain available until expended. Such sums as may be necessary may be transferred from the Food and Drug Administration salaries and expenses appropriation account without fiscal year limitation to such appropriation account for salaries and expenses with such fiscal year limitation. The sums transferred shall be available solely for the process for the review of biosimilar biological product applications.

(2) Collections and Appropriation Acts. —

(A) In General. — Subject to subparagraphs (C) and (D), the fees authorized by this section shall be collected and available in each fiscal year in an amount not to exceed the amount specified in appropriation Acts, or otherwise made available for obligation for such fiscal year.

(B) Use of Fees and ~~Limitation.~~ Limitations. — ~~The fees authorized~~

(i) In General. — The fees authorized by this section shall be available for a fiscal year beginning after fiscal year 2012 to defray the costs of the process for the review of biosimilar biological product applications (including such costs for an additional number of full-time equivalent positions in the Department of Health and Human Services to be engaged in such process), only if the Secretary allocates for such purpose an amount for such fiscal year (excluding amounts from fees collected under this section) no less than $20,000,000, multiplied by the adjustment factor applicable to the fiscal year involved.

(ii) Leasing and Necessary Equipment. — Beginning on October 1, 2023, the authorities under section 744G(9)(C) shall include only leasing and necessary scientific equipment.

(C) ~~Fee Collection During First Program Year. — Until the date of enactment of an Act making appropriations through September 30, 2013, for the salaries and expenses account of the Food and Drug Administration, fees authorized by this section for fiscal year 2013 may be collected and shall be credited to such account and remain available until expended.~~ Compliance. — The Secretary shall be considered to have met the requirements of subparagraph (B) in any fiscal year if the costs described in such subparagraph are not more than 15 percent below the level specified in such subparagraph.

(D) Provision for Early Payments ~~in Subsequent Years.~~. — Payment of fees authorized under this section for a fiscal year (after fiscal year 2013), prior to the due date for such fees, may be accepted by the Secretary in accordance with authority provided in advance in a prior year appropriations Act.

(3) Authorization of Appropriations. — For each of fiscal years ~~2013 through 2017~~ 2018 through 2022, there is authorized to be appropriated for fees under this section an amount equivalent to the total amount of fees assessed for such fiscal year under this section.

~~(f)~~ (g) **Collection of Unpaid Fees.** — In any case where the Secretary does not receive payment of a fee assessed under subsection (a) within 30 days after it is due, such fee shall be treated as a claim of the United States Government subject to subchapter II of chapter 37 of title 31, United States Code.

~~(g)~~ (h) **Written Requests for Waivers and Refunds.** — To qualify for consideration for a waiver under subsection ~~(c)~~ (d), or for a refund of any fee collected in accordance with subsection (a)(2)(A), a person shall submit to the Secretary a written request for such waiver or refund not later than 180 days after such fee is due.

~~(h)~~ (i) **Construction.** — This section may not be construed to require that the number of full-time equivalent positions in the Department of Health and Human Services, for officers, employers, and advisory committees not engaged in the process of the review of biosimilar biological product applications, be reduced to offset the number of officers, employees, and advisory committees so engaged.

Sec. 744I. [379j-53] Reauthorization; Reporting Requirements.*

(a) Performance Report. —

(1) General Requirements. — Beginning with fiscal year ~~2013~~ 2018, not later than 120 days after the end of each fiscal year for which fees are collected under this part, the Secretary shall prepare and submit to the Committee on Energy and Commerce of the House of Representatives and the Committee on Health, Education, Labor, and Pensions of the Senate a report concerning the progress of the Food and Drug Administration in achieving the goals identified in the letters descried in section 401(b) of the Biosimilar User Fee Amendments of ~~2012~~ 2017 during such fiscal year and the future plans of the Food and Drug Administration for meeting such goals. The report for a fiscal year shall include information on all previous cohorts for which the Secretary has not given a complete response on all biosimilar biological product applications and supplements in the cohort.

(2) Additional Information. —Beginning with fiscal year 2018, the report under this subsection shall include the progress of the Food and Drug Administration in achieving the goals, and future plans for meeting the goals, including —

(A) information on all previous cohorts for which the Secretary has not given a complete response on all biosimilar biological product applications and supplements in the cohort;

(B) the number of original biosimilar biological product applications filed per fiscal year, and the number of approvals issued by the agency for such applications; and

(C) the number of resubmitted original biosimilar biological product applications filed per fiscal year and the number of approvals letters issued by the agency for such applications.

(3) Real Time Reporting. —

(A) In General. — Not later than 30 calendar days after the end of the second quarter of fiscal year 2018, and not later than 30 calendar days after the end of each quarter of each fiscal year thereafter, the Secretary shall post the data described in subparagraph (B) for such quarter and on a cumulative basis for the fiscal year on the internet website of the Food and Drug Administration, and may remove duplicative data from the annual report under this subsection.

(B) Data. — The Secretary shall post the following data in accordance with subparagraph (A):

(i) The number and titles of draft and final guidance on topics related to the process for the review of biosimilars, and whether such guidances were required by statute or pursuant to a commitment under the letters described in section 401(b) of the Biosimilar User Fee Amendments of 2017.

(ii) The number and titles of public meetings held on topics related to the process for the review of biosimilars, and whether such meetings were required by statute or pursuant to a commitment under the letters described in section 401(b) of the Biosimilar User Fee Amendments of 2017.

(4) Rationale for BSUFA Program Changes. — Beginning with fiscal year 2020, the Secretary shall include in the annual report under paragraph (1) —

(A) data, analysis, and discussion of the changes in the number of full-time equivalents hired as agreed upon in the letters described in section 401(b) of the Biosimilar User Fee Amendments of 2017 and the number of full time equivalents funded by budget authority at the Food and Drug Administration by each division within the Center for Drug Evaluation and Research, the Center for Biologics Evaluation and Research, the Office of Regulatory Affairs, and the Office of the Commissioner;

(B) data, analysis, and discussion of the changes in the fee revenue amounts and costs for the process for the review of biosimilar biological product applications, including identifying drivers of such changes; and

* Ceases to be effective January 31, 2018.

(C) for each of the Center for Drug Evaluation and Research, the Center for Biologics Evaluation and Research, the Office of Regulatory Affairs, and the Office of the Commissioner, the number of employees for whom time reporting is required and the number of employees for whom time reporting is not required.

(5) Analysis. — For each fiscal year, the Secretary shall include in the report an analysis of the following:

(A) The difference between the aggregate number of biosimilar biological product applications and supplements filed and the aggregate number of approvals issued by the agency, accounting for —

(i) such applications filed during one fiscal year for which a decision is not scheduled to be made until the following fiscal year; and

(ii) the aggregate number of applications for each fiscal year that did not meet the goals identified by the letters described in section 401(b) of the Biosimilar User Fee Amendments of 2017 for the applicable fiscal year.

(B) Relevant data to determine whether the Center for Drug Evaluation and Research and the Center for Biologics Evaluation and Research have met the performance enhancement goals identified by the letters described in section 401(b) of the Biosimilar User Fee Amendments of 2017 for the applicable fiscal year.

(C) The most common causes and trends for external or other circumstances affecting the ability of the Secretary to meet review time and performance enhancement goals identified by the letters described in section 401(b) of the Biosimilar User Fee Amendments of 2017.

(b) Fiscal Report. — Not later than 120 days after the end of fiscal year ~~2013~~ 2018 and each subsequent fiscal year for which fees are collected under this part, the Secretary shall prepare and submit to the Committee on Energy and Commerce of the House of Representatives and the Committee on Health, Education, Labor, and Pensions of the Senate a report on the implementation of the authority for such fees during such fiscal year and the use, by the Food and Drug Administration, of the fees collected for such fiscal year.

(c) Corrective Action Report. — Beginning with fiscal year 2018, and for each fiscal year for which fees are collected under this part, the Secretary shall prepare and submit a corrective action report to the Committee on Energy and Commerce and Committee on Appropriations of the House of Representatives and the Committee on Health, Education, Labor, and Pensions and Committee on Appropriations of the Senate. The report shall include the following information, as applicable:

(1) Goals Met. — For each fiscal year, if the Secretary determines, based on the analysis under subsection (a)(5), that each of the goals identified by the letters described in section 401(b) of the Biosimilar User Fee Amendments of 2017 for the applicable fiscal year have been met, the corrective action report shall include recommendations on ways in which the Secretary can improve and streamline the biosimilar biological product application review process.

(2) Goals Missed. — For each of the goals identified by the letters described in section 401(b) of the Biosimilar User Fee Amendments of 2017 for the applicable fiscal year that the Secretary determines to not have been met, the corrective action report shall include —

(A) a justification for such determination and a description of the types of circumstances and trends, as applicable, under which biosimilar biological product applications missed the review goal times but were approved during the first cycle review, or review goals were missed; and

(B) with respect to performance enhancement goals that were not achieved, a description of efforts the Food and Drug Administration has put in place for the fiscal year in which the report is submitted to improve the ability of such agency to meet each such goal for the such fiscal year.

(d) Enhanced Communication. —

(1) Communications with Congress. — Each fiscal year, as applicable and requested, representatives from the Centers with expertise in the review of human drugs shall meet with representatives from the Committee on Health, Education, Labor, and Pensions of the Senate and the Committee on Energy and Commerce of the House of Representatives to report on the contents described in the reports under this section.

(2) Participation in Congressional Hearing. — Each fiscal year, as applicable and requested, representatives from the Food and Drug Administration shall participate in a public hearing before the Committee on Health, Education, Labor, and Pensions of the Senate and the Committee on Energy and Commerce of the House of Representatives, to report on the contents described in the reports under this section. Such hearing shall occur not later than 120 days after the end of each fiscal year for which fees are collected under this part.

~~(c)~~ (e) **Public Availability.** — The Secretary shall make the reports required under subsections (a) and (b) available to the public on the Internet Web site of the Food and Drug Administration.

~~**(d) Study.** —~~

~~**(1) In General.** — The Secretary shall contract with an independent accounting or consulting firm to study the workload volume and full costs associated with the process for the review of biosimilar biological product applications.~~

~~**(2) Interim Results.** — Not later than June 1, 2015, the Secretary shall publish, for public comment, interim results of the study described under paragraph (1).~~

~~**(3) Final Results.** — Not later than September 30, 2016, the Secretary shall publish, for public comment, the final results of the study described under paragraph (1).~~

~~(e)~~ (f) **Reauthorization.** —

(1) Consultation. — In developing recommendations to present to the Congress with respect to the goals described in subsection (a), and plans for meeting the goals, for the process for the review of biosimilar biological product applications for the first 5 fiscal years after fiscal year ~~2017~~ 2022, and for the reauthorization of this part for such fiscal years, the Secretary shall consult with —

(A) the Committee on Energy and Commerce of the House of Representatives;

(B) the Committee on Health, Education, Labor, and Pensions of the Senate;

(C) scientific and academic experts;

(D) health care professionals;

(E) representatives of patient and consumer advocacy groups; and

(F) the regulated industry.

(2) Public Review of Recommendations. — After negotiations with the regulated industry, the Secretary shall —

(A) present the recommendations developed under paragraph (1) to the congressional committees specified in such paragraph;

(B) publish such recommendations in the Federal Register;

(C) provide for a period of 30 days for the public to provide written comments on such recommendations;

(D) hold a meeting at which the public may present its views on such recommendations; and

(E) after consideration of such public views and comments, revise such recommendations as necessary.

(3) Transmittal of Recommendations. — Not later than January 15, 2017, the Secretary shall transmit to the Congress the revised recommendations under paragraph (2), a summary of the views and comments received under such paragraph, and any changes made to the recommendations in response to such views and comments.

Part 9 — Fees Relating to Outsourcing Facilities

Sec. 744J. [379j-61] Definitions.

In this part:

(1) The term "affiliate" has the meaning given such term in section 735(11).

(2) The term "gross annual sales" means the total worldwide gross annual sales, in United States dollars, for an outsourcing facility, including the sales of all the affiliates of the outsourcing facility.

(3) The term "outsourcing facility" has the meaning given to such term in section 503B(d)(4).

(4) The term "reinspection" means, with respect to an outsourcing facility, 1 or more inspections conducted under section 704 subsequent to an inspection conducted under such provision which identified noncompliance materially related to an applicable requirement of this Act, specifically to determine whether compliance has been achieved to the Secretary's satisfaction.

Sec. 744K. [379j-62] Authority to Assess and Use Outsourcing Facility Fees.

(a) Establishment and Reinspection Fees. —

(1) In General. — For fiscal year 2015 and each subsequent fiscal year, the Secretary shall, in accordance with this subsection, assess and collect —

(A) an annual establishment fee from each outsourcing facility; and

(B) a reinspection fee from each outsourcing facility subject to a reinspection in such fiscal year.

(2) Multiple Reinspections. — An outsourcing facility subject to multiple reinspections in a fiscal year shall be subject to a reinspection fee for each reinspection.

(b) Establishment and Reinspection Fee Setting. — The Secretary shall —

(1) establish the amount of the establishment fee and reinspection fee to be collected under this section for each fiscal year based on the methodology described in subsection (c); and

(2) publish such fee amounts in a Federal Register notice not later than 60 calendar days before the start of each such year.

(c) Amount of Establishment Fee and Reinspection Fee. —

(1) In General. — For each outsourcing facility in a fiscal year —

(A) except as provided in paragraph (4), the amount of the annual establishment fee under subsection (b) shall be equal to the sum of —

(i) $15,000, multiplied by the inflation adjustment factor described in paragraph (2); plus

(ii) the small business adjustment factor described in paragraph (3); and

(B) the amount of any reinspection fee (if applicable) under subsection (b) shall be equal to $15,000, multiplied by the inflation adjustment factor described in paragraph (2).

(2) Inflation Adjustment Factor. —

(A) In General. — For fiscal year 2015 and subsequent fiscal years, the fee amounts established in paragraph (1) shall be adjusted by the Secretary by notice, published in the Federal Register, for a fiscal year by the amount equal to the sum of —

(i) 1;

(ii) the average annual percent change in the cost, per full-time equivalent position of the Food and Drug Administration, of all personnel compensation and benefits paid with respect to such positions for the first 3 years of the preceding 4 fiscal years, multiplied by the proportion of personnel compensation and benefits costs to total costs of an average full-time equivalent position of the Food and Drug Administration for the first 3 years of the preceding 4 fiscal years; plus

(iii) the average annual percent change that occurred in the Consumer Price Index for urban consumers (U.S. City Average; Not Seasonally Adjusted; All items; Annual Index) for the first 3 years of the preceding 4 years of available data multiplied by the proportion of all costs other than personnel compensation and benefits costs to total costs of an average full-time equivalent position of the Food and Drug Administration for the first 3 years of the preceding 4 fiscal years.

(B) Compounded Basis. — The adjustment made each fiscal year under subparagraph (A) shall be added on a compounded basis to the sum of all adjustments made each fiscal year after fiscal year 2014 under subparagraph (A).

(3) Small Business Adjustment Factor. — The small business adjustment factor described in this paragraph shall be an amount established by the Secretary for each fiscal year based on the Secretary's estimate of —

(A) the number of small businesses that will pay a reduced establishment fee for such fiscal year; and

(B) the adjustment to the establishment fee necessary to achieve total fees equaling the total fees that the Secretary would have collected if no entity qualified for the small business exception in paragraph (4).

(4) Exception For Small Businesses. —

(A) In General. — In the case of an outsourcing facility with gross annual sales of $1,000,000 or less in the 12 months ending April 1 of the fiscal year immediately preceding the fiscal year in which the fees under this section are assessed, the amount of the establishment fee under subsection (b) for a fiscal year shall be equal to \1/3\ of the amount calculated under paragraph (1)(A)(i) for such fiscal year.

(B) Application. — To qualify for the exception under this paragraph, a small business shall submit to the Secretary a written request for such exception, in a format specified by the Secretary in guidance, certifying its gross annual sales for the 12 months ending April 1 of the fiscal year immediately preceding the fiscal year in which fees under this subsection are assessed. Any such application shall be submitted to the Secretary not later than April 30 of such immediately preceding fiscal year.

(5) Crediting of Fees. — In establishing the small business adjustment factor under paragraph (3) for a fiscal year, the Secretary shall —

(A) provide for the crediting of fees from the previous year to the next year if the Secretary overestimated the amount of the small business adjustment factor for such previous fiscal year; and

(B) consider the need to account for any adjustment of fees and such other factors as the Secretary determines appropriate.

(d) Use of Fees. — The Secretary shall make all of the fees collected pursuant to subparagraphs (A) and (B) of subsection (a)(1) available solely to pay for the costs of oversight of outsourcing facilities.

(e) Supplement Not Supplant. — Funds received by the Secretary pursuant to this section shall be used to supplement and not supplant any other Federal funds available to carry out the activities described in this section.

(f) Crediting and Availability of Fees. — Fees authorized under this section shall be collected and available for obligation only to the extent and in the amount provided in advance in appropriations Acts. Such fees are authorized to remain available until expended. Such sums as may be necessary may be transferred from the Food and Drug Administration salaries and expenses appropriation account without fiscal year limitation to such appropriation account for salaries and expenses with such fiscal year limitation. The sums transferred shall be available solely for the purpose of paying the costs of oversight of outsourcing facilities.

(g) Collection of Fees. —

(1) Establishment Fee. — An outsourcing facility shall remit the establishment fee due under this section in a fiscal year when submitting a registration pursuant to section 503B(b) for such fiscal year.

(2) Reinspection Fee. — The Secretary shall specify in the Federal Register notice described in subsection (b)(2) the manner in which reinspection fees assessed under this section shall be collected and the timeline for payment of such fees. Such a fee shall be collected after the Secretary has conducted a reinspection of the outsourcing facility involved.

(3) Effect of Failure to Pay Fees. —

(A) Registration. — An outsourcing facility shall not be considered registered under section 503B(b) in a fiscal year until the date that the outsourcing facility remits the establishment fee under this subsection for such fiscal year.

(B) Misbranding. — All drugs manufactured, prepared, propagated, compounded, or processed by an outsourcing facility for which any establishment fee or reinspection fee has not been paid, as required by this section, shall be deemed misbranded under section 502 until the fees owed for such outsourcing facility under this section have been paid.

(4) Collection of Unpaid Fees. — In any case where the Secretary does not receive payment of a fee assessed under this section within 30 calendar days after it is due, such fee shall be treated as a claim of the United States Government subject to provisions of subchapter II of chapter 37 of title 31, United States Code.

(h) Annual Report to Congress. — Not later than 120 calendar days after each fiscal year in which fees are assessed and collected under this section, the Secretary shall submit a report to the Committee on Health, Education, Labor, and Pensions of the Senate and the Committee on Energy and Commerce of the House of Representatives, to include a description of fees assessed and collected for such year, a summary description of entities paying the fees, a description of the hiring and placement of new staff, a description of the use of fee resources to support inspecting outsourcing facilities, and the number of inspections and reinspections of such facilities performed each year.

(i) Authorization of Appropriations. — For fiscal year 2014 and each subsequent fiscal year, there is authorized to be appropriated for fees under this section an amount equivalent to the total amount of fees assessed for such fiscal year under this section.

Subchapter D — Information and Education

Sec. 745. [379k] Information System.

The Secretary shall establish and maintain an information system to track the status and progress of each application or submission (including a petition, notification, or other similar form of request) submitted to the Food and Drug Administration requesting agency action.

Sec. 745A. [379k-1] Electronic Format for Submissions.

(a) Drugs and Biologics. —

(1) In General. — Beginning no earlier than 24 months after the issuance of a final guidance issued after public notice and opportunity for comment, submissions under subsection (b), (i), or (j) of section 505 of this Act or subsection (a) or (k) of section 351 of the Public Health Service Act shall be submitted in such electronic format as specified by the Secretary in such guidance.

(2) Guidance Contents. — In the guidance under paragraph (1), the Secretary may —

(A) provide a timetable for establishment by the Secretary of further standards for electronic submission as required by such paragraph; and

(B) set forth criteria for waivers of and exemptions from the requirements of this subsection.

(3) Exception — This subsection shall not apply to submissions described in section 561.

(b) Devices. —

(1) In General. — Beginning after the issuance of final guidance implementing this paragraph, presubmissions and submissions for devices under section 510(k), 513(f)(2)(A), 515(c), 515(d), 515(f), 520(g), 520(m), or 564 of this Act or section 351 of the Public Health Service Act, and any supplements to such presubmissions or submissions, shall include an electronic copy of such presubmissions or submissions.

(2) Guidance Contents. — In the guidance under paragraph (1), the Secretary may —

(A) provide standards for the electronic copy required under such paragraph; and

(B) set forth criteria for waivers of and exemptions from the requirements of this subsection.

(3) Presubmissions and Submissions Solely in Electronic Format. —

(A) In General. — Beginning on such date as the Secretary specifies in final guidance issued under subparagraph (C), presubmissions and submissions for devices described in paragraph (1) (and any appeals of action taken by the Secretary with respect to such presubmissions or submissions) shall be submitted solely in such electronic format as specified by the Secretary in such guidance.

(B) Draft Guidance. — The Secretary shall, not later than October 1, 2019, issue draft guidance providing for —

(i) any further standards for the submission by electronic format required under subparagraph (A);

(ii) a timetable for the establishment by the Secretary of such further standards; and

(iii) criteria for waivers of and exemptions from the requirements of this subsection.

(C) Final Guidance. — The Secretary shall, not later than 1 year after the close of the public comment period on the draft guidance issued under subparagraph (B), issue final guidance.

Sec. 746. [379l] Education.

(a) In General. — The Secretary shall conduct training and education programs for the employees of the Food and Drug Administration relating to the regulatory responsibilities and policies established by this Act, including programs for —

(1) scientific training;

(2) training to improve the skill of officers and employees authorized to conduct inspections under section 704;

(3) training to achieve product specialization in such inspections; and

(4) training in administrative process and procedure and integrity issues.

(b) Intramural Fellowships and Other Training Programs. — The Secretary, acting through the Commissioner, may, through fellowships and other training programs, conduct and support intramural research training for predoctoral and postdoctoral scientists and physicians. Any such fellowships and training programs under this section or under section 770(d)(2)(A)(ix) may include provision by such scientists and physicians of services on a voluntary and uncompensated basis, as the Secretary determines appropriate. Such scientists and physicians shall be subject to all legal and ethical requirements otherwise applicable to officers or employees of the Department of Health and Human Services.

Subchapter E — Environmental Impact Review

Sec. 749. [379o] Environmental Impact.

Notwithstanding any other provision of law, an environmental impact statement prepared in accordance with the regulations published in part 25 of title 21, Code of Federal Regulations (as in effect on August 31, 1997) in connection with an action carried out under (or a recommendation or report relating to) this Act, shall be considered to meet the requirements for a detailed statement under section 102(2)(C) of the National Environmental Policy Act of 1969 (42 U.S.C. 4332(2)(C)).

Subchapter F — National Uniformity for Nonprescription Drugs and Preemption for Labeling or Packaging of Cosmetics

Sec. 751. [379r] National Uniformity for Nonprescription Drugs.

(a) In General. — Except as provided in subsection (b), (c)(1), (d), (e), or (f), no State or political subdivision of a State may establish or continue in effect any requirement —

(1) that relates to the regulation of a drug that is not subject to the requirements of section 503(b)(1) or 503(f)(1)(A); and

(2) that is different from or in addition to, or that is otherwise not identical with, a requirement under this Act, the Poison Prevention Packaging Act of 1970 (15 U.S.C. 1471 et seq.), or the Fair Packaging and Labeling Act (15 U.S.C. 1451 et seq.).

(b) Exemption. —

(1) In General. — Upon application of a State or political subdivision thereof, the Secretary may by regulation, after notice and opportunity for written and oral presentation of views, exempt from subsection (a), under such conditions as may be prescribed in such regulation, a State or political subdivision requirement that —

(A) protects an important public interest that would otherwise be unprotected, including the health and safety of children;

(B) would not cause any drug to be in violation of any applicable requirement or prohibition under Federal law; and

(C) would not unduly burden interstate commerce.

(2) Timely Action. — The Secretary shall make a decision on the exemption of a State or political subdivision requirement under paragraph (1) not later than 120 days after receiving the application of the State or political subdivision under paragraph (1).

(c) Scope. —

(1) In General. — This section shall not apply to —

(A) any State or political subdivision requirement that relates to the practice of pharmacy; or

(B) any State or political subdivision requirement that a drug be dispensed only upon the prescription of a practitioner licensed by law to administer such drug.

(2) Safety or Effectiveness. — For purposes of subsection (a), a requirement that relates to the regulation of a drug shall be deemed to include any requirement relating to public information or any other form of public communication relating to a warning of any kind for a drug.

(d) Exceptions. —

(1) In General. — In the case of a drug described in subsection (a)(1) that is not the subject of an application approved under section 505 or section 507 (as in effect on the day before the date of enactment of the Food and Drug Administration Modernization Act of 1997 [November 21, 1997 — Ed.]) or a final regulation promulgated by the Secretary establishing conditions under which the drug is generally recognized as safe and effective and not misbranded, subsection (a) shall apply only with respect to a requirement of a State or political subdivision of a State that relates to the same subject as, but is different from or in addition to, or that is otherwise not identical with —

(A) a regulation in effect with respect to the drug pursuant to a statute described in subsection (a)(2); or

(B) any other requirement in effect with respect to the drug pursuant to an amendment to such a statute made on or after the date of enactment of the Food and Drug Administration Modernization Act of 1997.

(2) State Initiatives. — This section shall not apply to a State requirement adopted by a State public initiative or referendum enacted prior to September 1, 1997.

(e) No Effect on Product Liability Law. — Nothing in this section shall be construed to modify or otherwise affect any action or the liability of any person under the product liability law of any State.

(f) State Enforcement Authority. — Nothing in this section shall prevent a State or political subdivision thereof from enforcing, under any relevant civil or other enforcement authority, a requirement that is identical to a requirement of this Act.

Sec. 752. [379s] Preemption for Labeling or Packaging of Cosmetics.

(a) In General. — Except as provided in subsection (b), (d), or (e), no State or political subdivision of a State may establish or continue in effect any requirement for labeling or packaging of a cosmetic that is different from or in addition to, or that is otherwise not identical with, a requirement specifically applicable to a particular cosmetic or class of cosmetics under this Act, the Poison Prevention Packaging Act of 1970 (15 U.S.C. 1471 et seq.), or the Fair Packaging and Labeling Act (15 U.S.C. 1451 et seq.).

(b) Exemption. — Upon application of a State or political subdivision thereof, the Secretary may by regulation, after notice and opportunity for written and oral presentation of views, exempt from subsection (a), under such conditions as may be prescribed in such regulation, a State or political subdivision requirement for labeling or packaging that —

(1) protects an important public interest that would otherwise be unprotected;

(2) would not cause a cosmetic to be in violation of any applicable requirement or prohibition under Federal law; and

(3) would not unduly burden interstate commerce.

(c) Scope. — For purposes of subsection (a), a reference to a State requirement that relates to the packaging or labeling of a cosmetic means any specific requirement relating to the same aspect of such cosmetic as a requirement specifically applicable to that particular cosmetic or class of cosmetics under this Act for packaging or labeling, including any State requirement relating to public information or any other form of public communication.

(d) No Effect on Product Liability Law. — Nothing in this section shall be construed to modify or otherwise affect any action or the liability of any person under the product liability law of any State.

(e) State Initiative. — This section shall not apply to a State requirement adopted by a State public initiative or referendum enacted prior to September 1, 1997.

Subchapter G — Safety Reports

Sec. 756. [379v] Safety Report Disclaimers.

With respect to any entity that submits or is required to submit a safety report or other information in connection with the safety of a product (including a product that is a food, drug, device, dietary supplement, or cosmetic) under this Act (and any release by the Secretary of that report or information), such report or information shall not be construed to reflect necessarily a conclusion by the entity or the Secretary that the report or information constitutes an admission that the product involved malfunctioned, caused or contributed to an adverse experience, or otherwise caused or contributed to a death, serious injury, or serious illness. Such an entity need not admit, and may deny, that the report or information submitted by the entity constitutes an admission that the product involved malfunctioned, caused or contributed to an adverse health experience, or caused or contributed to a death, serious injury, or serious illness.

Subchapter H — Serious Adverse Event Reports

Sec. 760. [379aa] Serious Adverse Event Reporting for Nonprescription Drugs.

(a) Definitions — In this section:

(1) Adverse Event. — The term "adverse event" means any health-related event associated with the use of a nonprescription drug that is adverse, including —

(A) an event occurring from an overdose of the drug, whether accidental or intentional;

(B) an event occurring from abuse of the drug;

(C) an event occurring from withdrawal from the drug; and

(D) any failure of expected pharmacological action of the drug.

(2) Nonprescription Drug. — The term "nonprescription drug" means a drug that is—

(A) not subject to section 503(b); and

(B) not subject to approval in an application submitted under section 505.

(3) Serious Adverse Event. — The term "serious adverse event" is an adverse event that —

(A) results in —

(i) death;

(ii) a life-threatening experience;

(iii) inpatient hospitalization;

(iv) a persistent or significant disability or incapacity; or

(v) a congenital anomaly or birth defect; or

(B) requires, based on reasonable medical judgment, a medical or surgical intervention to prevent an outcome described under subparagraph (A).

(4) Serious Adverse Event Report. — The term "serious adverse event report" means a report that is required to be submitted to the Secretary under subsection (b).

(b) Reporting Requirement. —

(1) In General. — The manufacturer, packer, or distributor whose name (pursuant to section 502(b)(1) appears on the label of a nonprescription drug marketed in the United States (referred to in this section as the "responsible person") shall submit to the Secretary any report received of a serious adverse event associated with such drug when used in the United States, accompanied by a copy of the label on or within the retail package of such drug.

(2) Retailer. — A retailer whose name appears on the label described in paragraph (1) as a distributor may, by agreement, authorize the manufacturer or packer of the nonprescription drug to submit the required reports for such drugs to the Secretary so long as the retailer directs to the manufacturer or packer all adverse events associated with such drug that are reported to the retailer through the address or telephone number described in section 502(x).

(c) Submission of Reports. —

(1) Timing of Reports. — The responsible person shall submit to the Secretary a serious adverse event report no later than 15 business days after the report is received through the address or phone number described in section 502(x).

(2) New Medical Information. — The responsible person shall submit to the Secretary any new medical information, related to a submitted serious adverse event report that is received by the responsible person within 1 year of the initial report, no later than 15 business days after the new information is received by the responsible person.

(3) Consolidation of Reports. — The Secretary shall develop systems to ensure that duplicate reports of, and new medical information related to, a serious adverse event shall be consolidated into a single report.

(4) Exemption. — The Secretary, after providing notice and an opportunity for comment from interested parties, may establish an exemption to the requirements under paragraph (1) and (2) if the Secretary determines that such exemption would have no adverse effect on public health.

(d) Contents of Reports. — Each serious adverse event report under this section shall be submitted to the Secretary using the MedWatch form, which may be modified by the Secretary for nonprescription drugs, and may be accompanied by additional information.

(e) Maintenance and Inspection of Records. —

(1) Maintenance. — The responsible person shall maintain records related to each report of an adverse event received by the responsible person for a period of 6 years.

(2) Records Inspection. —

(A) In General. — The responsible person shall permit an authorized person to have access to records required to be maintained under this section, during an inspection pursuant to section 704.

(B) Authorized Person. — For purposes of this paragraph, the term "authorized person" means an officer or employee of the Department of Health and Human Services who has —

(i) appropriate credentials, as determined by the Secretary; and

(ii) been duly designated by the Secretary to have access to the records required under this section.

(f) Protected Information. — A serious adverse event report submitted to the Secretary under this section, including any new medical information submitted under subsection (c)(2), or an adverse event report voluntarily submitted to the Secretary shall be considered to be —

(1) a safety report under section 756 and may be accompanied by a statement, which shall be a part of any report that is released for public disclosure, that denies that the report or the records constitute an admission that the product involved caused or contributed to the adverse event; and

(2) a record about an individual under section 552a of title 5, United States Code (commonly referred to as the "Privacy Act of 1974") and a medical or similar file the disclosure of which would constitute a violation of section 552 of such title 5 (commonly referred to as the "Freedom of Information Act"), and shall not be publicly disclosed unless all personally identifiable information is redacted.

(g) Rule of Construction. — The submission of any adverse event report in compliance with this section shall not be construed as an admission that the nonprescription drug involved caused or contributed to the adverse event.

(h) Preemption. —

(1) In General. — No State or local government shall establish or continue in effect any law, regulation, order, or other requirement, related to a mandatory system for adverse event reports for nonprescription drugs, that is different from, in addition to, or otherwise not identical to, this section.

(2) Effect of Section. —

(A) In General. — Nothing in this section shall affect the authority of the Secretary to provide adverse event reports and information to any health, food, or drug officer o employee of any State, territory, or political subdivision of a State or territory, under a memorandum of understanding between the Secretary and such State, territory, or political subdivision.

(B) Personally-Identifiable Information. — Notwithstanding any other provision of law, personally-identifiable information in adverse event reports provided by the Secretary to any health, food, or drug officer or employee of any State, territory, or political subdivision of a State or territory, shall not —

(i) be made publicly available pursuant to any State or other law requiring disclosure of information or records; or

(ii) otherwise be disclosed or distributed to any party without the written consent of the Secretary and the person submitting such information to the Secretary.

(C) Use of Safety Reports. — Nothing in this section shall permit a State, territory, or political subdivision of a State, territory, to use any safety report received from the Secretary in a manner inconsistent with subsection (g) or section 756.

(i) Authorization of Appropriations. — There are authorized to be appropriated to carry out this section such sums as may be necessary.

Sec. 761. [379aa-1] Serious Adverse Event Reporting for Dietary Supplements.

(a) Definitions. — In this section:

(1) Adverse Event. — The term "adverse event" means any health-related event associated with the use of a dietary supplement that is adverse.

(2) Serious Adverse Event. — The term "serious adverse event" is an adverse event that —

(A) results in —

(i) death;

(ii) a life-threatening experience;

(ii) inpatient hospitalization;

(iv) a persistent or significant disability or incapacity; or

(v) a congenital anomaly or birth defect; or

(B) requires, based on reasonable medical judgment, a medical or surgical intervention to prevent an outcome described under subparagraph (A).

(3) Serious Adverse Event Report. — The term "serious adverse event report" means a report that is required to be submitted to the Secretary under subsection (b).

(b) Reporting Requirement. —

(1) In General. — The manufacturer, packer, or distributor of a dietary supplement whose name (pursuant to section 403(e)(1)) appears on the label of a dietary supplement marketed in the United States (referred to in this section as the "responsible person") shall submit to the Secretary any report received of a serious adverse event associated with such dietary supplement when used in the United States, accompanied by a copy of the label on or within the retail packaging of such dietary supplement.

(2) Retailer. — A retailer whose name appears on the label described in paragraph (1) as a distributor may, by agreement, authorize the manufacturer or packer of the dietary supplement to submit the required reports for such dietary supplements to the Secretary so long as the retailer directs to the manufacturer or packer all adverse events associated with such dietary supplement that are reported to the retailer through the address or telephone number described in section 403(y).

(c) Submission of Reports. —

(1) Timing of Reports. — The responsible person shall submit to the Secretary a serious adverse event report no later than 15 business days after the report is received through the address or phone number described in section 403(y).

(2) New Medical Information. — The responsible person shall submit to the Secretary any new medical information, related to a submitted serious adverse event report that is received by the responsible person within 1 year of the initial report, no later than 15 business days after the new information is received by the responsible person.

(3) Consolidation of Reports. — The Secretary shall develop systems to ensure that duplicate reports of, and new medical information related to, a serious adverse event shall be consolidated into a single report.

(4) Exemption. — The Secretary, after providing notice and an opportunity for comment from interested parties, may establish an exemption to the requirements under paragraph (1) and (2) if the Secretary determines that such exemption would have no adverse effect on public health.

(d) Contents of Reports. — Each serious adverse event report under this section shall be submitted to the Secretary using the MedWatch form, which may be modified by the Secretary for dietary supplements, any may be accompanied by additional information.

(e) Maintenance and Inspection of Reports. —

(1) Maintenance. — The responsible person shall maintain records related to each report of an adverse event received by the responsible person for a period of 6 years.

(2) Records Inspection. —

(A) In General. — The responsible person shall permit an authorized person to have access to records required to be maintained under this section during an inspection pursuant to section 704.

(B) Authorized Person. — For purposes of this paragraph, the term "authorized person" means an officer or employee of the Department of Health and Human Services, who has —

(i) appropriate credentials, as determined by the Secretary; and

(ii) been duly designated by the Secretary to have access to the records required under this section.

(f) Protected Information. — A serious adverse event report submitted to the Secretary under this section, including any new medical information submitted under subsection (c)(2), or an adverse event report voluntarily submitted to the Secretary shall be considered to be —

(1) a safety report under section 756 and may be accompanied by a statement, which shall be a part of any report that is released for public disclosure, that denies that the report or the records constitute an admission that the product involved caused or contributed to the adverse event; and

(2) a record about an individual under section 552a of title 5, United States Code (commonly referred to as the "Privacy Act of 1974") and a medical or similar file the disclosure of which would constitute a violation of section 552 of such title 5 (commonly referred to as the "Freedom of Information Act"), and shall not be publicly disclosed unless all personally identifiable information is redacted.

(g) Rule of Construction. — The submission of any adverse event report in compliance with this section shall not be construed as an admission that the dietary supplement involved caused or contributed to the adverse event.

(h) Preemption. —

(1) In General. — No State or local government shall establish or continue in effect any law, regulation, order, or other requirement, related to a mandatory system for adverse event reports for dietary supplements, that is different from, in addition to, or otherwise not identical to, this section.

(2) Effect of Section. —

(A) In General. — Nothing in this section shall affect the authority of the Secretary to provide adverse event reports and information to any health, food, or drug officer or employee of any State, territory, or political subdivision of a State or territory, under a memorandum of understanding between the Secretary and such State, territory, or political subdivision.

(B) Personally-Identifiable Information. — Notwithstanding any other provision of law, personally-identifiable information in adverse event reports provided by the Secretary to any health, food, or drug officer or employee of any State, territory, or political subdivision of a State or territory, shall not —

(i) be made publicly available pursuant to any State or other law requiring disclosure of information or records; or

(ii) otherwise be disclosed or distributed to any party without the written consent of the Secretary and the person submitting such information to the Secretary.

(C) Use of Safety Reports. — Nothing in this section shall permit a State, territory, or political subdivision of a State or territory, to use any safety report received from the Secretary in a manner inconsistent with subdivision (g) or section 756.

(i) Authorization of Appropriations. — There are authorized to be appropriated to carry out this section such sums as may be necessary.

Subchapter I — Reagan-Udall Foundation for the Food and Drug Administration

Sec. 770. [379dd] Establishment and Functions of the Foundation.

(a) In General. — A nonprofit corporation to be known as the Reagan-Udall Foundation for the Food and Drug Administration (referred to in this subchapter as the "Foundation") shall be established in accordance with this section.

The Foundation shall be headed by an Executive Director, appointed by the members of the Board of Directors under subsection (e). The Foundation shall not be an agency or instrumentality of the United States Government.

(b) Purpose of Foundation. — The purpose of the Foundation is to advance the mission of the Food and Drug Administration to modernize medical, veterinary, food, food ingredient, and cosmetic product development, accelerate innovation, and enhance product safety.

(c) Duties of the Foundation. — The Foundation shall —

(1) taking into consideration the Critical Path reports and priorities published by the Food and Drug Administration, identify unmet needs in the development, manufacture, and evaluation of the safety and effectiveness, including postapproval, of devices, including diagnostics, biologics, and drugs, and the safety of food, food ingredients, and cosmetics, and including the incorporation of more sensitive and predictive tools and devices to measure safety;

(2) establish goals and priorities in order to meet the unmet needs identified in paragraph (1);

(3) in consultation with the Secretary, identify existing and proposed Federal intramural and extramural research and development programs relating to the goals and priorities established under paragraph (2), coordinate Foundation activities with such programs, and minimize Foundation duplication of existing efforts;

(4) award grants to, or enter into contracts, memoranda of understanding, or cooperative agreements with, scientists and entities, which may include the Food and Drug Administration, university consortia, public-private partnerships, institutions of higher education, entities described in section 501(c)(3) of the Internal Revenue Code (and exempt from tax under section 501(a) of such Code), and industry, to efficiently and effectively advance the goals and priorities established under paragraph (2);

(5) recruit meeting participants and hold or sponsor (in whole or in part) meetings as appropriate to further the goals and priorities established under paragraph (2);

(6) release and publish information and data and, to the extent practicable, license, distribute, and release material, reagents, and techniques to maximize, promote, and coordinate the availability of such material, reagents, and techniques for use by the Food and Drug Administration, nonprofit organizations, and academic and industrial researchers to further the goals and priorities established under paragraph (2);

(7) ensure that —

(A) action is taken as necessary to obtain patents for inventions developed by the Foundation or with funds from the Foundation;

(B) action is taken as necessary to enable the licensing of inventions developed by the Foundation or with funds from the Foundation; and

(C) executed licenses, memoranda of understanding, material transfer agreements, contracts, and other such instruments, promote, to the maximum extent practicable, the broadest conversion to commercial and noncommercial applications of licensed and patented inventions of the Foundation to further the goals and priorities established under paragraph (2);

(8) provide objective clinical and scientific information to the Food and Drug Administration and, upon request, to other Federal agencies to assist in agency determinations of how to ensure that regulatory policy accommodates scientific advances and meets the agency's public health mission;

(9) conduct annual assessments of the unmet needs identified in paragraph (1); and

(10) carry out such other activities consistent with the purposes of the Foundation as the Board determines appropriate.

(d) Board of Directors. —

(1) Establishment. —

(A) In General. — The Foundation shall have a Board of Directors (referred to in this subchapter as the "Board"), which shall be composed of ex officio and appointed members in accordance with this subsection. All appointed members of the Board shall be voting members.

(B) Ex Officio Members. — The ex officio members of the Board shall be the following individuals or their designees:

(i) The Commissioner.

(ii) The Director of the National Institutes of Health.

(iii) The Director of the Centers for Disease Control and Prevention.

(iv) The Director of the Agency for Healthcare Research and Quality.

(C) Appointed Members. —

(i) In General. — The ex officio members of the Board under subparagraph (B) shall, by majority vote, appoint to the Board 14 individuals, of which 9 shall be from a list of candidates to be provided by the National Academy of Sciences and 5 shall be from lists of candidates provided by patient and consumer advocacy groups, professional scientific and medical societies, and industry trade organizations. Of such appointed members—

(I) 4 shall be representatives of the general pharmaceutical, device, food, cosmetic, and biotechnology industries;

(II) 3 shall be representatives of academic research organizations;

(III) 2 shall be representatives of patient or consumer advocacy organizations;

(IV) 1 shall be a representative of health care providers; and

(V) 4 shall be at-large members with expertise or experience relevant to the purpose of the Foundation.

(ii) Additional Members.—The Board, through amendments to the bylaws of the Foundation, may provide that the number of voting members of the Board shall be a number (to be specified in such amendment) greater than 14. Any Board positions that are established by any such amendment shall be appointed (by majority vote) by the individuals who, as of the date of such amendment, are voting members of the Board and persons so appointed may represent any of the categories specified in subclauses (I) through (V) of clause (i), so long as no more than 30 percent of the total voting members of the Board (including members whose positions are established by such amendment) are representatives of the general pharmaceutical, device, food, cosmetic, and biotechnology industries.

(iii) Requirements. —

(I) Expertise. — The ex officio members, acting pursuant to clause (i), and the Board, acting pursuant to clause (ii), shall ensure the Board membership includes individuals with expertise in areas including the sciences of developing, manufacturing, and evaluating the safety and effectiveness of devices, including diagnostics, biologics, and drugs, and the safety of food, food ingredients, and cosmetics.

(II) Federal Employees. — No employee of the Federal Government shall be appointed as a member of the Board under this subparagraph or under paragraph (3)(B). For purposes of this section, the term "employee of the Federal Government" does not include a special Government employee, as that term is defined in section 202(a) of title 18, United States Code.

(D) Initial Meeting. —

(i) In General. — Not later than 30 days after the date of the enactment of this subchapter, the Secretary shall convene a meeting of the ex officio members of the Board to —

(I) incorporate the Foundation; and

(II) appoint the members of the Board in accordance with subparagraph (C).

(ii) Service of Ex Officio Members. — Upon the appointment of the members of the Board under clause (i)(II) —

(I) the terms of service of the Director of the Centers for Disease Control and Prevention and of the Director of the Agency for Healthcare Research and Quality as ex officio members of the Board shall terminate; and

(II) the Commissioner and the Director of the National Institutes of Health shall continue to serve as ex officio members of the Board, but shall be nonvoting members.

(iii) Chair. — The ex officio members of the Board under subparagraph (B) shall designate an appointed member of the Board to serve as the Chair of the Board.

(2) Duties of Board. — The Board shall —

(A) establish bylaws for the Foundation that —

(i) are published in the Federal Register and available for public comment;

(ii) establish policies for the selection of the officers, employees, agents, and contractors of the Foundation;

(iii) establish policies, including ethical standards, for the acceptance, solicitation, and disposition of donations and grants to the Foundation and for the disposition of the assets of the Foundation, including appropriate limits on the ability of donors to designate, by stipulation or restriction, the use or recipient of donated funds;

(iv) establish policies that would subject all employees, fellows, and trainees of the Foundation to the conflict of interest standards under section 208 of title 18, United States Code;

(v) establish licensing, distribution, and publication policies that support the widest and least restrictive use by the public of information and inventions developed by the Foundation or with Foundation funds to carry out the duties described in paragraphs (6) and (7) of subsection (c), and may include charging cost-based fees for published material produced by the Foundation;

(vi) specify principles for the review of proposals and awarding of grants and contracts that include peer review and that are consistent with those of the Foundation for the National Institutes of Health, to the extent determined practicable and appropriate by the Board;

(vii) specify a cap on administrative expenses for recipients of a grant, contract, or cooperative agreement from the Foundation;

(viii) establish policies for the execution of memoranda of understanding and cooperative agreements between the Foundation and other entities, including the Food and Drug Administration;

(ix) establish policies for funding training fellowships, whether at the Foundation, academic or scientific institutions, or the Food and Drug Administration, for scientists, doctors, and other professionals who are not employees of regulated industry, to foster greater understanding of and expertise in new scientific tools, diagnostics, manufacturing techniques, and potential barriers to translating basic research into clinical and regulatory practice;

(x) specify a process for annual Board review of the operations of the Foundation; and

(xi) establish specific duties of the Executive Director;

(B) prioritize and provide overall direction to the activities of the Foundation;

(C) evaluate the performance of the Executive Director; and

(D) carry out any other necessary activities regarding the functioning of the Foundation.

(3) Terms and Vacancies. —

(A) Term. — The term of office of each member of the Board appointed under paragraph (1)(C)(i), and the term of office of any member of the Board whose position is established pursuant to paragraph (1)(C)(ii), shall be 4 years, except that —

(i) the terms of offices for the members of the Board initially appointed under paragraph (1)(C)(i) shall expire on a staggered basis as determined by the ex officio members; and

(ii) the terms of office for the per-sons initially appointed to positions established pursuant to paragraph (1) (C) (ii) may be made to expire on a staggered basis, as determined by the individuals who, as of the date of the amendment establishing such positions, are members of the Board.

(B) Vacancy. — Any vacancy in the membership of the Board —

(i) shall not affect the power of the remaining members to execute the duties of the Board; and

(ii) shall be filled by appointment by the appointed members described in paragraph (1)(C) by majority vote.

(C) Partial Term. — If a member of the Board does not serve the full term applicable under subparagraph (A), the individual appointed under subparagraph (B) to fill the resulting vacancy shall be appointed for the remainder of the term of the predecessor of the individual.

(D) Serving Past Term. — A member of the Board may continue to serve after the expiration of the term of the member until a successor is appointed.

(4) Compensation. — Members of the Board may not receive compensation for service on the Board. Such members may be reimbursed for travel, subsistence, and other necessary expenses incurred in carrying out the duties of the Board, as set forth in the bylaws issued by the Board.

(e) Incorporation. — The ex officio members of the Board shall serve as incorporators and shall take whatever actions necessary to incorporate the Foundation.

(f) Nonprofit Status. — In carrying out subsection (b), the Board shall establish such policies and bylaws under subsection (d), and the Executive Director shall carry out such activities under subsection (g), as may be necessary to ensure that the Foundation maintains status as an organization that —

(1) is described in subsection (c)(3) of section 501 of the Internal Revenue Code of 1986; and

(2) is, under subsection (a) of such section, exempt from taxation.

(g) Executive Director. —

(1) In General. — The Board shall appoint an Executive Director who shall serve at the pleasure of the Board. The Executive Director shall be responsible for the day-to-day operations of the Foundation and shall have such specific duties and responsibilities as the Board shall prescribe.

(2) Compensation. — The compensation of the Executive Director shall be fixed by the Board.

(h) Administrative Powers. — In carrying out this subchapter, the Board, acting through the Executive Director, may—

(1) adopt, alter, and use a corporate seal, which shall be judicially noticed;

(2) hire, promote, compensate, and discharge 1 or more officers, employees, and agents, as may be necessary, and define their duties;

(3) prescribe the manner in which —

(A) real or personal property of the Foundation is acquired, held, and transferred;

(B) general operations of the Foundation are to be conducted; and

(C) the privileges granted to the Board by law are exercised and enjoyed;

(4) with the consent of the applicable executive department or independent agency, use the information, services, and facilities of such department or agencies in carrying out this section;

(5) enter into contracts with public and private organizations for the writing, editing, printing, and publishing of books and other material;

(6) hold, administer, invest, and spend any gift, devise, or bequest of real or personal property made to the Foundation under subsection (i);

(7) enter into such other contracts, leases, cooperative agreements, and other transactions as the Board considers appropriate to conduct the activities of the Foundation;

(8) modify or consent to the modification of any contract or agreement to which it is a party or in which it has an interest under this subchapter;

(9) take such action as may be necessary to obtain patents and licenses for devices and procedures developed by the Foundation and its employees;

(10) sue and be sued in its corporate name, and complain and defend in courts of competent jurisdiction;

(11) appoint other groups of advisors as may be determined necessary to carry out the functions of the Foundation; and

(12) exercise other powers as set forth in this section, and such other incidental powers as are necessary to carry out its powers, duties, and functions in accordance with this subchapter.

(i) Acceptance of Funds from other Sources. — The Executive Director may solicit and accept on behalf of the Foundation, any funds, gifts, grants, devises, or bequests of real or personal property made to the Foundation, including from private entities, for the purposes of carrying out the duties of the Foundation.

(j) Service of Federal Employees. — Federal Government employees may serve on committees advisory to the Foundation and otherwise cooperate with and assist the Foundation in carrying out its functions, so long as such employees do not direct or control Foundation activities.

(k) Detail of Government Employees; Fellowships. —

(1) Detail from Federal Agencies. —

Federal Government employees may be detailed from Federal agencies with or without reimbursement to those agencies to the Foundation at any time, and such detail shall be without interruption or loss of civil service status or privilege. Each such employee shall abide by the statutory, regulatory, ethical, and procedural standards applicable to the employees of the agency from which such employee is detailed and those of the Foundation.

(2) Voluntary Service; Acceptance of Federal Employees. —

(A) Foundation. — The Executive Director of the Foundation may accept the services of employees detailed from Federal agencies with or without reimbursement to those agencies.

(B) Food and Drug Administration. — The Commissioner may accept the uncompensated services of Foundation fellows or trainees. Such services shall be considered to be undertaking an activity under contract with the Secretary as described in section 708.

(l) Annual Reports. —

(1) Reports to Foundation. — Any recipient of a grant, contract, fellowship, memorandum of understanding, or cooperative agreement from the Foundation under this section shall submit to the Foundation a report on an annual basis for the duration of such grant, contract, fellowship, memorandum of understanding, or cooperative agreement, that describes the activities carried out under such grant, contract, fellowship, memorandum of understanding, or cooperative agreement.

(2) Report to Congress and the FDA. — Beginning with fiscal year 2009, the Executive Director shall submit to Congress and the Commissioner an annual report that —

(A) describes the activities of the Foundation and the progress of the Foundation in furthering the goals and priorities established under subsection (c)(2), including the practical impact of the Foundation on regulated product development;

(B) provides a specific accounting of the source and use of all funds used by the Foundation to carry out such activities; and

(C) provides information on how the results of Foundation activities could be incorporated into the regulatory and product review activities of the Food and Drug Administration.

(m) Separation of Funds. — The Executive Director shall ensure that the funds received from the Treasury are managed as individual programmatic funds under subsection (i), according to best accounting practices.

(n) Funding. — From amounts appropriated to the Food and Drug Administration for each fiscal year, the Commissioner shall transfer not less than $500,000 and not more than $1,250,000, to the Foundation to carry out subsections (a), (b), and (d) through (m).

Sec. 771. [379dd-1] Location of Foundation.

The Foundation shall, if practicable, be located not more than 20 miles from the District of Columbia.

Sec. 772. [379dd-2] Activities of the Food and Drug Administration.

(a) In General. — The Commissioner shall receive and assess the report submitted to the Commissioner by the Executive Director of the Foundation under section 770(l)(2).

(b) Report to Congress. — Beginning with fiscal year 2009, the Commissioner shall submit to Congress an annual report summarizing the incorporation of the information provided by the Foundation in the report described under section 770(l) (2) and by other recipients of grants, contracts, memoranda of understanding, or cooperative agreements into regulatory and product review activities of the Food and Drug Administration.

(c) Extramural Grants. — The provisions of this subchapter and section 566 shall have no effect on any grant, contract, memorandum of understanding, or cooperative agreement between the Food and Drug Administration and any other entity entered into before, on, or after the date of the enactment of this subchapter.

Chapter VIII — Imports and Exports

Sec. 801. [381] Imports and Exports.

(a) The Secretary of the Treasury shall deliver to the Secretary of Health and Human Services, upon his request, samples of food, drugs, devices, tobacco products, and cosmetics which are being imported or offered for import into the United States, giving notice thereof to the owner or consignee, who may appear before the Secretary of Health and Human Services and have the right to introduce testimony. The Secretary of Health and Human Services shall furnish to the Secretary of the Treasury a list of establishments registered pursuant to subsection (i) of section 510 or section 905(h) and shall request that if any drugs and devices manufactured, prepared, propagated, compounded, or processed in an establishment not so registered are imported or offered for import into the United States, samples of such drugs, devices, or tobacco products be delivered to the Secretary of Health and Human Services, with notice of such delivery to the owner or consignee, who may appear before the Secretary of Health and Human Services and have the right to introduce testimony. If such article is subject to a requirement under section 760 or 761 and if the Secretary has credible evidence or information indicating that the responsible person (as defined in such section 760 or 761) has not complied with a requirement of such section 760 or 761 with respect to any such article, or has not allowed access to records described in such section 760 or 761, then such article shall be refused admission, except as provided in subsection (b) of this section. With respect to an article of food, if importation of such food is subject to, but not compliant with, the requirement under subsection (q) that such food be accompanied by a certification or other assurance that the food meets applicable requirements of this Act, then such article shall be refused admission. If it appears from the examination of such samples or otherwise that

(1) such article has been manufactured, processed, or packed under insanitary conditions or, in the case of a device, the methods used in, or the facilities or controls used for, the manufacture, packing, storage, or installation of the device do not conform to the requirements of section 520(f), or

(2) such article is forbidden or restricted in sale in the country in which it was produced or from which it was exported, or

(3) such article is adulterated, misbranded, or in violation of section 505 or the importer (as defined in section 805) is in violation of such section 805, or prohibited from introduction or delivery for introduction into interstate commerce under Section 301(ll), or

(4) the recordkeeping requirements under section 204 of the FDA Food Safety Modernization Act (other than the requirements, under subsection (f) of such section) have not been complied with regarding such articles,

then such article shall be refused admission, except as provided in subsection (b) of this section. The Secretary of the Treasury shall cause the destruction of any such article refused admission unless such article is exported, under regulations prescribed by the Secretary of the Treasury, within ninety days of the date of notice of such refusal or within such additional time as may be permitted pursuant to such regulations, except that the Secretary of Health and Human Services may destroy, without the opportunity for export, any drug refused admission under this section, if such drug is valued at an amount that is $2,500 or less (or such higher amount as the Secretary of the Treasury may set by regulation pursuant to section 498(a)(1) of the Tariff Act of 1930 (19 U.S.C. 1498(a)(1)) and was not brought into compliance as described under subsection (b). The Secretary of Health and Human Services shall issue regulations providing for notice and an opportunity to appear before the Secretary of Health and Human Services and introduce testimony, as described in the first sentence of this subsection, on destruction of a drug under the sixth sentence of this subsection. The regulations shall provide that prior to destruction, appropriate due process is available to the owner or cosignee seeking to challenge the decision to destroy the drug. Where the Secretary of Health and Human Services provides notice and an opportunity to appear and introduce testimony on the destruction of a drug, the Secretary of Health and Human Services shall store and, as applicable, dispose of the drug after the issuance of the notice, except that the owner and cosignee shall remain liable for costs pursuant to subsection (c). Such process may be combined with the notice and opportunity to appear before the Secretary and introduce testimony, as described in the first sentence of this subsection, as long as appropriate notice is provided to the owner or cosignee. Clause (2) of the third sentence of this subsection shall not be construed to prohibit the admission of narcotic drugs the importation of which is permitted under the Controlled Substances Import and Export Act.

(b) Pending decision as to the admission of an article being imported or offered for import, the Secretary of the Treasury may authorize delivery of such article to the owner or consignee upon the execution by him of a good and sufficient bond providing for the payment of such liquidated damages in the event of default as may be required pursuant to regulations of the Secretary of the Treasury. If it appears to the Secretary of Health and Human Services that (1) an article included within the provisions of clause (3) of subsection (a) of this section can, by relabeling or other action, be brought into compliance with the Act or rendered other than a food, drug, device, or cosmetic, or (2) with respect to an article described in subsection (a) relating to the requirements of section 760 or 761, the responsible person (as defined in section 760 or 761) can take action that would assure that the responsible person is in compliance with section 760 or 761, as the case may be. Final determination as to admission of such article may be deferred and, upon filing of timely written application by the owner or consignee and the execution by him of a bond as provided in the preceding provisions of this subsection, the Secretary may, in accordance with regulations, authorize the applicant, or, with respect to Clause (2), the responsible person, to perform such relabeling or other action specified in such authorization (including destruction or export of rejected articles or portions thereof, as may be specified in the Secretary's authorization). All such relabeling or other action pursuant to such authorization shall in accordance with regulations be under the supervision of an officer or employee of the Department of Health and Human Services designated by the Secretary, or an officer or employee of the Department of the Treasury designated by the Secretary of the Treasury.

(c) All expenses (including travel, per diem or subsistence, and salaries of officers or employees of the United States) in connection with the destruction provided for in subsection (a) of this section and the supervision of the relabeling or other action authorized under the provisions of subsection (b) of this section, the amount of such expenses to be determined in accordance with regulations, and all expenses in connection with the storage, cartage, or labor with respect to any article refused admission under subsection (a) of this section, shall be paid by the owner or consignee and, in default of such payment, shall constitute a lien against any future importations made by such owner or consignee.

(d) —

(1)

(A) Except as provided in paragraph (2) and section 804, no drug subject to section 503(b) or composed wholly or partly of insulin which is manufactured in a State and exported may be imported into the United States unless the drug is imported by the manufacturer of the drug.

(B) Except as authorized by the Secretary in the case of a drug that appears on the drug shortage list under section 506E or in the case of importation pursuant to section 804, no drug that is subject to section 503(b)(1) may be imported into the United States for commercial use if such drug is manufactured outside the United States, unless the manufacturer has authorized the drug to be marketed in the United States and has caused the drug to be labeled to be marketed in the United States.

(2) The Secretary may authorize the importation of a drug the importation of which is prohibited by paragraph (1) if the drug is required for emergency medical care.

(3) —

(A) Subject to subparagraph (B), no component of a drug, no component part or accessory of a device, or other article of device requiring further processing, which is ready or suitable for use for health-related purposes, and no article of a food additive, color additive, or dietary supplement, including a product in bulk form, shall be excluded from importation into the United States under subsection (a) if each of the following conditions is met:

(i) The importer of such article of a drug or device or importer of such article of a food additive, color additive, or dietary supplement submits to the Secretary, at the time of initial importation, a statement in accordance with the following:

(I) Such statement provides that such article is intended to be further processed by the initial owner or consignee, or incorporated by the initial owner or consignee, into a drug, biological product, device, food, food additive, color additive, or dietary supplement that will be exported by the initial owner or consignee from the United States in accordance with subsection (e) or section 802, or with section 351(h) of the Public Health Service Act.

(II) The statement identifies the manufacturer of such article and each processor, packer, distributor, or other entity that had possession of the article in the chain of possession of the article from the manufacturer to such importer of the article.

(III) The statement is accompanied by such certificates of analysis as are necessary to identify such article, unless the article is a device or is an article described in paragraph (4).

(ii) At the time of initial importation and before the delivery of such article to the importer or the initial owner or consignee, such owner or consignee executes a good and sufficient bond providing for the payment of such liquidated damages in the event of default as may be required pursuant to regulations of the Secretary of the Treasury.

(iii) Such article is used and exported by the initial owner or consignee in accordance with the intent described under clause (i)(I), except for any portions of the article that are destroyed.

(iv) The initial owner or consignee maintains records on the use or destruction of such article or portions thereof, as the case may be, and submits to the Secretary any such records requested by the Secretary.

(v) Upon request of the Secretary, the initial owner or consignee submits a report that provides an accounting of the exportation or destruction of such article or portions thereof, and the manner in which such owner or consignee complied with the requirements of this subparagraph.

(B) Notwithstanding subparagraph (A), the Secretary may refuse admission to an article that otherwise would be imported into the United States under such subparagraph if the Secretary determines that there is credible evidence or information indicating that such article is not intended to be further processed by the initial owner or consignee, or incorporated by the initial owner or consignee, into a drug, biological product, device, food, food additive, color additive, or dietary supplement that will be exported by the initial owner or consignee from the United States in accordance with subsection (e) or section 802, or with section 351(h) of the Public Health Service Act.

(C) This section may not be construed as affecting the responsibility of the Secretary to ensure that articles imported into the United States under authority of subparagraph (A) meet each of the conditions established in such subparagraph for importation.

(4) The importation into the United States of blood, blood components, source plasma, or source leukocytes or of a component, accessory, or part thereof is not permitted pursuant to paragraph (3) unless the importation complies with section 351(a) of the Public Health Service Act or the Secretary permits the importation under appropriate circumstances and conditions, as determined by the Secretary. The importation of tissue or a component or part of tissue is not permitted pursuant to paragraph (3) unless the importation complies with section 361 of the Public Health Service Act.

(e) —

(1) A food, drug, device, tobacco product or cosmetic intended for export shall not be deemed to be adulterated or misbranded under this Act, and a tobacco product intended for export shall not be deemed to be in violation of section 906(e), 907, 911, or 920(a), if it —

(A) accords to the specifications of the foreign purchaser,

(B) is not in conflict with the laws of the country to which it is intended for export,

(C) is labeled on the outside of the shipping package that it is intended for export, and

(D) is not sold or offered for sale in domestic commerce.

(2) Paragraph (1) does not apply to any device —

(A) which does not comply with an applicable requirement of section 514 or 515,

(B) which under section 520(g) is exempt from either such section, or

(C) which is a banned device under section 516,

unless, in addition to the requirements of paragraph (1), either

(i) the Secretary has determined that the exportation of the device is not contrary to public health and safety and has the approval of the country to which it is intended for export or

(ii) the device is eligible for export under section 802.

(3) A new animal drug that requires approval under section 512 shall not be exported pursuant to paragraph (1) if such drug has been banned in the United States.

(4) —

(A) Any person who exports a food, drug, animal drug, or device may request that the Secretary —

(i) certify in writing that the exported food, drug, animal drug, or device meets the requirements of paragraph (1) or section 802; or

(ii) certify in writing that the food, drug, animal drug, or device being exported meets the applicable requirements of this Act upon a showing that the food, drug or device meets the applicable requirements of this Act.

The Secretary shall issue such a certification within 20 days of the receipt of a request for such certification.

(B) If the Secretary issues a written export certification within the 20 days prescribed by subparagraph (A), a fee for such certification may be charged but shall not exceed $175 for each certification. Fees collected for a fiscal year pursuant to this subparagraph shall be credited to the appropriation account for salaries and expenses of the Food and Drug Administration and shall be available in accordance with appropriations Acts until expended without fiscal year limitation. Such fees shall be collected in each fiscal year in an amount equal to the amount specified in appropriations Acts for such fiscal year and shall only be collected and available for the costs of the Food and Drug Administration.

(C) For purposes of this paragraph, a certification by the Secretary shall be made on such basis, and in such form (including a publicly available listing) as the Secretary determines appropriate.

(D) With regard to fees pursuant to subparagraph (B) in connection with written export certifications for food:

(i) Such fees shall be collected and available solely for the costs of the Food and Drug Administration associated with issuing such certifications.

(ii) Such fees may not be retained in an amount that exceeds such costs for the respective fiscal year.

(E) —

(i)—

(I) If the Secretary denies a request for certification under subparagraph (A)(ii) with respect to a device manufactured in an establishment (foreign or domestic) registered under section 510, the Secretary shall provide in writing to the person seeking such certification the basis for such denial, and specifically identify the finding upon which such denial is based.

(II) If the denial of a request as described in subclause (I) is based on grounds other than an injunction proceeding pursuant to section 302, seizure action pursuant to section 304, or a recall designated Class I or Class II pursuant to part 7, title 21, Code of Federal Regulations, and is based on the facility being out of compliance with part 820 of title 21, Code of Federal Regulations, the Secretary shall provide a substantive summary of the specific grounds for noncompliance identified by the Secretary.

(III) With respect to a device manufactured in an establishment that has received a report under section 704(b), the Secretary shall not deny a request for certification as described in subclause (I) with respect to a device based solely on the issuance of that report if the owner, operator, or agent in charge of such establishment has agreed to a plan of correction in response to such report.

(ii)—

(I) The Secretary shall provide a process for a person who is denied a certification as described in clause (i)(I) to request a review that conforms to the standards of section 517A(b).

(II) Notwithstanding any previous review conducted pursuant to subclause (I), a person who has been denied a certification as described in clause (i)(I) may at any time request a review in order to present new information relating to actions taken by such person to address the reasons identified by the Secretary for the denial of certification, including evidence that corrective actions are being or have been implemented to address grounds for noncompliance identified by the Secretary.

(III) Not later than 1 year after the date of enactment of the FDA Reauthorization Act of 2017, the Secretary shall issue guidance providing for a process to carry out this subparagraph. Not later than 1 year after the close of the comment period for such guidance, the Secretary shall issue final guidance.

(iii)—

(I) Subject to subclause (II), this subparagraph applies to requests for certification on behalf of any device establishment registered under section 510, whether the establishment is located inside or outside of the United States, and regardless of whether such devices are to be exported from the United States.

(II) If an establishment described in subclause (I) is not located within the United States and does not demonstrate that the devices manufactured, prepared, propagated, compounded, or processed at such establishment are to be exported from the United States, this subparagraph shall apply only if—

(aa) the establishment has been inspected by the Secretary within 3 years of the date of the request; or

(bb) the establishment participates in an audit program in which the United States participates or the United States recognizes, an audit under such program has been conducted, and the findings of such audit are provided to the Secretary within 3 years of the date of the request.

(f) —

(1) If a drug (other than insulin, an antibiotic drug, an animal drug, or a drug exported under section 802) being exported in accordance with subsection (e) is being exported to a country that has different or additional labeling requirements or conditions for use and such country requires the drug to be labeled in accordance with those requirements or uses, such drug may be labeled in accordance with such requirements and conditions for use in the country to which such drug is being exported if it also is labeled in accordance with the requirements of this Act.

(2) If, pursuant to paragraph (1), the labeling of an exported drug includes conditions for use that have not been approved under this Act, the labeling must state that such conditions for use have not been approved under this Act. A drug exported under section 802 is exempt from this section.

(g) —

(1) With respect to a prescription drug being imported or offered for import into the United States, the Secretary, in the case of an individual who is not in the business of such importations, may not send a warning notice to the individual unless the following conditions are met:

(A) The notice specifies, as applicable to the importation of the drug, that the Secretary has made a determination that —

(i) importation is in violation of section 801(a) because the drug is or appears to be adulterated, misbranded, or in violation of section 505;

(ii) importation is in violation of section 801(a) because the drug is or appears to be forbidden or restricted in sale in the country in which it was produced or from which it was exported;

(iii) importation is or appears to be in violation of section 801(d)(1); or

(iv) importation otherwise is or appears to be in violation of Federal law.

(B) The notice does not specify any provision described in subparagraph (A) that is not applicable to the importation of the drug.

(C) The notice states the reasons underlying such determination by the Secretary, including a brief application to the principal facts involved of the provision of law described in subparagraph (A) that is the basis of the determination by the Secretary.

(2) For purposes of this section, the term "warning notice", with respect to the importation of a drug, means a communication from the Secretary (written or otherwise) notifying a person, or clearly suggesting to the person, that importing the drug for personal use is, or appears to be, a violation of this Act.

(h) —

(1) The Secretary shall give high priority to increasing the number of inspections under this section for the purpose of enabling the Secretary to inspect food offered for import at ports of entry into the United States, with the greatest priority given to inspections to detect the intentional adulteration of food.

(2) The Secretary shall give high priority to making necessary improvements to the information management systems of the Food and Drug Administration that contain information related to foods imported or offered for import into the United States for purposes of improving the ability of the Secretary to allocate resources, detect the intentional adulteration of food, and facilitate the importation of food that is in compliance with this Act.

(3) The Secretary shall improve linkages with other regulatory agencies of the Federal Government that share responsibility for food safety, and shall with respect to such safety improve linkages with the States and Indian tribes (as defined in section 4(e) of the Indian Self-Determination and Education Assistance Act (25 U.S.C. 450b(e))).

(i) —

(1) For use in inspections of food under this section, the Secretary shall provide for research on the development of tests and sampling methodologies —

(A) whose purpose is to test food in order to rapidly detect the adulteration of the food, with the greatest priority given to detect the intentional adulteration of food; and

(B) whose results offer significant improvements over the available technology in terms of accuracy, timing, or costs.

(2) In providing for research under paragraph (1), the Secretary shall give priority to conducting research on the development of tests that are suitable for inspections of food at ports of entry into the United States.

(3) In providing for research under paragraph (1), the Secretary shall as appropriate coordinate with the Director of the Centers for Disease Control and Prevention, the Director of the National Institutes of Health, the Administrator of the Environmental Protection Agency, and the Secretary of Agriculture.

(4) The Secretary shall annually submit to the Committee on Energy and Commerce of the House of Representatives, and the Committee on Health, Education, Labor, and Pensions of the Senate, a report describing the progress made in research under paragraph (1), including progress regarding paragraph (2).

(j) —

(1) If an officer or qualified employee of the Food and Drug Administration has credible evidence or information indicating that an article of food presents a threat of serious adverse health consequences or death to humans or animals, and such officer or qualified employee is unable to inspect, examine, or investigate such article upon the article being offered for import at a port of entry into the United States, the officer or qualified employee shall request the Secretary of Treasury to hold the food at the port of entry for a reasonable period of time, not to exceed 24 hours, for the purpose of enabling the Secretary to inspect, examine, or investigate the article as appropriate.

(2) The Secretary shall request the Secretary of Treasury to remove an article held pursuant to paragraph (1) to a secure facility, as appropriate. During the period of time that such article is so held, the article shall not be transferred by any person from the port of entry into the United States for the article, or from the secure facility to which the article has been removed, as the case may be. Subsection (b) does not authorize the delivery of the article pursuant to the execution of a bond while the article is so held.

(3) An officer or qualified employee of the Food and Drug Administration may make a request under paragraph (1) only if the Secretary or an official designated by the Secretary approves the request. An official may not be so designated unless the official is the director of the district under this Act in which the article involved is located, or is an official senior to such director.

(4) With respect to an article of food for which a request under paragraph (1) is made, the Secretary, promptly after the request is made, shall notify the State in which the port of entry involved is located that the request has been made, and as applicable, that such article is being held under this subsection.

(k) —

(1) If an article of food is being imported or offered for import into the United States, and the importer, owner, or consignee of the article is a person who has been debarred under section 306(b)(3), such article shall be held at the port of entry for the article, and may not be delivered to such person. Subsection (b) does not authorize the delivery of the article pursuant to the execution of a bond while the article is so held. The article shall be removed to a secure facility, as appropriate. During the period of time that such article is so held, the article shall not be transferred by any person from the port of entry into the United States for the article, or from the secure facility to which the article has been removed, as the case may be.

(2) An article of food held under paragraph (1) may be delivered to a person who is not a debarred person under section 306(b)(3) if such person affirmatively establishes, at the expense of the person, that the article complies with the requirements of this Act, as determined by the Secretary.

(l) If an article of food is being imported or offered for import into the United States, and such article is from a foreign facility for which a registration has not been submitted to the Secretary under section 415 (or for which a registration has been suspended under such section), such article shall be held at the port of entry for the article, and may not be delivered to the importer, owner, or consignee of the article, until the foreign facility is so registered. Subsection (b) does not authorize the delivery of the article pursuant to the execution of a bond while the article is so held. The article shall be removed to a secure facility, as appropriate. During the period of time that such article is so held, the article shall not be transferred by any person from the port of entry into the United States for the article, or from the secure facility to which the article has been removed, as the case may be.

(m) —

(1) In the case of an article of food that is being imported or offered for import into the United States, the Secretary, after consultation with the Secretary of the Treasury, shall by regulation require, for the purpose of enabling such article to be inspected at ports of entry into the United States, the submission to the Secretary of a notice providing the identity of each of the following: The article; the manufacturer and shipper of the article; if known within the specified period of time that notice is required to be provided, the grower of the article; the country from which the article originates; the country from which the article is shipped; any country to which the article has been refused entry; and the anticipated port of entry for the article. An article of food imported or offered for import without submission of such notice in accordance with the requirements under this paragraph shall be refused admission into the United States. Nothing in this section may be construed as a limitation on the port of entry for an article of food.

(2) —

(A) Regulations under paragraph (1) shall require that a notice under such paragraph be provided by a specified period of time in advance of the time of the importation of the article of food involved or the offering of the food for import, which period shall be no less than the minimum amount of time necessary for the Secretary to receive, review, and appropriately respond to such notification, but may not exceed five days. In determining the specified period of time required under this subparagraph, the Secretary may consider, but is not limited to consideration of, the effect on commerce of such period of time, the locations of the various ports of entry into the United States, the various modes of transportation, the types of food imported into the United States, and any other such consideration. Nothing in the preceding sentence may be construed as a limitation on the obligation of the Secretary to receive, review, and appropriately respond to any notice under paragraph (1).

(B) —

(i) If an article of food is being imported or offered for import into the United States and a notice under paragraph (1) is not provided in advance in accordance with the requirements under paragraph (1), such article shall be held at the port of entry for the article, and may not be delivered to the importer, owner, or consignee of the article, until such notice is submitted to the Secretary, and the Secretary examines the notice and determines that the notice is in accordance with the requirements under paragraph (1). Subsection (b) does not authorize the delivery of the article pursuant to the execution of a bond while the article is so held. The article shall be removed to a secure facility, as appropriate. During the period of time that such article is so held, the article shall not be transferred by any person from the port of entry into the United States for the article, or from the secure facility to which the article has been removed, as the case may be.

(ii) In carrying out clause (i) with respect to an article of food, the Secretary shall determine whether there is in the possession of the Secretary any credible evidence or information indicating that such article presents a threat of serious adverse health consequences or death to humans or animals.

(3) —

(A) This subsection may not be construed as limiting the authority of the Secretary to obtain information under any other provision of this Act.

(B) This subsection may not be construed as authorizing the Secretary to impose any requirements with respect to a food to the extent that it is within the exclusive jurisdiction of the Secretary of Agriculture pursuant to the Federal Meat Inspection Act (21 U.S.C. 601 et seq.), the Poultry Products Inspection Act (21 U.S.C. 451 et seq.), or the Egg Products Inspection Act (21 U.S.C. 1031 et seq.).

(n) —

(1) If a food has been refused admission under subsection (a), other than such a food that is required to be destroyed, the Secretary may require the owner or consignee of the food to affix to the container of the food a label that clearly and conspicuously bears the statement: "**United States: Refused Entry**".

(2) All expenses in connection with affixing a label under paragraph (1) shall be paid by the owner or consignee of the food involved, and in default of such payment, shall constitute a lien against future importations made by such owner or consignee.

(3) A requirement under paragraph (1) remains in effect until the Secretary determines that the food involved has been brought into compliance with this Act.

(o) If an article that is a device is being imported or offered for import into the United States, and the importer, owner, or consignee of such article does not, at the time of offering the article for import, submit to the Secretary a statement that identifies the registration under section 510(i) of each establishment that with respect to such article is required under such section to register with the Secretary, the article may be refused admission. If the article is refused admission for failure to submit such a statement, the article shall be held at the port of entry for the article, and may not be delivered to the importer, owner, or consignee of the article, until such a statement is submitted to the Secretary. Subsection (b) does not authorize the delivery of the article pursuant to the execution of a bond while the article is so held. The article shall be removed to a secure facility, as appropriate. During the period of time that such article is so held, the article shall not be transferred by any person from the port of entry into the United States for the article, or from the secure facility to which the article has been removed, as the case may be.

(p) —

(1) Not later than 36 months after the date of enactment of the Family Smoking Prevention and Tobacco Control Act, and annually thereafter, the Secretary shall submit to the Committee on Health, Education, Labor, and Pensions of the Senate and the Committee on Energy and Commerce of the House of Representatives, a report regarding —

(A) the nature, extent, and destination of United States tobacco product exports that do not conform to tobacco product standards established pursuant to this Act;

(B) the public health implications of such exports, including any evidence of a negative public health impact; and

(C) recommendations or assessments of policy alternatives available to Congress and the executive branch to reduce any negative public health impact caused by such exports.

(2) The Secretary is authorized to establish appropriate information disclosure requirements to carry out this subsection.

(q) Certifications Concerning Imported Foods. —

(1) In General. — The Secretary may require, as a condition of granting admission to an article of food imported or offered for import into the United States, that an entity described in paragraph (3) provide a certification, or such other assurances as the Secretary determines appropriate, that the article of food complies with applicable requirements of this Act. Such certification or assurances may be provided in the form of shipment-specific certificates, a listing of certified facilities that manufacture, process, pack, or hold such food, or in such other form as the Secretary may specify.

(2) Factors to Be Considered in Requiring Certification. — The Secretary shall base the determination that an article of food is required to have a certification described in paragraph (1) on the risk of the food, including —

(A) known safety risks associated with the food;

(B) known food safety risks associated with the country, territory, or region of origin of the food;

(C) a finding by the Secretary, supported by scientific, risk-based evidence, that —

(i) the food safety programs, systems, and standards in the country, territory, or region of origin of the food are inadequate to ensure that the article of food is as safe as a similar article of food that is manufactured, processed, packed, or held in the United States in accordance with the requirements of this Act; and

(ii) the certification would assist the Secretary in determining whether to refuse or admit the article of food under subsection (a); and

(D) information submitted to the Secretary in accordance with the process established in paragraph (7).

(3) Certifying Entities. — For purposes of paragraph (1), entities that shall provide the certification or assurances described in such paragraph are —

(A) an agency or a representative of the government of the country from which the article of food at issue originated, as designated by the Secretary; or

(B) such other persons or entities accredited pursuant to section 808 to provide such certification or assurance.

(4) Renewal and Refusal of Certifications. — The Secretary may—

(A) require that any certification or other assurance provided by an entity specified in paragraph (2) be renewed by such entity at such times as the Secretary determines appropriate; and

(B) refuse to accept any certification or assurance if the Secretary determines that such certification or assurance is not valid or reliable.

(5) Electronic Submission. — The Secretary shall provide for the electronic submission of certifications under this subsection.

(6) False Statements. — Any statement or representation made by an entity described in paragraph (2) to the Secretary shall be subject to section 1001 of title 18, United States Code.

(7) Assessment of Food Safety Programs, Systems, and Standards. — If the Secretary determines that the food safety programs, systems, and standards in a foreign region, country, or territory are inadequate to ensure that an article of food is as safe as a similar article of food that is manufactured, processed, packed, or held in the United States in accordance with the requirements of this Act, the Secretary shall, to the extent practicable, identify such inadequacies and establish a process by which the foreign region, country, or territory may inform the Secretary of improvements made to such food safety program, system, or standard and demonstrate that those controls are adequate to ensure that an article of food is as safe as a similar article of food that is manufactured, processed, packed, or held in the United States in accordance with the requirements of this Act.

(r) —

(1) The Secretary may require, pursuant to the regulations promulgated under paragraph (4)(A), as a condition of granting admission to a drug imported or offered for import into the United States, that the importer electronically submit information demonstrating that the drug complies with applicable requirements of this Act.

(2) The information described under paragraph (1) may include —

(A) information demonstrating the regulatory status of the drug, such as the new drug application, abbreviated new drug application, or investigational new drug or drug master file number;

(B) facility information, such as proof of registration and the unique facility identifier;

(C) indication of compliance with current good manufacturing practice, testing results, certifications relating to satisfactory inspections, and compliance with the country of export regulations; and

(D) any other information deemed necessary and appropriate by the Secretary to assess compliance of the article being offered for import.

(3) Information requirements referred to in paragraph (2)(C) may, at the discretion of the Secretary, be satisfied —

(A) through representation by a foreign government, if an inspection is conducted by a foreign government using standards and practices as determined appropriate by the Secretary;

(B) through representation by a foreign government or an agency of a foreign government recognized under section 809; or

(C) other appropriate documentation or evidence as described by the Secretary.

(4) —

(A) Not later than 18 months after the date of enactment of the Food and Drug Administration Safety and Innovation Act, the Secretary shall adopt final regulations implementing this subsection. Such requirements shall be appropriate for the type of import, such as whether the drug is for import into the United States for use in preclinical research or in a clinical investigation under an investigational new drug exemption under 505(i).

(B) In promulgating the regulations under subparagraph (A), the Secretary —

(i) may, as appropriate, take into account differences among importers and types of imports, and, based on the level of risk posed by the imported drug, provide for expedited clearance for those importers that volunteer to participate in partnership programs for highly compliant companies and pass a review of internal controls, including sourcing of foreign manufacturing inputs, and plant inspections; and

(ii) shall —

(I) issue a notice of proposed rulemaking that includes the proposed regulation;

(II) provide a period of not less than 60 days for comments on the proposed regulation; and

(III) publish the final regulation not less than 30 days before the effective date of the regulation.

(C) Notwithstanding any other provision of law, the Secretary shall promulgate regulations implementing this subsection only as described in subparagraph (B).

(s) Registration of Commercial Importers. —

(1) Registration. — The Secretary shall require a commercial importer of drugs —

(A) to be registered with the Secretary in a form and manner specified by the Secretary; and

(B) subject to paragraph (4), to submit, at the time of registration, a unique identifier for the principal place of business for which the importer is required to register under this subsection.

(2) Regulations. —

(A) In General. — The Secretary, in consultation with the Secretary of Homeland Security acting through U.S. Customs and Border Protection, shall promulgate regulations to establish good importer practices that specify the measures an importer shall take to ensure imported drugs are in compliance with the requirements of this Act and the Public Health Service Act.

(B) Procedure. — In promulgating a regulation under subparagraph (A), the Secretary shall —

(i) issue a notice of proposed rulemaking that includes the proposed regulation;

(ii) provide a period of not less than 60 days for comments on the proposed regulation; and

(iii) publish the final regulation not less than 30 days before the regulation's effective date.

(C) Restrictions. — Notwithstanding any other provision of Federal law, in implementing this subsection, the Secretary shall only promulgate regulations as described in subparagraph (B).

(D) Effective Date.— In establishing the effective date of the regulations under subparagraph (A), the Secretary shall, in consultation with the Secretary of Homeland Security acting through U.S. Customs and Border Protection, as determined appropriate by the Secretary of Health and Human Services, provide a reasonable period of time for an importer of a drug to comply with good importer practices, taking into account differences among importers and types of imports, including based on the level of risk posed by the imported product.

(3) Discontinuance of Registration. — The Secretary shall discontinue the registration of any commercial importer of drugs that fails to comply with the regulations promulgated under this subsection.

(4) Unique Facility Identifier. — The Secretary shall specify the unique facility identifier system that shall be used by registrants under paragraph (1). The requirement to include a unique facility identifier in a registration under paragraph (1) shall not apply until the date that the identifier system is specified by the Secretary under the preceding sentence.

(5) Exemptions. — The Secretary, by notice in the Federal Register, may establish exemptions from the requirements of this subsection.

Sec. 802. [382] Exports of Certain Unapproved Products.

(a) A drug or device —

(1) which, in the case of a drug —

(A) —

(i) requires approval by the Secretary under section 505 before such drug may be introduced or delivered for introduction into interstate commerce; or

(ii) requires licensing by the Secretary under section 351 of the Public Health Service Act or by the Secretary of Agriculture under the Act of March 4, 1913 (known as the Virus-Serum Toxin Act) before it may be introduced or delivered for introduction into interstate commerce;

(B) does not have such approval or license; and

(C) is not exempt from such sections or Act; and

(2) which, in the case of a device —

(A) does not comply with an applicable requirement under section 514 or 515;

(B) under section 520(g) is exempt from either such section; or

(C) is a banned device under section 516, is adulterated, misbranded, and in violation of such sections or Act unless the export of the drug or device is, except as provided in subsection (f), authorized under subsection (b), (c), (d), or (e) or section 801(e)(2). If a drug or device described in paragraphs (1) and (2) may be exported under subsection (b) and if an application for such drug or device under section 505 or 515 or section 351 of the Public Health Service Act was disapproved, the Secretary shall notify the appropriate public health official of the country to which such drug will be exported of such disapproval.

(b) —

(1) —

(A) A drug or device described in subsection (a) may be exported to any country, if the drug or device complies with the laws of that country and has valid marketing authorization by the appropriate authority —

(i) in Australia, Canada, Israel, Japan, New Zealand, Switzerland, or South Africa; or

(ii) in the European Union or a country in the European Economic Area (the countries in the European Union and the European Free Trade Association) if the drug or device is marketed in that country or the drug or device is authorized for general marketing in the European Economic Area.

(B) The Secretary may designate an additional country to be included in the list of countries described in clauses (i) and (ii) of subparagraph (A) if all of the following requirements are met in such country:

(i) Statutory or regulatory requirements which require the review of drugs and devices for safety and effectiveness by an entity of the government of such country and which authorize the approval of only those drugs and devices which have been determined to be safe and effective by experts employed by or acting on behalf of such entity and qualified by scientific training and experience to evaluate the safety and effectiveness of drugs and devices on the basis of adequate and well-controlled investigations, including clinical investigations, conducted by experts qualified by scientific training and experience to evaluate the safety and effectiveness of drugs and devices.

(ii) Statutory or regulatory requirements that the methods used in, and the facilities and controls used for —

(I) the manufacture, processing, and packing of drugs in the country are adequate to preserve their identity, quality, purity, and strength; and

(II) the manufacture, preproduction design validation, packing, storage, and installation of a device are adequate to assure that the device will be safe and effective.

(iii) Statutory or regulatory requirements for the reporting of adverse reactions to drugs and devices and procedures to withdraw approval and remove drugs and devices found not to be safe or effective.

(iv) Statutory or regulatory requirements that the labeling and promotion of drugs and devices must be in accordance with the approval of the drug or device.

(v) The valid marketing authorization system in such country or countries is equivalent to the systems in the countries described in clauses (i) and (ii) of subparagraph (A).

The Secretary shall not delegate the authority granted under this subparagraph.

(C) An appropriate country official, manufacturer, or exporter may request the Secretary to take action under subparagraph (B) to designate an additional country or countries to be added to the list of countries described in clauses (i) and (ii) of subparagraph (A) by submitting documentation to the Secretary in support of such designation. Any person other than a country requesting such designation shall include, along with the request, a letter from the country indicating the desire of such country to be designated.

(2) A drug described in subsection (a) may be directly exported to a country which is not listed in clause (i) or (ii) of paragraph (1)(A) if—

(A) the drug complies with the laws of that country and has valid marketing authorization by the responsible authority in that country; and

(B) the Secretary determines that all of the following requirements are met in that country:

(i) Statutory or regulatory requirements which require the review of drugs for safety and effectiveness by an entity of the government of such country and which authorize the approval of only those drugs which have been determined to be safe and effective by experts employed by or acting on behalf of such entity and qualified by scientific training and experience to evaluate the safety and effectiveness of drugs on the basis of adequate and well-controlled investigations, including clinical investigations, conducted by experts qualified by scientific training and experience to evaluate the safety and effectiveness of drugs.

(ii) Statutory or regulatory requirements that the methods used in, and the facilities and controls used for the manufacture, processing, and packing of drugs in the country are adequate to preserve their identity, quality, purity, and strength.

(iii) Statutory or regulatory requirements for the reporting of adverse reactions to drugs and procedures to withdraw approval and remove drugs found not to be safe or effective.

(iv) Statutory or regulatory requirements that the labeling and promotion of drugs must be in accordance with the approval of the drug.

(3) The exporter of a drug described in subsection (a) which would not meet the conditions for approval under this Act or conditions for approval of a country described in clause (i) or (ii) of paragraph (1)(A) may petition the Secretary for authorization to export such drug to a country which is not described in clause (i) or (ii) of paragraph (1)(A) or which is not described in paragraph (2). The Secretary shall permit such export if—

(A) the person exporting the drug—

(i) certifies that the drug would not meet the conditions for approval under this Act or the conditions for approval of a country described in clause (i) or (ii) of paragraph (1)(A); and

(ii) provides the Secretary with credible scientific evidence, acceptable to the Secretary, that the drug would be safe and effective under the conditions of use in the country to which it is being exported; and

(B) the appropriate health authority in the country to which the drug is being exported—

(i) requests approval of the export of the drug to such country;

(ii) certifies that the health authority understands that the drug is not approved under this Act or in a country described in clause (i) or (ii) of paragraph (1)(A); and

(iii) concurs that the scientific evidence provided pursuant to subparagraph (A) is credible scientific evidence that the drug would be reasonably safe and effective in such country.

The Secretary shall take action on a request for export of a drug under this paragraph within 60 days of receiving such request.

(c) A drug or device intended for investigational use in any country described in clause (i) or (ii) of subsection (b)(1)(A) may be exported in accordance with the laws of that country and shall be exempt from regulation under section 505(i) or 520(g).

(d) A drug or device intended for formulation, filling, packaging, labeling, or further processing in anticipation of market authorization in any country described in clause (i) or (ii) of subsection (b)(1)(A) may be exported for use in accordance with the laws of that country.

(e)—

(1) A drug or device which is used in the diagnosis, prevention, or treatment of a tropical disease or another disease not of significant prevalence in the United States and which does not otherwise qualify for export under this section shall, upon approval of an application, be permitted to be exported if the Secretary finds that the drug or device will not expose patients in such country to an unreasonable risk of illness or injury and the probable benefit to health from the use of the drug or device (under conditions of use prescribed, recommended, or suggested in the labeling or proposed labeling of the drug or device) outweighs the risk of injury or illness from its use, taking into account the probable risks and benefits of currently available drug or device treatment.

(2) The holder of an approved application for the export of a drug or device under this subsection shall report to the Secretary —

(A) the receipt of any credible information indicating that the drug or device is being or may have been exported from a country for which the Secretary made a finding under paragraph (1)(A) to a country for which the Secretary cannot make such a finding; and

(B) the receipt of any information indicating adverse reactions to such drug.

(3) —

(A) If the Secretary determines that —

(i) a drug or device for which an application is approved under paragraph (1) does not continue to meet the requirements of such paragraph; or

(ii) the holder of an approved application under paragraph (1) has not made the report required by paragraph (2),

the Secretary may, after providing the holder of the application an opportunity for an informal hearing, withdraw the approved application.

(B) If the Secretary determines that the holder of an approved application under paragraph (1) or an importer is exporting a drug or device from the United States to an importer and such importer is exporting the drug or device to a country for which the Secretary cannot make a finding under paragraph (1) and such export presents an imminent hazard, the Secretary shall immediately prohibit the export of the drug or device to such importer, provide the person exporting the drug or device from the United States prompt notice of the prohibition, and afford such person an opportunity for an expedited hearing.

(f) A drug or device may not be exported under this section —

(1) if the drug or device is not manufactured, processed, packaged, and held in substantial conformity with current good manufacturing practice requirements or does not meet international standards as certified by an international standards organization recognized by the Secretary;

(2) if the drug or device is adulterated under clause (1), (2)(A), or (3) of section 501(a) or subsection (c) or (d) of section 501;

(3) if the requirements of subparagraphs (A) through (D) of section 801(e)(1) have not been met;

(4) —

(A) if the drug or device is the subject of a notice by the Secretary or the Secretary of Agriculture of a determination that the probability of reimportation of the exported drug or device would present an imminent hazard to the public health and safety of the United States and the only means of limiting the hazard is to prohibit the export of the drug or device; or

(B) if the drug or device presents an imminent hazard to the public health of the country to which the drug or device would be exported;

(5) if the labeling of the drug or device is not —

(A) in accordance with the requirements and conditions for use in —

(i) the country in which the drug or device received valid marketing authorization under subsection (b); and

(ii) the country to which the drug or device would be exported; and

(B) in the language and units of measurement of the country to which the drug or device would be exported or in the language designated by such country; or

(6) if the drug or device is not promoted in accordance with the labeling requirements set forth in paragraph (5).

In making a finding under paragraph (4)(B), (5), or (6) the Secretary shall consult with the appropriate public health official in the affected country.

(g) The exporter of a drug or device exported under subsection (b)(1) shall provide a simple notification to the Secretary identifying the drug or device when the exporter first begins to export such drug or device to any country listed in clause (i) or (ii) of subsection (b)(1)(A). When an exporter of a drug or device first begins to export a drug or device to a country which is not listed in clause (i) or (ii) of subsection (b)(1)(A), the exporter shall provide a simple notification to the Secretary identifying the drug or device and the country to which such drug or device is being exported. Any exporter of a drug or device shall maintain records of all drugs or devices exported and the countries to which they were exported.

(h) For purposes of this section —

(1) a reference to the Secretary shall in the case of a biological product which is required to be licensed under the Act of March 4, 1913 (37 Stat. 832-833) (commonly known as the Virus-Serum Toxin Act) be considered to be a reference to the Secretary of Agriculture, and

(2) the term "drug" includes drugs for human use as well as biologicals under section 351 of the Public Health Service Act or the Act of March 4, 1913 (37 Stat. 832-833) (commonly known as the Virus-Serum Toxin Act).

(i) Insulin and antibiotic drugs may be exported without regard to the requirements in this section if the insulin and antibiotic drugs meet the requirements of section 801(e)(1).

Sec. 803. [383] Office of International Relations.

(a) There is established in the Department of Health and Human Services an Office of International Relations.

(b) In carrying out the functions of the office under subsection (a), the Secretary may enter into agreements with foreign countries to facilitate commerce in devices between the United States and such countries consistent with the requirements of this Act. In such agreements, the Secretary shall encourage the mutual recognition of —

(1) good manufacturing practice regulations promulgated under section 520(f), and

(2) other regulations and testing protocols as the Secretary determines to be appropriate.

(c) —

(1) The Secretary shall support the Office of the United States Trade Representative, in consultation with the Secretary of Commerce, in meetings with representatives of other countries to discuss methods and approaches to reduce the burden of regulation and harmonize regulatory requirements if the Secretary determines that such harmonization continues consumer protections consistent with the purposes of this Act.

(2) The Secretary shall support the Office of the United States Trade Representative, in consultation with the Secretary of Commerce, in efforts to move toward the acceptance of mutual recognition agreements relating to the regulation of drugs, biological products, devices, foods, food additives, and color additives, and the regulation of good manufacturing practices, between the European Union and the United States.

(3) —

(A) The Secretary shall regularly participate in meetings with representatives of other foreign governments to discuss and reach agreement on methods and approaches to harmonize regulatory requirements.

(B) In carrying out subparagraph (A), the Secretary may participate in appropriate fora, including the International Medical Device Regulators Forum, and may —

(i) provide guidance to such fora on strategies, policies, directions, membership, and other activities of a forum as appropriate;

(ii) to the extent appropriate, solicit, review, and consider comments from industry, academia, health care professionals, and patient groups regarding the activities of such fora; and

(iii) to the extent appropriate, inform the public of the Secretary's activities within such fora, and share with the public any documentation relating to a forum's strategies, policies, and other activities of such fora.

(4) With respect to devices, the Secretary may, when appropriate, enter into arrangements with nations regarding methods and approaches to harmonizing regulatory requirements for activities, including inspections and common international labeling symbols.

(5) Paragraphs (1) through (4) shall not apply with respect to products defined in section 201(ff).

Sec. 804. [384] Importation of Prescription Drugs.

(a) Definitions. — In this section:

(1) Importer. — The term "importer" means a pharmacist or wholesaler.

(2) Pharmacist. — The term "pharmacist" means a person licensed by a State to practice pharmacy, including the dispensing and selling of prescription drugs.

(3) Prescription Drug. — The term "prescription drug" means a drug subject to section 503(b), other than —

(A) a controlled substance (as defined in section 102 of the Controlled Substances Act (21 U.S.C. 802));

(B) a biological product (as defined in section 351 of the Public Health Service Act (42 U.S.C. 262));

(C) an infused drug (including a peritoneal dialysis solution);

(D) an intravenously injected drug;

(E) a drug that is inhaled during surgery; or

(F) a drug which is a parenteral drug, the importation of which pursuant to subsection (b) is determined by the Secretary to pose a threat to the public health, in which case section 801(d)(1) shall continue to apply.

(4) Qualifying Laboratory. — The term "qualifying laboratory" means a laboratory in the United States that has been approved by the Secretary for the purposes of this section.

(5) Wholesaler. —

(A) In General. — The term "wholesaler" means a person licensed as a wholesaler or distributor of prescription drugs in the United States under section 503(e)(2)(a).

(B) Exclusion. — The term "wholesaler" does not include a person authorized to import drugs under section 801(d)(1).

(b) Regulations. — The Secretary, after consultation with the United States Trade Representative and the Commissioner of Customs, shall promulgate regulations permitting pharmacists and wholesalers to import prescription drugs from Canada into the United States.

(c) Limitation. — The regulations under subsection (b) shall —

(1) require that safeguards be in place to ensure that each prescription drug imported under the regulations complies with section 505 (including with respect to being safe and effective for the intended use of the prescription drug), with sections 501 and 502, and with other applicable requirements of this Act;

(2) require that an importer of a prescription drug under the regulations comply with subsections (d)(1) and (e); and

(3) contain any additional provisions determined by the Secretary to be appropriate as a safeguard to protect the public health or as a means to facilitate the importation of prescription drugs.

(d) Information and Records. —

(1) In General. — The regulations under subsection (b) shall require an importer of a prescription drug under subsection (b) to submit to the Secretary the following information and documentation:

(A) The name and quantity of the active ingredient of the prescription drug.

(B) A description of the dosage form of the prescription drug.

(C) The date on which the prescription drug is shipped.

(D) The quantity of the prescription drug that is shipped.

(E) The point of origin and destination of the prescription drug.

(F) The price paid by the importer for the prescription drug.

(G) Documentation from the foreign seller specifying —

(i) the original source of the prescription drug; and

(ii) the quantity of each lot of the prescription drug originally received by the seller from that source.

(H) The lot or control number assigned to the prescription drug by the manufacturer of the prescription drug.

(I) The name, address, telephone number, and professional license number (if any) of the importer.

(J) —

(i) In the case of a prescription drug that is shipped directly from the first foreign recipient of the prescription drug from the manufacturer:

(I) Documentation demonstrating that the prescription drug was received by the recipient from the manufacturer and subsequently shipped by the first foreign recipient to the importer.

(II) Documentation of the quantity of each lot of the prescription drug received by the first foreign recipient demonstrating that the quantity being imported into the United States is not more than the quantity that was received by the first foreign recipient.

(III) —

(aa) In the case of an initial imported shipment, documentation demonstrating that each batch of the prescription drug in the shipment was statistically sampled and tested for authenticity and degradation.

(bb) In the case of any subsequent shipment, documentation demonstrating that a statistically valid sample of the shipment was tested for authenticity and degradation.

(ii) In the case of a prescription drug that is not shipped directly from the first foreign recipient of the prescription drug from the manufacturer, documentation demonstrating that each batch in each shipment offered for importation into the United States was statistically sampled and tested for authenticity and degradation.

(K) Certification from the importer or manufacturer of the prescription drug that the prescription drug —

(i) is approved for marketing in the United States and is not adulterated or misbranded; and

(ii) meets all labeling requirements under this Act.

(L) Laboratory records, including complete data derived from all tests necessary to ensure that the prescription drug is in compliance with established specifications and standards.

(M) Documentation demonstrating that the testing required by subparagraphs (J) and (L) was conducted at a qualifying laboratory.

(N) Any other information that the Secretary determines is necessary to ensure the protection of the public health.

(2) Maintenance by the Secretary. — The Secretary shall maintain information and documentation submitted under paragraph (1) for such period of time as the Secretary determines to be necessary.

(e) Testing. — The regulations under subsection (b) shall require —

(1) that testing described in subparagraphs (J) and (L) of subsection (d)(1) be conducted by the importer or by the manufacturer of the prescription drug at a qualified laboratory;

(2) if the tests are conducted by the importer —

(A) that information needed to —

(i) authenticate the prescription drug being tested; and

(ii) confirm that the labeling of the prescription drug complies with labeling requirements under this Act;

be supplied by the manufacturer of the prescription drug to the pharmacist or wholesaler; and

(B) that the information supplied under subparagraph (A) be kept in strict confidence and used only for purposes of testing or otherwise complying with this Act; and

(3) may include such additional provisions as the Secretary determines to be appropriate to provide for the protection of trade secrets and commercial or financial information that is privileged or confidential.

(f) Registration of Foreign Sellers. — Any establishment within Canada engaged in the distribution of a prescription drug that is imported or offered for importation into the United States shall register with the Secretary the name and place of business of the establishment and the name of the United States agent for the establishment.

(g) Suspension of Importation. — The Secretary shall require that importations of a specific prescription drug or importations by a specific importer under subsection (b) be immediately suspended on discovery of a pattern of importation of that specific prescription drug or by that specific importer of drugs that are counterfeit or in violation of any requirement under this section, until an investigation is completed and the Secretary determines that the public is adequately protected from counterfeit and violative prescription drugs being imported under subsection (b).

(h) Approved Labeling. — The manufacturer of a prescription drug shall provide an importer written authorization for the importer to use, at no cost, the approved labeling for the prescription drug.

(i) Charitable Contributions. — Notwithstanding any other provision of this section, section 801(d)(1) continues to apply to a prescription drug that is donated or otherwise supplied at no charge by the manufacturer of the drug to a charitable or humanitarian organization (including the United Nations and affiliates) or to a government of a foreign country.

(j) Waiver Authority for Importation by Individuals. —

(1) Declarations. — Congress declares that in the enforcement against individuals of the prohibition of importation of prescription drugs and devices, the Secretary should —

(A) focus enforcement on cases in which the importation by an individual poses a significant threat to public health; and

(B) exercise discretion to permit individuals to make such importations in circumstances in which —

(i) the importation is clearly for personal use; and

(ii) the prescription drug or device imported does not appear to present an unreasonable risk to the individual.

(2) Waiver Authority. —

(A) In General. — The Secretary may grant to individuals, by regulation or on a case-by-case basis, a waiver of the prohibition of importation of a prescription drug or device or class of prescription drugs or devices, under such conditions as the Secretary determines to be appropriate.

(B) Guidance on Case-by-Case Waivers. — The Secretary shall publish, and update as necessary, guidance that accurately describes circumstances in which the Secretary will consistently grant waivers on a case-by-case basis under subparagraph (A), so that individuals may know with the greatest practicable degree of certainty whether a particular importation for personal use will be permitted.

(3) Drugs Imported From Canada. — In particular, the Secretary shall by regulation grant individuals a waiver to permit individuals to import into the United States a prescription drug that —

(A) is imported from a licensed pharmacy for personal use by an individual, not for resale, in quantities that do not exceed a 90-day supply;

(B) is accompanied by a copy of a valid prescription;

(C) is imported from Canada, from a seller registered with the Secretary;

(D) is a prescription drug approved by the Secretary under chapter V;

(E) is in the form of a final finished dosage that was manufactured in an establishment registered under section 510; and

(F) is imported under such other conditions as the Secretary determines to be necessary to ensure public safety.

(k) Construction. — Nothing in this section limits the authority of the Secretary relating to the importation of prescription drugs, other than with respect to section 801(d)(1) as provided in this section.

(l) Effectiveness of Section. —

(1) Commencement of Program. — This section shall become effective only if the Secretary certifies to the Congress that the implementation of this section will —

(A) pose no additional risk to the public's health and safety; and

(B) result in a significant reduction in the cost of covered products to the American consumer.

(2) Termination of Program. —

(A) In General. — If, after the date that is 1 year after the effective date of the regulations under subsection (b) and before the date that is 18 months after the effective date, the Secretary submits to Congress a certification that, in the opinion of the Secretary, based on substantial evidence obtained after the effective date, the benefits of implementation of this section do not outweigh any detriment of implementation of this section, this section shall cease to be effective as of the date that is 30 days after the date on which the Secretary submits the certification.

(B) Procedure. — The Secretary shall not submit a certification under subparagraph (A) unless, after a hearing on the record under sections 556 and 557 of title 5, United States Code, the Secretary —

(i) —

(I) determines that it is more likely than not that implementation of this section would result in an increase in the risk to the public health and safety;

(II) identifies specifically, in qualitative and quantitative terms, the nature of the increased risk;

(III) identifies specifically the causes of the increased risk; and

(IV) —

(aa) considers whether any measures can be taken to avoid, reduce, or mitigate the increased risk; and

(bb) if the Secretary determines that any measures described in item (aa) would require additional statutory authority, submits to Congress a report describing the legislation that would be required;

(ii) identifies specifically, in qualitative and quantitative terms, the benefits that would result from implementation of this section (including the benefit of reductions in the cost of covered products to consumers in the United States, allowing consumers to procure needed medication that consumers might not otherwise be able to procure without foregoing other necessities of life); and

(iii) —

(I) compares in specific terms the detriment identified under clause (i) with the benefits identified under clause (ii); and

(II) determines that the benefits do not outweigh the detriment.

(m) Authorization of Appropriations. — There are authorized to be appropriated such sums as are necessary to carry out this section.

Sec. 805. [384a] Foreign Supplier Verification Program.

(a) In General. —

(1) Verification Requirement. — Except as provided under subsections (e) and (f), each importer shall perform risk-based foreign supplier verification activities for the purpose of verifying that the food imported by the importer or agent of an importer is —

(A) produced in compliance with the requirements of section 418 or section 419, as appropriate; and

(B) is not adulterated under section 402 or misbranded under section 403(w).

(2) Importer Defined. — For purposes of this section, the term "importer" means, with respect to an article of food —

(A) the United States owner or consignee of the article of food at the time of entry of such article into the United States; or

(B) in the case when there is no United States owner or consignee as described in subparagraph (A), the United States agent or representative of a foreign owner or consignee of the article of food at the time of entry of such article into the United States.

(b) Guidance. — Not later than 1 year after the date of enactment of the FDA Food Safety Modernization Act, the Secretary shall issue guidance to assist importers in developing foreign supplier verification programs.

(c) Regulations. —

(1) In General. — Not later than 1 year after the date of enactment of the FDA Food Safety Modernization Act, the Secretary shall promulgate regulations to provide for the content of the foreign supplier verification program established under subsection (a).

(2) Requirements. — The regulations promulgated under paragraph (1) —

(A) shall require that the foreign supplier verification program of each importer be adequate to provide assurances that each foreign supplier to the importer produces the imported food in compliance with —

(i) processes and procedures, including reasonably appropriate risk-based preventive controls, that provide the same level of public health protection as those required under section 418 or section 419 (taking into consideration variances granted under section 419), as appropriate; and

(ii) section 402 and section 403(w).

(B) shall include such other requirements as the Secretary deems necessary and appropriate to verify that food imported into the United States is as safe as food produced and sold within the United States.

(3) Considerations — In promulgating regulations under this subsection, the Secretary shall, as appropriate, take into account differences among importers and types of imported foods, including based on the level of risk posed by the imported food.

(4) Activities. — Verification activities under a foreign supplier verification program under this section may include monitoring records for shipments, lot-by-lot certification of compliance, annual on-site inspections, checking the hazard analysis and risk-based preventive control plan of the foreign supplier, and periodically testing and sampling shipments.

(d) Record Maintenance and Access. — Records of an importer related to a foreign supplier verification program shall be maintained for a period of not less than 2 years and shall be made available promptly to a duly authorized representative of the Secretary upon request.

(e) Exemption of Seafood, Juice, and Low-Acid Canned Food Facilities in Compliance with HACCP. — This section shall not apply to a facility if the owner, operator, or agent in charge of such facility is required to comply with, and is in compliance with, 1 of the following standards and regulations with respect to such facility:

(1) The Seafood Hazard Analysis Critical Control Points Program of the Food and Drug Administration.

(2) The Juice Hazard Analysis Critical Control Points Program of the Food and Drug Administration.

(3) The Thermally Processed Low-Acid Foods Packaged in Hermetically Sealed Containers standards of the Food and Drug Administration (or any successor standards).

The exemption under paragraph (3) shall apply only with respect to microbiological hazards that are regulated under the standards for Thermally Processed Low-Acid Foods Packaged in Hermetically Sealed Containers under part 113 of chapter 21, Code of Federal Regulations (or any successor regulations).

(f) Additional Exemptions. — The Secretary, by notice published in the Federal Register, shall establish an exemption from the requirements of this section for articles of food imported in small quantities for research and evaluation purposes or for personal consumption, provided that such foods are not intended for retail sale and are not sold or distributed to the public.

(g) Publication of List of Participants. — The Secretary shall publish and maintain on the Internet Web site of the Food and Drug Administration a current list that includes the name of, location of, and other information deemed necessary by the Secretary about, importers participating under this section.

Sec. 806. [384b] Voluntary Qualified Importer Program.

(a) In General. — Beginning not later than 18 months after the date of enactment of the FDA Food Safety Modernization Act, the Secretary shall —

(1) establish a program, in consultation with the Secretary of Homeland Security—

(A) to provide for the expedited review and importation of food offered for importation by importers who have voluntarily agreed to participate in such program; and

(B) consistent with section 808, establish a process for the issuance of a facility certification to accompany food offered for importation by importers who have voluntarily agreed to participate in such program; and

(2) issue a guidance document related to participation in, revocation of such participation in, reinstatement in, and compliance with, such program.

(b) Voluntary Participation. — An importer may request the Secretary to provide for the expedited review and importation of designated foods in accordance with the program established by the Secretary under subsection (a).

(c) Notice of Intent to Participate. — An importer that intends to participate in the program under this section in a fiscal year shall submit a notice and application to the Secretary of such intent at the time and in a manner established by the Secretary.

(d) Eligibility. — Eligibility shall be limited to an importer offering food for importation from a facility that has a certification described in subsection (a). In reviewing the applications and making determinations on such applications, the Secretary shall consider the risk of the food to be imported based on factors, such as the following:

(1) The known safety risks of the food to be imported.

(2) The compliance history of foreign suppliers used by the importer, as appropriate.

(3) The capability of the regulatory system of the country of export to ensure compliance with United States food safety standards for a designated food.

(4) The compliance of the importer with the requirements of section 805.

(5) The recordkeeping, testing, inspections and audits of facilities, traceability of articles of food, temperature controls, and sourcing practices of the importer.

(6) The potential risk for intentional adulteration of the food.

(7) Any other factor that the Secretary determines appropriate.

(e) Review and Revocation. — Any importer qualified by the Secretary in accordance with the eligibility criteria set forth in this section shall be reevaluated not less often than once every 3 years and the Secretary shall promptly revoke the qualified importer status of any importer found not to be in compliance with such criteria.

(f) False Statements. — Any statement or representation made by an importer to the Secretary shall be subject to section 1001 of title 18, United States Code.

(g) Definition. — For purposes of this section, the term "importer" means the person that brings food, or causes food to be brought, from a foreign country into the customs territory of the United States.

Sec. 807. [384c] Inspection of Foreign Food Facilities.

(a) Inspection. — The Secretary —

(1) may enter into arrangements and agreements with foreign governments to facilitate the inspection of foreign facilities registered under section 415; and

(2) shall direct resources to inspections of foreign facilities, suppliers, and food types, especially such facilities, suppliers, and food types that present a high risk (as identified by the Secretary), to help ensure the safety and security of the food supply of the United States.

(b) Effect of Inability to Inspect. — Notwithstanding any other provision of law, food shall be refused admission into the United States if it is from a foreign factory, warehouse, or other establishment of which the owner, operator, or agent in charge, or the government of the foreign country, refuses to permit entry of United States inspectors or other individuals duly designated by the Secretary, upon request, to inspect such factory, warehouse, or other establishment. For purposes of this subsection, such an owner, operator, or agent in charge shall be considered to have refused an inspection if such owner, operator, or agent in charge does not permit an inspection of a factory, warehouse, or other establishment during the 24-hour period after such request is submitted, or after such other time period, as agreed upon by the Secretary and the foreign factory, warehouse, or other establishment.

Sec. 808. [384d] Accreditation of Third-Party Auditors.

(a) Definitions. — In this section:

(1) Audit Agent. — The term "audit agent" means an individual who is an employee or agent of an accredited third-party auditor and, although not individually accredited, is qualified to conduct food safety audits on behalf of an accredited third-party auditor.

(2) Accreditation Body. — The term "accreditation body" means an authority that performs accreditation of third-party auditors.

(3) Third-Party Auditor. — The term "third-party auditor" means a foreign government, agency of a foreign government, foreign cooperative, or any other third party, as the Secretary determines appropriate in accordance with the model standards described in subsection (b)(2), that is eligible to be considered for accreditation to conduct food safety audits to certify that eligible entities meet the applicable requirements of this section. A third-party auditor may be a single individual. A third-party auditor may employ or use audit agents to help conduct consultative and regulatory audits.

(4) Accredited Third-Party Auditor. — The term "accredited third-party auditor" means a third-party auditor accredited by an accreditation body to conduct audits of eligible entities to certify that such eligible entities meet the applicable requirements of this section. An accredited third-party auditor may be an individual who conducts food safety audits to certify that eligible entities meet the applicable requirements of this section.

(5) Consultative Audit. — The term "consultative audit" means an audit of an eligible entity —

(A) to determine whether such entity is in compliance with the provisions of this Act and with applicable industry standards and practices; and

(B) the results of which are for internal purposes only.

(6) Eligible Entity. — The term "eligible entity" means a foreign entity, including a foreign facility registered under section 415, in the food import supply chain that chooses to be audited by an accredited third-party auditor or the audit agent of such accredited third-party auditor.

(7) Regulatory Audit. — The term "regulatory audit" means an audit of an eligible entity—

(A) to determine whether such entity is in compliance with the provisions of this Act; and

(B) the results of which determine —

(i) whether an article of food manufactured, processed, packed, or held by such entity is eligible to receive a food certification under section 801(q); or

(ii) whether a facility is eligible to receive a facility certification under section 806(a) for purposes of participating in the program under section 806.

(b) Accreditation System. —

(1) Accreditation Bodies. —

(A) Recognition of Accreditation Bodies. —

(i) In General. — Not later than 2 years after the date of enactment of the FDA Food Safety Modernization Act, the Secretary shall establish a system for the recognition of accreditation bodies that accredit third-party auditors to certify that eligible entities meet the applicable requirements of this section.

(ii) Direct Accreditation. — If, by the date that is 2 years after the date of establishment of the system described in clause (i), the Secretary has not identified and recognized an accreditation body to meet the requirements of this section, the Secretary may directly accredit third-party auditors.

(B) Notification. — Each accreditation body recognized by the Secretary shall submit to the Secretary a list of all accredited third-party auditors accredited by such body and the audit agents of such auditors.

(C) Revocation of Recognition as an Accreditation Body. — The Secretary shall promptly revoke the recognition of any accreditation body found not to be in compliance with the requirements of this section.

(D) Reinstatement. — The Secretary shall establish procedures to reinstate recognition of an accreditation body if the Secretary determines, based on evidence presented by such accreditation body, that revocation was inappropriate or that the body meets the requirements for recognition under this section.

(2) Model Accreditation Standards. — Not later than 18 months after the date of enactment of the FDA Food Safety Modernization Act, the Secretary shall develop model standards, including requirements for regulatory audit reports, and each recognized accreditation body shall ensure that third-party auditors and audit agents of such auditors meet such standards in order to qualify such third-party auditors as accredited third-party auditors under this section. In developing the model standards, the Secretary shall look to standards in place on the date of the enactment of this section for guidance, to avoid unnecessary duplication of efforts and costs.

(c) Third-Party Auditors. —

(1) Requirements for Accreditation as a Third-Party Auditor. —

(A) Foreign Governments. — Prior to accrediting a foreign government or an agency of a foreign government as an accredited third-party auditor, the accreditation body (or, in the case of direct accreditation under subsection (b)(1)(A)(ii), the Secretary) shall perform such reviews and audits of food safety programs, systems, and standards of the government or agency of the government as the Secretary deems necessary, including requirements under the model standards developed under subsection (b)(2), to determine that the foreign government or agency of the foreign government is capable of adequately ensuring that eligible entities or foods certified by such government or agency meet the requirements of this Act with respect to food manufactured, processed, packed, or held for import into the United States.

(B) Foreign Cooperatives and Other Third Parties. — Prior to accrediting a foreign cooperative that aggregates the products of growers or processors, or any other third party to be an accredited third-party auditor, the accreditation body (or, in the case of direct accreditation under subsection (b)(1)(A)(ii), the Secretary) shall perform such reviews and audits of the training and qualifications of audit agents used by that cooperative or party and conduct such reviews of internal systems and such other investigation of the cooperative or party as the Secretary deems necessary, including requirements under the model standards developed under subsection (b)(2), to determine that each eligible entity certified by the cooperative or party has systems and standards in use to ensure that such entity or food meets the requirements of this Act.

(2) Requirement to Issue Certification of Eligible Entities or Foods. —

(A) In General. — An accreditation body (or, in the case of direct accreditation under subsection (b)(1)(A)(ii), the Secretary) may not accredit a third-party auditor unless such third-party auditor agrees to issue a written and, as appropriate, electronic food certification, described in section 801(q), or facility certification under section 806(a), as appropriate, to accompany each food shipment for import into the United States from an eligible entity, subject to requirements set forth by the Secretary. Such written or electronic certification may be included with other documentation regarding such food shipment. The Secretary shall consider certifications under section 801(q) and participation in the voluntary qualified importer program described in section 806 when targeting inspection resources under section 421.

(B) Purpose of Certification. — The Secretary shall use certification provided by accredited third-party auditors to—

(i) determine, in conjunction with any other assurances the Secretary may require under section 801(q), whether a food satisfies the requirements of such section; and

(ii) determine whether a facility is eligible to be a facility from which food may be offered for import under the voluntary qualified importer program under section 806.

(C) Requirements for Issuing Certification. —

(i) In General. — An accredited third-party auditor shall issue a food certification under section 801(q) or a facility certification described under subparagraph (B) only after conducting a regulatory audit and such other activities that may be necessary to establish compliance with the requirements of such sections.

(ii) Provision of Certification. — Only an accredited third-party auditor or the Secretary may provide a facility certification under section 806(a). Only those parties described in 801(q)(3) or the Secretary may provide a food certification under 301(g).

(3) Audit Report Submission Requirements. —

(A) Requirements in General. — As a condition of accreditation, not later than 45 days after conducting an audit, an accredited third-party auditor or audit agent of such auditor shall prepare, and, in the case of a regulatory audit, submit, the audit report for each audit conducted, in a form and manner designated by the Secretary, which shall include—

(i) the identity of the persons at the audited eligible entity responsible for compliance with food safety requirements;

(ii) the dates of the audit;

(iii) the scope of the audit; and

(iv) any other information required by the Secretary that relates to or may influence an assessment of compliance with this Act.

(B) Records. — Following any accreditation of a third-party auditor, the Secretary may, at any time, require the accredited third-party auditor to submit to the Secretary an onsite audit report and such other reports or documents required as part of the audit process, for any eligible entity certified by the third-party auditor or audit agent of such auditor. Such report may include documentation that the eligible entity is in compliance with any applicable registration requirements.

(C) Limitation. — The requirement under subparagraph (B) shall not include any report or other documents resulting from a consultative audit by the accredited third-party auditor, except that the Secretary may access the results of a consultative audit in accordance with section 414.

(4) Requirements of Accredited Third-Party Auditors and Audit Agents of Such Auditors. —

(A) Risks to Public Health. — If, at any time during an audit, an accredited third-party auditor or audit agent of such auditor discovers a condition that could cause or contribute to a serious risk to the public health, such auditor shall immediately notify the Secretary of—

(i) the identification of the eligible entity subject to the audit; and

(ii) such condition.

(B) Types of Audits. — An accredited third-party auditor or audit agent of such auditor may perform consultative and regulatory audits of eligible entities.

(C) Limitations. —

(i) In General. — An accredited third party auditor may not perform a regulatory audit of an eligible entity if such agent has performed a consultative audit or a regulatory audit of such eligible entity during the previous 13-month period.

(ii) Waiver. — The Secretary may waive the application of clause (i) if the Secretary determines that there is insufficient access to accredited third-party auditors in a country or region.

(5) Conflicts of Interest. —

(A) Third-Party Auditors. — An accredited third-party auditor shall —

(i) not be owned, managed, or controlled by any person that owns or operates an eligible entity to be certified by such auditor;

(ii) in carrying out audits of eligible entities under this section, have procedures to ensure against the use of any officer or employee of such auditor that has a financial conflict of interest regarding an eligible entity to be certified by such auditor; and

(iii) annually make available to the Secretary disclosures of the extent to which such auditor and the officers and employees of such auditor have maintained compliance with clauses (i) and (ii) relating to financial conflicts of interest.

(B) Audit Agents. — An audit agent shall —

(i) not own or operate an eligible entity to be audited by such agent;

(ii) in carrying out audits of eligible entities under this section, have procedures to ensure that such agent does not have a financial conflict of interest regarding an eligible entity to be audited by such agent; and

(iii) annually make available to the Secretary disclosures of the extent to which such agent has maintained compliance with clauses (i) and (ii) relating to financial conflicts of interest.

(C) Regulations. — The Secretary shall promulgate regulations not later than 18 months after the date of enactment of the FDA Food Safety Modernization Act to implement this section and to ensure that there are protections against conflicts of interest between an accredited third-party auditor and the eligible entity to be certified by such auditor or audited by such audit agent. Such regulations shall include —

(i) requiring that audits performed under this section be unannounced;

(ii) a structure to decrease the potential for conflicts of interest, including timing and public disclosure, for fees paid by eligible entities to accredited third-party auditors; and

(iii) appropriate limits on financial affiliations between an accredited third-party auditor or audit agents of such auditor and any person that owns or operates an eligible entity to be certified by such auditor, as described in subparagraphs (A) and (B).

(6) Withdrawal of Accreditation.

(A) In General. — The Secretary shall withdraw accreditation from an accredited third-party auditor—

(i) if food certified under section 801(q) or from a facility certified under paragraph (2)(B) by such third-party auditor is linked to an outbreak of foodborne illness that has a reasonable probability of causing serious adverse health consequences or death in humans or animals;

(ii) following an evaluation and finding by the Secretary that the third-party auditor no longer meets the requirements for accreditation; or

(iii) following a refusal to allow United States officials to conduct such audits and investigations as may be necessary to ensure continued compliance with the requirements set forth in this section.

(B) Additional Basis for Withdrawal of Accreditation. — The Secretary may withdraw accreditation from an accredited third-party auditor in the case that such third-party auditor is accredited by an accreditation body for which recognition as an accreditation body under subsection (b)(1)(C) is revoked, if the Secretary determines that there is good cause for the withdrawal.

(C) Exception. — The Secretary may waive the application of subparagraph (A)(i) if the Secretary —

(i) conducts an investigation of the material facts related to the outbreak of human or animal illness; and

(ii) reviews the steps or actions taken by the third party auditor to justify the certification and determines that the accredited third-party auditor satisfied the requirements under section 801(q) of certifying the food, or the requirements under paragraph (2)(B) of certifying the entity.

(7) Reaccreditation. — The Secretary shall establish procedures to reinstate the accreditation of a third-party auditor for which accreditation has been withdrawn under paragraph (6) —

(A) if the Secretary determines, based on evidence presented, that the third-party auditor satisfies the requirements of this section and adequate grounds for revocation no longer exist; and

(B) in the case of a third-party auditor accredited by an accreditation body for which recognition as an accreditation body under subsection (b)(1)(C) is revoked —

(i) if the third-party auditor becomes accredited not later than 1 year after revocation of accreditation under paragraph (6)(A), through direct accreditation under subsection (b)(1)(A)(ii) or by an accreditation body in good standing; or

(ii) under such conditions as the Secretary may require for a third-party auditor under paragraph (6)(B).

(8) Neutralizing Costs. — The Secretary shall establish by regulation a reimbursement (user fee) program, similar to the method described in section 203(h) of the Agriculture Marketing Act of 1946, by which the Secretary assesses fees and requires accredited third-party auditors and audit agents to reimburse the Food and Drug Administration for the work performed to establish and administer the accreditation system under this section. The Secretary shall make operating this program revenue-neutral and shall not generate surplus revenue from such a reimbursement mechanism. Fees authorized under this paragraph shall be collected and available for obligation only to the extent and in the amount provided in advance in appropriation Acts. Such fees are authorized to remain available until expended.

(d) Recertification of Eligible Entities. — An eligible entity shall apply for annual recertification by an accredited third-party auditor if such entity —

(1) intends to participate in voluntary qualified importer program under section 806; or

(2) is required to provide to the Secretary a certification under section 801(q) for any food from such entity.

(e) False Statements. — Any statement or representation made —

(1) by an employee or agent of an eligible entity to an accredited third-party auditor or audit agent; or

(2) by an accredited third-party auditor to the Secretary, shall be subject to section 1001 of title 18, United States Code.

(f) Monitoring. To ensure compliance with the requirements of this section, the Secretary shall—

(1) periodically, or at least once every 4 years, reevaluate the accreditation bodies described in subsection (b)(1);

(2) periodically, or at least once every 4 years, evaluate the performance of each accredited third-party auditor, through the review of regulatory audit reports by such auditors, the compliance history as available of eligible entities certified by such auditors, and any other measures deemed necessary by the Secretary;

(3) at any time, conduct an onsite audit of any eligible entity certified by an accredited third-party auditor, with or without the auditor present; and

(4) take any other measures deemed necessary by the Secretary.

(g) Publicly Available Registry. — The Secretary shall establish a publicly available registry of accreditation bodies and of accredited third-party auditors, including the name of, contact information for, and other information deemed necessary by the Secretary about such bodies and auditors.

(h) Limitations. —

(1) No Effect on Section 704 Inspections. — The audits performed under this section shall not be considered inspections under section 704.

(2) No Effect on Inspection Authority. — Nothing in this section affects the authority of the Secretary to inspect any eligible entity pursuant to this Act.

Sec. 809. [384e] Recognition of Foreign Government Inspections.

(a) Inspection. — The Secretary —

(1) may enter into arrangements and agreements with a foreign government or an agency of a foreign government to recognize the inspection of foreign establishments registered under section 510(i) in order to facilitate risk-based inspections in accordance with the schedule established in ~~section 510(h)(3).~~ paragraph (2) or (3) of section 510(h).

(2) may enter into arrangements and agreements with a foreign government or an agency of a foreign government under this section only with a foreign government or an agency of a foreign government that the Secretary has determined as having the capability of conducting inspections that meet the applicable requirements of this Act; and

(3) shall perform such reviews and audits of drug safety programs, systems, and standards of a foreign government or agency for the foreign government as the Secretary deems necessary to determine that the foreign government or agency of the foreign government is capable of conducting inspections that meet the applicable requirements of this Act.

(b) Results of Inspection. — The results of inspections performed by a foreign government under this section may be used as —

(1) evidence of compliance with section 501(a)(2)(B) or section 801(r); and

(2) for any other purposes as determined appropriate by the Secretary.

Chapter IX – Tobacco Products

Sec. 900. [387] Definitions.

In this chapter:

(1) Additive. — The term "additive" means any substance the intended use of which results or may reasonably be expected to result, directly or indirectly, in its becoming a component or otherwise affecting the characteristic of any tobacco product (including any substances intended for use as a flavoring or coloring or in producing, manufacturing, packing, processing, preparing, treating, packaging, transporting, or holding), except that such term does not include tobacco or a pesticide chemical residue in or on raw tobacco or a pesticide chemical.

(2) Brand. — The term "brand" means a variety of tobacco product distinguished by the tobacco used, tar content, nicotine content, flavoring used, size, filtration, packaging, logo, registered trademark, brand name, identifiable pattern of colors, or any combination of such attributes.

(3) Cigarette. — The term "cigarette" —

(A) means a product that —

(i) is a tobacco product; and

(ii) meets the definition of the term "cigarette" in section 3(1) of the Federal Cigarette Labeling and Advertising Act; and

(B) includes tobacco, in any form, that is functional in the product, which, because of its appearance, the type of tobacco used in the filler, or its packaging and labeling, is likely to be offered to, or purchased by, consumers as a cigarette or as roll-your-own tobacco.

(4) Cigarette Tobacco. The term "cigarette tobacco" means any product that consists of loose tobacco that is intended for use by consumers in a cigarette. Unless otherwise stated, the requirements applicable to cigarettes under this chapter shall also apply to cigarette tobacco.

(5) Commerce. The term "commerce" has the meaning given that term by section 3(2) of the Federal Cigarette Labeling and Advertising Act.

(6) Counterfeit Tobacco Product. The term "counterfeit tobacco product" means a tobacco product (or the container or labeling of such a product) that, without authorization, bears the trademark, trade name, or other identifying mark, imprint, or device, or any likeness thereof, of a tobacco product listed in a registration under section 905(i)(1).

(7) Distributor. The term "distributor" as regards a tobacco product means any person who furthers the distribution of a tobacco product, whether domestic or imported, at any point from the original place of manufacture to the person who sells or distributes the product to individuals for personal consumption. Common carriers are not considered distributors for purposes of this chapter.

(8) Illicit Trade. The term "illicit trade" means any practice or conduct prohibited by law which relates to production, shipment, receipt, possession, distribution, sale, or purchase of tobacco products including any practice or conduct intended to facilitate such activity.

(9) Indian Country. The term "Indian country" has the meaning given such term in section 1151 of title 18, United States Code.

(10) Indian Tribe. The term "Indian tribe" has the meaning given such term in section 4(e) of the Indian Self-Determination and Education Assistance Act.

(11) Little Cigar. The term "little cigar" means a product that —

(A) is a tobacco product; and

(B) meets the definition of the term "little cigar" in section 3(7) of the Federal Cigarette Labeling and Advertising Act.

(12) Nicotine. — The term "nicotine" means the chemical substance named 3-(1-Methyl-2-pyrrolidinyl) pyridine or C[10]H[14]N[2], including any salt or complex of nicotine.

(13) Package. — The term "package" means a pack, box, carton, or container of any kind or, if no other container, any wrapping (including cellophane), in which a tobacco product is offered for sale, sold, or otherwise distributed to consumers.

(14) Retailer. — The term "retailer" means any person, government, or entity who sells tobacco products to individuals for personal consumption, or who operates a facility where self-service displays of tobacco products are permitted.

(15) Roll-Your-Own Tobacco. — The term "roll-your-own tobacco" means any tobacco product which, because of its appearance, type, packaging, or labeling, is suitable for use and likely to be offered to, or purchased by, consumers as tobacco for making cigarettes.

(16) Small Tobacco Product Manufacturer. — The term "small tobacco product manufacturer" means a tobacco product manufacturer that employs fewer than 350 employees. For purposes of determining the number of employees of a manufacturer under the preceding sentence, the employees of a manufacturer are deemed to include the employees of each entity that controls, is controlled by, or is under common control with such manufacturer.

(17) Smoke Constituent. — The term "smoke constituent" means any chemical or chemical compound in mainstream or sidestream tobacco smoke that either transfers from any component of the cigarette to the smoke or that is formed by the combustion or heating of tobacco, additives, or other component of the tobacco product.

(18) Smokeless Tobacco. — The term "smokeless tobacco" means any tobacco product that consists of cut, ground, powdered, or leaf tobacco and that is intended to be placed in the oral or nasal cavity.

(19) State; Territory. — The terms "State" and "Territory" shall have the meanings given to such terms in section 201.

(20) Tobacco Product Manufacturer. — The term "tobacco product manufacturer" means any person, including any repacker or relabeler, who —

(A) manufactures, fabricates, assembles, processes, or labels a tobacco product; or

(B) imports a finished tobacco product for sale or distribution in the United States.

(21) Tobacco Warehouse. —

(A) Subject to subparagraphs (B) and (C), the term "tobacco warehouse" includes any person —

(i) who —

(I) removes foreign material from tobacco leaf through nothing other than a mechanical process;

(II) humidifies tobacco leaf with nothing other than potable water in the form of steam or mist; or

(III) de-stems, dries, and packs tobacco leaf for storage and shipment;

(ii) who performs no other actions with respect to tobacco leaf; and

(iii) who provides to any manufacturer to whom the person sells tobacco all information related to the person's actions described in clause (i) that is necessary for compliance with this Act.

(B) The term "tobacco warehouse" excludes any person who —

(i) reconstitutes tobacco leaf;

(ii) is a manufacturer, distributor, or retailer of a tobacco product; or

(iii) applies any chemical, additive, or substance to the tobacco leaf other than potable water in the form of steam or mist.

(C) The definition of the term "tobacco warehouse" in subparagraph (A) shall not apply to the extent to which the Secretary determines, through rulemaking, that regulation under this chapter of the actions described in such subparagraph is appropriate for the protection of the public health.

(22) United States. — The term "United States" means the 50 States of the United States of America and the District of Columbia, the Commonwealth of Puerto Rico, Guam, the Virgin Islands, American Samoa, Wake Island, Midway Islands, Kingman Reef, Johnston Atoll, the Northern Mariana Islands, and any other trust territory or possession of the United States.

Sec. 901. [387a] FDA Authority Over Tobacco Products.

(a) In General. — Tobacco products, including modified risk tobacco products for which an order has been issued in accordance with section 911, shall be regulated by the Secretary under this chapter and shall not be subject to the provisions of chapter V.

(b) Applicability. — This chapter shall apply to all cigarettes, cigarette tobacco, roll-your-own tobacco, and smokeless tobacco and to any other tobacco products that the Secretary by regulation deems to be subject to this chapter.

(c) Scope. —

(1) In General. — Nothing in this chapter, or any policy issued or regulation promulgated thereunder, or in sections 101(a), 102, or 103 of title I, title II, or title III of the Family Smoking Prevention and Tobacco Control Act, shall be construed to affect, expand, or limit the Secretary's authority over (including the authority to determine whether products may be regulated), or the regulation of, products under this Act that are not tobacco products under chapter V or any other chapter.

(2) Limitation of Authority. —

(A) In General. — The provisions of this chapter shall not apply to tobacco leaf that is not in the possession of a manufacturer of tobacco products, or to the producers of tobacco leaf, including tobacco growers, tobacco warehouses, and tobacco grower cooperatives, nor shall any employee of the Food and Drug Administration have any authority to enter onto a farm owned by a producer of tobacco leaf without the written consent of such producer.

(B) Exception. — Notwithstanding subparagraph (A), if a producer of tobacco leaf is also a tobacco product manufacturer or controlled by a tobacco product manufacturer, the producer shall be subject to this chapter in the producer's capacity as a manufacturer. The exception in this subparagraph shall not apply to a producer of tobacco leaf who grows tobacco under a contract with a tobacco product manufacturer and who is not otherwise engaged in the manufacturing process.

(C) Rule of Construction. — Nothing in this chapter shall be construed to grant the Secretary authority to promulgate regulations on any matter that involves the production of tobacco leaf or a producer thereof, other than activities by a manufacturer affecting production.

(d) Rulemaking Procedures. — Each rulemaking under this chapter shall be in accordance with chapter 5 of title 5, United States Code. This subsection shall not be construed to affect the rulemaking provisions of section 102(a) of the Family Smoking Prevention and Tobacco Control Act.

(e) Center for Tobacco Products. — Not later than 90 days after the date of enactment of the Family Smoking Prevention and Tobacco Control Act, the Secretary shall establish within the Food and Drug Administration the Center for Tobacco Products, which shall report to the Commissioner of Food and Drugs in the same manner as the other agency centers within the Food and Drug Administration. The Center shall be responsible for the implementation of this chapter and related matters assigned by the Commissioner.

(f) Office to Assist Small Tobacco Product Manufacturers. — The Secretary shall establish within the Food and Drug Administration an identifiable office to provide technical and other nonfinancial assistance to small tobacco product manufacturers to assist them in complying with the requirements of this Act.

(g) Consultation Prior to Rulemaking. — Prior to promulgating rules under this chapter, the Secretary shall endeavor to consult with other Federal agencies as appropriate.

Sec. 902. [387b] Adulterated Tobacco Products.

A tobacco product shall be deemed to be adulterated if —

(1) it consists in whole or in part of any filthy, putrid, or decomposed substance, or is otherwise contaminated by any added poisonous or added deleterious substance that may render the product injurious to health;

(2) it has been prepared, packed, or held under insanitary conditions whereby it may have been contaminated with filth, or whereby it may have been rendered injurious to health;

(3) its package is composed, in whole or in part, of any poisonous or deleterious substance which may render the contents injurious to health;

(4) the manufacturer or importer of the tobacco product fails to pay a user fee assessed to such manufacturer or importer pursuant to section 919 by the date specified in section 919 or by the 30th day after final agency action on a resolution of any dispute as to the amount of such fee;

(5) it is, or purports to be or is represented as, a tobacco product which is subject to a tobacco product standard established under section 907 unless such tobacco product is in all respects in conformity with such standard;"

(6) —

(A) it is required by section 910(a) to have premarket review and does not have an order in effect under section 910(c)(1)(A)(i); or

(B) it is in violation of an order under section 910(c)(1)(A);

(7) the methods used in, or the facilities or controls used for, its manufacture, packing, or storage are not in conformity with applicable requirements under section 906(e)(1) or an applicable condition prescribed by an order under section 906(e)(2); or

(8) it is in violation of section 911.

SEC. 903. [387c] MISBRANDED TOBACCO PRODUCTS.

(a) IN GENERAL. — A tobacco product shall be deemed to be misbranded —

(1) if its labeling is false or misleading in any particular;

(2) if in package form unless it bears a label containing —

(A) the name and place of business of the tobacco product manufacturer, packer, or distributor;

(B) an accurate statement of the quantity of the contents in terms of weight, measure, or numerical count;

(C) an accurate statement of the percentage of the tobacco used in the product that is domestically grown tobacco and the percentage that is foreign grown tobacco; and

(D) the statement required under section 920(a), except that under subparagraph (B) reasonable variations shall be permitted, and exemptions as to small packages shall be established, by regulations prescribed by the Secretary;

(3) if any word, statement, or other information required by or under authority of this chapter to appear on the label or labeling is not prominently placed thereon with such conspicuousness (as compared with other words, statements, or designs in the labeling) and in such terms as to render it likely to be read and understood by the ordinary individual under customary conditions of purchase and use;

(4) if it has an established name, unless its label bears, to the exclusion of any other nonproprietary name, its established name prominently printed in type as required by the Secretary by regulation;

(5) if the Secretary has issued regulations requiring that its labeling bear adequate directions for use, or adequate warnings against use by children, that are necessary for the protection of users unless its labeling conforms in all respects to such regulations;

(6) if it was manufactured, prepared, propagated, compounded, or processed in an establishment not duly registered under section 905(b), 905(c), 905(d), or 905(h), if it was not included in a list required by section 905(i), if a notice or other information respecting it was not provided as required by such section or section 905(j), or if it does not bear such symbols from the uniform system for identification of tobacco products prescribed under section 905(e) as the Secretary by regulation requires;

(7) if, in the case of any tobacco product distributed or offered for sale in any State —

(A) its advertising is false or misleading in any particular; or

(B) it is sold or distributed in violation of regulations prescribed under section 906(d);

(8) unless, in the case of any tobacco product distributed or offered for sale in any State, the manufacturer, packer, or distributor thereof includes in all advertisements and other descriptive printed matter issued or caused to be issued by the manufacturer, packer, or distributor with respect to that tobacco product —

(A) a true statement of the tobacco product's established name as described in paragraph (4), printed prominently; and

(B) a brief statement of —

(i) the uses of the tobacco product and relevant warnings, precautions, side effects, and contraindications; and

(ii) in the case of specific tobacco products made subject to a finding by the Secretary after notice and opportunity for comment that such action is appropriate to protect the public health, a full description of the components of such tobacco product or the formula showing quantitatively each ingredient of such tobacco product to the extent required in regulations which shall be issued by the Secretary after an opportunity for a hearing;

(9) if it is a tobacco product subject to a tobacco product standard established under section 907, unless it bears such labeling as may be prescribed in such tobacco product standard; or

(10) if there was a failure or refusal —

(A) to comply with any requirement prescribed under section 904 or 908; or

(B) to furnish any material or information required under section 909.

(b) Prior Approval of Label Statements. — The Secretary may, by regulation, require prior approval of statements made on the label of a tobacco product to ensure that such statements do not violate the misbranding provisions of subsection (a) and that such statements comply with other provisions of the Family Smoking Prevention and Tobacco Control Act (including the amendments made by such Act). No regulation issued under this subsection may require prior approval by the Secretary of the content of any advertisement, except for modified risk tobacco products as provided in section 911. No advertisement of a tobacco product published after the date of enactment of the Family Smoking Prevention and Tobacco Control Act shall, with respect to the language of label statements as prescribed under section 4 of the Federal Cigarette Labeling and Advertising Act and section 3 of the Comprehensive Smokeless Tobacco Health Education Act of 1986 or the regulations issued under such sections, be subject to the provisions of sections 12 through 15 of the Federal Trade Commission Act.

Sec. 904. [387d] Submission of Health Information to the Secretary.

(a) Requirement. — Each tobacco product manufacturer or importer, or agents thereof, shall submit to the Secretary the following information:

(1) Not later than 6 months after the date of enactment of the Family Smoking Prevention and Tobacco Control Act, a listing of all ingredients, including tobacco, substances, compounds, and additives that are, as of such date, added by the manufacturer to the tobacco, paper, filter, or other part of each tobacco product by brand and by quantity in each brand and subbrand.

(2) A description of the content, delivery, and form of nicotine in each tobacco product measured in milligrams of nicotine in accordance with regulations promulgated by the Secretary in accordance with section 4(e) of the Federal Cigarette Labeling and Advertising Act.

(3) Beginning 3 years after the date of enactment of the Family Smoking Prevention and Tobacco Control Act, a listing of all constituents, including smoke constituents as applicable, identified by the Secretary as harmful or potentially harmful to health in each tobacco product, and as applicable in the smoke of each tobacco product, by brand and by quantity in each brand and subbrand. Effective beginning 3 years after such date of enactment, the manufacturer, importer, or agent shall comply with regulations promulgated under section 915 in reporting information under this paragraph, where applicable.

(4) Beginning 6 months after the date of enactment of the Family Smoking Prevention and Tobacco Control Act, all documents developed after such date of enactment that relate to health, toxicological, behavioral, or physiologic effects of current or future tobacco products, their constituents (including smoke constituents), ingredients, components, and additives.

(b) Data Submission. — At the request of the Secretary, each tobacco product manufacturer or importer of tobacco products, or agents thereof, shall submit the following:

(1) Any or all documents (including underlying scientific information) relating to research activities, and research findings, conducted, supported, or possessed by the manufacturer (or agents thereof) on the health, toxicological, behavioral, or physiologic effects of tobacco products and their constituents (including smoke constituents), ingredients, components, and additives.

(2) Any or all documents (including underlying scientific information) relating to research activities, and research findings, conducted, supported, or possessed by the manufacturer (or agents thereof) that relate to the issue of whether a reduction in risk to health from tobacco products can occur upon the employment of technology available or known to the manufacturer.

(3) Any or all documents (including underlying scientific or financial information) relating to marketing research involving the use of tobacco products or marketing practices and the effectiveness of such practices used by tobacco manufacturers and distributors. An importer of a tobacco product not manufactured in the United States shall supply the information required of a tobacco product manufacturer under this subsection.

(c) Time for Submission. —

(1) In General. — At least 90 days prior to the delivery for introduction into interstate commerce of a tobacco product not on the market on the date of enactment of the Family Smoking Prevention and Tobacco Control Act, the manufacturer of such product shall provide the information required under subsection (a).

(2) Disclosure of Additive. — If at any time a tobacco product manufacturer adds to its tobacco products a new tobacco additive or increases the quantity of an existing tobacco additive, the manufacturer shall, except as provided in paragraph (3), at least 90 days prior to such action so advise the Secretary in writing.

(3) Disclosure of Other Actions. — If at any time a tobacco product manufacturer eliminates or decreases an existing additive, or adds or increases an additive that has by regulation been designated by the Secretary as an additive that is not a human or animal carcinogen, or otherwise harmful to health under intended conditions of use, the manufacturer shall within 60 days of such action so advise the Secretary in writing.

(d) Data List. —

(1) In General. — Not later than 3 years after the date of enactment of the Family Smoking Prevention and Tobacco Control Act, and annually thereafter, the Secretary shall publish in a format that is understandable and not misleading to a lay person, and place on public display (in a manner determined by the Secretary) the list established under subsection (e).

(2) Consumer Research. — The Secretary shall conduct periodic consumer research to ensure that the list published under paragraph (1) is not misleading to lay persons. Not later than 5 years after the date of enactment of the Family Smoking Prevention and Tobacco Control Act, the Secretary shall submit to the appropriate committees of Congress a report on the results of such research, together with recommendations on whether such publication should be continued or modified.

(e) Data Collection. — Not later than 24 months after the date of enactment of the Family Smoking Prevention and Tobacco Control Act, the Secretary shall establish, and periodically revise as appropriate, a list of harmful and potentially harmful constituents, including smoke constituents, to health in each tobacco product by brand and by quantity in each brand and subbrand. The Secretary shall publish a public notice requesting the submission by interested persons of scientific and other information concerning the harmful and potentially harmful constituents in tobacco products and tobacco smoke.

Sec. 905. [387e] Annual Registration.

(a) Definitions. — In this section:

(1) Manufacture, Preparation, Compounding, or Processing. — The term "manufacture, preparation, compounding, or processing" shall include repackaging or otherwise changing the container, wrapper, or labeling of any tobacco product package in furtherance of the distribution of the tobacco product from the original place of manufacture to the person who makes final delivery or sale to the ultimate consumer or user.

(2) Name. — The term "name" shall include in the case of a partnership the name of each partner and, in the case of a corporation, the name of each corporate officer and director, and the State of incorporation.

(b) Registration by Owners and Operators. — On or before December 31 of each year, every person who owns or operates any establishment in any State engaged in the manufacture, preparation, compounding, or processing of a tobacco product or tobacco products shall register with the Secretary the name, places of business, and all such establishments of that person. If enactment of the Family Smoking Prevention and Tobacco Control Act occurs in the second half of the calendar year, the Secretary shall designate a date no later than 6 months into the subsequent calendar year by which registration pursuant to this subsection shall occur.

(c) Registration by New Owners and Operators. — Every person upon first engaging in the manufacture, preparation, compounding, or processing of a tobacco product or tobacco products in any establishment owned or operated in any State by that person shall immediately register with the Secretary that person's name, place of business, and such establishment.

(d) Registration of Added Establishments. — Every person required to register under subsection (b) or (c) shall immediately register with the Secretary any additional establishment which that person owns or operates in any State and in which that person begins the manufacture, preparation, compounding, or processing of a tobacco product or tobacco products.

(e) Uniform Product Identification System. — The Secretary may by regulation prescribe a uniform system for the identification of tobacco products and may require that persons who are required to list such tobacco products under subsection (i) shall list such tobacco products in accordance with such system.

(f) Public Access to Registration Information. — The Secretary shall make available for inspection, to any person so requesting, any registration filed under this section.

(g) Biennial Inspection of Registered Establishments. — Every establishment registered with the Secretary under this section shall be subject to inspection under section 704 or subsection (h), and every such establishment engaged in the manufacture, compounding, or processing of a tobacco product or tobacco products shall be so inspected by 1 or more officers or employees duly designated by the Secretary at least once in the 2-year period beginning with the date of registration of such establishment under this section and at least once in every successive 2-year period thereafter.

(h) Registration by Foreign Establishments. — Any establishment within any foreign country engaged in the manufacture, preparation, compounding, or processing of a tobacco product or tobacco products, shall register under this section under regulations promulgated by the Secretary. Such regulations shall require such establishment to provide the information required by subsection (i) and shall include provisions for registration of any such establishment upon condition that adequate and effective means are available, by arrangement with the government of such foreign country or otherwise, to enable the Secretary to determine from time to time whether tobacco products manufactured, prepared, compounded, or processed in such establishment, if imported or offered for import into the United States, shall be refused admission on any of the grounds set forth in section 801(a).

(i) Registration Information. —

(1) Product List. — Every person who registers with the Secretary under subsection (b), (c), (d), or (h) shall, at the time of registration under any such subsection, file with the Secretary a list of all tobacco products which are being manufactured, prepared, compounded, or processed by that person for commercial distribution and which have not been included in any list of tobacco products filed by that person with the Secretary under this paragraph or paragraph (2) before such time of registration. Such list shall be prepared in such form and manner as the Secretary may prescribe and shall be accompanied by —

(A) in the case of a tobacco product contained in the applicable list with respect to which a tobacco product standard has been established under section 907 or which is subject to section 910, a reference to the authority for the marketing of such tobacco product and a copy of all labeling for such tobacco product;

(B) in the case of any other tobacco product contained in an applicable list, a copy of all consumer information and other labeling for such tobacco product, a representative sampling of advertisements for such tobacco product, and, upon request made by the Secretary for good cause, a copy of all advertisements for a particular tobacco product; and

(C) if the registrant filing a list has determined that a tobacco product contained in such list is not subject to a tobacco product standard established under section 907, a brief statement of the basis upon which the registrant made such determination if the Secretary requests such a statement with respect to that particular tobacco product.

(2) Consultation with Respect to Forms. — The Secretary shall consult with the Secretary of the Treasury in developing the forms to be used for registration under this section to minimize the burden on those persons required to register with both the Secretary and the Tax and Trade Bureau of the Department of the Treasury.

(3) Biannual Report of Any Change in Product List. — Each person who registers with the Secretary under this section shall report to the Secretary once during the month of June of each year and once during the month of December of each year the following:

(A) A list of each tobacco product introduced by the registrant for commercial distribution which has not been included in any list previously filed by that person with the Secretary under this subparagraph or paragraph (1). A list under this subparagraph shall list a tobacco product by its established name and shall be accompanied by the other information required by paragraph (1).

(B) If since the date the registrant last made a report under this paragraph that person has discontinued the manufacture, preparation, compounding, or processing for commercial distribution of a tobacco product included in a list filed under subparagraph (A) or paragraph (1), notice of such discontinuance, the date of such discontinuance, and the identity of its established name.

(C) If since the date the registrant reported under subparagraph (B) a notice of discontinuance that person has resumed the manufacture, preparation, compounding, or processing for commercial distribution of the tobacco product with respect to which such notice of discontinuance was reported, notice of such resumption, the date of such resumption, the identity of such tobacco product by established name, and other information required by paragraph (1), unless the registrant has previously reported such resumption to the Secretary under this subparagraph.

(D) Any material change in any information previously submitted under this paragraph or paragraph (1).

(j) Report Preceding Introduction of Certain Substantially Equivalent Products Into Interstate Commerce. —

(1) In General. — Each person who is required to register under this section and who proposes to begin the introduction or delivery for introduction into interstate commerce for commercial distribution of a tobacco product intended for human use that was not commercially marketed (other than for test marketing) in the United States as of February 15, 2007, shall, at least 90 days prior to making such introduction or delivery, report to the Secretary (in such form and manner as the Secretary shall prescribe) —

(A) the basis for such person's determination that —

(i) the tobacco product is substantially equivalent, within the meaning of section 910, to a tobacco product commercially marketed (other than for test marketing) in the United States as of February 15, 2007, or to a tobacco product that the Secretary has previously determined, pursuant to subsection (a)(3) of section 910, is substantially equivalent and that is in compliance with the requirements of this Act; or

(ii) the tobacco product is modified within the meaning of paragraph (3), the modifications are to a product that is commercially marketed and in compliance with the requirements of this Act, and all of the modifications are covered by exemptions granted by the Secretary pursuant to paragraph (3); and

(B) action taken by such person to comply with the requirements under section 907 that are applicable to the tobacco product.

(2) Application to Certain Post-February 15, 2007, Products. — A report under this subsection for a tobacco product that was first introduced or delivered for introduction into interstate commerce for commercial distribution in the United States after February 15, 2007, and prior to the date that is 21 months after the date of enactment of the Family Smoking Prevention and Tobacco Control Act shall be submitted to the Secretary not later than 21 months after such date of enactment.

(3) Exemptions. —

(A) In General. — The Secretary may exempt from the requirements of this subsection relating to the demonstration that a tobacco product is substantially equivalent within the meaning of section 910, tobacco products that are modified by adding or deleting a tobacco additive, or increasing or decreasing the quantity of an existing tobacco additive, if the Secretary determines that —

(i) such modification would be a minor modification of a tobacco product that can be sold under this Act;

(ii) a report under this subsection is not necessary to ensure that permitting the tobacco product to be marketed would be appropriate for protection of the public health; and

(iii) an exemption is otherwise appropriate.

(B) Regulations. — Not later than 15 months after the date of enactment of the Family Smoking Prevention and Tobacco Control Act, the Secretary shall issue regulations to implement this paragraph.

Sec. 906. [387f] General Provisions Respecting Control of Tobacco Products.

(a) In General. — Any requirement established by or under section 902, 903, 905, or 909 applicable to a tobacco product shall apply to such tobacco product until the applicability of the requirement to the tobacco product has been changed by action taken under section 907, section 910, section 911, or subsection (d) of this section, and any requirement established by or under section 902, 903, 905, or 909 which is inconsistent with a requirement imposed on such tobacco product under section 907, section 910, section 911, or subsection (d) of this section shall not apply to such tobacco product.

(b) Information on Public Access and Comment. — Each notice of proposed rulemaking or other notification under section 907, 908, 909, 910, or 911 or under this section, any other notice which is published in the Federal Register with respect to any other action taken under any such section and which states the reasons for such action, and each publication of findings required to be made in connection with rulemaking under any such section shall set forth —

(1) the manner in which interested persons may examine data and other information on which the notice or findings is based; and

(2) the period within which interested persons may present their comments on the notice or findings (including the need therefore) orally or in writing, which period shall be at least 60 days but may not exceed 90 days unless the time is extended by the Secretary by a notice published in the Federal Register stating good cause therefore.

(c) Limited Confidentiality of Information. — Any information reported to or otherwise obtained by the Secretary or the Secretary's representative under section 903, 904, 907, 908, 909, 910, 911, or 704, or under subsection (e) or (f) of this section, which is exempt from disclosure under subsection (a) of section 552 of title 5, United States Code, by reason of subsection (b)(4) of that section shall be considered confidential and shall not be disclosed, except that the information may be disclosed to other officers or employees concerned with carrying out this chapter, or when relevant in any proceeding under this chapter.

(d) Restrictions. —

(1) In General. — The Secretary may by regulation require restrictions on the sale and distribution of a tobacco product, including restrictions on the access to, and the advertising and promotion of, the tobacco product, if the Secretary determines that such regulation would be appropriate for the protection of the public health. The Secretary may by regulation impose restrictions on the advertising and promotion of a tobacco product consistent with and to full extent permitted by the first amendment to the Constitution. The finding as to whether such regulation would be appropriate for the protection of the public health shall be determined with respect to the risks and benefits to the population as a whole, including users and nonusers of the tobacco product, and taking into account —

(A) the increased or decreased likelihood that existing users of tobacco products will stop using such products; and

(B) the increased or decreased likelihood that those who do not use tobacco products will start using such products. No such regulation may require that the sale or distribution of a tobacco product be limited to the written or oral authorization of a practitioner licensed by law to prescribe medical products.

(2) Label Statements. — The label of a tobacco product shall bear such appropriate statements of the restrictions required by a regulation under subsection (a) as the Secretary may in such regulation prescribe.

(3) Limitations. —

(A) In General. — No restrictions under paragraph (1) may —

(i) prohibit the sale of any tobacco product in face-to-face transactions by a specific category of retail outlets; or

(ii) establish a minimum age of sale of tobacco products to any person older than 18 years of age.

(B) Matchbooks. — For purposes of any regulations issued by the Secretary, matchbooks of conventional size containing not more than 20 paper matches, and which are customarily given away for free with the purchase of tobacco products, shall be considered as adult-written publications which shall be permitted to contain advertising. Notwithstanding the preceding sentence, if the Secretary finds that such treatment of matchbooks is not appropriate for the protection of the public health, the Secretary may determine by regulation that matchbooks shall not be considered adult-written publications.

(4) Remote Sales. —

(A) In General. — The Secretary shall —

(i) within 18 months after the date of enactment of the Family Smoking Prevention and Tobacco Control Act, promulgate regulations regarding the sale and distribution of tobacco products that occur through means other than a direct, face-to-face exchange between a retailer and a consumer in order to prevent the sale and distribution of tobacco products to individuals who have not attained the minimum age established by applicable law for the purchase of such products, including requirements for age verification; and

(ii) within 2 years after such date of enactment, issue regulations to address the promotion and marketing of tobacco products that are sold or distributed through means other than a direct, face-to-face exchange between a retailer and a consumer in order to protect individuals who have not attained the minimum age established by applicable law for the purchase of such products.

(B) Relation to Other Authority. — Nothing in this paragraph limits the authority of the Secretary to take additional actions under the other paragraphs of this subsection.

(e) Good Manufacturing Practice Requirements. —

(1) Methods, Facilities, and Controls to Conform. —

(A) In General. — In applying manufacturing restrictions to tobacco, the Secretary shall, in accordance with subparagraph (B), prescribe regulations (which may differ based on the type of tobacco product involved) requiring that the methods used in, and the facilities and controls used for, the manufacture, preproduction design validation (including a process to assess the performance of a tobacco product), packing, and storage of a tobacco product conform to current good manufacturing practice, or hazard analysis and critical control point methodology, as prescribed in such regulations to assure that the public health is protected and that the tobacco product is in compliance with this chapter. Such regulations may provide for the testing of raw tobacco for pesticide chemical residues regardless of whether a tolerance for such chemical residues has been established.

(B) Requirements. — The Secretary shall —

(i) before promulgating any regulation under subparagraph (A), afford the Tobacco Products Scientific Advisory Committee an opportunity to submit recommendations with respect to the regulation proposed to be promulgated;

(ii) before promulgating any regulation under subparagraph (A), afford opportunity for an oral hearing;

(iii) provide the Tobacco Products Scientific Advisory Committee a reasonable time to make its recommendation with respect to proposed regulations under subparagraph (A);

(iv) in establishing the effective date of a regulation promulgated under this subsection, take into account the differences in the manner in which the different types of tobacco products have historically been produced, the financial resources of the different tobacco product manufacturers, and the state of their existing manufacturing facilities, and shall provide for a reasonable period of time for such manufacturers to conform to good manufacturing practices; and

(v) not require any small tobacco product manufacturer to comply with a regulation under subparagraph (A) for at least 4 years following the effective date established by the Secretary for such regulation.

(2) Exemptions; Variances. —

(A) Petition. — Any person subject to any requirement prescribed under paragraph (1) may petition the Secretary for a permanent or temporary exemption or variance from such requirement. Such a petition shall be submitted to the Secretary in such form and manner as the Secretary shall prescribe and shall —

(i) in the case of a petition for an exemption from a requirement, set forth the basis for the petitioner's determination that compliance with the requirement is not required to assure that the tobacco product will be in compliance with this chapter;

(ii) in the case of a petition for a variance from a requirement, set forth the methods proposed to be used in, and the facilities and controls proposed to be used for, the manufacture, packing, and storage of the tobacco product in lieu of the methods, facilities, and controls prescribed by the requirement; and

(iii) contain such other information as the Secretary shall prescribe.

(B) Referral to the Tobacco Products Scientific Advisory Committee. — The Secretary may refer to the Tobacco Products Scientific Advisory Committee any petition submitted under subparagraph (A). The Tobacco Products Scientific Advisory Committee shall report its recommendations to the Secretary with respect to a petition referred to it within 60 days after the date of the petition's referral. Within 60 days after —

(i) the date the petition was submitted to the Secretary under subparagraph (A); or

(ii) the day after the petition was referred to the Tobacco Products Scientific Advisory Committee, whichever occurs later, the Secretary shall by order either deny the petition or approve it.

(C) Approval. — The Secretary may approve —

(i) a petition for an exemption for a tobacco product from a requirement if the Secretary determines that compliance with such requirement is not required to assure that the tobacco product will be in compliance with this chapter; and

(ii) a petition for a variance for a tobacco product from a requirement if the Secretary determines that the methods to be used in, and the facilities and controls to be used for, the manufacture, packing, and storage of the tobacco product in lieu of the methods, facilities, and controls prescribed by the requirement are sufficient to assure that the tobacco product will be in compliance with this chapter.

(D) Conditions. — An order of the Secretary approving a petition for a variance shall prescribe such conditions respecting the methods used in, and the facilities and controls used for, the manufacture, packing, and storage of the tobacco product to be granted the variance under the petition as may be necessary to assure that the tobacco product will be in compliance with this chapter.

(E) Hearing. — After the issuance of an order under subparagraph (B) respecting a petition, the petitioner shall have an opportunity for an informal hearing on such order.

(3) Compliance. — Compliance with requirements under this subsection shall not be required before the end of the 3-year period following the date of enactment of the Family Smoking Prevention and Tobacco Control Act.

(f) Research and Development. — The Secretary may enter into contracts for research, testing, and demonstrations respecting tobacco products and may obtain tobacco products for research, testing, and demonstration purposes.

Sec. 907. [387g] Tobacco Product Standards.

(a) In General. —

(1) Special Rules. —

(A) Special Rule for Cigarettes. — Beginning 3 months after the date of enactment of the Family Smoking Prevention and Tobacco Control Act, a cigarette or any of its component parts (including the tobacco, filter, or paper) shall not contain, as a constituent (including a smoke constituent) or additive, an artificial or natural flavor (other than tobacco or menthol) or an herb or spice, including strawberry, grape, orange, clove, cinnamon, pineapple, vanilla, coconut, licorice, cocoa, chocolate, cherry, or coffee, that is a characterizing flavor of the tobacco product or tobacco smoke. Nothing in this subparagraph shall be construed to limit the Secretary's authority to take action under this section or other sections of this Act applicable to menthol or any artificial or natural flavor, herb, or spice not specified in this subparagraph.

(B) Additional Special Rule. — Beginning 2 years after the date of enactment of the Family Smoking Prevention and Tobacco Control Act, a tobacco product manufacturer shall not use tobacco, including foreign grown tobacco, that contains a pesticide chemical residue that is at a level greater than is specified by any tolerance applicable under Federal law to domestically grown tobacco.

(2) Revision of Tobacco Product Standards. — The Secretary may revise the tobacco product standards in paragraph (1) in accordance with subsection (c).

(3) Tobacco Product Standards. —

(A) In General. — The Secretary may adopt tobacco product standards in addition to those in paragraph (1) if the Secretary finds that a tobacco product standard is appropriate for the protection of the public health.

(B) Determinations. —

(i) Considerations. — In making a finding described in subparagraph (A), the Secretary shall consider scientific evidence concerning —

(I) the risks and benefits to the population as a whole, including users and nonusers of tobacco products, of the proposed standard;

(II) the increased or decreased likelihood that existing users of tobacco products will stop using such products; and

(III) the increased or decreased likelihood that those who do not use tobacco products will start using such products.

(ii) Additional Considerations. — In the event that the Secretary makes a determination, set forth in a proposed tobacco product standard in a proposed rule, that it is appropriate for the protection of public health to require the reduction or elimination of an additive, constituent (including a smoke constituent), or other component of a tobacco product because the Secretary has found that the additive, constituent, or other component is or may be harmful, any party objecting to the proposed standard on the ground that the proposed standard will not reduce or eliminate the risk of illness or injury may provide for the Secretary's consideration scientific evidence that demonstrates that the proposed standard will not reduce or eliminate the risk of illness or injury.

(4) Content of Tobacco Product Standards. — A tobacco product standard established under this section for a tobacco product —

(A) shall include provisions that are appropriate for the protection of the public health, including provisions, where appropriate —

(i) for nicotine yields of the product;

(ii) for the reduction or elimination of other constituents, including smoke constituents, or harmful components of the product; or

(iii) relating to any other requirement under subparagraph(B);

(B) shall, where appropriate for the protection of the public health, include —

(i) provisions respecting the construction, components, ingredients, additives, constituents, including smoke constituents, and properties of the tobacco product;

(ii) provisions for the testing (on a sample basis or, if necessary, on an individual basis) of the tobacco product;

(iii) provisions for the measurement of the tobacco product characteristics of the tobacco product;

(iv) provisions requiring that the results of each or of certain of the tests of the tobacco product required to be made under clause (ii) show that the tobacco product is in conformity with the portions of the standard for which the test or tests were required; and

(v) a provision requiring that the sale and distribution of the tobacco product be restricted but only to the extent that the sale and distribution of a tobacco product may be restricted under a regulation under section 906(d);

(C) shall, where appropriate, require the use and prescribe the form and content of labeling for the proper use of the tobacco product; and

(D) shall require tobacco products containing foreign-grown tobacco to meet the same standards applicable to tobacco products containing domestically grown tobacco.

(5) Periodic Reevaluation of Tobacco Product Standards. — The Secretary shall provide for periodic evaluation of tobacco product standards established under this section to determine whether such standards should be changed to reflect new medical, scientific, or other technological data. The Secretary may provide for testing under paragraph (4)(B) by any person.

(6) Involvement of Other Agencies; Informed Persons. — In carrying out duties under this section, the Secretary shall endeavor to —

(A) use personnel, facilities, and other technical support available in other Federal agencies;

(B) consult with other Federal agencies concerned with standard setting and other nationally or internationally recognized standard setting entities; and

(C) invite appropriate participation, through joint or other conferences, workshops, or other means, by informed persons representative of scientific, professional, industry, agricultural, or consumer organizations who in the Secretary's judgment can make a significant contribution.

(b) Considerations by Secretary. —

(1) Technical Achievability. — The Secretary shall consider information submitted in connection with a proposed standard regarding the technical achievability of compliance with such standard.

(2) Other Considerations. — The Secretary shall consider all other information submitted in connection with a proposed standard, including information concerning the countervailing effects of the tobacco product standard on the health of adolescent tobacco users, adult tobacco users, or non-tobacco users, such as the creation of a significant demand for contraband or other tobacco products that do not meet the requirements of this chapter and the significance of such demand.

(c) Proposed Standards. —

(1) In General. — The Secretary shall publish in the Federal Register a notice of proposed rulemaking for the establishment, amendment, or revocation of any tobacco product standard.

(2) Requirements of Notice. — A notice of proposed rulemaking for the establishment or amendment of a tobacco product standard for a tobacco product shall —

(A) set forth a finding with supporting justification that the tobacco product standard is appropriate for the protection of the public health;

(B) invite interested persons to submit a draft or proposed tobacco product standard for consideration by the Secretary;

(C) invite interested persons to submit comments on structuring the standard so that it does not advantage foreign-grown tobacco over domestically grown tobacco; and

(D) invite the Secretary of Agriculture to provide any information or analysis which the Secretary of Agriculture believes is relevant to the proposed tobacco product standard.

(3) Finding. — A notice of proposed rulemaking for the revocation of a tobacco product standard shall set forth a finding with supporting justification that the tobacco product standard is no longer appropriate for the protection of the public health.

(4) Comment. — The Secretary shall provide for a comment period of not less than 60 days.

(d) Promulgation. —

(1) In General. — After the expiration of the period for comment on a notice of proposed rulemaking published under subsection (c) respecting a tobacco product standard and after consideration of comments submitted under subsections (b) and (c) and any report from the Tobacco Products Scientific Advisory Committee, the Secretary shall —

(A) if the Secretary determines that the standard would be appropriate for the protection of the public health, promulgate a regulation establishing a tobacco product standard and publish in the Federal Register findings on the matters referred to in subsection (c); or

(B) publish a notice terminating the proceeding for the development of the standard together with the reasons for such termination.

(2) Effective Date. — A regulation establishing a tobacco product standard shall set forth the date or dates upon which the standard shall take effect, but no such regulation may take effect before 1 year after the date of its publication unless the Secretary determines that an earlier effective date is necessary for the protection of the public health. Such date or dates shall be established so as to minimize, consistent with the public health, economic loss to, and disruption or dislocation of, domestic and international trade. In establishing such effective date or dates, the Secretary shall consider information submitted in connection with a proposed product standard by interested parties, including manufacturers and tobacco growers, regarding the technical achievability of compliance with the standard, and including information concerning the existence of patents that make it impossible to comply in the timeframe envisioned in the proposed standard. If the Secretary determines, based on the Secretary's evaluation of submitted comments, that a product standard can be met only by manufacturers requiring substantial changes to the methods of farming the domestically grown tobacco used by the manufacturer, the effective date of that product standard shall be not less than 2 years after the date of publication of the final regulation establishing the standard.

(3) Limitation on Power Granted to the Food and Drug Administration. — Because of the importance of a decision of the Secretary to issue a regulation —

(A) banning all cigarettes, all smokeless tobacco products, all little cigars, all cigars other than little cigars, all pipe tobacco, or all roll-your-own tobacco products; or

(B) requiring the reduction of nicotine yields of a tobacco product to zero, the Secretary is prohibited from taking such actions under this Act.

(4) Amendment; Revocation. —

(A) Authority. — The Secretary, upon the Secretary's own initiative or upon petition of an interested person, may by a regulation, promulgated in accordance with the requirements of subsection (c) and paragraph (2), amend or revoke a tobacco product standard.

(B) Effective Date. — The Secretary may declare a proposed amendment of a tobacco product standard to be effective on and after its publication in the Federal Register and until the effective date of any final action taken on such amendment if the Secretary determines that making it so effective is in the public interest.

(5) Referral to Advisory Committee. —

(A) In General. — The Secretary may refer a proposed regulation for the establishment, amendment, or revocation of a tobacco product standard to the Tobacco Products Scientific Advisory Committee for a report and recommendation with respect to any matter involved in the proposed regulation which requires the exercise of scientific judgment.

(B) Initiation of Referral. — The Secretary may make a referral under this paragraph —

(i) on the Secretary's own initiative; or

(ii) upon the request of an interested person that —

(I) demonstrates good cause for the referral; and

(II) is made before the expiration of the period for submission of comments on the proposed regulation.

(C) Provision of Data. — If a proposed regulation is referred under this paragraph to the Tobacco Products Scientific Advisory Committee, the Secretary shall provide the Advisory Committee with the data and information on which such proposed regulation is based.

(D) Report and Recommendation. — The Tobacco Products Scientific Advisory Committee shall, within 60 days after the referral of a proposed regulation under this paragraph and after independent study of the data and information furnished to it by the Secretary and other data and information before it, submit to the Secretary a report and recommendation respecting such regulation, together with all underlying data and information and a statement of the reason or basis for the recommendation.

(E) Public Availability. — The Secretary shall make a copy of each report and recommendation under subparagraph (D) publicly available.

(e) Menthol Cigarettes. —

(1) Referral; Considerations. — Immediately upon the establishment of the Tobacco Products Scientific Advisory Committee under section 917(a), the Secretary shall refer to the Committee for report and recommendation, under section 917(c)(4), the issue of the impact of the use of menthol in cigarettes on the public health, including such use among children, African-Americans, Hispanics, and other racial and ethnic minorities. In its review, the Tobacco Products Scientific Advisory Committee shall address the considerations listed in subsections (a)(3)(B)(i) and (b).

(2) Report and Recommendation. — Not later than 1 year after its establishment, the Tobacco Product Scientific Advisory Committee shall submit to the Secretary the report and recommendations required pursuant to paragraph (1).

(3) Rule of Construction. — Nothing in this subsection shall be construed to limit the Secretary's authority to take action under this section or other sections of this Act applicable to menthol.

(f) Dissolvable Tobacco Products. —

(1) Referral; Considerations. — The Secretary shall refer to the Tobacco Products Scientific Advisory Committee for report and recommendation, under section 917(c)(4), the issue of the nature and impact of the use of dissolvable tobacco products on the public health, including such use among children. In its review, the Tobacco Products Scientific Advisory Committee shall address the considerations listed in subsection (a)(3)(B)(i).

(2) Report and Recommendation. — Not later than 2 years after its establishment, the Tobacco Product Scientific Advisory Committee shall submit to the Secretary the report and recommendations required pursuant to paragraph (1).

(3) Rule of Construction. — Nothing in this subsection shall be construed to limit the Secretary's authority to take action under this section or other sections of this Act at any time applicable to any dissolvable tobacco product.

Sec. 908. [387h] Notification and Other Remedies.

(a) Notification. — If the Secretary determines that —

(1) a tobacco product which is introduced or delivered for introduction into interstate commerce for commercial distribution presents an unreasonable risk of substantial harm to the public health; and

(2) notification under this subsection is necessary to eliminate the unreasonable risk of such harm and no more practicable means is available under the provisions of this chapter (other than this section) to eliminate such risk, the Secretary may issue such order as may be necessary to assure that adequate notification is provided in an appropriate form, by the persons and means best suited under the circumstances involved, to all persons who should properly receive such notification in order to eliminate such risk. The Secretary may order notification by any appropriate means, including public service announcements. Before issuing an order under this subsection, the Secretary shall consult with the persons who are to give notice under the order.

(b) No Exemption from Other Liability. — Compliance with an order issued under this section shall not relieve any person from liability under Federal or State law. In awarding damages for economic loss in an action brought for the enforcement of any such liability, the value to the plaintiff in such action of any remedy provided under such order shall be taken into account.

(c) Recall Authority. —

(1) In General. — If the Secretary finds that there is a reasonable probability that a tobacco product contains a manufacturing or other defect not ordinarily contained in tobacco products on the market that would cause serious, adverse health consequences or death, the Secretary shall issue an order requiring the appropriate person (including the manufacturers, importers, distributors, or retailers of the tobacco product) to immediately cease distribution of such tobacco product. The order shall provide the person subject to the order with an opportunity for an informal hearing, to be held not later than 10 days after the date of the issuance of the order, on the actions required by the order and on whether the order should be amended to require a recall of such tobacco product. If, after providing an opportunity for such a hearing, the Secretary determines that inadequate grounds exist to support the actions required by the order, the Secretary shall vacate the order.

(2) Amendment of Order to Require Recall. —

(A) In General. — If, after providing an opportunity for an informal hearing under paragraph (1), the Secretary determines that the order should be amended to include a recall of the tobacco product with respect to which the order was issued, the Secretary shall, except as provided in subparagraph (B), amend the order to require a recall. The Secretary shall specify a timetable in which the tobacco product recall will occur and shall require periodic reports to the Secretary describing the progress of the recall.

(B) Notice. — An amended order under subparagraph (A) —

(i) shall not include recall of a tobacco product from individuals; and

(ii) shall provide for notice to persons subject to the risks associated with the use of such tobacco product. In providing the notice required by clause (ii), the Secretary may use the assistance of retailers and other persons who distributed such tobacco product. If a significant number of such persons cannot be identified, the Secretary shall notify such persons under section 705(b).

(3) Remedy Not Exclusive. — The remedy provided by this subsection shall be in addition to remedies provided by subsection (a).

Sec. 909. [387i] Records and Reports on Tobacco Products.

(a) In General. — Every person who is a tobacco product manufacturer or importer of a tobacco product shall establish and maintain such records, make such reports, and provide such information, as the Secretary may by regulation reasonably require to assure that such tobacco product is not adulterated or misbranded and to otherwise protect public health. Regulations prescribed under the preceding sentence —

(1) may require a tobacco product manufacturer or importer to report to the Secretary whenever the manufacturer or importer receives or otherwise becomes aware of information that reasonably suggests that one of its marketed tobacco products may have caused or contributed to a serious unexpected adverse experience associated with the use of the product or any significant increase in the frequency of a serious, expected adverse product experience;

(2) shall require reporting of other significant adverse tobacco product experiences as determined by the Secretary to be necessary to be reported;

(3) shall not impose requirements unduly burdensome to a tobacco product manufacturer or importer, taking into account the cost of complying with such requirements and the need for the protection of the public health and the implementation of this chapter;

(4) when prescribing the procedure for making requests for reports or information, shall require that each request made under such regulations for submission of a report or information to the Secretary state the reason or purpose for such request and identify to the fullest extent practicable such report or information;

(5) when requiring submission of a report or information to the Secretary, shall state the reason or purpose for the submission of such report or information and identify to the fullest extent practicable such report or information; and

(6) may not require that the identity of any patient or user be disclosed in records, reports, or information required under this subsection unless required for the medical welfare of an individual, to determine risks to public health of a tobacco product, or to verify a record, report, or information submitted under this chapter.

In prescribing regulations under this subsection, the Secretary shall have due regard for the professional ethics of the medical profession and the interests of patients. The prohibitions of paragraph (6) continue to apply to records, reports, and information concerning any individual who has been a patient, irrespective of whether or when he ceases to be a patient.

(b) Reports of Removals and Corrections. —

(1) In General. — Except as provided in paragraph (2), the Secretary shall by regulation require a tobacco product manufacturer or importer of a tobacco product to report promptly to the Secretary any corrective action taken or removal from the market of a tobacco product undertaken by such manufacturer or importer if the removal or correction was undertaken —

(A) to reduce a risk to health posed by the tobacco product; or

(B) to remedy a violation of this chapter caused by the tobacco product which may present a risk to health.

A tobacco product manufacturer or importer of a tobacco product who undertakes a corrective action or removal from the market of a tobacco product which is not required to be reported under this subsection shall keep a record of such correction or removal.

(2) Exception. — No report of the corrective action or removal of a tobacco product may be required under paragraph (1) if a report of the corrective action or removal is required and has been submitted under subsection (a).

Sec. 910. [387j] Application for Review of Certain Tobacco Products.

(a) In General. —

(1) New Tobacco Product Defined. — For purposes of this section the term "new tobacco product" means—

(A) any tobacco product (including those products in test markets) that was not commercially marketed in the United States as of February 15, 2007; or

(B) any modification (including a change in design, any component, any part, or any constituent, including a smoke constituent, or in the content, delivery or form of nicotine, or any other additive or ingredient) of a tobacco product where the modified product was commercially marketed in the United States after February 15, 2007.

(2) Premarket Review Required. —

(A) New Products. — An order under subsection (c)(1)(A)(i) for a new tobacco product is required unless—

(i) the manufacturer has submitted a report under section 905(j); and the Secretary has issued an order that the tobacco product —

(I) is substantially equivalent to a tobacco product commercially marketed (other than for test marketing) in the United States as of February 15, 2007; and

(II) is in compliance with the requirements of this Act; or

(ii) the tobacco product is exempt from the requirements of section 905(j) pursuant to a regulation issued under section 905(j)(3).

(B) Application to Certain Post-February 15, 2007, Products. — Subparagraph (A) shall not apply to a tobacco product —

(i) that was first introduced or delivered for introduction into interstate commerce for commercial distribution in the United States after February 15, 2007, and prior to the date that is 21 months after the date of enactment of the Family Smoking Prevention and Tobacco Control Act; and

(ii) for which a report was submitted under section 905(j) within such 21-month period, except that subparagraph (A) shall apply to the tobacco product if the Secretary issues an order that the tobacco product is not substantially equivalent.

(3) Substantially Equivalent Defined. —

(A) In General. — In this section and section 905(j), the term "substantially equivalent" or "substantial equivalence" means, with respect to the tobacco product being compared to the predicate tobacco product, that the Secretary by order has found that the tobacco product —

(i) has the same characteristics as the predicate tobacco product; or

(ii) has different characteristics and the information submitted contains information, including clinical data if deemed necessary by the Secretary, that demonstrates that it is not appropriate to regulate the product under this section because the product does not raise different questions of public health.

(B) Characteristics. — In subparagraph (A), the term "characteristics" means the materials, ingredients, design, composition, heating source, or other features of a tobacco product.

(C) Limitation. — A tobacco product may not be found to be substantially equivalent to a predicate tobacco product that has been removed from the market at the initiative of the Secretary or that has been determined by a judicial order to be misbranded or adulterated.

(4) Health Information. —

(A) Summary. — As part of a submission under section 905(j) respecting a tobacco product, the person required to file a premarket notification under such section shall provide an adequate summary of any health information related to the tobacco product or state that such information will be made available upon request by any person.

(B) Required Information. — Any summary under subparagraph (A) respecting a tobacco product shall contain detailed information regarding data concerning adverse health effects and shall be made available to the public by the Secretary within 30 days of the issuance of a determination that such tobacco product is substantially equivalent to another tobacco product.

(b) Application. —

(1) Contents. — An application under this section shall contain —

(A) full reports of all information, published or known to, or which should reasonably be known to, the applicant, concerning investigations which have been made to show the health risks of such tobacco product and whether such tobacco product presents less risk than other tobacco products;

(B) a full statement of the components, ingredients, additives, and properties, and of the principle or principles of operation, of such tobacco product;

(C) a full description of the methods used in, and the facilities and controls used for, the manufacture, processing, and, when relevant, packing and installation of, such tobacco product;

(D) an identifying reference to any tobacco product standard under section 907 which would be applicable to any aspect of such tobacco product, and either adequate information to show that such aspect of such tobacco product fully meets such tobacco product standard or adequate information to justify any deviation from such standard;

(E) such samples of such tobacco product and of components thereof as the Secretary may reasonably require;

(F) specimens of the labeling proposed to be used for such tobacco product; and

(G) such other information relevant to the subject matter of the application as the Secretary may require.

(2) Referral to Tobacco Products Scientific Advisory Committee. — Upon receipt of an application meeting the requirements set forth in paragraph (1), the Secretary —

(A) may, on the Secretary's own initiative; or

(B) may, upon the request of an applicant, refer such application to the Tobacco Products Scientific Advisory Committee for reference and for submission (within such period as the Secretary may establish) of a report and recommendation respecting the application, together with all underlying data and the reasons or basis for the recommendation.

(c) Action on Application. —

(1) Deadline. —

(A) In General. — As promptly as possible, but in no event later than 180 days after the receipt of an application under subsection (b), the Secretary, after considering the report and recommendation submitted under subsection (b)(2), shall —

(i) issue an order that the new product may be introduced or delivered for introduction into interstate commerce if the Secretary finds that none of the grounds specified in paragraph (2) of this subsection applies; or

(ii) issue an order that the new product may not be introduced or delivered for introduction into interstate commerce if the Secretary finds (and sets forth the basis for such finding as part of or accompanying such denial) that 1 or more grounds for denial specified in paragraph (2) of this subsection apply.

(B) Restrictions on Sale and Distribution. — An order under subparagraph (A)(i) may require that the sale and distribution of the tobacco product be restricted but only to the extent that the sale and distribution of a tobacco product may be restricted under a regulation under section 906(d).

(2) Denial of Application. — The Secretary shall deny an application submitted under subsection (b) if, upon the basis of the information submitted to the Secretary as part of the application and any other information before the Secretary with respect to such tobacco product, the Secretary finds that—

(A) there is a lack of a showing that permitting such tobacco product to be marketed would be appropriate for the protection of the public health;

(B) the methods used in, or the facilities or controls used for, the manufacture, processing, or packing of such tobacco product do not conform to the requirements of section 906(e);

(C) based on a fair evaluation of all material facts, the proposed labeling is false or misleading in any particular; or

(D) such tobacco product is not shown to conform in all respects to a tobacco product standard in effect under section 907, and there is a lack of adequate information to justify the deviation from such standard.

(3) Denial Information. — Any denial of an application shall, insofar as the Secretary determines to be practicable, be accompanied by a statement informing the applicant of the measures required to remove such application from deniable form (which measures may include further research by the applicant in accordance with 1 or more protocols prescribed by the Secretary).

(4) Basis for Finding. — For purposes of this section, the finding as to whether the marketing of a tobacco product for which an application has been submitted is appropriate for the protection of the public health shall be determined with respect to the risks and benefits to the population as a whole, including users and nonusers of the tobacco product, and taking into account—

(A) the increased or decreased likelihood that existing users of tobacco products will stop using such products; and

(B) the increased or decreased likelihood that those who do not use tobacco products will start using such products.

(5) Basis for Action. —

(A) Investigations. — For purposes of paragraph (2)(A), whether permitting a tobacco product to be marketed would be appropriate for the protection of the public health shall, when appropriate, be determined on the basis of well-controlled investigations, which may include 1 or more clinical investigations by experts qualified by training and experience to evaluate the tobacco product.

(B) Other Evidence. — If the Secretary determines that there exists valid scientific evidence (other than evidence derived from investigations described in subparagraph (A)) which is sufficient to evaluate the tobacco product, the Secretary may authorize that the determination for purposes of paragraph (2)(A) be made on the basis of such evidence.

(d) Withdrawal and Temporary Suspension. —

(1) In General. — The Secretary shall, upon obtaining, where appropriate, advice on scientific matters from the Tobacco Products Scientific Advisory Committee, and after due notice and opportunity for informal hearing for a tobacco product for which an order was issued under subsection (c)(1)(A)(i), issue an order withdrawing the order if the Secretary finds —

(A) that the continued marketing of such tobacco product no longer is appropriate for the protection of the public health;

(B) that the application contained or was accompanied by an untrue statement of a material fact;

(C) that the applicant —

(i) has failed to establish a system for maintaining records, or has repeatedly or deliberately failed to maintain records or to make reports, required by an applicable regulation under section 909;

(ii) has refused to permit access to, or copying or verification of, such records as required by section 704; or

(iii) has not complied with the requirements of section 905;

(D) on the basis of new information before the Secretary with respect to such tobacco product, evaluated together with the evidence before the Secretary when the application was reviewed, that the methods used in, or the facilities and controls used for, the manufacture, processing, packing, or installation of such tobacco product do not conform with the requirements of section 906(e) and were not brought into conformity with such requirements within a reasonable time after receipt of written notice from the Secretary of nonconformity;

(E) on the basis of new information before the Secretary, evaluated together with the evidence before the Secretary when the application was reviewed, that the labeling of such tobacco product, based on a fair evaluation of all material facts, is false or misleading in any particular and was not corrected within a reasonable time after receipt of written notice from the Secretary of such fact; or

(F) on the basis of new information before the Secretary, evaluated together with the evidence before the Secretary when such order was issued, that such tobacco product is not shown to conform in all respects to a tobacco product standard which is in effect under section 907, compliance with which was a condition to the issuance of an order relating to the application, and that there is a lack of adequate information to justify the deviation from such standard.

(2) Appeal. — The holder of an application subject to an order issued under paragraph (1) withdrawing an order issued pursuant to subsection (c)(1)(A)(i) may, by petition filed on or before the 30th day after the date upon which such holder receives notice of such withdrawal, obtain review thereof in accordance with section 912.

(3) Temporary Suspension. — If, after providing an opportunity for an informal hearing, the Secretary determines there is reasonable probability that the continuation of distribution of a tobacco product under an order would cause serious, adverse health consequences or death, that is greater than ordinarily caused by tobacco products on the market, the Secretary shall by order temporarily suspend the authority of the manufacturer to market the product. If the Secretary issues such an order, the Secretary shall proceed expeditiously under paragraph (1) to withdraw such application.

(e) Service of Order. — An order issued by the Secretary under this section shall be served —

(1) in person by any officer or employee of the department designated by the Secretary; or

(2) by mailing the order by registered mail or certified mail addressed to the applicant at the applicant's last known address in the records of the Secretary.

(f) Records. —

(1) Additional Information. — In the case of any tobacco product for which an order issued pursuant to subsection (c)(1)(A)(i) for an application filed under subsection (b) is in effect, the applicant shall establish and maintain such records, and make such reports to the Secretary, as the Secretary may by regulation, or by order with respect to such application, prescribe on the basis of a finding that such records and reports are necessary in order to enable the Secretary to determine, or facilitate a determination of, whether there is or may be grounds for withdrawing or temporarily suspending such order.

(2) Access to Records. — Each person required under this section to maintain records, and each person in charge of custody thereof, shall, upon request of an officer or employee designated by the Secretary, permit such officer or employee at all reasonable times to have access to and copy and verify such records.

(g) Investigational Tobacco Product Exemption for Investigational Use. — The Secretary may exempt tobacco products intended for investigational use from the provisions of this chapter under such conditions as the Secretary may by regulation prescribe.

Sec. 911. [387k] Modified-Risk Tobacco Products.

(a) In General. — No person may introduce or deliver for introduction into interstate commerce any modified risk tobacco product unless an order issued pursuant to subsection(g) is effective with respect to such product.

(b) Definitions. — In this section:

(1) Modified Risk Tobacco Product. — The term "modified risk tobacco product" means any tobacco product that is sold or distributed for use to reduce harm or the risk of tobacco-related disease associated with commercially marketed tobacco products.

(2) Sold or Distributed. —

(A) In General. — With respect to a tobacco product, the term "sold or distributed for use to reduce harm or the risk of tobacco-related disease associated with commercially marketed tobacco products" means a tobacco product —

(i) the label, labeling, or advertising of which represents explicitly or implicitly that —

(I) the tobacco product presents a lower risk of tobacco-related disease or is less harmful than one or more other commercially marketed tobacco products;

(II) the tobacco product or its smoke contains a reduced level of a substance or presents areduced exposure to a substance; or

(III) the tobacco product or its smoke does not contain or is free of a substance;

(ii) the label, labeling, or advertising of which uses the descriptors "light", "mild", or "low" or similar descriptors; or

(iii) the tobacco product manufacturer of which has taken any action directed to consumers through the media or otherwise, other than by means of the tobacco product's label, labeling, or advertising, after the date of enactment of the Family Smoking Prevention and Tobacco Control Act, respecting the product that would be reasonably expected to result in consumers believing that the tobacco product or its smoke may present a lower risk of disease or is less harmful than one or more commercially marketed tobacco products, or presents a reduced exposure to, or does not contain or is free of, a substance or substances.

(B) Limitation. — No tobacco product shall be considered to be "sold or distributed for use to reduce harm or the risk of tobacco-related disease associated with commercially marketed tobacco products", except as described in subparagraph (A).

(C) Smokeless Tobacco Product. — No smokeless tobacco product shall be considered to be 'sold or distributed for use to reduce harm or the risk of tobacco-related disease associated with commercially marketed tobacco products' solely because its label, labeling, or advertising uses the following phrases to describe such product and its use: "smokeless tobacco", "smokeless tobacco product", "not consumed by smoking", "does not produce smoke", "smokefree", "smoke-free", "without smoke", "no smoke", or "not smoke".

(3) Effective Date. — The provisions of paragraph (2)(A)(ii) shall take effect 12 months after the date of enactment of the Family Smoking Prevention and Tobacco Control Act for those products whose label, labeling, or advertising contains the terms described in such paragraph on such date of enactment. The effective date shall be with respect to the date of manufacture, provided that, in any case, beginning 30 days after such effective date, a manufacturer shall not introduce into the domestic commerce of the United States any product, irrespective of the date of manufacture, that is not in conformance with paragraph (2)(A)(ii).

(c) Tobacco Dependence Products. — A product that is intended to be used for the treatment of tobacco dependence, including smoking cessation, is not a modified risk tobacco product under this section if it has been approved as a drug or device by the Food and Drug Administration and is subject to the requirements of chapter V.

(d) Filing. — Any person may file with the Secretary an application for a modified risk tobacco product. Such application shall include—

(1) a description of the proposed product and any proposed advertising and labeling;

(2) the conditions for using the product;

(3) the formulation of the product;

(4) sample product labels and labeling;

(5) all documents (including underlying scientific information) relating to research findings conducted, supported, or possessed by the tobacco product manufacturer relating to the effect of the product on tobacco-related diseases and health-related conditions, including information both favorable and unfavorable to the ability of the product to reduce risk or exposure and relating to human health;

(6) data and information on how consumers actually use the tobacco product; and

(7) such other information as the Secretary may require.

(e) Public Availability. — The Secretary shall make the application described in subsection (d) publicly available (except matters in the application which are trade secrets or otherwise confidential, commercial information) and shall request comments by interested persons on the information contained in the application and on the label, labeling, and advertising accompanying such application.

(f) Advisory Committee. —

(1) In General. — The Secretary shall refer to the Tobacco Products Scientific Advisory Committee any application submitted under this section.

(2) Recommendations. — Not later than 60 days after the date an application is referred to the Tobacco Products Scientific Advisory Committee under paragraph (1), the Advisory Committee shall report its recommendations on the application to the Secretary.

(g) Marketing. —

(1) Modified Risk Products. — Except as provided in paragraph (2), the Secretary shall, with respect to an application submitted under this section, issue an order that a modified risk product may be commercially marketed only if the Secretary determines that the applicant has demonstrated that such product, as it is actually used by consumers, will —

(A) significantly reduce harm and the risk of tobacco-related disease to individual tobacco users; and

(B) benefit the health of the population as a whole taking into account both users of tobacco products and persons who do not currently use tobacco products.

(2) Special Rule for Certain Products. —

(A) In General. — The Secretary may issue an order that a tobacco product may be introduced or delivered for introduction into interstate commerce, pursuant to an application under this section, with respect to a tobacco product that may not be commercially marketed under paragraph (1) if the Secretary makes the findings required under this paragraph and determines that the applicant has demonstrated that —

(i) such order would be appropriate to promote the public health;

(ii) any aspect of the label, labeling, and advertising for such product that would cause the tobacco product to be a modified risk tobacco product under subsection (b) is limited to an explicit or implicit representation that such tobacco product or its smoke does not contain or is free of a substance or contains a reduced level of a substance, or presents a reduced exposure to a substance in tobacco smoke;

(iii) scientific evidence is not available and, using the best available scientific methods, cannot be made available without conducting long-term epidemiological studies for an application to meet the standards set forth in paragraph (1); and

(iv) the scientific evidence that is available without conducting long-term epidemiological studies demonstrates that a measurable and substantial reduction in morbidity or mortality among individual tobacco users is reasonably likely in subsequent studies.

(B) Additional Findings Required. — To issue an order under subparagraph A) the Secretary must also find that the applicant has demonstrated that —

(i) the magnitude of the overall reductions in exposure to the substance or substances which are the subject of the application is substantial, such substance or substances are harmful, and the product as actually used exposes consumers to the specified reduced level of the substance or substances;

(ii) the product as actually used by consumers will not expose them to higher levels of other harmful substances compared to the similar types of tobacco products then on the market unless such increases are minimal and the reasonably likely overall impact of use of the product remains a substantial and measurable reduction in overall morbidity and mortality among individual tobacco users;

(iii) testing of actual consumer perception shows that, as the applicant proposes to label and market the product, consumers will not be misled into believing that the product —

(I) is or has been demonstrated to be less harmful; or

(II) presents or has been demonstrated to present less of a risk of disease than 1 or more other commercially marketed tobacco products; and

(iv) issuance of an order with respect to the application is expected to benefit the health of the population as a whole taking into account both users of tobacco products and persons who do not currently use tobacco products.

(C) Conditions of Marketing. —

(i) In General. — Applications subject to an order under this paragraph shall be limited to a term of not more than 5 years, but may be renewed upon a finding by the Secretary that the requirements of this paragraph continue to be satisfied based on the filing of a new application.

(ii) Agreements by Applicant. — An order under this paragraph shall be conditioned on the applicant's agreement to conduct postmarket surveillance and studies and to submit to the Secretary the results of such surveillance and studies to determine the impact of the order on consumer perception, behavior, and health and to enable the Secretary to review the accuracy of the determinations upon which the order was based in accordance with a protocol approved by the Secretary.

(iii) Annual Submission. — The results of such postmarket surveillance and studies described in clause (ii) shall be submitted annually.

(3) Basis. — The determinations under paragraphs (1) and (2) shall be based on—

(A) the scientific evidence submitted by the applicant; and

(B) scientific evidence and other information that is made available to the Secretary.

(4) Benefit to Health of Individuals and of Population as a Whole. — In making the determinations under paragraphs (1) and (2), the Secretary shall take into account —

(A) the relative health risks to individuals of the tobacco product that is the subject of the application;

(B) the increased or decreased likelihood that existing users of tobacco products who would otherwise stop using such products will switch to the tobacco product that is the subject of the application;

(C) the increased or decreased likelihood that persons who do not use tobacco products will start using the tobacco product that is the subject of the application;

(D) the risks and benefits to persons from the use of the tobacco product that is the subject of the application as compared to the use of products for smoking cessation approved under chapter V to treat nicotine dependence; and

(E) comments, data, and information submitted by interested persons.

(h) Additional Conditions for Marketing. —

(1) Modified Risk Products. — The Secretary shall require for the marketing of a product under this section that any advertising or labeling concerning modified risk products enable the public to comprehend the information concerning modified risk and to understand the relative significance of such information in the context of total health and in relation to all of the diseases and health-related conditions associated with the use of tobacco products.

(2) Comparative Claims. —

(A) In General. — The Secretary may require for the marketing of a product under this subsection that a claim comparing a tobacco product to 1 or more other commercially marketed tobacco products shall compare the tobacco product to a commercially marketed tobacco product that is representative of that type of tobacco product on the market (for example the average value of the top 3 brands of an established regular tobacco product).

(B) Quantitative Comparisons. — The Secretary may also require, for purposes of subparagraph (A), that the percent (or fraction) of change and identity of the reference tobacco product and a quantitative comparison of the amount of the substance claimed to be reduced shall be stated in immediate proximity to the most prominent claim.

(3) Label Disclosure. —

(A) In General. — The Secretary may require the disclosure on the label of other substances in the tobacco product, or substances that may be produced by the consumption of that tobacco product, that may affect a disease or health-related condition or may increase the risk of other diseases or health-related conditions associated with the use of tobacco products.

(B) Conditions of Use. — If the conditions of use of the tobacco product may affect the risk of the product to human health, the Secretary may require the labeling of conditions of use.

(4) Time. — An order issued under subsection (g)(1) shall be effective for a specified period of time.

(5) Advertising. — The Secretary may require, with respect to a product for which an applicant obtained an order under subsection (g)(1), that the product comply with requirements relating to advertising and promotion of the tobacco product.

(i) Postmarket Surveillance and Studies. —

(1) In General. — The Secretary shall require, with respect to a product for which an applicant obtained an order under subsection (g)(1), that the applicant conduct postmarket surveillance and studies for such a tobacco product to determine the impact of the order issuance on consumer perception, behavior, and health, to enable the Secretary to review the accuracy of the determinations upon which the order was based, and to provide information that the Secretary determines is otherwise necessary regarding the use or health risks involving the tobacco product. The results of postmarket surveillance and studies shall be submitted to the Secretary on an annual basis.

(2) Surveillance Protocol. — Each applicant required to conduct a surveillance of a tobacco product under paragraph (1) shall, within 30 days after receiving notice that the applicant is required to conduct such surveillance, submit, for the approval of the Secretary, a protocol for the required surveillance. The Secretary, within 60 days of the receipt of such protocol, shall determine if the principal investigator proposed to be used in the surveillance has sufficient qualifications and experience to conduct such surveillance and if such protocol will result in collection of the data or other information designated by the Secretary as necessary to protect the public health.

(j) Withdrawal of Authorization. — The Secretary, after an opportunity for an informal hearing, shall withdraw an order under subsection (g) if the Secretary determines that —

(1) the applicant, based on new information, can no longer make the demonstrations required under subsection (g), or the Secretary can no longer make the determinations required under subsection (g);

(2) the application failed to include material information or included any untrue statement of material fact;

(3) any explicit or implicit representation that the product reduces risk or exposure is no longer valid, including if —

(A) a tobacco product standard is established pursuant to section 907;

(B) an action is taken that affects the risks presented by other commercially marketed tobacco products that were compared to the product that is the subject of the application; or

(C) any postmarket surveillance or studies reveal that the order is no longer consistent with the protection of the public health;

(4) the applicant failed to conduct or submit the postmarket surveillance and studies required under subsection (g)(2)(C)(ii) or subsection (i); or

(5) the applicant failed to meet a condition imposed under subsection (h).

(k) Chapter IV or V. — A product for which the Secretary has issued an order pursuant to subsection (g) shall not be subject to chapter IV or V.

(l) Implementing Regulations or Guidance. —

(1) Scientific Evidence. — Not than 2 years after the date of enactment of the Family Smoking Prevention and Tobacco Control Act, the Secretary shall issue regulations or guidance (or any combination thereof) on the scientific evidence required for assessment and ongoing review of modified risk tobacco products. Such regulations or guidance shall —

(A) to the extent that adequate scientific evidence exists, establish minimum standards for scientific studies needed prior to issuing an order under subsection (g) to show that a substantial reduction in morbidity or mortality among individual tobacco users occurs for products described in subsection(g)(1) or is reasonably likely for products described in subsection (g)(2);

(B) include validated biomarkers, intermediate clinical endpoints, and other feasible outcome measures, as appropriate;

(C) establish minimum standards for postmarket studies, that shall include regular and long-term assessments of health outcomes and mortality, intermediate clinical endpoints, consumer perception of harm reduction, and the impact on quitting behavior and new use of tobacco products, as appropriate;

(D) establish minimum standards for required postmarket surveillance, including ongoing assessments of consumer perception;

(E) require that data from the required studies and surveillance be made available to the Secretary prior to the decision on renewal of a modified risk tobacco product; and

(F) establish a reasonable timetable for the Secretary to review an application under this section.

(2) Consultation. — The regulations or guidance issued under paragraph (1) shall be developed in consultation with the Institute of Medicine, and with the input of other appropriate scientific and medical experts, on the design and conduct of such studies and surveillance.

(3) Revision. — The regulations or guidance under paragraph (1) shall be revised on a regular basis as new scientific information becomes available.

(4) New Tobacco Products. — Not later than 2 years after the date of enactment of the Family Smoking Prevention and Tobacco Control Act, the Secretary shall issue a regulation or guidance that permits the filing of a single application for any tobacco product that is a new tobacco product under section 910 and which the applicant seeks to commercially market under this section.

(m) Distributors. — Except as provided in this section, no distributor may take any action, after the date of enactment of the Family Smoking Prevention and Tobacco Control Act, with respect to a tobacco product that would reasonably be expected to result in consumers believing that the tobacco product or its smoke may present a lower risk of disease or is less harmful than one or more commercially marketed tobacco products, or presents a reduced exposure to, or does not contain or is free of, a substance or substances.

Sec. 912. [387l] Judicial Review.

(a) Right to Review. —

(1) In General. — Not later than 30 days after —

(A) the promulgation of a regulation under section 907 establishing, amending, or revoking a tobacco product standard; or

(B) a denial of an application under section 910(c), any person adversely affected by such regulation or denial may file a petition for judicial review of such regulation or denial with the United States Court of Appeals for the District of Columbia or for the circuit in which such person resides or has their principal place of business.

(2) Requirements. —

(A) Copy of Petition. — A copy of the petition filed under paragraph (1) shall be transmitted by the clerk of the court involved to the Secretary.

(B) Record of Proceedings. — On receipt of a petition under subparagraph (A), the Secretary shall file in the court in which such petition was filed —

(i) the record of the proceedings on which the regulation or order was based; and

(ii) a statement of the reasons for the issuance of such a regulation or order.

(C) Definition of Record. — In this section, the term "record" means —

(i) all notices and other matter published in the Federal Register with respect to the regulation or order reviewed;

(ii) all information submitted to the Secretary with respect to such regulation or order;

(iii) proceedings of any panel or advisory committee with respect to such regulation or order;

(iv) any hearing held with respect to such regulation or order; and

(v) any other information identified by the Secretary, in the administrative proceeding held with respect to such regulation or order, as being relevant to such regulation or order.

(b) Standard of Review. — Upon the filing of the petition under subsection (a) for judicial review of a regulation or order, the court shall have jurisdiction to review the regulation or order in accordance with chapter 7 of title 5, United States Code, and to grant appropriate relief, including interim relief, as provided for in such chapter. A regulation or denial described in subsection (a) shall be reviewed in accordance with section 706(2)(A) of title 5, United States Code.

(c) Finality of Judgment. — The judgment of the court affirming or setting aside, in whole or in part, any regulation or order shall be final, subject to review by the Supreme Court of the United States upon certiorari or certification, as provided in section 1254 of title 28, United States Code.

(d) Other Remedies. — The remedies provided for in this section shall be in addition to, and not in lieu of, any other remedies provided by law.

(e) Regulations and Orders Must Recite Basis in Record. — To judicial review, a regulation or order issued under section 906, 907, 908, 909, 910, or 916 shall contain a statement of the reasons for the issuance of such regulation or order in the record of the proceedings held in connection with its issuance.

Sec. 913. [387m] Equal Treatment of Retail Outlets.

The Secretary shall issue regulations to require that retail establishments for which the predominant business is the sale of tobacco products comply with any advertising restrictions applicable to retail establishments accessible to individuals under the age of 18.

Sec. 914. [387n] Jurisdiction of and Coordination with the Federal Trade Commission.

(a) Jurisdiction. —

(1) In General. — Except where expressly provided in this chapter, nothing in this chapter shall be construed as limiting or diminishing the authority of the Federal Trade Commission to enforce the laws under its jurisdiction with respect to the advertising, sale, or distribution of tobacco products.

(2) Enforcement. — Any advertising that violates this chapter or a provision of the regulations referred to in section 102 of the Family Smoking Prevention and Tobacco Control Act, is an unfair or deceptive act or practice under section 5(a) of the Federal Trade Commission Act and shall be considered a violation of a rule promulgated under section 18 of that Act.

(b) Coordination. — With respect to the requirements of section 4 of the Federal Cigarette Labeling and Advertising Act and section 3 of the Comprehensive Smokeless Tobacco Health Education Act of 1986 —

(1) the Chairman of the Federal Trade Commission shall coordinate with the Secretary concerning the enforcement of such Act as such enforcement relates to unfair or deceptive acts or practices in the advertising of cigarettes or smokeless tobacco; and

(2) the Secretary shall consult with the Chairman of such Commission in revising the label statements and requirements under such sections.

Sec. 915. [387o] Regulation Requirement.

(a) Testing, Reporting, and Disclosure. — Not later than 36 months after the date of enactment of the Family Smoking Prevention and Tobacco Control Act, the Secretary shall promulgate regulations under this Act that meet the requirements of subsection (b).

(b) Contents of Rules. — The regulations promulgated under subsection (a) —

(1) shall require testing and reporting of tobacco product constituents, ingredients, and additives, including smoke constituents, by brand and subbrand that the Secretary determines should be tested to protect the public health, provided that, for purposes of the testing requirements of this paragraph, tobacco products manufactured and sold by a single tobacco product manufacturer that are identical in all respects except the labels, packaging design, logo, trade dress, trademark, brand name, or any combination thereof, shall be considered as a single brand; and

(2) may require that tobacco product manufacturers, packagers, or importers make disclosures relating to the results of the testing of tar and nicotine through labels or advertising or other appropriate means, and make disclosures regarding the results of the testing of other constituents, including smoke constituents, ingredients, or additives, that the Secretary determines should be disclosed to the public to protect the public health and will not mislead consumers about the risk of tobacco-related disease.

(c) Authority. — The Secretary shall have the authority under this chapter to conduct or to require the testing, reporting, or disclosure of tobacco product constituents, including smoke constituents.

(d) Small Tobacco Product Manufacturers. —

(1) First Compliance Date. — The initial regulations promulgated under subsection (a) shall not impose requirements on small tobacco product manufacturers before the later of —

(A) the end of the 2-year period following the final promulgation of such regulations; and

(B) the initial date set by the Secretary for compliance with such regulations by manufacturers that are not small tobacco product manufacturers.

(2) Testing and Reporting Initial Compliance Period. —

(A) 4-Year Period. — The initial regulations promulgated under subsection (a) shall give each small tobacco product manufacturer a 4-year period over which to conduct testing and reporting for all of its tobacco products. Subject to paragraph (1), the end of the first year of such 4-year period shall coincide with the initial date of compliance under this section set by the Secretary with respect to manufacturers that are not small tobacco product manufacturers or the end of the 2-year period following the final promulgation of such regulations, as described in paragraph (1)(A). A small tobacco product manufacturer shall be required —

(i) to conduct such testing and reporting for 25 percent of its tobacco products during each year of such 4-year period; and

(ii) to conduct such testing and reporting for its largest-selling tobacco products (as determined by the Secretary) before its other tobacco products, or in such other order of priority as determined by the Secretary.

(B) Case-By-Case Delay. — Notwithstanding subparagraph (A), the Secretary may, on a case-by-case basis, delay the date by which an individual small tobacco product manufacturer must conduct testing and reporting for its tobacco products under this section based upon a showing of undue hardship to such manufacturer. Notwithstanding the preceding sentence, the Secretary shall not extend the deadline for a small tobacco product manufacturer to conduct testing and reporting for all of its tobacco products beyond a total of 5 years after the initial date of compliance under this section set by the Secretary with respect to manufacturers that are not small tobacco product manufacturers.

(3) Subsequent and Additional Testing and Reporting. — The regulations promulgated under subsection (a) shall provide that, with respect to any subsequent or additional testing and reporting of tobacco products required under this section, such testing and reporting by a small tobacco product manufacturer shall be conducted in accordance with the timeframes described in paragraph (2)(A), except that, in the case of a new product, or if there has been a modification described in section 910(a)(1)(B) of any product of a small tobacco product manufacturer since the last testing and reporting required under this section, the Secretary shall require that any subsequent or additional testing and reporting be conducted in accordance with the same timeframe applicable to manufacturers that are not small tobacco product manufacturers.

(4) Joint Laboratory Testing Services. — The Secretary shall allow any 2 or more small tobacco product manufacturers to join together to purchase laboratory testing services required by this section on a group basis in order to ensure that such manufacturers receive access to, and fair pricing of, such testing services.

(e) Extensions for Limited Laboratory Capacity. —

(1) In General. — The regulations promulgated under subsection (a) shall provide that a small tobacco product manufacturer shall not be considered to be in violation of this section before the deadline applicable under paragraphs (3) and (4), if—

(A) the tobacco products of such manufacturer are in compliance with all other requirements of this chapter; and

(B) the conditions described in paragraph (2) are met.

(2) Conditions. — Notwithstanding the requirements of this section, the Secretary may delay the date by which a small tobacco product manufacturer must be in compliance with the testing and reporting required by this section until such time as the testing is reported if, not later than 90 days before the deadline for reporting in accordance with this section, a small tobacco product manufacturer provides evidence to the Secretary demonstrating that—

(A) the manufacturer has submitted the required products for testing to a laboratory and has done so sufficiently in advance of the deadline to create a reasonable expectation of completion by the deadline;

(B) the products currently are awaiting testing by the laboratory; and

(C) neither that laboratory nor any other laboratory is able to complete testing by the deadline at customary, nonexpedited testing fees.

(3) Extension. — The Secretary, taking into account the laboratory testing capacity that is available to tobacco product manufacturers, shall review and verify the evidence submitted by a small tobacco product manufacturer in accordance with paragraph (2). If the Secretary finds that the conditions described in such paragraph are met, the Secretary shall notify the small tobacco product manufacturer that the manufacturer shall not be considered to be in violation of the testing and reporting requirements of this section until the testing is reported or until 1 year after the reporting deadline has passed, whichever occurs sooner. If, however, the Secretary has not made a finding before the reporting deadline, the manufacturer shall not be considered to be in violation of such requirements until the Secretary finds that the conditions described in paragraph (2) have not been met, or until 1 year after the reporting deadline, whichever occurs sooner.

(4) Additional Extension. — In addition to the time that may be provided under paragraph (3), the Secretary may provide further extensions of time, in increments of no more than 1 year, for required testing and reporting to occur if the Secretary determines, based on evidence properly and timely submitted by a small tobacco product manufacturer in accordance with paragraph (2), that a lack of available laboratory capacity prevents the manufacturer from completing the required testing during the period described in paragraph (3).

(f) Rule of Construction. — Nothing in subsection (d) or (e) shall be construed to authorize the extension of any deadline, or to otherwise affect any timeframe, under any provision of this Act or the Family Smoking Prevention and Tobacco Control Act other than this section.

Sec. 916. [387p] Preservation of State and Local Authority.

(a) In General. —

(1) Preservation. — Except as provided in paragraph (2)(A), nothing in this chapter, or rules promulgated under this chapter, shall be construed to limit the authority of a Federal agency (including the Armed Forces), a State or political subdivision of a State, or the government of an Indian tribe to enact, adopt, promulgate, and enforce any law, rule, regulation, or other measure with respect to tobacco products that is in addition to, or more stringent than, requirements established under this chapter, including a law, rule, regulation, or other measure relating to or prohibiting the sale, distribution, possession, exposure to, access to, advertising and promotion of, or use of tobacco products by individuals of any age, information reporting to the State, or measures relating to fire safety standards for tobacco products. No provision of this chapter shall limit or otherwise affect any State, tribal, or local taxation of tobacco products.

(2) Preemption of Certain State and Local Requirements. —

(A) In General. — No State or political subdivision of a State may establish or continue in effect with respect to a tobacco product any requirement which is different from, or in addition to, any requirement under the provisions of this chapter relating to tobacco product standards, premarket review, adulteration, misbranding, labeling, registration, good manufacturing standards, or modified risk tobacco products.

(B) Exception. — Subparagraph (A) does not apply to requirements relating to the sale, distribution, possession, information reporting to the State, exposure to, access to, the advertising and promotion of, or use of, tobacco products by individuals of any age, or relating to fire safety standards for tobacco products. Information disclosed to a State under subparagraph (A) that is exempt from disclosure under section 552(b)(4) of title 5, United States Code, shall be treated as a trade secret and confidential information by the State.

(b) Rule of Construction Regarding Product Liability. — No provision of this chapter relating to a tobacco product shall be construed to modify or otherwise affect any action or the liability of any person under the product liability law of any State.

Sec. 917. [387q] Tobacco Products Scientific Advisory Committee.

(a) Establishment. — Not later than 6 months after the date of enactment of the Family Smoking Prevention and Tobacco Control Act, the Secretary shall establish a 12-member advisory committee, to be known as the Tobacco Products Scientific Advisory Committee (in this section referred to as the "Advisory Committee").

(b) Membership. —

(1) In General. —

(A) Members. — The Secretary shall appoint as members of the Tobacco Products Scientific Advisory Committee individuals who are technically qualified by training and experience in medicine, medical ethics, science, or technology involving the manufacture, evaluation, or use of tobacco products, who are of appropriately diversified professional backgrounds. The committee shall be composed of—

(i) 7 individuals who are physicians, dentists, scientists, or health care professionals practicing in the area of oncology, pulmonology, cardiology, toxicology, pharmacology, addiction, or any other relevant specialty;

(ii) 1 individual who is an officer or employee of a State or local government or of the Federal Government;

(iii) 1 individual as a representative of the general public;

(iv) 1 individual as a representative of the interests of the tobacco manufacturing industry;

(v) 1 individual as a representative of the interests of the small business tobacco manufacturing industry, which position may be filled on a rotating, sequential basis by representatives of different small business tobacco manufacturers based on areas of expertise relevant to the topics being considered by the Advisory Committee; and

(vi) 1 individual as a representative of the interests of the tobacco growers.

(B) Nonvoting Members. — The members of the committee appointed under clauses (iv), (v), and (vi) of subparagraph (A) shall serve as consultants to those described in clauses (i) through (iii) of subparagraph (A) and shall be nonvoting representatives.

(C) Conflicts of Interest. — No members of the committee, other than members appointed pursuant to clauses (iv), (v), and (vi) of subparagraph (A) shall, during the member's tenure on the committee or for the 18-month period prior to becoming such a member, receive any salary, grants, or other payments or support from any business that manufactures, distributes, markets, or sells cigarettes or other tobacco products.

(2) Limitation. — The Secretary may not appoint to the Advisory Committee any individual who is in the regular full-time employ of the Food and Drug Administration or any agency responsible for the enforcement of this Act. The Secretary may appoint Federal officials as ex officio members.

(3) Chairperson. — The Secretary shall designate 1 of the members appointed under clauses (i), (ii), and (iii) of paragraph (1)(A) to serve as chairperson.

(c) Duties. — The Tobacco Products Scientific Advisory Committee shall provide advice, information, and recommendations to the Secretary —

(1) as provided in this chapter;

(2) on the effects of the alteration of the nicotine yields from tobacco products;

(3) on whether there is a threshold level below which nicotine yields do not produce dependence on the tobacco product involved; and

(4) on its review of other safety, dependence, or health issues relating to tobacco products as requested by the Secretary.

(d) Compensation; Support; FACA. —

(1) Compensation and Travel. — Members of the Advisory Committee who are not officers or employees of the United States, while attending conferences or meetings of the committee or otherwise engaged in its business, shall be entitled to receive compensation at rates to be fixed by the Secretary, which may not exceed the daily equivalent of the rate in effect under the Senior Executive Schedule under section 5382 of title 5, United States Code, for each day (including traveltime) they are so engaged; and while so serving away from their homes or regular places of business each member may be allowed travel expenses, including per diem in lieu of subsistence, as authorized by section 5703 of title 5, United States Code, for persons in the Government service employed intermittently.

(2) Administrative Support. — The Secretary shall furnish the Advisory Committee clerical and other assistance.

(3) Nonapplication of FACA. — Section 14 of the Federal Advisory Committee Act does not apply to the Advisory Committee.

(e) Proceedings of Advisory Panels and Committees. — The Advisory Committee shall make and maintain a transcript of any proceeding of the panel or committee. Each such panel and committee shall delete from any transcript made under this subsection information which is exempt from disclosure under section 552(b) of title 5, United States Code.

Sec. 918. [387r] Drug Products Used to Treat Tobacco Dependence.

(a) In General. — The Secretary shall —

(1) at the request of the applicant, consider designating products for smoking cessation, including nicotine replacement products as fast track research and approval products within the meaning of section 506;

(2) consider approving the extended use of nicotine replacement products (such as nicotine patches, nicotine gum, and nicotine lozenges) for the treatment of tobacco dependence; and

(3) review and consider the evidence for additional indications for nicotine replacement products, such as for craving relief or relapse prevention.

(b) Report on Innovative Products. —

(1) In General. — Not later than 3 years after the date of enactment of the Family Smoking Prevention and Tobacco Control Act, the Secretary, after consultation with recognized scientific, medical, and public health experts (including both Federal agencies and nongovernmental entities, the Institute of Medicine of the National Academy of Sciences, and the Society for Research on Nicotine and Tobacco), shall submit to the Congress a report that examines how best to regulate, promote, and encourage the development of innovative products and treatments (including nicotine-based and non-nicotine-based products and treatments) to better achieve, in a manner that best protects and promotes the public health—

(A) total abstinence from tobacco use;

(B) reductions in consumption of tobacco; and

(C) reductions in the harm associated with continued tobacco use.

(2) Recommendations. — The report under paragraph (1) shall include the recommendations of the Secretary on how the Food and Drug Administration should coordinate and facilitate the exchange of information on such innovative products and treatments among relevant offices and centers within the Administration and within the National Institutes of Health, the Centers for Disease Control and Prevention, and other relevant agencies.

Sec. 919. [387s] User Fees.

(a) Establishment of Quarterly Fee. — Beginning on the date of enactment of the Family Smoking Prevention and Tobacco Control Act, the Secretary shall in accordance with this section assess user fees on, and collect such fees from, each manufacturer and importer of tobacco products subject to this chapter. The fees shall be assessed and collected with respect to each quarter of each fiscal year, and the total amount assessed and collected for a fiscal year shall be the amount specified in subsection (b)(1) for such year, subject to subsection (c).

(b) Assessment of User Fee. —

(1) Amount of Assessment. — The total amount of user fees authorized to be assessed and collected under subsection (a) for a fiscal year is the following, as applicable to the fiscal year involved:

(A) For fiscal year 2009, $85,000,000 (subject to subsection (e)).

(B) For fiscal year 2010, $235,000,000.

(C) For fiscal year 2011, $450,000,000.

(D) For fiscal year 2012, $477,000,000.

(E) For fiscal year 2013, $505,000,000.

(F) For fiscal year 2014, $534,000,000.

(G) For fiscal year 2015, $566,000,000.

(H) For fiscal year 2016, $599,000,000.

(I) For fiscal year 2017, $635,000,000.

(J) For fiscal year 2018, $672,000,000.

(K) For fiscal year 2019 and each subsequent fiscal year, $712,000,000.

(2) Allocations of Assessment by Class of Tobacco Products. —

(A) In General. — The total user fees assessed and collected under subsection (a) each fiscal year with respect to each class of tobacco products shall be an amount that is equal to the applicable percentage of each class for the fiscal year multiplied by the amount specified in paragraph (1) for the fiscal year.

(B) Applicable Percentage. —

(i) In General. — For purposes of subparagraph (A), the applicable percentage for a fiscal year for each of the following classes of tobacco products shall be determined in accordance with clause (ii):

(I) Cigarettes.

(II) Cigars, including small cigars and cigars other than small cigars.

(III) Snuff.

(IV) Chewing tobacco.

(V) Pipe tobacco.

(VI) Roll-your-own tobacco.

(ii) Allocations. — The applicable percentage of each class of tobacco product described in clause (i) for a fiscal year shall be the percentage determined under section 625(c) of Public Law 108-357 for each such class of product for such fiscal year.

(iii) Requirement of Regulations. — Notwithstanding clause (ii), no user fees shall be assessed on a class of tobacco products unless such class of tobacco products is listed in section 901(b) or is deemed by the Secretary in a regulation under section 901(b) to be subject to this chapter.

(iv) Reallocations. — In the case of a class of tobacco products that is not listed in section 901(b) or deemed by the Secretary in a regulation under section 901(b) to be subject to this chapter, the amount of user fees that would otherwise be assessed to such class of tobacco products shall be reallocated to the classes of tobacco products that are subject to this chapter in the same manner and based on the same relative percentages otherwise determined under clause (ii).

(3) Determination of User Fee by Company. —

(A) In General. — The total user fee to be paid by each manufacturer or importer of a particular class of tobacco products shall be determined for each quarter by multiplying—

(i) such manufacturer's or importer's percentage share as determined under paragraph (4); by

(ii) the portion of the user fee amount for the current quarter to be assessed on all manufacturers and importers of such class of tobacco products as determined under paragraph (2).

(B) No Fee in Excess of Percentage Share. — No manufacturer or importer of tobacco products shall be required to pay a user fee in excess of the percentage share of such manufacturer or importer.

(4) Allocation of Assessment within Each Class of Tobacco Product. — The percentage share of each manufacturer or importer of a particular class of tobacco products of the total user fee to be paid by all manufacturers or importers of that class of tobacco products shall be the percentage determined for purposes of allocations under subsections (e) through (h) of section 625 of Public Law 108-357.

(5) Allocation for Cigars. — Notwithstanding paragraph (4), if a user fee assessment is imposed on cigars, the percentage share of each manufacturer or importer of cigars shall be based on the excise taxes paid by such manufacturer or importer during the prior fiscal year.

(6) Timing of Assessment. — The Secretary shall notify each manufacturer and importer of tobacco products subject to this section of the amount of the quarterly assessment imposed on such manufacturer or importer under this subsection for each quarter of each fiscal year. Such notifications shall occur not later than 30 days prior to the end of the quarter for which such assessment is made, and payments of all assessments shall be made by the last day of the quarter involved.

(7) Memorandum of Understanding. —

(A) In General. — The Secretary shall request the appropriate Federal agency to enter into a memorandum of understanding that provides for the regular and timely transfer from the head of such agency to the Secretary of the information described in paragraphs (2)(B)(ii) and (4) and all necessary information regarding all tobacco product manufacturers and importers required to pay user fees. The Secretary shall maintain all disclosure restrictions established by the head of such agency regarding the information provided under the memorandum of understanding.

(B) Assurances. — Beginning not later than fiscal year 2015, and for each subsequent fiscal year, the Secretary shall ensure that the Food and Drug Administration is able to determine the applicable percentages described in paragraph (2) and the percentage shares described in paragraph (4). The Secretary may carry out this subparagraph by entering into a contract with the head of the Federal agency referred to in subparagraph

(A) to continue to provide the necessary information.

(c) Crediting and Availability of Fees. —

(1) In General. — Fees authorized under subsection (a) shall be collected and available for obligation only to the extent and in the amount provided in advance in appropriations Acts, subject to paragraph (2)(D). Such fees are authorized to remain available until expended. Such sums as may be necessary may be transferred from the Food and Drug Administration salaries and expenses appropriation account without fiscal year limitation to such appropriation account for salaries and expenses with such fiscal year limitation.

(2) Availability. —

(A) In General. — Fees appropriated under paragraph (3) are available only for the purpose of paying the costs of the activities of the Food and Drug Administration related to the regulation of tobacco products under this chapter and the Family Smoking Prevention and Tobacco Control Act (referred to in this subsection as "tobacco regulation activities"), except that such fees may be used for the reimbursement specified in subparagraph (C).

(B) Prohibition Against Use of Other Funds. —

(i) In General. — Except as provided in clause (ii), fees collected under subsection (a) are the only funds authorized to be made available for tobacco regulation activities.

(ii) Startup Costs. — Clause (i) does not apply until October 1, 2009. Until such date, any amounts available to the Food and Drug Administration (excluding user fees) shall be available and allocated as needed to pay the costs of tobacco regulation activities.

(C) Reimbursement of Start-up Amounts. —

(i) In General. — Any amounts allocated for the start-up period pursuant to subparagraph (B)(ii) shall be reimbursed through any appropriated fees collected under subsection (a), in such manner as the Secretary determines appropriate to ensure that such allocation results in no net change in the total amount of funds otherwise available, for the period from October 1, 2008, through September 30, 2010, for Food and Drug Administration programs and activities (other than tobacco regulation activities) for such period.

(ii) Treatment of Reimbursed Amounts. — Amounts reimbursed under clause (i) shall be available for the programs and activities for which funds allocated for the start-up period were available, prior to such allocation, until September 30, 2010, notwithstanding any otherwise applicable limits on amounts for such programs or activities for a fiscal year.

(D) Fee Collected During Start-up Period. — Notwithstanding the first sentence of paragraph (1), fees under subsection (a) may be collected through September 30, 2009 under subparagraph B)(ii) and shall be available for obligation and remain available until expended. Such offsetting collections shall be credited to the salaries and expenses account of the Food and Drug Administration.

(E) Obligation of Start-up Costs in Anticipation of Available Fee Collections. — Notwithstanding any other provision of law, following the enactment of an appropriation for fees under this section for fiscal year 2010, or any portion thereof, obligations for costs of tobacco regulation activities during the start-up period may be incurred in anticipation of the receipt of offsetting fee collections through procedures specified in section 1534 of title 31, United States Code.

(3) Authorization of Appropriations. — For fiscal year 2009 and each subsequent fiscal year, there is authorized to be appropriated for fees under this section an amount equal to the amount specified in subsection (b)(1) for the fiscal year.

(d) Collection of Unpaid Fees. — In any case where the Secretary does not receive payment of a fee assessed under subsection (a) within 30 days after it is due, such fee shall be treated as a claim of the United States Government subject to subchapter II of chapter 37 of title 31, United States Code.

(e) Applicability to Fiscal Year 2009. — If the date of enactment of the Family Smoking Prevention and Tobacco Control Act occurs during fiscal year 2009, the following applies, subject to subsection (c):

(1) The Secretary shall determine the fees that would apply for a single quarter of such fiscal year according to the application of subsection (b) to the amount specified in paragraph (1)(A) of such subsection (referred to in this subsection as the "quarterly fee amounts").

(2) For the quarter in which such date of enactment occurs, the amount of fees assessed shall be a pro rata amount, determined according to the number of days remaining in the quarter (including such date of enactment) and according to the daily equivalent of the quarterly fee amounts. Fees assessed under the preceding sentence shall not be collected until the next quarter.

(3) For the quarter following the quarter to which paragraph (2) applies, the full quarterly fee amounts shall be assessed and collected, in addition to collection of the pro rata fees assessed under paragraph (2).

Sec. 920. [387t] Labeling, Recordkeeping, Records Inspection.

(a) Origin Labeling. —

(1) Requirement. — Beginning 1 year after the date of enactment of the Family Smoking Prevention and Tobacco Control Act, the label, packaging, and shipping containers of tobacco products other than cigarettes for introduction or delivery for introduction into interstate commerce in the United States shall bear the statement 'sale only allowed in the United States'. Beginning 15 months after the issuance of the regulations required by section 4(d) of the Federal Cigarette Labeling and Advertising Act (15 U.S.C. 1333), as amended by section 201 of Family Smoking Prevention and Tobacco Control Act, the label, packaging, and shipping containers of cigarettes for introduction or delivery for introduction into interstate commerce in the United States shall bear the statement 'Sale only allowed in the United States'.

(2) Effective Date. — The effective date specified in paragraph (1) shall be with respect to the date of manufacture, provided that, in any case, beginning 30 days after such effective date, a manufacturer shall not introduce into the domestic commerce of the United States any product, irrespective of the date of manufacture, that is not in conformance with such paragraph.

(b) Regulations Concerning Recordkeeping for Tracking and Tracing. —

(1) In General. — The Secretary shall promulgate regulations regarding the establishment and maintenance of records by any person who manufactures, processes, transports, distributes, receives, packages, holds, exports, or imports tobacco products.

(2) Inspection. — In promulgating the regulations described in paragraph (1), the Secretary shall consider which records are needed for inspection to monitor the movement of tobacco products from the point of manufacture through distribution to retail outlets to assist in investigating potential illicit trade, smuggling, or counterfeiting of tobacco products.

(3) Codes. — The Secretary may require codes on the labels of tobacco products or other designs or devices for the purpose of tracking or tracing the tobacco product through the distribution system.

(4) Size of Business. — The Secretary shall take into account the size of a business in promulgating regulations under this section.

(5) Recordkeeping by Retailers. — The Secretary shall not require any retailer to maintain records relating to individual purchasers of tobacco products for personal consumption.

(c) Records Inspection. — If the Secretary has a reasonable belief that a tobacco product is part of an illicit trade or smuggling or is a counterfeit product, each person who manufactures, processes, transports, distributes, receives, holds, packages, exports, or imports tobacco products shall, at the request of an officer or employee duly designated by the Secretary, permit such officer or employee, at reasonable times and within reasonable limits and in a reasonable manner, upon the presentation of appropriate credentials and a written notice to such person, to have access to and copy all records (including financial records) relating to such article that are needed to assist the Secretary in investigating potential illicit trade, smuggling, or counterfeiting of tobacco products. The Secretary shall not authorize an officer or employee of the government of any of the several States to exercise authority under the preceding sentence on Indian country without the express written consent of the Indian tribe involved.

(d) Knowledge of Illegal Transaction. —

(1) Notification. — If the manufacturer or distributor of a tobacco product has knowledge which reasonably supports the conclusion that a tobacco product manufactured or distributed by such manufacturer or distributor that has left the control of such person may be or has been —

(A) imported, exported, distributed, or offered for sale in interstate commerce by a person without paying duties or taxes required by law; or

(B) imported, exported, distributed, or diverted for possible illicit marketing, the manufacturer or distributor shall promptly notify the Attorney General and the Secretary of the Treasury of such knowledge.

(2) Knowledge Defined. — For purposes of this subsection, the term "knowledge" as applied to a manufacturer or distributor means —

(A) the actual knowledge that the manufacturer or distributor had; or

(B) the knowledge which a reasonable person would have had under like circumstances or which would have been obtained upon the exercise of due care.

(e) Consultation. — In carrying out this section, the Secretary shall consult with the Attorney General of the United States and the Secretary of the Treasury, as appropriate.

Chapter X — Miscellaneous

Sec. 1001. [391] Separability Clause.

If any provision of this Act is declared unconstitutional, or the applicability thereof to any person or circumstances is held invalid, the constitutionality of the remainder of the Act and the applicability thereof to other persons and circumstances shall not be affected thereby.

Sec. 1002. [392] Exemption of Meats and Meat Food Products.

(a) Meats and meat food products shall be exempt from the provisions of this Act to the extent of the application or the extension thereto of the Meat Inspection Act, approved March 4, 1907, as amended (21 U.S.C. 601 et seq.).

(b) Nothing contained in this Act shall be construed as in any way affecting, modifying, repealing, or superseding the provisions of section 351 of Public Health Service Act (42 U.S.C. 262) (relating to viruses, serums, toxins, and analogous products applicable to man); the virus, serum, toxin, and analogous products provisions, applicable to domestic animals, of the Act of Congress approved March 4, 1913 (21 U.S.C. 151 et seq.); the Filled Cheese Act of June 6, 1896 (U.S.C., 1934 ed., title 26, ch. 10), the Filled Milk Act of March 4, 1923 (21 U.S.C. 61 et seq.); or the Import Milk Act of February 15, 1927 (21 U.S.C. 141 et seq.).

Sec. 1003. [393] Food and Drug Administration.

(a) In General. — There is established in the Department of Health and Human Services the Food and Drug Administration (hereinafter in this section referred to as the "Administration").

(b) Mission. — The Administration shall —

(1) promote the public health by promptly and efficiently reviewing clinical research and taking appropriate action on the marketing of regulated products in a timely manner;

(2) with respect to such products, protect the public health by ensuring that —

(A) foods are safe, wholesome, sanitary, and properly labeled;

(B) human and veterinary drugs are safe and effective;

(C) there is reasonable assurance of the safety and effectiveness of devices intended for human use;

(D) cosmetics are safe and properly labeled; and

(E) public health and safety are protected from electronic product radiation;

(3) participate through appropriate processes with representatives of other countries to reduce the burden of regulation, harmonize regulatory requirements, and achieve appropriate reciprocal arrangements; and

(4) as determined to be appropriate by the Secretary, carry out paragraphs (1) through (3) in consultation with experts in science, medicine, and public health, and in cooperation with consumers, users, manufacturers, importers, packers, distributors, and retailers of regulated products.

(c) Interagency Collaboration. — The Secretary shall implement programs and policies that will foster collaboration between the Administration, the National Institutes of Health, and other science-based Federal agencies, to enhance the scientific and technical expertise available to the Secretary in the conduct of the duties of the Secretary with respect to the development, clinical investigation, evaluation, and postmarket monitoring of emerging medical therapies, including complementary therapies, and advances in nutrition and food science.

(d) Commissioner. —

(1) Appointment. — There shall be in the Administration a Commissioner of Food and Drugs (hereinafter in this section referred to as the "Commissioner") who shall be appointed by the President by and with the advice and consent of the Senate.

(2) General Powers. — The Secretary, through the Commissioner, shall be responsible for executing this Act and for—

(A) providing overall direction to the Food and Drug Administration and establishing and implementing general policies respecting the management and operation of programs and activities of the Food and Drug Administration;

(B) coordinating and overseeing the operation of all administrative entities within the Administration;

(C) research relating to foods, drugs, cosmetics, devices, and tobacco products in carrying out this Act;

(D) conducting educational and public information programs relating to the responsibilities of the Food and Drug Administration; and

(E) performing such other functions as the Secretary may prescribe.

(e) Technical and Scientific Review Groups. — The Secretary through the Commissioner of Food and Drugs may, without regard to the provisions of title 5, United States Code, governing appointments in the competitive service and without regard to the provisions of chapter 51 and subchapter III of chapter 53 of such title relating to classification and General Schedule pay rates, establish such technical and scientific review groups as are needed to carry out the functions of the Administration, including functions under the Federal Food, Drug, and Cosmetic Act, and appoint and pay the members of such groups, except that officers and employees of the United States shall not receive additional compensation for service as members of such groups.

(f) Agency Plan for Statutory Compliance. —

(1) In General. — Not later than 1 year after the date of enactment of the Food and Drug Administration Modernization Act of 1997 [November 21, 1997 — Ed.] the Secretary, after consultation with appropriate scientific and academic experts, health care professionals, representatives of patient and consumer advocacy groups, and the regulated industry, shall develop and publish in the Federal Register a plan bringing the Secretary into compliance with each of the obligations of the Secretary under this Act. The Secretary shall revise the plan biannually and shall revise the plan as necessary, in consultation with such persons.

(2) Objectives of Agency Plan. — The plan required by paragraph (1) shall establish objectives and mechanisms to achieve such objectives, including objectives related to —

(A) maximizing the availability and clarity of information about the process for review of applications and submissions (including petitions, notifications, and any other similar forms of request) made under this Act;

(B) maximizing the availability and clarity of information for consumers and patients concerning new products;

(C) implementing inspection and postmarket monitoring provisions of this Act;

(D) ensuring access to the scientific and technical expertise needed by the Secretary to meet obligations described in paragraph (1);

(E) establishing mechanisms, by July 1, 1999, for meeting the time periods specified in this Act for the review of all applications and submissions described in subparagraph (A) and submitted after the date of enactment of the Food and Drug Administration Modernization Act of 1997 [November 21, 1997 — Ed.]; and

(F) eliminating backlogs in the review of applications and submissions described in subparagraph (A), by January 1, 2000.

(g) Annual Report. — The Secretary shall annually prepare and publish in the Federal Register and solicit public comment on a report that —

(1) provides detailed statistical information on the performance of the Secretary under the plan described in subsection (f);

(2) compares such performance of the Secretary with the objectives of the plan and with the statutory obligations of the Secretary; and

(3) identifies any regulatory policy that has a significant negative impact on compliance with any objective of the plan or any statutory obligation and sets forth any proposed revision to any such regulatory policy.

(h) Annual Report Regarding Food. — Not later than February 1 of each year, the Secretary shall submit to Congress a report, including efforts to coordinate and cooperate with other Federal agencies with responsibilities for food inspections, regarding —

(1) information about food facilities including —

(A) the appropriations used to inspect facilities registered pursuant to section 415 in the previous fiscal year;

(B) the average cost of both a non-high-risk food facility inspection and a high-risk food facility inspection, if such a difference exists, in the previous fiscal year;

(C) the number of domestic facilities and the number of foreign facilities registered pursuant to section 415 that the Secretary inspected in the previous fiscal year;

(D) the number of domestic facilities and the number of foreign facilities registered pursuant to section 415 that were scheduled for inspection in the previous fiscal year and which the Secretary did not inspect in such year;

(E) the number of high-risk facilities identified pursuant to section 421 that the Secretary inspected in the previous fiscal year; and

(F) the number of high-risk facilities identified pursuant to section 421 that were scheduled for inspection in the previous fiscal year and which the Secretary did not inspect in such year.

(2) information about food imports including —

(A) the number of lines of food imported into the United States that the Secretary physically inspected or sampled in the previous fiscal year;

(B) the number of lines of food imported into the United States that the Secretary did not physically inspect or sample in the previous fiscal year; and

(C) the average cost of physically inspecting or sampling a line of food subject to this Act that is imported or offered for import into the United States; and

(3) information on the foreign offices of the Food and Drug Administration including —

(A) the number of foreign offices established; and

(B) the number of personnel permanently stationed in each foreign office.

(i) Public Availability of Annual Food Reports. — The Secretary shall make the reports required under subsection (h) available to the public on the Internet Web site of the Food and Drug Administration.

Sec. 1003a. [393a] Office of Pediatric Therapeutics.

(a) The Secretary of Health and Human Services shall establish an Office of Pediatric Therapeutics within the Food and Drug Administration.

(b) The Office of Pediatric Therapeutics shall be responsible for coordination and facilitation of all activities of the Food and Drug Administration that may have any effect on a pediatric population or the practice of pediatrics or may in any other way involve pediatric issues, including increasing pediatric access to medical devices.

(c) The staff of the Office of Pediatric Therapeutics shall coordinate with employees of the Department of Health and Human Services who exercise responsibilities relating to pediatric therapeutics and shall include —

(1) one or more additional individuals with expertise concerning ethical issues presented by the conduct of clinical research in the pediatric population;

(2) subject to subsection (d), one or more additional individuals with necessary expertise in a pediatric subpopulation that is, as determined through consideration of the reports and recommendations by the Institute of Medicine and the Comptroller General of the United States, less likely to be studied as a part of a written request issued under section 505A of the Federal Food, Drug, and Cosmetic Act or an assessment under section 505B of such Act;

(3) one or more additional individuals with expertise in pediatric epidemiology; and

(4) one or more additional individuals with expertise in pediatrics as may be necessary to perform the activities described in subsection (b).

(d) Neonatology Expertise — ~~For the 5-year period beginning on the date of enactment of this subsection, at~~ At least one of the individuals described in subsection (c)(2) shall have expertise in neonatology.

Sec. 1004. [394] Scientific Review Groups.

Without regard to the provisions of title 5, United States Code, governing appointments in the competitive service and without regard to the provisions of chapter 51 and subchapter III of chapter 53 of such title relating to classification and General Schedule pay rates, the Commissioner of Food and Drugs may —

(1) establish such technical and scientific review groups as are needed to carry out the functions of the Food and Drug Administration (including functions prescribed under this Act); and

(2) appoint and pay the members of such groups, except that officers and employees of the United States shall not receive additional compensation for service as members of such groups.

Sec. 1005. [395] Loan Repayment Program.

(a) In General. —

(1) Authority for Program. — Subject to paragraph (2), the Secretary shall carry out a program of entering into contracts with appropriately qualified health professionals under which such health professionals agree to conduct research, as employees of the Food and Drug Administration, in consideration of the Federal Government agreeing to repay, for each year of such service, not more than $20,000 of the principal and interest of the educational loans of such health professionals.

(2) Limitation. — The Secretary may not enter into an agreement with a health professional pursuant to paragraph (1) unless such professional —

(A) has a substantial amount of educational loans relative to income; and

(B) agrees to serve as an employee of the Food and Drug Administration for purposes of paragraph (1) for a period of not less than 3 years.

(b) Applicability of Certain Provisions. — With respect to the National Health Service Corps Loan Repayment Program established in subpart III of part D of title III of the Public Health Service Act, the provisions of such subpart shall, except as inconsistent with subsection (a) of this section, apply to the program established in such subsection in the same manner and to the same extent as such provisions apply to the National Health Service Corps Loan Repayment Program.

(c) Authorization of Appropriations. — For the purpose of carrying out this section, there are authorized to be appropriated such sums as may be necessary for each of the fiscal years 1994 through 1996.

Sec. 1006. [396] Practice of Medicine.

Nothing in this Act shall be construed to limit or interfere with the authority of a health care practitioner to prescribe or administer any legally marketed device to a patient for any condition or disease within a legitimate health care practitioner-patient relationship. This section shall not limit any existing authority of the Secretary to establish and enforce restrictions on the sale or distribution, or in the labeling, of a device that are part of a determination of substantial equivalence, established as a condition of approval, or promulgated through regulations. Further, this section shall not change any existing prohibition on the promotion of unapproved uses of legally marketed devices.

Sec. 1007. [397] Contracts for Expert Review.

(a) In General. —

(1) Authority. — The Secretary may enter into a contract with any organization or any individual (who is not an employee of the Department) with relevant expertise, to review and evaluate, for the purpose of making recommendations to the Secretary on, part or all of any application or submission (including a petition, notification, and any other similar form of request) made under this Act for the approval or classification of an article or made under section 351(a) of the Public Health Service Act (42 U.S.C. 262(a)) with respect to a biological product. Any such contract shall be subject to the requirements of section 708 relating to the confidentiality of information.

(2) Increased Efficiency and Expertise Through Contracts. — The Secretary may use the authority granted in paragraph (1) whenever the Secretary determines that use of a contract described in paragraph (1) will improve the timeliness of the review of an application or submission described in paragraph (1), unless using such authority would reduce the quality, or unduly increase the cost, of such review. The Secretary may use such authority whenever the Secretary determines that the use of such a contract will improve the quality of the review of an application or submission described in paragraph (1), unless using such authority would unduly increase the cost of such review. Such improvement in timeliness or quality may include providing the Secretary increased scientific or technical expertise that is necessary to review or evaluate new therapies and technologies.

(b) Review of Expert Review. —

(1) In General. — Subject to paragraph (2), the official of the Food and Drug Administration responsible for any matter for which expert review is used pursuant to subsection (a) shall review the recommendations of the organization or individual who conducted the expert review and shall make a final decision regarding the matter in a timely manner.

(2) Limitation. — A final decision by the Secretary on any such application or submission shall be made within the applicable prescribed time period for review of the matter as set forth in this Act or in the Public Health Service Act (42 U.S.C. 201 et seq.).

Sec. 1008. [398] Notices to States Regarding Imported Food.

(a) In General. — If the Secretary has credible evidence or information indicating that a shipment of imported food or portion thereof presents a threat of serious adverse health consequences or death to humans or animals, the Secretary shall provide notice regarding such threat to the States in which the food is held or will be held, and to the States in which the manufacturer, packer, or distributor of the food is located, to the extent that the Secretary has knowledge of which States are so involved. In providing notice to a State, the Secretary shall request the State to take such action as the State considers appropriate, if any, to protect the public health regarding the food involved.

(b) Rule of Construction. — Subsection (a) may not be construed as limiting the authority of the Secretary with respect to food under any other provision of this Act.

Sec. 1009. [399] Grants to Enhance Food Safety.

(a) In General. — The Secretary is authorized to make grants to eligible entities to —

(1) undertake examinations, inspections, and investigations, and related food safety activities under section 702;

(2) train to the standards of the Secretary for the examination, inspection, and investigation of food manufacturing, processing, packing, holding, distribution, and importation, including as such examination, inspection, and investigation relate to retail food establishments;

(3) build the food safety capacity of the laboratories of such eligible entity, including the detection of zoonotic diseases;

(4) build the infrastructure and capacity of the food safety programs of such eligible entity to meet the standards as outlined in the grant application; and

(5) take appropriate action to protect the public health in response to —

(A) a notification under section 1008, including planning and otherwise preparing to take such action; or

(B) a recall of food under this Act.

(b) Eligible Entities; Application. —

(1) In General. — In this section, the term "eligible entity" means an entity —

(A) that is —

(i) a State;

(ii) a locality;

(iii) a territory;

(iv) an Indian tribe (as defined in section 4(e) of the Indian Self-Determination and Education Assistance Act); or

(v) a nonprofit food safety training entity that collaborates with 1 or more institutions of higher education; and

(B) that submits an application to the Secretary at such time, in such manner, and including such information as the Secretary may reasonably require.

(2) Contents. — Each application submitted under paragraph (1) shall include —

(A) an assurance that the eligible entity has developed plans to engage in the types of activities described in subsection (a);

(B) a description of the types of activities to be funded by the grant;

(C) an itemization of how grant funds received under this section will be expended;

(D) a description of how grant activities will be monitored; and

(E) an agreement by the eligible entity to report information required by the Secretary to conduct evaluations under this section.

(c) Limitations. — The funds provided under subsection (a) shall be available to an eligible entity that receives a grant under this section only to the extent such entity funds the food safety programs of such entity independently of any grant under this section in each year of the grant at a level equal to the level of such funding in the previous year, increased by the Consumer Price Index. Such non-Federal matching funds may be provided directly or through donations from public or private entities and may be in cash or in-kind, fairly evaluated, including plant, equipment, or services.

(d) Additional Authority. — The Secretary may —

(1) award a grant under this section in each subsequent fiscal year without reapplication for a period of not more than 3 years, provided the requirements of subsection (c) are met for the previous fiscal year; and

(2) award a grant under this section in a fiscal year for which the requirement of subsection (c) has not been met only if such requirement was not met because such funding was diverted for response to 1 or more natural disasters or in other extenuating circumstances that the Secretary may determine appropriate.

(e) Duration of Awards. — The Secretary may award grants to an individual grant recipient under this section for periods of not more than 3 years. In the event the Secretary conducts a program evaluation, funding in the second year or third year of the grant, where applicable, shall be contingent on a successful program evaluation by the Secretary after the first year.

(f) Progress and Evaluation. —

(1) In General. — The Secretary shall measure the status and success of each grant program authorized under the FDA Food Safety Modernization Act (and any amendment made by such Act), including the grant program under this section. A recipient of a grant described in the preceding sentence shall, at the end of each grant year, provide the Secretary with information on how grant funds were spent and the status of the efforts by such recipient to enhance food safety. To the extent practicable, the Secretary shall take the performance of such a grant recipient into account when determining whether to continue funding for such recipient.

(2) No Duplication. — In carrying out paragraph (1), the Secretary shall not duplicate the efforts of the Secretary under other provisions of this Act or the FDA Food Safety Modernization Act that require measurement and review of the activities of grant recipients under either such Act.

(g) Supplement Not Supplant — Grant funds received under this section shall be used to supplement, and not supplant, non-Federal funds and any other Federal funds available to carry out the activities described in this section.

(h) Authorization of Appropriations. — For the purpose of making grants under this section, there are authorized to be appropriated such sums as may be necessary for fiscal years 2011 through 2015.

Sec. 1010. [399a] Office of the Chief Scientist.

(a) Establishment; Appointment. — The Secretary shall establish within the Office of the Commissioner an office to be known as the Office of the Chief Scientist. The Secretary shall appoint a Chief Scientist to lead such Office.

(b) Duties of the Office. — The Office of the Chief Scientist shall —

(1) oversee, coordinate, and ensure quality and regulatory focus of the intramural research programs of the Food and Drug Administration;

(2) track and, to the extent necessary, coordinate intramural research awards made by each center of the Administration or science-based office within the Office of the Commissioner, and ensure that there is no duplication of research efforts supported by the Reagan-Udall Foundation for the Food and Drug Administration;

(3) develop and advocate for a budget to support intramural research;

(4) develop a peer review process by which intramural research can be evaluated;

(5) identify and solicit intramural research proposals from across the Food and Drug Administration through an advisory board composed of employees of the Administration that shall include —

(A) representatives of each of the centers and the science-based offices within the Office of the Commissioner; and

(B) experts on trial design, epidemiology, demographics, pharmacovigilance, basic science, and public health; and

(6) develop postmarket safety performance measures that are as measurable and rigorous as the ones already developed for premarket review.

SEC. 1011. [399b] OFFICE OF WOMEN'S HEALTH.*

(a) ESTABLISHMENT. — There is established within the Office of the Commissioner, an office to be known as the Office of Women's Health (referred to in this section as the "Office"). The Office shall be headed by a director who shall be appointed by the Commissioner of Food and Drugs.

(b) PURPOSE. — The Director of the Office shall —

(1) report to the Commissioner of Food and Drugs on current Food and Drug Administration (referred to in this section as the "Administration") levels of activity regarding women's participation in clinical trials and the analysis of data by sex in the testing of drugs, medical devices, and biological products across, where appropriate, age, biological, and sociocultural contexts;

(2) establish short-range and long-range goals and objectives within the Administration for issues of particular concern to women's health within the jurisdiction of the Administration, including, where relevant and appropriate, adequate inclusion of women and analysis of data by sex in Administration protocols and policies;

(3) provide information to women and health care providers on those areas in which differences between men and women exist;

(4) consult with pharmaceutical, biologics, and device manufacturers, health professionals with expertise in women's issues, consumer organizations, and women's health professionals on Administration policy with regard to women;

(5) make annual estimates of funds needed to monitor clinical trials and analysis of data by sex in accordance with needs that are identified; and

(6) serve as a member of the Department of Health and Human Services Coordinating Committee on Women's Health (established under section 229(b)(4) of the Public Health Service Act).

(c) AUTHORIZATION OF APPROPRIATIONS. — For the purpose of carrying out this section, there are authorized to be appropriated such sums as may be necessary for each of the fiscal years 2010 through 2014.

SEC. 1012. [399c] IMPROVING THE TRAINING OF STATE, LOCAL, TERRITORIAL, AND TRIBAL FOOD SAFETY OFFICIALS.**

(a) TRAINING. — The Secretary shall set standards and administer training and education programs for the employees of State, local, territorial, and tribal food safety officials relating to the regulatory responsibilities and policies established by this Act, including programs for —

(1) scientific training;

(2) training to improve the skill of officers and employees authorized to conduct inspections under sections 702 and 704;

(3) training to achieve advanced product or process specialization in such inspections;

(4) training that addresses best practices;

(5) training in administrative process and procedure and integrity issues;

(6) training in appropriate sampling and laboratory analysis methodology; and

(7) training in building enforcement actions following inspections, examinations, testing, and investigations.

(b) PARTNERSHIPS WITH STATE AND LOCAL OFFICIALS. —

(1) IN GENERAL. — The Secretary, pursuant to a contract or memorandum of understanding between the Secretary and the head of a State, local, territorial, or tribal department or agency, is authorized and encouraged to conduct examinations, testing, and investigations for the purposes of determining compliance with the food safety provisions of this Act through the officers and employees of such State, local, territorial, or tribal department or agency.

(2) CONTENT. — A contract or memorandum described under paragraph (1) shall include provisions to ensure adequate training of such officers and employees to conduct such examinations, testing, and investigations. The contract or memorandum shall contain provisions regarding reimbursement. Such provisions may, at the sole discretion of the head of the other department or agency, require reimbursement, in whole or in part, from the Secretary for the examinations, testing, or investigations performed pursuant to this section by the officers or employees of the State, territorial, or tribal department or agency.

* This Section 1011 was enacted by Pub. L. No. 111-148, Title III, § 3509, Mar. 23, 2010, 124 Stat. 536.

** This Section 1011 was enacted by Pub. L. 111-353, Title II, § 209(a), Jan. 4, 2011, 124 Stat. 3945.

(3) Effect. — Nothing in this subsection shall be construed to limit the authority of the Secretary under section 702.

(c) Extension Service. — The Secretary shall ensure coordination with the extension activities of the National Institute of Food and Agriculture of the Department of Agriculture in advising producers and small processors transitioning into new practices required as a result of the enactment of the FDA Food Safety Modernization Act and assisting regulated industry with compliance with such Act.

(d) National Food Safety Training, Education, Extension, Outreach and Technical Assistance Program. —

(1) In General. — In order to improve food safety and reduce the incidence of foodborne illness, the Secretary shall, not later than 180 days after the date of enactment of the FDA Food Safety Modernization Act, enter into one or more memoranda of understanding, or enter into other cooperative agreements, with the Secretary of Agriculture to establish a competitive grant program within the National Institute for Food and Agriculture to provide food safety training, education, extension, outreach, and technical assistance to —

(A) owners and operators of farms;

(B) small food processors; and

(C) small fruit and vegetable merchant wholesalers.

(2) Implementation. — The competitive grant program established under paragraph (1) shall be carried out in accordance with section 405 of the Agricultural Research, Extension, and Education Reform Act of 1998.

(e) Authorization of Appropriations. — There are authorized to be appropriated such sums as may be necessary to carry out this section for fiscal years 2011 through 2015.

Sec. 1013. [399d] Employee Protections.

(a) In General. — No entity engaged in the manufacture, processing, packing, transporting, distribution, reception, holding, or importation of food may discharge an employee or otherwise discriminate against an employee with respect to compensation, terms, conditions, or privileges of employment because the employee, whether at the employee's initiative or in the ordinary course of the employee's duties (or any person acting pursuant to a request of the employee) —

(1) provided, caused to be provided, or is about to provide or cause to be provided to the employer, the Federal Government, or the attorney general of a State information relating to any violation of, or any act or omission the employee reasonably believes to be a violation of any provision of this Act or any order, rule, regulation, standard, or ban under this Act, or any order, rule, regulation, standard, or ban under this Act;

(2) testified or is about to testify in a proceeding concerning such violation;

(3) assisted or participated or is about to assist or participate in such a proceeding; or

(4) objected to, or refused to participate in, any activity, policy, practice, or assigned task that the employee (or other such person) reasonably believed to be in violation of any provision of this Act, or any order, rule, regulation, standard, or ban under this Act.

(b) Process. —

(1) In General. — A person who believes that he or she has been discharged or otherwise discriminated against by any person in violation of subsection (a) may, not later than 180 days after the date on which such violation occurs, file (or have any person file on his or her behalf) a complaint with the Secretary of Labor (referred to in this section as the "Secretary") alleging such discharge or discrimination and identifying the person responsible for such act. Upon receipt of such a complaint, the Secretary shall notify, in writing, the person named in the complaint of the filing of the complaint, of the allegations contained in the complaint, of the substance of evidence supporting the complaint, and of the opportunities that will be afforded to such person under paragraph (2).

(2) Investigation. —

(A) In General. — Not later than 60 days after the date of receipt of a complaint filed under paragraph (1) and after affording the complainant and the person named in the complaint an opportunity to submit to the Secretary a written response to the complaint and an opportunity to meet with a representative of the Secretary to present statements from witnesses, the Secretary shall initiate an investigation and determine whether there is reasonable cause to believe that the complaint has merit and notify, in writing, the complainant and the person alleged to have committed a violation of subsection (a) of the Secretary's findings.

(B) Reasonable Cause Found; Preliminary Order. — If the Secretary concludes that there is reasonable cause to believe that a violation of subsection (a) has occurred, the Secretary shall accompany the Secretary's findings with a preliminary order providing the relief prescribed by paragraph (3)(B). Not later than 30 days after the date of notification of findings under this paragraph, the person alleged to have committed the violation or the complainant may file objections to the findings or preliminary order, or both, and request a hearing on the record. The filing of such objections shall not operate to stay any reinstatement remedy contained in the preliminary order. Any such hearing shall be conducted expeditiously. If a hearing is not requested in such 30-day period, the preliminary order shall be deemed a final order that is not subject to judicial review.

(C) Dismissal of Complaint. —

(i) Standard for Complainant. — The Secretary shall dismiss a complaint filed under this subsection and shall not conduct an investigation otherwise required under subparagraph (A) unless the complainant makes a prima facie showing that any behavior described in paragraphs (1) through (4) of subsection (a) was a contributing factor in the unfavorable personnel action alleged in the complaint.

(ii) Standard for Employer. — Notwithstanding a finding by the Secretary that the complainant has made the showing required under clause (i), no investigation otherwise required under subparagraph (A) shall be conducted if the employer demonstrates, by clear and convincing evidence, that the employer would have taken the same unfavorable personnel action in the absence of that behavior.

(iii) Violation Standard. — The Secretary may determine that a violation of subsection (a) has occurred only if the complainant demonstrates that any behavior described in paragraphs (1) through (4) of subsection (a) was a contributing factor in the unfavorable personnel action alleged in the complaint.

(iv) Relief Standard. — Relief may not be ordered under subparagraph (A) if the employer demonstrates by clear and convincing evidence that the employer would have taken the same unfavorable personnel action in the absence of that behavior.

(3) Final Order. —

(A) In General. — Not later than 120 days after the date of conclusion of any hearing under paragraph (2), the Secretary shall issue a final order providing the relief prescribed by this paragraph or denying the complaint. At any time before issuance of a final order, a proceeding under this subsection may be terminated on the basis of a settlement agreement entered into by the Secretary, the complainant, and the person alleged to have committed the violation.

(B) Content of Order. — If, in response to a complaint filed under paragraph (1), the Secretary determines that a violation of subsection (a) has occurred, the Secretary shall order the person who committed such violation —

(i) to take affirmative action to abate the violation;

(ii) to reinstate the complainant to his or her former position together with compensation (including back pay) and restore the terms, conditions, and privileges associated with his or her employment; and

(iii) to provide compensatory damages to the complainant.

(C) Penalty. — If such an order is issued under this paragraph, the Secretary, at the request of the complainant, shall assess against the person against whom the order is issued a sum equal to the aggregate amount of all costs and expenses (including attorneys' and expert witness fees) reasonably incurred, as determined by the Secretary, by the complainant for, or in connection with, the bringing of the complaint upon which the order was issued.

(D) Bad Faith Claim. — If the Secretary finds that a complaint under paragraph (1) is frivolous or has been brought in bad faith, the Secretary may award to the prevailing employer a reasonable attorneys' fee, not exceeding $1,000, to be paid by the complainant.

(4) Action in Court. —

(A) In General. — If the Secretary has not issued a final decision within 210 days after the filing of the complaint, or within 90 days after receiving a written determination, the complainant may bring an action at law or equity for de novo review in the appropriate district court of the United States with jurisdiction, which shall have jurisdiction over such an action without regard to the amount in controversy, and which action shall, at the request of either party to such action, be tried by the court with a jury. The proceedings shall be governed by the same legal burdens of proof specified in paragraph (2)(C).

(B) Relief. — The court shall have jurisdiction to grant all relief necessary to make the employee whole, including injunctive relief and compensatory damages, including —

(i) reinstatement with the same seniority status that the employee would have had, but for the discharge or discrimination;

(ii) the amount of back pay, with interest; and

(iii) compensation for any special damages sustained as a result of the discharge or discrimination, including litigation costs, expert witness fees, and reasonable attorney's fees.

(5) Review. —

(A) In General. — Unless the complainant brings an action under paragraph (4), any person adversely affected or aggrieved by a final order issued under paragraph (3) may obtain review of the order in the United States Court of Appeals for the circuit in which the violation, with respect to which the order was issued, allegedly occurred or the circuit in which the complainant resided on the date of such violation. The petition for review must be filed not later than 60 days after the date of the issuance of the final order of the Secretary. Review shall conform to chapter 7 of title 5, United States Code. The commencement of proceedings under this subparagraph shall not, unless ordered by the court, operate as a stay of the order.

(B) No Judicial Review. — An order of the Secretary with respect to which review could have been obtained under subparagraph (A) shall not be subject to judicial review in any criminal or other civil proceeding.

(6) Failure to Comply with Order. — Whenever any person has failed to comply with an order issued under paragraph (3), the Secretary may file a civil action in the United States district court for the district in which the violation was found to occur, or in the United States district court for the District of Columbia, to enforce such order. In actions brought under this paragraph, the district courts shall have jurisdiction to grant all appropriate relief including, but not limited to, injunctive relief and compensatory damages.

(7) Civil Action to Require Compliance. —

(A) In General. — A person on whose behalf an order was issued under paragraph (3) may commence a civil action against the person to whom such order was issued to require compliance with such order. The appropriate United States district court shall have jurisdiction, without regard to the amount in controversy or the citizenship of the parties, to enforce such order.

(B) Award. — The court, in issuing any final order under this paragraph, may award costs of litigation (including reasonable attorneys' and expert witness fees) to any party whenever the court determines such award is appropriate.

(c) Effect of Section. —

(1) Other Laws. — Nothing in this section preempts or diminishes any other safeguards against discrimination, demotion, discharge, suspension, threats, harassment, reprimand, retaliation, or any other manner of discrimination provided by Federal or State law.

(2) Rights of Employees. — Nothing in this section shall be construed to diminish the rights, privileges, or remedies of any employee under any Federal or State law or under any collective bargaining agreement. The rights and remedies in this section may not be waived by any agreement, policy, form, or condition of employment.

(d) Enforcement. — Any nondiscretionary duty imposed by this section shall be enforceable in a mandamus proceeding brought under section 1361 of title 28, United States Code.

(e) Limitation. — Subsection (a) shall not apply with respect to an employee of an entity engaged in the manufacture, processing, packing, transporting, distribution, reception, holding, or importation of food who, acting without direction from such entity (or such entity's agent), deliberately causes a violation of any requirement relating to any violation or alleged violation of any order, rule, regulation, standard, or ban under this Act.

Sec. 1014. [399g] Food and Drug Administration Intercenter Institutes.

(a) In General.—The Secretary shall establish one or more Intercenter Institutes within the Food and Drug Administration (referred to in this section as an "Institute") or a major disease area or areas. With respect to the major disease area of focus of an Institute, such Institute shall develop and implement processes for coordination of activities, as applicable to such major disease area or areas, among the Center for Drug Evaluation and Re-search, the Center for Biologics Evaluation and Research, and the Center for Devices and Radiological Health (for the purposes of this section, referred to as the "Centers"). Such activities may include—

(1) coordination of staff from the Centers with diverse product expertise in the diagnosis, cure, mitigation, treatment, or prevention of the specific diseases relevant to the major disease area of focus of the Institute;

(2) streamlining, where appropriate, the review of medical products to diagnose, cure, mitigate, treat, or prevent the specific diseases relevant to the major disease area of focus of the Institute, applying relevant standards under sections 505, 510(k), 513(f)(2), and 515 of this Act and section 351 of the Public Health Service Act, and other applicable authorities;

(3) promotion of scientific programs within the Centers related to the major disease area of focus of the Institute;

(4) development of programs and enhancement of strategies to recruit, train, and provide continuing education opportunities for the personnel of the Centers with expertise related to the major disease area of focus of the Institute;

(5) enhancement of the interactions of the Centers with patients, sponsors, and the external biomedical community regarding the major disease area of focus of the Institute; and

(6) facilitation of the collaborative relationships of the Centers with other agencies within the Department of Health and Human Services regarding the major disease area of focus of the Institute.

(b) Public Process.—The Secretary shall provide a period for public comment during the time that each Institute is being implemented.

(c) Timing.—The Secretary shall establish at least one Institute under subsection (a) before the date that is 1 year after the date of enactment of the 21st Century Cures Act [December 13, 2016 —Ed.].

(d) Termination of Institutes.—The Secretary may terminate any Institute established pursuant to this section if the Secretary determines such Institute is no longer benefitting the public health. Not less than 60 days prior to so terminating an Institute, the Secretary shall provide public notice, including the rationale for such termination.

APPENDIX: SELECTED SECTIONS OF OTHER ACTS AND STATUTES

PUBLIC HEALTH SERVICE ACT

42 U.S.C. §§ 262, 264, 266, 282, 284, 289a-2, 289g-5

42 U.S.C. § 262. Regulation of Biological Products.

(a) Biologics License. —

(1) No person shall introduce or deliver for introduction into interstate commerce any biological product unless —

(A) a biologics license under this subsection or subsection (k) is in effect for the biological product; and

(B) each package of the biological product is plainly marked with —

(i) the proper name of the biological product contained in the package;

(ii) the name, address, and applicable license number of the manufacturer of the biological product; and

(iii) the expiration date of the biological product.

(2) —

(A) The Secretary shall establish, by regulation, requirements for the approval, suspension, and revocation of biologics licenses.

(B) Pediatric Studies. — A person that submits an application for a license under this paragraph shall submit to the Secretary as part of the application any assessments required under section 505B of the Federal Food, Drug, and Cosmetic Act.

(C) The Secretary shall approve a biologics license application —

(i) on the basis of a demonstration that —

(I) the biological product that is the subject of the application is safe, pure, and potent; and

(II) the facility in which the biological product is manufactured, processed, packed, or held meets standards designed to assure that the biological product continues to be safe, pure, and potent; and

(ii) if the applicant (or other appropriate person) consents to the inspection of the facility that is the subject of the application, in accordance with subsection (c) of this section.

(D) Postmarket Studies and Clinical Trials; Labeling; Risk Evaluation and Mitigation. A person that submits an application for a license under this paragraph is subject to Sections 505(o), 505(p), and 505-1 of the Federal Food, Drug, and Cosmetic Act.

(E) -

(i) The Secretary may rely upon qualified data summaries to support the approval of a supplemental application, with respect to a qualified indication for a drug, submitted under this subsection, if such supplemental application complies with the requirements of subparagraph (B) of section 505(c)(5) of the Federal Food, Drug, and Cosmetic Act.

(ii) In this subparagraph, the terms 'qualified indication' and 'qualified data summary' have the meanings given such terms in section 505(c)(5) of the Federal Food, Drug, and Cosmetic Act.

(3) The Secretary shall prescribe requirements under which a biological product undergoing investigation shall be exempt from the requirements of paragraph (1).

(b) Falsely Labeling or Marking Package or Container; Altering Label or Mark. — No person shall falsely label or mark any package or container of any biological product or alter any label or mark on the package or container of the biological product so as to falsify the label or mark.

(c) Inspection of Establishment for Propagation and Preparation. — Any officer, agent, or employee of the Department of Health and Human Services, authorized by the Secretary for the purpose, may during all reasonable hours enter and inspect any establishment for the propagation or manufacture and preparation of any biological product.

(d) Recall of Product Presenting Imminent Hazard; Violations. —

(1) Upon a determination that a batch, lot, or other quantity of a product licensed under this section presents an imminent or substantial hazard to the public health, the Secretary shall issue an order immediately ordering the recall of such batch, lot, or other quantity of such product. An order under this paragraph shall be issued in accordance with section 554 of Title 5.

(2) Any violation of paragraph (1) shall subject the violator to a civil penalty of up to $100,000 per day of violation. The amount of a civil penalty under this paragraph shall, effective December 1 of each year beginning 1 year after the effective date of this paragraph, be increased by the percent change in the Consumer Price Index for the base quarter of such year over the Consumer Price Index for the base quarter of the preceding year, adjusted to the nearest 1/10 of 1 percent. For purposes of this paragraph, the term "base quarter", as used with respect to a year, means the calendar quarter ending on September 30 of such year and the price index for a base quarter is the arithmetical mean of such index for the 3 months comprising such quarter.

(e) Interference with Officers. — No person shall interfere with any officer, agent, or employee of the Service in the performance of any duty imposed upon him by this section or by regulations made by authority thereof.

(f) Penalties for Offenses. — Any person who shall violate, or aid or abet in violating, any of the provisions of this section shall be punished upon conviction by a fine not exceeding $500 or by imprisonment not exceeding one year, or by both such fine and imprisonment, in the discretion of the court.

(g) Construction with Other Laws. — Nothing contained in this chapter shall be construed as in any way affecting, modifying, repealing, or superseding the provisions of the Federal Food, Drug, and Cosmetic Act.

(h) Exportation of Partially Processed Biological Products. — A partially processed biological product which —

(1) is not in a form applicable to the prevention, treatment, or cure of diseases or injuries of man;

(2) is not intended for sale in the United States; and

(3) is intended for further manufacture into final dosage form outside the United States,

shall be subject to no restriction on the export of the product under this chapter or the Federal Food, Drug, and Cosmetic Act, if the product is manufactured, processed, packaged, and held in conformity with current good manufacturing practice requirements or meets international manufacturing standards as certified by an international standards organization recognized by the Secretary and meets the requirements of section 801(e)(1) of the Federal Food, Drug, and CosmeticAct (21 U.S.C. 381(e)).

(i) Definition; Application. — In this section:

(1) The term "biological product" means a virus, therapeutic serum, toxin, antitoxin, vaccine, blood, blood component or derivative, allergenic product, protein (except any chemically synthesized polypeptide) or analogous product, or arsphenamine or derivative of arsphenamine (or any other trivalent organic arsenic compound), applicable to the prevention, treatment, or cure of a disease or condition of human beings.

(2) The term "biosimilar" or "biosimilarity", in reference to a biological product that is the subject of an application under subsection (k), means —

(A) that the biological product is highly similar to the reference product notwithstanding minor differences in clinically inactive components; and

(B) there are no clinically meaningfully differences between the biological product and the reference product in terms of the safety, purity, and potency of the product.

(3) The term "interchangeable" or "interchangeability", in reference to a biological product that is shown to meet the standards described in subsection (k)(4), means that the biological product may be substituted for the reference product without the intervention of the health care provider who prescribed the reference product.

(4) The term "reference product" means the single biological product licensed under subsection (a) against which a biological product is evaluated in an application submitted under subsection (k).

(j) Application of Federal Food, Drug, and Cosmetic Act. — The Federal Food, Drug, and Cosmetic Act, including the requirements under sections 505(o), 505(p), and 505-1 such Act, applies to a biological product subject to regulation under this section, except that a product for which a license has been approved under subsection (a) shall not be required to have an approved application under section 355 of Title 21.

(k) Licensure of Biological Products as Biosimilar or Interchangeable. —

(1) In General. — Any person may submit an application for licensure of a biological product under this subsection.

(2) Content. —

(A) In General. —

(i) Required Information. — An application submitted under this subsection shall include information demonstrating that —

(I) the biological product is biosimilar to a reference product based upon data derived from —

(aa) analytical studies that demonstrate that the biological product is highly similar to the reference product notwithstanding minor differences in clinically inactive components;

(bb) animal studies (including the assessment of toxicity); and

(cc) a clinical study or studies (including the assessment of immunogenicity and pharmacokinetics or pharmacodynamics) that are sufficient to demonstrate safety, purity, and potency in 1 or more appropriate conditions of use for which the reference product is licensed and intended to be used and for which licensure is sought for the biological product;

(II) the biological product and reference product utilize the same mechanism or mechanisms of action for the condition or conditions of use prescribed, recommended, or suggested in the proposed labeling, but only to the extent the mechanism or mechanisms of action are known for the reference product;

(III) the condition or conditions of use prescribed, recommended, or suggested in the labeling proposed for the biological product have been previously approved for the reference product;

(IV) the route of administration, the dosage form, and the strength of the biological product are the same as those of the reference product; and

(V) the facility in which the biological product is manufactured, processed, packed, or held meets standards designed to assure that the biological product continues to be safe, pure, and potent.

(ii) Determination by Secretary. — The Secretary may determine, in the Secretary's discretion, that an element described in clause (i)(I) is unnecessary in an application submitted under this subsection.

(iii) Additional Information. — An application submitted under this subsection —

(I) shall include publicly-available information regarding the Secretary's previous determination that the reference product is safe, pure, and potent; and

(II) may include any additional information in support of the application, including publicly-available information with respect to the reference product or another biological product.

(B) Interchangeability. — An application (or a supplement to an application) submitted under this subsection may include information demonstrating that the biological product meets the standards described in paragraph (4).

(3) Evaluation by Secretary. — Upon review of an application (or a supplement to an application) submitted under this subsection, the Secretary shall license the biological product under this subsection if —

(A) the Secretary determines that the information submitted in the application (or the supplement) is sufficient to show that the biological product —

(i) is biosimilar to the reference product; or

(ii) meets the standards described in paragraph (4), and therefore is interchangeable with the reference product; and

(B) the applicant (or other appropriate person) consents to the inspection of the facility that is the subject of the application, in accordance with subsection (c).

(4) Safety Standards for Determining Interchangeability. — Upon review of an application submitted under this subsection or any supplement to such application, the Secretary shall determine the biological product to be interchangeable with the reference product if the Secretary determines that the information submitted in the application (or a supplement to such application) is sufficient to show that —

(A) the biological product —

(i) is biosimilar to the reference product; and

(ii) can be expected to produce the same clinical result as the reference product in any given patient; and

(B) for a biological product that is administered more than once to an individual, the risk in terms of safety or diminished efficacy of alternating or switching between use of the biological product and the reference product is not greater than the risk of using the reference product without such alternation or switch.

(5) General Rules. —

(A) One Reference Product Per Application. — A biological product, in an application submitted under this subsection, may not be evaluated against more than 1 reference product.

(B) Review. — An application submitted under this subsection shall be reviewed by the division within the Food and Drug Administration that is responsible for the review and approval of the application under which the reference product is licensed.

(C) Risk Evaluation and Mitigation Strategies. — The authority of the Secretary with respect to risk evaluation and mitigation strategies under the Federal Food, Drug, and Cosmetic Act shall apply to biological products licensed under this subsection in the same manner as such authority applies to biological products licensed under subsection (a).

(6) Exclusivity for First Interchangeable Biological Product. — Upon review of an application submitted under this subsection relying on the same reference product for which a prior biological product has received a determination of interchangeability for any condition of use, the Secretary shall not make a determination under paragraph (4) that the second or subsequent biological product is interchangeable for any condition of use until the earlier of —

(A) 1 year after the first commercial marketing of the first interchangeable biosimilar biological product to be approved as interchangeable for that reference product;

(B) 18 months after —

(i) a final court decision on all patents in suit in an action instituted under subsection (l)(6) against the applicant that submitted the application for the first approved interchangeable biosimilar biological product; or

(ii) the dismissal with or without prejudice of an action instituted under subsection (l)(6) against the applicant that submitted the application for the first approved interchangeable biosimilar biological product; or

(C) —

(i) 42 months after approval of the first interchangeable biosimilar biological product if the applicant that submitted such application has been sued under subsection (l)(6) and such litigation is still ongoing within such 42-month period; or

(ii) 18 months after approval of the first interchangeable biosimilar biological product if the applicant that submitted such application has not been sued under subsection (l)(6).

For purposes of this paragraph, the term "final court decision" means a final decision of a court from which no appeal (other than a petition to the United States Supreme Court for a writ of certiorari) has been or can be taken.

(7) Exclusivity for Reference Product. —

(A) Effective Date of Biosimilar Application Approval. — Approval of an application under this subsection may not be made effective by the Secretary until the date that is 12 years after the date on which the reference product was first licensed under subsection (a).

(B) Filing Period. — An application under this subsection may not be submitted to the Secretary until the date that is 4 years after the date on which the reference product was first licensed under subsection (a).

(C) First Licensure. — Subparagraphs (A) and (B) shall not apply to a license for or approval of —

(i) a supplement for the biological product that is the reference product; or

(ii) a subsequent application filed by the same sponsor or manufacturer of the biological product that is the reference product (or a licensor, predecessor in interest, or other related entity) for —

(I) a change (not including a modification to the structure of the biological product) that results in a new indication, route of administration, dosing schedule, dosage form, delivery system, delivery device, or strength; or

(II) a modification to the structure of the biological product that does not result in a change in safety, purity, or potency.

(8) GUIDANCE DOCUMENTS. —

(A) IN GENERAL. — The Secretary may, after opportunity for public comment, issue guidance in accordance, except as provided in subparagraph (B)(i), with section 701(h) of the Federal Food, Drug, and Cosmetic Act with respect to the licensure of a biological product under this subsection. Any such guidance may be general or specific.

(B) PUBLIC COMMENT. —

(i) IN GENERAL. — The Secretary shall provide the public an opportunity to comment on any proposed guidance issued under subparagraph (A) before issuing final guidance.

(ii) INPUT REGARDING MOST VALUABLE GUIDANCE. — The Secretary shall establish a process through which the public may provide the Secretary with input regarding priorities for issuing guidance.

(C) NO REQUIREMENT FOR APPLICATION CONSIDERATION. — The issuance (or non-issuance) of guidance under subparagraph (A) shall not preclude the review of, or action on, an application submitted under this subsection.

(D) REQUIREMENT FOR PRODUCT CLASS-SPECIFIC GUIDANCE. — If the Secretary issues product class-specific guidance under subparagraph (A), such guidance shall include a description of —

(i) the criteria that the Secretary will use to determine whether a biological product is highly similar to a reference product in such product class; and

(ii) the criteria, if available, that the Secretary will use to determine whether a biological product meets the standards described in paragraph (4).

(E) CERTAIN PRODUCT CLASSES. —

(i) GUIDANCE. — The Secretary may indicate in a guidance document that the science and experience, as of the date of such guidance, with respect to a product or product class (not including any recombinant protein) does not allow approval of an application for a license as provided under this subsection for such product or product class.

(ii) MODIFICATION OR REVERSAL. — The Secretary may issue a subsequent guidance document under subparagraph (A) to modify or reverse a guidance document under clause (i).

(iii) NO EFFECT ONABILITY TO DENY LICENSE. — Clause (i) shall not be construed to require the Secretary to approve a product with respect to which the Secretary has not indicated in a guidance document that the science and experience, as described in clause (i), does not allow approval of such an application.

(l) PATENTS. —

(1) CONFIDENTIAL ACCESS TO SUBSECTION (k) APPLICATION. —

(A) APPLICATION OF PARAGRAPH. — Unless otherwise agreed to by a person that submits an application under subsection (k) (referred to in this subsection as the "subsection (k) applicant") and the sponsor of the application for the reference product (referred to in this subsection as the "reference product sponsor"), the provisions of this paragraph shall apply to the exchange of information described in this subsection.

(B) IN GENERAL. —

(i) PROVISION OF CONFIDENTIAL INFORMATION. — When a subsection (k) applicant submits an application under subsection (k), such applicant shall provide to the persons described in clause (ii), subject to the terms of this paragraph, confidential access to the information required to be produced pursuant to paragraph (2) and any other information that the subsection (k) applicant determines, in its sole discretion, to be appropriate (referred to in this subsection as the "confidential information").

(ii) RECIPIENTS OF INFORMATION. — The persons described in this clause are the following:

(I) OUTSIDE COUNSEL. — One or more attorneys designated by the reference product sponsor who are employees of an entity other than the reference product sponsor (referred to in this paragraph as the "outside counsel", provided that such attorneys do not engage, formally or informally, in patent prosecution relevant or related to the reference product.

(II) IN-HOUSE COUNSEL. — One attorney that represents the reference product sponsor who is an employee of the reference product sponsor, provided that such attorney does not engage, formally or informally, in patent prosecution relevant or related to the reference product.

(iii) Patent Owner Access. — A representative of the owner of a patent exclusively licensed to a reference product sponsor with respect to the reference product and who has retained a right to assert the patent or participate in litigation concerning the patent may be provided the confidential information, provided that the representative informs the reference product sponsor and the subsection (k) applicant of his or her agreement to be subject to the confidentiality provisions set forth in this paragraph, including those under clause (ii).

(C) Limitation on Disclosure. — No person that receives confidential information pursuant to subparagraph (B) shall disclose any confidential information to any other person or entity, including the reference product sponsor employees, outside scientific consultants, or other outside counsel retained by the reference product sponsor, without the prior written consent of the subsection (k) applicant, which shall not be unreasonably withheld.

(D) Use of Confidential Information. — Confidential information shall be used for the sole and exclusive purpose of determining, with respect to each patent assigned to or exclusively licensed by the reference product sponsor, whether a claim of patent infringement could reasonably be asserted if the subsection (k) applicant engaged in the manufacture, use, offering for sale, sale, or importation into the United States of the biological product that is the subject of the application under subsection (k).

(E) Ownership of Confidential Information. — The confidential information disclosed under this paragraph is, and shall remain, the property of the subsection (k) applicant. By providing the confidential information pursuant to this paragraph, the subsection (k) applicant does not provide the reference product sponsor or the outside counsel any interest in or license to use the confidential information, for purposes other than those specified in subparagraph (D).

(F) Effect of Infringement Action. — In the event that the reference product sponsor files a patent infringement suit, the use of confidential information shall continue to be governed by the terms of this paragraph until such time as a court enters a protective order regarding the information. Upon entry of such order, the subsection (k) applicant may redesignate confidential information in accordance with the terms of that order. No confidential information shall be included in any publicly-available complaint or other pleading. In the event that the reference product sponsor does not file an infringement action by the date specified in paragraph (6), the reference product sponsor shall return or destroy all confidential information received under this paragraph, provided that if the reference product sponsor opts to destroy such information, it will confirm destruction in writing to the subsection (k) applicant.

(G) Rule of Construction. — Nothing in this paragraph shall be construed —

(i) as an admission by the subsection (k) applicant regarding the validity, enforceability, or infringement of any patent; or

(ii) as an agreement or admission by the subsection (k) applicant with respect to the competency, relevance, or materiality of any confidential information.

(H) Effect of Violation. — The disclosure of any confidential information in violation of this paragraph shall be deemed to cause the subsection (k) applicant to suffer irreparable harm for which there is no adequate legal remedy and the court shall consider immediate injunctive relief to be an appropriate and necessary remedy for any violation or threatened violation of this paragraph.

(2) Subsection (k) Application Information. — Not later than 20 days after the Secretary notifies the subsection (k) applicant that the application has been accepted for review, the subsection (k) applicant—

(A) shall provide to the reference product sponsor a copy of the application submitted to the Secretary under subsection (k), and such other information that describes the process or processes used to manufacture the biological product that is the subject of such application; and

(B) may provide to the reference product sponsor additional information requested by or on behalf of the reference product sponsor.

(3) List and Description of Patents. —

(A) List by Reference Product Sponsor. — Not later than 60 days after the receipt of the application and information under paragraph (2), the reference product sponsor shall provide to the subsection (k) applicant—

(i) a list of patents for which the reference product sponsor believes a claim of patent infringement could reasonably be asserted by the reference product sponsor, or by a patent owner that has granted an exclusive license to the reference product sponsor with respect to the reference product, if a person not licensed by the reference product sponsor engaged in the making, using, offering to sell, selling, or importing into the United States of the biological product that is the subject of the subsection (k) application; and

(ii) an identification of the patents on such list that the reference product sponsor would be prepared to license to the subsection (k) applicant.

(B) List and Description by Subsection (k) Applicant. — Not later than 60 days after receipt of the list under subparagraph (A), the subsection (k) applicant —

(i) may provide to the reference product sponsor a list of patents to which the subsection (k) applicant believes a claim of patent infringement could reasonably be asserted by the reference product sponsor if a person not licensed by the reference product sponsor engaged in the making, using, offering to sell, selling, or importing into the United States of the biological product that is the subject of the subsection (k) application;

(ii) shall provide to the reference product sponsor, with respect to each patent listed by the reference product sponsor under subparagraph (A) or listed by the subsection (k) applicant under clause (i)—

(I) a detailed statement that describes, on a claim by claim basis, the factual and legal basis of the opinion of the subsection (k) applicant that such patent is invalid, unenforceable, or will not be infringed by the commercial marketing of the biological product that is the subject of the subsection (k) application; or

(II) a statement that the subsection (k) applicant does not intend to begin commercial marketing of the biological product before the date that such patent expires; and

(iii) shall provide to the reference product sponsor a response regarding each patent identified by the reference product sponsor under subparagraph (A)(ii).

(C) Description by Reference Product Sponsor. — Not later than 60 days after receipt of the list and statement under subparagraph (B), the reference product sponsor shall provide to the subsection (k) applicant a detailed statement that describes, with respect to each patent described in subparagraph (B)(ii)(I), on a claim by claim basis, the factual and legal basis of the opinion of the reference product sponsor that such patent will be infringed by the commercial marketing of the biological product that is the subject of the subsection (k) application and a response to the statement concerning validity and enforceability provided under subparagraph (B)(ii)(I).

(4) Patent Resolution Negotiations. —

(A) In General. — After receipt by the subsection (k) applicant of the statement under paragraph (3)(C), the reference product sponsor and the subsection (k) applicant shall engage in good faith negotiations to agree on which, if any, patents listed under paragraph (3) by the subsection (k) applicant or the reference product sponsor shall be the subject of an action for patent infringement under paragraph (6).

(B) Failure to Reach Agreement. — If, within 15 days of beginning negotiations under subparagraph (A), the subsection (k) applicant and the reference product sponsor fail to agree on a final and complete list of which, if any, patents listed under paragraph (3) by the subsection (k) applicant or the reference product sponsor shall be the subject of an action for patent infringement under paragraph (6), the provisions of paragraph (5) shall apply to the parties.

(5) Patent Resolution if No Agreement. —

(A) Number of Patents. — The subsection (k) applicant shall notify the reference product sponsor of the number of patents that such applicant will provide to the reference product sponsor under subparagraph (B)(i)(I).

(B) Exchange of Patent Lists. —

(i) In General. — On a date agreed to by the subsection (k) applicant and the reference product sponsor, but in no case later than 5 days after the subsection (k) applicant notifies the reference product sponsor under subparagraph (A), the subsection (k) applicant and the reference product sponsor shall simultaneously exchange —

(I) the list of patents that the subsection (k) applicant believes should be the subject of an action for patent infringement under paragraph (6); and

(II) the list of patents, in accordance with clause (ii), that the reference product sponsor believes should be the subject of an action for patent infringement under paragraph (6).

(ii) Number of Patents Listed by Reference Product Sponsor. —

(I) In General. — Subject to subclause (II), the number of patents listed by the reference product sponsor under clause (i)(II) may not exceed the number of patents listed by the subsection (k) applicant under clause (i)(I).

(II) Exception. — If a subsection (k) applicant does not list any patent under clause (i)(I), the reference product sponsor may list 1 patent under clause (i)(II).

(6) Immediate Patent Infringement Action. —

(A) Action if Agreement on Patent List. — If the subsection (k) applicant and the reference product sponsor agree on patents as described in paragraph (4), not later than 30 days after such agreement, the reference product sponsor shall bring an action for patent infringement with respect to each such patent.

(B) Action if No Agreement on Patent List. — If the provisions of paragraph (5) apply to the parties as described in paragraph (4)(B), not later than 30 days after the exchange of lists under paragraph (5)(B), the reference product sponsor shall bring an action for patent infringement with respect to each patent that is included on such lists.

(C) Notification and publication of Complaint. —

(i) Notification to Secretary. — Not later than 30 days after a complaint is served to a subsection (k) applicant in an action for patent infringement described under this paragraph, the subsection (k) applicant shall provide the Secretary with notice and a copy of such complaint.

(ii) Publication by Secretary. — The Secretary shall publish in the Federal Register notice of a complaint received under clause (i).

(7) Newly Issued or Licensed Patents. — In the case of a patent that —

(A) is issued to, or exclusively licensed by, the reference product sponsor after the date that the reference product sponsor provided the list to the subsection (k) applicant under paragraph (3)(A); and

(B) the reference product sponsor reasonably believes that, due to the issuance of such patent, a claim of patent infringement could reasonably be asserted by the reference product sponsor if a person not licensed by the reference product sponsor engaged in the making, using, offering to sell, selling, or importing into the United States of the biological product that is the subject of the subsection (k) application, not later than 30 days after such issuance or licensing, the reference product sponsor shall provide to the subsection (k) applicant a supplement to the list provided by the reference product sponsor under paragraph (3)(A) that includes such patent, not later than 30 days after such supplement is provided, the subsection (k) applicant shall provide a statement to the reference product sponsor in accordance with paragraph (3)(B), and such patent shall be subject to paragraph (8).

(8) Notice of Commercial Marketing and Preliminary Injunction. —

(A) Notice of Commercial Marketing. — The subsection (k) applicant shall provide notice to the reference product sponsor not later than 180 days before the date of the first commercial marketing of the biological product licensed under subsection (k).

(B) Preliminary Injunction. — After receiving the notice under subparagraph (A) and before such date of the first commercial marketing of such biological product, the reference product sponsor may seek a preliminary injunction prohibiting the subsection (k) applicant from engaging in the commercial manufacture or sale of such biological product until the court decides the issue of patent validity, enforcement, and infringement with respect to any patent that is—

(i) included in the list provided by the reference product sponsor under paragraph (3)(A) or in the list provided by the subsection (k) applicant under paragraph (3)(B); and

(ii) not included, as applicable, on—

(I) the list of patents described in paragraph (4); or

(II) the lists of patents described in paragraph (5)(B).

(C) Reasonable Cooperation. — If the reference product sponsor has sought a preliminary injunction under subparagraph (B), the reference product sponsor and the subsection (k) applicant shall reasonably cooperate to expedite such further discovery as is needed in connection with the preliminary injunction motion.

(9) Limitation on Declaratory Judgment Action. —

(A) Subsection (k) Application Provided. — If a subsection (k) applicant provides the application and information required under paragraph (2)(A), neither the reference product sponsor nor the subsection (k) applicant may, prior to the date notice is received under paragraph (8)(A), bring any action under section 2201 of title 28, United States Code, for a declaration of infringement, validity, or enforceability of any patent that is described in clauses (i) and (ii) of paragraph (8)(B).

(B) Subsequent Failure to Act by Subsection (k) Applicant. — If a subsection (k) applicant fails to complete an action required of the subsection (k) applicant under paragraph (3)(B)(ii), paragraph (5), paragraph (6)(C)(i), paragraph (7), or paragraph (8)(A), the reference product sponsor, but not the subsection (k) applicant, may bring an action under section 2201 of title 28, United States Code, for a declaration of infringement, validity, or enforceability of any patent included in the list described in paragraph (3)(A), including as provided under paragraph (7).

(C) Subsection (k) Application Not Provided. — If a subsection (k) applicant fails to provide the application and information required under paragraph (2)(A), the reference product sponsor, but not the subsection (k) applicant, may bring an action under section 2201 of title 28, United States Code, for a declaration of infringement, validity, or enforceability of any patent that claims the biological product or a use of the biological product.

(m) Pediatric Studies. —

(1) Application of Certain Provisions. — The provisions of subsections (a), (d), (e), (f), (h), (i), (j), (k), (l), (p), and (q) of section 505A of the Federal Food, Drug, and Cosmetic Act shall apply with respect to the extension of a period under paragraphs (2) and (3) to the same extent and in the same manner as such provisions apply with respect to the extension of a period under subsection (b) or (c) of section 505A of the Federal Food, Drug, and Cosmetic Act.

(2) Market Exclusivity for New Biological Products. — If, prior to approval of an application that is submitted under subsection (a), the Secretary determines that information relating to the use of a new biological product in the pediatric population may produce health benefits in that population, the Secretary makes a written request for pediatric studies (which shall include a timeframe for completing such studies), the applicant agrees to the request, such studies are completed using appropriate formulations for each age group for which the study is requested within any such timeframe, and the reports thereof are submitted and accepted in accordance with section ~~505A(d)(3)~~ 505A(d)(4) of the Federal Food, Drug, and Cosmetic Act —

(A) the periods for such biological product referred to in subsection (k)(7) are deemed to be 4 years and 6 months rather than 4 years and 12 years and 6 months rather than 12 years; and

(B) if the biological product is designated under section 526 for a rare disease or condition, the period for such biological product referred to in section 527(a) is deemed to be 7 years and 6 months rather than 7 years.

(3) Market Exclusivity for Already-Marketed Biological Products. — If the Secretary determines that information relating to the use of a licensed biological product in the pediatric population may produce health benefits in that population and makes a written request to the holder of an approved application under subsection (a) for pediatric studies (which shall include a timeframe for completing such studies), the holder agrees to the request, such studies are completed using appropriate formulations for each age group for which the study is requested within any such timeframe, and the reports thereof are submitted and accepted in accordance with section ~~505A(d)(3)~~ 505A(d)(4) of the Federal Food, Drug, and Cosmetic Act —

(A) the periods for such biological product referred to in subsection (k)(7) are deemed to be 4 years and 6 months rather than 4 years and 12 years and 6 months rather than 12 years; and

(B) if the biological product is designated under section 526 for a rare disease or condition, the period for such biological product referred to in section 527(a) is deemed to be 7 years and 6 months rather than 7 years.

(4) Exception. — The Secretary shall not extend a period referred to in paragraph (2)(A), (2)(B), (3)(A), or (3)(B) if the determination under section ~~505A(d)(3)~~ 505A(d)(4) is made later than 9 months prior to the expiration of such period.

(n) Date of Approval in the Case of Recommended Controls Under the CSA. —

(1) In General. — In the case of an application under subsection (a) with respect to a biological product for which the Secretary provides notice to the sponsor that the Secretary intends to issue a scientific and medical evaluation and recommend controls under the Controlled Substances Act, approval of such application shall not take effect until the interim final rule controlling the biological product is issued in accordance with section 201(j) of the Controlled Substances Act.

(2) Date of Approval. — For purposes of this section, with respect to an application described in paragraph (1), references to the date of approval of such application, or licensure of the product subject to such application, shall mean the later of —

(A) the date an application is approved under subsection (a); or

(B) the date of issuance of the interim final rule controlling the biological product.

42 U.S.C. § 264. Regulations to Control Communicable Diseases.

(a) Promulgation and Enforcement by Surgeon General. — The Surgeon General, with the approval of the Secretary, is authorized to make and enforce such regulations as in his judgment are necessary to prevent the introduction, transmission, or spread of communicable diseases from foreign countries into the States or possessions, or from one State or possession into any other State or possession. For purposes of carrying out and enforcing such regulations, the Surgeon General may provide for such inspection, fumigation, disinfection, sanitation, pest extermination, destruction of animals or articles found to be so infected or contaminated as to be sources of dangerous infection to human beings, and other measures, as in his judgment may be necessary.

(b) Apprehension, Detention, or Conditional Release of Individuals. — Regulations prescribed under this section shall not provide for the apprehension, detention, or conditional release of individuals except for the purpose of preventing the introduction, transmission, or spread of such communicable diseases as may be specified from time to time in Executive orders of the President upon the recommendation of the Secretary, in consultation with the Surgeon General.

(c) Application of Regulations to Persons Entering from Foreign Countries. — Except as provided in subsection (d) of this section, regulations prescribed under this section, insofar as they provide for the apprehension, detention, examination, or conditional release of individuals, shall be applicable only to individuals coming into a State or possession from a foreign country or a possession.

(d) —

(1) Apprehension and Examination of Persons Reasonably Believed to Be Infected. — Regulations prescribed under this section may provide for the apprehension and examination of any individual reasonably believed to be infected with a communicable disease in a qualifying stage and

(A) to be moving or about to move from a State to another State; or

(B) to be a probable source of infection to individuals who, while infected with such disease in a qualifying stage, will be moving from a State to another State.

Such regulations may provide that if upon examination any such individual is found to be infected, he may be detained for such time and in such manner as may be reasonably necessary. For purposes of this subsection, the term "State" includes, in addition to the several States, only the District ofColumbia.

(2) For purposes of this subsection, the term "qualifying stage", with respect to a communicable disease, means that such disease

(A) is in a communicable stage; or

(B) is in a precommunicable stage, if the disease would be likely to cause a public health emergency if transmitted to other individuals.

(e) Nothing in this section or section 266 of this title, or the regulations promulgated under such sections, may be construed as superseding any provision under State law (including regulations and including provisions established by political subdivisions of States), except to the extent that such a provision conflicts with an exercise of Federal authority under this section or section 266 of this title.

42 U.S.C. § 266. Special Quarantine Powers in Time of War.

To protect the military and naval forces and war workers of the United States, in time of war, against any communicable disease specified in Executive orders as provided in subsection (b) of section 264 of this title, the Secretary, in consultation with the Surgeon General, is authorized to provide by regulations for the apprehension and examination, in time of war, of any individual reasonably believed

(1) to be infected with such disease and

(2) to be a probable source of infection to members of the armed forces of the United States or to individuals engaged in the production or transportation of arms, munitions, ships, food, clothing, or other supplies for the armed forces.

Such regulations may provide that if upon examination any such individual is found to be so infected, he may be detained for such time and in such manner as may be reasonably necessary.

42 U.S.C. § 282. Director of National Institutes of Health.

(a) Appointment. The National Institutes of Health shall be headed by the Director of NIH who shall be appointed by the President by and with the advice and consent of the Senate. The Director of NIH shall perform functions as provided under subsection (b) and as the Secretary may otherwise prescribe.

(b) Duties and Authority. In carrying out the purposes of section 301, the Secretary, acting through the Director of NIH —

(1) shall carry out this title, including being responsible for the overall direction of the National Institutes of Health and for the establishment and implementation of general policies respecting the management and operation of programs and activities within the National Institutes of Health.;

(2) shall coordinate and oversee the operation of the national research institutes, national centers, and administrative entities within the National Institutes of Health;

(3) shall, in consultation with the heads of the national research institutes and national centers, be responsible for program coordination across the national research institutes and national centers, including conducting priority-setting reviews, to ensure that the research portfolio of the National Institutes of Health is balanced and free of unnecessary duplication, and takes advantage of collaborative, cross-cutting research;

(4) shall assemble accurate data to be used to assess research priorities, including:

(A) information to better evaluate scientific opportunity, public health burdens, and progress in reducing health disparities; and

(B) data on study populations of clinical research, funded by or conducted at each national research institute and national center, which—

(i) specifies the inclusion of—

(I) women;

(II) members of minority groups;

(III) relevant age categories, including pediatric subgroups; and

(IV) other demographic variables as the Director of the National Institutes of Health determines appropriate;

(ii) is disaggregated by research area, condition, and disease categories; and

(iii) is to be made publicly available on the Internet website of the National Institutes of Health;

(5) shall ensure that scientifically based strategic planning is implemented in support of research priorities as determined by the agencies of the National Institutes of Health, and through the development, implementation, and updating of the strategic plan developed under subsection (m);

(6) shall ensure that the resources of the National Institutes of Health are sufficiently allocated for research projects identified in strategic plans;

(7) —

(A) shall, through the Division of Program Coordination, Planning, and Strategic Initiatives —

(i) identify research that represents important areas of emerging scientific opportunities, rising public health challenges, or knowledge gaps that deserve special emphasis and would benefit from conducting or supporting additional research that involves collaboration between 2 or more national research institutes or national centers, or would otherwise benefit from strategic coordination and planning;

(ii) include information on such research in reports under section 403; and

(iii) in the case of such research supported with funds referred to in subparagraph (B) —

(I) require as appropriate that proposals include milestones and goals for the research;

(II) require that the proposals include timeframes for funding of the research; and

(III) ensure appropriate consideration of proposals for which the principal investigator is an individual who has not previously served as the principal investigator of research conducted or supported by the National Institutes of Health;

(B)

(i) may, with respect to funds reserved under section 402A(e)(1) for the Common Fund, allocate such funds to the national research institutes and national centers for conducting and supporting research that is identified under subparagraph (A); and

(ii) shall, with respect to funds appropriated to the Common Fund pursuant to section 402(a)(2), allocate such funds to the national research institutes and national centers for making grants for pediatric research that is identified under subparagraph (A); and

(C) may assign additional functions to the Division in support of responsibilities identified in subparagraph (A), as determined appropriate by the Director;

(8) shall, in coordination with the heads of the national research institutes and national centers, ensure that such institutes and centers —

(A) preserve an emphasis on investigator-initiated research project grants, including with respect to research involving collaboration between 2 or more such institutes or centers;

(B) when appropriate, maximize investigator-initiated research project grants in their annual research portfolios;

(C) foster collaboration between clinical research projects funded by the respective national research institutes and national centers that—

(i) conduct research involving human subjects; and

(ii) collect similar data; and

(D) encourage collaboration described in subparagraph (C) to—

(i) allow for an increase in the number of subjects studied; and

(ii) utilize diverse study populations, with special consideration to biological, social, and other determinants of health that contribute to health disparities;

(9) shall ensure that research conducted or supported by the National Institutes of Health is subject to review in accordance with section 492 and that, after such review, the research is reviewed in accordance with section 492A(a)(2) by the appropriate advisory council under section 406 before the research proposals are approved for funding;

(10) shall have authority to review and approve the establishment of all centers of excellence recommended by the national research institutes;

(11) **(A)** shall oversee research training for all of the national research institutes and National Research Service Awards in accordance with section 487; and

(B) may conduct and support research training —

(i) for which fellowship support is not provided under section 487; and

(ii) that does not consist of residency training of physicians or other health professionals;

(12) may, form funds appropriated under section 402A(b), reserve funds to provide for research on matters that have not received significant funding relative to other matters, to respond to new issues and scientific emergencies, and to act on research opportunities of high priority;

(13) may, subject to appropriations Acts, collect and retain registration fees obtained from third parties to defray expenses for scientific, educational, and research-related conferences;

(14) for the national research institutes and administrative entities within the National Institutes of Health —

(A) may acquire, construct, improve, repair, operate, and maintain, at the site of such institutes and entities, laboratories, and other research facilities, other facilities, equipment, and other real or personal property, and

(B) may acquire, without regard to the Act of March 3, 1877 (40 U.S.C. 34) by lease or otherwise through the Administrator of General Services, buildings or parts of buildings in the District of Columbia or communities located adjacent to the District of Columbia for use for a period not to exceed ten years;

(15) may secure resources for research conducted by or through the National Institutes of Health;

(16) may, without regard to the provision of title 5, United States Code, governing appointments in the competitive service, and without regard to the provisions of chapter 51 and subchapter III of chapter 53 of such title [5 USC §§ 5101 et seq. and 5331 et seq.] relating to classification and General Schedule pay rates, establish such technical and scientific peer review groups and scientific program advisory committees as are needed to carry out the requirements of this title and appoint and pay the members of such groups, except that officers and employees of the United States shall not receive additional compensation for service as members of such groups.

(17) may secure for the National Institutes of Health consultation services and advice of persons from the United States or abroad;

(18) may use, with their consent, the services, equipment, personnel, information, and facilities of other Federal, State, or local public agencies, with or without reimbursement therefor;

(19) may, for purposes of study, admit and treat at facilities of the National Institutes of Health individuals not otherwise eligible for such treatment;

(20) may accept voluntary and uncompensated services;

(21) may perform such other administrative functions as the Secretary determines are needed to effectively carry out this title;

(22) may appoint physicians, dentists, and other health care professionals, subject to the provisions of title 5, United States Code, relating to appointments and classifications in the competitive service, and may compensate such professional subject to the provisions of chapter 74 of title 38, United States Code; and

(23) shall designate a contact point or office to help innovators and physicians identify sources of funding available for pediatric medical device development;

(24) implement the Cures Acceleration Network described in section 287a of this title; and

(25) may require recipients of National Institutes of Health awards to share scientific data, to the extent feasible, generated from such National Institutes of Health awards in a manner that is consistent with all applicable Federal laws and regulations, including such laws and regulations for the protection of—

(A) human research participants, including with respect to privacy, security, informed consent, and protected health information; and

(B) proprietary interests, confidential commercial information, and the intellectual property rights of the funding recipient.

The Federal Advisory Committee Act shall not apply to the duration of a peer review group appointed under paragraph (16). The members of such a group shall be individuals who by virtue of their training or experience are eminently qualified to perform the review functions of such group. Nor more than one-fourth of the members of any such group shall be officers or employees of the United States

(c) - (h) [Text not included. — Ed.]

(i) Information on Clinical Trials for Drugs for Serious or Life-Threatening Disease and Conditions.

(1) —

(A) The Secretary, acting through the Director of NIH, shall establish, maintain, and operate a data bank of information on clinical trials for drugs for serious or life-threatening disease and conditions in the subsection referred to as the "data bank". The activities of the data bank shall be integrated and coordinated with related activities of other agencies of the Department of Health and Human Services, and to the extent practicable, coordinated with other data banks containing similar information.

(B) The Secretary shall establish the data bank after consultation with the Commissioner of Food and Drugs, the directors of the appropriate agencies of the National Institutes of Health (including the National Library of Medicine), and the Director of the Centers for Disease Control and Prevention.

(2) In carrying out paragraph (1), the Secretary shall collect, catalog, store, and disseminate the information described in such paragraph. The Secretary shall disseminate such information through information systems, which shall include toll-free telephone communications, available to individuals with serious or life-threatening disease and conditions, to other members of the public, to health care providers, and to researchers.

(3) The data bank shall include the following:

(A) A registry of clinical trials (whether federally or privately funded) of experimental treatments for serious or life-threatening diseases and conditions under regulations promulgated pursuant to section 505(i) of the Federal Food, Drug, and Cosmetic Act, which provides a description of the purpose of each experimental drug, either with the consent of the protocol sponsor, or when a trial to test effectiveness begins. Information provided shall consist of eligibility criteria for participation in the clinical trials, a description of the location of trial sites, a point of contact for those wanting to enroll in the trial, and a description of whether, and through what procedure, the manufacturer or sponsor of the investigation of a new drug will respond to requests for protocol exception, with appropriate safeguards, for single-patient and expanded protocol use of the new drug, particularly in children, and shall be in a form that can be readily understood by members of the public. Such information shall be forwarded to the data bank by the sponsor of the trial not later than 21 days after the approval of the protocol.

(B) Information pertaining to experimental treatments for serious or life-threatening diseases and conditions that may be available—

(i) Under a treatment investigational new drug application that has been submitted to the Secretary under section 561(c) of the Federal Food, Drug, and Cosmetic Act or

(ii) as a Group C cancer drug (as defined by the National Cancer Institute).

The data bank may also include information pertaining to the results of clinical trials of such treatments, with the consent of the sponsor, including information concerning potential toxicities or adverse effects associated with the use or administration of such experimental treatments.

(4) The data bank shall not include information relating to an investigation if the sponsor has provided a detailed certification to the Secretary that disclosure of such information would substantially interfere with the timely enrollment of subjects in the investigation, unless the Secretary, after the receipt of the certification, provides the sponsor with a detailed written determination that such disclosure would not substantially interfere with such enrollment.

(5) Fees collected under section 736 of the Federal Food, Drug, and Cosmetic Act shall not be used in carrying out this subsection.

(j) Expanded Clinical Trial Registry Data Bank. —

(1) Definitions; Requirement. —

(A) Definitions. — In this subsection:

(i) Applicable Clinical Trial. — The term "applicable clinical trial" means an applicable device clinical trial or an applicable drug clinical trial.

(ii) Applicable Device Clinical Trial. — The term "applicable device clinical trial" means —

(I) a prospective clinical study of health outcomes comparing an intervention with a device subject to section 510(k), 515, or 520(m) of the Federal Food, Drug, and Cosmetic Act against a control in human subjects (other than a small clinical trial to determine the feasibility of a device, or a clinical trial to test prototype devices where the primary outcome measure relates to feasibility and not to health outcomes); and

(II) a pediatric postmarket surveillance as required under section 522 of the Federal Food, Drug, and Cosmetic Act.

(iii) Applicable Drug Clinical Trial. —

(I) In General. — The term "applicable drug clinical trial" means a controlled clinical investigation, other than a phase I clinical investigation, of a drug subject to section 505 of the Federal Food, Drug, and Cosmetic Act or to section 351 of this Act.

(II) Clinical Investigation. — For purposes of subclause (I), the term "clinical investigation" has the meaning given that term in section 312.3 of title 21, Code of Federal Regulations (or any successor regulation).

(III) Phase I. — For purposes of subclause (I), the term "phase I" has the meaning given that term in section 312.21 of title 21, Code of Federal Regulations (or any successor regulation).

(iv) Clinical Trial Information. — The term "clinical trial information" means, with respect to an applicable clinical trial, those data elements that the responsible party is required to submit under paragraph (2) or under paragraph (3).

(v) Completion Date. — The term "completion date" means, with respect to an applicable clinical trial, the date that the final subject was examined or received an intervention for the purposes of final collection of data for the primary outcome, whether the clinical trial concluded according to the prespecified protocol or was terminated.

(vi) Device. — The term "device" means a device as defined in section 201(h) of the Federal Food, Drug, and Cosmetic Act.

(vii) Drug. — The term "drug" means a drug as defined in section 201(g) of the Federal Food, Drug, and Cosmetic Act or a biological product as defined in section 351 of this Act.

(viii) Ongoing. — The term "ongoing" means, with respect to a clinical trial of a drug or a device and to a date, that—

(I) 1 or more patients is enrolled in the clinical trial; and

(II) the date is before the completion date of the clinical trial.

(ix) Responsible Party. — The term "responsible party", with respect to a clinical trial of a drug or device, means —

(I) the sponsor of the clinical trial (as defined in section 50.3 of title 21, Code of Federal Regulations (or any successor regulation)); or

(II) the principal investigator of such clinical trial if so designated by a sponsor, grantee, contractor, or awardee, so long as the principal investigator is responsible for conducting the trial, has access to and control over the data from the clinical trial, has the right to publish the results of the trial, and has the ability to meet all of the requirements under this subsection for the submission of clinical trial information.

(B) Requirement. — The Secretary shall develop a mechanism by which the responsible party for each applicable clinical trial shall submit the identity and contact information of such responsible party to the Secretary at the time of submission of clinical trial information under paragraph (2).

(2) Expansion of Clinical Trial Registry Data Bank with Respect to Clinical Trial Information. —

(A) In General. —

(i) Expansion of Data Bank. — To enhance patient enrollment and provide a mechanism to track subsequent progress of clinical trials, the Secretary, acting through the Director of NIH, shall expand, in accordance with this subsection, the clinical trials registry of the data bank described under subsection (i)(1) (referred to in this subsection as the "registry data bank"). The Director of NIH shall ensure that the registry data bank is made publicly available through the Internet.

(ii) Content. — The clinical trial information required to be submitted under this paragraph for an applicable clinical trial shall include —

(I) descriptive information, including —

(aa) a brief title, intended for the lay public;

(bb) a brief summary, intended for the lay public;

(cc) the primary purpose;

(dd) the study design;

(ee) for an applicable drug clinical trial, the study phase;

(ff) study type;

(gg) the primary disease or condition being studied, or the focus of the study;

(hh) the intervention name and intervention type;

(ii) the study start date;

(jj) the expected completion date;

(kk) the target number of subjects; and

(ll) outcomes, including primary and secondary outcome measures;

(II) recruitment information, including —

(aa) eligibility criteria;

(bb) gender;

(cc) age limits;

(dd) whether the trial accepts healthy volunteers;

(ee) overall recruitment status;

(ff) individual site status; and

(gg) in the case of an applicable drug clinical trial, if the drug is not approved under section 505 of the Federal Food, Drug, and Cosmetic Act or licensed under section 351 of this Act, specify whether or not there is expanded access to the drug under section 561 of the Federal Food, Drug, and Cosmetic Act for those who do not qualify for enrollment in the clinical trial and how to obtain information about such access;

(III) location and contact information, including—

(aa) the name of the sponsor;

(bb) the responsible party, by official title; and

(cc) the facility name and facility contact information (including the city, State, and zip code for each clinical trial location, or a tollfree number through which such location information may be accessed); and

(IV) administrative data (which the Secretary may make publicly available as necessary), including—

(aa) the unique protocol identification number;

(bb) other protocol identification numbers, if any; and

(cc) the Food and Drug Administration IND/IDE protocol number and the record verification date.

(iii) Modifications. — The Secretary may by regulation modify the requirements for clinical trial information under this paragraph, if the Secretary provides a rationale for why such a modification improves and does not reduce such clinical trial information.

(B) Format and Structure. —

(i) Searchable Categories. — The Director of NIH shall ensure that the public may, in addition to keyword searching, search the entries in the registry data bank by 1 or more of the following criteria:

(I) The disease or condition being studied in the clinical trial, using Medical Subject Headers (MESH) descriptors.

(II) The name of the intervention, including any drug or device being studied in the clinical trial.

(III) The location of the clinical trial

(IV) The age group studied in the clinical trial, including pediatric subpopulations.

(V) The study phase of the clinical trial.

(VI) The sponsor of the clinical trial, which may be the National Institutes of Health or another Federal agency, a private industry source, or a university or other organization.

(VII) The recruitment status of the clinical trial.

(VIII) The National Clinical Trial number or other study identification for the clinical trial.

(ii) Additional Searchable Category. — Not later than 18 months after the date of the enactment of the Food and Drug Administration Amendments Act of 2007, the Director of NIH shall ensure that the public may search the entries of the registry data bank by the safety issue, if any, being studied in the clinical trial as a primary or secondary outcome.

(iii) Other Elements. — The Director of NIH shall also ensure hat the public may search the entries of the registry data bank by such other elements as the Director deems necessary on an ongoing basis.

(iv) Format. — The Director of the NIH shall ensure that the registry data bank is easily used by the public, and that entries are easily compared.

(C) Data Submission. — The responsible party for an applicable clinical trial, including an applicable drug clinical trial for a serious or life-threatening disease or condition, that is initiated after, or is ongoing on the date that is 90 days after, the date of the enactment of the Food and Drug Administration Amendments Act of 2007, shall submit to the Director of NIH for inclusion in the registry data bank the clinical trial information described in of subparagraph (A)(ii) not later than the later of —

(i) 90 days after such date of enactment;

(ii) 21 days after the first patient is enrolled in such clinical trial; or

(iii) in the case of a clinical trial that is not for a serious or life-threatening disease or condition and that is ongoing on such date of enactment, 1 year after such date of enactment.

(D) Posting of Data. —

(i) Applicable Drug Clinical Trial. — The Director of NIH shall ensure that clinical trial information for an applicable drug clinical trial submitted in accordance with this paragraph is posted in the registry data bank not later than 30 days after such submission.

(ii) Applicable Device Clinical Trial. — The Director of NIH shall ensure that clinical trial information for an applicable device clinical trial submitted in accordance with this paragraph is posted publicly in the registry data bank —

(I) not earlier than the date of clearance under section 510(k) of the Federal Food, Drug, and Cosmetic Act, or approval under section 515 or 520(m) of such Act, as applicable, for a device that was not previously cleared or approved, and not later than 30 days after such date, unless the responsible party affirmatively requests that the Director of the National Institutes of Health publicly post such clinical trial information for an applicable device clinical trial prior to such date of clearance or approval; or

(II) for a device that was previously cleared or approved, not later than 30 days after the clinical trial information under paragraph (3)(C) is required to be posted by the Secretary.

(iii) Option to Make Certain Clinical Trial Information Available Earlier.—The Director of the National Institutes of Health shall inform responsible parties of the option to request that clinical trial information for an applicable device clinical trial be publicly posted prior to the date of clearance or approval, in accordance with clause (ii)(I).

(iv) Combination Products.—An applicable clinical trial for a product that is a combination of drug, device, or biological product shall be considered—

(I) an applicable drug clinical trial, if the Secretary determines under section 503(g) of the Federal Food, Drug, and Cosmetic Act that the primary mode of action of such product is that of a drug or biological product; or

(II) an applicable device clinical trial, if the Secretary determines under such section that the primary mode of action of such product is that of a device.

(3) Expansion of Registry Data Bank to Include Results of Clinical Trials. —

(A) Linking Registry Data Bank to Existing Results. —

(i) In General. — Beginning not later than 90 days after the date of the enactment of the Food and Drug Administration Amendments Act of 2007, for those clinical trials that form the primary basis of an efficacy claim or are conducted after the drug involved is approved or after the device involved is cleared or approved, the Secretary shall ensure that the registry data bank includes links to results information as described in clause (ii) for such clinical trial —

(I) not earlier than 30 days after the date of the approval of the drug involved or clearance or approval of the device involved; or

(II) not later than 30 days after the results information described in clause (ii) becomes publicly available.

(ii) Required Information. —

(I) FDA Information. — The Secretary shall ensure that the registry data bank includes links to the following information:

(aa) If an advisory committee considered at a meeting an applicable clinical trial, any posted Food and Drug Administration summary document regarding such applicable clinical trial.

(bb) If an applicable drug clinical trial was conducted under section 505A or 505B of the Federal Food, Drug, and Cosmetic Act, a link to the posted Food and Drug Administration assessment of the results of such trial.

(cc) Food and Drug Administration public health advisories regarding the drug or device that is the subject of the applicable clinical trial, if any.

(dd) For an applicable drug clinical trial, the Food and Drug Administration action package for approval document required under section 505(l)(2) of the Federal Food, Drug, and Cosmetic Act.

(ee) For an applicable device clinical trial, in the case of a premarket application under section 515 of the Federal Food, Drug, and Cosmetic Act, the detailed summary of information respecting the safety and effectiveness of the device required under section 520(h)(1) of such Act, or, in the case of a report under section 510(k) of such Act, the section 510(k) summary of the safety and effectiveness data required under section 807.95(d) of title 21, Code of Federal Regulations (or any successor regulation).

(II) NIH Information. — The Secretary shall ensure that the registry data bank includes links to the following information:

(aa) Medline citations to any publications focused on the results of an applicable clinical trial.

(bb) The entry for the drug that is the subject of an applicable drug clinical trial in the National Library of Medicine database of structured product labels, if available.

(iii) Results for Existing Data Bank Entries. — The Secretary may include the links described in clause (ii) for data bank entries for clinical trials submitted to the data bank prior to enactment of the Food and Drug Administration Amendments Act of 2007, as available.

(B) Inclusion of Results. — The Secretary, acting through the Director of NIH, shall —

(i) expand the registry data bank to include the results of applicable clinical trials (referred to in this subsection as the "registry and results data bank");

(ii) ensure that such results are made publicly available through the Internet;

(iii) post publicly a glossary for the lay public explaining technical terms related to the results of clinical trials; and

(iv) in consultation with experts on risk communication, provide information with the information included under subparagraph (C) in the registry and results data bank to help ensure that such information does not mislead the patients or the public.

(C) Basic Results. — Not later than 1 year after the date of the enactment of the Food and Drug Administration Amendments Act of 2007, the Secretary shall include in the registry and results data bank the following elements for drugs that are approved under section 505 of the Federal Food, Drug, and Cosmetic Act or licensed under section 351 of this Act and devices that are cleared under section 510(k) of the Federal Food, Drug, and Cosmetic Act or approved under section 515 or 520(m) of such Act:

(i) Demographic And Baseline Characteristics of Patient Sample. — A table of the demographic and baseline data collected overall and for each arm of the clinical trial to describe the patients who participated in the clinical trial, including the number of patients who dropped out of the clinical trial and the number of patients excluded from the analysis, if any.

(ii) Primary and Secondary Outcomes. — The primary and secondary outcome measures as submitted under paragraph (2)(A)(ii)(I)(ll), and a table of values for each of the primary and secondary outcome measures for each arm of the clinical trial, including the results of scientifically appropriate tests of the statistical significance of such outcome measures.

(iii) Point of Contact. — A point of contact for scientific information about the clinical trial results.

(iv) Certain Agreements. — Whether there exists an agreement (other than an agreement solely to comply with applicable provisions of law protecting the privacy of participants) between the sponsor or its agent and the principal investigator (unless the sponsor is an employer of the principal investigator) that restricts in any manner the ability of the principal investigator, after the completion date of the trial, to discuss the results of the trial at a scientific meeting or any other public or private forum, or to publish in a scientific or academic journal information concerning the results of the trial.

(D) Expanded Registry and Results Data Bank. —

(i) Expansion by Rulemaking. — To provide more complete results information and to enhance patient access to and understanding of the results of clinical trials, not later than 3 years after the date of the enactment of the Food and Drug Administration Amendments Act of 2007, the Secretary shall by regulation expand the registry and results data bank as provided under this subparagraph.

(ii) Clinical Trials. —

(I) Approved Products. — The regulations under this subparagraph shall require the inclusion of the results information described in clause (iii) for —

(aa) each applicable drug clinical trial for a drug that is approved under section 505 of the Federal Food, Drug, and Cosmetic Act or licensed under section 351 of this Act; and

(bb) each applicable device clinical trial for a device that is cleared under section 510(k) of the Federal Food, Drug, and Cosmetic Act or approved under section 515 or 520(m) of such Act.

(II) Unapproved Products. — The regulations under this subparagraph shall establish whether or not the results information described in clause (iii) shall be required for —

(aa) an applicable drug clinical trial for a drug that is not approved under section 505 of the Federal Food, Drug, and Cosmetic Act and not licensed under section 351 of this Act (whether approval or licensure was sought or not); and

(bb) an applicable device clinical trial for a device that is not cleared under section 510(k) of the Federal Food, Drug, and Cosmetic Act and not approved under section 515 or section 520(m) of such Act (whether clearance or approval was sought or not).

(iii) Required Elements. — The regulations under this subparagraph shall require, in addition to the elements described in subparagraph (C), information within each of the following categories:

(I) A summary of the clinical trial and its results that is written in non-technical, understandable language for patients, if the Secretary determines that such types of summary can be included without being misleading or promotional.

(II) A summary of the clinical trial and its results that is technical in nature, if the Secretary determines that such types of summary can be included without being misleading or promotional.

(III) The full protocol or such information on the protocol for the trial as may be necessary to help to evaluate the results of the trial.

(IV) Such other categories as the Secretary determines appropriate.

(iv) Results Submission. — The results information described in clause (iii) shall be submitted to the Director of NIH for inclusion in the registry and results data bank as provided by subparagraph (E), except that the Secretary shall by regulation determine —

(I) whether the 1-year period for submission of clinical trial information described in subparagraph (E)(i) should be increased from 1 year to a period not to exceed 18 months;

(II) whether the clinical trial information described in clause (iii) should be required to be submitted for an applicable clinical trial for which the clinical trial information described in subparagraph (C) is submitted to the registry and results data bank before the effective date of the regulations issued under this subparagraph; and

(III) in the case when the clinical trial information described in clause (iii) is required to be submitted for the applicable clinical trials described in clause (ii)(II), the date by which such clinical trial information shall be required to be submitted, taking into account —

(aa) the certification process under subparagraph (E)(iii) when approval, licensure, or clearance is sought; and

(bb) whether there should be a delay of submission when approval, licensure, or clearance will not be sought.

(v) Additional Provisions. — The regulations under this subparagraph shall also establish —

(I) a standard format for the submission of clinical trial information under this paragraph to the registry and results data bank;

(II) additional information on clinical trials and results that is written in nontechnical, understandable language for patients;

(III) considering the experience under the pilot quality control project described in paragraph (5)(C), procedures for quality control, including using representative samples, with respect to completeness and content of clinical trial information under this subsection, to help ensure that data elements are not false or misleading and are non-promotional;

(IV) the appropriate timing and requirements for updates of clinical trial information, and whether and, if so, how such updates should be tracked;

(V) a statement to accompany the entry for an applicable clinical trial when the primary and secondary outcome measures for such clinical trial are submitted under paragraph (4)(A) after the date specified for the submission of such information in paragraph (2)(C); and

(VI) additions or modifications to the manner of reporting of the data elements established under subparagraph (C).

(vi) Consideration of World Health Organization Data Set. — The Secretary shall consider the status of the consensus data elements set for reporting clinical trial results of the World Health Organization when issuing the regulations under this subparagraph.

(vii) Public Meeting. — The Secretary shall hold a public meeting no later than 18 months after the date of the enactment of the Food and Drug Administration Amendments Act of 2007 to provide an opportunity for input from interested parties with regard to the regulations to be issued under this subparagraph.

(E) Submission of Results Information. —

(i) In General. — Except as provided in clauses (iii), (iv), (v), and (vi) the responsible party for an applicable clinical trial that is described in clause (ii) shall submit to the Director of NIH for inclusion in the registry and results data bank the clinical trial information described in subparagraph (C) not later than 1 year, or such other period as may be provided by regulation under subparagraph (D), after the earlier of —

(I) the estimated completion date of the trial as described in paragraph (2)(A)(ii)(I)(jj); or

(II) the actual date of completion.

(ii) Clinical Trials Described. — An applicable clinical trial described in this clause is an applicable clinical trial subject to —

(I) paragraph (2)(C); and

(II) —

(aa) subparagraph (C); or

(bb) the regulations issued under subparagraph (D).

(iii) Delayed Submission of Results with Certification. — If the responsible party for an applicable clinical trial submits a certification that clause (iv) or (v) applies to such clinical trial, the responsible party shall submit to the Director of NIH for inclusion in the registry and results data bank the clinical trial information described in subparagraphs (C) and (D) as required under the applicable clause.

(iv) Seeking Initial Approval of a Drug or Device. — With respect to an applicable clinical trial that is completed before the drug is initially approved under section 505 of the Federal Food, Drug, and Cosmetic Act or initially licensed under section 351 of this Act, or the device is initially cleared under section 510(k) or initially approved under section 515 or 520(m) of the Federal Food, Drug, and Cosmetic Act, the responsible party shall submit to the Director of NIH for inclusion in the registry and results data bank the clinical trial information described in subparagraphs (C) and (D) not later than 30 days after the drug or device is approved under such section 505, licensed under such section 351, cleared under such section 510(k), or approved under such section 515 or 520(m), as applicable.

(v) Seeking Approval of a New Use for the Drug or Device. —

(I) In General. — With respect to an applicable clinical trial where the manufacturer of the drug or device is the sponsor of an applicable clinical trial, and such manufacturer has filed, or will file within 1 year, an application seeking approval under section 505 of the Federal Food, Drug, and Cosmetic Act, licensing under section 351 of this Act, or clearance under section 510(k), or approval under section 515 or 520(m), of the Federal Food, Drug, and Cosmetic Act for the use studied in such clinical trial (which use is not included in the labeling of the approved drug or device), then the responsible party shall submit to the Director of NIH for inclusion in the registry and results data bank the clinical trial information described in subparagraphs (C) and (D) on the earlier of the date that is 30 days after the date —

(aa) the new use of the drug or device is approved under such section 505, licensed under such section 351, cleared under such section 510(k), or approved under such section 515 or 520(m);

(bb) the Secretary issues a letter, such as a complete response letter, not approving the submission or not clearing the submission, a not approvable letter, or a not substantially equivalent letter for the new use of the drug or device under such section 505, 351, 510(k), 515, or 520(m); or

(cc) except as provided in subclause (III), the application or premarket notification under such section 505, 351, 510(k), 515, or 520(m) is withdrawn without resubmission for no less than 210 days.

(II) Requirement that Each Clinical Trial in Application be Treated the Same. — If a manufacturer makes a certification under clause (iii) that this clause applies with respect to a clinical trial, the manufacturer shall make such a certification with respect to each applicable clinical trial that is required to be submitted in an application or report for licensure, approval, or clearance (under section 351 of this Act or section 505, 510(k), 515, or 520(m) of the Federal Food, Drug, and Cosmetic Act, as applicable) of the use studied in the clinical trial.

(III) Two-year Limitation. — The responsible party shall submit to the Director of NIH for inclusion in the registry and results data bank the clinical trial information subject to subclause (I) on the date that is 2 years after the date a certification under clause (iii) was made to the Director of NIH, if an action referred to in item (aa), (bb), or (cc) of subclause (I) has not occurred by such date.

(vi) Extensions. — The Director of NIH may provide an extension of the deadline for submission of clinical trial information under clause (i) if the responsible party for the trial submits to the Director a written request that demonstrates good cause for the extension and provides an estimate of the date on which the information will be submitted. The Director of NIH may grant more than one such extension for a clinical trial.

(F) Notice to Director of NIH. — Commissioner of Food and Drugs shall notify the Director of NIH when there is an action described in subparagraph (E)(iv) or item (aa), (bb), or (cc) of subparagraph (E)(v)(I) with respect to an application or a report that includes a certification required under paragraph (5)(B) of such action not later than 30 days after such action.

(G) Posting of Data. — The Director of NIH shall ensure that the clinical trial information described in subparagraphs (C) and (D) for an applicable clinical trial submitted in accordance with this paragraph is posted publicly in the registry and results database not later than 30 days after such submission.

(H) Waivers Regarding Certain Clinical Trial Results. — The Secretary may waive any applicable requirements of this paragraph for an applicable clinical trial, upon a written request from the responsible party, if the Secretary determines that extraordinary circumstances justify the waiver and that providing the waiver is consistent with the protection of public health, or in the interest of national security. Not later than 30 days after any part of a waiver is granted, the Secretary shall notify, in writing, the appropriate committees of Congress of the waiver and provide an explanation for why the waiver was granted.

(I) Adverse Events. —

(i) Regulations. — Not later than 18 months after the date of the enactment of the Food and Drug Administration Amendments Act of 2007, the Secretary shall by regulation determine the best method for including in the registry and results data bank appropriate results information on serious adverse and frequent adverse events for drugs described in subparagraph (C) in a manner and form that is useful and not misleading to patients, physicians, and scientists.

(ii) Default. — If the Secretary fails to issue the regulation required by clause (i) by the date that is 24 months after the date of the enactment of the Food and Drug Administration Amendments Act of 2007, clause (iii) shall take effect.

(iii) Additional Elements. — Upon the application of clause (ii), the Secretary shall include in the registry and results data bank for drugs described in subparagraph (C), in addition to the clinical trial information described in subparagraph (C), the following elements:

(I) Serious Adverse Events. — A table of anticipated and unanticipated serious adverse events grouped by organ system, with number and frequency of such event in each arm of the clinical trial.

(II) Frequent Adverse Events. — A table of anticipated and unanticipated adverse events that are not included in the table described in subclause (I) that exceed a frequency of 5 percent within any arm of the clinical trial, grouped by organ system, with number and frequency of such event in each arm of the clinical trial.

(iv) Posting of Other Information. — In carrying out clause (iii), the Secretary shall, in consultation with experts in risk communication, post with the tables information to enhance patient understanding and to ensure such tables do not mislead patients or the lay public.

(v) Relation To Subparagraph (c). — Clinical trial information included in the registry and results data bank pursuant to this subparagraph is deemed to be clinical trial information included in such data bank pursuant to subparagraph (C).

(4) Additional Submissions of Clinical Trial Information. —

(A) Voluntary Submissions. — A responsible party for a clinical trial that is not an applicable clinical trial, or that is an applicable clinical trial that is not subject to paragraph (2)(C), may submit complete clinical trial information described in paragraph (2) or paragraph (3) provided the responsible party submits clinical trial information for each applicable clinical trial that is required to be submitted under section 351 or under section 505, 510(k), 515, or 520(m) of the Federal Food, Drug, and Cosmetic Act in an application or report for licensure, approval, or clearance of the drug or device for the use studied in the clinical trial.

(B) Required Submissions. —

(i) In General. —

Notwithstanding paragraphs (2) and (3) and subparagraph (A), in any case in which the Secretary determines for a specific clinical trial described in clause (ii) that posting in the registry and results data bank of clinical trial information for such clinical trial is necessary to protect the public health —

(I) the Secretary may require by notification that such information be submitted to the Secretary in accordance with paragraphs (2) and (3) except with regard to timing of submission;

(II) unless the responsible party submits a certification under paragraph (3)(E)(iii), such information shall be submitted not later than 30 days after the date specified by the Secretary in the notification; and

(III) failure to comply with the requirements under subclauses (I) and (II) shall be treated as a violation of the corresponding requirement of such paragraphs.

(ii) Clinical Trials Described. — Aclinical trial described in this clause is —

(I) an applicable clinical trial for a drug that is approved under section 505 of the Federal Food, Drug, and Cosmetic Act or licensed under section 351 of this Act or for a device that is cleared under section 510(k) of the Federal Food, Drug, and Cosmetic Act or approved under section 515 or section 520(m) of such Act, whose completion date is on or after the date 10 years before the date of the enactment of the Food and Drug Administration Amendments Act of 2007; or

(II) an applicable clinical trial that is described by both by paragraph (2)(C) and paragraph (3)(D)(ii)(II)).

(C) Updates to Clinical Trial Data Bank. —

(i) Submission of Updates. — The responsible party for an applicable clinical trial shall submit to the Director of NIH for inclusion in the registry and results data bank updates to reflect changes to the clinical trial information submitted under paragraph (2). Such updates —

(I) shall be provided not less than once every 12 months, unless there were no changes to the clinical trial information during the preceding 12-month period;

(II) shall include identification of the dates of any such changes;

(III) not later than 30 days after the recruitment status of such clinical trial changes, shall include an update of the recruitment status; and

(IV) not later than 30 days after the completion date of the clinical trial, shall include notification to the Director that such clinical trial is complete.

(ii) Public Availability of Updates. — The Director of NIH shall make updates submitted under clause (i) publicly available in the registry data bank. Except with regard to overall recruitment status, individual site status, location, and contact information, the Director of NIH shall ensure that updates to elements required under subclauses (I) to (V) of paragraph (2)(A)(ii) do not result in the removal of any information from the original submissions or any preceding updates, and information in such databases is presented in a manner that enables users to readily access each original element submission and to track the changes made by the updates. The Director of NIH shall provide a link from the table of primary and secondary outcomes required under paragraph (3)(C)(ii) to the tracked history required under this clause of the primary and secondary outcome measures submitted under paragraph (2)(A)(ii)(I)(ll).

(5) Coordination and Compliance. —

(A) Clinical Trials Supported by Grants from Federal Agencies. —

(i) Grants from Certain Federal Agencies. — If an applicable clinical trial is funded in whole or in part by a grant from any agency of the Department of Health and Human Services, including the Food and Drug Administration, the National Institutes of Health, or the Agency for Healthcare Research and Quality, any grant or progress report forms required under such grant shall include a certification that the responsible party has made all required submissions to the Director of NIH under paragraphs (2) and (3).

(ii) Verification by Federal Agencies. — The heads of the agencies referred to in clause (i), as applicable, shall verify that the clinical trial information for each applicable clinical trial for which a grantee is the responsible party has been submitted under paragraphs (2) and (3) before releasing any remaining funding for a grant or funding for a future grant to such grantee.

(iii) Notice and Opportunity to Remedy. — If the head of an agency referred to in clause (i), as applicable, verifies that a grantee has not submitted clinical trial information as described in clause (ii), such agency head shall provide notice to such grantee of such non-compliance and allow such grantee 30 days to correct such non-compliance and submit the required clinical trial information.

(iv) Consultation with Other Federal Agencies. — The Secretary shall —

(I) consult with other agencies that conduct research involving human subjects in accordance with any section of part 46 of title 45, Code of Federal Regulations (or any successor regulations), to determine if any such research is an applicable clinical trial; and

(II) develop with such agencies procedures comparable to those described in clauses (i), (ii), and (iii) to ensure that clinical trial information for such applicable clinical trial is submitted under paragraphs (2) and (3).

(B) Certification to Accompany Drug, Biological Product, and Device Submissions. — At the time of submission of an application under section 505 of the Federal Food, Drug, and Cosmetic Act, section 515 of such Act, section 520(m) of such Act, or section 351 of this Act, or submission of a report under section 510(k) of such Act, such application or submission shall be accompanied by a certification that all applicable requirements of this subsection have been met. Where available, such certification shall include the appropriate National Clinical Trial control numbers.

(C) Quality Control. —

(i) Pilot Quality Control Project. — Until the effective date of the regulations issued under paragraph (3)(D), the Secretary, acting through the Director of NIH and the Commissioner of Food and Drugs, shall conduct a pilot project to determine the optimal method of verification to help to ensure that the clinical trial information submitted under paragraph (3)(C) is non-promotional and is not false or misleading in any particular under subparagraph (D). The Secretary shall use the publicly available information described in paragraph (3)(A) and any other information available to the Secretary about applicable clinical trials to verify the accuracy of the clinical trial information submitted under paragraph (3)(C).

(ii) Notice of Compliance. — If the Secretary determines that any clinical trial information was not submitted as required under this subsection, or was submitted but is false or misleading in any particular, the Secretary shall notify the responsible party and give such party an opportunity to remedy such noncompliance by submitting the required revised clinical trial information not later than 30 days after such notification.

(D) Truthful Clinical Trial Information. —

(i) In General. — The clinical trial information submitted by a responsible party under this subsection shall not be false or misleading in any particular.

(ii) Effect. — Clause (i) shall not have the effect of—

(I) requiring clinical trial information with respect to an applicable clinical trial to include information from any source other than such clinical trial involved; or

(II) requiring clinical trial information described in paragraph (3)(D) to be submitted for purposes of paragraph (3)(C).

(E) Public Notices. —

(i) Notice of Violations. — If the responsible party for an applicable clinical trial fails to submit clinical trial information for such clinical trial as required under paragraphs (2) or (3), the Director of NIH shall include in the registry and results data bank entry for such clinical trial a notice —

(I) that the responsible party is not in compliance with this Act by —

(aa) failing to submit required clinical trial information; or

(bb) submitting false or misleading clinical trial information;

(II) of the penalties imposed for the violation, if any; and

(III) whether the responsible party has corrected the clinical trial information in the registry and results data bank.

(ii) Notice of Failure to Submit Primary and Secondary Outcomes. — If the responsible party for an applicable clinical trial fails to submit the primary and secondary outcomes as required under section 2(A)(ii)(I)(ll), the Director of NIH shall include in the registry and results data bank entry for such clinical trial a notice that the responsible party is not in compliance by failing to register the primary and secondary outcomes in accordance with this act, and that the primary and secondary outcomes were not publicly disclosed in the database before conducting the clinical trial.

(iii) Failure to Submit Statement. — The notice under clause (i) for a violation described in clause (i)(I)(aa) shall include the following statement: 'The entry for this clinical trial was not complete at the time of submission, as required by law. This may or may not have any bearing on the accuracy of the information in the entry.'.

(iv) Submission of False Information Statement. — The notice under clause (i) for a violation described in clause (i)(I)(bb) shall include the following statement: 'The entry for this clinical trial was found to be false or misleading and therefore not in compliance with the law.

(v) Non-Submission of Statement. — The notice under clause (ii) for a violation described in clause (ii) shall include the following statement: 'The entry for this clinical trial did not contain information on the primary and secondary outcomes at the time of submission, as required by law. This may or may not have any bearing on the accuracy of the information in the entry.

(vi) Compliance Searches. — The Director of NIH shall provide that the public may easily search the registry and results data bank for entries that include notices required under this subparagraph.

(6) Limitation on Disclosure of Clinical Trial Information. —

(A) In General. — Nothing in this subsection (or under section 552 of title 5, United States Code) shall require the Secretary to publicly disclose, by any means other than the registry and results data bank, information described in subparagraph (B).

(B) Information Described. — Information described in this subparagraph is —

(i) information submitted to the Director of NIH under this subsection, or information of the same general nature as (or integrally associated with) the information so submitted; and

(ii) information not otherwise publicly available, including because it is protected from disclosure under section 552 of title 5, United States Code.

(7) Authorization of Appropriations. — There are authorized to be appropriated to carry out this subsection $10,000,000 for each fiscal year.

(k) Day Care Service for The Employees of the National Institutes of Health.

(1) The Director of NIH may establish a program to provide day care service for the employees of the National Institutes of Health similar to those services provided by other Federal agencies (including the availability of day care service on a 24-hour-a-day basis).

(2) Any day care provider at the National Institutes of Health shall establish a sliding scale of fees that takes into consideration the income and needs of the employee.

(3) For purposes regarding the provision of day care services, the Director of NIH may enter into rental or lease purchase agreements.

(l) Council of Councils.

(1) Establishment. Not later than 90 days after the date of the enactment of the National Institutes of Health Reform Act of 2006 [January 15, 2007 — Ed.], the Director of NIH shall establish within the Office of the Director an advisory council to be known as the "Council of Councils" (referred to in this subsection as the "Council") for the purpose of advising the Director on matters related to the policies and activities of the Division of Program Coordination, Planning, and Strategic Initiatives, including making recommendations with respect to the conduct and support of research described in subsection (b)(7).

(2) Membership.

(A) In General. The Council shall be composed of 27 members selected by the Director of NIH with approval from the Secretary from among the list of nominees under subparagraph (C).

(B) Certain Requirements. In selecting the members of the Council, the Director of NIH shall ensure —

(i) the representation of a broad range of disciplines and perspectives; and

(ii) the ongoing inclusion of at least 1 representative from each national research institute whose budget is substantial relative to a majority of the other institutes.

(C) Nomination. The Director of NIH shall maintain an updated list of individuals who have been nominated to serve on the Council, which list shall consist of the following:

(i) For each national research institute and national center, 3 individuals nominated by the head of such institute or center from among the members of the advisory council of the institute or center, of which —

(I) two shall be scientists; and

(II) one shall be from the general public or shall be a leader in the field of public policy, law, health policy, economics, or management.

(ii) For each office within the Division of Program Coordination, Planning, and Strategic Initiatives, 1 individual nominated by the head of such office.

(iii) Members of the Council of Public Representatives.

(2) Terms. [Probably should be (3). — Ed.]

(A) In General. The term of service for a member of the Council shall be 6 years, except as provided in subparagraphs (B) and (C).

(B) Terms of Initial Appointees. Of the initial members selected for the Council, the Director of NIH shall designate —

(i) nine for a term of 6 years;

(ii) nine for a term of 4 years; and

(iii) nine for a term of 2 years.

(C) Vacancies. Any member appointed to fill a vacancy occurring before the expiration of the term for which the member's predecessor was appointed shall be appointed only for the remainder of that term. A member may serve after the expiration of that member's term until a successor has taken office.

(m) National Institutes of Health Strategic Plan.—

(1) In General. —Not later than 2 years after the date of enactment of the 21st Century Cures Act [December 13, 2016 —Ed.], and at least every 6 years thereafter, the Director of the National Institutes of Health shall develop and submit to the appropriate committees of Congress and post on the Internet website of the National Institutes of Health, a coordinated strategy (to be known as the "National Institutes of Health Strategic Plan") to provide direction to the biomedical research investments made by the National Institutes of Health, to facilitate collaboration across the institutes and centers, to leverage scientific opportunity, and to advance biomedicine.

(2) Requirements. —The strategy under paragraph (1) shall—

(A) identify strategic research priorities and objectives across biomedical research, including—

(i) an assessment of the state of biomedical and behavioral research, including areas of opportunity with respect to basic, clinical, and translational research;

(ii) priorities and objectives to ad vance the treatment, cure, and prevention of health conditions;

(iii) emerging scientific opportunities, rising public health challenges, and scientific knowledge gaps; and

(iv) the identification of near-, mid-, and long-term scientific needs;

(B) consider, in carrying out subparagraph (A) —

(i) Disease burden in the United States and the potential for return on investment to the United States;

(ii) rare diseases and conditions;

(iii) biological, social, and other determinants of health that contribute to health disparities; and

(iv) other factors the Director of National Institutes of Health determines appropriate;;

(C) include multi-institute priorities, including coordination of research among institutes and centers;

(D) include strategic priorities for funding research through the Common Fund, in accordance with section 402A(c)(1)(C);

(E) address the National Institutes of Health's proposed and ongoing activities related to training and the biomedical workforce; and

(F) Describe opportunities for collaboration with other agencies and departments, as appropriate.

(3) Use of Plans.—Strategic plans developed and updated by the national research institutes and national centers of the National Institutes of Health shall be prepared regularly and in such a manner that such plans will be informed by the strategic plans developed and updated under this subsection. Such plans developed by and updated by the naional research institutes and national centers shall have a common template.

(4) Consultation.—The Director of National Institutes of Health shall develop the strategic plan under paragraph (1) in consultation with the directors of the national research institutes and national centers, researchers, patient advocacy groups, and industry leaders.

(n) Unique Research Initiatives.—

(1) In General. —The Director of NIH may approve, after consideration of a proposal under paragraph (2)(A), requests by the national research institutes and centers, or program officers within the Office of the Director to engage in transactions other than a contract, grant, or cooperative agreement with respect to projects that carry out—

(A) the Precision Medicine Initiative under section 498E; or

(B) section 402(b)(7), except that not more than 50 percent of the funds available for a fiscal year through the Common Fund under section 402A(c)(1) for purposes of carrying out such section 402(b)(7) may be used to engage in such other transactions.

(2) Requirements. —The authority provided under this subsection may be used to conduct or support high impact cutting-edge research described in paragraph (1) using the other transactions authority described in such paragraph if the institute, center, or office—

(A) submits a proposal to the Director of NIH for the use of such authority before conducting or supporting the research, including why the use of such authority is essential to promoting the success of the project;

(B) receives approval for the use of such authority from the Director of NIH; and

(C) for each year in which the institute, center, or office has used such authority in accordance with this subsection, submits a report to the Director of NIH on the activities of the institute, center, or office relating to such research.

42 U.S.C. § 284m. Program for Pediatric Studies of Drugs.

(a) List of Priority Issues in Pediatric Therapeutics. —

(1) In General. — Not later than one year after the date of the enactment of the Best Pharmaceuticals for Children Act of 2007, the Secretary, acting through the Director of the National Institutes of Health and in consultation with the Commissioner of Food and Drugs and experts in pediatric research, shall develop and publish a priority list of needs in pediatric therapeutics, including drugs, biological products, or indications that require study. The list shall be revised every three years.

(2) Consideration of Available Information.* — In developing and prioritizing the list under paragraph (1), the Secretary shall consider —

(A) therapeutic gaps in pediatrics that may include developmental pharmacology, pharmacogenetic determinants of drug response, metabolism of drugs and biologics in children, and pediatric clinical trials;

(B) particular pediatric diseases, disorders or conditions where more complete knowledge and testing of therapeutics, including drugs and biologics and identification of biomarkers for such diseases, disorders, or conditions, may be beneficial in pediatric populations; and

(C) the adequacy of necessary infrastructure to conduct pediatric pharmacological research, including research networks and trained pediatric investigators.

(b) Pediatric Studies and Research. — The Secretary, acting through the National Institutes of Health, shall award funds to entities that have the expertise to conduct pediatric clinical trials or other research (including qualified universities, hospitals, laboratories, contract research organizations, practice groups, federally funded programs such as pediatric pharmacology research units, other public or private institutions, or individuals) to enable the entities to conduct the drug studies or other research on the issues described in subsection (a). The Secretary may use contracts, grants, or other appropriate funding mechanisms to award funds under this subsection.

(c) Process for Proposed Pediatric Study Requests and Labeling Changes. —

(1) Submission of Proposed Pediatric Study Request. — The Director of the National Institutes of Health shall, as appropriate, submit proposed pediatric study requests for consideration by the Commissioner of Food and Drugs for pediatric studies of a specific pediatric indication identified under subsection (a). Such a proposed pediatric study request shall be made in a manner equivalent to a written request made under subsection (b) or (c) of section 505A of the Federal Food, Drug, and Cosmetic Act, or section 351(m) of this Act, including with respect to the information provided on the pediatric studies to be conducted pursuant to the request. The Director of the National Institutes of Health may submit a proposed pediatric study request for a drug for which —

(A) —

(i) there is an approved application under section 505(j) of the Federal Food, Drug, and Cosmetic Act or section 351(k) of this Act; or

(ii) there is a submitted application that could be approved under the criteria of such section; and

(B) there remains no patent listed pursuant to section 505(b)(1) of the Federal Food, Drug, and Cosmetic Act, and every three-year and five-year period referred to in subsection (c)(3)(E)(ii), (c)(3)(E)(iii), (c)(3)(E)(iv), (j)(5)(F)(ii), (j)(5)(F)(iii), or (j)(5)(F)(iv) of section 505 of the Federal Food, Drug, and Cosmetic Act, or applicable twelve-year period referred to in section 351(k)(7) of this Act, and any seven-year period referred to in section 527 of the Federal Food, Drug, and Cosmetic Act has ended for at least one form of the drug; and

* Ed. note.—Sec. 501 of the FDA Reauthorization Act of 2017 amends subsection (a)(2)(A)(ii), possibly using an unofficial version of the text wherein subparagraph (a)(2)(A) reads "(a)(2)(A) shall consider—", followed by subparagraphs (i), (ii), and (iii), which do not exist in official versions of the statute.

(C) additional studies are needed to assess the safety and effectiveness of the use of the drug in the pediatric population.

(2) Written Request to Holders of Approved Applications. — The Commissioner of Food and Drugs, in consultation with the Director of the National Institutes of Health, may issue a written request based on the proposed pediatric study request for the indication or indications submitted pursuant to paragraph (1) (which shall include a timeframe for negotiations for an agreement) for pediatric studies concerning a drug identified under subsection (a) to all holders of an approved application for the drug. Such a written request shall be made in a manner equivalent to the manner in which a written request is made under subsection (b) or (c) of section 505A of the Federal Food, Drug, and Cosmetic Act or section 351(m) of this Act, including with respect to information provided on the pediatric studies to be conducted pursuant to the request and using appropriate formulations for each age group for which the study is requested.

(3) Requests for Proposals. — If the Commissioner of Food and Drugs does not receive a response to a written request issued under paragraph (2) not later than 30 days after the date on which a request was issued, the Secretary, acting through the Director of the National Institutes of Health and in consultation with the Commissioner of Food and Drugs, shall publish a request for proposals to conduct the pediatric studies described in the written request in accordance with subsection (b).

(4) Disqualification. — A holder that receives a first right of refusal shall not be entitled to respond to a request for proposals under paragraph (3).

(5) Contracts, Grants, or Other Funding Mechanisms. — A contract, grant, or other funding may be awarded under this section only if a proposal is submitted to the Secretary in such form and manner, and containing such agreements, assurances, and information as the Secretary determines to be necessary to carry out this section.

(6) Reporting of Studies. —

(A) In General. — On completion of a pediatric study in accordance with an award under this section, a report concerning the study shall be submitted to the Director of the National Institutes of Health and the Commissioner of Food and Drugs. The report shall include all data generated in connection with the study, including a written request if issued.

~~**(B) Availability of Reports.** — Each report submitted under subparagraph (A) shall be considered to be in the public domain (subject to section 505A(d)(4) of the Federal Food, Drug, and Cosmetic Act) and shall be assigned a docket number by the Commissioner of Food and Drugs. An interested person may submit written comments concerning such pediatric studies to the Commissioner of Food and Drugs, and the written comments shall become part of the docket file with respect to each of the drugs.~~

<u>**(B) Availability of Reports.** —</u>

<u>**(i) In General.** — Each report submitted under subparagraph (A) shall be considered to be in the public domain (subject to section 505A(d)(4) of the Federal Food, Drug, and Cosmetic Act) and not later than 90 days after submission of such report, shall be—</u>

<u>**(I)** posted on the internet website of the National Institutes of Health in a manner that is accessible and consistent with all applicable Federal laws and regulations, including such laws and regulations for the protection of—</u>

<u>**(aa)** human research participants, including with respect to privacy, security, informed consent, and protected health information; and</u>

<u>**(bb)** proprietary interests, confidential commercial information, and intellectual property rights; and</u>

<u>**(II)** assigned a docket number by the Commissioner of Food and Drugs and made available for the submission of public comments.</u>

<u>**(ii) Submission of Comments.** — An interested person may submit written comments concerning such pediatric studies to the Commissioner of Food and Drugs, and the submitted comments shall become part of the docket file with respect to each of the drugs.</u>

(C) Action by Commissioner. — The Commissioner of Food and Drugs shall take ~~appropriate action in response to the reports submitted under subparagraph (A) in accordance with paragraph (7).~~ <u>action in a timely and appropriate manner in response to the reports submitted under subparagraph (A), in accordance with paragraph (7).</u>

(7) Requests for Labeling Change. — ~~During~~ Within the 180-day period after the date on which a report is submitted under paragraph (6)(A), the Commissioner of Food and Drugs shall —

(A) review the report and such other data as are available concerning the safe and effective use in the pediatric population of the drug studied;

(B) negotiate with the holders of approved applications for the drug studied for any labeling changes that the Commissioner of Food and Drugs determines to be appropriate and requests the holders to make; and

(C) —

(i) ~~place in the public docket file a copy of the report and of~~ include in the public docket file a reference to the location of the report on the internet website of the National Institutes of Health and a copy of any requested labeling changes; and

(ii) publish ~~in the Federal Register and~~ through a posting on the Web site of the Food and Drug Administration a summary of the report and a copy of any requested labeling changes.

(8) Dispute Resolution. —

(A) Referral to Pediatric Advisory Committee. — If, not later than the end of the 180-day period specified in paragraph (7), the holder of an approved application for the drug involved does not agree to any labeling change requested by the Commissioner of Food and Drugs under that paragraph, the Commissioner of Food and Drugs shall refer the request to the Pediatric Advisory Committee.

(B) Action by the Pediatric Advisory Committee. — Not later than 90 days after receiving a referral under subparagraph (A), the Pediatric Advisory Committee shall —

(i) review the available information on the safe and effective use of the drug in the pediatric population, including study reports submitted under this section; and

(ii) make a recommendation to the Commissioner of Food and Drugs as to appropriate labeling changes, if any.

(9) FDA Determination. — Not later than 30 days after receiving a recommendation from the Pediatric Advisory Committee under paragraph (8)(B)(ii) with respect to a drug, the Commissioner of Food and Drugs shall consider the recommendation and, if appropriate, make a request to the holders of approved applications for the drug to make any labeling change that the Commissioner of Food and Drugs determines to be appropriate.

(10) Failure to Agree. — If a holder of an approved application for a drug, within 30 days after receiving a request to make a labeling change under paragraph (9), does not agree to make a requested labeling change, the Commissioner of Food and Drugs may deem the drug to be misbranded under the Federal Food, Drug, and Cosmetic Act.

(11) No Effect on Authority. — Nothing in this subsection limits the authority of the United States to bring an enforcement action under the Federal Food, Drug, and Cosmetic Act when a drug lacks appropriate pediatric labeling. Neither course of action (the Pediatric Advisory Committee process or an enforcement action referred to in the preceding sentence) shall preclude, delay, or serve as the basis to stay the other course of action.

~~**(d) Dissemination of Pediatric Information.** — Not later than one year after the date of the enactment of the Best Pharmaceuticals for Children Act of 2007, the Secretary, acting through the Director of the National Institutes of Health, shall study the feasibility of establishing a compilation of information on pediatric drug use and report the findings to Congress.~~

~~**(e)**~~ **(d) Authorization of Appropriations.** —

(1) In General. — There are authorized to be appropriated to carry out this section, $25,000,000 for each of fiscal years ~~2013 through 2017~~ 2018 through 2022.

(2) Availability. — Any amount appropriated under paragraph (1) shall remain available to carry out this section until expended.

42 U.S.C. § 289g-5. Precision Medicine Initiative.

(a) In General. —The Secretary is encouraged to establish and carry out an initiative, to be known as the "Precision Medicine Initiative" (in this section referred to as the "Initiative"), to augment efforts to address disease prevention, diagnosis, and treatment.

(b) Components. —The Initiative described under subsection (a) may include—

(1) developing a network of scientists to assist in carrying out the purposes of the Initiative;

(2) developing new approaches for addressing scientific, medical, public health, and regulatory science issues;

(3) applying genomic technologies, such as whole genomic sequencing, to provide data on the molecular basis of disease;

(4) collecting information voluntarily provided by a diverse cohort of individuals that can be used to better understand health and disease; and

(5) other activities to advance the goals of the Initiative, as the Secretary determines appropriate.

(c) Authority of the Secretary.—In carrying out this section, the Secretary may—

(1) coordinate with the Secretary of Energy, private industry, and others, as the Secretary determines appropriate, to identify and address the advanced supercomputing and other advanced technology needs for the Initiative;

(2) develop and utilize public-private partnerships; and

(3) leverage existing data sources.

(d) Requirements.—In the implementation of the Initiative under subsection (a), the Secretary shall—

(1) ensure the collaboration of the National Institutes of Health, the Food and Drug Administration, the Office of the National Coordinator for Health Information Technology, and the Office for Civil Rights of the Department of Health and Human Services;

(2) comply with existing laws and regulations for the protection of human subjects involved in research, including the protection of participant privacy;

(3) implement policies and mechanisms for appropriate secure data sharing across systems that include protections for privacy and security of data;

(4) consider the diversity of the cohort to ensure inclusion of a broad range of participants, including consideration of biological, social, and other determinants of health that contribute to health disparities;

(5) ensure that only authorized individuals may access controlled or sensitive, identifiable biological material and associated information collected or stored in connection with the Initiative; and

(6) on the appropriate Internet website of the Department of Health and Human Services, identify any entities with access to such information and provide information with respect to the purpose of such access, a summary of the research project for which such access is granted, as applicable, and a description of the biological material and associated information to which the entity has access.

(e) Report.—Not later than 1 year after the date of enactment of the 21st Century Cures Act [December 13, 2016 —Ed.], the Secretary shall submit a report on the relevant data access policies and procedures to the Committee on Health, Education, Labor, and Pensions of the Senate and the Committee on Energy and Commerce of the House of Representatives. Such report shall include steps the Secretary has taken to consult with experts or other heads of departments or agencies of the Federal Government in the development of such policies.

TITLE I OF THE DRUG PRICE COMPETITION AND PATENT TERM RESTORATION ACT OF 1984

35 U.S.C. §§ 156, 271, 282-85
[WAXMAN-HATCH PATENT PROVISIONS]

35 U.S.C. § 156. EXTENSION OF PATENT TERM.

(a) The term of a patent which claims a product, a method of using a product, or a method of manufacturing a product shall be extended in accordance with this section from the original expiration date of the patent, which shall include any patent term adjustment granted under section 154(b), if —

(1) the term of the patent has not expired before an application is submitted under subsection (d)(1) for its extension;

(2) the term of the patent has never been extended under subsection (e)(1) of this section;

(3) an application for extension is submitted by the owner of record of the patent or its agent and in accordance with the requirements of paragraphs (1) through (4) of subsection (d);

(4) the product has been subject to a regulatory review period before its commercial marketing or use;

(5) —

(A) except as provided in subparagraph (B) or (C), the permission for the commercial marketing or use of the product after such regulatory review period is the first permitted commercial marketing or use of the product under the provision of law under which such regulatory review period occurred;

(B) in the case of a patent which claims a method of manufacturing the product which primarily uses recombinant DNA technology in the manufacture of the product, the permission for the commercial marketing or use of the product after such regulatory review period is the first permitted commercial marketing or use of a product manufactured under the process claimed in the patent; or

(C) for purposes of subparagraph (A), in the case of a patent which —

(i) claims a new animal drug or a veterinary biological product which

(I) is not covered by the claims in any other patent which has been extended, and

(II) has received permission for the commercial marketing or use in non-food-producing animals and in food-producing animals, and

(ii) was not extended on the basis of the regulatory review period for use in non-food-producing animals, the permission for the commercial marketing or use of the drug or product after the regulatory review period for use in food-producing animals is the first permitted commercial marketing or use of the drug or product for administration to a food-producing animal.

The product referred to in paragraphs (4) and (5) is hereinafter in this section referred to as the "approved product".

(b) Except as provided in subsection (d)(5)(F), the rights derived from any patent the term of which is extended under this section shall during the period during which the term of the patent is extended —

(1) in the case of a patent which claims a product, be limited to any use approved for the product —

(A) before the expiration of the term of the patent —

(i) under the provision of law under which the applicable regulatory review occurred, or

(ii) under the provision of law under which any regulatory review described in paragraph (1), (4), or (5) of subsection (g) occurred, and

(B) on or after the expiration of the regulatory review period upon which the extension of the patent was based;

(2) in the case of a patent which claims a method of using a product, be limited to any use claimed by the patent and approved for the product —

(A) before the expiration of the term of the patent —

(i) under any provision of law under which an applicable regulatory review occurred, and

(ii) under the provision of law under which any regulatory review described in paragraph (1), (4), or (5) of subsection (g) occurred, and

(B) on or after the expiration of the regulatory review period upon which the extension of the patent was based; and

(3) in the case of a patent which claims a method of manufacturing a product, be limited to the method of manufacturing as used to make —

(A) the approved product, or

(B) the product if it has been subject to a regulatory review period described in paragraph (1), (4), or (5) of subsection (g).

As used in this subsection, the term "product" includes an approved product.

(c) The term of a patent eligible for extension under subsection (a) shall be extended by the time equal to the regulatory review period for the approved product which period occurs after the date the patent is issued, except that —

(1) each period of the regulatory review period shall be reduced by any period determined under subsection (d)(2)(B) during which the applicant for the patent extension did not act with due diligence during such period of the regulatory review period;

(2) after any reduction required by paragraph (1), the period of extension shall include only one-half of the time remaining in the periods described in paragraphs (1)(B)(i), (2)(B)(i), (3)(B)(i), (4)(B)(i), and (5)(B)(i) of subsection (g);

(3) if the period remaining in the term of a patent after the date of the approval of the approved product under the provision of law under which such regulatory review occurred when added to the regulatory review period as revised under paragraphs (1) and (2) exceeds fourteen years, the period of extension shall be reduced so that the total of both such periods does not exceed fourteen years; and

(4) in no event shall more than one patent be extended under subsection (e)(1) for the same regulatory review period for any product.

(d) —

(1) To obtain an extension of the term of a patent under this section, the owner of record of the patent or its agent shall submit an application to the Director. Except as provided in paragraph (5), such an application may only be submitted within the sixty-day period beginning on the date the product received permission under the provision of law under which the applicable regulatory review period occurred for commercial marketing or use, or in the case of a drug product described in subsection (i), within the sixty-day period beginning on the covered date (as defined in subsection (i)). The application shall contain —

(A) the identity of the approved product and the Federal statute under which regulatory review occurred;

(B) the identity of the patent for which an extension is being sought and the identity of each claim of such patent which claims the approved product or a method of using or manufacturing the approved product;

(C) information to enable the Director to determine under subsections (a) and (b) the eligibility of a patent for extension and the rights that will be derived from the extension and information to enable the Director and the Secretary of Health and Human Services or the Secretary of Agriculture to determine the period of the extension under subsection (g);

(D) a brief description of the activities undertaken by the applicant during the applicable regulatory review period with respect to the approved product and the significant dates applicable to such activities; and

(E) such patent or other information as the Director may require.

(2) —

(A) Within 60 days of the submittal of an application for extension of the term of a patent under paragraph (1), the Director shall notify —

(i) the Secretary of Agriculture if the patent claims a drug product or a method of using or manufacturing a drug product and the drug product is subject to the Virus-Serum-Toxin Act, and

(ii) the Secretary of Health and Human Services if the patent claims any other drug product, a medical device, or a food additive or color additive or a method of using or manufacturing such a product, device, or additive and if the product, device, and additive are subject to the Federal Food, Drug, and Cosmetic Act,

of the extension application and shall submit to the Secretary who is so notified a copy of the application. Not later than 30 days after the receipt of an application from the Director, the Secretary receiving the application shall review the dates contained in the application pursuant to paragraph (1)(C) and determine the applicable regulatory review period, shall notify the Director of the determination, and shall publish in the Federal Register a notice of such determination.

(B) —

(i) If a petition is submitted to the Secretary making the determination under subparagraph (A), not later than 180 days after the publication of the determination under subparagraph (A), upon which it may reasonably be determined that the applicant did not act with due diligence during the applicable regulatory review period, the Secretary making the determination shall, in accordance with regulations promulgated by such Secretary, determine if the applicant acted with due diligence during the applicable regulatory review period. The Secretary making the determination shall make such determination not later than 90 days after the receipt of such a petition. For a drug product, device, or additive subject to the Federal Food, Drug, and Cosmetic Act or the Public Health Service Act, the Secretary may not delegate the authority to make the determination prescribed by this clause to an office below the Office of the Director of Food and Drugs. For a product subject to the Virus-Serum-Toxin Act, the Secretary of Agriculture may not delegate the authority to make the determination prescribed by this clause to an office below the Office of the Assistant Secretary for Marketing and Inspection Services.

(ii) The Secretary making a determination under clause (i) shall notify the Director of the determination and shall publish in the Federal Register a notice of such determination together with the factual and legal basis for such determination. Any interested person may request, within the 60-day period beginning on the publication of a determination, the Secretary making the determination to hold an informal hearing on the determination. If such a request is made within such period, such Secretary shall hold such hearing not later than 30 days after the date of the request, or at the request of the person making the request, not later than 60 days after such date. The Secretary who is holding the hearing shall provide notice of the hearing to the owner of the patent involved and to any interested person and provide the owner and any interested person an opportunity to participate in the hearing. Within 30 days after the completion of the hearing, such Secretary shall affirm or revise the determination which was the subject of the hearing and shall notify the Director of any revision of the determination and shall publish any such revision in the Federal Register.

(3) For the purposes of paragraph (2)(B), the term "due diligence" means that degree of attention, continuous directed effort, and timeliness as may reasonably be expected from, and are ordinarily exercised by, a person during a regulatory review period.

(4) An application for the extension of the term of a patent is subject to the disclosure requirements prescribed by the Director.

(5) —

(A) If the owner of record of the patent or its agent reasonably expects that the applicable regulatory review period described in paragraph (1)(B)(ii), (2)(B)(ii), (3)(B)(ii), (4)(B)(ii), or (5)(B)(ii) of subsection (g) that began for a product that is the subject of such patent may extend beyond the expiration of the patent term in effect, the owner or its agent may submit an application to the Director for an interim extension during the period beginning 6 months, and ending 15 days, before such term is due to expire. The application shall contain —

(i) the identity of the product subject to regulatory review and the Federal statute under which such review is occurring;

(ii) the identity of the patent for which interim extension is being sought and the identity of each claim of such patent which claims the product under regulatory review or a method of using or manufacturing the product;

(iii) information to enable the Director to determine under subsection (a)(1), (2), and (3) the eligibility of a patent for extension;

(iv) a brief description of the activities undertaken by the applicant during the applicable regulatory review period to date with respect to the product under review and the significant dates applicable to such activities; and

(v) such patent or other information as the Director may require.

(B) If the Director determines that, except for permission to market or use the product commercially, the patent would be eligible for an extension of the patent term under this section, the Director shall publish in the Federal Register a notice of such determination, including the identity of the product under regulatory review, and shall issue to the applicant a certificate of interim extension for a period of not more than 1 year.

(C) The owner of record of a patent, or its agent, for which an interim extension has been granted under subparagraph (B), may apply for not more than 4 subsequent interim extensions under this paragraph, except that, in the case of a patent subject to subsection (g)(6)(C), the owner of record of the patent, or its agent, may apply for only 1 subsequent interim extension under this paragraph. Each such subsequent application shall be made during the period beginning 60 days before, and ending 30 days before, the expiration of the preceding interim extension.

(D) Each certificate of interim extension under this paragraph shall be recorded in the official file of the patent and shall be considered part of the original patent.

(E) Any interim extension granted under this paragraph shall terminate at the end of the 60-day period beginning on the date on which the product involved receives permission for commercial marketing or use, except that, if within that 60-day period the applicant notifies the Director of such permission and submits any additional information under paragraph (1) of this subsection not previously contained in the application for interim extension, the patent shall be further extended, in accordance with the provisions of this section —

(i) for not to exceed 5 years from the date of expiration of the original patent term; or

(ii) if the patent is subject to subsection (g)(6)(C), from the date on which the product involved receives approval for commercial marketing or use.

(F) The rights derived from any patent the term of which is extended under this paragraph shall, during the period of interim extension —

(i) in the case of a patent which claims a product, be limited to any use then under regulatory review;

(ii) in the case of a patent which claims a method of using a product, be limited to any use claimed by the patent then under regulatory review; and

(iii) in the case of a patent which claims a method of manufacturing a product, be limited to the method of manufacturing as used to make the product then under regulatory review.

(e) —

(1) a determination that a patent is eligible for extension may be made by the Director solely on the basis of the representations contained in the application for the extension. If the Director determines that a patent is eligible for extension under subsection (a) and that the requirements of paragraphs (1) through (4) of subsection (d) have been complied with, the Director shall issue to the applicant for the extension of the term of the patent a certificate of extension, under seal, for the period prescribed by subsection (c). Such certificate shall be recorded in the official file of the patent and shall be considered as part of the original patent.

(2) If the term of a patent for which an application has been submitted under subsection (d)(1) would expire before a certificate of extension is issued or denied under paragraph (1) respecting the application, the Director shall extend, until such determination is made, the term of the patent for periods of up to one year if he determines that the patent is eligible for extension.

(f) For purposes of this section:

(1) The term "product" means:

(A) A drug product.

(B) Any medical device, food additive, or color additive subject to regulation under the Federal Food, Drug, and Cosmetic Act.

(2) The term "drug product" means the active ingredient of —

(A) a new drug, antibiotic drug, or human biological product (as those terms are used in the Federal Food, Drug, and Cosmetic Act and the Public Health Service Act), or

(B) a new animal drug or veterinary biological product (as those terms are used in the Federal Food, Drug, and Cosmetic Act and the Virus-Serum-Toxin Act) which is not primarily manufactured using recombinant DNA, recombinant RNA, hybridoma technology, or other processes involving site specific genetic manipulation techniques, including any salt or ester of the active ingredient, as a single entity or in combination with another active ingredient.

(3) The term "major health or environmental effects test" means a test which is reasonably related to the evaluation of the health or environmental effects of a product, which requires at least six months to conduct, and the data from which is submitted to receive permission for commercial marketing or use. Periods of analysis or evaluation of test results are not to be included in determining if the conduct of a test required at least six months.

(4) —

(A) Any reference to section 351 is a reference to section 351 of the Public Health Service Act.

(B) Any reference to section 503, 505, 512, or 515 is a reference to section 503, 505, 512, or 515 of the Federal Food, Drug, and Cosmetic Act.

(C) Any reference to the Virus-Serum-Toxin Act is a reference to the Act of March 4, 1913 (21 U.S.C. 151-158).

(5) The term "informal hearing" has the meaning prescribed for such term by section 201(y) of the Federal Food, Drug, and Cosmetic Act.

(6) The term "patent" means a patent issued by the United States Patent and Trademark Office.

(7) The term "date of enactment" as used in this section means September 24, 1984, for a human drug product, a medical device, food additive, or color additive.

(8) The term "date of enactment" as used in this section means the date of enactment of the Generic Animal Drug and Patent Term Restoration Act for an animal drug or a veterinary biological product.

(g) For purposes of this section, the term "regulatory review period" has the following meanings:

(1) —

(A) In the case of a product which is a new drug, antibiotic drug, or human biological product, the term means the period described in subparagraph (B) to which the limitation described in paragraph (6) applies.

(B) The regulatory review period for a new drug, antibiotic drug, or human biological product is the sum of—

(i) the period beginning on the date an exemption under subsection (i) of section 505 or subsection (d) of section 507 became effective for the approved product and ending on the date an application was initially submitted for such drug product under section 351, 505, or 507, and

(ii) the period beginning on the date the application was initially submitted for the approved product under section 351, subsection (b) of section 505, or section 507 and ending on the date such application was approved under such section.

(2) —

(A) In the case of a product which is a food additive or color additive, the term means the period described in subparagraph (B) to which the limitation described in paragraph (6) applies.

(B) The regulatory review period for a food or color additive is the sum of—

(i) the period beginning on the date a major health or environmental effects test on the additive was initiated and ending on the date a petition was initially submitted with respect to the product under the Federal Food, Drug, and Cosmetic Act requesting the issuance of a regulation for use of the product, and

(ii) the period beginning on the date a petition was initially submitted with respect to the product under the Federal Food, Drug, and Cosmetic Act requesting the issuance of a regulation for use of the product, and ending on the date such regulation became effective or, if objections were filed to such regulation, ending on the date such objections were resolved and commercial marketing was permitted or, if commercial marketing was permitted and later revoked pending further proceedings as a result of such objections, ending on the date such proceedings were finally resolved and commercial marketing was permitted.

(3) —

(A) In the case of a product which is a medical device, the term means the period described in subparagraph (B) to which the limitation described in paragraph (6) applies.

(B) The regulatory review period for a medical device is the sum of—

(i) the period beginning on the date a clinical investigation on humans involving the device was begun and ending on the date an application was initially submitted with respect to the device under section 515, and

(ii) the period beginning on the date an application was initially submitted with respect to the device under section 515 and ending on the date such application was approved under such Act or the period beginning on the date a notice of completion of a product development protocol was initially submitted under section 515(f)(5) and ending on the date the protocol was declared completed under section 515(f)(6).

(4) —

(A) In the case of a product which is a new animal drug, the term means the period described in subparagraph (B) to which the limitation described in paragraph (6) applies.

(B) The regulatory review period for a new animal drug product is the sum of—

(i) the period beginning on the earlier of the date a major health or environmental effects test on the drug was initiated or the date an exemption under subsection (j) of section 512 became effective for the approved new animal drug product and ending on the date an application was initially submitted for such animal drug product under section 512, and

(ii) the period beginning on the date the application was initially submitted for the approved animal drug product under subsection (b) of section 512 and ending on the date such application was approved under such section.

(5) —

(A) In the case of a product which is a veterinary biological product, the term means the period described in subparagraph (B) to which the limitation described in paragraph (6) applies.

(B) The regulatory period for a veterinary biological product is the sum of—

(i) the period beginning on the date the authority to prepare an experimental biological product under the Virus-Serum-Toxin Act became effective and ending on the date an application for a license was submitted under the Virus-Serum-Toxin Act, and

(ii) the period beginning on the date an application for a license was initially submitted for approval under the Virus-Serum-Toxin Act and ending on the date such license was issued.

(6) A period determined under any of the preceding paragraphs is subject to the following limitations:

(A) If the patent involved was issued after the date of the enactment of this section, the period of extension determined on the basis of the regulatory review period determined under any such paragraph may not exceed five years.

(B) If the patent involved was issued before the date of the enactment of this section and—

(i) no request for an exemption described in paragraph (1)(B) or (4)(B) was submitted and no request for the authority described in paragraph (5)(B) was submitted,

(ii) no major health or environmental effects test described in paragraph (2)(B) or (4)(B) was initiated and no petition for a regulation or application for registration described in such paragraph was submitted, or

(iii) no clinical investigation described in paragraph (3) was begun or product development, protocol described in such paragraph was submitted,

before such date for the approved product the period of extension determined on the basis of the regulatory review period determined under any such paragraph may not exceed five years.

(C) If the patent involved was issued before the date of the enactment of this section and if an action described in subparagraph (B) was taken before the date of the enactment of this section with respect to the approved product and the commercial marketing or use of the product has not been approved before such date, the period of extension determined on the basis of the regulatory review period determined under such paragraph may not exceed two years or in the case of an approved product which is a new animal drug or veterinary biological product (as those terms are used in the Federal Food, Drug, and Cosmetic Act or the Virus-Serum-Toxin Act), three years.

(h) The Director may establish such fees as the Director determines appropriate to cover the costs to the Office of receiving and acting upon applications under this section.

(i) —

(1) For purposes of this section, if the Secretary of Health and Human Services provides notice to the sponsor of an application or request for approval, conditional approval, or indexing of a drug product for which the Secretary intends to recommend controls under the Controlled Substances Act, beginning on the covered date, the drug product shall be considered to —

(A) have been approved or indexed under the relevant provision of the Public Health Service Act or the Federal Food, Drug, and Cosmetic Act; and

(B) have permission for commercial marketing or use.

(2) In this subsection, the term "covered date" means the later of —

(A) the date an application is approved —

(i) under section 351(a)(2)(C) of the Public Health Service Act; or

(ii) under section 505(b) or 512(c) of the Federal Food, Drug, and Cosmetic Act;

(B) the date an application is conditionally approved under section 571(b) of the Federal Food, Drug, and Cosmetic Act;

(C) the date a request for indexing is granted under section 572(d) of the Federal Food, Drug, and Cosmetic Act; or

(D) the date of issuance of the interim final rule controlling the drug under section 201(j) of the Controlled Substances Act.

35 U.S.C. § 271. Infringement of Patent.

(a) Except as otherwise provided in this title, whoever without authority makes, uses, offers to sell, or sells any patented invention, within the United States or imports into the United States any patented invention during the term of the patent therefor, infringes the patent.

(b) Whoever actively induces infringement of a patent shall be liable as an infringer.

(c) Whoever offers to sell or sells within the United States or imports into the United States a component of a patented machine, manufacture, combination or composition, or a material or apparatus for use in practicing a patented process, constituting a material part of the invention, knowing the same to be especially made or especially adapted for use in an infringement of such patent, and not a staple article or commodity of commerce suitable for substantial noninfringing use, shall be liable as a contributory infringer.

(d) No patent owner otherwise entitled to relief for infringement or contributory infringement of a patent shall be denied relief or deemed guilty of misuse or illegal extension of the patent right by reason of his having

(1) derived revenue from acts which if performed by another without his consent would constitute contributory infringement of the patent;

(2) licensed or authorized another to perform acts which if performed without his consent would constitute contributory infringement of the patent;

(3) sought to enforce his patent rights against infringement or contributory infringement;

(4) refused to license or use any rights to the patent; or

(5) conditioned the license of any rights to the patent or the sale of the patented product on the acquisition of a license to rights in another patent or purchase of a separate product,

unless, in view of the circumstances, the patent owner has market power in the relevant market for the patent or patented product on which the license or sale is conditioned.

(e) —

(1) It shall not be an act of infringement to make, use, offer to sell, or sell within the United States or import into the United States a patented invention (other than a new animal drug or veterinary biological product (as those terms are used in the Federal Food, Drug, and Cosmetic Act and the Act of March 4, 1913) which is primarily manufactured using recombinant DNA, recombinant RNA, hybridoma technology, or other processes involving site specific genetic manipulation techniques) solely for uses reasonably related to the development and submission of information under a Federal law which regulates the manufacture, use, or sale of drugs or veterinary biological products.

(2) It shall be an act of infringement to submit —

(A) an application under section 505(j) of the Federal Food, Drug, and Cosmetic Act or described in section 505(b)(2) of such Act for a drug claimed in a patent or the use of which is claimed in a patent,

(B) an application under section 512 of such Act or under the Act of March 4, 1913 (21 U.S.C. 151-158) for a drug or veterinary biological product which is not primarily manufactured using recombinant DNA, recombinant RNA, hybridoma technology, or other processes involving site specific genetic manipulation techniques and which is claimed in a patent or the use of which is claimed in a patent, or

(C) —

(i) with respect to a patent that is identified in the list of patents described in section 351(l)(3) of the Public Health Service Act (including as provided under section 351(l)(7) of such Act), an application seeking approval of a biological product, or

(ii) if the applicant for the application fails to provide the application and information required under section 351(l)(2)(A) of such Act, an application seeking approval of a biological product for a patent that could be identified pursuant to section 351(l)(3)(A)(i) of such Act,

if the purpose of such submission is to obtain approval under such Act to engage in the commercial manufacture, use, or sale of a drug, veterinary biological product, or biological product claimed in a patent or the use of which is claimed in a patent before the expiration of such patent.

(3) In any action for patent infringement brought under this section, no injunctive or other relief may be granted which would prohibit the making, using, offering to sell, or selling within the United States or importing into the United States of a patented invention under paragraph (1).

(4) For an act of infringement described in paragraph (2) —

(A) the court shall order the effective date of any approval of the drug or veterinary biological product involved in the infringement to be a date which is not earlier than the date of the expiration of the patent which has been infringed,

(B) injunctive relief may be granted against an infringer to prevent the commercial manufacture, use, offer to sell, or sale within the United States or importation into the United States of an approved drug, veterinary biological product, or biological product,

(C) damages or other monetary relief may be awarded against an infringer only if there has been commercial manufacture, use, offer to sell, or sale within the United States or importation into the United States of an approved drug, veterinary biological product, or biological product, and

(D) the court shall order a permanent injunction prohibiting any infringement of the patent by the biological product involved in the infringement until a date which is not earlier than the date of the expiration of the patent that has been infringed under paragraph (2)(C), provided the patent is the subject of a final court decision, as defined in section 351(k)(6) of the Public Health Service Act, in an action for infringement of the patent under section 351(l)(6) of such Act, and the biological product has not yet been approved because of section 351(k)(7) of such Act.

The remedies prescribed by subparagraphs (A), (B), (C), and (D) are the only remedies which may be granted by a court for an act of infringement described in paragraph (2), except that a court may award attorney fees under section 285.

(5) Where a person has filed an application described in paragraph (2) that includes a certification under subsection (b)(2)(A)(iv) or (j)(2)(A)(vii)(IV) of section 505 of the Federal Food, Drug, and Cosmetic Act (21 U.S.C. 355), and neither the owner of the patent that is the subject of the certification nor the holder of the approved application under subsection (b) of such section for the drug that is claimed by the patent or a use of which is claimed by the patent brought an action for infringement of such patent before the expiration of 45 days after the date on which the notice given under subsection (b)(3) or (j)(2)(B) of such section was received, the courts of the United States shall, to the extent consistent with the Constitution, have subject matter jurisdiction in any action brought by such person under section 2201 of title 28 for a declaratory judgment that such patent is invalid or not infringed.

(6) —

(A) Subparagraph (B) applies, in lieu of paragraph (4), in the case of a patent —

(i) that is identified, as applicable, in the list of patents described in section 351(l)(4) of the Public Health Service Act or the lists of patents described in section 351(l)(5)(B) of such Act with respect to a biological product; and

(ii) for which an action for infringement of the patent with respect to the biological product —

(I) was brought after the expiration of the 30-day period described in subparagraph (A) or (B), as applicable, of section 351(l)(6) of such Act; or

(II) was brought before the expiration of the 30-day period described in subclause (I), but which was dismissed without prejudice or was not prosecuted to judgment in good faith.

(B) In an action for infringement of a patent described in subparagraph (A), the sole and exclusive remedy that may be granted by a court, upon a finding that the making, using, offering to sell, selling, or importation into the United States of the biological product that is the subject of the action infringed the patent, shall be a reasonable royalty.

(C) The owner of a patent that should have been included in the list described in section 351(l)(3)(A) of the Public Health Service Act, including as provided under section 351(l)(7) of such Act for a biological product, but was not timely included in such list, may not bring an action under this section for infringement of the patent with respect to the biological product.

(f) —

(1) Whoever without authority supplies or causes to be supplied in or from the United States all or a substantial portion of the components of a patented invention, where such components are uncombined in whole or in part, in such manner as to actively induce the combination of such components outside of the United States in a manner that would infringe the patent if such combination occurred within the United States, shall be liable as an infringer.

(2) Whoever without authority supplies or causes to be supplied in or from the United States any component of a patented invention that is especially made or especially adapted for use in the invention and not a staple article or commodity of commerce suitable for substantial noninfringing use, where such component is uncombined in whole or in part, knowing that such component is so made or adapted and intending that such component will be combined outside of the United States in a manner that would infringe the patent if such combination occurred within the United States, shall be liable as an infringer.

(g) Whoever without authority imports into the United States or offers to sell, sells, or uses within the United States a product which is made by a process patented in the United States shall be liable as an infringer, if the importation, offer to sell, sale, or use of the product occurs during the term of such process patent. In an action for infringement of a process patent, no remedy may be granted for infringement on account of the noncommercial use or retail sale of a product unless there is no adequate remedy under this title for infringement on account of the importation or other use, offer to sell, or sale of that product. A product which is made by a patented process will, for purposes of this title, not be considered to be so made after —

(1) it is materially changed by subsequent processes; or

(2) it becomes a trivial and nonessential component of another product.

(h) As used in this section, the term "whoever" includes any State, any instrumentality of a State, and any officer or employee of a State or instrumentality of a State acting in his official capacity. Any State, and any such instrumentality, officer, or employee, shall be subject to the provisions of this title in the same manner and to the same extent as any nongovernmental entity.

(i) As used in this section, an "offer for sale" or an "offer to sell" by a person other than the patentee, or any designee of the patentee, is that in which the sale will occur before the expiration of the term of the patent.

35 U.S.C. § 282. Presumption of Validity; Defenses.

A patent shall be presumed valid. Each claim of a patent (whether in independent, dependent, or multiple dependent form) shall be presumed valid independently of the validity of other claims; dependent or multiple dependent claims shall be presumed valid even though dependent upon an invalid claim. Notwithstanding the preceding sentence, if a claim to a composition of matter is held invalid and that claim was the basis of a determination of nonobviousness under section 103(b)(1), the process shall no longer be considered nonobvious solely on the basis of section 103(b)(1). The burden of establishing invalidity of a patent or any claim thereof shall rest on the party asserting such invalidity.

The following shall be defenses in any action involving the validity or infringement of a patent and shall be pleaded:

(1) Noninfringement, absence of liability for infringement or unenforceability,

(2) Invalidity of the patent or any claim in suit on any ground specified in part II of this title as a condition for patentability,

(3) Invalidity of the patent or any claim in suit for failure to comply with any requirement of sections 112 or 251 of this title,

(4) Any other fact or act made a defense by this title.

In actions involving the validity or infringement of a patent the party asserting invalidity or noninfringement shall give notice in the pleadings or otherwise in writing to the adverse party at least thirty days before the trial, of the country, number, date, and name of the patentee of any patent, the title, date, and page numbers of any publication to be relied upon as anticipation of the patent in suit or, except in actions in the United States Court of Federal Claims, as showing the state of the art, and the name and address of any person who may be relied upon as the prior inventor or as having prior knowledge of or as having previously used or offered for sale the invention of the patent in suit. In the absence of such notice proof of the said matters may not be made at the trial except on such terms as the court requires. Invalidity of the extension of a patent term or any portion thereof under section 154(b) or 156 of this title because of the material failure —

(1) by the applicant for the extension, or

(2) by the Director,

to comply with the requirements of such section shall be a defense in any action involving the infringement of a patent during the period of the extension of its term and shall be pleaded. A due diligence determination under section 156(d)(2) is not subject to review in such an action.

35 U.S.C. § 283. Injunction.

The several courts having jurisdiction of cases under this title may grant injunctions in accordance with the principles of equity to prevent the violation of any right secured by patent, on such terms as the court deems reasonable.

35 U.S.C. § 284. Damages.

Upon finding for the claimant the court shall award the claimant damages adequate to compensate for the infringement, but in no event less than a reasonable royalty for the use made of the invention by the infringer, together with interest and costs as fixed by the court.

When the damages are not found by a jury, the court shall assess them. In either event the court may increase the damages up to three times the amount found or assessed. Increased damages under this paragraph shall not apply to provisional rights under section 154(d) of this title.

The court may receive expert testimony as an aid to the determination of damages or of what royalty would be reasonable under the circumstances.

35 U.S.C. § 285. Attorney Fees.

The court in exceptional cases may award reasonable attorney fees to the prevailing party.

FDA MODERNIZATION ACT OF 1997

SEC. 121. POSITRON EMISSION TOMOGRAPHY.

(a) [Text not included. — Ed.]

(b) —

(2) SUNSET. — Section 501(a)(2)(C) of the Federal Food, Drug, and Cosmetic Act (21 U.S.C. 351(a)(2)(C)) shall not apply 4 years after the date of enactment of this Act or 2 years after the date on which the Secretary of Health and Human Services establishes the requirements described in subsection (c)(1)(B), whichever is later.

(c) REQUIREMENTS FOR REVIEW OF APPROVAL PROCEDURES AND CURRENT GOOD MANUFACTURING PRACTICES FOR POSITRON EMISSION TOMOGRAPHY. —

(1) PROCEDURES AND REQUIREMENTS. —

(A) IN GENERAL. — In order to take account of the special characteristics of positron emission tomography drugs and the special techniques and processes required to produce these drugs, not later than 2 years after the date of enactment of this Act, the Secretary of Health and Human Services shall establish —

(i) appropriate procedures for the approval of positron emission tomography drugs pursuant to section 505 of the Federal Food, Drug, and Cosmetic Act (21 U.S.C. 355); and

(ii) appropriate current good manufacturing practice requirements for such drugs.

(B) CONSIDERATIONS AND CONSULTATION. — In establishing the procedures and requirements required by subparagraph (A), the Secretary of Health and Human Services shall take due account of any relevant differences between not-for-profit institutions that compound the drugs for their patients and commercial manufacturers of the drugs. Prior to establishing the procedures and requirements, the Secretary of Health and Human Services shall consult with patient advocacy groups, professional associations, manufacturers, and physicians and scientists licensed to make or use positron emission tomography drugs.

(2) SUBMISSION OF NEW DRUG APPLICATIONS AND ABBREVIATED NEW DRUG APPLICATIONS. —

(A) IN GENERAL. — Except as provided in subparagraph (B), the Secretary of Health and Human Services shall not require the submission of new drug applications or abbreviated new drug applications under subsection (b) or (j) of section 505 (21 U.S.C. 355), for compounded positron emission tomography drugs that are not adulterated drugs described in section 501(a)(2)(C) of the Federal Food, Drug, and Cosmetic Act (21 U.S.C. 351(a)(2)(C)) (as amended by subsection (b)), for a period of 4 years after the date of enactment of this Act, or for 2 years after the date on which the Secretary establishes procedures and requirements under paragraph (1), whichever is longer.

(B) EXCEPTION. — Nothing in this Act shall prohibit the voluntary submission of such applications or the review of such applications by the Secretary of Health and Human Services. Nothing in this Act shall constitute an exemption for a positron emission tomography drug from the requirements of regulations issued under section 505(i) of the Federal Food, Drug, and Cosmetic Act (21 U.S.C. 355(i)).

(d) [Text not included. — Ed.]

(e) DEFINITION. — As used in this section, the term "compounded positron emission tomography drug" has the meaning given the term in section 201 of the Federal Food, Drug, and Cosmetic Act (21 U.S.C. 321).

SEC. 125. INSULIN AND ANTIBIOTICS.

(a) – (c) [Text not included. — Ed.]

(d) TRANSITION. —

(1) IN GENERAL. — An application that was approved by the Secretary of Health and Human Services before the date of the enactment of this Act for the marketing of an antibiotic drug under section 507 of the Federal Food, Drug, and Cosmetic Act (21 U.S.C. 357), as in effect on the day before the date of the enactment of this Act, shall, on and after such date of enactment, be considered to be an application that was submitted and filed under section 505(b) of such Act (21 U.S.C. 355(b)) and approved for safety and effectiveness under section 505(c) of such Act (21 U.S.C. 355(c)), except that if such application for marketing was in the form of an abbreviated application, the application shall be considered to have been filed and approved under section 505(j) of such Act (21 U.S.C. 355(j)).

(2) Exception. — The following subsections of section 505 (21 U.S.C. 355) shall not apply to any application for marketing in which the drug that is the subject of the application contains an antibiotic drug and the antibiotic drug was the subject of any application for marketing received by the Secretary of Health and Human Services under section 507 of such Act (21 U.S.C. 357) before the date of the enactment of this Act:

(A) —

(i) Subsections (c)(2), (d)(6), (e)(4), (j)(2)(A)(vii), (j)(2)(A)(viii), (j)(2)(B), (j)(4)(B), and (j)(4)(D); and

(ii) The third and fourth sentences of subsection (b)(1) (regarding the filing and publication of patent information); and

(B) Subsections (b)(2)(A), (b)(2)(B), (b)(3), and (c)(3) if the investigations relied upon by the applicant for approval of the application were not conducted by or for the applicant and for which the applicant has not obtained a right of reference or use from the person by or for whom the investigations were conducted.

(3) Publication. — For purposes of this section, the Secretary is authorized to make available to the public the established name of each antibiotic drug that was the subject of any application for marketing received by the Secretary for Health and Human Services under section 507 of the Federal Food, Drug, and Cosmetic Act (21 U.S.C. 357) before the date of enactment of this Act.

(e) [Text not included. — Ed.]

Sec. 308. Glass and Ceramic Ware.

(a) In General. — The Secretary may not implement any requirement which would ban, as an unapproved food additive, lead and cadmium based enamel in the lip and rim area of glass and ceramic ware before the expiration of one year after the date such requirement is published.

(b) Lead and Cadmium Based Enamel. — Unless the Secretary determines, based on available data, that lead and cadmium based enamel on glass and ceramic ware —

(1) which has less than 60 millimeters of decorating area below the external rim, and

(2) which is not, by design, representation, or custom of usage intended for use by children, is unsafe, the Secretary shall not take any action before January 1, 2003, to ban lead and cadmium based enamel on such glass and ceramic ware. Any action taken after January 1, 2003, to ban such enamel on such glass and ceramic ware as an unapproved food additive shall be taken by regulation and such regulation shall provide that such products shall not be removed from the market before 1 year after publication of the final regulation.

Sec. 413. Food and Drug Administration Study of Mercury Compounds in Drugs and Food.

(a) [Text not included. — Ed.]

(b) Study. — The Secretary of Health and Human Services, acting through the Food and Drug Administration, shall conduct a study of the effect on humans of the use of mercury compounds in nasal sprays. Such study shall include data from other studies that have been made of such use.

(c) Study of Mercury Sales. —

(1) Study. — The Secretary of Health and Human Services, acting through the Food and Drug Administration and subject to appropriations, shall conduct, or shall contract with the Institute of Medicine of the National Academy of Sciences to conduct, a study of the effect on humans of the use of elemental, organic, or inorganic mercury when offered for sale as a drug or dietary supplement. Such study shall, among other things, evaluate —

(A) the scope of mercury use as a drug or dietary supplement; and

(B) the adverse effects on health of children and other sensitive populations resulting from exposure to, or ingestion or inhalation of, mercury when so used.

In conducting such study, the Secretary shall consult with the Administrator of the Environmental Protection Agency, the Chair of the Consumer Product Safety Commission, and the Administrator of the Agency for Toxic Substances and Disease Registry, and, to the extent the Secretary believes necessary or appropriate, with any other Federal or private entity.

(2) Regulations. — If, in the opinion of the Secretary, the use of elemental, organic, or inorganic mercury offered for sale as a drug or dietary supplement poses a threat to human health, the Secretary shall promulgate regulations restricting the sale of mercury intended for such use. At a minimum, such regulations shall be designed to protect the health of children and other sensitive populations from adverse effects resulting from exposure to, or ingestion or inhalation of, mercury. Such regulations, to the extent feasible, should not unnecessarily interfere with the availability of mercury for use in religious ceremonies.

FDA AMENDMENTS ACT OF 2007

TITLE I — PRESCRIPTION DRUG USER FEE AMENDMENTS OF 2007

SEC. 101. SHORT TITLE; REFERENCES IN TITLE; FINDING.

(a) SHORT TITLE. — This title may be cited as the "Prescription Drug User Fee Amendments of 2007".

(b) REFERENCES IN TITLE. — Except as otherwise specified, amendments made by this title to a section or other provision of law are amendments to such section or other provision of the Federal Food, Drug, and Cosmetic Act (21 U.S.C. 301 et seq.).

(c) FINDING. — The Congress finds that the fees authorized by the amendments made in this title will be dedicated toward expediting the drug development process and the process for the review of human drug applications, including postmarket drug safety activities, as set forth in the goals identified for purposes of part 2 of subchapter C of chapter VII of the Federal Food, Drug, and Cosmetic Act, in the letters from the Secretary of Health and Human Services to the Chairman of the Committee on Health, Education, Labor, and Pensions of the Senate and the Chairman of the Committee on Energy and Commerce of the House of Representatives, as set forth in the Congressional Record.

SEC. 106. SUNSET DATES.

(a) AUTHORIZATION. — The amendments made by sections 102, 103, and 104 cease to be effective October 1, 2012.

(b) REPORTING REQUIREMENTS. — The amendment made by section 105 ceases to be effective January 31, 2013.

SEC. 107. EFFECTIVE DATE.

The amendments made by this title shall take effect on October 1, 2007, or the date of the enactment of this Act, whichever is later, except that fees under part 2 of subchapter C of chapter VII of the Federal Food, Drug, and Cosmetic Act shall be assessed for all human drug applications received on or after October 1, 2007, regardless of the date of the enactment of this Act.

SEC. 108. SAVINGS CLAUSE.

Notwithstanding section 509 of the Prescription Drug User Fee Amendments of 2002 (21 U.S.C. 379g note), and notwithstanding the amendments made by this title, part 2 of subchapter C of chapter VII of the Federal Food, Drug, and Cosmetic Act, as in effect on the day before the date of the enactment of this title, shall continue to be in effect with respect to human drug applications and supplements (as defined in such part as of such day) that on or after October 1, 2002, but before October 1, 2007, were accepted by the Food and Drug Administration for filing with respect to assessing and collecting any fee required by such part for a fiscal year prior to fiscal year 2008.

TITLE II — MEDICAL DEVICE USER FEE AMENDMENTS OF 2007

SEC. 201. SHORT TITLE; REFERENCES IN TITLE; FINDING.

(a) SHORT TITLE. — This title may be cited as the "Medical Device User Fee Amendments of 2007".

(b) REFERENCES IN TITLE. — Except as otherwise specified, amendments made by this title to a section or other provision of law are amendments to such section or other provision of the Federal Food, Drug, and Cosmetic Act (21 U.S.C. 301 et seq.).

(c) FINDING. — The Congress finds that the fees authorized under the amendments made by this title will be dedicated toward expediting the process for the review of device applications and for assuring the safety and effectiveness of devices, as set forth in the goals identified for purposes of part 3 of subchapter C of chapter VII of the Federal Food, Drug, and Cosmetic Act in the letters from the Secretary of Health and Human Services to the Chairman of the

Committee on Health, Education, Labor, and Pensions of the Senate and the Chairman of the Committee on Energy H. and Commerce of the House of Representatives, as set forth in the Congressional Record.

Sec. 214. Savings Clause.

Notwithstanding section 107 of the Medical Device User Fee and Modernization Act of 2002 (Public Law 107–250), and notwithstanding the amendments made by this subtitle, part 3 of subchapter C of chapter VII of the Federal Food, Drug, and Cosmetic Act (21 U.S.C. 379i et seq.), as in effect on the day before the date of the enactment of this subtitle, shall continue to be in effect with respect to premarket applications, premarket reports, premarket notification submissions, and supplements (as defined in such part as of such day) that on or after October 1, 2002, but before October 1, 2007, were accepted by the Food and Drug Administration for filing with respect to assessing and collecting any fee required by such part for a fiscal year prior to fiscal year 2008.

Sec. 215. Additional Authorization of Appropriations for Postmarket Safety Information.

For the purpose of collecting, developing, reviewing, and evaluating postmarket safety information on medical devices, there are authorized to be appropriated to the Food and Drug Administration, in addition to the amounts authorized by other provisions of law for such purpose —

(1) $7,100,000 for fiscal year 2008;

(2) $7,455,000 for fiscal year 2009;

(3) $7,827,750 for fiscal year 2010;

(4) $8,219,138 for fiscal year 2011; and

(5) $8,630,094 for fiscal year 2012.

Sec. 216. Effective Date.

The amendments made by this subtitle shall take effect on October 1, 2007, or the date of the enactment of this Act, whichever is later, except that fees under part 3 of subchapter C of chapter VII of the Federal Food, Drug, and Cosmetic Act shall be assessed for all premarket applications, premarket reports, supplements, 30-day notices, and premarket notification submissions received on or after October 1, 2007, regardless of the date of the enactment of this Act.

Sec. 217. Sunset Clause.

The amendments made by this subtitle cease to be effective October 1, 2012, except that section 738A of the Federal Food, Drug, and Cosmetic Act (regarding annual performance and financial reports) ceases to be effective January 31, 2013.

Sec. 225. Report by Government Accountability Office.

(a) In General. — The Comptroller General of the United States shall conduct a study on the appropriate use of the process under section 510(k) of the Federal Food, Drug, and Cosmetic Act as part of the device classification process to determine whether a new device is as safe and effective as a classified device.

(b) Consideration. — In determining the effectiveness of the premarket notification and classification authority under section 510(k) and subsections (f) and (i) of section 513 of the Federal Food, Drug, and Cosmetic Act, the study under subsection (a) shall consider the Secretary of Health and Human Services's evaluation of the respective intended uses and technologies of such devices, including the effectiveness of such Secretary's comparative assessment of technological characteristics such as device materials, principles of operations, and power sources.

(c) Report. —Not later than 1 year after the date of the enactment of this Act, the Comptroller General shall complete the study under subsection (a) and submit to the Congress a report on the results of such study.

Sec. 229. Study of Nosocomial Infections Relating to Medical Devices.

(a) In General. — The Comptroller General of the United States shall conduct a study on —

(1) the number of nosocomial infections attributable to new and reused medical devices; and

(2) the causes of such nosocomial infections, including the following:

(A) Reprocessed single-use devices.

(B) Handling of sterilized medical devices.

(C) In-hospital sterilization of medical devices.

(D) Health care professionals' practices for patient examination and treatment.

(E) Hospital-based policies and procedures for infection control and prevention.

(F) Hospital-based practices for handling of medical waste.

(G) Other causes.

(b) Report. — Not later than 1 year after the date of the enactment of this Act, the Comptroller General shall complete the study under subsection (a) and submit to the Congress a report on the results of such study.

(c) Definition. — In this section, the term "nosocomial infection" means an infection that is acquired while an individual is a patient at a hospital and was neither present nor incubating in the patient prior to receiving services in the hospital.

Sec. 230. Report by the Food and Drug Administration Regarding Labeling Information on the Relationship Between the Use of Indoor Tanning Devices and Development of Skin Cancer or Other Skin Damage.

(a) In General. —The Secretary of Health and Human Services (referred to in this section as the "Secretary"), acting through the Commissioner of Food and Drugs, shall determine —

(1) whether the labeling requirements for indoor tanning devices, including the positioning requirements, provide sufficient information to consumers regarding the risks that the use of such devices pose for the development of irreversible damage to the eyes and skin, including skin cancer; and

(2) —

(A) whether modifying the warning label required on tanning beds to read, "Ultraviolet radiation can cause skin cancer", or any other additional warning, would communicate the risks of indoor tanning more effectively; or

(B) whether there is no warning that would be capable of adequately communicating such risks.

(b) Consumer Testing. — In making the determinations under subsection (a), the Secretary shall conduct appropriate consumer testing to determine consumer understanding of label warnings.

(c) Report. — Not later than 1 year after the date of the enactment of this Act, the Secretary shall submit to the Congress a report that provides the determinations under subsection (a). In addition, the Secretary shall include in the report the measures being implemented by the Secretary to significantly reduce the risks associated with indoor tanning devices.

Title III — Pediatric Medical Device Safety and Improvement Act of 2007

Sec. 301. Short Title.

This title may be cited as the "Pediatric Medical Device Safety and Improvement Act of 2007".

Sec. 304. Encouraging pediatric Medical Device Research.

(a) [Text not included. — Ed.]

(b) Plan for Pediatric Medical Device Research. —

(1) In General. — Not later than 180 days after the date of the enactment of this Act, the Secretary of Health and Human Services, acting through the Commissioner of Food and Drugs, the Director of the National Institutes of Health, and the Director of the Agency for Healthcare Research and Quality, shall submit to the Committee on Health, Education, Labor, and Pensions of the Senate and the Committee on Energy and Commerce of the House of Representatives a plan for expanding pediatric medical device research and development. In developing such plan, the Secretary of Health and Human Services shall consult with individuals and organizations with appropriate expertise in pediatric medical devices.

(2) Contents. — The plan under paragraph (1) shall include —

(A) the current status of federally funded pediatric medical device research;

(B) any gaps in such research, which may include a survey of pediatric medical providers regarding unmet pediatric medical device needs, as needed; and

(C) a research agenda for improving pediatric medical device development and Food and Drug Administration clearance or approval of pediatric medical devices, and for evaluating the short- and long-term safety and effectiveness of pediatric medical devices.

Sec. 305. Demonstrating Grants for Improving Pediatric Device Availability.

(a) In General. —

(1) Request for Proposals. — Not later than 90 days after the date of the enactment of this Act, the Secretary of Health and Human Services shall issue a request for proposals for 1 or more grants or contracts to nonprofit consortia for demonstration projects to promote pediatric device development.

(2) Determination on Grants or Contracts. — Not later than 180 days after the date the Secretary of Health and Human Services issues a request for proposals under paragraph (1), the Secretary shall make a determination on the grants or contracts under this section.

(b) Application. — A nonprofit consortium that desires to receive a grant or contract under this section shall submit an application to the Secretary of Health and Human Services at such time, in such manner, and containing such information as the Secretary may require.

(c) Use of Funds. — A nonprofit consortium that receives a grant or contract under this section shall facilitate the development, production, and distribution of pediatric medical devices by —

(1) encouraging innovation and connecting qualified individuals with pediatric device ideas with potential manufacturers;

(2) mentoring and managing pediatric device projects through the development process, including product identification, prototype design, device development, and marketing;

(3) connecting innovators and physicians to existing Federal and non-Federal resources, including resources from the Food and Drug Administration, the National Institutes of Health, the Small Business Administration, the Department of Energy, the Department of Education, the National Science Foundation, the Department of Veterans Affairs, the Agency for Healthcare Research and Quality, and the National Institute of Standards and Technology;

(4) assessing the scientific and medical merit of proposed pediatric device projects; ~~and~~

(5) providing assistance and advice as needed on business development, personnel training, prototype development, postmarket needs, and other activities consistent with the purposes of this section~~.~~; and

(6) providing regulatory consultation to the device sponsors in support of the submission of an application for a pediatric device, where appropriate.

(d) Coordination. —

(1) National Institutes of Health. — Each consortium that receives a grant or contract under this section shall —

(A) coordinate with the National Institutes of Health's pediatric device contact point or office, designated under section 402(b)(23) of the Public Health Service Act, as added by section 304(a) of this Act; and

(B) provide to the National Institutes of Health any identified pediatric device needs that the consortium lacks sufficient capacity to address or those needs in which the consortium has been unable to stimulate manufacturer interest.

(2) Food and Drug Administration. — Each consortium that receives a grant or contract under this section shall coordinate with the Commissioner of Food and Drugs and device companies to facilitate the application for approval or clearance of devices labeled for pediatric use.

(3) Effectiveness and Outcomes. — Each consortium that receives a grant or contract under this section shall annually report to the Secretary of Health and Human Services on the status of pediatric device development, production, and distribution that has been facilitated by the consortium.

(e) Authorization of Appropriations. — There are authorized to be appropriated to carry out this section $6,000,000 for each of fiscal years ~~2008 through 2012~~ <u>2018 through 2022</u>.

Title IV — Pediatric Research Equity Act of 2007

Sec. 401. Short Title.

This title may be cited as the "Pediatric Research Equity Act of 2007".

Sec. 404. Government Accountability Office Report.

Not later than January 1, 2011, the Comptroller General of the United States, in consultation with the Secretary of Health and Human Services, shall submit to the Congress a report that addresses the effectiveness of sections 505A and 505B of the Federal Food, Drug, and Cosmetic Act (21 U.S.C. 355a, 355c) and section 409I of the Public Health Service Act (42 U.S.C. 284m) in ensuring that medicines used by children are tested and properly labeled. Such report shall include —

(1) the number and importance of drugs and biological products for children that are being tested as a result of the amendments made by this title and title V and the importance for children, health care providers, parents, and others of labeling changes made as a result of such testing;

(2) the number and importance of drugs and biological products for children that are not being tested for their use notwithstanding the provisions of this title and title V and possible reasons for the lack of testing;

(3) the number of drugs and biological products for which testing is being done and labeling changes required, including the date labeling changes are made and which labeling changes required the use of the dispute resolution process established pursuant to the amendments made by this title, together with a description of the outcomes of such process, including a description of the disputes and the recommendations of the Pediatric Advisory Committee;

(4) any recommendations for modifications to the programs established under sections 505A and 505B of the Federal Food, Drug, and Cosmetic Act (21 U.S.C. 355a) and section 409I of the Public Health Service Act (42 U.S.C. 284m) that the Secretary determines to be appropriate, including a detailed rationale for each recommendation; and

(5) —

(A) the efforts made by the Secretary to increase the number of studies conducted in the neonate population; and

(B) the results of those efforts, including efforts made to encourage the conduct of appropriate studies in neonates by companies with products that have sufficient safety and other information to make the conduct of the studies ethical and safe.

Title V — Best Pharmaceuticals for Children Act of 2007

Sec. 501. Short Title.

This title may be cited as the "Best Pharmaceuticals for Children Act of 2007".

Sec. 509. Reauthorization of Best Pharmaceuticals for Children Act.

(a) – (e) [Text not included. — Ed.]

(f) Effective Date and Limitation for Rule Relating to Toll-Free Number for Adverse Events on Labeling for Human Drug Products. —

(1) In General. —Notwithstanding subchapter II of chapter 5, and chapter 7, of title 5, United States Code (commonly known as the "Administrative Procedure Act") and any other provision of law, the proposed rule issued by the Commissioner of Food and Drugs entitled "Toll-Free Number for Reporting Adverse Events on Labeling for Human Drug Products," 69 Fed. Reg. 21778, (April 22, 2004) shall take effect on January 1, 2008, unless such Commissioner issues the final rule before such date.

(2) Limitation. — The proposed rule that takes effect under subsection (a), or the final rule described under subsection (a), shall, notwithstanding section 17(a) of the Best Pharmaceuticals for Children Act (21 U.S.C. 355b(a)), not apply to a drug —

(A) for which an application is approved under section 505 of the Federal Food, Drug, and Cosmetic Act (21 U.S.C. 355);

(B) that is not described under section 503(b)(1) of such Act (21 U.S.C. 353(b)(1)); and

(C) the packaging of which includes a toll-free number through which consumers can report complaints to the manufacturer or distributor of the drug.

Title IX — Enhanced Authorities Regarding Postmarket Safety of Drugs

Subtitle A — Postmarket Studies and Surveillance

Sec. 904. Benefit-Risk Assessments.

Not later than 1 year after the date of the enactment of this Act, the Commissioner of Food and Drugs shall submit to the Congress a report on how best to communicate to the public the risks and benefits of new drugs and the role of the risk evaluation and mitigation strategy in assessing such risks and benefits. As part of such study, the Commissioner may consider the possibility of including in the labeling and any direct-to-consumer advertisements of a newly approved drug or indication a unique symbol indicating the newly approved status of the drug or indication for a period after approval.

Sec. 905. Active Postmarket Risk Identification and Analysis.

(a) [Text not included. — Ed.]

(b) Rule of Construction. — Nothing in this section or the amendment made by this section shall be construed to prohibit the lawful disclosure or use of data or information by an entity other than as described in paragraph (4)(B) or (4)(G) of section 505(k) of the Federal Food, Drug, and Cosmetic Act, as added by subsection (a).

(c) Report to Congress. — Not later than 4 years after the date of the enactment of this Act, the Secretary shall report to the Congress on the ways in which the Secretary has used the active postmarket risk identification and analysis system described in paragraphs (3) and (4) of section 505(k) of the Federal Food, Drug, and Cosmetic Act, as added by subsection (a), to identify specific drug safety signals and to better understand the outcomes associated with drugs marketed in the United States

(d) Authorization of Appropriations. — To carry out activities under the amendment made by this section for which funds are made available under section 736 of the Federal Food, Drug, and Cosmetic Act (21 U.S.C. 379h), there are authorized to be appropriated to carry out the amendment made by this section, in addition to such funds, $25,000,000 for each of fiscal years 2008 through 2012.

(e) GAO Report. — Not later than 18 months after the date of the enactment of this Act, the Comptroller General of the United States shall evaluate data privacy, confidentiality, and security issues relating to accessing, transmitting, and maintaining data for the active postmarket risk identification and analysis system described in paragraphs (3) and (4) of section 505(k) of the Federal Food, Drug, and Cosmetic Act, as added by subsection (a), and make recommendations to the Committee on Energy and Commerce of the House of Representatives and the Committee on Health, Education, Labor and Pensions of the Senate, and any other congressional committees of relevant jurisdiction, regarding the need for any additional legislative or regulatory actions to ensure privacy, confidentiality, and security of this data or otherwise address privacy, confidentiality, and security issues to ensure the effective operation of such active postmarket identification and analysis system.

Sec. 906. Statement for Inclusion in Direct-to-Consumer Advertisements of Drugs.

(a) [Text not included. -- Ed.]

(b) Study. —

(1) In General. — In the case of direct-to-consumer television advertisements, the Secretary of Health and Human Services, in consultation with the Advisory Committee on Risk Communication under section 567 of the Federal Food, Drug, and Cosmetic Act (as added by section 917), shall, not later than 6 months after the date of the enactment of this Act, conduct a study to determine if the statement in section 502(n) of such Act (as added by subsection (a)) required with respect to published direct-to-consumer advertisements is appropriate for inclusion in such television advertisements.

(2) Content. — As part of the study under paragraph (1), such Secretary shall consider whether the information in the statement described in paragraph (1) would detract from the presentation of risk information in a direct-to-consumer television advertisement. If such Secretary determines the inclusion of such statement is appropriate in direct-to-consumer television advertisements, such Secretary shall issue regulations requiring the implementation of such statement in direct-to-consumer television advertisements, including determining a reasonable length of time for displaying the statement in such advertisements. The Secretary shall report to the appropriate committees of Congress the findings of such study and any plans to issue regulations under this paragraph.

Sec. 907. No Effect on Veterinary Medicine.

This subtitle, and the amendments made by this subtitle, shall have no effect on the use of drugs approved under section 505 of the Federal Food, Drug, and Cosmetic Act by, or on the lawful written or oral order of, a licensed veterinarian within the context of a veterinarian-client-patient relationship, as provided for under section 512(a)(5) of such Act.

Sec. 908. Authorization of Appropriations.

(a) In General. — For carrying out this subtitle and the amendments made by this subtitle, there is authorized to be appropriated $25,000,000 for each of fiscal years 2008 through 2012.

(b) Relation to Other Funding. — The authorization of appropriations under subsection (a) is in addition to any other funds available for carrying out this subtitle and the amendments made by this subtitle.

Sec. 909. Effective Date and Applicability.

(a) Effective Date. — This subtitle takes effect 180 days after the date of the enactment of this Act.

(b) Drugs Deemed to Have Risk Evaluation and Mitigation Strategies. —

(1) In General. — A drug that was approved before the effective date of this Act is, in accordance with paragraph (2), deemed to have in effect an approved risk evaluation and mitigation strategy under section 505–1 of the Federal Food, Drug, and Cosmetic Act (as added by section 901) (referred to in this section as the "Act") if there are in effect on the effective date of this Act elements to assure safe use —

(A) required under section 314.520 or section 601.42 of title 21, Code of Federal Regulations; or

(B) otherwise agreed to by the applicant and the Secretary for such drug.

(2) Elements of Strategy; Enforcement. — The approved risk evaluation and mitigation strategy in effect for a drug under paragraph (1) —

(A) is deemed to consist of the timetable required under section 505–1(d) and any additional elements under subsections (e) and (f) of such section in effect for such drug on the effective date of this Act; and

(B) is subject to enforcement by the Secretary to the same extent as any other risk evaluation and mitigation strategy under section 505–1 of the Act, except that sections 303(f)(4) and 502(y) and (z) of the Act (as added by section 902) shall not apply to such strategy before the Secretary has completed review of, and acted on, the first assessment of such strategy under such section 505–1.

(3) Submission. — Not later than 180 days after the effective date of this Act, the holder of an approved application for which a risk evaluation and mitigation strategy is deemed to be in effect under paragraph (1) shall submit to the Secretary a proposed risk evaluation and mitigation strategy. Such proposed strategy is subject to section 505–1 of the Act as if included in such application at the time of submission of the application to the Secretary.

Subtitle B — Other Provisions to Ensure Drug Safety and Surveillance

Sec. 919. Response to the Institute of Medicine.

(a) In General. — Not later than 1 year after the date of the enactment of this title, the Secretary shall issue a report responding to the 2006 report of the Institute of Medicine entitled "The Future of Drug Safety—Promoting and Protecting the Health of the Public".

(b) Content of Report. — The report issued by the Secretary under subsection (a) shall include —

(1) an update on the implementation by the Food and Drug Administration of its plan to respond to the Institute of Medicine report described under such subsection; and (2) an assessment of how the Food and Drug Administration has implemented —

(A) the recommendations described in such Institute of Medicine report; and

(B) the requirement under section 505–1(c)(2) of the Federal Food, Drug, and Cosmetic Act (as added by this title), that the appropriate office responsible for reviewing a drug and the office responsible for postapproval safety with respect to the drug work together to assess, implement, and ensure compliance with the requirements of such section 505–1.

Title X — Food Safety

Sec. 1001. Findings.

Congress finds that —

(1) the safety and integrity of the United States food supply are vital to public health, to public confidence in the food supply, and to the success of the food sector of the Nation's economy;

(2) illnesses and deaths of individuals and companion animals caused by contaminated food —

(A) have contributed to a loss of public confidence in food safety; and

(B) have caused significant economic losses to manufacturers and producers not responsible for contaminated food items;

(3) the task of preserving the safety of the food supply of the United States faces tremendous pressures with regard to —

(A) emerging pathogens and other contaminants and the ability to detect all forms of contamination;

(B) an increasing volume of imported food from a wide variety of countries; and

(C) a shortage of adequate resources for monitoring and inspection;

(4) according to the Economic Research Service of the Department of Agriculture, the United States is increasing the amount of food that it imports such that —

(A) from 2003 to 2007, the value of food imports has increased from $45,600,000,000 to $64,000,000,000; and

(B) imported food accounts for 13 percent of the average American diet including 31 percent of fruits, juices, and nuts, 9.5 percent of red meat, and 78.6 percent of fish and shellfish; and

(5) the number of full-time equivalent Food and Drug Administration employees conducting inspections has decreased from 2003 to 2007.

Sec. 1002. Ensuring the Safety of Pet Food.

(a) Processing and Ingredient Standards. — Not later than 2 years after the date of the enactment of this Act, the Secretary of Health and Human Services (referred to in this title as the "Secretary"), in consultation with the Association of American Feed Control Officials and other relevant stakeholder groups, including veterinary medical associations, animal health organizations, and pet food manufacturers, shall by regulation establish —

(1) ingredient standards and definitions with respect to pet food;

(2) processing standards for pet food; and

(3) updated standards for the labeling of pet food that include nutritional and ingredient information.

(b) Early Warning Surveillance Systems and Notification During Pet Food Recalls. — Not later than 1 year after the date of the enactment of this Act, the Secretary shall establish an early warning and surveillance system to identify adulteration of the pet food supply and outbreaks of illness associated with pet food. In establishing such system, the Secretary shall —

(1) consider using surveillance and monitoring mechanisms similar to, or in coordination with, those used to monitor human or animal health, such as the Foodborne Diseases Active Surveillance Network (FoodNet) and PulseNet of the Centers for Disease Control and Prevention, the Food Emergency Response Network of the Food and Drug Administration and the Department of Agriculture, and the National Animal Health Laboratory Network of the Department of Agriculture;

(2) consult with relevant professional associations and private sector veterinary hospitals;

(3) work with the National Companion Animal Surveillance Program, the Health Alert Network, or other notification networks as appropriate to inform veterinarians and relevant stakeholders during any recall of pet food; and

(4) use such information and conduct such other activities as the Secretary deems appropriate.

Sec. 1003. Ensuring Efficient and Effective Communications During a Recall.

The Secretary shall, during an ongoing recall of human or pet food regulated by the Secretary —

(1) work with companies, relevant professional associations, and other organizations to collect and aggregate information pertaining to the recall;

(2) use existing networks of communication, including electronic forms of information dissemination, to enhance the quality and speed of communication with the public; and

(3) post information regarding recalled human and pet foods on the Internet Web site of the Food and Drug Administration in a single location, which shall include a searchable database of recalled human foods and a searchable database of recalled pet foods, that is easily accessed and understood by the public.

Sec. 1004. State and Federal Cooperation.

(a) In General. — The Secretary shall work with the States in undertaking activities and programs that assist in improving the safety of food, including fresh and processed produce, so that State food safety programs and activities conducted by the Secretary function in a coordinated and cost-effective manner. With the assistance provided under subsection (b), the Secretary shall encourage States to —

(1) establish, continue, or strengthen State food safety programs, especially with respect to the regulation of retail commercial food establishments; and

(2) establish procedures and requirements for ensuring that processed produce under the jurisdiction of State food safety programs is not unsafe for human consumption.

(b) Assistance. — The Secretary may provide to a State, for planning, developing, and implementing such a food safety program —

(1) advisory assistance;

(2) technical assistance, training, and laboratory assistance (including necessary materials and equipment); and

(3) financial and other assistance.

(c) Service Agreements. — The Secretary may, under an agreement entered into with a Federal, State, or local agency, use, on a reimbursable basis or otherwise, the personnel, services, and facilities of the agency to carry out the responsibilities of the agency under this section. An agreement entered into with a State agency under this subsection may provide for training of State employees.

Sec. 1005. Reportable Food Registry.

(a) Findings. — Congress makes the following findings:

(1) In 1994, Congress passed the Dietary Supplement Health and Education Act of 1994 (Public Law 103–417) to provide the Food and Drug Administration the legal framework which is intended to ensure that dietary supplements are safe and properly labeled foods.

(2) In 2006, Congress passed the Dietary Supplement and Nonprescription Drug Consumer Protection Act (Public Law 109–462) to establish a mandatory reporting system of serious adverse events for nonprescription drugs and dietary supplements sold and consumed in the United States.

(3) The adverse event reporting system created under the Dietary Supplement and Nonprescription Drug Consumer Protection Act is intended to serve as an early warning system for potential public health issues associated with the use of these products.

(4) A reliable mechanism to track patterns of adulteration in food would support efforts by the Food and Drug Administration to target limited inspection resources to protect the public health.

(e) Effective Date. — The requirements of section 417(d) of the Federal Food, Drug, and Cosmetic Act, as added by subsection (a), shall become effective 1 year after the date of the enactment of this Act.

(f) Guidance. — Not later than 9 months after the date of the enactment of this Act, the Secretary shall issue a guidance to industry about submitting reports to the electronic portal established under section 417 of the Federal Food, Drug, and Cosmetic Act (as added by this section) and providing notifications to other persons in the supply chain of an article of food under such section 417.

(g) Effect. — Nothing in this title, or an amendment made by this title, shall be construed to alter the jurisdiction between the Secretaries of Agriculture and of Health and Human Services, under applicable statutes and regulations.

Sec. 1006. Enhanced Aquaculture and Seafood Inspection.

(a) Findings. — Congress finds the following:

(1) In 2007, there has been an overwhelming increase in the volume of aquaculture and seafood that has been found to contain substances that are not approved for use in food in the United States.

(2) As of May 2007, inspection programs are not able to satisfactorily accomplish the goals of ensuring the food safety of the United States.

(3) To protect the health and safety of consumers in the United States, the ability of the Secretary to perform inspection functions must be enhanced.

(b) Heightened Inspections. — The Secretary is authorized to enhance, as necessary, the inspection regime of the Food and Drug Administration for aquaculture and seafood, consistent with obligations of the United States under international agreements and United States law.

(c) Report to Congress. — Not later than 180 days after the date of the enactment of this Act, the Secretary shall submit to Congress a report that —

(1) describes the specifics of the aquaculture and seafood inspection program;

(2) describes the feasibility of developing a traceability system for all catfish and seafood products, both domestic and imported, for the purpose of identifying the processing plant of origin of such products; and

(3) provides for an assessment of the risks associated with particular contaminants and banned substances.

(d) Partnerships with States. — Upon the request by any State, the Secretary may enter into partnership agreements, as soon as practicable after the request is made, to implement inspection programs to Federal standards regarding the importation of aquaculture and seafood.

Sec. 1007. Consultation Regarding Genetically Engineered Seafood Products.

The Commissioner of Food and Drugs shall consult with the Assistant Administrator of the National Marine Fisheries Service of the National Oceanic and Atmospheric Administration to produce a report on any environmental risks associated with genetically engineered seafood products, including the impact on wild fish stocks.

Sec. 1008. Sense of Congress.

It is the sense of Congress that —

(1) it is vital for Congress to provide the Food and Drug Administration with additional resources, authorities, and direction with respect to ensuring the safety of the food supply of the United States;

(2) additional inspectors are required to improve the Food and Drug Administration's ability to safeguard the food supply of the United States;

(3) because of the increasing volume of international trade in food products the Secretary should make it a priority to enter into agreements with the trading partners of the United States with respect to food safety; and

(4) Congress should work to develop a comprehensive response to the issue of food safety.

Sec. 1009. Annual Report to Congress.

The Secretary shall, on an annual basis, submit to the Committee on Health, Education, Labor, and Pensions and the Committee on Appropriations of the Senate and the Committee on Energy and Commerce and the Committee on Appropriations of the House of Representatives a report that includes, with respect to the preceding 1-year period —

(1) the number and amount of food products regulated by the Food and Drug Administration imported into the United States, aggregated by country and type of food;

(2) a listing of the number of Food and Drug Administration inspectors of imported food products referenced in paragraph (1) and the number of Food and Drug Administration inspections performed on such products; and

(3) aggregated data on the findings of such inspections, including data related to violations of the Federal Food, Drug, and Cosmetic Act (21 U.S.C. 201 et seq.), and enforcement actions used to follow-up on such findings and violations.

Sec. 1010. Publication of Annual Reports.

(a) In General. — The Commissioner of Food and Drugs shall annually submit to Congress and publish on the Internet Web site of the Food and Drug Administration, a report concerning the results of the Administration's pesticide residue monitoring program, that includes —

(1) information and analysis similar to that contained in the report entitled "Food and Drug Administration Pesticide Program Residue Monitoring 2003" as released in June of 2005;

(2) based on an analysis of previous samples, an identification of products or countries (for imports) that require special attention and additional study based on a comparison with equivalent products manufactured, distributed, or sold in the United States (including details on the plans for such additional studies), including in the initial report (and subsequent reports as determined necessary) the results and analysis of the Ginseng Dietary Supplements Special Survey as described on page 13 of the report entitled "Food and Drug Administration Pesticide Program Residue Monitoring 2003";

(3) information on the relative number of interstate and imported shipments of each tested commodity that were sampled, including recommendations on whether sampling is statistically significant, provides confidence intervals or other related statistical information, and whether the number of samples should be increased and the details of any plans to provide for such increase; and

(4) a description of whether certain commodities are being improperly imported as another commodity, including a description of additional steps that are being planned to prevent such smuggling.

(b) Initial Reports. — Annual reports under subsection (a) for fiscal years 2004 through 2006 may be combined into a single report, by not later than June 1, 2008, for purposes of publication under subsection (a). Thereafter such reports shall be completed by June 1 of each year for the data collected for the year that was 2-years prior to the year in which the report is published.

(c) Memorandum of Understanding. — The Commissioner of Food and Drugs, the Administrator of the Food Safety and Inspection Service, the Department of Commerce, and the head of the Agricultural Marketing Service shall enter into a memorandum of understanding to permit inclusion of data in the reports under subsection (a) relating to testing carried out by the Food Safety and Inspection Service and the Agricultural Marketing Service on meat, poultry, eggs, and certain raw agricultural products, respectively.

Sec. 1011. Rule of Construction.

Nothing in this title (or an amendment made by this title) shall be construed to affect —

(1) the regulation of dietary supplements under the Dietary Supplement Health and Education Act of 1994 (Public Law 103–417); or

(2) the adverse event reporting system for dietary supplements created under the Dietary Supplement and Nonprescription Drug Consumer Protection Act (Public Law 109–462).

Sec. 1011. Office of Women's Health.

(a) Establishment. — There is established within the Office of the Commissioner, an office to be known as the Office of Women's Health (referred to in this section as the "Office"). The Office shall be headed by a director who shall be appointed by the Commissioner of Food and Drugs.

(b) Purpose. — The Director of the Office shall —

(1) report to the Commissioner of Food and Drugs on current Food and Drug Administration (referred to in this section as the "Administration") levels of activity regarding women's participation in clinical trials and the analysis of data by sex in the testing of drugs, medical devices, and biological products across, where appropriate, age, biological, and sociocultural contexts;

(2) establish short-range and long-range goals and objectives within the Administration for issues of particular concern to women's health within the jurisdiction of the Administration, including, where relevant and appropriate, adequate inclusion of women and analysis of data by sex in Administration protocols and policies;

(3) provide information to women and health care providers on those areas in which differences between men and women exist;

(4) consult with pharmaceutical, biologics, and device manufacturers, health professionals with expertise in women's issues, consumer organizations, and women's health professionals on Administration policy with regard to women;

(5) make annual estimates of funds needed to monitor clinical trials and analysis of data by sex in accordance with needs that are identified; and

(6) serve as a member of the Department of Health and Human Services Coordinating Committee on Women's Health (established under section 229(b)(4) of the Public Health Service Act).

(c) Authorization of Appropriations. — For the purpose of carrying out this section, there are authorized to be appropriated such sums as may be necessary for each of the fiscal years 2010 through 2014.

Title XI — Other Provisions

Subtitle A — In General

Sec. 1103. Improving Genetic Test Safety and Quality.

(a) Report. — If the Secretary's Advisory Committee on Genetics, Health, and Society does not complete and submit the Regulatory Oversight of Genetic/Genomic Testing Report & Action Recommendations to the Secretary of Health and Human Services (referred to in this section as the "Secretary") by July of 2008, the Secretary shall enter into a contract with the Institute of Medicine to conduct a study to assess the overall safety and quality of genetic tests and prepare a report that includes recommendations to improve Federal oversight and regulation of genetic tests. Such study shall take into consideration relevant reports by the Secretary's Advisory Committee on Genetics, Health, and Society and other groups and shall be completed not later than 1 year after the date on which the Secretary entered into such contract.

(b) Rule of Construction. — Nothing in this section shall be construed as requiring Federal efforts with respect to regulatory oversight of genetic tests to cease or be limited or delayed pending completion of the report by the Secretary's Advisory Committee on Genetics, Health, and Society or the Institute of Medicine.

Sec. 1105. Severability Clause.

If any provision of this Act, an amendment made this Act, or the application of such provision or amendment to any person or circumstance is held to be unconstitutional, the remainder of this Act, the amendments made by this Act, and the application of the provisions of such to any person or circumstances shall not be affected thereby.

Subtitle B — Antibiotic Access and Innovation

Sec. 1112. Orphan Antibiotic Drugs.

(a) Public Meeting. — The Commissioner of Food and Drugs shall convene a public meeting regarding which serious and life threatening infectious diseases, such as diseases due to gram-negative bacteria and other diseases due to antibiotic-resistant bacteria, potentially qualify for available grants and contracts under section 5(a) of the Orphan Drug Act (21 U.S.C. 360ee(a)) or other incentives for development.

Sec. 1114. Report.

Not later than January 1, 2012, the Comptroller General of the United States shall submit a report to the Committee on Health, Education, Labor, and Pensions of the Senate and the Committee on Energy and Commerce of the House of Representatives that examines whether and how this subtitle has—

(1) encouraged the development of new antibiotics and other drugs; and

(2) prevented or delayed timely generic drug entry into the market.

FAMILY SMOKING PREVENTION AND TOBACCO CONTROL ACT

Sec. 2. Findings.

The Congress finds the following:

(1) The use of tobacco products by the Nation's children is a pediatric disease of considerable proportions that results in new generations of tobacco-dependent children and adults.

(2) A consensus exists within the scientific and medical communities that tobacco products are inherently dangerous and cause cancer, heart disease, and other serious adverse health effects.

(3) Nicotine is an addictive drug.

(4) Virtually all new users of tobacco products are under the minimum legal age to purchase such products.

(5) Tobacco advertising and marketing contribute significantly to the use of nicotine-containing tobacco products by adolescents.

(6) Because past efforts to restrict advertising and marketing of tobacco products have failed adequately to curb tobacco use by adolescents, comprehensive restrictions on the sale, promotion, and distribution of such products are needed.

(7) Federal and State governments have lacked the legal and regulatory authority and resources they need to address comprehensively the public health and societal problems caused by the use of tobacco products.

(8) Federal and State public health officials, the public health community, and the public at large recognize that the tobacco industry should be subject to ongoing oversight.

(9) Under article I, section 8 of the Constitution, the Congress is vested with the responsibility for regulating interstate commerce and commerce with Indian tribes.

(10) The sale, distribution, marketing, advertising, and use of tobacco products are activities in and substantially affecting interstate commerce because they are sold, marketed, advertised, and distributed in interstate commerce on a nationwide basis, and have a substantial effect on the Nation's economy.

(11) The sale, distribution, marketing, advertising, and use of such products substantially affect interstate commerce through the health care and other costs attributable to the use of tobacco products.

(12) It is in the public interest for Congress to enact legislation that provides the Food and Drug Administration with the authority to regulate tobacco products and the advertising and promotion of such products. The benefits to the American people from enacting such legislation would be significant in human and economic terms.

(13) Tobacco use is the foremost preventable cause of premature death in America. It causes over 400,000 deaths in the United States each year, and approximately 8,600,000 Americans have chronic illnesses related to smoking.

(14) Reducing the use of tobacco by minors by 50 percent would prevent well over 10,000,000 of today's children from becoming regular, daily smokers, saving over 3,000,000 of them from premature death due to tobacco-induced disease. Such a reduction in youth smoking would also result in approximately $75,000,000,000 in savings attributable to reduced health care costs.

(15) Advertising, marketing, and promotion of tobacco products have been especially directed to attract young persons to use tobacco products, and these efforts have resulted in increased use of such products by youth. Past efforts to oversee these activities have not been successful in adequately preventing such increased use.

(16) In 2005, the cigarette manufacturers spent more than $13,000,000,000 to attract new users, retain current users, increase current consumption, and generate favorable long-term attitudes toward smoking and tobacco use.

(17) Tobacco product advertising often misleadingly portrays the use of tobacco as socially acceptable and healthful to minors.

(18) Tobacco product advertising is regularly seen by persons under the age of 18, and persons under the age of 18 are regularly exposed to tobacco product promotional efforts.

(19) Through advertisements during and sponsorship of sporting events, tobacco has become strongly associated with sports and has become portrayed as an integral part of sports and the healthy lifestyle associated with rigorous sporting activity.

(20) Children are exposed to substantial and unavoidable tobacco advertising that leads to favorable beliefs about tobacco use, plays a role in leading young people to overestimate the prevalence of tobacco use, and increases the number of young people who begin to use tobacco.

(21) The use of tobacco products in motion pictures and other mass media glamorizes its use for young people and encourages them to use tobacco products.

(22) Tobacco advertising expands the size of the tobacco market by increasing consumption of tobacco products including tobacco use by young people.

(23) Children are more influenced by tobacco marketing than adults: more than 80 percent of youth smoke three heavily marketed brands, while only 54 percent of adults, 26 and older, smoke these same brands.

(24) Tobacco company documents indicate that young people are an important and often crucial segment of the tobacco market. Children, who tend to be more price sensitive than adults, are influenced by advertising and promotion practices that result in drastically reduced cigarette prices.

(25) Comprehensive advertising restrictions will have a positive effect on the smoking rates of young people.

(26) Restrictions on advertising are necessary to prevent unrestricted tobacco advertising from undermining legislation prohibiting access to young people and providing for education about tobacco use.

(27) International experience shows that advertising regulations that are stringent and comprehensive have a greater impact on overall tobacco use and young people's use than weaker or less comprehensive ones.

(28) Text only requirements, although not as stringent as a ban, will help reduce underage use of tobacco products while preserving the informational function of advertising.

(29) It is in the public interest for Congress to adopt legislation to address the public health crisis created by actions of the tobacco industry.

(30) The final regulations promulgated by the Secretary of Health and Human Services in the August 28, 1996, issue of the Federal Register (61 Fed. Reg. 44615-44618) for inclusion as part 897 of title 21, Code of Federal Regulations, are consistent with the first amendment to the United States Constitution and with the standards set forth in the amendments made by this subtitle for the regulation of tobacco products by the Food and Drug Administration, and the restriction on the sale and distribution of, including access to and the advertising and promotion of, tobacco products contained in such regulations are substantially related to accomplishing the public health goals of this division.

(31) The regulations described in paragraph 30 will directly and materially advance the Federal Government's substantial interest in reducing the number of children and adolescents who use cigarettes and smokeless tobacco and in preventing the life-threatening health consequences associated with tobacco use. An overwhelming majority of Americans who use tobacco products begin using such products while they are minors and become addicted to the nicotine in those products before reaching the age of 18. Tobacco advertising and promotion play a crucial role in the decision of these minors to begin using tobacco products. Less restrictive and less comprehensive approaches have not and will not be effective in reducing the problems addressed by such regulations. The reasonable restrictions on the advertising and promotion of tobacco products contained in such regulations will lead to a significant decrease in the number of minors using and becoming addicted to those products.

(32) The regulations described in paragraph (30) impose no more extensive restrictions on communication by tobacco manufacturers and sellers than are necessary to reduce the number of children and adolescents who use cigarettes and smokeless tobacco and to prevent the life-threatening health consequences associated with tobacco use. Such regulations are narrowly tailored to restrict those advertising and promotional practices which are most likely to be seen or heard by youth and most likely to entice them into tobacco use, while affording tobacco manufacturers and sellers ample opportunity to convey information about their products to adult consumers.

(33) Tobacco dependence is a chronic disease, one that typically requires repeated interventions to achieve long-term or permanent abstinence.

(34) Because the only known safe alternative to smoking is cessation, interventions should target all smokers to help them quit completely.

(35) Tobacco products have been used to facilitate and finance criminal activities both domestically and internationally. Illicit trade of tobacco products has been linked to organized crime and terrorist groups.

(36) It is essential that the Food and Drug Administration review products sold or distributed for use to reduce risks or exposures associated with tobacco products and that it be empowered to review any advertising and labeling for such products. It is also essential that manufacturers, prior to marketing such products, be required to demonstrate that such products will meet a series of rigorous criteria, and will benefit the health of the population as a whole, taking into account both users of tobacco products and persons who do not currently use tobacco products.

(37) Unless tobacco products that purport to reduce the risks to the public of tobacco use actually reduce such risks, those products can cause substantial harm to the public health to the extent that the individuals, who would otherwise not consume tobacco products or would consume such products less, use tobacco products purporting to reduce risk. Those who use products sold or distributed as modified risk products that do not in fact reduce risk, rather than quitting or reducing their use of tobacco products, have a substantially increased likelihood of suffering disability and premature death. The costs to society of the widespread use of products sold or distributed as modified risk products that do not in fact reduce risk or that increase risk include thousands of unnecessary deaths and injuries and huge costs to our health care system.

(38) As the National Cancer Institute has found, many smokers mistakenly believe that "low tar" and "light" cigarettes cause fewer health problems than other cigarettes. As the National Cancer Institute has also found, mistaken beliefs about the health consequences of smoking "low tar" and "light" cigarettes can reduce the motivation to quit smoking entirely and thereby lead to disease and death.

(39) Recent studies have demonstrated that there has been no reduction in risk on a population-wide basis from "low tar" and "light" cigarettes, and such products may actually increase the risk of tobacco use.

(40) The dangers of products sold or distributed as modified risk tobacco products that do not in fact reduce risk are so high that there is a compelling governmental interest in ensuring that statements about modified risk tobacco products are complete, accurate, and relate to the overall disease risk of the product.

(41) As the Federal Trade Commission has found, consumers have misinterpreted advertisements in which one product is claimed to be less harmful than a comparable product, even in the presence of disclosures and advisories intended to provide clarification.

(42) Permitting manufacturers to make unsubstantiated statements concerning modified risk tobacco products, whether express or implied, even if accompanied by disclaimers would be detrimental to the public health.

(43) The only way to effectively protect the public health from the dangers of unsubstantiated modified risk tobacco products is to empower the Food and Drug Administration to require that products that tobacco manufacturers sold or distributed for risk reduction be reviewed in advance of marketing, and to require that the evidence relied on to support claims be fully verified.

(44) The Food and Drug Administration is a regulatory agency with the scientific expertise to identify harmful substances in products to which consumers are exposed, to design standards to limit exposure to those substances, to evaluate scientific studies supporting claims about the safety of products, and to evaluate the impact of labels, labeling, and advertising on consumer behavior in order to reduce the risk of harm and promote understanding of the impact of the product on health. In connection with its mandate to promote health and reduce the risk of harm, the Food and Drug Administration routinely makes decisions about whether and how products may be marketed in the United States.

(45) The Federal Trade Commission was created to protect consumers from unfair or deceptive acts or practices, and to regulate unfair methods of competition. Its focus is on those marketplace practices that deceive or mislead consumers, and those that give some competitors an unfair advantage. Its mission is to regulate activities in the marketplace. Neither the Federal Trade Commission nor any other Federal agency except the Food and Drug Administration possesses the scientific expertise needed to implement effectively all provisions of the Family Smoking Prevention and Tobacco Control Act.

(46) If manufacturers state or imply in communications directed to consumers through the media or through a label, labeling, or advertising, that a tobacco product is approved or inspected by the Food and Drug Administration or complies with Food and Drug Administration standards, consumers are likely to be confused and misled. Depending upon the particular language used and its context, such a statement could result in consumers being misled into believing that the product is endorsed by the Food and Drug Administration for use or in consumers being misled about the harmfulness of the product because of such regulation, inspection, approval, or compliance.

(47) In August 2006 a United States district court judge found that the major United States cigarette companies continue to target and market to youth. USA v. Philip Morris, USA, Inc., et al. (Civil Action No. 99-2496(GK), August 17, 2006).

(48) In August 2006 a United States district court judge found that the major United States cigarette companies dramatically increased their advertising and promotional spending in ways that encourage youth to start smoking subsequent to the signing of the Master Settlement Agreement in 1998. USA v. Philip Morris, USA, Inc., et al. (Civil Action No. 99-2496(GK), August 17, 2006).

(49) In August 2006 a United States district court judge found that the major United States cigarette companies have designed their cigarettes to precisely control nicotine delivery levels and provide doses of nicotine sufficient to create and sustain addiction while also concealing much of their nicotine-related research. USA v. Philip Morris, USA, Inc., et al. (Civil Action No. 99-2496(GK), August 17, 2006).

Sec. 3. Purpose.

The purposes of this division are —

(1) to provide authority to the Food and Drug Administration to regulate tobacco products under the Federal Food, Drug, and Cosmetic Act (21 U.S.C. 301 et seq.), by recognizing it as the primary Federal regulatory authority with respect to the manufacture, marketing, and distribution of tobacco products as provided for in this division;

(2) to ensure that the Food and Drug Administration has the authority to address issues of particular concern to public health officials, especially the use of tobacco by young people and dependence on tobacco;

(3) to authorize the Food and Drug Administration to set national standards controlling the manufacture of tobacco products and the identity, public disclosure, and amount of ingredients used in such products;

(4) to provide new and flexible enforcement authority to ensure that there is effective oversight of the tobacco industry's efforts to develop, introduce, and promote less harmful tobacco products;

(5) to vest the Food and Drug Administration with the authority to regulate the levels of tar, nicotine, and other harmful components of tobacco products;

(6) in order to ensure that consumers are better informed, to require tobacco product manufacturers to disclose research which has not previously been made available, as well as research generated in the future, relating to the health and dependency effects or safety of tobacco products;

(7) to continue to permit the sale of tobacco products to adults in conjunction with measures to ensure that they are not sold or accessible to underage purchasers;

(8) to impose appropriate regulatory controls on the tobacco industry;

(9) to promote cessation to reduce disease risk and the social costs associated with tobacco-related diseases; and

(10) to strengthen legislation against illicit trade in tobacco products.

Sec. 4. Scope and Effect.

(a) Intended Effect. — Nothing in this division (or an amendment made by this division) shall be construed to —

(1) establish a precedent with regard to any other industry, situation, circumstance, or legal action; or

(2) affect any action pending in Federal, State, or tribal court, or any agreement, consent decree, or contract of any kind.

(b) Agricultural Activities. — The provisions of this division (or an amendment made by this division)which authorize the Secretary to take certain actions with regard to tobacco and tobacco products shall not be construed to affect any authority of the Secretary of Agriculture under existing law regarding the growing, cultivation, or curing of raw tobacco.

(c) Revenue Activities. — The provisions of this division (or an amendment made by this division) which authorize the Secretary to take certain actions with regard to tobacco products shall not be construed to affect any authority of the Secretary of the Treasury under chapter 52 of the Internal Revenue Code of 1986.

Sec. 5. Severability.

If any provision of this division, of the amendments made by this division, or of the regulations promulgated under this division (or under such amendments), or the application of any such provision to any person or circumstance is held to be invalid, the remainder of this division, such amendments and such regulations, and the application of such provisions to any other person or circumstance shall not be affected and shall continue to be enforced to the fullest extent possible.

Sec. 6. Modification of Deadlines for Secretarial Action.

(a) Delayed Commencement of Dates for Secretarial Action. —

(1) In General. — Except as provided in subsection (c), with respect to any time periods specified in this division (or in an amendment made by this division) that begin on the date of enactment of this Act, within which the Secretary of Health and Human Services is required to carry out and complete specified activities, the calculation of such time periods shall commence on the date described in subsection (b).

(2) Limitation. — Subsection (a) shall only apply with respect to obligations of the Secretary of Health and Human Services that must be completed within a specified time period and shall not apply to the obligations of any other person or to any other provision of this division (including the amendments made by this division)that do not create such obligations of the Secretary and are not contingent on actions by the Secretary.

(b) Date Described. — The date described in this subsection is the first day of the first fiscal quarter following the initial 2 consecutive fiscal quarters of fiscal year 2010 for which the Secretary of Health and Human Services has collected fees under section 919 of the Federal Food, Drug, and Cosmetic Act (as added by section 101).

(c) Exception. — Subsection (a) shall not apply to any time period (or date) contained —

(1) in section 102, except that the reference to "180 days" in subsection (a)(1) of such section shall be deemed to be "270 days"; and

(2) in sections 201 through 204 (or the amendments made by any such sections).

(d) Adjustment. — The Secretary of Health and Human Services may extend or reduce the duration of one or more time periods to which subsection (a) applies if the Secretary determines appropriate, except that no such period shall be extended for more than 90 days.

Title I – Authority of the Food and Drug Administration

Sec. 102. Final Rule.

(a) Cigarettes and Smokeless Tobacco. —

(1) In General. — On the first day of publication of the Federal Register that is 180 days or more after the date of enactment of this Act, the Secretary of Health and Human Services shall publish in the Federal Register a final rule regarding cigarettes and smokeless tobacco, which —

(A) is deemed to be issued under chapter 9 of the Federal Food, Drug, and Cosmetic Act, as added by section 101 of this division; and

(B) shall be deemed to be in compliance with all applicable provisions of chapter 5 of title 5, United States Code, and all other provisions of law relating to rulemaking procedures.

(2) Contents of Rule. — Except as provided in this subsection, the final rule published under paragraph (1), shall be identical in its provisions to part 897 of the regulations promulgated by the Secretary of Health and Human Services in the August 28, 1996, issue of the Federal Register (61 Fed. Reg. 44615-44618). Such rule shall —

(A) provide for the designation of jurisdictional authority that is in accordance with this subsection in accordance with this division and the amendments made by this division;

(B) strike Subpart C — Labels and section 897.32(c);

(C) strike paragraphs (a), (b), and (i) of section 897.3 and insert definitions of the terms "cigarette", "cigarette tobacco", and "smokeless tobacco" as defined in section 900 of the Federal Food, Drug, and Cosmetic Act;

(D) insert "or roll-your-own paper" in section 897.34(a) after "other than cigarettes or smokeless tobacco";

(E) include such modifications to section 897.30(b), if any, that the Secretary determines are appropriate in light of governing First Amendment case law, including the decision of the Supreme Court of the United States in Lorillard Tobacco Co. v. Reilly (533 U.S. 525 (2001));

(F) become effective on the date that is 1 year after the date of enactment of this Act; and

(G) amend paragraph(d) of section 897.16 to read as follows:

"(d)(1) Except as provided in subparagraph (2), no manufacturer, distributor, or retailer may distribute or cause to be distributed any free samples of cigarettes, smokeless tobacco, or other tobacco products (as such term is defined in section 201 of the Federal Food, Drug, and Cosmetic Act).

"(2)(A) Subparagraph (1) does not prohibit a manufacturer, distributor, or retailer from distributing or causing to be distributed free samples of smokeless tobacco in a qualified adult-only facility.

"(B) This subparagraph does not affect the authority of a State or local government to prohibit or otherwise restrict the distribution of free samples of smokeless tobacco.

"(C) For purposes of this paragraph, the term "qualified adult-only facility" means a facility or restricted area that —

"(i) requires each person present to provide to a law enforcement officer (whether on or off duty) or to a security guard licensed by a governmental entity government-issued identification showing a photograph and at least the minimum age established by applicable law for the purchase of smokeless tobacco;

"(ii) does not sell, serve, or distribute alcohol;

"(iii) is not located adjacent to or immediately across from (in any direction) a space that is used primarily for youth-oriented marketing, promotional, or other activities;

"(iv) is a temporary structure constructed, designated, and operated as a distinct enclosed area for the purpose of distributing free samples of smokeless tobacco in accordance with this subparagraph;

"(v) is enclosed by a barrier that —

"(I) is constructed of, or covered with, an opaque material (except for entrances and exits);

"(II) extends from no more than 12 inches above the ground or floor (which area at the bottom of the barrier must be covered with material that restricts visibility but may allow airflow) to at least 8 feet above the ground or floor (or to the ceiling); and

"(III) prevents persons outside the qualified adult-only facility from seeing into the qualified adult-only facility, unless they make unreasonable efforts to do so; and

"(vi) does not display on its exterior —

"(I) any tobacco product advertising;

"(II) a brand name other than in conjunction with words for an area or enclosure to identify an adult-only facility; or

"(III) any combination of words that would imply to a reasonable observer that the manufacturer, distributor, or retailer has a sponsorship that would violate section 897.34(c).

"(D) Distribution of samples of smokeless tobacco under this subparagraph permitted to be taken out of the qualified adult-only facility shall be limited to 1 package per adult consumer containing no more than 0.53 ounces (15 grams) of smokeless tobacco. If such package of smokeless tobacco contains individual portions of smokeless tobacco, the individual portions of smokeless tobacco shall not exceed 8 individual portions and the collective weight of such individual portions shall not exceed 0.53 ounces (15 grams). Any manufacturer, distributor, or retailer who distributes or causes to be distributed free samples also shall take reasonable steps to ensure that the above amounts are limited to one such package per adult consumer per day.

"(3) Notwithstanding subparagraph (2), no manufacturer, distributor, or retailer may distribute or cause to be distributed any free samples of smokeless tobacco —

"(A) to a sports team or entertainment group; or

"(B) at any football, basketball, baseball, soccer, or hockey event or any other sporting or entertainment event determined by the Secretary to be covered by this subparagraph.

"(4) The Secretary shall implement a program to ensure compliance with this paragraph and submit a report to the Congress on such compliance not later than 18 months after the date of enactment of the Family Smoking Prevention and Tobacco Control Act.

"(5) Nothing in this paragraph shall be construed to authorize any person to distribute or cause to be distributed any sample of a tobacco product to any individual who has not attained the minimum age established by applicable law for the purchase of such product."

(3) Amendments to Rule. — Prior to making amendments to the rule published under paragraph (1), the Secretary shall promulgate a proposed rule in accordance with chapter 5 of title 5, United States Code.

(4) Rule of Construction. — Except as provided in paragraph (3), nothing in this section shall be construed to limit the authority of the Secretary to amend, in accordance with chapter 5 of title 5, United States Code, the regulation promulgated pursuant to this section, including the provisions of such regulation relating to distribution of free samples.

(5) Enforcement of Retail Sale Provisions. — The Secretary of Health and Human Services shall ensure that the provisions of this division, the amendments made by this division, and the implementing regulations (including such provisions, amendments, and regulations relating to the retail sale of tobacco products) are enforced with respect to the United States and Indian tribes.

(6) Qualified Adult-Only Facility. — A qualified adult-only facility (as such term is defined in section 897.16(d) of the final rule published under paragraph (1)) that is also a retailer and that commits a violation as a retailer shall not be subject to the limitations in section 103(q) and shall be subject to penalties applicable to a qualified adult-only facility.

(7) Congressional Review Provisions. — Section 801 of title 5, United States Code, shall not apply to the final rule published under paragraph (1).

(b) Limitation on Advisory Opinions. — As of the date of enactment of this Act, the following documents issued by the Food and Drug Administration shall not constitute advisory opinions under section 10.85(d)(1) of title 21, Code of Federal Regulations, except as they apply to tobacco products, and shall not be cited by the Secretary of Health and Human Services or the Food and Drug Administration as binding precedent:

(1) The preamble to the proposed rule in the document titled "Regulations Restricting the Sale and Distribution of Cigarettes and Smokeless Tobacco Products to Protect Children and Adolescents" (60 Fed. Reg. 41314-41372 (August 11, 1995)).

(2) The document titled "Nicotine in Cigarettes and Smokeless Tobacco Products is a Drug and These Products Are Nicotine Delivery Devices Under the Federal Food, Drug, and Cosmetic Act" (60 Fed. Reg. 41453-41787 (August 11, 1995)).

(3) The preamble to the final rule in the document titled "Regulations Restricting the Sale and Distribution of Cigarettes and Smokeless Tobacco to Protect Children and Adolescents" (61 Fed. Reg. 44396-44615 (August 28, 1996)).

(4) The document titled "Nicotine in Cigarettes and Smokeless Tobacco is a Drug and These Products are Nicotine Delivery Devices Under the Federal Food, Drug, and Cosmetic Act; Jurisdictional Determination" (61 Fed. Reg. 44619-45318 (August 28, 1996)).

Sec. 103. Conforming and Other Amendments to General Provisions.

(a) – (o) [Text not included. — Ed.]

(p) Rule of Construction. — Nothing in this section is intended or shall be construed to expand, contract, or otherwise modify or amend the existing limitations on State government authority over tribal restricted fee or trust lands.

(q) Guidance and Effective Dates. —

(1) In General. — The Secretary of Health and Human Services shall issue guidance —

(A) defining the term "repeated violation", as used in section 303(f)(8) of the Federal Food, Drug, and Cosmetic Act (21 U.S.C. 333(f)(8)) as amended by subsection(c), as including at least 5 violations of particular requirements over a 36-month period at a particular retail outlet that constitute a repeated violation and providing for civil penalties in accordance with paragraph(2);

(B) providing for timely and effective notice by certified or registered mail or personal delivery to the retailer of each alleged violation at a particular retail outlet prior to conducting a followup compliance check, such notice to be sent to the location specified on the retailer's registration or to the retailer's registered agent if the retailer has provider such agent information to the Food and Drug Administration prior to the violation;

(C) providing for a hearing pursuant to the procedures established through regulations of the Food and Drug Administration for assessing civil money penalties, including at a retailer's request a hearing by telephone or at the nearest regional or field office of the Food and Drug Administration, and providing for an expedited procedure for the administrative appeal of an alleged violation;

(D) providing that a person may not be charged with a violation at a particular retail outlet unless the Secretary has provided notice to the retailer of all previous violations at that outlet;

(E) establishing that civil money penalties for multiple violations shall increase from one violation to the next violation pursuant to paragraph (2) within the time periods provided for in such paragraph;

(F) providing that good faith reliance on the presentation of a false government-issued photographic identification that contains a date of birth does not constitute a violation of any minimum age requirement for the sale of tobacco products if the retailer has taken effective steps to prevent such violations, including —

(i) adopting and enforcing a written policy against sales to minors;

(ii) informing its employees of all applicable laws;

(iii) establishing disciplinary sanctions for employee noncompliance; and

(iv) requiring its employees to verify age by way of photographic identification or electronic

(G) providing for the Secretary, in determining whether to impose a no-tobacco-sale order and in determining whether to compromise, modify, or terminate such an order, to consider whether the retailer has taken effective steps to prevent violations of the minimum age requirements for the sale of tobacco products, including the steps listed in subparagraph (F).

(2) Penalties for Violations. —

(A) In General. —The amount of the civil penalty to be applied for violations of restrictions promulgated under section 906(d), as described in paragraph (1), shall be as follows:

(i) With respect to a retailer with an approved training program, the amount of the civil penalty shall not exceed —

(I) in the case of the first violation, $0.00 together with the issuance of a warning letter to the retailer;

(II) in the case of a second violation within a 12-month period, $250;

(III) in the case of a third violation within a 24-month period, $500;

(IV) in the case of a fourth violation within a 24-month period, $2,000;

(V) in the case of a fifth violation within a 36-month period, $5,000; and

(VI) in the case of a sixth or subsequent violation within a 48-month period, $10,000 as determined by the Secretary on a case-by-case basis.

(ii) With respect to a retailer that does not have an approved training program, the amount of the civil penalty shall not exceed —

(I) in the case of the first violation, $250;

(II) in the case of a second violation within a 12-month period, $500;

(III) in the case of a third violation within a 24-month period, $1,000;

(IV) in the case of a fourth violation within a 24-month period, $2,000;

(V) in the case of a fifth violation within a 36-month period, $5,000; and

(VI) in the case of a sixth or subsequent violation within a 48-month period, $10,000 as determined by the Secretary on a case-by-case basis.

(B) Training Program. — For purposes of subparagraph (A), the term "approved training program" means a training program that complies with standards developed by the Food and Drug Administration for such programs.

(C) Consideration of State Penalties. — The Secretary shall coordinate with the States in enforcing the provisions of this Act and, for purposes of mitigating a civil penalty to be applied for a violation by a retailer of any restriction promulgated under section 906(d), shall consider the amount of any penalties paid by the retailer to a State for the same violation.

(3) General Effective Date. — The amendments made by paragraphs (2), (3), and (4)of subsection (c) shall take effect upon the issuance of guidance described in paragraph (1) of this subsection.

(4) Special Effective Date. — The amendment made by subsection (c)(1) shall take effect on the date of enactment of this Act.

(5) Package Label Requirements. — The package label requirements of paragraphs (3) and (4) of section 903(a) of the Federal Food, Drug, and Cosmetic Act (as amended by this division) shall take effect on the date that is 12 months after the date of enactment of this Act. The package label requirements of paragraph (2) of such section 903(a) for cigarettes shall take effect on the date that is 15 months after the issuance of the regulations required by section 4(d) of the Federal Cigarette Labeling and Advertising Act (15 U.S.C. 1333), as amended by section 201 of this division. The package label requirements of paragraph (2) of such section 903(a) for tobacco products other than cigarettes shall take effect on the date that is 12 months after the date of enactment of this Act. The effective date shall be with respect to the date of manufacture, provided that, in any case, beginning 30 days after such effective date, a manufacturer shall not introduce into the domestic commerce of the United States any product, irrespective of the date of manufacture, that is not in conformance with section 903(a) (2), (3), and (4) and section 920(a) of the Federal Food, Drug, and Cosmetic Act.

(6) Advertising Requirements. — The advertising requirements of section 903(a)(8) of the Federal Food, Drug, and Cosmetic Act (as amended by this division) shall take effect on the date that is 12 months after the date of enactment of this Act.

Sec. 104. Study on Raising the Minimum Age to Purchase Tobacco Products.

The Secretary of Health and Human Services shall —

(1) convene an expert panel to conduct a study on the public health implications of raising the minimum age to purchase tobacco products; and

(2) not later than 5 years after the date of enactment of this Act, submit a report to the Congress on the results of such study.

Sec. 105. Enforcement Action Plan for Advertising and Promotion Restrictions.

(a) Action Plan. —

(1) Development. — Not later than 6 months after the date of enactment of this Act, the Secretary of Health and Human Services(in this section referred to as the "Secretary") shall develop and publish an action plan to enforce restrictions adopted pursuant to section 906 of the Federal Food, Drug, and Cosmetic Act, as added by section 101(b) of this division, or pursuant to section 102(a) of this division, on promotion and advertising of menthol and other cigarettes to youth.

(2) Consultation. — The action plan required by paragraph(1) shall be developed in consultation with public health organizations and other stakeholders with demonstrated expertise and experience in serving minority communities.

(3) Priority. — The action plan required by paragraph(1) shall include provisions designed to ensure enforcement of the restrictions described in paragraph(1) in minority communities.

(b) State and Local Activities. —

(1) Information on Authority. — Not later than 3 months after the date of enactment of this Act, the Secretary shall inform State, local, and tribal governments of the authority provided to such entities under section 5(c) of the Federal Cigarette Labeling and Advertising Act, as added by section 203 of this division, or preserved by such entities under section 916 of the Federal Food, Drug, and Cosmetic Act, as added by section 101(b) of this division.

(2) Community Assistance. — At the request of communities seeking assistance to prevent underage tobacco use, the Secretary shall provide such assistance, including assistance with strategies to address the prevention of underage tobacco use in communities with a disproportionate use of menthol cigarettes by minors.

Sec. 106. Studies of Progress and Effectiveness.

(a) FDA Report. — Not later than 3 years after the date of enactment of this Act, and not less than every 2 years thereafter, the Secretary of Health and Human Services shall submit to the Committee on Health, Education, Labor, and Pensions of the Senate and the Committee on Energy and Commerce of the House of Representatives, a report concerning —

(1) the progress of the Food and Drug Administration in implementing this division, including major accomplishments, objective measurements of progress, and the identification of any areas that have not been fully implemented;

(2) impediments identified by the Food and Drug Administration to progress in implementing this division and to meeting statutory timeframes;

(3) data on the number of new product applications received under section 910 of the Federal Food, Drug, and Cosmetic Act and modified risk product applications received under section 911 of such Act, and the number of applications acted on under each category; and

(4) data on the number of full time equivalents engaged in implementing this division.

(b) GAO Report. — Not later than 5 years after the date of enactment of this Act, the Comptroller General of the United States shall conduct a study of, and submit to the Committees described in subsection(a) a report concerning —

(1) the adequacy of the authority and resources provided to the Secretary of Health and Human Services for this division to carry out its goals and purposes; and

(2) any recommendations for strengthening that authority to more effectively protect the public health with respect to the manufacture, marketing, and distribution of tobacco products.

(c) Public Availability. — The Secretary of Health and Human Services and the Comptroller General of the United States, respectively, shall make the reports required under subsection(a) and(b) available to the public, including by posting such reports on the respective Internet websites of the Food and Drug Administration and the Government Accountability Office.

Title III – Prevention of Illicit Trade in Tobacco Products

* * *

Sec. 302. Study and Report.

(a) Study. — The Comptroller General of the United States shall conduct a study of cross-border trade in tobacco products to —

(1) collect data on cross-border trade in tobacco products, including illicit trade and trade of counterfeit tobacco products and make recommendations on the monitoring of such trade;

(2) collect data on cross-border advertising (any advertising intended to be broadcast, transmitted, or distributed from the United States to another country) of tobacco products and make recommendations on how to prevent or eliminate, and what technologies could help facilitate the elimination of, cross-border advertising; and

(3) collect data on the health effects(particularly with respect to individuals under 18 years of age) resulting from cross-border trade in tobacco products, including the health effects resulting from —

(A) the illicit trade of tobacco products and the trade of counterfeit tobacco products; and

(B) the differing tax rates applicable to tobacco products.

(b) Report. — Not later than 18 months after the date of enactment of this Act, the Comptroller General of the United States shall submit to the Committee on Health, Education, Labor, and Pensions of the Senate and the Committee on Energy and Commerce of the House of Representatives a report on the study described in subsection(a).

(c) Definition. — In this section:

(1) The term "cross-border trade" means trade across a border of the United States, a State or Territory, or Indian country.

(2) The term "Indian country" has the meaning given to such term in section 1151 of title 18, United States Code.

(3) The terms "State" and "Territory" have the meanings given to those terms in section 201 of the Federal Food, Drug, and Cosmetic Act (21 U.S.C. 321).

FOOD SAFETY MODERNIZATION ACT

Sec. 103. Hazard Analysis and Risk-Based Preventive Controls.

(a) – (b) [Text not included. — Ed.]

(c) Rulemaking. —

(1) Proposed Rulemaking. —

(A) In General. — Not later than 9 months after the date of enactment of this Act, the Secretary of Health and Human Services (referred to in this subsection as the "Secretary") shall publish a notice of proposed rulemaking in the Federal Register to promulgate regulations with respect to —

(i) activities that constitute on-farm packing or holding of food that is not grown, raised, or consumed on such farm or another farm under the same ownership for purposes of section 415 of the Federal Food, Drug, and Cosmetic Act (21 U.S.C. 350d), as amended by this Act; and

(ii) activities that constitute on-farm manufacturing or processing of food that is not consumed on that farm or on another farm under common ownership for purposes of such section 415.

(B) Clarification. — The rulemaking described under subparagraph (A) shall enhance the implementation of such section 415 and clarify the activities that are included as part of the definition of the term "facility" under such section 415. Nothing in this Act authorizes the Secretary to modify the definition of the term "facility" under such section.

(C) Science-Based Risk Analysis. — In promulgating regulations under subparagraph (A), the Secretary shall conduct a science-based risk analysis of —

(i) specific types of on-farm packing or holding of food that is not grown, raised, or consumed on such farm or another farm under the same ownership, as such packing and holding relates to specific foods; and

(ii) specific on-farm manufacturing and processing activities as such activities relate to specific foods that are not consumed on that farm or on another farm under common ownership.

(D) Authority with Respect to Certain Facilities. —

(i) In General. — In promulgating the regulations under subparagraph (A), the Secretary shall consider the results of the science-based risk analysis conducted under subparagraph (C), and shall exempt certain facilities from the requirements in section 418 of the Federal Food, Drug, and Cosmetic Act (as added by this section), including hazard analysis and preventive controls, and the mandatory inspection frequency in section 421 of such Act (as added by section 201), or modify the requirements in such sections 418 or 421, as the Secretary determines appropriate, if such facilities are engaged only in specific types of on-farm manufacturing, processing, packing, or holding activities that the Secretary determines to be low risk involving specific foods the Secretary determines to be low risk.

(ii) Limitation. — The exemptions or modifications under clause (i) shall not include an exemption from the requirement to register under section 415 of the Federal Food, Drug, and Cosmetic Act (21 U.S.C. 350d), as amended by this Act, if applicable, and shall apply only to small businesses and very small businesses, as defined in the regulation promulgated under section 418(n) of the Federal Food, Drug, and Cosmetic Act (as added under subsection (a)).

(2) Final Regulations. — Not later than 9 months after the close of the comment period for the proposed rulemaking under paragraph (1), the Secretary shall adopt final rules with respect to —

(A) activities that constitute on-farm packing or holding of food that is not grown, raised, or consumed on such farm or another farm under the same ownership for purposes of section 415 of the Federal Food, Drug, and Cosmetic Act (21 U.S.C. 350d), as amended by this Act;

(B) activities that constitute on-farm manufacturing or processing of food that is not consumed on that farm or on another farm under common ownership for purposes of such section 415; and

(C) the requirements under sections 418 and 421 of the Federal Food, Drug, and Cosmetic Act, as added by this Act, from which the Secretary may issue exemptions or modifications of the requirements for certain types of facilities.

(d) Small Entity Compliance Policy Guide. — Not later than 180 days after the issuance of the regulations promulgated under subsection (n) of section 418 of the Federal Food, Drug, and Cosmetic Act (as added by subsection (a)), the Secretary shall issue a small entity compliance policy guide setting forth in plain language the requirements of such section 418 and this section to assist small entities in complying with the hazard analysis and other activities required under such section 418 and this section.

(e) [Text not included. — Ed.]

(f) No Effect on HACCP Authorities. — Nothing in the amendments made by this section limits the authority of the Secretary under the Federal Food, Drug, and Cosmetic Act (21 U.S.C. 301 et seq.) or the Public Health Service Act (42 U.S.C. 201 et seq.) to revise, issue, or enforce Hazard Analysis Critical Control programs and the Thermally Processed Low-Acid Foods Packaged in Hermetically Sealed Containers standards.

(g) Dietary Supplements. — Nothing in the amendments made by this section shall apply to any facility with regard to the manufacturing, processing, packing, or holding of a dietary supplement that is in compliance with the requirements of sections 402(g)(2) and 761 of the Federal Food, Drug, and Cosmetic Act (21 U.S.C. 342(g)(2), 379aa-1).

(h) Updating Guidance Relating to Fish and Fisheries Products Hazards and Controls. — The Secretary shall, not later than 180 days after the date of enactment of this Act, update the Fish and Fisheries Products Hazards and Control Guidance to take into account advances in technology that have occurred since the previous publication of such Guidance by the Secretary.

(i) Effective Dates. —

(1) General Rule. — The amendments made by this section shall take effect 18 months after the date of enactment of this Act.

(2) Flexibility for Small Businesses. — Notwithstanding paragraph (1) —

(A) the amendments made by this section shall apply to a small business (as defined in the regulations promulgated under section 418(n) of the Federal Food, Drug, and Cosmetic Act (as added by this section)) beginning on the date that is 6 months after the effective date of such regulations; and

(B) the amendments made by this section shall apply to a very small business (as defined in such regulations) beginning on the date that is 18 months after the effective date of such regulations.

Sec. 104. Performance Standards.

(a) In General. — The Secretary shall, in coordination with the Secretary of Agriculture, not less frequently than every 2 years, review and evaluate relevant health data and other relevant information, including from toxicological and epidemiological studies and analyses, current Good Manufacturing Practices issued by the Secretary relating to food, and relevant recommendations of relevant advisory committees, including the Food Advisory Committee, to determine the most significant foodborne contaminants.

(b) Guidance Documents and Regulations. — Based on the review and evaluation conducted under subsection (a), and when appropriate to reduce the risk of serious illness or death to humans or animals or to prevent adulteration of the food under section 402 of the Federal Food, Drug, or Cosmetic Act (21 U.S.C. 342) or to prevent the spread by food of communicable disease under section 361 of the Public Health Service Act (42 U.S.C. 264), the Secretary shall issue contaminant-specific and science-based guidance documents, including guidance documents regarding action levels, or regulations. Such guidance, including guidance regarding action levels, or regulations —

(1) shall apply to products or product classes;

(2) shall, where appropriate, differentiate between food for human consumption and food intended for consumption by animals other than humans; and

(3) shall not be written to be facility-specific.

(c) No Duplication of Efforts. — The Secretary shall coordinate with the Secretary of Agriculture to avoid issuing duplicative guidance on the same contaminants.

(d) Review. — The Secretary shall periodically review and revise, as appropriate, the guidance documents, including guidance documents regarding action levels, or regulations promulgated under this section.

Sec. 108. National Agriculture and Food Defense Strategy.

(a) Development and Submission of Strategy. —

(1) In General. — Not later than 1 year after the date of enactment of this Act, the Secretary of Health and Human Services and the Secretary of Agriculture, in coordination with the Secretary of Homeland Security, shall prepare and transmit to the relevant committees of Congress, and make publicly available on the Internet Web sites of the Department of Health and Human Services and the Department of Agriculture, the National Agriculture and Food Defense Strategy.

(2) Implementation Plan. — The strategy shall include an implementation plan for use by the Secretaries described under paragraph (1) in carrying out the strategy.

(3) Research. — The strategy shall include a coordinated research agenda for use by the Secretaries described under paragraph (1) in conducting research to support the goals and activities described in paragraphs (1) and (2) of subsection (b).

(4) Revisions. — Not later than 4 years after the date on which the strategy is submitted to the relevant committees of Congress under paragraph (1), and not less frequently than every 4 years thereafter, the Secretary of Health and Human Services and the Secretary of Agriculture, in coordination with the Secretary of Homeland Security, shall revise and submit to the relevant committees of Congress the strategy.

(5) Consistency with Existing Plans. — The strategy described in paragraph (1) shall be consistent with —

(A) the National Incident Management System;

(B) the National Response Framework;

(C) the National Infrastructure Protection Plan;

(D) the National Preparedness Goals; and

(E) other relevant national strategies.

(b) Components. —

(1) In General. — The strategy shall include a description of the process to be used by the Department of Health and Human Services, the Department of Agriculture, and the Department of Homeland Security —

(A) to achieve each goal described in paragraph (2); and

(B) to evaluate the progress made by Federal, State, local, and tribal governments towards the achievement of each goal described in paragraph (2).

(2) Goals. — The strategy shall include a description of the process to be used by the Department of Health and Human Services, the Department of Agriculture, and the Department of Homeland Security to achieve the following goals:

(A) Preparedness Goal. — Enhance the preparedness of the agriculture and food system by —

(i) conducting vulnerability assessments of the agriculture and food system;

(ii) mitigating vulnerabilities of the system;

(iii) improving communication and training relating to the system;

(iv) developing and conducting exercises to test decontamination and disposal plans;

(v) developing modeling tools to improve event consequence assessment and decision support; and

(vi) preparing risk communication tools and enhancing public awareness through outreach.

(B) Detection Goal. — Improve agriculture and food system detection capabilities by —

(i) identifying contamination in food products at the earliest possible time; and

(ii) conducting surveillance to prevent the spread of diseases.

(C) Emergency Response Goal. — Ensure an efficient response to agriculture and food emergencies by —

(i) immediately investigating animal disease outbreaks and suspected food contamination;

(ii) preventing additional human illnesses;

(iii) organizing, training, and equipping animal, plant, and food emergency response teams of —

(I) the Federal Government; and

(II) State, local, and tribal governments;

(iv) designing, developing, and evaluating training and exercises carried out under agriculture and food defense plans; and

(v) ensuring consistent and organized risk communication to the public by —

(I) the Federal Government;

(II) State, local, and tribal governments; and

(III) the private sector.

(D) Recovery Goal. — Secure agriculture and food production after an agriculture or food emergency by —

(i) working with the private sector to develop business recovery plans to rapidly resume agriculture, food production, and international trade;

(ii) conducting exercises of the plans described in subparagraph (C) with the goal of long-term recovery results;

(iii) rapidly removing, and effectively disposing of —

(I) contaminated agriculture and food products; and

(II) infected plants and animals; and

(iv) decontaminating and restoring areas affected by an agriculture or food emergency.

(3) Evaluation. — The Secretary, in coordination with the Secretary of Agriculture and the Secretary of Homeland Security, shall —

(A) develop metrics to measure progress for the evaluation process described in paragraph (1)(B); and

(B) report on the progress measured in subparagraph (A) as part of the National Agriculture and Food Defense strategy described in subsection (a)(1).

(c) Limited Distribution. — In the interest of national security, the Secretary of Health and Human Services and the Secretary of Agriculture, in coordination with the Secretary of Homeland Security, may determine the manner and format in which the National Agriculture and Food Defense strategy established under this section is made publicly available on the Internet Web sites of the Department of Health and Human Services, the Department of Homeland Security, and the Department of Agriculture, as described in subsection (a)(1).

Sec. 109. Food and Agriculture Coordinating Councils.

The Secretary of Homeland Security, in coordination with the Secretary of Health and Human Services and the Secretary of Agriculture, shall within 180 days of enactment of this Act, and annually thereafter, submit to the relevant committees of Congress, and make publicly available on the Internet Web site of the Department of Homeland Security, a report on the activities of the Food and Agriculture Government Coordinating Council and the Food and Agriculture Sector Coordinating Council, including the progress of such Councils on —

(1) facilitating partnerships between public and private entities to help coordinate and enhance the protection of the agriculture and food system of the United States;

(2) providing for the regular and timely interchange of information between each council relating to the security of the agriculture and food system (including intelligence information);

(3) identifying best practices and methods for improving the coordination among Federal, State, local, and private sector preparedness and response plans for agriculture and food defense; and

(4) recommending methods by which to protect the economy and the public health of the United States from the effects of —

(A) animal or plant disease outbreaks;

(B) food contamination; and

(C) natural disasters affecting agriculture and food.

SEC. 110. BUILDING DOMESTIC CAPACITY.

(a) IN GENERAL. —

(1) INITIAL REPORT. — The Secretary, in coordination with the Secretary of Agriculture and the Secretary of Homeland Security, shall, not later than 2 years after the date of enactment of this Act, submit to Congress a comprehensive report that identifies programs and practices that are intended to promote the safety and supply chain security of food and to prevent outbreaks of foodborne illness and other food-related hazards that can be addressed through preventive activities. Such report shall include a description of the following:

(A) Analysis of the need for further regulations or guidance to industry.

(B) Outreach to food industry sectors, including through the Food and Agriculture Coordinating Councils referred to in section 109, to identify potential sources of emerging threats to the safety and security of the food supply and preventive strategies to address those threats.

(C) Systems to ensure the prompt distribution to the food industry of information and technical assistance concerning preventive strategies.

(D) Communication systems to ensure that information about specific threats to the safety and security of the food supply are rapidly and effectively disseminated.

(E) Surveillance systems and laboratory networks to rapidly detect and respond to foodborne illness outbreaks and other food-related hazards, including how such systems and networks are integrated.

(F) Outreach, education, and training provided to States and local governments to build State and local food safety and food defense capabilities, including progress implementing strategies developed under sections 108 and 205.

(G) The estimated resources needed to effectively implement the programs and practices identified in the report developed in this section over a 5-year period.

(H) The impact of requirements under this Act (including amendments made by this Act) on certified organic farms and facilities (as defined in section 415 (21 U.S.C. 350d).

(I) Specific efforts taken pursuant to the agreements authorized under section 421(c) of the Federal Food, Drug, and Cosmetic Act (as added by section 201), together with, as necessary, a description of any additional authorities necessary to improve seafood safety.

(2) BIENNIAL REPORTS. — On a biennial basis following the submission of the report under paragraph (1), the Secretary shall submit to Congress a report that —

(A) reviews previous food safety programs and practices;

(B) outlines the success of those programs and practices;

(C) identifies future programs and practices; and

(D) includes information related to any matter described in subparagraphs (A) through (H) of paragraph (1), as necessary.

(b) RISK-BASED ACTIVITIES. — The report developed under subsection (a)(1) shall describe methods that seek to ensure that resources available to the Secretary for food safety-related activities are directed at those actions most likely to reduce risks from food, including the use of preventive strategies and allocation of inspection resources. The Secretary shall promptly undertake those risk-based actions that are identified during the development of the report as likely to contribute to the safety and security of the food supply.

(c) CAPABILITY FOR LABORATORY ANALYSES; RESEARCH. — The report developed under subsection (a)(1) shall provide a description of methods to increase capacity to undertake analyses of food samples promptly after collection, to identify new and rapid analytical techniques, including commercially-available techniques that can be employed at ports of entry and by Food Emergency Response Network laboratories, and to provide for well-equipped and staffed laboratory facilities and progress toward laboratory accreditation under section 422 of the Federal Food, Drug, and Cosmetic Act (as added by section 202).

(d) INFORMATION TECHNOLOGY. — The report developed under subsection (a)(1) shall include a description of such information technology systems as may be needed to identify risks and receive data from multiple sources, including foreign governments, State, local, and tribal governments, other Federal agencies, the food industry, laboratories, laboratory networks, and consumers. The information technology systems that the Secretary describes shall also provide for the integration of the facility registration system under section 415 of the Federal Food, Drug, and Cosmetic Act (21 U.S.C. 350d), and the prior notice system under section 801(m) of such Act (21 U.S.C. 381(m)) with other information technology systems that are used by the Federal Government for the processing of food offered for import into the United States.

(e) Automated Risk Assessment. — The report developed under subsection (a)(1) shall include a description of progress toward developing and improving an automated risk assessment system for food safety surveillance and allocation of resources.

(f) Traceback and Surveillance Report. — The Secretary shall include in the report developed under subsection (a)(1) an analysis of the Food and Drug Administration's performance in foodborne illness outbreaks during the 5-year period preceding the date of enactment of this Act involving fruits and vegetables that are raw agricultural commodities (as defined in section 201(r) (21 U.S.C. 321(r)) and recommendations for enhanced surveillance, outbreak response, and traceability. Such findings and recommendations shall address communication and coordination with the public, industry, and State and local governments, as such communication and coordination relates to outbreak identification and traceback.

(g) Biennial Food Safety and Food Defense Research Plan. — The Secretary, the Secretary of Agriculture, and the Secretary of Homeland Security shall, on a biennial basis, submit to Congress a joint food safety and food defense research plan which may include studying the long-term health effects of foodborne illness. Such biennial plan shall include a list and description of projects conducted during the previous 2-year period and the plan for projects to be conducted during the subsequent 2-year period.

(h) Effectiveness of Programs Administered by the Department of Health and Human Services. —

(1) In General. — To determine whether existing Federal programs administered by the Department of Health and Human Services are effective in achieving the stated goals of such programs, the Secretary shall, beginning not later than 1 year after the date of enactment of this Act —

(A) conduct an annual evaluation of each program of such Department to determine the effectiveness of each such program in achieving legislated intent, purposes, and objectives; and

(B) submit to Congress a report concerning such evaluation.

(2) Content. — The report described under paragraph (1)(B) shall —

(A) include conclusions concerning the reasons that such existing programs have proven successful or not successful and what factors contributed to such conclusions;

(B) include recommendations for consolidation and elimination to reduce duplication and inefficiencies in such programs at such Department as identified during the evaluation conduct under this subsection; and

(C) be made publicly available in a publication entitled "Guide to the U.S. Department of Health and Human Services Programs".

(i) Unique Identification Numbers. —

(1) In General. — Not later than 1 year after the date of enactment of this Act, the Secretary, acting through the Commissioner of Food and Drugs, shall conduct a study regarding the need for, and challenges associated with, development and implementation of a program that requires a unique identification number for each food facility registered with the Secretary and, as appropriate, each broker that imports food into the United States. Such study shall include an evaluation of the costs associated with development and implementation of such a system, and make recommendations about what new authorities, if any, would be necessary to develop and implement such a system.

(2) Report. — Not later than 15 months after the date of enactment of this Act, the Secretary shall submit to Congress a report that describes the findings of the study conducted under paragraph (1) and that includes any recommendations determined appropriate by the Secretary.

Sec. 111. Sanitary Transportation of Food.

(a) In General. — Not later than 18 months after the date of enactment of this Act, the Secretary shall promulgate regulations described in section 416(b) of the Federal Food, Drug, and Cosmetic Act (21 U.S.C. 350e(b)).

(b) Food Transportation Study. — The Secretary, acting through the Commissioner of Food and Drugs, shall conduct a study of the transportation of food for consumption in the United States, including transportation by air, that includes an examination of the unique needs of rural and frontier areas with regard to the delivery of safe food.

Sec. 112. Food Allergy and Anaphylaxis Management.

(a) Definitions. — In this section:

(1) Early Childhood Education Program. — The term "early childhood education program" means —

(A) a Head Start program or an Early Head Start program carried out under the Head Start Act (42 U.S.C. 9831 et seq.);

(B) a State licensed or regulated child care program or school; or

(C) a State prekindergarten program that serves children from birth through kindergarten.

(2) ESEA Definitions. — The terms "local educational agency", "secondary school", "elementary school", and "parent" have the meanings given the terms in section 9101 of the Elementary and Secondary Education Act of 1965 (20 U.S.C. 7801).

(3) School. — The term "school" includes public —

(A) kindergartens;

(B) elementary schools; and

(C) secondary schools.

(4) Secretary. — The term "Secretary" means the Secretary of Health and Human Services.

(b) Establishment of Voluntary Food Allergy and Anaphylaxis Management Guidelines. —

(1) Establishment. —

(A) In General. — Not later than 1 year after the date of enactment of this Act, the Secretary, in consultation with the Secretary of Education, shall —

(i) develop guidelines to be used on a voluntary basis to develop plans for individuals to manage the risk of food allergy and anaphylaxis in schools and early childhood education programs; and

(ii) make such guidelines available to local educational agencies, schools, early childhood education programs, and other interested entities and individuals to be implemented on a voluntary basis only.

(B) Applicability of FERPA. — Each plan described in subparagraph (A) that is developed for an individual shall be considered an education record for the purpose of section 444 of the General Education Provisions Act (commonly referred to as the "Family Educational Rights and Privacy Act of 1974") (20 U.S.C. 1232g).

(2) Contents. — The voluntary guidelines developed by the Secretary under paragraph (1) shall address each of the following and may be updated as the Secretary determines necessary:

(A) Parental obligation to provide the school or early childhood education program, prior to the start of every school year, with —

(i) documentation from their child's physician or nurse —

(I) supporting a diagnosis of food allergy, and any risk of anaphylaxis, if applicable;

(II) identifying any food to which the child is allergic;

(III) describing, if appropriate, any prior history of anaphylaxis;

(IV) listing any medication prescribed for the child for the treatment of anaphylaxis;

(V) detailing emergency treatment procedures in the event of a reaction;

(VI) listing the signs and symptoms of a reaction; and

(VII) assessing the child's readiness for self-administration of prescription medication; and

(ii) a list of substitute meals that may be offered to the child by school or early childhood education program food service personnel.

(B) The creation and maintenance of an individual plan for food allergy management, in consultation with the parent, tailored to the needs of each child with a documented risk for anaphylaxis, including any procedures for the self-administration of medication by such children in instances where —

(i) the children are capable of self-administering medication; and

(ii) such administration is not prohibited by State law.

(C) Communication strategies between individual schools or early childhood education programs and providers of emergency medical services, including appropriate instructions for emergency medical response.

(D) Strategies to reduce the risk of exposure to anaphylactic causative agents in classrooms and common school or early childhood education program areas such as cafeterias.

(E) The dissemination of general information on life-threatening food allergies to school or early childhood education program staff, parents, and children.

(F) Food allergy management training of school or early childhood education program personnel who regularly come into contact with children with life-threatening food allergies.

(G) The authorization and training of school or early childhood education program personnel to administer epinephrine when the nurse is not immediately available.

(H) The timely accessibility of epinephrine by school or early childhood education program personnel when the nurse is not immediately available.

(I) The creation of a plan contained in each individual plan for food allergy management that addresses the appropriate response to an incident of anaphylaxis of a child while such child is engaged in extracurricular programs of a school or early childhood education program, such as non-academic outings and field trips, before- and after-school programs or before- and after-early child education program programs, and school-sponsored or early childhood education program-sponsored programs held on weekends.

(J) Maintenance of information for each administration of epinephrine to a child at risk for anaphylaxis and prompt notification to parents.

(K) Other elements the Secretary determines necessary for the management of food allergies and anaphylaxis in schools and early childhood education programs.

(3) Relation to State Law. — Nothing in this section or the guidelines developed by the Secretary under paragraph (1) shall be construed to preempt State law, including any State law regarding whether students at risk for anaphylaxis may self-administer medication.

(c) School-Based Food Allergy Management Grants. —

(1) In General. — The Secretary may award grants to local educational agencies to assist such agencies with implementing voluntary food allergy and anaphylaxis management guidelines described in subsection (b).

(2) Application. —

(A) In General. — To be eligible to receive a grant under this subsection, a local educational agency shall submit an application to the Secretary at such time, in such manner, and including such information as the Secretary may reasonably require.

(B) Contents. — Each application submitted under subparagraph (A) shall include —

(i) an assurance that the local educational agency has developed plans in accordance with the food allergy and anaphylaxis management guidelines described in subsection (b);

(ii) a description of the activities to be funded by the grant in carrying out the food allergy and anaphylaxis management guidelines, including —

(I) how the guidelines will be carried out at individual schools served by the local educational agency;

(II) how the local educational agency will inform parents and students of the guidelines in place;

(III) how school nurses, teachers, administrators, and other school-based staff will be made aware of, and given training on, when applicable, the guidelines in place; and

(IV) any other activities that the Secretary determines appropriate;

(iii) an itemization of how grant funds received under this subsection will be expended;

(iv) a description of how adoption of the guidelines and implementation of grant activities will be monitored; and

(v) an agreement by the local educational agency to report information required by the Secretary to conduct evaluations under this subsection.

(3) Use of Funds. — Each local educational agency that receives a grant under this subsection may use the grant funds for the following:

(A) Purchase of materials and supplies, including limited medical supplies such as epinephrine and disposable wet wipes, to support carrying out the food allergy and anaphylaxis management guidelines described in subsection (b).

(B) In partnership with local health departments, school nurse, teacher, and personnel training for food allergy management.

(C) Programs that educate students as to the presence of, and policies and procedures in place related to, food allergies and anaphylactic shock.

(D) Outreach to parents.

(E) Any other activities consistent with the guidelines described in subsection (b).

(4) Duration of Awards. — The Secretary may award grants under this subsection for a period of not more than 2 years. In the event the Secretary conducts a program evaluation under this subsection, funding in the second year of the grant, where applicable, shall be contingent on a successful program evaluation by the Secretary after the first year.

(5) Limitation on Grant Funding. — The Secretary may not provide grant funding to a local educational agency under this subsection after such local educational agency has received 2 years of grant funding under this subsection.

(6) Maximum Amount of Annual Awards. — A grant awarded under this subsection may not be made in an amount that is more than $50,000 annually.

(7) Priority. — In awarding grants under this subsection, the Secretary shall give priority to local educational agencies with the highest percentages of children who are counted under section 1124(c) of the Elementary and Secondary Education Act of 1965 (20 U.S.C. 6333(c)).

(8) Matching Funds. —

(A) In General. — The Secretary may not award a grant under this subsection unless the local educational agency agrees that, with respect to the costs to be incurred by such local educational agency in carrying out the grant activities, the local educational agency shall make available (directly or through donations from public or private entities) non-Federal funds toward such costs in an amount equal to not less than 25 percent of the amount of the grant.

(B) Determination of Amount of Non-Federal Contribution. — Non-Federal funds required under subparagraph (A) may be cash or in kind, including plant, equipment, or services. Amounts provided by the Federal Government, and any portion of any service subsidized by the Federal Government, may not be included in determining the amount of such non-Federal funds.

(9) Administrative Funds. — A local educational agency that receives a grant under this subsection may use not more than 2 percent of the grant amount for administrative costs related to carrying out this subsection.

(10) Progress and Evaluations. — At the completion of the grant period referred to in paragraph (4), a local educational agency shall provide the Secretary with information on how grant funds were spent and the status of implementation of the food allergy and anaphylaxis management guidelines described in subsection (b).

(11) Supplement, Not Supplant. — Grant funds received under this subsection shall be used to supplement, and not supplant, non-Federal funds and any other Federal funds available to carry out the activities described in this subsection.

(12) Authorization of Appropriations. — There is authorized to be appropriated to carry out this subsection $30,000,000 for fiscal year 2011 and such sums as may be necessary for each of the 4 succeeding fiscal years.

(d) Voluntary Nature of Guidelines. —

(1) In General. — The food allergy and anaphylaxis management guidelines developed by the Secretary under subsection (b) are voluntary. Nothing in this section or the guidelines developed by the Secretary under subsection (b) shall be construed to require a local educational agency to implement such guidelines.

(2) Exception. — Notwithstanding paragraph (1), the Secretary may enforce an agreement by a local educational agency to implement food allergy and anaphylaxis management guidelines as a condition of the receipt of a grant under subsection (c).

Sec. 114. Requirement for Guidance Relating to Post Harvest Processing of Raw Oysters.

(a) In General. — Not later than 90 days prior to the issuance of any guidance, regulation, or suggested amendment by the Food and Drug Administration to the National Shellfish Sanitation Program's Model Ordinance, or the issuance of any guidance or regulation by the Food and Drug Administration relating to the Seafood Hazard Analysis Critical Control Points Program of the Food and Drug Administration (parts 123 and 1240 of title 21, Code of Federal Regulations (or any successor regulations), where such guidance, regulation or suggested amendment relates to post harvest processing for raw oysters, the Secretary shall prepare and submit to the Committee on Health, Education, Labor, and Pensions of the Senate and the Committee on Energy and Commerce of the House of Representatives a report which shall include —

(1) an assessment of how post harvest processing or other equivalent controls feasibly may be implemented in the fastest, safest, and most economical manner;

(2) the projected public health benefits of any proposed post harvest processing;

(3) the projected costs of compliance with such post harvest processing measures;

(4) the impact post harvest processing is expected to have on the sales, cost, and availability of raw oysters;

(5) criteria for ensuring post harvest processing standards will be applied equally to shellfish imported from all nations of origin;

(6) an evaluation of alternative measures to prevent, eliminate, or reduce to an acceptable level the occurrence of foodborne illness; and

(7) the extent to which the Food and Drug Administration has consulted with the States and other regulatory agencies, as appropriate, with regard to post harvest processing measures.

(b) Limitation. — Subsection (a) shall not apply to the guidance described in section 103(h).

(c) Review and Evaluation. — Not later than 30 days after the Secretary issues a proposed regulation or guidance described in subsection (a), the Comptroller General of the United States shall —

(1) review and evaluate the report described in (a) and report to Congress on the findings of the estimates and analysis in the report;

(2) compare such proposed regulation or guidance to similar regulations or guidance with respect to other regulated foods, including a comparison of risks the Secretary may find associated with seafood and the instances of those risks in such other regulated foods; and

(3) evaluate the impact of post harvest processing on the competitiveness of the domestic oyster industry in the United States and in international markets.

(d) Waiver. — The requirement of preparing a report under subsection (a) shall be waived if the Secretary issues a guidance that is adopted as a consensus agreement between Federal and State regulators and the oyster industry, acting through the Interstate Shellfish Sanitation Conference.

(e) Public Access. — Any report prepared under this section shall be made available to the public.

Sec. 115. Port Shopping.

Until the date on which the Secretary promulgates a final rule that implements the amendments made by section 308 of the Public Health Security and Bioterrorism Preparedness and Response Act of 2002, (Public Law 107-188), the Secretary shall notify the Secretary of Homeland Security of all instances in which the Secretary refuses to admit a food into the United States under section 801(a) of the Federal Food, Drug, and Cosmetic Act (21 U.S.C. 381(a)) so that the Secretary of Homeland Security, acting through the Commissioner of Customs and Border Protection, may prevent food refused admittance into the United States by a United States port of entry from being admitted by another United States port of entry, through the notification of other such United States ports of entry.

Sec. 116. Alcohol-Related Facilities.

(a) In General. — Except as provided by sections 102, 206, 207, 302, 304, 402, 403, and 404 of this Act, and the amendments made by such sections, nothing in this Act, or the amendments made by this Act, shall be construed to apply to a facility that —

(1) under the Federal Alcohol Administration Act (27 U.S.C. 201 et seq.) or chapter 51 of subtitle E of the Internal Revenue Code of 1986 (26 U.S.C. 5001 et seq.) is required to obtain a permit or to register with the Secretary of the Treasury as a condition of doing business in the United States; and

(2) under section 415 of the Federal Food, Drug, and Cosmetic Act (21 U.S.C. 350d) is required to register as a facility because such facility is engaged in manufacturing, processing, packing, or holding 1 or more alcoholic beverages, with respect to the activities of such facility that relate to the manufacturing, processing, packing, or holding of alcoholic beverages.

(b) Limited Receipt and Distribution of Non-Alcohol Food. — Subsection (a) shall not apply to a facility engaged in the receipt and distribution of any non-alcohol food, except that such paragraph shall apply to a facility described in such paragraph that receives and distributes non-alcohol food, provided such food is received and distributed —

(1) in a prepackaged form that prevents any direct human contact with such food; and

(2) in amounts that constitute not more than 5 percent of the overall sales of such facility, as determined by the Secretary of the Treasury.

(c) Rule of Construction. — Except as provided in subsections (a) and (b), this section shall not be construed to exempt any food, other than alcoholic beverages, as defined in section 214 of the Federal Alcohol Administration Act (27 U.S.C. 214), from the requirements of this Act (including the amendments made by this Act).

Title II — Improving Capacity to Detect and Respond to Food Safety Problems

Sec. 202. Laboratory Accreditation for Analyses of Food.

(a) [Text not included. — Ed.]

(b) Food Emergency Response Network. — The Secretary, in coordination with the Secretary of Agriculture, the Secretary of Homeland Security, and State, local, and tribal governments shall, not later than 180 days after the date of enactment of this Act, and biennially thereafter, submit to the relevant committees of Congress, and make publicly available on the Internet Web site of the Department of Health and Human Services, a report on the progress in implementing a national food emergency response laboratory network that —

(1) provides ongoing surveillance, rapid detection, and surge capacity for large-scale food-related emergencies, including intentional adulteration of the food supply;

(2) coordinates the food laboratory capacities of State, local, and tribal food laboratories, including the adoption of novel surveillance and identification technologies and the sharing of data between Federal agencies and State laboratories to develop national situational awareness;

(3) provides accessible, timely, accurate, and consistent food laboratory services throughout the United States;

(4) develops and implements a methods repository for use by Federal, State, and local officials;

(5) responds to food-related emergencies; and

(6) is integrated with relevant laboratory networks administered by other Federal agencies.

Sec. 203. Integrated Consortium of Laboratory Networks.

(a) In General. — The Secretary of Homeland Security, in coordination with the Secretary of Health and Human Services, the Secretary of Agriculture, the Secretary of Commerce, and the Administrator of the Environmental Protection Agency, shall maintain an agreement through which relevant laboratory network members, as determined by the Secretary of Homeland Security, shall —

(1) agree on common laboratory methods in order to reduce the time required to detect and respond to foodborne illness outbreaks and facilitate the sharing of knowledge and information relating to animal health, agriculture, and human health;

(2) identify means by which laboratory network members could work cooperatively —

(A) to optimize national laboratory preparedness; and

(B) to provide surge capacity during emergencies; and

(3) engage in ongoing dialogue and build relationships that will support a more effective and integrated response during emergencies.

(b) Reporting Requirement. — The Secretary of Homeland Security shall, on a biennial basis, submit to the relevant committees of Congress, and make publicly available on the Internet Web site of the Department of Homeland Security, a report on the progress of the integrated consortium of laboratory networks, as established under subsection (a), in carrying out this section.

Sec. 204. Enhancing Tracking and Tracing of Food and Recordkeeping.

(a) Pilot Projects. —

(1) In General. — Not later than 270 days after the date of enactment of this Act, the Secretary of Health and Human Services (referred to in this section as the "Secretary"), taking into account recommendations from the Secretary of Agriculture and representatives of State departments of health and agriculture, shall establish pilot projects in coordination with the food industry to explore and evaluate methods to rapidly and effectively identify recipients of food to prevent or mitigate a foodborne illness outbreak and to address credible threats of serious adverse health consequences or death to humans or animals as a result of such food being adulterated under section 402 of the Federal Food, Drug, and Cosmetic Act (21 U.S.C. 342) or misbranded under section 403(w) of such Act (21 U.S.C. 343(w)).

(2) Content. — The Secretary shall conduct 1 or more pilot projects under paragraph (1) in coordination with the processed food sector and 1 or more such pilot projects in coordination with processors or distributors of fruits and vegetables that are raw agricultural commodities. The Secretary shall ensure that the pilot projects under paragraph (1) reflect the diversity of the food supply and include at least 3 different types of foods that have been the subject of significant outbreaks during the 5-year period preceding the date of enactment of this Act, and are selected in order to —

(A) develop and demonstrate methods for rapid and effective tracking and tracing of foods in a manner that is practicable for facilities of varying sizes, including small businesses;

(B) develop and demonstrate appropriate technologies, including technologies existing on the date of enactment of this Act, that enhance the tracking and tracing of food; and

(C) inform the promulgation of regulations under subsection (d).

(3) Report. — Not later than 18 months after the date of enactment of this Act, the Secretary shall report to Congress on the findings of the pilot projects under this subsection together with recommendations for improving the tracking and tracing of food.

(b) Additional Data Gathering. —

(1) In General. — The Secretary, in coordination with the Secretary of Agriculture and multiple representatives of State departments of health and agriculture, shall assess —

(A) the costs and benefits associated with the adoption and use of several product tracing technologies, including technologies used in the pilot projects under subsection (a);

(B) the feasibility of such technologies for different sectors of the food industry, including small businesses; and

(C) whether such technologies are compatible with the requirements of this subsection.

(2) Requirements. — To the extent practicable, in carrying out paragraph (1), the Secretary shall —

(A) evaluate domestic and international product tracing practices in commercial use;

(B) consider international efforts, including an assessment of whether product tracing requirements developed under this section are compatible with global tracing systems, as appropriate; and

(C) consult with a diverse and broad range of experts and stakeholders, including representatives of the food industry, agricultural producers, and nongovernmental organizations that represent the interests of consumers.

(c) Product Tracing System. — The Secretary, in consultation with the Secretary of Agriculture, shall, as appropriate, establish within the Food and Drug Administration a product tracing system to receive information that improves the capacity of the Secretary to effectively and rapidly track and trace food that is in the United States or offered for import into the United States. Prior to the establishment of such product tracing system, the Secretary shall examine the results of applicable pilot projects and shall ensure that the activities of such system are adequately supported by the results of such pilot projects.

(d) Additional Recordkeeping Requirements for High Risk Foods. —

(1) In General. — In order to rapidly and effectively identify recipients of a food to prevent or mitigate a foodborne illness outbreak and to address credible threats of serious adverse health consequences or death to humans or animals as a result of such food being adulterated under section 402 of the Federal Food, Drug, and Cosmetic Act or misbranded under section 403(w) of such Act, not later than 2 years after the date of enactment of this Act, the Secretary shall publish a notice of proposed rulemaking to establish recordkeeping requirements, in addition to the requirements under section 414 of the Federal Food, Drug, and Cosmetic Act (21 U.S.C. 350c) and subpart J of part 1 of title 21, Code of Federal Regulations (or any successor regulations), for facilities that manufacture, process, pack, or hold foods that the Secretary designates under paragraph (2) as high-risk foods. The Secretary shall set an appropriate effective date of such additional requirements for foods designated as high risk that takes into account the length of time necessary to comply with such requirements. Such requirements shall —

(A) relate only to information that is reasonably available and appropriate;

(B) be science-based;

(C) not prescribe specific technologies for the maintenance of records;

(D) ensure that the public health benefits of imposing additional recordkeeping requirements outweigh the cost of compliance with such requirements;

(E) be scale-appropriate and practicable for facilities of varying sizes and capabilities with respect to costs and recordkeeping burdens, and not require the creation and maintenance of duplicate records where the information is contained in other company records kept in the normal course of business;

(F) minimize the number of different recordkeeping requirements for facilities that handle more than 1 type of food;

(G) to the extent practicable, not require a facility to change business systems to comply with such requirements;

(H) allow any person subject to this subsection to maintain records required under this subsection at a central or reasonably accessible location provided that such records can be made available to the Secretary not later than 24 hours after the Secretary requests such records; and

(I) include a process by which the Secretary may issue a waiver of the requirements under this subsection if the Secretary determines that such requirements would result in an economic hardship for an individual facility or a type of facility;

(J) be commensurate with the known safety risks of the designated food;

(K) take into account international trade obligations;

(L) not require —

(i) a full pedigree, or a record of the complete previous distribution history of the food from the point of origin of such food;

(ii) records of recipients of a food beyond the immediate subsequent recipient of such food; or

(iii) product tracking to the case level by persons subject to such requirements; and

(M) include a process by which the Secretary may remove a high-risk food designation developed under paragraph (2) for a food or type of food.

(2) Designation of High-Risk Foods. —

(A) In General. — Not later than 1 year after the date of enactment of this Act, and thereafter as the Secretary determines necessary, the Secretary shall designate high-risk foods for which the additional recordkeeping requirements described in paragraph (1) are appropriate and necessary to protect the public health. Each such designation shall be based on —

(i) the known safety risks of a particular food, including the history and severity of foodborne illness outbreaks attributed to such food, taking into consideration foodborne illness data collected by the Centers for Disease Control and Prevention;

(ii) the likelihood that a particular food has a high potential risk for microbiological or chemical contamination or would support the growth of pathogenic microorganisms due to the nature of the food or the processes used to produce such food;

(iii) the point in the manufacturing process of the food where contamination is most likely to occur;

(iv) the likelihood of contamination and steps taken during the manufacturing process to reduce the possibility of contamination;

(v) the likelihood that consuming a particular food will result in a foodborne illness due to contamination of the food; and

(vi) the likely or known severity, including health and economic impacts, of a foodborne illness attributed to a particular food.

(B) List of High-Risk Foods. — At the time the Secretary promulgates the final rules under paragraph (1), the Secretary shall publish the list of the foods designated under subparagraph (A) as high-risk foods on the Internet website of the Food and Drug Administration. The Secretary may update the list to designate new high-risk foods and to remove foods that are no longer deemed to be high-risk foods, provided that each such update to the list is consistent with the requirements of this subsection and notice of such update is published in the Federal Register.

(3) Protection of Sensitive Information. — In promulgating regulations under this subsection, the Secretary shall take appropriate measures to ensure that there are effective procedures to prevent the unauthorized disclosure of any trade secret or confidential information that is obtained by the Secretary pursuant to this section, including periodic risk assessment and planning to prevent unauthorized release and controls to —

(A) prevent unauthorized reproduction of trade secret or confidential information;

(B) prevent unauthorized access to trade secret or confidential information; and

(C) maintain records with respect to access by any person to trade secret or confidential information maintained by the agency.

(4) Public Input. — During the comment period in the notice of proposed rulemaking under paragraph (1), the Secretary shall conduct not less than 3 public meetings in diverse geographical areas of the United States to provide persons in different regions an opportunity to comment.

(5) Retention of Records. — Except as otherwise provided in this subsection, the Secretary may require that a facility retain records under this subsection for not more than 2 years, taking into consideration the risk of spoilage, loss of value, or loss of palatability of the applicable food when determining the appropriate timeframes.

(6) Limitations. —

(A) Farm to School Programs. — In establishing requirements under this subsection, the Secretary shall, in consultation with the Secretary of Agriculture, consider the impact of requirements on farm to school or farm to institution programs of the Department of Agriculture and other farm to school and farm to institution programs outside such agency, and shall modify the requirements under this subsection, as appropriate, with respect to such programs so that the requirements do not place undue burdens on farm to school or farm to institution programs.

(B) Identity-Preserved Labels with Respect to Farm Sales of Food that is Produced and Packaged on A Farm. — The requirements under this subsection shall not apply to a food that is produced and packaged on a farm if —

(i) the packaging of the food maintains the integrity of the product and prevents subsequent contamination or alteration of the product; and

(ii) the labeling of the food includes the name, complete address (street address, town, State, country, and zip or other postal code), and business phone number of the farm, unless the Secretary waives the requirement to include a business phone number of the farm, as appropriate, in order to accommodate a religious belief of the individual in charge of such farm.

(C) Fishing Vessels. — The requirements under this subsection with respect to a food that is produced through the use of a fishing vessel (as defined in section 3(18) of the Magnuson-Stevens Fishery Conservation and Management Act (16 U.S.C. 1802(18))) shall be limited to the requirements under subparagraph (F) until such time as the food is sold by the owner, operator, or agent in charge of such fishing vessel.

(D) Commingled Raw Agricultural Commodities. —

(i) Limitation on Extent of Tracing. — Recordkeeping requirements under this subsection with regard to any commingled raw agricultural commodity shall be limited to the requirements under subparagraph (F).

(ii) Definitions. — For the purposes of this subparagraph—

(I) the term "commingled raw agricultural commodity" means any commodity that is combined or mixed after harvesting, but before processing;

(II) the term "commingled raw agricultural commodity" shall not include types of fruits and vegetables that are raw agricultural commodities for which the Secretary has determined that standards promulgated under section 419 of the Federal Food, Drug, and Cosmetic Act (as added by section 105) would minimize the risk of serious adverse health consequences or death; and

(III) the term "processing" means operations that alter the general state of the commodity, such as canning, cooking, freezing, dehydration, milling, grinding, pasteurization, or homogenization.

(E) Exemption of Other Foods. — The Secretary may, by notice in the Federal Register, modify the requirements under this subsection with respect to, or exempt a food or a type of facility from, the requirements of this subsection (other than the requirements under subparagraph (F), if applicable) if the Secretary determines that product tracing requirements for such food (such as bulk or commingled ingredients that are intended to be processed to destroy pathogens) or type of facility is not necessary to protect the public health.

(F) Recordkeeping Regarding Previous Sources and Subsequent Recipients. — In the case of a person or food to which a limitation or exemption under subparagraph (C), (D), or (E) applies, if such person, or a person who manufactures, processes, packs, or holds such food, is required to register with the Secretary under section 415 of the Federal Food, Drug, and Cosmetic Act (21 U.S.C. 350d) with respect to the manufacturing, processing, packing, or holding of the applicable food, the Secretary shall require such person to maintain records that identify the immediate previous source of such food and the immediate subsequent recipient of such food.

(G) Grocery Stores. — With respect to a sale of a food described in subparagraph (H) to a grocery store, the Secretary shall not require such grocery store to maintain records under this subsection other than records documenting the farm that was the source of such food. The Secretary shall not require that such records be kept for more than 180 days.

(H) Farm Sales to Consumers. — The Secretary shall not require a farm to maintain any distribution records under this subsection with respect to a sale of a food described in subparagraph (I) (including a sale of a food that is produced and packaged on such farm), if such sale is made by the farm directly to a consumer.

(I) Sale of a Food. — A sale of a food described in this subparagraph is a sale of a food in which —

(i) the food is produced on a farm; and

(ii) the sale is made by the owner, operator, or agent in charge of such farm directly to a consumer or grocery store.

(7) No Impact on Non-High-Risk Foods. — The recordkeeping requirements established under paragraph (1) shall have no effect on foods that are not designated by the Secretary under paragraph (2) as high-risk foods. Foods described in the preceding sentence shall be subject solely to the recordkeeping requirements under section 414 of the Federal Food, Drug, and Cosmetic Act (21 U.S.C. 350c) and subpart J of part 1 of title 21, Code of Federal Regulations (or any successor regulations).

(e) Evaluation and Recommendations. —

(1) Report. — Not later than 1 year after the effective date of the final rule promulgated under subsection (d)(1), the Comptroller General of the United States shall submit to Congress a report, taking into consideration the costs of compliance and other regulatory burdens on small businesses and Federal, State, and local food safety practices and requirements, that evaluates the public health benefits and risks, if any, of limiting —

(A) the product tracing requirements under subsection (d) to foods identified under paragraph (2) of such subsection, including whether such requirements provide adequate assurance of traceability in the event of intentional adulteration, including by acts of terrorism; and

(B) the participation of restaurants in the recordkeeping requirements.

(2) Determination and Recommendations. — In conducting the evaluation and report under paragraph (1), if the Comptroller General of the United States determines that the limitations described in such paragraph do not adequately protect the public health, the Comptroller General shall submit to Congress recommendations, if appropriate, regarding recordkeeping requirements for restaurants and additional foods, in order to protect the public health.

(f) Farms. —

(1) Request for Information. — Notwithstanding subsection (d), during an active investigation of a foodborne illness outbreak, or if the Secretary determines it is necessary to protect the public health and prevent or mitigate a foodborne illness outbreak, the Secretary, in consultation and coordination with State and local agencies responsible for food safety, as appropriate, may request that the owner, operator, or agent of a farm identify potential immediate recipients, other than consumers, of an article of the food that is the subject of such investigation if the Secretary reasonably believes such article of food —

(A) is adulterated under section 402 of the Federal Food, Drug, and Cosmetic Act;

(B) presents a threat of serious adverse health consequences or death to humans or animals; and

(C) was adulterated as described in subparagraph (A) on a particular farm (as defined in section 1.227 of chapter 21, Code of Federal Regulations (or any successor regulation)).

(2) Manner of Request. — In making a request under paragraph (1), the Secretary, in consultation and coordination with State and local agencies responsible for food safety, as appropriate, shall issue a written notice to the owner, operator, or agent of the farm to which the article of food has been traced. The individual providing such notice shall present to such owner, operator, or agent appropriate credentials and shall deliver such notice at reasonable times and within reasonable limits and in a reasonable manner.

(3) Delivery of Information Requested. — The owner, operator, or agent of a farm shall deliver the information requested under paragraph (1) in a prompt and reasonable manner. Such information may consist of records kept in the normal course of business, and may be in electronic or non-electronic format.

(4) Limitation. — A request made under paragraph (1) shall not include a request for information relating to the finances, pricing of commodities produced, personnel, research, sales (other than information relating to shipping), or other disclosures that may reveal trade secrets or confidential information from the farm to which the article of food has been traced, other than information necessary to identify potential immediate recipients of such food. Section 301(j) of the Federal Food, Drug, and Cosmetic Act and the Freedom of Information Act shall apply with respect to any confidential commercial information that is disclosed to the Food and Drug Administration in the course of responding to a request under paragraph (1).

(5) Records. — Except with respect to identifying potential immediate recipients in response to a request under this subsection, nothing in this subsection shall require the establishment or maintenance by farms of new records.

(g) No Limitation on Commingling of Food. — Nothing in this section shall be construed to authorize the Secretary to impose any limitation on the commingling of food.

(h) Small Entity Compliance Guide. — Not later than 180 days after promulgation of a final rule under subsection (d), the Secretary shall issue a small entity compliance guide setting forth in plain language the requirements of the regulations under such subsection in order to assist small entities, including farms and small businesses, in complying with the recordkeeping requirements under such subsection.

(i) Flexibility for Small Businesses. — Notwithstanding any other provision of law, the regulations promulgated under subsection (d) shall apply —

(1) to small businesses (as defined by the Secretary in section 103, not later than 90 days after the date of enactment of this Act) beginning on the date that is 1 year after the effective date of the final regulations promulgated under subsection (d); and

(2) to very small businesses (as defined by the Secretary in section 103, not later than 90 days after the date of enactment of this Act) beginning on the date that is 2 years after the effective date of the final regulations promulgated under subsection (d).

Sec. 205. Surveillance.

(a) Definition of Foodborne Illness Outbreak. — In this Act, the term "foodborne illness outbreak" means the occurrence of 2 or more cases of a similar illness resulting from the ingestion of a certain food.

(b) Foodborne Illness Surveillance Systems. —

(1) In General. — The Secretary, acting through the Director of the Centers for Disease Control and Prevention, shall enhance foodborne illness surveillance systems to improve the collection, analysis, reporting, and usefulness of data on foodborne illnesses by —

(A) coordinating Federal, State and local foodborne illness surveillance systems, including complaint systems, and increasing participation in national networks of public health and food regulatory agencies and laboratories;

(B) facilitating sharing of surveillance information on a more timely basis among governmental agencies, including the Food and Drug Administration, the Department of Agriculture, the Department of Homeland Security, and State and local agencies, and with the public;

(C) developing improved epidemiological tools for obtaining quality exposure data and microbiological methods for classifying cases;

(D) augmenting such systems to improve attribution of a foodborne illness outbreak to a specific food;

(E) expanding capacity of such systems, including working toward automatic electronic searches, for implementation of identification practices, including fingerprinting strategies, for foodborne infectious agents, in order to identify new or rarely documented causes of foodborne illness and submit standardized information to a centralized database;

(F) allowing timely public access to aggregated, de-identified surveillance data;

(G) at least annually, publishing current reports on findings from such systems;

(H) establishing a flexible mechanism for rapidly initiating scientific research by academic institutions;

(I) integrating foodborne illness surveillance systems and data with other biosurveillance and public health situational awareness capabilities at the Federal, State, and local levels, including by sharing foodborne illness surveillance data with the National Biosurveillance Integration Center; and

(J) other activities as determined appropriate by the Secretary.

(2) Working Group. — The Secretary shall support and maintain a diverse working group of experts and stakeholders from Federal, State, and local food safety and health agencies, the food and food testing industries, consumer organizations, and academia. Such working group shall provide the Secretary, through at least annual meetings of the working group and an annual public report, advice and recommendations on an ongoing and regular basis regarding the improvement of foodborne illness surveillance and implementation of this section, including advice and recommendations on —

(A) the priority needs of regulatory agencies, the food industry, and consumers for information and analysis on foodborne illness and its causes;

(B) opportunities to improve the effectiveness of initiatives at the Federal, State, and local levels, including coordination and integration of activities among Federal agencies, and between the Federal, State, and local levels of government;

(C) improvement in the timeliness and depth of access by regulatory and health agencies, the food industry, academic researchers, and consumers to foodborne illness aggregated, de-identified surveillance data collected by government agencies at all levels, including data compiled by the Centers for Disease Control and Prevention;

(D) key barriers at Federal, State, and local levels to improving foodborne illness surveillance and the utility of such surveillance for preventing foodborne illness;

(E) the capabilities needed for establishing automatic electronic searches of surveillance data; and

(F) specific actions to reduce barriers to improvement, implement the working group's recommendations, and achieve the purposes of this section, with measurable objectives and timelines, and identification of resource and staffing needs.

(3) Authorization of Appropriations. — To carry out the activities described in paragraph (1), there is authorized to be appropriated $24,000,000 for each fiscal years 2011 through 2015.

(c) Improving Food Safety and Defense Capacity at the State and Local Level. —

(1) In General. — The Secretary shall develop and implement strategies to leverage and enhance the food safety and defense capacities of State and local agencies in order to achieve the following goals:

(A) Improve foodborne illness outbreak response and containment.

(B) Accelerate foodborne illness surveillance and outbreak investigation, including rapid shipment of clinical isolates from clinical laboratories to appropriate State laboratories, and conducting more standardized illness outbreak interviews.

(C) Strengthen the capacity of State and local agencies to carry out inspections and enforce safety standards.

(D) Improve the effectiveness of Federal, State, and local partnerships to coordinate food safety and defense resources and reduce the incidence of foodborne illness.

(E) Share information on a timely basis among public health and food regulatory agencies, with the food industry, with health care providers, and with the public.

(F) Strengthen the capacity of State and local agencies to achieve the goals described in section 108.

(2) Review. — In developing of the strategies required by paragraph (1), the Secretary shall, not later than 1 year after the date of enactment of the FDA Food Safety Modernization Act, complete a review of State and local capacities, and needs for enhancement, which may include a survey with respect to —

(A) staffing levels and expertise available to perform food safety and defense functions;

(B) laboratory capacity to support surveillance, outbreak response, inspection, and enforcement activities;

(C) information systems to support data management and sharing of food safety and defense information among State and local agencies and with counterparts at the Federal level; and

(D) other State and local activities and needs as determined appropriate by the Secretary.

(d) Food Safety Capacity Building Grants. — Section 317R(b) of the Public Health Service Act (42 U.S.C. 247b-20(b)) is amended —

(1) by striking "2002" and inserting "2010"; and

(2) by striking "2003 through 2006" and inserting "2011 through 2015".

Sec. 206. Mandatory Recall Authority.

(a) – (d) [Text not included. — Ed.]

(e) GAO Review. —

(1) In General. — Not later than 90 days after the date of enactment of this Act, the Comptroller General of the United States shall submit to Congress a report that —

(A) identifies State and local agencies with the authority to require the mandatory recall of food, and evaluates use of such authority with regard to frequency, effectiveness, and appropriateness, including consideration of any new or existing mechanisms available to compensate persons for general and specific recall-related costs when a recall is subsequently determined by the relevant authority to have been an error;

(B) identifies Federal agencies, other than the Department of Health and Human Services, with mandatory recall authorityandexamines use of thatauthority with regard to frequency, effectiveness, andappropriateness, including any new or existing mechanisms available to compensate persons for general and specific recall-related costs when a recall is subsequently determined by the relevant agency to have been an error;

(C) considers models for farmer restitution implemented in other nations in cases of erroneous recalls; and

(D) makes recommendations to the Secretary regarding use of the authority under section 423 of the Federal Food, Drug, and Cosmetic Act (as added by this section) to protect the public health while seeking to minimize unnecessary economic costs.

(2) Effect of Review. — If the Comptroller General of the United States finds, after the review conducted under paragraph (1), that the mechanisms described in such paragraph do not exist or are inadequate, then, not later than 90 days after the conclusion of such review, the Secretary of Agriculture shall conduct a study of the feasibility of implementing a farmer indemnification program to provide restitution to agricultural producers for losses sustained as a result of a mandatory recall of an agricultural commodity by a Federal or State regulatory agency that is subsequently determined to be in error. The Secretary of Agriculture shall submit to the Committee on Agriculture of the House of Representatives and the Committee on Agriculture, Nutrition, and Forestry of the Senate a report that describes the results of the study, including any recommendations.

(f) Annual Report to Congress. —

(1) In General. — Not later than 2 years after the date of enactment of this Act and annually thereafter, the Secretary of Health and Human Services (referred to in this subsection as the "Secretary") shall submit a report to the Committee on Health, Education, Labor, and Pensions of the Senate and the Committee on Energy and Commerce of the House of Representatives on the use of recall authority under section 423 of the Federal Food, Drug, and Cosmetic Act (as added by subsection (a)) and any public health advisories issued by the Secretary that advise against the consumption of an article of food on the ground that the article of food is adulterated and poses an imminent danger to health.

(2) Content. — The report under paragraph (1) shall include, with respect to the report year —

(A) the identity of each article of food that was the subject of a public health advisory described in paragraph (1), an opportunity to cease distribution and recall under subsection (a) of section 423 of the Federal Food, Drug, and Cosmetic Act, or a mandatory recall order under subsection (b) of such section;

(B) the number of responsible parties, as defined in section 417 of the Federal Food, Drug, and Cosmetic Act, formally given the opportunity to cease distribution of an article of food and recall such article, as described in section 423(a) of such Act;

(C) the number of responsible parties described in subparagraph (B) who did not cease distribution of or recall an article of food after given the opportunity to cease distribution or recall under section 423(a) of the Federal Food, Drug, and Cosmetic Act;

(D) the number of recall orders issued under section 423(b) of the Federal Food, Drug, and Cosmetic Act; and

(E) a description of any instances in which there was no testing that confirmed adulteration of an article of food that was the subject of a recall under section 423(b) of the Federal Food, Drug, and Cosmetic Act or a public health advisory described in paragraph (1).

Sec. 208. Decontamination and Disposal Standards and Plans.

(a) In General. — The Administrator of the Environmental Protection Agency (referred to in this section as the "Administrator"), in coordination with the Secretary of Health and Human Services, Secretary of Homeland Security, and Secretary of Agriculture, shall provide support for, and technical assistance to, State, local, and tribal governments in preparing for, assessing, decontaminating, and recovering from an agriculture or food emergency.

(b) Development of Standards. — In carrying out subsection (a), the Administrator, in coordination with the Secretary of Health and Human Services, Secretary of Homeland Security, Secretary of Agriculture, and State, local, and tribal governments, shall develop and disseminate specific standards and protocols to undertake clean-up, clearance, and recovery activities following the decontamination and disposal of specific threat agents and foreign animal diseases.

(c) Development of Model Plans. — In carrying out subsection (a), the Administrator, the Secretary of Health and Human Services, and the Secretary of Agriculture shall jointly develop and disseminate model plans for —

(1) the decontamination of individuals, equipment, and facilities following an intentional contamination of agriculture or food; and

(2)the disposal of large quantities of animals, plants, or food products that have been infected or contaminated by specific threat agents and foreign animal diseases.

(d) Exercises. — In carrying out subsection (a), the Administrator, in coordination with the entities described under subsection (b), shall conduct exercises at least annually to evaluate and identify weaknesses in the decontamination and disposal model plans described in subsection (c). Such exercises shall be carried out, to the maximum extent practicable, as part of the national exercise program under section 648(b)(1) of the Post-Katrina Emergency Management Reform Act of 2006 (6 U.S.C. 748(b)(1)).

(e) Modifications. — Based on the exercises described in subsection (d), the Administrator, in coordination with the entities described in subsection (b), shall review and modify as necessary the plans described in subsection (c) not less frequently than biennially.

(f) Prioritization. — The Administrator, in coordination with the entities described in subsection (b), shall develop standards and plans under subsections (b) and (c) in an identified order of priority that takes into account —

(1) highest-risk biological, chemical, and radiological threat agents;

(2) agents that could cause the greatest economic devastation to the agriculture and food system; and

(3) agents that are most difficult to clean or remediate.

Sec. 209. Improving the Training of State, Local, Territorial, and Tribal Food Safety Officials.

(a) [Text not included. — Ed.]

(b) National Food Safety Training , Education, Extension, Outreach, and Technical Assistance Program. — Title IV of the Agricultural Research, Extension, and Education Reform Act of 1998 is amended by inserting after section 404 (7 U.S.C. 7624) the following:

"Sec. 405. National Food Safety Training, Education, Extension, Outreach, and Technical Assistance Program.

"(a) In General. — The Secretary shall award grants under this section to carry out the competitive grant program established under section 1011(d) of the Federal Food, Drug, and Cosmetic Act, pursuant to any memoranda of understanding entered into under such section.

"(b) Integrated Approach. — The grant program described under subsection (a) shall be carried out under this section in a manner that facilitates the integration of food safety standards and guidance with the variety of agricultural production systems, encompassing conventional, sustainable, organic, and conservation and environmental practices.

"(c) Priority. — In awarding grants under this section, the Secretary shall give priority to projects that target small and medium-sized farms, beginning farmers, socially disadvantaged farmers, small processors, or small fresh fruit and vegetable merchant wholesalers.

"(d) Program Coordination. —

"(1) In General. — The Secretary shall coordinate implementation of the grant program under this section with the National Integrated Food Safety Initiative.

"(2) Interaction. — The Secretary shall —

"(A) in carrying out the grant program under this section, take into consideration applied research, education, and extension results obtained from the National Integrated Food Safety Initiative; and

"(B) in determining the applied research agenda for the National Integrated Food Safety Initiative, take into consideration the needs articulated by participants in projects funded by the program under this section.

"(e) Grants. —

"(1) In General. — In carrying out this section, the Secretary shall make competitive grants to support training, education, extension, outreach, and technical assistance projects that will help improve public health by increasing the understanding and adoption of established food safety standards, guidance, and protocols.

"(2) Encouraged Features. — The Secretary shall encourage projects carried out using grant funds under this section to include co-management of food safety, conservation systems, and ecological health.

"(3) Maximum Term and Size of Grant. —

"(A) In General. — A grant under this section shall have a term that is not more than 3 years.

"(B) Limitation on Grant Funding. — The Secretary may not provide grant funding to an entity under this section after such entity has received 3 years of grant funding under this section.

"(f) Grant Eligibility. —

"(1) In General. — To be eligible for a grant under this section, an entity shall be —

"(A) a State cooperative extension service;

"(B) a Federal, State, local, or tribal agency, a nonprofit community-based or non-governmental organization, or an organization representing owners and operators of farms, small food processors, or small fruit and vegetable merchant wholesalers that has a commitment to public health and expertise in administering programs that contribute to food safety;

"**(C)** an institution of higher education (as defined in section 101(a) of the Higher Education Act of 1965 (20 U.S.C. 1001(a))) or a foundation maintained by an institution of higher education;

"**(D)** a collaboration of 2 of more eligible entities described in this subsection; or

"**(E)** such other appropriate entity, as determined by the Secretary.

"**(2) Multistate Partnerships.** — Grants under this section may be made for projects involving more than 1 State.

"**(g) Regional Balance.** — In making grants under this section, the Secretary shall, to the maximum extent practicable, ensure —

"**(1)** geographic diversity; and

"**(2)** diversity of types of agricultural production.

"**(h) Technical Assistance.** — The Secretary may use funds made available under this section to provide technical assistance to grant recipients to further the purposes of this section.

"**(i) Best Practices and Model Programs.** — Based on evaluations of, and responses arising from, projects funded under this section, the Secretary may issue a set of recommended best practices and models for food safety training programs for agricultural producers, small food processors, and small fresh fruit and vegetable merchant wholesalers.

"**(j) Authorization of Appropriations.** — For the purposes of making grants under this section, there are authorized to be appropriated such sums as may be necessary for fiscal years 2011 through 2015.".

Sec. 210. Enhancing Food Safety.

(a) [Text not included. — Ed.]

(b) Centers of Excellence. — Part P of the Public Health Service Act (42 U.S.C. 280g et seq.) is amended by adding at the end the following:

"Sec. 399V-5. Food Safety Integrated Centers of Excellence.

"**(a) In General.** — Not later than 1 year after the date of enactment of the FDA Food Safety Modernization Act, the Secretary, acting through the Director of the Centers for Disease Control and Prevention and in consultation with the working group described in subsection (b)(2), shall designate 5 Integrated Food Safety Centers of Excellence (referred to in this section as the 'Centers of Excellence') to serve as resources for Federal, State, and local public health professionals to respond to foodborne illness outbreaks. The Centers of Excellence shall be headquartered at selected State health departments.

"**(b) Selection of Centers of Excellence.** —

"**(1) Eligible Entities.** — To be eligible to be designated as a Center of Excellence under subsection (a), an entity shall —

"**(A)** be a State health department;

"**(B)** partner with 1 or more institutions of higher education that have demonstrated knowledge, expertise, and meaningful experience with regional or national food production, processing, and distribution, as well as leadership in the laboratory, epidemiological, and environmental detection and investigation of foodborne illness; and

"**(C)** provide to the Secretary such information, at such time, and in such manner, as the Secretary may require.

"**(2) Working Group.** — Not later than 180 days after the date of enactment of the FDA Food Safety Modernization Act, the Secretary shall establish a diverse working group of experts and stakeholders from Federal, State, and local food safety and health agencies, the food industry, including food retailers and food manufacturers, consumer organizations, and academia to make recommendations to the Secretary regarding designations of the Centers of Excellence.

"**(3) Additional Centers of Excellence.** — The Secretary may designate eligible entities to be regional Food Safety Centers of Excellence, in addition to the 5 Centers designated under subsection (a).

"**(c) Activities.** — Under the leadership of the Director of the Centers for Disease Control and Prevention, each Center of Excellence shall be based out of a selected State health department, which shall provide assistance to other regional, State, and local departments of health through activities that include —

"(1) providing resources, including timely information concerning symptoms and tests, for frontline health professionals interviewing individuals as part of routine surveillance and outbreak investigations;

"(2) providing analysis of the timeliness and effectiveness of foodborne disease surveillance and outbreak response activities;

"(3) providing training for epidemiological and environmental investigation of foodborne illness, including suggestions for streamlining and standardizing the investigation process;

"(4) establishing fellowships, stipends, and scholarships to train future epidemiological and food-safety leaders and to address critical workforce shortages;

"(5) training and coordinating State and local personnel;

"(6) strengthening capacity to participate in existing or new foodborne illness surveillance and environmental assessment information systems; and

"(7) conducting research and outreach activities focused on increasing prevention, communication, and education regarding food safety.

"(d) Report to Congress. — Not later than 2 years after the date of enactment of the FDA Food Safety Modernization Act, the Secretary shall submit to Congress a report that—

"(1) describes the effectiveness of the Centers of Excellence; and

"(2) provides legislative recommendations or describes additional resources required by the Centers of Excellence.

"(e) Authorization of Appropriations. — There is authorized to be appropriated such sums as may be necessary to carry out this section.

"(f) No Duplication of Effort. — In carrying out activities of the Centers of Excellence or other programs under this section, the Secretary shall not duplicate other Federal foodborne illness response efforts.".

Title III — Improving the Safety of Imported Food

Sec. 305. Building Capacity of Foreign Governments with Respect to Food Safety.

(a) In General. — The Secretary shall, not later than 2 years of the date of enactment of this Act, develop a comprehensive plan to expand the technical, scientific, and regulatory food safety capacity of foreign governments, and their respective food industries, from which foods are exported to the United States.

(b) Consultation. — In developing the plan under subsection (a), the Secretary shall consult with the Secretary of Agriculture, Secretary of State, Secretary of the Treasury, the Secretary of Homeland Security, the United States Trade Representative, and the Secretary of Commerce, representatives of the food industry, appropriate foreign government officials, nongovernmental organizations that represent the interests of consumers, and other stakeholders.

(c) Plan. — The plan developed under subsection (a) shall include, as appropriate, the following:

(1) Recommendations for bilateral and multilateral arrangements and agreements, including provisions to provide for responsibility of exporting countries to ensure the safety of food.

(2) Provisions for secure electronic data sharing.

(3) Provisions for mutual recognition of inspection reports.

(4) Training of foreign governments and food producers on United States requirements for safe food.

(5) Recommendations on whether and how to harmonize requirements under the Codex Alimentarius.

(6) Provisions for the multilateral acceptance of laboratory methods and testing and detection techniques.

(d) Rule of Construction. — Nothing in this section shall be construed to affect the regulation of dietary supplements under the Dietary Supplement Health and Education Act of 1994 (Public Law 103-417).

Sec. 306. Inspection of Foreign Food Facilities.

(a) [Text not included. — Ed.]

(b) Inspection by the Secretary of Commerce. —

(1) In General. — The Secretary of Commerce, in coordination with the Secretary of Health and Human Services, may send 1 or more inspectors to a country or facility of an exporter from which seafood imported into the United States originates. The inspectors shall assess practices and processes used in connection with the farming, cultivation, harvesting, preparation for market, or transportation of such seafood and may provide technical assistance related to such activities.

(2) Inspection Report. —

(A) In General. — The Secretary of Health and Human Services, in coordination with the Secretary of Commerce, shall —

(i) prepare an inspection report for each inspection conducted under paragraph (1);

(ii) provide the report to the country or exporter that is the subject of the report; and

(iii) provide a 30-day period during which the country or exporter may provide a rebuttal or other comments on the findings of the report to the Secretary of Health and Human Services.

(B) Distribution and Use of Report. — The Secretary of Health and Human Services shall consider the inspection reports described in subparagraph (A) in distributing inspection resources under section 421 of the Federal Food, Drug, and Cosmetic Act, as added by section 201.

Sec. 308. Foreign Offices of the Food and Drug Administration.

(a) In General. — The Secretary shall establish offices of the Food and Drug Administration in foreign countries selected by the Secretary, to provide assistance to the appropriate governmental entities of such countries with respect to measures to provide for the safety of articles of food and other products regulated by the Food and Drug Administration exported by such country to the United States, including by directly conducting risk-based inspections of such articles and supporting such inspections by such governmental entity.

(b) Consultation. — In establishing the foreign offices described in subsection (a), the Secretary shall consult with the Secretary of State, the Secretary of Homeland Security, and the United States Trade Representative.

(c) Report. — Not later than October 1, 2011, the Secretary shall submit to Congress a report on the basis for the selection by the Secretary of the foreign countries in which the Secretary established offices, the progress which such offices have made with respect to assisting the governments of such countries in providing for the safety of articles of food and other products regulated by the Food and Drug Administration exported to the United States, and the plans of the Secretary for establishing additional foreign offices of the Food and Drug Administration, as appropriate.

Sec. 309. Smuggled Food.

(a) In General. — Not later than 180 days after the enactment of this Act, the Secretary shall, in coordination with the Secretary of Homeland Security, develop and implement a strategy to better identify smuggled food and prevent entry of such food into the United States.

(b) Notification to Homeland Security. — Not later than 10 days after the Secretary identifies a smuggled food that the Secretary believes would cause serious adverse health consequences or death to humans or animals, the Secretary shall provide to the Secretary of Homeland Security a notification under section 417(n) of the Federal Food, Drug, and Cosmetic Act (21 U.S.C. 350f(k)) describing the smuggled food and, if available, the names of the individuals or entities that attempted to import such food into the United States.

(c) Public Notification. — If the Secretary —

(1) identifies a smuggled food;

(2) reasonably believes exposure to the food would cause serious adverse health consequences or death to humans or animals; and

(3) reasonably believes that the food has entered domestic commerce and is likely to be consumed,

the Secretary shall promptly issue a press release describing that food and shall use other emergency communication or recall networks, as appropriate, to warn consumers and vendors about the potential threat.

(d) Effect of Section. — Nothing in this section shall affect the authority of the Secretary to issue public notifications under other circumstances.

(e) Definition. — In this subsection, the term "smuggled food" means any food that a person introduces into the United States through fraudulent means or with the intent to defraud or mislead.

21st CENTURY CURES ACT

Title II—Development

Subtitle B—Advancing Precision Medicine

Sec. 2014. Data Sharing

[Sec. (a), omitted here, codified at Sec. 402(b) of the P.H.S.A. (42 U.S.C. 282(b)) —Ed.]

(b) Confidentiality.—Nothing in the amendments made by subsection (a) authorizes the Secretary of Health and Human Services to disclose any information that is a trade secret, or other privileged or confidential information, described in section 552(b)(4) of title 5, United States Code, or section 1905 of title 18, United States Code, or be construed to require recipients of grants or cooperative agreements through the National Institutes of Health to share such information.

Subtitle D—National Institutes of Health Planning and Administration

Sec. 2036. High-risk, High-Reward Research.

[Sec. (a), omitted here, codified at Sec. 402(n) of the P.H.S.A. (42 U.S.C. 282(n)). –Ed.]

(b) Report to Congress.—Not later than September 30, 2020, the Secretary of Health and Human Services, acting through the Director of the National Institutes of Health, shall conduct an evaluation of the activities under subsection (n) of section 402 of the Public Health Service Act (42 U.S.C. 282), as added by subsection (a), and submit a report to the Committee on Health, Education, Labor, and Pensions of the Senate and the Committee on Energy and Commerce of the House of Representatives on the results of such evaluation.

(c) Duties of Directors of Institutes.—Section 405(b)(1) of the Public Health Service Act (42 U.S.C. 284(b)(1)) is amended—

(1) by redesignating subparagraphs (C) through (L) as subparagraphs (D) through (M), respectively; and

(2) by inserting after subparagraph (B), the following:

"(C) shall, as appropriate, conduct and support research that has the potential to transform the scientific field, has inherently higher risk, and that seeks to address major current challenges;".

Subtitle E—Advancement of the National Institutes of Health Research and Data Access

Sec. 2052. Compliance Activities Reports.

(a) Definitions.—In this section:

(1) Applicable Clinical Trial.—The term "applicable clinical trial" has the meaning given the term in section 402(j) of the Public Health Service Act (42 U.S.C. 282(j)).

(2) Secretary.—The term "Secretary" means the Secretary of Health and Human Services.

(b) Report on Activities to Encourage Compliance.— Not later than 2 years after the date of enactment of this Act, the Secretary, acting through the Director of the National Institutes of Health and in collaboration with the Commissioner of Food and Drugs, shall submit to the Committee on Health, Education, Labor, and Pensions of the Senate and the Committee on Energy and Commerce of the House of Representatives, a report that describes education and outreach, guidance, enforcement, and other activities undertaken to encourage compliance with section 402(j) of the Public Health Service Act (42 U.S.C. 282(j)).

(c) Reports on Clinical Trials.—

(1) In General.—Not later than 2 years after the final compliance date under the final rule implementing section 402(j) of the Public Health Service Act, and every 2 years thereafter for the next 4 years, the Secretary, acting through the Director of the National Institutes of Health and in collaboration with the Commissioner of Food and Drugs, shall submit to the Committee on Health, Education, Labor, and Pensions of the Senate and the Committee on Energy and Commerce of the House of Representatives, a report describing—

(A) the total number of applicable clinical trials with complete data bank registration information registered during the period for which the report is being prepared (broken down by each year of such reporting period);

(B) the total number of applicable clinical trials registered during the period for which the report is being prepared for which results have been submitted to the data bank (broken down by each year of such reporting period);

(C) the activities undertaken by the Secretary to educate responsible persons about data bank registration and results submission requirements, including through issuance of guidance documents, informational meetings, and training sessions; and

(D) the activities described in the report submitted under subsection (b).

(2) Actions to Enforce Compliance.—After the Secretary has undertaken the educational activities described in paragraph (1)(C), the Secretary shall include in subsequent reports submitted under paragraph (1) the number of actions taken by the Secretary during the period for which the report is being prepared to enforce compliance with data bank registration and results submission requirements.

Title III—Development

Subtitle A—Patient-Focused Drug Development

Sec. 3002. Patient-Focused Drug Development Guidance.

(a) Publication of Guidance Documents.— Not later than 180 days after the date of enactment of this Act, the Secretary of Health and Human Services (referred to in this section as the "Secretary"), acting through the Commissioner of Food and Drugs, shall develop a plan to issue draft and final versions of one or more guidance documents, over a period of 5 years, regarding the collection of patient experience data, and the use of such data and related information in drug development. Not later than 18 months after the date of enactment of this Act, the Secretary shall issue a draft version of at least one such guidance document. Not later than 18 months after the public comment period on the draft guidance ends, the Secretary shall issue a revised draft guidance or final guidance.

(b) Patient Experience Data.— For purposes of this section, the term "patient experience data" has the meaning given such term in section 569C of the Federal Food, Drug, and Cosmetic Act (as added by section 3001).

(c) Contents.— The guidance documents described in subsection (a) shall address—

(1) methodological approaches that a person seeking to collect patient experience data for submission to, and proposed use by, the Secretary in regulatory decisionmaking may use, that are relevant and objective and ensure that such data are accurate and representative of the intended population, including methods to collect meaningful patient input throughout the drug development process and methodological considerations for data collection, reporting, management, and analysis;

(2) methodological approaches that may be used to develop and identify what is most important to patients with respect to burden of disease, burden of treatment, and the benefits and risks in the management of the patient's disease;

(3) approaches to identifying and developing methods to measure impacts to patients that will help facilitate collection of patient experience data in clinical trials;

(4) methodologies, standards, and technologies to collect and analyze clinical outcome assessments for purposes of regulatory decisionmaking;

(5) how a person seeking to develop and submit proposed draft guidance relating to patient experience data for consideration by the Secretary may submit such proposed draft guidance to the Secretary;

(6) the format and content required for submissions under this section to the Secretary, including with respect to the information described in paragraph (1);

(7) how the Secretary intends to respond to submissions of information described in paragraph (1), if applicable, including any timeframe for response when such submission is not part of a regulatory application or other submission that has an associated timeframe for response; and

(8) how the Secretary, if appropriate, anticipates using relevant patient experience data and related information, including with respect to the structured risk-benefit assessment framework described in section 505(d) of the Federal Food, Drug, and Cosmetic Act (21 U.S.C. 355(d)), to inform regulatory decisionmaking.

Subtitle B—Advancing New Drug Therapies

Sec. 3011. Qualification of Drug Development Tools.

[Sec. (a), omitted here, codified at Sec. 507(a)-(e) of the F.D.C.A. (21 U.S.C. 357 (a)-(e))—Ed.]

(b) Guidance.—

(1) In General.—The Secretary of Health and Human Services (referred to in this section as the "Secretary") shall, in consultation with biomedical research consortia (as defined in subsection (e) of section 507 of the Federal Food, Drug, and Cosmetic Act (as added by subsection (a)) and other interested parties through a collaborative public process, issue guidance to implement such section 507 that—

(A) provides a conceptual framework describing appropriate standards and scientific approaches to support the development of biomarkers delineated under the taxonomy established under paragraph (3);

(B) with respect to the qualification process under such section 507—

(i) describes the requirements that entities seeking to qualify a drug development tool under such section shall observe when engaging in such process;

(ii) outlines reasonable timeframes for the Secretary's review of letters, qualification plans, or full qualification packages submitted under such process; and

(iii) establishes a process by which such entities or the Secretary may consult with biomedical research consortia and other individuals and entities with expert knowledge and insights that may assist the Secretary in the review of qualification plans and full qualification submissions under such section; and

(C) includes such other information as the Secretary determines appropriate.

(2) Timing.—Not later than 3 years after the date of the enactment of this Act, the Secretary shall issue draft guidance under paragraph (1) on the implementation of section 507 of the Federal Food, Drug, and Cosmetic Act (as added by subsection (a)). The Secretary shall issue final guidance on the implementation of such section not later than 6 months after the date on which the comment period for the draft guidance closes.

(3) Taxonomy.—

(A) In General.—For purposes of informing guidance under this subsection, the Secretary shall, in consultation with biomedical research consortia and other interested parties through a collaborative public process, establish a taxonomy for the classification of biomarkers (and related scientific concepts) for use in drug development.

(B) Public Availability.—Not later than 2 years after the date of the enactment of this Act, the Secretary shall make such taxonomy publicly available in draft form for public comment. The Secretary shall finalize the taxonomy not later than 1 year after the close of the public comment period.

(c) Meeting and Report.—

(1) Meeting.—Not later than 2 years after the date of the enactment of this Act, the Secretary shall convene a public meeting to describe and solicit public input regarding the qualification process under section 507 of the Federal Food, Drug, and Cosmetic Act, as added by subsection (a).

(2) Report.—Not later than 5 years after the date of the enactment of this Act, the Secretary shall make publicly available on the Internet website of the Food and Drug Administration a report. Such report shall include, with respect to the qualification process under section 507 of the Federal Food, Drug, and Cosmetic Act, as added by subsection (a), information on—

(A) the number of requests submitted, as a letter of intent, for qualification of a drug development tool (as defined in subsection (e) of such section 507);

(B) the number of such requests accepted and determined to be eligible for submission of a qualification plan or full qualification package (as such terms are defined in subsection (e) of such section 507), respectively;

(C) the number of such requests for which external scientific experts were utilized in the development of a qualification plan or review of a full qualification package;

(D) the number of qualification plans and full qualification packages, respectively, submitted to the Secretary; and

(E) the drug development tools qualified through such qualification process, specified by type of tool, such as a biomarker or clinical outcome assessment (as such terms are defined in subsection (e) of such section 507).

Subtitle C—Modern Trial Design and Evidence Development

Sec. 3021. Novel Clinical Trial Designs.

(a) Proposals for Use of Novel Clinical Trial Designs for Drugs and Biological Products.—For purposes of assisting sponsors in incorporating complex adaptive and other novel trial designs into proposed clinical protocols and applications for new drugs under section 505 of the Federal Food, Drug, and Cosmetic Act (21 U.S.C. 355) and biological products under section 351 of the Public Health Service Act (42 U.S.C. 262), the Secretary of Health and Human Services (referred to in this section as the "Secretary") shall conduct a public meeting and issue guidance in accordance with subsection (b).

(b) Guidance Addressing Use of Novel Clinical Trial Designs.—

(1) In General.—The Secretary, acting through the Commissioner of Food and Drugs, shall update or issue guidance addressing the use of complex adaptive and other novel trial design in the development and regulatory review and approval or licensure for drugs and biological products.

(2) Contents.—The guidance under paragraph (1) shall address—

(A) the use of complex adaptive and other novel trial designs, including how such clinical trials proposed or submitted help to satisfy the substantial evidence standard under section 505(d) of the Federal Food, Drug, and Cosmetic Act (21 U.S.C. 355(d));

(B) how sponsors may obtain feedback from the Secretary on technical issues related to modeling and simulations prior to—

(i) completion of such modeling or simulations; or

(ii) the submission of resulting information to the Secretary;

(C) the types of quantitative and qualitative information that should be submitted for review; and

(D) recommended analysis methodologies.

(3) Public Meeting.—Prior to updating or issuing the guidance required by paragraph (1), the Secretary shall consult with stakeholders, including representatives of regulated industry, academia, patient advocacy organizations, consumer groups, and disease research foundations, through a public meeting to be held not later than 18 months after the date of enactment of this Act.

(4) Timing.—The Secretary shall update or issue a draft version of the guidance required by paragraph (1) not later than 18 months after the date of the public meeting required by paragraph (3) and finalize such guidance not later than 1 year after the date on which the public comment period for the draft guidance closes.

Subtitle D—Patient Access to Therapies and Information

Sec. 3033. Accelerated Approval for Regenerative Advanced Therapies.

[Sec. (a), omitted here, codified at Sec. 506(g) of the F.D.C.A. (21 U.S.C. 356(g)). —Ed.]

(b) Rule of Construction.—Nothing in this section and the amendments made by this section shall be construed to alter the authority of the Secretary of Health and Human Services—

(1) to approve drugs pursuant to the Federal Food, Drug, and Cosmetic Act (21 U.S.C. 301 et seq.) and section 351 of the Public Health Service Act (42 U.S.C. 262) as authorized prior to the date of enactment of the 21st Century Cures Act [December 13, 2016 —Ed.], including the standards of evidence, and applicable conditions, for approval under such Acts; or

(2) to alter the authority of the Secretary to require postapproval studies pursuant to such Acts, as authorized prior to the date of enactment of the 21st Century Cures Act [December 13, 2016 —Ed.].

[Sec. (c), omitted here, codified at Sec. 506(e)(1) of the F.D.C.A. (21 U.S.C. 356(e)(1)). —Ed.]

Sec. 3034. Guidance Regarding Devices Used in the Recovery, Isolation, or Delivery of Regenerative Advanced Therapies.

(a) Draft Guidance.—Not later than 1 year after the date of enactment of the 21st Century Cures Act [December 13, 2016 —Ed.], the Secretary of Health and Human Services, acting through the Commissioner of Food and Drugs, shall issue draft guidance clarifying how, in the context of regenerative advanced therapies, the Secretary will evaluate devices used in the recovery, isolation, or delivery of regenerative advanced therapies. In doing so, the Secretary shall specifically address—

(1) how the Food and Drug Administration intends to simplify and streamline regulatory requirements for combination device and cell or tissue products;

(2) what, if any, intended uses or specific attributes would result in a device used with a regenerative therapy product to be classified as a class III device;

(3) when the Food and Drug Administration considers it is necessary, if ever, for the intended use of a device to be limited to a specific intended use with only one particular type of cell; and

(4) application of the least burdensome approach to demonstrate how a device may be used with more than one cell type.

(b) Final Guidance.—Not later than 12 months after the close of the period for public comment on the draft guidance under subsection (a), the Secretary of Health and Human Services shall finalize such guidance.

Sec. 3038. Combination Product Innovation.

[Sec. (a) and (b), omitted here, codified at Sec. 503(g) of the F.D.C.A. (21 U.S.C. 353(g)) and Sec. 520(h)(4) of the F.D.C.A. (21 U.S.C. 360j(h)(4)). —Ed.]

(c) Variations from CGMP Streamlined Approach.— Not later than 18 months after the date of enactment of this Act, the Secretary of Health and Human Services (referred to in this subsection as the "Secretary") shall identify types of combination products and manufacturing processes with respect to which the Secretary proposes that good manufacturing processes may be adopted that vary from the requirements set forth in section 4.4 of title 21, Code of Federal Regulations (or any successor regulations) or that the Secretary proposes can satisfy the requirements in section 4.4 through alternative or stream- lined mechanisms. The Secretary shall identify such types, variations from such requirements, and such mechanisms, in a proposed list published in the Federal Register. After a public comment period regarding the appropriate good manufacturing practices for such types, the Secretary shall publish a final list in the Federal Register, notwithstanding section 553 of title 5, United States Code. The Secretary shall evaluate such types, variations, and mechanisms using a risk-based approach. The Secretary shall periodically review such final list.

Subtitle E—Antimicrobial Innovation and Stewardship

Sec. 3044. Susceptibility Test Interpretive Criteria for Microorganisms; Antimicrobial Susceptibility Testing Devices.

[Sec. (a), codified at Sec. 511A of the F.D.C.A.; Sec. (b)(1), repealing Section 1111 of the Food and Drug Administration Amendments Act of 2007 (42 U.S.C. 247d-5a); Sec. (b)(2), codified at Sec. 502 of the F.D.C.A. (21 U.S.C. 352); and Sec. (b)(3), codified at Sec. 514 (c)(1)(A) of the F.D.C.A. (21 U.S.C. 360(c)(1)(A)), omitted here. -Ed.]

(c) Report to Congress.— Not later than 2 years after the date of enactment of this Act, the Secretary of Health and Human Services shall submit to the Committee on Health, Education, Labor, and Pensions of the Senate and the Committee on Energy and Commerce of the House of Representatives a report on the progress made in implementing section 511A of the Federal Food, Drug, and Cosmetic Act (21 U.S.C. 360a), as added by subsection (a).

(d) Requests for Updates to Interpretive Criteria Website.— Chapter 35 of title 44, United States Code, shall not apply to the collection of information from interested parties regarding updating the lists established under section 511A(b) of the Federal Food, Drug, and Cosmetic Act and posted on the Interpretive Criteria Website established under section 511A(c) of such Act.

Subtitle G—Improving Scientific Expertise and Outreach at FDA

Sec. 3072. Hiring Authority for Scientific, Technical, and Professional Personnel.

[Sec. (a), codified at Sec. 714A of the F.D.C.A. (21 U.S.C. 379d-3A), omitted here. –Ed.]

(b) GAO Study and Report.—

(1) In General.—The Comptroller General of the United States shall conduct a study of the ability of the Food and Drug Administration to hire, train, and retain qualified scientific, technical, and professional staff, not including contractors, necessary to fulfill the mission of the Food and Drug Administration to protect and promote public health. Not later than January 1, 2022, the Comptroller General shall submit a report on such study to the Committee on Health, Education, Labor, and Pensions of the Senate and the Committee on Energy and Commerce of the House of Representatives.

(2) Contents of Study.—The Comptroller General shall include in the study and report under paragraph (1)—

(A) information about the progress of the Food and Drug Administration in recruiting and retaining qualified scientific, technical, and professional staff outstanding in the field of biomedical research, clinical research evaluation, and biomedical product assessment;

(B) the extent to which critical staffing needs exist at the Food and Drug Administration, and barriers to hiring, training, and retaining qualified staff, if any;

(C) an examination of the recruitment and retention strategies of the Food and Drug Administration, including examining any strategic workforce plan, focused on improving scientific, technical, and professional staff recruitment and retention; and

(D) recommendations for potential improvements that would address staffing needs of the Food and Drug Administration.

CPSIA information can be obtained
at www.ICGtesting.com
Printed in the USA
FFOW04n0238050218
44887834-45078FF